Advance Praise for
Bank Asset and Liability Management

"Like the author's book *The Bond and Money Markets: Strategy, Trading, Analysis*, this is again a superb example how a financial book should be written! Not only has Moorad managed to write another hit, but as with the previous book he has managed to show workable illustrations so that a novice or a full-blown professional can make good use of the examples – either for understanding the subject better or for simply brushing up on one's memory. The book comes highly recommended!"

Tibor Szigeti
Fixed Income Analytics
Bloomberg L.P., London

"Again, Moorad Choudhry takes his readers beyond the older books in the market that simply list a string of facts, and into a world of highly practical and up-to-the-minute concepts and strategies. Bank asset–liability management is about knowing when and how to use all the tools available. The modern practitioner can't be limited to just managing rate and liquidity risk, but must be highly versed in securitisation and other balance sheet techniques. This book tackles the whole spectrum."

Peter Eisenhardt
Head of Short Term Fixed Income Origination
Debt Capital Markets
Bank of America N.A.

"Professor Choudhry has written a comprehensive guide providing invaluable insights into bank asset and liability management. The subject matter is delivered in an accessible and refreshingly clear manner. This latest publication is an essential read for anyone involved in the industry. Moorad delivers financial theories in a practical and entertaining package."

Mark Williams (Director)
and **Wei Lieh Goh**
Hedge Fund Derivatives
KBC Financial Products, London

"A complete representation of the asset–liability management challenge facing the bank risk manager, the best practice to deploy and the mitigating tools available. A thoroughly well-researched piece."

Remi Bola
Chief Operating Officer
Asset Backed Solutions
The Law Debenture Corporation plc

"A highly readable text which serves as an essential primer for both market practitioners and academics alike to help understand the rapidly evolving risk management techniques used by Treasury and Money Market desks. The author uses real-world examples throughout, and includes extensive and up-to-date coverage of current financing products and the regulatory environment."

Adam Sutton
Head of European Repo
Global Funding Desk
Bank of America, London

"A brilliant and comprehensive account of all the various disciplines that make up the art of bank asset–liability management. Professor Choudhry brings together the instruments, the procedures and the strategies that are vital knowledge for any successful risk manager or ALCO member. This book will be appreciated and respected by all bankers in all fields. A fantastic work! Every bank should have a copy of this book."

Mohamoud Barre Dualeh
Private Banking Unit
Abu Dhabi Commercial Bank, UAE

"*Bank Asset And Liability Management* offers a clear, insightful perspective of the global banking and liquidity markets. It covers all the major products in just the right level of detail and is written in a practical, accessible style. This book is a great reference tool for all finance professionals. Really, really impressive."

Bhavin Parmar
Securities Finance Trader
ABN Amro Bank N.V., London

"An informative account of banking ALM from the point of view of the market practitioner. The author brings together all the various strands that make up this important discipline in a technical yet accessible way"

Shahid Ikram
Head of UK Sovereign bonds and G7 hedge fund
Morley Fund Management IT, London

"Moorad Choudhry has managed to update and include the most relevant and practical knowledge required for ALM in a modern financial institution, especially with Basle II requirements and adoption looming ahead in 2008. Balance sheet management, financial markets and credit risk management, coupled with regulatory capital implications, are important considerations that are well addressed in this book that anybody looking to learn about or have a handy guide on ALM will find useful!"

Lee Ka Shao
Managing Director, Head of Investments
DBS Bank Limited, Singapore

Bank
Asset and Liability Management
Management

Strategy, Trading, Analysis

Bank Asset and Liability Management

Strategy, Trading, Analysis

Moorad Choudhry
With contributions from Andrew Oliver, Jaffar Hussain,
Kevin Zhuoshi Liu, Rod Pienaar, Abukar Ali and Suleman Baig

John Wiley & Sons (Asia) Pte Ltd

Published in 2007 by John Wiley & Sons (Asia) Pte Ltd
2 Clementi Loop, #02-01, Singapore 129809

Other Wiley Editorial Offices

John Wiley & Sons, Inc., 111 River Street, Hoboken, NJ 07030, USA
John Wiley & Sons Ltd, The Atrium, Southern Gate, Chichester P019 8SQ, England
John Wiley & Sons (Canada) Ltd, 5353 Dundas Street West, Suite 400, Toronto,
Ontario M9B 6HB, Canada
John Wiley & Sons Australia Ltd, 42 McDougall Street, Milton, Queensland 4064, Australia
Wiley-VCH, Boschstrasse 12, D-69469 Weinheim, Germany

Library of Congress Cataloging-in-Publication Data
978-0-470-82135-0

Typeset in 10.5/13 points, Times by Paul Lim
Printed in Singapore by Markono Print Media Pte Ltd
10 9 8 7 6

For Lindsay
We should have met years ago...

Contents

Foreword		xi
Preface		xiii
About the Author		xxiii
Part I	**Banking business, bank capital and debt market instruments**	**1**
Chapter 1	Bank business and bank capital	3
Chapter 2	Financial statements and ratio analysis	29
Chapter 3	The money markets	47
Chapter 4	The bond instrument	133
Part II	**Bank treasury asset–liability management**	**209**
Chapter 5	Asset–liability management I	211
Chapter 6	Asset–liability management II	247
Chapter 7	ALM trading principles	305
Chapter 8	Asset–liability management III: The ALCO	327
Chapter 9	The yield curve	339
Chapter 10	The determinants of the swap spread and understanding the term premium	451
Chapter 11	Introduction to relative spread analysis	477
Part III	**Financial instruments, applications and hedging**	**491**
Chapter 12	Repo instruments	493
Chapter 13	Money market derivatives	539
Chapter 14	Interest-rate swaps and overnight-index swaps	625
Chapter 15	Hedging using bond futures contracts	713
Chapter 16	Credit risk and credit derivatives	745
Chapter 17	Value-at-Risk (VaR) and credit VaR	833

Part IV	**Funding and balance sheet management using securitisation and structured credit vehicles**	**881**
Chapter 18	Introduction to securitisation	887
Chapter 19	Structured, synthetic and repackaged funding vehicles	921
Chapter 20	Mortgage-backed securities and covered bonds	961
Chapter 21	Asset-backed securities	999
Chapter 22	Collateralised debt obligations	1021
Chapter 23	Synthetic collateralised debt obligations	1059
Chapter 24	Synthetic mortgage-backed securities	1139
Chapter 25	Structured investment vehicles	1147
Part V	**Bank regulatory capital**	**1161**
Chapter 26	Bank regulatory capital and the Basel rules	1165
Chapter 27	A primer on Basel II	1195
Part VI	**Treasury middle office operations**	**1241**
Chapter 28	Funding and Treasury procedures for banking corporations	1243
Part VII	**Applications software enclosed with the book**	**1261**
Chapter 29	Applications software and spreadsheet models	1263
Appendix	Financial markets arithmetic	1277
Glossary		1315
Index		1383

Foreword

Asset and liability management (ALM) is a key aspect of risk management in the financial services industry. The business of financial services firms is risk and return, using their skills in the measurement of risks to make profits. In modern finance, this often involves using complex products. The types of risks taken by firms are often complex and hidden, reflecting the financial products on offer and the wider marketplace. As such, when analysing risks, it is important to think about the firm's balance sheet holistically. A firm's ALM Committee (ALCO) uses this *modus operandi*, managing its assets and liabilities, and supervising liquidity, credit, market and operational risks, in short prudential matters, at the most senior level.

Financial services firms, especially banks, are essential to the global economy. Therefore, ALM is a major aspect of their operations. Liquidity, the ability of a firm to generate money at often short notice and ideally low cost to meet a liability when it falls due, is important to the stability and smooth running of the global financial system. Poor planning has an impact beyond the individual financial institution. In similar vein, market risk, including yield curve and gap risks, requires thoughtful management, including monitoring and reporting.

There is no single metric that gives a full picture of these risks. The assessment of liquidity risk needs thinking about on- and off-balance sheet items. The management of market risk is complicated. These risks often overlap. ALM accepts this by monitoring them simultaneously. The process is as much qualitative as quantitative. Some observers even compare ALM to an art, not dissimilar to stress testing. ALCOs have to think about future market scenarios, the probability of these events occurring and their impact, and take action to mitigate these risks. In addition to making sure that the firm can withstand any event, including a stress, the Committee has to allocate assets and liabilities in order to meet certain objectives, profits and returns on equity (ROE) and the discipline of liquidity management.

ALM specialists have a wide variety of products and techniques to mitigate risk. Some tools, for example securitisation, have been around for years. Some techniques use fairly new products, for example credit derivatives. Moorad's magisterial work brings all the issues into a single publication. The book is written in an easy to understand manner, ideal for both practitioners and regulators. The book is also practical for those who want to learn ALM. There is something for every stakeholder in this book.

Irving Henry
Director
British Bankers' Association

Preface

As Sir Arthur Conan Doyle would have put it, so elementary a form of literature as the textbook on financial economics hardly deserves the dignity of a preface. It is possible, though, to bring some instant clarity to the purpose of such a book if we open with a few words here.

The traditional view of a bank is that of a financial institution that is in the business of taking deposits and advancing loans, and which makes its money from the difference in interest rate paid and received on these two products. While this quaint image would have been true a few hundred years ago, it is decidedly incomplete today. The modern banking institution is a complex beast, which in many cases operates in a wide range of products and services and across international markets. Banks are the cornerstone of the global economy, and at the highest level the banking sector influences, and is influenced by, macroeconomic trends such as GDP growth, central bank base interest rates, equity and debt capital markets activity, and the supply and demand for investments and credit.

However, notwithstanding our first statement that banks now engage in many complex activities outside traditional borrowing and lending, we must remember that at the core of *all* capital markets activity lies the need to bring together the suppliers of capital with the borrowers of capital. This was the original business logic behind the very first banks, so in that respect very little has changed! There is much other activity surrounding this basic function in the markets, but this need is paramount. Hence a key ingredient in bank strategy is the management of its assets and liabilities. It is this that is the subject of this book: Asset and Liability Management (ALM). These days there are a large number of instruments, in cash and derivative form, that make up a bank's assets and liabilities. No matter. For the ALM desk in a bank, the cash assets and liabilities are king and must be managed prudently. That there is more to this than may meet the eye is apparent immediately from the thickness of this book!

Let us set the scene further with some discussion on banks.

Introduction

Banking operations encompass a wide range of activities, all of which contribute to the asset and liability profile of a bank. Table P.1 shows selected banking activities, and the type of risk exposure they represent. The terms used in the table, such as "market risk", are explained elsewhere in this book. In Chapter 2 we discuss elementary aspects of financial analysis, using key financial ratios, that are used to examine the profitability and asset quality of a bank. We also discuss bank regulation and the concept of bank capital.

Service or function	Revenue generated	Risk
Lending		
– Retail	Interest income, fees	Credit, Market
– Commercial	Interest income, fees	Credit, Market
– Mortgage	Interest income, fees	Credit, Market
– Syndicated	Trading, interest income, fees	Credit, Market
Credit cards	Interest income, fees	Credit, Operational
Project finance	Interest income, fees	Credit
Trade finance	Interest income, fees	Credit, Operational
Cash management		
– Processing	Fees	Operational
– Payments	Fees	Credit, Operational
Custodian	Fees	Credit, Operational
Private banking	Commission income, interest income, fees	Operational
Asset management	Fees, performance payments	Credit, Market, Operational
Capital markets		
– Investment banking	Fees	Credit, Market
– Corporate finance	Fees	Credit, Market
– Equities	Trading income, fees	Credit, Market
– Bonds	Trading income, interest income, fees	Credit, Market
– Foreign exchange	Trading income, fees	Credit, Market
– Derivatives	Trading income, interest income, fees	Credit, Market

Table P.1 Selected banking activities and services

Before considering the concept of ALM, all readers should be familiar with the way a bank's earnings and performance are reported in its financial statements. A bank's income statement will break down the earnings by type, as we have defined in Table P.1. So we need to be familiar with interest income, trading income and so on. The other side of an income statement is the costs, such as operating expenses and bad loan provisions.

That the universe of banks encompasses many different varieties of beast is evident from the way they earn their money. Traditional banking institutions, perhaps typified by a regional bank in the United States or a building society in the United Kingdom, will generate a much greater share of their revenues through net interest income than trading income, and vice versa for an investment bank such as Lehman International or Merrill Lynch. The latter firms will earn a greater share of their revenues through fees and trading income.

During 2004 a regional European bank reported the following earnings breakdown, as shown in Table P.2.

Core operating income	% share
Net interest income	62
Fees and commissions	27
Trading income	11

Table P.2 European regional bank, earnings structure 2004
Source: Author's notes.

However, this breakdown varies widely across regions and banks, and in fact would be reversed at an investment bank whose core operating activity was market-making and proprietary trading.

Let us consider now the different types of income stream and costs.

Interest income

Interest income, or net interest income (NII), is the main source of revenue for the majority of banks worldwide. As we saw from Table P.2, it can form upwards of 60% of operating income, and for smaller banks and building societies it reaches 80% or more.

NII is generated from lending activity and interest-bearing assets, the "net" return is this interest income minus the cost of funding the loans. Funding, which is a cost to the bank, is obtained from a wide variety of sources. For many banks, deposits are a key source of funding, as well as one of the cheapest. They are generally short-term, though, or available on demand, so they must be supplemented with longer term funding. Other sources of funds include senior debt, in the form of bonds, securitised bonds and money market paper.

NII is sensitive to both credit risk and market risk. Market risk, which we will look at later, is essentially interest-rate risk for loans and deposits. Interest-rate risk will be driven by the maturity structure of the loan book, as well as the match (or mismatch) between the maturity of the loans against the maturity of the funding. This is known as the interest-rate gap.

Fees and commissions

Banks generate fee income as a result of the provision of services to customers. Fee income is very popular with bank senior management because it is less volatile and not susceptible to market risk like trading income or even NII. There is also no credit risk because the fees are often paid up front. There are other benefits as well, such as the opportunity to build up a diversified customer base for this additional range of services, but these are of less concern to a bank ALM desk.

Fee income uses less capital and also carries no market risk, but does carry other risks such as operational risk.

Trading income

Banks generate trading income through trading activity in financial products such as equities (shares), bonds and derivative instruments. This includes acting as a dealer or market-maker in these products, as well as taking proprietary positions for speculative purposes. Running positions in securities (as opposed to derivatives) in some cases generates interest income, some banks strip this out of the capital gain made when the security is traded to profit, while others include it as part of overall trading income.

Trading income is the most volatile income source for a bank. It also carries relatively high market risk, as well as not inconsiderable credit risk. Many banks, although by no means all, use the Value-at-Risk (VaR) methodology to measure the risk arising from trading activity, which gives a statistical measure of expected losses to the trading portfolio under certain selected market scenarios.

Costs

Bank operating costs comprise staff costs, as well as other costs such as premises, information technology and equipment costs. Further significant elements of cost are provisions for loan losses, which are a charge against the loan revenues of the bank. The provision is based on a subjective measure by management of how much of the loan portfolio can be expected to be repaid by the borrower.

The capital markets

Capital markets is the term used to describe the market for raising and investing finance. The economies of developed countries and a large number of developing countries are based on financial systems that contain investors and borrowers, *markets* and trading arrangements. A market can be one in the traditional sense such as an exchange where financial instruments are bought and sold on a trading floor, or it may refer to one where participants deal with each other over the telephone or via electronic screens. The basic principles are the same in any type of market. There are two primary users of the capital markets: lenders and borrowers. The source of lenders' funds is, to a large extent, the personal sector made up of household savings and those acting as their investment managers such as life assurance companies and pension funds. The borrowers are made up of the government, local governments and companies (called corporates). There is a basic conflict in the financial objectives of borrowers and lenders, in that those who are investing funds wish to remain *liquid*, which means they have easy access to their investments. They also wish to maximise the return on their investment. A borrower, on the other hand, will wish to generate maximum net profit on its activities, which will require continuous investment in plant, equipment, human resources and so on. Such investment will therefore need to be as long-term as possible. Government borrowing, as well, is often related to long-term projects such as the construction of schools, hospitals and roads. So while investors wish to have ready access to their cash and invest short, borrowers desire funding to be as long as possible. The economist John Hicks[1] referred to this conflict as the "constitutional weakness" of financial markets, especially when there is no conduit through which to reconcile the needs of lenders and borrowers. To facilitate the efficient operation of financial markets and the price mechanism,

[1] Hicks, J. 1939, *Value and Capital*, Oxford University Press, Oxford.

intermediaries exist to bring together the needs of lenders and borrowers. A bank is the best example of this. Banks accept deposits from investors, which make up the *liability* side of their balance sheet, and lend funds to borrowers, which form the *assets* on their balance sheet. If a bank builds up a sufficiently large asset and liability base, it will be able to meet the needs of both investors and borrowers, as it can maintain liquidity to meet investors' requirements, as well as create long-term assets to meet the needs of borrowers. The bank is exposed to two primary risks in carrying out its operations, one that a large number of investors decide to withdraw their funds at the same time (a "run" on the bank), or that large numbers of borrowers go bankrupt and default on their loans. In acting as a financial intermediary, the bank reduces the risks it is exposed to by spreading and pooling risk across a wide asset and liability base.

Corporate borrowers wishing to finance investment can raise capital in various ways. The main methods are:

- continued reinvestment of the profits generated by a company's current operations;
- selling shares in the company, known as equity capital, equity securities or *equity*, which confirm on buyers a share in ownership of the company. The shareholders as owners have the right to vote at general meetings of the company, as well as the right to share in the company's profits by receiving dividends;
- borrowing money from a bank, via a bank loan. This can be a short-term loan such as an overdraft, or a longer term loan over two, three, five years or even longer. Bank loans can be at either a fixed or more usually, variable rate of interest;
- borrowing money by issuing debt securities, in the form of *bills*, *commercial paper* and *bonds* that subsequently trade in the debt capital market.

The first method may not generate sufficient funds, especially if a company is seeking to expand by growth or acquisition of other companies. In any case a proportion of annual after-tax profits will need to be paid out as dividends to shareholders. Selling further shares is not always popular among existing shareholders as it dilutes the extent of their ownership; there are also a host of other factors to consider, including if there is any appetite in the market for that company's shares. A bank loan is often inflexible, and the interest rate charged by the bank may be comparatively high for all but the highest quality companies. However, it is often the first source of corporate finance. We say comparatively, because there is often a cheaper way for corporates to borrow money: by tapping the bond and money markets. And that is where banks come in.

Layout of the book

Bank Asset and Liability Management is written in seven parts, covering the various different but related aspects of bank ALM. These are:

Part I – Banking business, bank capital and debt market instruments
Part II – Bank treasury asset–liability management
Part III – Financial instruments, applications and hedging
Part IV – Funding and balance-sheet management using securitisation and structured credit vehicles
Part V – Regulatory capital and the Basel rules
Part VI – Treasury middle office operations
Part VII– Applications software enclosed with the book.

For newcomers to the market there is a primer on financial market arithmetic located in the Appendix, as well as a Glossary of market terms.

Highlights of the book include:

- a detailed look at ALM activity and operation as undertaken by banks and securities houses, including risk management and management reporting;
- comprehensive coverage of the money markets;
- a look at the syndicated loan market;
- the use of securitisation in balance sheet management;
- applications of synthetic structured finance securities;
- yield curve analysis, the determinants of the swap spread and understanding the term premium;
- the role of the ALM committee (ALCO);
- coverage of market instruments including interest-rate derivatives (FRAs, futures, caps, floors and swaps) and credit derivatives, and their use and application for hedging purposes;
- calculating the credit risk exposure hedge notional amount;
- the latest developments in structured funding vehicles;
- description and analysis of structured credit products including collateralised debt obligations (CDOs) and structured investment vehicles (SIVs), and their application in ALM;

- the process of structuring a securitisation deal;
- synthetic CDO note pricing and tranche correlation; and
- a look at the Basel II regulatory capital rules and its implications.

The book also features a contribution from Andrew Oliver of KBC Financial Products in London, who wrote the chapter on Treasury middle office operations. This is an important element in overall ALM for banks and we are pleased to have Mr Oliver's expert opinion on this subject. Parts of the chapters on credit derivatives and CDOs were co-authored with Abukar Ali of Bloomberg L.P., Richard Pereira of JPMorgan Chase and Jaffar Hussein of the Saudi National Commercial Bank, and my grateful thanks to them.

The accompanying CD-R features software co-written with Kevin Zhuoshi Liu, Rod Pienaar, Suleman Baig, Abukar Ali, Stuart Turner and Didier Joannas, and again my grateful thanks to them.

As ever, the intention is to remain accessible and practical throughout. We hope this aim has been achieved. Comments on the text are most welcome and should be sent to the author care of John Wiley & Sons (Asia) Ltd.

Acknowledgments and special thanks

With thanks to Luis Perez and Zhuoshi Liu for assistance with the Errata, much appreciated.

Big, big, emotional hug to the **Raynes Park Footy Boys** (Abubakar, Abukar, Anuk, Clax, Farooq, Harry, Kevin, Khurram, Mohamoud, Richard and Rod, plus honourary members Melvin Chan, Mike Brand, Brian Eales and Carol Alexander) – you are total legends and I love you like my own brother. *A Solid Bond In Your Heart.*

Salaam Aleikum to Adnan Jaffery at Citigroup, Bhavin Parmar at ABN Amro and Ali Mahdavi at Bloomberg. David Walters, I have high hopes for you, all the best. El Gunista get some desk sweets in mate… Thanks to Suraj Gohil and Bruno Pajusco at KBC FP for expert help on all matters CDS… Special thanks to Anne Carter as always for help with the proofing process, you are an absolute darling. Mr James Harrison, as you can see when I can't remember the numbers in the calculations I just use *x* and *y*..!

Thanks to the Teesside 5-a-side boys including Jonno, Cooper, Dick, Walker and Pie – your attitude is spot on, and it's my privilege and pleasure to know you.

Thanks to the publishing Dream Team that is Janis Soo, Paul Lim and Edward Caruso, you guys can make *any* book look good. Awesome – thank you.

Thanks to that other Dream Team which is any group of capital markets lawyers led by the legendary Jim Croke – the man is a demon!

EDG United thank you for the swansong… Also thanks to a company of youth on the football field for their first-class teamwork, the essence of success in any endeavour: Mark Burgess, Frank Spiteri, John Key, Russell Betteridge, Sam McArthur, Richard Silver, Hirak Chakravorty, Henrik Ljungstrom, Petch Pompili, Vladan Ognjenovic, Bilal Mannaa, Adam Hockley, Paul Muttett and Philip Cooper.

Finally, thank you to Terry Williams, Andrew Calvy, John Marshall, Ray Saunders, Anthony Goodin, Damon Carter, Rich Lynn, Neil Lewis, Stuart Medlen, Michael Nicoll, Jonathan Rossington, Alan Fulling, Sean Murphy and Michael Beddow for demonstrating consistently the unquantifiable, yet vital, characteristic that is the ability to inspire. Quintessential Best of British.

Or, as Justin Rockberger would say – "Be up for it!"

I beg that readers indulge me as I list my eight desert-island discs:

1. *Lean On Me!*, Redskins
2. *My Sweet Lord,* George Harrison
3. *Rattlesnakes*, Lloyd Cole and The Commotions
4. *Still Ill*, The Smiths
5. *Don't Let Me Down*, The Beatles
6. *I Can't Help Myself*, Orange Juice
7. *A Lover Sings*, Billy Bragg
8. *Speak Like A Child*, The Style Council

And, after nine years…that's yer lot! Goodbye…

Moorad

Moorad Choudhry
Surrey, England
30 January 2007

About the Author

Moorad Choudhry is Head of Treasury at KBC Financial Products in London. He is a Visiting Professor at the Department of Economics, London Metropolitan University; a Visiting Research Fellow at the ICMA Centre, University of Reading; a Senior Fellow at the Centre for Mathematical Trading and Finance, Cass Business School; a Fellow of the Global Association of Risk Professionals, a Fellow of the Institute of Sales and Marketing Management; a Fellow of the Securities and Investment Institute and a member of the Chartered Institute of Bankers. He is on the Editorial Board of the *Journal of Structured Finance*.

I must frankly admit that, if I had known beforehand the labour which this book entailed, I should never have been courageous enough to commence it.

– Isabella Beeton, *Mrs Beeton's Household Guide*,
Ward, Lock & Co., c.1861

PART

I

Banking Business, Bank Capital and Debt Market Instruments

Part I is something of a primer on banking, and is designed to set the scene for beginners, be they students or practitioners. We need to be familiar with the nature of banking business, as well as the types of instruments used in money market trading. We also need to be familiar with banking capital and financial statements, the former preparatory to a discussion of regulatory capital and the Basel rules, the latter simply for general knowledge purposes. So the first part of this book covers all these areas.

We begin with a look at the fundamentals of banking business, and the different elements of bank capital. This is essentially an introduction into the nature of banking. We then look at financial statements, which comprise balance sheet and profit and loss account. The contents of this chapter may appear more at home in a textbook on accounting, but an understanding of ratio analysis is vital for the ALM practitioner, who is concerned with issues such as return on capital.

The remainder of Part I looks at financial market debt instruments, which are the main products issued and traded by banks. Chapter 3 discusses money market instruments and Chapter 4 is concerned with capital market instruments or bonds. For undergraduate students and junior practitioners we cover elements of financial arithmetic, which are essential to an understanding of ALM, in the Appendix at the back of the book.

"[Cassandra is] a bit like me – an achiever. I've always been an achiever ......I've never actually achieved anything, mind...but I've always been up there with a shout."

– Derek 'Del-Boy' Trotter, "The Jolly Boys Outing"
Only Fools and Horses
BBC TV 1989

CHAPTER

1

Bank Business and Bank Capital

Banking has a long and honourable history. Today it encompasses a wide range of activities, of varying degrees of complexity. Whatever the precise business, the common denominators of all banking activities are those of risk, return and the bringing together of the providers of capital. Return on capital is the focus of banking activity. The coordination of all banking activity could be said to be the focus of asset and liability management (ALM), although some practitioners will give ALM a narrower focus. Either way, we need to be familiar with the wide-ranging nature of banking business, and the importance of bank capital. This then acts as a guide for what follows.

In this introductory chapter of the first part of the book, we place ALM in context by describing the financial markets and the concept of bank capital. Subsequent chapters look at money market instruments and the basics of bank financial statements. We begin with a look at the business of banking. We then consider the different types of revenue generated by a bank, the concept of the banking book and the trading book, and financial statements. The chapter concludes with an introduction to the money market, the key area of involvement for an ALM desk.

Banking business

We introduced the different aspects of banking business in the Preface. For the largest banks these aspects are widely varying in nature. For our purposes we may group them together in the form shown in Figure 1.1. Put very simply, "retail" or "commercial" banking covers the more traditional lending and trust activities, while "investment" banking covers trading activity and fee-based income such as stock exchange listing and mergers and acquisition (M&A). The one common objective of all banking activity is return on capital. Depending on the degree of risk it represents, a particular activity will be required to achieve a specified return on the capital it uses. The issue of banking capital is vital to an appreciation of the banking business; entire new business lines (such as securitisation) have been originated in response to a need to generate more efficient use of capital.

As we can see from Figure 1.1, the scope of banking business is vast. The activities range from essentially plain vanilla activity, such as corporate

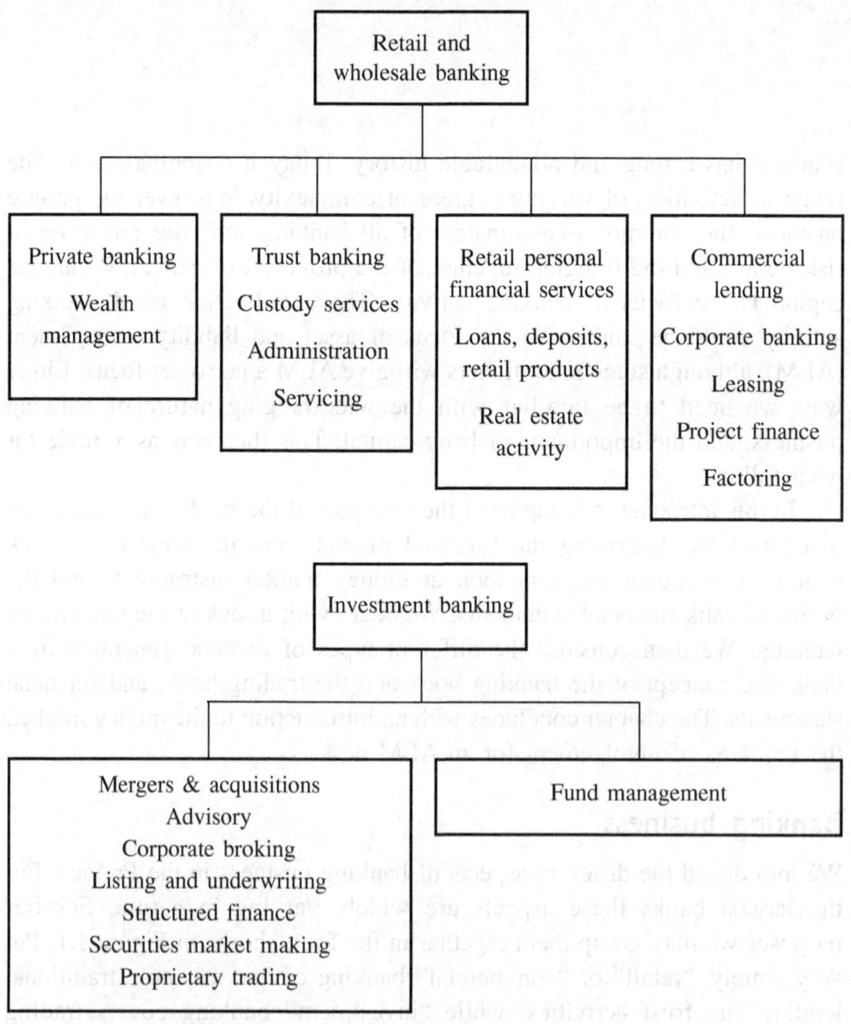

Figure 1.1 Scope of banking activities

lending, to complex transactions such as securitisation and hybrid products trading. There is a vast literature on all these activities, so we do not need to cover them here. However, it is important to have a basic general knowledge of the basic products, so subsequent chapters will introduce these.

ALM is concerned with, among other things, the efficient management of banking capital. It therefore concerns itself with all banking operations, even if the day-to-day contact between the ALM desk (or Treasury desk) with other parts of the bank is remote. The ALM desk will be responsible for the treasury and money markets activities of the entire bank. So if we wish, we could draw a box with ALM in it around the whole of Figure 1.1. This is not to say that the ALM function does all these activities; rather, it is just to make clear that all the various activities represent assets and liabilities for the bank, and one central function is responsible for this side of these activities.

For capital management purposes a bank's business is organised into a "banking book" and a "trading book". We consider them next; first though, a word on bank capital.

Capital

Bank capital is the equity of the bank. It is important as it is the cushion that absorbs any unreserved losses that the bank incurs. By acting as this cushion, it enables the bank to continue operating and thus avoid insolvency or bankruptcy during periods of market correction or economic downturn. When the bank suffers a loss or writes off a loss-making or otherwise economically untenable activity, the capital is used to absorb the loss. This can be done by eating into reserves, freezing dividend payments or (in more extreme scenarios) a write-down of equity capital. In the capital structure, the rights of capital creditors, including equity holders, are subordinated to senior creditors and deposit holders.

Banks occupy a vital and pivotal position in any economy, as suppliers of credit and financial liquidity, so bank capital is important. As such, banks are heavily regulated by central monetary authorities, and their capital is subject to regulatory rules governed by the Bank for International Settlements (BIS), based in Basel, Switzerland. For this reason its regulatory capital rules are often called the Basel rules. Under the original Basel rules ("Basel I") a banking institution was required to hold a minimum capital level of 8% against the assets on its book.[1] Total capital is comprised of:

---

[1] There is more to this than just this simple statement, and we consider this in chapters 26 and 27.

- equity capital;
- reserves;
- retained earnings;
- preference share issue proceeds;
- hybrid capital instruments;
- subordinated debt.

Capital is split into Tier 1 capital and Tier 2 capital. The first three items above comprise Tier 1 capital while the remaining items are Tier 2 capital.

The quality of the capital in a bank reflects its mix of Tier 1 and 2 capital. Tier 1 or "core capital" is the highest quality capital, as it is not obliged to be repaid, and moreover there is no impact on the bank's reputation if it is not repaid. Tier 2 is considered lower quality as it is not "loss absorbing"; it is repayable and also of shorter-term than equity capital. Assessing the financial strength and quality of a particular banking institution often requires calculating key capital ratios for the bank and comparing these to market averages and other benchmarks.

Analysts use a number of ratios to assess bank capital strength. Some of the more common ones are shown in Table 1.1.

Ratio	Calculation	Notes
Core capital ratio	Tier 1 capital/ Risk-weighted assets	A key ratio monitored in particular by rating agencies as a measure of high-quality non-repayable capital, available to absorb losses incurred by the bank
Tier 1 capital ratio	Eligible Tier 1 capital/ Risk-weighted assets	Another important ratio monitored by investors and rating agencies. Represents the amount of high-quality, non-repayable capital available to the bank
Total capital ratio	Total capital/ Risk-weighted assets	Represents total capital available to the bank
Off-balance sheet risk to total capital	Off-balance sheet and contingent risk/ Total capital	Measure of adequacy of capital against off-balance sheet risk including derivatives exposure and committed, undrawn credit lines

Table 1.1 Bank analysis ratios for capital strength
Source: Higson (1995)

Banking and trading books

Banks and financial institutions make a distinction between their activities for capital management, including regulatory capital, purposes. Activities are split into the "banking book" and the "trading book". Put simply, the banking book holds the more traditional banking activities such as commercial banking; for example, loans and deposits. This would cover lending to individuals as well as corporates and other banks, and so will interact with investment banking business.[2] The trading book records wholesale market transactions, such as market making and proprietary trading in bonds and derivatives. Again speaking simply, the primary difference between the two books is that the over-riding principle of the banking book is one of "buy and hold"; that is, a long-term acquisition. Assets may be held on the book for up to 30 years or longer. The trading book is just that, it employs a trading philosophy so that assets may be held for very short terms, less than one day in some cases. The regulatory capital and accounting treatment of each book differs. The primary difference here is that the trading book employs the "mark-to-market" approach to record profit and loss (p&l), which is the daily "marking" of an asset to its market value. An increase or decrease in the mark on the previous day's mark is recorded as an unrealised profit or loss on the book: on disposal of the asset, the realised profit or loss is the change in the mark at disposal compared to its mark at purchase.

The banking book

Traditional banking activity such as deposits and loans is recorded in the banking book. Accounting treatment for the banking book follows the accrual concept, which is accruing interest cash flows as they occur. There is no mark-to-market. The banking book holds assets for which both corporate and retail counterparties as well as banking counterparties are represented. So it is the type of business activity that dictates whether it is placed in the banking book, not the type of counterparty or which department of the bank is conducting it. Assets and liabilities in the banking book generate interest-rate and credit risk exposure for the bank. They also create liquidity and term mismatch ("gap") risks. Liquidity refers to the ease with which an asset can be transformed into cash, as well as to the ease with which funds can be raised in the market. So we see that "liquidity risk" actually refers to two related but separate issues.

[2] For a start, there will be a commonality of clients. A corporate client will borrow from a bank, and may also retain the bank's underwriting or structured finance departments to arrange a share issue or securitisation for it.

All these risks form part of ALM. Interest-rate risk management is a critical part of Treasury policy and ALM, while credit risk policy will be set and dictated by the credit policy of the bank. Gap risk creates an excess or shortage of cash, which must be managed. This is the cash management part of ALM. There is also a mismatch risk associated with fixed-rate and floating-rate interest liabilities. The central role of the financial markets is to enable cash management and interest-rate management to be undertaken efficiently. ALM of the banking book will centre on interest-rate risk management and hedging, and liquidity management. Note how there is no "market risk" for the banking book in principle, because there is no marking-to-market. However, the interest rate exposure of the book creates an exposure that is subject to market movements in interest rates, so in reality the banking book is indeed exposed to market risk.

Trading book

Wholesale market activity, including market making and proprietary trading, is recorded in the trading book. Assets on the trading book can be expected to have a high turnover, although not necessarily so, and are marked-to-market daily. The counterparties to this trading activity can include other banks and financial institutions such as hedge funds, corporates and central banks. Trading book activity generates the same risk exposure as that on the banking book, including market risk, credit risk and liquidity risk. It also creates a need for cash management. Much trading book activity involves derivative instruments, as opposed to "cash" products. Derivatives include futures, swaps and options. These can be equity, interest-rate, credit, commodity, foreign exchange (FX), weather and other derivatives. Derivatives are known as "off-balance sheet" instruments because they are recorded off the (cash) balance sheet. Their widespread use and acceptance has greatly improved the efficiency of the risk exposure hedging process, for banks and other institutions alike.

Off-balance sheet transactions refer to "contingent liabilities", which are so-called because they refer to a future exposure contracted now. These are not only derivatives contracts such as interest-rate swaps or writing an option, but include guarantees such as a credit line to a third-party customer or a group subsidiary company. These represent a liability for the bank that may be required to be honoured at some future date. In most cases they do not generate cash inflow or outflow at inception, unlike a cash transaction, but represent future exposure. If a credit line is drawn on, it represents a cash outflow and that transaction is then recorded on the balance sheet.

EXAMPLE 1.1 The first banks[3]

Banks have a long and interesting history, and for many centuries have been the leader for economies to follow. The first records of banks come from Ancient Greece. Many private and civic entities conducted various financial transactions in the temple banks. These included loans, deposits, currency exchanges and coin validation. There is also evidence of credit, which was when a Greek port would write a credit note in exchange for the payment of a client. The port would hold the money in the temple for the customer who paid him the money, and he could collect the money in another city when he cashed in the credit note. This would save him having to carry around the gold all the time, because he could collect the money in a different city. This gave rise to a risk of being unbalanced in money at certain times. In Ancient Rome the art of banking was developed to include charging interest on loans, and paying interest on deposits.

The first bank to offer most of the basic banking functions known today was the *Bank of Barcelona* in Spain. Founded by merchants in 1401, this bank held deposits, exchanged currency, and carried out lending operations. It also introduced the bank cheque. Modern banking was introduced in what is now Italy. In the 15th century the Lombards, a group of bankers from the north of Italy began to apply accounting to work around a religious moral repugnance of usury. Accounting principles were used to keep a record of loans, and the loan was paid back "voluntarily". The oldest surviving bank today is *Monte dei Paschi di Siena*, which opened in 1472.

Modern British economic and financial history is usually traced back to the coffee houses of London. The London Royal Exchange was established in 1565 as a centre of commerce for the City of London, and trading of all sorts of commodities took place on its floors. Banking offices at that time were usually located near centers of trade, like the Royal Exchange. In London, individuals could now participate in the lucrative East India trade by purchasing

[3] This section was co-written with Darrell Hellmuth, Year 10, Wilmington Grammar School, Dartford, Kent, and Dan Slater, 2nd year mathematics, University College, Oxford.

bills of credit from these banks, but the price they received for commodities was dependent on the ships returning and on the cargo they carried. The commodities market was very volatile for this reason.

Aside from the central Bank of England, which was founded in 1694, early English banks were privately owned goldsmiths rather than stock-issuing firms. Bank failures were common; so in the early 19th century, stock-issuing banks, with a larger capital base, were encouraged as a means of stabilising the industry. By 1833 these corporate banks were permitted to accept and transfer deposits in London, although they were prohibited from issuing money, a prerogative monopolised by the Bank of England. Corporate banking flourished after legislation in 1858 approved limited liability for stock-issuing banks.

c. 3000 – c. 2000 BC	Development of Banking in Mesopotamia
c. 350 BC	Many banking services offered in Ancient Greece
476 AD	Roman Empire falls. Coins cease to be used as medium of exchange in Britain
1232 – 1253	Gold coins are issued by several Italian states
1401	Bank of Barcelona founded
1403	Charging interest on loans is ruled legal in Florence
1407	Bank of St George, Genoa, founded
1585	Bank of Genoa founded
1587	Banco di Rialto, Venice, founded
1600	The London East India Company is founded
c. 1660	Goldsmiths' receipts become banknotes in England
1694	Bank of England is founded

Table 1.2 Timeline
Source: YieldCurve.com (www.yieldcurve.com)

Financial statements and ratios

A key information tool for bank analysis is the financial statement, which is comprised of the balance sheet and the profit & loss (p&l) account. Assets on the balance sheet should equal the assets on a bank's ALM report, while receipt of revenue (such as interest and fees income) and payout of costs during a specified period is recorded in the p&l report or income statement.

The balance sheet

The balance sheet is a statement of a company's assets and liabilities as determined by accounting rules. It is a snapshot of a particular point in time, and so by the time it is produced it is already out of date. However, it is an important information statement. A number of management information ratios are used when analysing the balance sheet and these are considered in the next chapter.

In Chapter 2 we use an hypothetical example to illustrate balance sheets. For a bank, there are usually four parts to a balance sheet, as it is split to show separately:

- lending and deposits, or traditional bank business;
- trading assets;
- treasury and interbank assets;
- off-balance sheet assets;
- long-term assets, including fixed assets, shares in subsidiary companies, together with equity and Tier 2 capital.

This is illustrated in Table 1.3. The actual balance sheet of a retail or commercial bank will differ significantly from that of an investment bank, due to the relative importance of their various business lines, but the basic layout will be similar.

Assets	Liabilities
Cash	Short-term liabilities
Loans	Deposits
Financial instruments (long)	Financial instruments (short)
Fixed assets	Long-dated debt
Off-balance sheet (receivables)	Equity
	Off-balance sheet (liabilities)

Table 1.3 Components of a bank balance sheet

Profit & loss report

The income statement for a bank is the p&l report and it records all the income, and losses, during a specified period of time. A bank income statement will show revenues that can be accounted for as either net interest income, fees and commissions, and trading income. The precise mix of these sources will reflect the type of banking institution and the business lines it operates in. Revenue is offset by operating (non-interest) expenses, loan loss provisions, trading losses and tax expense.

A more "traditional" commercial bank such as a United Kingdom (UK) building society will have a much higher dependence on interest revenues than an investment bank that engages in large-scale wholesale capital market business. Investment banks have a higher share of revenue comprised of trading and fee income. Table 1.4 shows the components of a UK retails bank's income statement.

	%	Expressed as percentage of
Core operating income	100	
Net interest income	64	/ core operating income
Commissions and fee income	31	/ core operating income
Trading income	8	/ core operating income
+ Net other operating income	8	/ core operating income
– Operating expenses	61	/ revenues
Personnel	38	/ revenues
Other, depreciation		
– Loan loss provisions	23	/ pre-provision net income
= Net operating income		
+ Other non-operating income		
= Profit before tax		
– Tax		
= Net income		
– Minority interest		
= Attributable income		

Table 1.4 Components of a bank income statement, typical structure for a retail bank
Source: Bank financial statements.

The composition of earnings varies widely among different institutions, Figure 1.2 shows the breakdown for a UK building society and the UK branch of a US investment bank in 2005, as reported in their financial accounts for that year.

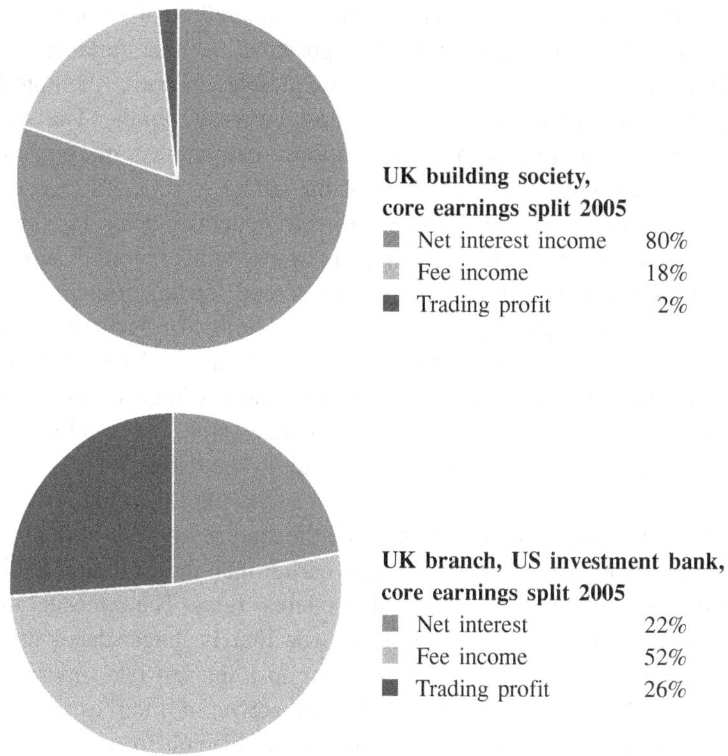

Figure 1.2 Composition of earnings
Source: Bank financial statements.

Net interest income

The traditional source of revenue for retail banks, net interest income (NII) remains as such today (see Figure 1.2). NII is driven by lending and interest-earning asset volumes and the net yield available on these assets after taking into account the cost of funding. While the main focus is on the loan book, the ALM desk will also concentrate on the bank's investment portfolio. The latter will include coupon receipts from money market and bond market assets, and dividends received from any equity holdings.

The cost of funding is a key variable in generating overall NII. For a retail bank the cheapest source of funds is deposits, especially non-interest-bearing deposits such as cheque accounts.[4] Even in an era of high-street competition, the interest payable on short-term liabilities such as instant access deposits is far below the wholesale market interest rate. This is a funding advantage for retail banks when compared to investment banks, which generally do not have a retail deposit base. Other funding sources include capital markets (senior debt), wholesale markets (the interbank money market), securitised markets and covered bonds. The overall composition of funding significantly affects net interest margin, and if constrained, can reduce the activities of the bank.

The risk profile of the asset classes that generate yields for the bank should lead to a range of net interest margins being reported across the sector, such that a bank with a strong unsecured lending franchise should seek significantly higher yields than one investing in secured mortgage loans; this reflects the different risk profiles of the assets. The proportion of NIBLs will also have a significant impact on the net interest margin of the institution. While a high net interest margin is desirable, it should also be an adequate return for the risk incurred in holding the assets.

Bank NII is sensitive to both credit risk and market risk. Interest income is sensitive to changes in interest rates and the maturity profile of the balance sheet. Banks that have assets that mature earlier than their funding liabilities will gain from an environment of rising interest rates. The opposite applies where the asset book has a maturity profile that is longer-dated than the liability book. Note that in a declining or low interest-rate environment, banks may suffer from negative NII irrespective of their asset–liability maturity profile, as it becomes more and more difficult to pass on interest rate cuts to depositors.

While investment banks are less sensitive to changes in rates, as their overall NII expectations are low due to their lower reliance on NII itself, their trading book will also be sensitive to changes in interest rates.

Fee and commission income

Fee revenue is generated from the sale and provision of financial services to customers. The level of fees and commission will be communicated in advance to customers. Fee income, separate from trading income and known as non-interest income, is desirable for banks because it represents a stable

[4] These are referred to as *NIBLs* (non-interest bearing liabilities).

source of revenue that is not exposed to market risk. It is also attractive because it provides an opportunity for the bank to cross-sell new products and services to existing customers, and the provision of these services does not expose the bank to additional credit or market risk. Fee income represents diversification in a bank's revenue base.

Note that although fee-based business may not expose the bank to market risk directly, it does bring with it other risks, and these can include indirect exposure to market risk.[5] In addition, an ability to provide fee-based financial services may require significant investment in infrastructure and human resources.

Trading income

Trading income arises from the capital gain earned from buying and selling financial instruments. These instruments include both cash and derivative (off-balance sheet) instruments, and can arise from undertaking market-making business, which in theory is undertaken to meet client demands, and from proprietary business for the bank's own trading book. Note that interest income earned while holding assets on the trading book should really be considered as NII and not trading income, but sometimes this is not stripped out from the overall trading book p&l. There is no uniformity of approach among banks in this regard.

Trading income is the most volatile form of bank revenue. Even a record of consistent profit in trading over a long period is no guarantee of future losses arising out of market corrections or simply making the wrong bet on financial markets. Trading activity was the first type of banking activity whose risk exposure was measured using the VaR methodology, which replaced duration-based risk measures in the 1990s.

Operating expenses

Banking operating costs typically contain the human resources costs (remuneration and other personnel-related expenses) together with other operating costs such as premises and infrastructure costs, depreciation charges and goodwill.[6] Cost is generally measured as a proportion of revenue. A number of cost–income ratios are used by analysts, some of which are given in Table 1.5.

---

5 For example, a strategy pursued by banks in the 1990s was to merge with or acquire insurance companies, so-called *bancassurance* groups. Although much insurance business is fee-based, the acquisition of insurance portfolios brought with it added market risk to the banking group.

6 These are accounting terms common to all corporate entities, and are not just used to describe bank operating costs.

Ratio	Calculation	Notes
Pre-tax ROE	Pre-tax income / Average shareholders' equity	Measures the pre-tax return on equity. A measure above 20% is viewed as above average and strong
ROE	Attributable net income / Average shareholders' equity	Measures return on equity. A measure above 10% is considered strong
ROA	Net income / Average assets	Measures return on assets. A measure above 1% is considered strong
Cost–income ratio	Non-interest costs / Total net revenues	Non-interest costs minus non-cash items such as goodwill or depreciation of intengible assets. The cost to produce one unit of net interest and non-interest income. The lower the ratio, the more efficient the bank
Net interest margin	Net interest income / Average earning assets	The difference between tax-equivalent yield on earning assets and the rate paid on funds to support those assets, divided by average earning assets
Loan loss provision	Loan-loss provision / Pre-provision, pre-tax income	The proportion of pre-tax income that is being absorbed by loan losses. This is the credit cost of conducting the business
Non-interest income	Non-interest income / Net revenues	Non-interest income includes service charges on deposits, trust fees, advisory fees, servicing fees, net trading profits from trading books, and commissions and fees from off-balance sheet items. Generally, the higher the ratio, the greater the bank's sensitivity to changes in interest rates

Table 1.5 Common bank cost–income ratios

The return on equity (ROE) measure is probably the most commonly encountered, and is usually part of bank strategy, with a target ROE level stated explicitly in management objectives. Note that there is a difference between the accounting ROE and the market return on equity; the latter is calculated as a price return, rather like a standard p&l calculation, which is taken as the difference between market prices between two dates. During the 1990s, and certainly into 2005, the average required ROE was in the order of 15% or higher, with investment banks usually set a higher target of 20%, 22%, or even higher for certain higher risk business. The ROE target needs to reflect the relative risk of different business activity.

The return on assets (ROA) is another common measure of performance. This is calculated as follows:

$$\frac{\text{Current income (Interest income + Fees)}}{\text{Asset value}}.$$

Both financial statement p&l reports and measures such as ROE and ROA are bland calculations of absolute values. They do not make any adjustment for relative risk exposure so cannot stand too much comparison with the equivalent figures of another institution. This is because the risk exposure, not to mention the specific type of business activity, will differ from one bank to another. However, there are general approximate values that serve as benchmarks for certain sectors, such as the 15% ROE level we stated above. Banks also calculate risk-adjusted ratios.

Provisions

Banks expect a percentage of loan assets, and other assets, to suffer loss or become unrecoverable completely. Provisions are set aside out of reserves to cover for these losses each year, and are a charge against the loan revenues of the bank. The size of the provision taken is a function of what write-offs may be required against the loan portfolio in the current portfolio in the current period and in the future, and the size and adequacy of loan loss reserves currently available. In some jurisdictions there are regulatory requirements that dictate the minimum size of the provision.

Provisions fund the bank's loan loss reserve, and the reserve will grow in size when the bank provides more for expected credit losses than the actual amount that is written off. If the bank believes subsequently that the size of the reserve built up is in excess to what is currently required, it may write back a percentage of it.

The money markets

The money markets are part of the global financial system. The various markets that make up this system are all, in one form or another, channels through which fund flows between the users and the suppliers of capital move. This flow of funds takes place in different markets, depending on the characteristics of the funds themselves and the needs of the market participants. The money market is where transactions in short-term funds take place. This is the borrowing and lending of funds that have a repayment date of within 12 months of the loan start date. However, the money market is not just made up of loans or cash products. As we shall see, there is a wide range of instruments used in the market, both cash and *derivative*, and it is these products and the uses to which they are put that are a significant focus of this book.

So, the money market is the centre in which market participants, which can be governments, banks, other corporate institutions, fund managers or individuals, meet to transform a short-term shortage (or surplus) of funds into a surplus (or shortage). As such, the money market enables market participants to manage their liquidity positions.

The suppliers of funds in financial systems worldwide are generally commercial banks, as well as savings institutions such as money market mutual funds. Other institutions such as local authorities and corporations are also long of cash at certain times. The borrowers of funds include the government, banks (again), local authorities and corporations (also, again).

In terms of trading volumes the money markets are the largest and most active market in the world. As money market securities are securities with maturities of up to 12 months, they are short-term debt obligations. Money market debt is an important part of the global financial markets, and facilitates the smooth running of the banking industry, as well as providing working capital for industrial and commercial corporate institutions. The diversity of the money market is such that it provides market users with a wide range of opportunities and funding possibilities, and the market is characterised by the range of products that can be traded within it. Money market instruments allow issuers to raise funds for short-term periods at relatively low interest rates. These issuers include sovereign governments, who issue Treasury bills, corporates issuing commercial paper, and banks issuing bills and certificates of deposit. At the same time investors are attracted to the market because the instruments are highly liquid and carry relatively low credit risk. The Treasury bill (T-bill) market in any country is that country's lowest risk instrument, and consequently carries the lowest yield of any debt instrument. Indeed, the first market that develops in any country is frequently the T-bill market.

Although the money market has traditionally been defined as the market for instruments maturing in one year or less, frequently the money market desks of banks trade instruments with maturities of up to two or three years, both cash and off-balance sheet.[7] In addition to the cash instruments that go to make up the market, the money markets also consist of a wide range of over-the-counter off-balance sheet derivative instruments. These instruments are used mainly to establish future borrowing and lending rates, and to hedge or change existing interest-rate exposure. This activity is carried out by both banks, central banks and corporates. The main derivatives are short-term interest rate futures, forward rate agreements, and short-dated interest rate swaps. But as we shall see, other derivatives like total return swaps are also used.

Financial transactions

Irrespective of the market we are speaking of, all financial systems exist to facilitate one basic transaction: the moving of funds from cash-rich entities to cash-poor ones. This transaction involves the exchange of money for financial assets, or an interest in a financial asset. This exchange can be undertaken directly between participants, via an intermediary or indirectly.

Direct finance

This involves two parties, one of which lends funds directly to the other for an agreed term and rate of interest. This transaction is shown in Figure 1.3. The funds can be lent in exchange for security (known as *collateral*) or on an *unsecured* basis. Direct financing is the simplest method for undertaking a financial transaction. Its drawbacks are that parties must know about each other and each other's requirements; they must also possess sufficient information on their counterparties such that they are satisfied in entering into the transaction. For this reason, direct financing, while very common among larger institutions or where the central government is involved, often gives way to financing via intermediaries.

---

7 The author has personal experience in market-making on a desk that combined cash and derivative instruments of up to two years' maturity, as well as government bonds of up to three years' maturity. In his current capacity on the Treasury desk he is part of trades in loans and deposits and overnight-index swaps of up to 18 months' maturity and medium-term notes (MTNs) of up to 24 months' maturity.

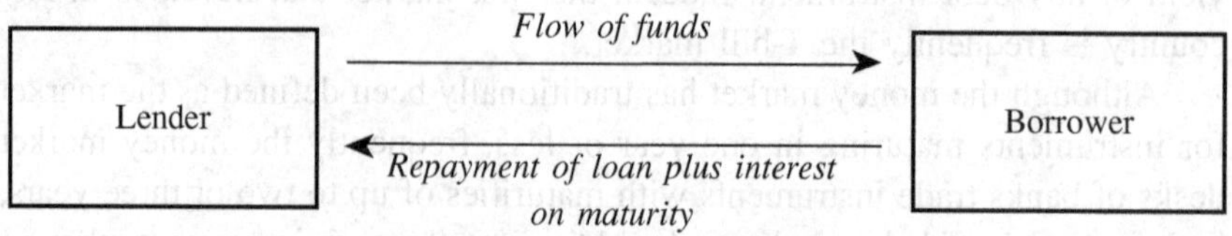

Figure 1.3 Direct financing

Financing via intermediary

In terms of volume, the majority of money market transactions are carried out in semi-direct form, via intermediaries. We include banks among our list of intermediaries, which can be distinguished into two types:

- Brokers: a broker simply acts to bring lenders and borrowers together, and charges a commission for doing so. However, the involvement of a broker introduces greater transparency and information into the market.
- Market-makers: known as *dealers* in the US market, who also serve as intermediaries between borrowers and lenders, but take the cash position onto their own books and charge a two-way price in this cash to all other market participants. As such, dealers run a risk exposure position in the cash they own directly, as their profit depends on the value of the cash, which fluctuates in line with market dynamics and supply and demand.

Of course, the same institution can act in both capacities, according to who its counterparties are or what market it is trading in.

This transaction is illustrated in Figure 1.4.

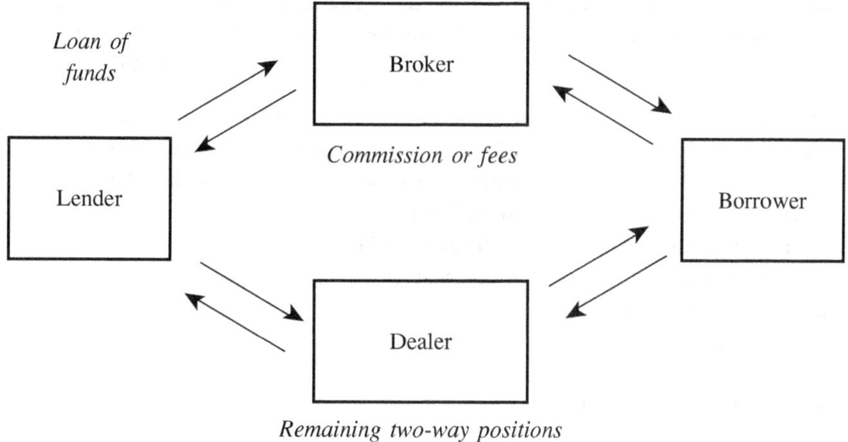

Figure 1.4 Intermediary financing

Indirect financing

The existence of an active secondary market in money market securities reflects the extent of indirect financing. This covers a number of areas, such as banks issuing their own securities to fund their loans to corporates and individuals, and the trading of these securities after the initial finance has been raised. Financial intermediaries that are part of this market include commercial banks, insurance companies, credit institutions such as automobile manufacturer credit arms, finance companies, savings and loan associations (known as building societies in the United Kingdom), pension funds, mutual funds and so on. Their role in the market is to act essentially as both borrowers and lenders themselves in a way that serves the market's ultimate borrowers and lenders. Table 1.6 lists the types of firms involved in indirect financing.

Deposit-taking institutions	Contractual institutions	Wholesale market counterparties
Commercial banks	Life insurance companies	Investment banks
Retail banks	Life assurance companies	Securities houses ("Broker-Dealers")
Non-banking institutions:	Pension fund managers	Brokers
– Savings & Loan ("Building Societies")	Mutual funds ("Unit Trusts")	
– Credit Unions	Investment trust companies	
Mutual funds ("Unit Trusts")		
– Money market funds		
Finance companies		
Government-lending institutions		

Table 1.6 Financial institutions and intermediaries active in the money markets

Characteristics of the money market

The money market, worldwide, acts as a channel through which market participants exchange financial assets for cash, or raise cash on a secured and unsecured basis. Its key defining point is that it serves short-term needs. This is the short-term financing needs of participants who are short cash, and the short-term investment needs of participants who are temporarily long cash. Figure 1.5 shows a stylised structure of the money market as it would exist in most countries.

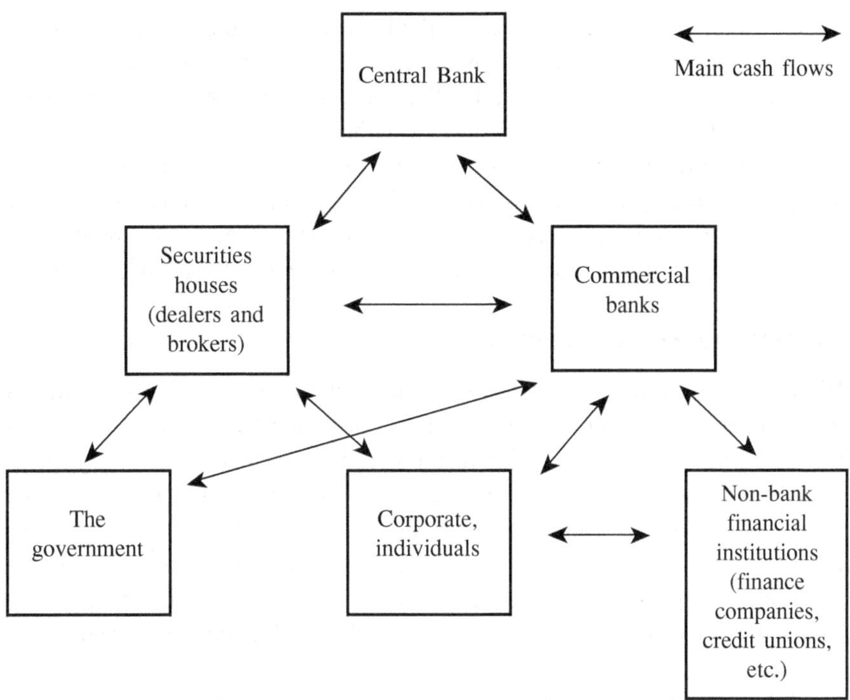

Figure 1.5 The structure of the money market

Interest rates set in the money market (well, one key interest rate) act as benchmarks and guidelines for all other rates used. The importance of the money markets to this activity is often over-looked, but cannot be denied.

The size of the market means that it, in most countries and certainly in all developed economies, carries considerable breadth and depth. It is possible to transact very large volumes of business and for this not to impact the money market in an observable way. Like most financial markets these days, money market dealing is "over-the-counter", meaning it is not conducted on an exchange but over the telephone or computer terminal.

Interest rates in the money market – the rates at which participants borrow and lend funds – are set by the market and reflect a number of factors, from macroeconomic issues such as global supply and demand, to more market-specific issues such as liquidity and transparency. There are a large number of interest rates, for different products and different counterparties. The cornerstone of the market's various rates is the T-bill rate. T-bills are issued by the government to raise short-term cash (the typical maturity is 90 days). Because the bills are backed by the government, they carry no (or little) default risk. Hence the rates payable on these bills are the lowest in any market. All other rates in the market (and the bond market) will be at a positive spread over the T-bill rate.

In the following chapters we look in detail at the various instruments that go to make up the money markets. For beginners, we include a primer on financial markets arithmetic in the Appendix at the back of the book. This is required background for an understanding of interest rate mechanics.

Money market conventions

We will see from the following pages that many money market instruments trade under similar market conventions. For example, for most currencies the basis used to calculate interest on a loan assumes a 360-day year, although sterling is an important exception to this. Again, while it is the norm for many currencies to float freely, their exchange rates to other currencies set by market supply and demand, some other important currencies are pegged to the US dollar and move with that currency. A very small number of currencies are not convertible and cannot be traded in the market.

Table 1.7 shows the characteristics of a sample of world currencies. It serves to highlight the individual detail differences that exist in the market. Terms such as "day-count" and "value date" will be fully explained in the following chapters.

Practitioners with access to Bloomberg can look up individual currency details by selecting:

[Ticker] [Currency yellow key] DES <Go>.

We show this page for Australian dollars, Brazilian reals and Egyptian pounds in Figures 1.6, 1.7 and 1.8 respectively.

Country	Currency	FX rate	Day-count	Spot FX value date
Argentina	Peso	Free-floating	ACT/360	T+2
Australia	Dollar	Free-floating	ACT/365	T+2
Brazil	Real	Free-floating	ACT/360	T+3
Canada	Dollar	Free-floating	ACT/365 (domestic)	T+1
			ACT/360 (int'l)	T+2
Czech Republic	Koruna	Free-floating	ACT/360	T+2
Denmark	Krone	Free-floating	ACT/360	T+2
Egypt	Pound	Free-floating	ACT/360	T+2
Euro Area[1]	Euro	Free-floating	ACT/360	T+2
Hong Kong	Dollar	Pegged to USD, HKD 7.70 per USD 1	ACT/365	T+2
Hungary	Forint	Managed floating	ACT/360	T+2
Japan	Yen	Free-floating	ACT/360	T+2
Estonia	Kroon	Pegged to euro	ACT/360	T+2
Latvia	Lats	Pegged to Special Drawing Right (SDR)[2]	ACT/360	T+2
Lithuania	Litas	Pegged to euro, LTL 3.4528 to EUR 1	ACT/360	T+2
Malaysia	Ringgit	Pegged to US dollar	ACT/365	T+2
New Zealand	Dollar	Free-floating	ACT/365	T+2
Norway	Krone	Free-floating	ACT/360	T+2
Poland	Zloty	Free-floating	ACT/365	T+2
Singapore	Dollar	Managed floating	ACT/365	T+2
South Africa	Rand	Free-floating	ACT/365	T+2
South Korea	Won	Free-floating	ACT/365	T+2
Switzerland	Franc	Free-floating	ACT/360	T+2
Taiwan	Dollar	Free-floating	ACT/365	T+2
Thailand	Baht	Free-floating	ACT/365	T+2
United Kingdom	Pound	Free-floating	ACT/365	T+2
United States	Dollar	Free-floating	ACT/360	T+2

1 Austria, Belgium, Finland, France, Germany, Greece, Ireland, Italy, Luxembourg, Netherlands, Portugal, Slovenia and Spain.

2 The "currency" of the International Monetary Fund.

Table 1.7 Selected global currency conventions
Sources: Bloomberg L.P. and Reuters

```
AUD ↓  .7495  +.0056  TTOL .7493/.7497 TTOL        Curncy DES
At 9:35 Op .7448  Hi .7498 Lo .7441  Prev .7439      Value 4/21/04
                     Description                       Page 1/1
AUD-USD        AUSTRALIAN DOLLAR SPOT           1 Dollar = 100 Cents
The Australian dollar is the official currency of the Commonwealth of Australia.
The conventional market quotation is the number of US dollars per Australian
dollar.  It is an independent, free-floating currency.
1)Economic Statistics                AUSTRALIA
9)  GDP                190200 12/31/03   Region:    Pacific Rim
10) Unemploymnt Rate      5.6 03/31/04   Capital:   Canberra
11) CPI                 142.80 12/31/03   Population          19.55 12/31/02
12) Total Foreign De    360688 09/30/03   Area:        2966155
13) Exports (MLN)     11639.00 02/29/04   4)MAPS  Map
14) Imports (MLN)     13355.00 02/29/04   5)CDR   Calendar
2)News,Research & Market Information    Quick Statistics
15) Current News                         6)GPO 52Wk High     0.80 02/18/04
16) Bond Market News                           52Wk Low      0.61 04/21/03
17) Equity Market News                   History Since    12/13/83
18) Economic News                        Day count        ACT/365
19) Economist Intelligence Unit          Value Date       04/21/04
20) Economic Releases
                                         7)PCS  Composite(NY)
3)Related Instruments                    8)VOTE
Australia 61 2 9777 8600     Brazil 5511 3048 4500     Europe 44 20 7330 7500     Germany 49 69 920410
Hong Kong 852 2977 6000 Japan 81 3 3201 8900 Singapore 65 6212 1000 U.S. 1 212 318 2000 Copyright 2004 Bloomberg L.P.
                                                                   G926-802-0 19-Apr-04  9:35:26
```

Figure 1.6 Bloomberg page DES for Australian dollars


```
BRL     2.9130Y as of close  4/16                      Curncy DES
                     Description                       Page 1/3
USD-BRL        BRAZILIAN REAL SPOT              1 Real = 100 Centavos
The Brazilian real is the official currency of the Federative Republic of
Brazil.  The conventional market quotation is the number of reals per US dollar.
It is an independent free-floating currency.
1)Economic Statistics                  BRAZIL
9)  GDP% Qtr/Qtr          1.50 12/31/03   Region:    South America
10) Unemploymnt Rate      7.08 11/30/02   Capital:   Brasilia
11) CPI                    .12 03/31/04   Population          179.91 12/31/02
12) Government Debt  926680.65 02/29/04   Area:        3286500
13) Total revenue      13053.0 11/30/99   4)MAPS  Map
14) Total Expenditur   12742.0 11/30/99   5)CDR   Calendar
2)News,Research & Market Information    Quick Statistics
15) Current News                         6)GPO 52Wk High       3.11 08/04/03
16) Equity Market News                         52Wk Low        2.77 01/13/04
17) Economist Intelligence Unit          History Since    1/15/92
18) Economic Statistics                  Day count        ACT/360
19) IMF Data                             Value Date       04/22/04
20) Related Instruments
                                         7)PCS  Composite(NY)
3)Related Instruments                    8)VOTE
Australia 61 2 9777 8600     Brazil 5511 3048 4500     Europe 44 20 7330 7500     Germany 49 69 920410
Hong Kong 852 2977 6000 Japan 81 3 3201 8900 Singapore 65 6212 1000 U.S. 1 212 318 2000 Copyright 2004 Bloomberg L.P.
                                                                   G926-802-0 19-Apr-04  9:35:52
```

Figure 1.7 Bloomberg page DES for Brazilian real

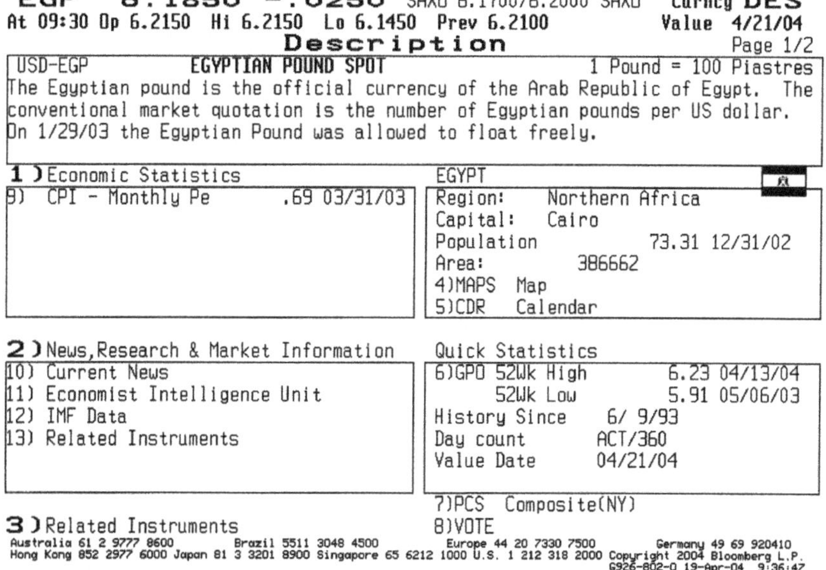

Figure 1.8 Bloomberg page DES for Egyptian pound

CHAPTER 2

Financial Statements and Ratio Analysis

As essential background we present an introductory chapter on financial statements and ratio analysis. Practitioners may wish to skip this chapter and move straight to the introduction to ALM in Chapter 5.

Firm financial structure and company accounts

A corporate entity or *firm* is governed by the types of equity capital it can issue as stipulated in its *memorandum* and *articles of association*. In the past, in the UK market at least, firms would issue different classes of shares, including "A" shares that carried restricted voting rights. However, this was not encouraged by the Stock Exchange and the most common form of share in the market is the *ordinary share*, which is known as *common stock* in the US market. The holders of ordinary shares are entitled to certain privileges, including the right to vote in the running of the company, the right to dividend payments and the right to subscribe to further shares ahead of non-shareholders, in the event of a new issue. Dividends are only payable after liabilities to all other parties with a claim on the company, including bondholders, have been discharged. Shares are issued with a par value, but this has no relevance to their analysis and is frequently for a token amount such as £0.10 or £0.25.

We begin by considering the financial structure of the firm, which traditionally was of vital importance to shareholders. We can consider the importance to shareholders of the financial structure of a firm by comparing the interests of shareholders with those of bondholders. Unlike shareholders, bondholders have a prior contractual claim on the firm. This means that as and when the contractual claim is covered, bondholders have no further interest in the firm. Put another way, as long as the firm is able to meet its contractual commitments, which are interest and principal payments owing to creditors, bondholders will be satisfied.[1] On the other hand, shareholders have what is known as a *residual* claim on the firm. As its owners, they will be concerned about the overall value of the firm and that this is being maximised. Hence they are (in theory) keenly concerned with the financial structure of their firm, as well as its long-term prospects.

We begin therefore, with a review of company accounts. Firms are required by law to produce accounts, originally under the belief that owners should be kept informed about how the directors are managing the company. In the United Kingdom for example this is stipulated in section 226 of the *Companies Act 1985*, which updated previous versions of the Act.

The balance sheet

The balance sheet is a snapshot in time of the asset value of a company. We are familiar with the two sources of corporate financing in a developed economy; namely, debt finance sourced from lenders including banks, finance houses and directly from the market through bond issues; and equity finance sourced from shareholders and retained profits. Put simply, once a corporate entity has repaid all its debt financing, remaining funds are the property of the shareholders. Hence we may state:

$$\text{Assets} - \text{Liabilities} = \text{Shareholders' funds.}$$

Again in simple terms, the valuation of one share in the company is a function of the total assets of the company less the liabilities. So, as a firm's assets decrease in value, shareholders will experience a decrease in their share value, while the opposite occurs if there is an increase in firm assets. This explains why a corporate balance sheet always balances.

Company balance sheets may be put together using one of three different approaches; namely, *historic cost book value*, *current cost* or *market value*. Equity analysts' preference is for the market value basis, which records the value of assets and liabilities in the balance sheet using current market values. For liabilities this is relatively straightforward to undertake if the firm is listed on an exchange and there is a liquid market in its shares; the net value of the firm can be taken to be the difference between the market value of the firm's ordinary shares and the *book value* of the shares. The

[1] This is perhaps too simplistic: bondholders will also be concerned if any developments affect the *perceived* ability of the firm to meet its future liabilities, such as a change of credit rating. Such events will affect the value of the bonds issued by the firm, which is why they will be of concern to bondholders.

latter is the par value of the shares together with the share premium and accumulated retained earnings. It is more problematic to determine a market value for firm assets, however; for instance, what is the market value of two-year-old photocopying machines? In fact the majority of incorporated institutions do not have their shares traded on an exchange and so a market value balance sheet is rarely released.

The most common balance sheet approach uses the historic cost book value approach, in which assets and liabilities are valued at their original cost, known as historic cost. The net worth of the company is calculated as the sum of the share capital and retained profits (reserves). It is rare to observe balance sheets presented using the current cost book value approach, which values assets at current replacement cost.

An hypothetical company balance sheet is shown in Figure 2.1.

Note that the balance sheet orders assets and liabilities in terms of their maturity. Fixed assets are recorded first, followed by current assets less current liabilities. This value, the net current assets, indicates if the company is able to cover its short-term liabilities with its current assets. The net current asset value is added to fixed assets value, resulting in the value of the firm's assets less current liabilities. The balance sheet then records long-term liabilities, and subtracted from the previous figure, shows the total value of the company once all liabilities have been discharged. This is also known as shareholders' funds, and would be distributed to them in the event that the firm was wound up at this point. Shareholders' funds are represented by the capital and reserves entries. Share capital is the sum of the issued share par value and the share premium. These are defined as follows:

- paid-up share capital – the nominal value of the shares, which represents the total liabilities of the shareholders in the event of winding up, and which has been paid by shareholders;
- share premium – the difference between market value of the shares and the nominal or par value.

The entry for "profit and loss account" sometimes appears as *retained earnings*. This is the accumulated profit over the life of the company that has not been paid out as dividend to shareholders, but has been reinvested back into the company. The profit and loss account is part of the firm's reserves, and its calculation is arrived at via a separate financial statement.

Balance sheet as at 31 December 2005		
	£m	£m
Fixed assets		675
Long-term investments		98
		773
Current assets		
Stock	365	
Debtors	523	
Cash	18	
	906	
Short-term liabilities		
Creditors	355	
Short-dated loans	109	
Bank overdraft	88	
Corporation tax	91	
Planned dividend	66	
	709	
Net current assets		197
Total assets less current liabilities		970
Liabilities falling due after 12 months		
Creditors	28	
Long-dated debt, bonds	400	(428)
Net assets		542
Share capital		
Ordinary shares issued		170
Preference shares		30
		200
Capital and reserves		
Paid-up capital	25	
Share premium	109	
Profit and loss account (reserves)	208	342
Shareholders' funds		542

Fixed assets include items such as factory buildings, property holdings and so on. Short-term liabilities are those falling due within 12 months.

Figure 2.1 Hypothetical corporate balance sheet

The profit and loss (p&l) account

The p&l account, also known as the *income statement*, shows the profit generated by a firm, separating out the amount paid to shareholders and that retained in the company. Hence the p&l account is also a statement of retained earnings. Unlike the balance sheet, which is a snapshot in time, the income statement is a rolling total of retained profit from the last accounting period to the current one. Generally this period is one year.

The calculation of the p&l account[2] is relatively straightforward, recording income less expenses. A firm's income is generated from its business activities, and so excludes share capital or loan funding. The expenses are the daily costs of running the business, and so exclude items such as plant and machinery, which are considered "capital" expenditure and recorded as fixed assets in the balance sheet. Due to the different accounting conventions and bases in use, it is possible for two identical companies to produce very different p&l statements. This is a complex and vast subject, well outside the scope of this book, and so we will not enter into it. A good overview of accounting principles in the context of corporate finance is given in Higson (1995).

An hypothetical p&l statement is shown at Figure 2.2.

In the context of a p&l statement the *net profit* is the gross profit minus business operating expenses. This is an accurate measure of the profit that the firm's managers have generated. The more efficiently managers run the business, the lower its expenses will be, and correspondingly the higher the net profit will be. Tax expenses are outside the control of the firm's managers and so appear afterwards. *Extraordinary items* are deemed to be those generating income that are outside the ordinary business activities of the company, and are expected to be one-off or rare occurrences. This might include the disposal of a subsidiary, for example.

---

[2] Strictly speaking, it is a profit *or* loss account, as the firm would have made one or the other in the accounting period.

	£m	£m	£m
Operating revenue	737		
Operating costs	(389)		
Gross operating profit		348	
Expenses			
Administration	(19)		
Sales	(67)		
Financial	(27)		
		(113)	
Net profit		235	
Taxation		(78)	
Profit on ordinary activities after tax		157	
Extraordinary items		—	
		157	
Dividends			30
Retained profit			127
Retained profit brought forward			81
Retained profit carried forward			208

Figure 2.2 Hypothetical corporate p&l statement

Consolidated accounts

Consolidated accounts are produced when a company has one or more subsidiaries; the accounts of the individual undertakings are combined into a single consolidated account for shareholders. In the United Kingdom this is required under the *Companies Act 1985*, based on the belief that a company's business will be closely linked to that of any subsidiary that it owns, and therefore its shareholders require financial statements on the combined entity. At the same time the subsidiaries also produce their balance sheet and p&l account.

Ratio analysis

Ratio analysis is used heavily in bank financial analysis. In this section we present a review of the general application of ratio analysis and its use in peer group analysis.

Overview of ratio analysis

A number of performance measures are used as management information in the financial analysis of corporations. Generally they may be calculated from published accounts. The following key indicators are used by most listed companies to monitor their performance:

- return on capital employed;
- profit on sales;
- sales multiple on capital employed;
- sales multiple of fixed assets;
- sales per employee;
- profit per employee.

These indicators are all related and it is possible to measure the impact of an improvement in one of them on the others. Return on capital employed (ROCE) is defined in a number of ways, the two most common being return on net assets (RONA) and return on equity (ROE). RONA measures the overall return on capital irrespective of the long-term source of that capital, while ROE measures return on shareholders' funds only, thereby ignoring interest payments to providers of debt capital. Focusing on RONA, which gives an indication of the return generated from net assets (that is, fixed assets and current assets minus current liabilities), analysts frequently split this into return on sales and sales multiples. Such measures are commonly calculated for quoted and unquoted companies, and are used in the comparison of performance between different companies.

We illustrate the calculation and use of these ratios in the next section.

Using ratio analysis

In Figures 2.3 and 2.4 we show the published accounts for a fictitious financial institution, Constructa plc. These are the balance sheet and p&l account. From the information in the accounts we are able to calculate the RONA, return on sales and sales multiples ratios, shown in Table 2.1. Notes to the accounts are given in Figure 2.5.

	Notes	2000	1999	1998
		£m	£m	£m
Fixed assets		97.9	88.2	79.4
Current assets				
Stock		80.6	67.3	65.4
Debtors	(2)	44.3	40.5	39.6
Cash		2.4	2.7	1.4
		127.3	110.5	106.4
Creditors: amounts due within one year	(3)	104.8	85.8	70.0
Net current assets		22.5	24.7	36.4
Total assets less current liabilities		120.4	112.9	115.8
Creditors: amounts due after one year	(3)	31.4	36.9	35.5
		89.0	76.0	80.3
Capital and reserves				
Paid-up share capital	(4)	15.0	15.0	15.0
Share premium account		45.5	37.2	46.1
Profit and loss account		28.5	23.8	19.2
Shareholders' funds		89.0	76.0	80.3

Note: Explanantions for (2), (3) and (4) are given in Figure 2.5.

Figure 2.3 Constructa plc balance sheet for the year ended 31 December 2000

	Notes	2000	1999	1998
		£m	£m	£m
Turnover		251.6	233.7	211.0
Cost of sales		118.2	109.3	88.7
Gross profit		133.4	124.4	122.3
Operating expenses		109.0	102.7	87.9
Operating profit		24.4	21.7	34.4
Interest payable	(1)	7.6	6.2	7.1
Profit before tax		16.8	15.5	27.3
Tax liability		5.04	4.65	8.19
Shareholders' profit		11.8	10.8	19.1
Dividends		7.1	6.2	8.5
Reserves		4.7	4.6	10.6
Earnings per share		7.87	7.27	12.7

Note: Explanation for (1) is in Figure 2.5.

Figure 2.4 Constructa plc p&l account for the year ended 31 December 2000

	2000	1999	1998
	£m	£m	£m
(1) Interest payable			
Bank loans and short-term loans	5.8	4.1	5.4
Hire purchase	1.0	1.0	1.0
Leases and other loans	0.8	1.1	0.7
	7.6	6.2	7.1
(2) Debtors			
Trade debtors	34.3	31.8	32.1
Other debtors	10	8.7	7.5
	44.3	40.5	39.6

(3) Creditors: amounts due within one year			
Bank loans	31.7	26.0	21.1
Bond	7.0	7.0	7.0
Trade creditors	30.6	28.4	19.4
Tax and national insurance	10.8	6.8	3.8
Leases	3.5	2.6	11.7
Other creditors	8.9	4.1	1.4
Accruals	6.8	5.8	1.6
Dividend	5.5	5.1	4.0
	104.8	85.8	70.0
(3) Creditors: amounts due after one year			
Bank loans	12.1	11.8	10.2
Bond	7.0	7.0	7.0
Leases	8.9	9.4	9.1
Other creditors	3.4	8.7	9.2
	31.4	36.9	35.5

(4) Paid-up share capital
10p ordinary shares, 150 million

Figure 2.5 Constructa plc: notes to the accounts

Ratio	Calculation	2000	1999	1998
RONA %	(3)/(5) × 100	20.3%	19.2%	29.7%
Return on sales %	(3)/(4) × 100	9.7%	9.3%	16.3%
Sales multiple (x)	(4)/(5)	2.1x	2.1x	1.8x
	Source	**£m**	**£m**	**£m**
(1) Profit before tax	p&l account	16.8	15.5	27.3
(2) Interest payable	p&l account	7.6	6.2	7.1
(3) Profit before interest and tax	(1) + (2)	24.4	21.7	34.4
(4) Sales ("turnover")	p&l account	251.6	233.7	211.0
(5) Net assets	Balance sheet	120.4	112.9	115.8

Table 2.1 Constructa plc RONA ratio measures

From Table 2.1 we see that Constructa's RONA measure was 20.3% in 2000; however, on its own this figure is meaningless. In order to gauge the relative importance of this measure we would have to compare it to previous years' figures, to see if any trend was visible. Other useful comparisons would be to the same measure for Constructa's competitor companies, as well as industry sector averages. From the information available here, it is possible only to make an historical comparison. We see that the measure has fallen considerably from the 29.7% figure in 1998, but that the most recent year has improved from the year before. The sales margin shows exactly the same pattern; however, the sales generation figure has not decreased. During a period of falling return such as this, which is commonly encountered during a recession, a company would analyse its asset base, with a view to increasing the sales generation ratio and countering the decrease in decreasing margin ratio.

This illustration is a very basic one. Any management-level ratio analysis would need to look at a higher level if it is to provide any meaningful insight. We consider this in the next section.

Management-level ratio analysis

Return on equity (ROC)

We now consider a number of performance measures that are used in corporate-level analysis. Table 2.2 shows performance for a UK-listed company in terms of ROE. The terms we have considered, together with a few we have not, are shown as a historical trend. "Asset turnover" refers to the sales generation or sales multiple, while "leverage factor" is a measure of the *gearing* level, which we consider shortly.

Performance measure	**1999**	**1998**	**1997**	**1996**	**1995**
Asset turnover (sales generation)	2.01	1.97	1.85	1.91	1.79
Return on net sales	4.26%	4.43%	3.99%	4.77%	4.12%
Return on net assets(1)	8.56%	8.73%	7.38%	9.11%	7.37%
Leverage factor (gearing)	2.43	2.54	2.83	2.95	2.71
Return on equity(2)	20.80%	22.17%	20.89%	26.87%	19.97%

(1) This is Asset turnover × Return on net sales.

(2) This is Return on Net assets × Leverage factor.

Table 2.2 UK plc corporate performance 1995–1999

Our analysis of the anonymous UK plc shows how ROE is linked to RONA, which we illustrated in the earlier analysis. How do the figures turn out for the hypothetical bank Constructa plc? These are listed in Table 2.3.

Ratio	Calculation	2000	1999	1998
RONA %	See Table 2.1	20.3%	19.2%	29.7%
Return on sales %	See Table 2.1	9.7%	9.3%	16.3%
Sales multiple (x)	See Table 2.1	2.1x	2.1x	1.8x
ROE %	(6)/(7) × 100	13.26%	14.21%	23.78%
Gearing (x)	(5)/(7)	1.35x	1.49x	1.44x
	Source	**£m**	**£m**	**£m**
(1) Profit before tax	p&l account	16.8	15.5	27.3
(2) Interest payable	p&l account	7.6	6.2	7.1
(3) Profit before interest and tax	(1) + (2)	24.4	21.7	34.4
(4) Sales ("turnover")	p&l account	251.6	233.7	211.0
(5) Net assets	Balance sheet	120.4	112.9	115.8
(6) Shareholders' profit	p&l account	11.8	10.8	19.1
(7) Shareholders' funds	Balance sheet	89.0	76.0	80.3

Table 2.3 Constructa plc corporate-level ratios

Unlike our actual examples from the anonymous UK plc, the ratios for Constructa plc do not work out as a product of lower level ratios. This is because different profit measures have been used to calculate the RONA and ROE; this is deliberate. With RONA we wish to measure the profit generated by the business irrespective of the source of funds used in generating this profit. ROE on the other hand measures profit attributable to shareholders, so we use the profit after tax and interest figure. The actual results illustrate a downtrend in the ROE and senior management will be concerned about this. However, this is outside the scope of this chapter. We consider gearing next.

Gearing

In Table 2.2 we encountered a leverage ratio, known as gearing in the United Kingdom. We also observed that gearing combined with RONA results in

ROE. Put simply, gearing is the ratio of debt capital to equity capital, and measures the extent of indebtedness of a company. Gearing ratios are used by analysts and investors because they indicate the impact on ordinary shareholders' earnings of a change in operating profit. For a company with high gearing, such a change in profit can have a disproportionate impact on shareholders' earnings because more of the profit has to be used to service debt. There is no one "right" level of gearing, but at some point the level will be high enough to raise both shareholders' and rating agency concerns, as doubts creep in about the company's ability to meet its debt interest obligations.[3] The acceptable level of gearing for any company is dependent on a number of issues, including the type of business it is involved in, the average gearing level across similar companies, the stage of the business cycle (companies with high gearing levels are more at risk if the economy is heading into recession), the level of and outlook for interest rates and so on. The common view is that a firm with a historically good track record, and which is less prone to the effects of changes in the business cycle, can afford to be more highly geared than a company that does not boast these features.

As the values for debt and equity capital can be measured in more than one way, so a company's gearing level can take more than one value. We illustrate this below. Table 2.4 shows hypothetical company results.

	£m
Short-term debt	190
Long-term debt	250
Preference shares	35
Shareholders' funds	500
Cash at bank	89
Market value of long-term debt	276
Market value of shareholders' funds	2,255

Table 2.4 Hypothetical company results

3 A good illustration of this was the experience of telecommunications companies after they borrowed heavily in the debt capital market to pay for so-called "third-generation" mobile phone licences, which were auctioned off by respective European governments. As a result of the multi-billion dollar sums involved in the purchase of each licence, some of the telecoms companies saw their credit ratings downgraded by Moody's and S&P (in the case of BT plc, to one level above non-investment grade) as concerns were raised about their resulting high gearing levels.

From the data in Table 2.4 it is possible to calculate a number of different gearing ratios. These are shown in Table 2.5. So any individual measure of gearing is essentially meaningless unless it is also accompanied by a note of how it was calculated.

Measure	Gearing
Long-term debt / Equity [250/(35 + 595)]	39.7%
Short-term and long-term debt / Shareholders' funds [(190 + 250) / 595]	74.0%
Short-term and long-term debt less cash at bank / Shareholders' funds [(190 + 250 − 89) / 595]	59.0%
Market value of long-term debt / Market value of equity [276 / 1,977]	14.0%

Table 2.5 Gearing ratios

Market-to-book and price–earnings ratio

The remaining performance measures we wish to consider are the market-to-book ratio (MB) and the price–earnings or p/e ratio. It was not possible to calculate these for the hypothetical Constructa plc because we did not have a publicly quoted share price for it.[4] However, these ratios are widely used and quoted by analysts and investors. For valuation purposes, they are used to obtain an estimated value of a company or subsidiary. Provided we have data for shareholders' earnings and shareholders' funds, as well as MB and p/e figures for comparable companies, it is possible to calculate an approximation of fair market value for an unquoted company.

The p/e ratio is considered to be an important performance indicator and for stock exchange-listed companies it is quoted in, for example, the London *Financial Times*. It is given by:

$$p/e = \frac{P_{share}}{EPS}, \tag{2.1}$$

[4] Not every "public listed company" (plc) actually has its shares quoted on the stock exchange. It is possible for a company to be a plc without having quoted shares.

where P_{share} is the market price of the company's shares and EPS is the earnings per share. For quoted companies both these values may be obtained with ease.

The p/e ratio is an indication of the price that investors are prepared to pay for a company's shares in return for its current level of earnings. It relates shareholder profit to the market value of the company. Companies that are in "high-growth" sectors, such as (during the late 1990s) the "dot.com" or technology sector, are observed generally to have high p/e ratios, while companies in low-growth sectors will have lower p/e ratios. This illustrates one important factor of p/e ratio analysis: an individual figure on its own is of no real use; rather, it is the sector average as well as the overall level of the stock market that are important considerations for the investor. In the *Financial Times* the company pages list the p/e ratio for each industry sector, thus enabling investors to compare specific company p/e ratios with the sector level and the market level.[5] The *p/e relative* is calculated by comparing specific and industry-level p/e ratios, given in (2.2), which is an indication of where investors rate the company in relation to the industry it is operating in, or the market as a whole.

$$p/e \text{ relative} = \frac{p/e_{company}}{p/e_{market}} \tag{2.2}$$

A very high p/e relative for a specific company may indicate a highly rated company and one that is a sector leader. However, it may also indicate, and this is very topical, a "glamour" company that is significantly overvalued and overdue for a correction and decline in its share price.

The MB ratio relates a company's market value to shareholder funds value. If we see the p/e ratio as emanating from the p&l account, then the MB ratio emanates from the balance sheet. It is given by:

$$MB = ROE\% \times p/e \ ratio. \tag{2.3}$$

We consider the MB and p/e ratios in the context of business valuation in the next section.

[5] These figures are not listed in the Monday edition of the *Financial Times*, which contains other relevant data.

Corporate valuation

We have noted how for a company listed on a stock exchange, it is straightforward to know its market value: its share price. However, for subsidiaries and divisions of quoted companies or unquoted companies, a proper market value is not so simple to obtain. In this section we provide an introduction of how analysis from within a "peer group" of companies may be used to obtain an estimated valuation for unquoted companies.

We wish to calculate an estimated market share price for Constructa plc, our hypothetical banking institution. Assume that we are fortunate to observe a peer group that consists of three other banks of comparable size and performance, operating in a similar line of business as Constructa plc. The three companies are known as "X", "Y" and "Z". Table 2.6 shows the financial data and key performance indicators for the year 2000 for each of these three companies.

	X plc	Y plc	Z plc
Turnover £m	821.4	369.7	211.3
Profit before interest and tax £m	97.6	41.9	18.7
Net profit (profit after interest and tax) £m	56.2	26.7	15.4
Book value of shareholders' funds £m	331.2	219.6	46.9
Shares in issue	167m	55m	48m
Share market price	712p	408p	926p
Return on sales % (1)	11.88	11.33%	8.85%
Earnings per share (2)	33.7p	48.5p	32.1p
p/e ratio (3)	21.1	8.4	28.8
Book value per share (4)	198p	399p	97.7p
MB ratio (5)	3.6	1.02	9.5

(1) Return on sales is [profit before interest and tax / turnover]
(2) Earnings per share (EPS) is [net profit / number of shares in issue]
(3) The p/e ratio is [share price / earnings per share]
(4) Book value per share is [book value of shareholders' funds / number of shares in issue]
(5) MB ratio is [share market price / book value per share]

Table 2.6 Comparable company financial indicators, year 2000

The next step is to use this observed data in conjunction with Constructa plc data to obtain a range of possible values for the latter's market value. First, we calculate the mean p/e and MB ratios of the three peer group companies, and then from the range of ratios for these companies we calculate the estimated Constructa plc values, using that company's own earnings per share value. In this way, we obtain a highest and lowest possible market valuation and a mean valuation. We have not previously calculated a book value per share for Constructa plc, so this is done now; the result is 59.3 pence, obtained by dividing the shareholders' funds figure of £89 million by the number of shares (150 million).

The mean value p/e and MB ratios are shown in Table 2.7, together with the range of possible market values for Constructa plc using each method.

	Mean value	X plc	Y plc	Z plc
p/e ratio	19.4	21.1	8.4	28.8
MB ratio	4.7	3.6	1.02	9.5
Constructa plc		**Mean value**	**High value**	**Low value**
Valuation using p/e ratio				
EPS	7.87			
p/e ratio		19.4	28.8	8.4
Share market value[(1)]		152.7p	226.7p	66.1p
Valuation using MB ratio				
Book value per share	59.3p			
MB ratio		4.7	9.5	1.02
Share market value[(2)]		278.7p	563.4p	60.5p

[(1)] Obtained by multiplying EPS by the p/e ratio.
[(2)] Obtained by multiplying book value per share by the MB ratio.

Table 2.7 Peer group company ratios, mean values and Constructa plc market valuation

In this approach we obtain a mean value for the Constructa plc share price of £1.53 or £2.79, depending on which method we use. It is a subjective issue as to which approach is the better one, and the motivation of the analyst undertaking the calculation is key. In practice, analysts will consider a peer group with a greater number of companies, which usually results in a wider range of possible values. Of course, the true market valuation for any good is the price at which there is both a buyer and seller for it, and similarly the true value for a company will lie somewhere in between the high and low limits that arise from using the method we have just described.

References and bibliography

Fama, E. 1965, "The Behaviour of Stock Market Prices", *Journal of Business*, January, pp. 34–105.

Fama, E. and French, K. 1992, "The Cross-section of Expected Stock Returns", *Journal of Finance*, June, pp. 427–465.

Fisher, I. 1930, *Theory of Interest*, Macmillan, London.

Higson, C. 1995, *Business Finance*, 2nd edition, Butterworths, Oxford.

Mills, R. and Robertson, J. 1995, *Fundamentals of Managerial Accounting and Finance*, Mars Business Associates.

Modigliani, F. and Miller, M. 1961, "Dividend Policy, Growth and the Valuation of Shares", *Journal of Business*, 34, pp. 411–433.

Van Horne, J. 1995, *Financial Management and Policy*, 10th edition, Prentice Hall, New Jersey.

Sharpe, W., Alexander, G. and Bailey, J. 1995, *Investments*, Prentice-Hall, New Jersey.

CHAPTER

3

The Money Markets

Part of the global debt capital markets, the money markets are a separate market in their own right. Money market securities are defined as debt instruments with an original maturity of less than one year, although it is common to find that the maturity profile of banks' money market desks runs out to two years.

Money markets exist in every market economy, which is practically every country in the world. They are often the first element of a developing capital market. In every case they comprise securities with maturities of up to 12 months. Money market debt is an important part of the global capital markets, and facilitates the smooth running of the banking industry, as well as providing working capital for industrial and commercial corporate institutions. The market provides users with a wide range of opportunities and funding possibilities, and the market is characterised by the diverse range of products that can be traded within it. Money market instruments allow issuers, including financial organisations and corporates, to raise funds for short-term periods at relatively low interest rates. These issuers include sovereign governments, who issue T-bills, corporates issuing commercial paper, and banks issuing bills and certificates of deposit. At the same time investors are attracted to the market because the instruments are highly liquid and carry relatively low credit risk. The T-bill market in any country is that country's lowest risk instrument, and consequently carries the lowest yield of any debt instrument. Indeed, the first market that develops in any country is usually the T-bill market. Investors in the money market include banks, local authorities, corporations, money market investment funds and mutual funds, and individuals.

In addition to cash instruments, the money markets also consist of a wide range of exchange-traded and over-the-counter off-balance sheet derivative instruments. These instruments are used mainly to establish future borrowing and lending rates, and to hedge or change existing interest-rate exposure. This activity is carried out by both banks, central banks and corporates. The main derivatives are short-term interest rate futures, forward rate agreements, and short-dated interest rate swaps such as overnight-index swaps.

In this chapter we review the cash instruments traded in the money market, including the loan market. In further chapters we review the market in repurchase agreements and the market in money market derivative instruments, including interest-rate futures and forward-rate agreements.

Introduction

The cash instruments traded in money markets include the following:

- time deposits;
- T-bills;
- certificates of deposit;
- commercial paper;
- bankers acceptances;
- bills of exchange.

In addition money market desks may also trade repo and take part in stock borrowing and lending activities. These products are covered in a separate chapter.

T-bills are used by sovereign governments to raise short-term funds, while certificates of deposit (CDs) are used by banks to raise finance. The other instruments are used by corporates and occasionally banks. Each instrument represents an obligation on the borrower to repay the amount borrowed on the maturity date together with interest if this applies. The instruments above fall into one of two main classes of money market securities: those quoted on a *yield* basis and those quoted on a *discount* basis. These two terms are discussed later in this chapter. A *repurchase agreement* or "repo" is also a money market instrument and is considered in a separate chapter.

Figure 3.17 on page 84 shows the composition by product type of the money markets in the United Kingdom in 2000.

The calculation of interest in the money markets often differs from the calculation of accrued interest in the corresponding bond market. Generally, the day-count convention in the money market is the exact number of days that the instrument is held over the number of days in the year. In the UK sterling market the year base is 365 days, so the interest calculation for sterling money market instruments is given by (3.1):

$$i = \frac{n}{365} \quad . \tag{3.1}$$

However, the great majority of currencies, including the US dollar and the euro, calculate interest on a 360-day base so the denominator in (3.1) would be changed accordingly. The process by which an interest rate quoted on one basis is converted to one quoted on the other basis is shown in Appendix 3.1. Those markets that calculate interest based on a 365-day year are also listed at Appendix 3.1.

Dealers will want to know the interest day-base for a currency before dealing it in FX or money markets. Bloomberg users can use screen DCX to look up the number of days of an interest period. For instance, Figure 3.1 on page 50 shows screen DCX for the US dollar market, for a loan taken out for value on 7 May 2004 for a straight three-month period. Ordinarily this would mature on 7 August 2004; however, from Figure 3.1 we see that this is not a good day so the loan will actually mature on 9 August 2004. Also from Figure 3.1 we see that this period is actually 94 days, and 92 days under the 30/360-day convention (a bond market accrued interest convention). The number of business days is 64, we also see that there is a public holiday on the 31 May.

For the same loan taken out in Singapore dollars, look at Figure 3.2 on page 50. This shows that the same loan taken out for value on 7 May will actually mature on 10 August, because 9 August 2004 is a public holiday in that market.

Settlement of money market instruments can be for value today (generally only when traded in before midday), tomorrow or two days forward, known as *spot*.

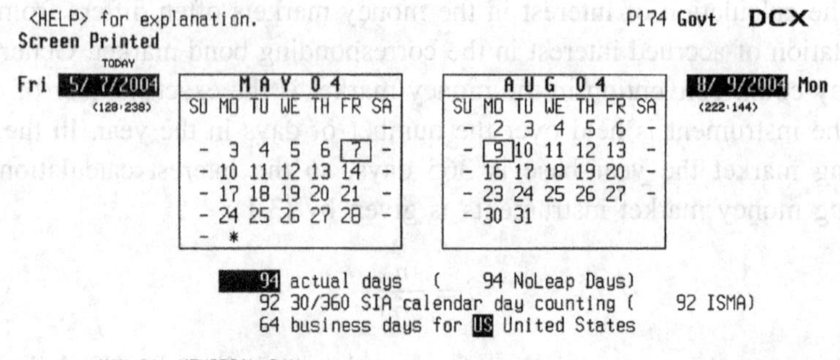

Figure 3.1 Bloomberg screen DCX used for US dollar market, three-month loan taken out 7 May 2004

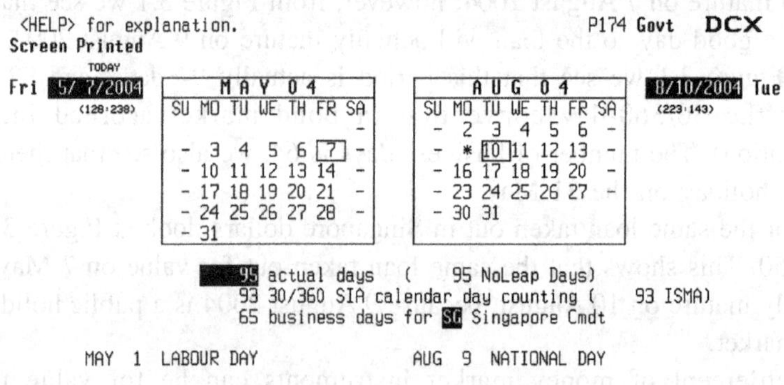

Figure 3.2 Bloomberg screen DCX for Singapore dollar market, three-month loan taken out 7 May 2004

Figure 3.3 shows London money market rates as they appear in the *Financial Times* for 11 March 2004. Also, Figure 3.17 on page 84 shows the composition of the London money markets by instrument dealing volume, as at November 2000.

UK INTEREST RATES

Mar 10	Over-night	7 days notice	One month	Three months	Six months	One year
Interbank Sterling	$3\frac{13}{16} - 3\frac{9}{16}$	$3\frac{7}{8} - 3\frac{3}{4}$	$4\frac{1}{8} - 4$	$4\frac{9}{32} - 4\frac{5}{32}$	$4\frac{7}{16} - 4\frac{5}{16}$	$4\frac{5}{8} - 4\frac{1}{2}$
BBA Sterling	$3\frac{3}{4}$	$3\frac{7}{8}$	$4\frac{1}{8}$	$4\frac{9}{32}$	$4\frac{13}{32}$	$4\frac{19}{32}$
Sterling CDs			$4\frac{1}{8} - 4\frac{1}{16}$	$4\frac{1}{4} - 4\frac{7}{32}$	$4\frac{3}{8} - 4\frac{11}{32}$	$4\frac{17}{32} - 4\frac{1}{2}$
Treasury Bills			$4 - 3\frac{15}{16}$	$4\frac{1}{16} - 4$		
Bank Bills			$4\frac{3}{32} - 4\frac{1}{32}$	$4\frac{7}{32} - 4\frac{5}{32}$		
†Local authority deps.		$4\frac{1}{16} - 3\frac{15}{16}$	$4\frac{1}{8} - 4$	$4\frac{1}{4} - 4\frac{1}{8}$	$4\frac{3}{8} - 4\frac{1}{4}$	$4\frac{5}{8} - 4\frac{1}{2}$
Discount Market deps	$3\frac{7}{8} - 3\frac{11}{16}$	$4 - 3\frac{13}{16}$				

Av. tndr rate of discount Mar 4, 4.0651pc. ECGD fixed rate Stlg. Export Finance. make up day Feb 27,2003. Agreed rate for period Feb 25 2004 to Mar 25, 2004, Scheme III 5.30pc. Reference rate for period Jan 31, 2004 to Feb 27, 2004, Scheme IV & V 4.164%. Finance House Base Rate 4.5pv for Feb 2004
UK clearing bank base lending rate 4 per cent from Feb 5, 2004 Source: Reuters, RBS, †Tradition (UK) Ltd.

	Up to 1 month	1-3 month	3-6 months	6-9 months	9-12 months
Certs of Tax dep. (£100,000)	¼	3	3	3	3

Certs of Tax dep. under £100,000 is ¼pc. Deposits withdrawn for cash 0pc.

Figure 3.3 London sterling money market rates.
Extract from the *Financial Times*, 11 March 2004

Securities quoted on a yield basis

By convention, money market products are quoted either as discount instruments or yield instruments. However, the products trade with regard to liquidity and credit quality, and the quote convention has no impact on this (although quotes frequently need to be converted from one basis to another in order to compare true yields). Two of the instruments listed in the previous section are yield-based instruments, and we discuss them first.

Money market deposits

These are fixed-interest term deposits of up to one year with banks and securities houses. They are also known as *time deposits* or *clean deposits*. They are not negotiable so they cannot be liquidated before maturity. The interest rate on the deposit is fixed for the term and related to the London Interbank Offer Rate (Libor) of the same term. Interest and capital are paid on maturity.

Libor

The term Libor or "LIBOR" comes from London Interbank Offered Rate and is the interest rate at which one London bank offers funds to another London bank of acceptable credit quality in the form of a cash deposit. The rate is "fixed" by the British Bankers' Association (BBA) at 11 a.m. every business day morning (in practice the fix is usually about 20 minutes later) by taking the average of the rates supplied by member banks. The term Libid is the bank's "bid" rate; that is, the rate at which it pays for funds in the London market. The quote spread for a selected maturity is therefore the difference between Libor and Libid. The convention in London is to quote the two rates as Libor–Libid, thus matching the yield convention for other instruments. In some other markets the quote convention is reversed. Euribor is the interbank rate offered for euros as reported by the European Central Bank, fixed in Brussels.[1]

Figure 3.4 shows the Libor fixing page from the BBA on Bloomberg, for the Libor rate fix on 31 August 2004.

BBAM1 N1211a Govt **BBAM**

BRITISH BANKERS' ASSOCIATION

Page 1 of 4

08/31 11:03 GMT [BRITISH BANKERS ASSOCIATION LIBOR RATES] 3750

[31/08/04] RATES AT 11:00 LONDON TIME 31/08/2004 31/08 10:39 GMT

CCY	USD	GBP	CAD	EUR	JPY	EUR 365
O/N	1.62500	4.69375	2.03500	2.07625	SN0.03375	2.10509
1WK	1.57375	4.78625	2.06000	2.06863	0.03500	2.09736
2WK	1.58375	4.82156	2.12333	2.06938	0.03625	2.09812
1MO	1.67000	4.85375	2.16333	2.07575	0.03813	2.10458
2MO	1.73000	4.89500	2.23833	2.09300	0.04563	2.12207
3MO	1.80000	4.96250	2.32000	2.11313	0.05188	2.14248
4MO	1.86000	5.00250	2.38333	2.13300	0.05500	2.16263
5MO	1.92125	5.04125	2.44667	2.14925	0.05838	2.17910
6MO	1.99000	5.07625	2.51000	2.16575	0.06300	2.19583
7MO	2.04875	5.10625	2.56500	2.18450	0.06875	2.21484
8MO	2.10000	5.13625	2.61667	2.20138	0.07313	2.23195
9MO	2.15000	5.16375	2.66667	2.22000	0.07875	2.25083
10MO	2.20000	5.18750	2.71167	2.24438	0.08450	2.27555
11MO	2.25000	5.20750	2.76167	2.26800	0.08875	2.29950
12MO	2.30000	5.22750	2.81167	2.29575	0.09313	2.32764

Figure 3.4 BBA Libor fixing page, 31 August 2004

[1] Thanks to Dan Cunningham at KBC Bank London for clearing up the concept of an act/365 day-count Libor fix for the euro…sort of counter-intuitive, eh?

Euribor

The official euro fixing is known as Euribor, which is set in Brussels at 1100 hours local time each euro business day. This should not be confused with the euro Libor fixing. The fixing operates in the same way as Libor, with a panel of Euribor banks contributing their rates each morning. The average rate of all contributions is taken as the fix.

Figure 3.5 shows the main menu page for euro fixing on Bloomberg, which is EBF. The rates fix page is shown in Figure 3.6, which is the fix for 11 June 2004. The fix is for spot value, and this is confirmed on the page, where we see that the value date is 15 June 2004, two business days later. The same menu page can be used to access both Euribor and the EONIA fix, which is the euro overnight interest rate.[2] This is shown at Figure 3.7, again for 11 June 2004. This shows the same fixings seen in Figure 3.6, as well as the previous days' fixing and the EONIA rate fixing at the bottom of the screen.

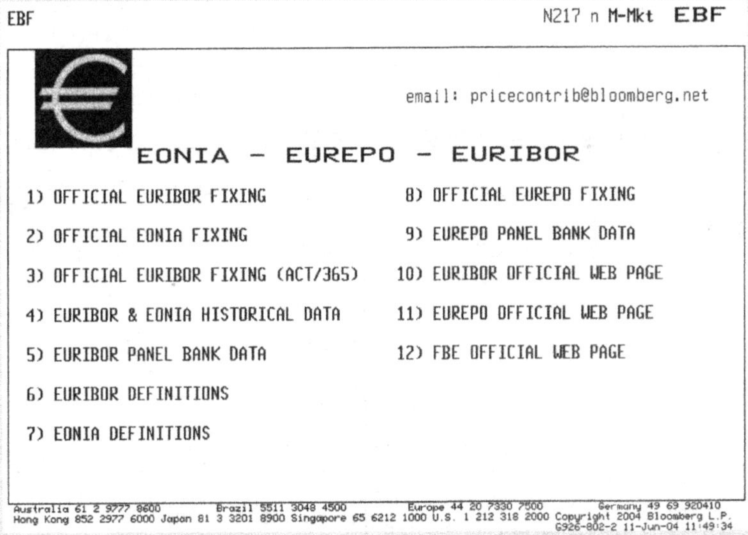

EBF N217 n M-Mkt **EBF**

email: pricecontrib@bloomberg.net

EONIA – EUREPO – EURIBOR

1) OFFICIAL EURIBOR FIXING	8) OFFICIAL EUREPO FIXING
2) OFFICIAL EONIA FIXING	9) EUREPO PANEL BANK DATA
3) OFFICIAL EURIBOR FIXING (ACT/365)	10) EURIBOR OFFICIAL WEB PAGE
4) EURIBOR & EONIA HISTORICAL DATA	11) EUREPO OFFICIAL WEB PAGE
5) EURIBOR PANEL BANK DATA	12) FBE OFFICIAL WEB PAGE
6) EURIBOR DEFINITIONS	
7) EONIA DEFINITIONS	

Australia 61 2 9777 8600 Brazil 5511 3048 4500 Europe 44 20 7330 7500 Germany 49 69 920410
Hong Kong 852 2977 6000 Japan 81 3 3201 8900 Singapore 65 6212 1000 U.S. 1 212 318 2000 Copyright 2004 Bloomberg L.P.
G926-802-2 11-Jun-04 11:49:34

Figure 3.5 Euribor menu page EBF on Bloomberg

---

[2] EONIA is the rate used with regard to an overnight-index swap (OIS), which we discuss in Chapter 14.

1 N121 a M-Mkt **EBF**
Screen Printed

EUROPEAN BANKING FEDERATION Page 1 of 1

06/11 12:48 GMT [EURIBOR FBE/ACI] 248

EURIBOR RATES ACT/360 AT 11H00 BRUSSELS TIME 11/06/2004 11/06 09:12 GMT

		ACT/ 360	
	1WK	2.054	[FIXED]
	2WK	2.058	VALUE DATE 15/06/04
	3WK	2.070	[EURIBOR NOTE ON PAGE 47893]
	1MO	2.078	
	2MO	2.093	
	3MO	2.112	
	4MO	2.148	
	5MO	2.177	[WARNING] EITHER EURIBOR FBE,
	6MO	2.199	NOR EURIBOR ACI, NOR THE EURIBO
	7MO	2.240	PANEL BANKS, NOR THE EURIBOR
	8MO	2.280	STEERING COMMITTEE, NOR MONEYLI
	9MO	2.312	TELERATE LTD CAN BE HELD LIABLE
[HISTORY] THIS CAN BE	10MO	2.345	FOR ANY IRREGULARITY OR
DOWNLOADED FROM THE	11MO	2.390	INACCURACY OF THE EURIBOR RATE.
WEBSITE WWW.EURIBOR.ORG	12MO	2.426	(FOR DETAILS SEE PAGE 47896)

Figure 3.6 Euribor rates fix page, 11 June 2004

4 N2N299 M-Mkt **EBF**
Screen Printed
11:47 **EURIBOR & EONIA FIXINGS** PAGE 1 / 1

EURIBOR ACT/360	RATE	PREVIOUS RATE	TIME	EURIBOR ACT/365	RATE	PREVIOUS RATE	TIME
1) 1 WK	2.054	2.054	10:12	17) 1 WK	2.083	2.083	10:12
2) 2 WK	2.058	2.058	10:12	18) 2 WK	2.087	2.087	10:12
3) 3 WK	2.070	2.069	10:12	19) 3 WK	2.099	2.098	10:12
4) 1 MTH	2.078	2.077	10:12	20) 1 MTH	2.107	2.106	10:12
5) 2 MTH	2.093	2.093	10:12	21) 2 MTH	2.122	2.122	10:12
6) 3 MTH	2.112	2.109	10:12	22) 3 MTH	2.141	2.138	10:12
7) 4 MTH	2.148	2.132	10:12	23) 4 MTH	2.178	2.162	10:12
8) 5 MTH	2.177	2.155	10:12	24) 5 MTH	2.207	2.185	10:12
9) 6 MTH	2.199	2.178	10:12	25) 6 MTH	2.230	2.208	10:12
10) 7 MTH	2.240	2.211	10:12	26) 7 MTH	2.271	2.242	10:12
11) 8 MTH	2.280	2.247	10:12	27) 8 MTH	2.312	2.278	10:12
12) 9 MTH	2.312	2.281	10:12	28) 9 MTH	2.344	2.313	10:12
13) 10 MTH	2.345	2.313	10:12	29) 10 MTH	2.378	2.345	10:12
14) 11 MTH	2.390	2.349	10:12	30) 11 MTH	2.423	2.382	10:12
15) 12 MTH	2.426	2.386	10:12	31) 12 MTH	2.460	2.419	10:12
EONIA	TODAY'S RATE	PREVIOUS RATE	TIME		in millions of EURO		
16) EONIA	2.030	2.030	6/10	32) EONIA VOLUME	27567		6/10

Eonia updates at 7 PM CET
Use ER <GO> to monitor additional European money market rates.

Figure 3.7 Euribor and EONIA rates fix page, 11 June 2004

The effective rate on a money market deposit is the annual equivalent interest rate for an instrument with a maturity of less than one year.

EXAMPLE 3.1 Rate of return

A sum of £250,000 is deposited for 270 days, at the end of which the total proceeds are £261,000. What are the simple and effective rates of return on a 365-day basis?

$$\text{Simple rate of return} = \left(\frac{\text{Total proceeds}}{\text{Initial investment}} - 1\right) \times \frac{M}{n}$$

$$= \left(\frac{261{,}000}{250{,}000} - 1\right) \times \frac{365}{270}$$

$$= 5.9481\%$$

$$\text{Effective rate of return} = \left(\frac{\text{Total proceeds}}{\text{Initial investment}}\right)^{\frac{M}{n}} - 1$$

$$= \left(\frac{261{,}000}{250{,}000}\right)^{\frac{365}{270}} - 1$$

$$= 5.9938\%$$

Certificates of Deposit

Certificates of deposit (CDs) are receipts from banks for deposits that have been placed with them. They were first introduced in the US dollar market in 1964, and in the sterling market in 1958. The deposits themselves carry a fixed rate of interest related to Libor and have a fixed term to maturity, so they cannot be withdrawn before then. However, the certificates themselves can be traded in a secondary market; that is, they are negotiable.[3] CDs are therefore very similar to negotiable money market deposits, although the yields are about 0.15% below the equivalent deposit rates because of the

[3] A small number of CDs are non-negotiable.

added benefit of liquidity. Most CDs issued are of between one and three months' maturity, although they do trade in maturities of one to five years. Interest is paid on maturity except for CDs lasting longer than one year, where interest is paid annually or occasionally, semi-annually.

Banks, investment banks and building societies issue CDs to raise funds to finance their business activities. A CD will have a stated interest rate and fixed maturity date, and can be issued in any denomination. On issue a CD is sold for face value, so the settlement proceeds of a CD on issue are always equal to its nominal value. The interest is paid, together with the face amount, on maturity. The interest rate is sometimes called the *coupon*, but unless the CD is held to maturity this will not equal the yield, which is of course the current rate available in the market and varies over time. The largest group of CD investors are banks, money market funds, corporates and local authority treasurers.

Unlike coupons on bonds, which are paid in rounded amounts, CD coupon is calculated to the exact day.

CD yields

The coupon quoted on a CD is a function of the credit quality of the issuing bank, and its expected liquidity level in the market, and of course the maturity of the CD, as this will be considered relative to the money market yield curve. As CDs are issued by banks as part of their short-term funding and liquidity requirement, issue volumes are driven by the demand for bank loans and the availability of alternative sources of funds for bank customers. The credit quality of the issuing bank is the primary consideration however; in the sterling market the lowest yield is paid by "clearer" CDs, which are CDs issued by the clearing banks such as the Royal Bank of Scotland, HSBC and Barclays Bank plc. In the US market "prime" CDs, issued by highly rated domestic banks, trade at a lower yield than non-prime CDs. In both markets CDs issued by foreign banks such as French or Japanese banks will trade at higher yields.

Euro-CDs, which are CDs issued in a different currency to that of the home currency, also trade at higher yields in the US because of reserve and deposit insurance restrictions.

If the current market price of the CD, including accrued interest, is P and the current quoted yield is r, the yield can be calculated given the price, using (3.2):

$$r = \left(\frac{M}{P} \times \left(1 + C\left(\frac{N_{im}}{B}\right)\right) - 1\right) \times \left(\frac{B}{N_{sm}}\right). \tag{3.2}$$

The price can be calculated given the yield using (3.3):

$$P = M \times \left(1 + C\left(\frac{N_{im}}{B}\right)\right) / \left(1 + r\left(\frac{N_{sm}}{B}\right)\right) \quad (3.3)$$
$$= F / \left(1 + r\left(\frac{N_{sm}}{B}\right)\right)$$

where

C is the quoted coupon on the CD
M is the face value of the CD
B is the year day-basis (365 or 360)
F is the maturity value of the CD
N_{im} is the number of days between issue and maturity
N_{sm} is the number of days between settlement and maturity.

After issue a CD can be traded in the secondary market. The secondary market in CDs in developed economies is very liquid, and CDs will trade at the rate prevalent at the time, which will invariably be different from the coupon rate on the CD at issue. When a CD is traded in the secondary market, the settlement proceeds will need to take into account interest that has accrued on the paper and the different rate at which the CD has now been dealt. The formula for calculating the settlement figure is given in (3.4), which applies to the sterling market and its 365-day count basis.

$$\text{Proceeds} = \frac{\text{M} \times \text{Tenor} \times \text{C} \times 100 + 36{,}500}{\text{Days remaining} \times r \times 100 + 36{,}500} \quad (3.4)$$

The settlement figure for a new issue CD is of course, its face value…![4]

The *tenor* of a CD is the life of the CD in days, while *days remaining* is the number of days left to maturity from the time of trade.

The return on holding a CD is given by (3.5):

$$R = \left(\frac{(1 + \text{Purchase yield} \times (\text{Days from purchase to maturity/B}))}{1 + \text{Sale yield} \times (\text{Days from sale to maturity/B})} - 1\right) \times \left(\frac{B}{\textit{Days held}}\right). \quad (3.5)$$

[4] With thanks to Del Boy during the time he was at Tradition for pointing out this very obvious fact after I'd just bought a sizeable chunk of Japanese bank CDs…

EXAMPLE 3.2 CD settlement proceeds

A three-month CD is issued on 6 September 2005 and matures on 6 December 2005 (maturity of 91 days). It has a face value of £20,000,000 and a coupon of 5.45%. What are the total maturity proceeds?

Proceeds = 20 million × (1 + 0.0545 × 91/365) = £20,271,753.42

What is the secondary market proceeds on 11 October if the yield for short 60-day paper is 5.60%?

$$P = \frac{20.271\text{m}}{(1 + 0.056 \times 56/365)} = £20{,}099{,}066.64$$

On 18 November the yield on short three-week paper is 5.215%. What rate of return is earned from holding the CD for the 38 days from 11 October to 18 November?

$$R = \left(\frac{1 + 0.0560 \times 56/365}{1 + 0.05215 \times 38/365} - 1\right) \times \frac{365}{38} = 9.6355\%$$

CDs issued with more than one coupon

CDs issued for a maturity of greater than one year pay interest on an annual basis. The longest-dated CDs are issued with a maturity of five years. The price of a CD paying more than one coupon therefore depends on all the intervening coupons before maturity, valued at the current yield. Consider a CD that has four more coupons remaining to be paid, the last of which will be paid on maturity together with the face value of the CD. The value of this last coupon will be:

$$M \times C \times \frac{n_{3\text{–}4}}{B} \tag{3.6}$$

where $n_{3\text{–}4}$ is the number of days between the third and fourth (last) coupon dates and C is the coupon rate on the CD. The maturity proceeds of the CD are therefore:

$$M\left(1 + C \times \frac{n_{3\text{–}4}}{B}\right). \tag{3.7}$$

The present value of this amount to the date of the second coupon payment is therefore its discounted value using the current yield *r*, given by (3.8):

$$P_2 = \frac{M\left(1 + C \times \frac{n_{3-4}}{B}\right)}{1 + r \times \frac{n_{3-4}}{B}} \quad . \tag{3.8}$$

This value is then added to the actual cash flow received on the same date; that is, the second coupon date, which is given by:

$$M \times C \times \frac{n_{2-3}}{B} \quad . \tag{3.9}$$

The total of these two amounts is given by (3.10):

$$P_1 = \mathrm{M} \times \left(\frac{\left(1 + C \times \frac{n_{3-4}}{B}\right)}{\left(1 + r \times \frac{n_{3-4}}{B}\right)} + C \times \frac{n_{2-3}}{B} \right) \quad . \tag{3.10}$$

This amount is then discounted again to obtain the present value on the first coupon date at the current yield *r*, and added to the total cash flow. This process is repeated so that the final total amount can be discounted to the purchase date, at the current yield.

In general for a CD with *N* coupon payments remaining the price is given by (3.11):

$$P = M\left(\frac{1}{A_N} + \left(\frac{C}{B} \times \sum_{k=1}^{N}\left(\frac{n_{k-1;k}}{A_k}\right)\right)\right) \tag{3.11}$$

where

$$A_k = \left(1 + r \times \frac{n_{p1}}{B}\right)\left(1 + r \times \frac{n_{1-2}}{B}\right)\left(1 + r \times \frac{n_{2-3}}{B}\right)\ldots\left(1 + r \times \frac{n_{k-1;k}}{B}\right)$$

$n_{k-1;k}$ is the number of days between the (*k*–1)th coupon and the *k*th coupon
n_{p1} is the number of days between purchase date and the first coupon.

An example of the way CDs and time deposits are quoted on screen is shown in Figure 3.8 on page 60, which shows one of the rates screens displayed by Tullett & Tokyo, money brokers in London, on a Bloomberg screen. Essentially the same screen is displayed also on Reuters. The screen has been reproduced with permission from Tulletts and Bloomberg. The screen displays sterling interbank and CD bid and offer rates for maturities up to one year as at 10 November 2003. The maturity marked "O/N" is the over-night rate, which at that time was 3.3125–3.375. The maturity marked "T/N" is "tom-next", or "tomorrow-to-the-next", which is the over-night rate for deposits commencing tomorrow. As we noted earlier, the liquidity of CDs means that they trade at a lower yield to deposits, and this can be seen from Figure 3.8, although on the day this snapshot was taken the spread below the cash rate was relatively narrow. The bid–offer convention in sterling is that the rate at which the market maker will pay for funds – its borrowing rate – is placed on the left. This is the same for both CDs and deposits, so a six-month CD would be sold at 4.08%, which means that funds are borrowed at 4.08%, while a six-month time deposit is lent at 4.13%.

This is a reversal of the traditional sterling market convention of placing the offered rate on the left-hand side.

GRAB Comdty TTDE

11:24 TULLETT & TOKYO PAGE 1 / 1

GBP Cash Deposits	Euro-Sterling Bid	Ask	Time
1) T/N	3.4500	3.5500	7:20
2) 1 Week	3.6600	3.7100	7:20
3) 2 Week	3.7000	3.7400	7:32
4) 3 Week	3.7100	3.7600	7:32
5) 1 Month	3.7300	3.7700	9:31
6) 2 Month	3.8300	3.8700	7:20
7) 3 Month	3.9100	3.9400	9:31
8) 4 Month	3.9700	4.0100	7:20
9) 5 Month	4.0400	4.0800	7:32
10) 6 Month	4.0900	4.1300	7:54
11) 7 Month	4.1500	4.1900	7:52
12) 8 Month	4.2200	4.2600	7:52
13) 9 Month	4.2700	4.3100	7:52
14) 10 Month	4.3300	4.3700	7:52
15) 11 Month	4.3900	4.4300	7:54
16) 12 Month	4.4500	4.4900	7:54
Cash Deposits - Domestic Interbank			
17) O/N	3.3125	3.3750	11:16
18) 1 Week	3.5600	3.5950	11:01
19) 1 Month	3.7175	3.7513	7:11

GBP Cash Deposits	Domestic Interbank (cont'd) Bid	Ask	Time
20) 2 Month	3.8150	3.8700	7:11
21) 3 Month	3.9050	3.9362	9:31
22) 4 Month	3.9650	4.0062	7:11
23) 5 Month	4.0000	4.0625	7:11
24) 6 Month	4.0950	4.1575	7:51
25) 9 Month	4.2925	4.3463	7:51
26) 12 Month	4.4300	4.5025	7:51
GBP Certificate of Deposits			
27) 1 Month	3.7300	3.7500	7:38
28) 2 Month	3.8000	3.8200	9:29
29) 3 Month	3.8900	3.9100	7:09
30) 4 Month	3.9500	3.9800	7:09
31) 5 Month	4.0100	4.0400	7:51
32) 6 Month	4.0800	4.1000	7:09
33) 9 Month	4.2600	4.2800	8:27
34) 10 Month	4.3200	4.3400	8:27
35) 11 Month	4.3900	4.4100	8:27
36) 12 Month	4.4500	4.4700	8:27

Australia 61 2 9777 8600 Brazil 5511 3048 4500 Europe 44 20 7330 7500 Germany 49 69 920410
Hong Kong 852 2977 6000 Japan 81 3 3201 8900 Singapore 65 6212 1000 U.S. 1 212 318 2000
G657-802-0 10-Nov-03 11:24:35

Figure 3.8 Tullett and Tokyo brokers sterling money markets screen, 10 November 2003

EXAMPLE 3.3 CD with four coupon payments remaining

A CD is purchased with the following terms:

Face value: €1 million
Coupon: 8.00% semi-annual
Maturity date: 15 September 2003
Settlement date: 17 January 2002
Current yield: 7.00%

What amount is paid for the CD?

The coupon date prior to purchase was on 17 September 2001. Note that 15 September in that year falls on a weekend, so the coupon rolls on to the next working day. The future coupon dates are 15 March and 16 September 2002, and 17 March and 15 September 2003. The number of days between coupon dates are $n_{0-1} = 179$, $n_{p-1} = 57$, $n_{1-2} = 185$, $n_{2-3} = 182$ and $n_{3-4} = 182$.

Price =

$$\frac{1 \text{ million} \times (1 + 0.08 \times \frac{182}{360})}{(1 + 0.07 \times \frac{57}{360})(1 + 0.07 \times \frac{185}{360})(1 + 0.07 \times \frac{182}{360})(1 + 0.07 \times \frac{182}{360})}$$

$$+ \frac{1 \text{ million} \times (1 + 0.08 \times \frac{182}{360})}{(1 + 0.07 \times \frac{57}{360})(1 + 0.07 \times \frac{185}{360})(1 + 0.07 \times \frac{182}{360})}$$

$$+ \frac{1 \text{ million} \times (1 + 0.08 \times \frac{182}{360})}{(1 + 0.07 \times \frac{57}{360})(1 + 0.07 \times \frac{185}{360})}$$

$$+ \frac{1 \text{ million} \times (1 + 0.08 \times \frac{182}{360})}{(1 + 0.07 \times \frac{57}{360})}$$

The price of the CD for settlement on the date given is therefore €1,042,449.80.

US Dollar market rates

T-bills

The T-bill market in the United States is the most liquid and transparent debt market in the world. Consequently, the bid–offer spread on them is very narrow. The Treasury issues bills at a weekly auction each Monday, made up of 91-day and 182-day bills. Every fourth week the Treasury also issues 52-week bills as well. As a result there are large numbers of T-bills outstanding at any one time. The interest earned on T-bills is not liable to state and local income taxes. T-bill rates are the lowest in the dollar market (as indeed any bill market is in respective domestic environment) and as such represent the corporate financier's *risk-free* interest rate.

Federal funds

Commercial banks in the US are required to keep reserves on deposit at the Federal Reserve. Banks with reserves in excess of required reserves can lend these funds to other banks, and these interbank loans are called *federal funds,* or *fed funds,* and are usually overnight loans. Through the fed funds market, commercial banks with excess funds are able to lend to banks that are short of reserves, thus facilitating liquidity. The transactions are very large denominations, and are lent at the *fed funds rate*, which is a very volatile interest rate because it fluctuates with market shortages.

Prime rate

The *prime interest rate* in the United States is often said to represent the rate at which commercial banks lend to their most creditworthy customers. In practice, many loans are made at rates below the prime rate, so the prime rate is not the best rate at which highly rated firms may borrow. Nevertheless, the prima rate is a benchmark indicator of the level of US money market rates, and is often used as a reference rate for floating-rate instruments. As the market for bank loans is highly competitive, all commercial banks quote a single prime rate, and the rate for all banks changes simultaneously.

Securities quoted on a discount basis

The remaining money market instruments are all quoted on a *discount* basis, and so are known as "discount" instruments. This means that they are issued on a discount to face value, and are redeemed on maturity at face value. T-bills, bills of exchange, bankers' acceptances and commercial paper are examples of money market securities that are quoted on a discount basis; that is, they are sold on the basis of a discount to par. The difference between the price paid at the time of purchase and the redemption value (par) is the interest earned by the holder of the paper. Explicit interest is not paid on discount instruments, rather interest is reflected implicitly in the difference between the discounted issue price and the par value received at maturity.

T-bills

T-bills are short-term government "IOUs" of short duration, often three-month maturity. For example, if a bill is issued on 10 January it will mature on 10 April. Bills of one-month and six-month maturity are issued in certain markets, but only rarely by the UK Treasury. On maturity the holder of a T-bill receives the par value of the bill by presenting it to the Central Bank. In the United Kingdom most such bills are denominated in sterling but issues are also made in euros. In a capital market, T-bill yields are regarded as the *risk-free* yield, as they represent the yield from short-term government debt. In emerging markets they are often the most liquid instruments available for investors.

A sterling T-bill with £10 million face value issued for 91 days will be redeemed on maturity at £10 million. If the three-month yield at the time of issue is 5.25%, the price of the bill at issue is:

$$P = \frac{10 \text{ m}}{(1 + 0.0525 \times \frac{91}{365})} = £9{,}870{,}800.69.$$

In the UK market the interest rate on discount instruments is quoted as a *discount rate* rather than a yield. This is the amount of discount expressed as an annualised percentage of the face value, and not as a percentage of the original amount paid. By definition the discount rate is always lower than the corresponding yield. If the discount rate on a bill is d, then the amount of discount is given by (3.12):

$$d_{value} = M \times d \times n/B \tag{3.12}$$

where B is the day-count basis.

The price P paid for the bill is the face value minus the discount amount, given by (3.13):

$$P = 100\left(1 - \frac{d \times (N_{sm}/365)}{100}\right). \tag{3.13}$$

If we know the yield on the bill, then we can calculate its price at issue by using the simple present value formula, as shown in (3.14):

$$P = M/(1 + r(N_{sm}/365)). \tag{3.14}$$

The discount rate d for T-bills is calculated using (3.15):

$$d = (1 - P) \times B/n \tag{3.15}$$

where n is the T-bill number of days.

The relationship between discount rate and true yield is given by (3.16):

$$d = \frac{r}{(1 + r \times \frac{n}{B})} \tag{3.16}$$

$$r = \frac{d}{1 + d \times \frac{n}{B}}.$$

EXAMPLE 3.4 T-bill price and yield

A 91-day £100 T-bill is issued with a yield of 4.75%. What is its issue price?

$$P = \left(\frac{£100}{1 + 0.0475\left(\frac{91}{365}\right)}\right)$$

$$= £98.80$$

A UK T-bill with a remaining maturity of 39 days is quoted at a discount of 4.95%. What is the equivalent yield?

$$r = \frac{0.0495}{1 - 0.0495\left(\frac{39}{365}\right)}$$

$$= 4.976\%$$

If a T-bill is traded in the secondary market, the settlement proceeds from the trade are calculated using (3.17):

$$\text{Proceeds} = M - \left(\frac{M \times \text{Days remaining} \times d}{B \times 100}\right). \qquad (3.17)$$

Bond equivalent yield

In the UK market the yields on government bonds that have a maturity of less than one year are compared to the yields of T-bills; however, before the comparison can be made the yield on a bill must be converted to a "bond equivalent" yield. Therefore the bond equivalent yield of a T-bill is the coupon of a theoretical gilt trading at par that has an identical maturity date. If the bill has 182 days or less until maturity, the calculation required is the conventional conversion from discount rate to yield.

If there are more than 182 days remaining to maturity on the bill, the calculation must take into account the fact that an equivalent bond would pay a coupon during the period as well as on maturity. To convert the yield to a bond equivalent we use (3.18):

$$rm = \frac{-\frac{n}{365} + \left[\left(\frac{n}{365}\right)^2 + 2 \times \left(\frac{n}{365} - \frac{1}{2}\right) \times \left(\frac{1}{1 - d \times n/365} - 1\right)\right]^{1/2}}{\left(\frac{n}{365} - \frac{1}{2}\right)} \qquad (3.18)$$

where d is the discount rate and rm is the bond equivalent yield.

If 29 February falls in the 12-month period that begins on the purchase date, 365 is replaced by 366.

Note that if there is a bill and a bond that mature on the same day in a period under 182 days, the bond-equivalent yield will not be precisely the same as the yield quoted for the bond in its final coupon period, although it is a very close approximation. This is because the bond is quoted on actual/actual basis, so its yield is actually made up of 2× the actual number of days in the interest period.

Conversely, bonds that have a remaining maturity of less than one year are often quoted in terms of an equivalent money market yield so that their return can be compared to money market yields. For example, the US Treasury security, the $1^3/_4$% 2004, was issued on 31 December 2002 and matured on 31 December 2004. On 5 May 2004, for settlement on 6 May, the bond was priced to yield 1.628%. This is shown in Figure 3.9 on page 66, which is the Bloomberg screen YA for calculating yield-to-maturity. However, for this bond at this time, a more approporiate screen to calculate yield is ME, which shows the money market equivalent yield for the bond. We see from Figure 3.10 on page 66 that this yield is 1.598%.

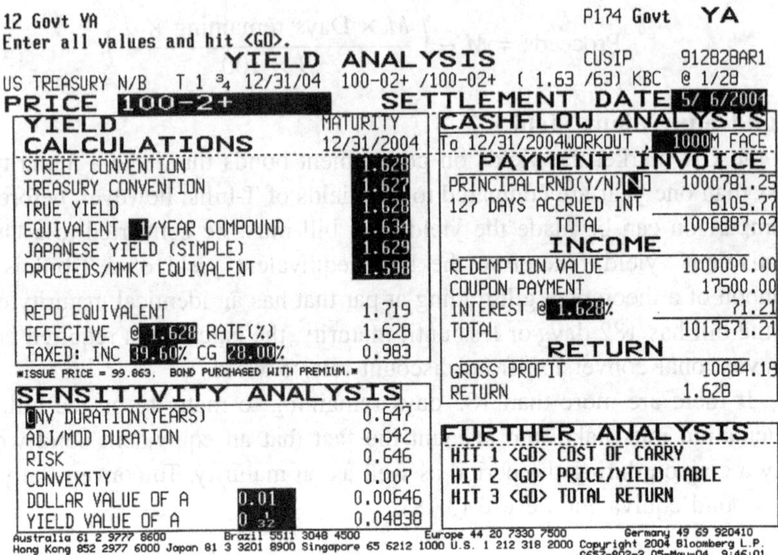

Figure 3.9 Bloomberg screen YA for US Treasury $1^3/_4\%$ 2004 bond, as at 5 May 2004

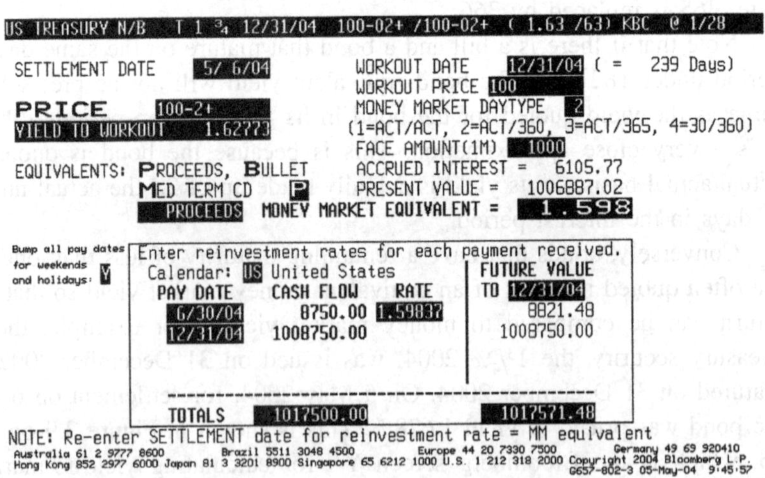

Figure 3.10 Bloomberg screen ME for US Treasury $1^3/_4\%$ 2004 bond, as at 5 May 2004, showing money market equivalent yield

Bankers acceptances

A bankers acceptance is a written promise issued by a borrower to a bank to repay borrowed funds. The lending bank lends funds and in return accepts the bankers acceptance. The acceptance is negotiable and can be sold in the secondary market. The investor who buys the acceptance can collect the loan on the day that repayment is due. If the borrower defaults, the investor has legal recourse to the bank that made the first acceptance. Bankers acceptances are also known as *bills of exchange, bank bills, trade bills* or *commercial bills.*

Essentially, bankers acceptances are instruments created to facilitate commercial trade transactions. The instrument is called a *bankers acceptance* because a bank accepts the ultimate responsibility to repay the loan to its holder. The use of bankers acceptances to finance commercial transactions is known as *acceptance financing*. The transactions in which acceptances are created include the import and export of goods; the storage and shipping of goods between two overseas countries, where neither the importer nor the exporter is based in the home country;[5] and the storage and shipping of goods between two entities based at home. Acceptances are discount instruments and are purchased by banks, local authorities and money market investment funds. The creation of a bankers acceptance is illustrated in Example 3.5.

The rate that a bank charges a customer for issuing a bankers acceptance is a function of the rate at which the bank thinks it will be able to sell it in the secondary market. A commission is added to this rate. For ineligible bankers acceptances (see below) the issuing bank will add an amount to offset the cost of the additional reserve requirements.

EXAMPLE 3.5 Illustrating the creation of a bankers acceptance in the sterling market

The following fictitious institutions are involved in this process:

- PCTools plc, a firm in London that sells information technology equipment, including personal computers, laptops and so on;
- Rony Ltd, a manufacturer of personal computers (PCs) based in Japan;
- ABC Bank plc, a clearing bank based in London;

[5] A bankers acceptance created to finance such a transaction is known as a *third-party acceptance.*

- Samurai Bank, a bank based in Japan;
- XYZ Bank plc, another bank based in London;
- Thistle Investors plc, a money market fund based in Edinburgh.

PCTools and Rony Ltd are to enter into a deal in which PCTools will purchase (that is, import) a consignment of PCs with a transaction value of £1 million; however, Rony Ltd is concerned about the ability of PCTools to make payment on the PCs when they are delivered. To get around this uncertainty both parties decided to fund the transaction using acceptance financing. The terms of the transaction are that payment must be made by PCTools within 60 days after the PCs have been shipped to the United Kingdom. In determining whether it is willing to accept the £1 million, it must calculate the present value of the amount because it will not be receiving this sum until 60 days after shipment. Therefore it agrees to the following terms:

- PCTools arranges with its bankers, ABC Bank plc, to issue a letter of credit (LOC, also known as a *time draft*). The LOC states that ABC Bank plc will guarantee the payment of £1 million that PCTools must make to Rony 60 days after shipment. The LOC is sent by ABC Bank plc to Rony's bankers, who are Samurai Bank. On receipt of the LOC, Samurai Bank notifies Rony, who will then transport the PCs. After the PCs are shipped, Rony presents the shipping documents to Samurai Bank and receives the present value of £1 million. This completes the transaction for Rony Ltd.
- Samurai Bank presents the LOC and the shipping documents to ABC Bank plc. The latter will stamp the LOC as "accepted", thus creating a bankers acceptance. This means that ABC Bank plc agrees to pay the holder of the bankers acceptance the sum of £1 million on the maturity date. PCTools will receive the shipping documents so that it can then take delivery of the PCs once it signs a note or financing arrangement with ABC Bank plc.

At this point the holder of the bankers acceptance is Samurai Bank. It has two choices open to it: it may retain the bankers acceptance as an investment in its loan portfolio, or it may request that ABC Bank plc makes a payment of the present value of £1 million. Let us assume that Samurai elects to request payment of the present value of £1 million.

At this point, the holder of the bankers acceptance is ABC Bank plc. It also has two choices to retain the bankers acceptance as an investment, or to sell it to an investor. Again, we assume that it chooses the latter, and one of its clients, Thistle Investors, is interested in a high-quality instrument with the same maturity as the bankers acceptance. ABC Bank plc sells the acceptance to Thistle Investments at the present value of £1 million, calculated using the appropriate discount rate for paper of that maturity and credit quality. Alternatively, it may have sold the acceptance to another bank, such as XYZ Bank plc, that also runs a book in acceptances.

In either case, on maturity of the bankers acceptance, its holder presents it to ABC Bank plc and receives the maturity value of £1 million, which the bank in turn recovers from PCTools plc. The holder of a bankers acceptance is exposed to credit risk on two fronts: the risk that the original borrower is unable to pay the face value of the acceptance, and the risk that the accepting bank will not be able to redeem the paper.

For this reason the rate paid on a bankers acceptance will be on average 10–25 basis points higher than the equivalent maturity T-bill. Someone trading in acceptances though will need to know the identity and credit risk of the original borrower as well as the accepting bank.

Eligible bankers acceptance

An accepting bank that chooses to retain a bankers acceptance in its portfolio may be able to use it as collateral for a loan obtained from the central bank during open market operations; for example, the Bank of England in the United Kingdom and the Federal Reserve in the United States. Not all acceptances are eligible to be used as collateral in this way, as they must meet certain criteria set by the central bank. The main requirement for eligibility is that the acceptance must be within a certain maturity band (a maximum of six months in the United States and three months in the United Kingdom), and that it must have been created to finance a self-liquidating commercial transaction. In the United States eligibility is also important because the Federal Reserve imposes a reserve requirement on funds raised via bankers acceptances that are ineligible.

Bankers acceptances sold by an accepting bank are potential liabilities of the bank, but the reserve imposes a limit on the amount of eligible bankers acceptances that a bank may issue. Bills eligible for deposit at a central bank enjoy a better rate than ineligible bills, and also act as a benchmark for prices in the secondary market.

Commercial paper

Commercial paper (CP) is a short-term money market funding instrument issued by corporates. In most markets, including the United States and United Kingdom, it is a discount instrument. Companies' short-term capital and *working* capital requirement is usually sourced directly from banks, in the form of bank loans. An alternative short-term funding instrument is CP, which is available to corporates that have a sufficiently strong credit rating. CP is a short-term unsecured promissory note. The issuer of the note promises to pay its holder a specified amount on a specified maturity date. CP normally has a zero coupon and trades at a *discount* to its face value. The discount represents interest to the investor in the period to maturity. CP is typically issued in bearer form, although some issues are in registered form.

In the London market, CP was not introduced until the mid-1980s. In the United States, however, the market was developed in the late nineteenth century, and as early as 1922 there were 2,200 issuers of CP with $700 million outstanding. In 2005 there was just over $1 trillion outstanding. After its introduction in the United Kingdom in 1986, CP was subsequently issued in other European countries.

Originally the CP market was restricted to borrowers with a high credit rating, and although lower-rated borrowers do now issue CP, sometimes by obtaining credit enhancements or setting up collateral arrangements, issuance in the market is still dominated by highly rated companies. The majority of issues are very short-term, from 30 to 90 days in maturity; it is extremely rare to observe paper with a maturity of more than 270 days or nine months. This is because of regulatory requirements in the United States,[6] which states that debt instruments with a maturity of less than 270 days need not be registered. Companies therefore issue CP with a maturity lower than nine months and so avoid the administration costs associated with registering issues with the SEC.

[6] This is the Securities Act of 1933. Registration is with the Securities and Exchange Commission.

	USCP	ECP
Currency	US dollar	Any Euro currency
Maturity	1–270 days	2–365 days
Common maturity	30–50 days	30–90 days
Interest	Zero coupon, issued at discount	Zero-coupon, issued at discount
Quotation	On a discount rate basis	On a yield basis
Settlement	T + 0	T + 2
Registration	Bearer form	Bearer form
Negotiable	Yes	Yes

Table 3.1 Comparison of USCP and ECP

There are two major markets: the US dollar market with an outstanding amount in 2005 just under $1.3 trillion, and the Eurocommercial paper (EuroCP or ECP) market with outstanding value of $470 billion at the end of 2005.[7] CP markets are wholesale markets, and transactions are typically very large size. In the United States over one-third of all CP is purchased by money market unit trusts, known as mutual funds; other investors include pension fund managers, retail or commercial banks, local authorities and corporate treasurers. Table 3.1 is a summary of the main differences between the USCP and ECP markets.

Although there is a secondary market in CP, little trading activity takes place since investors generally hold CP until maturity. This is to be expected because investors purchase CP that match their specific maturity requirement. In fact, issuers are frequently contacted by investors in a "reverse enquiry", asking for specific maturity date issuance of their CP. When an investor does wish to sell paper, it can be sold back to the dealer or, where the issuer has placed the paper directly in the market (and not via an investment bank), it can be sold back to the issuer.

CP programmes

The issuers of CP are often divided into two categories of company: banking and financial institutions and non-financial companies. The majority of CP issues are by financial companies. Financial companies include not only banks but also the financing arms of corporates such as General Motors, Ford Motor Credit, British Airways plc and Daimler-Chrysler Financial.

[7] *Source*: Morgan Stanley International.

Most of the issuers have strong credit ratings, but lower-rated borrowers have tapped the market, often after arranging credit support from a higher rated company, such as a *letter of credit* from a bank, or by arranging collateral for the issue in the form of high-quality assets such as Treasury bonds. CP issued with credit support is known as *credit-supported commercial paper*, while paper backed with assets is known naturally enough, as *asset-backed commercial paper*. Paper that is backed by a bank letter of credit is termed *LOC paper*. Although banks charge a fee for issuing letters of credit, borrowers are often happy to arrange for this, since by so doing they are able to tap the CP market. The yield paid on an issue of CP will be lower than a commercial bank loan.

Although CP is a short-dated security, typically of three- to six-month maturity, it is issued within a longer-term programme, usually for three to five years for euro paper; US CP programmes are often open-ended. For example, a company might arrange a five-year CP programme with a limit of $500 million. Once the programme is established the company can issue CP up to this amount, say for maturities of 30 or 60 days. The programme is continuous and new CP can be issued at any time, daily if required. The total amount in issue cannot exceed the limit set for the programme. A CP programme can be used by a company to manage its short-term liquidity; that is, its working capital requirements. New paper can be issued whenever a need for cash arises, and for an appropriate maturity.

Issuers often roll over their funding and use funds from a new issue of CP to redeem a maturing issue. There is a risk that an issuer might be unable to roll over the paper where there is a lack of investor interest in the new issue. To provide protection against this risk issuers often arrange a stand-by line of credit from a bank, normally for all of the CP programme, to draw against in the event that it cannot place a new issue. This is known as a *liquidity facility*, and is charged for by the liquidity bank.

There are two methods by which CP is issued: *direct-issued* or *direct paper* and *dealer-issued* or *dealer paper*. Direct paper is sold by the issuing firm directly to investors, and no agent bank or securities house is involved. It is common for financial companies to issue CP directly to their customers, often because they have continuous programmes and because they constantly roll-over their paper. It is therefore cost-effective for them to have their own sales arm and to sell their CP direct. The treasury arms of certain non-financial companies also issue direct paper; this includes, for example, British Airways plc corporate treasury, which runs a continuous direct CP programme, used to provide short-term working capital for the company.

Dealer paper is paper that is sold using a banking or securities house intermediary. In the United States, dealer CP is effectively dominated by investment banks, as retail (commercial) banks were until recently forbidden from underwriting CP. This restriction has since been removed and now both investment banks and CP underwrite dealer paper.

CP yields

CP is a discount instrument. There have been issues of coupon CP in the Euro market, but this is unusual, as well as floating-rate coupon CP in both the US and Euro markets. Usually though, CP is sold at a discount to its maturity value, and the difference between this maturity value and the purchase price is the interest earned by the investor. The CP day-count base is 360 days in the US and euro markets, and 365 days in the UK market. The paper is quoted on a discount yield basis, in the same manner as T-bills. The yield on CP follows that of other money market instruments and is a function of the short-dated yield curve. The yield on CP is higher than the T-bill rate; this is due to the credit risk that the investor is exposed to when holding CP, for tax reasons (in certain jurisdictions interest earned on T-bills is exempt from income tax) and because of the lower level of liquidity available in the CP market. CP also pays a higher yield than CD, due to the lower liquidity of the CP market.

ECP trades on a yield basis, similar to a CD. The expressions below illustrate the relationship between true yield and discount rate:

$$P = \frac{M}{1 + r \times (\text{Days/year})} \tag{3.19}$$

$$rd = \frac{r}{1 + r \times (\text{Days/year})} \tag{3.20}$$

$$r = \frac{rd}{1 - rd \times (\text{Days/year})} \tag{3.21}$$

where M is the face value of the instrument, rd is the discount rate and r the true yield.

Asset-backed commercial paper

The rise in securitisation has led to the growth of short-term instruments backed by the cash flows from other assets, known as *asset-backed commercial paper* (ABCP). Securitisation is the practice of using the cash flows from a specified asset, such as residential mortgages, car loans or commercial bank loans, as backing for an issue of bonds. A detailed introduction is given in Chapter 18. The assets themselves are transferred from the original owner (the *originator*) to a specially created legal entity known as a *special purpose vehicle* (SPV), so as to make them separate and bankruptcy-remote from the originator. In the meantime, the originator is able to benefit from capital market financing, often charged at a lower rate of interest than that earned by the originator on its assets. Securitised products are not money market instruments, and although ABCP is, most textbooks treat ABCP as part of the structured products market rather than as a money market product. It is nevertheless a money market product.

Generally, securitisation is used as a funding instrument by companies for three main reasons: it offers lower cost funding compared with traditional bank loan or bond financing; it is a mechanism by which assets such as corporate loans or mortgages can be removed from the balance sheet, thus improving the lender's return on assets or return on equity ratios; and it increases a borrower's funding options. When entering into securitisation, an entity may issue term securities against assets into the public or private market, or it may issue CP via a SPV known as a *conduit*. These conduits are usually sponsored by commercial banks.[8]

Entities usually access the CP market in order to secure permanent financing, rolling over individual issues as part of a longer-term *programme* and using interest-rate swaps to arrange a fixed rate if required. Conventional CP issues are typically supported by a line of credit from a commercial bank, and so this form of financing is in effect a form of bank funding. Issuing ABCP enables an originator to benefit from money market financing that it might otherwise not have access to because its credit rating is not sufficiently strong. A bank may also issue ABCP for balance sheet or funding reasons. ABCP trades, however, exactly as conventional CP. The administration and legal treatment is more onerous because of the need to establish the CP trust structure and issuing SPV. The servicing of an ABCP

[8] An SPV in the capital markets is usually called an SPV, whereas for some reason in the asset-backed money markets it is called a conduit.

programme follows that of conventional CP and is carried out by the same entities, these include the "Trust" arm of banks such as HSBC, Deutsche Bank and the Bank of New York.

Example 3.6 on page 80 details an hypothetical ABCP issue and typical structure.

Basic characteristics

An ABCP conduit has the following features:

- it is a bankruptcy-remote legal entity that issues CP to finance a purchase of assets from a seller of assets;
- the interest on the CP issued by the conduit, and its principal on maturity, will be paid out of the receipts on the assets purchased by the conduit;
- conduits have also been set up to exploit credit arbitrage opportunities, such as raising finance at Libor to invest in high-quality assets such as investment-grade rated structured finance securities that pay above Libor.

The assets that can be funded via a conduit programme are many and varied; to date they have included:

- trade receivables and equipment lease receivables;
- credit card receivables;
- auto loans and leases;
- corporate loans, franchise loans and mortgage loans;
- real-estate leases;
- investment-grade rated structured finance bonds such as asset-backed securities (ABS), mortgage-backed securities (MBS) and CDO notes;
- future (expected) cash flows.

Conduits are classified into a "programme type", which refers to the make-up of the underlying asset portfolio. This can be *single-seller* or *multi-seller*, which indicates how many institutions or entities are selling assets to the conduit. They are also designated as *funding* or securities *credit arbitrage* vehicles. A special class of conduit known as a structured investment vehicle (SIV, sometimes called a special investment vehicle) also exists. It issues both CP and medium-term notes (MTNs), and these are usually credit arbitrage vehicles, and are described in Chapter 25.

Credit enhancement and liquidity support

To make the issue of liabilities from a conduit more appealing to investors (or to secure a particular credit rating), a programme sponsor will usually arrange some form of credit enhancement and/or back-up borrowing facility. Generally, two types of credit enhancement are used, either "pool-specific" enhancement or "programme-wide". The first arrangement will cover only losses on a specific named part of the asset pool, and cannot be used to cover losses in any other part of the asset pool. Programme-wide credit enhancement is a fungible layer of credit protection that can be drawn on to cover losses from the start or if any pool-specific facility has been used up.

Pool-specific credit-enhancement instruments include the following:

- over-collateralisation: the nominal value of the underlying assets exceeds that of the issued paper;
- surety bond: a guarantee of repayment from a sponsor or other bank;
- letter of credit: a stand-by facility that the issuer can use to draw funds from;
- irrevocable loan facility;
- excess cash, invested in eligible instruments such as T-bills.

The size of a pool-specific credit-enhancement facility is quoted as a fixed percentage of the asset pool. Programme-wide credit enhancement is in the same form as pool-specific enhancement, and acts as a second layer of credit protection. It may be provided by a third party such as a commercial bank as well as by the sponsor.

Liquidity support is separate from credit enhancement. While credit-enhancement facilities cover losses due to asset default, liquidity providers undertake to make available funds should these be required for reasons other than asset default. A liquidity line is drawn on, if required, to ensure timely repayment of maturing CP. This might occur because of market disruption (such that the issuer could not place new CP in the market), an inability of the issuer to roll maturing CP, or because of asset and liability mismatches. This last item is the least serious situation, and reflects that in many cases long-dated assets are used to back short-dated liabilities, and cash flow dates often do not match. The availability of a liquidity arrangement provides comfort to investors that CP will be repaid in full and on time, and is usually arranged with a commercial bank. It is usually provided as a loan agreement, of an amount equal to 100% of the face amount of CP issued, under which the liquidity provider agrees to lend funds to the conduit as required. The security for the liquidity line comes from the underlying assets.

Figure 3.11 illustrates a typical ABC structure issuing to the US CP and Euro CP markets. Figure 3.12 on page 78 shows a multi-seller conduit set up to issue in the Euro CP market.

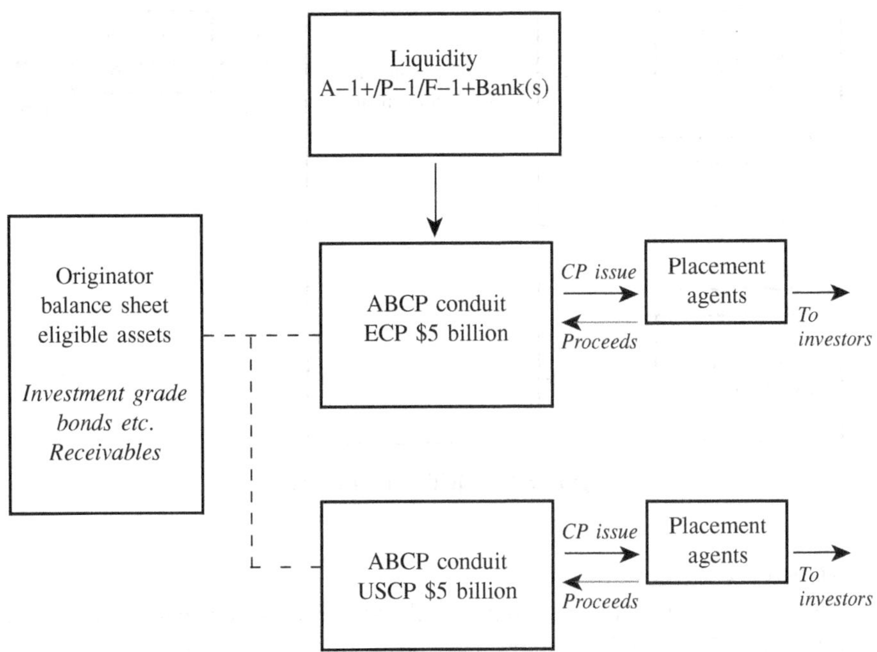

Figure 3.11 Single-seller conduit (see also Figure 19.1)

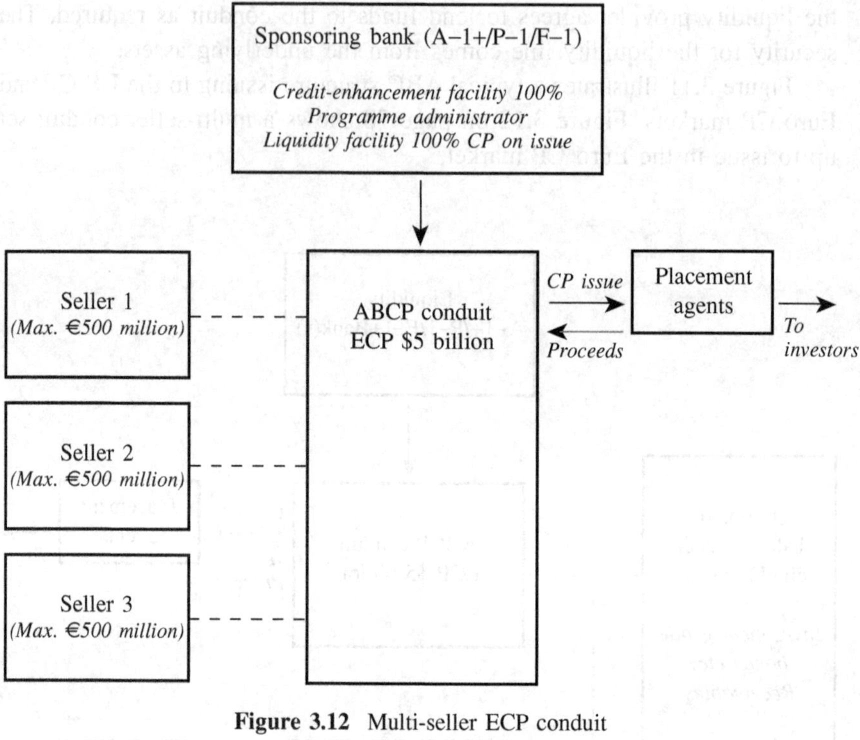

Figure 3.12 Multi-seller ECP conduit

Market volumes

The CP market is a large and liquid market in which capital is raised efficiently. The ABCP markets have also grown such that they represent considerable depth and liquidity. For instance, as at 31 March 2004, the US CP market had $1.28 trillion of outstanding paper, of which $650 billion was ABCP. Figure 3.13 shows the trend in volume, with the increasing share of ABCP apparent.

The EuroCP market has also been experiencing growth. Figure 3.14 shows the ECP market figures outstandings at the end of Quarter 1, 2004, while Figure 3.15 on page 80 shows the Euro ABCP market as a percentage of the total ECP market.

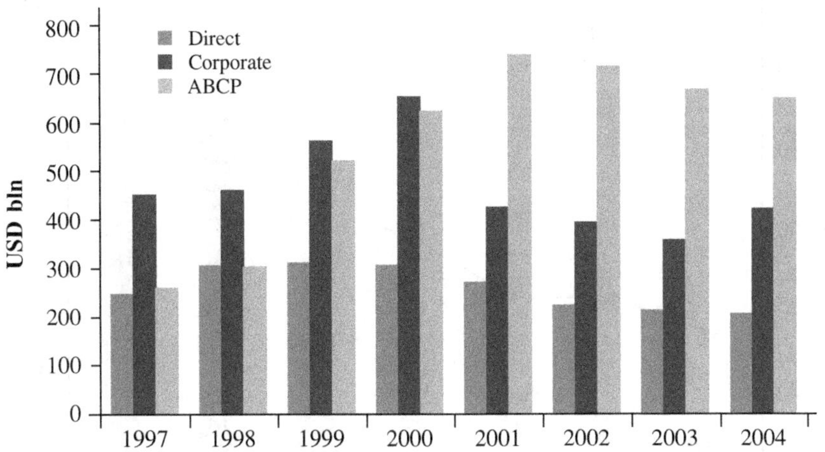

Figure 3.13 Total US CP market volumes, 2004
Source: Merrill Lynch. Reprinted with permission.

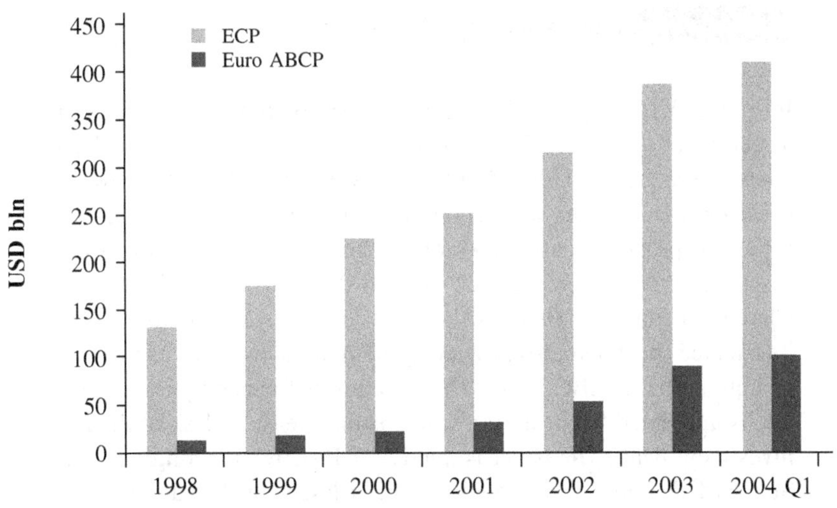

Figure 3.14 ECP market outstanding, 2004
Source: Merrill Lynch. Reprinted with permission.

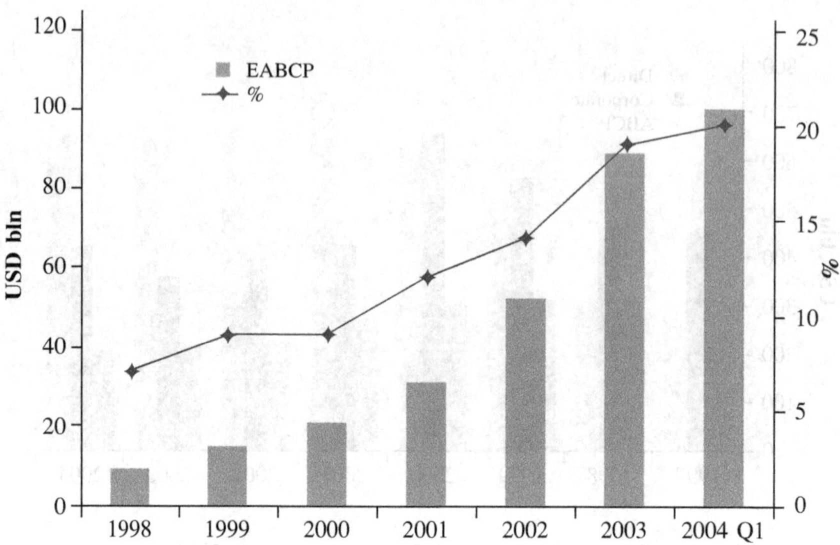

Figure 3.15 Euro ABCP market as share of total ECP market, 2004
Source: Merrill Lynch. Reprinted with permission.

EXAMPLE 3.6 Illustration of ABCP structure

In Figure 3.16 on page 82 we illustrate an hypothetical example of a securitisation of bank loans in an ABCP structure. The loans have been made by ABC Bank plc and are secured on borrowers' specified assets. They are denominated in sterling. These might be a lien on property, cash flows of the borrowers' business or other assets. The bank makes a "true sale" of the loans to an SPV, named Claremont Finance. This has the effect of removing the loans from its balance sheet and also protecting them in the event of bankruptcy or liquidation of ABC Bank. The SPV raises finance by issuing CP, via its appointed CP dealer(s), which is the Treasury desk of the MC investment bank. The paper is rated A–1/P–1 by the rating agencies Standard & Poors and Moody's, and is issued in US dollars. The liability of the CP is met by the cash flow from the original ABC Bank loans.

ABC manager is the SPV manager for Claremont Finance, a subsidiary of ABC Bank. Liquidity for Claremont Finance is provided by ABC Bank, which also acts as the hedge provider. The hedge is effected by means of a swap agreement between Claremont and ABC Bank; in fact, ABC will fix a currency swap with a swap bank counterparty, who is most likely to be the swap desk of the MC investment bank. The trustee for the transaction is Trust Bank Limited, who acts as a security trustee and represents the investors in the event of default.

The term sheet for the structure might look as follows:

Programme facility limit:	USD500 million
Facility term:	The facility is available on an uncommitted basis renewable annually by the agreement of the SPV manager and the security trustee. It has a final termination date five years from first issue.
Tenor of paper:	Seven days to 270 days.
Prepayment guarantee:	In the event of pre-payment of a loan, the seller will provide Claremont Finance with a guaranteed rate of interest for the relevant interest period.
Hedge agreement:	Claremont Finance will enter into currency and interest-rate swaps with the hedge provider to hedge any interest-rate or currency risk that arises.
Events of default:	Under event of default the issuance programme will cease and in certain events will lead to Claremont Finance to pay loan collections into a segregated specific collection account. Events of default can include non-payment by Claremont Finance under the transaction documentation, insolvency or ranking of charge (where the charge ceases to be a first ranking charge over the assets of Claremont Finance).
Loans guarantee:	Loans purchased by Claremont Finance will meet a range of eligibility criteria,

specified in the transaction offering circular. These criteria will include requirements on the currency of the loans, their term to maturity, confirmation that they can be assigned, that they are not in arrears, and so on.

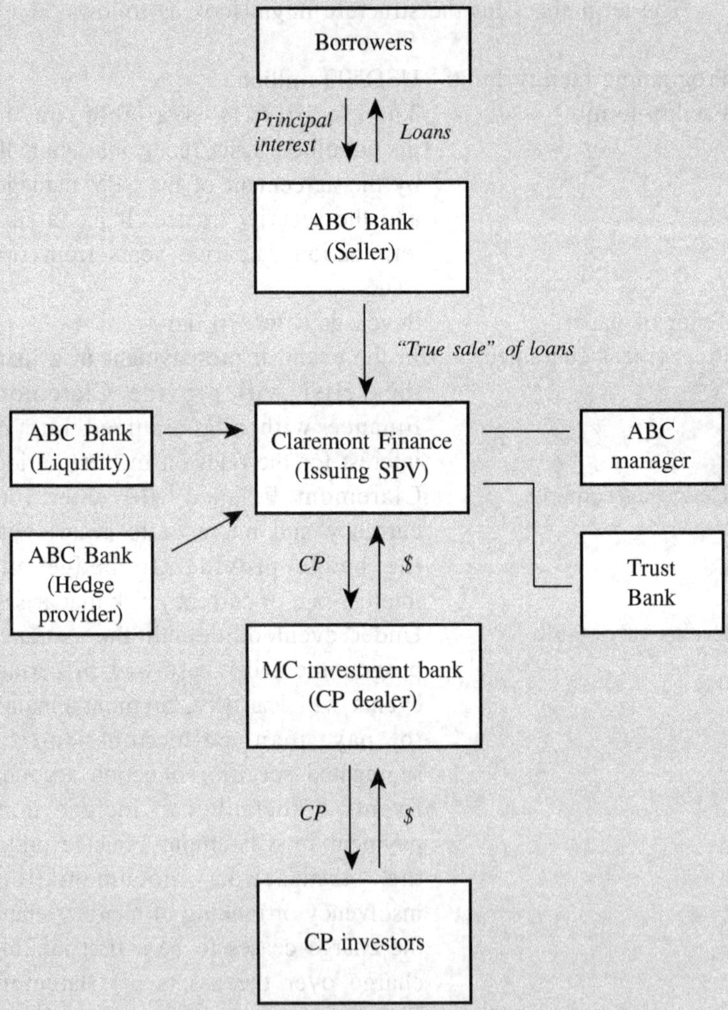

Figure 3.16 "Claremont Finance" ABCP structure

EXAMPLE 3.7 CP calculations

1. A 60-day CP note has a nominal value of £100,000. It is issued at a discount of $7^1/_2\%$ per annum. The discount is calculated as:

$$Dis = \frac{£100{,}000\ (0.075 \times 60)}{365}$$

$$= £1{,}232.88.$$

The issue price for the CP is therefore £100,000 – £1,232, or £98,768. The money market yield on this note at the time of issue is:

$$\left(\frac{365 \times 0.075}{365 - (0.075 \times 60)}\right) \times 100\% = 7.594\%.$$

Another way to calculate this yield is to measure the capital gain (the discount) as a percentage of the CP's cost, and to convert this from a 60-day yield to a one-year (365-day) yield, as shown below:

$$r = (1{,}232/98{,}768) \times (365/60) \times 100\%$$
$$= 7.588\%.$$

2. ABC plc wishes to issue CP with 90 days to maturity. The investment bank managing the issue advises that the discount rate should be 9.5%. What should the issue price be, and what is the money market yield for investors?

$$Dis = \frac{100\ (0.095 \times 90)}{365}$$

$$= 2.342$$

The issue price will be 97.658.
The yield to investors will be:

$$(2.342/97.658) \times (365/90) \times 100\% = 9.725\%.$$

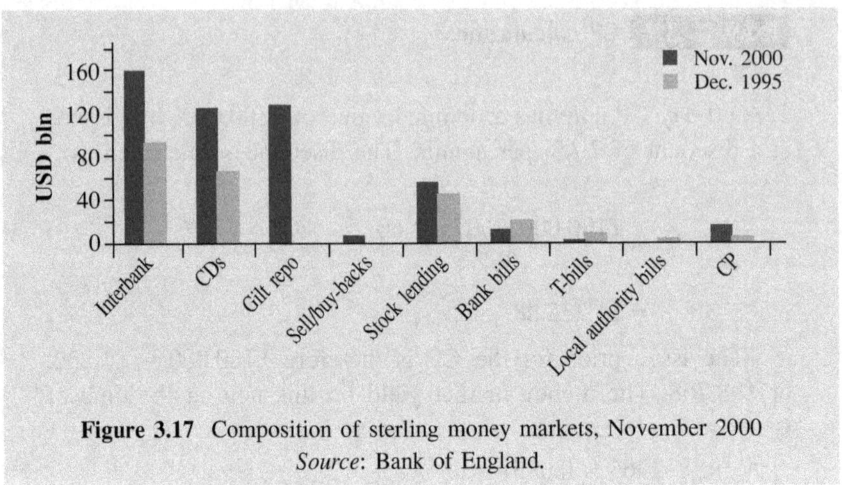

Figure 3.17 Composition of sterling money markets, November 2000
Source: Bank of England.

Extendable note commercial paper

Extendable CP is a recent development in the ABCP market and a number of conduits have been set up, or restructured, to enable them to issue it.[9] In many cases extendable CP acts as a back-up or substitute to the conventional bank liquidity line on a conduit. In this section we describe a generic extendable ABCP vehicle.

Extendable notes

Before we describe an extendable note ABCP structure, we should consider the form that the notes themselves take. Extendable notes are short-term liabilities issued by CP conduits in the normal way, but with certain structural features that enable them to act more as liquidity reserve facilities than a typical CP liability.

Extendable notes are issued in the following form:

- secured liquidity notes (SLNs);
- collateralised callable notes (CCNs).

SLNs are also referred to variously as *liquidity notes, structured liquidity notes* and *extendable commercial paper notes*. An SLN issued by a conduit

[9] The first extendable ABCP issue was in 2002, from a number of vehicles including ABN Amro "Tulip" conduit and AIG's Orchard Park and Bluegrass conduits.

is a secured note issued with a formal maturity date of up to 397 days from original issuance. (As such, its maturity exceeds the 270 or 364 days maximum maturity of US dollar or euro paper respectively.) The key aspect of the SLN, however, is that its *expected* maturity date is shorter than the formal maturity date. The last expected maturity date of the note will be a function of the underlying assets in the vehicle, and the nature of the cash flows associated with these assets. Generally, the issuer is free to set the expected maturity date in line with its requirements, up to a maximum term in line with the formal maturity date.

On the expected maturity date of the SLN, the issuer will repay the note principal and interest, usually through a roll-over issue of new SLNs. At that point, the note is no different from a normal issue of ABCP. However, if for any reason a new issue of SLNs cannot be placed, then the SLN will not be repaid and instead it will be extended until its final maturity date. This is in effect similar to a liquidity facility; if the SLN cannot be rolled over, underlying assets must be sold to cover repayment on the formal maturity date. So, for instance, if an SLN is issued with expected maturity of 90 days, and on the 90th day new SLNs cannot be issued, the SLN remains outstanding from the 91st to the 397th day. During the 307-day period after the expected repay date, underlying assets are sold, or amortise, and the proceeds are used to repay the SLNs on or before the 397th day.

The advantage of the SLN facility over a traditional bank liquidity line is that the credit-rating agencies assess the cash flow from the underlying assets (needed to repay the SLNs) for the end of the extension period. Hence, no bank liquidity would be required until this period, which would reduce the liquidity fee. Investors also view the extension of SLNs to be an unexpected occurrence, and would treat the initial issue to be normal ABCP in terms of required return.

Therefore, an SLN is essentially an ABCP issue with an extension feature at the option of the issuer. The most common occurrence is for SLNs to be issued with 90- or 180-day maturities, with a legal final maturity date of 397 days.

A CCN is a collateralised callable note issued with a final maturity date, again for a maximum of 397 days. The CCN has a call option that can be exercised by the issuer on a date prior to the final maturity date. The expected call date will depend on the nature of the cash flows of the underlying assets, but will be for a period inside the 397-day maximum. On the call date, the CCN will be called by the issuance of new CCNs. Again, this is similar to conventional ABCP. If new CCNs cannot be issued, then the CCN will not be called and it remains outstanding to its final maturity date. Unlike with an SLN, there is a yield penalty: if the issue is not called when expected, its yield is increased (by anything from 10 to 25 basis points) for the remaining term. If the CCN is not called, underlying assets must be realised to repay the proceeds on final maturity.

Investor perspective

In economic terms CCNs are identical to SLNs, although investors may view CCNs as more favourable because there is no extension risk associated with them. Also, from the point of view of a credit-rating agency, a callable note that is not called can be considered a not abnormal occurrence, while the extension of a SLN could be construed to be a serious negative occurrence.

Where the market has a reasonable idea of the likelihood of an extended note facility actually being used, it is better able to determine how much of a return premium should be demanded by investors. For instance, the view among investors is that the ABN Amro "Tulip" and the Citibank "Dakota" vehicles are highly unlikely to exercise their extension facilities, hence this paper is treated more or less as conventional ABCP.[10]

Issuer benefits

By structuring, or restructuring, a conduit with an extendable note facility, issuers can reduce their overall cost of funding. It also gives them more flexibility with managing their liquidity requirements and allows for unexpected occurrences.

The main advantages of an extendable note facility are:

- the freedom of having a one-year liquidity facility at lower cost than a normal liquidity line;
- the flexibility to issue to any term within the 397-day period;
- favourable credit-rating agency treatment, who view the extendable notes as 397-day liabilities, thus any liquidity back-up need not kick in until then;

[10] In addition, the Dakota programme stipulates a number of triggers under which the extended note facility will kick in, connected with cash flows on a Citibank credit card ABS programme called Master Trust I. If these triggers, which relate to excess interest spread and the underlying asset principal repayment rate, are breached, the Dakota notes will be extended. By measuring the likelihood of these triggers kicking in, investors can gauge the possibility of the SLNs being extended.

- if backed with a traditional liquidity facility, or (in synthetic ABCP programmes) a guaranteed total-return swap contract (TRS), the extended note facility is viewed very favourably by investors and traded as conventional ABCP.

The credit-rating agencies consider its liquidity management capabilities as an essential component when making their rating assessment of a bank. Typically, a rating agency will analyse the following factors in assigning a bank's rating:

- diversity of funding sources;
- structure and maturity of liabilities;
- balance sheet flexibility;
- ability to access the markets for funding in time of correction or illiquidity.

The addition of an extendable note facility to a bank's ABCP funding vehicles should strengthen the above points from the perspective of the ratings agencies. In fact, a number of banks have set up extendable note ABCP vehicles, or restructured existing vehicles to issue both straight and extendable ABCP. These banks include Citibank, Sumitomo, Banco Santander, CDC Ixis, Bear Stearns and State Street.

Conduit structuring

It is possible to structure a CP vehicle to issue straight and extendable CP from inception or to modify an existing vehicle for subsequent extendable note issuance. In the case of existing conduits that are set up to issue extendable paper, the restructuring can be effected by allowing extendable notes to be issued that are backed with:

- a facility to liquidate or amortise underlying assets within the extension period; market value risk of assets not being able to cover liabilities can be hedged through over-collateralisation, or a swap arrangement that pays out on any underperformance;
- setting up a TRS with a highly rated counterparty or guaranteed by another bank that supports the extendable notes on final maturity;
- a traditional bank liquidity facility that is drawn on to repay notes on final maturity.

A traditional bank liquidity facility is the most expensive option, as it carries with it a standing fee that is payable irrespective of whether the line is ever drawn on.

For existing vehicles, legal documentation describing the conduit structure (the issue and paying agency agreement and the placement agreement or "private placement memorandum") would need to be re-drafted and executed. The redrafted documents would describe the new facility to issue both extendable and straight ABCP.

Figure 3.18 illustrates the structure diagram for a multi-seller, multi-SPV combined ABCP and extendable note programme.

Commercial paper dealing sheet

The Treasury or money markets desk will keep a note of all liabilities of the vehicle so that they are aware of the roll-over schedule on each CP maturity. In Figure 3.19 we show a typical dealing sheet for an ABCP programme, as at 10 August 2004.

The dealing sheet shows data on each issue, with the name of the dealer, the term, discount rate, term to maturity, remaining term and so on. We see that there is a timetable of continuous issuance, with the next roll-over of paper due on 8 September 2004.

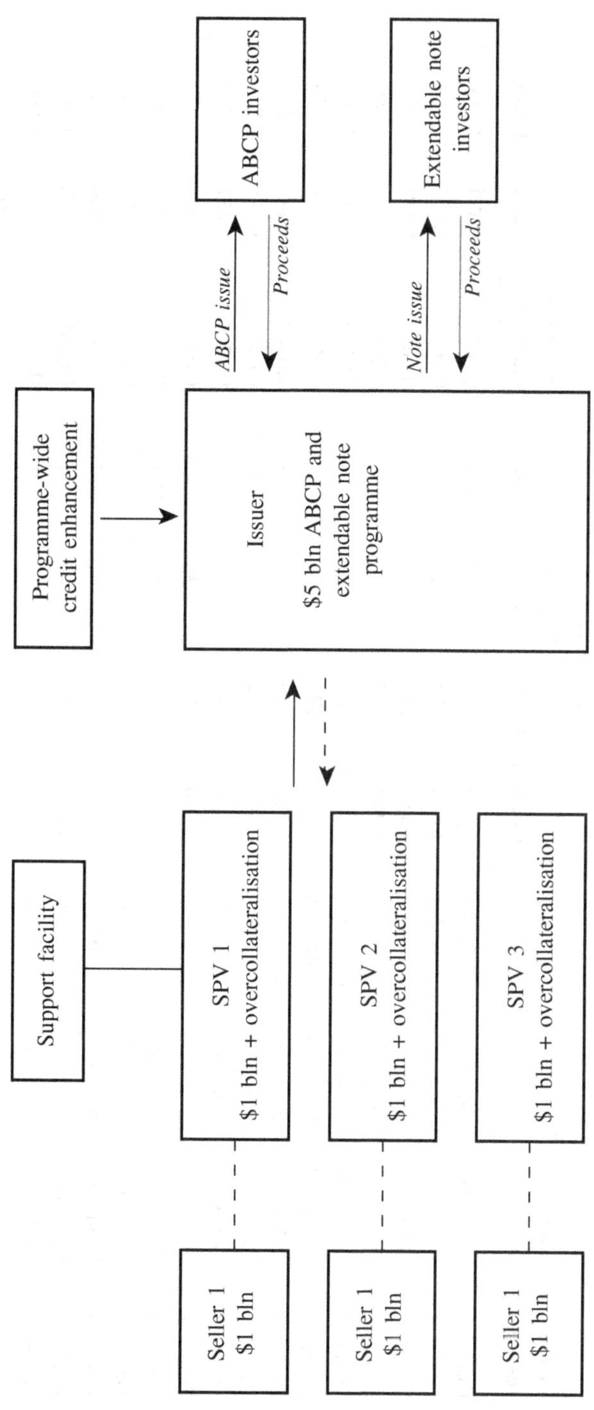

Figure 3.18 Combined ABCP/Extendable note programme

ABC Funding plc
CP dealing sheet

			1,558,180,000	1.435		38.69	23,055	0.089		1.576
10-Aug-04 10-Aug-04	**Value date**	**Maturity date**	**Nominal funds**	**Coupon**	**Term**	**Days to re-fix**	**bpv**	**Modified duration**	**p&l**	**Libor**
Dealer 1	29-Jul-04	8-Sep-04	15,828,000	1.500	41	29	99.63	0.0629	679	1.568
Dealer 2	8-Jul-04	8-Sep-04	75,000,000	1.480	62	29	472.18	0.0630	4,161	1.568
Dealer 1	10-Mar-04	8-Sep-04	21,123,000	1.150	182	29	133.42	0.0632	5,579	1.568
Dealer 1	14-Jul-04	9-Sep-04	94,223,000	1.490	57	30	618.93	0.0657	4,874	1.569
Dealer 3	11-Mar-04	9-Sep-04	61,351,000	1.130	182	30	404.44	0.0659	17,745	1.569
Dealer 2	15-Mar-04	10-Sep-04	81,462,000	1.140	179	31	559.33	0.0687	24,061	1.570
Dealer 3	17-Mar-04	13-Sep-04	40,230,000	1.140	180	34	309.37	0.0769	13,440	1.574
Dealer 2	12-Jul-04	14-Sep-04	50,133,000	1.490	64	35	397.92	0.079	3,415	1.576
Dealer 3	16-Mar-04	14-Sep-04	4,000,000	1.150	182	35	31.86	0.0796	1,357	1.576
Dealer 1	18-Jun-04	15-Sep-04	92,500,000	1.550	89	36	759.07	0.0821	2,068	1.577
Dealer 1	16-Mar-04	17-Sep-04	113,696,000	1.150	185	38	999.14	0.0879	42,971	1.580
Dealer 1	24-Jun-04	20-Sep-04	71,278,000	1.590	88	41	682.13	0.096	-387	1.584
Dealer 1	22-Jun-04	20-Sep-04	50,000,000	1.550	90	41	478.69	0.096	1,644	1.584
Dealer 2	20-Jul-04	21-Sep-04	45,121,000	1.530	63	42	444.41	0.0985	2,478	1.586
Dealer 2	8-Jul-04	5-Oct-04	77,159,000	1.600	89	56	1054.78	0.1367	589	1.606
Dealer 2	6-Jul-04	5-Oct-04	41,164,000	1.570	91	56	562.88	0.1367	2,003	1.606
Dealer 2	1-Jul-04	5-Oct-04	50,000,000	1.620	96	56	683.37	0.137	-985	1.606
Dealer 1	9-Aug-04	7-Oct-04	87,733,000	1.620	59	58	1247.05	0.142	-1,445	1.608

Dealer 2	5-Aug-04	7-Oct-04	226,655,000	1.650	63	58	3220.76	0.1421	−13,393	1.608
Dealer 3	15-Jul-04	14-Oct-04	59,240,000	1.600	91	65	955.59	0.1613	2,011	1.621
Dealer 3	12-Jul-04	15-Oct-04	40,168,000	1.580	95	66	659.05	0.164	2,834	1.623
Dealer 2	20-Apr-04	19-Oct-04	46,429,000	1.260	182	70	815.13	0.1756	30,228	1.631
Dealer 2	23-Jun-04	21-Dec-04	35,195,000	1.660	120	72	634.71	0.180	−1,603	1.635
Dealer 3	28-Jun-04	25-Dec-04	10,056,000	1.670	119	76	192.32	0.191	−527	1.643
Dealer 3	25-Jun-04	25-Dec-04	48,274,000	1.670	122	76	923.24	0.191	−2,531	1.643
Dealer 3	5-Aug-04	7-Jan-05	20,162,000	1.860	155	150	791.75	0.3927	−4,652	1.801
			1,558,180,000	1.435					$152,355	1.576
Liquidity maturity									−$55,001	

Next	8-Sep-04	15,828,000
Rollover schedule	8-Sep-04	75,000,000
	8-Sep-04	21,123,000

	Value date	Maturity date	CP rate	Issue price	CP nominal	Actual cash	Real interest	Term	Days to maturity
Nominal value									
Calculator	28 Aug 04	1 Jan 05	2.100%	99.253333%	251,880,709.30	250,000,000.00	2.1157980%	128	114

Figure 3.19 Hypothetical ABCP programme dealing sheet, for data as at 10 August 2004

EXAMPLE 3.8 Money markets clearing in CREST

The Central Moneymarkets Office (CMO) was the clearing system for the London money markets. It supports the settlement of sterling- and euro-denominated money markets instruments. The CMO was originally developed by the Bank of England but merged with CREST, the London market equity settlement system in July 2000; hence, CMO is now operated by CRESTCo on behalf of the Bank of England. The CREST mechanism provides secure facilities for what is termed the *immobilisation* and transfer of bills, CDs and CP. Settling through CREST means that the clearing system is *dematerialised*; that is, by computer book-entry transfer, obviating the need for physical settlement.

CREST settlement

When settled through CREST, money market instruments are immobilised within the CERST Depository operated by the Bank of England on behalf of CRESTCo. The instrument is lodged into CREST by the issuing and paying agent (IPA), which acts as agent for the issuer of the paper. It is usually an appointed agent bank. Lodgement usually is into the account of the primary dealer, against payment sent via CREST. The primary dealer may retain the instruments in its CREST account, or they may be passed onto other members.

CREST settlement occurs on the same day of issue, between 08.30 and 17.00 hours. This same-day settlement is termed *London Good Delivery*. The service supports the transfer of instruments against sterling or euro payment; paper may be used as collateral against loans or in repo within the CREST mechanism, which assists in maintaining market liquidity. Once paper is lodged in CREST it is of course dematerialised, but it may be withdrawn into physical form before it matures. However, this is rare. Paper may also be transferred to Euroclear, which maintains an account at CREST. When an instrument matures, CREST will automatically transfer it to the IPA, in return for the redemption proceeds.

Only CREST members may lodge instruments into the CREST facility. As at May 2003 there were 31 members of the service, which included the main commercial banks such as RBoS, Lloyds TSB, Barclays, JPMorgan Chase and Citigroup.

Money market screens on Bloomberg

Market professionals such as those on the money market trading desks of banks make extensive use of the Bloomberg system for trading and analytics. In this section we illustrate some key Bloomberg screens.

A good overview screen is BTMM. Figures 3.20 and 3.21 on page 94 show this screen for the US dollar and sterling markets. As we can see, this page is a "composite" of a number of rates and market sectors; for instance, the US "Fed Funds" rate[11] is in the top-left corner, while US Treasury bond yields, swap rates and futures rates are also shown. A slightly different layout is adopted for the UK markets, in Figure 3.21, which has T-bill rates as well.

GRAB Corp BTMM

Change Country US TREASURY & MONEY MARKETS 11:34:49

11/7	FED FUNDS	
BID/ASK	15/16	1
LST/OPEN	1	1
HIGH/LOW	1	1

US T-BILL YIELD/PRICE				
4W	0.93	-0.00	0.92	0.91
3M	0.95	-0.00	0.94	0.93
6M	1.06	0.01	1.05	1.04

EURO$DEP		
3M	1 3/32	1 1/8
6M	1 5/32	1 7/32
1Y	1 1/2	1 9/16

	REVERSE	REPO
O/N	0.96	0.95
1W	1.00	0.95
2W	1.00	0.95
1M	1.00	0.95

DJIA	9809.79	-47.18
S&P 500 FUT	1050.40	-8.10
CCMP	1970.74	-5.63

US BONDS YLD/BID/ASK/CHG				
1 5/8 10/31/05	2.008	99-08	99-08+	00
2 3/8 08/16/06	2.463	99-24	99-24+	00
3 1/8 10/16/08	3.431	98-19+	98-20	00
4 1/4 08/15/13	4.434	98-16+	98-17+	01
5 3/8 02/15/31	5.246	101-26	101-27	03

DEALER CP	
15D	1.030
30D	1.050
60D	1.060
90D	1.100
120D	1.120
180D	1.170

90D EUR$ FUT	
DEC	98.79
MAR	98.57
JUN	98.19
SEP	97.75
DEC	97.29
MAR	96.89

FUNDS FUT	
NOV	98.99
DEC	98.99
JAN	98.98
FEB	98.94
MAR	98.88
APR	98.81

LIBOR FIX	
1W	1.09375
1M	1.12000
2M	1.17000
3M	1.18000
4M	1.21000
5M	1.24000
6M	1.27000
1Y	1.57500

SPOT FOREX	
JPY	108.5800
EUR	1.1486
GBP	1.6745
CHF	1.3696
MXN	10.9845

KRCRB	251.03	2.39

30Y MBS			
GNMA 5.5	100-13	100-14	00
GOLD 5.5	99-30	99-31	00
FNMA 5.5	99-30	99-31	00

LONG BOND FUT		
CBT	107-04	- 07

CRUDE,FUEL OIL		
WTI	30.85	0.59

SWAP RATES	
5Y	3.869
10Y	4.856

BANK RATES	
PRIME	4.00
BLR	2.75

Date/Time			Indicator			BN Survey	Actual	Prior	Revised
11/13 13:30	US	1)	Trade Balance		(SEP)	-$40.2B	- -	-$39.2B	- -
11/13 13:30	US	2)	Import Price Index	(MoM)	(OCT)	0.5%	- -	-0.5%	- -
11/13 13:30	US	3)	Import Price Index	(YoY)	(OCT)	- -	- -	0.8%	- -
11/13 13:30	US	4)	Initial Jobless Claims		(NOV8)	364K	- -	348K	- -

Australia 61 2 9777 8600 Brazil 5511 3048 4500 Europe 44 20 7330 7500 Germany 49 69 920410
Hong Kong 852 2977 6000 Japan 81 3 3201 8900 Singapore 65 6212 1000 U.S. 1 212 318 2000 Copyright 2003 Bloomberg L.P.
G657-802-0 10-Nov-03 11:34:49

Figure 3.20 Bloomberg screen BTMM US for US dollar rates, 10 November 2003

[11] This is in effect the US base interest rate, it is the rate at which the Federal Reserve lends funds to the primary Federal Reserve dealing banks.

GRAB Corp **BTMM**

Change Country | UNITED KINGDOM - TSY & MONEY MARKETS | 11:35:11

DEP DOMESTIC		EURO	LIBOR		SWAPS		
O/N	3.3438	3.3438	1M	3.81156	1YR	4.51	4.53
1WK	3.5625	3.6850	2M	3.88500	1.5Y	4.70	4.73
2WK	3.7188	3.7200	3M	3.97625	2YR	4.87	4.91
3WK	3.6562	3.7350	4M	4.04250	3YR	5.08	5.09
1MO	3.7344	3.7450	5M	4.10500	4YR	5.18	5.19
2MO	3.8425	3.8500	6M	4.17250	5YR	5.22	5.25
3MO	3.9362	3.9300	7M	4.23375	6YR	5.25	5.27
6MO	4.1262	4.1100	8M	4.29500	7YR	5.26	5.28
9MO	4.3194	4.2900	9M	4.35375	8YR	5.26	5.28
12MO	4.4550	4.4700	10M	4.41500	9YR	5.26	5.28
			11M	4.47500	10YR	5.26	5.28
			12M	4.53891			

FRAs	
1X4	4.0580
2X5	4.1905
3X6	4.2935
4X7	4.3970
5X8	4.5170
6X9	4.6100
9X12	4.8880
1X7	4.2605
2X8	4.3700
3X9	4.4780
6X12	4.7755
12X18	5.2130
12X24	5.3820

T-BILLS	
1M	3.740
2M	3.800
3M	3.900
1YR	4.028

GILTS		
2Y	4.583	-0.062
3Y	4.754	-0.055
5Y	4.918	-0.052
6Y	4.976	-0.047
7Y	5.026	-0.038
10Y	5.054	-0.025
15Y	5.067	-0.024
20Y	5.020	-0.009
30Y	4.880	0.005

SPOT FOREX	
GBP	1.6746
EUR	1.1487
€/GBP	.6859
£/CHF	2.2940
£/JPY	181.8050

BASE RT
3.750

COMMODITIES		
GOLD	383.60	0.55
SILVER	5.03	-0.03
BRENT	28.81	0.10

CRUDE/FUEL OIL	
WTI	30.85

FUTURES		
0LA	95.91	0.01
G A	114.19	0.22

FTSE100	4360.30	-16.60
FTSE350	2198.30	-8.30

Date/Time			Indicator			BN Survey	Actual	Prior	Revised
11/10 0:01	UK	1)	Land Registry residential property price report						
11/10 9:30	UK	2)	PPI Input s.a.	(MoM)	(OCT)	0.7%	1.6%	-1.2%	-1.1%
11/10 9:30	UK	3)	PPI Input s.a.	(YoY)	(OCT)	0.7%	1.8%	0.5%	0.7%
11/10 9:30	UK	4)	PPI Output n.s.a.	(MoM)	(OCT)	0.2%	0.1%	0.1%	0.0%

Figure 3.21 Screen BTMM UK for sterling money rates, 10 November 2003

A selection of money rates can also be seen using page MMR. Figure 3.22 shows this page for the sterling market. Money market yield curves are accessed from the main MMCV screen. The menu page is shown in Figure 3.23, while the sterling curve is shown in Figure 3.24 on page 96. This can also be viewed as a table, which we illustrate in Figure 3.25.

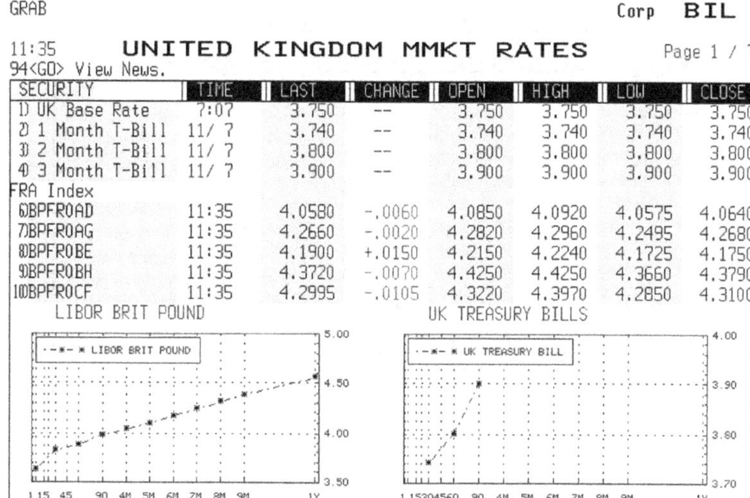

GRAB Corp BIL

11:35 UNITED KINGDOM MMKT RATES Page 1 / 7

94<GO> View News.

SECURITY	TIME	LAST	CHANGE	OPEN	HIGH	LOW	CLOSE
1) UK Base Rate	7:07	3.750	--	3.750	3.750	3.750	3.750
2) 1 Month T-Bill	11/ 7	3.740	--	3.740	3.740	3.740	3.740
3) 2 Month T-Bill	11/ 7	3.800	--	3.800	3.800	3.800	3.800
4) 3 Month T-Bill	11/ 7	3.900	--	3.900	3.900	3.900	3.900
FRA Index							
6)BPFR0AD	11:35	4.0580	-.0060	4.0850	4.0920	4.0575	4.0640
7)BPFR0AG	11:35	4.2660	-.0020	4.2820	4.2960	4.2495	4.2680
8)BPFR0BE	11:35	4.1900	+.0150	4.2150	4.2240	4.1725	4.1750
9)BPFR0BH	11:35	4.3720	-.0070	4.4250	4.4250	4.3660	4.3790
10)BPFR0CF	11:35	4.2995	-.0105	4.3220	4.3970	4.2850	4.3100

Australia 61 2 9777 8600 Brazil 5511 3048 4500 Europe 44 20 7330 7500 Germany 49 69 920410
Hong Kong 852 2977 6000 Japan 81 3 3201 8900 Singapore 65 6212 1000 U.S. 1 212 318 2000 Copyright 2003 Bloomberg L.P.
G657-802-0 10-Nov-03 11:35:41

Figure 3.22 Sterling money rates page MMR as at 10 November 2003

GRAB M-Mkt MMCV

Enter curve selections and hit <GO>

MMKT SINGLE MARKET CURVES Page 1/4

LIBOR FIXINGS
1)Australian Dollar-M9
2)British Pound -M10
3)Canadian Dollar -M11
4)Dutch Guilder -M12
5)German Mark -M13
6)EURO Libor -M14
7)French Franc -M15
8)Italian Lira -M16
9)Japanese Yen -M17
10)Portuguese Escudo-M18
11)Swiss Franc -M19
12)Spanish Peseta -M20
13)US Dollar -M21
14)EURO Libor -M76
15)Eurolibor Act/365-M95

U.S. CURVES
16)Dealer CP (A1+/P1-M1
17)Dealer CP (A1/P1)-M2
18)Dealer CP Split -M3
19)Dealer CP (A2/P2)-M4
20)Dealer CP (A3/P3)-M5
21)DI CP (A1+/P1) -M6
22)DI CP (A1/P1) -M7
23)DI CP (A2/P2) -M8
24)Term Fed Funds -M22
25)US Discount Notes-M47
26)U.S. T-bills -M48
27)CDs (A1+/P1) -M58
28)CDs (A1/P1) -M59
29)Asset Backed CP 1-M60
30)Asset Backed CP 2-M61
31)Fed H15 Financial-M62
32)Fed H15 Non-Finan-M63
33)H15 A2/P2 Non-Fin-M71

(Continued)
34)US Govt Repo -M74
35)US Govt Rev Repo -M75
36)GE Capital DI CP -M101
37)USD ECP (A1+/P1) -M107
38)USD ECP (A1/P1) -M108
39)US Deposits -M130

Argentina
40)Baibor IntBank-Pe-M64

Australia
41)Aust. Bank Bills -M23
42)AUD Deposit Rates-M97

Austria
43)Vienna Interbank -M40

Australia 61 2 9777 8600 Brazil 5511 3048 4500 Europe 44 20 7330 7500 Germany 49 69 920410
Hong Kong 852 2977 6000 Japan 81 3 3201 8900 Singapore 65 6212 1000 U.S. 1 212 318 2000 Copyright 2003 Bloomberg L.P.
G657-802-0 10-Nov-03 11:36:12

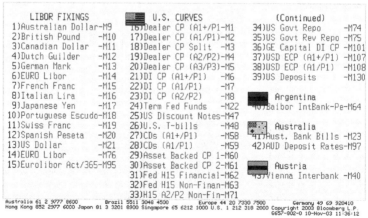

Figure 3.23 Main menu page for screen MMCV

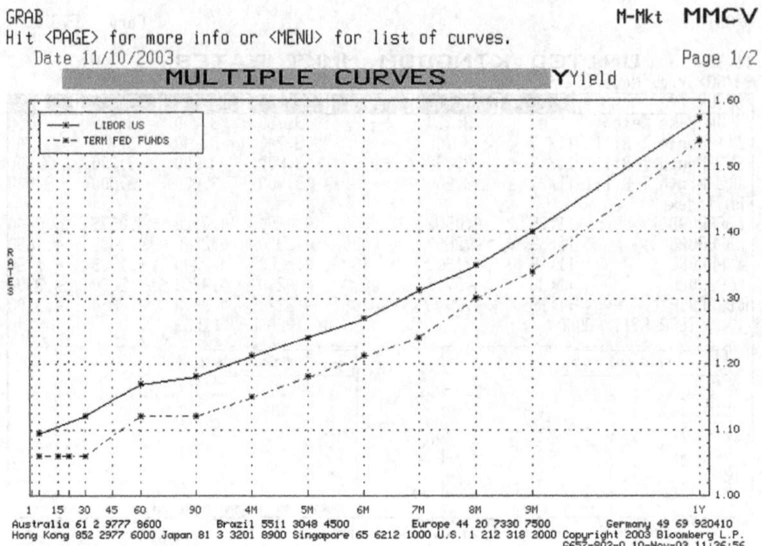

Figure 3.24 UK sterling money market yield curves as at 10 November 2003

GRAB M-Mkt MMCV
Hit <PAGE> for graph or <MENU> for list of curves.
Page 2/2

MULTIPLE CURVES

Date 11/10/2003

	11:29 LIBOR US	11/07 TERM FED FUNDS	
	Yield	Yield	Yield
1 DAY			
7 DAY	1.09375	1.06000	
15 DAY		1.06000	
21 DAY		1.06000	
30 DAY	1.12000	1.06000	
45 DAY			
60 DAY	1.17000	1.12000	
90 DAY	1.18000	1.12000	
4 MONTH	1.21000	1.15000	
5 MONTH	1.24000	1.18000	
6 MONTH	1.27000	1.21000	
7 MONTH	1.31000	1.24000	
8 MONTH	1.35000	1.30000	
9 MONTH	1.40000	1.34000	
1 YEAR	1.57500	1.54000	

Australia 61 2 9777 8600 Brazil 5511 3048 4500 Europe 44 20 7330 7500 Germany 49 69 920410
Hong Kong 852 2977 6000 Japan 81 3 3201 8900 Singapore 65 6212 1000 U.S. 1 212 318 2000 Copyright 2003 Bloomberg L.P.
G657-802-0 10-Nov-03 11:37:19

Figure 3.25 UK sterling money market yield curves, table format

Press 98<GO> to make a copy, 99<GO> to clear news alerts. Govt **MMR**
94<GO> View News.
14:44 **ASSET BACKED CP RATES** Page 1 / 1

TOP TOP TIER (A1+/P1/F1+)			TOP TIER (A1/P1/F1)		
1	↓1.77	-.05	1	↓1.77	-.06
7	↓1.77	-.02	7	↓1.79	-.03
15	1.78	--	15	1.81	--
21	↓1.78	-.02	21	↓1.80	-.02
30	↓1.78	-.01	30	↓1.79	-.01
45	1.81	--	45	1.83	--
60	↑1.86	+.01	60	↑1.88	+.01
90	↑1.94	+.01	90	↑1.95	+.01
120	↓2.00	--	120	2.01	--
150	↑2.06	+.01	150	↑2.07	+.01
180	↑2.11	+.01	180	↑2.12	+.01
210	2.13	+.01	210	1.92	--
240	2.06	+.05	240	2	+.01
270	2.16	+.06	270	2.18	+.06

FOR HISTORICAL RATES TYPE:
ALLX ACPA <GO> ALLX ACPB <GO>

Australia 61 2 9777 8600 Brazil 5511 3048 4500 Europe 44 20 7330 7500 Germany 49 69 920410
Hong Kong 852 2977 6000 Japan 81 3 3201 8900 Singapore 65 6212 1000 U.S. 1 212 318 2000
G926-802-2 04-Oct-04 14:44:09

Figure 3.26 USD ABCP rates as at 4 October 2004, top-tier dealer placed paper

Figure 3.26 shows ABCP rates for the US dollar market for paper that has been placed via dealers. Note the different rates for top-top-tier (A1+/P1/F1+) and top-tier paper (A1/P1/F1). More information on the money market yield curve is given in Chapter 9.

BBVA money market rate screens on Bloomberg

Money market rates and prices are available from a wide range of sources and vendors. Banks and brokers post live and indicative prices on Bloomberg, Reuters, Telerate and other systems. Generally, bank rates are not available to all users, as they are usually made exclusive to registered clients.

Banco Bilbao Vizcaya Argentaria (BBVA), headquartered in Madrid, Spain, is a bank that makes its screens available to all users. It posts rates on all major vendor systems. Figures 3.27 to 3.31 show the bank's main money market menu pages on Bloomberg, which is BBVC. With the kind of permission of BBVA, for illustration purposes we show a sample of their pages here, as at 16 June 2004, for the following currencies, instruments and interest rates:

- USD deposits;
- USD overnight-interest swaps;
- EUR government bond repo;
- EUR overnight-interest swaps.

Generally, customers will check broker screens such as those of GarbanICAP and Tullett & Tokyo at the same time as they are looking at their banker's rates.

```
BBVC                                          P174 n Govt   BBVC

BBVA                       Banco Bilbao Vizcaya Argentaria
                           Global Markets
                           Via de los Poblados s/n
                           28033 Madrid  Spain
                           Tel: 34 91 537 8224/8285

        SHORT TERM INTEREST RATE TRADING

    SHORT TERM DERIVATIVES               REPO RATES
 1) EUR SWAPS (EONIA)                 9) EUR
 2) EUR FRAs
 3) USD SWAPS OIS                        T-BILLS TRADING
 4) USD FRAs                         10) Spanish T-Bills
    COMMERCIAL PAPER RATES           11) DTC Dutch T-Bills
 5) ECP                              12) BOTS Italian T-Bills
    DEPOSIT RATES                    13) CTZ Italian T-Bills
 6) EUR                                  OTHER
 7) GBP                              14) Specific Repos
 8) USD                              15) To Request Information

Australia 61 2 9777 8600        Brazil 5511 3048 4500        Europe 44 20 7330 7500        Germany 49 69 920410
Hong Kong 852 2977 6000 Japan 81 3 3201 8900 Singapore 65 6212 1000 U.S. 1 212 318 2000 Copyright 2004 Bloomberg L.P.
                                                                              G657-802-2 16-Jun-04 10:15:41
```

Figure 3.27 Money market rates menu page for BBVA

8 P1P300 Govt BBVC

9:36 BBVA PAGE 1 / 1

USD DEPOSIT RATES

	RATES	BID	ASK	TIME
1)	O/N	1.2900	1.3200	7:43
2)	T/N	1.2700	1.3000	7:20
3)	S/N	1.2700	1.3000	7:20
4)	1 WEEK	1.2700	1.3000	7:44
5)	2 WEEK	1.2700	1.3000	7:44
6)	3 WEEK	1.2700	1.3000	7:44
7)	1 MONTH	1.2800	1.3100	9:21
8)	2 MONTH	1.4100	1.4700	7:20
9)	3 MONTH	1.5100	1.5700	7:20
10)	4 MONTH	1.6000	1.6600	9:26
11)	5 MONTH	1.6800	1.7400	8:52
12)	6 MONTH	1.7800	1.8400	8:22
13)	7 MONTH	1.8600	1.9200	7:22
14)	8 MONTH	1.9300	1.9900	7:31
15)	9 MONTH	2.0100	2.0700	8:22
16)	10 MONTH	2.0800	2.1400	9:27
17)	11 MONTH	2.1700	2.2300	9:28
18)	1 YEAR	2.2400	2.3000	9:03

Figure 3.28 USD deposit rates on BBVA rates page, 16 June 2004

3 P1P300 Govt BBVC

10:15 BBVA PAGE 1 / 1

USD SWAPS OIS

	RATES	BID	ASK	TIME
1)	1 WEEK	1.0000	1.0300	6/09
2)	2 WEEK	1.0000	1.0300	6/09
3)	3 WEEK	1.0000	1.0300	6/09
4)	1 MONTH	1.1350	1.1650	6/11
5)	2 MONTH	1.2800	1.3100	6/11
6)	3 MONTH	1.4050	1.4350	6/11
7)	4 MONTH	1.5250	1.5550	6/11
8)	5 MONTH	1.6450	1.6750	6/11
9)	6 MONTH	1.7500	1.7800	6/11
10)	7 MONTH	1.8550	1.8850	6/11
11)	8 MONTH	1.9450	1.9750	6/11
12)	9 MONTH	2.0300	2.0600	6/11
13)	10 MONTH	2.1250	2.1550	6/11
14)	11 MONTH	2.2150	2.2450	6/11
15)	12 MONTH	2.3000	2.3300	6/11

ACT/360

Figure 3.29 USD overnight-index swaps (OIS) on BBVA page, 16 June 2004

9 P1P300 Govt **BBVC**

10:16 **BBVA** PAGE 1 / 1

EUR REPO RATES

	RATES	BID	ASK	TIME
1)	O/N	1.8000	1.7500	6/08
2)	T/N	2.0000	1.9800	6/08
3)	1 WEEK	1.9600	1.9300	6/08
4)	2 WEEK	1.9900	1.9700	6/08
5)	1 MONTH	1.9900	1.9700	6/08
6)	2 MONTH	2.0000	1.9800	6/08
7)	3 MONTH	2.0000	1.9800	6/08
8)	4 MONTH	2.0100	1.9900	6/08
9)	5 MONTH	2.0400	2.0100	6/08
10)	6 MONTH	2.0600	2.0300	6/08
11)	9 MONTH	2.1400	2.1100	6/08
12)	1 YEAR	2.2500	2.2200	6/08

Australia 61 2 9777 8600 Brazil 5511 3048 4500 Europe 44 20 7330 7500 Germany 49 69 920410
Hong Kong 852 2977 6000 Japan 81 3 3201 8900 Singapore 65 6212 1000 U.S. 1 212 318 2000 Copyright 2004 Bloomberg L.P.
G657-802-2 16-Jun-04 10:16:12

Figure 3.30 EUR government bond repo rates on BBVA page, 16 June 2004

1 P1P300 Govt **BBVC**

9:35 **BBVA** PAGE 1 / 1

EUR SWAPS (EONIA)

	RATES	BID	ASK	TIME
1)	1 WEEK	2.0350	2.0650	8:22
2)	2 WEEK	2.0300	2.0600	8:14
3)	3 WEEK	2.0300	2.0600	8:14
4)	1 MONTH	2.0350	2.0550	5:00
5)	2 MONTH	2.0400	2.0600	5:00
6)	3 MONTH	2.0440	2.0640	8:51
7)	4 MONTH	2.0540	2.0740	8:51
8)	5 MONTH	2.0690	2.0890	9:27
9)	6 MONTH	2.0950	2.1150	8:51
10)	7 MONTH	2.1180	2.1380	9:27
11)	8 MONTH	2.1420	2.1620	9:27
12)	9 MONTH	2.1730	2.1930	9:27
13)	10 MONTH	2.2070	2.2270	9:27
14)	11 MONTH	2.2430	2.2630	9:27
15)	12 MONTH	2.2800	2.3000	9:27
16)	15 MONTH	2.3850	2.4050	9:28
17)	18 MONTH	2.4960	2.5160	9:34
18)	21 MONTH	2.6040	2.6240	9:33
19)	2 YEAR	2.7100	2.7300	9:34

Quote: Annual Settlement & Compounding vs. EONIA Day Count: ACT/360

Australia 61 2 9777 8600 Brazil 5511 3048 4500 Europe 44 20 7330 7500 Germany 49 69 920410
Hong Kong 852 2977 6000 Japan 81 3 3201 8900 Singapore 65 6212 1000 U.S. 1 212 318 2000 Copyright 2004 Bloomberg L.P.
G657-802-2 02-Jul-04 9:35:46

Figure 3.31 EUR overnight-index swaps (EONIA) on BBVA page, 16 June 2004

Foreign exchange markets

The market in foreign exchange is an excellent example of a liquid, transparent and immediate global financial market. Rates in the foreign exchange (FX) markets move at an extremely rapid pace and one might say that trading in FX is a different discipline to bond trading or money markets trading. There is a considerable literature on the FX markets, as it is a separate subject in its own right. However, some banks organise their forward FX desk as part of the money market desk and not the foreign exchange desk, necessitating its inclusion in this book. For this reason we present an overview summary of FX in this chapter, both spot and forward.

The quotation for currencies generally follows the ISO convention, which is also used by the SWIFT and Reuters dealing systems, and is the three-letter code used to identify a currency, such as USD for US dollar and GBP for sterling. The rate convention is to quote everything in terms of one unit of the US dollar, so that the dollar and Swiss franc rate is quoted as USD/CHF, and is the number of Swiss francs to one US dollar. The exception is for sterling, which is quoted as GBP/USD and is the number of US dollars to the pound. This rate is also known as "cable". The rate for euros has been quoted both ways round – for example, EUR/USD – although some banks, such as the Royal Bank of Scotland in the United Kingdom, quote euros to the pound; that is, GBP/EUR.

The complete list of currency codes is given in Appendix 3.2.

Spot exchange rates

A *spot* FX trade is an outright purchase or sale of one currency against another currency, with delivery two working days after the trade date. Non-working days do not count, so a trade on a Friday is settled on the following Tuesday. There are some exceptions to this – for example, trades of US dollar against Canadian dollar are settled the next working day – and note that in some currencies, generally in the Middle East, markets are closed on Friday but open on Saturday. A settlement date that falls on a public holiday in the country of one of the two currencies is delayed for settlement by that day. An FX transaction is possible between any two currencies; however, to reduce the number of quotes that need to be made the market generally quotes only against the US dollar or occasionally against sterling or euro, so that the exchange rate between two non-dollar currencies is calculated from the rate for each currency against the dollar. The resulting exchange rate is known as the *cross-rate*. Cross-rates themselves are also traded between banks in addition to dollar-based rates. This is usually because the relationship between two rates is closer than that of either against the dollar; for example, the Swiss franc moves more closely in line with the euro than against the dollar, so in practice one observes that the dollar / Swiss franc rate is more a function of the euro / franc rate.

The spot FX quote is a two–way bid-offer price, just as in the bond and money markets, and indicates the rate at which a bank is prepared to buy the base currency against the variable currency; this is the "bid" for the variable currency, so it is the lower rate. The other side of the quote is the rate at which the bank is prepared to sell the base currency against the variable currency. For example, a quote of 1.6245–1.6255 for GBP/USD means that the bank is prepared to buy sterling for $1.6245, and to sell sterling for $1.6255. The convention in the FX market is uniform across countries, unlike the money markets. Although the money market convention for bid–offer quotes is for example, $5^1/_2$%–$5^1/_4$%, meaning that the "bid" for paper – the rate at which the bank will lend funds, say, in the CD market – is the higher rate and always on the left, this convention is reversed in certain countries. In the FX markets the convention is always the same one just described.

The difference between the two sides in a quote is the bank's dealing spread. Rates are quoted to 1/100th of a cent, known as a *pip*. In the quote above, the spread is 10 pips; however, this amount is a function of the size of the quote number, so that the rate for USD/JPY at, say, 110.10–110.20, indicates a spread of 0.10 yen. Generally, only the pips in the two rates are quoted, so that, for example, the quote above would be simply "45–55". The "big figure" is not quoted.

EXAMPLE 3.9 Exchange cross-rates

Consider the following two spot rates:

EUR/USD	1.0566-1.0571
AUD/USD	0.7034-0.7039.

The EUR/USD dealer buys euros and sells dollars at 1.0566 (the left side), while the AUD/USD dealer sells Australian dollars and buys US dollars at 0.7039 (the right side). To calculate the rate at which the bank buys euros and sells Australian dollars, we need to do

1.0566 / 0.7039 = 1.4997

which is the rate at which the bank buys euros and sells Australian dollars. In the same way, the rate at which the bank sells euros and buys Australian dollars is given by:

1.0571/0.7034 or 1.5028.

Therefore the spot EUR/AUD rate is 1.4997–1.5028.

The derivation of cross-rates can be depicted in the following way. If we assume two exchange rates XXX/YYY and XXX/ZZZ, the cross-rates are:

YYY/ZZZ = XXX/ZZZ ÷ XXX/YYY
ZZZ/YYY = XXX/YYY ÷ XXX/ZZZ

Given two exchange rates, YYY/XXX and XXX/ZZZ, the cross-rates are:

YYY/ZZZ = YYY/XXX × XXX/ZZZ
ZZZ/YYY = 1 ÷ (YYY/XXX × XXX/ZZZ).

Figure 3.32 shows the Bloomberg major currency FX monitor, page FXC, as at 10 May 2004.

<HELP> for explanation, <MENU> for similar functions. P174 **Comdty FXC**

Screen Printed
14:42
Mon 5/10

KEY CROSS CURRENCY RATES

	USD	EUR	JPY	GBP	CHF	CAD	AUD	NZD	HKD	NOK	SEK
SEK	7.7315	9.1436	6.8059	13.723	5.9288	5.5436	5.3544	4.6679	.99122	1.1226	....
NOK	6.8874	8.1453	6.0628	12.225	5.2815	4.9384	4.7698	4.1582	.88300	....	.89082
HKD	7.8000	9.2246	6.8662	13.845	5.9813	5.5928	5.4019	4.7092	....	1.1325	1.0089
NZD	1.6563	1.9588	1.4580	2.9400	1.2701	1.1876	1.1471	....	.21235	.24049	.21423
AUD	1.4439	1.7077	1.2711	2.5630	1.1073	1.0353	....	.87178	.18512	.20965	.18676
CAD	1.3947	1.6494	1.2277	2.4755	1.0695	....	.96586	.84202	.17880	.20249	.18039
CHF	1.3041	1.5422	1.1479	2.3147	....	.93504	.90312	.78732	.16719	.18934	.16867
GBP	.56338	.66628	.49593	....	.43202	.40396	.39017	.34014	.07223	.08180	.07287
JPY	113.60	134.35	....	201.64	87.113	81.454	78.674	68.586	14.564	16.494	14.693
EUR	.84556	....	.74433	1.5009	.64841	.60629	.58559	.51051	.10841	.12277	.10937
USD	....	1.1827	.88028	1.7750	.76684	.71703	.69255	.60375	.12821	.14519	.12934
			(x100)								

Spot Enter 1M,2M etc. for forward rates E EURO D Default Currencies
Hit -1,-2...<Page> for previous days A Show all

monitoring enabled: decrease increase no change BLOOMBERG Composite
Australia 61 2 9777 8600 Brazil 5511 3048 4500 Europe 44 20 7330 7500 Germany 49 69 920410
Hong Kong 852 2977 6000 Japan 81 3 3201 8900 Singapore 65 6212 1000 U.S. 1 212 318 2000
0 10-May-04 14:42:34

Figure 3.32 Bloomberg major currency monitor page, 10 May 2004

Forward exchange rates

Forward outright

The spot exchange rate is the rate for immediate delivery (notwithstanding that actual delivery is two days forward). A *forward contract* or simply *forward* is an outright purchase or sale of one currency in exchange for another currency for settlement on a specified date at some point in the future. The exchange rate is quoted in the same way as the spot rate, with the bank buying the base currency on the bid side and selling it on the offered side. In some emerging markets no liquid forward market exists so forwards are settled in cash against the spot rate on the maturity date. These *non-deliverable forwards* are considered at the end of this section.

Although some commentators have stated that the forward rate may be seen as the market's view of where the spot rate will be on the maturity date of the forward transaction, this is incorrect. A forward rate is calculated on the current interest rates of the two currencies involved, and the principle of no-arbitrage pricing ensures that there is no profit to be gained from simultaneous (and opposite) dealing in spot and forward. Consider the following strategy:

- borrow US dollars for six months starting from the spot value date;
- sell dollars and buy sterling for value spot;
- deposit the long sterling position for six months from the spot value date;
- sell forward today the sterling principal and interest that mature in six months' time into dollars.

The market will adjust the forward price so that the two initial transactions if carried out simultaneously will generate a zero profit/loss. The forward rates quoted in the trade will be calculated on the six months deposit rates for dollars and sterling; in general, the calculation of a forward rate is given as (3.22).

$$Fwd = Spot \times \frac{(1 + \text{Variable currency deposit rate} \times \frac{Days}{B})}{(1 + \text{Base currency deposit rate} \times \frac{Days}{B})}. \quad (3.22)$$

The year day-count base B will be either 365 or 360, depending on the convention for the currency in question.

So, in other words, a forward is more a deposit instrument than an FX instrument.

EXAMPLE 3.10 Forward rate

90-day GBP deposit rate: 5.75%
90-day USD deposit rate: 6.15%
Spot GBP/USD rate: 1.6315 (mid-rate)

The forward rate is given by:

$$1.6315 \times \frac{(1 + 0.0575 \times \frac{90}{365})}{(1 + 0.0615 \times \frac{90}{360})} = 1.6296.$$

Therefore to deal forward the GBP/USD mid-rate is 1.6296, so in effect £1 buys $1.6296 in three months' time, as opposed to $1.6315 today. Under different circumstances sterling may be worth more in the future than at the spot date.

Example 3.11 Forward rate arbitrage

The following rates are quoted to a bank:

USD/CHF	spot:	1.4810–1.4815
	3-month swap:	116-111
USD	3-month deposit rates:	7.56–7.43
CHF	3-month deposit rates:	4.62–4.50.

The bank requires funding of CHF10 million for three months (91 days). It deals on the above rates and does the following:

- it borrows USD6,749,915.63 for 91 days from spot at 7.56%;
- at the end of the 91 days the bank repays the principal plus the interest, which is a total of USD6,880,324.00;
- the bank "buys and sells" USD against CHF at a swap price of 11, based on the spot rate of 1.4815; that is:
  - the bank sells USD6,749,915.63 / buys CHF10 million spot at 1.4815;
  - the bank buys USD6,880,324 / sells CHF10,116,828.42 for three months forward at 1.4704.

The net USD cash flows result in a zero balance.

The effective cost of borrowing is therefore interest of CHF 116,828.41 on a principal sum of CHF10 million for 91 days, which is:

$$\frac{116,828}{10,000,000} \times \frac{360}{91} = 4.57\%.$$

The net effect is therefore a CHF10 million borrowing at 4.57%, which is 5 basis points lower than the 4.62% quote at which the bank could borrow directly in the market. If the bank had not actually required funding but was able to deposit the Swiss francs at a higher rate than 4.57%, it would have been able to lock in a profit.

Forward swaps

The calculation given above illustrates how a forward rate is calculated and quoted in theory. In practice, as spot rates change rapidly, often many times even in one minute, it would be tedious to keep recalculating the forward rate so often. Therefore banks quote a forward spread over the spot rate, which can then be added or subtracted to the spot rate as it changes. This spread is known as the *swap points*. An approximate value for the number of swap points is given by (3.23) below:

$$\text{Forward swap} \approx \text{Spot} \times \text{Deposit rate differential} \times \frac{Days}{B}. \quad (3.23)$$

The approximation is not accurate enough for forwards maturing more than 30 days from now, in which case another equation must be used. This is given as (3.24). It is also possible to calculate an approximate deposit rate differential from the swap points by rearranging (3.23).

$$Fwd\ swap = Spot \times \frac{(\text{Variable currency depo rate} \times \frac{Days}{B} - \text{Base currency depo rate} \times \frac{Days}{B})}{(1 + \text{Base currency depo rate} \times \frac{Days}{B})} \quad (3.24)$$

EXAMPLE 3.12 Forward swap points

Spot EUR/USD: 1.0566–1.0571
Forward swap: 0.0125–0.0130
Forward outright: 1.0691–1.0701

The forward outright is the spot price + the swap points, so in this case:

$$1.0691 = 1.0566 + 0.0125$$
$$1.0701 = 1.0571 + 0.0130.$$

Spot EUR/USD rate: 0.9501
31-day EUR rate: 3.15%
31-day USD rate: 5.95%

$$Fwd\ swap = 0.9501 \times \frac{(0.0595 \times \frac{31}{360} - 0.0315 \times \frac{31}{360})}{(1 + 0.0315 \times \frac{31}{360})} = 0.0024$$

or +24 points.

The swap points are quoted as two-way prices in the same way as spot rates. In practice a middle spot price is used and then the forward swap spreads around the spot quote. The difference between the interest rates of the two currencies will determine the magnitude of the swap points and whether they are added or subtracted from the spot rate. When the swap points are positive and the forwards trader applies a bid–offer spread to quote a two-way price, the left-hand side of the quote is smaller than the right-hand side as usual. When the swap points are negative, the trader must quote a "more negative" number on the left and a "more positive" number on the right-hand side. The "minus" sign is not shown, however, so that the left-hand side may appear to be the larger number. Basically, when the swap price appears larger on the right, it means that it is negative and must be subtracted from the spot rate and not added.

Forwards traders are in fact interest rate traders rather than foreign exchange traders; although they will be left with positions that arise from customer orders, in general they will manage their book based on their view of short-term deposit rates in the currencies they are trading. Generally, a forward trader expecting the interest rate differential to move in favour of the base currency – for example, a rise in base currency rates or a fall in the variable currency rate – will "buy and sell" the base currency. This is equivalent to borrowing the base currency and depositing in the variable currency. The relationship between interest rates and forward swaps means that banks can take advantage of different opportunities in different markets. For instance, assume that a bank requires funding in one currency but is able to borrow in another currency at a relatively cheaper rate. It may wish to borrow in the second currency and use a forward contract to convert the borrowing to the first currency. It will do this if the all-in cost of borrowing is less than the cost of borrowing directly in the first currency.

Forward cross-rates

A forward cross-rate is calculated in the same way as spot cross-rates. The formulas given for spot cross-rates can be adapted to forward rates.

Forward–forwards

A forward–forward swap is a deal between two forward dates rather than from the spot date to a forward date; this is the same terminology and meaning as in the bond markets, where a forward or a forward–forward interest rate is the zero-coupon interest rate between two points both beginning in the future. In the foreign exchange market, an example would be a contract to sell sterling three months forward and buy it back in six months. Here, the swap is for the three-month period between the three-month date and the six-month date. The reason a bank or corporate might do this is to hedge a forward exposure or because of a particular view it has on forward rates, or, in effect, deposit rates.

EXAMPLE 3.13 Forward–forward contract

GBP/USD spot rate:	1.6315–20
3-month swap:	45–41
6-month swap:	135–125

If a bank wished to sell GBP three months forward and buy it back six months forward, this is identical to undertaking one swap to buy GBP spot and sell GBP three months forward, and another to sell GBP spot and buy it six months forward. Swaps are always quoted as the quoting bank buying the base currency forward on the bid side, and selling the base currency forward on the offered side; the counterparty bank can "buy and sell" GBP "spot against three months" at a swap price of –45, with settlement rates of spot and (spot − 0.0045). It can "sell and buy" GBP "spot against six months" at the swap price of −125 with settlement rates of spot and (spot − 0.0125). It can therefore do both simultaneously, which implies a difference between the two forward prices of (−125) − (–45) = –90 points. Conversely, the bank can "buy and sell" GBP "three months against six months" at a swap price of (−135) − (–41) or –94 points. The two-way price is therefore 94–90 (we ignore the negative signs).

Long-dated forward contracts

The formula for calculating a forward rate was given earlier (see 3.23). This formula applies to any period that is under one year, hence the adjustment of the deposit rate by the fraction of the day-count. However, if a forward contract is traded for a period greater than one year, the formula must be adjusted to account for the fact that deposit rates are compounded if they are in effect for more than one year. To calculate a long-dated forward rate, in theory (3.25) on page 110 should be used. In practice the formula may not give an answer to the required accuracy, because it does not consider reinvestment risk. To get around this it is necessary to use spot (zero-coupon) rates in the formula. However, the market in long-dated forward contracts is not as liquid as the sub-one-year market, so banks may not be as keen to quote a price.

$$\textit{Long-dated forward} = \textit{Spot} \times \frac{(1 + \text{Variable currency deposit rate})^N}{(1 + \text{Base currency deposit rate})^N} \tag{3.25}$$

where N is the contract's maturity in years.

Non-deliverable forward

A market in *non-deliverable forwards* was established first in Latin American currencies and then in certain Asian currencies, as organisations interested in investing and trading with counterparties in countries in these areas were constrained by local exchange control regulations and by the absence of a forward foreign exchange market in the currencies of the countries concerned. A non-deliverable forward (NDF) is conceptually similar to an outright forward foreign exchange transaction. In essence a (notional) principal amount, forward foreign exchange rate and forward delivery date are all agreed at the time of the trade. In the case of an NDF, however, there is no physical exchange of principal amount; the deal is agreed on the basis that net settlement will be made in US dollars, or another fully convertible currency, to reflect any differential between the agreed forward rate and the actual exchange rate on the agreed forward date. An NDF therefore is a cash-settled outright forward and is more similar to a *contract for difference* than a conventional forward.

A fixing methodology is agreed when the NDF is contracted. It specifies how a fixing spot rate is to be determined on the fixing date, which is normally one or two business days before settlement. Generally, the fixing spot rate is based on a reference page on Reuters or Telerate. Settlement is made in the major currency, paid to or by the counterparty, and reflects the differential between the agreed NDF forward rate and the fixing rate. Using an NDF a corporate can hedge any forward exposure in the currency even though no forward market is available. As NDFs are cash-settled instruments with no exchange of principal amount involved, settlement risk is reduced and the credit risk is therefore lower than for a conventional forward contract.

In Asia, NDF markets developed through 1995 and 1996 in several currencies including the Korean won, Taiwan dollar, Philippine peso and Indian rupee.

Once an NDF currency becomes fully convertible then the need for a non-deliverable market falls away, as a deliverable offshore forward market then develops. This has happened with certain Latin American currencies such as the Argentina peso. As the economies of the other emerging markets develop, investors may focus on other currencies such as those of South Asia and south-east Asia. In Eastern Europe, as economies have transformed into market economies, their currencies have also become fully convertible, such that in 2004 the Russian rouble was the only major Eastern European currency that still needed to be traded as an NDF.

Example 3.14 Non-deliverable forward

During 1998 a fund manager has invested $2 million in the Taiwanese stock market for one year. She expects the stock market to rise but is concerned about potential Taiwan dollar (TWD) depreciation. She wishes to hedge her foreign exchange exposure using an NDF. A USD/TWD non-deliverable forward rate of 35.00 is agreed between the fund manager and her bank for a notional principal of $2 million. There are three possible outcomes in one year's time: the TWD may have reached the forward rate, depreciated further or appreciated relative to the forward rate. These scenarios are shown in Table 3.2 below.

	Outcome A	Outcome B	Outcome C
TWD	Depreciated	–	Appreciated
Fixing spot rate	35.3	35	34.7
Equivalent rate	USD1,983,002.83	USD2 million	USD2,017,291.07
Settlement	Bank pays customer USD16,997.17	No net payment	Customer pays bank USD17,291.07

Table 3.2 Example of non-deliverable forward

Whatever the outcome, the fund manager has achieved the objective of her Taiwan dollar exposure at 35.00. In outcome A, the hedge has worked in the fund manager's favour and when she physically sells the Taiwan dollars in the spot market, she will be compensated for the higher rate by the proceeds of the NDF received from the bank. In outcome C the fund manager can achieve a better rate in the spot market, but this is negated by the payment required on the NDF.

Deposits and loans

Banks are financial institutions that are licensed to take deposits. A financial institution that is not licensed by the national regulator may not advertise for or accept deposits from either wholesale or retail customers. The regulator is most commonly the central bank. National central banks take their direction from the BIS in Basel, although there are regional variations in approach and direction between different central banks.[12] In this section we discuss the bank loan market.

Wholesale deposits and loans

The majority of market participants in the deposit business are banks, although credit unions, trust companies and the subsidiaries of insurance companies and fund managers also operate in this business. Banks generally offer the following types of deposit:

- Demand deposit: this is a deposit that may be withdrawn on request, with no notice. A cheque account is an example of a demand deposit. Typically, the rate of interest paid on a demand deposit is negligible, or zero.
- Notice deposit: this is a deposit that requires notice to be given by the depositor before any or all of the balance can be withdrawn. These usually attract a rate of interest that is not a token one.
- Term deposit: also known as *time deposits*, these are accounts that are created for a fixed period of time, and cannot be drawn down until

[12] Note that in a group company situation, it is necessary for a subsidiary (such as a securities house or derivatives trading entity) to have their own banking license if they wish to undertake deposit business.

expiry of the term. An example would be a two-year fixed term account opened at a high-street bank. These usually attract the highest rate of interest. Term accounts may pay a fixed interest rate or a floating-rate that is reset periodically.

Loans in the wholesale market also exist in a number of different forms. Medium- and large-size corporates will be able to draw down on an overdraft facility, also known as a *credit line.* This is an on-demand borrowing facility. Fixed-term loans are also offered, and large-size loans may be taken in the syndicated loans market, which we consider in a separate section. A credit line may be offered on an unsecured or secured basis, although smaller size or new businesses are generally only offered the latter.

A credit line is usually set up with a *commitment fee*, which is a standing fee payable irrespective of whether the line is used or not. This might be 10, 20 or 30 basis points or more of the notional amount, usually payable quarterly in advance, and recognises that the provision of credit facilities by a bank attracts a capital charge for the bank and so incurs a cost even if it is not used.

Eurocurrency market

The Eurocurrency market is the market in cross-border deposits and loans. Essentially, any deposit or loan that is placed with or taken out from a bank that is in a different currency to the domicile currency of the bank branch that is accepting the business is a Eurocurrency transaction.[13] The overseas market in US dollars, or Eurodollars, is the largest segment of the euro market by volume. Example 3.15 on page 114 describes the creation of a Eurodollar deposit.

[13] In other words, the currency and domicile of the local branch do not have to have anything to do with "Europe" or the euro-currency area to be a Eurocurrency transaction. A deposit of Singapore dollars made at the Dubai branch of Citigroup would be a Eurocurrency deposit. The origins of the market lie in the foreign currency restrictions of many countries that existed in the 1960s and 1970s, as well as the growth in volume of "Petrodollar" deposits after the rise in oil prices in 1974. Although foreign currency restrictions were removed in the 1980s and had disappeared in market economies by the 1990s, the market continued to thrive and is a primary factor behind the ease with which international trade flows and currency movements are facilitated today.

EXAMPLE 3.15 Eurodollar deposit: hypothetical illustration

A United Arab Emirates-incorporated corporate, UAE Ltd, has previously placed USD100 million on a fixed-term deposit with the Bank of New York in New York. This deposit matures today; however, UAE Ltd does not require the funds now and desires to place the funds on deposit for a further 12 months. However, the London branch of ABN Amro bank offers an interest rate that is higher than the rollover quote from the Bank of New York, so the treasurer at UAE Ltd decides to place the deposit there.

UAE Ltd also had a demand deposit account with the Bank of New York in New York. At the time that the time deposit matures, it instructs the bank to transfer this demand deposit to the account of ABN Amro in New York. This creates the Eurodollar deposit. In effect the Bank of New York has transferred ownership of the demand deposit to ABN Amro. The demand deposit itself – that is, the funds that it represents – remains with the Bank of New York. ABN Amro on the other hand is custodian of a USD100 million demand deposit on which it will pay interest to UAE Ltd.

The creation of deposits and loans forms part of the overall money market transactions of both the Bank of New York and ABN Amro, and they will manage net surplus or shortages in the money market; that is, they will lay off any surplus and bring in any required funding. This business will be undertaken with a large number of banks in both the domestic and Eurocurrency markets.

Syndicated loans

Traditional bank-lending business, while very important from a global economic as well as customer point of view, is no longer a major source of revenue for many banks. This is because the margins on lending, and the spread between deposits and loans, the two sources of earnings in loan business, have become progressively squeezed in a very competitive environment. The use of the balance sheet as a source of income is not encouraged in bank strategy, and customers who do require lending lines are frequently targeted to engage in other forms of business as part of the overall relationship.

Nevertheless, loan business remains large scale. That does not mean loans remain on an originating bank's balance sheet for their entire life; as we shall see, securitisation, secondary market trading and other techniques are frequently employed to reduce or eliminate the capital impact of balance sheet loans. However, ultimately, the loan business remains important, if only from a customer relationship point of view, for retail and commercial banks.

Lending business

Syndicated lending is where a group of banks participate in a large-size loan to a corporate entity. The aggregate size of a loan can be very large, with $1 billion not uncommon, and is spread across the banks in the syndicate. The syndicated loan market is very large, and in terms of nominal size it easily outranks the corporate bond market (see Figure 3.33).

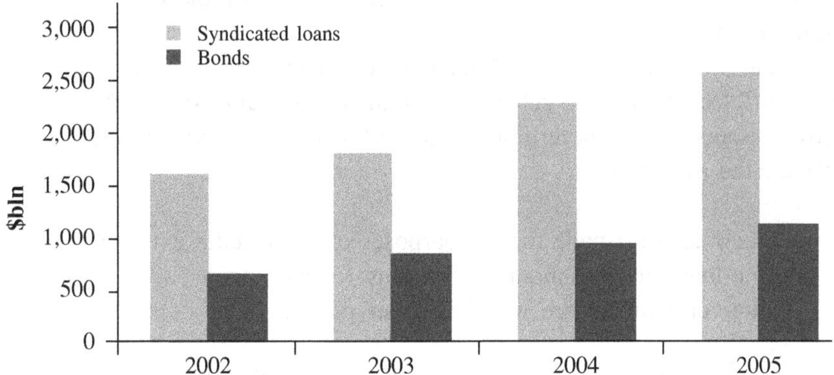

Figure 3.33 Issuance in syndicated loan and corporate bond markets, USD, EUR, JPY and GBP investment grade
Source: BIS 2006.

Although spreads in the loan market have reduced to the extent where this is no longer lucrative business for banks, the importance of advancing credit in furthering customer relationships means that it will continue to be a large-scale market. Loans remain a primary source of corporate financing for a number of other reasons, including:

- lack of alternatives: many corporate borrowers lack the size, presence, name and/or credit-rating quality to access the bond market;

- flexibility: loans (like bonds) can be arranged to specific customer requirements, but unlike bonds they do not need to meet as stringent requirements with regard to documentation and facilitation for secondary market trading;
- more straightforward clearing (settlement) arrangements;
- client confidentiality: there is less publicity in the loan market and lower level of name recognition in the secondary loan market.

A primary difference between the loan and bond market, the lack of tradeability of the former in a secondary market, no longer applies. For USD-denominated loans, and to a lesser-extent for EUR- and GBP-loans, it is now possible to trade loans in a secondary market, although liquidity is variable. The growth in securitisation has contributed to the development of a secondary market, as originators of asset-backed securities, backed with bank-loan underlying collateral, source their deals with loans of acceptable type and quality.

Figure 3.34 shows a list of loans made to the UK telecoms company British Telecom plc. We select one of them, the July 2007 maturity, for closer inspection. The description page for this loan is shown in Figure 3.35. We see the following:

- the loan was made for the purposes of refinancing existing debt;
- the loan rate is 3-month Libor plus 15 basis points;
- the commitment fee was 4.12 basis points.

The loan size is comparatively small at GBP110 million, and this was spread out across a syndicate of 10 banks. The banks in the syndicate are shown in Figure 3.36 on page 118, with the lead manager and agent bank being Citigroup.

We show the DES page from Bloomberg for a loan made to Nordic Telephone in Figure 3.37 on page 119, now trading in the secondary market.

<HELP> for explanation. P174 **Corp** **TKL**
Page to view more data. Click on columns to sort. 94<GO> to edit columns.

Loan Facilities Page 1/1

BRITEL (16 Found) Type All | Status All | Exclude None

Issuer	Effective Dt	Tranche	Loan Type	Maturity	Curr	Loan Status
1)INFONET SERVICES	08/17/99		REVOLVER	08/17/05	USD	SIGNED
2)INFONET SERVICES	08/17/99		TERM	06/30/06	USD	SIGNED
3)INFONET SERVICES	08/17/99	*	FACILITY	06/30/06	USD	SIGNED
4)INFONET SERVICES	08/17/99	B	TERM	06/30/06	USD	SIGNED
5)ESAT TELECOM	09/02/99		REVOLVER	09/02/04	EUR	SIGNED
6)ESAT DIGIFONE	02/29/00		TERM	12/31/06	IEP	SIGNED
7)BRIT TELECOM PLC	06/13/00		REVOLVER	06/12/01	GBP	A&R
8)BRIT TELECOM PLC	08/23/00		FACILITY	08/22/02	GBP	REPLACED
9)BRIT TELECOM PLC	08/23/00	A	REVOLVER/TERM	08/22/02	GBP	REPLACED
10)BRIT TELECOM PLC	08/23/00	B	REVOLVER/TERM	08/22/02	GBP	REPLACED
11)BRIT TELECOM PLC	07/30/01		REVOLVER	07/29/02	GBP	RETIRED
12)BRIT TELECOM PLC	07/26/02		REVOLVER	07/25/03	GBP	REPLACED
13)BRIT TELECOM PLC	07/28/03		REVOLVER	07/26/04	GBP	REPLACED
14)BT GROUP PLC	07/26/04		REVOLVER	07/25/05	GBP	REPLACED
15)BT GROUP PLC	07/25/05		REVOLVER	07/24/06	GBP	SIGNED
16)BT GROUP PLC	01/31/06		REVOLVER	01/31/11	GBP	SIGNED

Australia 61 2 9777 8600 Brazil 5511 3048 4500 Europe 44 20 7330 7500 Germany 49 69 920410
Hong Kong 852 2977 6000 Japan 81 3 3201 8900 Singapore 65 6212 1000 U.S. 1 212 318 2000 Copyright 2006 Bloomberg L.P.
0 01-Jun-06 7:58:41

Figure 3.34 List of outstanding loans for UK telecoms entity BT plc, as at 1 June 2006

Menu P174 **Corp** **DES**
Enter 99<GO> for options. <HELP> for Disclaimer

TRANCHE LOAN DESCRIPTION Page 1 of 1

Tranche# LN225658 Tranche BRITEL Maturity 07/24/06 Country GB
Cusip# Type REVOLVER Mkt Type EURO
Facility# Amend N.A. Issue Status SIGNED

Issue Information	Bank Group	Info @ Close
Borrower BT GROUP PLC	Ld Arranger C	GB LIBOR +15.000BP
Industry Telephone - Integrated	Agent C	Comm Fee 4.12BP
Calc Type (99) *NO CALCULATIONS*	Participants 55<GO>	
Fac/Trnch Amts GBP 110MM /110MM	**Assignment Info**	
Purpose REFINANCE DEBT	Min Pc	
Effective Date 07/25/05	Increment	
Amt Available 110MM	Fee	
	Retain	**Current Sprd & Fees**
	Tranche Ratings	Interest Typ FLOATER
	S&P NA	Int Freqncy QTRLY
	Moody's NA	Current Base LIBOR
	FI NA	Reset Freq QTRLY
	Senior Debt Ratings	
Sub Limit Borrowings	S & P A-	
Not Applicable	MOODY Baa1	

FAC REPLACES {LN175926 Corp DES<GO>}. 1 YEAR TERM OUT OPTION.

Australia 61 2 9777 8600 Brazil 5511 3048 4500 Europe 44 20 7330 7500 Germany 49 69 920410
Hong Kong 852 2977 6000 Japan 81 3 3201 8900 Singapore 65 6212 1000 U.S. 1 212 318 2000 Copyright 2006 Bloomberg L.P.
0 01-Jun-06 8:04:20

Figure 3.35 Bloomberg DES page for BT syndicated loan maturing July 2007

55 P174 Corp **DES**
<Menu> for PREVIOUS

Loan Participants Page 1/ 1
7/25/05

BT GROUP PLC (BRITEL L 7/24/06) Not Priced

Agent(s)	Citigroup
Arranger(s)	ABN AMRO Bank NV Bank of Tokyo-Mitsubishi UFJ Ltd Barclays Capital BayernLB Deutsche Bank AG HSBC Lloyds TSB Group PLC Royal Bank of Scotland Societe Generale
Bookrunner	Citigroup
Mandated Arranger	Citigroup

Australia 61 2 9777 8600 Brazil 5511 3048 4500 Europe 44 20 7330 7500 Germany 49 69 920410
Hong Kong 852 2977 6000 Japan 81 3 3201 8900 Singapore 65 6212 1000 U.S. 1 212 318 2000 Copyright 2006 Bloomberg L.P.
0 01-Jun-06 8:04:38

Figure 3.36 Syndicate banks for BT loan

EXAMPLE 3.16 Loan issue traded in secondary market

We describe here a syndicated loan that was trading in the secondary market as at 1 June 2006. The obligor is Nordic Telephone company, and the particular loan is the "B" tranche of the January 2014 syndicated loan. The details are shown in Figure 3.37, which is Bloomberg's DES page for this tranche. The tranche is large in size, at EUR 1.85 billion, and the purpose of the loan was to facilitate an acquisition. Although the loan was effective from 12 January 2006, it was not actually drawn down until 12 May 2006.

The syndicate group is shown in Figure 3.38 on page 120. Note that the arranging bank, SEB Bank, is not actually one of the five lending banks. One could describe its role as that of "relationship bank". The joint lead managers were Deutsche Bank and JPMorgan. As this loan was trading in the secondary market on 1 June 2006, there was a yield analysis page for it on Bloomberg, which is shown in Figure 3.39 on page 120. This shows that, with a price at par, the loan spread is 275 basis points. This is as per the loan's original terms, confirmed in Figure 3.37. The offer price for the loan on 1 June 2006 was above par, as seen on a dealer bank's price page, shown in Figure 3.40 on page 121. We observe a number of loans listed on this page, with two-way bid and offer prices. The Nordic Telephone loan B tranche (as well as the C tranche), identified by its Bloomberg ticker "TDC", is seen priced at 101.50–101.75. The spread at the offer price of 101.75 is 246 basis points, and this is seen in Figure 3.41 on page 121. This is the yield analysis page with the new offer price of 101.75 entered in the price field.

```
DES                                                              P174 Corp   DES
Enter 99<GO> for options. <HELP> for Disclaimer
              TRANCHE LOAN DESCRIPTION                           Page  1 of  6
Tranche#  LN253818 Tranche  B1  TDCDC     Maturity 01/12/14         Country  DK
Cusip#             Type TERM              Mkt Type EURO             Credit Agreement
Facility# LN253806 Amend            N.A.  Issue Status  SIGNED
           Issue Information              Bank Group               Info @ Close
Borrower  NORDIC TELEPHONE CO APS        Ld Arranger JOINT          EURIBOR  +275.000BP
Industry  Specified Purpose Acquis       Agent DB,JPM               Comm Fee  37.50BP
Calc Type  ( 533) TERM-TYPE:COM LOAN     Participants 55<GO>
Fac/Trnch Amts EUR 9600MM    /1850MM       Assignment Info
Purpose  ACQUISITION                     Min Pc     EUR 1MM
Effective Date      01/12/06             Increment
Outstanding         1850MM               Fee        EUR 1500
Alt Crncy Opt       Yes  22<GO>          Retain     EUR 2.5MM       Current Sprd & Fees
Secured/Guarantee Yes                       Tranche Ratings         EURIBOR   + 275.00BP
Governing Law       GB                   S&P        NA              Commit       62.50BP
Drawdown Date       05/12/06             Moody's    NA
                                         FI         NA
                                          Senior Debt Ratings
      Sub Limit Borrowings               S & P      NA
            Not Applicable               MOODY      NA
SPONSORS: APAX, BLACKSTONE, KKR, PERMIRA, PROVIDENCE.
Australia 61 2 9777 8600          Brazil 5511 3048 4500          Europe 44 20 7330 7500          Germany 49 69 920410
Hong Kong 852 2977 6000 Japan 81 3 3201 8900 Singapore 65 6212 1000 U.S. 1 212 318 2000 Copyright 2006 Bloomberg L.P.
                                                                                      3 01-Jun-06 10:05:24
```

Figure 3.37 Nordic Telephone syndicated loan tranche "B" details

55 P174 Corp **DES**

<Page> for more. <Menu> for PREVIOUS

Loan Participants Page 1/ 2

1/12/06 Amount

NORDIC TELEPHONE (TDCDC L 1/12/14) B1 Not Priced %

Agent(s)	Deutsche Bank AG	
	JP Morgan	
Arranger(s)	Skandinaviska Enskilda Banken	
Bookrunner	Barclays Capital	
	Credit Suisse	
	Deutsche Bank AG	
	JP Morgan	
	Royal Bank of Scotland	
Collateral Agent(s)	JP Morgan	
Lender(s)	Barclays Capital	20.00
	Credit Suisse	20.00
	Deutsche Bank AG	20.00
	JP Morgan	20.00
	Royal Bank of Scotland	20.00
Mandated Arranger	Barclays Capital	

Australia 61 2 9777 8600 Brazil 5511 3048 4500 Europe 44 20 7330 7500 Germany 49 69 920410
Hong Kong 852 2977 6000 Japan 81 3 3201 8900 Singapore 65 6212 1000 U.S. 1 212 318 2000 Copyright 2006 Bloomberg L.P.
3 01-Jun-06 10:05:44

Figure 3.38 Syndicate group

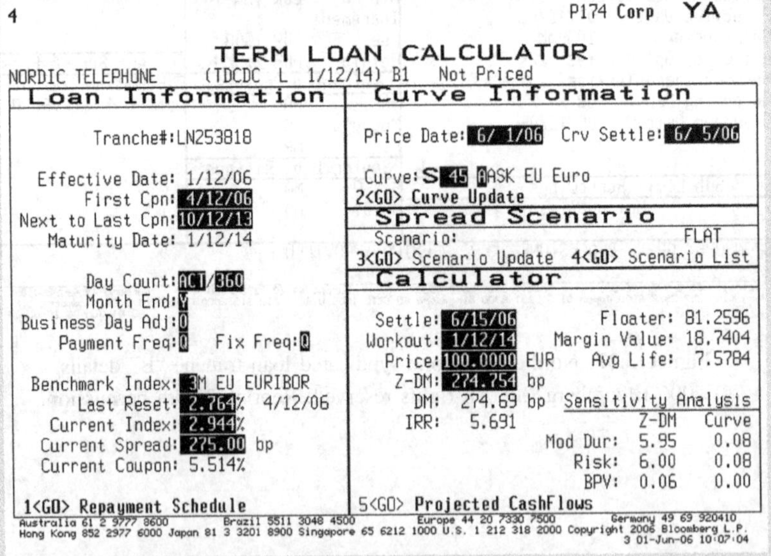

Figure 3.39 Nordic Telephone syndicated loan tranche "B", yield analysis, price par

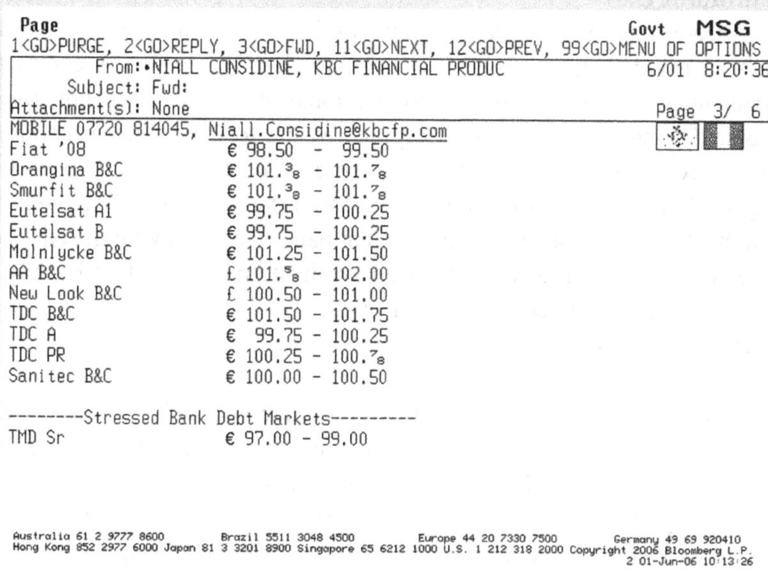

Page | Govt MSG
1<GO>PURGE, 2<GO>REPLY, 3<GO>FWD, 11<GO>NEXT, 12<GO>PREV, 99<GO>MENU OF OPTIONS

From: •NIALL CONSIDINE, KBC FINANCIAL PRODUC 6/01 8:20:36
Subject: Fwd:
Attachment(s): None Page 3/ 6

MOBILE 07720 814045, Niall.Considine@kbcfp.com

Fiat '08	€ 98.50 - 99.50
Orangina B&C	€ 101.$^3/_8$ - 101.$^7/_8$
Smurfit B&C	€ 101.$^3/_8$ - 101.$^7/_8$
Eutelsat A1	€ 99.75 - 100.25
Eutelsat B	€ 99.75 - 100.25
Molnlycke B&C	€ 101.25 - 101.50
AA B&C	£ 101.$^5/_8$ - 102.00
New Look B&C	£ 100.50 - 101.00
TDC B&C	€ 101.50 - 101.75
TDC A	€ 99.75 - 100.25
TDC PR	€ 100.25 - 100.$^7/_8$
Sanitec B&C	€ 100.00 - 100.50

--------Stressed Bank Debt Markets---------

TMD Sr	€ 97.00 - 99.00

Figure 3.40 Dealer bank secondary loan prices, 1 June 2006

4 P174 Corp YA

TERM LOAN CALCULATOR

NORDIC TELEPHONE (TDCDC L 1/12/14) B1 Not Priced

Loan Information

Tranche#: LN253818

Effective Date: 1/12/06
First Cpn: 4/12/06
Next to Last Cpn: 10/12/13
Maturity Date: 1/12/14

Day Count: ACT/360
Month End: Y
Business Day Adj: 0
Payment Freq: Q Fix Freq: Q

Benchmark Index: 3M EU EURIBOR
Last Reset: 2.764% 4/12/06
Current Index: 2.944%
Current Spread: 275.00 bp
Current Coupon: 5.514%

1<GO> Repayment Schedule

Curve Information

Price Date: 6/ 1/06 Crv Settle: 6/ 5/06

Curve: S 45 AASK EU Euro
2<GO> Curve Update

Spread Scenario

Scenario: FLAT
3<GO> Scenario Update 4<GO> Scenario List

Calculator

Settle: 6/15/06 Floater: 83.0096
Workout: 1/12/14 Margin Value: 18.7404
Price: 101.7500 EUR Avg Life: 7.5784
Z-DM: 245.905 bp
DM: 246.72 bp
IRR: 5.411

Sensitivity Analysis

	Z-DM	Curve
Mod Dur:	5.97	0.13
Risk:	6.13	0.14
BPV:	0.06	0.00

5<GO> Projected CashFlows

Figure 3.41 Nordic Telephone syndicated loan tranche "B" yield analysis, price 101.75 as at 1 June 2006

Terminology

A syndicated loan is essentially a plain vanilla bank loan to a borrower that has been divided up between two or more lending banks. A contractual agreement, which is similar to a conventional loan agreement, governs the terms and conditions of the loan. Typically, the loan will pay floating-rate interest, reset monthly, quarterly or semi-annually.[14] The syndicate is comprised of a pool of banks that have shared the risk out among them; one of the banks will be the lead bank or agent bank that deals with the customer. There is no formal agreement between syndicate members; that is, they are not contractually obliged to each other.

The types of loan are:

- *Term loan*: a conventional fixed-term loan with a fixed maturity date. The borrower may draw down the entire loan immediately or borrow only a portion of it in an initial *tranche*, with further drawdowns being made via further tranches if necessary. The loan may be repaid as a bullet payment on maturity or in segments during its life if it is an amortising loan.
- *Revolving credit line*: under a revolver facility the borrower may draw down any amount up to the maximum, but can then repay parts or all of it at any time, before then drawing down again if needed.
- *Liquidity line*: this is also known as a stand-by credit line and is usually arranged to act as a back-up if needed. The borrower is not expected to draw on the line but may do if he or she wishes. A standing fee is payable irrespective of whether the line is used or not.

Note also the term *leveraged loan*. There is no single definition of this in the market. We prefer to define it as a loan that carries an interest rate of more than 100 basis points over Libor, although some market participants define it as a loan that is taken out by a sub-investment grade-rated borrower. Leveraged loans are commonly traded in the secondary market but remain a relatively small market compared to other securitised assets. Because fixed and revolver loans are not usually drawn down all in one go, individual tranches are identified by the letters A, B and so on (for example, see Figure 3.35). Each tranche may have a different maturity date and also a different interest-rate spread. Compared to bonds, loans are generally ranked higher in the capital structure, so will be senior debt or even senior

[14] Some loans pay interest that is reset every two months.

secured debt. They can also be pre-paid without any cost or penalty to the borrower, which is an advantage if the borrower wants to refinance at lower interest rates.

The terms and conditions of a loan are described in the loan term sheet. Figures 3.36 and 3.37 (DES pages) show the type of detail that is listed in a loan term sheet.

Syndication and pricing

The syndication process is similar to that for a bond underwriting in the Eurobond market. The syndicate lead manager or book runner is the lead bank, while the agent bank is the one that deals with the borrower for the life of the loan. Often these are the same bank. The lead manager will contact other banks and invite them to join the syndicate. The final syndication group will parcel out the loan among themselves according to their appetite for the deal.

The pricing for the deal involves a number of factors, and will affect banks in the syndicate differently. The syndicated lending group at the lead manager's bank will liaise with the credit department to arrive at the final lending margin. The former manages the customer relationship while the latter undertakes the formal credit analysis for the deal with respect to the borrower as a credit risk. The actual return on a loan, or yield, will differ for participating syndicate banks. This is because there are other issues, such as commitment fees, and whether the line is drawn down and to what extent, that influence the yield for syndicate members. If a line is drawn on immediately, the commitment fee has less of an impact on final yield because the actual lending margin comes into effect. If not, the commitment fee impacts the final yield.

We can consider this issue in reverse order; that is, assuming a given margin on a loan, what is the impact in terms of yield? Imagine an hypothetical loan with the following terms:

Nominal:	GBP600,000,000
Term:	7 years
Margin:	Libor + 100 basis points
Arrangement fee:	50 basis points
Commitment fee:	12.5 basis points per annum
Agency fee:	1 basis point per annum.

The loan begins to be repayable after five years, when it will amortise down in equal amounts to maturity.

The actual return received will depend on how much of the loan is drawn down and at what time. Let us assume that an immediate tranche of GBP100 million is taken and then one year later the remaining GBP500 million is taken. This is illustrated in Figure 3.42.

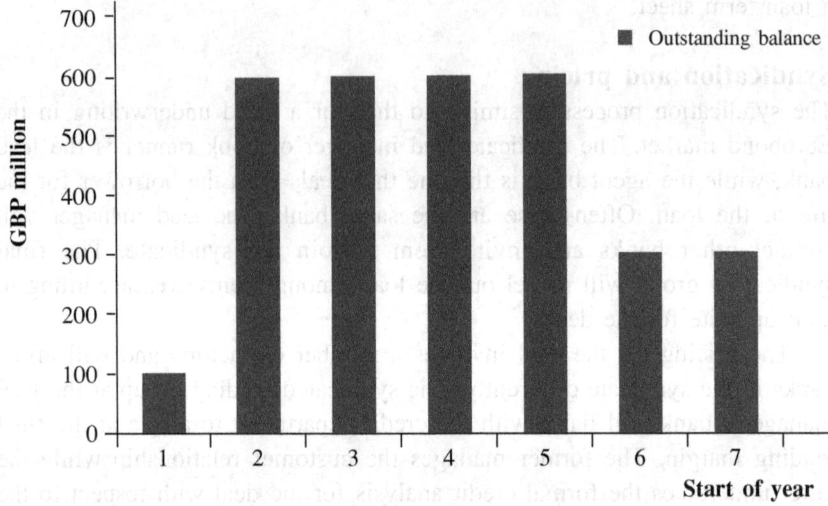

Figure 3.42 Loan drawdown schedule

On this basis, the loan earns:

- annual interest of Libor plus 100 basis points, GBP100 million for year 1, GBP600 million for years 2–5 and then on the lower amount as the loan starts to be paid down;
- the commitment fee; this is charged on any unused part of the line, and is paid up-front; as such it is charged on GBP500 million for the first year only. As it is paid up-front the calculated amount is discounted;
- the agency fee; this is charged at the start of each year on the entire nominal amount of the line.

The total cost to the borrower is the above, together with the (one-off) arrangement fee. For the lead manager, the process is arrived at in reverse, and the total costs are averaged out over the year to produce a basis point spread for the margin. This requires some assumptions on the amount of drawdown of the loan.

Syndicate members do not receive the same amount. They would receive only the elements that apply to them (for example, only the agent bank receives the agency fee). At the start of the process, the lead manager underwrites the entire loan, and then parcels out the risk exposure to syndicate banks.

Internal transfer pricing

The traditional business of banking – the bilateral loan – is priced on the basis of an internal transfer price that takes into account all the various business lines of the bank. The transfer mechanism is a high-level process that links the commercial side of the business with group-level asset–liability management. We call this mechanism the transfer price or funds transfer pricing (FTP) process. If we consider a bank to be a collective of different business lines, all of which have access to one overall set of resources (the bank's capital), the FTP process is the means by which the cost of this capital can be charged at the right rate to each business line; the business lines will have their own target rates of return over this capital charge. The target rate of return varies according to the risk-reward profile of the business line; generally, the higher the risk exposure taken, the higher the return on capital must be.

Each business line has a different approach, process and risk profile. The FTP process will seek to net these differences with regard to each business line's requirement for funds. Funds are allocated where needed and laid off where there is a surplus. Note that this is an *internal* process or mechanism: the Treasury or ALM desk will manage the external process in the money markets. The FTP process applies this internally in the bank. Unlike the Treasury desk, it has one source of funds: the Treasury desk. The cost to the Treasury of its funds will be the external bank cost. FTP will add a margin to this cost, which is known as the *commercial margin* or *transfer price*. This can be viewed as the internal market price of the bank's funds.[15] This margin might range from 5 to 100 basis points over Libor.

The commercial margin is designed to reflect that there is a cost (to the bank) of doing business, and that this cost needs to be passed on to business lines within the bank to enforce discipline in the lending process. That is, managers need to be aware that the cost of doing business is not zero, and that any business that does not produce an appropriate rate of return must be

[15] Not all banks apply an internal transfer price. Some banks lend to internal businesses and group companies at the market rate.

discouraged. The transfer price can be thought of as the breakeven cost of doing business, and any business activity that does not reach this breakeven rate needs to be discontinued or not initiated. Business activity that is seen as additional risk may be set a target return over the breakeven transfer price, while business that is viewed as the core activity of the bank may have to generate the breakeven rate only.

Leveraged loans

Leveraged loans have been variously defined as loans paying a rate of Libor plus 100 basis points or more, or loans made to sub-investment grade-rated borrowers. Some market participants define them to be both of these. They are usually senior and secured obligations with maturity terms of 5–10 years. In comparison to other asset classes the leveraged loan market would be classed as small, but has witnessed rapid growth. Figure 3.43 shows this growth during the period 1990–2003.

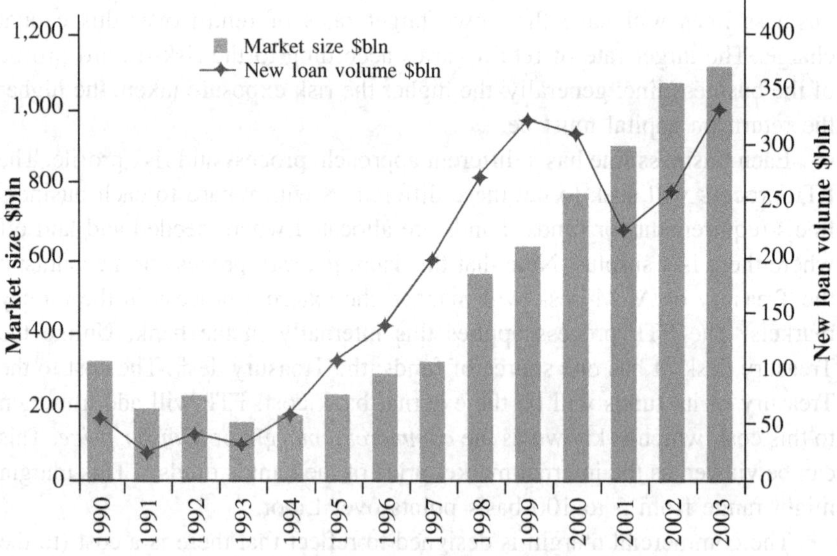

Fig 3.43 Growth of leveraged loan market
Source: Merrill Lynch research, 2004.

The growth in the market has been due to growth in the sub-investment grade debt market, as investors sought higher returns and more diverse risk-return profiles. They are a source of high-yield debt for institutional investors, as well as assets in securitisation structures such as collateralised debt obligations, which are often originated by third-party fund managers. The development of a liquid secondary trading market in leveraged loans has been significant in attracting third-party investors. As such, the market now features elements of infrastructure more commonly associated with mature capital markets such as the bond markets; these include competitive market-maker quotes, formal credit ratings, third-party administrators and formal relative value processes.

While the risk-return profile of the leveraged loan secondary market remains attractive to institutional investors, we can expect it to continue its growth pattern. Factors that are considered attractive to investors include a perceived low returns volatility compared to high-yield bonds and other assets. This may be due to:

- a floating-rate interest basis: syndicated leveraged loans pay interest on a floating-rate basis, usually on a three-month or six-month Libor basis. This renders interest-rate risk exposure negligible for investor purposes;
- prepayment feature: loans may be repaid early at short notice and usually without penalty, and their average life is considerably lower than the legal final maturity of most loans. A low duration maturity means loans exhibit low volatility;
- security protection: leveraged loans are usually both secured and also senior obligations of the obligor. This makes them the lowest exposure liabilities of the obligor, and perceived as lower risk compared to other sub-investment grade assets.

In the secondary market, loans are sold without accrued interest, so there is no concept of a "dirty" price. The interest accrued at the time of sale is paid out to the buyer at the time of the coupon payment, usually by the loan administrator or agent bank.

The leveraged loan product is either a funded commitment or an unfunded commitment. An unfunded commitment is a revolving credit facility or a letter of credit (LOC) that is not drawn initially and then drawn down over time. They are usually required to back up CP programmes, a trade receivables programme and other ongoing business activity. An analogy could be made with credit cards, which once set up can be drawn on and repaid at any time and to any amount up to the credit limit.

Funded commitments may be described under the following:

- term loan: a fixed-term loan with a specified drawdown and repayment pattern;
- amortising loans, also known as "A" term loans, which are of 5–7 years maturity;
- institutional term loans, known as "B", "C" and "D" term loans, which are created specifically for institutional investors and have longer maturities;
- second-lien loans, which are senior loans but rank second behind other senior loans of the obligor.

The loans themselves feature compliance covenants that are a set of tests which the issuer is required to meet in order for the loan to be effected. These are tests of financial ability, such as interest coverage tests (cash flows divided by interest charge) and leverage tests (debt outstanding divided by cash flow or total capitalisation). Some loans combine features of loans and bonds in that they are floating-rate liabilities and repayable, but do not have a loan covenant and feature a prepayment charge. These are known as hybrid term loans.

Appendices

APPENDIX 3.1

Currencies using a money market year base of 365 days:

- sterling
- Hong Kong dollar
- Malaysian ringgit
- Singapore dollar
- South African rand
- Taiwan dollar
- Thai baht.

In addition, the domestic markets, but not the international markets, of the following currencies also use a 365-day base:

- Australian dollar
- Canadian dollar
- Japanese yen
- New Zealand dollar.

To convert an interest rate i quoted on a 365-day basis to one quoted on a 360-day basis (i^*) use the expressions given in (3.26):

$$i = i^* \times (365/360) \tag{3.26}$$

$$i^* = i \times (360/365).$$

Appendix 3.2 Country SWIFT/ISO currency codes

Country	Currency	Code
Abu Dhabi	UAE dirham	AED
Albania	lek	ALL
Algeria	dinar	DZD
Angola	kwanza	AON
Argentina	peso	ARS
Australia	Australian $	AUD
Austria	euro	EUR
	schilling	ATS
Bahamas	Bahama $	BSD
Bahrain	dinar	BHD
Bangladesh	taka	BDT
Belarus	rouble	BYR
Belgium	euro	EUR
	Belgian franc	BEF
Bermuda	Bermuda $	BMD
Bolivia	boliviano	BOB
Brazil	real	BRL
Brunei	Brunei $	BND
Bulgaria	lev	BGL
Burkina Faso	CFA franc	XOF
Burundi	Burundi franc	BIF
Cambodia	riel	KHR
Cameroon	CFA franc	XAF
Canada	Canadian $	CAD
Canary Islands	euro	EUR
	Spanish peseta	ESP
Central African Rep.	CFA franc	XAF
Chad	CFA franc	XAF
Chile	peso	CLP
China	renmimbi/yuan	CNY
Colombia	peso	COP
Costa Rica	colon	CRC
Croatia	kuna	HRK
Cuba	peso	CUP
Cyprus	Cyprus £	CYP
Czech Rep.	koruna	CZK
Denmark	krone	DKK
Dubai	UAE dirham	AED
Ecuador	sucre	ECS
Egypt	Egyptian £	EGP
Equatorial Guinea	CFA franc	XAF
Estonia	kroon	EEK
Ethiopia	birr	ETB
EMU	euro	EUR
Finland	euro	EUR
	markka	FIM
France	euro	EUR
	French franc	FRF
Gambia	dalasi	GMD
Germany	euro	EUR
	mark	DEM
Ghana	cedi	GHC
Gibraltar	Gibraltar £	GIP
Great Britain	pound	GBP
Greece	euro	EUR
Greenland	Danish krone	DKK
Grenada	E.Caribbean $	XCD
Guatemala	quetzal	GTQ
Guinea Rep.	Guinean franc	GNF
Haiti	gourde	HTG
Honduras	lempira	HNL
Hong Kong	HK $	HKD
Hungary	forint	HUF
Iceland	krona	ISK
India	rupee	INR
Indonesia	rupiah	IDR
Iran	rial	IRR
Iraq	dinar	IQD
Irish Republic	euro	EUR
	punt	IEP

Israel	shekel	ILS
Italy	euro	EUR
	lira	ITL
Ivory Coast	CFA franc	XOF
Jamaica	Jamaican $	JMD
Japan	yen	JPY
Jordan	dinar	JOD
Kenya	shilling	KES
Korea (North)	won	KPW
Korea (South)	won	KRW
Kuwait	dinar	KWD
Lebanon	Lebanese £	LBP
Libya	dinar	LYD
Liechtenstein	Swiss franc	CHF
Luxembourg	euro	EUR
	franc	LUF
Macao	pataca	MOP
Macedonia	denar	MKD
Madeira	euro	EUR
Malagasy Rep.	franc	MGF
Malawi	kwacha	MWK
Malaysia	ringgitt	MYR
Maldives	rufiyaa	MVR
Mali	CFA franc	XOF
Malta	lira	MTL
Martinique	euro	EUR
	French franc	FRF
Mauritania	ouguiya	MRO
Mauritius	rupee	MUR
Mexico	peso nuevo	MXN
Morocco	dirham	MAD
Namibia	rand	NAD
Nepal	rupee	NPR
Netherlands	euro	EUR
	guilder	NLG
New Zealand	NZ dollar	NZD
Nigeria	naira	NGN
Norway	krone	NOK
Oman	riyal	OMR
Pakistan	rupee	PKR
Peru	solnuevo	PEN
Philippines	peso	PHP
Poland	zloty	PLN
Portugal	euro	EUR
	escudo	PTE
Qatar	riyal	QAR
Romania	leu	ROL
Russia	rouble	RUB
Rwanda	franc	RWF
Saudi Arabia	riyal	SAR
Senegal	CFA franc	XOF
Seychelles	rupee	SCR
Sierra Leone	leone	SLL
Singapore	Singapore $	SGD
Slovakia	koruna	SKK
Slovenia	euro	EUR
	tolar	SIT
Solomon Is.	$	SBD
Somalia	shilling	SOS
South Africa	rand	ZAR
Spain	euro	EUR
	peseta	ESP
Sri Lanka	rupee	LKR
St Lucia	E.Caribbean $	XCD
Sudan	dinar	SDD
Sudan	Sudanese £	SDP
Surinam	S. guilder	SRG
Swaziland	lilangeni	SZL
Sweden	krona	SEK
Switzerland	Swiss franc	CHF
Syria	Syrian £	SYP
Taiwan	NT$	TWD
Tanzania	shilling	TZS
Thailand	baht	THB
Togo	CFA franc	XOF
Trinidad & Tobago	TT $	TTD
Tunisia	dinar	TND

Turkey	lira	TRL	Venezuela	bolivar	VEB
Turkmenistan	manat	TMM	Vietnam	dong	VND
Uganda	shilling	UGX	Virgin Is, USA	US $	USD
Ukraine	hryvna	UAH	Yemen	rial	YER
UAE	dirham	AED	Yugoslavia	dinar	YUM
Uruguay	peso	UYP	Zambia	kwacha	ZMK
USA	US $	USD	Zimbabwe	Zimbabwe $	ZWD

References and bibliography

Bishop, P. and Dixon, D. 1992, *Foreign Exchange Handbook*, McGraw-Hill, New York.

Choudhry, M. 2004, *The Money Markets Handbook*, John Wiley & Sons, Singapore.

Cook, T. and Rowe, T. 1986, (eds), *Instruments of the Money Market*, 6th edition, Federal Reserve Bank of Richmond.

Grabbe, J. 1986, *International Financial Markets*, Elsevier, Oxford.

Sarver, E. 1990, *The Eurocurrency Market Handbook*, New York Institute of Finance, New York.

Stigum, M. 1995, *The Money Market*, 4th edition, Irwin, New York.

Teasdale, A. 2004, "The Process of Securitisation", *Journal of Bond Trading and Management*, Volume 2, Number 1, October, www.YieldCurve.com.

Walmsley, J. 1992, *The Foreign Exchange and Money Markets Guide*, Wiley, New York.

CHAPTER

4

The Bond Instrument

The ALM desk of a bank does not concern itself solely with money market instruments. It also needs to be aware of, and be familiar with, bond instruments, for example, when dealing with bonds as loan collateral, or when managing bonds such as floating-rate notes as part of a liquidity book portfolio. For this reason we present now a primer on fixed income instruments. This is necessary background knowledge for ALM practitioners.

Bonds are debt-capital market instruments that represent a cash flow payable during a specified time period heading into the future. This cash flow represents the interest payable on the loan and the loan redemption. So, essentially, a bond is a loan, albeit one that is tradeable in a secondary market. This differentiates bond-market securities from commercial bank loans.

In the analysis that follows, bonds are assumed to be default-free, which means that there is no possibility that the interest payments and principal repayment will not be made. Such an assumption is accurate when one is referring to government bonds such as US Treasuries, UK gilts, Japanese JGBs, and so on. However, it is unreasonable when applied to bonds issued by corporates or lower-rated sovereign borrowers. Nevertheless, it is still relevant to understand the valuation and analysis of bonds that are default-free, as the pricing of bonds that carry default risk is based on the price of risk-free government securities. Essentially, the price investors charge borrowers that are not of risk-free credit standing is the price of government securities plus some credit risk premium.

Bond-market basics

All bonds are described in terms of their issuer, maturity date and coupon. For a default-free conventional, or "plain vanilla", bond this will be the essential information required. Non-vanilla bonds are defined by further characteristics such as their interest basis, flexibilities in their maturity date, credit risk and so on. Different types of bonds are described in the author's book *Fixed Income Markets* (John Wiley & Sons 2004).

Figure 4.1 shows screen DES from the Bloomberg system. This page describes the key characteristics of a bond. From Figure 4.1, we see a description of a bond issued by the Singapore government, the 4.625% of 2010. It tells us the following bond characteristics:

Issue date:	July 2000
Coupon:	4.625%
Maturity date:	1 July 2010
Issue currency:	Singapore dollars
Issue size:	SGD 3.4 million
Credit rating:	AAA/Aaa.

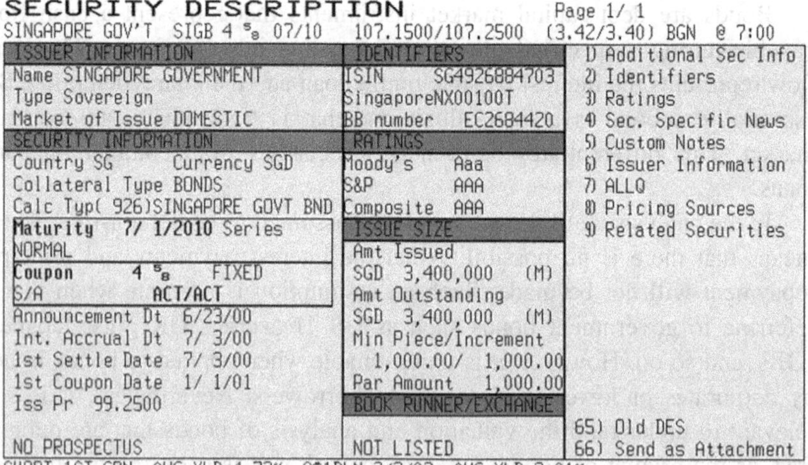

Figure 4.1 Bloomberg screen DES showing details of $4^5/_8$% 2010 issued by the Republic of Singapore, as at 20 October 2003

Calling up screen DES for any bond, provided it is supported by Bloomberg, will provide us with its key details. Later on, we will see how non-vanilla bonds include special features that investors take into consideration in their analysis.

We will consider the essential characteristics of bonds later in this chapter. First, we review the capital market; the essential principles of finance, the time value of money, are described in the Appendix at the back of the book.

Capital market participants

The debt capital markets exist because of the financing requirements of governments and corporates. The source of capital is varied, but the total supply of funds in a market is made up of personal or household savings, business savings and increases in the overall money supply. Growth in the money supply is a function of the overall state of the economy, and interested readers may wish to consult the references at the end of this chapter which includes several standard economic texts. Individuals save out of their current income for future consumption, while business savings represent retained earnings. The entire savings stock represents the capital available in a market. The requirements of savers and borrowers differs significantly, in that savers have a short-term investment horizon while borrowers prefer to take a longer-term view. The "constitutional weakness" of what would otherwise be *unintermediated* financial markets led, from an early stage, to the development of financial intermediaries.

Financial intermediaries

In its simplest form a financial intermediary is a broker or agent. Today we would classify the broker as someone who acts on behalf of the borrower or lender, buying or selling a bond as instructed. However, intermediaries originally acted between borrowers and lenders in placing funds as required. A broker would not simply on-lend funds that have been placed with it, but would accept deposits and make loans as required by its customers. This resulted in the first banks. A retail bank deals mainly with the personal financial sector and small businesses, and in addition to loans and deposits also provides cash transmission services. A retail bank is required to maintain a minimum cash reserve, to meet potential withdrawals, but the remainder of its deposit base can be used to make loans. This does not mean that the total size of its loan book is restricted to what it has taken in deposits: loans can also be funded in the wholesale market. An investment bank will deal with governments, corporates and institutional investors. Investment banks perform an agency role for their customers, and are the primary vehicle through which a corporate will borrow funds in the bond markets. This is part of the bank's corporate finance function; it will also act as wholesaler in the bond markets, a function known as market-making. The bond-issuing function of an investment bank, by which the bank will issue bonds on behalf of a customer and pass the funds raised to this customer, is known as origination. Investment banks will also carry out a range of other functions for institutional customers, including export finance, corporate advisory and fund management.

Other financial intermediaries will trade not on behalf of clients but for their own book. These include arbitrageurs and speculators. Usually such market participants form part of investment banks.

Investors

There is a large variety of players in the bond markets, each trading some or all of the different instruments available to suit their own purposes. We can group the main types of investors according to the time horizon of their investment activity.

Short-term institutional investors. These include banks and building societies, money market fund managers, central banks and the Treasury desks of some types of corporates. Such bodies are driven by short-term investment views, often subject to close guidelines, and will be driven by the total return available on their investments. Banks will have an additional requirement to maintain *liquidity*, often in fulfilment of regulatory authority rules, by holding a proportion of their assets in the form of easily tradeable short-term instruments.

Long-term institutional investors. Typically, these types of investors include pension funds and life assurance companies. Their investment horizon is long-term, reflecting the nature of their liabilities; often they will seek to match these liabilities by holding long-dated bonds.

Mixed horizon institutional investors. This is possibly the largest category of investors and will include general insurance companies and most corporate bodies. Like banks and financial sector companies, they are also very active in the primary market, issuing bonds to finance their operations.

Market professionals. This category includes the banks and specialist financial intermediaries mentioned above, firms that one would not automatically classify as "investors" although they will also have an investment objective. Their time horizon will range from one day to the very long term. They include the proprietary trading desks of investment banks, as well as bond market makers in securities houses and banks who are providing a service to their customers. Proprietary traders will actively position themselves in the market in order to gain trading profit; for example, in response to their view on where they think interest rate levels are headed. These participants will trade direct with other market professionals and investors, or via brokers. Market-makers or *traders* (also called *dealers* in the United States) are wholesalers in the bond markets; they make two-way prices in selected bonds. Firms will not necessarily be active market-makers in all types of bonds, smaller firms often specialise in certain sectors. In a two-way quote the *bid price* is the price at which the market-maker will buy stock, so it is the price the investor will receive when selling stock. The *offer price* or *ask price* is the price at which investors can buy stock from the market-maker. As one might expect the bid price is always higher than the offer price, and it is this *spread* that represents the theoretical profit to the market-maker. The bid–offer spread set by the market-maker is determined by several factors, including supply and demand and liquidity considerations for that particular stock, the trader's view on market direction and *volatility,* as well as that of the stock itself and the presence of any market intelligence. A large bid–offer spread reflects low liquidity in the stock, as well as low demand.

Markets

Markets are that part of the financial system where capital market transactions, including the buying and selling of securities, takes place. A market can describe a traditional stock exchange, a physical trading floor where securities trading occurs. Many financial instruments are traded over the telephone or electronically over computer links; these markets are known as *over-the-counter* (OTC) markets. A distinction is made between financial instruments of up to one year's maturity and instruments of over one year's maturity. Short-term instruments make up the *money market* while all other instruments are deemed to be part of the *capital market*. There is also a distinction made between the *primary market* and the *secondary market*. A new issue of bonds made by an investment bank on behalf of its client is made in the primary market. Such an issue can be a *public* offer, in which anyone can apply to buy the bonds, or a *private* offer where the customers of the investment bank are offered the stock. The secondary market is the market in which existing bonds and shares are subsequently traded.

Overview of the main bond markets

So far we have established that bonds are debt capital market instruments, which means that they represent loans taken out by governments and corporations. The duration of any particular loan will vary from two years to 30 years or longer. Here we introduce just a small proportion of the different bond instruments that trade in the market, plus a few words on different country markets.

Domestic and international bonds

In any market there is a primary distinction between *domestic* bonds and other bonds. Domestic bonds are issued by borrowers domiciled in the country of issue, and in the currency of the country of issue. Generally they trade only in their original market. A *Eurobond* is issued across national boundaries and can be in any currency, which is why they are also sometimes called *international* bonds. It is now more common for Eurobonds to be referred to as international bonds, to avoid confusion with "euro bonds", which are bonds denominated in *euros*, the currency of 12 countries of the European Union (EU). As an issue of Eurobonds is not restricted in terms of currency or country, the borrower is not restricted as to its nationality either. There are also *foreign* bonds, which are domestic bonds issued by foreign borrowers. An example of a foreign bond is a *Bulldog*, which is a sterling bond issued for trading in the UK market by a foreign borrower. The equivalent foreign bonds in other countries include *Yankee* bonds (the United States), *Samurai* bonds (Japan), *Alpine* bonds (Switzerland) and *Matador* bonds (Spain).

There are detail differences between these bonds; for example, in the frequency of interest payments that each one makes and the way the interest payment is calculated. Some bonds, such as domestic bonds, pay their interest *net*, which means net of a withholding tax such as income tax. Other bonds including Eurobonds make *gross* interest payments.

Government bonds

As their name suggests government bonds are issued by a government or *sovereign*. Government bonds in any country form the foundation for the entire domestic debt market. This is because the government market will be the largest in relation to the market as a whole. Government bonds also represent the best *credit risk* in any market as people do not expect the government to go bankrupt. As discussed in Chapter 4 of the author's book *Structured Credit Products* (John Wiley & Sons 2010), professional institutions that analyse borrowers in terms of their credit risk always rate the government in any market as the highest credit available. While this may sometimes not be the case, it is usually a good rule of thumb.[1] The government bond market is usually also the most *liquid* in the domestic market due to its size, and it will form the benchmark against which other borrowers are rated. Generally, but not always, the yield offered on government debt will be the lowest in that market. Table 4.1 on page 140 is a comparison of different sovereign bond markets conventions; the respective yield curves for each of these markets as of June 2004 are given in Table 4.2 on page 141.

The United States

Government bonds in the United States are known as *Treasuries*. Bonds issued with an original maturity of between two and ten years are known as *notes* (as in "Treasury note"), while those issued with an original maturity of over ten years are known as *bonds*. In practice there is no real difference between notes and bonds and they trade the same way in the market. Treasuries pay semi-annual coupons. The US Treasury market is the largest single bond market anywhere and trades on a 24-hour basis all around the world. A large proportion of Treasuries are held by foreign governments and corporations. It is a very liquid and *transparent* market.

The United Kingdom

The UK government issues bonds known as *gilt-edged securities* or *gilts*.[2] The gilt market is another very liquid and transparent market, with prices being very competitive. Many of the more esoteric features of gilts, such as "tick" pricing (where prices are quoted in 32nds and not decimals) and *special ex-dividend* trading, have recently been removed in order to harmonise the market with euro government bonds. Gilts still pay coupon on

[1] Occasionally one may come across a corporate entity that one may view as better rated in terms of credit risk compared to the government of the country in which the company is domiciled. However, the main rating agencies will not rate a corporate entity at a level higher than its country of domicile.

[2] This is because early gilt issues are said to have been represented by certificates that were edged with gold leaf, hence the term gilt-edged. In fact, the story is almost certainly apocryphal and it is unlikely that gilt certificates were ever edged with gold!

	Credit rating	Maturity range	Dealing mechanism	Benchmark bonds	Issuance	Coupon and day-count basis
Australia	AAA	2–15 years	OTC dealer network	5, 10 years	Auction	Semi-annual, act/act
Canada	AAA	2–30 years	OTC dealer network	3, 5, 10 years	Auction, subscription	Semi-annual, act/act
France	AAA	BTAN: 1–7 years OAT: 10–30 years	OTC dealer network. Bonds listed on Paris Stock Exchange	BTAN: 2 & 5 years OAT: 10 & 30 years	Dutch auction	BTAN: Semi-annual, act/act OAT: Annual, act/act
Germany	AAA	OBL: 2, 5 years BUND: 10, 30 years	OTC dealer network. Listed on stock exchange	The most recent issue	Combination of Dutch auction and proportion of each issue allocated on fixed basis to institutions	Annual, act/act
South Africa	A	2–30 years	OTC dealer network. Listed on Johannesburg SE	2, 7, 10 and 20 years	Auction	Semi-annual, act/365
Singapore	AAA	2–15 years	OTC dealer network	1, 5, 10 and 15 years	Auction	Semi-annual, act/act
Taiwan	AA–	2–30 years	OTC dealer network	2, 5, 10, 20 and 30 years	Auction	Annual, act/act
United Kingdom	AAA	2–35 years	OTC dealer network	5, 10 and 30 years	Auction, subsequent issue by "tap" subscription	Semi-annual, act/act
United States	AAA	2–20 years	OTC dealer network	2, 5 and 10 years	Auction	Semi-annual, act/act

Table 4.1 Selected government bond market conventions

Source: Choudhry (2004).

Term (years)	Australia	Canada	France	Germany	South Africa	Singapore	Taiwan	UK	US
1	5.2154	2.749	2.3291	2.3747	4.71	0.937		4.9599	
2	5.2259	3.394	2.8375	2.7184	9.351	1.157	1.449	5.1033	2.7034
3	5.3451	2.6339	3.1998	3.0609				5.1633	3.1129
4	5.482	3.937	3.4966	3.3998	10.025			5.1685	
5	5.5761	4.2684	3.7222	3.6425		2.3085	2.3243	4.6946	3.9406
7	5.735	4.0704	4.014	4.0465		2.9583		5.2042	
10	5.8888	4.9984	4.395	4.3708	10.468	3.3355	3.0608	5.1863	4.8135
15	5.941		4.709			3.8989	3.1635	5.1504	
20		5.2426	4.776	4.8365	9.605		3.3507	4.9885	
30		5.4447	4.98	4.9481			3.5571	4.8596	5.3878

Table 4.2 Selected government bond markets, yield curves as at 21 June 2004
Source: Bloomberg L.P.

a semi-annual basis though, unlike euro paper. The UK government also issues bonds known as *index-linked* gilts whose interest and redemption payments are linked to the rate of inflation. There are also older gilts with peculiar features such as no redemption date and quarterly paid coupons.

Germany

Government bonds in Germany are known as *bunds*, BOBLs or *Schatze*. These terms refer to the original maturity of the paper and has little effect on trading patterns. Bunds pay coupon on an annual basis and are, of course, now denominated in euros.

Non-conventional bonds

The definition of bonds given earlier in this chapter referred to conventional or *plain vanilla* bonds. There are many variations on vanilla bonds and we can introduce a few of them here.

Floating-rate notes (FRNs). The bond market is often referred to as the *fixed income* market, or the *fixed interest* market in the United Kingdom. FRNs do not have a fixed coupon at all but instead link their interest payments to an external reference, such as the three-month bank lending rate. Bank interest rates will fluctuate constantly during the life of the bond and so an FRN's cash flows are not known with certainty. Usually, FRNs pay a fixed margin or *spread* over the specified reference rate; occasionally, the spread is not fixed and such a bond is known as a *variable rate note*. Because FRNs pay coupons based on the three-month or six-month bank rate they are essentially money market instruments and are treated by bank dealing desks as such.

Index-linked bonds. An index-linked bond, as its coupon and redemption payment, or possibly just either one of these, is linked to a specified index. When governments issue index-linked bonds the cash flows are linked to a price index such as consumer or commodity prices. Corporates have issued index-linked bonds that are connected to inflation or a stock market index.

Zero-coupon bonds. Certain bonds do not make any coupon payments at all and these are known as *zero-coupon bonds*. A zero-coupon bond or *strip* has only cash flow, the redemption payment on maturity. If we assume that the maturity payment is, say, $100 per cent or *par* the issue price will be at a discount to par. Such bonds are also known therefore as *discounted* bonds.

The difference between the price paid on issue and the redemption payment is the interest realised by the bondholder. As we will discover when we look at strips this has certain advantages for investors, the main one being that there are no coupon payments to be invested during the bond's life. Both governments and corporates issue zero-coupon bonds. Conventional coupon-bearing bonds can be *stripped* into a series of individual cash flows, which would then trade as separate zero-coupon bonds. This is a common practice in government bond markets such as Treasuries or gilts where the borrowing authority does not actually issue strips, and they have to be created via the stripping process.

Amortising bonds. A conventional bond will repay on maturity the entire nominal sum initially borrowed on issue. This is known as a *bullet* repayment (which is why vanilla bonds are sometimes known as bullet bonds). A bond that repays portions of the borrowing in stages during its life is known as an *amortising* bond.

Bonds with embedded options. Some bonds include a provision in their offer particulars that gives either the bondholder and/or the issuer an option to enforce early redemption of the bond. The most common type of option embedded in a bond is a *call feature*. A call provision grants the issuer the right to redeem all or part of the debt before the specified maturity date. An issuing company may wish to include such a feature as it allows it to replace an old bond issue with a lower coupon rate issue if interest rates in the market have declined. As a call feature allows the issuer to change the maturity date of a bond it is considered harmful to the bondholder's interests; therefore the market price of the bond at any time will reflect this. A call option is included in all asset-backed securities based on mortgages, for obvious reasons (asset-backed bonds are considered in a later chapter). A bond issue may also include a provision that allows the investor to change the maturity of the bond. This is known as a *put feature* and gives the bondholder the right to sell the bond back to the issuer at par on specified dates. The advantage to the bondholder is that if interest rates rise after the issue date, thus depressing the bond's value, the investor can realise par value by *putting* the bond back to the issuer. A *convertible* bond is an issue giving the bondholder the right to exchange the bond for a specified amount of shares (equity) in the issuing company. This feature allows the investor to take advantage of favourable movements in the price of the issuer's shares. The presence of embedded options in a bond makes valuation more complex compared to plain vanilla bonds, and will be considered separately.

Bond warrants. A bond may be issued with a *warrant* attached to it, which entitles the bondholder to buy more of the bond (or a different bond issued by the same borrower) under specified terms and conditions at a later date. An issuer may include a warrant in order to make the bond more attractive to investors. Warrants are often detached from their host bond and traded separately.

Finally, there is a large class of bonds known as *asset-backed securities*. These are bonds formed from pooling together a set of loans such as mortgages or car loans and issuing bonds against them. The interest payments on the original loans serve to back the interest payable on the asset-backed bond. We will look at these instruments in some detail in Part IV.

Bond pricing and yield: The traditional approach

Bond pricing

The interest rate that is used to discount a bond's cash flows (and therefore called the discount rate) is the rate required by the bondholder. This is therefore known as the bond's yield. The yield on the bond will be determined by the market and is the price demanded by investors for buying it, which is why it is sometimes called the bond's return. The required yield for any bond will depend on a number of political and economic factors, including what yield is being earned by other bonds of the same class. Yield is always quoted as an annualised interest rate, so that for a bond paying semi-annually exactly half of the annual rate is used to discount the cash flows.

The fair price of a bond is the present value of all its cash flows. Therefore, when pricing a bond, we need to calculate the present value of all the coupon interest payments and the present value of the redemption payment, and sum these. The price of a conventional bond that pays annual coupons can therefore be given by (4.1):

$$P = \frac{C}{(1+r)} + \frac{C}{(1+r)^2} + \frac{C}{(1+r)^3} + \cdots \frac{C}{(1+r)^N} + \frac{M}{(1+r)^N}$$

$$= \sum_{n=1}^{N} \frac{C}{(1+r)^N} + \frac{M}{(1+r)^N} \tag{4.1}$$

where

P is the price
C is the annual coupon payment

r is the discount rate (therefore, the required yield)
N is the number of years to maturity (therefore, the number of interest periods in an annually paying bond; for a semi-annual bond the number of interest periods is $N \times 2$)
M is the maturity payment or par value (usually 100% of currency).

For long-hand calculation purposes, the first half of (4.1) is usually simplified and is sometimes encountered in one of the two ways shown in (4.2):

$$P = C\left[\frac{1 - \left[\frac{1}{(1+r)^N}\right]}{r}\right] \tag{4.2}$$

or

$$P = \frac{C}{r}\left[1 - \frac{1}{(1+r)^N}\right].$$

The price of a bond that pays semi-annual coupons is given by the expression in (4.3), which is our earlier expression modified to allow for the twice-yearly discounting:

$$\begin{aligned} P &= \frac{C/2}{(1+\frac{1}{2}r)} + \frac{C/2}{(1+\frac{1}{2}r)^2} + \frac{C/2}{(1+\frac{1}{2}r)^3} + \cdots \frac{C/2}{(1+\frac{1}{2}r)^{2N}} + \frac{M}{(1+\frac{1}{2}r)^{2N}} \\ &= \sum_{t=1}^{2T} \frac{C/2}{(1+\frac{1}{2}r)^N} + \frac{M}{(1+\frac{1}{2}r)^{2N}} \\ &= \frac{C}{r}\left[1 - \frac{1}{(1+\frac{1}{2}r)^{2N}}\right] + \frac{M}{(1+\frac{1}{2}r)^{2N}}. \end{aligned} \tag{4.3}$$

Note how we set $2N$ as the power to which to raise the discount factor, as there are two interest payments every year for a bond that pays semi-annually. Therefore, a more convenient function to use might be the number of interest periods in the life of the bond, as opposed to the number of years to maturity, which we could set as n, allowing us to alter the equation for a semi-annually paying bond as:

$$P = \frac{C}{r}\left[1 - \frac{1}{(1+\frac{1}{2}r)^{2N}}\right] + \frac{M}{(1+\frac{1}{2}r)^{2N+1}}. \tag{4.4}$$

The formula in (4.4) calculates the fair price on a coupon-payment date, so that there is no accrued interest incorporated into the price. It also assumes that there is an even number of coupon-payment dates remaining before maturity. The concept of accrued interest is an accounting convention, and treats coupon interest as accruing every day that the bond is held; this amount is added to the discounted present value of the bond (the *clean* price) to obtain the market value of the bond, known as the *dirty* price.

The date used as the point for calculation is the settlement date for the bond, the date on which a bond will change hands after it is traded. For a new issue of bonds, the settlement date is the day when the stock is delivered to investors and payment is received by the bond issuer. The settlement date for a bond traded in the secondary market is the day that the buyer transfers payment to the seller of the bond and when the seller transfers the bond to the buyer. Different markets will have different settlement conventions. For example, Australian government bonds normally settle two business days after the trade date (the notation used in bond markets is "T + 2"), whereas Eurobonds settle on T + 3. The term *value date* is sometimes used in place of settlement date. However, the two terms are not strictly synonymous. A settlement date can only fall on a business date, so that an Australian government bond traded on a Friday will settle on a Tuesday (T + 2). However, a value date can sometimes fall on a non-business day; for example, when accrued interest is being calculated.

If there is an odd number of coupon-payment dates before maturity, the formula at (4.4) is modified as shown in (4.5):

$$P = \frac{C}{r}\left[1 - \frac{1}{(1 + {}^{1}\!/_{2}r)^{2N+1}}\right] + \frac{M}{(1 + {}^{1}\!/_{2}r)^{2N+1}}. \tag{4.5}$$

The standard formula also assumes that the bond is traded for a settlement on a day that is precisely one interest period before the next coupon payment. The price formula is adjusted if dealing takes place in between coupon dates. If we take the value date for any transaction, we then need to calculate the number of calendar days from this day to the next coupon date. We then use the following ratio i when adjusting the exponent for the discount factor:

$$i = \frac{\text{Days from value date to next coupon date}}{\text{Days in the interest period}}.$$

The number of days in the interest period is the number of calendar days between the last coupon date and the next one, and it will depend on the day-count basis used for that specific bond. The price formula is then modified as shown at (4.6).

$$P = \frac{C}{(1+r)^i} + \frac{C}{(1+r)^{1+i}} + \frac{C}{(1+r)^{2+i}} + \cdots \frac{C}{(1+r)^{n-1+i}} + \frac{M}{(1+r)^{n-1+i}} \tag{4.6}$$

where the variables C, M, n and r are as before. Note that (4.6) assumes r for an annually paying bond and is adjusted to $r/2$ for a semi-annually paying bond.

EXAMPLE 4.1 Practical calculations

In these examples we illustrate the long-hand price calculation, using both expressions for the calculation of the present value of the annuity stream of a bond's cash flows.

4.1 (a)

Calculate the fair pricing of a US Treasury, the 4% of February 2014, which pays semi-annual coupons, with the following terms:

C = \$4.00 per \$100 nominal
M = \$100
N = 10 years (that is, the calculation is for value on 17 February 2004)
r = 4.048%

$$P = \frac{\$4.00}{0.04048}\left\{1 - \frac{1}{[1 + \tfrac{1}{2}(0.04048)]^{20}}\right\} + \frac{\$100}{[1 + \tfrac{1}{2}(0.04048)]^{20}}$$
$$= \$32.628 + \$66.981$$
$$= \$99.609 \text{ or } 99\text{-}19+$$

The fair price of the Treasury is \$99-19+, which is composed of the present value of the stream of coupon payments (\$32.628) and the present value of the return of the principal (\$66.981).

This yield calculation is shown in Figure 4.2 on page 148, the Bloomberg YA page for this security. We show the price shown as 99-19+ for settlement on 17 February 2004, the date it was issued.

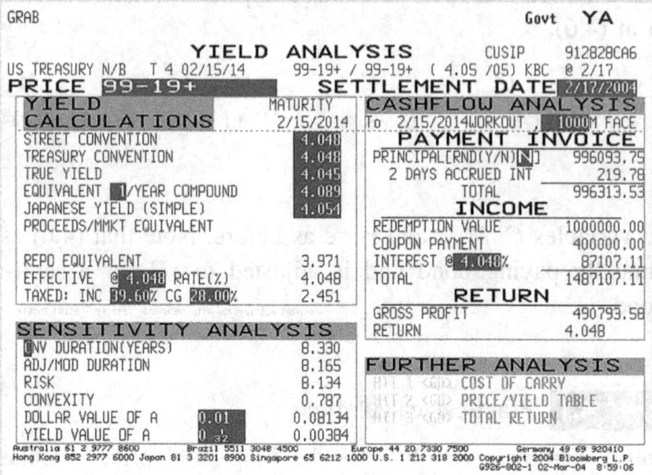

GRAB
Govt YA
YIELD ANALYSIS
CUSIP 912828CA6
US TREASURY N/B T 4 02/15/14 99-19+ / 99-19+ (4.05 /05) KBC @ 2/17
PRICE 99-19+
SETTLEMENT DATE 2/17/2004
YIELD CALCULATIONS
MATURITY 2/15/2014
STREET CONVENTION 4.048
TREASURY CONVENTION 4.048
TRUE YIELD 4.045
EQUIVALENT 1/YEAR COMPOUND 4.089
JAPANESE YIELD (SIMPLE) 4.054
PROCEEDS/MMKT EQUIVALENT
REPO EQUIVALENT 3.971
EFFECTIVE @ 4.048 RATE(%) 4.048
TAXED: INC 39.60% CG 28.00% 2.451
CASHFLOW ANALYSIS
To 2/15/2014WORKOUT , 1000M FACE
PAYMENT INVOICE
PRINCIPAL[RND(Y/N)N] 996093.75
2 DAYS ACCRUED INT 219.78
TOTAL 996313.53
INCOME
REDEMPTION VALUE 1000000.00
COUPON PAYMENT 400000.00
INTEREST @ 4.048% 87107.11
TOTAL 1487107.11
RETURN
GROSS PROFIT 490793.58
RETURN 4.048
SENSITIVITY ANALYSIS
CNV DURATION(YEARS) 8.330
ADJ/MOD DURATION 8.165
RISK 8.134
CONVEXITY 0.787
DOLLAR VALUE OF A 0.01 0.08134
YIELD VALUE OF A 0 1/32 0.00384
FURTHER ANALYSIS
COST OF CARRY
PRICE/YIELD TABLE
TOTAL RETURN
Australia 61 2 9777 8600 Brazil 5511 3048 4500 Europe 44 20 7330 7500 Germany 49 69 920410
Hong Kong 852 2977 6000 Japan 81 3 3201 8900 Singapore 65 6212 1000 U.S. 1 212 318 2000 Copyright 2004 Bloomberg L.P.
G926-802-1 02-Mar-04 8:59:06

Figure 4.2 Bloomberg YA page for yield analysis

4.1(b)

What is the price of a 5% coupon sterling bond with precisely five years to maturity, with semi-annual coupon payments, if the yield required is 5.40%?

As the cash flows for this bond are 10 semi-annual coupons of £2.50 and a redemption payment of £100 in 10, six-month periods from now, the price of the bond can be obtained by solving the following expression, where we substitute $C = 2.5$, $n = 10$ and $r = 0.027$ into the price equation (the values for C and r reflect the adjustments necessary for a semi-annual paying bond).

$$P = 2.5\left[\frac{1-\left[\frac{1}{(1.027)^{10}}\right]}{0.027}\right] + \frac{100}{(1.027)^{10}}$$

$$= 21.65574 + 76.61178$$

$$= £98.26752$$

The price of the bond is £98.2675 per \$100 nominal.

4.1(c)

What is the price of a 5% coupon euro bond with five years to maturity paying annual coupons, again with a required yield of 5.4%?

In this case there are five periods of interest, so we may set $C = 5$, $n = 5$, with $r = 0.05$.

$$P = 5\left[\frac{1-\left[\frac{1}{(1.054)^5}\right]}{0.054}\right] + \frac{100}{(1.054)^5}$$
$$= 21.410121 + 76.877092$$
$$= £98.287213$$

Note how the annual-paying bond has a slightly higher price for the same required annualised yield. This is because the semi-annual paying sterling bond has a higher effective yield than the euro bond, resulting in a lower price.

4.1(d)

Consider our 5% sterling bond again, but this time the required yield has risen and is now 6%. This makes $C = 2.5$, $n = 10$ and $r = 0.03$.

$$P = 2.5\left[\frac{1-\left[\frac{1}{(1.03)^{10}}\right]}{0.03}\right] + \frac{100}{(1.03)^{10}}$$
$$= 21.325507 + 74.409391$$
$$= £95.7349$$

As the required yield has risen, the discount rate used in the price calculation is now higher, and the result of the higher discount is a lower present value (price).

4.1(e)

Calculate the price of our sterling bond, still with five years to maturity, but offering a yield of 5.1%.

$$P = 2.5\left[\frac{1-\left[\frac{1}{(1.0255)^5}\right]}{0.0255}\right] + \frac{100}{(1.0255)^5}$$

$$= 21.823737 + 77.739788$$

$$= £99.563523$$

To satisfy the lower required yield of 5.1%, the price of the bond has fallen to £99.56 per £100.

4.1(f)

Calculate the price of the 5% sterling bond one year later, with precisely four years left to maturity and with the required yield still at the original 5.40%. This sets the terms in 4.1(b) unchanged, except now $n = 8$.

$$P = 2.5\left[\frac{1-\left[\frac{1}{(1.027)^8}\right]}{0.027}\right] + \frac{100}{(1.027)^8}$$

$$= 17.773458 + 80.804668$$

$$= £98.578126$$

The price of the bond is £98.58. Compared to 4.1(b) this illustrates how, other things being equal, the price of a bond will approach par (£100 per cent) as it approaches maturity.

There also exist *perpetual* or *irredeemable* bonds that have no redemption date, so that interest on them is paid indefinitely. They are also known as undated bonds. An example of an undated bond is the 3½% War Loan, a UK gilt originally issued in 1916 to help pay for the 1914–1918 war effort. Most undated bonds date from a long time in the past and it is unusual to see them issued today. In structure, the cash flow from an undated bond can be viewed as a continuous annuity. The fair price of such a bond is given from (4.1) by setting $N = \infty$, such that:

$$P = \frac{C}{r}. \tag{4.7}$$

In most markets, bond prices are quoted in decimals, in minimum increments of 1/100,000. This is the case with Eurobonds, euro-denominated bonds and gilts, for example. Certain markets – including the US Treasury market and South African and Indian government bonds, for example – quote prices in ticks, where the minimum increment is 1/32nd. One tick is therefore equal to 0.03125. A US Treasury might be priced at "98-05" which means "98 and five ticks". This is equal to 98 and 5/32nds, which is 98.15625.

Example 4.2 Bond consideration

What is the total consideration for £5 million nominal of a gilt, where the price is 114.50? The price of the gilt is £114.50 per £100, so the consideration is:

$$1.145 \times 5{,}000{,}000 = £5{,}725{,}000.$$

What consideration is payable for $5 million nominal of a US Treasury, quoted at an all-in price of 99-16? The US Treasury price is 99-16, which is equal to 99 and 16/32, or 99.50 per $100. The consideration is therefore:

$$0.9950 \times 5{,}000{,}000 = \$4{,}975{,}000.$$

If the price of a bond is below par, the total consideration is below the nominal amount, whereas if it is priced above par the consideration will be above the nominal amount.

Bonds that do not pay a coupon during their life are known as zero-coupon bonds or strips, and the price for these bonds is determined by modifying (4.1) to allow for the fact that $C = 0$. We know that the only cash flow is the maturity payment, so we may set the price as:

$$P = \frac{M}{(1 + r)^N} \tag{4.8}$$

where M and r are as before and N is the number of years to maturity. The important factor is to allow for the same number of interest periods as coupon bonds of the same currency. That is, even though there are no actual coupons, we calculate prices and yields on the basis of a quasi-coupon period. For a US dollar or a sterling zero-coupon bond, a five-year zero-coupon bond would be assumed to cover ten quasi-coupon periods, which would set the price equation as:

$$P = \frac{M}{(1 + {}^1\!/_2 r)^n}. \tag{4.9}$$

We have to note carefully the quasi-coupon periods in order to maintain consistency with conventional bond pricing.

EXAMPLE 4.3 Zero-coupon bond consideration

4.3(a)

Calculate the price of a gilt strip with a maturity of precisely five years, where the required yield is 5.40%.

These terms allow us to set $N = 5$ so that $n = 10$, $r = 0.054$ (and $r/2 = 0.027$), with $M = 100$ as usual.

$$P = \frac{100}{(1.027)^{10}}$$

$$= £76.611782$$

4.3(b)

Calculate the price of a French government zero-coupon bond with precisely five years to maturity, with the same required yield of 5.40%.

$$P = \frac{100}{(1.054)^5}$$

$$= £76.877092$$

An examination of the bond price formula tells us that the yield and price for a bond are closely related. A key aspect of this relationship is that the price changes in the opposite direction to the yield. This is because the price of the bond is the net present value of its cash flows; if the discount rate used in the present value calculation increases, the present values of the cash flows will decrease. This occurs whenever the yield level required by bondholders increases. In the same way, if the required yield decreases, the price of the bond will rise. This property was observed in Example 4.2. As the required yield decreased, the price of the bond increased, and we observed the same relationship when the required yield was raised.

The relationship between any bond's price and yield at any required yield level is illustrated in Figure 4.3, which is obtained if we plot the yield against the corresponding price; this shows a convex curve. In practice, the curve is not quite as perfectly convex as illustrated in Figure 4.3; the diagram is representative.

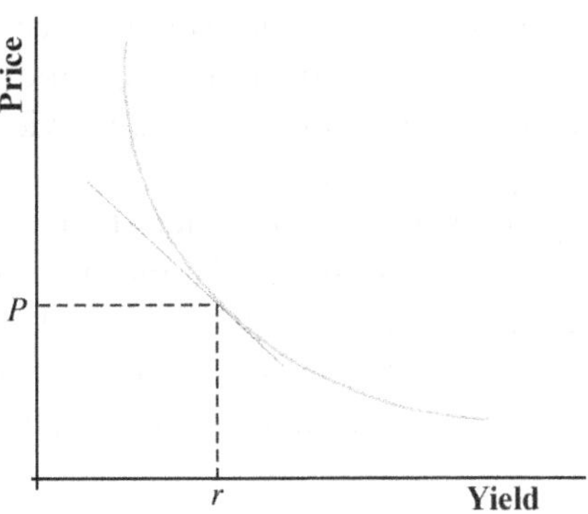

Figure 4.3 The price/yield relationship

Summary of the price/yield relationship

- At issue, if a bond is priced at par, its coupon will equal the yield that the market requires from the bond.
- If the required yield rises above the coupon rate, the bond price will decrease.
- If the required yield goes below the coupon rate, the bond price will increase.

Bond yield

We have observed how to calculate the price of a bond using an appropriate discount rate known as the bond's yield. We can reverse this procedure to find the yield of a bond where the price is known, which would be equivalent to calculating the bond's internal rate of return (IRR). The IRR calculation is taken to be a bond's yield to maturity or redemption yield, and is one of various yield measures used in the markets to estimate the return generated from holding a bond. In most markets, bonds are generally traded on the basis of their prices but because of the complicated patterns of cash flows that different bonds can have, they are generally compared in terms of their yields. This means that a market-maker will usually quote a two-way price at which he or she will buy or sell a particular bond, but it is the yield at which the bond is trading that is important to the market maker's customer. This is because a bond's price does not actually tell us anything useful about what we are getting. Remember, that in any market there will be a number of bonds with different issuers, coupons and terms to maturity. Even in a homogenous market such as the Treasury market, different bonds and notes will trade according to their own specific characteristics. To compare bonds in the market, therefore, we need the yield on any bond and it is yields that we compare, not prices.

The yield on any investment is the interest rate that will make the present value of the cash flows from the investment equal to the initial cost (price) of the investment. Mathematically, the yield on any investment, represented by r, is the interest rate that satisfies equation (4.10) below, which is simply the bond price equation we've already reviewed.

$$P = \sum_{n=1}^{N} \frac{C_n}{(1 + r)^n} \tag{4.10}$$

But as we have noted there are other types of yield measure used in the market for different purposes. The simplest measure of the yield on a bond is the current yield, also known as the flat yield, interest yield or running yield. The running yield is given by (4.11):

$$rc = \frac{C}{P} \times 100 \tag{4.11}$$

where

rc is the current yield.

In (4.11) C is not expressed as a decimal. Current yield ignores any capital gain or loss that might arise from holding and trading a bond, and it does not consider the time value of money. It essentially calculates the bond coupon income as a proportion of the price paid for the bond, and to be accurate would have to assume that the bond was more like an annuity rather than a fixed-term instrument.

The current yield is useful as a "rough-and-ready" interest-rate calculation; it is often used to estimate the cost of, or profit from, a short-term holding of a bond. For example, if other short-term interest rates such as the one-week or three-month rates are higher than the current yield, holding the bond is said to involve a running cost. This is also known as *negative carry* or *negative funding*. The term is used by bond traders and market-makers and leveraged investors. The carry on a bond is a useful measure for all market practitioners as it illustrates the cost of holding or funding a bond. The funding rate is the bondholder's short-term cost of funds. A private investor could also apply this to a short-term holding of bonds.

The yield to maturity (YTM) or gross redemption yield is the most frequently used measure of return from holding a bond.[3] YTM takes into account the pattern of coupon payments, the bond's term to maturity and the capital gain (or loss) arising over the remaining life of the bond. We saw from our bond price formula in the previous section that these elements were all related and were important components determining a bond's price. If we set the IRR for a set of cash flows to be the rate that applies from a start-date to an end-date we can assume the IRR to be the YTM for those cash flows. The YTM therefore is equivalent to the IRR on the bond, the rate that equates the value of the discounted cash flows on the bond to its current price. The calculation assumes that the bond is held until maturity and therefore it is the cash flows to maturity that are discounted in the calculation. It also employs the concept of the time value of money.

As we would expect, the formula for YTM is essentially that for calculating the price of a bond. For a bond paying annual coupons, the YTM is calculated by solving equation (4.11). Note that the expression in (4.11) has two variable parameters: the price P and yield r. It cannot be rearranged to solve for yield r explicitly and, in fact, the only way to solve for the yield is to use the process of numerical iteration. The process involves estimating a value for r and calculating the price associated with the estimated yield. If the calculated price is higher than the price of the bond at the time, the yield estimate is lower than the actual yield, and so it must be adjusted until it converges to the level that corresponds with the bond price.[4] For the YTM of a semi-annual coupon bond, we have to adjust the formula to allow for the semi-annual payments, shown in (4.13) on page 158.

To differentiate redemption yield from other yield and interest-rate measures described in this book, we henceforth refer to it as *rm*.

---

[3] In this book the terms "yield to maturity" and "gross redemption yield" are used synonymously. The latter term is encountered in sterling markets.

[4] Bloomberg also uses the term "yield-to-workout", where "workout" refers to the maturity date for the bond.

EXAMPLE 4.4 YTM for semi-annual coupon bond

A semi-annual paying bond has a dirty price of \$98.50, an annual coupon of 6% and there is exactly one year before maturity. The bond therefore has three remaining cash flows, comprising two coupon payments of \$3 each and a redemption payment of \$100. Equation 4.12 can be used with the following inputs:

$$98.50 = \frac{3.00}{(1 + {}^1\!/_2 rm)} + \frac{103.00}{(1 + {}^1\!/_2 rm)^2}.$$

Note that we use half of the YTM value *rm* because this is a semi-annual paying bond. The expression above is a quadratic equation, which is solved using the standard solution for quadratic equations, which is noted below.

$$ax^2 + bx + c = 0$$

$$x = \frac{-b \pm \sqrt{b^2 - 4ac}}{2a}$$

In our expression, if we let $x = (1 + rm/2)$, we can rearrange the expression as follows:

$$98.50x^2 - 3.0x - 103.00 = 0.$$

We then solve for a standard quadratic equation, and there will be two solutions, only one of which gives a positive redemption yield. The positive solution is $rm/2 = 0.037929$ so that $rm =$ 7.5859%.

As an example of the iterative solution method, suppose that we start with a trial value for *rm* of $r_1 = 7\%$ and plug this into the right-hand side of Equation 4.12. This gives a value for the right-hand side of:

$$\text{RHS}_1 = 99.050,$$

which is higher than the left-hand side (LHS = 98.50); the trial value for *rm* was therefore too low. Suppose then that we try next $r_2 = 8\%$ and use this as the right-hand side of the equation. This gives:

$$\text{RHS}_2 = 98.114$$

which is lower than the LHS. Because RHS_1 and RHS_2 lie on either side of the LHS value we know that the correct value for *rm* lies between 7% and 8%. Using the formula for linear interpolation,

$$rm = r_1 + (r_2 - r_1)\frac{RHS_1 - LHS}{RHS_1 - RHS_2},$$

our linear approximation for the redemption yield is $rm = 7.587\%$, which is near the exact solution.

Note that the redemption yield, as discussed earlier in this section, is the gross redemption yield, the yield that results from payment of coupons without deduction of any withholding tax. The net redemption yield is obtained by multiplying the coupon rate C by (1 − Marginal tax rate). The net yield is what will be received if the bond is traded in a market where bonds pay coupon net, which means net of a withholding tax. The net redemption yield is always lower than the gross redemption yield.

We have noted the difference between calculating redemption yield on the basis of both annual and semi-annual coupon bonds. Analysis of bonds that pay semi-annual coupons incorporates semi-annual discounting of semi-annual coupon payments. This is appropriate for most UK and US bonds. However, government bonds in most of continental Europe and most Eurobonds pay annual coupon payments, and the appropriate method of calculating the redemption yield is to use annual discounting. The two yield measures are not therefore directly comparable. We could make a Eurobond directly comparable with a UK gilt by using semi-annual discounting of the Eurobond's annual coupon payments. Alternatively, we could make the gilt comparable with the Eurobond by using annual discounting of its semi-annual coupon payments. The price/yield formulas for different discounting possibilities we encounter in the markets are listed below (as usual we assume that the calculation takes place on a coupon payment date so that accrued interest is zero).

Semi-annual discounting of annual payments:

$$P_d = \frac{C}{(1 + {}^1\!/_2 rm)^2} + \frac{C}{(1 + {}^1\!/_2 rm)^4} + \frac{C}{(1 + {}^1\!/_2 rm)^6} + \cdots \frac{C}{(1 + {}^1\!/_2 rm)^{2N}} + \frac{M}{(1 + rm)^{2N}}. \tag{4.12}$$

Annual discounting of semi-annual payments:

$$P_d = \frac{C/2}{(1 + {}^1/_2 rm)^{\frac{1}{2}}} + \frac{C/2}{(1 + rm)} + \frac{C/2}{(1 + {}^1/_2 rm)^{\frac{3}{2}}} + \cdots \frac{C/2}{(1 + rm)^N} + \frac{M}{(1 + rm)^N}. \tag{4.13}$$

Consider a bond with a dirty price of 97.89, a coupon of 6% and five years to maturity. This bond would have the following gross redemption yields under the different yield-calculation conventions:

Discounting	Payments	YTM (%)
Semi-annual	Semi-annual	6.500
Annual	Annual	6.508
Semi-annual	Annual	6.428
Annual	Semi-annual	6.605

This proves what we have already observed; namely, that the coupon and discounting frequency will affect the redemption yield calculation for a bond. We can see that increasing the frequency of discounting will lower the yield, while increasing the frequency of payments will raise the yield. When comparing yields for bonds that trade in markets with different conventions, it is important to convert all the yields to the same calculation basis.

Intuitively we might think that doubling a semi-annual yield figure will give us the annualised equivalent; in fact, this will result in an inaccurate figure due to the multiplicative effects of discounting and one that is an underestimate of the true annualised yield. The correct procedure for producing an annualised yields from semi-annual and quarterly yields is given by the expressions below.

The general conversion expression is given by (4.14):

$$rm_a = (1 + \text{Interest rate})^m - 1 \tag{4.14}$$

where m is the number of coupon payments per year.

Specifically, we can convert between yields using the expressions given in (4.15) and (4.16).

$$rm_a = [(1 + {}^1\!/_2 rm_s)^2 - 1]$$
$$rm_s = [(1 + rm_a)^{\frac{1}{2}} - 1] \times 2 \qquad (4.15)$$

$$rm_a = [(1 + {}^1\!/_4 rm_q)^4 - 1]$$
$$rm_q = [(1 + rm_a)^{\frac{1}{4}} - 1] \times 4 \qquad (4.16)$$

where rm_q, rm_s and rm_a are, respectively, the quarterly, semi-annually and annually compounded YTM.

EXAMPLE 4.5 Bond yield comparison

A UK gilt paying semi-annual coupons and a maturity of 10 years has a quoted yield of 4.89%. A European government bond of similar maturity is quoted at a yield of 4.96%. Which bond has the higher effective yield?

The effective annual yield of the gilt is:

$$rm = (1 + [{}^1\!/_2 \bullet 0.0489])^2 - 1 = 4.9498\%$$

therefore, the gilt does indeed have the lower yield.

The market convention is sometimes simply to double the semi-annual yield to obtain the annualised yields, despite the fact that this produces an inaccurate result. It is only acceptable to do this for rough calculations. An annualised yield obtained by multiplying the semi-annual yield by two is known as a bond equivalent yield.

While YTM is the most commonly used measure of yield, it has one major disadvantage: implicit in its calculation is the assumption that each coupon payment as it becomes due is reinvested at the rate rm. This is clearly unlikely, due to the fluctuations in interest rates over time and as the bond approaches maturity. In practice, the measure itself will not equal the actual return from holding the bond, even if it is held to maturity. That said, the market standard is to quote bond returns as YTMs, bearing the key assumptions behind the calculation in mind.

Another disadvantage of this measure of return arises where investors do not hold bonds to maturity. The redemption yield measure will not be of great value where the bond is not being held to redemption. Investors might then be interested in other measures of return, which we can look at later.

To reiterate then, the redemption yield measure assumes that:

- the bond is held to maturity;
- all coupons during the bond's life are reinvested at the same (redemption yield) rate.

Therefore the YTM can be viewed as an assumed YTM. Even then the actual realised YTM would be different from expected or anticipated yield and is closest to reality perhaps where an investor buys a bond on first issue and holds the YTM figure because of the inapplicability of the second condition above.

In addition, as coupons are discounted at the yield specific for each bond, it actually becomes inaccurate to compare bonds using this yield measure. For instance, the coupon cash flows that occur in two years' time from both a two-year and five-year bond will be discounted at different rates (assuming we do not have a flat yield curve). This would occur because the YTM for a five-year bond is invariably different from the YTM for a two-year bond. However, it would clearly not be correct to discount a two-year cash flow at different rates, because we can see that the present value calculated today of a cash flow in two years' time should be the same whether it is sourced from a short- or long-dated bond. Even if the first condition noted above for the YTM calculation is satisfied, it is clearly unlikely for any but the shortest maturity bond that all coupons will be reinvested at the same rate. Market interest rates are in a state of constant flux and would thus affect money reinvestment rates. Therefore, although YTM is the main market measure of bond levels, it is not a true interest rate. However, despite the limitations presented by its assumptions, the YTM is the main measure of return used in the markets. We explore the concept of a true interest rate, the zero-coupon rate in Chapter 3 of the author's book *Fixed Income Markets*.

Market yield measures

In Figure 4.2 we saw the Bloomberg page YA, used for yield analysis of fixed-income instruments. Readers will notice from this figure that there are a number of different measures of yield shown on the page, all related to the standard YTM calculation. This is because different markets and instruments use slightly different conventions when calculating YTM.

All market yield measures define a bond's maturity date as the date when the final principal amount becomes due. This is almost invariably the stated maturity date of the bond, but in certain cases this date may fall on a non-business day, so the following working date is used instead.

Otherwise there are subtle differences in the way the different measures are calculated, although they may still give the same result. Here we explain these differences:

- *Street convention*: the standard YTM calculation.
- *True yield*: this is the standard YTM calculated with coupon dates moved whenever they fall on a non-business day, to the next valid business day. Moving this date is pertinent to the yield measure because it affects the number of days in an interest period.
- *Treasury convention*: the yield calculated using simple interest for the first coupon period, and compounded interest for subsequent interest periods. Assume an actual/actual accrued interest basis (this term is explained in the next section).
- *Consortium yield*: this is used for bonds that use an actual/365 day-count basis, it assume 182.5 days in each (semi-annual) interest period.
- *DMO yield*: a yield associated with United Kingdom gilts, the street convention equivalent as defined by the UK Debt Management Office.
- *Equivalent/year compound*: this is the street convention method adjusted for actual cash flow and compounding frequency; it uses the actual date of cash flows as they would be received;
- *Japanese yield*: This is a simple yield calculation using the annualised cash flow, expressed as a percentage of the original clean price used at purchase.
- *Money market equivalent*: this is the yield of the bond but adjusted to make it equate to money market yield conventions. It would only be used for a bond that had less than 365 days left to maturity. This calculation compounds the remaining coupon payments to the maturity date, and this total amount is used to calculate a yield, based on simple interest, quoted using the present value of the total cash flows. It assumes an actual/360 day-count basis.
- *Repo equivalent*: this is the yield calculated with interest accumulated on an overnight basis, with bond priced fixed, and assuming actual/360 day-count basis.

- *Effective rate*: the bond yield realised by investing coupon income at a specified reinvestment rate from now until maturity.

Investors will use the yield measure appropriate to the market and instrument they are analysing.

Accrued interest, clean and dirty bond prices

Our discussion of bond pricing up to now has ignored coupon interest. All bonds (except zero-coupon bonds) accrue interest on a daily basis, and this is then paid out on the coupon date. The calculation of bond prices using present value analysis does not account for coupon interest or *accrued interest*. In all major bond markets, the convention is to quote price as a *clean price*. This is the price of the bond as given by the net present value of its cash flows, but excluding coupon interest that has accrued on the bond since the last dividend payment. As all bonds accrue interest on a daily basis, even if a bond is held for only one day, interest will have been earned by the bondholder. However, we have referred already to a bond's *all-in* price, which is the price that is actually paid for the bond in the market. This is also known as the *dirty price* (or *gross price*), which is the clean price of a bond plus accrued interest. In other words, the accrued interest must be added to the quoted price to get the total consideration for the bond.

Accruing interest compensates the seller of the bond for giving up all of the next coupon payment even though he or she will have held the bond for part of the period since the last coupon payment. The clean price for a bond will move with changes in market interest rates; assuming that this is constant in a coupon period, the clean price will be constant for this period. However, the dirty price for the same bond will increase steadily from one interest payment date until the next. On the coupon date, the clean and dirty prices are the same and the accrued interest is zero. Between the coupon payment date and the next ex-dividend date the bond is traded cum dividend, so that the buyer gets the next coupon payment. The seller is compensated for not receiving the next coupon payment by receiving accrued interest instead. This is positive and increases up to the next ex-dividend date, at which point the dirty price falls by the present value of the amount of the coupon payment. The dirty price at this point is below the clean price, reflecting the fact that accrued interest is now negative. This is because after the ex-dividend date the bond is traded "ex-dividend"; the seller not the buyer receives the next coupon and the buyer has to be compensated for not receiving the next coupon by means of a lower price for holding the bond.

The net interest accrued since the last ex-dividend date is determined as follows:

$$AI = C \times \left[\frac{N_{xt} - N_{xc}}{Day\ base}\right] \tag{4.17}$$

where

AI	is the next accrued interest
C	is the bond coupon
N_{xt}	is the number of days between the ex-dividend date and the date for the calculation
N_{xc}	is the number of days between the ex-dividend date and the coupon payment date (seven business days for UK gilts)
Day base	is the day-count base (365 or 360).

Interest accrues on a bond from and including the last coupon date up to and excluding what is called the value date. The value date is almost always the settlement date for the bond, or the date when a bond is passed to the buyer and the seller receives payment. Interest does not accrue on bonds whose issuer has subsequently gone into default. Bonds that trade without accrued interest are said to be trading flat or clean. By definition therefore:

Clean price of a bond = Dirty price – Accrued interest.

For bonds that are trading ex-dividend, the accrued coupon is negative and would be subtracted from the clean price. The calculation is given by (4.18) below:

$$AI = -C \times \frac{\text{Days to } next \text{ coupon}}{Day\ base}. \tag{4.18}$$

Certain classes of bonds – for example, US Treasuries and Eurobonds – do not have an ex-dividend period and therefore trade cum dividend right up to the coupon date.

The accrued-interest calculation for a bond is dependent on the day-count basis specified for the bond in question. When bonds are traded in the market, the actual consideration that changes hands is made up of the clean price of the bond together with the accrued interest that has accumulated on the bond since the last coupon payment; these two components make up the dirty price of the bond. When calculating the accrued interest, the market will use the appropriate day-count convention for that bond. A particular market will apply one of five different methods to calculate accrued interest:

actual/365	Accrued = Coupon × days/365
actual/360	Accrued = Coupon × days/360
actual/actual	Accrued = Coupon × days/actual number of days in the interest period
30/360	See below
30E/360	See below.

When determining the number of days in between two dates, include the first date but not the second; thus, under the actual/365 convention, there are 37 days between 4 August and 10 September. The last two conventions assume 30 days in each month; so, for example, there are "30 days" between 10 February and 10 March. Under the 30/360 convention, if the first date falls on the 31st, it is changed to the 30th of the month, and if the second date falls on the 31st *and* the first date is on the 30th or 31st, the second date is changed to the 30th. The difference under the 30E/360 method is that if the second date falls on the 31st of the month, it is automatically changed to the 30th.

The accrued interest day-count basis for selected country bond markets is given in Table 4.3.

Market	Coupon frequency	Day-count basis	Ex-dividend period
Australia	Semi-annual	actual / actual	Yes
Austria	Annual	actual / actual	No
Belgium	Annual	actual / actual	No
Canada	Semi-annual	actual / actual	No
Denmark	Annual	30E/360	Yes
Eurobonds	Annual	30/360	No
France	Annual	actual / actual	No
Germany	Annual	actual / actual	No
Eire	Annual	actual / actual	No
Italy	Annual	actual / actual	No
New Zealand	Semi-annual	actual / actual	Yes
Norway	Annual	actual / 365	Yes
Spain	Annual	actual / actual	No
Sweden	Annual	30E/360	Yes
Switzerland	Annual	30E/360	No
United Kingdom	Semi-annual	actual / actual	Yes
United States	Semi-annual	actual / actual	No

Table 4.3 Selected country market accrued interest day-count basis

Van Deventer and Imai (1997) present an effective critique of the accrued interest concept, believing essentially that it is an arbitrary construct that has little basis in economic reality. In their book they state: "The amount of accrued interest bears no relationship to the current level of interest rates".

This is quite true, the accrued interest on a bond that it is traded in the secondary market at any time is not related to the current level of interest rates, and is the same irrespective of where current rates are. As Example 4.6 on page 166 makes clear, the accrued interest on a bond is a function of its coupon, which reflects the level of interest rates at the time the bond was issued. Accrued interest is therefore an accounting concept only, but at least it serves to recompense the holder for interest earned during the period the bond was held. It is conceivable that the calculation could be adjusted for present value but, at the moment, accrued interest is the convention that is followed in the market.

EXAMPLE 4.6 Accrued interest calculations

4.6(a): Accrual calculation for 7% Treasury 2002

This gilt has coupon dates of 7 June and 7 December each year. £100 nominal of the bond is traded for value on 27 August 1998. What is the accrued interest on the value date?

On the value date, 81 days have passed since the last coupon date. Under the old system for gilts, act/365, the calculation was:

$$7 \times 81/365 = 1.55342.$$

Under the current system of act/act, which came into effect for gilts in November 1998, the accrued calculation uses the actual number of days between the two coupon dates, giving us:

$$7 \times 81/183 \times 0.5 = 1.54918.$$

4.6(b)

Mansur buys £25,000 nominal of the 7% 2002 gilt for value on 27 August 1998, at a price of 102.4375. How much does he actually pay for the bond?

The clean price of the bond is 102.4375. The dirty price of the bond is: 102.4375 + 1.55342 = 103.99092.

The total consideration is therefore:

$$1.0399092 \times 25{,}000 = £25{,}997.73.$$

Example 4.6(c)

A Norwegian government bond with a coupon of 8% is purchased for settlement on 30 July 1999 at a price of 99.50. Assume that this is seven days before the coupon date and therefore the bond trades ex-dividend. What is the all-in price?

The accrued interest = $-8 \times 7/365 = -0.153424$

The all-in price is therefore 99.50 − 0.1534 = 99.3466

Example 4.6(d)

A bond has coupon payments on 1 June and 1 December each year. What is the day-base count if the bond is traded for value date on 30 October, 31 October and 1 November 1999, respectively? There are 183 days in the interest period.

	30 October	31 October	1 November
Act/365	151	152	153
Act/360	151	152	153
Act/Act	151	152	153
30/360	149	150	151
30E/360	149	150	150

Floating-rate notes

Floating-rate notes (FRNs) are bonds that do not pay a fixed coupon, but instead pay coupon that changes in line with another specified reference interest rate. The FRN market in countries such as the US and UK is large and well-developed; floating-rate bonds are particularly popular with ALM desks at banks where they are held as part of a the liquidity book.

With the exception of its coupon arrangement, an FRN is similar to a conventional bond. Maturity lengths for FRNs range from two years to over 30 years. The coupon on a floating-rate bond "floats" in line with market interest rates. According to the payment frequency, which is usually quarterly or semi-annually, the coupon is re-fixed in line with a money market index such as Libor. Often an FRN will pay a spread over Libor, and this spread is fixed through the life of the bond. For example a sterling FRN issued by the Nationwide Building Society in the United Kingdom maturing in August 2008 pays semi-annual coupons at a rate of Libor plus 5.7 basis points. This means that every six months the coupon is set in line with the 6-month Libor rate, plus the fixed spread.

The rate with which the FRN coupon is set is known as the *reference rate*. This will be 1-month, 3-month or 6-month Libor or another interest rate index. In the US market FRNs frequently set their coupons in line with the T-bill rate. The spread over the reference note is called the *index spread.* The index spread is the number of basis points over the reference rate; in a few cases the index spread is negative, so it is subtracted from the reference rate.

Yield measurement

As the coupon on an FRN is reset every time it is paid, the bond's cash flows cannot be determined with certainty in advance. It is not possible therefore to calculate a conventional YTM measure for an FRN. Instead the markets use a measure called the *discounted margin* to estimate the return received from holding a floating-rate bond. The discounted margin measures the life of the bond, assuming that the reference rate stays at a constant level throughout. The assumption of a stable reference rate is key to enabling the calculation to be made, and although it is slightly unrealistic it does enable comparisons to be made between yields on different bonds. In addition, the discount margin method also suffers from the same shortcoming as the conventional redemption yield calculation; namely, the assumption of a stable discount rate.

To calculate discounted margin, select a reference rate and assume that this remains unchanged up to the bond's maturity date. The common practice is to set the rate at its current level. The bond's margin or index spread is then added to this reference rate (or subtracted if the spread is negative). With a "fixed" rate in place, it is possible to determine the FRN's cash flows, which are then discounted at the fixed rate selected. The correct discount rate will be the one that equates the present values of the discounted cash flows to the bond's price. Since the reference rate is fixed, we need to alter the margin element in order to obtain the correct result. When we have equated the NPV to the price at a selected discount rate, we know what the discounted margin for the bond is.

Due to the way that each coupon is reset every quarter or every six months, FRNs trade very close to par (100%) and on the coupon reset date the price is always par. For any floater with a LIBOR spread if the credit spread has changed since issued the FRN will trade at a price other than par. When a floating-rate bond is priced at par the discounted margin is identical to the fixed spread over the reference rate. Note that some FRNs feature a spread over the reference rate that itself is floating; such bonds are known as *variable rate notes*.

EXAMPLE 4.7 FRN yield

Consider a floating-rate note trading at a price of £99.95 per cent. The bond pays semi-annual coupons at 6-month Libor plus 10 basis points and has precisely three years to maturity (so that the discount margin calculation is carried out for value on a coupon date). Table 4.4 shows the present value calculations, from which we can see that at the price of 99.95 this represents a discounted margin of 12 basis points on an annualised basis.

In our calculation the 6-month Libor rate is 5.50%, so we assume that this rate stays constant for the life of the bond. As this is an annual rate, the semi-annual equivalent for our purposes is

3-year FRN
Price: 99.95
6-mo Libor + 10 basis points
Libor 5.5%

				PV of cash flows: at selected spread over reference rate (bps)					
Interest period (*n*)	**Libor$_{6mo}$**	**s/a**	**Cash flow**	**10**	**11**	**12**	**13**	**14**	**15**
1	5.50%	2.75%	2.80	2.72374	2.72360	2.72347	2.72334	2.72321	2.72307
2	5.50%	2.75%	2.80	2.64955	2.64929	2.64903	2.64878	2.64852	2.64826
3	5.50%	2.75%	2.80	2.57738	2.57701	2.57663	2.57625	2.57589	2.57550
4	5.50%	2.75%	2.80	2.50718	2.50669	2.50621	2.50572	2.50523	2.50474
5	5.50%	2.75%	2.80	2.43889	2.43830	2.43771	2.43711	2.43652	2.43593
6	5.50%	2.75%	102.80	87.10326	87.07785	87.05244	87.02704	87.00166	86.97628
		Net Present Value		100.00000	99.97274	**99.94549**	99.91824	99.89103	99.86378
		PV calculated using:		1.028	1.02805	1.0281	1.02815	1.0282	1.02825
		C / (1 + Ref rate + Margin)^n							

Calculation carried out on coupon date

Table 4.4 Discounted margin calculation for an FRN

2.75%. There are two coupon payments per year, so that there are six interest periods and six remaining cash flows until maturity. As we have assumed a constant reference rate, we can set the bond coupons and redemption payment, shown as "cash flow" in the table. Each coupon payment is half of the annual reference rate plus half the annual spread. This works out as 2.75% plus 5 basis points, which is a semi-annual coupon of £2.80. The last cash flow is the final coupon of £2.80 plus the redemption payment of £100.00. We then discount all the cash flows at the selected margin levels until we find a level that results in a net present value to equal the current bond price. From the table we see that the price equates to a discounted margin of 6 basis points on a semi-annual basis, or 12 basis points annually.

Yield calculation using Bloomberg pages

The main page used on Bloomberg to calculate bond yields is YA, which is also suitable for FRN securities. Figure 4.4 shows page YA used for the Ford Motor Credit FRN maturing in June 2005.

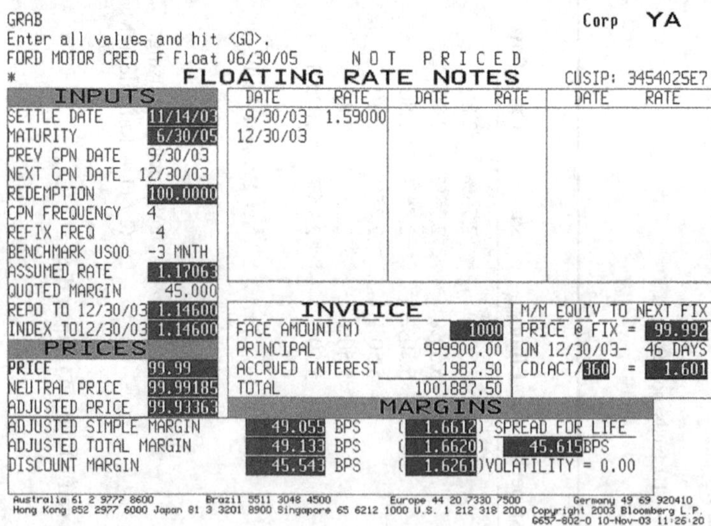

Figure 4.4 Ford Motor Credit June 2005 floating-rate bond yield analysis on Bloomberg page YA, 10 November 2003

The relevant fields for FRNs are as follows:

- refix freq: the number of times that the coupon is reset each year; this is a static data field;
- benchmark: the reference index or security to which the bond is linked, of which the most common is Libor; this is a static data field;
- assumed rate: the assumed average rate of the benchmark for all future rate refixes. This rate is based on the current level of the reference benchmark, and is the assumed rate used to calculate the present values of the cash flows, to determine the discount margin for the security;
- quoted margin: the basis point spread above the benchmark reference rate; in the example in Figure 4.4, the spread is 45 basis points above three-month Libor for the Ford Motor Credit FRN. Unless the bond is a variable rate note, this is a static data field;
- repo to: the next rate refix date and the assumed repo funding rate for the period from settlement to the next refix. The rate is specified by the user, and is the funding rate used to calculate the adjusted price;
- index to: the assumed benchmark rate for the period from settlement to the next coupon date. It is used to calculate present value of the current coupon in discounted margin calculation. Where the period between the settlement date and the next coupon is less than the bond's refix frequency, the rate assumed may not be appropriate to use for the discounted margin calculation, so the user may select a more suitable rate in this field.

For FRNs that have a cap, floor or collar on their interest yield, the user must adjust the assumed rate, entering the relevant rate that results from imposition of the cap or floor.

The YA page calculates three prices for FRNs. The price used can be that resulting either from treating the bond as a conventional bond or as a money market instrument. The price fields are:

- price: this is the current market price, specified by the user. It defaults using the price link that is set for the particular Bloomberg terminal;
- neutral price: the price that results in the same discount margin as calculated to the next coupon date and not the settlement date. This is used to determine value if trading the bond after the next coupon date, so this is in effect the next coupon forward trade price;

- adjusted price: the fair value or breakeven price of the bond to the next coupon refix date; it is used when funding the bond to this date in the repo market. For a fixed-rate bond this function is carried out by COC (cost-of-carry) on the same YA page;
- price @ fix: the price of the bond on the coupon refix date;
- on: the number of days between the settlement date to the next coupon date; a static field;
- CD (Act/xxx): the day-count basis used for the bond, which defaults to its normal market convention. In Figure 4.4 this is Act/365, the sterling money market day-count basis.

Yields on FRNs are usually expressed as a margin spread over the reference rate. Page YA calculates the following margins, as basis points and as effective yield:

- adjusted simple margin: referred to as ASM, the simple margin comprised of the quoted spread over the reference rate together with the difference between the adjusted bond price and par. The combined spread is amortised over the bond's term to maturity;
- adjusted total margin: the ASM plus the interest earned from investing any surplus gain if the difference between par and the adjusted price is below par. The assumed interest rate is used to calculate the gain;
- discount margin: the margin spread, when compared against the base reference index rate, that results in the present value of the cash flows being equal to the dirty bond price. The discount rate is the assumed rate plus the discount margin itself. In other words, this is the equivalent "yield-to-maturity" of the note;
- spread for life: the spread above or below the reference rate (quoted margin) and any capital gain resulting from convergence of the bond price to par of maturity. The latter will be negative if the current price is above par; it is calculated as a percentage gain and discounted over the term to maturity;
- volatility: the relative change in the discount margin for a 100 basis points change in the assumed interest rate.

Bond instruments and interest-rate risk

We discuss here the sensitivity of bond prices to changes in market interest rates, the key concepts of duration and convexity.

Duration

Bonds pay a part of their total return during their lifetime, in the form of coupon interest, so that the term to maturity does not reflect the true period over which the bond's return is earned. Additionally, if we wish to gain an idea of the trading characteristics of a bond, and compare this to other bonds of, say, similar maturity, term to maturity is insufficient and so we need a more accurate measure. A plain vanilla coupon bond pays out a proportion of its return during the course of its life, in the form of coupon interest. If we were to analyse the properties of a bond, we should conclude quite quickly that its maturity neither gives us a great deal of indication as to how much of its return is paid out during its life, nor any idea of the timing or size of its cash flows, and hence its sensitivity to moves in market interest rates. For example, if comparing two bonds with the same maturity date but different coupons, the higher coupon bond provides a larger proportion of its return in the form of coupon income than does the lower coupon bond. The higher coupon bond provides its return at a faster rate; its value is theoretically therefore less subject to subsequent fluctuations in interest rates.

We may wish to calculate an average of the time to receipt of a bond's cash flows, and use this measure as a more realistic indication of maturity. However, cash flows during the life of a bond are not all equal in value, so a more accurate measure would be to take the average time to receipt of a bond's cash flows, but weighted in the form of the cash flows' present value. This is, in effect, duration. We can measure the speed of payment of a bond, and hence its price risk relative to other bonds of the same maturity, by measuring the average maturity of the bond's cash flow stream. Bond analysts use duration to measure this property (it is sometimes known as Macaulay's duration, after its inventor, who first introduced it in 1938).[5] Duration is the weighted average time until the receipt of cash flows from a bond, where the weights are the present values of the cash flows, measured in years. When he introduced the concept, Macaulay used the duration measure as an alternative for the length of time that a bond investment had remaining to maturity.

---

[5] Macaulay, F., "Some Theoretical Problems Suggested by the Movements of Interest Rates, Bond Yields and Stock Prices in the United States Since 1865", National Bureau of Economic Research, NY, 1938. Although it is frequently quoted, it's rare to meet someone who has actually read this work. However, it remains a fascinating treatise and is well worth reading; it is available from Risk Classics publishing, under the title *Interest Rates, Bond Yields and Stock Prices in the United States Since 1856.*

Deriving the duration formula

Recall that the price/yield formula for a plain vanilla bond is as given in Equation (4.19) below, assuming complete years to maturity paying annual coupons, and with no accrued interest at the calculation date. The YTM reverts to the symbol r in this section.

$$P = \frac{C}{(1+r)} + \frac{C}{(1+r)^2} + \frac{C}{(1+r)^3} + \dots \frac{C}{(1+r)^N} + \frac{M}{(1+r)^N} \tag{4.19}$$

If we take the first derivative of this expression we obtain (4.20):

$$\frac{dP}{dr} = \frac{(-1)C}{(1+r)^2} + \frac{(-2)C}{(1+r)^3} + \dots + \frac{(-n)C}{(1+r)^{n+1}} + \frac{(-n)M}{(1+r)^{n+1}}. \tag{4.20}$$

If we rearrange (4.20), we will obtain the expression in (4.21), which is our equation to calculate the approximate change in price for a small change in yield.

$$\frac{dP}{dr} = \frac{1}{(1+r)}\left[\frac{1C}{(1+r)} + \frac{2C}{(1+r)^2} + \dots + \frac{nC}{(1+r)^n} + \frac{nM}{(1+r)^n}\right]\frac{1}{P} \tag{4.21}$$

Readers may feel a sense of familiarity regarding the expression in brackets in equation (4.21), as this is the weighted average time to maturity of the cash flows from a bond, where the weights are, as in our example above, the present values of each cash flow. The expression in (4.21) gives us the approximate measure of the change in price for a small change in yield. If we divide both sides of (4.21) by P we obtain the expression for the approximate percentage price change, given in (4.22):

$$\frac{dP}{dr}\frac{1}{P} = -\frac{1}{(1+r)}\left[\frac{1C}{(1+r)} + \frac{2C}{(1+r)^2} + \dots + \frac{nC}{(1+r)^n} + \frac{nM}{(1+r)^n}\right]\frac{1}{P}. \tag{4.22}$$

If we divide the bracketed expression in (4.22) by the current price of the bond P, we obtain the definition of Macaulay's duration, given in (4.23):

$$D = \frac{\frac{1C}{(1+r)} + \frac{2C}{(1+r)^2} + \dots + \frac{nC}{(1+r)^n} + \frac{nM}{(1+r)^n}}{P}. \tag{4.23}$$

Equation (4.23) is simplified using Σ as shown by (4.24):

$$D = \frac{\sum_{n=1}^{N} \frac{nC_n}{(1+r)^n}}{P} \tag{4.24}$$

where C represents the bond cash flow at time n.

Example 4.8 calculates the Macaulay duration for an hypothetical bond, the 8% 2009 annual coupon bond.

EXAMPLE 4.8 Macaulay duration calculation (1)

Calculating the Macaulay duration for the 8% 2009 annual coupon bond:

Issued:	30 September 1999
Maturity:	30 September 2009
Price:	102.497
Yield:	7.634%

Period (*n*)	Cash flow	PV at current yield*	n × PV
1	8	7.43260	7.4326
2	8	6.90543	13.81086
3	8	6.41566	19.24698
4	8	5.96063	23.84252
5	8	5.53787	27.68935
6	8	5.14509	30.87054
7	8	4.78017	33.46119
8	8	4.44114	35.529096
9	8	4.12615	37.13535
10	108	51.75222	517.5222
Total		102.49696	746.540686

* Calculated as C/(1 + r)n

Macaulay duration = 746.540686 / 102.497
= 7.283539998 years

Modified duration = 7.28354 / 1.07634
= 6.76695

Table 4.5 Duration calculation for the 8% 2009 bond

The Macaulay duration value given by (4.24) is measured in years. An interesting observation by Burghardt (1994, p. 90) is that, "measured in years, Macaulay's duration is of no particular use to anyone". This is essentially correct. However, as a risk measure and hedge calculation measure, duration transformed into modified duration was the primary measure of interest-rate risk used in the markets, and is still widely used despite the advent of the VaR measure for market risk.

If we substitute the expression for Macaulay duration (4.23) into Equation (4.22) for the approximate percentage change in price, we obtain (4.25) below:

$$\frac{dP}{dr}\frac{1}{P} = -\frac{1}{(1+r)}D. \tag{4.25}$$

This is the definition of modified duration, given as (4.26):

$$MD = \frac{D}{(1+r)}. \tag{4.26}$$

Modified duration is clearly related to duration, then. In fact we can use it to indicate that, for small changes in yield, a given change in yield results in an inverse change in bond price. We can illustrate this by substituting (4.26) into (4.25), giving us (4.27).

$$\frac{dP}{dr}\frac{1}{P} = -MD \tag{4.27}$$

If we are determining duration long-hand, there is another arrangement we can use to shorten the procedure. Instead of Equation (4.19), we use (4.28) as the bond price formula, which calculates price based on a bond being comprised of an annuity stream and a redemption payment, and summing the present values of these two elements. Again we assume an annual coupon bond priced on a date that leaves a complete number of years to maturity and with no interest accrued.

$$P = C\left[\frac{1 - \frac{1}{(1+r)^n}}{r}\right] + \frac{M}{(1+r)^n} \tag{4.28}$$

This expression calculates the price of a bond as the present value of the stream of coupon payments and the present value of the redemption payment. If we take the first derivative of (4.28) and then divide this by the current price of the bond P, the result is another expression for the modified duration formula, given in (4.29).

$$MD = \frac{\frac{C}{r^2}\left[1 - \frac{1}{(1+r)^n}\right] + \frac{n\left(M - \frac{C}{r}\right)}{(1+r)^{n+1}}}{P} \tag{4.29}$$

We have already shown that modified duration and duration are related; to obtain the expression for Macaulay duration from (4.29) we multiply it by $(1 + r)$. This short-hand formula is demonstrated below in Example 4.9 for the same hypothetical bond, the annual coupon 8% 2009.

EXAMPLE 4.9 Macaulay duration calculation (2)

The 8% 2009 bond: using equation (4.29) for the modified duration calculation.

Coupon:	8%, annual basis
Yield:	7.634%
n:	10
Price:	102.497

Substituting the above terms into the equation we obtain:

$$MD = \frac{\frac{8}{(0.07634^2)}\left[1 - \frac{1}{(1.07634)^{10}}\right] + \frac{10\left(100 - \frac{8}{0.07634}\right)}{(1.07634)^{11}}}{102.497}$$

$MD = 6.76695.$

To obtain the Macaulay duration we multiply the modified duration by $(1 + r)$, in this case 1.07634, which gives us a value of 7.28354 years.

For an irredeemable bond, duration is given by:

$$D = \frac{1}{rc} \tag{4.30}$$

where $rc = (C/P_d)$ is the *running yield* (or *current yield*) of the bond.

This follows from Equation (4.24) as $N \rightarrow \infty$, recognising that for an irredeemable bond $r = rc$. Equation (4.30) on page 177 provides the limiting value to duration. For bonds trading at or above par, duration increases with maturity and approaches this limit from below. For bonds trading at a discount to par, duration increases to a maximum at around 20 years and then declines towards the limit given by (4.30) on page 177. So, in general, duration increases with maturity, with an upper bound given by (4.30).

Properties of Macaulay duration

A bond's duration is always less than its maturity. This is because some weight is given to the cash flows in the early years of the bond's life, which brings forward the average time at which cash flows are received. In the case of a zero-coupon bond, there is no present value weighting of the cash flows, for the simple reason that there are no cash flows, and duration for a zero-coupon bond is equal to its term to maturity. Duration varies with coupon, yield and maturity. The following three factors imply higher duration for a bond:

- the lower the coupon;
- the lower the yield;
- broadly, the longer the maturity.

Duration increases as coupon and yield decrease. As the coupon falls, more of the relative weight of the cash flows is transferred to the maturity date and this causes duration to rise. Because the coupon on index-linked bonds is generally much lower than on vanilla bonds, this means that the duration of index-linked bonds will be much higher than for vanilla bonds of the same maturity. As yield increases, the present values of all future cash flows fall, but the present values of the more distant cash flows fall relatively more than those of the nearer cash flows. This has the effect of increasing the relative weight given to nearer cash flows and hence of reducing duration.

The effect of the coupon frequency. As we have already stated, certain bonds such as most Eurobonds pay coupon annually compared to, say, gilts, which pay semi-annual coupons. Again thinking of our duration fulcrum, if we imagine that every coupon is divided into two parts, with one part paid a half-period earlier than the other, this will represent a shift in weight to the left, as part of the coupon is paid earlier. Thus, increasing the coupon frequency shortens duration and, of course, decreasing coupon frequency has the effect of lengthening duration.

Duration as maturity approaches. Using our definition of duration we can see that initially it will decline slowly, and then at a more rapid pace as a bond approaches maturity.

Duration of a portfolio. Portfolio duration is a weighted average of the duration of the individual bonds. The weights are the present values of the bonds divided by the full price of the entire portfolio, and the resulting duration calculation is often referred to as a "market-weighted" duration. This approach is, in effect, similar to the duration calculation for a single bond. Portfolio duration has the same application as duration for an individual bond, and can be used to structure an immunised portfolio.

Modified duration and bond hedging

Although it is common for newcomers to the market to think intuitively of duration, much as Macaulay originally did, as a proxy measure for the time to maturity of a bond, such an interpretation is to miss the main point of duration, which is a measure of price volatility or interest-rate risk.

Using the first term of a Taylor's expansion of the bond price function,[6] we can show the following relationship between price volatility and the duration measure, which is expressed as (4.31) below:

$$\Delta P = -\left[\frac{1}{(1+r)}\right] \times \text{Macaulay duration} \times \text{Change in yield} \qquad (4.31)$$

where r is the yield to maturity for an annual-paying bond (for a semi-annual coupon bond, we use r/2). If we combine the first two components of the right-hand side, we obtain the definition of modified duration. Equation (4.31) expresses the approximate percentage change in price as being equal to the modified duration multiplied by the change in yield. We saw in the previous section how the formula for Macaulay duration could be modified to obtain the modified duration for a bond. There is a clear relationship between the two measures. From the Macaulay duration of a bond can be derived its modified duration, which gives a measure of the sensitivity of a bond's price to small changes in yield. As we have seen, the relationship between modified duration and duration is given by (4.32):

---

[6] For an accessible explanation of the Taylor expansion, see Butler, C. 1998, *Mastering Value-at-Risk*, FT Prentice Hall, London, pp. 112–14. See also Appendix 4.1.

$$MD = \frac{D}{1 + r} \tag{4.32}$$

where *MD* is the modified duration in years. However, it also measures the approximate change in bond price for a 1% change in bond yield. For a bond that pays semi-annual coupons, the equation becomes:

$$MD = \frac{D}{1 + {}^1\!/_2 r}\,. \tag{4.33}$$

This means that the following relationship holds between modified duration and bond prices:

$$\Delta P = -MD \times \Delta r \times P. \tag{4.34}$$

In the UK markets, the term *volatility* is sometimes used to refer to modified duration, but this is becoming increasingly uncommon to avoid confusion with option markets' use of the same term, which often refers to implied volatility and is something different.

EXAMPLE 4.10 Using modified duration

An 8% annual coupon bond is trading at par with a duration of 2.74 years. If yields rise from 8% to 8.50%, then the price of the bond will fall by:

$$\begin{aligned}\Delta P &= -D \times \frac{\Delta(r)}{1 + r} \times P \\ &= -\ (2.74) \times \left(\frac{0.005}{1.080}\right) \times 100 \\ &= -£1.2685.\end{aligned}$$

That is, the price of the bond will now be £98.7315.

The modified duration of a bond with a duration of 2.74 years and yield of 8% is obviously:

$$\text{MD} = \frac{2.74}{1.08}$$

which gives us *MD* equal to 2.537 years.

In the earlier example of the five-year bond with a duration of 4.31 years, the modified duration can be calculated to be 3.99. This tells us that for a 1% move in the YTM, the price of the bond will move (in the opposite direction) by 3.99%.

A formal derivation of the modified duration expression is given in Appendix 4.2.

We can use modified duration to approximate bond prices for a given yield change. This is illustrated with the following expression:

$$\Delta P = -MD \times (\Delta r) \times P. \tag{4.35}$$

For a bond with a modified duration of 3.24, priced at par, an increase in yield of 1 basis point (100 basis points = 1%) leads to a fall in the bond's price of:

$$\Delta P = (-3.24/100) \times (+0.01) \times 100.00$$
$$\Delta P = \$0.0399, \text{ or } 3.99 \text{ cents.}$$

In this case, 3.99 cents is the basis point value (BPV) of the bond, which is the change in the bond price given a 1 basis point change in the bond's yield. The BPV of a bond can be calculated using (4.36):

$$BPV = \frac{MD}{100} \times \frac{P}{100}. \tag{4.36}$$

BPVs are used in hedging bond positions. To hedge a bond position requires an opposite position to be taken in the hedging instrument. So, if we are long a 10-year bond, we may wish to sell short a similar 10-year bond as a hedge against it. Similarly, a short position in a bond will be hedged through a purchase of an equivalent amount of the hedging instrument. In fact, there are a variety of hedging instruments available, both on- and off-balance sheet. Once the hedge is put on, any loss in the primary position should, in theory, be offset by a gain in the hedge position, and vice-versa. The objective of a hedge is to ensure that the price change in the primary instrument is equal to the price change in the hedging instrument. If we are hedging a position with another bond, we use the BPVs of each bond to calculate the amount of the hedging instrument required. This is important because each bond will have different BPVs, so that to hedge a long position in, say, £1 million nominal of a 30-year bond does not mean we simply sell £1 million of another 30-year bond. This is because the BPVs of the two bonds will almost certainly be different. Also, there may not be another 30-year bond in that particular bond. What if we have to hedge with a 10-year bond? How much nominal of this bond would be required?

We need to know the ratio given in (4.37) to calculate the nominal hedge position.

$$\frac{BPV_p}{BPV_h} \tag{4.37}$$

where

BPV_p is the BPV of the primary bond (the position to be hedged)
BPV_h is the BPV of the hedging instrument.

The *hedge ratio* is used to calculate the size of the hedge position and is given in (4.38):

$$\frac{BPV_p}{BPV_h} \times \frac{\text{Change in yield for primary bond position}}{\text{Change in yield for hedge instrument}} . \tag{4.38}$$

The second ratio in (4.38) is sometimes called the *yield beta*. Example 4.11 illustrates the use of the hedge ratio.

EXAMPLE 4.11 Calculating hedge size using BPV

A trader holds a long position of £1 million of the 8% 2019 bond. The modified duration of the bond is 11.14692 and its price is 129.87596. The BPV of this bond is therefore 0.14477. The trader decides, to protect against a rise in interest rates, to hedge the position using the 0% 2009 bond, which has a BPV of 0.05549. If we assume that the yield beta is 1, what nominal value of the zero-coupon bond must be sold in order to hedge the position?

The hedge ratio is:

$$(0.14477/0.05549) \times 1 = 2.60894.$$

Therefore, to hedge £1 million of the 20-year bond the trader shorts £2,608,940 of the zero-coupon bond. If we use the respective BPVs to see the net effect of a 1 basis point rise in yield, the loss on the long position is approximately equal to the gain in the hedge position.

EXAMPLE 4.12 The nature of the modified duration approximation

Bond:		8% 2009
Maturity (years):		10
Modified duration:		6.76695
Price duration of basis point:		0.06936
Yield:	6.00%	114.72017
	6.50%	110.78325
	7.00%	107.02358
	7.50%	103.43204
	7.99%	100.0671311
	8.00%	100.00000
	8.01%	99.932929
	8.50%	96.71933
	9.00%	93.58234
	10.00%	87.71087

Yield change	Price change	Estimate using price duration
down 1 bp	0.06713	0.06936
up 1 bp	0.06707	0.06936

Table 4.6 Nature of the modified duration approximation

Table 4.6 shows the change in price for one of our hypothetical bonds, the 8% 2009, for a selection of yields. We see that for a 1 basis point change in yield, the change in price given by the dollar duration figure, while not completely accurate, is a reasonable estimation of the actual change in price. For a large move, however, say 200 basis points, the approximation is significantly in error and analysts will not use it. Notice also for our hypothetical bond how the dollar duration value, calculated from the modified-duration measurement, underestimates the change in price resulting from a fall in yields but overestimates the price change for a rise in yields. This is a reflection of the price/yield relationship for this bond. Some bonds will have a more pronounced convex relationship between price and yield, and the modified-duration calculation will underestimate the price change resulting from both a fall or a rise in yields.

Convexity

Duration can be regarded as a first-order measure of interest-rate risk: it measures the slope of the present value/yield profile. It is, however, only an approximation of the actual change in bond price given a small change in YTM. This is the same for modified duration, which describes the price sensitivity of a bond to small changes in yield. However, as Figure 4.5 illustrates, the approximation is an underestimate of the actual price at the new yield. This is the weakness of the duration measure.

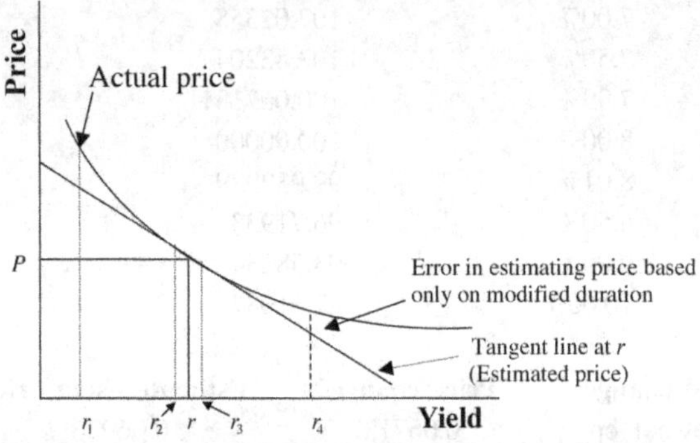

Figure 4.5 Approximation of the bond price change using modified duration
Reproduced with permission from Fabozzi, F. (1997), *Fixed Income Mathematics*, McGraw-Hill, New York.

Convexity is a second-order measure of interest-rate risk; it measures the curvature of the present value/yield profile. Convexity can be regarded as an indication of the error we make when using duration and modified duration, as it measures the degree to which the curvature of a bond's price/yield relationship diverges from the straight-line estimation. The convexity of a bond is positively related to the dispersion of its cash flows; thus, other things being equal, if one bond's cash flows are more spread out in time than another's, then it will have a higher dispersion and hence a higher convexity. Convexity is also positively related to duration.

The second-order differential of the bond price equation with respect to the redemption yield r is:

$$\frac{\Delta P}{P} = \frac{1}{P}\frac{\Delta P}{P}(\Delta r) + \frac{1}{2P}\frac{\Delta^2 P}{\Delta r^2}(\Delta r)^2 \tag{4.39}$$

$$= -MD(\Delta r) + \frac{CV}{2}(\Delta r)^2$$

where CV is the convexity.

From Equation (4.39), convexity is the rate at which price variation to yield changes with respect to yield. That is, it describes a bond's modified duration changes with respect to changes in yield. It can be approximated by expression (4.40):

$$CV = 10^8\left(\frac{\Delta P'}{P} + \frac{\Delta P''}{P}\right) \tag{4.40}$$

where

$\Delta P'$ is the change in bond price if yield increases by 1 basis point (0.01)
$\Delta P''$ is the change in bond price if yield decreases by 1 basis point (0.01).

Appendix 4.3 provides the mathematical derivation of the formula.

EXAMPLE 4.13 Convexity calculation

A 5% annual coupon is trading at par with three years to maturity. If the yield increases from 5.00 to 5.01%, the price of the bond will fall (using the bond price equation) to:

$$P'_d = \frac{5}{(0.0501)}\left[1 - \frac{1}{(1.0501)^3}\right] + \frac{100}{(1.0501)^3}$$
$$= 99.97277262$$

or by $\Delta P'_d = -0.02722737$. If the yield falls to 4.99%, the price of the bond will rise to:

$$P''_d = \frac{5}{(0.0499)}\left[1 - \frac{1}{(1.0499)^3}\right] + \frac{100}{(1.0499)^3}$$
$$= 100.0272376$$

or by $P''_d = 0.027237584$. Therefore:

$$CV = 5^8\left(\frac{-0.0272284}{100} + \frac{0.0281623}{100}\right)$$
$$= 10.206.$$

The unit of measurement for convexity using (4.40) is the number of interest periods. For annual coupon bonds this is equal to the number of years; for bonds paying coupon on a different frequency we use (4.41) to convert the convexity measure to years.

$$CV_{years} = \frac{CV}{C^2} \tag{4.41}$$

The convexity measure for a zero-coupon bond is given by (4.42):

$$CV = \frac{n(n+1)}{(1+r)^2}. \tag{4.42}$$

Convexity is a second-order approximation of the change in price resulting from a change in yield. This is given by:

$$\Delta P = {}^1/_2 \times CV \times (\Delta r)^2 . \tag{4.43}$$

The reason we multiply the convexity by half to obtain the convexity adjustment is because the second term in the Taylor expansion contains the coefficient $^1/_2$. The convexity approximation is obtained from a Taylor expansion of the bond price formula. An illustration of Taylor expansion of the bond price/yield equation is given in Appendix 4.1.

The formula is the same for a semi-annual coupon bond.

Note that the value for convexity given by the expressions above will always be positive; that is, the approximate price change due to convexity is positive for both yield increases and decreases.

EXAMPLE 4.14 Applying the convexity adjustments

4.14(a):

A 5% annual coupon bond is trading at par with a modified duration of 2.639 and convexity of 9.57. If we assume a significant market correction and yields rise from 5% to 7%, the price of the bond will fall by:

$$\Delta P_d = -MD \times (\Delta r) \times P_d + \frac{CV}{2} \times (\Delta r)^2 \times P_d$$

$$= -(2.639) \times (0.02) \times 100 + \frac{9.57}{2} \times (0.02)^2 \times 100$$

$$= -5.278 + 0.1914$$

$$= -\$5.0866$$

to \$94.9134. The first-order approximation, using the modified-duration value of 2.639, is –\$5.278, which is an overestimation of the fall in price by \$0.1914.

4.14(b)

The 5% 2009 bond is trading at a price of £96.23119 (a yield of 5.50%) and has precisely 10 years to maturity. If the yield rises to 7.50%, a change of 200 basis points, the percentage price change due to the convexity effect is given by:

$$(0.5) \times 96.23119 \times (0.02)^2 \times 100 = 1.92462\%.$$

If we use an HP calculator to find the price of the bond at the new yield of 7.50% we see that it is £82.83980, a change in price of 13.92%. The convexity measure of 1.92462% is an approximation of the error we would make when using the modified-duration value to estimate the price of the bond following the 200 basis point rise in yield.

If the yield of the bond were to fall by 200 basis points, the convexity effect would be the same, as given by the expression in (4.43).

In example (4.14b) we saw that the price change estimated using modified duration will be quite inaccurate, and that the convexity measure is the approximation of the size of the inaccuracy. The magnitude of the price change as estimated by both duration and convexity is obtained by summing the two values. However, it only makes any significant difference if the change in yield is very large. If we take our hypothetical bond again, the 5% 2009 bond, its modified duration is 7.64498. If the yield rises by 200 basis points, the approximation of the price change given by modified duration and convexity is:

$$\text{Modified duration} = 7.64498 \times 2 = -15.28996$$
$$\text{Convexity} = 1.92462.$$

Note that the modified duration is given as a negative value, because a rise in yields results in a fall in price. This gives us a net percentage price change of 13.36534. As we saw in Example (4.14b), the actual percentage price change is 13.92%. So, in fact, using the convexity adjustment has given us a noticeably more accurate estimation. Let us examine the percentage price change resulting from a fall in yields of 1.50% from the same starting yield of 5.50%. This is a decrease in yield of 150 basis points, so our convexity measurement needs to be recalculated. The convexity value is:

$$(0.5) \times 96.23119 \times (0.0150)^2 \times 100 = 1.0826\%.$$

So the price change is based on:

Modified duration = 7.64498 × 1.5 = 11.46747
Convexity = 1.0826.

This gives us a percentage price change of 12.55007. The actual price change was 10.98843%, so here the modified duration estimate is actually closer! This illustrates that the convexity measure is effective for larger yield changes only. Example (4.15) shows us that for very large changes, a closer approximation for bond price volatility is given by combining the modified duration and convexity measures.

EXAMPLE 4.15 Convexity adjustments (2)

The hypothetical bond is the 5% 2009, again trading at a yield of 5.50% and priced at 96.23119. If the yield rises to 8.50%, a change of 300 basis points, the percentage price change due to the convexity effect is given by:

$$(0.5) \times 96.23119 \times (0.03)^2 \times 100 = 4.3304\%.$$

Meanwhile, as before, the modified duration of the bond at the initial yield is 7.64498. At the new yield of 8.50% the price of the bond is 77.03528 (check by using an HP calculator).

The price change can be approximated using:

Modified duration = 7.64498 × 3.0 = −22.93494
Convexity = 4.3304.

This gives a percentage price change of 18.60454%. The actual percentage price change was 19.9477%, but our estimate is still closer than that obtained using only the modified-duration measure.

The continuing error reflects the fact that convexity is also a dynamic measure and changes with yield changes; the effect of a large yield movement compounds the inaccuracy given by convexity.

EXAMPLE 4.16 Using Microsoft Excel®

The Excel® spreadsheet package has two duration functions, *Duration* and *Mduration*, which can be used for the two main measures. Not all installations of the software may include these functions, which have to be installed using the "Analysis ToolPak" add-in macro. The syntax required for using these functions is the same in both cases, and for Macaulay duration it is:

Duration (settlement, maturity, coupon, yield, frequency, basis).

The dates that are used in the syntax for Excel® version 5 are serial dates, so the user may need to use the separate function available to convert conventional date formats to the serial date for Excel®. All later versions of Excel® recognise conventional date formats. The other parameters are:

- settlement: the settlement date;
- maturity: the maturity date;
- coupon: the coupon level;
- yield: the YTM;
- frequency: annual or semi-annual;
- basis: the day-count basis.

Once the parameters have been set up, Excel® will calculate the duration and modified duration for you.

Convexity is an attractive property for a bond to have. What level of premium will be attached to a bond's higher convexity? This is a function of the current yield levels in the market as well as market volatility. Remember that modified duration and convexity are functions of yield level, and that the effect of both is magnified at lower yield levels. As well as the relative level, investors will value convexity higher if the current market conditions are volatile. The cash effect of convexity is noticeable only for large moves in yield. If an investor expects market yields to move only by relatively small amounts, he or she will attach a lower value to convexity; and vice-versa for large movements in yield. Therefore the yield premium attached to a bond with higher convexity will vary according to market expectations of the future size of interest-rate changes.

For a conventional vanilla bond, convexity is almost always positive. Negative convexity resulting from a bond with a concave price/yield profile would not be an attractive property for a bondholder. The most common occurrence of negative convexity in the cash markets is with callable bonds.

We illustrated that for most bonds, and certainly when the convexity measure is high, the modified-duration measurement for interest-rate risk becomes more inaccurate for large changes in yield. In such situations it becomes necessary to use the approximation given by the convexity equation, to measure the error we have made in estimating the price change based on modified duration only.

The following are the main convexity properties for conventional vanilla bonds.

A fall in yields leads to an increase in convexity. A decrease in bond yield leads to an increase in the bond's convexity; this is a property of positive convexity. Equally, a rise in yields leads to a fall in convexity.

For a given term to maturity, higher coupon results in lower convexity. For any given redemption yield and term to maturity, the higher a bond's coupon, the lower its convexity. Therefore, among bonds of the same maturity, zero-coupon bonds have the highest convexity.

For a given modified duration, higher coupon results in higher convexity. For any given redemption yield and modified duration, a higher coupon results in a higher convexity. Contrast this with the earlier property; in this case, for bonds of the same modified duration, zero-coupon bonds have the lowest convexity.

Option-adjusted spread analysis

The modified duration and convexity methods are suitable only for the analysis of conventional fixed income instruments with known fixed cash flows and a maturity date. They are not satisfactory for use with bonds that contain embedded options, such as callable bonds, or instruments with unknown final redemption dates, such as mortgage-backed bonds.[7] For these and other bonds that exhibit uncertainties in their cash flow pattern and redemption date, so-called option-adjusted measures are used. The most common of these is option-adjusted spread (OAS). The techniques were developed to allow for the uncertain cash flow structure of non-vanilla fixed income instruments, and to model the effect of the option element of such bonds. A complete description of OAS is outside the scope of this book, so we present only an overview of the basic concepts. An accessible account of this technique is given in Windas (1993).

Option-adjusted spread analysis uses simulated interest-rate paths as part of its calculation of bond yield and convexity. Therefore an OAS model is a stochastic model. The OAS refers to the yield spread between a callable or mortgage-backed bond and a government benchmark bond. The government bond chosen ideally will have similar coupon and duration values. Thus the OAS is an indication of the value of the option element of the bond, as well as the premium required by investors in return for accepting the default risk of the corporate bond. When OAS is measured as a spread between two bonds of similar default risk, the yield difference between the bonds reflects the value of the option element only. This is rare, and the market convention is to measure OAS over the equivalent benchmark government bond. OAS is used in the analysis of corporate bonds that incorporate call or put provisions, as well as mortgage-backed securities with prepayment risk. For both applications the spread is calculated as the number of basis points over the yield of the government bond that would equate the price of both bonds.

The essential components of the OAS technique are as follows:

- a simulation method such as Monte Carlo is used to generate sample interest-rate paths, and a cash flow pattern generated for each interest-rate path;
- the value of the bond for each of the future possible rate paths is found, by discounting in the normal manner each of the bond's cash flows at the relevant interest rate (plus a spread) along the points of each path. This produces a range of values for the bond, and for a given price the OAS is the spread at which the average of the range of values equates the given price.

[7] The term "embedded" is used because the option element of the bond cannot be stripped out and traded separately; for example, the call option inherent in a callable bond.

Thus OAS is a general stochastic model, with discount rates derived from the standard benchmark term structure of interest rates. This is an advantage over more traditional methods in which a single discount rate is used. The calculated spread is a spread over risk-free forward rates, accounting for both interest rate uncertainty and the price of default risk. OAS provides more realistic analysis than the traditional YTM approach. It has been widely adopted by investors since its introduction in the late 1980s.

A theoretical framework

All bond instruments are characterised by the promise to pay a stream of future cash flows. The term structure of interest rates and associated discount function is crucial to the valuation of any debt security, and underpins any valuation framework.[8] Armed with the term structure we can value any bond, assuming it is liquid and default-free, by breaking it down into a set of cash flows and valuing each cash flow with the appropriate discount factor. Further characteristics of any bond, such as an element of default risk or embedded option, are valued incrementally over its discounted cash flow valuation.

Valuation under known interest rate environments

We show in Chapter 9 how forward rates can be calculated using the no-arbitrage argument. We use this basic premise to introduce the concept of OAS. Consider the spot interest rates for two interest periods:

Term (interest periods)	Spot rate
1	5%
2	6%

We can determine that the one-period interest rate starting one period from now is 7.009%. This is the implied one-period forward rate.

We may use the spot rate term structure to value a default-free zero-coupon bond, so for example a two-period bond would be priced at \$89.[9]

[8] The term structure of interest rates is the spot rate yield curve; spot rates are viewed as identical to zero-coupon bond interest rates where there is a market of liquid zero-coupon bonds along regular maturity points. As such a market does not exist anywhere, the spot rate yield curve is considered a theoretical construct, which is most closely equated by the zero-coupon term structure derived from the prices of default-free liquid government bonds (see Chapter 9).

[9] \$100/(1.06)2 = \$88.9996.

Using the forward rate we obtain the same valuation, which is exactly what we expect.[10]

This framework can be used to value other types of bonds. Let us say we wish to calculate the price of a two-period bond that has the following cash flow stream:

Period 1	\$5
Period 2	\$105.

The price of this bond is calculated to be \$98.21.[11] This would be the bond's fair value if it were liquid and default-free. Assume, however, that the bond is a corporate bond and carries an element of default risk, and is priced at \$97. What spread over the risk-free price does this indicate? We require the spread over the implied forward rate that would result in a discounted price of \$97. Using iteration, this is found to be 67.6 basis points.[12] The calculation is:

$$P = \frac{5}{1 + (0.05+0.00676)} + \frac{105}{[1 + (0.05+0.00676)] \times [1 + (0.07009+0.00676)]}$$

$$= 97.00.$$

The spread of 67.6 basis points is implied by the observed market price of the bond, and is the spread over the expected path of interest rates. Another way of considering this is that it is the spread premium earned by holding the corporate bond instead of a risk-free bond with identical cash flows.

This framework can be used to evaluate relative value. For example, if the average sector spread of bonds with similar credit risk is observed to be 73 basis points, a fairer value for our example bond might be:

$$P = \frac{5}{1 + (0.05+0.0073)} + \frac{105}{[1 + (0.05+0.0073)] \times [1 + (0.07009+0.0073)]}$$

$$= 96.905$$

which would indicate that our bond is overvalued.

---

[10] $\$100/(1.05) \times (1.07009) = \$89.$

[11] $[\$5/1.05 + \$105/(1.05) \times (1.07009)] = \$98.21.$

[12] For students, problems requiring the use of iteration can be found using the 'Goal Seek' function in Microsoft Excel, under the 'Tools' menu.

The approach just described is the OAS methodology in essence and provides the OAS spread under conditions of no uncertainty. This approach is preferable to the traditional one of comparing redemption yields; whereas the latter uses a single discount rate, the OAS approach uses the correct spot rate for each period's cash flow.

However, our interest lies with conditions of interest rate uncertainty. In practice, the future path of interest rates is not known with certainty. The range of possible values of future interest rates is a large one, although the probability of higher or lower rates that are very far away from current rates is low. For this reason the OAS calculation is based on the most likely future interest-rate path among the universe of possible rate paths. This is less relevant for vanilla bonds, but for securities whose future cash flow is contingent on the level of future interest rates, such as mortgage-backed bonds, it is very important. The first step, then, is to describe the interest-rate process in terms that capture the character of its dynamics.[13]

Ideally the analytical framework under conditions of uncertainty would retain the arbitrage-free character of our earlier discussion. But by definition the evolution of interest rates will not match the calculated forward rate, thus creating arbitrage conditions. This is not surprising. For instance, if the calculated one-period forward rate shown above actually turns out to be 7.50%, the maturity value of the bond at the end of period 2 would be \$100.459 rather than \$100. This means that there was an arbitrage opportunity at the original price of \$89. For the bond price to have been arbitrage-free at the start of period 1, it would have been priced at \$88.59.[14]

This shows that as interest rates can follow a large number of different paths, of varying possibility, so bond prices can assume a number of fair values. The ultimate arbitrage-free price is as unknown as future interest rate levels! Let us look then at how the OAS methodology uses the most likely interest-rate path when calculating fair values.

---

[13] This is interest rate modelling, an extensive and complex, not to mention heavily researched, subject. We present it here in accessible, intuitive terms.

[14] The price of the bond at the start of the period is \$89, shown earlier. This is worth (89 × 1.05) or \$93.45 at the end of period 1, and hence \$100 at the end of period 2 (93.45 × 1.07009). However, if an investor at the time of rolling over the one-period bond can actually invest at 7.50%, this amount will mature to (93.45 × 1.075) or \$100.459. In this situation, *in hindsight* the arbitrage-free price of the bond at the start of period 1 would be 100/(1.05 × 1.075) or \$88.59.

Valuation under uncertain interest-rate environments

We begin by assuming that the current spot rate term structure is consistent with bond prices of zero option-adjusted spreads, so that their price is the average expected for all possible evolutions of the future interest-rate. By assuming this we may state that the most likely future interest-rate path, which lies in the centre of the range of all possible interest rate paths, will be a function of interest rate volatility. Here we use volatility to mean the average annual percentage deviation of interest rates around their mean value. So an environment of 0% volatility would be one of interest rate certainty and would generate only one possible arbitrage-free bond price. This is a worthwhile scenario, since it enables us to generalise the example in the previous section as the arbitrage-free model in times of uncertainty, but when volatility is 0%.

A rise in volatility generates a range of possible future paths around the expected path. The actual expected path that corresponds to a zero-coupon bond price incorporating zero OAS is a function of the dispersion of the range of alternative paths around it. This dispersion is the result of the dynamics of the interest-rate process, so this process must be specified for the current term structure. We can illustrate this with a simple binomial model example. Consider again the spot rate structure shown early on. Assume that there are only two possible future interest-rate scenarios, outcome 1 and outcome 2, both of equal probability. The dynamics of the short-term interest rate are described by a constant drift rate a, together with a volatility rate σ. These two parameters describe the evolution of the short-term interest rate. If outcome 1 occurs, the one-period interest rate one period from now will be:

$$5\% \times \exp(a + \sigma)$$

while if outcome 2 occurs, the period 1 rate will become:

$$5\% \times \exp(a - \sigma).$$

In Figure 4.6 on page 196 we present the possible interest-rate paths under conditions of 0% and 25% volatility levels, and maintain our assumption that the current spot rate structure price for a risk-free zero-coupon bond is identical to the price generated using the structure to obtain a zero option-adjusted spread. To maintain the no-arbitrage condition, we know that the price of the bond at the start of period 1 must be \$89, so we calculate the implied drift rate by an iterative process (Figure 4.6).

At 0% volatility the prices generated by the up and down moves are equal, because the future interest rates are equal. Hence the forward rate is the same as before: 7.009%. When there is a multiple interest-rate path scenario, the fair value of the bond is determined as the average of the discounted values for each rate path. Under conditions of certainty (0% volatility), the price of the bond is, not surprisingly, unchanged at both paths. The average of these is obviously \$89. Under 25% volatility the up-move interest rate is 7.889% and the down-move rate is 6.144%. The average of these rates is 7.017%. We can check the values by calculating the value of the bond at each outcome (or "node") and then obtaining the average of these values; this is shown to be \$89.

Readers can view the simple spreadsheet used to calculate the rates in Table 4.7, with the iterative process undertaken using the Microsoft Excel 'Goal Seek' function. The table also shows the cell references.

Term (interest periods)	Spot Rate
1	5.00%
2	6.00%
1v1 fwd rate	7.009%

0% volatility
Implied drift rate 33.776%

Expected future rate under zero volatility is 7.009%

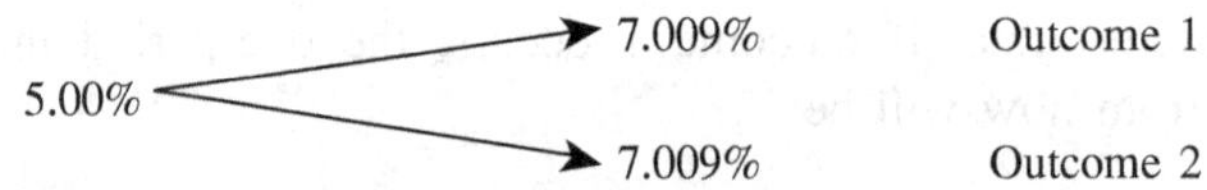

Probability of up-move and down-move is identical at 50%

25% volatility
Implied drift rate 20.61%

Expected future rate under zero volatility is 7.017%

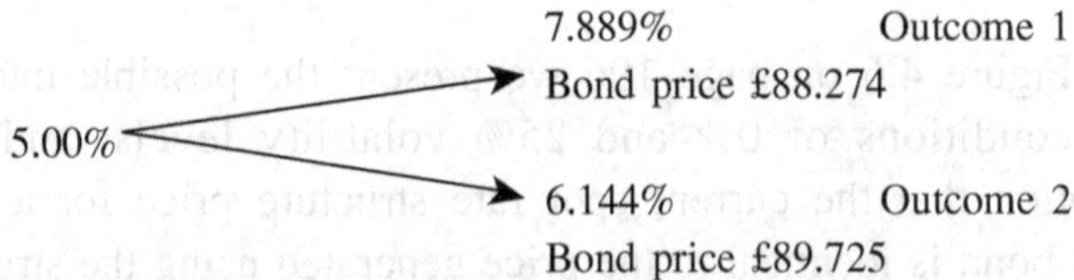

Probability of up-move and down-move is identical at 50%

Figure 4.6 Expected interest rate paths under conditions of uncertainty

Price	89						
Period 1 rate	1.05						
Volatility	0.25						
Drift	0.206054017						
Up state	0.078891779	1.0788918	Bond price	88.2740022	Average	88.9996	
Down state	0.061440979	1.061441		89.72528584			
					Fwd rate %	0.070166379	

	F	G	H	I	J	K	L
17							
18	Price	89					
19	Period 1 rate	1.05					
20	Volatility	0.25					
21	Drift	0.206054017					
22							
23							
24	Up state	=0.05*EXP(G21+G20)	=1+G24	Bond price	=100/(G19*H24)	Average	=(J24+J25)/2
25	Down state	=0.05*EXP(G21-H19)	=1+G25	=100/(G19*H25)			
26							
27						Fwd rate %	=(G24+G25)/2

Table 4.7 Calculating interest-rate paths using Microsoft Excel

We now consider the corporate bond with \$5 and \$105 cash flows at the end of periods 1 and 2 respectively. In an environment of certainty, the bond price of \$97 implied an OAS of 67.6 basis points (bps). In the uncertain environment we can use the same process as above to determine the spread implied by the same price. The process involves discounting the cash flows across each path with the spread added, to determine the price at each node. The price of the bond is the average of all the resulting prices; this is then compared to the observed market price (or required price). If the calculated price is lower than the market price, then a higher spread is required, and if the calculated price is higher than the market price, then the spread is too high and must be lowered.

Applying this approach to the model in Figure 4.6, under the 0% volatility the spread implied by the price of \$97 is, unsurprisingly, 67.6 basis points. In the 25% volatility environment, however, this spread results in a price of \$97.296, which is higher than the observed price. This suggests the spread is too low. By iteration we find that the spread that generates a price of \$97 is 89.76 basis points, which is the bond's OAS. This is shown below.

Outcome 1:

$$P = \frac{5}{1 + (0.05+0.00897)} + \frac{105}{[1 + (0.05+0.00897)] \times [1+ (0.07889+0.00897)]}$$

$$= \$95.865$$

Outcome 2:

$$P = \frac{5}{1 + (0.05+0.00897)} + \frac{105}{[1 + (0.05+0.00897)] \times [1+ (0.06144+0.00897)]}$$

$$= \$98.135$$

The calculated price is the average of these two values and is [(95.87 + 98.13)/2] or \$97 as required. The OAS of 89.76 basis points in the binomial model is a measure of the value attached to the option element of the bond at 25% volatility.

The final part of this discussion introduces the value of the embedded option in a bond. Our example bond from earlier is now semi-annually paying and carries a coupon value of 7%. It has a redemption value of \$101.75. Assume that the bond is callable at the end of period 1, and that it is advantageous for the issuer to call the bond at this point if interest rates fall below 7%. We assume further that the bond is trading at the fair value implied by the discounting calculation earlier. With a principal nominal amount of $101.75, this suggests a market price of (101.75/97.00) or $104.89. We require the OAS implied by this price now that there is an embedded option element in the bond. Under conditions of 0% volatility the value of the call is zero, as the option is out-of-the-money when interest rates are above 7%. In these circumstances the bond behaves exactly as before, and the OAS remains 67.6 basis points. However, in the 25% volatility environment it becomes advantageous to the issuer to call the bond in the down-state environment, as rates are below 7%. In fact we can calculate that the spread over the interest rate paths that would produce an average price of 104.89 is 4 basis points, which means that the option carries a cost to the bond issuer of (67.6 – 4) or 63.6 basis points.

OAS analysis for an hypothetical corporate callable bond and Treasury bond

We conclude with an illustration of the OAS technique. Consider a five-year semi-annual corporate bond with a coupon of 8%. The bond incorporates a call feature that allows the issuer to call it after two years, and is currently priced at $104.25. This is equivalent to a yield to maturity of 6.979%. We wish to measure the value of the call feature to the issuer, and we can do this using the OAS technique. Assume that a five-year Treasury security also exists with a coupon of 8%, and is priced at $109.11, a yield of 5.797%. The higher yield of the corporate bond reflects the market-required premium, due to the corporate bond's default risk and call feature.

The valuation of both securities is shown in Table 4.8.

Bond	Price	Yield
Corporate bond	104.25	6.979%
Treasury 8% 2006	109.11	5.797%

OAS Spread 110.81 bps

Period	YTM	Date	Spot rate	Discount factor	Cash flow	Present value	OAS-adjusted spot rate	PV of OAS-adjusted cash flows
0	5.000	25-Feb-2001	5.000	1				
1	5.000	27-Aug-2001	5.069	0.97521333	4	3.901125962	6.177	3.88016
2	5.150	25-Feb-2002	5.225	0.95034125	4	3.798913929	6.333	3.75822
3	5.200	26-Aug-2002	5.277	0.92582337	4	3.699381343	6.385	3.64011
4	5.250	25-Feb-2003	5.329	0.90137403	4	3.600632571	6.437	3.52394
5	5.374	25-Aug-2003	5.463	0.87567855	4	3.495761898	6.571	3.40300
6	5.500	25-Feb-2004	5.597	0.84928019	4	3.389528778	6.705	3.28196
7	5.624	25-Aug-2004	5.734	0.82277146	4	3.281916075	6.842	3.16080
8	5.750	25-Feb-2005	5.870	0.79585734	4	3.173623771	6.978	3.04022
9	5.775	25-Aug-2005	5.895	0.77285090	4	3.079766213	7.003	2.93453
10	5.800	27-Feb-2006	5.920	0.74972455	104	77.6869373	7.028	73.62754
						109.1075878		**104.25049**

Table 4.8 OAS analysis for corporate callable bond and Treasury bond

Our starting point is the redemption yield curve, from which we calculate the current spot rate term structure. This was done using RATE software (included in the CD-R at the back of this book) and is shown in column 4. Using the spot rate structure, we calculate the present value of the Treasury security's cash flows, which is shown in column 7. We wish to calculate the OAS that equates the price of the Treasury to that of the corporate bond. By iteration, this is found to be 110.81 basis points. This is the semi-annual OAS spread. The annualised OAS spread is double this. With the OAS spread added to the spot rates for each period, the price of the Treasury matches that of the corporate bond, as shown in column 9. The adjusted spot rates are shown in column 8.

Figure 4.7 illustrates the yield curve for the Treasury security and the corporate bond.

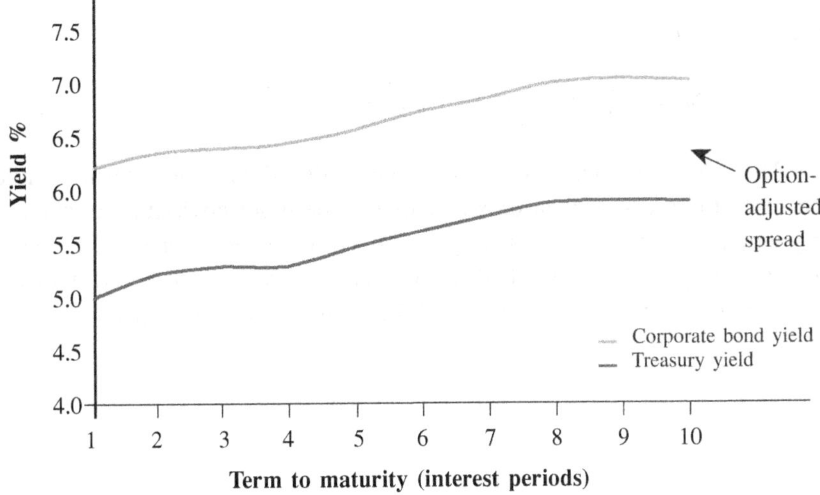

Figure 4.7 Yield curves illustrating OAS yield spread

Appendices

Appendix 4.1 Taylor expansion of the price/yield function

We summarise the bond price formula as (A4.1.1), where C represents all the cash flows from the bond, including the redemption payment.

$$\mathrm{P} = \sum_{n=1}^{N} \frac{C_n}{(1+r)^n} \tag{A4.1.1}$$

We therefore derive the following:

$$\frac{dP}{dr} = -\sum_{n=1}^{N} \frac{C_n \times n}{(1+r)^{n+1}} \tag{A4.1.2}$$

$$\frac{d^2P}{dr^2} = \sum_{n=1}^{N} \frac{C_n \times n(n+1)}{(1+r)^{n+2}} \quad . \tag{A4.1.3}$$

This then gives us:

$$\Delta P = \left[\frac{dP}{dr}\Delta r\right] + \left[\frac{1}{2!}\frac{d^2P}{dr^2}(\Delta r)^2\right] + \left[\frac{1}{3!}\frac{d^3P}{dr^3}(\Delta r)^3\right] + \ldots \tag{A4.1.4}$$

The first expression in (A4.1.4) is the modified duration measure, while the second expression measures convexity. The more powerful the changes in yield, the more expansion is required to approximate the change to greater accuracy. Expression (A4.1.4) therefore gives us the equations for modified duration and convexity, shown by (A4.1.5) and (A4.1.6), respectively.

$$MD = -\frac{dP \,/\, dr}{P} \tag{A4.1.5}$$

$$CV = -\frac{d^2P \,/\, dr^2}{P} \tag{A4.1.6}$$

We can therefore state the following:

$$\frac{\Delta P}{P} = \left[-(MD)\Delta r\right] + \left[\frac{1}{2}(CV)(\Delta r)^2\right] + \text{residual error} \tag{A4.1.7}$$

$$\Delta P = -\left[P(MD)\Delta r\right] + \left[\frac{P}{2}(CV)(\Delta r)^2\right] + \text{residual error.} \tag{A4.1.8}$$

APPENDIX 4.2 Formal derivation of modified-duration measure

Given that duration is defined as:

$$D = \frac{\sum_{n=1}^{N} \frac{nC_n}{(1+r)^n}}{P}, \tag{A4.2.1}$$

if we differentiate P with respect to r we obtain:

$$\frac{dP}{dr} = -\sum_{n=1}^{N} nC_n(1+r)^{-n-1}. \tag{A4.2.2}$$

Multiplying (A4.2.2) by $(1 + r)$ we obtain:

$$(1+r)\frac{dP}{dr} = -\sum_{n=1}^{N} nC_n(1+r)^{-n}. \tag{A4.2.3}$$

We then divide the expression by P giving us:

$$\frac{dP}{dr}\frac{1+r}{P} = -\sum_{n=1}^{N} \frac{nC_n}{(1+r)^n P} = -D. \tag{A4.2.4}$$

If we then define modified duration as $D/(1 + r)$ then:

$$-\frac{dP}{dr}\frac{1}{P} = MD. \tag{A4.2.5}$$

Thus, modified duration measures the proportionate impact on the price of a bond resulting from a change in its yield. The sign in (A4.2.5) is negative because of the inverse relationship between bond prices and yields (that is, rising yields result in falling prices). So if a bond has a modified duration of 6.767, then a rise in yield of 1% means that the price of the bond will fall by 6.767%. As we discuss in the main text, however, this is an approximation only and is progressively more inaccurate for greater changes in yield.

Appendix 4.3 Measuring convexity

The modified duration of a plain vanilla bond is:

$$MD = \frac{D}{(1+r)} . \qquad (A4.3.1)$$

We know that:

$$\frac{dP}{dr}\frac{1}{P} = -MD. \qquad (A4.3.2)$$

This shows that for a percentage change in the yield, we have an inverse change in the price by the amount of the modified-duration value.

If we multiply both sides of (A4.3.2) by any particular change in the bond yield, given by dr, we obtain expression (A4.3.3):

$$\frac{dP}{P} = -MD \times dr . \qquad (A4.3.3)$$

Using the first two terms of a Taylor expansion, we obtain an approximation of the bond price change, given by (A4.3.4).

$$dP = \frac{dP}{dr}dr + \frac{1}{2}\frac{d^2P}{dr^2}(\mathrm{dr})^2 + \text{Approximation error} \qquad (A4.3.4)$$

If we divide both sides of (A4.3.4) by P to obtain the percentage price change, the result is the expression in (A4.3.5):

$$\frac{dP}{P} = \frac{dP}{dr}\frac{1}{2}dr + \frac{1}{2}\frac{d^2P}{dr^2}(\mathrm{dr})^2 + \frac{\text{Approximation error}}{P} . \qquad (A4.3.5)$$

The first component of the right-hand side of (A4.3.4) is the expression in (A4.3.3), which is the cash price change given by the duration value. Therefore, equation (A4.3.4) is the approximation of the price change. Equation (A4.3.5) is the approximation of the price change as given by the modified-duration value. The second component in both expressions is the second derivative of the bond price equation. This second derivative captures the convexity value of the price/yield relationship and is the cash value given by convexity. As such, it is referred to as dollar convexity in the US markets. The dollar convexity is stated as (A4.3.6):

$$CV_{dollar} = \frac{d^2P}{dr^2} . \qquad (A4.3.6)$$

If we multiply the dollar convexity value by the square of a bond's yield change, we obtain the approximate cash value change in price resulting from the convexity effect. This is shown by (A4.3.7):

$$dP = (CV_{dollar})(dr)^2. \tag{A4.3.7}$$

If we then divide the second derivative of the price equation by the bond price, we obtain a measure of the percentage change in bond price as a result of the convexity effect. This is the measure known as convexity and is the convention used in virtually all bond markets. This is given by the expression at (A4.3.8):

$$CV = \frac{d^2P}{dr^2}\frac{1}{2}. \tag{A4.3.8}$$

To measure the amount of the percentage change in bond price as a result of the convex nature of the price/yield relationship we can use (A4.3.9):

$$\frac{dP}{P} = \frac{1}{2}CV(dr)^2. \tag{A4.3.9}$$

For long-hand calculations note that the second derivative of the bond price equation is (A4.3.10), which can be simplified to (A4.3.12). The usual assumptions apply to the expressions, that the bond pays annual coupons and has a precise number of interest periods to maturity. If the bond pays semi-annually the yield value r is replaced by $r/2$:

$$\frac{d^2P}{dr^2} = \sum_{n=1}^{N}\frac{n(n+1)C}{(1+r)^{n+2}} + \frac{n(n+1)M}{(1+r)^{n+2}}. \tag{A4.3.10}$$

Alternatively, we differentiate to the second order the bond price equation as given by (A4.3.11), giving us the alternative expression (A4.3.12):

$$P = \frac{C}{r}\left[1 - \frac{1}{(1+r)^n}\right] + \frac{100}{(1+r)^n}. \tag{A4.3.11}$$

$$\frac{d^2P}{dr^2} = \frac{2C}{r^3}\left[1 - \frac{1}{(1+r)^n}\right] - \frac{2C}{r^2(1+r)^{n+1}} + \frac{n(n+1)(100 - \frac{C}{r})}{(1+r)^{n+2}}. \tag{A4.3.12}$$

EXAMPLE A4.3.1 Convexity adjustments (3)

Consider a three-year bond with (annual) coupon of 5% and yield of 5%. At a price of par we have:

$$\frac{dP}{dr} = -\left[\frac{5}{(1.05)^2} + \frac{5(2)}{(1.05)^3} + \frac{105(3)}{(1.05)^4}\right] = 263.9048$$

$$D = \frac{dP}{dr}\left[\frac{1+r}{P}\right] = 263.9048\left[\frac{1.05}{100}\right] = 2.771$$

$$MD = \frac{2.771}{1.05} = 2.639$$

$$\frac{d^2P}{dr^2} = \left[\frac{5(1)(2)}{(1.05)^3} + \frac{5(2)(3)}{(1.05)^4} + \frac{105(3)(4)}{(1.05)^5}\right] = 957.3179$$

$$CV = \frac{d^2P \;/\; dr^2}{P} = \frac{957.3179}{100} = 9.573.$$

References and bibliography

Allen, S.L. and Kleinstein, A.D. 1991, *Valuing Fixed Income Investments and Derivative Securities*, New York Institute of Finance, New York.

Bierwag, G.O. 1977, "Immunisation, Duration and the Term Structure of Interest Rates", *Journal of Financial and Quantitative Analysis*, December, pp. 725–741.

Bierwag, G.O. 1978, "Measures of Duration", *Economic Inquiry 16*, October, pp.497–507.

Burghardt, G. 1994, *The Treasury Bond Basis*, McGraw-Hill, New York.

Fabozzi, F. 1989, *Bond Markets, Analysis and Strategies*, Prentice Hall, New Jersey, Chapter 2.

Fabozzi, F. 1993, *Bond Markets, Analysis and Strategies*, 2nd edition, Prentice Hall, New Jersey.

Fabozzi, F. 1997, *Fixed Income Mathematics*, 3rd edition, McGraw-Hill, New York, pp. 190–192.

Fabozzi, F. (editor), 1997, *The Handbook of Fixed Income Securities*, 5th edition, McGraw-Hill, New York.

Fabozzi, F. 1998a, *Valuation of Fixed Income Securities and Derivatives*, 3rd edition, FJF Associates, New Hope, PA.

Fabozzi, F. 1998b, *Treasury Securities and Derivatives*, FJF Associates, New Hope, PA.

Garbade, K. 1996, *Fixed Income Analytics*, MIT Press, Massachusettes, Chapters 3, 4 and 12.

Higson, C. 1995, *Business Finance*, Butterworth, Oxford.

Macaulay, F. 1999, *The Movements of Interest Rates, Bond Yields and Stock Prices in the United States Since 1856*, RISK Classics Library, London.

Martellini L., Priaulet, D. and Priaulet, S. 2004, *Fixed Income Securities*, John Wiley & Sons, Chichester, Sussex.

Questa, G. 1999, *Fixed Income Analysis for the Global Financial Market*, John Wiley & Sons, Chichester, Sussex.

Stigum, M. and Robinson, F. 1996, *Money Market and Bond Calculations*, Irwin, New York.

Sundaresan, S. 1997, *Fixed Income Markets and their Derivatives*, South-Western, Cincinnati.

Van Deventer, D. and Imai, K. 1997, *Financial Risk Analytics*, Irwin, New York, pp. .9–11

Weston, J.F. and Copeland, T.E. 1986, *Managerial Finance*, Dryden, Oxford.

Windas, T. 1993, *Option-adjusted Spread Analysis*, Bloomberg Press, Princeton.

Mail sent. Index MSG

1<GO>PURGE, 2<GO>REPLY, 3<GO>FWD, 11<GO>NEXT, 12<GO>PREV, 99<GO>MENU OF OPTIONS

From: •DEREK TAYLOR, KING & SHAXSON LTD 5/25 11:01:49

Subject: Re:

Attachment(s): None Page 1/ 1

020 7929 8484 DEREK 020 7929 8483 MARC

HAVE YOU GOT THE LIMIT FOR BARCLAYS YET, ITS ONLY TAKEN ABOUT 12YEARS

LOVE DEL

Australia 61 2 9777 8600 Brazil 5511 3048 4500 Europe 44 20 7330 7500 Germany 49 69 920410
Hong Kong 852 2977 6000 Japan 81 3 3201 8900 Singapore 65 6212 1000 U.S. 1 212 318 2000 Copyright 2006 Bloomberg L.P.
0 25-May-06 11:02:27

PART II

Bank Treasury Asset–Liability Management

Having introduced the market instruments, we are in a position to introduce the basics of asset–liability management (ALM). In Part II we review the main strands of the discipline, including a look at the role of the ALM Committee (ALCO) and ALCO reporting. We also consider the yield curve, relative value analysis, determinants of the swap spread and the expected magnitude of the term premium, all of which feed into ALM decision-making.

We describe the ALM function in four chapters. In Chapter 5 we introduce basic concepts, such as liquidity, gap and the cost of funds. This is illustrated with case studies that show how an hypothetical medium-sized bond and derivatives trading house, which we call XYZ Securities Limited, would structure its ALM policy. There are also case studies that illustrate how XYZ would use floating-rate notes (FRNs) and sovereign bond portfolios as part of its treasury management. Chapter 6 develops these concepts with real-world illustrations. We take an interlude with Chapter 7 which introduces the basic techniques of money market trading and hedging; these are essential elements in the daily ALM process. Finally we describe in detail the function of the bank ALM committee or ALCO, in Chapter 8.

CHAPTER

5

Asset–Liability Management I

Asset–liability management (ALM) is a generic term that is used to refer to a number of things by different market participants. We believe however that it should be used to denote specifically the high-level management of a bank's assets and liabilities; as such it is a strategy-level discipline and not a tactical one. It may be set within a bank's Treasury division by its asset–liability committee (ALCO). The principle function of the ALM desk is to manage interest-rate risk and liquidity risk. It will also set overall policy for credit risk and credit risk management, although tactical-level credit policy is set at a lower level within credit committees. Although the basic tenets of ALM would seem to apply more to commercial banking rather than investment banking, in reality it is applied to both functions. A trading desk still deals in assets and liabilities, and these must be managed for interest-rate risk and liquidity risk. In a properly integrated banking function the ALM desk must have a remit overseeing all aspects of a bank's operations.

In this chapter we introduce the key ALM concepts of liquidity, management policy and the internal cost of funds.

Basic concepts

In financial markets two main strands of risk management are interest-rate risk and liquidity risk. ALM practice is concerned with managing this risk. Interest-rate risk exists in two strands. The first strand is the more obvious one, the risk of changes in asset–liability value due to changes in interest rates. Such a change impacts the cash flows of assets and liabilities, or rather their present value, because financial instruments are valued with reference to market interest rates. The second strand is that associated with optionality, which arises with products such as early redeemable loans. The other main type of risk that ALM seeks to manage is liquidity risk, which refers both to the liquidity of markets and the ease with which assets can be translated to cash.

ALM is conducted primarily at an overview, balance sheet level. The risk that is managed is an aggregate, group-level risk. This makes sense because one could not manage a viable banking business by leaving interest-rate and liquidity risk management at individual operating levels. We illustrate this in Figure 5.1, which highlights the cornerstones of ALM. Essentially, interest-rate risk exposure is managed at the group level by the Treasury desk. The drivers are the different currency interest rates, with each exposure being made up of the net present value (NPV) of cash flow as it changes with movements in interest rates. The discount rate used to calculate the NPV is the prevailing market rate for each time bucket in the term structure.

The interest-rate exposure arises because rates fluctuate from day to day, and continuously over time. The primary risk is that of interest-rate reset, for floating-rate assets and liabilities. The secondary risk is liquidity risk: unless assets and liabilities are matched by amount and term, assets must be funded on a continuous rolling basis. Equally, the receipt of funds must be placed on a continuous basis. Whether an asset carries a fixed or floating-rate reset will determine its exposure to interest-rate fluctuations. Where an asset is marked at a fixed rate, a rise in rates will reduce its NPV and so reduce its value to the bank. This is intuitively easy to grasp, even without recourse to financial arithmetic, because we can see that the asset is now paying a below-market rate of interest. Or we can think of it as a loss due to opportunity cost foregone, since the assets are earning below what they could earn if they were employed elsewhere in the market. The opposite applies if there is a fall in rates: this causes the NPV of the asset to rise. For assets marked at a floating-rate of interest, the risk exposure to fluctuating rates is lower, because the rate receivable on the asset will reset at periodic intervals, which will allow for changes in market rates.

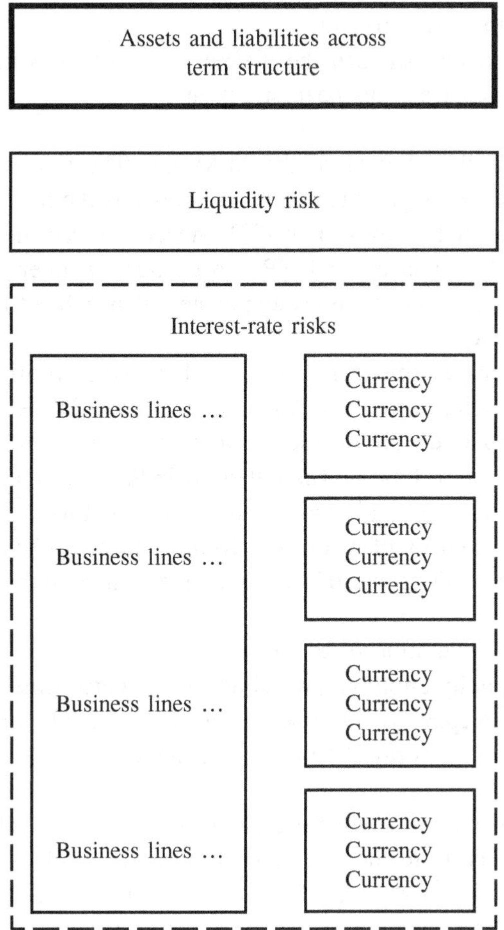

Figure 5.1 Cornerstone of ALM philosophy

We speak of risk exposure as being for the group as a whole. This exposure must therefore aggregate the net risk of all the bank's operating business. Even for the simplest banking operation, we can see that this will produce a net mismatch between assets and liabilities, because different business lines will have differing objectives for their individual books. This mismatch will manifest itself in two ways:

- the mismatch between the different terms of assets and liabilities across the term structure;
- the mismatch between the different interest rates that each asset or liability contract has been struck at.

This mismatch is known as the ALM *gap*. The first type is referred to as the *liquidity gap*, while the second is known as the *interest-rate gap*. We value assets and liabilities at their NPV; hence, we can measure the overall sensitivity of the balance sheet NPV to changes in interest rates. As such ALM is an art that encompasses aggregate balance sheet risk management at the group level.

Figure 5.2 shows the aggregate group-level ALM profile for a securities and derivatives trading house based in London. There is a slight term mismatch as no assets are deemed to have "overnight" maturity whereas a significant portion of funding (liabilities) is in the overnight term. One thing we do not know from looking at Figure 5.2 is how this particular institution is defining the maturity of its assets.[1] To place these in the relevant maturity buckets, one can adopt one of two approaches, namely:

- the actual duration of the assets;
- the "liquidity duration", which is the estimated time it would take the firm to dispose of its assets in an enforced or "firesale" situation, such as a withdrawal from the business.

Each approach has its adherents, and we believe that actually there is no "right" way. It is up to the individual institution to adopt one method and then consistently adhere to it. The second approach has the disadvantage, however, of being inherently subjective – the estimate of the time taken to dispose of an asset book is not an exact science and is little more than educated guesswork. Nevertheless, for long-dated and/or illiquid assets, it is at least a workable method that enables practitioners to work around a specified ALM framework with regard to structuring the liability profile.

[1] This report is discussed in full in the Case Study later in the chapter.

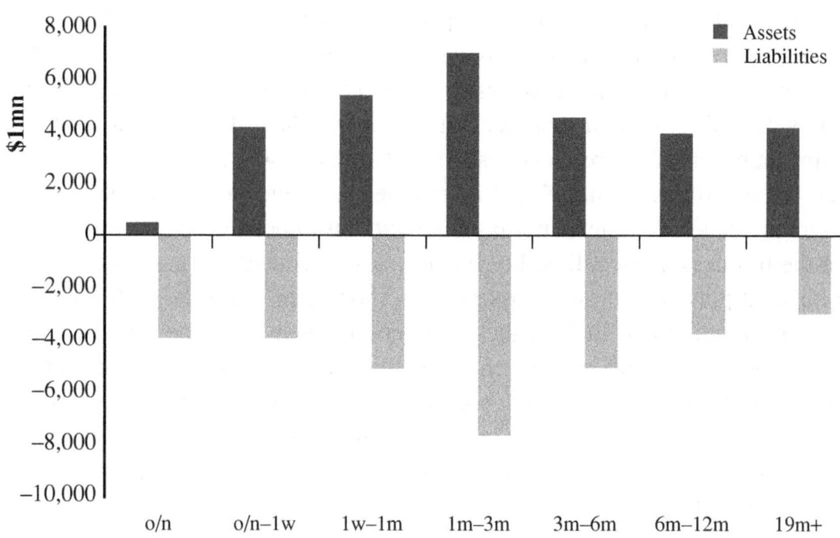

Figure 5.2 Securities and derivatives trading house ALM profile

Liquidity gap

There is an obvious risk exposure arising because of liquidity mismatch of assets and liabilities. The maturity terms will not match, which creates the liquidity gap. The amount of assets and liabilities maturing at any one time will also not match (although overall, as we saw in Chapter 2, by definition assets must equal liabilities). Liquidity risk is the risk that a bank will not be able to refinance assets as liabilities become due, for any reason.[2] To manage this, the bank will hold a large portion of assets in very liquid form.[3] A surplus of assets over liabilities creates a funding requirement. If there is a surplus of liabilities, the bank will need to find efficient uses for those funds. In either case, the bank has a liquidity gap. This liquidity can be projected over time, so that one knows what the situation is each morning, based on net expiring assets and liabilities. The projection will change daily of course, due to new business undertaken each day.

---

[2] The reasons can be macro-level ones, affecting most or all market participants, or more firm- or sector-specific. The former might be a general market correction that causes the supply of funds to dry up, and would be a near-catastrophe situation. The latter is best illustrated with the example of Barings plc in 1995: when it went bust overnight due to large, hitherto covered-up losses on the Simex exchange, the supply of credit to similar institutions was reduced or charged at much higher rates, albeit only temporarily, as a result.

[3] Such assets would be very short-term, risk-free assets such as T-bills.

We could eliminate liquidity gap risk by matching assets and liabilities across each time bucket. Actually, at individual loan level this is a popular strategy: if we can invest in an asset paying 5.50% for three months and fund this with a three-month loan costing 5.00%, we have locked in a 50-basis point gain that is interest-rate risk free. However, while such an approach can be undertaken at individual asset level, it would not be possible at an aggregate level, or at least not possible without imposing severe restrictions on the business. Hence, liquidity risk is a key consideration in ALM. A bank with a surplus of long-term assets over short-term liabilities will have an ongoing requirement to fund the assets continuously, and there is the ever-present risk that funds may not be available as and when they are required. The concept of a future funding requirement is itself a driver of interest-rate risk, because the bank will not know what the future interest rates at which it will deal will be.[4] So a key part of ALM involves managing and hedging this forward liquidity risk.

Definition and illustration

To reiterate then, the liquidity gap is the difference in maturity between assets and liabilities at each point along the term structure. Because for many banks ALM concerns itself with a medium-term management of risk, this will not be beyond a five-year horizon, and in many cases will be considerably less than this. Note from Figure 5.2 how the longest-dated time bucket in the ALM profile extends out to only "12-month plus", so that all liabilities longer than one year were grouped in one time bucket. This recognises that most liabilities are funded in the money markets, although a proportion of funding will be much longer term, up to 30 years or so.

For each point along the term structure at which a gap exists, there is (liquidity) gap risk exposure. This is the risk that funds cannot be raised as required, or that the rate payable on these funds is prohibitive.[5] To manage this risk, a bank must perforce:

- disperse the funding profile (the liability profile) over more than just a short period of time. For example, it would be excessively risky to concentrate funding in just the overnight to one-week time bucket, so a bank will spread the profile across a number of time buckets. Figure

[4] It can of course lock in future funding rates with forward-starting loans, which is one way to manage liquidity risk.

[5] Of course the opposite applies: the gap risk refers to an excess of liabilities over assets.

5.3 shows the liability profile for a European multi-currency asset-backed CP programme, with liabilities extending from one month to one year;

- manage expectations so that large-size funding requirements are diarised well in advance, as well as not planned for times of low liquidity such as the Christmas and New Year period;
- hold a significant proportion of assets in the form of very liquid instruments such as very short term cash loans, T-bills and high-quality short-term bank CDs.

Observing the last guideline allows a bank to maintain a reserve of liquidity in the event of a funding crisis, because such assets can be turned into cash at very short notice.

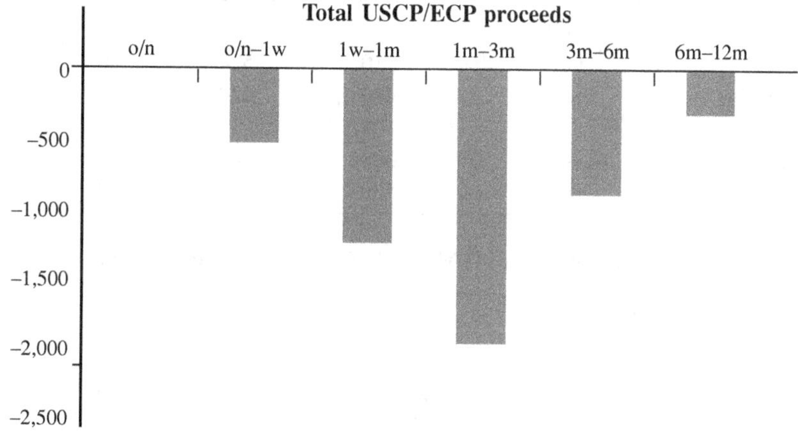

Figure 5.3 CP programme liability profile

The size of the liquidity gap at any one time is never more than a snapshot in time, because it is constantly changing as new commitments are entered into on both the asset and liability side. For this reason some writers speak of a "static" gap and a "dynamic" gap, but in practice one recognises that there is only ever a dynamic gap, because the position changes daily. Hence we will refer only to one liquidity gap.

A further definition is the "marginal" gap, which is the difference between the change in assets and change in liabilities during a specified time period. This is also known as the "incremental" gap. If the change in assets is greater than the change in liabilities, this is a positive marginal gap, while if the opposite applies this is a negative marginal gap.[6]

We illustrate these values in Table 5.1. This is a simplified asset–liability profile from a regional European bank, showing gap and marginal gap at each time period. Note that the liabilities have been structured to produce an "ALM Smile", which is recognised to follow prudent business practice. Generally, no more than 20% of the total funding should be in the overnight to one-week time bucket, and similarly for the 9–12 month bucket. The marginal gap is measured as the difference between the change in assets and the change in liabilities from one period to the next.

Figure 5.4 shows the graphical profile of the numbers in Table 5.1; and Figure 5.2 shown earlier illustrates the "ALM Smile".

	One week	One month	3–month	6–month	9–12 month	> 12months	Total
Assets	10	90	460	710	520	100	1890
Liabilities	100	380	690	410	220	90	1890
Gap	–90	–290	–230	300	300	10	
Marginal gap		200	–60	–530	0	290	

Table 5.1 Simplified ALM profile for regional European bank

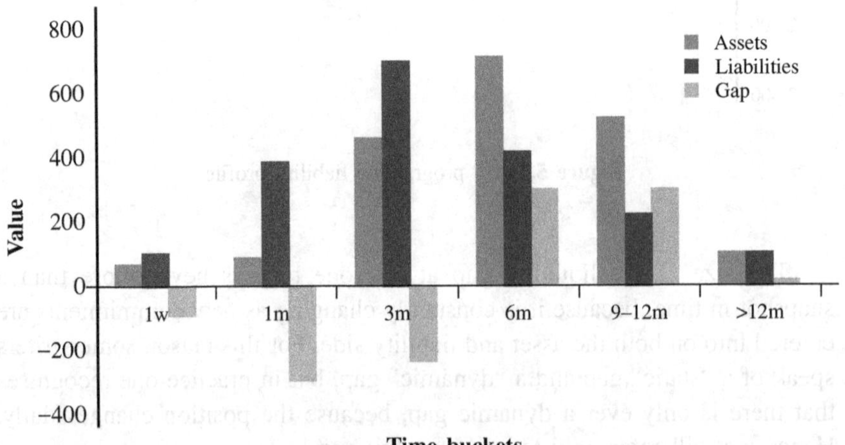

Figure 5.4 ALM time profile

[6] Note that this terminology is not a universal convention.

Liquidity risk

Liquidity risk exposure arises from normal banking operations. That is, it exists irrespective of the type of funding gap, be it excess assets over liabilities for any particular time bucket or an excess of liabilities over assets. In other words, there is a funding risk in any case, either funds must be obtained or surplus assets laid off. The liquidity risk in itself generates interest-rate risk, due to the uncertainty of future interest rates. This can be managed through hedging, and we discuss interest-rate hedging in chapters 13, 14 and 15.

If assets are floating-rate, there is less concern over interest-rate risk because of the nature of the interest-rate reset. This also applies to floating-rate liabilities, but only insofar that these match floating-rate assets. Floating-rate liabilities issued to fund fixed-rate assets create forward risk exposure to rising interest rates. Note that even if both assets and liabilities are floating-rate, they can still generate interest-rate risk. For example, if assets pay six-month Libor and liabilities pay three-month Libor, there is an interest-rate spread risk between the two terms. Such an arrangement has eliminated liquidity risk, but not interest-rate spread risk.

Liquidity risk can be managed by matching assets and liabilities, or by setting a series of rolling term loans to fund a long-dated asset. Generally, however, banks will have a particular view of future market conditions, and manage the ALM book in line with this view. This would leave in place a certain level of liquidity risk.

Matched book

The simplest way to manage liquidity and interest-rate risk is the matched book approach, also known as cash matching. This is actually very rare to observe in practice, even among conservative institutions such as the smaller UK building societies. In matched book, assets and liabilities, and their time profiles, are matched as closely as possible. This includes allowing for the amortisation of assets.[7] As well as matching maturities and time profiles, the interest-rate basis for both assets and liabilities will be matched. That is, fixed loans to fund fixed-rate assets, and the same for floating-rate assets and liabilities. Floating-rate instruments will further need to match the period of each interest-rate reset, to eliminate spread risk.

---

[7] Many bank assets, such as residential mortgages and credit-card loans, are repaid before their legal maturity date. Thus the size of the asset book is constantly amortising.

Under a matched book, also known as *cash flow matching*, in theory there is no liquidity gap. Locking in terms and interest rate bases will also lock in profit. For instance, a six-month fixed-rate loan is funded with a six-month fixed-rate deposit. This would eliminate both liquidity and interest-rate risk. In a customer-focused business it will not be possible to precisely match assets and liabilities, but from a macro-level it should be possible to match the profiles fairly closely, by netting total exposure on both sides and matching this. Of course, it may not be desirable to run a matched book, as this would mean the ALM book was not taking any view at all on the path of future interest rates. Hence a part of the banking book is usually left unmatched, and it is this part that will benefit (or lose out) if rates go the way they are expected to (or not!).

Managing the gap with undated assets and liabilities

We have described a scenario of liquidity management where the maturity date of both assets and liabilities is known with certainty. A large part of retail and commercial banking operations revolves around assets that do not have an explicit maturity date however. These include current account overdrafts and credit card balances. They also include drawn and undrawn lines of credit. The volume of these is a function of general economic conditions, and can be difficult to predict. Banks will need to be familiar with their clients' behaviour and their requirements over time to be able to assess when and for how long these assets will be utilised.

Undated assets are balanced on the other side by non-dated liabilities, such as non-interest-bearing liabilities (NIBLs), which include cheque accounts and instant-access deposit accounts. The latter frequently attract very low rates of interest, and are usually included in the NIBL total. Undated liabilities are treated in different ways by banks; the most common treatment places these funds in the shortest time bucket, the overnight to one-week bucket. However, this means the firm's gap and liquidity profile can be highly volatile and unpredictable, which places greater strain on ALM management. For this reason some bank's take the opposite approach and place these funds in the longest-dated bucket, the greater-than-12-month bucket. A third approach is to split the total undated liabilities into a "core" balance and an "unstable" balance, and place the first in the long-dated bucket and the second in the shortest dated bucket. The amount recognised as the core balance will need to be analysed over time, to make sure that it is accurate.

Managing liquidity

Managing liquidity gaps and the liquidity process is a continuous, dynamic one because the ALM profile of a bank changes on a daily basis. Liquidity management is the term used to describe this continuous process of raising and laying off funds, depending on whether one is long or short cash that day.

The basic premise is a simple one: the bank must be "squared off" by the end of each day, which means that the net cash position is zero. Thus, liquidity management is both very short-term, as well as projected over the long term, because every position put on today creates a funding requirement in the future on its maturity date. The ALM desk must be aware of their future funding or excess cash positions and act accordingly, whether this means raising funds now or hedging forward interest-rate risk.

The basic case: the funding gap

A funding requirement is dealt on the day it occurs. The decision on how it will be treated will factor the term that is put on, as well as allowing for any new assets put on that day. As funding is arranged, the gap at that day will be zero. The next day there will be a new funding requirement or surplus, depending on the net position of the book.

This is illustrated in Figure 5.5 on page 222. Starting from a flat position on the first day (t_0) we observe a gap (the dotted line) on t_1, which is closed by putting on funding to match the asset maturity. The amount of funding to raise, and the term to run it to, will take into account the future gap as well as that day's banking activities. So at t_2 we observe a funding excess, which is then laid off. We see at t_3 that the assets invested in run beyond the maturity of the liabilities at t_2, so we have a funding requirement again at t_3. The decision on the term and amount will be based on the market view of the ALM desk. A matched book approach may well be taken where the desk does not have a strong view, or if its view is at odds with market consensus.

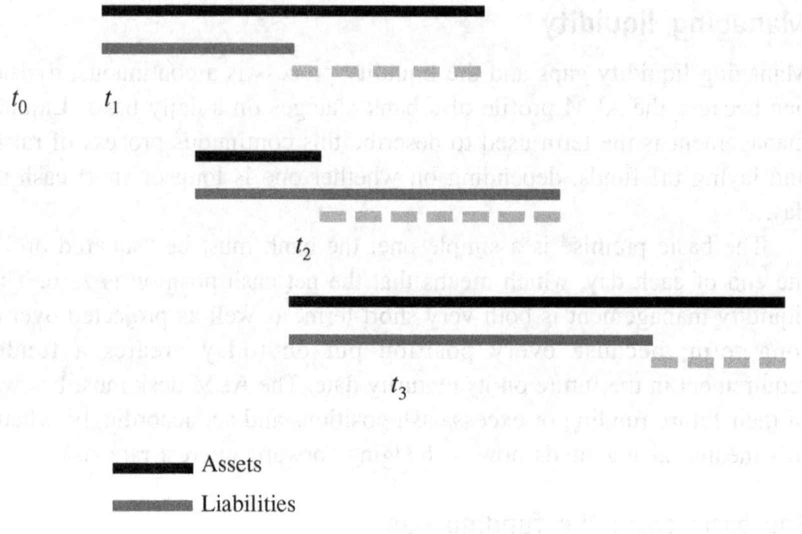

Figure 5.5 Funding position on a daily basis

There are also external factors to take into account. For instance, the availability of funds in the market may be limited, due to both macro-level issues and to the bank's own ability to raise funds. The former might be during times of market correction or recession (a "credit crunch"), while the latter includes the bank's credit lines with market counterparties. Also some funds will have been raised in the capital markets and this cash will cover part of the funding requirement. In addition, the ALM desk must consider the cost of the funds it is borrowing; if, for example, it thought that interest rates in the short term, and for short-term periods, were going to fall, it might cover the gap with only short-term funds so it can then refinance at the expected lower rates. The opposite might be done if the desk thought rates would rise in the near future.

Running a liquidity gap over time, beyond customer requirements, would reflect a particular view of the ALM desk. So maintaining a consistently underfunded position suggests that interest rates are expected to decline, at which longer-term funds can be taken at cost. Maintaining an over-funded gap would imply that the bank thinks rates will be rising, and so longer-term funds are locked in now at lower interest rates. Even if the net position is dictated by customer requirements (for example, customers placing more on deposit than they take out in loans), the bank can still manage the resultant gap in the wholesale market.

Excess liabilities generally is a rare scenario in a bank and it is not, under most circumstances, a desirable position to be in. This is because the bank will have target return on capital ratios to achieve, and this requires that funds be put to work, so to speak, by acquiring assets. In the case of equity capital it is imperative that these funds are properly employed.[8] The exact structure of the asset book will depend on the bank's view on interest rates and the yield curve generally. The shape of the yield curve and expectations on this will also influence the structure and tenor of the asset book. The common practice is to spread assets across the term structure, with varying maturities. There will also be investments made with a forward start date, to lock in rates in the forward curve now. Equally, some investments will be made for very short periods so that if interest rates rise, when the funds are reinvested they will benefit from the higher rates.

The basic case: illustration

The basic case is illustrated in Table 5.2, in two scenarios. In the first scenario, the longest-dated gap is −130, so the bank puts on funding for +130 to match this tenor of three periods. The gap at period t_2 is −410, so this is matched with a 2-period tenor funding position of +280. This leaves a gap of −180 at period t_1, which is then funded with a 1-period loan. The net position is zero at each period ("squared off"), and the book has been funded with three bullet fixed-term loans. The position is not a matched book as such, although there is now no liquidity risk exposure.

In the second case, the gap is increasing from period 1 to period 2. The first period is funded with a three-period and a two-period borrowing of +50 and +200 respectively. The gap at t_2 needs to be funded with a position that is not needed *now*. The bank can cover this with a forward-start loan of +390 at t_1 or can wait and act at t_2. If it does the latter it may still wish to hedge the interest-rate exposure.[9]

[8] The firm's capital will be invested in risk-free assets such as government T-bills or, in some cases, bank CDs. It will not be lent out in normal banking operations because the ALM desk will not want to put capital in a credit-risk investment.

[9] We look at the mechanics of this, using different derivative instruments, in chapters 13, 14 and 15.

(i)

Time	t_1	t_2	t_3
Assets	970	840	1,250
Liabilities	380	430	1,120
Gap	−590	−410	−130
Borrow 1: tenor 3 periods	130	130	130
Borrow 2: tenor 2 periods	280	280	
Borrow 3: tenor 1 periods	180		
Total funding	+590	+410	+130
Squared off	0	0	0

(ii)

Time	t_1	t_2	t_3
Assets	970	840	1,250
Liabilities	720	200	1,200
Gap	−250	−640	−50
Borrow 1: tenor 3 periods	50	50	50
Borrow 2: tenor 2 periods	200	200	
Borrow 3: tenor 1 periods	0	390	
Total funding	+250	+640	+50
Squared off	0	0	0

Table 5.2 Funding the liquidity gap: two examples

The liquidity ratio

The *liquidity ratio* is the ratio of assets to liabilities. It is a short-term ratio, usually calculated for the money market term only; that is, up to one year. Under most circumstances, and certainly under a positive yield curve environment, it would be expected to be above 1.00; however, this is less common at the very short end because the average tenor of assets is often greater than the average tenor of liabilities. So in the one-month to three-month period, and perhaps out to six months, the ratio may well be less than one. This reflects the fact that short-term borrowing is used to fund longer-term assets.

A ratio of below one is inefficient from an RoE point of view. It represents an opportunity cost of return foregone. To manage it, banks may invest more funds in the very short term, but this also presents its own problems because the return on these assets may not be sufficient. This is especially true in a positive yield curve environment. This is one scenario where a matched book approach will be prudent, because the bank should be able to lock in a bid–offer spread in the very short end of the yield curve.[10] A more risky approach would be to lend in the short term and fund these in the long term, but this would create problems because the term premium in the yield curve will make borrowing in the long term expensive relative to the return on short-dated assets (unless we have an inverted yield curve). There is also the liquidity risk associated with the more frequent rolling over of assets compared to liabilities. We see then, that maintaining the liquidity ratio carries something of a cost for banks.

CASE STUDY 5.1 Hypothetical derivatives trading house ALM policy and profile

We conclude this introduction to the basic concept of ALM with a look at the ALM policy and profile of a hypothetical securities and derivatives trading house, which we will call XYZ Securities Limited. The business is a financial institution based in London, with a number of business lines in FX, equity, and credit derivatives trading and market-making. We outline the various firm-wide policies on ALM, cash management, liquidity and investment that have been formalised at XYZ Securities.

[10] In addition, the bank will be able to raise funds at Libid, or at worst at Li-mid, while it should be able to lend at Libor in interbank credit quality assets. Li-mid is an unofficial term and refers to the mid-rate between Libid and Libor.

XYZ Securities Limited

Funding and ALM

This note outlines the approach to managing the asset–liability profile that is generated by the funding requirements of XYZ Securities Limited ("XYZ"). The principal source of funding is the parent bank. Funds are also taken from a variety of external sources (prime brokerage, bank lines, TRS and repo lines, a repo conduit and an ABCP programme). The overall management of the ALM profile is centralised within XYZ Treasury desk.

The key objective of the Treasury desk is to undertake prudent management of XYZ's funding requirement, with regard to liquidity management, interest-rate management (gap profile) and funding diversification. This process includes management information and reporting. The primary deliverable of the Treasury desk is the ALM report. This is presented in Table 5.3 on page 233.

ALM report

The ALM profile of all combined XYZ business lines is shown in Table 5.3. The report comprises the following segments:

- the ALM report;
- asset liquidity profile;
- liabilities.

We consider each part next.

ALM report

This report summarises the total funding requirement of each of XYZ's business lines. The business lines are: FX, interest-rate and credit derivatives market-making; equity derivatives proprietary trading, asset management and equity brokerage. The funding is profiled against the asset profile to produce the firm-wide ALM profile. Liability represents the funding taken by each business line. They are set out in accordance with the maturity term structure of each constituent loan of the total funding requirement. The maturity buckets used are:

- overnight
- overnight – one week
- one week – one month
- one month – three months
- three months – six months
- six months – 12 months
- over 12 months.

The asset pool is distributed along the same maturity buckets in accordance with certain assumptions. These assumptions are concerned with the expected turnover of assets in each business, and the time estimated to liquidate the business under enforced conditions.[11] Underneath the ALM profile is the gap profile (see Figure 5.6 on page 233). Gap is defined as the difference between assets and liabilities per maturity bucket; it shows how the liability profile differs from the asset profile. It is also a snapshot that reflects where the forward funding requirement lies at the time of the snapshot.

Asset liquidity profile

This report is a detailed breakdown of the funding requirement of each business line. Assets and liabilities are split according to desk within each business line, set out by maturity profile.

Liabilities

This is the detailed liability profile breakdown of all the business lines. Funding is split into term structure of liabilities. A separate table is given for each business line. There is also a detailed breakdown of use of funds from each source of funds.

Aims and objectives

Historically, the funding of XYZ business was concentrated overwhelmingly on a very short-term basis. This reflected primarily the short-term trading nature of XYZ's assets, which meant that the asset profile was effectively changing on a high frequency. Over time, XYZ's business evolved into dealing in more longer-term

[11] The percentage breakdown that reflects senior management assumptions of the maturity profile of assets is an input into the ALM report.

asset classes and as a consequence XYZ moved to funding in the longer-term to more adequately match its asset profile. The Treasury objective is based on the following reasoning:

- to minimise forward funding gap;
- to term out the funding away from the very short-dated tenors used hitherto;
- to construct an ALM profile that recognises the differing requirements of individual business lines. For example, the market-making businesses are expected to have a more flexible liquidity profile than the asset management business. Hence, the liability profile of the former will be concentrated along the short end of the funding term structure when compared to the latter;
- to even out the liability profile such that no one maturity bucket contains more than 20% of the total funding requirement. This will be treated as a funding limit.

A 20% gap limit will apply to the overall XYZ funding requirement.

Application of cost of funds

The effect of terming out funding is to produce a cost of funds that is not explicitly observable without calculation. That is, the cost of funds must be determined as a pooled or weighted-average cost of funds (WAC). XYZ uses a simplified version of this calculation that is essentially the interest charged on each loan as a proportion of the total borrowing, or, put another way, the daily interest payable on all loans divided by the total notional amount. This is standard market practice and is used, for example, at a number of European investment banks. Treasury applies the WAC interest rate to each business line.

XYZ Securities Limited

Funding and ALM: enhanced procedures

As XYZ increases in size and complexity, it becomes necessary to implement a more sophiscated ALM approach. This is described below.

ALM report

The ALM report summarises the total funding requirement of each of XYZ's business lines. The funding is profiled against the asset profile to produce the firm-wide ALM profile. Liability represents the funding taken by each business line. They are set out in accordance with the maturity term structure of each constituent loan of the total funding requirement. The asset pool is distributed along the same maturity buckets in accordance with certain assumptions. These assumptions are concerned with the expected turnover of assets in each business, and the time estimated to liquidate the business under enforced conditions. Underneath the ALM profile is shown the gap profile. Gap is defined as the difference between assets and liabilities per maturity bucket; it shows how the liability profile differs from the asset profile. It is also a snapshot that reflects where the forward funding requirement lies at the time of the snapshot.

Aims and objectives

The aims and objectives remain the same as described on pages 227-8.

Modifications and updates

The new ALM policy includes the following improvements:

- the ALM profile of XYZ has been structured in line with market good practice, with more accurate matching of liabilities to assets; it now resembles a banking ALM profile more accurately;
- the overnight funding profile of XYZ, which represented significant liquidity risk, has now been transformed such that

overnight funding now represents 13% of overall funding, compared with over 40% at the start of the new policy;
- the 20% gap limit has been formalised and put in place, and now is a formal limit that is observed by Treasury;
- there is regular weekly reporting of ALM and funding for XYZ (see Table 5.3 and Figure 5.6);
- greater diversity in funding sources has been achieved, with bank lines in place for XYZ access to unsecured, un-guaranteed funding, secured funding using repo and total return swaps, a repo conduit and an asset-backed CP programme.

The Treasury desk is charged with implementing market best practice with regard to ALM and funding policy.

Funding cost allocation

The major change in policy is now a move from a WAC-funding cost allocation to each of the business lines to a Treasury "pool" funding method.[12] In this approach, all funding, both overnight and term loans, is placed in a central Treasury pool. These funds are lent out, on an overnight basis, to the various business lines in accordance with their funding requirement. This removes interest-rate risk hedging considerations from the business lines and places them with Treasury. All business lines receive the same funding rate, the overnight Libor rate, so no business line has a funding cost advantage over another.

Treasury moves from being a cost-centre to a profit-centre, with any savings it makes in structuring the funding, below that of Libor-flat at which it lends funds, being retained within it.

Interest-rate hedge

Under the new funding regime, all interest-rate risk exposure generated when putting on term loans is hedged within the Treasury book. The policy is as follows:

- Treasury has an interest-rate exposure limit of USD30,000 total interest-rate risk, measured as present value of a basis point (PVBP, or "DV01"), for all time buckets greater than 30 days.

[12] This approach is described fully in Chapter 28.

- This exposure is generated by the use of term loans. Exposure is offset by lending funds in matching terms, running the liquidity book of CP, CDs, sovereign bonds and FRNs.
- Remaining DV01 is hedged using Eurodollar, Bund and short-sterling futures contracts.

The interest-rate exposure is monitored daily and subject to dynamic hedging as term loans are replaced.

Cash management

Cash management at XYZ is undertaken by the Treasury desk. Its aim is to undertake prudent management of XYZ's funding requirement, with regard to liquidity management, interest-rate management (gap profile and gap risk) and funding diversification. It is also responsible for producing management information and ALM reporting. The Treasury desk carries out its responsibilities working in conjunction with the middle office and back office. The back office reports each day's funding requirement, and the funding itself is carried out by Treasury in accordance with its view. The middle office reports the funding allocated to each line of business as part of regular p&l reporting.

The objective of ALM policy is to apply market-standard guidelines to the XYZ business and to follow prudent market practice. It is also to make the whole funding process more transparent with regard to management reporting and to centralise funding into one desk within the group.

ALM and funding report

The firm-wide ALM report is shown in Table 5.3 and Figure 5.6. From Table 5.6 we observe the following:

- the "gap" is defined as the absolute value of the assets and liabilities added together, which, because liabilities are reported as negative numbers, is essentially assets minus liabilities;
- the funding within each time bucket is reported as a percent of total funding. This is a key control measure, as prudent ALM policy suggests that the liability profile should be humped in shape ("the ALM Smile"), so that each bucket should not hold more than approximately 15–20% of the total funding;

- the next control value is the "gap as percent of total gap". This is noted to prevent an excessive forward gap developing in one time bucket;
- the key control measure is the gap as percent of total funding, which at XYZ is set at a 20% limit. We see that on this date there was no breach of this limit in any of the time buckets;
- the report also lists cumulative assets and liabilities, as well as the "net gap", which is the sum of the two cumulative values for each time bucket.

We observe that the ALM profile at XYZ follows roughly the ALM Smile shape that is recommended as the ideal profile over the term structure, and accepted good business practice.

	o/n	o/n–1	1w–1m	1m–3m	3m–6m	6m–12m	12m+	**Total**
Assets	481	4,104	5,325	6,954	4,478	3,845	4,128	29,315
Liabilities	–3,947	–844	–5,107	–7,579	–5,053	–3,799	–2,986	(29,315)
Gap	3,466	3,260	218	625	575	46	1,142	9,332
Percent of total funding	13%	3%	17%	26%	17%	13%	10%	100%
Gap as % of total gap	37%	35%	2%	7%	6%	0%	12%	100%
Gap as % of total funding	12%	11%	1%	2%	2%	0%	4%	
Gap limit	20%	20%	20%	20%	20%	20%	20%	
Limit breach	–	–	–	–	–	–	–	
Cumulative assets	481	4,585	9,910	16,864	21,342	25,187	29,315	
Cumulative liabilities	–3,947	–4,791	–9,898	–1,747	–22,530	–26,329	–29,315	
Net gap	–3,466	–206	12	–613	–1,188	–1,142	0	

Table 5.3 XYZ Securities Limited ALM report and profile

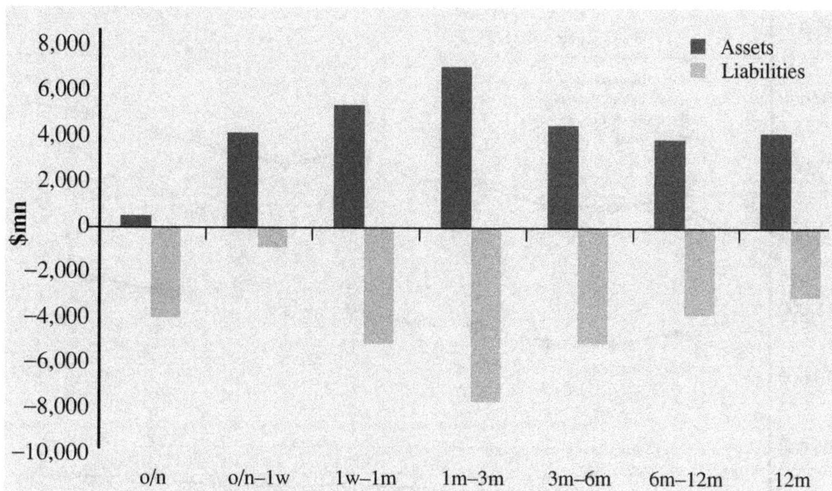

Figure 5.6 XYZ Securities Limited gap profile

The firm-wide funding report is shown in Figure 5.7. This is reported in graphical form to observe adherence to funding limits and indicate breaches. Unlike the ALM report, which is produced by Treasury (a front-office function), the funding report is produced by the bank's Middle Office, which is a control function. Figure 5.8 shows the breakdown by business line.

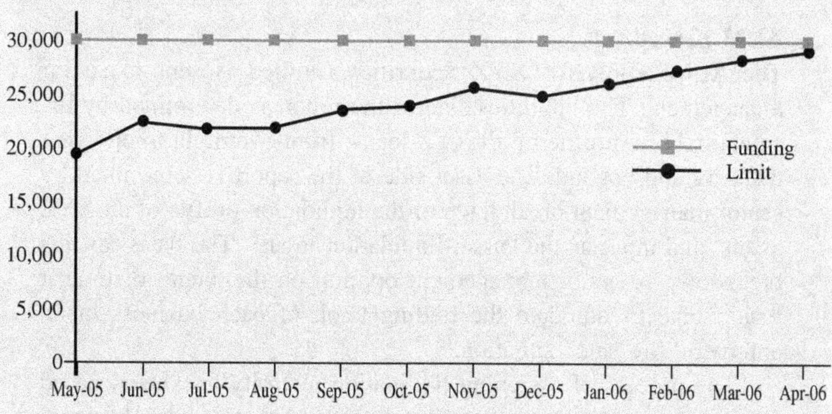

Figure 5.7 XYZ Securities Limited funding usage and limit report

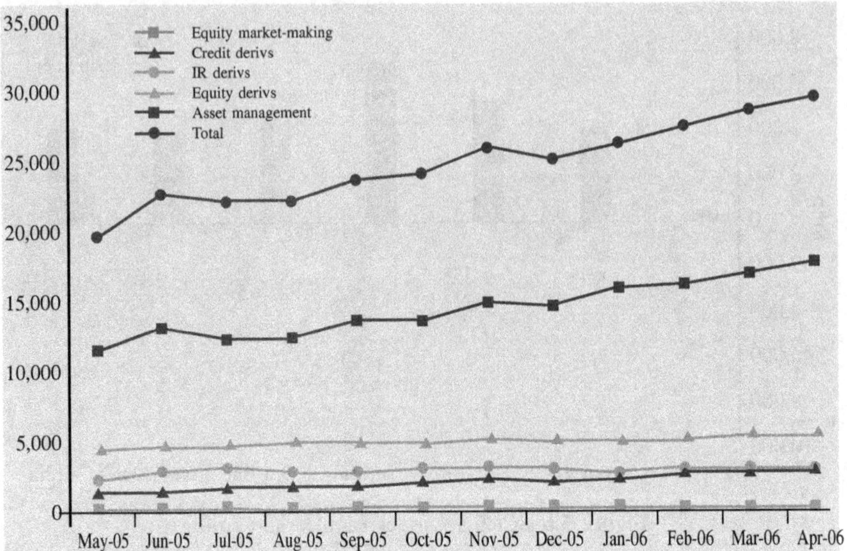

Figure 5.8 XYZ Securities Limited funding usage by business line

ALM reporting

XYZ Treasury follows the ALM policy previously described to and approved by senior management. One strand of the ALM discipline is the regular reporting of the firm's ALM profile, by means of the ALM report. This is produced by Treasury using data recorded by itself as well as data from Middle Office (MO).

ALM procedures

The ALM report for XYZ Securities Limited is sent to senior management. The liabilities side of the report is determined by the actual liability profile of all XYZ loans, from overnight to one-year maturity and beyond. The asset side of the report is determined by senior management breakdown of the liquidation profile of all XYZ assets, and input as the "asset-liquidation input". The basis for this breakdown is senior management opinion on the length of time it would take to liquidate the trading book of each business in an enforced "fire sale" situation.[13]

The process of assigning liquidation maturity buckets is based on the subjective view of senior management. For each business line, senior management ask the question, "What reasonable time

[13] The liquidity duration of the asset pool is unrelated to the actual duration of the assets themselves.

period would it take to liquidate positions if it were decided to close down the business?" The answer to this question is a function of the secondary market trading liquidity of the assets in question.[14] Hence, for frequently traded assets such as Eurobonds, we assume that one week would be sufficient time to trade out of all assets. For business lines with illiquid assets, such as some part of the asset management book, a longer time period (specifically in this case, in excess of one year) is noted. Management allocate this estimated time period in the same time buckets as we have established for the liabilities.

We assume that assets equal liabilities.

The procedure for compiling the report is as follows:

- Treasury compiles its own funding report, independent of MO, from its own record of overnight and term funding for XYZ. The procedure for creating this document is documented internally;
- the Treasury report is used to populate the "Liabilities" segment on the ALM report. This segment lists the current funding profile (liabilities) of XYZ by business line;
- senior management will instruct any change to the asset liquidation breakdown, otherwise these values are retained;
- the "asset liquidity profile" segment is linked directly to the asset liquidation segment (for the asset side) and liabilities input segment (for the liability side).

The ALM graph is automatically updated when the input tabs are populated.

The Treasury liquidity book

Following conventional banking business practice, XYZ Treasury maintains a liquidity book of T-bills, CDs, sovereign bonds and bank FRNs. The firm's capital as well as a proportion of long-term cash is held in the liquidity book.

In the next case study we set out the firm's policy for maintaining the FRN book.

[14] In practice, other factors (such as whether the market was aware that this was an enforced sale or not) would also influence this timing but cannot be factored into any estimation.

CASE STUDY 5.2 XYZ Securities liquidity book: FRN portfolio

Banks maintain a pool of low-risk FRNs issued by other banks and building societies as part of their reserve and liquidity requirements. This well-established practice is favoured because of low capital requirements against these assets and because it enables institutions that are funded at sub-Libor to hold Libor-plus floating-rate assets with funding locked in.

The XYZ Treasury desk is able to secure sub-Libor funding via its commercial paper vehicle. Within the parent group funding limit of USD30 billion, Treasury maintains a low-risk portfolio of bank and building society assets to employ spare capacity by holding a low-risk, locked-in funding portfolio of bank and building society FRNs.

Objectives of the business activity

To maintain a portfolio of short- to medium-dated bank and building society FRNs, all rated A or better, and held to maturity. These will be FRNs paying a spread over three-month Libor, and denominated in USD, EUR or GBP.

Bonds are funded in their own currency by means of three-month CP issued from the CP conduit, funded at sub-Libor. There is no gap funding risk.

Motivation behind the business

A portfolio of bank and building society FRNs enables XYZ Securities Ltd to:

- earn a low-risk but material return over locked-in funding;
- utilise spare capacity in funding availability.

Bonds will be purchased at par or below par so there is no capital loss if held to maturity.

Building society paper carries particular value relative to their credit rating. There has never been a default in the history of the building society movement (traditionally building societies merge or are taken over if in any financial difficulty) and this implies that their financial risk warrants stronger than the A-rating they receive. In effect, XYZ would carry bank risk (AA-rated) for A-rated return.

Booking procedure

The FRN book is held in a separate trading book within the Treasury book, in order to ring-fence the match-funded positions. The booking procedure is shown in Figure 5.9.

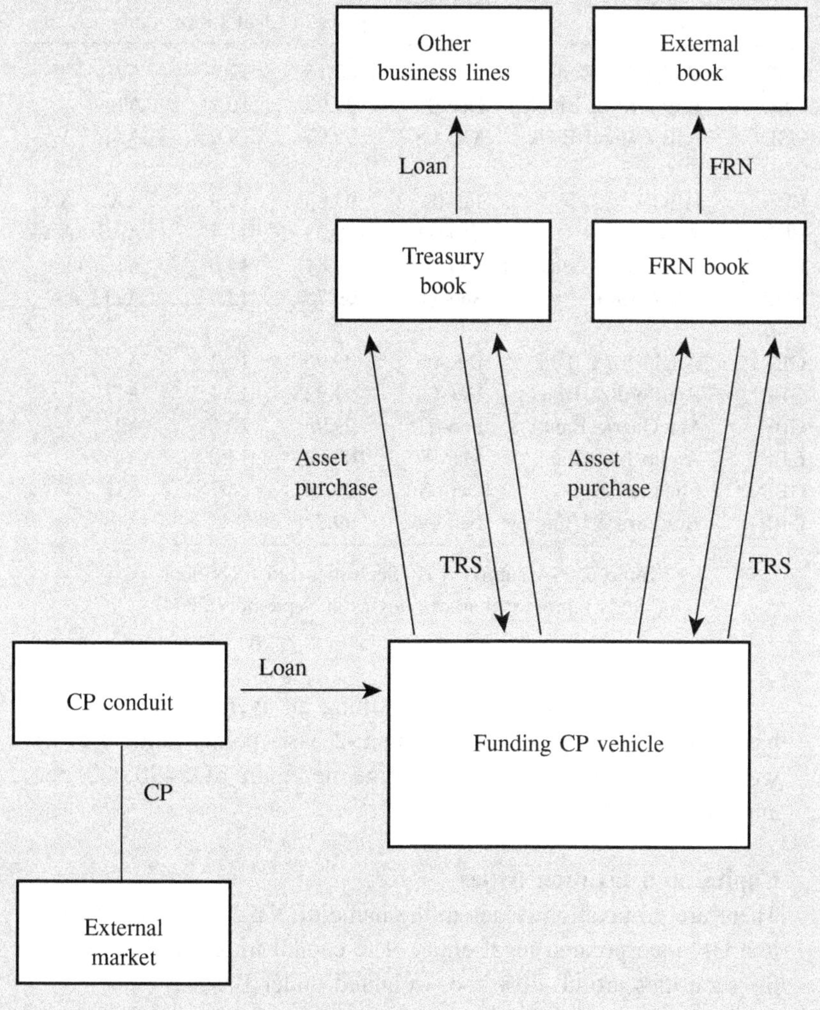

Figure 5.9 FRN book: schematic of booking cash flows

Expected return

Assume that the portfolio stands at USD350 million. A sample of the securities held in the book is shown in Table 5.4, all funded using 3-month CP issuance. This eliminates gap funding risk as the bonds all pay quarterly coupon.

Currency	Bond	Maturity	Offer price	Spread 3-m Libor	Rating
USD	Kaupthing Bank	Feb-07	100.15	12.9	A2
USD	Bradford & Bingley	Dec-07	99.935	16.7	A1
USD	NIB Capital Bank	Mar-08	99.94	9.0	AA3 / AA–
EUR	HBOS	Jun-09	99.835	9.9	AA2 / AA
EUR	ANZ	Sep-09	100.03	11.4	AA3 / AA–
EUR	Alliance & Leicester	Sep-09	99.81	14.0	A1 / A+
EUR	ABN Amro	Sep-11	99.75	13.4	Aa3 / AA–
GBP	Anglo Irish Bank	Dec-06	99.96	10.3	A2
GBP	Bradford & Bingley	Dec-06	99.925	13.4	A1
GBP	MacQuarie Bank	Feb-07	99.95	12.6	A2
GBP	Anglo Irish Bank	Mar-07	100.02	14.0	A2
GBP	Fin Danish	Oct-08	99.92	14.7	A1
GBP	Bradford & Bingley	Feb-09	99.725	19.5	A1

Table 5.4 Assumed XYZ Securities Ltd FRN book (yields represent market rates as at September 2004)

For a $350 million portfolio earning an average spread of 12 basis points, the net p&l (assuming L-2 basis points funding cost) would be approximately an average net gain of $490,000 per annum.

Capital and taxation issues

There are no taxation issues in the name of XYZ Securities, which is a UK-incorporated legal entity. The capital implications are that the securities are all 20% risk-weighted under Basel I.

Sovereign bond portfolio for interest-rate hedging

Using XYZ Securities again as our hypothetical bank, we now consider a bond portfolio maintained for ALM hedging purposes by XYZ Treasury. The Treasury desk maintains a liquidity book of US Treasury, German Bund and UK gilts. This is also used to facilitate a repo business, as well as reduce the quantity of interest-rate futures needed as part of the interest-rate exposure hedge.

Description of the product/business activity

XYZ Treasury is required to fund a large size of the firm-wide funding requirement in term loans, as part of prudent ALM. The resulting DV01 exposure is managed using Eurodollar futures. It has also established a US government bond portfolio as a lower cost means of managing the DV01 risk. The objective is to manage the DV01 exposure of the Treasury book by buying very short-dated Treasury notes and strips, which sets up an income stream that is diversified from other sources and that represents zero credit risk. This is achieved by:

- establishing a portfolio of very short-dated US Treasuries and Treasury strips on the balance sheet (maximum maturity recommended 1–1.5 years, majority in three- to six-months);
- placing the composition of the book as:
    - 200m, 3-m
    - 300m, 6-m
    - 50m, 1-year;
- having the average maturity of portfolio at around the six-month tenor;
- funding these in Treasury repo, under the standard GMRA legal agreement;[15]
- holding Treasury securities and Treasury strips to maturity to generate a steady income stream. With ultra-short-dated strips, this also benefits from the pull-to-par effect on mark-to-market.

All funding is locked into maturity, thus there is no gap risk.

[15] See Chapter 12 on repo.

Objectives of the business

The sovereign bond book is business that:

- allows XYZ to undertake cheaper hedging of its interest-rate risk (DV01), complementing the standard arrangement using Eurodollar, Euribor and short sterling futures;
- establishes a risk-free portfolio that generates a funding gain for XYZ;
- enables XYZ to use a AAA risk-free portfolio for use in setting up total-return swaps (TRSs) and repo lines with market counterparties.

The benefits to XYZ of holding such a portfolio include:

- earning the spread between yield and funding cost; a bonus that is not available when using Eurodollar futures for DV01 hedging, which do not earn any income. XYZ also saves on the commission and margin costs associated with maintaining Eurodollar futures positions;
- using the business to set up dealing relationships with bank counterparties that could then be used as sources of additional funding if required, adding to the diversity of funding (required as part of the Treasury remit);
- assisting Treasury in undertaking ALM objectives through lower cost hedging of DV01 risk, compared to futures, which impose a cost on the book.

Expected return

The fundamental gain is the removal of the requirement to hold Eurodollar futures. In a rising interest-rate environment, this will significantly reduce hedging costs.

Net profit in the first full year is upwards of $250,000–$280,000 funding gain on a £350 million average position (10–12 basis points on average per trade). This does not take into account any mark-to-market profit that is realised on Treasury bonds and strips.

Capital and taxation issues

Treasury securities are 0% risk-weighted under Basel I (and II), except where they create DV01 risk when the charge is 0.7%. However, if held for interest-rate risk hedging purposes (as is the case here), they may actually reduce overall capital requirements.

Profitable risk-free trade examples observed on 1 July 2004

Below are examples of hypothetical funding trades that were observed on July 2004 that generated a risk-free funding gain, rates as at 1 July 2004 (data source: Bloomberg LP). This shows where value was obtained from holding a book of Treasuries in the first instance. The following positions all yielded funding profit:

- buy the 2% November 2004 Treasury at a yield of 1.597% and hold to maturity, and repo to maturity at a rate of 1.56%. This is a locked-in gain of 3.70 basis points for the term to maturity, on a position of USD150 million a profit of USD24,800;
- buy the 31 July 2004 strip at a yield of 1.568% and repo to maturity at 1.28%, a spread of 28.8 basis points at risk-free locked-in funding. On a position of USD200 million this represents positive p&l of USD48,000 – this is risk-free income.
- the ability to take advantage of special rates for stocks we are long in. On 1 July a position in 1% May 2005 Treasury could be funded cheaper than normal repo ("GC") due to special status, by 7–8 basis points. So the gain on holding that stock would be around this amount for the term of the trade, as our funding cost in repo would be lower by this amount. It would be an objective of the Treasury desk to be aware of stocks expected to go special and act accordingly.

These opportunities are not frequent but they do occur, as shown above. As the book is primarily designed to hedge, trading is infrequent and only undertaken as opportunities arise.

Risks

There is no gap (funding) risk and no credit risk.

As the positions are held on a Trading book, and not the Banking book, they are marked-to-market. The desk expects volatility in short-dated government bonds to be lower than for the term loans they are hedging, but volatility is a risk exposure and there may be periods when the desk will experience mark-to-market losses.

CASE STUDY 5.3 XYZ Securities UK gilt portfolio

Commercial banks and building societies are natural holders of government bonds such as gilts, for the following reasons:

- for liquidity purposes, as gilts are the most liquid instruments in the UK market;
- as an instrument in which to invest the firm's capital reserves;
- for income generation purposes, given the favourable funding costs of gilt repo and the zero credit and liquidity risk;
- to intermediate between gilt, stock loan and interbank markets in CDs;
- to benefit from being long in gilts that go "special" and can be funded at anything from 25 basis points to 2–3% cheaper than "general collateral" (GC) repo;
- to establish an asset pool that receives favourable capital treatment (0% risk-weighted under Basel I and Basel II).

The benefits to XYZ Securities Ltd of holding such a portfolio would include some of the above, as well as the following:

- earning the spread between yield and funding cost;
- using the business to set up dealing relationships with bank counterparties that could then be used as sources of additional funding if required, adding to the diversity of funding (required as part of the Treasury remit);
- assisting Treasury to undertake ALM objectives.

Business line

This is a UK government bond portfolio at XYZ Treasury. The objective is to maintain an income stream that is diversified from current sources and that is also relatively low risk, but stable. This is achieved by:

- establishing a portfolio of very short-dated gilts and gilt strips on the balance sheet (the maximum maturity recommended is one year, the majority in three- to six-months). The expected make-up of the book might be:

  - ➤ 125m, 3-m
  - ➤ 200m, 6-m
  - ➤ 25m, 1-year
  - ➤ average maturity of the portfolio in the first year would be around the six-month mark;
- funding these in gilt repo, under the GMRA agreement and also funding using TRS under ISDA if required;
- the repo funding margin for gilts in the wholesale market, which is often 0%. With zero or a very low margin or "haircut", all positions will be virtually fully funded;
- holding gilts and gilt strips to maturity to generate a steady income stream. With ultra-short-dated strips, we also benefit from the pull-to-par effect.

Market rates

Table 5.5 on pages 245-6 shows income yields and funding rates as at 2 June 2004. This shows where value could be obtained from holding a book of gilts in the first instance. For example, all the following positions yielded funding profit:

- holding gilts and funds in general collateral (GC); depending on the specific stock and the term of funding arranged, a gain ranging from 15 to 50–60 basis points;
- holding strips to maturity; for example, a gain of approximately 35 basis points for Dec 04 Principal strip at 1w or 2w funding. Locked-in funding gain (buy 6-m strip and fund in 6-m) of 9 basis points for the Dec 04 strip – this is risk-free income;
- holding strips at 3-, 6- and 9-month maturities as longer-dated bills and holding to maturity. Funding will be locked in if available or rolled:
  - ➤ for example, as at 2 June 2004, XYZ Securities Ltd purchased the Sep 04 coupon strip at 4.34% and funded in the one-week term at 4.15% (and ran the resultant funding gap risk – but this gilt had a strong pull-to-par effect. If funding is no longer profitable in the short dates, XYZ would have sold the gilt for a probable realised mark-to-market profit)
  - ➤ coupon strips are bid for in repo by the main market-makers, thereby reducing liquidity risk in these products

- taking advantage of special rates for stocks XYZ when long in. On 2 June 2004, a position in the 9.5% 2005 gilt was funded cheaper due to special status, from 35 basis points (down from 50 basis points the week before). The 6.75% 2004 gilt was being funded at 100 basis points cheaper than GC. So the gain on holding that stock would be significant, as the funding cost in repo would be very low. It would be an objective of the Treasury desk to be aware of stocks expected to go special and act accordingly.

Risks

The principal risk is funding roll-over (gap risk). Where possible XYZ Treasury will lock in funding with an expected holding period of positions, but will also look to take advantage of markets rates as appropriate and roll over funding. Gap risk will be managed in the normal way as part of overall Treasury operations. Gaps will be put on to reflect the interest-rate and yield curve view of the desk.

There is no credit risk.

The interest-rate risk and gap risk is managed as a standard banking ALM or cash book. The objective is to set up an income stream position at low risk, but if necessary DV01 risk would be managed where deemed necessary using 90-day sterling futures, overnight-index swap (OIS) or short-dated swaps. XYZ can also sell out of positions where it expects significant market movement (for example, a central bank base rate hike). The main objective, however, is to establish an income stream, in line with a view on short-term interest rates. Hedging would only be carried out when necessary for short-term periods (say, ahead of a data release or anticipated high volatility).

The interest-rate risk for longer-dated stocks is shown in Table 5.5 below, measured as DV01 (dollar-value of loss for a 1 basis point rise in yields). Longer-dated stocks expose XYZ Securities Ltd to greater interest-rate risk position when marking-to-market.

Market rates

GC rates 2 Jun

1w	4.15	4.10	4m	4.40	4.30
2w	4.25	4.15	5m	4.43	4.33
3w	4.25	4.15	6m	4.50	4.40
1m	4.15	4.15	9m	4.67	4.57
2m	4.28	4.18	1y	4.78	4.68
3m	4.32	4.22			

Source: HBOS screen

Gilt yields 2 Jun	GRY%	DV01	**Special rates**
5% Jun 04	5.05		
6T Nov 04	4.33	0.00416	100 basis points
9H Apr 05	4.668	0.00817	30 basis points cheaper than GC
8H Dec 05	4.818	0.014	25 basis points cheaper, down from 1.5%
7T Sep 06	4.945	0.02141	
7H Dec 06	4.966	0.02364	10 basis points

Sources: Butler Securities / KSBB screens.

Gilt strip yields 2 Jun

	GRY %	DV01
P Jun 04	3.78	
C Sep 04	4.342	0.00195
C Dec 04	4.509	0.00432
C Mar 05	4.633	0.00664
C Jun 05	4.744	0.00888
C Sep 05	4.829	0.01107
P Dec 05	4.85	0.01321

Source: Bloomberg.

Table 5.5 Market rates as at 2 June 2004

Bibliography

Gup, B.E. and Brooks, R. 1993, *Interest Rate Risk Management*, New York, NY: Irwin.

CHAPTER

6

Asset–Liability Management II

In our second introductory chapter, we delve deeper, or more accurately wider, into ALM. The art of asset and ALM is essentially one of risk management and capital management, and although the day-to-day activities are run at the desk level, overall direction is given at the highest level of a banking institution. The risk exposures in a banking environment are multi-dimensional, as we have seen they encompass interest-rate risk, liquidity risk, credit risk and operational risk. Interest-rate risk is one type of market risk. Risks associated with moves in interest rates and levels of liquidity[1] are those that result in adverse fluctuations in earnings levels due to changes in market rates and bank funding costs. By definition, banks' earnings levels are highly sensitive to moves in interest rates and the cost of funds in the wholesale market. ALM covers the set of techniques used to manage interest rate and liquidity risks; it also deals with the structure of the bank's balance sheet, which is heavily influenced by funding and regulatory constraints and profitability targets.

In this chapter we review the concept of balance sheet management, the role of the ALM desk, liquidity risk and maturity gap risk. We also review a basic gap report. The increasing use of *securitisation* and the responsibility of the ALM desk in enhancing the return on assets on the balance sheet is also introduced. For readers who are interested in developing their knowledge further, as usual we list a selection of articles and publications in the bibliography.

[1] In this chapter the term *liquidity* is used to refer to funding liquidity.

Introduction

For newcomers to the subject, an excellent introduction to the primary activity of banking is contained in a supplement in *The Economist* entitled "The Business of Banking".[2] Those who are complete beginners may wish to refer to this article. In this section we provide an overview of the main business of banking before considering the subject of ALM.

One of the major areas of decision-making in a bank involves the maturity of assets and liabilities. Typically, longer-term interest rates are higher than shorter-term rates; that is, it is common for the yield curve in the short-term (say 0–3 year range) to be positively sloping. To take advantage of this banks usually raise a large proportion of their funds from the short-dated end of the yield curve and lend out these funds for longer maturities at higher rates. The spread between the borrowing and lending rates is in principle the bank's profit. The obvious risk from such a strategy is that the level of short-term rates rises during the term of the loan, so that when the loan is refinanced the bank makes a lower profit or a net loss. Managing this risk exposure is the key function of an ALM desk. As well as managing the interest-rate risk itself, banks also match assets with liabilities – thus locking in a profit – and diversify their loan book, to reduce exposure to one sector of the economy.

Another risk factor is liquidity. From a banking and Treasury point of view the term *liquidity* means funding liquidity, or the "nearness" of money. The most liquid asset is cash money. Banks bear several interrelated liquidity risks, including the risk of being unable to pay depositors on demand, an inability to raise funds in the market at reasonable rates and an insufficient level of funds available with which to make loans. Banks keep only a small portion of their assets in the form of cash, because this earns no return for them. In fact, once they have met the minimum cash level requirement, which is something set down by international regulation, they will hold assets in the form of other instruments. Therefore the ability to meet deposit withdrawals depends on a bank's ability to raise funds in the market. The market and the public's perception of a bank's financial position heavily influences liquidity. If this view is very negative, the bank may be unable to raise funds and consequently be unable to meet withdrawals or loan demand. Thus liquidity management is running a bank in a way that maintains confidence in its financial position. The assets of the banks that

[2] *The Economist*, 30 October 1999.

are held in near-cash instruments, such as T-bills and clearing bank CDs, must be managed with liquidity considerations in mind. The asset book on which these instruments are held is sometimes called the *liquidity book*.

Basic concepts

In the era of stable interest rates that preceded the breakdown of the Bretton–Woods agreement, ALM was a more straightforward process, constrained by regulatory restrictions and the saving and borrowing pattern of bank customers.[3] The introduction of the negotiable CD by Citibank in the 1960s enabled banks to diversify both their investment and funding sources. With this there developed the concept of the *interest margin*, which is the spread between the interest earned on assets and that paid on liabilities. This led to the concept of the *interest gap* and the management of the gap, which is the cornerstone of modern-day ALM. The increasing volatility of interest rates, and the rise in absolute levels of rates themselves, made gap management a vital part of running the banking book. This development meant that banks could no longer rely permanently on the traditional approach of borrowing short (funding short) to lend long, as a rise in the level of short-term rates would result in funding losses. The introduction of derivative instruments such as FRAs and swaps in the early 1980s removed the previous uncertainty and allowed banks to continue the traditional approach while hedging against medium-term uncertainty.

Foundations of ALM

The general term *asset and liability management* entered common usage from the mid-1970s onwards. In the changing interest-rate environment, it became imperative for banks to manage both assets and liabilities simultaneously, in order to minimise interest rate and liquidity risk and maximise interest income. ALM is a key component of any financial

[3] For instance, in the US banking sector the terms on deposit accounts were fixed by regulation, and there were restrictions on the geographic base of customers and the interest rates that could be offered. Interest-rate volatility was also low. In this environment, ALM consisted primarily of asset management, in which the bank would use depositors' funds to arrange the asset portfolio that was most appropriate for the liability portfolio. This involved little more than setting aside some of the assets in non-interest reserves at the central bank authority and investing the balance in short-term securities, while any surplus outside of this would be lent out at very short-term maturities.

institution's overall operating strategy. ALM is defined in terms of four key concepts, which are described below.

The first is *liquidity*, which in an ALM context does not refer to the ease with which an asset can be bought or sold in the secondary market, but the ease with which assets can be converted into cash.[4] A banking book is required by the regulatory authorities to hold a specified minimum share of its assets in the form of very liquid instruments. Liquidity is very important to any institution that accepts deposits because of the need to meet customer demand for instant-access funds. In terms of a banking book the most liquid assets are overnight funds, while the least liquid are medium-term bonds. Short-term assets such as T-bills and CDs are also considered to be very liquid.

The second key concept is the money market *term structure* of interest rates. The shape of the yield curve at any one time, and expectations as to its shape in the short- and medium-term, impact to a significant extent on the ALM strategy employed by a bank. Market risk in the form of *interest-rate sensitivity* is significant, in the form of present-value sensitivity of specific instruments to changes in the level of interest rates, as well as the sensitivity of floating-rate assets and liabilities to changes in rates. Another key factor is the *maturity profile* of the book. The maturities of assets and liabilities can be matched or unmatched; although the latter is more common the former is not uncommon, depending on the specific strategies that are being employed. Matched assets and liabilities lock in return in the form of the spread between the funding rate and the return on assets. The maturity profile, the absence of a locked-in spread and the yield curve combine to determine the total interest-rate risk of the banking book.

The fourth key concept is *default risk*: the risk exposure that borrowers will default on interest or principal payments that are due to the banking institution.

These issues are placed in context in the simple hypothetical situation described in Example 6.1 "ALM considerations".

[4] The marketability definition of liquidity is also important in ALM. Less liquid financial instruments must offer a yield premium compared to liquid instruments.

Example 6.1 ALM considerations

Assume that a bank may access the markets for three-month and six-month funds, whether for funding or investment purposes. The rates for these terms are shown in Table 6.1. Assume no bid–offer spreads. The ALM manager also expects the three-month Libor rate in three-months to be 5.10%. The bank can usually fund its book at Libor, while it is able to lend at Libor plus 1%.

Term	Libor	Bank rate
90-day	5.50%	6.50%
180-day	5.75%	6.75%
Expected 90-day rate in 90 days' time	5.10%	6.10%
3v6 FRA[1]	6.60%	

[1] FRA – forward rate agreement

Table 6.1 Hypothetical money market rates

The bank could adopt any of the following strategies, or a combination of them:

- Borrow three-month funds at 5.50% and lend this out in the three-month period at 6.50%. This locks in a return of 1% for a three-month period.
- Borrow six-month funds at 5.75% and lend in the six-month at 6.75%; again this earns a locked-in spread of 1%.
- Borrow three-month funds at 5.50% and lend this in the six-month term at 6.75%. This approach would require the bank to re-fund the loan in three months' time, which it expects to be able to do at 5.10%. This approach locks in a return of 1.25% in the first three-month period, and an expected return of 1.65% in the second three-month period. The risk of this tactic is that the three-month rate in three months does not fall as expected by the ALM manager, reducing profits and possibly leading to loss.
- Borrow in the six-month at 5.75% and lend these for a three-month period at 6.50%. After this period, lend the funds in the three-month or six-month period. This strategy does not tally with the ALM manager's view, however, who expects a fall in rates and so should not wish to be long of funds in three months' time.

- Borrow three-month funds at 5.50% and again lend this in the six-month period at 6.75%. To hedge the gap risk, the ALM manager simultaneously buys a 3v6 FRA to lock in the three-month rate in three months' time. The first period spread of 1.25% is guaranteed, but the FRA guarantees only a spread of 15 basis points in the second period. This is the cost of the hedge (and also suggests that the market does not agree with the ALM manager's assessment of where rates will be three months from now!), the price the bank must pay for reducing uncertainty, the lower spread return. Alternatively, the bank could lend in the six-month period, funding initially in the three-month, and buy an interest-rate cap with a ceiling rate of 6.60% and pegged to Libor, the rate at which the bank can actually fund its book.

Although simplistic, these scenarios serve to illustrate what is possible, and indeed there are many other strategies that could be adopted. The approaches described in the last option show how derivative instruments can be used actively to manage the banking book, and the cost that is associated with employing them.

Liquidity and gap management

We noted in Chapter 5 that the simplest approach to ALM is to match assets with liabilities. For a number of reasons, which include the need to meet client demand and to maximise return on capital, this is not practical and banks must adopt more active ALM strategies. One of the most important of these is the role of the gap, and gap management. This term describes the practice of varying the asset and liability gap in response to expectations about the future course of interest rates and the shape of the yield curve. Simply put, this means increasing the gap when interest rates are expected to rise, and decreasing it when rates are expected to decline. The gap here is the difference between floating-rate assets and liabilities, but gap management must also be pursued when one of these elements is fixed rate.

Such an approach is of course an art and not a science. Gap management assumes that the ALM manager is proved to be correct in his or her prediction of the future direction of rates and the yield curve.[5] Views that

[5] Or, is proved to be correct at least three times out of five!

turn out to be incorrect can lead to an unexpected widening or narrowing of the gap spread, and losses. The ALM manager must choose the level of trade-off between risk and return.

Gap management also assumes that the profile of the banking book can be altered with relative ease. This is not always the case, and even today may still present problems, although the evolution of a liquid market in off-balance sheet interest-rate derivatives has eased this problem somewhat. Historically it has always been difficult to change the structure of the book, as many loans cannot be liquidated instantly and fixed-rate assets and liabilities cannot be changed to floating-rate ones. Client relationships must also be observed and maintained – this is a key banking issue. For this reason it is much more common for ALM managers to use off-balance sheet products when dynamically managing the book. For example, FRAs can be used to hedge gap exposure, while interest-rate swaps are used to alter an interest basis from fixed to floating, or vice-versa. The last strategy presented in Example 6.1 presented, albeit simplistically, the use that could be made of derivatives. The widespread use of derivatives has enhanced the opportunities available to ALM managers, as well as the flexibility with which the banking book can be managed, but it has also contributed to the increase in competition and the reduction in margins and bid–offer spreads.

Interest-rate risk and source: Banking book

The Banking book

Traditionally, ALM has been concerned with the Banking book. The conventional techniques of ALM were developed for application to a bank's banking book; that is, the lending and deposit-taking transactions. The core banking activity will generate either an excess of funds, when the receipt of deposits outweighs the volume of lending the bank has undertaken, or a shortage of funds, when the reverse occurs. This mis-match is balanced via financial transactions in the wholesale market. The Banking book generates both interest-rate and liquidity risks, which are then monitored and managed by the ALM desk. Interest-rate risk is the risk that the bank suffers losses due to adverse movements in market interest rates. Liquidity risk is the risk that the bank cannot generate sufficient funds when required; the most extreme version of this is when there is a "run" on the bank, and the bank cannot raise the funds required when depositors withdraw their cash.

Note that the asset side of the Banking book, which is the loan portfolio, also generates credit risk.

The ALM desk will be concerned with risk management that focuses on the quantitative management of the liquidity and interest-rate risks inherent in a Banking book. The major areas of ALM include:

- *measurement and monitoring of liquidity and interest-rate risk.* This includes setting up targets for earnings and volume of transactions, and setting up and monitoring interest-rate risk limits;
- *funding and control of any constraints on the balance sheet.* This includes liquidity constraints, debt policy and *capital adequacy* ratio and solvency;
- *hedging of liquidity and interest-rate risk.*

Interest-rate risk

Put simply, interest-rate risk is defined as the potential impact, adverse or otherwise, on the net asset value of a financial institution's balance sheet and earnings resulting from a change in interest rates. Risk exposure exists whenever there is a maturity date mis-match between assets and liabilities, or between principal and interest cash flows. Interest-rate risk is not necessarily a negative thing; for instance, changes in interest rates that increase the net asset value of a banking institution would be regarded as positive. For this reason, active ALM seeks to position a banking book to gain from changes in rates. The Bank for International Settlements (BIS) splits interest-rate risk into two elements: *investment risk* and *income risk.* The first risk type is the term for potential risk exposure arising from changes in the market value of fixed interest-rate cash instruments and off-balance sheet instruments, and is also known as *price risk.* Investment risk is perhaps best exemplified by the change in value of a plain vanilla bond following a change in interest rates, and from Chapter 4 we know that there is an inverse relationship between changes in rates and the value of such bonds (see Example 4.1). Income risk is the risk of loss of income when there is a non-synchronous change in deposit and funding rates, and it this risk that is known as gap risk.

ALM covering the formulation of interest-rate risk policy is usually the responsibility of what is known as the asset–liability committee or ALCO, which is made up of senior management personnel including the Finance Director and the heads of Treasury and Risk Management. ALCO sets bank policy for balance sheet management and the likely impact on revenue of various scenarios that it considers may occur. The size of ALCO will depend on the complexity of the balance sheet and products traded, and the amount of management information available on individual products and desks.

The process employed by ALCO for ALM will vary according to the particular internal arrangement of the institution. A common procedure involves a monthly presentation to ALCO of the impact of different interest-rate scenarios on the balance sheet. This presentation may include:

- an analysis of the difference between the actual net interest income (NII) for the previous month and the amount that was forecast at the previous ALCO meeting. This is usually presented as a gap report, broken by maturity buckets and individual products;
- the result of discussion with business unit heads on the basis of the assumptions used in calculating forecasts and impact of interest-rate changes; scenario analysis usually assumes an unchanging book position between now and one month later, which is essentially unrealistic;
- a number of interest-rate scenarios, based on assumptions of (a) what is expected to happen to the shape and level of the yield curve, and (b) what may happen to the yield curve; for example, extreme scenarios. Essentially, this exercise produces a value for the forecasted NII due to changes in interest rates;
- an update of the latest actual revenue numbers.

Specific new or one-off topics may be introduced at ALCO as circumstances dictate; for example, the presentation of the approval process for the introduction of a new product or business line.

Sources of interest-rate risk

Assets on the balance sheet are affected by absolute changes in interest rates, as well as increases in the volatility of interest rates. For instance, fixed-rate assets will fall in value in the event of a rise in rates, while funding costs will rise. This decreases the margins available. We noted that the way to remove this risk was to lock in assets with matching liabilities; however, this is not only not always possible, but also sometimes undesirable, as it prevents the ALM manager from taking a view on the yield curve. In a falling interest-rate environment, deposit-taking institutions may experience a decline in available funds, requiring new funding sources that may be accessed at less favourable terms. Liabilities are also impacted by a changing interest-rate environment.

There are five primary sources of interest-rate risk inherent in an ALM book, which are described below.

Gap risk is the risk that revenue and earnings decline as a result of changes in interest rates, due to the difference in the maturity profile of assets, liabilities and off-balance sheet instruments. Another term for gap risk is *mismatch risk*. An institution with gap risk is exposed to changes in the level of the yield curve, a so-called *parallel shift*, or a change in the shape of the yield curve or *pivotal shift*. Gap risk is measured in terms of short- or long-term risk, which is a function of the impact of rate changes on earnings for a short or long period. Therefore the maturity profile of the book, and the time to maturity of instruments held on the book, will influence whether the bank is exposed to short-term or long-term gap risk.

Yield curve risk is the risk that non-parallel or pivotal shifts in the yield curve cause a reduction in NII. The ALM manager will change the structure of the book to take into account their views on the yield curve. For example, a book with a combination of short-term and long-term asset- or liability-maturity structures[6] is at risk from a yield curve inversion, sometimes known as a *twist* in the curve.

Basis risk arises from the fact that assets are often priced off one interest rate, while funding is priced off another interest rate. Taken one step further, hedge instruments are often linked to a different interest rate to that of the product they are hedging. In the US market the best example of basis risk is the difference between the prime rate and Libor. Term loans in the United States are often set at prime, or a relationship to prime, while bank funding is usually based on the Eurodollar market and linked to Libor. However, the prime rate is what is known as an "administered" rate and does not change on a daily basis, unlike Libor. While changes in the two rates are positively correlated, they do not change by the same amount, which means that the spread between them changes regularly. This results in the spread earned on a loan product changing over time. Figure 6.1 illustrates the change in spread during 2005–2006.

---

[6] This describes a *barbell* structure, but this is really a bond market term.

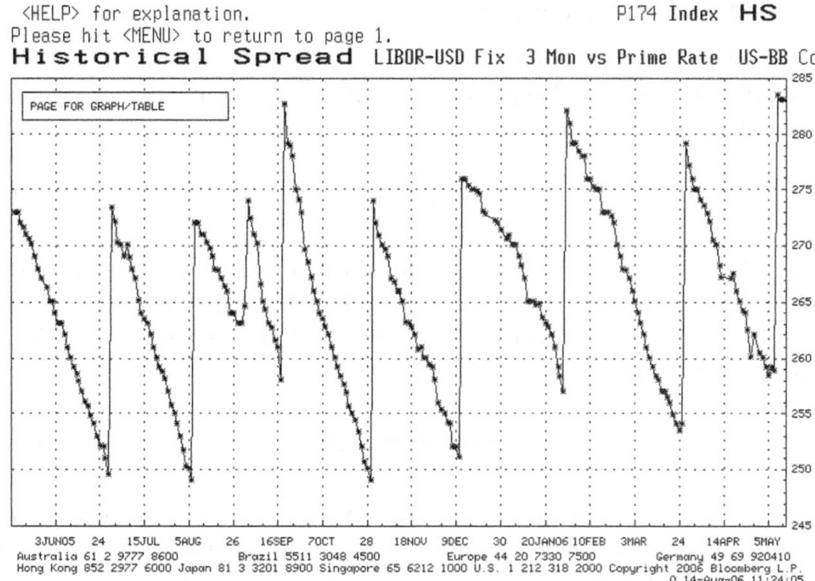

Figure 6.1 Change in spread between the 3-month prime rate and 3-month Libor 2005–06.

Another risk for deposit-taking institutions such as clearing banks is ***run-off risk***, associated with the non-interest bearing liabilities (NIBLs) of such banks. The level of interest rates at any one time represents an opportunity cost to depositors who have funds in such facilities. However, in a rising interest-rate environment, this opportunity cost rises and depositors will withdraw these funds, available at immediate notice, resulting in an outflow of funds for the bank. The funds may be taken out of the banking system completely; for example, for investment in the stock market. This risk is significant and therefore sufficient funds must be maintained at short notice, which is an opportunity cost for the bank itself.

Many banking products entitle the customer to terminate contractual arrangements ahead of the stated maturity term; this is sometimes referred to as ***option risk***. This is another significant risk as products such as CDs, cheque account balances and demand deposits can be withdrawn or liquidated at no notice, which is a risk to the level of NII should the option inherent in the products be exercised.

Gap and net interest income

We noted earlier that gap is a measure of the difference in interest-rate sensitivity of assets and liabilities that revalue at a particular date, expressed as a cash value. Put simply it is:

$$Gap = A_{ir} - L_{ir} \tag{6.1}$$

where A_{ir} and L_{ir} are the interest-rate sensitive assets and interest-rate-sensitive liabilities. Where $A_{ir} > L_{ir}$ the banking book is described as being *positively gapped*, and when $A_{ir} < L_{ir}$ the book is said to be *negatively gapped.* The change in NII is given by:

$$\Delta NII = Gap \times \Delta r \tag{6.2}$$

where r is the relevant interest rate used for valuation. The NII of a bank that is positively gapped will increase as interest rates rise, and will decrease as rates decline. This describes a banking book that is asset sensitive; the opposite, when a book is negatively gapped, is known as liability sensitive. The NII of a negatively gapped book will increase when interest rates decline. The value of a book with zero gap is immune to changes in the level of interest rates. The shape of the banking book at any one time is a function of customer demand, the treasury manager's operating strategy, and view of future interest rates.

Gap analysis is used to measure the difference between interest-rate-sensitive assets and liabilities, over specified time periods. Another term for this analysis is *periodic gap*, and the common expression for each time period is maturity *bucket*. For a commercial bank the typical maturity buckets are:

- 0–3 months;
- 3–12 months;
- 1–5 years;
- > 5 years.

Another common approach is to group assets and liabilities by the buckets or grid points of the *Riskmetrics* VaR methodology (see Chapter 17). Any combination of time periods may be used, however. For instance, certain US commercial banks place assets, liabilities and off-balance sheet items in terms of *known maturities*, *judgemental maturities* and *market-driven maturities*. These are defined as:

- *known maturities*: fixed-rate loans and CDs;
- *judgemental maturities*: passbook savings accounts, demand deposits, credit cards, non-performing loans;
- *market-driven maturities*: option-based instruments such as mortgages, and other interest-rate sensitive assets.

The other key measure is *cumulative gap*, defined as the sum of the individual gaps up to one-year maturity. Banks traditionally use the cumulative gap to estimate the impact of a change in interest rates on NII.

Assumptions of gap analysis

A number of assumptions are made when using gap analysis, assumptions that may not reflect reality in practice. These include:

- the key assumption that interest rate changes manifest themselves as a parallel shift in the yield curve; in practice, changes do not occur as a parallel shift, giving rise to basis risk between short-term and long-term assets;
- the expectation that contractual repayment schedules are met; if there is a fall in interest rates, prepayments of loans by borrowers who wish to refinance their loans at lower rates will have an impact on NII. Certain assets and liabilities have option features that are exercised as interest rates change, such as letters of credit and variable rate deposits; early repayment will impact a bank's cash flow;
- that repricing of assets and liabilities takes place in the mid-point of the time bucket;
- the expectation that all loan payments will occur on schedule; in practice, certain borrowers will repay the loan earlier.

Recognised weaknesses of the gap approach include:

- no incorporation of future growth, or changes in the asset–liability mix;
- no consideration of the time value of money;
- arbitrary setting of time periods.

Limitations notwithstanding, gap analysis is used extensively. Gup and Brooks (1993, pp. 59) state the following reasons for the continued popularity of gap analysis:

- it was the first approach introduced to handle interest-rate risk, and provides reasonable accuracy;
- the data required to perform the analysis are already compiled for the purposes of regulatory reporting;
- the gaps can be calculated using simple spreadsheet software;
- it is easier (and cheaper) to implement than more sophisticated techniques;
- it is straightforward to demonstrate and explain to senior management and shareholders.

Although there are more sophisticated methods available, gap analysis remains in widespread use.

The ALM desk

The ALM desk or unit is a specialised business unit that fulfils a range of functions. Its precise remit is a function of the type of the activities of the financial institution that it is a part of. Let us consider the main types of activities that are carried out.

If an ALM unit has a profit target of zero, it will act as a cost centre with a responsibility to minimise operating costs. This would be consistent with a strategy that emphasises commercial banking as the core business of the firm, and where ALM policy is concerned purely with hedging interest-rate and liquidity risk.

The next level is where the ALM unit is responsible for minimising the cost of funding. That would allow the unit to maintain an element of exposure to interest-rate risk, depending on the view that was held as to the future level of interest rates. As we noted above, the core banking activity generates either an excess or shortage of funds. To hedge away all of the excess or shortage, while removing interest-rate exposure, has an opportunity cost associated with it since it eliminates any potential gain that might arise from movements in market rates. Of course, without a complete hedge, there is an exposure to interest-rate risk. The ALM desk is responsible for monitoring and managing this risk, and of course is credited with any cost savings in the cost of funds that arise from the exposure. The saving may be measured as the difference between the funding costs of a full hedging policy and the actual policy that the ALM desk adopts. Under this policy, interest-rate risk limits are set which the ALM desk ensures the bank's operations do not breach.

The final stage of development is to turn the ALM unit into a profit centre, with responsibility for optimising the funding policy within specified limits. The limits may be set as *gap* limits, VaR limits or by another measure, such as level of earnings volatility. Under this scenario the ALM desk is responsible for managing all financial risk.

The final development of the ALM function has resulted in it taking on a more active role. The previous paragraphs described the three stages of development that ALM has undergone, although all three versions are part of the "traditional" approach. Practitioners are now beginning to think of ALM as extending beyond the risk management field, and responsible for adding value to the net worth of the bank, through proactive positioning of the book and hence, the balance sheet. That is, in addition to the traditional function of managing liquidity risk and interest-rate risk, ALM should be concerned with managing the regulatory capital of the bank and with actively positioning the balance sheet to maximise profit. The latest developments mean that the there are now financial institutions that run a much more sophisticated ALM operation than that associated with a traditional banking book.

Let us review now the traditional and developed elements of an ALM function.

Traditional ALM

Generally, a bank's ALM function has in the past been concerned with managing the risk associated with the banking book. This does not mean that this function is now obsolete, rather that additional functions have now been added to the ALM role. There are a large number of financial institutions that adopt the traditional approach; indeed, the nature of their operations would not lend themselves to anything more. We can summarise the role of the traditional ALM desk as follows:

Interest-rate risk management. This is the interest-rate risk arising from the operation of the banking book. It includes net interest income sensitivity analysis, typified by maturity gap and duration gap analysis, and the sensitivity of the book to parallel changes in the yield curve. The ALM desk will monitor the exposure and position the book in accordance with the limits as well as its market view. Smaller banks, or subsidiaries of banks that are based overseas, often run no interest-rate risk; that is, there is no short gap in their book. Otherwise the ALM desk is responsible for hedging the interest-rate risk or positioning the book in accordance with its view.

Liquidity and funding management. There are regulatory requirements that dictate the proportion of banking assets that must be held as short-term instruments. The liquidity book in a bank is responsible for running the portfolio of short-term instruments. The exact make-up of the book is however the responsibility of the ALM desk, and will be a function of the desk's view of market interest rates, as well as its opinion on the relative value of one asset over another. For example, it may decide to move some assets into short-dated government bonds, above what it normally holds, at the expense of high-quality CDs, or vice-versa.

Reporting on hedging of risks. The ALM fulfils a senior management information function by reporting on a regular basis on the extent of the bank's risk exposure. This may be in the form of a weekly hardcopy report, or via some other medium.

Setting up risk limits. The ALM unit will set limits, implement them and enforce them, although it is common for an independent "middle office" risk function to monitor compliance with limits.

Capital requirement reporting. This function involves the compilation of reports on capital usage and position limits as a percentage of capital allowed, and the reporting to regulatory authorities.

All financial institutions will carry out the activities described above.

EXAMPLE 6.2 Gap analysis

Maturity gap analysis measures the cash difference or *gap* between the absolute values of the assets and liabilities that are sensitive to movements in interest rates. Therefore the analysis measures the relative interest-rate sensitivities of the assets and liabilities, and thus determines the risk profile of the bank with respect to changes in rates. The *gap ratio* is given as (6.3):

$$Gap\ ratio = \frac{Interest\text{-}rate\ sensitive\ assets}{Interest\text{-}rate\ sensitive\ liabilities} \quad (6.3)$$

and measures whether there are more interest-rate sensitive assets than liabilities. A gap ratio higher than one for example, indicates that a rise in interest rates will increase the NPV of the book, thus raising the return on assets at a rate higher than the rise in the cost of funding. This also results in a higher income spread. A gap ratio lower than one indicates a rising funding cost. *Duration gap* analysis measures the impact on the net worth of the bank due to changes in interest rates by focusing on changes in market value of either assets or liabilities. This is because duration measures the percentage change in the market value of a single security for a 1% change in the underlying yield of the security (strictly speaking, this is *modified duration* but the term for the original "duration" is now almost universally used to refer to modified duration). The duration gap is defined as (6.4):

$$Duration\ gap = Duration\ of\ assets - w(Duration\ of\ liabilities) \quad (6.4)$$

where w is the percentage of assets funded by liabilities. Hence, the duration gap measures the effects of the change in the net worth of the bank. A higher duration gap indicates a higher interest rate exposure. As duration only measures the effects of a linear change in the interest rate – that is, a parallel shift yield curve change – banks with portfolios that include a significant amount of instruments with elements of optionality, such as callable bonds, asset-backed securities and convertibles, also use the *convexity* measure of risk exposure to adjust for the inaccuracies that arise in duration over large yield changes.

Developments in ALM

A greater number of financial institutions are enhancing their risk management function by adding to the responsibilities of the ALM function. These have included enhancing the role of the head of Treasury and the ALCO, using other risk exposure measures such as the option-adjusted spread and VaR, and integrating the traditional interest-rate risk management with credit risk and operational risk. The increasing use of credit derivatives has facilitated this integrated approach to risk management.

The additional roles of the ALM desk can include:

- using the VaR tool to assess risk exposure;
- integrating market risk and credit risk;
- using new *risk-adjusted* measures of return;
- optimising portfolio return;
- proactively managing the balance sheet; this includes giving direction on the securitisation of assets (removing them from the balance sheet), hedging credit exposure using credit derivatives, and actively enhancing returns from the liquidity book, such as entering into stock lending and repo.

An expanded ALM function will by definition expand the role of the Treasury function and the ALCO. This may see the Treasury function becoming active "portfolio managers" of the bank's book. The ALCO, traditionally composed of risk managers from across the bank as well as the senior member of the ALM desk or liquidity desk, is responsible for assisting the head of Treasury and the Finance Director in the risk management process. In order to fulfil the new enhanced function the Treasurer will require a more strategic approach to his or her function, as many of the decisions with running the bank's entire portfolio will be closely connected with the overall direction that the bank wishes to take. These are Board-level decisions.

Liquidity and interest-rate risk

The liquidity gap

Liquidity risk arises because a bank's portfolio will consist of assets and liabilities with different sizes and maturities. When assets are greater than resources from operations, a funding gap will exist that needs to be sourced in the wholesale market. When the opposite occurs, the excess resources must be invested in the market. The differences between the assets and liabilities is called the *liquidity gap*. For example, if a bank has long-term commitments that have arisen from its dealings and its resources are exceeded by these commitments, and have a shorter maturity, there is both an immediate and a future deficit. The liquidity risk for the bank is that, at any time, there are not enough resources, or funds available in the market, to balance the assets.

Liquidity management has several objectives; possibly the most important is to ensure that deficits can be funded under all foreseen circumstances, and without incurring prohibitive costs. In addition there are regulatory requirements that force a bank to operate certain limits, and state that short-term assets be in excess of short-run liabilities, in order to provide a safety net of highly liquid assets. Liquidity management is also concerned with funding deficits and investing surpluses, with managing and growing the balance sheet, and with ensuring that the bank operates within regulatory and in-house limits. In this section we review the main issues concerned with liquidity and interest-rate risk.

The liquidity gap is the difference, at all future dates, between assets and liabilities of the banking portfolio. Gaps generate liquidity risk. When liabilities exceed assets, there is an excess of funds. An excess does not of course generate liquidity risk, but it does generate interest-rate risk, because the present value of the book is sensitive to changes in market rates. When assets exceed liabilities, there is a funding deficit and the bank has long-term commitments that are not currently funded by existing operations. The liquidity risk is that the bank requires funds at a future date to match the assets. The bank is able to remove any liquidity risk by locking in maturities, but of course there is a cost involved as it will be dealing at longer maturities.[7]

Gap risk and limits

Liquidity gaps are measured by taking the difference between outstanding balances of assets and liabilities over time. At any point a positive gap between assets and liabilities is equivalent to a deficit, and this is measured as a cash amount. The *marginal gap* is the difference between the changes of assets and liabilities over a given period. A positive marginal gap means that the variation of value of assets exceeds the variation of value of liabilities. As new assets and liabilities are added over time, as part of the ordinary course of business, the gap profile changes.

The gap profile is tabulated or charted (or both) during and at the end of each day as a primary measure of risk. For illustration, a tabulated gap report is shown in Table 6.2 on page 266 and is an actual example from a UK banking institution. It shows the assets and liabilities grouped into maturity *buckets* and the net position for each bucket. It is a snapshot today of the exposure, and hence funding requirement of the bank for future maturity periods.

[7] This assumes a conventional upward-sloping yield curve.

	Time periods											
	Total		0–6 months		6–12 months		1–3 years		3–7 years		7+ years	
Assets	40,533	6.17%	28,636	6.08%	3,801	6.12%	4,563	6.75%	2,879	6.58%	654	4.47%
Liabilities	40,533	4.31%	30,733	4.04%	3,234	4.61%	3,005	6.29%	2,048	6.54%	1,513	2.21%
Net cumulative positions	0	1.86%	(2,097)		567		1,558		831		(859)	
Margin on total assets:			2.58%									
Average margin on total assets:			2.53%									

Table 6.2 Example gap profile: UK bank

Table 6.2 is very much a summary report, because the maturity gaps are very wide. For risk management purposes the buckets would be much narrower; for instance, the period between zero and 12 months might be split into 12 different maturity buckets. An example of a more detailed gap report is shown in Table 6.3 on pages 268–9, which is from another UK banking institution. Note that the overall net position is zero, because this is a balance sheet and therefore, not surprisingly, it balances. However, along the maturity buckets or grid points there are net positions which are the gaps that need to be managed.

Limits on a banking book can be set in terms of gap limits. For example, a bank may set a six-month gap limit of £10 million. The net position of assets and maturities expiring in six months' time could then not exceed £10 million. An example of a gap limit report is shown at Figure 6.2 on page 270, with the actual net gap positions shown against the gap limits for each maturity. Again this is an actual limit report from a UK banking institution.

The maturity gap can be charted to provide an illustration of net exposure, and an example is shown in Figure 6.3 on page 270, from yet another UK banking institution. In some firms' reports both the assets and the liabilities are shown for each maturity point, but in our example only the net position is shown. This net position is the gap exposure for that maturity point. A second example, used by the overseas subsidiary of a Middle Eastern commercial bank, which has no funding lines in the interbank market and so does not run short positions, is shown in Figure 6.4 on page 271, while the gap report for a UK high-street bank is shown in Figure 6.5 on page 271. Note the large short gap under the maturity labelled "non-int"; this stands for *non-interest bearing liabilities* and represents the balance of current accounts (cheque or "checking" accounts), which are funds that attract no interest and are in theory very short-dated (because they are demand deposits, so may be called at instant notice).

ASSETS	Total (£m)	Up to 1 month	1–3 months	3–6 months	6 months to 1 year
Cash & interbank loans	2,156.82	1,484.73	219.36	448.90	3.84
CDs purchased	1,271.49	58.77	132.99	210.26	776.50
FRNs purchased	936.03	245.62	586.60	12.68	26.13
Bank bills	314.35	104.09	178.36	31.90	0.00
Other loans	13.00	0.00	1.00	0.00	0.00
Debt securities/gilts	859.45	0.00	25.98	7.58	60.05
Fixed-rate mortgages	4,180.89	97.72	177.37	143.13	964.98
Variable & capped rate mortgages	14,850.49	14,850.49	0.00	0.00	0.00
Commercial loans	271.77	96.62	96.22	56.52	0.86
Unsecured lending and leasing	3,720.13	272.13	1,105.20	360.03	507.69
Other assets	665.53	357.72	0.00	18.77	5.00
	29,239.95	17,567.91	2,523.06	1,289.77	2,345.05
Swaps	9,993.28	3,707.34	1,462.32	1,735.59	1,060.61
FRAs	425.00	0.00	50.00	0.00	220.00
Futures	875.00	0.00	300.00	0.00	175.00
TOTAL	40,533.24	21,275.24	4,335.38	3,025.36	3,800.66
LIABILITIES (£m)					
Bank deposits	3,993.45	2,553.85	850.45	233.03	329.06
CDs issued	1,431.42	375.96	506.76	154.70	309.50
CP & Euro	508.46	271.82	128.42	108.21	0.00
Subordinated debt	275.00	0.00	0.00	0.00	0.00
Eurobonds + other	2,582.24	768.75	1,231.29	121.94	53.86
Customer deposits	17,267.55	15,493.65	953.60	311.70	340.50
Other liabilities (incl capital/reserves)	3,181.83	1,336.83	0.00	0.00	741.72
	29,239.96	20,800.86	3,670.52	929.58	1,774.64
Swaps	9,993.28	1,754.70	1,657.59	1,399.75	1,254.24
FRAs	425.00	0.00	150.00	70.00	55.00
Futures	875.00	0.00	0.00	300.00	150.00
TOTAL	40,533.24	22,555.56	5,478.11	2,699.33	3,233.89
Net Positions	0.00	–1,351.09	–1,234.54	265.58	583.48

1–2 years	2–3 years	3–4 years	4–5 years	5–6 years	6–7 years	7–8 years	8–9 years	9–10 years	10+ years
0.00	0.00	0.00	0.00	0.00	0.00	0.00	0.00	0.00	0.00
92.96	0.00	0.00	0.00	0.00	0.00	0.00	0.00	0.00	0.00
45.48	0.00	0.00	19.52	0.00	0.00	0.00	0.00	0.00	0.00
0.00	0.00	0.00	0.00	0.00	0.00	0.00	0.00	0.00	0.00
7.00	0.00	1.00	0.00	0.00	2.00	2.00	0.00	0.00	0.00
439.06	199.48	26.81	100.50	0.00	0.00	0.00	0.00	0.00	0.00
1,452.91	181.86	661.36	450.42	22.78	4.30	3.65	3.10	2.63	14.67
0.00	0.00	0.00	0.00	0.00	0.00	0.00	0.00	0.00	0.00
2.16	1.12	3.64	8.85	1.06	0.16	0.17	0.16	4.23	0.00
694.86	400.84	195.19	79.98	25.45	14.06	10.03	10.44	10.82	33.42
0.00	0.00	0.00	0.00	0.00	0.00	0.00	0.00	0.00	284.03
2,734.43	783.31	888.00	659.26	49.28	20.53	15.85	13.71	17.68	332.12
344.00	146.50	537.60	649.00	70.00	5.32	200.00	75.00	0.00	0.00
5.00	150.00	0.00	0.00	0.00	0.00	0.00	0.00	0.00	0.00
400.00	0.00	0.00	0.00	0.00	0.00	0.00	0.00	0.00	0.00
3,483.43	1,079.81	1,425.60	1,308.26	119.28	25.84	215.85	88.71	17.68	332.12
21.07	1.00	0.00	5.00	0.00	0.00	0.00	0.00	0.00	0.00
60.00	20.00	3.50	1.00	0.00	0.00	0.00	0.00	0.00	0.00
0.00	0.00	0.00	0.00	0.00	0.00	0.00	0.00	0.00	0.00
0.00	0.00	0.00	0.00	0.00	0.00	200.00	75.00	0.00	0.00
9.77	13.16	150.43	150.53	0.00	7.51	0.00	0.00	0.00	75.00
129.10	6.60	24.90	0.00	7.50	0.00	0.00	0.00	0.00	0.00
0.00	0.00	0.00	0.00	0.00	0.00	0.00	0.00	0.00	1,103.28
219.93	40.76	178.83	156.53	7.50	7.51	200.00	75.00	0.00	1,178.28
1,887.97	281.44	905.06	770.52	15.76	6.48	7.27	8.13	13.06	31.30
150.00	0.00	0.00	0.00	0.00	0.00	0.00	0.00	0.00	0.00
425.00	0.00	0.00	0.00	0.00	0.00	0.00	0.00	0.00	0.00
2,682.90	322.20	1,083.90	927.05	23.26	13.99	207.27	83.13	13.06	1,209.58
929.10	803.46	341.70	404.88	104.28	11.85	8.58	5.57	4.62	-877.45

Table 6.3 Detailed gap profile: UK bank

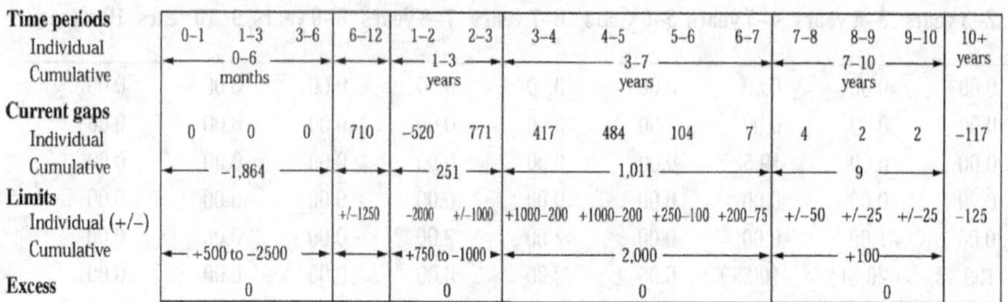

Time periods														
Individual	0–1	1–3	3–6	6–12	1–2	2–3	3–4	4–5	5–6	6–7	7–8	8–9	9–10	10+ years
Cumulative	0–6 months				1–3 years		3–7 years				7–10 years			
Current gaps														
Individual	0	0	0	710	−520	771	417	484	104	7	4	2	2	−117
Cumulative	−1,864				251		1,011				9			
Limits														
Individual (+/−)				+/-1250	-2000	+/-1000	+1000-200	+1000-200	+250-100	+200-75	+/-50	+/-25	+/-25	-125
Cumulative	+500 to −2500				+750 to −1000		2,000				+100			
Excess	0				0		0				0			

Figure 6.2 Gap limit report

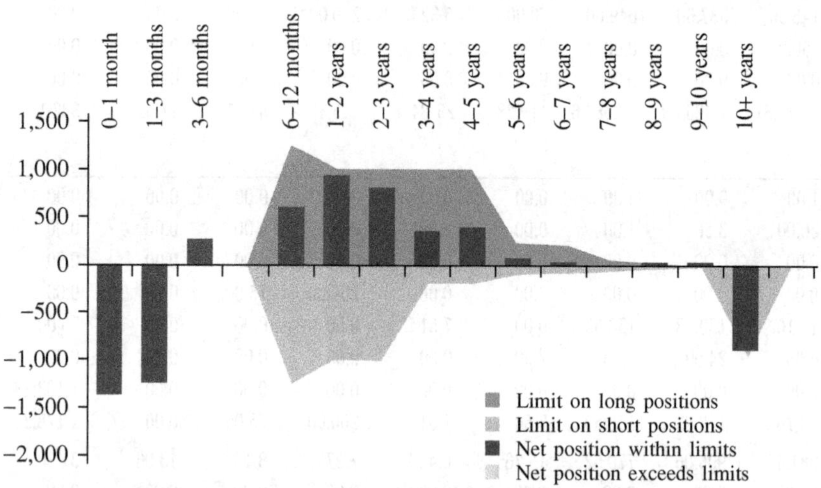

Figure 6.3 Gap maturity profile in graphical form

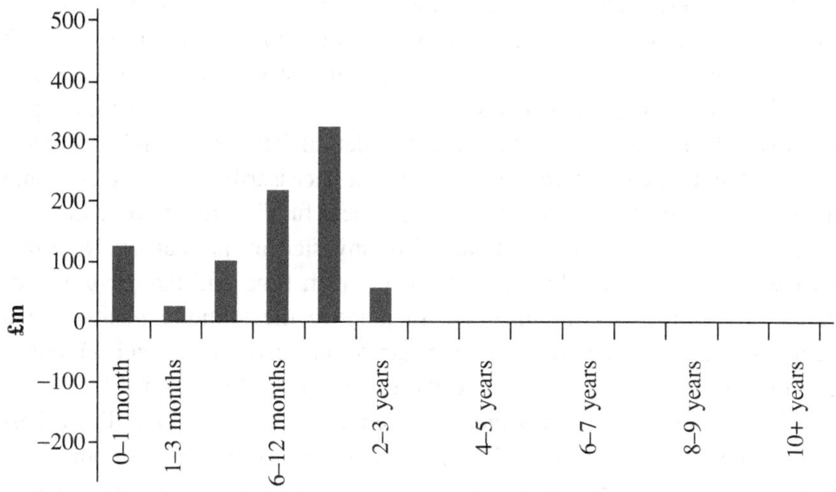

Figure 6.4 Gap maturity profile, bank with no short funding allowed

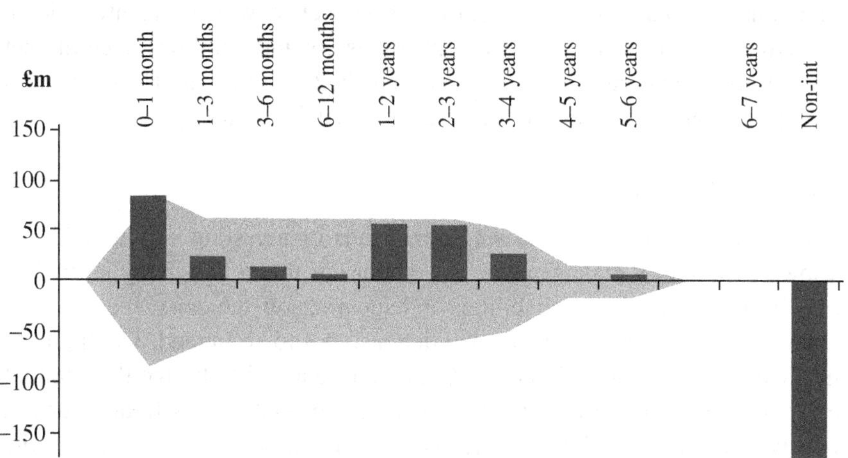

Figure 6.5 Gap maturity profile, UK high-street bank

Gaps represent cumulative funding required at all dates. The cumulative funding is not necessarily identical to the new funding required at each period, because the debt issued in previous periods is not necessarily amortised at subsequent periods. The new funding between, for example, months 3 and 4 is not the accumulated deficit between months 2 and 4 because the debt contracted at month 3 is not necessarily amortised at month 4. Marginal gaps may be identified as the new funding required or the new excess funds of the period that should be invested in the market. Note that all the reports are snapshots at a fixed point in time and the picture is of course a continuously moving one. In practice the liquidity position of a bank cannot be characterised by one gap at any given date, and the entire gap profile must be used to gauge the extent of the book's profile.

The liquidity book may decide to match its assets with its liabilities. This is known as *cash matching* and occurs when the time profiles of both assets and liabilities are identical. By following such a course the bank can lock in the spread between its funding rate and the rate at which it lends cash, and run a guaranteed profit. Under cash matching, the liquidity gaps will be zero. Matching the profile of both legs of the book is done at the overall level; that is, cash matching does not mean that deposits should always match loans. This would be difficult as both result from customer demand, although an individual purchase of, say, a CD can be matched with an identical loan. Nevertheless, the bank can elect to match assets and liabilities once the net position is known, and keep the book matched at all times. However, it is highly unusual for a bank to adopt a cash matching strategy.

Liquidity management

The continuous process of raising new funds or investing surplus funds is known as liquidity management. If we consider that a gap today is funded, thus balancing assets and liabilities and squaring-off the book, the next day a new deficit or surplus is generated that also has to be funded. The liquidity management decision must cover the amount required to bridge the gap that exists the following day, as well as position the book across future dates in line with the bank's view on interest rates. Usually in order to define the maturity structure of debt a target profile of resources is defined. This may be done in several ways. If the objective of ALM is to replicate the asset profile with resources, the new funding should contribute to bringing the resources profile closer to that of the assets; that is, more of a matched book looking forward. This is the lowest risk option. Another target profile may be imposed on the bank by liquidity constraints. This may arise if, for example the bank has a limit on borrowing lines in the market so that it could not raise a certain amount each week or month. For instance, if the maximum that could be raised in one week by a bank is £10 million, the maximum period liquidity gap is constrained by that limit. The ALM desk will manage the book in line with the target profile that has been adopted, which requires it to try to reach the required profile over a given time horizon.

Figure 6.6 is a liquidity analysis for a UK bank, showing the maturity of funding going forward and where liquidity requirements arise.

Managing the banking book's liquidity is a dynamic process, as loans and deposits are known at any given point, but new business will be taking place continuously and the profile of the book looking forward must be continuously re-balanced to keep it within the target profile. There are several factors that influence this dynamic process, the most important of which are reviewed below.

Demand deposits

Deposits placed on demand at the bank, such as current accounts (known in the United States as "checking accounts") have no stated maturity and are available on demand at the bank. Technically they are referred to as "non-interest-bearing liabilities" because the bank pays no or very low rates of interest on them, so they are effectively free funds. The balance of these funds can increase or decrease throughout the day without any warning, although in practice the balance is quite stable. There are a number of ways that a bank can choose to deal with these balances. These are:

- to group all outstanding balances into one maturity bucket at a future date that is the preferred time horizon of the bank, or a date beyond this. This would then exclude them from the gap profile. Although this is considered unrealistic because it excludes the current account balances from the gap profile, it is nevertheless a fairly common approach;
- to rely on an assumed rate of amortisation for the balances, say 5% or 10% each year;
- to divide deposits into stable and unstable balances, of which the core deposits are set as a permanent balance. The amount of the core balance is set by the bank based on a study of the total balance volatility pattern over time. The excess over the core balance is then viewed as very short-term debt. This method is reasonably close to reality as it is based on historical observations;

- to make projections based on observable variables that are correlated with the outstanding balances of deposits. For instance, such variables could be based on the level of economic growth plus an error factor based on the short-term fluctuations in the growth pattern.

Pre-set contingencies

A bank will have committed lines of credit, the utilisation of which depends on customer demand. Contingencies generate outflows of funds that are by definition uncertain, as they are contingent upon some event; for example, the willingness of the borrower to use a committed line of credit. The usual way for a bank to deal with these unforeseen fluctuations is to use statistical data based on past observation to project a future level of activity.

Prepayment options of existing assets

Where the maturity schedule is stated in the terms of a loan, it may still be subject to uncertainty because of prepayment options. This is similar to the prepayment risk associated with a mortgage-backed bond. An element of prepayment risk renders the actual maturity profile of a loan book to be uncertain; banks often calculate an "effective maturity schedule" based on prepayment statistics instead of the theoretical schedule. There are also a range of prepayment models that may be used, the simplest of which use constant prepayment ratios to assess the average life of the portfolio. The more sophisticated models incorporate more parameters, such as one that bases the prepayment rate on the interest rate differential between the loan rate and the current market rate, or the time elapsed since the loan was taken out.

Interest cash flows

Assets and liabilities generate interest cash inflows and outflows, as well as the amortisation of principal. The interest payments must be included in the gap profile as well.

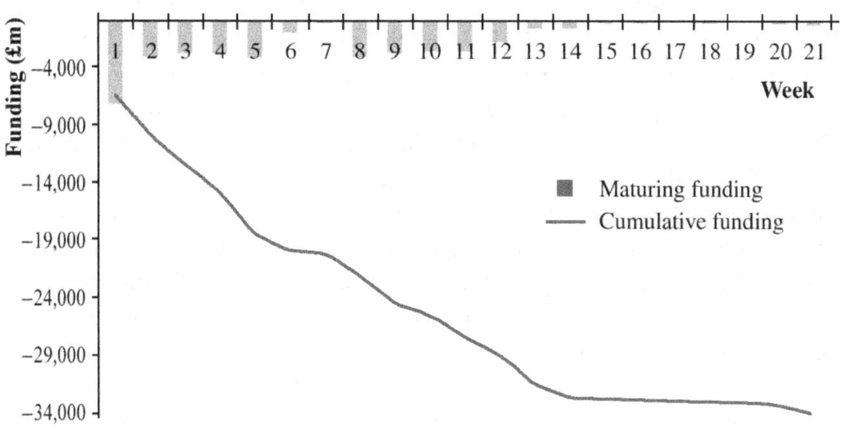

Figure 6.6 Liquidity analysis – example of UK bank profile of maturity of funding

Interest-rate gap

The interest-rate gap is the standard measure of the exposure of the banking book to interest-rate risk. The interest-rate gap for a given period is defined as the difference between fixed-rate assets and fixed-rate liabilities. It can also be calculated as the difference between interest-rate sensitive assets and interest-rate liabilities. Both differences are identical in value when total assets are equal to total liabilities, but will differ when the balance sheet is not balanced. This only occurs intra-day, when, for example, a short position has not been funded yet. The general market practice is to calculate interest-rate gap as the difference between assets and liabilities. The gap is defined in terms of the maturity period that has been specified for it.

The convention for calculating gaps is important for interpretation. The "fixed-rate" gap is the opposite of the "variable-rate" gap when assets and liabilities are equal. They differ when assets and liabilities do not match and there are many reference rates. When there is a deficit, the "fixed-rate gap" is consistent with the assumption that the gap will be funded through liabilities for which the rate is unknown. This funding is then a variable-rate liability and is the bank's risk, unless the rate has been locked in beforehand. The same assumption applies when the banks run a cash surplus position, and the interest rate for any period in the future is unknown. The gap position at a given time bucket is sensitive to the interest rate that applies to that period.

The gap is calculated for each discrete time bucket, so there is a net exposure for, say, 0–1 month, 1–3 months and so on. Loans and deposits do not, except at the time of being undertaken, have precise maturities like that, so they are "mapped" to a time bucket in terms of their relative weighting. For example, a £100 million deposit that matures in 20 days' time will have most of its balance mapped to the three-week time bucket, but a smaller amount will also be allocated to the two-week bucket. Interest-rate risk is measured as the change in present value of the deposit, at each grid point, given a 1 basis point change in the interest rate. So a £10 million one-month CD that was bought at 6.50% will have its present value move upwards if on the next day the one-month rate moves down by a basis point.

The net change in present value for a 1 basis point move is the key measure of interest-rate risk for a banking book and this is what is usually referred to as a "gap report", although strictly speaking it is not. The correct term for such a report is a "PVBP" or "DV01" report, which are acronyms for "present value of a basis point" and "dollar value of a 01 [1 basis point]" respectively. The calculation of interest-rate sensitivity assumes a *parallel shift* in the yield curve; that is, that every maturity point along the term structure moves by the same amount (here one basis point) and in the same direction. An example of a PVBP report is given in Table 6.4, split by different currency books, but with all values converted to sterling.

	1 day	1 week	1 month	2 months	3 months	6 months	12 months	2 years
GBP	8,395	6,431	9,927	8,856	(20,897)	(115,303)	(11,500)	(237,658)
USD	1,796	(903)	10,502	12,941	16,784	17,308	(13,998)	(18,768)
Euro	1,026	1,450	5,105	2,877	(24,433)	(24,864)	(17,980)	(9,675)
Total	11,217	6,978	25,534	24,674	(28,546)	(122,859)	(43,478)	(266,101)

	3 years	4 years	5 years	7 years	10 years	15 years	20 years	30 years
GBP	(349,876)	(349,654)	5,398	(5,015)	(25,334)	(1,765)	(31,243)	(50,980)
USD	(66,543)	(9,876)	(1,966)	237	2,320	(5,676)	(1,121)	0
Euro	(11,208)	(3,076)	1,365	1,122	3,354	(545)	(440)	(52)
Total	(427,627)	(362,606)	4,797	(3,656)	(19,660)	(7,986)	(32,804)	(51,032)

GBP total: (1,160,218); USD total: (56,963); Euro total: (75,974); Grand total: (1,293,155)
All figures in £.

Table 6.4 Banking book PVBP grid report

The basic concept in the gap report is the NPV of the banking book, which is introduced in Appendix 6.1. The PVBP report measures the difference between the market values of assets and liabilities in the banking book. To calculate NPV we require a discount rate, and it represents a *mark-to-market* of the book. The rates used are always the zero-coupon rates derived from the government bond yield curve, although some adjustment should be made to this to allow for individual instruments.

Gaps may be calculated as differences between outstanding balances at one given date, or as differences of variations of those balances over a time period. A gap number calculated from variations is known as a *margin gap*. The cumulative margin gaps over a period of time, plus the initial difference in assets and liabilities at the beginning of the period are identical to the gaps between assets and liabilities at the end of the period.

The interest-rate gap differs from the liquidity gap in a number of ways; note that:

- whereas for liquidity gap all assets and liabilities must be accounted for, only those that have a fixed rate are used for the interest-rate gap;
- the interest-rate gap cannot be calculated unless a period has been defined because of the fixed-rate/variable-rate distinction. The interest-rate gap is dependent on a maturity period and an original date.

The primary purpose in compiling the gap report is to determine the sensitivity of the interest margin to changes in interest rates. As we noted earlier the measurement of the gap is always "behind the curve" as it is a historical snapshot; the actual gap is a dynamic value as the banking book continually undertakes day-to-day business.

Portfolio modified duration gap

From Chapter 4 we know that modified duration measures the change in the market price of a financial instrument that results from a given change in market interest rates. The duration gap of a net portfolio value is a measure of the interest-rate sensitivity of a portfolio of financial instruments and is the difference between the weighted-average duration of assets and liabilities, adjusted for the net duration of any off-balance sheet instruments. Hence it measures the percentage change in the net portfolio value that is expected to occur if interest rates change by 1%.

The net portfolio value, given by the NPV of the book, is the market value of assets A minus the market value of the liabilities L, plus or minus the market value OBS of off-balance sheet instruments, shown by (6.5):

$$NPV = A - L \pm \text{OBS}. \qquad (6.5)$$

To calculate the duration gap of the NPV, we obtain the modified duration of each instrument in the portfolio and weight this by the ratio of its market value to the net value of the portfolio. This is done for assets, liabilities and off-balance sheet instruments. The modified duration of the portfolio is given by (6.6):

$$MD_{NPV} = MD_A - MD_l \pm MD_{OBS}. \qquad (6.6)$$

The modified duration of the NPV may be used to estimate the expected change in the market value of the portfolio for a given change in interest rates, shown by (6.7):

$$\Delta NPV = NPV' - MD_{NPV} \times \Delta r. \qquad (6.7)$$

It is often problematic to obtain an accurate value for the market value of every instrument in a banking book. In practice book values often are used to calculate the duration gap when market values are not available. This may result in inaccurate results when actual market values differ from book values by a material amount.

The other points to note about duration gap analysis are:

- the analysis uses modified duration to calculate the change in NPV and therefore provides an accurate estimate of price sensitivity of instruments for only small changes in interest rates. For a change in rates of more than, say, 50 basis points the sensitivity measure given by modified duration will be significantly in error;
- the duration gap analysis, like the maturity gap model, assumes that interest rates change in a parallel shift, which is clearly unrealistic.

As with the maturity gap analysis, the duration gap is favoured in ALM application because it is easily understood and summarises a banking book's interest-rate exposure in one convenient number.

Critique of the traditional approach

Traditionally, the main approach of ALM is concentrated on the interest sensitivity and NPV sensitivity of a bank's loan/deposit book. The usual interest sensitivity report is the maturity gap report, which we reviewed briefly earlier. The maturity gap report is not perfect, however, and can be said to have the following drawbacks:

- the repricing intervals chosen for gap analysis are ultimately arbitrary, and there may be significant mismatches within a repricing interval. For instance, a common repricing interval chosen is the one-year gap and the 1–3-year gap; there are (albeit extreme) circumstances when mismatches would go undetected by the model. Consider a banking book that is composed solely of liabilities that reprice in one month's time, and an equal cash value of assets that reprice in 11 months' time. The one-year gap of the book (assuming no other positions) would be zero, implying no risk to net interest income. In fact, under our scenario the net interest income is significantly at risk from a rise in interest rates;
- maturity gap models assume that interest rates change by a uniform magnitude and direction. For any given change in the general level of interest rates, however, it is more realistic for different maturity interest rates to change by different amounts, what is known as a non-parallel shift;
- maturity gap models assume that principal cash flows do not change when interest rates change. Therefore it is not possible effectively to incorporate the impact of options embedded in certain financial instruments. Instruments such as mortgage-backed bonds and convertibles do not fall accurately into a gap analysis, as only their first-order risk exposure is captured.

Notwithstanding these drawbacks, the gap model is widely used as it is easily understood in the commercial banking and mortgage industry, and its application does not require a knowledge of sophisticated financial modelling techniques.

The cost of funding

Banks can choose to set up their Treasury function as either a cost centre or a profit centre. Most of the discussion up to now has assumed a profit centre arrangement, with the Treasury desk also responsible for market-making of money market instruments and being expected to position the bank's ALM requirement and trade money markets to profit. Some institutions set the Treasury function up simply to arrange the firm's funding requirement, so that it is not expected to generate profit.

In such an arrangement, the question arises as what the Treasury desk should charge the firm's lines of business for their funds. Consider a broker–dealer firm that operated the following lines of business:

- a corporate bond market-making desk;
- an equity derivatives trading desk;
- an investment portfolio that holds ABS, MBS and CDO securities for the medium term;
- a business that offers structured derivatives products, on a leveraged basis, to clients that wish to invest in hedge fund of funds or other alternative assets.

Each of these lines of business will have a different funding requirement; for example, the market-making desk would expect to have a frequent turnover of its portfolio and so its liquidity profile would be fairly short-dated. It could be funded using short-term borrowing, no more than one-week to one-month, with much funding on an overnight to one-week basis. The client-focused business would have a longer-dated asset profile, and so should be funded using a mixture of short-, medium- and long-dated funds. Assuming a positive-sloping yield curve, the term structure effect means that the client-focused business would have a higher cost of funds. However, the Treasury desk would not fund each desk separately (it could, but that would be inefficient and wasteful of resources). Hence, what charge should be made to the desks for their funds?

One option is for banks to use a weighted-average cost (WAC or WACC) of funds, sometimes called a "blended" or "pooled" rate, and this rate is passed on to the whole firm.

The cost of borrowing

There are two approaches with regard to the transfer price for loans. The first approach refers to existing assets and liabilities, and charges a cost for each loan as a proportion of the total. The second, and more common approach, is to define an optimum funding solution and use this as the cost of funds. In practice this will be the blended rate.

Using the existing resources has the appeal of simplicity. However, it raises the problems we encountered at the start of this section: each type of resource has a different cost. We could define a maturity term for all assets and match each term loan to assets of identical maturity. But this is not effective in practice. For instance, if an asset can be identified that has a precise maturity profile, then one can fund it to matching dates, either with one loan or a set of loans that all roll off in order until the final maturity date. But to do this for every asset would be impractical.

Hence a "weighted-average cost of capital" (WACC) is used.

The blended cost of funds

For fixed-rate loans, the cost of funds is explicit, but when more than one loan is taken out, the funding cost will depend on the combination of amounts borrowed and their respective maturity dates. For instance, consider a funding arrangement for USD100 that is comprised of:

- 40 borrowed for two years;
- 60 borrowed for one year.

The relevant interest rates are the zero-coupon interest rates for one- and two-year loans. The transfer price to use for the overall funding of 100 in the first 12 months is the average cost of the funds of these two loans. It is in fact given by the discount rate that would equate the present value of the future values of each loan equal to the original amount borrowed. The future value is of course the maturity amount, which is the original principal plus interest. To be strictly accurate, we assume that the loans are zero-coupon loans and the interest rates charged are zero-coupon interest rates.

The future cash flows on the above arrangement are:

- $60\ (1 + r_1)$ in year 1;
- $40\ (1 + r_2)^2$ in year 1 and year 2.

So the WACC is given by the rate rw such that:

$$100 = 60(1 + r_1)/(1 + rw) + 40(1 + r_2)^2 \ / \ (1 + rw)^2\ .$$

This discount rate will obviously lie somewhere between r_1 and r_2. A "back of the envelope" solution to this can be to calculate a lincar approximation of the formula above, namely:

$$100 = 60(1 + r_1 - rw) + 40(1 + 2r_2 - 2rw)$$

$$rw = (60 \times r_1 + 40 \times 2 \times r_2) / (60 + 2 \times 40).$$

The rate rw is the weighted average of the two rates r_1 and r_2, which we took to be the one- and two-year zero-coupon rates respectively. The weighting used refers to the size of the loan in proportion to the total and its maturity. As a rough rule of thumb, a one-year rate rolled over in a two-tear period would be weighed at twice the two-year one. If we imagine that r_1 is 4% and r_2 is 5%, then rw in this case will be nearer to r_2, because it is the longest-dated loan, but pulling in the other direction is the fact that the one-year loan in our example was for a larger sum.

In practice, even very large commercial banks and investment banks calculate their WACC as the daily interest payment on each loan outstanding, added together, and then divided by the total nominal amount of all loans.

We illustrate the concept of the WACC in practical fashion in Table 6.5 on pages 284–5. This shows a USD500 million funding requirement that has been arranged as three loans, namely:

- overnight USD200 million at 1.05%;
- one-week loan of USD200 million at 1.07%;
- three-month loan of USD100 million at 1.15%.

The spreadsheet shows the calculation of the WACC on a more scientific basis than the "back of the envelope" approach, as it takes into account the term structure effect of the loans (as we go further out along the term structure, we pay a higher rate of interest). However, the result is very close to the simple approach. The WACC for these three loans is shown to be 1.146%.

For students, repeat the spreadsheet in Table 6.6 on pages 286–7 with the formulas used in each cell shown instead of the value.

EXAMPLE 6.3 Position management

Starting the day with a flat position, a money market interbank desk transacts the following deals:

1. £100 million borrowing from 16/9/99 to 7/10/99 (3 weeks) at 6.375%;

2. £60 million borrowing from 16/9/99 to 16/10/99 (1 month) at 6.25%;
3. £110 million loan from 16/9/99 to 18/10/99 (32 days) at 6.45%.

The desk reviews its cash position and the implications for refunding and the interest-rate risk, bearing in mind the following:

- There is an internal overnight rollover limit of £40 million (net).
- The bank's economist feels more pessimistic about a rise in interest rates than most others in the market, and has recently given an internal seminar on the dangers of inflation in the United Kingdom as a result of recent increases in the level of average earnings.
- Today there are some important figures being released including inflation (CPI) data. If today's CPI figures exceed market expectations, the dealer expects a tightening of monetary policy by *at least* 0.50% almost immediately.
- A broker's estimate of daily market liquidity for the next few weeks is one of low shortage, with little central bank intervention required, and hence low volatilities and rates in the overnight rate.
- Brokers' screens indicate the following term repo rates:

O/N	6.350%–6.300%
1 week	6.390%–6.340%
2 week	6.400%–6.350%
1 month	6.410%–6.375%
2 month	6.500%–6.450%
3 month	6.670%–6.620%

- The indication for a 1v2 FRA is:

1v2 FRA	6.680%–6.630%

- The quote for an 11-day forward borrowing in three weeks' time (the "21v32 rate") is 6.50% bid. The book's exposure looks like this:

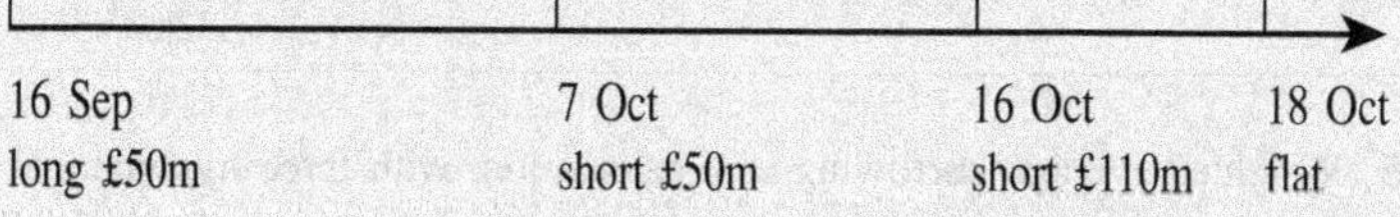

WACC calculation

Term (days)			Interest rate % pa (Libor fix)	0.002777778 Amount of interest (accrued) 1 o/n Amount of interest
1	o/n	200,000,000	1.05%	5,833.33
7	1wk	200,000,000	1.07%	5,944.44
90	3mth	100,000,000	1.15%	3,194.44
		500,000,000		1.078%
				14,972.22
			Period	1
				0.0030%
			Overall cost of funds – WAC measure	1.146%
			Total interest	1,432,055.56
				0.002777778
				Amount of interest (accrued)

SAME CALCULATION – as above – but using the effective cost of funds

Term (days)			WAC rate	1 o/n Amount of interest
1	o/n	200,000,000	1.1456%	6,364.69
7	1wk	200,000,000	1.1456%	6,364.69
90	3mth	100,000,000	1.1456%	3,182.35
		500,000,000		1.146%
				15,911.73
			Period	1
				0.0032%
			Overall cost of funds	1.146%
				1,432,055.56

Table 6.5 Weighted-average borrowing cost calculation, with three hypothetical loans

0.01944444	0.25			
7	90			
1wk	3mth			
–	–	1	0	0
41,611.11	–	1	1	0
22,361.11	287,500.00	1	1	1
1.097%	1.150%	500,000,000.00	300,000,000.00	100,000,000.00
63,972.22	287,500.00	366,444.44		
6	83			
0.0183%	0.2651%	0.2864%		

0.01944444	0.25			
7	90			
1wk	3mth			
–	–	1	0	0
44,552.84	–	1	1	0
22,276.42	286,411.11	1	1	1
1.146%	1.146%	500,000,000.00	300,000,000.00	100,000,000.00
66,829.26	286,411.11	369,152.10		
6	83			
0.0191%	0.2641%	0.2864%		

Cell	B	C	D	E	F	G	H
3					=F4/360	=G5/360	=H5/360
4					Amount of interest (accrued)		
5					1	7	90
6					o/n	1wk	3mth
7	Term (days)		Interest rate %pa	Amount of interest (Libor fix)			
8	1	o/n	200,000,000	1.05%	=$E8*(F$5/360)*$D8 *IF(F$5>$B8,0,1)	=$E8*(G$5/360)*$D8 *IF(G$5>$B8,0,1)	=$E8*(H$5/360)*$D8 *IF(H$5>$B8,0,1)
9	7	1wk	200,000,000	1.07%	=$E9*(F$5/360)*$D9 *IF(F$5>$B9,0,1)	=$E9*(G$5/360)*$D9 *IF(G$5>$B9,0,1)	=$E9*(H$5/360)*$D9 *IF(H$5>$B9,0,1)
10	90	3mth	100,000,000	1.15%	=$E10*(F$5/360)*$D10 *IF(F$5>$B10,0,1)	=$E10*(G$5/360)*$D10 *IF(G$5>$B10,0,1)	=$E10*(H$5/360)*$D10 *IF(H$5>$B10,0,1)
11							
12			=SUM(D8:D10)		=(SUM(F$8:F$10)/K12) *360/F$5	=(SUM(G$8:G$10)/L12) *360/G$5	=(SUM(H$8:H$10)/M12) *360/H$5
13					=SUM(F8:F10)	=SUM(G8:G10)	=SUM(H8:H10)
14				Period	=F5-E5	=G5-F5	=H5-G5
15							
16					=F12*F14/360	=G12*G14/360	=H12*H14/360
17							
18	Overall cost of funds – WAC measure				=I16*360/90		
19							
20				Total interest	=F18*90/360*D12		
21							
22					=F24/360	=G24/360	=H24/360
23					Amount of interest (accrued)		
24	**SAME CALCULATION – as above – but using the effective cost of funds**						
25					o/n	1wk	3mth
26	Term (days)			WAC rate	Amount of interest		
27	1	o/n	200,000,000	=$F$18	=$E27*(F$5/360)*$D27 *IF(F$5>$B27,0,1)	=$E27*(G$5/360)*$D27 *IF(G$5>$B27,0,1)	=$E27*(H$5/360)*$D27 *IF(H$5>$B27,0,1)
28	7	1wk	200,000,000	=$F$18	=$E28*(F$5/360)*$D28 *IF(F$5>$B28,0,1)	=$E28*(G$5/360)*$D28 *IF(G$5>$B28,0,1)	=$E28*(H$5/360)*$D28 *IF(H$5>$B28,0,1)
29	90	3mth	100,000,000	=$F$18	=$E29*(F$5/360)*$D29 *IF(F$5>$B29,0,1)	=$E29*(G$5/360)*$D29 *IF(G$5>$B29,0,1)	=$E29*(H$5/360)*$D29 *IF(H$5>$B29,0,1)
30							
31			500,000,000		=(SUM(F27:F29)/K31) *360/F$5	=(SUM(G27:G29)/L31) *360/G$5	=(SUM(H27:H29)/M31) *360/H$5
32					=SUM(F27:F29)	=SUM(G27:G29)	=SUM(H27:H29)
33				Period	=F24-E24	=G24-F24	=H24-G24
34							
35					=F31*F33/360	=G31*G33/360	=H31*H33/360
36							
37			Overall cost of funds		=I35*360/90		
38							
39					=F37*90/360*D31		

Table 6.6 WACC calculation showing Excel formula

I	J	K	L	M
		=IF(F8<>0,1,0)	=IF(G8<>0,1,0)	1
		=IF(F9<>0,1,0)	=IF(G9<>0,1,0)	1
		=IF(F10<>0,1,0)	=IF(G10<>0,1,0)	1
		=SUMPRODUCT (K8:K10,$D$8:$D$10)	=SUMPRODUCT (L8:L10,$D$8:$D$10)	=SUMPRODUCT (M8:M10,$D$8:$D$10)
=SUM(F13:H13)				
=SUM(F16:H16)				
		1	7	90
		1	1	1
		1	1	1
		1	1	1
		=SUMPRODUCT (K27:K29,$D$8:$D$10)	=SUMPRODUCT (L27:L29,$D$8:$D$10)	=SUMPRODUCT (M27:M29,$D$8:$D$10)
=SUM(F32:H32)				
=SUM(F35:H35)				

What courses of action are open to the desk, bearing in mind that the book needs to be squared off such that the position is flat each night?

Possible solutions

Investing early surplus

From a cash management point of view, the desk has a £50 million surplus from 16/9 up to 7/10. This needs to be invested. It may be able to negotiate a 6.31% loan with the market for an overnight term, or a 6.35% term desposit for one week to 6.38% for one month.

The overnight roll is the most flexible but offers a worse rate, and if the desk expects the overnight rate to remain both low and stable (due to forecasts of low market shortages), it may not opt for this course of action.

However, it may make sense from an interest-rate risk point of view. If the desk agrees with the bank's economist, it should be able to benefit from rolling at higher rates soon – possibly in the next three weeks. Therefore it may not want to lock in a term rate now, and the overnight roll would match this view. However, it exposes them to lower rates, if their view is wrong, which will limit the extent of the positive funding spread. The market itself appears neutral about rate changes in the next month, but appears to factor in a rise thereafter.

The forward "gap"

Looking forward, the book is currently on course to exceed the £40 million overnight position limit on 7/10, when the refunding requirement is £50 million. The situation gets worse on 16/10 (for two days) when the refunding requirement is £110 million. The desk needs to fix a term deal before those dates to carry it over until 18/10 when the funding position reverts to zero. A borrowing from 7/10 to 18/10 of £50 million will reduce the rollover requirement to within limit.

However, given that interest rates will rise, should the Treasury desk wait until the 7th to deal in the cash? Not if it has a firm view. It may end up paying as much as 6.91% or higher for the funding (after the 0.50% rate rise). So it would be better to transact now a forward starting repo to cover the period, thus locking in the benefits obtainable from today's yield curve. The market rate for a 21×32 day repo is quoted at 6.50%. This reflects the market's consensus that rates may rise in about a month's time. However, the desk's own expectation is of a larger rise, hence its own logic suggests trading in the forward loan. This strategy will pay dividends if their view is right, as it limits the extent of funding loss.

An alternative means of protecting the interest-rate risk alone is to *buy* a 1v2 month FRA for 6.68%. This does not exactly match the gap, but should act as an effective hedge. If there is a rate rise, the book gains from the FRA profit. Note that the cash position still needs to be squared off. Should the desk deal before or after the inflation announcement? That is, of course, down to it, but most dealers like, if at all possible, to sit tight ahead of releases of key economic data.

Generic ALM policy for different banks

The management of interest-rate risk is a fundamental ingredient of commercial banking. Bank shareholders require comfort that interest-rate risk is measured and managed in a satisfactory manner. A common approach to risk management involves the following:

- the preparation and adoption of a high-level interest-rate risk policy at managing board level; this sets general guidelines on the type and extent of risk exposure that can be taken on by the bank;
- setting limits on the risk exposure levels of the banking book; this can be by product type, desk, geographic area and so on, and will be along the maturity spectrum;
- actively measuring the level of interest-rate risk exposure at regular, specified intervals;
- reporting to senior management on general aspects of risk management, risk exposure levels, limit breaches and so on;
- monitoring of risk management policies and procedures by an independent "middle office" risk function.

The risk management approach adopted by banks will vary according to their specific markets and appetite for risk. Certain institutions will have their activities set out or proscribed for them under regulatory rules. For instance, building societies in the United Kingdom are prohibited from trading in certain instruments under the regulator's guidelines.[8] In this section we present, purely for the purposes of illustration, the ALM policies of three hypothetical banks, called Bank S, Bank M and Bank L. These are respectively, a small banking entity with assets of £500 million, a medium-sized bank with assets of £2.5 billion and a large bank with assets of £10 billion. The following serves to demonstrate the differing approaches that can be taken according to the environment that a financial institution operates in.

ALM policy for Bank S (assets = £500 million)

The aim of the ALM policy for Bank S is to provide guidelines on risk appetite, revenue targets and rates of return, as well as risk management policy. Areas that may be covered include capital ratios, liquidity, asset mix, rate-setting policy for loans and deposits, and investment guidelines for the banking portfolio. The key objectives should include:

- to maintain capital ratios at the planned minimum, and to ensure safety of the deposit base;
- to generate a satisfactory revenue stream, both for income purposes and to further protect the deposit base.

The responsibility for overseeing the operations of the bank to ensure that these objectives are achieved is lodged with the ALM Committee. This body monitors the volume and mix of the bank's assets and funding (liabilities), and ensures that this asset mix follows internal guidelines with regard to banking liquidity, capital adequacy, asset base growth targets, risk exposure and return on capital. The norm is for the committee to meet on a monthly basis; at a minimum the membership of the committee will include the finance director, head of Treasury and risk manager. For a bank the size of Bank S the ALM committee membership will possibly be extended to the chief executive, the head of the loans business and the chief operating officer.

As a matter of course the committee will wish to discuss and review the following on a regular basis:

- overall macroeconomic conditions;

[8] This is the UK Financial Services Authority, which was established as a "super regulator" for all financial market activities in 2000, through a merger of all the industry-specific regulatory authorities.

- financial results and key management ratios, such as share price analysis and rates of return on capital and equity;
- the bank's view on the likely direction of short-term interest rates;
- the current lending strategy, and suggestions for changes to this, as well as the current funding strategy;
- any anticipated changes to the volume and mix of the loan book, and that of the main sources of funding; in addition, the appropriateness or otherwise of alternative sources of funding;
- suggestions for any alteration to the bank's ALM policy;
- the maturity gap profile and anticipated and suggested changes to it.

The committee will also wish to consider the interest rates offered currently on loans and deposits, and whether these are still appropriate.

Interest-rate sensitivity is monitored and confirmed as lying within specified parameters; these parameters are regularly reviewed and adjusted if deemed necessary according to changes in the business cycle and economic conditions. Measured using the following ratio:

$$A_{ir} \; / \; L_{ir}$$

typical risk levels would be expected to lie between 90–120% for the maturity period 0–90 days, and between 80–110% for the maturity period over 90 days and less than 365 days.

Put simply, the objective of Bank S would be to remain within specified risk parameters at all times, and to maintain as consistent a level of earnings as possible (and one that is immune to changes in the stage of the business cycle).

ALM policy for Bank M (assets = £2.5 billion)

Bank M is our hypothetical "medium-sized" banking institution. Its ALM policy would be overseen by an ALCO. Typically, the following members of senior management would be expected to be members of the ALCO:

- deputy chief executive
- finance director
- head of retail banking
- head of corporate banking
- head of Treasury
- head of risk management
- head of internal audit

together with others such as product specialists who are called to attend as and when required. The finance director will often chair the meeting.

The primary responsibilities of the Bank M ALCO are detailed below.

Objectives

The ALCO is tasked with reviewing the bank's overall funding strategy. Minutes are taken at each meeting, and decisions taken are recorded on the minutes and circulated to attendees and designated key staff. ALCO members are responsible for undertaking regular reviews of the following:

- minutes of the previous meeting;
- the ratio of the interest-rate-sensitive assets to liabilities, gap reports, risk reports and the funding position;
- the bank's view on the expected level of interest rates, and how the book should be positioned with respect to this view; and related to this, the ALCO view on anticipated funding costs in the short- and medium-term;
- stress testing in the form of "what if?" scenarios, to check the effect on the Banking book of specified changes in market conditions; and the change in parameters that may be required if there is a change in market conditions or risk tolerance;
- the current interest rates for loans and deposits, to ensure that these are in accordance with the overall lending and funding strategy;
- the maturity distribution of the liquidity book (expected to be comprised of T-bills, CDs and very short-dated government bonds); the current liquidity position and the expected position in the short and medium term.

As the ALCO meets on a regular monthly basis, it may not be the case that every aspect of their responsibility is discussed at every meeting; the agenda is set by the chair of the meeting in consultation with committee members. The policies adopted by ALCO should be dynamic and flexible, and capable of adaptation to changes in operating conditions. Any changes will be made on agreement of committee members. Generally, any exceptions to agreed policy can only be with the agreement of the CEO and ALCO itself.

Interest-rate risk policy

The objective will be to keep earnings volatility resulting from an upward or downward move in interest rates to a minimum. To this end, at each ALCO meeting members will review risk and position reports and discuss these in the light of the risk policy. Generally, the six-month and 12-month A_{ir}/L_{ir} cumulative ratio will lie in the range of 90–110%. A significant move outside this range will most likely be subject to corrective action. The committee will also consider the results of various scenario analyses on the book, and if these tests indicate a potential earnings impact of greater than, say, 10%, instructions may be given to alter the shape and maturity profile of the book.

Liquidity policy

A primary responsibility of the ALCO is to ensure that an adequate level of liquidity is maintained at all times. We define liquidity as:

> ... the ability to meet anticipated and unanticipated operating cash needs, loan demand, and deposit withdrawals, without incurring a sustained negative impact on profitability.
>
> Gup and Brooks (1993), p. 238

Generally, a Bank M-type operation would expect to have a target level for loans to deposits of around 75–85%, and a loans to core deposits ratio of 85–95%. The loan/deposit ratio is reported to ALCO and reviewed on a monthly basis, and a reported figure significantly outside these ranges (say, by 5% or more) will be reviewed and asked to be adjusted to bring it back into line with ALCO policy.

ALM policy for Bank L (assets = £10 billion)

The management policy for ALM at a larger entity will build on that described for a medium-sized financial institution. If Bank L is a group company, the policy will cover the consolidated balance sheet as well as individual subsidiary balance sheets; the committee will provide direction on the management of assets and liabilities, and the off-balance sheet instruments used to manage interest-rate and credit risk. A well-functioning management process will be proactive and concentrate on direction in response to anticipated changes in operating conditions, rather than reactive responses to changes that have already taken place. The primary objectives will be to maximise shareholder value, with target returns on capital of 15–22%.

The responsibility for implementing and overseeing the ALM management policy will reside with the ALCO. The ALCO will establish the operating guidelines for ALM, and review these guidelines on a periodic basis. The committee will meet on a more frequent basis than would be the case for Bank M, usually on a fortnightly basis. As well as this, it will set policies governing liquidity and funding objectives, investment activities and interest-rate risk. It will also oversee the activities of the investment banking division. The head of the ALM desk will prepare the interest-rate risk sensitivity report and present it to the ALCO.

Interest-rate risk management

The ALCO will establish an interest-rate risk policy that sets direction on acceptable levels of interest-rate risk. This risk policy is designed to guide management in the evaluation of the impact of interest-rate risk on the bank's earnings. The extent of risk exposure is a function of the maturity profile of the balance sheet, as well as the frequency of repricing, the level of loan prepayments and funding costs. Managing interest-rate risk is, in effect, the adjustment of risk exposure upwards or downwards, which will be in response to ALCO's views on the future direction of interest rates. As part of the risk management process the committee will monitor the current risk exposure and duration gap, using rate sensitivity analysis and simulation modelling to assess whether the current level of risk is satisfactory.

Measuring interest-rate risk

Notwithstanding the widespread adoption of VaR as the key market risk measurement tool, funding books such as repo books continue to use the gap report as a key measure of interest-rate risk exposure. This enables ALCO to view the risk sensitivity along the maturity structure. Cumulative gap positions, and the ratio of assets revaluation to liabilities revaluation, are calculated and compared to earnings levels on the current asset/liability position. Generally, the 90-day, six-month and one-year gap positions are the most significant points along the term structure at which interest-rate risk exposure is calculated. The ratio of gap to earnings assets will be set at the ±15% to ±20% level.

As it is a traditional duration-based approach, gap reporting is a static measure that measures risk sensitivity at one specific point in time. It for this reason that banks combine a VaR measure as well, or only use VaR. We discuss the VaR measure in Chapter 17.

Simulation modelling

Simulation modelling is a procedure that measures the potential impact on the banking book, and hence earnings levels, of a user-specified change in interest rates and/or a change in the shape of the book itself. This process enables senior management to gauge the risk associated with particular strategies. Put simply the process is to:

- construct a "base" balance sheet and income statement as the starting point (this is derived from the current shape of the banking book, and any changes expected from current growth trends that have been projected forward);
- assess the impact on the balance sheet of changes under selected scenarios; these might be no change in rates; a 100 basis point and 250 basis point upward parallel shift in the yield curve; a 100 basis point and 250 basis point downward parallel shift; a 25 basis point steepening and flattening of the yield curve, between the three-month and the three-year maturity points; a combination of a parallel shift with a pivotal shift at a selected point; an increase or decrease in three-month T-bill yield volatility levels; and a 20 basis point change in swap spreads;
- compare the difference in earnings resulting from any of the scenarios to the anticipated earnings stream under the current environment.

Generally, the committee will have set guidelines about the significance of simulation results; for example, there may be a rule that a 100 basis point change in interest rates should not impact NII by more than 10%. If results indicate such an impact, ALCO will determine if the current risk strategy is satisfactory or whether adjustments are necessary.

Securitisation

It is common for ALM units in banks to take responsibility for a more proactive balance sheet management role, and *securitisation* is a good example of this. Securitisation is a process undertaken by banks both to realise additional value from assets held on the balance sheet, as well as to remove them from the balance sheet entirely, thus freeing up lending lines. Essentially it involves selling assets on the balance sheet to third-party investors. In principle the process is straightforward, as assets that are sold generate cash flows in the future, which provide the return to investors who have purchased the securitised assets. To control the risk exposure for investors, the uncertainty associated with certain asset cash flows is controlled or re-engineered, and there are a range of ways that this may be done.

For balance sheet management one of the principal benefits of securitisation is to save or reduce capital charges through the sale of assets. The other added benefit of course is that the process generates additional return for the issuing bank; therefore, securitisation is not only a method by which capital charges may be saved, but an instrument in its own right that enables a bank to increase its return on capital.

The securitisation process

For an introduction to asset-backed instruments readers should refer to recent literature such as Fabozzi and Choudhry (2004). In this section we consider the implications of securitisation from the point of view of asset and liability management. The subject is considered in greater detail in Part IV.

The basic principle of securitisation is to sell assets to investors, usually through a medium known as a special purpose vehicle (SPV) or some other intermediate structure, and to provide the investors with a fixed or floating-rate return on the assets they have purchased; the cash flows from the original assets are used to provide this return. It is rare, though not totally unknown, for the investors to buy the assets directly, instead a class of securities is created to represent the assets and the investors purchase these securities. The most common type of assets that are securitised include mortgages, car loans, and credit card loans. However, in theory virtually any asset that generates a cash flow that can be predicted or modelled may be securitised. The vehicle used is constructed so that securities issued against the asset base have a risk-return profile that is attractive to the investors that are being targeted.

To benefit from diversification asset types are usually pooled, and this pool then generates a range of interest payments, principal repayments and principal prepayments. The precise nature of the cash flows is uncertain because of the uncertainty of payment and prepayment patterns, and also because of the occurrence of loan defaults and delays in payment. However, the pooling of a large number of loans means that cash flow fluctuation can be ironed out to a large extent, sufficient to issues notes against. The cash flows generated by the pool of assets are re-routed to investors through a dedicated structure, and a credit rating for the issue is usually requested from one or more of the private credit agencies. Most asset-backed securities carry investment-grade credit ratings, up to triple-A or double-A, mainly because of various credit insurance facilities that are set up to guarantee the bonds. The securitisation structure disassociates the quality of the original cash flows from the quality of the flows accruing to investors. In many cases the original borrowers are not aware that the process has occurred and notice no difference in the way their loan is handled. The credit rating on the securitisation issue has no bearing on the rating of the selling bank and often will be different.

Benefits of securitisation

Securitising assets produces a double benefit for the issuing bank. Those assets which are sold to investors generate a saving in the cost of required capital for the bank, as they are no longer on the balance sheet, so the bank's capital requirement is reduced. Second, if the credit rating of the issued securities is higher than that of the originating bank, there is a potential gain in the funding costs of the bank. For example, if the securities issued are triple-A rated, a double-A-rated bank will have lower funding costs for those securities. The bank benefits from paying a lower rate on the borrowed funds than if it had borrowed those funds directly in the market. This has led to strong growth in, for example, the specialised "credit card" banks in the United States, where banks such as Capital One, First USA and MBNA Bank have benefited from triple-A-rated funding levels and low capital charges. It is doubtful if such banks could have grown as rapidly as they did without securitisation. Although there is a cost associated with securitising assets, which include the direct issue transaction costs and the cost of running the payment structure, these are outweighed by the benefits obtained from the process.

The major benefit of securitisation is reduced funding costs. Several factors influence such costs. These include:

- the lower cost of funds due to the enhanced credit rating of the issued bonds. The extent of this gain is a function of current spreads in the market and the current rating of the originating bank, and will fluctuate in line with market conditions;
- the saving in capital charges obtained from reducing the size of assets on the balance sheet. This decreases the minimum earnings required to ensure an adequate return for shareholders, in effect improving return on capital at a stroke.

The costs of the process include:

- those associated with setting up the issuing structure, and subsequently the payment mechanism that channels cash flows to investors. These costs are a function of the structure and risk of the original assets; the higher the risk of the original assets, the higher the cost of insuring the cash flows for investors;
- the legal costs of origination, plus operating costs and servicing costs.

However, the reduction in funding costs obtained as a result of securitisation should significantly outweigh the cost of the process itself. In order to determine whether a securitisation is feasible, as well as the impact on the return on capital, the originating bank will conduct a cost and benefit analysis prior to embarking on the process. This is frequently the responsibility of the ALM unit.

EXAMPLE 6.4 Securitisation transaction: Illustration of economics

We illustrate the impact of securitising the balance sheet with a hypothetical example from ABC Bank plc. The bank has a mortgage book of £100 million, and under Basel I the regulatory weight for this asset is 50%. The capital requirement is therefore £4 million (that is, 8% × 0.5% × £100 million). The capital is comprised of equity, estimated to cost 25% and subordinated debt, which has a cost of 10.2%. The cost of straight debt is 10%. The ALM desk reviews a securitisation of 10% of the asset book, or £10 million. The loan book has a fixed duration of 20 years, but its effective duration is estimated at seven years, due to refinancings and early repayment. The net return from the loan book is 10.2%.

The ALM desk decides on a securitised structure that is made up of two classes of security, subordinated notes and senior notes. The subordinated notes will be granted a single-A rating due to their higher risk, while the senior notes are rated triple-A. Given such ratings the required rate of return for the subordinated notes is 10.61%, and that of the senior notes is 9.80%. The senior notes have a lower cost than the current balance sheet debt, which has a cost of 10%. To obtain a single-A rating, the subordinated notes need to represent at least 10% of the securitised amount.

The costs associated with the transaction are the initial cost of issue and the yearly servicing cost, estimated at 0.20% of the securitised amount. The summary information is given at Table 6.7.

ABC Bank plc	
Current funding	
Cost of equity	25%
Cost of subordinated debt	10.20%
Cost of debt	10%
Mortgage book	
Net yield	10.20%
Duration	7 years
Balance outstanding	100 million
Proposed structure	
Securitised amount	10 million
Senior securities:	
Cost	9.80%
Weighting	90%
Maturity	10 years
Subordinated notes:	
Cost	10.61%
Weighting	10%
Maturity	10 years
Servicing costs	0.20%

Table 6.7 ABC Bank plc mortgage loan book and securitisation proposal

A bank's cost of funding is the average cost of all the funds it employed. The funding structure in our example is capital 4%, divided into 2% equity at 25%, 2% subordinated debt at 10.20%, and 96% debt at 10%. The weighted funding cost F therefore is:

$$F_{\text{balance sheet}}$$
$$= 96\% \times 10\% + ((8\% \times 50\%) \times (25\% \times 50\%) + (10.20\% \times 50\%))$$
$$= 10.30\%.$$

This average rate is consistent with the 25% before-tax return on equity given at the start. If the assets do not generate this return, the received return will change accordingly, since it is the end result of the bank's profitability. As currently the assets generate only 10.20%, they are currently performing below shareholder expectations. The return actually obtained by shareholders is such that the average cost of funds is identical to the 10.20% return on assets. We may calculate this return to be:

Asset return = 10.20%
= (96% × 10%) + 8% × 50% × (*ROE* × 50% + 10.20% × 50%).

Solving this relationship we obtain an ROE of 19.80%, which is lower than shareholder expectations. In theory the bank would find it impossible to raise new equity in the market because its performance would not compensate shareholders for the risk they are incurring by holding the bank's paper. Therefore any asset that is originated by the bank would have to be securitised, which would also be expected to raise the shareholder return. The ALM desk proceeds with the securitisation, issuing £9 million of the senior securities and £1 million of the subordinated notes. The bonds are placed by an investment bank with institutional investors. The outstanding balance of the loan book decreases from £100 million to £90 million. The weighted assets are therefore £45 million. Therefore the capital requirement for the loan book is now £3.6 million, a reduction from the original capital requirement of £400,000, which can be used for expansion in another area, a possible route for which is given in Table 6.8.

Outstanding balances	Value (£m)	Capital required (£m)
Initial loan book	100	4
Securitised amount	10	0.4
Senior securities	9	Sold
Subordinated notes	1	Sold
New loan book	90	3.6
Total asset	90	
Total weighted assets	45	3.6

Table 6.8 Impact of securitisation on the balance sheet

The benefit of the securitisation is the reduction in the cost of funding. The funding cost as a result of securitisation is the weighted cost of the senior notes and the subordinated notes, together with the annual servicing cost. The cost of the senior securities is 9.80%, while the subordinated notes have a cost of 10.61% (for simplicity here we ignore any differences in the duration and amortisation profiles of the two bonds). This is calculated as:

$$(90\% \times 9.80\%) + (10\% \times 10.61\%) + 0.20\% \ = \ 10.08\%.$$

This overall cost is lower than the target funding cost obtained direct from the balance sheet, which was 10.30%. This is the quantified benefit of the securitisation process. Note that the funding cost obtained through securitisation is lower than the yield on the loan book. Therefore the original loan can be sold to the SPV structure, issuing the securities for a gain.

Appendix

APPENDIX 6.1 NPV and Value-at-Risk (VaR)

The NPV of a banking book is an appropriate target of interest-rate policy because it captures all future cash flows and is equal to the discounted value of future margins when the discount rate is the cost of all debt. The sensitivity of the NPV is derived from the duration of the assets and liabilities. Therefore we may write the change in NPV as below:

$$\frac{\Delta NPV}{\Delta r} = \left(\frac{1}{(1+r)}\right)(-D_A MV_A + D_L MV_L) \tag{A6.1.1}$$

where D_A is the duration of assets and MV_A is the market value of assets. (A6.1.1) is applicable when only one interest rate is used for reference. The sensitivity with respect to the interest rate r is known. It is then possible to derive the VaR from these simple relationships above. With one interest rate we are interested in the maximum variation of the NPV that results from a change in the reference interest rate. The volatility of the NPV can be derived from its sensitivity and from the interest-rate volatility. If we set S_r as the sensitivity of the NPV with respect to the interest rate r, the volatility of the NPV is given by:

$$\sigma(NPV) = S_r \times \sigma(r). \tag{A6.1.2}$$

Once the volatility is known, the maximum change at a given confidence level is obtained as a multiple of the volatility. The multiple is based on assumptions with respect to the shape of the distribution of interest rates. Under a curve of the normal distribution, a multiple of 1.96 provides the maximum expected change at a 2.5% two-tailed confidence level, so that we are able to say that the VaR of the book is as given by:

$$\text{VaR} = 1.96 \times S_r \times \sigma(r). \tag{A6.1.3}$$

Where there is more than one interest rate, the variation of the NPV can be approximated as a linear combination of the variations due to a change of each interest rate. This is written as:

$$NPV = S_r \times \Delta r + S_s \times \Delta s + S_t \times \Delta t + L \qquad \text{(A6.1.4)}$$

where r, s and t are the different interest rates. Since all interest rate changes are uncertain, the volatility of the NPV is the volatility of a sum of random variables. Deriving the volatility of this sum requires assumptions on correlations between interest rates.

This problem is identical to the general problem of measuring the market risk of a portfolio when bearing in mind that its change in market value arises as a result of changes generated by the random variations of market parameters. The main concern is to calculate the volatility of the mark-to-market value of the portfolio, expressed as the sum of the random changes of the mark-to-market values of the various individual transactions. These random changes can be interdependent, in the same way that the underlying market parameters are. The volatility of the value of the portfolio depends upon the sensitivities of individual transactions, upon the volatilities of the individual market parameters and also upon their interdependency, if any exists. The methodology that calculates this volatility is known as *delta-VaR*. This is based on the delta sensitivity of the portfolio to changes in market interest rates.

References and bibliography

Asset & Liability Management, RISK Books, London (1998).

Bitner, J. 1992, *Successful Bank Asset–Liability Management*, John Wiley & Sons, New Jersey.

Butler, C. 1998, *Mastering Value-at-Risk*, FT Prentice Hall, London.

Cornyn, A. and Mays, E. (eds) 1997, *Interest Rate Risk Models: Theory and Practice*, Glenlake Publishing/Fitzroy Dearborn Publishers, Chicago, IL, chapters 6 and 15.

Fabozzi, F. and Konishi, A. 1996, *The Handbook of Asset/Liability Management*, revised edition, Irwin McGraw-Hill, New York, chapters 3, 6, 7, 8 and 12.

Fabozzi, F. and Choudhry. M. 2004, *Handbook of European Structured Financial Products*, John Wiley & Sons, New Jersey.

Gup, B. and Brooks, R. 1993, *Interest Rate Risk Management*, Irwin, New York.

Howe, D. 1992, *A Guide to Managing Interest-Rate Risk*, New York Institute of Finance, New York.

Johnson, H. 1994, *Bank Asset/Liability Management*, Probus Publishing, New York.

Kamakura Corporation 1998, *Asset & Liability Management: A Synthesis of New Methodologies*, Risk Publications, London.

Koch, T. 1988, *Bank Management*, Dryden Press, New York.

Marshall, J. and Bansal, V.K. 1992, *Financial Engineering*, New York Institute of Finance, New York, Chapter 20.

Schaffer, S. 1991, "Interest Rate Risk", *Business Review*, Federal Reserve Bank of Philadelphia, May–June, pp. 17–27.

Sinkey, J. 1992, *Commercial Bank Financial Management*, 4th edition, Macmillan, London.

Stevenson, B. and Fadil, M. 1995, "Modern Portfolio Theory: Can it Work for Commercial Loans?", *Commercial Lending Review*, 10(2), Spring, pp. 4–12, London.

Stigum, M. 1990, *The Money Market*, 3rd edition, Dow Jones Irwin, New York.

Toevs, A. and Haney, W. 1984, *Measuring and Managing Interest Rate Risk*, Morgan Stanley publication, New York.

Toevs, A. and Haney, W. 1986, "Measuring and Managing Interest Rate Risk: A Guide to Asset/Liability Models Used in Banks and Thrifts", in Platt, R. (ed.) 1986, *Controlling Interest Rate Risk, New Techniques and Applications for Money Management*, John Wiley & Sons, New Jersey.

Wilson, J.S.G. (ed.) 1988, *Managing Banks' Assets and Liabilities*, Euromoney Publications, London.

CHAPTER

7

ALM Trading Principles

In this chapter we introduce the basics of trading and hedging as employed by an ALM desk. The instruments and techniques used form the fundamental building blocks of ALM, and this subject is central to this book.[1] Our purpose here is to acquaint the newcomer to the market with the essentials; further recommended reading is in the bibliography.

The ALM and money markets desk has a vital function on the trading floor, supporting the fixed-interest sales desk, hedging new issues, and working with the swaps and over-the-counter (OTC) options desks. In some banks and securities houses it will be placed within the Treasury or money markets areas, whereas other firms will organise it as an entirely separate function. Wherever it is organised, the need for clear and constant communication between the ALM desk and other operating areas of the bank is paramount. We presented an overview of ALM, liquidity and interest-rate strategy in the previous chapter; here we look at specific uses of money market products like deposits and repo in the context of yield enhancement and market-making.

Trading approach

The yield curve and interest rate expectations

When the yield curve is positively sloped, the conventional approach is to fund the book at the short end of the curve and lend at the long end. In essence therefore if the yield curve resembled that shown in Figure 7.1 a

---

1 And a very large and interesting book it has turned out to be! ☺

bank would borrow, say, one-week funds while simultaneously lending out at, say, the three-month maturity. This is known as *funding short*. A bank can effect the economic equivalent of borrowing at the short end of the yield curve and lending at the longer end through repo transactions – in our example, a one-week repo and a three-month reverse repo. The bank then continuously rolls over its funding at one-week intervals for the three-month period. This is also known as *creating a tail*; here the "tail" is the gap between one week and three months – the interest-rate "gap" that the bank is exposed to. During the course of the trade, as the reverse repo has locked in a loan for three months, the bank is exposed to interest-rate risk should the slope or shape of the yield curve change. In this case if short-dated interest rates rise, the bank may see its profit margin shrink or turn into a funding loss.

As we will discuss further in Chapter 9, there are a number of hypotheses advanced to explain the shape of the yield curve at any particular time. A steeply positively shaped curve may indicate that the market expects interest rates to rise over the longer term, although this is also sometimes given as the reason for an inverted curve with regard to shorter-term rates. Generally speaking, trading volumes are higher in a positively sloping yield curve environment, compared to a flat or negative-shaped curve.

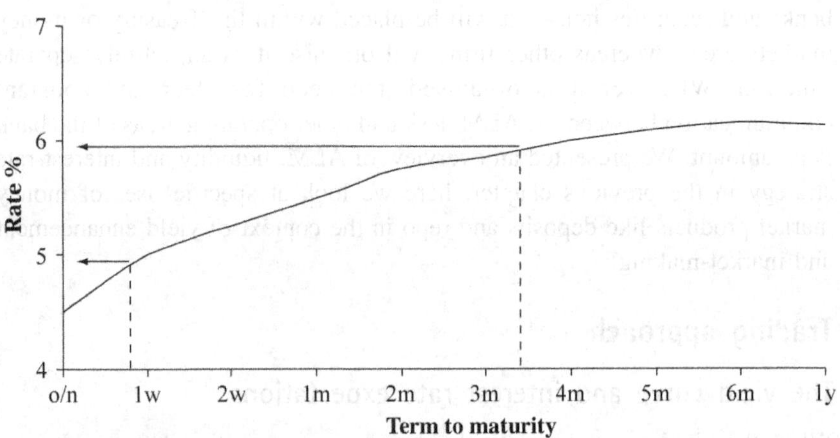

Figure 7.1 Positive yield curve funding

In the case of an inverted yield curve, a bank will (all else being equal) lend at the short end of the curve and borrow at the longer end. This is known as *funding long* and is shown in Figure 7.2.

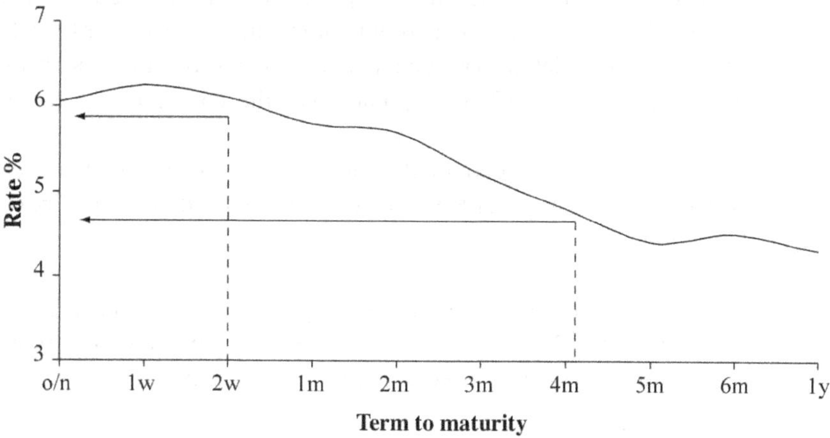

Figure 7.2 Negative yield curve funding

The example in Figure 7.2 shows a short cash position of two-week maturity against a long cash position of four-month maturity. The interest rate gap of 10 weeks is the book's interest rate exposure. The inverted shape of the yield curve may indicate market expectations of a fall in short-term interest rates. Further along the yield curve the market may expect a benign inflationary environment, which is why the premium on longer-term returns is lower than normal.

Credit intermediation by the repo desk

The government bond repo market will trade at a lower rate than other money market instruments, reflecting its status as a secured instrument and the best credit. This allows the spreads between markets of different credits to be exploited. The following are examples of credit intermediation trades:

- a repo dealer lends general collateral currently trading at a spread below Libor, and uses the cash to buy CDs trading at a smaller spread below Libor;
- a repo dealer borrows specific collateral in the stock-lending market, paying a fee, and sells the stock in the repo market at the general collateral (GC) rate; the cash is then lent in the interbank market at

a higher rate; for instance, through the purchase of a clearing bank CD. The CD is used as collateral in the stock loan transaction. A bank must have dealing relationships with both the stock loan and repo markets to effect this trade. An example of the trade that could be put on using this type of intermediation is shown in Figure 7.3 for the UK gilt market; the details are given below, and show that the bank would stand to gain 17 basis points over the course of the three-month trade;

- a repo dealer trades repo in the GC market, and using this cash reverses in emerging market collateral at a spread, say, 400 basis points higher.

These are only three examples of the way that repo can be used to exploit the interest-rate differentials that exist between markets of varying credit qualities, and between the secured and unsecured markets.

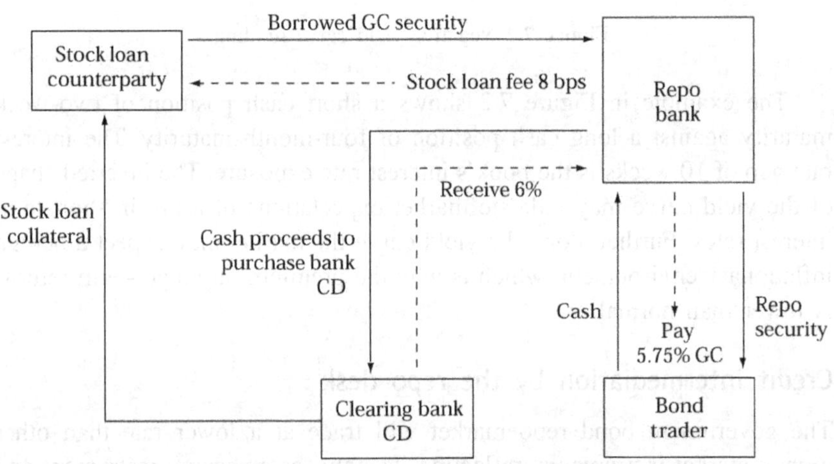

Figure 7.3 Intermediation between stock loan and repo markets; an example using UK gilts

Figure 7.3 shows the potential gains that can be made by a repo dealing bank (market-maker) that has access to both the stock loan and general collateral repo market. It illustrates the rates available in the gilt market on 31 October 2000 for three-month maturities, which were:

- 3-month GC repo 5.83 – 5.75%
- 3-month clearing bank CD $6\,{}^{1}/_{32}$ – 6.00%.

The stock loan fee for this term was quoted at 5–10 basis points, with the actual fee paid being 8 basis points. Therefore the repo trader borrows GC stock for three months, and offers this in repo at 5.75%;[2] the cash proceeds are then used to purchase a clearing bank CD at 6.00%. This CD is used as collateral in the stock loan. The profit is market risk-free as the terms are locked, although there is an element of credit risk in holding the CD. On these terms in £100 million stock the profit for the three-month period is approximately £170,000.

The main consideration for the dealing bank is the capital requirements of the trade. Gilt repo is zero-weighted for capital purposes, and indeed clearing bank CDs are accepted by the Bank of England for liquidity purposes, so the capital cost is not onerous. The bank will need to ensure that it has sufficient credit lines for the repo and CD counterparties.

Yield curve trading: the role of the repo funding desk

We describe here a first-principles type of *relative value* trading common on fixed-interest desks, and the role played by the repo desk in funding the trade. If a trader believes that the shape of the yield curve is going to change, thus altering the yield *spread* between two bonds of differing maturities, they can position the book to benefit from such a move. A yield spread arbitrage trade is not market directional; that is, it is not necessarily dependent on the direction that the market moves in, but rather the move in the shape of the yield curve. As long as the trade is *duration weighted* there is no first-order interest-rate risk involved, although there is second-order risk in that if the shape of the yield curve changes in the opposite direction to that expected, the trader will suffer a loss.

Consider the yield spread between two hypothetical bonds, one of two-year and the other of five-year maturity; the trader believes that this spread will widen in the near future. The trade therefore looks like this:

- buy £x million of the two-year bond and fund in repo;
- sell £y million of the five-year bond and cover in reverse repo.

[2] The repo dealer is the market-maker, and so offers stock in repo at the offered side, which is 5.75%. However, this trade still turns in a profit if the bank dealt at another market-maker's bid side of 5.83%, with a profit of 9 basis points on the cash sum. Rates are quoted from King & Shaxson Bond Brokers Limited.

The nominal amount of the five-year bond will be a ratio of the respective *basis point values* multiplied by the amount of the two-year bond.

The trader will arrange the repo transaction simultaneously (or instruct the repo desk to do so). The funding for both bonds forms an important part of the rationale for the trade. As repo rates can be fixed for the anticipated term of the trade, the trader will know the net funding cost – irrespective of any change in market levels or yield spreads – and this cost is the breakeven cost for the trade. A disciplined trader will have a time horizon for the trade, and the trade will be reviewed if the desired spread increase has not occurred by the expected time. In the case of the repo, however, the repo trader may wish to fix this at a shorter interval than the initial time horizon, and roll over as necessary. This will depend on the trader's (or repo desk's) view of repo rates.

Figure 7.4 illustrates the yield curve considerations involved.

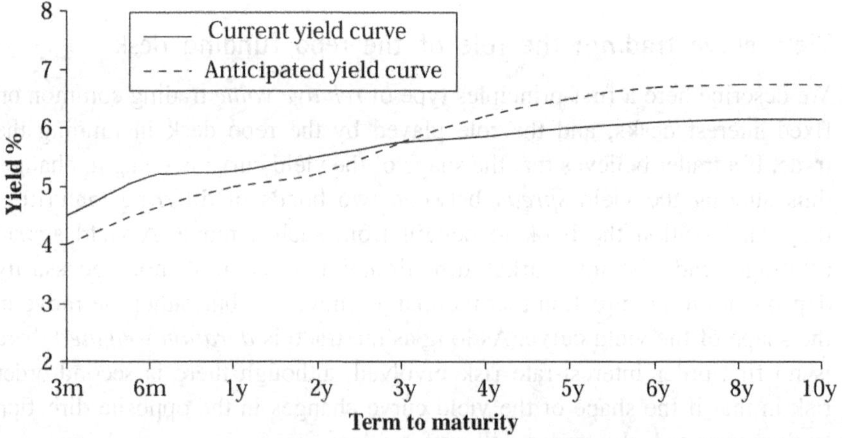

Figure 7.4 Yield curve relative value analysis

The solid curve in Figure 7.4 represents the yield curve at the time the trade is put on, while the dotted curve shows the curve that is *anticipated* by the trader at the end of their time horizon for the trade. If this proves correct, at this point profit is taken and the trade is unwound. The increase in the two-year versus five-year spread is the profit made from the trade, minus the net funding.

This yield curve spread trade is an example of relative value trading. There are many variations on this, including trades spanning different currencies and markets.

For example, around the spring of 1999 the spread between 10-year UK gilts and 10-year German bunds had narrowed from a high of 160 basis points six months previously to a level of 91 basis points. A trader looking at this may believe that this spread will widen out again in the near future. To reflect this view, a trade can be put on in which the trader sells the gilt and buys the bund in anticipation of the change in spread. Both trades are funded/covered in the respective repo markets. The net funding cost is a vital consideration of whether the trade should be put on or not; any anticipation of the widening of bond yield spread must take the funding into account. A trade such as this also requires that the trader has a view on the currency exchange rate, as any profit from the trade could be reduced or eliminated by adverse movements in the exchange rate.

Note that disciplined trading will require a "stop-loss" point at which the trade will be unwound if the trader's view is proved incorrect. This is usually half the anticipated gain; for example, if the trader has an objective to take profit if spreads change in their favour by, say, 10 basis points, the stop-loss will be put on at five basis points, or even less, should the trade not prove successful.[3]

Figure 7.5 illustrates the starting point for the trade.

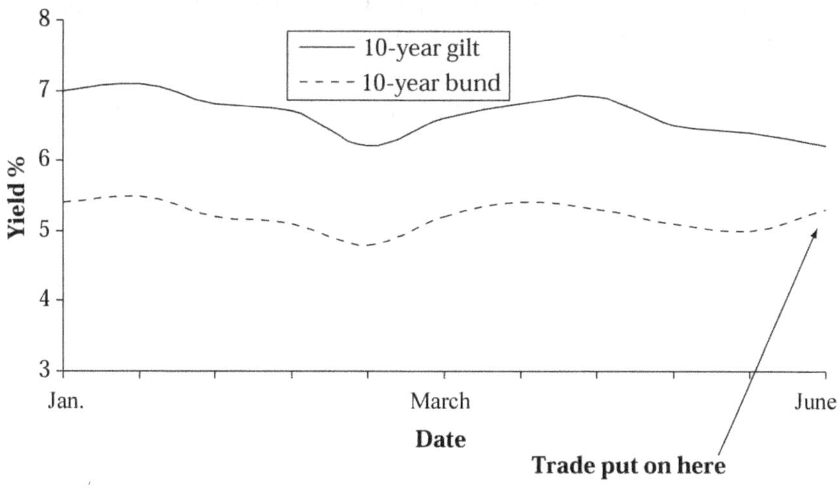

Figure 7.5 Further relative value considerations

[3] It is easier to say this than it is to do it!

EXAMPLE 7.1 Spread trade repo funding calculator

The spreadsheet shown in Figure 7.6 calculates the net funding cost associated with running a spread position of two bonds, and was written by Dr Didier Joannas. It comprises an Excel front-end and Visual Basic program. The bonds shown in the spreadsheet are gilts. The user selects which bonds to enter into the spreadsheet; the first half shows benchmark bonds, which represent the short position of a trade, and the bond that is taken on as the long position is entered into a cell in the lower half. The specific repo rate that applies to each bond is also entered, as is the term of the trade. The calculator then works out the net funding, if this is negative it represents the trader's break-even cost for the trade. Any combination of bonds can be selected. The spreadsheet also calculates each bond's basis point value (bpv) and bpv ratio, because of course this is used to determine the nominal value of the bond positions. A spread trade is first-order risk neutral because both the long and short positions are duration-weighted. Note that a trade made up of a long position in the 8.50% 2005, against a short position in the 8% 2021, makes a 1.29 basis point gain in funding over a 30-day period, so that if the yield curve stays unchanged during that time, which admittedly is unlikely, the trade would still make a net gain for the book, composed of the funding profit. The funding of bond trades is a vital ingredient in devising trade strategy.

The spreadsheet is available on the CD-R at the back of this book.

Yield Spread | 18Feb00 21Feb00 | Settlement

UK gilt					Yield	bpv	3	5	10	20	Funding in pence	Repo rate	TERM 23Feb00	Basis points gain 2	Days
SHORT															
2	103.24	103.75	7.00	07-Jun-02	5.234	2.08	2 40	1	–1	–50	0.09	**5**	103.740	0.04	98
3	107.50	107	8.00	10-Jun-03	5.638	2.86	3	–39	–42	–91	–0.18	**5.9**	106.991	–0.06	101
5	114.66	116.0625	8.50	07-Dec-05	5.244	4.59		5	–2	–51	–0.17	**5.5**	116.051	–0.04	98
10	104.30	104	5.75	07-Dec-09	5.221	7.39			10	–49	–0.18	**5.5**	104.000	–0.02	98
20	141.82	143.5625	8.00	07-Jun-21	4.730	11.86					–0.72	**6**	143.566	–0.06	98
30	120.60	120.03125	6.00	07-Dec-28	4.720	17.92					0.11	**4.5**	120.028	0.01	98

	LONG		Cpn	Maturity	Yield	bpv	Benchmark	Spread	bpv ratio	Funding forward gain	spread		Repo rate	23Feb00	2	Days
UK	114.66	116.0625	8.5	07-Dec-05	5.24389915	5.41	**20**	51.39	0.45631285	0.14	51.54	0.44	**4.5**	116.045	0.08	98
UK	141.82	143.5625	8	07-Jun-21	4.72997011	17.23	**30**	1.04	0.96180726	–0.04	0.99	–0.6490288	**5.5**	143.562	–0.04	98
UK	103.24	103.75	7	07-Jun-02	5.2336894	2.19	**10**	1.28	0.2958155	–0.06	1.22	–0.1901567	**5.5**	103.743	–0.09	98

Figure 7.6 Spread trade funding calculator
© Didier Joannas.

EXAMPLE 7.2 Bond spread trade and funding considerations: Example from the gilt market

The UK gilt yield curve for 1 November 2000 is shown in Figure 7.7. This is the Bloomberg screen "IYC". The trader believes that the spread between the two-year benchmark bond, the UK Treasury 7% 2002 and the five-year bond, the UK Treasury 8.5% 2005, will widen, and put on a spread position, sometimes referred to as a *swap* or *switch*[4] that is long the two-year and short the five-year. The respective bond yields also suit this trade because the inverted yield curve produces a higher return for the two-year stock. If we assume the trader goes long of £10 million of the 7% 2002 bond, Bloomberg screen "SW" can be used to calculate the equivalent nominal amount of five-year bond to short. From Figure 7.8 we see that this is £3.23 million nominal. This ratio is calculated using the respective basis point values for each stock, which Bloomberg terms the *risk* values. This calculation basis is user-selected, as shown by the number "4" being entered in the box marked "Swap Type" in Figure 7.8. The two-year bond has a redemption yield of 5.732%, against the yield on the five-year of 5.565%; a yield pick-up of 16.7 basis points. The trader has one-month and three-month horizon periods; that is, the trade will be reviewed at these points in time. The funding element is crucial. The trader obtains the following specific repo rates from a repo market-maker:

One-month	8.5% 2005	5.82–5.77%
	7% 2002	5.78–5.70%
Three-month	8.5% 2005	5.83–5.75%
	7% 2002	5.77–5.72%.

The trader uses Bloomberg screen "CCS" to check the funding, inserting the rates given above. This shows the net funding cost and breakeven amount for the trade; any widening of spread must be by at least the breakeven amount to account for the funding cost. The calculations are shown in Figure 7.9 on page 316. If the yield spread has widened by the trader's target after one month or three months, the trade is unwound and profit taken. If the spread has not widened by that amount after one month, the trade is reviewed and may be continued, but if it has narrowed by the stop-loss amount at any time it is immediately unwound.

[4] Not to be confused with a swap, the derivative instrument.

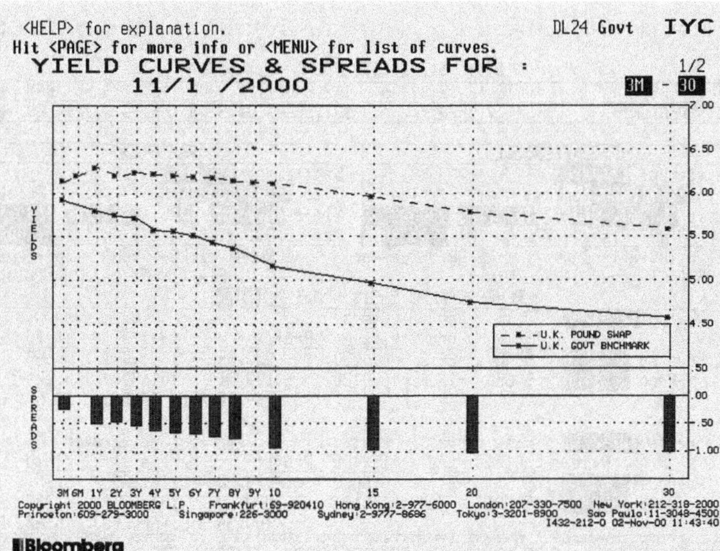

Figure 7.7 Bloomberg screen IYC showing yield curve

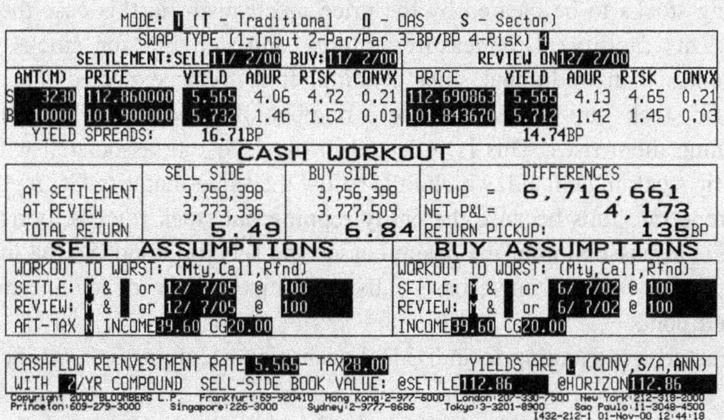

Figure 7.8 Bloomberg screen SW showing bond spread trade calculation

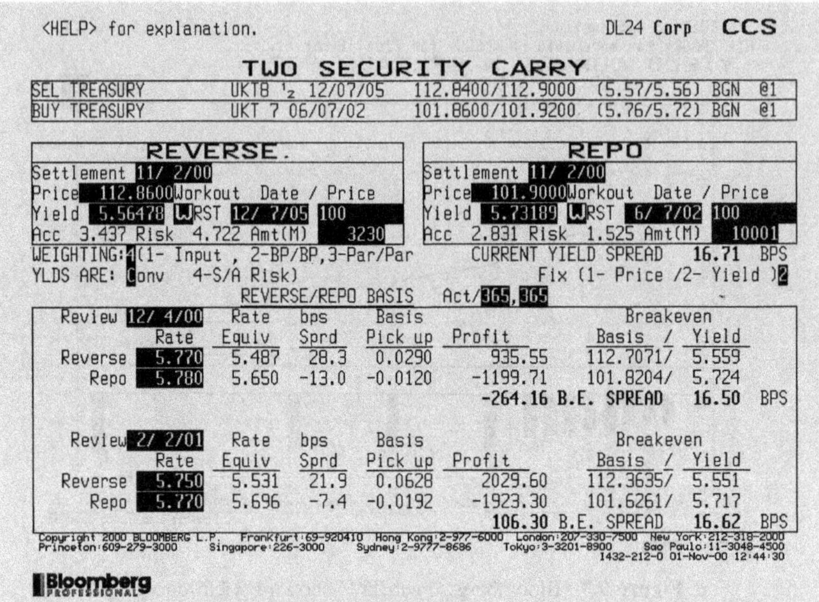

Figure 7.9 Bloomberg screen CCS showing bond spread trade repo funding

Repo market specials trading

The existence of an open repo market allows the demand for borrowing and lending stocks to be cleared by the price mechanism, in this case the repo rate. This facility also measures supply and demand for stocks more efficiently than traditional stock lending. It is to be expected that when specific stocks are in demand, for a number of reasons, the premium on obtaining them rises. This is reflected in the repo rate associated with the specific stock in demand, which falls below the same-maturity GC repo rate. The repo rate falls because the entity repoing out stock (that is, borrowing cash) is in possession of the desired asset: the specific bond. So the interest rate payable by this counterparty falls, as compensation for lending out the desired bond.

Factors contributing to individual securities becoming *special* include:

- government bond auctions; the bond to be issued is shorted by market-makers in anticipation of new supply of stock and due to client demand;
- outright short selling, whether deliberate position-taking on the trader's view, or market-makers selling stock on client demand;

- hedging, including bond underwriters who will short the benchmark government bond that the corporate bond is priced against;
- derivatives trading such as basis ("cash-and-carry") trading creating demand for a specific stock.

Natural holders of government bonds can benefit from issues *going special*, which is when the demand for specific stocks is such that the rate for borrowing them is reduced. The lower repo rate reflects the premium for borrowing the stock. Note that the party borrowing the special stock is lending cash; it is the rate payable on the cash that they have lent which is depressed.

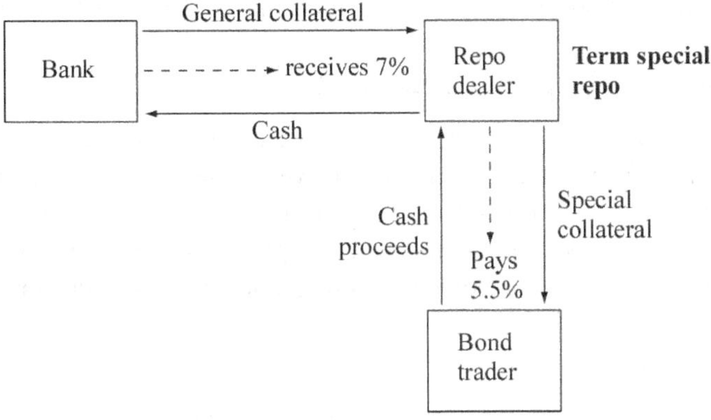

Figure 7.10 Funding gain from the repo of a special stock

The holder of a stock that has gone special can obtain cheap funding for the issue itself, by lending it out. Alternatively, the holder can lend the stock and obtain cash in exchange in a repo, for which the rate payable is lower than the interbank rate. These funds can then be lent out as either secured funding (in a repo), or as unsecured funding, enabling the special stock holder to lock in a funding profit. For example, consider a situation where a repo dealer holds an issue that is trading at 5.5% in one-week repo. The equivalent general collateral (GC) rate is 7%, making the specific issue very special. By lending the stock out the dealer can lock in the profit by lending one-week cash at 7%, or at a higher rate in the interbank market. This is illustrated in Figure 7.10.

There is a positive correlation between the extent to which a stock trades expensive to the yield curve and the degree to which it trades special in repo. Theory would predict this, since traders will maintain short positions for bonds with high funding (repo) costs only if the anticipated fall in the price of the bond is large enough to cover this funding premium. When stock is perceived as being expensive, for example after an auction announcement, this creates a demand for short positions and hence greater demand for the paper in repo. At other times the stock may go tight in the repo market, following which it will tend to be bid higher in the *cash* market as traders closed out existing shorts (which had become expensive to finance). At the same time traders and investors may attempt to buy the stock outright since it will now be cheap to finance in repo. The link between dearness in the cash market and special status in the repo market flows both ways.

An analysis of special repo rates

In this chapter we have looked at why certain bonds may go special in the repo market. The subject is not extensively researched in the academic literature, and empirical results are scarce. In this section we consider some further issues associated with special repo rates, concentrating on the Treasury and gilt markets for observations and anecdotal illustrations.

Introduction

In government markets there are specific rates for every security, and the highest of these rates is essentially the GC rate. The repo rate on a specific named bond issue becomes *special* when it is trading at over, say, 10–15 basis points below the GC rate for stock of equivalent credit quality and from the same issuer. A special rate is a manifestation of the demand for the specific stock from dealers in the market, most commonly because they are covering a short position in that stock. The measure of a security's *specialness* is the spread in basis points below the equivalent-maturity GC rate. In government markets, which are characterised by an easily defined GC rate, there is invariably a number of stocks that are special. In the US Treasury market the most liquid benchmark securities, known as *on-the-run* issues, are usually special to a certain extent. This contrasts with the UK gilt market where the current benchmark is only rarely special. Since a bond can be marked as "special" when trading anywhere from a (relatively) small premium away from the GC rate as well as down to a negative rate, special status does not necessarily signify great shortages; a stock can go in and out of being special from one day to the next.

Figure 7.11 is an illustration of the fluctuation of the extent of specialness for the 10-year gilt benchmark during 2000–2001. Specialness is measured in basis points below the overnight GC rate. The benchmark bond, a status assigned by the market in this instance as the bond also being the cheapest-to-deliver bond for the gilt future, changed from the $5\,^3/_4\%$ 2009 stock to the $6\,^1/_4\%$ 2010 stock during this time.

As we noted in the previous section, special status for a bond can arise for a number of reasons. Whatever the background factors are, a bond will go special because of a shortage of supply in the market, and the extent of specialness will reflect the amount of shortage as well as the inability of owners of stock to make it available for lending in repo.

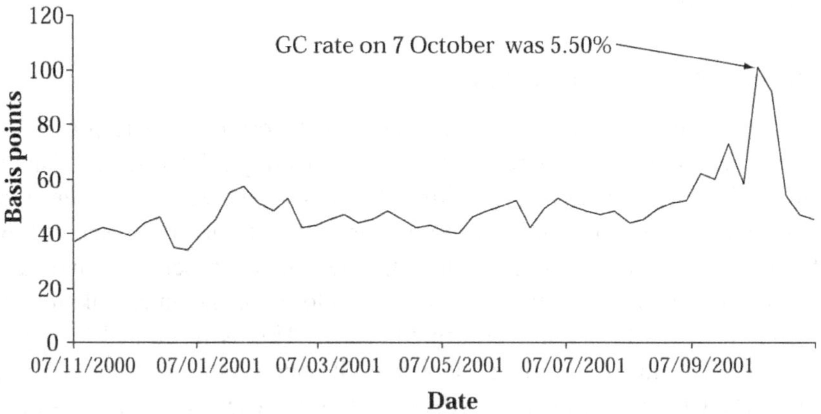

Figure 7.11 Extent of specialness for 10-year benchmark gilt, overnight repo rates

The specific repo rate on a particular stock also reflects in part, the price volatility of that stock in the market, and this volatility may influence the margin level for that stock in repo. Although in theory government stocks all have the same credit risk, the differing market risk may result in variations in margin levels. The general rule is that stocks of high modified duration are generally traded with higher margin.[5] A high demand to cover short stock positions using reverse repo can depress repo rates to special levels, and has

[5] This depends on the counterparty. Professional wholesale market counterparties in the gilt market frequently enter into short-term repo with no margin, irrespective of the stock being given up as collateral. Where the counterparty is not as "trusted", margin will be taken or dealers may offer to trade via tri-party arrangements.

been observed for some time; for example, see Cornell and Shapiro (1989) for an illustration using the Treasury long bond in 1986. This is not surprising when viewed in terms of orthodox economic theory, as the supply and demand equilibrium for individual stocks is reached via the interest rate in reverse repo. Amihud and Mendelson (1991) state that in the US Treasury market most on-the-run securities, as the most liquid stocks, are used for both hedging and speculative purposes, and therefore dealers frequently maintain large short position in these bonds. The current US Treasury benchmarks are almost always to some extent special for this reason. Due to the constant issue in the Treasury market, the market shifts its active trading into each successive on-the-run security, as it is issued. A reduced level of cash market trading (as a stock ceases to become the benchmark) can also lead to specialness.

The market-determined repo rate

Viewed purely as a loan of cash and using the theory of forward prices, the overnight repo rate would be identical to the overnight interest rate. This is summarised in Appendix 7.1. This, of course, ignores the existence of collateral and the impact this has on the repo rate. Duffie (1996) shows how the upper level on repo rates is the GC rate. Market observation indicates that the overnight GC rate is at, or very close to, the interbank market overnight rate, which is for unsecured funds.[6] This is illustrated in Figure 7.12, which compares sterling Libor and GC rates in the overnight during 2001. The GC rate tracks the interbank rate very closely, and on occasion is seen to lie above it. This reflects the supply and demand for short-date repo compared to interbank borrowing and lending. Where specific repo rates start to diverge from the GC rate and become special, market participants who are long of the stock can make risk-free gain from repoing out the stock at the reduced interest rate, and investing the cash proceeds into GC or the interbank market. The interest amount paid out in the reverse repo trade will be below that received in the repo or interbank trade. As Duffie states (1996, p. 503) this is not an arbitrage trade because the profit potential of the trade is a function of the amount of stock that is held and which is repoed out. Duffie also confirms market practice that trading repo, whether one is long of the special bond or not, is a speculative rather than arbitrage activity,

---

6 See Choudhry (2001) *The Bond and Money Markets*, Butterworth-Heinemann, Oxford, Chapter 10, section 10.1, for observations and reasoning on why overnight GC repo is very close to interbank overnight in the gilt market.

since the market does not know whether individual stocks will go special, the extent of their specialness and when they will cease being special.

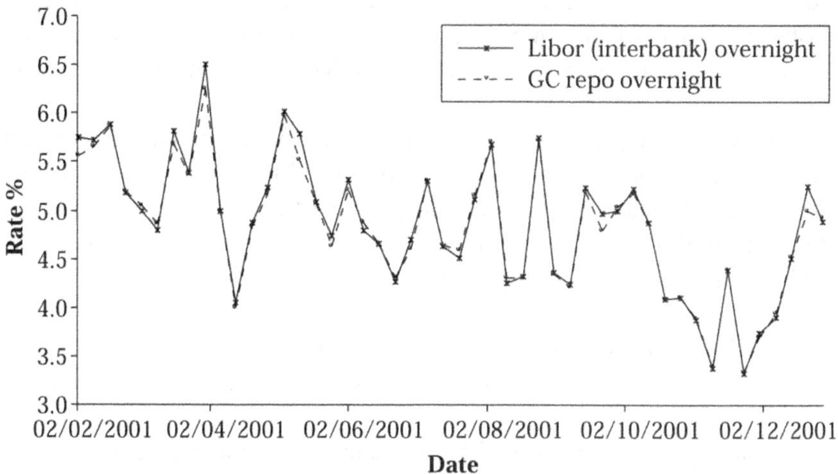

Figure 7.12 Sterling overnight Libor and GC repo rates compared, February–December 2001

Source: British Bankers Association.

Repo rates therefore reflect the individual supply and demand of specific stocks *whenever a specific stock is requested or offered as collateral* (as opposed to a trade stated at the outset as a GC trade), with the upper level being the GC rate. A large demand for a specific stock in reverse repo will result in the stock going special unless the stock is made available either in the stock-lending market or very shortly afterwards in the repo market. If no stock is available in either market, perhaps because the overall issue size is small or institutional holders are unable or unwilling to release supply to the market, the repo rate will become special. Hence the specific repo rate is the market clearing price for supply and demand for that stock.

Matched book trading in repo

The growth and development of repo markets has led to repo match book trading desks. Essentially this is market-making in repo; dealers make two-way trading prices in various securities, irrespective of their underlying positions. In fact the term "matched book" is a misnomer; most matched books are deliberately mismatched as part of a view on the short-term yield curve. Another commonly encountered definition of the term "matched book" is of a bank that trades repo solely to cover its long and short bond positions, and does not enter into trades for other reasons.[7] It is *not* matching cash lent and borrowed, however, or trading to profit from the bid–offer spread, and not any sundry other definitions that have been given in previous texts.

Traders running a matched book put on positions to take advantage of (1) short-term interest-rate movements and (2) anticipated supply and demand in the underlying stock. Many of the trading ideas and strategies described in this book are examples of matched book trading. Matched book trading can involve the following types of trade:

- taking a view on interest rates; for example, the dealer bids for one-month GC and offers three-month GC, expecting the yield curve to invert;
- taking a view on specials; for example, the trader borrows stock in the stock-lending market for use in repo once (as they expect) it goes *special*;
- credit intermediation; for example, a dealer reverses in Brady bonds from a Latin American bank, at a rate of Libor +200 and offers this stock to a US money market investor at a rate of Libor +20.

Principals and principal intermediaries with large volumes of repos and reverse repos, such as the market-makers mentioned above, are said to be running matched books. An undertaking to provide two-way prices is made to provide customers with a continuous financing service for long and short positions and also as part of proprietary trading. Traders will mismatch positions in order to take advantage of a combination of two factors, which are short-term interest rate movements and anticipated supply/demand in the underlying bond.

Hedging tools

For dealers who are not looking to trade around term mismatch or other spreads, there is more than one way to hedge the repo trade. The best hedge for any trade is an exact offsetting trade. This is not always possible, nor

[7] Thanks to Del-boy at King & Shaxson Bond Brokers Limited for pointing this out, although I still reckon that my definition is the right one!

indeed always desirable as it may reduce profit, or may use up valuable capital and credit lines. However, the advantage of a similar offsetting trade is that it reduces *basis risk* exposure. The residual risk will be that between, say, GC and special or interest-rate gap risk.

It is the interest-rate risk exposure that the repo trader may need to hedge. This is part of managing the book and will be considered in more detail in the next chapter, as the considerations are similar to other money market desks. Here we introduce the main hedging tools. They are covered in greater depth in Part III.

Interest-rate futures

A forward term interest-rate gap exposure can be hedged using interest rate futures. These instruments are introduced in Chapter 13. In the sterling market the instrument will typically be the 90-day short sterling future traded on LIFFE. A strip of futures can be used to hedge the term gap. The trader buys futures contracts to the value of the exposure and for the term of the gap. Any change in cash rates should be hedged by offsetting moves in futures prices.

Forward rate agreements

FRAs are similar in concept to interest-rate futures and are also off-balance sheet instruments. Under an FRA a buyer agrees notionally to borrow and a seller to lend a specified notional amount at a fixed rate for a specified period; the contract to commence on an agreed date in the future. On this date (the "fixing date") the actual rate is taken and, according to its position versus the original trade rate, the borrower or lender will receive an interest payment on the notional sum equal to the difference between the trade rate and the actual rate. The sum paid over is present-valued as it is transferred at the start of the notional loan period, whereas in a cash market trade interest would be handed over at the end of the loan period. As FRAs are off-balance sheet contracts no actual borrowing or lending of cash takes place, hence the use of the term "notional". In hedging an interest-rate gap in the cash period, the trader will buy an FRA contract that equates to the term gap for a nominal amount equal to their exposure in the cash market. Should rates move against them in the cash market, the gain on the FRA should (in theory) compensate for the loss in the cash trade.

Further detail on FRAs is given in Chapter 13 of this book.

Interest-rate swaps

An interest-rate swap is an off-balance sheet agreement between two parties to make periodic interest payments to each other. Payments are on a predetermined set of dates in the future, based on a notional principal amount; one party is the *fixed-rate payer*, the rate agreed at the start of the swap, and the other party is the *floating-rate payer*, the floating-rate being determined during the life of the swap by reference to a specific market rate or index. There is no exchange of principal, only of the interest payments on this principal amount. Note that our description is for a plain vanilla swap contract; it is common to have variations on this theme – for instance *floating–floating* swaps where both payments are floating-rate, as well as *cross-currency* swaps where there is an exchange of an equal amount of different currencies at the start- and end-dates for the swap.

An interest-rate swap can be used to hedge the fixed-rate risk arising from the purchase of a bond during a repo arbitrage or spread trade. The terms of the swap should match the payment dates and maturity date of the bond. The idea is to match the cash flows from the bond with equal and opposite payments in the swap contract, which will hedge the bond position. For example, if a trader has purchased a bond, they will be receiving fixed-rate coupon payments on the nominal value of the bond. To hedge this position the trader buys a swap contract for the same nominal value in which they will be paying the same fixed-rate payment; the net cash flow is a receipt of floating interest-rate payments. A bond issuer, on the other hand, may issue bonds of a particular type because of the investor demand for such paper, but prefer to have the interest exposure on debt in some other form. So, for example, a UK company issues fixed-rate bonds denominated in, say, Australian dollars, swaps the proceeds into sterling and pays floating-rate interest on the sterling amount. As part of the swap it will be receiving fixed-rate Australian dollars; which neutralises the exposure arising from the bond issue. At the termination of the swap (which must coincide with the maturity of the bond) the original currency amounts are exchanged back, enabling the issuer to redeem the holders of the bond in Australian dollars.

Swaps are discussed in detail in Chapter 14. For a readable and accessible introduction to interest-rate swaps and their applications see Decovny (1998). Another quality article is the one by Ramamurthy (1998), while a more technical approach is given in Jarrow and Turnbull (2000). The mother of all swaps books is Das (1994), which is worth purchasing just to make the bookshelf look impressive. The author also suggests (but will leave a recommendation to someone else!) Fabozzi, Mann and Choudhry (2002), which includes a very accessible and comprehensive chapter on swaps.

Appendix

APPENDIX 7.1 Confirming the forward interest rate

The forward price that drives the repo rate suggests that the latter should be equal to the overnight rate. This of course ignores the impact of the existence of collateral. The argument is the standard no-arbitrage one, which we summarise here. As usual we assume no bid–offer spreads.

A bond is trading at a price of P and the overnight interest rate for cash borrowing or lending is r. Assuming we are able to short the bond at P, the funding cost for the overnight forward price is:

$$P_{fwd} = P(1 + r). \qquad \text{(A7.1.1)}$$

This price is based on the principle of no-arbitrage, because if we had

$$P_{fwd} > P(1 + r) \qquad \text{(A7.1.2)}$$

it would be possible to undertake the following:

- purchase the bond at price P;
- agree forward delivery;
- borrow funds at rate r to fund the trade.

The repayment of borrowed funds is at $(1 + r)$. The bond is delivered at the forward date and given (A7.1.2) above. We know that this would yield a profit of:

$$P_{fwd} - P(1 + r) > 0.$$

This would be a risk-free profit and so cannot be allowed under market no-arbitrage principles. A similar argument is used to demonstrate that we cannot have

$$P_{fwd} < P(1 + r)$$

because traders would then short the bond today and simultaneously buy the bond for forward delivery, investing sale proceeds at the interest rate of r. This would yield a risk-free profit of $P(1 + r) - P_{fwd} > 0$.

Applying the same reasoning to the repo market, the forward price P_{fwd} would be given from the repo rate r_{repo} and is $P_{fwd} = P(1 + r_{repo})$. This implies that $r_{repo} = r$.

References and bibliography

Amihud, Y. and Mendelson, H. 1991, "Liquidity, Maturity and the Yields on U.S. Government Securities, *Journal of Finance*, Vol. 4, pp. 1411–25.

Beim, D. 1992, "Estimating bond liquidity", cited in Duffie (1996).

Cornell, B. 1993, "Adverse Selection, Squeezes, and the Bid-ask Spread on Treasury Securities", *Journal of Fixed Income* June, pp. 39–47.

Cornell, B. and Shapiro, A. 1989, "The Mispricing of US Treasury Bonds: A Case Study", *Review of Financial Studies 3*, Vol. 3, pp. 297–310.

Das, S. 1994, *Swaps and Financial Derivatives*, 2nd edition, IFR Books, London.

Decovny, S. 1998, *Swaps,* 2nd edition, FT Prentice Hall, London.

Duffie, D. 1996, "Special Repo Rates", *Journal of Finance*, Vol. LI, No. 2, June, pp. 492–526.

Fabozzi, F., Mann, S. and Choudhry, M. 2002, *The Global Money Markets*, John Wiley & Sons, New Jersey.

Jarrow, R. and Turnbull, S. 2000, *Derivative Securities*, 2nd edition, South-Western College Publishing, Cincinnati, Chapter 14.

Ramamurthy, S. 1998, "Hedging Fixed-income Securities with Interest-rate Swaps", in Fabozzi, F. (ed.), *Perspectives on Interest Rate Risk Management for Money Managers and Traders*, FJF Associates, New Hope, PA.

CHAPTER 8

Asset–Liability Management III: The ALCO

The third and final strand of our look at traditional ALM considers the reporting process, often overseen by the ALM committee (ALCO). The ALCO will have a specific remit to oversee all aspects of ALM, from the front-office money market function to back-office operations and middle-office reporting and risk management. In this chapter we consider the salient features of ALCO procedures.

ALCO policy

The ALCO is responsible for setting, and implementing, the ALM policy. Its composition varies in different banks but usually includes heads of business lines, as well as director-level staff such as the finance director. The ALCO also sets hedging policy.

The ALM process may be undertaken by the Treasury desk, ALM desk or another dedicated function within the bank. In traditional commercial banks it will be responsible for management reporting to the ALCO. The ALCO will consider the report in detail at regular meetings, usually weekly. Main points of interest in the ALCO report include variations in interest income, the areas that experienced fluctuations in income and what the latest short-term income projections are. The ALM report will link these three strands across the group entity and also to each individual business line. That is, it will consider macro-level factors driving variations in interest income as well as specific desk-level factors. The former includes changes in the shape and level of the yield curve, while the latter will include new business, customer behaviour and so on. Of necessity the ALM report is a detailed, large document.

Table 8.1 is a summary overview of the responsibilities of the ALCO, and is essentially a banking ALM strategic overview.

Mission	Components
ALCO management and reporting	Formulating ALM strategy Management reporting ALCO agenda and minutes Assessing liquidity, gap and interest-rate risk reports Scenario planning and analysis Interest income projection
Asset management	Managing bank liquidity book (CDs, Bills) Managing the FRN book Investing bank capital
ALM strategy	Yield curve analysis Money market trading
Funding and liquidity management	Liquidity policy Managing funding and liquidity risk Ensuring funding diversification Managing lending of funds
Risk management	Formulating hedging policy Interest-rate risk exposure management Implementing hedging policy using cash and derivative instruments
Internal treasury function	Formulating transfer pricing system and level Funding group entities Calculating the cost of capital

Table 8.1 ALCO main mission

The ALCO will meet on a regular basis; the frequency depends on the type of institution but is usually once a month. The composition of the ALCO also varies by institution but may be comprised of the heads of Treasury, Trading and Risk Management, as well as the finance director. Representatives from the credit committee and loan syndication may also be present. A typical agenda would consider all the elements listed in Table 8.1. Thus the meeting will discuss and generate action points on the following:

- Management reporting: this will entail analysing the various management reports and either signing off on them or agreeing to items for actioning. The issues to consider include lending margin, interest income, variance from last projection, customer business and future business. Current business policy with regard to lending and portfolio management will be reviewed and either continued or adjusted.
- Business planning: existing asset (and liability) books will be reviewed, and future business direction drawn up. This will consider the performance of existing business, most importantly with regard to return on capital. The existing asset portfolio will be analysed from a risk-reward perspective, and a decision taken to continue or modify all lines of business. Any proposed new business will be discussed and if accepted in principle will be moved on to the next stage.[1] At this stage any new business will be assessed for projected returns, revenue and risk exposure.
- Hedging policy: overall hedging policy will consider the acceptance of risk exposure, existing risk limits and the use of hedging instruments. The latter also includes use of derivative instruments. Many bank ALM desks find that their hedging requirements can be met using plain vanilla products such as interest-rate swaps and exchange-traded short-money futures contracts. The use of options, and even vanilla instruments such as FRAs,[2] is much less common than one might think. Hedging policy takes into account the cash book revenue level, current market volatility levels and the overall cost of hedging. On occasion, certain exposures may be left unhedged

---

1 New business will follow a long process of approval, typically involving all the relevant front, middle- and back-office departments of the bank, and culminating in a "new products committee" meeting at which the proposed new line of business will be either approved, sent back to the sponsoring department for modification or rejected.

2 See Chapter 13. But, as a well-known old boy from the market is fond of saying, "Hedging is for gardeners!"

because the cost associated with hedging them is deemed prohibitive (this includes the actual cost of putting on the hedge as well as the opportunity cost associated with expected reduced income from the cash book). Of course, hedging policy is formulated in coordination with overall funding and liquidity policy. Its final form must consider the bank's views of the following:

- expectations on the future level and direction of interest rates;
- balancing the need to manage and control risk exposure with the need to maximise revenue and income;
- the level of risk aversion, and how much risk exposure the bank is willing to accept.

The ALCO is dependant on management reporting from the ALM or Treasury desk. The reports may be compiled by the Treasury middle office. The main report is the overall ALM report, showing the composition of the bank's ALM book. This was discussed in Chapter 5. Other reports will look at specific business lines, and will consider the return on capital generated by these businesses. These reports will need to break down aggregate levels of revenue and risk by business line. Reports will also drill down by product type, across business lines. Other reports will consider the gap, the gap risk, the VaR or DV01 (interest-rate risk) report and credit risk exposures. Overall, the reporting system must be able to isolate revenues, return and risk by country sector, business line and product type. There is also an element of scenario planning; that is, expected performance under various specified macro- and micro-level market conditions.

Figure 8.1 illustrates the general reporting concept.

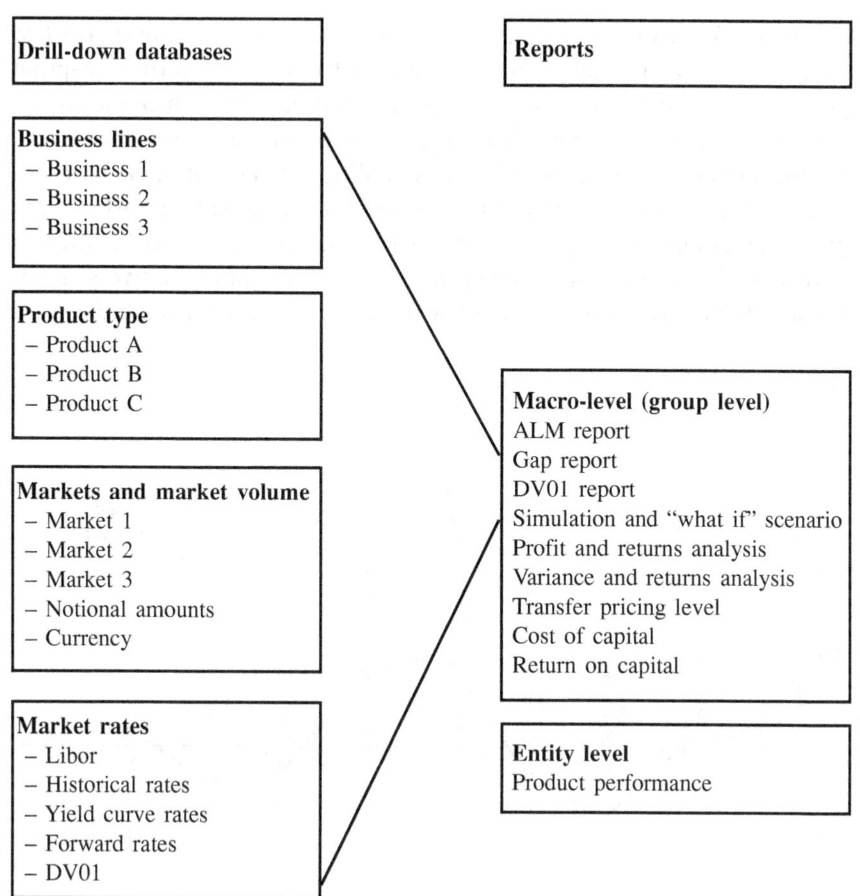

Figure 8.1 ALCO reporting input and output

ALCO reporting

We now provide a flavour of the reporting that is provided to, and analysed by, the ALCO. This is a generalisation, reports will of course vary by the type of the institution and the nature of its business.

In Chapter 5 we showed an example of a macro-level ALM report. The ALCO will also consider macro-level gap and liquidity reports compiled for product and market. The interest-rate gap, being simply the difference between assets and liabilities, is easily set into these parameters. For management reporting purposes the report will attempt to show a dynamic profile, but its chief limitation is that it is always a snapshot of a fixed point in time, and therefore strictly speaking will always be out-of-date.

Figure 8.2 shows a typical dynamic gap, positioned in a desired ALM "Smile", with the projected interest-rate gaps based on the current snapshot profile. This report shows the future funding requirement, which the ALCO can give direction on what reflects their view on future interest-rate levels. It also shows where the sensitivity to falling interest rates, in terms of revenue, lies because it shows the volume of assets. Again, the ALCO can give instructions on hedging if they expect interest income to be affected adversely. The x-axis is the time buckets from overnight out to two years or beyond. Banks use different time buckets to suit their own requirements.[3]

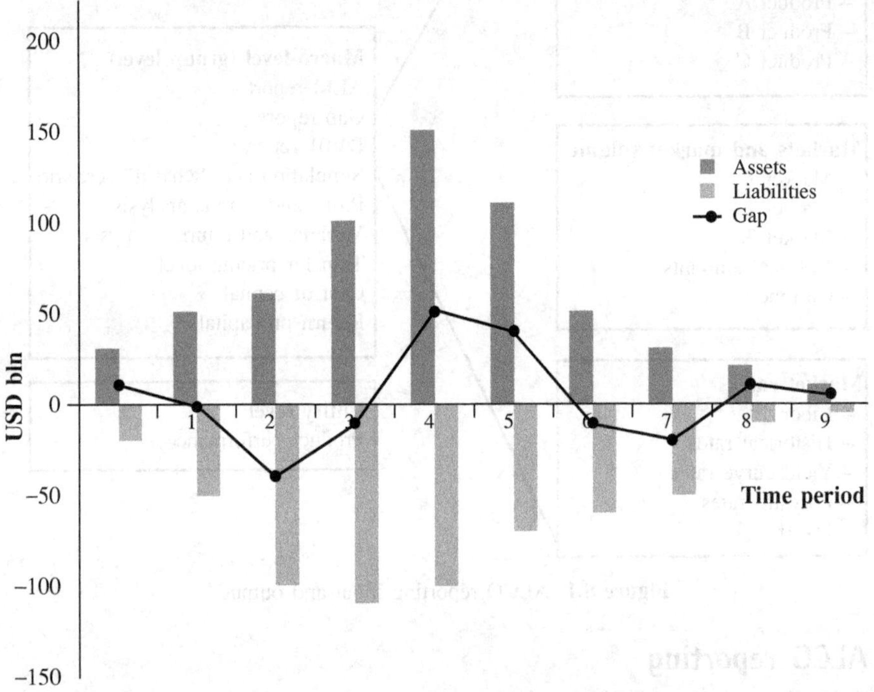

Figure 8.2 ALM and expected liquidity and interest-rate gap, snapshot profile

[3] For example, a bank may have the "overnight" time bucket on its own, or incorporate it into an "overnight to one-week" period. Similarly, banks may have each period from one month to 12 in their own separate buckets, or may place some periods into combined time periods. There is no "correct" way.

Figure 8.3 shows the same report with a breakdown by product (or market – the report would have a similar layout). We use a hypothetical sample of different business lines. Using this format the ALCO can observe which assets and liabilities are producing the gaps, which is important because it shows if products (or markets) are fitting into overall bank policy. Equally, policy can be adjusted if required in response to what the report shows. So the ALCO can see what proportion of total assets is represented by each business line, and which line has the greatest forward funding requirement. The same report is shown again in Figure 8.4 on page 334, but this time with the breakdown by type of interest rate, fixed or variable.

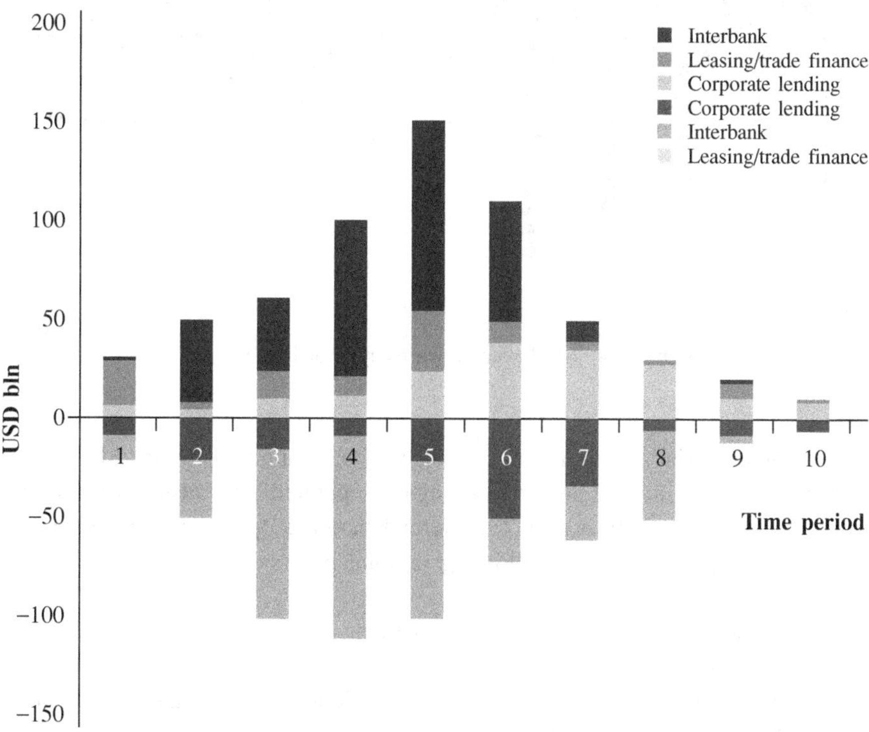

Figure 8.3 ALM breakdown by product (or market) segment

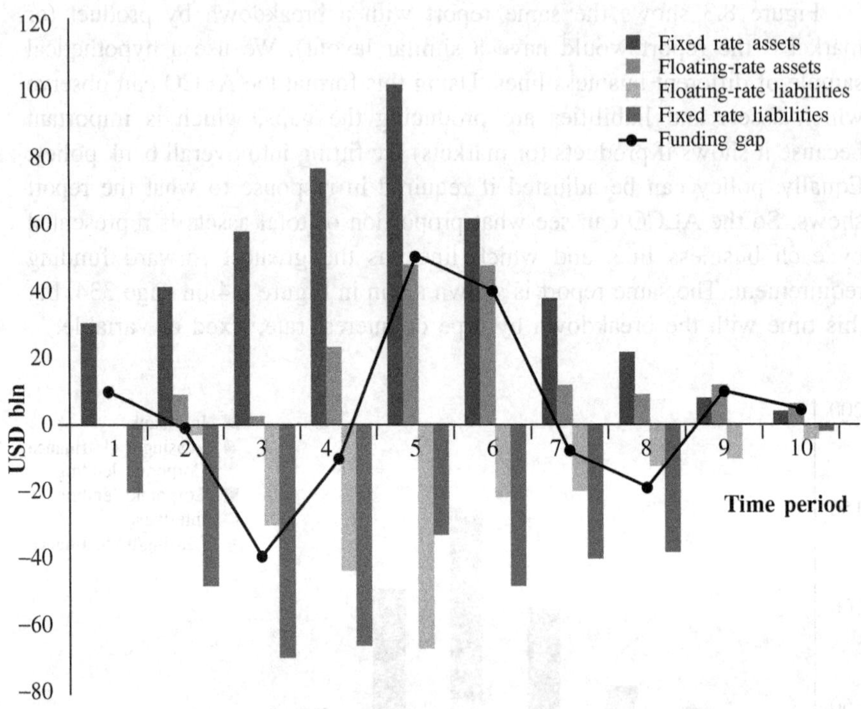

Figure 8.4 ALM breakdown by type of interest rate

Another variation of this report that will be examined by the ALCO is a breakdown by income and margin, again separated into business lines or markets as required. In a pure commercial banking operation the revenue-type mix will comprise the following (among others):

- the bid–offer spread between borrowing and lending in the interbank market;
- corporate lending margin; that is, the loan rate over and above the bank's cost of funds;
- trading income;
- fixed fees charged for services rendered.

The ALCO will receive an income breakdown report, split by business line. The x-axis in such a report would show the margin level for each time period; that is, it shows the margin of the lending rate over the cost of funds by each time bucket. Figure 8.5 is another type of income report, which shows the volumes and income spread by business line. The spread is shown in basis points and is an average for that time bucket (across all loans and deposits for that bucket). The volumes will be those reported in the main ALM report (Figure 8.2), but this time with the margin contribution per time period. As we might expect, the spread levels per product across time are roughly similar. They will differ more markedly by product time. The latter report is shown in Figure 8.6 on page 336, which is more useful because it shows the performance of each business line. In general, the ALCO will prefer low volumes and high margin as a combination, because lower volumes consume less capital. However, some significant high-volume business (such as interbank money market operations) operates at relatively low margin.

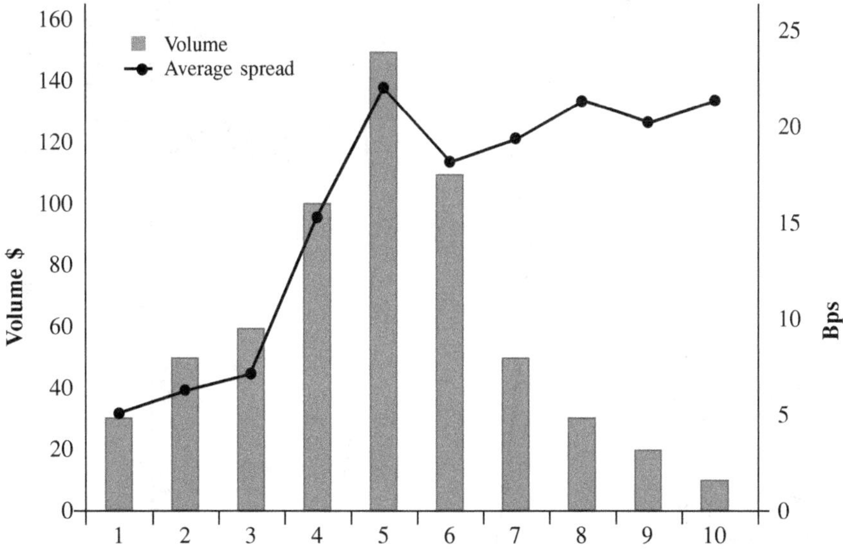

Figure 8.5 Asset profile volume and average income spread

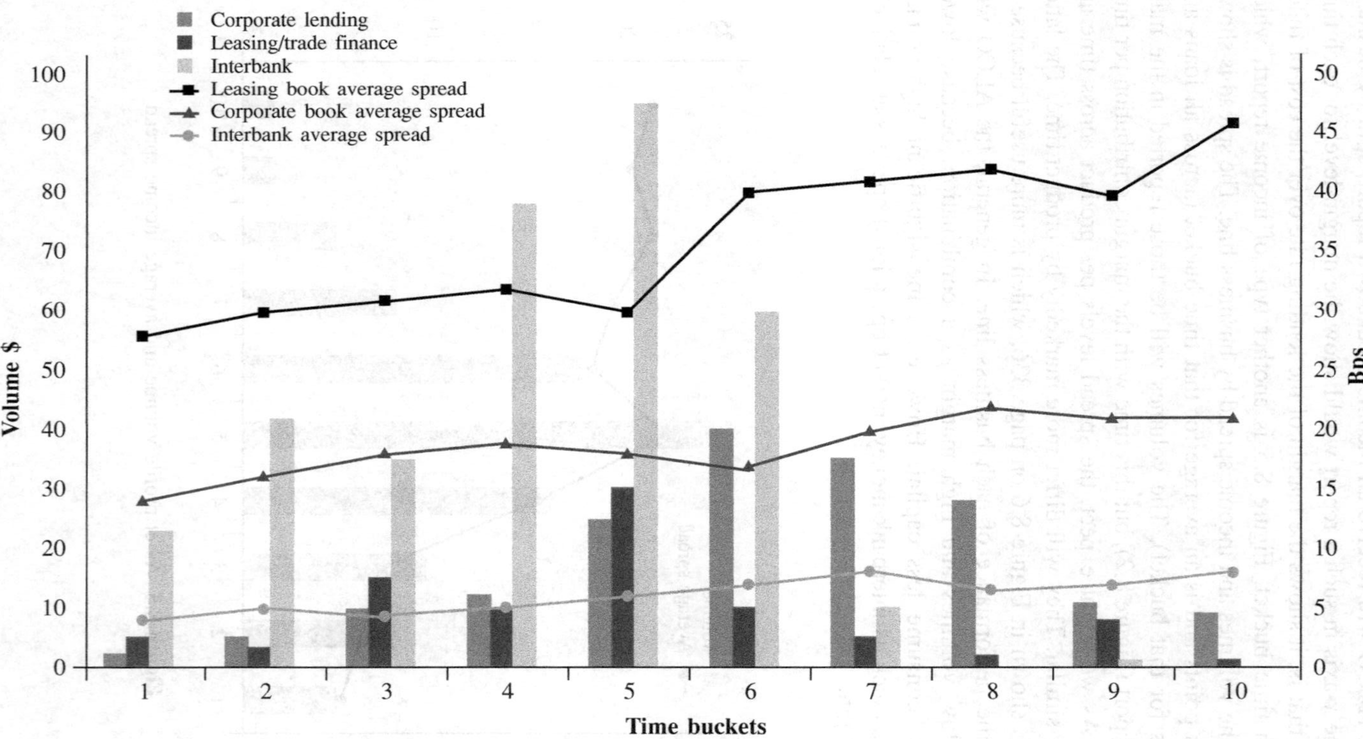

Figure 8.6 Business lines and average income spread

The income and return reports viewed by ALCO requires that it checks if bank policy with regard to lending and money market trading is being adhered to. Essentially, these reports are providing information on the risk-return profile of the bank. The ideal combination is the lowest possible risk for the highest possible return, although of course low-risk business carries the lowest return. The level of trade-off that the bank is comfortable with is what the ALCO will set in its direction and strategy. With regard to volumes and bank business, it might be thought that the optimum mix is high volume mixed with a high-income margin. However, high-volume business consumes the most capital, so there will be another trade-off with regard to use of capital.

The rate of interest is always the most important single variable in an advanced market economy.

— Anatole Kaletsky, "Economic View",
The Times, 26 June 2006

The long-term government bond yield is the single most important financial variable in any market economy, setting the tone for equity and house prices, governing business investment decisions and establishing the discount rate for pension liabilities and insurance policies.

– Anatole Kaletsky, "Economic View",
The Times, 22 February 2005

CHAPTER

9

The Yield Curve

Understanding and appreciating the yield curve is important to all capital market participants. It is especially important to debt capital market participants, and especially, especially important to bank ALM practitioners. So if you are reading this book it is safe to assume that the yield curve is a very important subject! This is a long chapter but well worth getting to grips with. In it, we discuss basic concepts of the yield curve, as well as its uses and interpretation. We show how to calculate the zero-coupon (or spot) and forward yield curve, and present the main theories that seek to explain its shape and behaviour. We will see that the spread of different curves to another, such as the swap curve compared to the government curve, is itself important and we seek to explain the determinants of these spreads in the next chapter. We begin with an introduction to the curve and interest rates.

Importance of the yield curve

Banks deal in interest rates and credit risk. These are the two fundamental tenets of banking, today as they were when banking first began. The first of these, interest rates, is an explicit measure of the cost of borrowing money and is encapsulated in the yield curve. For bankers, understanding the behaviour and properties of the yield curve is an essential part of the ALM process. The following are some, but not all, of the reasons why this is so:

- changes in interest rates have a direct impact on bank revenue; the yield curve captures the current state of term interest rates, and also presents the current market expectation of future interest rates;

- the interest-rate gap reflects the state of bank borrowing and lending; gaps along the term structure are sensitive to changes in the shape and slope of the yield curve;
- current and future trading strategy, including the asset allocation and credit policy decision, will impact interest-rate risk exposure and therefore will take into account the shape and behaviour of the yield curve.

We can see then that understanding and appreciating the yield curve is a vital part of ALM operations. This chapter is a detailed look at the curve from the banker's viewpoint. It is divided into two parts, Part I on interest rates and interpreting the yield curve, and Part II on dynamic aspects and fitting the curve.

Part I

The money market yield curve

The main measure of return associated with holding debt market assets is the yield-to-maturity (YTM) or *gross redemption yield*. In developed markets, as well as certain emerging economies, there is usually a large number of bonds trading at one time, at different yields and with varying terms to maturity. Investors and traders frequently examine the relationship between the yields on bonds that are in the same class; plotting yields of bonds that differ only in their term to maturity produces what is known as a *yield curve*. The yield curve is an important indicator and knowledge source of the state of a debt capital market. It is sometimes referred to as the *term structure of interest rates*, but strictly speaking this is not correct, as this term should be reserved for the zero-coupon yield curve only. We shall examine this in detail later.

Much of the analysis and pricing activity that takes place in the capital markets revolves around the yield curve. The yield curve describes the relationship between a particular redemption yield and a bond's maturity. Plotting the yields of bonds along the term structure will give us our yield curve. It is very important that only bonds from the same class of issuer or with the same degree of liquidity are used when plotting the yield curve; for example, a curve may be constructed for UK gilts or for AA-rated sterling Eurobonds, but not a mixture of both, because gilts and Eurobonds are bonds from different class issuers. The primary yield curve in any domestic capital market is the government bond yield curve, so for example in the US market it is the US Treasury yield curve. With the advent of the euro currency in

12 countries of the European Union, in theory any euro-currency government bond can be used to plot a euro yield curve. In practice only bonds from the same government are used, as for various reasons different country bonds within euro-land trade at different yields.

Outside the government bond markets yield curves are plotted for money-market instruments, off-balance sheet instruments; in fact, virtually all debt market instruments. Money market instruments trade on a simple yield basis, as the cash market is comprised essentially of bullet interest payment securities. So the money market yield curve is simple to construct. The "Libor curve" for money markets is the main measure of money market return, and in theory goes out to 12 months only. In fact, money market derivatives frequently trade out to 18 months and even two years. We show in Figures 9.1 and 9.2 on page 342 the Bloomberg screen for Libor fixing and a broker's screen (Garban ICAP) for US dollar overnight-index swaps (OIS) swaps. These show that the maximum accepted maturity for the money market yield curve is 24 months. Another money market yield curve, in fact the most widely used by participants, is the exchange-traded futures curve for short-dated deposits; for instance, the Eurodollar curve or the short-sterling curve. This is taken as the most reliable and liquid indicator of expected money market rates. Figure 9.3 on page 342 shows the Eurodollar curve as at 10 May 2004.

1 P3007a **Govt** **BBAM**
Screen Printed

BRITISH BANKERS'
ASSOCIATION
Page 1 of 4

05/10 13:34 GMT [BRITISH BANKERS ASSOCIATION LIBOR RATES] 3750
[10/05/04] RATES AT 11:00 LONDON TIME 10/05/2004 10/05 11:18 GMT

CCY	USD	GBP	CAD	EUR	JPY	EUR 365
O/N	1.05250	4.27875	2.07000	2.00125	SN0.03250	2.02905
1WK	1.08000	4.32813	2.06833	2.04613	0.03375	2.07455
2WK	1.08125	4.37500	2.07000	2.05063	0.03500	2.07911
1MO	1.10000	4.40500	2.07500	2.06263	0.03750	2.09128
2MO	1.16000	4.43875	2.08500	2.08038	0.04313	2.10927
3MO	1.24000	4.47188	2.10833	2.08950	0.04750	2.11852
4MO	1.34000	4.52750	2.13167	2.10613	0.05075	2.13538
5MO	1.43750	4.59500	2.15833	2.12275	0.05525	2.15223
6MO	1.53000	4.65625	2.20000	2.14038	0.05975	2.17011
7MO	1.62000	4.70750	2.23833	2.16150	0.06250	2.19152
8MO	1.71250	4.76375	2.27500	2.19150	0.06750	2.22194
9MO	1.81000	4.82125	2.32667	2.22363	0.07188	2.25451
10MO	1.89375	4.86875	2.37000	2.25275	0.07750	2.28404
11MO	1.98125	4.91625	2.41000	2.27788	0.08438	2.30952
12MO	2.07000	4.95875	2.46333	2.31538	0.08875	2.34754

Figure 9.1 Bloomberg screen BBAM, daily Libor fixing page, as at 10 May 2004

ICAU2 P1P300 Govt **ICAU**
Screen Printed
14:34 **USD OIS – ICAU** PAGE 1 / 1

	USD OIS	Ask	Bid	Time
1)	1 Month	1.0230	1.0030	14:12
2)	2 Month	1.0670	1.0470	14:12
3)	3 Month	1.1350	1.1150	14:26
4)	4 Month	1.2430	1.2230	14:31
5)	5 Month	1.3220	1.3020	14:31
6)	6 Month	1.4030	1.3830	14:31
7)	7 Month	1.4920	1.4720	14:31
8)	8 Month	1.5810	1.5600	14:34
9)	9 Month	1.6680	1.6470	14:34
10)	10 Month	1.7490	1.7290	14:34
11)	11 Month	1.8280	1.8070	14:34
12)	12 Month	1.9120	1.8920	14:34
13)	15 Month	2.1590	2.1390	14:34
14)	18 Month	2.3900	2.3690	14:34
15)	21 Month	2.6120	2.5920	14:34
16)	24 Month	2.8010	2.7810	14:34

Australia 61 2 9777 8600 Brazil 5511 3048 4500 Europe 44 20 7330 7500 Germany 49 69 920410
Hong Kong 852 2977 6000 Japan 81 3 3201 8900 Singapore 65 6212 1000 U.S. 1 212 318 2000
0 10-May-04 14:34:21

Figure 9.2 Bloomberg screen ICAU2, Garban ICAP broker's price screen for US dollar OIS swaps, 10 May 2004

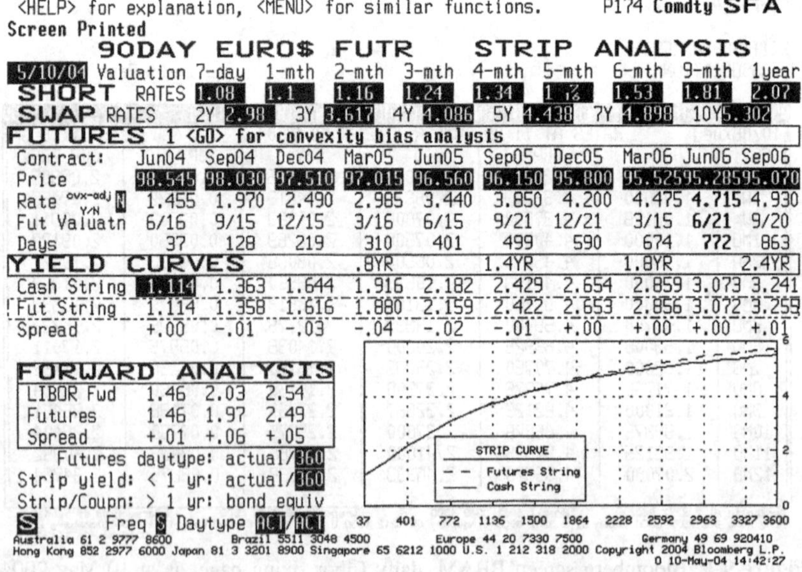

<HELP> for explanation, <MENU> for similar functions. P174 Comdty SFA
Screen Printed
90DAY EURO$ FUTR STRIP ANALYSIS
5/10/04 Valuation 7-day 1-mth 2-mth 3-mth 4-mth 5-mth 6-mth 9-mth 1year
SHORT RATES 1.08 1.1 1.16 1.24 1.34 1 7/16 1.53 1.81 2.07
SWAP RATES 2Y 2.98 3Y 3.617 4Y 4.086 5Y 4.438 7Y 4.898 10Y 5.302
FUTURES 1 <GO> for convexity bias analysis
Contract: Jun04 Sep04 Dec04 Mar05 Jun05 Sep05 Dec05 Mar06 Jun06 Sep06
Price 98.545 98.030 97.510 97.015 96.560 96.150 95.800 95.525 95.285 95.070
Rate cvx-adj Y/N N 1.455 1.970 2.490 2.985 3.440 3.850 4.200 4.475 4.715 4.930
Fut Valuatn 6/16 9/15 12/15 3/16 6/15 9/21 12/21 3/15 6/21 9/20
Days 37 128 219 310 401 499 590 674 772 863
YIELD CURVES .8YR 1.4YR 1.8YR 2.4YR
Cash String 1.114 1.363 1.644 1.916 2.182 2.429 2.654 2.859 3.073 3.241
Fut String 1.114 1.358 1.616 1.880 2.159 2.422 2.653 2.856 3.072 3.259
Spread +.00 -.01 -.03 -.04 -.02 -.01 +.00 +.00 +.00 +.01
FORWARD ANALYSIS
LIBOR Fwd 1.46 2.03 2.54
Futures 1.46 1.97 2.49
Spread +.01 +.06 +.05
Futures daytype: actual/360
Strip yield: < 1 yr: actual/360
Strip/Coupn: > 1 yr: bond equiv
S Freq S Daytype ACT/ACT
STRIP CURVE
Futures String
Cash String
6
4
2
0
37 401 772 1136 1500 1864 2228 2592 2963 3327 3600
Australia 61 2 9777 8600 Brazil 5511 3048 4500 Europe 44 20 7330 7500 Germany 49 69 920410
Hong Kong 852 2977 6000 Japan 81 3 3201 8900 Singapore 65 6212 1000 U.S. 1 212 318 2000 Copyright 2004 Bloomberg L.P.
0 10-May-04 14:42:27

Figure 9.3 Eurodollar yield curve, 10 May 2004

Figure 9.4 shows the interbank fixings for HKD and SGD, and the AUD deposit rates as at 6 September 2004, as money market yield curves on Bloomberg screen MMCV.

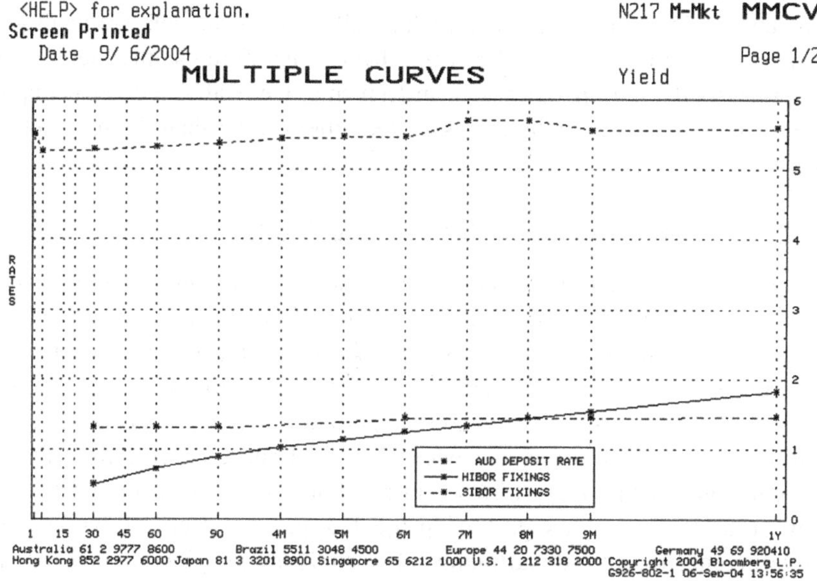

Figure 9.4 Bloomberg screen MMCV, interbank fixings for HKD and SGD, and AUD deposit rates as at 6 September 2004

The principles behind the money market yield curve are exactly the same as those behind the longer-dated bond market yield curve. So in this chapter we will consider the YTM yield curve and how to derive spot and forward yields from a current redemption yield curve.

Using the yield curve

Let us first consider the main uses of the yield curve. All participants in the debt capital markets have an interest in the current shape and level of the yield curve, as well as what this information implies for the future. The main uses are summarised below.

Setting the yield for all debt market instruments

The yield curve essentially fixes the cost of money over the maturity term structure. The yields of government bonds from the shortest maturity instrument to the longest set the benchmark for yields for all other debt instruments in the market, around which all debt instruments are analysed. Issuers of debt (and their underwriting banks) therefore use the yield curve to price bonds and all other debt instruments. Generally, the zero-coupon yield curve is used to price new issue securities, rather than the redemption yield curve.

Acting as an indicator of future yield levels

As we discuss later in this chapter, the yield curve assumes certain shapes in response to market expectations of future interest rates. Bond market participants analyse the present shape of the yield curve in an effort to determine the implications regarding the future direction of market interest rates. This is perhaps one of the most important functions of the yield curve, and it is as much an art as a science. The yield curve is scrutinised for its information content, not just by bond traders and fund managers, but also by corporate financiers as part of project appraisal. Central banks and government treasury departments also analyse the yield curve for its information content, not just regarding forward interest rates but also with regard to expected inflation levels.

Measuring and comparing returns across the maturity spectrum

Portfolio managers use the yield curve to assess the relative value of investments across the maturity spectrum. The yield curve indicates the returns that are available at different maturity points and is therefore very important to fixed-income fund managers, who can use it to assess which point of the curve offers the best return relative to other points.

Indicating relative value between different bonds of similar maturity

The yield curve can be analysed to indicate which bonds are cheap or dear to the curve. Placing bonds relative to the zero-coupon yield curve helps to highlight which bonds should be bought or sold either outright or as part of a bond spread trade.

Pricing interest-rate derivative securities

The price of derivative securities revolves around the yield curve. At the short-end, products such as forward rate agreements (FRAs) are priced off the futures curve, but futures rates reflect the market's view on forward three-month cash deposit rates. At the longer end, interest-rate swaps are priced off the yield curve, while hybrid instruments that incorporate an option feature such as convertibles and callable bonds also reflect current yield curve levels. The "risk-free" interest rate, which is one of the parameters used in option pricing, is the T-bill rate or short-term government repo rate, both constituents of the money market yield curve.

Yield-to-maturity (YTM) yield curve

The most commonly occurring yield curve is the YTM yield curve. The equation used to calculate the YTM was shown in Chapter 4 (4.1). The curve itself is constructed by plotting the YTM against the term to maturity for a group of bonds of the same class. Three different examples are shown in Figure 9.5 on page 346. Bonds used in constructing the curve will only rarely have an exact number of whole years to redemption; however, it is often common to see yields plotted against whole years on the x-axis. This is because once a bond is designated the *benchmark* for that term, its yield is taken to be the representative yield. For example, the then 10-year benchmark bond in the UK gilt market, the 5% Treasury 2012, maintained its benchmark status throughout 2002 and into 2003, even as its term to maturity fell below ten years. The YTM yield curve is the most commonly observed curve simply because YTM is the most frequent measure of return used. The business sections of daily newspapers, where they quote bond yields at all, usually quote bond yields to maturity.

As we might expect, given the source data from which it is constructed, the YTM yield curve contains some inaccuracies. We have already come across the main weakness of the YTM measure, which is the assumption of a constant rate for coupon reinvestment during the bond's life at the redemption yield level. Since market rates will fluctuate over time, it will not be possible to achieve this (a feature known as *reinvestment risk*). Only zero-coupon bondholders avoid reinvestment risk as no coupon is paid during the life of a zero-coupon bond.

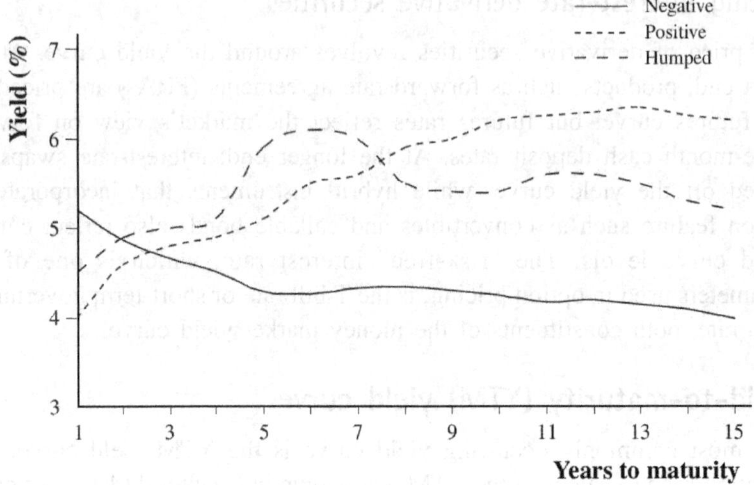

Figure 9.5 YTM yield curves

The YTM yield curve does not distinguish between different payment patterns that may result from bonds with different coupons; that is, the fact that low-coupon bonds pay a higher portion of their cash flows at a later date than high-coupon bonds of the same maturity. The curve also assumes an even cash flow pattern for all bonds. Therefore in this case cash flows are not discounted at the appropriate rate for the bonds in the group being used to construct the curve. To get around this, bond analysts may sometimes construct a *coupon yield curve,* which plots YTM against term to maturity for a group of bonds with the same coupon. This may be useful when a group of bonds contains some with very high coupons; high coupon bonds often trade "cheap to the curve"; that is, they have higher yields than corresponding bonds of the same maturity but lower coupon. This is usually because of reinvestment risk and, in some markets, for tax reasons.

For the reasons we have discussed the market often uses other types of yield curve for analysis when the YTM yield curve is deemed unsuitable.

That there are a number of yield curves that can be plotted, each relevant to its own market, can be seen from Figure 9,6, which shows the curves that can be selected for the US dollar market, from screen IYC on Bloomberg. We see that curves can be selected for US Treasuries, US dollar swaps, strips, agency securities, and so on. Figure 9.7 shows the curves for Treasuries, interest-rate swaps and strips as at August 2003.

GRAB Govt **IYC**
Enter curve selection <go>

SINGLE YIELD CURVE
Curves for UNITED STATES Page 1 / 1

1)	US Treasury Actives	I25
2)	US On/Off The Run Govt	I111
3)	US Government Strips	I39
4)	US Treas. Inflation Index	I169
5)	US Dollar Swap Rates	I52
6)	US Dollar Swap Spreads	I48
7)	US Swap Act/360	I205
8)	US Swap Spreads Act/360	I207
9)	US Agency	I26
10)	US Fannie Mae Benchmarks	I168
11)	US Freddie Mac Notes	I197
12)	US FHLB Issues	I199
13)	Supranational Eurodollar	I27
14)	World Bank Global	I80
15)	BMA-FNMA Benchmark	I252
16)	BMA-FHLMC Reference	I267

Australia 61 2 9777 8600 Brazil 5511 3048 4500 Europe 44 20 7330 7500 Germany 49 69 920410
Hong Kong 852 2977 6000 Japan 81 3 3201 8900 Singapore 65 6212 1000 U.S. 1 212 318 2000 Copyright 2003 Bloomberg L.P.
G657-802-2 15-Aug-03 8:37:53

Figure 9.6 US menu page from screen IYC on Bloomberg

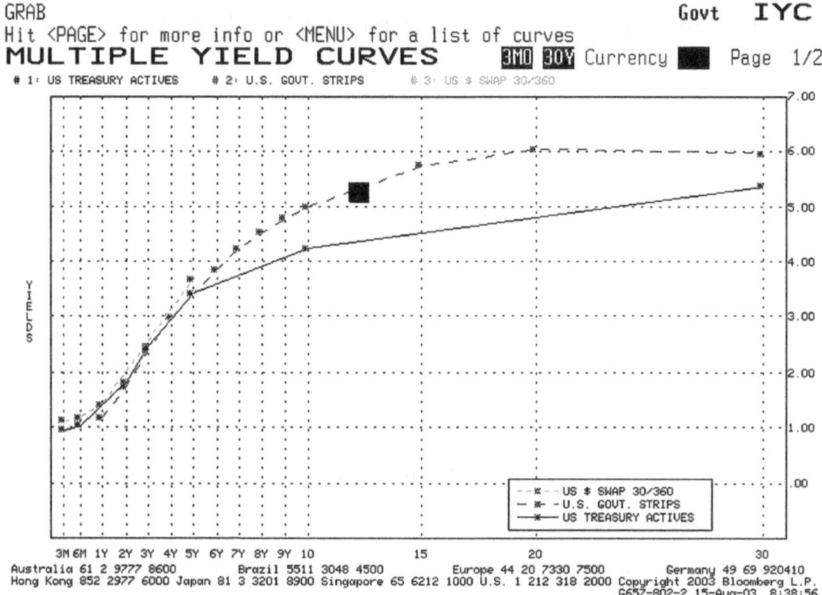

Figure 9.7 US yield curves, August 2003

We discuss next the various types of curve that can be plotted.

The coupon yield curve

The *coupon yield curve* is a plot of the YTM against term to maturity for a group of bonds with the same coupon. If we were to construct such a curve we would see that in general high-coupon bonds trade at a discount (have higher yields) relative to low-coupon bonds, because of reinvestment risk and for tax reasons (in the United Kingdom, for example, on gilts the coupon is taxed as income tax, while any capital gain is exempt from capital gains tax; even in jurisdictions where capital gain on bonds is taxable, this can often be deferred whereas income tax cannot). It is frequently the case that yields vary considerably with coupons for the same term to maturity, and with term to maturity for different coupons. Put another way, usually we observe different coupon curves not only at different levels but also with different shapes. Distortions arise in the YTM curve if no allowance is made for coupon differences. For this reason bond analysts frequently draw a line of "best fit" through a plot of redemption yields, because the coupon effect in a group of bonds will produce a curve with humps and troughs. Figure 9.8 shows a hypothetical set of coupon yield curves. However, since in any group of bonds it is unusual to observe bonds with the same coupon along the entire term structure this type of curve is relatively rare.

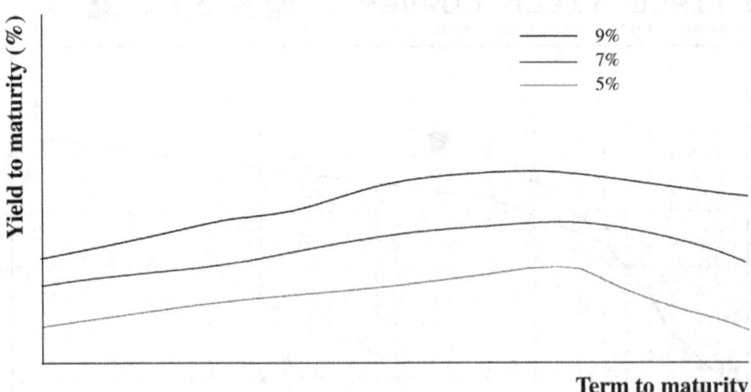

Figure 9.8 Coupon yield curves

The par yield curve

The *par yield curve* is not usually encountered in secondary market trading; however, it is often constructed for use by corporate financiers and others in the new issues or *primary* market. The par yield curve plots YTM against term to maturity for current bonds trading at par.[1] The par yield is therefore equal to the coupon rate for bonds priced at par or near to par, as the YTM for bonds priced exactly at par is equal to the coupon rate. Those involved in the primary market will use a par yield curve to determine the required coupon for a new bond that is to be issued at par. This is because investors prefer not to pay over par for a new-issue bond, so the bond requires a coupon that will result in a price at or slightly below par.

The par yield curve can be derived directly from bond yields when bonds are trading at or near par. If bonds in the market are trading substantially away from par then the resulting curve will be distorted. It is then necessary to derive it by iteration from the spot yield curve. As we would observe at almost any time, it is rare to encounter bonds trading at par for any particular maturity. The market therefore uses actual non-par vanilla bond yield curves to derive *zero-coupon yield curves* and then constructs hypothetical par yields that would be observed were there any par bonds being traded.

The zero-coupon (or spot) yield curve

The *zero-coupon* (or *spot*) *yield curve* plots zero-coupon yields (or spot yields) against term to maturity. A zero-coupon yield is the yield prevailing on a bond that has no coupons. In the first instance if there is a liquid zero-coupon bond market we can plot the yields from these bonds if we wish to construct this curve. However, it is not necessary to have a set of zero-coupon bonds in order to construct the curve, as we can derive it from a coupon or par yield curve; in fact, in many markets where no zero-coupon bonds are traded, a spot yield curve is derived from the conventional YTM yield curve. This is of course a *theoretical* zero-coupon (spot) yield curve, as opposed to the *market* or *observed* spot curve that can be constructed using the yields of actual zero-coupon bonds trading in the market.[2]

---

1 Par price for a bond is almost invariably 100%. Certain bonds have par defined as 1,000 per 1,000 nominal of paper.

2 It is common to see the terms spot rate and zero-coupon rate used synonymously. However, the spot rate is a theoretical construct and cannot be observed in the market. The definition of the spot rate, which is the rate of return on a single cash flow that has been dealt today and is received at some point in the future, comes very close to that of the yield on a zero-coupon bond, which can be observed directly in the market. Zero-coupon rates can therefore be taken to be spot rates in practice, which is why the terms are frequently used interchangeably.

Basic concepts

Spot yields must comply with equation (9.1). This equation assumes annual coupon payments and that the calculation is carried out on a coupon date so that accrued interest is zero.

$$P_d = \sum_{n=1}^{N} \frac{C}{(1 + rs_n)^n} + \frac{M}{(1 + rs_N)^N}$$
$$= \sum_{n=1}^{N} C \times df_n + M \times df_N \tag{9.1}$$

where

rs_n is the spot or zero-coupon yield on a bond with n years to maturity
df is the corresponding *discount factor.*

In (9.1) rs_1 would be the current one-year spot yield, rs_2 the current two-year spot yield and so on. Theoretically the spot yield for a particular term to maturity is the same as the yield on a zero-coupon bond of the same maturity, which is why spot yields are also known as zero-coupon yields.

This last is an important result, as spot yields can be derived from redemption yields that have been observed in the market.

As with the yield to redemption yield curve, the spot yield curve is commonly used in the market. It is viewed as the true term structure of interest rates because there is no reinvestment risk involved; the stated yield is equal to the actual annual return. That is, the yield on a zero-coupon bond of n years maturity is regarded as the true n-year interest rate. Because the observed government bond redemption yield curve is not considered to be the true interest rate, analysts often construct a theoretical spot yield curve. Essentially, this is done by breaking down each coupon bond being observed into its constituent cash flows, which become a series of individual zero-coupon bonds. For example, £100 nominal of a 5% two-year bond (paying annual coupons) is considered equivalent to £5 nominal of a one-year zero-coupon bond and £105 nominal of a two-year zero-coupon bond.

Let us assume that in the market there are 30 bonds all paying annual coupons. The first bond has a maturity of one year, the second bond of two years and so on out to 30 years. We know the price of each of these bonds, and we wish to determine what the prices imply about the market's estimate of future interest rates. We naturally expect interest rates to vary over time, but that all payments being made on the same date are valued using the same rate. For the one-year bond we know its current price and the amount of the payment (comprised of one coupon payment and the redemption proceeds) we will receive at the end of the year; therefore we can calculate the interest rate for the first year: assume the one-year bond has a coupon of 5%. If the bond is priced at par and we invest £100 today we will receive £105 in one year's time, hence the rate of interest is apparent and is 5%. For the two-year bond we use this interest rate to calculate the future value of its current price in one year's time: *this is how much we would receive if we had invested the same amount in the one-year bond.* However, the two-year bond pays a coupon at the end of the first year; if we subtract this amount from the future value of the current price, the net amount is what we should be giving up in one year in return for the one remaining payment. From these numbers we can calculate the interest rate in year 2.

Assume that the two-year bond pays a coupon of 6% and is priced at 99.00. If the 99.00 were invested at the rate we calculated for the one-year bond (5%), it would accumulate £103.95 in one year, made up of the £99 investment and interest of £4.95. On the payment date in one year's time, the one-year bond matures and the two-year bond pays a coupon of 6%. If everyone expected that at this time the two-year bond would be priced at more than 97.95 (which is 103.95 minus 6.00), then no investor would buy the one-year bond, since it would be more advantageous to buy the two-year bond and sell it after one year for a greater return. Similarly, if the price was less than 97.95 no investor would buy the two-year bond, as it would be cheaper to buy the shorter bond and then buy the longer-dated bond with the proceeds received when the one-year bond matures. Therefore the two-year bond must be priced at exactly 97.95 in 12 months' time. For this £97.95 to grow to £106.00 (the maturity proceeds from the two-year bond, comprising the redemption payment and coupon interest), the interest rate in year 2 must be 8.20%. We can check this by using the present value formula covered earlier. At these two interest rates, the two bonds are said to be in equilibrium.

This is an important result and shows that (in theory) there can be no arbitrage opportunity along the yield curve; using interest rates available today the return from buying the two-year bond must equal the return from buying the one-year bond and rolling over the proceeds (or *reinvesting*) for another year. This is the known as the *breakeven principle*, the law of no-arbitrage.

Using the price and coupon of the three-year bond we can calculate the interest rate in year 3 in precisely the same way. Using each of the bonds in turn, we can link together the *implied one-year rates* for each year up to the maturity of the longest-dated bond. The process is known as *boot-*

strapping. The "average" of the rates over a given period is the spot yield for that term: in the example given above, the rate in year 1 is 5% and in year 2 it is 8.20%. An investment of £100 at these rates would grow to £113.61. This gives a total percentage increase of 13.61% over two years, or 6.588% per annum (the average rate is not obtained by simply dividing 13.61 by 2, but – using our present value relationship again – by calculating the square root of "1 plus the interest rate" and then subtracting 1 from this number). Thus, the one-year yield is 5% and the two-year yield is 8.20%.

In real-world markets it is not necessarily as straightforward as this; for instance, on some dates there may be several bonds maturing, with different coupons, and on some dates there may be no bonds maturing. It is most unlikely that there will be a regular spacing of bond redemptions exactly one year apart. For this reason it is common for analysts to use a software model to calculate the set of implied spot rates which best fits the market prices of the bonds that do exist in the market. For instance, if there are several one-year bonds, each of their prices may imply a slightly different rate of interest. We choose the rate which gives the smallest average price error. In practice all bonds are used to find the rate in year 1, all bonds with a term longer than one year are used to calculate the rate in year 2, and so on. The zero-coupon curve can also be calculated directly from the coupon yield curve using a method similar to that described above; in this case the bonds would be priced at par and their coupons set to the par yield values.

The zero-coupon yield curve is ideal to use when deriving implied forward rates, which we consider next, and defining the term structure of interest rates. It is also the best curve to use when determining the *relative value*, whether cheap or dear, of bonds trading in the market, and when pricing new issues, irrespective of their coupons. However, it is not an absolutely accurate indicator of average market yields because most bonds are not zero-coupon bonds.

Zero-coupon discount factors

Having introduced the concept of the zero-coupon curve in the previous paragraph, we can illustrate more formally the mathematics involved. When deriving spot yields from redemption yields, we view conventional bonds as being made up of an *annuity*, which is the stream of fixed coupon payments, and a zero-coupon bond, which is the redemption payment on maturity. To derive the rates we can use (9.1), setting $P_d = M = 100$ and $C = rm_N$ as shown in (9.2) below. This has the coupon bonds trading at par, so that the coupon is equal to the yield. So we have:

$$
\begin{aligned}
100 &= rm_N \times \sum_{n=1}^{N} df_n + 100 \times df_n \\
&= rm_N \times A_N + 100 \times df_N
\end{aligned}
\tag{9.2}
$$

where rm_N is the par yield for a term to maturity of N years, where df_n the discount factor is the fair price of a zero-coupon bond with a par value of £1 and a term to maturity of N years, and where

$$A_N = \sum_{n=1}^{N} df_n = A_{N-1} + df_N \tag{9.3}$$

is the fair price of an annuity of £1 per year for N years (with A_0 by convention). Substituting (9.3) into (9.2) and rearranging will give us the expression below for the N-year discount factor, shown in (9.4):

$$df_N = \frac{1 - rm_N \times A_{N-1}}{1 + rm_N}. \tag{9.4}$$

If we assume one-year, two-year and three-year redemption yields for bonds priced at par to be 5%, 5.25% and 5.75% respectively, we will obtain the following solutions for the discount factors:

$$df_1 = \frac{1}{1 + 0.05} = 0.95238$$

$$df_2 = \frac{1 - (0.0525)(0.95238)}{1 + 0.0525} = 0.90261$$

$$df_3 = \frac{1 - (0.0575)(0.95238 + 0.90261)}{1 + 0.0575} = 0.84476.$$

We can confirm that these are the correct discount factors by substituting them back into equation (9.2); this gives us the following results for the one-year, two-year and three-year par value bonds (with coupons of 5%, 5.25% and 5.75% respectively):

$$
\begin{aligned}
100 &= 105 \times 0.95238 \\
100 &= 5.25 \times 0.95238 + 105.25 \times 0.90261 \\
100 &= 5.75 \times 0.95238 + 5.75 \times 0.90261 + 105.75 \times 0.84476.
\end{aligned}
$$

Now that we have found the correct discount factors it is relatively straightforward to calculate the spot yields using equation (9.1), and this is shown below:

$$df_1 = \frac{1}{(1+rs_1)} = 0.95238 \text{ which gives } rs_1 = 5.0\%$$

$$df_2 = \frac{1}{(1+rs_2)} = 0.90261 \text{ which gives } rs_2 = 5.256\%$$

$$df_3 = \frac{1}{(1+rs_3)} = 0.84476 \text{ which gives } rs_3 = 5.784\%.$$

Equation (9.1) discounts the n-year cash flow (comprising the coupon payment and/or principal repayment) by the corresponding n-year spot yield. In other words, rs_n is the *time-weighted rate of return* on an n-year bond. Thus as we said in the previous section the spot yield curve is the correct method for pricing or valuing any cash flow, including an irregular cash flow, because it uses the appropriate discount factors. That is, it matches each cash flow to the discount rate that applies to the time period in which the cash flow is paid. Compare this to the approach for the YTM procedure discussed earlier, which discounts all cash flows by the same yield to maturity. This illustrates neatly why the N-period zero-coupon interest rate is the true interest rate for an N-year bond.

The expressions above are solved algebraically in the conventional manner, although those wishing to use a spreadsheet application such as Microsoft Excel® can input the constituents of each equation into individual cells and solve using the "Tools" and "Goal Seek" functions.[3]

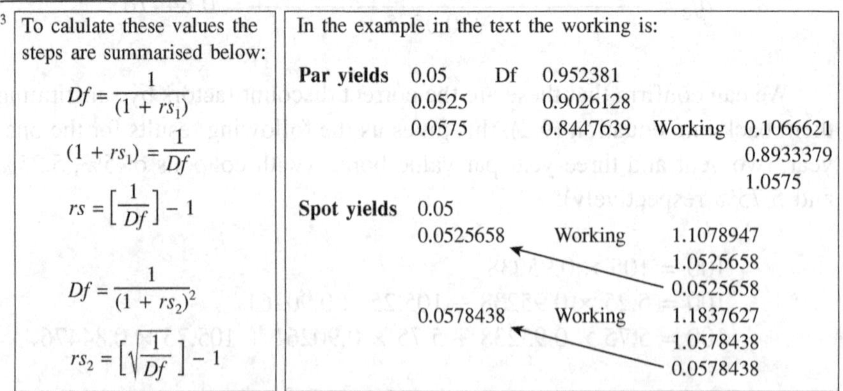

[3] To calulate these values the steps are summarised below:

$$Df = \frac{1}{(1 + rs_1)}$$

$$(1 + rs_1) = \frac{1}{Df}$$

$$rs = \left[\frac{1}{Df}\right] - 1$$

$$Df = \frac{1}{(1 + rs_2)^2}$$

$$rs_2 = \left[\sqrt{\frac{1}{Df}}\right] - 1$$

In the example in the text the working is:

Par yields	0.05	Df	0.952381		
	0.0525		0.9026128		
	0.0575		0.8447639	Working	0.1066621
					0.8933379
					1.0575
Spot yields	0.05				
	0.0525658		Working		1.1078947
					1.0525658
					0.0525658
	0.0578438		Working		1.1837627
					1.0578438
					0.0578438

With special thanks to Praveen Murthy, iflexsolutions, for pointing out an arithmetic error when this appeared in my earlier book, *Analysing and Interpreting the Yield Curve*.

Example 9.1 Zero-coupon yields

Consider the following zero-coupon market rates:

One-year (1y):	5.000%
2y:	5.271%
3y:	5.598%
4y:	6.675%
5y:	7.213%.

Calculate the zero-coupon discount factors and the prices and yields of:

(a) a 6% two-year bond;
(b) a 7% five-year bond.

Assume both are annual coupon bonds.

The zero-coupon discount factors are:

1y: $1/1.05 = 0.95238095$
2y: $1/(1.05271)^2 = 0.90236554$
3y: $1/(1.05598)^3 = 0.84924485$
4y: $1/(1.06675)^4 = 0.77223484$
5y: $1/(1.07213)^5 = 0.70593182$.

The price of the 6% two-year bond is then calculated in the normal fashion using present values of the cash flows:

$$(6 \times 0.95238095) \times (106 \times 0.90236554) = 101.365.$$

The YTM is 5.263%, obtained using the iterative method, with a spreadsheet function such as Microsoft Excel® "Goal Seek" or a Hewlett Packard (HP) calculator.

The price of the 7% five-year bond is:

$$(7 \times 0.95238095) + (7 \times 0.90236554) + (7 \times 0.84924485) + (7 \times 0.77223484) + (107 \times 0.70593182) = 99.869.$$

The yield to maturity is 7.05%.

FORMULA SUMMARY

Example 9.1 illustrates that if the zero-coupon discount factor for n years is df_n and the par yield for N years is rp, then the expression in (9.5) is always true.

$$(rp \times df_1) + (rp \times df_2) + \ldots + (rp \times df_N) + (1 \times df_N) = 1$$

$$rp \times (df_1 + df_2 + \ldots + df_N) = 1 - df_N \tag{9.5}$$

$$rp = \frac{1 - df_N}{\sum_{n=1}^{N} df_N}$$

Using spot rates in bond analysis

The convention in the markets is to quote the yield on a non-government bond as a certain *spread* over the yield on the equivalent maturity government bond, usually using gross redemption yields. Traders and investment managers will assess the relative merits of holding the non-government bond based on the risk associated with the bond's issuer and the magnitude of its yield spread. For example, in the United Kingdom at the beginning of 2003 companies such as National Grid, Severn Trent Water, Abbey National plc and Tesco plc issued sterling-denominated bonds, all of which paid a certain spread over the equivalent gilt bond.[4] Figure 9.9 shows the yield spreads of corporate bonds of different rating sectors in the USD, EUR and GBP markets in 2005 and 2006, relative to the government yield curve. Yield source is Bloomberg L.P. in all cases.

[4] The spread is, of course, not fixed and fluctuates with market conditions and supply and demand. Special thanks to Nick Wallis, University of Nottingham Business School, for his assistance in the preparation of Figure 9.9.

USD Eurobond yield spreads, September 2005

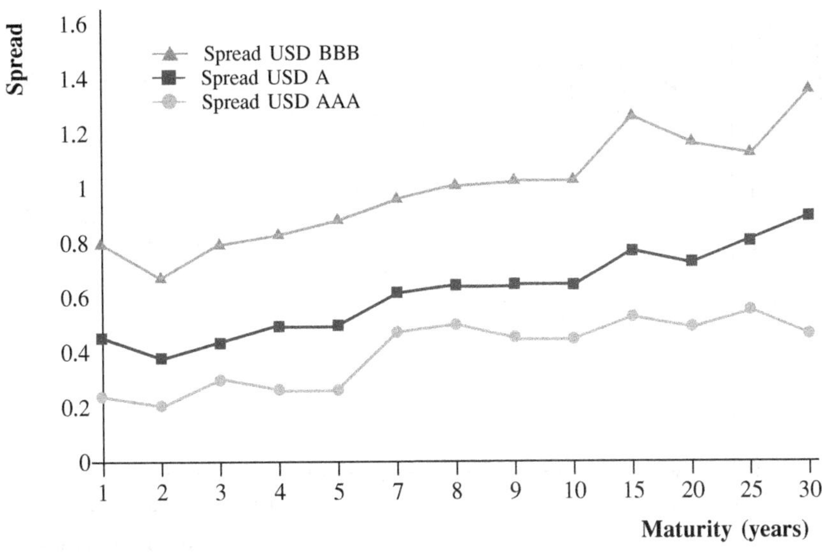

USD Eurobond yield spreads, September 2006

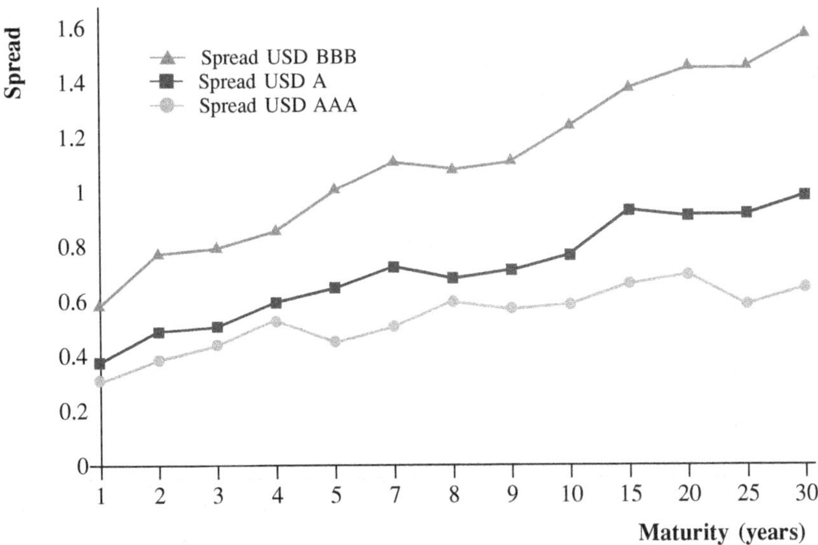

Figure 9.9(i) USD Eurobond yield spreads, 6 September 2005 and 6 September 2006

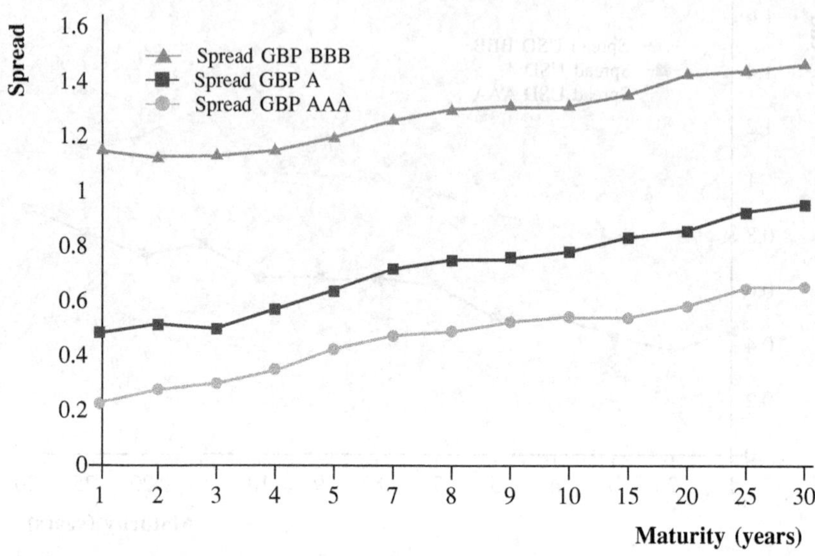

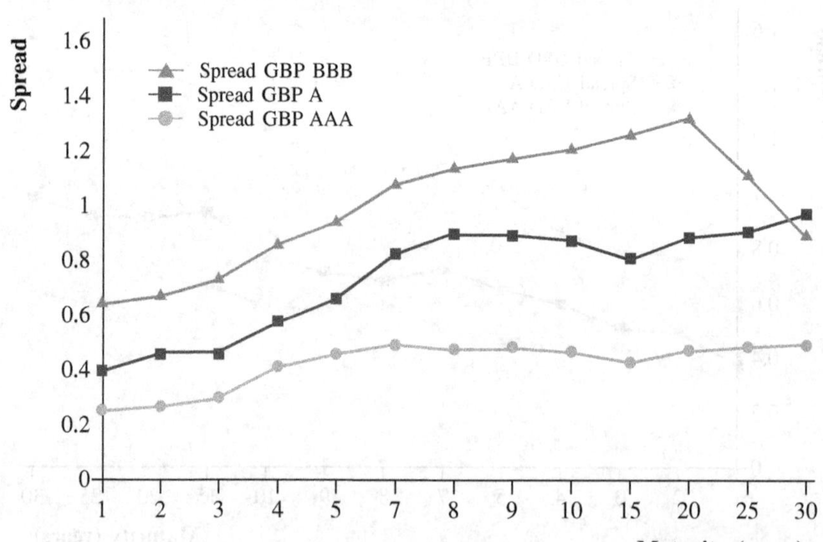

Figure 9.9(ii) GBP Eurobond yield spreads, 6 September 2005 and 6 September 2006

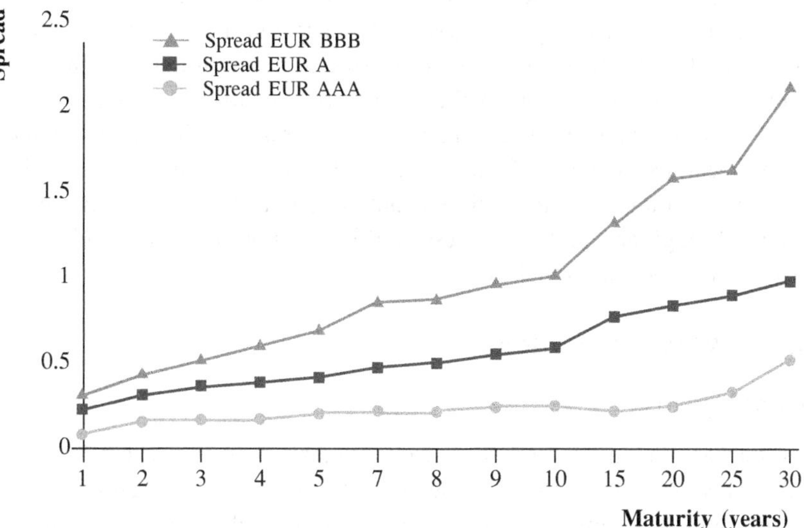

Figure 9.9(iii) EUR Eurobond yield spreads, 6 September 2006

Traditionally, investors will compare the redemption yield of the bond they are analysing with the redemption yield of the equivalent government bond. Just as with the redemption yield measure, however, there is a flaw with this measure, in that the spread quoted is not really comparing like-for-like, as the yields do not reflect the true term structure given by the spot rate curve. There is an additional flaw if the cash flow stream of the two bonds do not match, which in practice they will do only rarely.

Therefore the correct method for assessing the yield spread of a corporate bond is to replicate its cash flows with those of a government bond, which can be done in theory by matching the cash flows of the corporate bond with a package of government zero-coupon bonds of the same nominal value. If no zero-coupon bond market exists, the cash flows can be matched synthetically by valuing a coupon bond's cash flows on a zero-coupon basis. The corporate bond's price is of course the sum of the present value of all its cash flows, which should be valued at the spot rates in place for each cash flow's maturity. It is the yield spread of each individual cash flow over the equivalent maturity government spot rate that is then taken to be the true yield spread.

This measure is known in US markets as the *zero-volatility spread* or *static spread*, and it is a measure of the spread that would be realised over the government spot rate yield curve if the corporate bond were to be held to maturity. It is therefore a different measure to the traditional spread, as it is not taken over one point on the (redemption yield) curve but over the whole term to maturity. The zero-volatility spread is that spread which equates the present value of the corporate bond's cash flows to its price, where the discount rates are each relevant government spot rate. The spread is found through an iterative process, and it is a more realistic yield spread measure than the traditional one.

The forward yield curve

Forward yields

Most transactions in the market are for immediate delivery, which is known as the *cash* market, although some markets also use the expression *spot* market, which is more common in foreign exchange. Cash market transactions are settled straight away, with the purchaser of a bond being entitled to interest from the settlement date onwards.[5] There is a large market in *forward* transactions, which are trades carried out today for a forward settlement date. For financial transactions that are forward transactions, the parties to the trade agree today to exchange a security for cash at a future date, but at a price agreed today. So the *forward rate* applicable to a bond is the spot bond yield as at the forward date. That is, it is the yield of a zero-coupon bond that is purchased for settlement at the forward date. It is derived today, using data from a present-day yield curve, so it is not correct to consider forward rates to be a prediction of the spot rates as at the forward date.

Forward rates can be derived from spot interest rates. Such rates are then known as *implied* forward rates, since they are implied by the current range of spot interest rates. The *forward* (or *forward–forward*) *yield curve* is a plot of forward rates against term to maturity. Forward rates satisfy expression (9.6):

[5] We refer to "immediate" settlement, although of course there is a delay between trade date and settlement date, which can be anything from one day to seven days, or even longer in some markets. The most common settlement period is known as "spot" and is two business days.

$$P_d = \frac{C}{(1 + {}_0rf_1)} + \frac{C}{(1 + {}_0rf_1)(1 + {}_0rf_2)} + \ldots + \frac{M}{(1 + {}_0rf_1) \ldots (1 + {}_{N-1}rf_N)}$$

$$= \sum_{n=1}^{N} \frac{C}{\prod_{n=1}^{n}(1 + {}_{i-1}rf_i)} + \frac{M}{\prod_{n=1}^{N}(1 + {}_{i-1}rf_i)} \tag{9.6}$$

where ${}_{n-1}rf_n$ is the implicit forward rate (or forward–forward rate) on a one-year bond maturing in year N.

As a forward or forward–forward yield is implied from spot rates, the forward rate is a forward zero-coupon rate. Comparing (9.1) and (9.6) we see that the spot yield is the *geometric mean* of the forward rates, as shown below:

$$(1 + rs_n)^n = (1 + {}_0rf_1)(1 + {}_1rf_2) \ldots (1 + {}_{n-1}rf_n). \tag{9.7}$$

This implies the following relationship between spot and forward rates:

$$\begin{aligned}(1 + {}_{n-1}rf_n) &= \frac{(1 + rs_n)^n}{(1 + rs_{n-1})^{n-1}} \\ &= \frac{df_{n-1}}{df_n}.\end{aligned} \tag{9.8}$$

Using the spot yields we calculated in the earlier paragraph we can derive the implied forward rates from (9.8). For example, the two-year and three-year forward rates are given by:

$$(1 + {}_1rf_2) = \frac{(1 + 0.05256)^2}{(1 + 0.05)} = 5.5138\%$$

$$(1 + {}_2rf_3) = \frac{(1 + 0.05778)^3}{(1 + 0.05256)^2} = 6.8479\%.$$

Using our expression gives us ${}_0rf_1$ equal to 5%, ${}_1rf_2$ equal to 5.514% and ${}_2rf_3$ as 6.8479%. This means, for example, that given current spot yields, which we calculated from the one-year, two-year and three-year bond redemption yields (which were priced at par), the market is expecting the yield on a bond with one year to mature in three years' time to be 6.8479% (that is, the three-year one-period forward–forward rate is 6.8479%).

The relationship between the par yields, spot yields and forward rates is shown in Table 9.1 on page 362.

Year	Coupon yield (%)	Zero-coupon yield (%)	Forward rate (%)
1	5.000	5.000	5.000
2	5.250	5.2566	5.5138
3	5.750	5.7844	6.8479

Table 9.1 Coupon, spot and forward yields

Figure 9.10 highlights our results for all three yield curves graphically. This illustrates another important property of the relationship between the three curves, in that as the original coupon yield curve was positively sloping, so the spot and forward yield curves lie above it. The reasons behind this will be considered later in the chapter.

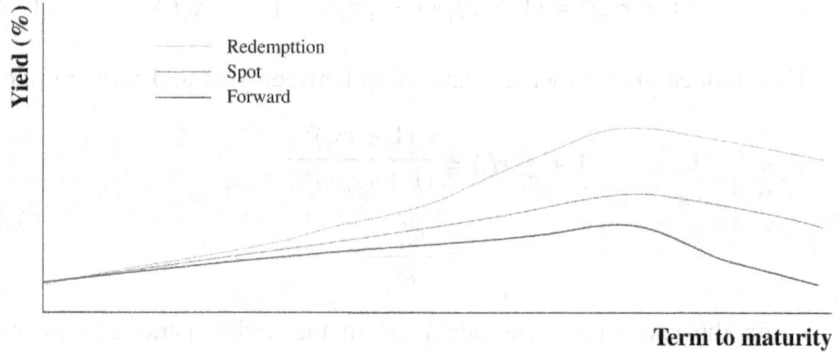

Figure 9.10 Redemption, spot and forward yield curves: traditional analysis

Let us now consider the following example. Suppose that a two-year bond with cash flows of £5.25 at the end of year 1 and £105.25 at the end of year 2 is trading at par, hence it has a redemption yield (indeed, a par yield) of 5.25% (this is the bond in Table 9.1 above). As we showed in the section on zero-coupon yields and the idea of the breakeven principle, in order to be regarded as equivalent to this a pure zero-coupon bond or discount bond making a lump-sum payment at the end of year 2 only (so with no cash flow at the end of year 1) would require a rate of return of 5.256%, which is the spot yield. That is, for the same investment of £100 the maturity value would have to be £110.7895 (this figure is obtained by multiplying 100 by $((1 + 0.052566)^2)$).

This illustrates why the zero-coupon curve is important to corporate financiers involved in new bond issues. If we know the spot yields, then we can calculate the coupon required on a new three-year bond that is going to be issued at par in this interest-rate environment by making the following calculation:

$$100 = \frac{C}{(1.05)} + \frac{C}{(1.05269)^2} + \frac{C + 100}{(1.05778)^3}.$$

This is solved in the conventional algebraic manner to give C equal to 5.75%.

The relationship between spot rates and forward rates was shown in (9.8). We can illustrate it as follows. If the spot yield is the *average return*, then the forward rate can be interpreted as the *marginal return*. If the marginal return between years 2 and 3 increases from 5.514% to 6.848%, then the average return increases from 5.256% up to the three-year spot yield of 5.784% as shown below:

$$\{[1.052566)^2\ (1.068479)]^{1/3} - 1\} = 0.057844$$

or 5.778%, as shown in Table 9.1.

FORMULA SUMMARY

The forward zero-coupon rate from interest period a to period b is given by (9.9):

$$_a rf_b = \left[\frac{(1 + rs_b)^b}{(1 + rs_a)^a} \right]^{1/(b-a)} - 1 \tag{9.9}$$

where rs_a and rs_b are the a and b period spot rates respectively.

The forward rate from interest period a to period $(a + 1)$ is given by (9.10):

$$_a rf_{a+1} = \frac{(1 + rs_{a+1})^{a+1}}{(1 + rs_a)^a} - 1. \tag{9.10}$$

Calculating spot rates from forward rates

The previous section showed the relationship between spot and forward rates. Just as we have derived forward rates from spot rates based on this mathematical relationship, it is possible to reverse this and calculate spot rates from forward rates. If we are presented with a forward yield curve, plotted from a set of one-period forward rates, we can use this to construct a spot yield curve. Equation (9.7) states the relationship between spot and forward rates, rearranged as (9.11) to solve for the spot rate:

$$rs_n = [(1 + {}_1rf_1) \times (1 + {}_2rf_1) \times (1 + {}_3rf_1) \times \ldots \times (1 + {}_nrf_1)]^{1/n} - 1 \tag{9.11}$$

where ${}_1rf_1$, ${}_2rf_1$, ${}_3rf_1$ are the one-period versus two-period, two-period versus three-period forward rates up to the $(n - 1)$ period versus n-period forward rates.

Remember to adjust (9.11) as necessary if dealing with forward rates relating to a deposit of a different interest period. If we are dealing with the current six-month spot rate and implied six-month forward rates, the relationship between these and the n-period spot rate is given by (9.11) in the same way as if we were dealing with the current one-year spot rate and implied one-year forward rates.

EXAMPLE 9.2(i) Spot rates

The one-year cash market yield is 5.00%. Market expectations have priced one-year rates in one year's time at 5.95% and in two years' time at 7.25%. What is the current three-year spot rate that would produce these forward rate views?

To calculate this we assume an investment strategy dealing today at forward rates, and calculate the return generated from this strategy. The return after a three-year period is given by the future value relationship, which in this case is $1.05 \times 1.0595 \times 1.0725 = 1.1931$.

The three-year spot rate is then obtained by:

$$\left(\frac{1.1931}{1}\right)^{1/3} - 1 = 6.062\%.$$

9.2(ii) Forward rates

Consider the following six-month implied forward rates, when the six-month spot rate is 4.0000%.

$_1rf_1$	4.0000%
$_2rf_1$	4.4516%
$_3rf_1$	5.1532%
$_4rf_1$	5.6586%
$_5rf_1$	6.0947%
$_6rf_1$	7.1129%

An investor is debating between purchasing a three-year zero-coupon bond at a price of £72.79481 per £100 nominal, or buying a six-month zero-coupon bond and then rolling over her investment every six months for the three-year term. If the investor were able to reinvest her proceeds every six months at the actual forward rates in place today, what would her proceeds be at the end of the three-year term? An investment of £72.79481 at the spot rate of 4% and then reinvested at the forward rates in our table over the next three years would yield a terminal value of:

$$72.79481 \times (1.04)(1.044516)(1.051532)(1.056586)(1.060947)(1.071129) = 100.$$

This merely reflects our spot and forward rates relationship, in that if all the forward rates are indeed realised, our investor's £72.79 will produce a terminal value that matches the investment in a three-year zero-coupon bond priced at the three-year spot rate. This illustrates the relationship between the three-year spot rate, the six-month spot rate and the implied six-month forward rates. So what is the three-year zero-coupon bond trading at? Using (9.11) the solution to this is given by:

$$rs_6 = [(1.04)(1.044516)(1.051532)(1.056586)(1.060947)(1.071129)]^{1/6} - 1 = 5.4346\%$$

which solves our three-year spot rate rs_6 as 5.4346%. Of course, we could have also solved for rs_6 using the conventional price/yield formula for zero-coupon bonds; however, the calculation above illustrates the relationship between spot and forward rates.

An important note on spot and forward rates

Forward rates that exist at any one time reflect everything that is known in the market *up to that point*. Certain market participants may believe that the forward rate curve is a forecast of the future spot rate curve. This is implied by the *unbiased expectations hypothesis* that we consider below. In fact there is no direct relationship between the forward rate curve and the spot rate curve; for an excellent analysis of this see Jarrow (1996). It is possible, for example, for the forward rate curve to be upward sloping at the same time that short-dated spot rates are expected to decline.

To view the forward rate curve as a predictor of rates is a misuse of it. The derivation of forward rates reflects all currently known market information. Assuming that all developed country markets are at least in a semi-strong form,[6] to preserve market equilibrium there can only be one set of forward rates from a given spot rate curve. However, this does not mean that such rates are a prediction because the instant after they have been calculated new market knowledge may become available that alters the market's view of future interest rates. This will cause the forward rate curve to change.

Forward rates are important because they are needed if we are to make prices today for dealing at a future date. For example, a bank's corporate customer may wish to fix today the interest rate payable on a loan that begins in one year from now; what rate does the bank quote? The forward rate is used by market-makers to quote prices for dealing today, and is the best *expectation* of future interest rates given everything that is known in the market up to now, but it is not a prediction of future spot rates. What would happen if a bank was privy to insider information; for example, it knew that central bank base rates would be changed very shortly? A bank in possession of such information (if we ignore the ethical implications) would not quote forward rates based on the spot rate curve, but would quote rates that reflected its insider knowledge.

---

6 See Fama (1970).

Bond valuation using forward rates

That there is a relationship between spot rates and implied forward rates should tell us that, in theory, there is no difference in valuing a conventional bond with either spot rates or forward rates. The present value of a cash flow C received in period n using forward rates is given by (9.12):

$$PV_C = \frac{C}{(1 + rs_1)(1 + {}_1rf_1)(1 + {}_2rf_1) \ldots (1 + {}_nrf_1)}. \qquad (9.12)$$

Therefore we use (9.12) to assemble the expression for valuing an N-period term bond using implied forward rates, with coupon C, given in (9.13). Note that we use the six-month or one-year spot rates and the six-month or one-year implied forward rates for the forward dates according to whether the bond pays annual or semi-annual coupons. Equation (9.13) assumes an exact number of interest periods to maturity.

$$P_d = \frac{C}{(1 + rs_1)} + \frac{C}{(1 + rs_1)(1 + {}_0rf_1)} + \frac{C}{(1 + rs_1)(1 + {}_1rf_1)(1 + {}_2rf_1)} + \ldots$$
$$+ \frac{C + M}{(1 + rs_1)(1 + {}_1rf_1)(1 + {}_2rf_1) \ldots (1 + {}_Nrf_1)} \qquad (9.13)$$

Although bond analysts may use either spot or implied forward rates to present-value cash flow streams, the final valuation will be the same regardless of whichever rates are used.

The annuity yield curve

Life assurance companies and other providers of personal pensions are users of the *annuity yield curve*, which is a plot of annuity yields against term to maturity. The *annuity yield* is the implied yield on an annuity where the annuity is valued using spot yields. In (9.2) above we decomposed a bond into an annuity and a zero-coupon discounted bond. We used the spot yield to price the discount bond component. Now we are concerned with the annuity or pure coupon component.

The value of the annuity component of a bond is given by (9.14):

$$A_N = \sum_{n=1}^{N} \frac{C}{(1 + rs_n)^n} = \sum_{n=1}^{N} C \times df_n \qquad (9.14)$$
$$= C \times A_N$$

where rs_n and df_n are the n-period spot rate and discount factor, as defined earlier, and A_N is the fair price of an N-year annuity of £1. However, A_N is also given by the standard formula (9.15):

$$A_N = \frac{1}{ra_N}\left[1 - \frac{1}{(1 + ra_N)^N}\right] \qquad (9.15)$$

where ra_N is the annuity yield on an N-year annuity.

Again using the same rates as before, consider a three-year bond with a coupon of 5.75%. To obtain the value of the annuity portion of the bond we would use (9.14) to give us:

$$\begin{aligned} A_3 &= \frac{5.75}{1.05} + \frac{5.75}{(1.05269)^2} + \frac{5.75}{(1.05778)^3} \\ &= 15.52. \end{aligned}$$

This indicates a value for A_3 of £2.70, obtained by dividing 15.52 by 5.75. We can then use this value to solve for the annuity yield ra using (9.15) or using annuity tables; in this case the three-year annuity yield is 5.46%.

The relationship between the spot and annuity yield curves will depend on the level of market rates. With a positive-sloping spot yield curve, the annuity yield is below the end-of-period spot yield; with a negative-sloping spot yield curve, the annuity yield curve lies above it. With a low-coupon bond the present value will be dominated by the terminal payment and the annuity curve will lie close to the spot curve; with a high-coupon bond the two curves will be further apart.

The Term Structure

We have already referred to the yield curve or *term structure of interest rates*. Strictly speaking only a spot rate yield curve is a term structure, but one sometimes encounters the two expressions being used synonymously. At any time t there will be a set of coupon and/or zero-coupon bonds with different terms to maturity and cash flow streams. There will be certain fixed maturities that are not represented by actual bonds in the market, as there will be more than one bond maturing at or around the same redemption date. It is this paucity of data in selected parts of the curve that makes fitting the term structure problematic at times. We illustrate by considering the bootstrapping approach to fitting the term structure.

The bootstrapping approach using discount factors[7]

In this section we describe how to obtain zero-coupon and forward rates from the yields available from coupon bonds, using the *bootstrapping* technique. In a government bond market such as US Treasuries, the bonds are considered to be default-free. The rates from a government bond yield curve describe the risk-free rates of return available in the market *today*; however, they also *imply* (risk-free) rates of return for future time periods. These implied future rates, known as *implied forward rates*, or simply *forward rates*, can be derived from a given discount function or spot yield curve using bootstrapping. This term reflects the fact that each calculated spot rate is used to determine the next period spot rate, in successive steps.

We illustrate the technique using discount factors. Once we have obtained the discount curve, it is a straightforward process to obtain the spot rate curve, as we saw earlier when we described the relationship that exists between discount factors, spot rates and forward rates.

A t-period discount factor is the present value of \$1 that is payable at the end of period t. Essentially it is the present value relationship expressed in terms of \$1. If $d(t)$ is the t-year discount factor, then the five-year discount factor at a discount rate of 6% is given by:

$$d(5) = \frac{1}{(1 + 0.06)^5} = 0.747258.$$

The set of discount factors for the time period from one day to 30 years (or longer) is termed the *discount function*. Discount factors are used to price any financial instrument that is comprised of a future cash flow. For example, if the six-month discount factor is 0.98756, the current value of the maturity payment of a 7% semi-annual coupon bond due for receipt in six months' time is given by 0.98756 × 103.50 or 102.212.

In addition, discount factors may be used to calculate the future value of any current investment. From the example above, \$0.98756 would be worth \$1 in six months' time, so by the same principle a present sum of \$1 would be worth at the end of six months:

$$1/d(5) = 1/0.98756 = 1.0126.$$

[7] For beginners, an introduction to discount factors is given in the Appendix at the back of this book.

As we saw earlier in the chapter, the interrelationship between discount factors and spot and rates means we may obtain discount factors from current bond prices. Assume a hypothetical set of semi-annual coupon bonds and bond prices as given in Table 9.2, and assume further that the first bond matures in precisely six months' time. All other bonds then mature at six-month intervals.

Coupon	Maturity date	Price
7%	7/6/2001	101.65
8%	7/12/2001	101.89
6%	7/6/2002	100.75
6.50%	7/12/2002	100.37

Table 9.2 Hypothetical set of bonds and bond prices

Taking the first bond, this matures in precisely six months' time, and its final cash flow will be 103.50, comprised of the $3.50 final coupon payment and the $100 redemption payment. The market-observed price of this bond is $101.65, which allows us to calculate the six-month discount factor as:

$$d(0.5) \times 103.50 = 101.65$$

which gives us $d(0.5)$ equal to 0.98213.

From this step we can calculate the discount factors for the following six-month periods. The second bond in Table 9.2, the 8% 2001, has the following cash flows:

- $4 in six months' time
- $104 in one year's time.

The price of this bond is 101.89, the bond's present value, and this is comprised of the sum of the present values of the bond's total cash flows. So we are able to set the following:

$$101.89 = 4 \times d(0.5) + 101 \times d(1).$$

However, we already know $d(0.5)$ to be 0.98213, which leaves only one unknown in the above expression. Therefore we may solve for $d(1)$ and this is shown to be 0.94194.

If we carry on with this procedure for the remaining two bonds, using successive discount factors, we obtain the complete set of discount factors as shown in Table 9.3. The continuous function for the two-year period is shown as the discount function in Figure 9.11.

Coupon	Maturity date	Term (years)	Price	*d(n)*
7%	7/6/2001	0.5	101.65	0.98213
8%	7/12/2001	1	101.89	0.94194
6%	7/6/2002	1.5	100.75	0.92211
6.50%	7/12/2002	2	100.37	0.88252

Table 9.3 Discount factors calculated using the bootstrapping technique

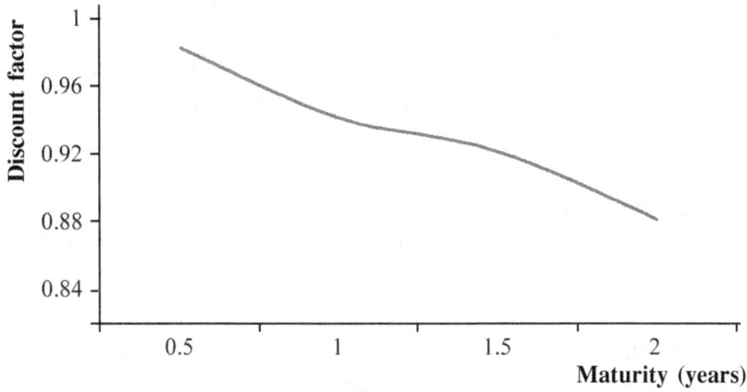

Figure 9.11 Discount function

Once we have the discount function we are able to compute the zero-coupon rates and hence also the forward rates. As a result, we can fit the yield curve from the discount function.

The theoretical approach described above is neat and appealing, but in practice there are a number of issues that will complicate the attempt to extract zero-coupon rates from bond yields. The main problem is that it is highly unlikely that we will have a set of bonds that are both precisely six months (or one interest) apart in maturity and priced precisely at par. We also require our procedure to fit as smooth a curve as possible. Setting our coupon bonds at a price of par simplified the analysis in our illustration of bootstrapping, so in reality we need to apply more advanced techniques. A basic approach for extracting zero-coupon bond prices is described in Choudhry (2004b).

EXAMPLE 9.3 Forward rates: Breakeven principle

Consider the following spot yields:

1y: 10%
2y: 12%.

Assume that a bank's client wishes to lock in *today* the cost of borrowing one-year funds in one year's time. The solution for the bank (and the mechanism to enable the bank to quote a price to the client) involves raising one-year funds at 10% and investing the proceeds for two years at 12%. The no-arbitrage principle means that the same return must be generated from both fixed rate and reinvestment strategies.

In effect, we can look at the issue in terms of two alternative investment strategies, both of which must provide the same return.

Strategy 1: Invest funds for two years at 12%.
Strategy 2: Invest funds for one year at 10%, and reinvest the proceeds for a further year at the forward rate calculated today.

The forward rate for strategy 2 is the rate that will be quoted to the client. Using the present value relationship we know that the proceeds from strategy 1 are:

$$FV = (1 + r_2)^2$$

while the proceeds from strategy 2 would be:

$$FV = (1 + r_1) \times (1 + R).$$

We know from the no-arbitrage principle that the proceeds from both strategies will be the same, therefore this enables us to set:

$$(1 + r_2)^2 = (1 + r_1)(1 + R)$$

$$R = \frac{(1 + r_2)^2}{(1 + r_1)} - 1$$

This enables us to calculate the forward rate that can be quoted to the client (together with any spread that the bank might add) as follows:

$$(1 + 0.12)^2 = (1 + 0.10) \times (1 + R)$$
$$(1 + R) = (1 + 0.12)^2 / (1 + 0.10)$$
$$(1 + R) = 1.14036$$
$$R = 14.04\%.$$

This rate is the one-year forward–forward rate, or the implied forward rate.

EXAMPLE 9.4 Simple calculation of the forward rate from zero-coupon rate

A highly rated customer asks you to fix a yield at which he could issue a two-year zero-coupon USD Eurobond in three years' time. At this time the US Treasury zero-coupon rates were:

1y:	6.25%
2y:	6.75%
3y:	7.00%
4y:	7.125%
5y:	7.25%.

Ignoring borrowing spreads over these benchmark yields, as a market-maker you could cover the exposure created by borrowing funds for five years on a zero-coupon basis and placing these funds in the market for three years before lending them on to your client. Assume annual interest compounding (even if none is actually paid out during the life of the loans).

$$\text{Borrowing rate for five years: } \left[\frac{R_5}{100}\right] = 0.0725$$

$$\text{Lending rate for three years: } \left[\frac{R_3}{100}\right] = 0.0700$$

The key arbitrage relationship is:

Total cost of funding = Total return on investments

$$(1 + R_5)^5 = (1 + R_3)^3 \times (1 + R_{3\times5})^2.$$

Therefore the breakeven forward yield is:

$$(1 + R_{3\times5})^2 = \frac{(1 + 0.0725)^5}{(1 + 0.0700)^3}$$

$$(1 + R_{3\times5}) = \sqrt{\left[\frac{(1 + 0.0725)^5}{(1 + 0.0700)^3}\right]}$$

$$R_{3\times5} = \sqrt{\left[\frac{(1 + 0.0725)^5}{(1 + 0.0700)^3}\right]} - 1$$

$$= 7.63\%.$$

EXAMPLE 9.5 Forward rate calculation for money market term

Consider two positions:

- the borrowing of £100 million from 5 November for 30 days at 5.875%;
- a loan of £100 million from 5 November for 60 days at 6.125%.

The two positions can be viewed as a 30-day forward 30-day interest-rate exposure (a 30- versus 60-day forward rate). It is usually referred to as an interest-rate *gap* position. What forward rate must be used if the trader wished to hedge this exposure?

The 30-day by 60-day forward rate can be calculated using the following formula:

$$rf_i = \left[\left(\frac{1 + \left(rs_{L\%} \cdot \frac{n_L}{B}\right)}{1 + \left(rs_{S\%} \cdot \frac{n_S}{B}\right)}\right) - 1\right] \times \frac{B}{n_L - n_S}$$

where

rf_i	is the forward rate
$rs_{L\%}$	is the long-period rate
$rs_{S\%}$	is the short-period rate
n_L	is the long-period term in days
n_S	is the short-period term in days
B	is the day-count base, either 360 or 365.

Using this formula we obtain a 30v60 day forward rate of 6.3443%.

This interest-rate exposure can be hedged using interest-rate futures or FRAs. Either method is an effective hedging mechanism, although the trader must be aware of:

- *basis* risk that exists between cash market rates and the forward rates implied by futures and FRAs;
- dates mismatched between the expiry of futures contracts and the maturity dates of the cash market transactions.

EXAMPLE 9.6 Rough-and-ready calculation method

(a)

Given the following zero-coupon yields, what does the par yield curve look like?

Term	Zero-coupon yield	Par yield	
1-year	4.5000	4.5	
2-year	4.7800	4.77	
3-year	5.1250	5.1	
4-year	5.3640	5.32	
5-year	5.8210	5.74	
		Discount factor	
1-year	1/(1.045)	0.956938	
2-year	1/(1.0478)^2	0.910842	
3-year	1/(1.05125)^3	0.860760	
4-year	1/(1.053640)^4	0.811393	
5-year	1/(1.058210)^5	0.753600	
1-year par yield			4.50%
2-year par yield	1–0.910842/(0.956939+0.910842)	0.047734718	4.77%
3-year par yield	1–0.86076/(0.956938+0.910842+0.86076)	0.051030954	5.10%
4-year par yield	1–0.811393/(0.956938+0.910842+0.86076 +0.811393)	0.053279822	5.32%
5-year par yield	1–0.753600/(0.956938+0.910842+0.86076 +0.811393+0.753600)	0.057388635	5.74%

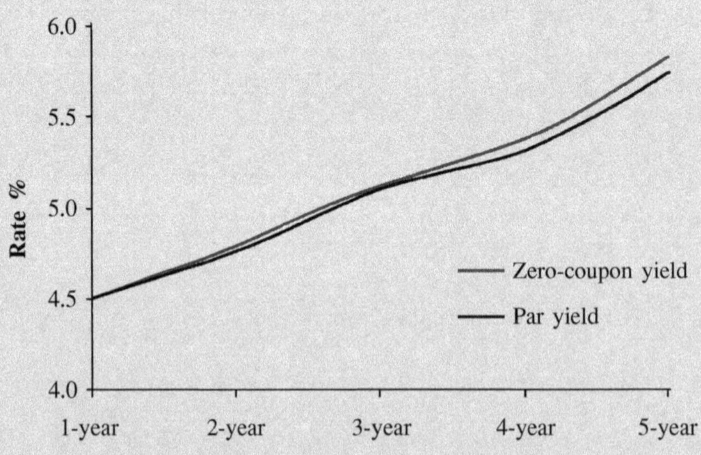

Figure 9.12(i) Par and zero-coupon curves

(b)

Given the same zero-coupon yield curve as above, what are the one-year versus two-year, two-year versus three-year, three-year versus four-year and the four-year versus five-year forward–forward yields?

The zero-coupon discount factors are the same as before.

Term	Zero-coupon yield	Discount factor
1-year	4.5000	0.956938
2-year	4.7800	0.910842
3-year	5.1250	0.860760
4-year	5.3640	0.811393
5-year	5.8210	0.753600

1-year versus 2-year fwd–fwd yield		
= (0.956938 / 0.910842) – 1	0.050608119	5.06%
2-year versus 3-year fwd–fwd yield		
= (0.910842 / 0.860760) – 1	0.058183466	5.81%
3-year versus 4-year fwd–fwd yield		
= (0.860760 / 0.811393) – 1	0.06084228	6.08%
4-year versus 5-year fwd–fwd yield		
= (0.811393 / 0.753600) – 1	0.076689225	7.67%

Figure 9.12(ii) Forward rates calculation

(c)

The one-year market interest rate is at 4.50%. Market expectations are for a rise in the one-year rate to 5.00% in the next year and 5.50% in the year following that. Given this consensus, what should the current two-year and three-year zero-coupon yields be?

2-year zero-coupon yield = $(1.045 \times 1.05)^{1/2} - 1$
= 0.47497 = 4.75%

3-year zero-coupon yield = (1.045 × 1.05 × 1.055)^1/3 – 1
= 1.049992 = 5.00%

CASE STUDY 9.1 Deriving a discount function[8]

In this example we present a traditional bootstrapping technique for deriving a discount function for yield curve fitting purposes. This technique has been called "naïve" (for instance, see James and Webber 2000, p. 129) because it suffers from a number of drawbacks; for example, it results in an unrealistic forward rate curve, which means that it is unlikely to be used in practice. This does not mean that the method does not have practical application though. We review the drawbacks at the end of the case study.

Today is 14 July 2000. The following rates are observed in the market. We assume that the day-count basis for the cash instruments and swaps is act/365. Construct the money market discount function.

Money market rates	*Rate (%)*	*Expiry*	*Days*
One month (1-m)	$4\ ^{7}/_{32}$	14/8/00	31
3-m	$4\ ^{1}/_{4}$	16/10/00	94
6-m	$4\ ^{1}/_{2}$	15/1/01	185
Futures prices			
Sep-00	95.60	20/9/00	68
Dec-00	95.39	20/12/00	159
Mar-01	95.25	21/3/01	250
Jun-01	94.80	20/6/01	341
Swap rates			
One year (1y)	4.95	16/7/01	367
2y	5.125	15/7/02	731
3y	5.28	14/7/03	1095
4y	5.55	14/7/04	1461
5y	6.00	14/7/05	1826

Creating the discount function

Using the cash money market rates we can create discount factors up to a maturity of six months, using the expression below:

[8] In this illustration, the discount function is derived using interest- rate data from two off-balance-sheet-derivative instruments, futures and swaps, as well as money market deposit rates. For readers unfamiliar with these products, futures and swaps are covered in chapters 13 and 14.

$$df = \frac{1}{(1 + r \times \frac{days}{365})}.$$

The resulting discount factors are shown below.

From	*To*	*Days*	*r%*	*df*
14/7/00	14/8/00	31	$4\,^{7}/_{32}$	0.99642974
	16/10/00	94	$4\,^{1}/_{4}$	0.98917329
	15/1/01	185	$4\,^{1}/_{2}$	0.97770040

We can also calculate forward discount factors from the rates implied in the futures prices, which are shown below.

From	*To*	*Days*	*r%*	*df*
20/9/00	20/12/00	91	4.40	0.98914917
20/12/00	21/3/01	91	4.61	0.98863717
21/3/01	20/6/01	91	4.75	0.98829614
20/6/01	19/9/01	91	5.20	0.98720154

In order to convert these values into zero-coupon discount factors, we need first to derive a cash "stub" rate up to the expiry of the first futures contract. The most straightforward way to do this is by linear interpolation of the one-month and three-month rates, as shown in Figure 9.13 below.

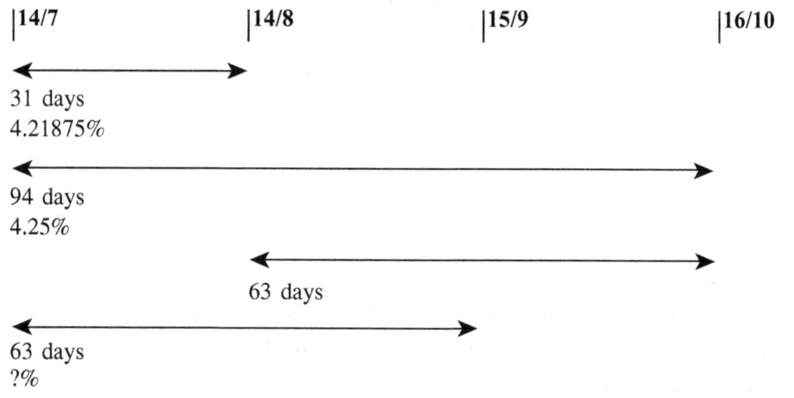

Figure 9.13 Linear interpolation of money market and futures rates

For instance, the calculation for the term marked is:

$$4.21875 + \left((4.25 - 4.21875) \times \tfrac{32}{63}\right) = 4.235\%.$$

Converting this to a discount factor:

$$\frac{1}{1 + (0.04235143 \times \frac{63}{365})} = 0.99274308.$$

From the futures implied forward rates, the zero-coupon discount factors are calculated by successive multiplication of the individual discount factors. These are shown below.

From	*To*	*Days*	*df*
14/7/00	20/9/00	68	0.99172819
	20/12/00	159	0.98172542
	21/3/01	250	0.96992763
	20/6/01	341	0.960231459
	19/9/01	432	0.948925494

For the interest-rate swap rates, to calculate discount factors for the relevant dates we use the bootstrapping technique.

1-y swap

We assume a par swap, the present value is known to be 100, and as we know the future value as well, we are able to calculate the one-year zero-coupon rate as shown from the one-year swap rate:

$$df_1 = \frac{1}{1 + r} = \frac{100}{104.95}$$

$$= 0.95283468.$$

2-y swap

The coupon payment occurring at the end of period 1 can be discounted back using the one-year discount factor above, leaving a zero-coupon structure as before.

$$df_2 = \frac{100 - \mathrm{C} \times df_1}{105.125}$$

This gives df_2 equal to 0.91379405.

The same process can be employed for the three-, four- and five-year par swap rates to calculate the appropriate discount factors:

$$df_3 = \frac{100 - C \times (df_1 + df_2)}{105.28}.$$

This gives df_3 equal to 0.87875624. The discount factors for the four-year and five-year maturities, calculated in the same way, are 0.82899694 and 0.77835621 respectively.

The full discount function is given in Table 9.4 and illustrated graphically in Figure 9.14 on page 382.

From	To	Days	Zero-coupon (%)	Discount factor	Source
14/07/2000	14/08/2000	31	4.21875	0.99642974	Money market
	20/09/2000	68	4.23500	0.992168	Money market
	16/10/2000	94	4.25000	0.98917329	Money market
	20/12/2000	159	4.38000	0.98172542	Futures
	15/01/2001	185	4.50000	0.97777004	Money market
	21/03/2001	250	4.55000	0.96992763	Futures
	20/06/2001	341	4.73000	0.96023145	Futures
	16/07/2001	367	4.95000	0.95283468	Swap
	19/09/2001	432	5.01000	0.94892549	Futures
	15/07/2002	731	5.12500	0.91379405	Swap
	14/07/2003	1095	5.28000	0.87875624	Swap
	15/07/2004	1461	5.58000	0.82899694	Swap
	15/07/2005	1826	6.10000	0.77835621	Swap

Table 9.4 Discount factors

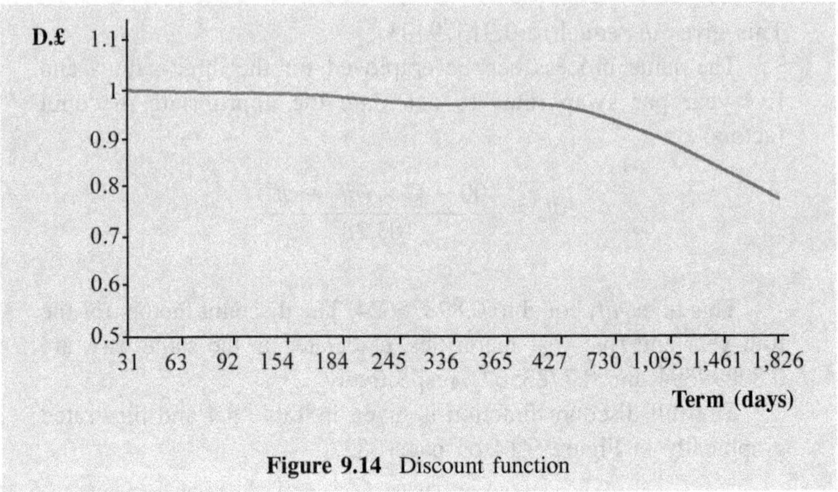

Figure 9.14 Discount function

Critique of the traditional technique

The method used to derive the discount function in the case study used three different price sources to produce an integrated function and hence yield curve. However, there is no effective method by which the three separate curves, which are shown in Figure 9.15, can be integrated into one complete curve. The result is that a curve formed from the three separate curves will exhibit distinct kinks or steps at the points at which one data source is replaced by another data source.

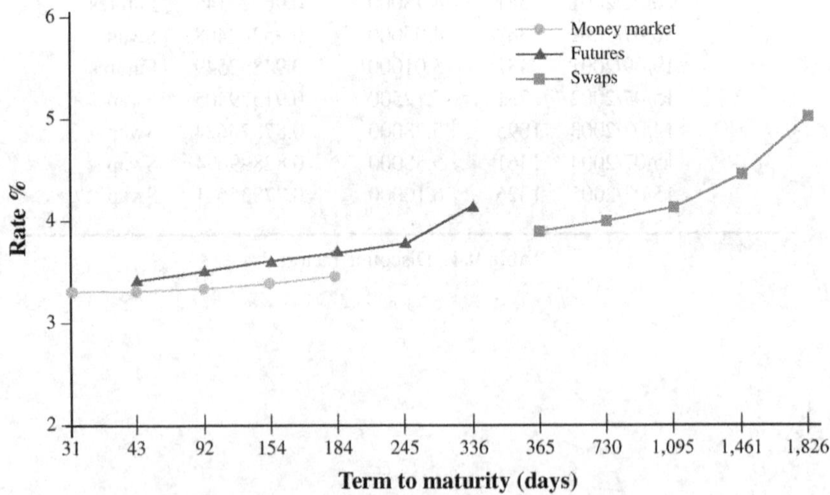

Figure 9.15 Comparison of money market curves

The money market and swap rates incorporate a credit risk premium, reflecting the fact that interbank market counterparties carry an element of default risk. This means that money market rates lie above government repo rates. Futures rates do not reflect default risk, as they are exchange-traded contracts and the exchange clearing house takes on counterparty risk for each transaction. However, futures rates are treated as one-point period rates, in effect making them equivalent to FRA rates. In practice, as the cash flow from FRAs is received as a discounted payoff at one point, whereas futures contract trades require a daily margin payment, a *convexity adjustment* is required to convert futures accurately to FRA rates. This adjustment is considered in Choudhry (2004b).

Swap rates also incorporate an element of credit risk, although generally they are considered lower risk as they are off-balance sheet instruments and no principal is at risk. As liquid swap rates are only available for set maturity points, linear interpolation is used to plot points in between available rates. This results in an unstable forward rate curve calculated from the spot rate curve (see James and Webber 2000), due to the interpolation effect. Nevertheless, market-makers in certain markets price intermediate-dated swaps based on this linear interpolation method. Another drawback is that the bootstrapping method uses near-maturity rates to build up the curve to far-maturity rates. One of the features of a spot curve derived in this way is that even small changes in short-term rates cause excessive changes in long-dated spot rates, and oscillations in the forward curve. Finally, money market rates beyond the "stub" period are not considered once the discount factor to the stub date is calculated, so their impact is not felt.

For these reasons the traditional technique is not used very often in the markets, although its use, especially for analysis purposes, is not uncommon.

Spot and forward rates in the market

Using spot rates

The concepts discussed in this chapter are important and form a core part of debt markets analysis. It may appear that the content is largely theoretical, especially since many markets do not trade zero-coupon instruments and so spot rates are therefore not observable in practice; however, the concept of the spot rate is an essential part of bond (and other instruments') pricing. In the first instance we are already aware that bond redemption yields do not reflect a true interest rate for that maturity, for which we use the spot rate.

For relative value purposes, traders and portfolio managers frequently compare a bond's actual market price to its theoretical price, calculated using specific zero-coupon yields for each cash flow, and determine whether the bond is "cheap" or "dear". Even where there is some misalignment between the theoretical price of a bond and the actual price, the decision to buy or sell may be based on judgemental factors, since there is often no zero-coupon instrument against which to effect an arbitrage trade. In a market where no zero-coupon instruments are traded, the spot rates used in the analysis are theoretical and are not represented by actual market prices. Traders therefore often analyse bonds in terms of relative value against each other, and the redemption yield curve, rather than against their theoretical zero-coupon-based price.

What considerations apply where a zero-coupon bond market exists alongside a conventional coupon-bond market? In such a case, in theory arbitrage trading is possible if a bond is priced above or below the price suggested by zero-coupon rates. For example, a bond priced above its theoretical price could be sold, and zero-coupon bonds that equated its cash-flow stream could be purchased; the difference in price is the arbitrage profit. Or a bond trading below its theoretical price could be purchased and its coupons "stripped" and sold individually as zero-coupon bonds; the proceeds from the sale of the zero-coupon bonds would then exceed the purchase price of the coupon bond. In practice, the existence of both markets equalises prices between both markets so that arbitrage is no longer possible, although opportunities will still occasionally present themselves.

Using forward rates

Newcomers to the markets frequently experience confusion when first confronted with forward rates. Do they represent the market's expectation of where interest rates will actually be when the forward date arrives? If forward rates are a predictor of future interest rates, exactly how good are they at making this prediction? Empirical evidence[9] suggests that in fact forward rates are not accurate predictors of future interest rates, frequently over-stating them by a considerable margin. If this is the case, should we attach any value or importance to forward rates?

The value of forward rates does not lie, however, in its track record as a market predictor, but moreover in its use as a hedging tool. As we illustrate in Example 9.3 the forward rate is calculated on the basis that if we are to

---

[9] Including Fama (1976).

price, say, a cash deposit with a forward starting date, but we wish to deal today, the return from the deposit will be exactly the same as if we invested for a start date today and rolled over the investment at the forward date. The forward rate allows us to lock in a dealing rate now. Once we have dealt today, it is irrelevant what the actual rate pertaining to the forward date is – we have already dealt. Therefore forward rates are better called *hedge* rates, as they allow us to lock in a dealing rate for a future period, thus removing uncertainty.

The existence of forward prices in the market also allows us to make an investment decision, based on our view compared to the market view. The forward rate implied by, say, government bond prices is in effect the market's view of future interest rates. If we happen not to agree with this view, we will deal accordingly. In effect we are comparing our view on future interest rates with that of the market, and making our investment decision based on this comparison.

Analysing and interpreting the yield curve

From observing yield curves in different markets at any time, we notice that a yield curve can adopt one of four basic shapes. These are:

- *normal* or *conventional*: in which yields are at "average" levels and the curve slopes gently upwards as maturity increases;
- *upward sloping* or *positive* or *rising*: in which yields are at historically low levels, with long rates substantially greater than short rates;
- *downward sloping* or *inverted* or *negative*: in which yield levels are very high by historical standards, but long-term yields are significantly lower than short rates;
- *humped*: where yields are high with the curve rising to a peak in the medium-term maturity area, and then sloping downwards at longer maturities.

Sometimes yield curves will incorporate a mixture of the above features.

A great deal of effort is expended by bond analysts and economists in analysing and interpreting yield curves. There is often considerable information content associated with any curve at any time. For example, Figure 9.16 on page 386 shows the UK gilt redemption yield curve at three different times in the ten years from June 1989 to June 1999. What does the shape of each curve tell us about the UK debt market, and the UK economy at each particular time?

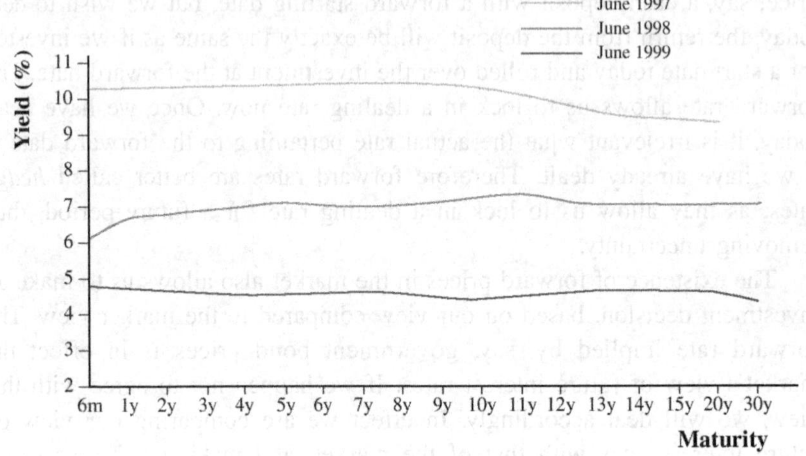

Figure 9.16 UK gilt redemption yield curves

In this section we will consider the various explanations that have been put forward to explain the shape of the yield curve at any one time. None of the theories can adequately explain everything about yield curves and the shapes they assume at any time, so generally observers seek to explain specific curves using a combination of the accepted theories. This subject is a large one; indeed, we could devote several books to it, so at this stage we will introduce the main ideas; readers wishing to read about this in further degree may consult the author's book *Advanced Fixed Income Analysis* (Elsevier 2004).

The existence of a yield curve itself indicates that there is a cost associated with funds of different maturities, otherwise we would observe a flat yield curve. The fact that we very rarely observe a flat yield suggests that investors require different rates of return depending on the maturity of the instrument they are holding. In this section we review the main theories that have been put forward to explain the shape of the yield curve, which all have fairly long-dated antecedents.

An excellent account of the term structure is given in *Theory of Financial Decision Making* by Jonathan Ingersoll (1987), Chapter 18. In fact it is worth purchasing this book just for Chapter 18 alone. Another quality account of the term structure is by Shiller (1990). In the following section we provide an introductory review of the research on this subject to date.

The expectations hypothesis

The expectations hypothesis suggests that bondholders' expectations determine the course of future interest rates. There are two main competing versions of this hypothesis, the *local expectations hypothesis* and the *unbiased expectations hypothesis*. The *return-to-maturity expectations* hypothesis and *yield-to-maturity expectations* hypothesis are also referred to (see Ingersoll 1987). The local expectations hypothesis states that all bonds of the same class, but differing in term to maturity, will have the same expected holding period rate of return. This suggests that a six-month bond and a 20-year bond will produce the same rate of return, on average, over the stated holding period. So if we intend to hold a bond for six months, we will receive the same return no matter what specific bond we buy. The author feels that this theory is not always the case or relevant, despite being mathematically neat; however, it is worth spending a few moments discussing it and related points. Generally, holding period returns from longer-dated bonds are on average higher than those from short-dated bonds. Intuitively we would expect this, with longer-dated bonds offering higher returns to compensate for their higher price volatility (risk). The local expectations hypothesis would not agree with the conventional belief that investors, being risk averse, require higher returns as a reward for taking on higher risk; in addition, it does not provide any insight about the shape of the yield curve. An article by Cox, Ingersoll and Ross (1981) shows that the local expectations hypothesis best reflected equilibrium between spot and forward yields. This was demonstrated using a feature known as Jensen's inequality, which is described in Appendix 9.1 at the end of this chapter. Robert Jarrow (1996) states:

> ... in an economic equilibrium, the returns on ... similar maturity zero-coupon bonds cannot be too different. If they were too different, no investor would hold the bond with the smaller return. This difference could not persist in an economic equilibrium.
>
> Jarrow (1996), p. 50

This reflects economic logic, but in practice other factors can impact on holding period returns between bonds that do not have similar maturities. For instance, investors will have restrictions as to which bonds they can hold; for example, banks and building societies are required to hold short-dated bonds for liquidity purposes. In an cnvironment of economic disequilibrium, these investors would still have to hold shorter-dated bonds, even if the holding period return was lower.

So although it is economically neat to expect that the return on a long-dated bond is equivalent to rolling over a series of shorter-dated bonds, it is often observed that longer-term (default-free) returns exceed annualised short-term default-free returns. So an investor who continuously rolled over a series of short-dated zero-coupon bonds would most likely receive a lower return than if she had invested in a long-dated zero-coupon bond. Rubinstein (1999) gives an excellent, accessible explanation of why this should be so. The reason is that compared to the theoretical model, in reality future spot rates are not known with certainty. This means that short-dated zero-coupon bonds are more attractive to investors for two reasons; first, they are more appropriate instruments to use for hedging purposes, and second they are more liquid instruments, in that they may be more readily converted back into cash than long-dated instruments. With regard to hedging, consider an exposure to rising interest rates. If the yield curve shifts upwards at some point in the future, the price of long-dated bonds will fall by a greater amount. This is a negative result for holders of such bonds, whereas the investor in short-dated bonds will benefit from rolling over his funds at the (new) higher rates. With regard to the second issue, Rubinstein (1999) states:

> ... it can be shown that in an economy with risk-averse individuals, uncertainty concerning the timing of aggregate consumption, the partial irreversibility of real investments (longer-term physical investments cannot be converted into investments with earlier payouts without sacrifice), [and] ... real assets with shorter-term payouts will tend to have a "liquidity" advantage.
>
> Rubinstein (1999), pp. 84–5

Therefore the demand for short-term instruments is frequently higher, and hence short-term returns are often lower than long-term returns.

The *pure* or *unbiased expectations hypothesis* is more commonly encountered and states that current implied forward rates are unbiased estimators of future spot interest rates.[10] It assumes that investors act in a way that eliminates any advantage of holding instruments of a particular maturity. Therefore if we have a positive-sloping yield curve, the unbiased

[10] For original discussion, see Lutz (1940) and Fisher (1986), although he formulated his ideas earlier.

expectations hypothesis states that the market expects spot interest rates to rise. Equally, an inverted yield curve is an indication that spot rates are expected to fall. If short-term interest rates are expected to rise, then longer yields should be higher than shorter ones to reflect this. If this were not the case, investors would only buy the shorter-dated bonds and roll over the investment when they matured. Likewise, if rates are expected to fall then longer yields should be lower than short yields. The unbiased expectations hypothesis states that the long-term interest rate is a geometric average of expected future short-term rates. This was in fact the theory that was used to derive the forward yield curve using (9.5) and (9.7) previously. This gives us:

$$(1 + rs_N)^N = (1 + rs_1)(1 + {}_1rf_2) \ldots (1 + {}_{N-1}rf_N) \qquad (9.16)$$

or

$$(1 + rs_N)^N = (1 + rs_{N-1})^{N-1}(1 + {}_{N-1}rf_N) \qquad (9.17)$$

where rs_N is the spot yield on a N-year bond and ${}_{n-1}rf_n$ is the implied one-year rate n years ahead. For example, if the current one-year spot rate is rs_1 and the market is expecting the one-year rate in a year's time to be ${}_1rf_2 =$ 5.539%, then the market is expecting a £100 investment in two one-year bonds to yield:

$$£100(1.05)(1.05539) = £110.82$$

after two years. To be equivalent to this an investment in a two-year bond has to yield the same amount, implying that the current two-year rate is rs_2 as shown below:

$$£100(1 + rs_2)^2 = £110.82$$

which gives us rs_2 equal to 5.27%, and gives us the correct future value as shown below:

$$£100(1.0527)^2 = £110.82.$$

This result must be so, to ensure no arbitrage opportunities exist in the market and in fact we showed as much earlier in the chapter when we considered forward rates. According to the unbiased expectations hypothesis therefore the forward rate ${}_0rf_2$ is an unbiased predictor of the spot rate ${}_2rs_1$

observed one period later; on average the forward rate should equal the subsequent spot rate. The hypothesis can be used to explain any shape in the yield curve.

A rising yield curve is therefore explained by investors expecting short-term interest rates to rise; that is, ${}_1rf_2 > rs_2$. A falling yield curve is explained by investors expecting short-term rates to be lower in the future. A humped yield curve is explained by investors expecting short-term interest rates to rise and long-term rates to fall. Expectations, or views on the future direction of the market, are a function mainly of the expected rate of inflation. If the market expects inflationary pressures in the future, the yield curve will be positively shaped, while if inflation expectations are inclined towards disinflation, then the yield curve will be negative. However, several empirical studies, including one by Fama (1976), have shown that forward rates are essentially biased predictors of future spot interest rates, and often over-estimate future levels of spot rates. The unbiased hypothesis has also been criticised for suggesting that investors can forecast (or have a view on) very long-dated spot interest rates, which might be considered slightly unrealistic. As yield curves in most developed country markets exist to a maturity of up to 30 years or longer, such criticisms may have some substance. Are investors able to forecast interest rates 10, 20 or 30 years into the future? Perhaps not, nevertheless this is indeed the information content of, say, a 30-year bond; since the yield on the bond is set by the market, it is valid to suggest that the market has a view on inflation and future interest rates for up to 30 years forward.

The expectations hypothesis is stated in more than one way; we have already encountered the local expectations hypothesis. Other versions include the *return-to-maturity* expectations hypothesis, which states that the total return from holding a zero-coupon bond to maturity will be equal to the total return that is generated by holding a short-term instrument and continuously rolling it over the same maturity period. A related version, the *yield-to-maturity* hypothesis, states that the periodic return from holding a zero-coupon bond will be equal to the return from rolling over a series of coupon bonds, but refers to the annualised return earned each year rather than the total return earned over the life of the bond. This assumption enables a zero-coupon yield curve to be derived from the redemption yields of coupon bonds. The unbiased expectations hypothesis of course states that forward rates are equal to the spot rates expected by the market in the future. The Cox, Ingersoll and Ross article suggests that only the local expectations hypothesis describes a model that is purely arbitrage-free, as under the other scenarios it would be possible to employ certain investment strategies that would produce returns in excess of what was implied by today's yields. Although it has been suggested[11] that the differences between the local and the unbiased hypotheses are not material, a model that describes such a scenario would not reflect investors' beliefs, which is why further research is ongoing in this area.

The unbiased expectations hypothesis does not by itself explain all the shapes of the yield curve or the information content contained within it, so it is often tied in with other explanations, including the liquidity preference theory. For a description on testing the unbiased expectations hypothesis, see Appendix 9.2.

Liquidity preference theory

Intuitively we might feel that longer maturity investments are more risky than shorter ones. Investors lending money for a five-year term will usually demand a higher rate of interest than if they were to lend the same customer money for a five-week term. This is because borrowers may not be able to repay the loan over the longer time period as they may, for instance, have gone bankrupt in that period. For this reason longer-dated yields should be higher than short-dated yields, to recompense the lender for the higher risk exposure during the term of the loan.[12] This is a logical argument.

We can consider this theory in terms of inflation expectations as well. Where inflation is expected to remain roughly stable over time, the market would anticipate a positive yield curve. However, the expectations hypothesis cannot by itself explain this phenomenon, as under stable inflationary conditions one would expect a flat yield curve. The risk inherent in longer-dated investments, or the *liquidity preference theory*, seeks to explain a positive-shaped curve. Generally, borrowers prefer to borrow over as long a term as possible, while lenders will wish to lend over as short a term as possible. Therefore, as we first stated, lenders have to be compensated for lending over the longer term; this compensation is considered a premium for a loss in *liquidity* for the lender. The premium is increased the further the investor lends across the term structure, so that the longest-dated investments will, all else being equal, have the highest yield. So the liquidity preference theory states that the yield curve should almost always be upward sloping, reflecting bondholders' preference for the liquidity and lower risk of shorter-dated bonds. An inverted yield curve

[11] For example, see Campbell (1986) and Livingstone (1990).

[12] For original discussion, see Hicks (1946).

could still be explained by the liquidity preference theory when it is combined with the unbiased expectations hypothesis. A *humped* yield curve might be viewed as a combination of an inverted yield curve together with a positive-sloping liquidity preference curve.

The difference between a yield curve explained by unbiased expectations and an actual observed yield curve is sometimes referred to as the *liquidity premium*. This refers to the fact that in some cases short-dated bonds are easier to transact in the market than long-term bonds. It is difficult to quantify the effect of the liquidity premium, which in any cases is not static and fluctuates over time. The liquidity premium is so-called because, in order to induce investors to hold longer-dated securities, the yields on such securities must be higher than those available on short-dated securities, which are more liquid and may be converted into cash more easily. The liquidity premium is the compensation required for holding less liquid instruments. If longer-dated securities then provide higher yields, as is suggested by the existence of the liquidity premium, they should generate on average higher total returns over an investment period. This is not consistent with the local expectations hypothesis. More formally we can write:

$$0 = L_1 < L_2 < L_3 < \ldots < L_n$$

$$\text{and } (L_2 - L_1) > (L_3 - L_2) > \ldots (L_n - L_{n-1})$$

where L is the premium for a bond with term to maturity of n years, which states that the premium increases as the term to maturity rises and that an otherwise flat yield curve will have a positively sloping curve, with the degree of slope steadily decreasing as we extend along the yield curve. This is consistent with observation of yield curves under "normal" conditions.

The expectations hypothesis assumes that forward rates are equal to the expected future spot rates; that is, as shown in (9.18):

$$_{n-1}rf_n = E(_{n-1}rs_n) \tag{9.18}$$

where $E()$ is the expectations operator for the current period. This assumption implies that the forward rate is an unbiased predictor of the future spot rate, as we suggested in the previous paragraph. Liquidity preference theory, on the other hand, recognises the possibility that the forward rate may contain an element of liquidity premium that declines over time as the period approaches, given by (9.19):

$$_{n-1}rf_n > E(_{n-1}rs_n). \tag{9.19}$$

If there was uncertainty in the market about the future direction of spot rates and hence where the forward rate should lie, (9.19) is adjusted to give the reverse inequality.

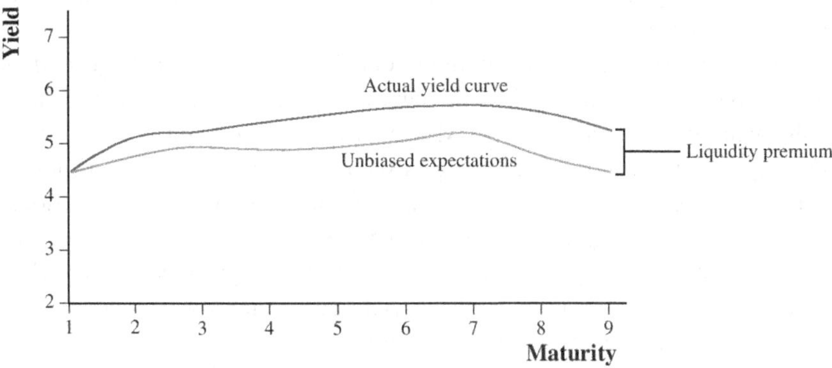

Figure 9.17 Yield curve explained by expectations hypothesis and liquidity preference

Money substitute hypothesis

A particular explanation of short-dated bond yield curves has been attempted by Kessel (1965). In the *money substitute* theory, short-dated bonds are regarded as substitutes for holding cash. Investors hold only short-dated market instruments because these are viewed as low or negligible risk. As a result the yields of short-dated bonds are depressed due to the increased demand and lie below longer-dated bonds. Borrowers, on the other hand, prefer to issue debt for longer maturities, and on as few occasions as possible to minimise costs. Therefore the yields of longer-dated paper are driven upwards due to a combination of increased supply and lower liquidity. In certain respects the money substitute theory is closely related to the liquidity preference theory, and by itself does not explain inverted or humped yield curves.

Segmentation hypothesis

The capital markets are made up of a wide variety of users, each with different requirements. Certain classes of investors will prefer dealing at the short-end of the yield curve, while others will concentrate on the longer end of the market. The *segmented markets* theory suggests that activity is concentrated in certain specific areas of the market, and that there are no interrelationships between these parts of the market; the relative amounts of funds invested in each of the maturity spectrum causes differentials in supply and demand, which results in humps in the yield curve. That is, the shape of the yield curve is determined by supply and demand for certain specific maturity investments, each of which has no reference to any other part of the curve.

For example, banks and building societies concentrate a large part of their activity at the short end of the curve, required by the routine of daily cash management (central to ALM) and for regulatory purposes (part of liquidity requirements). Fund managers such as pension funds and insurance companies are active at the long end of the market. Few institutional investors, the theory posits, have any preference for medium-dated assets. This behaviour on the part of investors will lead to high prices (low yields) at both the short and long ends of the yield curve and lower prices (higher yields) in the middle of the term structure.

Since according to the segmented markets hypothesis a separate market exists for specific maturities along the term structure, interest rates for these maturities are set by supply and demand.[13] Where there is no demand for a particular maturity, the yield will lie above other segments. Market participants do not hold bonds in any other area of the curve outside their area of interest[14] so that short-dated and long-dated bond yields exist independently of each other. The segmented markets theory is usually illustrated by reference to banks and life insurance companies. Banks' and building societies' Treasury desks hold their funds in short-dated instruments, usually no longer than five years in maturity. This is because of the nature of retail banking operations, with a large volume of instant access funds being deposited in banks, and also for regulatory purposes. Holding short-term, liquid bonds enables banks to meet any sudden or unexpected demand for funds from customers. The classic theory suggests that as banks invest their funds in short-dated bonds, the yields on these bonds are driven down. When they then liquidate part of their holding, perhaps to meet higher demand for loans, the yields are driven up and prices of the bonds fall. This affects the short end of the yield curve but not the long end.

The segmented markets theory can be used to explain any particular shape of the yield curve, although it fits best perhaps with positive-sloping curves. However, it cannot be used to interpret the yield curve whatever

---

[13] See Culbertson (1957).

[14] For example, retail and commercial banks hold bonds in the short dates, while life assurance companies hold long-dated bonds.

shape it may be, and therefore it offers no information content during analysis. By definition, the theory suggests that bonds with different maturities are not perfect substitutes for each other. This is because different bonds would have different holding period returns, making them imperfect substitutes of one another.[15] As a result of bonds being imperfect substitutes, markets are segmented according to maturity.

The segmentations hypothesis is a reasonable explanation of certain features of a conventional positively sloping yield curve, but by itself it is not sufficient. There is no doubt that banks and building societies have a requirement to hold securities at the short end of the yield curve, as much for regulatory purposes as for yield considerations; however, other investors are probably more flexible and will place funds where value is deemed to exist. Nonetheless, the higher demand for benchmark securities does drive down yields along certain segments of the curve.

A slightly modified version of the market segmentation hypothesis is known as the *preferred habitat theory*. This suggests that different market participants have an interest in specified areas of the yield curve, but can be induced to hold bonds from other parts of the maturity spectrum if there is sufficient incentive. Hence banks may at certain times hold longer-dated bonds once the price of these bonds falls to a certain level, making the return on the bonds worth the risk involved in holding them. Similar considerations may persuade long-term investors to hold short-dated debt. So higher yields will be required to make bondholders shift out of their usual area of interest. This theory essentially recognises the flexibility that investors have, outside regulatory or legal requirements (such as the terms of an institutional fund's objectives), to invest in whatever part of the yield curve they identify value.

Humped yield curves

When plotting a yield curve of all the bonds in a certain class, it is common to observe humped yield curves. These usually occur for a variety of reasons. In line with the unbiased expectations hypothesis, humped curves will be observed when interest rates are expected to rise over the next several periods and then decline. On other occasions humped curves can result from skewed expectations of future interest rates. This is when the market believes that fairly constant future interest rates are likely, but also believes that there is a small probability for lower rates in the medium term. The other common explanation for humped curves is the preferred habitat theory.

[15] See footnote 12.

The combined theory

The explanation for the shape of the yield curve at any time is more likely to be described by a combination of the pure expectations hypothesis and the liquidity preference theory, and possibly one or two other theories. Market analysts often combine the unbiased expectations hypothesis and the liquidity preference theory into an "eclectic" theory. The result is fairly consistent with any shape of yield curve, and is also a predictor of rising interest rates. In the combined theory the forward interest rate is equal to the expected future spot rate, together with a quantified liquidity premium. This is shown in (9.20):

$$_0rf_i = E(\,_{i-1}rs_1) + L_i \tag{9.20}$$

where L_i is the liquidity premium for a term to maturity of i. The size of the liquidity premium is expected to increase with increasing maturity.[16] An illustration is given in Example 9.7.

EXAMPLE 9.7 Positive yield curve with constant expected future interest rates

Consider the interest rate structure in Table 9.5.

Period n	0	1	2	3	4	5
$E(rs)$		4.5%	4.5%	4.5%	4.5%	4.5%
Forward rate $_0rf_n$		5.0%	5.5%	6.0%	6.5%	7.5%
Spot rate rs_n	5.0%	5.3%	5.8%	6.2%	6.8%	7.0%

Table 9.5 Positive yield curve with constant expected future rates

The current term structure is positively sloping since the spot rates increase with increasing maturity. However, the market expects future spot rates to be constant at 4.5%. The forward and spot rates are also shown; however, the forward rate is a function of the expected spot rate and the liquidity premium. This premium is equal to 0.50% for the first year, 1.0% in the second and so on.

[16] So that $L_i > L_{i-1}$.

The combined theory is consistent with an inverted yield curve. This will apply even when the liquidity premium is increasing with maturity; for example, where the expected future spot interest rate is declining. Typically, this would be where there was a current term structure of falling yields along the term structure. The spot rates might be declining where the fall in the expected future spot rate exceeds the corresponding increase in the liquidity premium.

The flat yield curve

The conventional theories do not seek to explain a flat yield curve. Although it is rare to observe flat curves in a market, certainly for any length of time, at times they do emerge in response to peculiar economic circumstances. In the conventional thinking, a flat curve is not tenable because investors should in theory have no incentive to hold long-dated bonds over shorter-dated bonds when there is no yield premium, so that as they sell off long-dated paper the yield at the long end should rise, producing an upward-sloping curve. In the previous circumstances of a flat curve, analysts have produced different explanations for their existence. In November 1988 the US Treasury yield curve was flat relative to the recent past; researchers contended that this was the result of the market's view that long-dated yields would fall as bond prices rallied upwards.[17] One recommendation is to buy longer maturities when the yield curve is flat, in anticipation of lower long-term interest rates, which is the direct opposite to the view that a flat curve is a signal to sell long bonds. In the case of the US market in 1988, long bond yields did in fact fall by approximately 2% in the following 12 months. This would seem to indicate that one's view of future long-term rates should be behind the decision to buy or sell long bonds, rather than the shape of the yield curve itself. A flat curve may well be more heavily influenced by supply and demand factors than anything else, with the majority opinion eventually winning out and forcing a change in the curve to a more conventional shape.

Yield curves as a function of the stochastic behaviour of interest rates

As a result of research into the behaviour of asset prices more recent explanations for the shape of the yield curve have sought to describe it as

[17] See Levy (1999).

reflecting the behaviour of interest rates and the process that interest rates follow. These explanations are termed *stochastic processes*. A stochastic process is one where random phenomena evolve over time, and these may be asset prices, interest rates, returns on an investment portfolio and so on. Under these explanations then, yield curves reflect the following:

- bond yields follow a stochastic process over time, and hence the yield curve reflects this;
- bond yields at any one time satisfy the no-arbitrage pricing rule for spot and forward rates.

The model of the term structure as being an arbitrage-free stochastic process evolved with option pricing theory and is described in Choudhry (2004a).[18] Such models sought to describe the term structure in terms of the short-term interest rate only, more recent models describe the whole term structure as part of a stochastic process.[19] This subject is key to yield curve modelling and is discussed further in Choudhry (2004b).

Further views on the yield curve

In our discussion of present values, spot and forward interest rates assumed an economist's world of the *perfect market* (also sometimes called the *frictionless* financial market). Such a perfect capital market is characterised by:

- perfect information;
- no taxes;
- bullet maturity bonds;
- no transaction costs.

Of course, in practice markets are not completely perfect. However, assuming perfect markets makes the discussion of spot and forward rates and the term structure easier to handle. When we analyse yield curves for their information content, we have to remember that the markets that they represent are not perfect, and that frequently we observe anomalies that are not explained by the conventional theories.

At any one time it is probably more realistic to suggest that a range of factors contributes to the yield curve being one particular shape. For

[18] See Black and Scholes (1973) and Merton (1973) for original discussion.

[19] For example, see Heath, Jarrow and Morton (1992).

instance, short-term interest rates are greatly influenced by the availability of funds in the money market. The slope of the yield curve (usually defined as the 10-year yield minus the three-month interest rate) is also a measure of the degree of tightness of government monetary policy. A low, upward-sloping curve is often thought to be a sign that an environment of cheap money, due to a more loose monetary policy, is to be followed by a period of higher inflation and higher bond yields. Equally, a high downward-sloping curve is taken to mean that a situation of tight credit, due to more strict monetary policy, will result in falling inflation and lower bond yields. Inverted yield curves have often preceded recessions; for instance, *The Economist* in an article from April 1998 remarked that in the United States every recession since 1955 bar one had been preceded by a negative yield curve. The analysis is the same: if investors expect a recession they also expect inflation to fall, so the yields on long-term bonds will fall relative to short-term bonds. Hence the conventional explanation for an inverted yield curve is that the markets and the investment community expect either a slow-down of the economy, or an outright recession.[20] In this case one would expect the monetary authorities to ease the money supply by reducing the base interest rate in the near future; hence, an inverted curve. At the same time, a reduction of short-term interest rates will affect short-dated bonds and these are sold off by investors, further raising their yield.

While the conventional explanation for negative yield curves is an expectation of economic slow-down, on occasion other, structural, factors will be involved. In the United Kingdom in the period July 1997–June 1999 the gilt yield curve was inverted.[21] There was no general view that the economy was heading for recession, however. In fact, the new Labour government inherited an economy believed to be in good health. Instead the explanation behind the inverted shape of the gilt yield curve focused on two other factors: first, the handing of responsibility for setting interest rates to the Monetary Policy Committee (MPC) of the BoE, and second, the expectation that the United Kingdom would over the medium term abandon sterling and join the euro currency. The yield curve in this time suggested that the market expected the MPC to be successful and keep inflation at a

[20] A recession is formally defined as two successive quarters of falling output in the domestic economy.

[21] Although the curve briefly went positively sloped out to 7–8 years in July 1999, it very quickly reverted to being inverted throughout the term structure, and remained so until certain restrictions on the need for institutional investors to hold long-dated gilts were lifted by the government in 2002.

level around 2.5% over the long term (its target is actually a 1% range either side of 2.5%),[22] and also that sterling interest rates would need to come down over the medium term as part of *convergence* with interest rates in euroland. These are both medium-term expectations, however, and in the author's view not logical at the short-end of the yield curve. In fact, the term structure moved to a positive-sloped shape up to the 6–7-year area, before inverting out to the long-end of the curve, in June 1999. This is a more logical shape for the curve to assume, but it was short-lived and returned to being inverted after the two-year term.

There is therefore significant information content in the yield curve, and economists and bond analysts will consider the shape of the curve as part of their policymaking and investment advice. The shape of parts of the curve, whether the short-end or long-end, as well that of the entire curve, can serve as useful predictors of future market conditions. As part of an analysis it is also worthwhile considering the yield curves across several different markets and currencies. For instance, the interest-rate swap curve, and its position relative to that of the government bond yield curve, is also regularly analysed for its information content. In developed country economies the swap market is invariably as liquid as the government bond market, if not more liquid, and so it is common to see the swap curve analysed when making predictions about, say, the future level of short-term interest rates.

Government policy will influence the shape and level of the yield curve, including policy on public-sector borrowing, debt management and open-market operations. The market's perception of the size of public-sector debt will influence bond yields; for instance, an increase in the level of debt can lead to an increase in bond yields across the maturity range. Open-market operations, which refer to the daily operation by the BoE to control the level of the money supply (to which end the BoE purchases short-term bills and also engages in repo dealing), can have a number of effects. In the short-term it can tilt the yield curve both upwards and downwards; longer term, changes in the level of the base rate will affect yield levels. An anticipated rise in base rates can lead to a drop in prices for short-term bonds, whose yields will be expected to rise – this can lead to a temporary inverted curve. Finally, debt management policy will influence the yield curve. Much government debt is rolled over as it matures, but the maturity of the replacement debt can have a significant influence on the yield curve in the

[22] From 2004 the BoE adopted the European Unions' harmonised consumer price index (CPI) inflation measure, and its target rate for the CPI is now 2%.

form of humps in the market segment in which the debt is placed, if the debt is priced by the market at a relatively low price and hence high yield.

Interpreting the yield curve

We illustrate some of the points we have raised here using yield curves from the UK gilt market during the 1990s. It is of course easier to analyse them for their information content in hindsight than it might have been at the time, but these observations help illustrate the general conclusions that can be made during real-time analysis.

To begin, consider the observed yield curves for January and June 1990 in Figures 9.18 and 9.19 on page 402.[23]

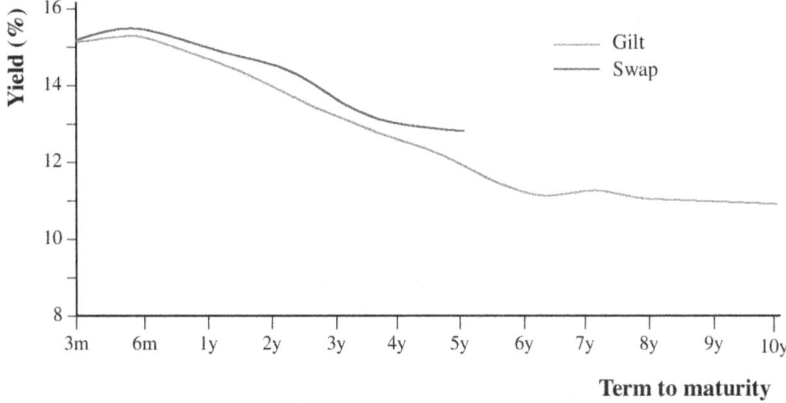

Figure 9.18 Sterling curves January 1990

The yield curve for the first date suggests declining short-term rates and this is indicated by the yield curve for June 1990. The prediction is approximately accurate.

[23] All government yield curves shown are fitted par yield curves, using the BoE's internal model (see Mastronikola (1991) and Anderson and Sleath (1999)), except where indicated. Source data is from the BoE. The other curve is the interest-rate swap curve, also called the Libor curve, for sterling swaps. In practice, interest-rate swaps are priced off the government yield curve, and reflect the market's view of interbank credit risk, as the swap rate is payable by a bank (or corporate) viewed as having an element of credit risk. All swap curves are drawn using interest data from Bloomberg.

That the yield curves were inverted is not surprising, given that the UK economy was shortly to enter an economic recession; however, at that date – January 1990 – it had not yet begun. The evidence of GDP output data is that the recession took place during 1990–91. The markets were therefore expecting some loosening of monetary policy, given the economic slowdown during 1989. There was an additional anomaly in that during 1988 the government had been paying off public-sector debt, leading some commentators to suggest that gilt supply would be reduced in coming years. This may have contributed to the depressed yields at the long end in January 1990 but almost certainly had less influence in June 1990, when the recession was underway.

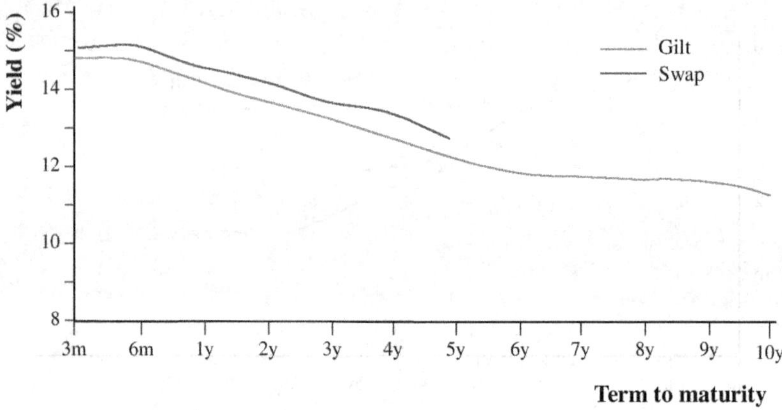

Figure 9.19 Sterling curves June 1990

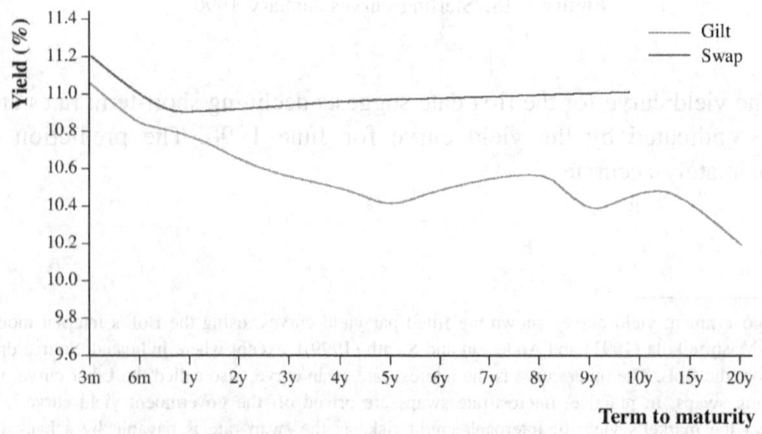

Figure 9.20 Sterling curves June 1991

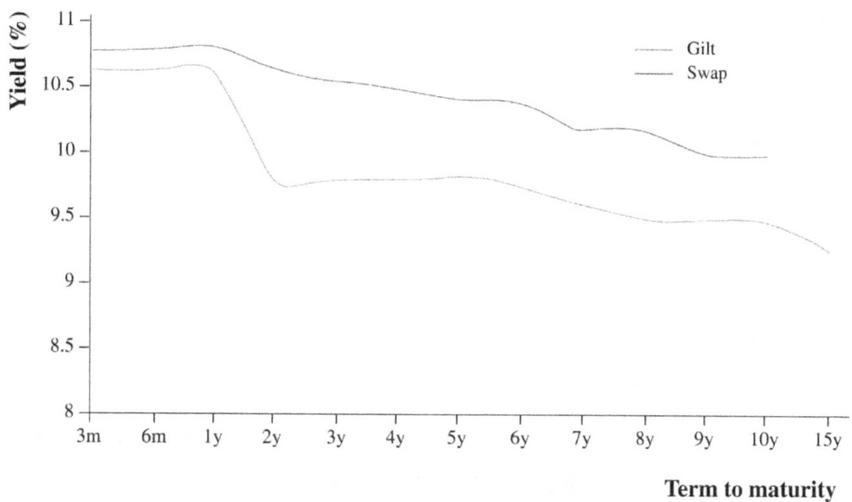

Figure 9.21 Sterling curves January 1992

Consider the same curves for June 1991 and January 1992, shown as Figures 9.20 and 9.21 respectively. In this case the money market has priced swaps to give a different shaped yield curve; does this mean that the money market has a different view of forward rates to government bond investors? Observing the yield curves for January 1992 suggests not: the divergence in the swap curve reflects credit considerations that price long maturity corporate rates at increasing yield spreads. This is common during recessions, and indeed the curves reflect recession conditions in the UK economy at the time, as predicted by the yield curves during 1990. Another indicator is the continuation of the wide swap spread as the term to maturity increases to ten years, rather than the conventional mirroring of the government curve. Note also that the short-term segment of the swap curve in June 1991 (Figure 9.20) matches the government yield curve, indicating that the market agreed with the short-term forward rate prediction of the government curve.

During 1992, as the UK economy came out of recession, the government yield curve changed from inverted to steadily positive, while the swap curve mirrored the shape of the government curve. The swap spread itself has declined, to no more than 10 basis points at the short end. This was most pronounced shortly after sterling fell out of the European Union's exchange rate mechanism. The curves for November 1992 are shown in Figure 9.22.

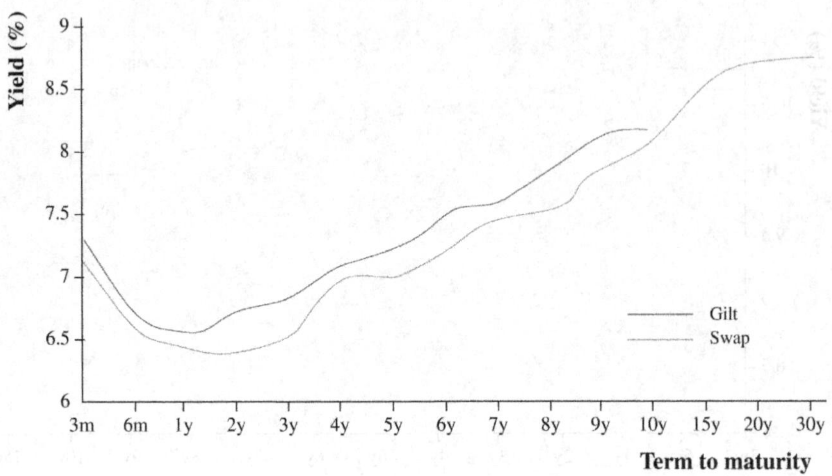

Figure 9.22 5 November 1992

Both yield curves had reverted to being purely positively sloping by January 1993.

The illustrations used are examples where government yield curves were shown to be accurate predictors of the short-term rates that followed, more so than the swap curve. This is to be expected: the government or benchmark yield curve is the cornerstone of the debt markets, and is used by the market to price all other debt instruments, including interest-rate swaps. This reflects both the liquidity of the government market and its risk-free status.

Another example illustrating that the yield curve is an accurate predictive indicator of the economy can be seen in the US market. The general assessment of an inverted yield curve is that it is a signal for lower interest rates, lower inflation levels and a recession. An examination of Figure 9.23, which shows US market data, would appear to prove the yield curve's accuracy in this regard; it shows how an inverted curve has "predicted" all the previous recessions in recent US history.

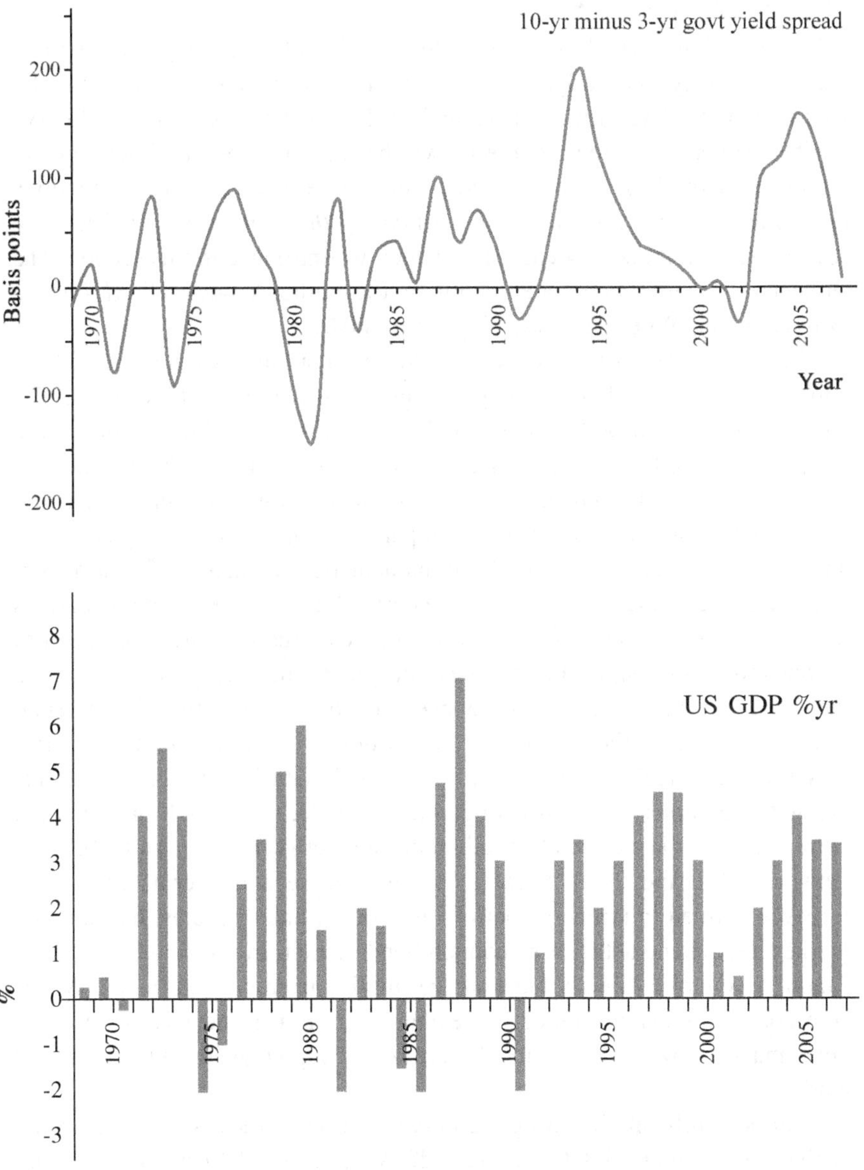

Figure 9.23 USD yield curve spread (10-year minus 3-year) and US GDP
Source: HBOS/Datastream.

Fitting the yield curve

When graphing a yield curve, we plot a series of discrete points of yield against maturity. Similarly, for the term structure of interest rates, we plot spot rates for a fixed time period against that time period. The yield curve itself however is a smooth curve drawn through these points. Therefore we require a method that allows us to fit the curve as accurately as possible, known as *yield curve modelling* or *estimating the term structure*. There are several ways to model a yield curve, which we introduce in this section. The subject is covered in greater depth in the author's book *Fixed Income Markets* (John Wiley & Sons, Singapore 2004).

Ideally, the fitted yield curve should be a continuous function, with no gaps in the curve, while passing through the observed yield vertices. The curve also needs to be "smooth", as kinks in it will produce sudden sharp jumps in derived forward rates. We have stated how it is possible to calculate a set of discrete discount factors or a continuous discount function. It has been shown that the discount function, par yield curve, spot rate yield curve and forward rate curve are all related mathematically, such that if one knows any one of these, the other three can be derived. In practice, in many markets it is not possible usually to observe the curves directly, hence they need to be derived from coupon bond prices and yields. In attempting to model a yield curve from bond yields we need to consider the two fundamental issues introduced above. First is the problem of gaps in the maturity spectrum, as in reality there will not be a bond maturing at regular intervals along the complete term structure. For example, in the UK gilt market, currently there is no bond at all maturing between 2017 and 2021, or between 2021 and 2028. Second, as we have seen the term structure is formally defined in terms of spot or zero-coupon interest rates, but in many markets there is no actual zero-coupon bond market. In such cases spot rates cannot be inferred directly but must be implied from coupon bonds. Where zero-coupon bonds are traded, for example in the US and UK government bond markets, we are able to observe zero-coupon yields directly in the market.

Further problems in fitting the curve arise from these two issues. How is the gap in maturities to be tackled? Analysts need to choose between "smoothness" and "responsiveness" of the curve estimate. Most models opt for a smooth fitting; however, enough flexibility should be retained to allow for true movements in the term structure where indicated by the data. Should the yield curve be estimated from the discount function or, say, the par yield curve? There are other practical factors to consider as well, such as the effect of withholding tax on coupons, and the size of bond coupons themselves. Issues connected with estimating the yield curve are outside the scope of this book; here we confine ourselves to simply introducing the main methods that are used.

Interpolation

The simplest method that is employed to fit a curve is *linear interpolation*, which involves drawing a straight line joining each pair of yield vertices. To calculate the yield for one vertex we use (9.21):

$$rm_t = rm_i + \frac{t - n_i}{n_{i+1} - n_i} \times (rm_{i+1} - rm_i) \qquad (9.21)$$

where rm_t is the yield being estimated and n is the number of years to maturity for yields that are observed. For example, consider the following redemption yields:

1 month:	4.00%
2 years:	5.00%
4 years:	6.50%
10 years:	6.75%

If we wish to estimate the six-year yield we calculate it using (9.21), which is:

$$rm_{6y} = 6.50\% + \frac{6 - 4}{10 - 6} \times 6.75\% - 6.5\%$$

$$= 6.5833\%.$$

The limitations of using linear interpolation are that first the curve can have sharp angles at the vertices where two straight lines meet, resulting in unreasonable jumps in the derived forward rates. Second, and more fundamentally, being a straight-line method, it assumes that the yield between two vertices should automatically be rising (in a positive yield curve environment) or falling. This assumption can lead to gross inaccuracies in the fitted curve.

Another approach is to use *logarithmic interpolation*, which involves applying linear interpolation to the natural logarithms of the corresponding discount factors. Therefore given any two discount factors we can calculate an intermediate discount factor using (9.22):

$$ln(df_t) = ln(df_{n_i}) + \frac{t - n_i}{n_{i-1} - n_i} \times [ln(df_{n_{i+1}}) - ln(df_{n_i})]. \qquad (9.22)$$

To calculate the six-year yield from the same yield structure above, we use the following procedure:

- calculate the discount factors for years 4 and 10, and then take the natural logarithms of these discount factors;
- perform a linear interpolation on these logarithms;
- take the anti-log of the result, to get the implied interpolated discount factor;
- calculate the implied yield in this discount factor.

Using (9.22) we obtain a six-year yield of 6.6388%. The logarithmic interpolation method reduces the sharpness of angles on the curve and so makes it smoother, but it retains the other drawbacks of the linear interpolation method.

Polynomial models[24]

The most straightforward method for estimating the yield curve involves fitting a single polynomial in time. For example, a model might use an F-order polynomial, illustrated in (9.23):

$$rm_i = \alpha + \beta_1 n_i + \beta_2 N_i^2 + \ldots + \beta_F N_i^F + u_i \qquad (9.23)$$

where

rm_i is the yield to maturity of the i-th bond
N_i is the term to maturity of the i-th bond
α, β_i are coefficients of the polynomial
u_i is the residual error on the i-th bond.

To determine the coefficients of the polynomial we minimise the sum of the squared residual errors, given by:

$$\sum_i^T u_i^2 \qquad (9.24)$$

where T is the number of bonds used. This is represented graphically in Figure 9.24.

[24] These are standard econometric techniques. For an excellent account see Campbell et al. (1997).

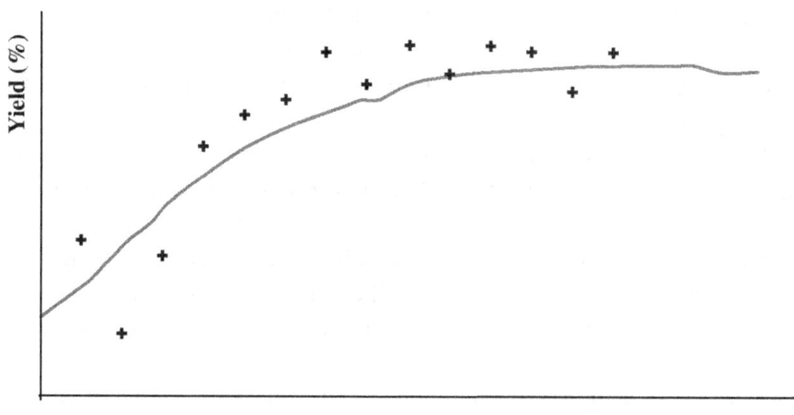

Figure 9.24 Polynomial curve fitting

The type of curve that results is a function of the order of the polynomial F. If F is too large the curve will not be smooth, but will be in effect too "responsive", such that the curve runs through every point, known as being "over-fitted". The extreme of this is given when $F = T - 1$. If F is too small the curve will be an over-estimation.

The method described above has been supplanted by a more complex method, which fits different polynomials over different but overlapping terms to maturity. The fitted curves are then spliced together to produce a single smooth curve over the entire term structure. This is known as a *spline* curve and is the one most commonly encountered in the markets. For an accessible introduction to spline techniques see James and Webber (2000) and Choudhry et al. (2001).

The limitation of the polynomial method is that a blip in the observed series of vertices, for instance a vertex which is out of line with others in the series, produces a "wobbled" shape, causing wild oscillations in the corresponding forward yields. This can result in the calculation of negative long-dated forward rates.

Cubic splines

The cubic spline method involves connecting each pair of yield vertices by fitting a unique cubic equation between them. This results in a yield curve where the whole curve is represented by a chain of cubic equations, instead of a single polynomial. This technique adds some "stiffness" to the yield curve, while at the same time preserving its smoothness.[25]

Using the same example as before, we wish to fit the yield curve from 0 to 10 years.

There are four observed vertices, so we require three cubic equations, $rm(_{i,t})$, each one connecting two adjacent vertices n_i and n_{i+1} as follows:

$$rm_{(0,t)} = a_0 n_3 + b_0 n_2 + c_0 n + d_0, \text{ which connects vertex } n_0 \text{ with } n_1$$
$$rm_{(1,t)} = a_1 n_3 + b_1 n_2 + c_1 n + d_1, \text{ which connects vertex } n_1 \text{ with } n_2$$
$$rm_{(2,t)} = a_2 n_3 + b_2 n_2 + c_2 n + d_2, \text{ which connects vertex } n_2 \text{ with } n_3$$

where a, b, c, and d are unknowns. The equations each contain four unknowns (the coefficients a to d), and there are three equations, so we require 12 conditions in all to solve the system. The cubic spline method imposes certain conditions on the curves that makes it possible to solve the system. The solution for this set is summarised in Appendix 9.3.

The three cubic equations for the data in this example are:

$$rm_{(0,t)} = 0.022 \times n^3 + 0.413 \times n + 4.000 \text{ for vertices } n_0 - n_1$$
$$rm_{(1,t)} = -0.047 \times n^3 + 0.411 \times n^2 - 0.410 \times n + 4.548 \text{ for vertices } n_1 - n_2$$
$$rm_{(2,t)} = 0.008 \times n^3 - 0.249 \times n^2 + 2.230 \times n + 1.029 \text{ for vertices } n_2 - n_3.$$

Using a cubic spline produces a smoother curve for both the spot rates and the forward rates, while the derived forward curve will have fewer "kinks" in it.

To calculate the estimated yield for the six-year maturity we apply the third cubic equation, which spans the 4–10-year vertices, which is:

$$rm_{(2,t)} = 0.008 \times 6^3 - 0.249 \times 6^2 + 2.230 \times 6 + 1.029 = 7.173\%.$$

From Appendix 9.3 it is clear that simply to fit a four-vertex spline requires the inversion of a fairly large matrix. In practice, more efficient mathematical techniques, known as basis splines or *B-splines,* are typically used when there are a larger number of observed yield vertices. This produces results that are very close to what we would obtain by simple matrix inversion.

---

[25] In case you're wondering, a spline is a tool used by a carpenter to draw smooth curves.

Regression models

A variation on polynomial fitting is regression analysis. In this method bond prices are used as the dependent variable, with the coupon and maturity cash flows of the bonds being the independent variables. This is given by (9.25):

$$P_{di} = \beta_1 c_{1i} + \beta_2 c_{2i} + \ldots + \beta_N (C_{Ni} + M) + u_i \qquad (9.25)$$

where

P_{di} is the dirty price of the *i*-th bond
C_{Ni} is the coupon of the *i*-th bond in period *n*
β_N is the coefficient of the regression equation
u_i is the residual error in the *i*-th bond.

In fact, the coefficient in (9.25) is an estimate of the discount factor, as shown by (9.26) and can be used to generate the spot interest rate curve.

$$\beta_n = df_n = \frac{1}{(1 + rs_n)^n} \qquad (9.26)$$

In the form shown, (9.25) cannot be estimated directly. This is because individual coupon payment dates will differ across different bonds, and in a semi-annual coupon market there will be more coupons than bonds available. In practice therefore the term structure is divided into specific dates, known as *grid points*, along the entire maturity term; coupon payments are then allocated between two grid points. The allocation between two points is done in such a way so that the present value of the coupon is not altered. This is shown in Figure 9.25.

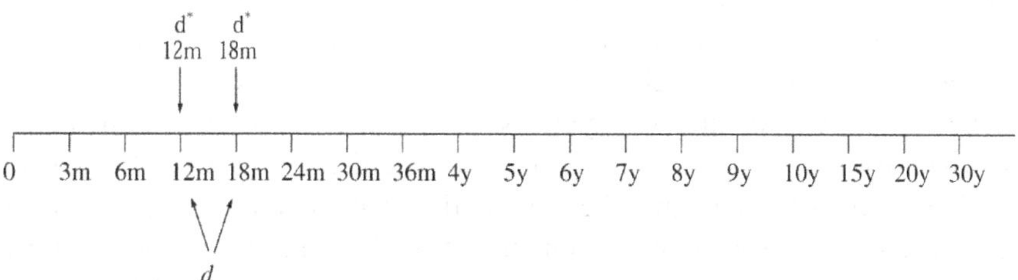

Figure 9.25 Grid point allocation in regression analysis

Note how there are more grid points at the short end of the term structure, with progressively fewer points as we reach the longer end. This is because the preponderance of the data is invariably at the shorter end of the curve, which makes yield curve fitting more difficult. At the long end however the shortage of data, due to the relative lack of issues, makes curve estimation more inaccurate.

The actual regression equation that is used in the analysis is given in (9.27) where d_{ni} represents the grid points.

$$P_{di} = \beta_1 d_{1i} + \beta_2 d_{2i} + \ldots + \beta_N (d_{Ni} + M) + u_i \tag{9.27}$$

The two methodologies described above are the most commonly encountered in the market. Generally, models used to estimate the term structure generally fall into two distinct categories: these being the ones that estimate the structure using the par yield curve and those that fit it using a discount function. This is examined in greater detail in Choudhry (2004a).

Part II

A further look at spot and forward rates

We now continue the analysis begun in this chapter; using more technical terminology. First we illustrate basic concepts, which is followed by a discussion of yield curve analysis and the term structure of interest rates.

Basic concepts

We are familiar with two types of fixed-income securities, *zero-coupon bonds*, also known as *discount bonds* or *strips*, and *coupon bonds*. A zero-coupon bond makes a single payment on its maturity date, while a coupon bond makes regular interest payments at regular dates up to and including its maturity date. A coupon bond may be regarded as a set of strips, with each coupon payment and the redemption payment on maturity being equivalent to a zero-coupon bond maturing on that date. This is not a purely academic concept, which is illustrated by events that occurred before the advent of the formal market in US Treasury strips, when a number of investment banks traded the cash flows of Treasury securities as separate zero-coupon securities.[26] The literature we review in this section is set in a market of default-free bonds, whether they are zero-coupon bonds or coupon bonds. The market is assumed to be liquid so that bonds may be freely bought and sold. Prices of bonds are determined by the economy-wide supply and demand for the bonds at any time, so they are *macroeconomic* and not set by individual bond issuers or traders.

Zero-coupon bonds

A zero-coupon bond is the simplest form of fixed-income security. It is an issue of debt, the issuer promising to pay the face value of the debt to the bondholder on the date the bond matures. There are no coupon payments during the life of the bond, so it is a discount instrument, issued at a price that is below the face or *principal* amount. We denote as $P(t, T)$, the price of a discount bond at time t that matures at time T, with $T \geqslant t$. The term to maturity of the bond is denoted with n, where $n = T - t$. The price increases over time until the maturity date when it reaches the maturity or *par* value. If the par value of the bond is £1, then the YTM of the bond at time t is denoted by $r(t, T)$, where r is actually "one plus the percentage yield" that is earned by holding the bond from t to T. We have:

$$P(t,T) = \frac{1}{[r(t,T)]^n}. \tag{9.28}$$

The yield may be obtained from the bond price and is given by:

$$r(t,T) = \left[\frac{1}{P(t,T)}\right]^{1/n} \tag{9.29}$$

which is sometimes written as:

$$r(t, T) = P(t\ T)^{-(1/n)}. \tag{9.30}$$

[26] These banks included Merrill Lynch, Lehman Brothers and Salomon Brothers, among others (Fabozzi 1993). The term "strips" comes from Separate Trading of Registered Interest and Principal of Securities, the name given when the official market was introduced by the Treasury. The banks would purchase Treasuries, which would then be deposited in a safe custody account. Receipts were issued against each cash flow from each Treasury, and these receipts traded as individual zero-coupon securities. The market-making banks earned profit due to the arbitrage difference in the price of the original coupon bond and the price at which the individual strips were sold. The US Treasury formalised trading in strips after 1985, after legislation had been introduced that altered the tax treatment of such instruments. The market in UK gilt strips trading began in December 1997. Strips are also traded in France, Germany, the Netherlands, among other countries.

Analysts and researchers frequently work in terms of logarithms of yields and prices, or continuously compounded rates. One advantage of this is that it converts the non-linear relationship in (9.29) into a linear relationship.[27]

The bond price at time t_2 where $t < t_2 < T$ is given by:

$$P(t_2, T) = P(t, T)e^{(t_2 - t)r(t, T)} \tag{9.31a}$$

which is consistent, given that the bond price equation in continous time is:

$$P(t, T) = e^{-r(t, T)(T-t)} \tag{9.31b}$$

so that the yield is given by:

$$r(t, T) = -\log\left(\frac{P(t, T)}{n}\right) \tag{9.32}$$

which is sometimes written as:

$$\log r(t, T) = -\left(\frac{1}{n}\right)\log P(t, T). \tag{9.33}$$

The expression in (9.31) includes the exponential function, hence the use of the term continuously compounded.

The *term structure of interest rates* is the set of zero-coupon yields at time t for all bonds ranging in maturity from $(t, t+1)$ to $(t, t+m)$ where the bonds have maturities of $\{0, 1, 2, \ldots, m\}$. A good definition of the term structure of interest rates is given by Sundaresan, who states that it:

> ... refers to the relationship between the yield to maturity of default-free zero coupon securities and their maturities.
>
> Sundaresan (1997), p. 176

---

[27] A linear relationship in X would be a function $Y = f(X)$, in which the X values change via a power or index of 1 only and are not multiplied or divided by another variable or variables. So, for example, terms such as X^2, $\sqrt{X}$ and other similar functions are not linear in X, nor are terms such as XZ or X/Z where Z is another variable. In econometric analysis, if the value of Y is solely dependent on the value of X, then its rate of change with respect to X, or the derivative of Y with respect to X, denoted dY/dX, is independent of X. Therefore if $Y = 5X$, then $dY/dX = 5$, which is independent of the value of X. However, if $Y = 5X^2$, then $dY/dX = 10X$, which is not independent of the value of X. Hence this function is not linear in X. The classic regression function $E(Y|X_i) = \alpha + \beta X_i$ is a linear function with slope b and intercept a and the regression "curve" is represented geometrically by a straight line.

The *yield curve* is a plot of the set of yields for $r(t, t+1)$ to $r(t, t+m)$ against m at time t. For example, Figures 9.26–9.28 on pages 416–17 show the log zero-coupon yield curve for US Treasury strips, UK gilt strips and French OAT strips on 27 September 2000. Each of the curves exhibit peculiarities in their shape, although the most common type of curve is gently upward-sloping, as is the French curve. The UK curve is inverted.

Coupon bonds

The majority of bonds in the market make coupon payments during their lives, and such bonds may be viewed as a package of individual zero-coupon bonds. The coupons have a nominal value that is a percentage of the nominal value of the bond itself, with steadily longer maturity dates, while the final redemption payment has the nominal value of the bond itself and is redeemed on the maturity date. We denote a bond issued at time i and maturing at time T as having a w-element vector of payment dates: $(t_1, t_2, \ldots, t_{w-1}, T)$ and matching date payments $C_1, C_2, \ldots, C_{w-1}, C_w$. In academic literature these coupon payments are assumed to be made in continuous time, so that the stream of coupon payments is given by a positive function of time $C(t)$, $i < t \leqslant T$. Investors that purchase a bond at time t, that matures at time T and pays $P(t, T)$ will receive the coupon payments as long as they continue to hold the bond.[28]

[28] Theoretically, this is the discounted clean price of the bond. For coupon bonds in practice, unless the bond is purchased for value on a coupon date, it will be traded with interest accrued. The interest that has accrued on a pro-rata basis from the last coupon date is added to the clean price of the bond, to give the market "dirty" price that is actually paid by the purchaser.

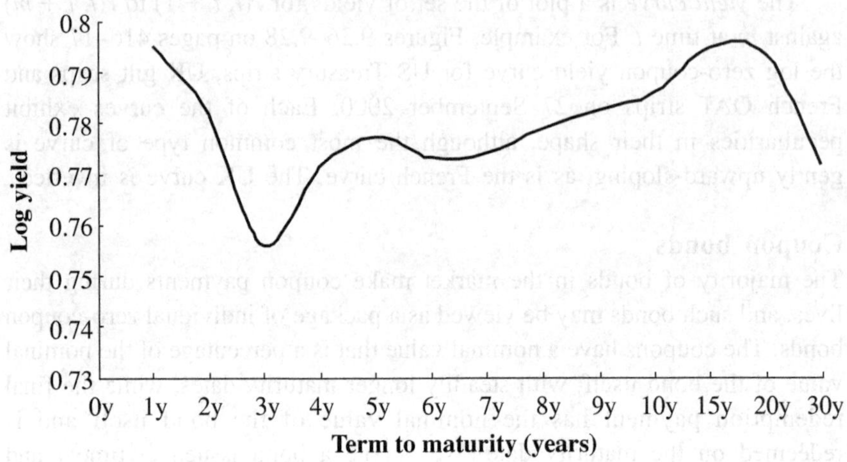

Figure 9.26 US Treasury zero-coupon yield curve in September 2000
Yield source: Bloomberg L.P.

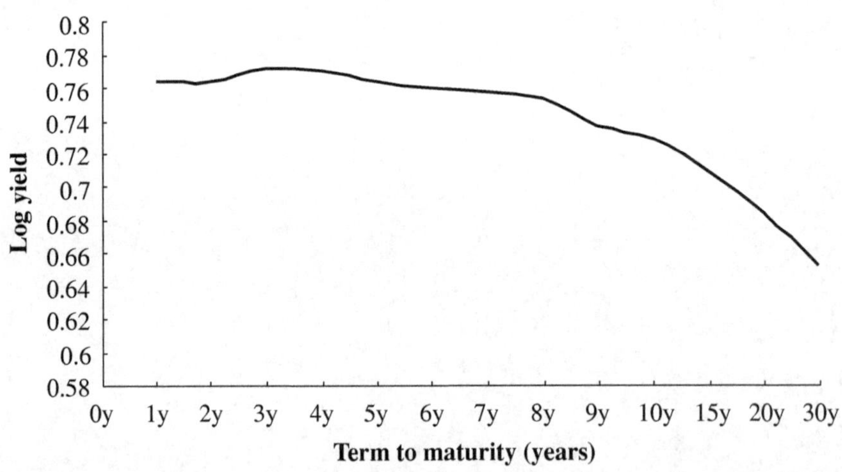

Figure 9.27 UK gilt zero-coupon yield curve in September 2000
Yield source: Bloomberg L.P.

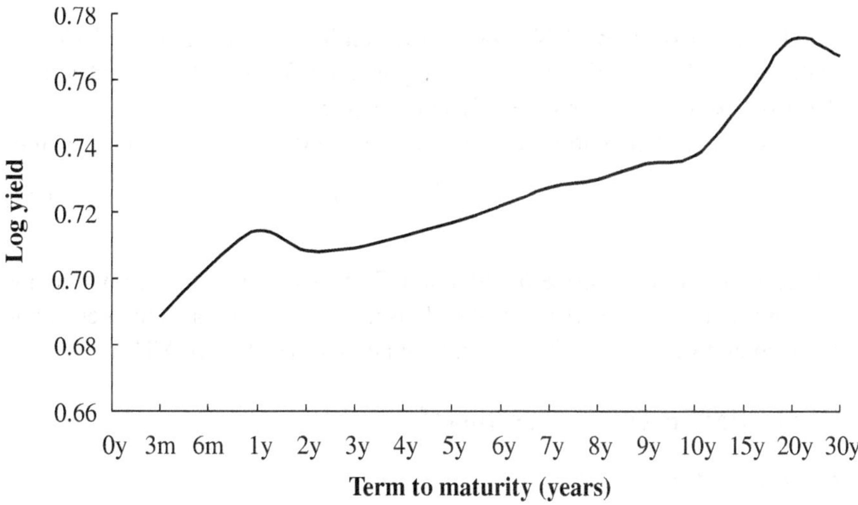

Figure 9.28 US Treasury zero-coupon yield curve in September 2000
Yield source: Bloomberg L.P.

The YTM at time t of a bond that matures at T is the interest rate that relates the price of the bond to the future returns on the bond; that is, the rate that *discounts* the bond's cash flow stream C_w to its price $P(t, T)$. This is given by:

$$P(t,T) = \sum_{t_i > t} C_i e^{-(t_i - t)r(t,T)} \qquad (9.34)$$

which says that the bond price is given by the present value of the cash flow stream of the bond, discounted at the rate $r(t, T)$. A zero-coupon (9.34) reduces to (9.31b). In academic literature where coupon payments are assumed to be made in continuous time, the Σ summation in (9.34) is replaced by the $\int$ integral. We will look at this shortly.

In some texts the plot of the YTM at time t for the term of the bonds m is described as the term structure of interest rates; but it is generally accepted that the term structure is the plot of zero-coupon rates only. Plotting yields to maturity is generally described as graphically depicting the yield curve, rather than the term structure. Of course, given the law of one price, there is a relationship between the YTM yield curve and the zero-coupon term structure, and given the first one can derive the second.

The expression in (9.34) obtains the continuously compounded yield to maturity $r(t, T)$. It is the use of the exponential function that enables us to describe the yield as continuously compounded.

The market frequently uses the measure known as *current yield,* which is:

$$rc = \frac{C}{P_d} \times 100 \tag{9.35}$$

where P_d is the dirty price of the bond. The measure is also known as the *running yield* or *flat yield.* Current yield is not used to indicate the interest rate or discount rate and therefore should not be mistaken for the YTM.

Bond price in continuous time[29]

Fundamental concepts

In this section, we present an introduction to the bond price equation in continuous time. The necessary background on price processes is introduced in Choudhry (2001), readers will see the logic in this as we introduce term structure modeling there.

Let us consider a trading environment where bond prices evolve in a w-dimensional process:

$$X(t) = [X_1(t), X_2(t), X_3(t), \ldots, X_w(t)], \ t > 0 \tag{9.36}$$

where the random variables are termed *state variables* that reflect the state of the economy at any point in time. The markets assume that the state variables evolve through a process described as geometric Brownian motion or a Weiner process. It is therefore possible to model the evolution of these variables, in the form of a stochastic differential equation.

The market assumes that the cash flow stream of assets such as bonds and equities is a function of the stated variables. A bond is characterised by its coupon process:

---

[29] This section follows a similar approach as seen in Avellaneda and Lawrence (2000), Baxter and Rennie (1996), Neftci (2000), Cambell et al. (1997), Ross (1999), and Shiller (1990), among others. These are all excellent texts of very high quality, and are strongly recommended. For an accessible and highly readable introduction, Ross's book is worth buying for Chapter 4 alone, as is Avellaneda's for his Chapter 12. For a general introduction to the main pricing concepts, see Campbell et al. (1997), Chapter 10. Chapter 3 in Jarrow (1996) is an accessible introduction for discrete-time bond pricing. Sundaresan (1997) is an excellent overview text on the fixed-income market as a whole, and is highly recommended. Further recommended references are given in the bibliography and selected references at the end of the chapter.

$$C(t) = \tilde{C}[X_1(t), X_2(t), X_3(t), \ldots, X_w(t), t]. \tag{9.37}$$

The coupon process represents the cash flow that the investor receives during the time that they hold the bond. Over a small incremental increase in time of dt from the time t, the investor can purchase $1 + C(t)dt$ units of the bond at the end of the period $t + dt$. Assume that there is a very short-term discount security such as a T-bill that matures at $t + dt$, and during this period the investor receives a return of $r(t)$. This rate is the annualised short-term interest rate or *short rate*, which, in the mathematical analysis is defined as the rate of interest charged on a loan that is taken out at time t and which matures almost immediately. For this reason the rate is also known as the *instantaneous rate*. The short rate is given by:

$$r(t) = r(t, t) \tag{9.38}$$

and:

$$r(t) = -\frac{\partial}{\partial T} \log P(t, t). \tag{9.39}$$

If we continuously reinvest the short-term security such as the T-bill at this short rate, we obtain a cumulative amount that is the original investment multiplied by (9.38).[30]

$$M(t) = \exp\left[\int_0^t r(s)\,ds\right] \tag{9.40}$$

where M is a money market account that offers a return of the short rate $r(t)$.

If we say that the short rate is constant, making $r(t) = r$, then the price of a risk-free bond that pays £1 on maturity at time T is given by:

$$P(t, T) = e^{-r(T-t)}. \tag{9.41a}$$

What (9.41a) states is that the bond price is simply a function of the continuously compounded interest rate, with the right-hand side of (9.41a) being the discount factor at time t. At $t = T$ the discount factor will be 1, which is the redemption value of the bond and hence the price of the bond at this time.

---

[30] This expression uses the integral operator. The integral is the tool used in mathematics to calculate sums of an infinite number of objects; that is, where the objects are uncountable. This is different to the Σ operator, which is used for a countable number of objects. For a readable and accessible review of the integral and its use in quantitative finance, see Neftci (2000), pp. 59–66; we briefly introduce it in Appendix 9.4.

Let us now consider the following scenario. A market participant may undertake the following:

- it can invest $r^{-r(T-t)}$ units cash in a money market account today, which will have grown to a sum of £1 at time T;
- it can purchase the risk-free zero-coupon bond today, which has a maturity value of £1 at time T.

The market participant can invest in either instrument, both of which we know beforehand to be risk-free, and both of which have identical payouts at time T and have no cash flow between now and time T. As interest rates are constant, a bond that paid out £1 at T must have the same value as the initial investment in the money market account, which is $e_t^{-r(T-t)}$. Therefore equation (9.41a) must apply. This is a restriction placed on the zero-coupon bond price by the requirement for markets to be arbitrage-free.

If the bond was not priced at this level, arbitrage opportunities would present themselves. Consider if the bond was priced higher than $e_t^{-r(T-t)}$. In this case, an investor could sell short the bond and invest the sale proceeds in the money market account. On maturity at time T, the short position will have a value of $-$£1 (negative, because the investor is short the bond) while the money market will have accumulated £1, which the investor can use to pay the proceeds on the zero-coupon bond. However, investors will have surplus funds because at time t:

$$P(t, T) - e^{-r(T-t)} > 0$$

and so will have profited from the transaction at no risk to themselves.

The same applies if the bond is priced below $e_t^{-r(T-t)}$. In this case, the investor borrows $e_t^{-r(T-t)}$ and buys the bond at its price $P(t, T)$. On maturity, the bond pays £1, which is used to repay the loan amount; however, the investor will gain because:

$$e^{-r(T-t)} - P(t, T) > 0.$$

Therefore the only price at which no arbitrage profit can be made is if:

$$P(t, T) = e^{-r(T-t)}. \tag{9.41b}$$

In academic literature, the price of a zero-coupon bond is given in terms of the evolution of the short-term interest rate, in what is termed the *risk-neutral measure*.[31] The short rate $r(t)$ is the interest rate earned on a money

[31] This is part of the *arbitrage pricing theory*. For detail on this see Cox et al. (1985), while Duffie (1992) gives a fuller treatment.

market account or short-dated risk-free security such as the T-bill suggested above, and it is assumed to be continuously compounded. This makes the mathematical treatment simpler. With a zero-coupon bond we assume a payment on maturity of 1 (say \$1 or £1), a one-off cash flow payable on maturity at time T. The value of the zero-coupon bond at time t is therefore given by:

$$P(t, T) = \exp\left(-\int_t^T r(s)\,ds\right) \tag{9.42}$$

which is the redemption value of 1 divided by the value of the money market account, given by (9.42).

The bond price for a coupon bond is given in terms of its yield as:

$$P(t, T) = \exp(-(T - t)r(T - t)) \tag{9.43}$$

Expression (9.42) is very commonly encountered in academic literature. Its derivation is not so frequently occurring, however, and we present it in Appendix 9.6, which is a summary of the description given in Ross (1999). This reference is highly recommended reading. It is also worth referring to Neftci (2000), Chapter 18.

The expression (9.42) represents the zero-coupon bond pricing formula when the spot rate is continuous or *stochastic*, rather than constant. The rate $r(s)$ is the risk-free return earned during the very short or *infinitesimal* time interval $(t, t + dt)$. The rate is used in the expressions for the value of a money market account (9.41) and the price of a risk-free zero-coupon bond (9.43).

Stochastic rates in continuous time

In the academic literature, the bond price given by (9.43) evolves as a *martingale* process under the risk-neutral probability measure $\tilde{P}$. This is an advanced branch of fixed-income mathematics, and is outside the scope of this book; however, it is discussed in an introductory fashion in Chapter 5 of Choudhry (2001).[32] For the purposes of this analysis, the bond price is given as:

$$P(t, T) = E_t^{\tilde{P}}\left[e^{-\int_t^T r(s)\,ds}\right] \tag{9.44}$$

[32] Interested readers should consult Nefcti (2000), Chapters 2, 17–18, another accessible text is Baxter and Rennie (1996), while Duffie (1992) is a leading-edge reference for those with a strong background in mathematics.

where the right-hand side of (9.44) is viewed as the randomly evolved *discount factor* used to obtain the present value of the £1 maturity amount. Expression (9.44) also states that bond prices are dependent on the entire spectrum of short-term interest rates $r(s)$ in the future during the period $t < s < T$. This also implies that the term structure at time t contains all the information available on short rates in the future.[33]

From (9.44), we say that the function $T \to P_t^T$, $t < T$, is the discount curve (or *discount function*) at time t. Avellaneda and Lawrence (2000) note that the markets usually replace the term $(T - t)$ with a term meaning *time to maturity*, so the function becomes:

$$\tau \to P_t^{t+\tau},\ \tau > 0, \text{ where } \tau = (T - t).$$

Under a constant spot rate, the zero-coupon bond price is given by:

$$P(t, T) = e^{-r(t,\, T)(T-t)}. \tag{9.45}$$

From (9.44) and (9.45) we can derive a relationship between the yield $r(t, T)$ of the zero-coupon bond and the short rate $r(t)$, if we equate the two right-hand sides, namely:

$$e^{-r(T,\, t)(T-t)} = E_t^{\tilde{P}}\left[e^{-\int_t^T r(s)\,ds}\right]. \tag{9.46}$$

Taking the logarithm of both sides we obtain:

$$r(t, T) = \frac{-\log E_t^{\tilde{P}}\left[e^{-\int_t^T r(s)\,ds}\right]}{T-t}. \tag{9.47}$$

This describes the yield on a bond as the average of the spot rates that apply during the life of the bond, and under a constant spot rate the yield is equal to the spot rate.

With a zero-coupon bond and assuming that interest rates are positive, $P(t, T)$ is less than or equal to 1. The yield of the bond is, as we have noted, the continuously compounded interest rate that equates the bond price to the discounted present value of the bond at time t. This is given by:

$$r(t, T) = -\frac{\log(P(t, T))}{T-t} \tag{9.48}$$

---

[33] This is related to the view of the short rate evolving as a martingale process. For a derivation of (9.44) see Neftci (2000), page 417.

so we obtain:

$$P(t, T) = e^{-(T-t)r(T-t)}. \tag{9.49}$$

In practice, this means that investors will earn $r(t, T)$ if they purchase the bond at t and hold it to maturity.

Coupon bonds

Using the same principles as in the previous section, we can derive an expression for the price of a coupon bond in the same terms of a risk-neutral probability measure of the evolution of interest rates. Under this analysis, the bond price is given by:

$$P_c = 100.E_t^{\tilde{P}}\left(e^{-\int_t^{t_N} r(s)ds}\right) + \sum_{n:t_n>t}^{N} \frac{C}{w} E_t^{\tilde{P}}\left(e^{-\int_t^{t_n} r(s)ds}\right) \tag{9.50}$$

where

P_c is the price of a coupon bond
C is the bond coupon
t_n is the coupon date, with $n \leqslant N$, and $t = 0$ at the time of valuation
w is the coupon frequency[34]

and where 100 is used as the convention for *principal* or bond nominal value (that is, prices are quoted per cent, or per 100 nominal).

Expression (9.50) is written in some texts as:

$$P_c = 100e^{-rN} + \int_n^N Ce^{-rn}\, dt. \tag{9.51}$$

We can simplify (9.50) by substituting Df to denote the discount factor part of the expression and assuming an annual coupon, which gives us:

$$P = 100.Df_N + \sum_{n:t_n>t}^{N} C.DF_n\ , \tag{9.52}$$

which states that the market value of a risk-free bond on any date is determined by the discount function on that date.

---

[34] Conventional or *plain vanilla bonds* pay coupon on an annual or semi-annual basis. Other bonds, notably certain FRNs and mortgage- and other asset-backed securities also pay coupon on a monthly basis, depending on the structuring of the transaction.

We know from Chapter 4 that the actual price paid in the market for a bond includes accrued interest from the last coupon date, so that the price given by (9.52) is known as the clean price and the traded price, which includes accrued interest, is the *dirty price.*

Forward rates

An investor can combine positions in bonds of differing maturities to guarantee a rate of return that begins at a point in the future. That is, the trade ticket is written at time t but covers the period T to $T + 1$ where $t < T$ (sometimes written as beginning at T_1 and ending at T_2, with $t < T_1 < T_2$). The interest rate earned during this period is known as the *forward rate.*[35] The mechanism by which this forward rate can be guaranteed is described in Example 9.8 below, following Jarrow (1996) and Campbell et al. (1997).

EXAMPLE 9.8 The forward rate

An investor buys at time t one unit of a zero-coupon bond maturing at time T, priced at $P(t, T)$ and simultaneously sells $P(t, T)/P(t, T + 1)$ bonds that mature at $T + 1$. From Table 9.6, we can see that the net result of these transactions is a zero cash flow. At time T there is a cash inflow of 1, and then at time $T + 1$ there is a cash outflow of $P(t, T)/P(t, T + 1)$. These cash flows are identical to a loan of funds made during the period T to $T + 1$, contracted at time t. The interest rate on this loan is given by $P(t, T)/P(t, T + 1)$, which is therefore the forward rate. That is:

$$f(t, T) = \frac{P(t, T)}{P(t, T + 1)}. \tag{9.53}$$

Together with our earlier relationships on bond price and yield, from (9.53), we can define the forward rate in terms of yield, with the return earned during the period $(T, T + 1)$ being:

$$f(t, T, T + 1) = \frac{1}{(P(t, T + 1) / P(t, T))} = \frac{(r(t, T + 1))^{(T+1)}}{r(t, T)^{T}}. \tag{9.54}$$

35 See the footnote on page 639 of Shiller (1990) for a fascinating insight to the origin of the term "forward rate", which Mr Shiller ascribes to John Hicks in his book *Value and Capital*, 2nd edition, Oxford University Press (1946).

From (9.53), we can obtain a bond price equation in terms of the forward rates that hold from t to T:

$$P(t,T) = \frac{1}{\prod_{k=t}^{T-1} f(t,k)} \tag{9.55}$$

Transactions	Time t	T	$T+1$
Buy 1 unit of T-period bond	$-P(t,T)$	$+1$	
Sell $P(t,T)/P(t,T+1)$ of $T+1$ period bonds	$+[(P(t,T)/P(t,T+1)] \times P(t,T+1)$		$-(P(t,T)/P(t,T+1)$
Net cash flows	0	$+1$	$-(P(t,T)/P(t,T+1)$

Table 9.6 Breaking down the forward rate principle

A derivation of this expression can be found in Jarrow (1996), Chapter 3. Equation (9.55) states that the price of a zero-coupon bond is equal to the nominal value, here assumed to be 1, receivable at time T after it has been discounted at the set of forward rates that apply from t to T.[36]

When calculating a forward rate, it is as if we are transacting at an interest rate today that is applicable at the forward start date; in other words, we are trading a forward contract. The law of one price, or no-arbitrage, is used to calculate the rate. For a loan that begins at T and matures at $T + 1$, similarly to the way we described in Example 9.8, consider the purchase of a $T + 1$ period bond and the sale of p amount of the T-period bond. The cash net cash position at t must be zero, so p is given by:

$$p = \frac{P(t,T+1)}{P(t,T)}$$

[36] The symbol $\prod$ means "take the product of", and is defined as $\prod_{i=1}^{n} x_i = x_1 \cdot x_2 \cdot \text{L} \cdot x_n$, so that $\prod_{k=t}^{T-1} f(t,k) = f(t,t) \cdot f(t,t+1) \cdot \text{L} \cdot f(t,T-1)n$, which is the result of multiplying the rates that are obtained when the index k runs from t to $T - 1$.

and to avoid arbitrage, the value of p must be the price of the T + 1-period bond at time T. Therefore the forward yield is given by:

$$f(t, T+1) = -\frac{\log P(t, T+1) - \log P(t, T)}{(T+1) - T}. \tag{9.56}$$

If the period between T and the maturity of the later-dated bond is reduced, we now have bonds that mature at T and T_2, and $T_2 = T + \Delta t$. The incremental change in time Δt becomes progressively smaller until we obtain an instantaneous forward rate, which is given by:

$$f(t, T) = -\frac{\partial}{\partial T} \log P(t, T). \tag{9.57}$$

This rate is defined as the forward rate and is the price today of forward borrowing at time T. The forward rate for borrowing today where $T = t$ is equal to the instantaneous short rate $r(t)$. At time t, the spot and forward rates for the period (t, t) will be identical, while at other maturity terms they will differ.

For all points other than at (t, t) the forward rate yield curve will lie above the spot rate curve if the spot curve is positively sloping. The opposite applies if the spot rate curve is downward-sloping. Campbell et al. (1997, pp. 400–1) observe that this property is a standard one for marginal and average cost curves. That is, when the cost of a marginal unit (say, of production) is above that of an average unit, then the average cost will increase with the addition of a marginal unit. This results in the average cost rising when the marginal cost is above the average cost. Equally, the average cost per unit will decrease when the marginal cost lies below the average cost.

EXAMPLE 9.9 The spot and forward yield curves

From the discussion in this section, we can see that it is possible to calculate bond prices, spot and forward rates provided that we have a set of only one of these parameters. Therefore, given the following set of zero-coupon rates observed in the market, given in Table 9.7, we calculate the corresponding forward rates and zero-coupon bond prices as shown. The initial term structure is upward-sloping. The two curves are illustrated in Figure 9.29(a).

There are technical reasons why the theoretical forward rate has a severe kink in at the later maturity.

Term to maturity (0, *T*)	Spot rate $r(0, T)$*	Forward rate $f(0, T)$*	Bond price $P(0, T)$
0			1
1	1.054	1.054	0.94877
2	1.055	1.056	0.89845
3	1.0563	1.059	0.8484
4	1.0582	1.064	0.79737
5	1.0602	1.068	0.7466
6	1.0628	1.076	0.69386
7	1.06553	1.082	0.64128
8	1.06856	1.0901	0.58833
9	1.07168	1.0972	0.53631
10	1.07526	1.1001	0.48403
11	1.07929	1.1205	0.43198

* Interest rates are given as $(1 + r)$

Table 9.7 Hypothetical zero-coupon yield and forward rates

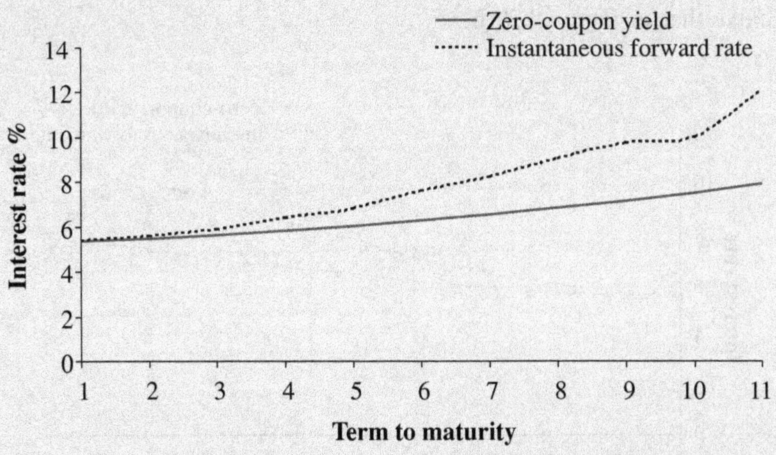

Table 9.29(a) Hypothetical zero-coupon and forward yield curves

Essentially, the relationship between the spot and forward rate curve is as stated by Campbell et al. (1997). The forward rate curve lies above the spot rate curve if the latter is increasing, and it lies below it if the spot rate curve is decreasing. This relationship can be shown mathematically. The forward rate or *marginal rate of return* is equal to the spot rate or *average rate of return* plus the rate of increase of the spot rate, multiplied by the sum of the increases between t and T. If the spot rate is constant (a flat curve), the forward rate curve will be equal to it.

However, an increasing spot rate curve does not always result in an increasing forward curve, only one that lies above it. It is possible for the forward curve to be increasing or decreasing while the spot rate is increasing. If the spot rate reaches a maximum level and then stays constant, or falls below this high point, the forward curve will begin to decrease at a maturity point *earlier* than the spot curve high point. In the example in Figure 9.29(a), the rate of increase in the spot rate in the last period is magnified when converted to the equivalent forward rate. If the last spot rate is below the previous-period rate, the forward rate curve would look like that in Figure 9.29(b).

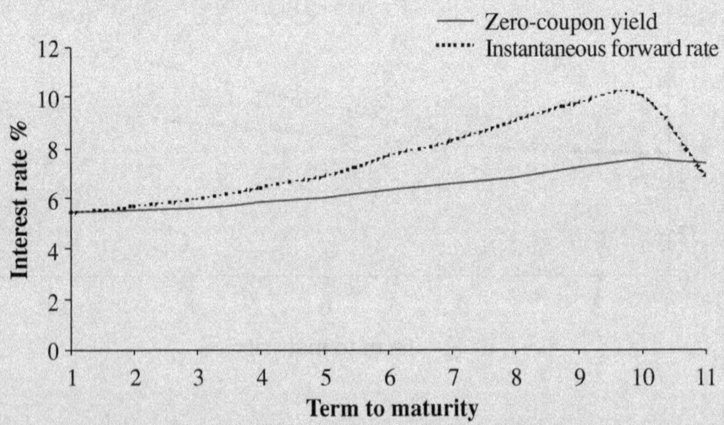

Figure 9.29(b) Hypothetical spot and forward yield curves

Calculating spot rates in practice

Researchers have applied econometric techniques to the problem of extracting a zero-coupon term structure from coupon bond prices. The most well-known approaches are described in McCulloch (1971, 1975), Schaefer (1981), Nelson and Siegel (1987), Deacon and Derry (1994), Adams and Van Deventer (1994), and Waggoner (1997), to name but a few. The most accessible article is probably the one by Deacon and Derry.[37] In addition, a good overview of all the main approaches is contained in James and Webber (2000), and chapters 15–18 of their book provide an excellent summary of the research highlights to date.

We have noted that a coupon bond may be regarded as a portfolio of zero-coupon bonds. By treating a set of coupon bonds as a larger set of zero-coupon bonds, we can extract an implied zero-coupon interest-rate structure from the yields on the coupon bonds.

If the actual term structure is observable, so that we know the prices of zero-coupon bonds of £1 nominal value $P_1, P_2, \ldots, P_N$, then the price P_C of a coupon bond of nominal value £1 and coupon C is given by:

$$P_C = P_1C + P_2C + \cdots + P_N(1 + C). \tag{9.58}$$

Conversely, if we observe the coupon bond yield curve so that we know the prices $P_{C1}, P_{C2}, \ldots, P_{CN}$, then we may use (9.58) to extract the implied zero-coupon term structure. We begin with the one-period coupon bond, for which the price is:

$$P_{C1} = P_1(1 + C)$$

so that:

$$P_1 = \frac{P_{C1}}{(1+C)}. \tag{9.59}$$

This process is repeated. Once we have the set of zero-coupon bond prices $P_1, P_2, \ldots, P_{N21}$ we obtain P_N using:

$$P_N = \frac{P_{CN} + P_{N-1}C - \text{L} - P_1C}{1+C}. \tag{9.60}$$

[37] This is in the author's opinion. Those with a good grounding in econometrics will find all these references both readable and accessible. Further recommended references are given in the bibliography and selected readings at the end of this chapter.

At this point we apply a regression technique known as *ordinary least squares* (OLS) to fit the term structure. OLS and regression techniques are summarised in Choudhry (2001),

Expression (9.58) restricts the prices of coupon bonds to be precise functions of the other coupon bond prices. In fact, this is unlikely in practice because specific bonds will be treated differently according to liquidity, tax effects and so on. For this reason we add an *error term* to (9.58) and estimate the value using cross-sectional regression against all the other bonds in the market. If we say that these bonds are numbered $i = 1, 2, \ldots, I$ then the regression is given by:

$$P_{CN} = P_1 C_i + P_2 C_i + \cdots + P_{N_i}(1 + C_i) + u_i \tag{9.61}$$

for $i = 1, 2, \ldots, I$ and where C_i is the coupon on the ith bond and N_i is the maturity of the ith bond. In (9.61), the regressor parameters are the coupon payments at each interest period date, and the coefficients are the prices of the zero-coupon bonds P_1 to P_N where $j = 1, 2, \ldots, N$. The values are obtained using OLS as long as we have a complete term structure and that $I \geqslant N$.

In practice, we will not have a complete term structure of coupon bonds and so we are not able to identify the coefficients in (9.61). McCulloch (1971, 1975) described a *spline estimation* method, which assumes that zero-coupon bond prices vary smoothly with term to maturity. In this approach we define P_N, a function of maturity $P(N)$, as a *discount function* given by:

$$P(N) = 1 + \sum_{j=1}^{J} a_j f_j(N). \tag{9.62}$$

The function $f_j(N)$ is a known function of maturity N, and the coefficients a_j must be estimated. We arrive at a regression equation by substituting (9.62) into (9.61) to give us (9.64), which can be estimated using OLS:

$$\prod_i = \sum_{j=1}^{J} a_j X_{ij} + u_i, \quad i = 1, 2, \ldots, I \tag{9.63}$$

where:

$$\prod_i \equiv P_{C_i N_i} - 1 - C_i N_i$$

$$X_{ij} \equiv f_j(N_i) + C_i \textstyle\sum_{l=1}^{N_i} f_j(l).$$

The function $f_j(N)$ is usually specified by setting the discount function as a polynomial. In certain texts, including McCulloch, this is carried out by applying what is known as a *spline* function. Considerable academic research has gone into the use of spline functions as a yield curve fitting technique; however, we are not able to go into the required level of detail here, which is outside the scope of this book. Please refer to the selected bibliography for further information. For a specific discussion on using regression techniques for spline curve fitting methods, see Suits et al. (1978).

Introduction to bond analysis using spot rates and forward rates in continuous time

This section analyses further the relationship between spot and forward rates and the yield curve.

The spot and forward rate relationship

In the discussion to date, we have assumed discrete time intervals and interest rates in discrete time. Here we consider the relationship between spot and forward rates in continuous time. For this we assume the mathematical convenience of a continuously compounded interest rate.

We start by saying that at the interest rate r, compounded using e^r, an initial investment of M earning $r(t, T)$ over the period $T - t$ (initial investment at time t and for maturity at T, where $T > t$), would have a value of $Me^{r(t,T)(T-t)}$ on maturity.[38] If we denote the initial value M_t and the maturity value M_T, then we can state $M_t e^{r(t,T)(T-t)} = M_T$ and therefore the continuously compounded yield, defined as the continuously compounded interest rate $r(t, T)$, can be shown to be:

$$r(t,T) = \frac{\log(M_T / M_t)}{T - t}. \tag{9.64}$$

We can then formulate a relationship between the continuously compounded interest rate and yield. It can be shown that

$$M_T = M_t e^{\int_t^T r(s)ds} \tag{9.65}$$

where $r(s)$ is the instantaneous spot interest rate and is a function of time.

[38] e is the mathematical constant 2.7182818 ... and it can be shown that an investment of £1 at time t will have grown to e on maturity at time T (during the period $T - t$) if it is earning an interest rate of $1/(T - t)$ continuously compounded.

It can further be shown that the continuously compounded yield is actually the equivalent of the average value of the continuously compounded interest rate. In addition it can be shown that:

$$r(t,T) = \frac{\int_t^T r(s)\,ds}{T-t}. \tag{9.66}$$

In a continuous time environment we do not assume discrete time intervals over which interest rates are applicable, rather a period of time in which a borrowing of funds would be repaid instantaneously. So we define the forward rate $f(t, s)$ as the interest rate applicable for borrowing funds where the deal is struck at time t; the actual loan is made at s (with $s > t$) and repayable almost instantaneously. In mathematics the period $s - t$ is described as infinitesimally small. The spot interest rate is defined as the continuously compounded yield or interest rate $r(t, T)$. In an environment of no arbitrage, the return generated by investing at the forward rate $f(t, s)$ over the period $s - t$ must be equal to that generated by investing initially at the spot rate $r(t, T)$. So we may set:

$$e^{\int_t^T f(t,s)\,ds} = e^{r(t)dt} \tag{9.67}$$

which enables us to derive an expression for the spot rate itself, which is

$$r(t,T) = \frac{\int_t^T f(t,s)\,ds}{T-t}. \tag{9.68}$$

The relationship described by (9.68) states that the spot rate is given by the *arithmetic* average of the forward rates $f(t, s)$ where $t < s < T$. How does this differ from the relationship in a discrete time environment? We know that the spot rate in such a framework is the *geometric* average of the forward rates,[39] and this is the key difference in introducing the continuous time structure. Equation (9.68) can be rearranged to:

$$r(t,T)(T-t) = \int_t^T f(t,s)\,ds \tag{9.69}$$

and this is used to show (by differentiation) the relationship between spot and forward rates, given below:

$$f(t,s) = r(t,T) + (T-t)\frac{dr(t,T)}{dT}. \tag{9.70}$$

[39] To be precise, if we assume annual compounding, the relationship is one plus the spot rate is equal to the geometric average of one plus the forward rates.

If we assume we are dealing today (at time 0) for maturity at time T, then the expression for the spot rate becomes:

$$r(0,T) = \frac{\int_t^T f(0,s)\,ds}{T} \tag{9.71}$$

so we can write:

$$r(0,T)\cdot T = \int_t^T f(0,s)\,ds. \tag{9.72}$$

This is illustrated in Figure 9.30 which is a diagrammatic representation showing that the spot rate $r(0, T)$ is the average of the forward rates from 0 to T, using the hypothetical value of 5% for $r(0, T)$. Figure 9.30 also shows the area represented by (9.72).

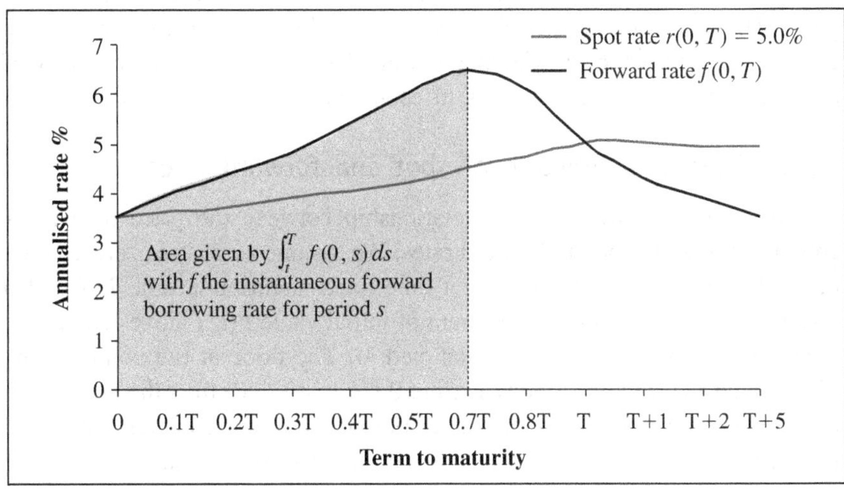

Figure 9.30 Diagrammatic representation of the relationship between spot and forward rate

What (9.70) implies is that if the spot rate increases, then by definition the forward rate (or *marginal* rate, as it has been suggested that it may be called[40]) will be greater. From (9.70) we deduce that the forward rate will be equal to the spot rate plus a value that is the product of the *rate* of increase

[40] For example, see Section 10.1 of Campbell, Lo and Mackinlay (1997), Chapter 10 of which is an excellent and accessible study of the term structure, and provides proofs of some of the results discussed here. This book is written in a very readable style and is worth purchasing for Chapter 10 alone.

of the spot rate and the time period $(T - t)$. In fact, the conclusions simply confirm what we already discovered in the discrete time analysis described earlier in this chapter: the forward rate for any period will lie above the spot rate if the spot rate term structure is increasing, and will lie below the spot rate if it is decreasing. In a constant spot rate environment, the forward rate will be equal to the spot rate.

However, it is not as simple as that. An increasing spot rate term structure only implies that the forward rate lies above the spot rate, but not that the forward rate structure is itself also *increasing*. In fact, one can observe the forward rate term structure to be increasing or decreasing while spot rates are increasing. As the spot rate is the average of the forward rates, it can be shown that in order to accommodate this, forward rates must in fact be *decreasing* before the point at which the spot rate reaches its highest point. This confirms market observation. An illustration of this property is given in Appendix 9.6. As Campbell et al. (1997) state, this is a property of average and marginal cost curves in economics.

Bond prices as a function of spot and forward rates[41]

In this section we describe the relationship between the price of a zero-coupon bond and spot and forward rates. We assume a risk-free zero-coupon bond of nominal value £1, priced at time t and maturing at time T. We also assume a money market bank account of initial value $P(t, T)$ invested at time t. The money market account is denoted M. The price of the bond at time t is denoted $P(t, T)$ and if today is time 0 (so that $t > 0$) then the bond price today is unknown and a random factor (similar to a future interest rate). The bond price can be related to the spot rate or forward rate that is in force at time t.

Consider the scenario below, used to derive the risk-free zero-coupon bond price.[42]

The continuously compounded *constant* spot rate is r as before. An investor has a choice of purchasing the zero-coupon bond at price $P(t, T)$, which will return the sum of £1 at time T or of investing this same amount of cash in the money market account, and this sum would have grown to £1 at time T. We know that the value of the money market account is given by $Me^{r(t,T)(T-t)}$. If M must have a value of £1 at time T, then the function $e^{-r(t,T)(T-t)}$ must give the present value of £1 at time t and therefore the value of the zero-coupon bond is given by:

---

[41] For more detail on this see Neftci (2000), Chapter 18, Section 3. This is also an excellent, readable text.

[42] This approach is also used in Campbell et al. (1997).

$$P(t,T) = e^{-r(t,T)(T-t)}. \tag{9.73}$$

If the same amount of cash that could be used to buy the bond at t, invested in the money market account, does *not* return £1 then arbitrage opportunities will result. If the price of the bond exceeded the discount function $e^{-r(t,T)(T-t)}$ then the investor could short the bond and invest the proceeds in the money market account. At time T the bond position would result in a cash outflow of £1, while the money market account would be worth £1. However, the investor would gain because in the first place $P(t,T) - e^{-r(t,T)(T-t)} > 0$. Equally, if the price of the bond was below $e^{-r(t,T)(T-t)}$ then the investor would borrow $e^{-r(t,T)(T-t)}$ in cash and buy the bond at price $P(t,T)$. On maturity the bond would return £1, the proceeds would be used to repay the loan. However, the investor would gain because $e^{-r(t,T)(T-t)} - P(t,T) > 0$. To avoid arbitrage opportunities we must therefore have:

$$P(t,T) = e^{-r(t,T)(T-t)}. \tag{9.74}$$

Following the relationship between spot and forward rates it is also possible to describe the bond price in terms of forward rates.[43] We show the result here only. First we know that

$$P(t,T)e^{\int_t^T f(t,s)ds} = 1 \tag{9.75}$$

because the maturity value of the bond is £1, and we can rearrange (9.75) to give:

$$P(t,T) = e^{-\int_t^T f(t,s)ds}. \tag{9.76}$$

Expression (9.76) states that the bond price is a function of the range of forward rates that apply for all $f(t,s)$; that is, the forward rates for all time periods s from t to T (where $t < s < T$, and where s is infinitesimally small). The forward rate $f(t,s)$ that results for each s arises as a result of a random or *stochastic* process that is assumed to start today at time 0. Therefore the bond price $P(t,T)$ also results from a random process, in this case all the random processes for all the forward rates $f(t,s)$.

The zero-coupon bond price may also be given in terms of the spot rate $r(t,T)$, as shown in (9.74). From our earlier analysis we know that:

$$P(t,T)e^{r(t,T)(T-t)} = 1 \tag{9.77}$$

[43] For instance, see Campbell et al. (1997), Section 4.2.

which is rearranged to give the zero-coupon bond price equation

$$P(t,T) = e^{-r(t,T)(T-t)} \tag{9.78}$$

as before.

Equation (9.78) describes the bond price as a function of the spot rate only, as opposed to the multiple processes that apply for all the forward rates from t to T. As the bond has a nominal value of £1 the value given by (9.78) is the discount factor for that term; the range of zero-coupon bond prices would give us the discount function.

Conclusions

What is the importance of this result for our understanding of the term structure of interest rates? First, we see (again, but here in continuous time) that spot rates, forward rates and the discount function are all closely related, and given one we can calculate the remaining two. More significantly, we may model the term structure either as a function of the spot rate only, described as a stochastic process, or as a function of all of the forward rates $f(t, s)$ for each period s in the period (t, T), described by multiple random processes. The first yield curve models adopted the first approach, while a later development described the second approach.

Appendices

Appendix 9.1 Jensen's inequality and the shape of the yield curve

In Cox, Ingersoll and Ross (1981) an analysis on the shape of the term structure used a feature known as *Jensen's inequality* to illustrate that the expectations hypothesis was consistent with forward rates being an indicator of future spot rates. Jensen's inequality states that the expected value of the reciprocal of a variable is not identical to the reciprocal of the expected value of that variable. Following this, if the expected holding period returns on a set of bonds are all equal, the expected holding period returns on the bonds cannot then be equal over any other holding period. Applying this in practice, consider two zero-coupon bonds, a one-year bond with a yield of 11.11% and a two-year zero-coupon bond with a yield of 11.8034%. The prices of the bonds are as follows:

1 year: 90
2 year: 80.

Assume that the price of the two-year bond in one year's time can be either 86.89 or 90.89, with identical probability. At the end of year 1, the total return generated by the two-year bond will be either (86.89/80) 8.6125% or (90.89/80) 13.6125%, while at this point the (now) one-year bond will offer a return of either (100/86.89) 15.089% or (100/90.89) 10.023%. The two possible prices have been set deliberately so as to ensure that the expected return over one year for the two-year bond is equal to the return available today on the one-year bond, which is 11.11% as we noted at the start. The return expected on the two-year bond is indeed the same (provided either of the two prices is available); that is [(0.5) × (86.89/80) + (0.5) × (90.89/80)], or 11.11%. Therefore it cannot also be true that the certain return over two years for the two-year bond is equal to the expected return for two years from rolling over the investment in the one-year bond. At the start of the period the two-year bond has a guaranteed return of [100/80] 25% over its lifetime. However, investing in the one-year bond and then reinvesting at the one-year period after the first year will produce a return that is higher than this, as shown:

$$11.11\% \times [(0.5) \times (100/86.89) + (0.5) \times (100/90.89)]$$

or 25.063%. Under this scenario, investors cannot expect equality of returns for all bonds over all investment horizons.

APPENDIX 9.2 Testing the unbiased expectations hypothesis

For empirical studies testing the unbiased expectations hypothesis see Kessel (1965) and Fama (1976). If we consider the expectations hypothesis to be true then the forward rate ${}_0rf_2$ should be an accurate predictor of the spot rate in period 2. Put another way, the mean of ${}_0rf_2$ should be equal to the mean of ${}_1rs_1$. In previous studies (Fama 1976) it has been shown that forward rates are in fact biased upwards in their estimates of future spot rates. That is, ${}_0rf_2$ is usually higher than the mean of ${}_1rs_1$. This bias tends to be magnified the further one moves along the term structure. We can test the unbiased expectations hypothesis by determining if the following condition holds:

$$ {}_1rs_1 = p + q\,({}_0rf_2). \tag{A9.2.1} $$

In an environment where we upheld the expectations hypothesis, then p should be equal to zero and q equal to one. Outside of the very short end of the yield curve, there is no evidence that this is true. Another approach, adopted by Fama (1984), involved subtracting the current spot rate rs_1 from both sides of equation (A9.2.1) and testing whether:

$$ {}_1rs_1 - {}_0rs_1 = p + q({}_0rf_2 - {}_0rs_1). \tag{A9.2.2} $$

If the hypothesis were accurate, we would again have p equal to zero and q equal to one. This is because ${}_1rs_1 - {}_0rs_1$ is the change in the spot rate predicted by the hypothesis. The left-hand side of (A9.2.2) is the actual change in the spot rate, which must equal the right-hand side of the equation if the hypothesis is true. Evidence from the earlier studies mentioned has suggested that q is a positive number less than one. This of course is not consistent with the unbiased expectations hypothesis. However, the studies indicate that the prediction of changes in future spot rates is linked to actual changes that occur. This suggests then that forward rates are indeed based on the market's view of future spot rates, but not in a completely unbiased manner.

An earlier study was conducted by Meiselman (1962), referred to as his error-learning model. According to this, if the unbiased expectations hypothesis is true, forward rates are not then completely accurate forecasts of future spot rates. The study tested whether (A9.2.3) was true.

$$ {}_1rf_n - {}_0rf_n = p + q\,{}_1rs_1 - {}_0rf_2 \tag{A9.2.3} $$

If the hypothesis is true then p should be equal to zero and q should be positive. The error-learning model suggests a positive correlation between forward rates, but this would hold in an environment where the unbiased expectations hypothesis did not apply.

The empirical evidence suggests that the predictions of future spot rates reflected in forward rates is related to subsequent actual spot rates. So forward rates *do* include an element of market interest-rate forecasts. However, this would indicate more a biased expectations theory, rather than the pure unbiased expectations hypothesis.

APPENDIX 9.3 Cubic spline interpolation

There are four observed vertices in the example quoted in the main text, which requires three cubic equations, $rm_{(i,t)}$, each one connecting two adjacent vertices, n_i and n_{i+1}, as follows:

$rm_{(0,t)} = a_0 n^3 + b_0 n^2 + c_0 n + d_0$, connecting vertex n_0 with n_1

$rm_{(1,t)} = a_1 n^3 + b_1 n^2 + c_1 n + d_1$, connecting vertex n_1 with n_2

$rm_{(2,t)} = a_2 n^3 + b_2 n^2 + c_2 n + d_2$, connecting vertex n_2 with n_3

where a, b, c and d are unknowns. The three equations require 12 conditions in all. The cubic spline method imposes the following set of conditions on the curves: Each cubic equation must pass through its own pair of vertices. Thus, for the first equation:

$$a_0 n_0^3 + b_0 n_0^2 + c_0 n_0 + d_0 = 4.00$$

$$a_0 n_1^3 + b_0 n_1^2 + c_0 n_1 + d_0 = 5.00.$$

For the second and third equations:

$$a_1 n_1^3 + b_1 n_1^2 + c_1 n_1 + d_1 = 5.00$$

$$a_1 n_2^3 + b_1 n_2^2 + c_1 n_2 + d_1 = 6.50$$

$$a_2 n_2^3 + b_2 n_2^2 + c_2 n_2 + d_2 = 6.50$$

$$a_2 n_3^3 + b_2 n_3^2 + c_2 n_3 + d_2 = 6.75.$$

The resulting yield curve should be smooth at the point where one cubic equation joins with the next one. This is achieved by requiring the slope and the convexity of adjacent equations to be equal at the point where they meet, ensuring a smooth rollover from one equation to the next. Mathematically, the first and second derivatives of all adjacent equations must be equal at the point where the equations meet.

Thus, at vertex n_1:

$$3a_0n_1^2 + 2b_0n_1 + 1 = 3a_1n_1^2 + 2b_1n_1 + 1 \text{ (the first derivative)}$$

$$6a_0n_1 + 2 = 6a_1n_1 + 2 \text{ (the second derivative).}$$

And at vertex n_2:

$$3a_1n_2^2 + 2b_1n_2 + 1 = 3a_2n_2^2 + 2b_2n_2 + 1 \text{ (the first derivative)}$$

$$6a_1n_2 + 2 = 6a_2n_2 + 2 \text{ (the second derivative).}$$

Finally, we may impose the condition that the splines tail off flat at the end vertices, or more formally we state mathematically that the second derivatives should be zero at the end points:

$$6a_0n_0 + 2 = 0 \text{ (first spline starts flat)}$$

$$6a_2n_3 + 2 = 0 \text{ (second spline ends flat).}$$

These constraints together give us a system of 12 equations from which we can solve for the 12 unknown coefficients. The solution is usually reached using matrices, where the equations are expressed in matrix form. This is shown below.

$$\begin{bmatrix} n_0^3 & n_0^2 & n_0 & 1 & 0 & 0 & 0 & 0 & 0 & 0 & 0 & 0 \\ n_1^3 & n_1^2 & n_1 & 1 & 0 & 0 & 0 & 0 & 0 & 0 & 0 & 0 \\ 0 & 0 & 0 & 0 & n_1^3 & n_1^2 & n_1 & 1 & 0 & 0 & 0 & 0 \\ 0 & 0 & 0 & 0 & n_2^3 & n_2^2 & n_2 & 1 & 0 & 0 & 0 & 0 \\ 0 & 0 & 0 & 0 & 0 & 0 & 0 & 0 & n_2^3 & n_2^2 & n_2 & 1 \\ 0 & 0 & 0 & 0 & 0 & 0 & 0 & 0 & n_3^3 & n_3^2 & n_3 & 1 \\ 3n_1^2 & 2n_1 & 1 & 0 & -3n_1^2 & -2n_1 & -1 & 0 & 0 & 0 & 0 & 0 \\ 6n_1 & 2 & 0 & 0 & -6n_1 & -2 & 0 & 0 & 0 & 0 & 0 & 0 \\ 0 & 0 & 0 & 0 & 3n_2^2 & 2n_2 & 1 & 0 & -3n_2^2 & -2n_1 & -1 & 0 \\ 0 & 0 & 0 & 0 & 6n_2 & 2 & 0 & 0 & -6n_2 & -2 & 0 & 0 \\ 6n_0 & 2 & 0 & 0 & 0 & 0 & 0 & 0 & 0 & 0 & 0 & 0 \\ 0 & 0 & 0 & 0 & 0 & 0 & 0 & 0 & 6n_3 & 2 & 0 & 0 \end{bmatrix} \times \begin{bmatrix} a_0 \\ b_0 \\ c_0 \\ d_0 \\ a_1 \\ b_1 \\ c_1 \\ d_1 \\ a_2 \\ b_2 \\ c_2 \\ d_2 \end{bmatrix} = \begin{bmatrix} 4 \\ 5 \\ 6.5 \\ 6.75 \\ 0 \\ 0 \\ 0 \\ 0 \\ 0 \\ 0 \\ 0 \\ 0 \end{bmatrix}$$

Figure A9.3.1 Cubic spline interpolation matrix

In matrix notation we have:

$$[n] \times [\text{Coefficients}] = [rm],$$

therefore the solution is:

$$[\text{Coefficients}] = [n]^{-1} \times [rm].$$

Inverting the matrix n and then pre-multiplying rm with the resulting inverse, we obtain the array of required coefficients:

Coefficients = [0.022, 0.000, 0.413, 4.000, –0.047, 0.411, –0.410, 4.548, 0.008, –0.249, 2.230, 1.029].

So the three cubic equations are specified as:

$rm_{(0,t)} = 0.022 \times n^3 + 0.413 \times n + 4.000$ for vertices $n_0 - n_1$

$rm_{(1,t)} = -0.047 \times n^3 + 0.411 \times n^2 - 0.410 \times n + 4.548$ for vertices $n_1 - n_2$

$rm_{(2,t)} = 0.008 \times n^3 - 0.249 \times n^2 + 2.230 \times n + 1.029$ for vertices $n_2 - n_3$.

APPENDIX 9.4 The integral

The approach used to define integrals begins with an approximation involving a countable number of objects, which is then gradually transformed into an uncountable number of objects. A common form of integral is the Riemann integral.

Given a calculable or *deterministic* function that has been graphed for a period of time, let us say we require the area represented by this graph. The function is $f(t)$ and it is graphed over the period $[0, T]$. The area of the graph is given by the integral:

$$\int_0^T f(s)\,ds \tag{A9.4.1}$$

which is the area represented by the graph. This can be calculated using the Riemann integral, for which the area represented is shown in Figure 9.4.1.

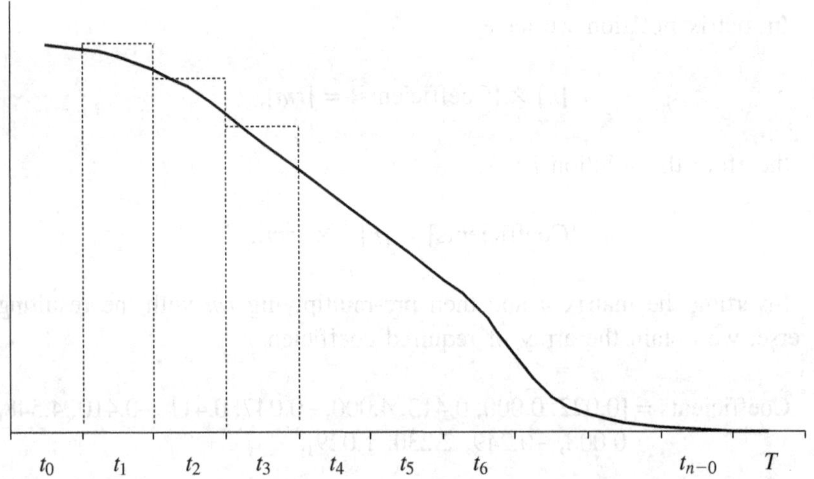

Figure A9.4.1 Illustrating the calculation of area by applying integration

To make the calculation, the time interval is separated into an n of intervals, given by:

$$t_0 = 0 < t_1 < t_2 < \cdots < t_{n-1} < t_n < T.$$

The approximate area under the graph is given by the sum of the area of each of the rectangles, for which we assume each segment outside the graph is compensated by the area under the line that is not captured by any of the rectangles. Therefore we can say that an approximating measure is described by:

$$\sum_{i=0}^{n} f\left(\frac{t_i + t_{i-1}}{2}\right)(t_i - t_{i-1}). \qquad \text{(A9.4.2)}$$

This states that the area under the graph can be approximated by taking the sum of the n rectangles, which are created from the base x-axis that begins from t_0 through to T_n and the y-axis as height, described as:

$$f((t_i + t_{i-1})/2).$$

This approximation only works if a sufficiently small base has been used for each interval, and if the function $f(t)$ is a smooth function; that is, it does not experience sudden swings or kinks.

The definition of the Riemann integral is, given that:

$$\max_i |t_i + t_{i-1}| \to 0,$$

defined by the limit:

$$\sum_{i=0}^{n} f\left(\frac{t_i + t_{i-1}}{2}\right)(t_i - t_{i-1}) \to \int_0^T f(s)\,ds. \qquad \text{(A9.4.3)}$$

If the approximation is not sufficiently accurate, we can adjust it by making the intervals smaller still, which will make the approximation closer. This approach cannot be used if the function is not smooth. In mathematics, this requirement is stated by saying that the function must be integrable or Riemann integrable.

Other integral forms are also used, a good introduction to these is given in Neftci (2000), Chapter 4.

APPENDIX 9.5 The derivation of the bond price equation in continuous time

This section summarises the approach described in Ross (1999), on pp. 54–6. This is an excellent reference, very readable and accessible, and is highly recommended. We replace Ross's use of investment at time 0 for maturity at time t with the terms t and T respectively, which is consistent with the price equations given in the main text. We also use the symbol M for the maturity value of the money market account, again to maintain consistency with the expressions used in this chapter.

Assume a continuously compounded interest rate $r(s)$ that is payable on a money market account at time s. This is the instantaneous interest rate at time s. Assume further that an investor places x in this account at time s; after a very short time period of time h, the account would contain:

$$x_h \approx x(1 + r(s)h). \tag{A9.5.1}$$

Assume that $M(T)$ is the amount that will be in the account at time T if an investor deposits £1 at time t. To calculate $M(T)$ in terms of the spot rate $r(s)$, where $t \leqslant s \leqslant T$, for an incremental change in time of h, we have:

$$M(s + h) \approx M(s)(1 + r(s)h) \tag{A9.5.2}$$

which leads us to:

$$M(s + h) - M(s) \approx M(s)r(s)h \tag{A9.5.3}$$

and:

$$\frac{M(s+h) - M(s)}{h} \approx M(s)r(s). \tag{A9.5.4}$$

The approximation given by (A9.5.3) turns into an equality as the time represented by h becomes progressively smaller. At the limit given as h approaches zero, we say:

$$M'(s) = M(s)r(s) \tag{A9.5.5}$$

which can be rearranged to give:

$$\frac{M'(s)}{M(s)} = r(s). \tag{A9.5.6}$$

From expression (A9.5.6), we imply that in a continuous time process:

$$\int_t^T \frac{M'(s)}{M(s)}\,ds = \int_t^T r(s)\,ds \qquad \text{(A9.5.7)}$$

and that:

$$\log(M(T)) - \log(M(t)) = \int_t^T r(s)\,ds. \qquad \text{(A9.5.8)}$$

However, we deposited £1 at time t, that is $M(t) = 1$, so from (A9.5.8), we obtain the value of the money market account at T to be:

$$M(T) = \exp\left(\int_t^T r(s)\,ds\right) \qquad \text{(A9.5.9)}$$

which was our basic equation shown as (9.41).

Let us now introduce a risk-free zero-coupon bond that has a maturity value of £1 when it is redeemed at time T. If the spot rate is constant, then the price at time t of this bond is given by:

$$P(t, T) = e^{-r(T-t))} \qquad \text{(A9.5.10)}$$

where r is the continuously compounded instantaneous interest rate. The right-hand side of (A9.5.10) is the expression for the present value of £1, payable at time T, discounted at time t at the continuously compounded, constant interest rate r.

So we say that $P(t, T)$ is the present value at time t of £1 to be received at time T. Since a deposit of $1/M(T)$ at time t will have a value of 1 at time T, we are able to say that:

$$P(t, T) = \frac{1}{M(T)} = \exp\left(-\int_t^T r(s)\,ds\right). \qquad \text{(A9.5.11)}$$

If we say that the *average* of the spot interest rates from t to T is denoted by $rf(T)$, so we have $rf(T) = \frac{1}{T}\int_t^T r(s)\,ds$, then the function $rf(T)$ is the term structure of interest rates.

APPENDIX 9.6 Illustration of forward rate structure when the spot rate structure is increasing

We assume the spot rate $r(0, T)$ is a function of time and is increasing to a high point at $\bar{T}$. It is given by:

$$r(0,T) = \frac{\int_0^T f(0,s)\,ds}{T}. \tag{A9.6.1}$$

At its high point the function is neither increasing nor decreasing, so we may write:

$$\frac{dr(0,\bar{T})}{dT} = 0 \tag{A9.6.2}$$

and therefore the second derivative with respect to T will be:

$$\frac{d^2 r(0,\bar{T})}{dT^2} < 0. \tag{A9.6.3}$$

From (9.70) and (A9.6.2) we may state:

$$f(0,\bar{T}) = r(0,\bar{T}) \tag{A9.6.4}$$

and from (A9.6.3) and (A9.6.4) the second derivative of the spot rate is:

$$\frac{d^2 r(0,\bar{T})}{dT^2} = \left[\frac{df(0,\bar{T})}{dT} - \frac{dr(0,\bar{T})}{dT}\right]\frac{1}{T} < 0 \tag{A9.6.5}$$

From (A9.6.2) we know the spot rate function is zero at $\bar{T}$ so the derivative of the forward rate with respect to T would therefore be:

$$\frac{df(0,\bar{T})}{dT} < 0 \tag{A9.6.6}$$

So in this case the forward rate is decreasing at the point $\bar{T}$ when the spot rate is at its maximum value. This is illustrated hypothetically in Figure 9.29 and it is common to observe the forward rate curve decreasing as the spot rate is increasing.

References and bibliography

Adams, K. and Van Deventer, D. 1994, "Fitting Yield Curves and Forward Rate Curves with Maximum Smoothness", *Journal of Fixed Income,* 4, pp. 52–62.

Anderson, N. and Sleath, J. 1999, *Bank of England Quarterly Bulletin*, November.

Avellaneda, M. and Laurence, P. 2000, *Quantitative Modelling of Derivative Securities*, Chapman & Hall/CRC, London, chapters 10–12.

Baxter, M. and Rennie, A. 1996, *Financial Calculus*, Cambridge University Press, Cambridge, Chapter 5.

Black, F. and Scholes, M. 1973, "The Pricing of Options and Corporate Liability", *Journal of Political Economy*, 81, May–June, pp. 637–59.

Brennan, M. and Schwartz, E. 1979, "A Continuous Time Approach to the Pricing of Bonds", *Journal of Banking and Finance,* 3, p. 134 *ff.*

Brennan, M. and Schwartz, E. 1980, "Conditional Predictions of Bond Prices and Returns", *Journal of Finance,* 35, p. 405 *ff.*

Brooks, C. 2004, *Introductory Econometrics for Finance*, Cambridge University Press.

Campbell, J. 1986, "A Defence of Traditional Hypotheses about the Term Structure of Interest Rates", *Journal of Finance*, March, pp. 183–93.

Campbell, J., Lo, A. and MacKinlay, A. 1997, *The Econometrics of Financial Markets*, Princeton UP, Princeton, New Jersey, chapters 10–11.

Choudhry, M. 1998, "The Information Content of the United Kingdom Gilt Yield Curve", unpublished MBA assignment, Henley Management College.

Choudhry, M. 2001, *Bond Market Securities*, FT Prentice Hall, London.

Choudhry, M., Joannas, D., Pereira, R. and Pienaar, R. 2001, *Capital Markets Instruments*, FT Prentice Hall, London.

Choudhry, M. 2004a, *Advanced Fixed Income Analysis*, Elsevier, Oxford.

Choudhry, M. 2004b, *Fixed Income Markets*, John Wiley & Sons, Singapore.

Cox, J., Ingersoll, J.E. and Ross, S.A. 1981, "A Re-examination of Traditional Hypothesis about the Term Structure of Interest Rates", *Journal of Finance*, 36, September, pp. 769–99.

Cox, J., Ingersoll, J. and Ross, S. 1985, "An Inter-Temporal General Equilibrium Model of Asset Prices", *Econometrica*, 53, pp. 81–90.

Culbertson, J.M. 1957, "The Term Structure of Interest Rates," *Quarterly Journal of Economics,* 71, November 7, pp. 485–517.

Deacon, M. and Derry, A. 1994, "Estimating the Term Structure of Interest Rates", *Bank of England Working Paper Series,* No. 24, July.

Duffie, D. 1992, *Dynamic Asset Pricing Theory*, Princeton University Press, Princeton.

Fabozzi, F. 1993, *Bond Markets, Analysis and Strategies*, 2nd edition, Prentice Hall, New Jersey.

Fabozzi, F. 1997, *Fixed Income Mathematics*, McGraw-Hill, New York.

Fama, E.F. 1970, "Efficient Capital Markets: A Review of Theory and Empirical Work", *Journal of Finance*, Vol. 25, pp. 383–417.

Fama, E.F. 1976, "Forward Rates as Predictors of Future Spot Interest Rates", *Journal of Financial Economics*, Vol. 3, No. 4, October, pp. 361–77.

Fama, E.F. 1984, "The Information in the Term Structure," *Journal of Financial Economics*, 13, December, pp. 509–28.

Fisher, I. 1986, "Appreciation of Interest", *Publications of the American Economic Association*, August, pp. 23–39.

Gujarati, D. 1999, *Basic Econometrics*, 3rd edition, McGraw-Hill, New York.

Heath, D., Jarrow, R. and Morton, A. 1992, "Bond Pricing and the Term Structure of Interest Rates", *Journal of Financial and Quantitative Analysis*, 25, pp. 419–40.

Hicks, J. 1946, *Value and Capital*, 2nd edition, Oxford University Press, Oxford.

Ingersoll, J. 1987, *Theory of Financial Decision Making*, Rowman & Littlefield, Princeton, Chapter 18, Savage, MA.

James, J. and Webber, N. 2000, *Interest Rate Modelling*, John Wiley & Sons, Chichester.

Jarrow, R. 1981, "Liquidity Premiums and the Expectations Hypothesis", *Journal of Banking and Finance* 5(4), pp. 539–46.

Jarrow, R. 1996, *Modelling Fixed Income Securities and Interest Rate Options*, McGraw-Hill, New York.

Kessel, R.A. 1965, "The Cyclical Behaviour of the Term Structure of Interest Rates", *Essays in Applied Price Theory*, University of Chicago.

Kitter, G. 1999, Investment Mathematics for Finance and Treasury Professionals, Wiley, London, chapters 3 and 5.

Levy, H. 1999, *Introduction to Investments*, 2nd edition, South-Western College Publishing, Cincinatti.

Livingstone, M. 1990, *Money and Capital Markets*, Prentice Hall, New Jersey, pp. 254–6.

Lutz, F. 1940, "The Structure of Interest Rates", *Quarterly Journal of Economics*, November, pp. 36–63.

Mastronikola, K. 1991, "Yield Curves for Gilt-edged Stocks: A New Model", *Bank of England Discussion Paper* (*Technical Series*), No. 49.

McCulloch, J. 1971, "Measuring the Term Structure of Interest Rates", *Journal of Business*, 44, pp. 19–31.

McCulloch, J. 1975, "The Tax-Adjusted Yield Curve", *Journal of Finance*, 30, pp. 811–30.

McCulloch, J.H. 1975, "An Estimate of the Liquidity Premium," *Journal of Political Economy*, 83, Jan.–Feb., pp. 95–119.

Merton, R. 1973, "Theory of Rational Option Pricing", *Bell Journal of Economics and Management Science*, 4, Spring, pp. 141–83.

Meiselman, D. 1962, *The Term Structure of Interest Rates*, Prentice Hall, New Jersey.

Neftci, S. 2000, *An Introduction to the Mathematics of Financial Derivatives*, 2nd edition, Academic Press, San Francisco, Chapter 18.

Nelson, C. and Siegel, A. 1987, "Parsimonious Modelling of Yield Curves, *Journal of Business*, 60(4), pp. 473–89.

Ross, Sheldon M. 1999, *An Introduction to Mathematical Finance*, Cambridge University Press, Cambridge.

Rubinstein, M. 1999, *Rubinstein on Derivatives*, RISK, London, pp. 84–5.

Ryan, R. (ed.) 1997, *Yield Curve Dynamics*, Glenlake Publishing Company, Chicago.

Schaefer, S. 1981, "Measuring a Tax-Specific Term Structure of Interest Rates in the Market for British Government Securities", *Economic Journal*, 91, pp. 415–38.

Shiller, R. 1990, "The Term Structure of Interest Rates", in Friedman, B. and Hahn, F. (eds), *Handbook of Monetary Economics*, North-Holland, Amsterdam, Chapter 13.

Suits, D., Mason, A. and Chan, L. 1978, "Spline Functions Fitted by Standard Regression Methods", *Review of Economics and Statistics*, 60, pp. 132–39.

Sundaresan, S. 1997, *Fixed Income Markets and Their Derivatives*, South-Western, Cincinnati.

The Economist 1998, "Admiring Those Shapely Curves", 4 April, p. 117.

The Economist 2000, "Out of Debt", 12 February, pp. 44–9.

Van Deventer, D. and Imai, K. 1997, *Financial Risk Analytics*, Irwin, New York.

Van Horne, J. 1995, *Financial Management and Policy*, 10th edition, Prentice Hall, New Jersey.

Waggoner, D. 1997, "Spline Methods for Extracting Interest Rate Curves from Coupon Bond Prices", *Working Paper, Federal Reserve Bank of Atlanta*, 97–10.

Windas, T. 1993, *An Introduction to Option-adjusted Spread Analysis*, Bloomberg Publishing, Princeton.

In addition, interested readers may wish to consult the following recommended references on term structure analysis.

Constantinides, G. 1992, "A Theory of the Nominal Term Structure of Interest Rates", *The Review of Financial Studies*, 5(4), pp. 531–52.

Cox, J., Ingersoll, J. and Ross, S. 1981, "A Re-examination of Traditional Hypotheses about the Term Structure of Interest Rates", *Journal of Finance*, 36, pp. 769–99.

Cox, J., Ingersoll, J. and Ross, S. 1985, "A Theory of the Term Structure of Interest Rates", *Econometrica*, 53, pp. 385–407.

Culbertson, J. 1957, "The Term Structure of Interest Rates", *Quarterly Journal of Economics*, LXXI, pp. 489–504.

McCulloch, J.H. 1993, "A Reexamination of Traditional Hypotheses about the Term Structure: A Comment", *Journal of Finance*, 63(2), pp. 779–89.

Stambaugh, R. 1988, "The Information in Forward Rates: Implications for Models of the Term Structure", *Journal of Financial Economics*, 21, pp. 41–70.

Shiller, R., Cambell, J. and Schoenholtz, K. 1983, "Forward Rates and Future Policy: Interpreting the Term Structure of Interest Rates", *Brookings Papers on Economic Activity*, 1, pp. 173–223.

Hold On
You're moving way too fast
For me, wait and see.
Don't go
Don't leave me behind
I'm scared, for us

Someday, The Sun
Is going to shine on you

I saw you
Grow up with me
We were running
Through the sand and trees…
Hang on
Don't go away -
I know I let you down.

Someday, The Sun
Is going to shine on you

– Red Son, "Palestine"
The Promised Land EP (Jackfruit Records) 1998

CHAPTER

10

The Determinants of the Swap Spread and Understanding the Term Premium

In the previous chapter we looked in detail at the yield curve. An important hedging tool in ALM operations is the interest-rate swap, which is described in detail in Chapter 14. In this chapter, we consider an important issue for interest-rate analysis, the swap spread. Specifically, we look at the spread of the swap curve over the government bond yield curve and the relationship between the two yield curves. This subject is important because the swap spread is an indicator value in the market, as well as an indicator of the overall health of the economy. Understanding the determinants of the swap spread is important for ALM practitioners for this reason.

In the second part of this chapter we look at a related area: the magnitude of the term premium. Given "normal" market conditions, what should the extent of the term premium of the (under normal conditions positively sloping) yield curve be? We also consider the impact of macro-level geo-political factors on the swap spread.

The determinants of the swap spread

Interest-rate swaps, which are described in Chapter 14, are an important ALM and risk management tool in banking markets. The rate payable on a swap represents bank risk, if we assume that a swap is paying (receiving) the fixed swap rate on one leg and receiving (paying) Libor-flat on the other leg. If one of the counterparties is not a bank, then either leg is adjusted to account for the different counterparty risk; usually the floating leg will have a spread added to Libor. We can see that this produces a swap curve that lies above the government bond yield curve, if we compare Figure 10.1 with

Figure 10.2. Figure 10.1 is the USD swap rates page from Tullett & Tokyo brokers, and Figure 10.2 is the US Treasury yield curve, both as at 3 July 2006. The higher rates payable on swaps represents the additional risk premium associated with bank risk compared to government risk. The spread itself is the number of basis points the swap rate lies above the equivalent-maturity government bond yield, quoted on the same interest basis.

2 P1P122 Govt **TTIS**

200<Go> to view in Launchpad

10:10 **TULLETT & TOKYO** PAGE 1 / 2

USD Swaps	Bid	Ask	Time	USD Swaps	Bid	Ask	Time
IMM SWAPS				19) 15 Year	5.7380	5.7780	1:46
1) 1st	5.6900	5.7100	10:08	20) 20 Year	5.8060	5.8460	1:46
2) 2nd	5.6580	5.6790	10:08	21) 25 Year	5.8080	5.8490	3:02
3) 3rd	5.6150	5.6350	10:10	22) 30 Year	5.7740	5.8150	1:46
4) 4th	5.5800	5.6000	10:01	SEMI-ANNUAL SWAPS			
ANNUAL SWAPS				23) 2 Year	5.6310	5.6710	7/03
5) 1 Year	5.6770	5.6970	9:36	24) 3 Year	5.6120	5.6520	7/03
6) 2 Year	5.6240	5.6650	7/03	25) 4 Year	5.6210	5.6610	7:16
7) 3 Year	5.6070	5.6480	7/03	26) 5 Year	5.6410	5.6810	0:01
8) 4 Year	5.6180	5.6590	7:16	27) 6 Year	5.6600	5.7000	0:01
9) 5 Year	5.6390	5.6790	0:01	28) 7 Year	5.6770	5.7170	0:01
10) 6 Year	5.6560	5.6970	0:01	29) 8 Year	5.6910	5.7310	0:01
11) 7 Year	5.6740	5.7150	0:01	30) 9 Year	5.7080	5.7480	0:01
12) 8 Year	5.6890	5.7300	0:01	31) 10 Year	5.7270	5.7670	7:40
13) 9 Year	5.7070	5.7470	0:01	32) 11 Year	5.7370	5.7770	0:01
14) 10 Year	5.7250	5.7650	7:40	33) 12 Year	5.4570	5.4970	1:46
15) 11 Year	5.7350	5.7760	0:01	34) 13 Year	5.7620	5.8020	0:01
16) 12 Year	5.4520	5.4920	1:46	35) 14 Year	5.7720	5.8120	0:01
17) 13 Year	5.7610	5.8020	0:01	LIVE Treasury Mid-Yields &			
18) 14 Year	5.7700	5.8110	0:01	Treasury Swap Spreads -> SMKR<GO>			

Australia 61 2 9777 8600 Brazil 5511 3048 4500 Europe 44 20 7330 7500 Germany 49 69 920410
Hong Kong 852 2977 6000 Japan 81 3 3201 8900 Singapore 65 6212 1000 U.S. 1 212 318 2000 Copyright 2006 Bloomberg L.P.
2 04-Jul-06 10:10:46

Figure 10.1 Tullet & Tokyo brokers USD interest-rate swaps page on Bloomberg, as at 3 July 2006

<HELP> for explanation. P122 Govt **IYC**
Cancel: Screen not saved

YIELD CURVE – US TREASURY ACTIVES Page 2/2
DATE 7/ 4/06

	DESCRIPTION	PRICE	SRC	UPDATE	YIELD	HEDGED YIELD
3MO	1) B 0 09/28/06	B 4.8900	BGN	4:00	5.0158	5.0158
6MO	2) B 0 12/28/06	B 5.0700	BGN	4:00	5.2711	5.2711
1YR	3)					
2YR	4) T 5 1/8 06/30/08	B 99.9063	BGN	4:00	5.1748	5.1748
3YR	5) T 4 7/8 05/15/09	B 99.2969	BGN	4:00	5.1400	5.1400
4YR	6)					
5YR	7) T 5 1/8 06/30/11	B100.0625	BGN	4:00	5.1104	5.1104
6YR	8)					
7YR	9)					
8YR	10)					
9YR	11)					
10YR	12) T 5 1/8 05/15/16	B 99.7813	BGN	4:00	5.1527	5.1527
15YR	13)					
20YR	14)					
30YR	15) T 4 1/2 02/15/36	B 89.4531	BGN	4:00	5.2017	5.2017
1MO	16) B 0 07/27/06	B 4.5500	BGN	4:00	4.6261	4.6261

To change price source for securities, use <FMPS>.
To change price source for swaps, use <XDF>.
Yields are based on STANDARD settlement and are Conventional

Australia 61 2 9777 8600 Brazil 5511 3048 4500 Europe 44 20 7330 7500 Germany 49 69 920410
Hong Kong 852 2977 6000 Japan 81 3 3201 8900 Singapore 65 6212 1000 U.S. 1 212 318 2000 Copyright 2006 Bloomberg L.P.
3 04-Jul-06 10:30:31

Figure 10.2 US Treasury yield curve as at 3 July 2006

In theory, the swap spread represents only the additional credit risk of the interbank market above the government market. However, as the spread is variable, it is apparent that other factors influence it. An ALM desk will want to be aware of these factors, because they influence swap rates. Swaps are an important risk hedging tool, if not the most important, for banks so it becomes necessary for practitioners to have an appreciation of what drives swap spreads.

Historical pattern

If we plot swap spreads over the last ten years, we note that they have tightened in the last five years or so. Figure 10.3 on page 454 shows the spread for USD and GBP for the period 1997 to the first quarter of 2006.

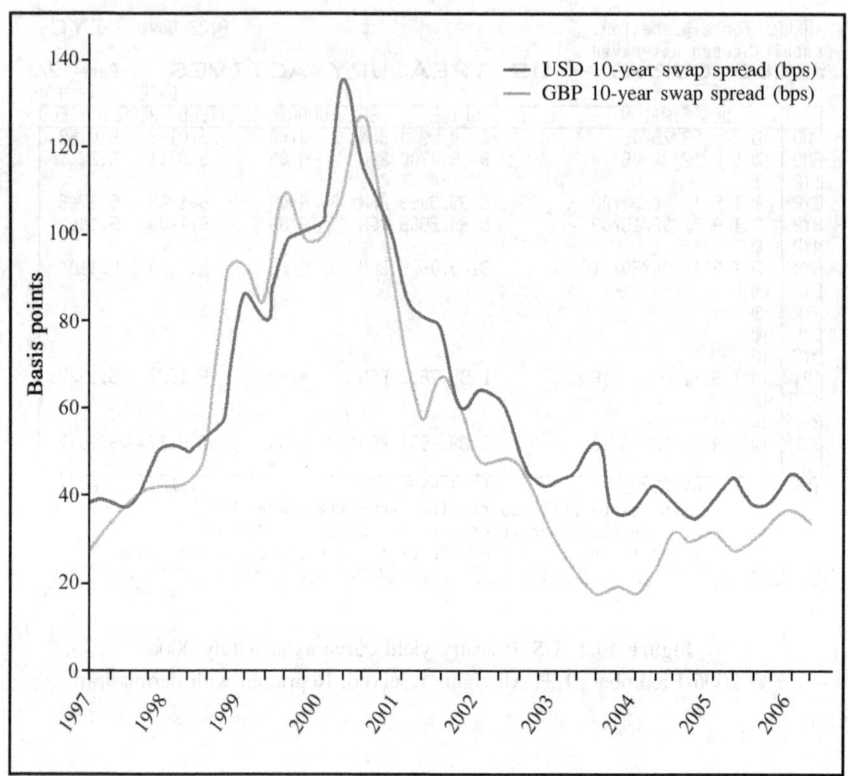

Figure 10.3 USD and GBP interest-rate swap spreads over government curve, 1997–2006

Yield source: Bloomberg L.P.

We see that spreads have reduced in recent years. The highest spread for both currencies was reached during 2000, when the 10-year sterling swap spread peaked at around 140 basis points above the gilt yield. The tightest spreads were reached during 2003, when the 10-year sterling spread reached around 15 basis points towards the end of that year. At the beginning of 2006 sterling spreads were still lower than the 10-year average of 55 basis points. This implies that the perceived risk premium for the capital markets has fallen.

Note how the change in spread levels coincides with macro-level factors and occurrences. For instance, spreads have moved in line with:

- the Asian currency crisis of 1997;
- the Russian government bond default and collapse of the Long Term Capital Management (LTCM) hedge fund in 1998;
- the "dot.com" crash in 2000;
- the subsequent loosening of monetary policy after the dot.com crash and the events of 9/11.

This indicates to us, if just superficially, that swap spreads react to macro-level factors that are perceived by the market to affect their business risk, credit risk and liquidity risk. Spreads also reflect supply and demand, as well as the absolute level of base interest rates.

Determinants of the spread

We have already noted that in theory the swap spread, representing interbank counterparty risk, should reflect only the market's perception of bank risk over and above government risk. Bank risk is captured in the Libor rate – the rate paid by banks on unsecured deposits to other banks.[1] So in other words, the swap spread is meant to adequately compensate against the risk of bank default. The Libor rate is the floating-rate paid against the fixed rate in the swap transaction, and moves with the perception of bank risk. As we implied in the previous section though, it would appear that other factors influence the swap spread. We can illustrate this better by comparing the swap spread for 10-year quarterly paying swaps with the spread between 3-month Libor and the 3-month general collateral (GC)) repo rate. The GC rate is the risk-free borrowing rate, whereas the Libor rate represents bank risk again. In theory, the spread between 3-month Libor and the GC rate should therefore move closely with the swap spread for quarterly resetting swaps, as both represent bank risk. A look at Figure 10.4 on page 456 shows us that this is not the case. Figure 10.4 compares the two spreads in the US dollar market, but we do not need to calculate the correlation or the R^2 for the two sets of numbers. Even on cursory observation we can see that the correlation is not high. Therefore we conclude that other factors, in addition to perceived bank default risk, drive one or both spreads. These other factors influence swap rates and government bond yields, and hence the swap spread, and we consider them below.

---

[1] In theory. In fact, banks are more likely to pay Li-mid to other banks, and the biggest banks pay Libid. But we can safely ignore this for the purposes of our discussion here.

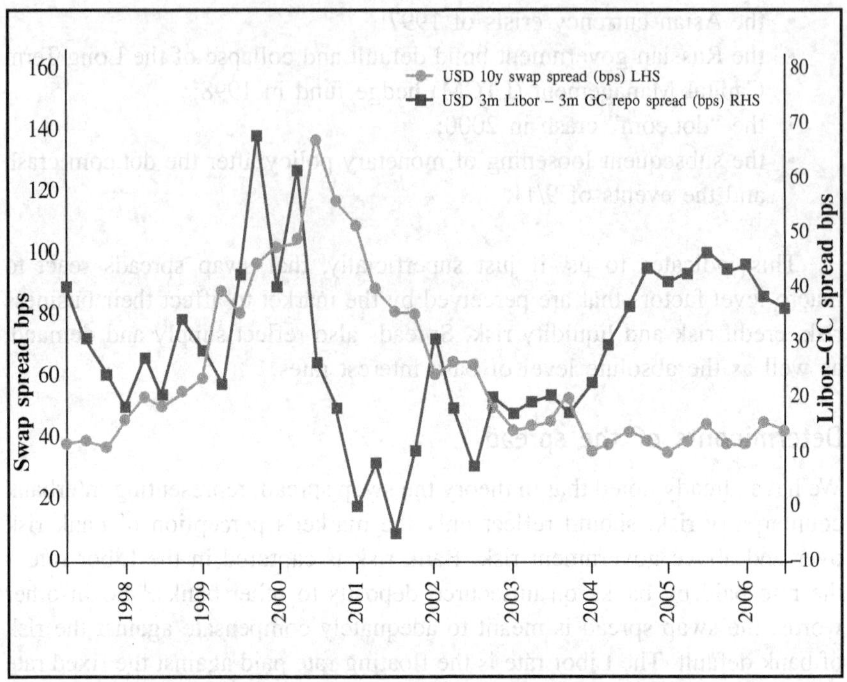

Figure 10.4 Comparison of USD 10-year swap spread and 3-month Libor–GC repo spread
Yield source: Bloomberg L.P.

Level and slope of the yield curve

The magnitude of the swap spread is influenced by the absolute level of base interest rates. If the base rate is 10%, so that the government short-term rate is around 10%, with longer-term rates being recorded higher, the spread tends to be greater than that seen if the base rate is 5%. The shape of the yield curve has even greater influence. When the curve is positively sloping, under the expectations hypothesis (see Chapter 9) investors will expect future rates to be higher; hence, floating-rates are expected to rise. This would suggest the swap spread will narrow. The opposite happens if the yield curve inverts.

Figure 10.5 shows the GBP 10-year swap spread compared to the GBP gilt yield curve spread (10-year gilt yield minus 2-year yield). We see that the slope of the curve has influenced the swap spread; as the slope is narrowing, swap spreads are increasing and vice-versa.

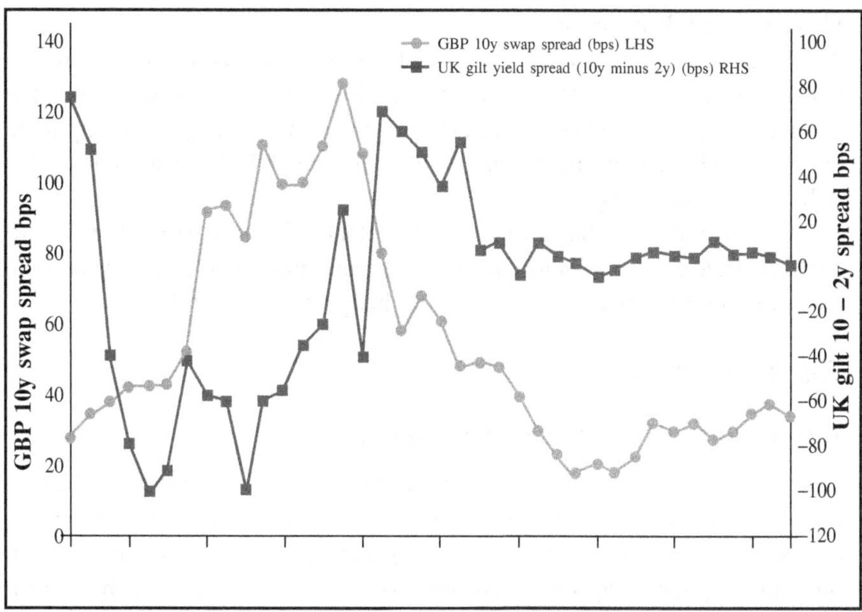

Figure 10.5 GBP swap spreads and gilt spreads compared 1997–2006
Yield source: Bloomberg L.P.

Supply and demand

The swap spread is influenced greatly by supply and demand for swaps. For example, greater trading volume in cash market instruments increases the need for hedging instruments, which will widen swap spreads. The best example of this is corporate bond issuance; as volumes increase, the need for underwriters to hedge issues increases. However, greater bond issuance also has another impact, as issuers seek to swap their fixed-rate liabilities to floating-rate. This also increases demand for swaps.

Market volatility

As suggested by Figure 10.3, swap spreads widen during times of market volatility. This may be in times of market uncertainty (for example, the future direction of base rates or possible inversion of the yield curve) or in times of market shock such as 9/11. In some respects spread widening during periods of volatility reflects the perception of increased bank default risk. It also reflects the "flight to quality" that occurs during times of volatility or market correction: this is the increased demand for risk-free assets such as government bonds that drives their yields lower and hence swap spreads wider.

Government borrowing

The level of government borrowing influences government bond yields, so perforce it will also impact swap spreads. If borrowing is viewed as being in danger of getting out of control, or the government runs persistently large budget deficits, government bond yields will rise. All else being equal, this will lead to narrowing swap spreads.

We can see then that a number of factors influence swap spreads. An ALM or Treasury desk should be aware of these and assess them because the swap rate represents a key funding and hedging rate for a bank.

The term premium

The magnitude of the term premium

From our reading of Chapter 9 we know that a positively sloping yield curve is to be expected under transparent, liquid market conditions. A combination of the expectations hypothesis, the liquidity premium and the inflation premium explains why this is so; longer-dated assets yield a higher return than shorter-dated assets. Thus in most circumstances we expect the one-month rate to be higher than the one-week rate, and the three-month rate to be higher than both the one-week and the one-month rates. This is confirmed in Figure 10.6, which shows the Libor curves for USD and sterling on 25 May 2006.

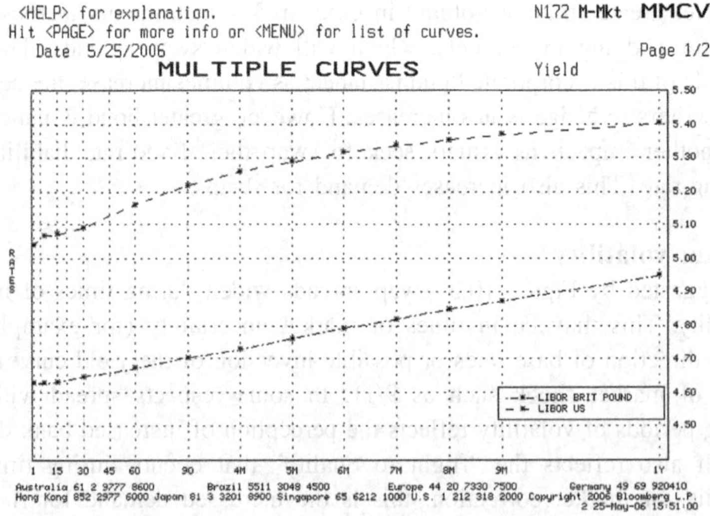

Figure 10.6 USD and GBP curves in Bloomberg; as at 25 May 2006

We expect that the rate on a longer term will be higher than that on a shorter-term, unless we have an inverted yield curve. This is because under most circumstances lenders demand a higher return for longer-dated loans as compensation for the increased inflation and credit risk exposure of longer-dated assets. But what should the magnitude of this term premium be? By how much more should a three-month deposit pay compared to a one-month deposit?

The answer to this question is not fixed, and is a function of a number of factors. In a developed economy that is not subject to high inflation, the most important of these factors is probably future interest-rate expectations. If we allow for this factor, we can conclude that a reasonable term premium under "normal" market conditions for the three-month rate compared to the central bank base rate is in the order of between 12 and 20 basis points. We choose the three-month rate because it is traded on a liquid futures contract (the Eurodollar and short-sterling contracts for USD and GBP respectively and the Euribor contract for the euro) and so we can analyse the market's forward rate expectations for this tenor deposit. But the basic principles will apply to any maturity. Of course, there is no such thing as a "normal" market condition, the term premium will fluctuate daily and always reflect the interaction of a number of factors.

Illustration

On 25 May 2005 we observe the following rates for USD:

Fed funds rate (overnight): 3.00%
Three-month Libor fix: 3.31%.

The three-month rate is 31 basis points above the overnight rate.

The same rates for pounds sterling are:

BoE base rate: 4.75%
Three-month Libor fix: 4.87%.

The three-month rate here is at a much lower spread, only 12 basis points.

Fast-forwarding one year later to 25 May 2006, we observe the following rates:

Fed funds rate (overnight): 5.00%
Three-month Libor fix: 5.22%

BoE base rate: 4.50%
Three-month Libor fix: 4.705%.

The spreads here are 22 basis points for USD and 20.5 basis points for sterling.

We need to look at market expectations for an explanation of these term premiums. In May 2005 the market was expecting a continuation of the gradual, "measured"[2] interest raises, in clips of 25 basis points, at each meeting of the Federal Reserve.[3] This is reflected in the positively sloping yield curve for USD money markets, as shown in Figure 10.7. It is confirmed in Figure 10.8, a graph of the Fed Funds rate for the period May 2005–May 2006, which shows that the rate was moved upwards by 25 basis points at every Fed meeting up until the one on 10 May 2006, which raised the rate to 5.00%. Lenders will require the premium to reflect the expectations of higher interest rates – hence the three-month term premium in May 2005 was 31 basis points. Figure 10.9 on page 462 shows the USD three-month Libor rate history for the same period.

[2] This was the US Federal Reserve's own term to describe its rate-setting policy. Figure 10.10 on page 462 shows the extent of this measured approach, with steady 25 basis point hikes from June 2004 through to June 2006.

[3] The Federal Reserve's Open Market Committee (FOMC), which sets the USD base rate, meets every six weeks or so.

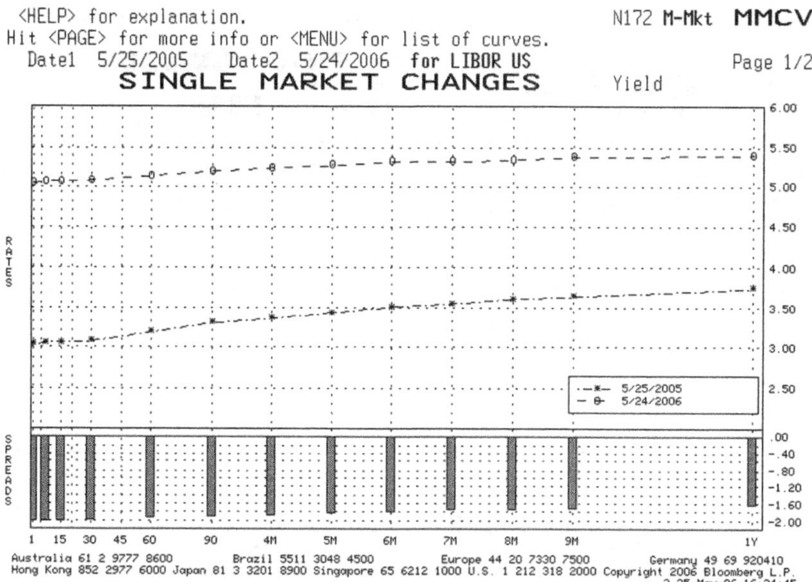

Figure 10.7 Positively sloping USD money market curves, as at 25 May 2006

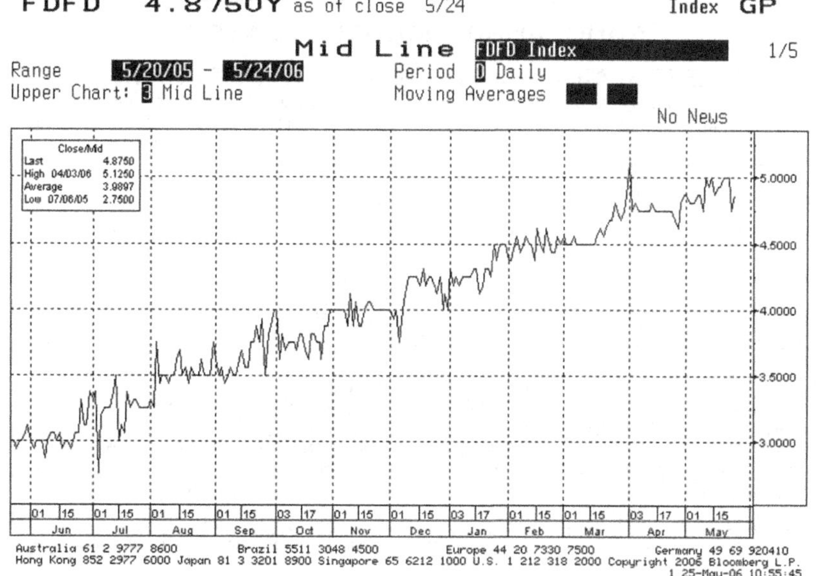

Figure 10.8 Fed Funds rate for May 2005–May 2006

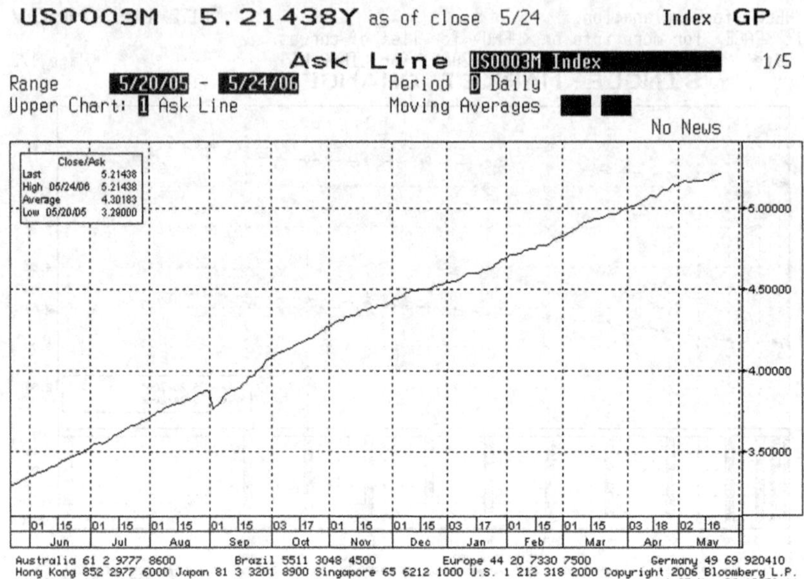

Figure 10.9 USD 3-month Libor rate, May 2005–May 2006

FOMC N172 n Govt **FOMC**

FOMC ANNOUNCEMENT DATES

Historical Change In Monetary Policy and Yield Curve Reaction

2005 FOMC Schedule of Meetings				2006 FOMC Schedule of Meetings			
Date	Rate %	Risk Assessment (Growth/Prices)	Time	Date	Rate %	Risk Assessment (Growth/Prices)	Time
Start	2.25	Balanced		Start	4.25		
1) Feb 02	2.50	Balanced	2:17	9) Jan 31	4.50	Balanced	2:14
2) Mar 22	2.75	Balanced	2:17	10) Mar 28	4.75	Balanced	2:17
3) May 03	3.00	Balanced	2:16	11) May 10	5.00	Data Dependent	2:17
4) Jun 30	3.25	Balanced	2:15	12) Jun 29	-.--		-:--
5) Aug 09	3.50	Balanced	2:17	13) Aug 08	-.--		-:--
6) Sep 20	3.75	Balanced	2:17	14) Sep 20	-.--		-:--
7) Nov 01	4.00	Balanced	2:18	15) Oct 24	-.--		-:--
8) Dec 13	4.25	Balanced	2:13	16) Dec 12	-.--		-:--

Other Fed Related Options and Functions

17) US TREASURIES DAILY YIELD CURVE
18) 2000-2006 FOMC STATEMENTS
19) 1996-2006 FOMC MINUTES RELEASES
20) FEDERAL RESERVE <FOMC> WEBSITE
21) FED SPEECH CALENDAR
22) HISTORICAL RATES AND BIAS
23) FED FUNDS FUTURES
24) TOP FED NEWS - FEDU <GO>
25) FOMC DESCRIPTION - FOMM <GO>
26) CENTRAL BANK RATES - CBRT <GO>
* CLICK ON ANNOUNCEMENT FOR CORRESPONDING SURVEY

Australia 61 2 9777 8600 Brazil 5511 3048 4500 Europe 44 20 7330 7500 Germany 49 69 920410
Hong Kong 852 2977 6000 Japan 81 3 3201 8900 Singapore 65 6212 1000 U.S. 1 212 318 2000 Copyright 2006 Bloomberg L.P.
0 26-May-06 17:45:18

Figure 10.10 FOMC rate-setting history, 2005–2006

Contrast the situation with pound sterling. In May 2005, the prevailing market sentiment was that the next move in base rates would be downwards. This is shown in the money market yield curve for 25 May 2005, which shows an inverted curve at Figure 10.11.

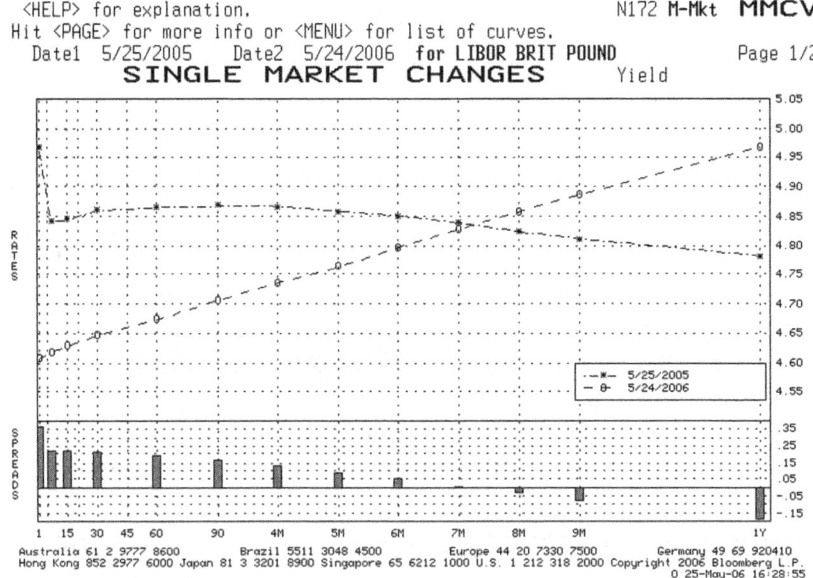

Fig 10.11 GBP money market curves, 2005–2006

Note that the curve slopes gently upwards before then inverting, implying that the market expected the cut in rates to be in a period more than three months from now. However, the term premium was only 12 basis points, reflecting the negative curve. Figures 10.12 and 10.13 show the rates histories for the BoE base rate and GBP three-month Libor.

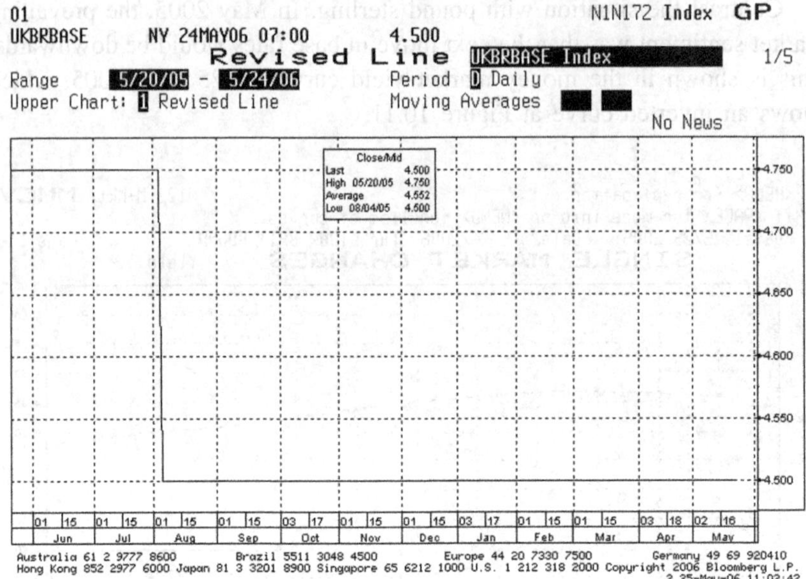

Figure 10.12 GBP base rate history, May 2005–May 2006

Figure 10.13 GBP 3-month Libor history, May 2005–May 2006

So we see that the term premium reflects the market expectations of future rates, and in an environment where the expectations are for higher rates the premium will be higher. The opposite applies where the expectation is for lower base rates.

This begs the question, what should the term premium be in a "neutral" interest-rate environment. That is, what should a lender demand for term funds lent out when the market does not expect rates to be stable over the next 12 months and not move up or down?

We can look at the 90-day money futures contracts for an idea of when this is the case. In May 2006, the outlook for base rates in USD and GBP was fairly stable. In the United States, the consenus was that rates would either top out at 5.00% or be raised one more time to 5.25% at the 29 June 2006 FOMC meeting. This is shown by the Eurodollar curve, which gives us the market expecations for forward 3-month deposit rates. Figure 10.14 shows the Eurodollar curve as at 25 May 2006.

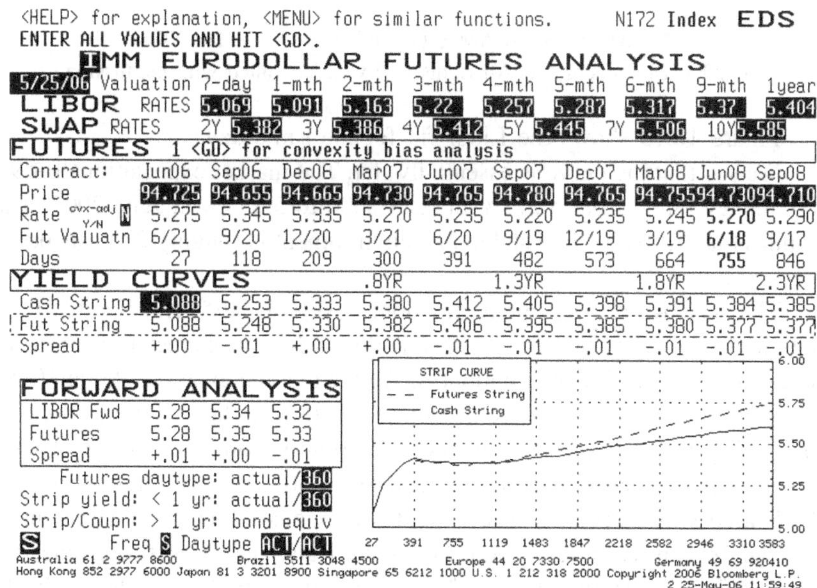

Figure 10.14 Eurodollars futures curve, as at 25 May 2006

200<GO>to view this page in Launchpad N299 Govt **BBAM**

BRITISH BANKERS' ASSOCIATION Page 1 of 4

05/25 10:58 GMT [REUTERS] [BBA LIBOR RATES] Telerate Successor Page 3750

[25/05/06] RATES AT 11:00 LONDON TIME 25/05/2006 Alternative to LIBOR01

CCY	USD	GBP	CAD	EUR	JPY	EUR 365
O/N	5.04250	4.62500	4.25000	2.61250	SN0.13625	2.64878
1WK	5.06875	4.62750	4.26667	2.62688	0.14000	2.66336
2WK	5.07375	4.63375	4.27000	2.63875	0.14500	2.67540
1MO	5.09063	4.64938	4.27333	2.75388	0.15125	2.79213
2MO	5.16313	4.67375	4.28167	2.86000	0.20750	2.89972
3MO	5.22000	4.70500	4.29167	2.91125	0.27000	2.95168
4MO	5.25688	4.73125	4.29500	2.96050	0.31000	3.00162
5MO	5.28750	4.76250	4.29917	3.01513	0.34625	3.05701
6MO	5.31688	4.79125	4.31167	3.05850	0.37938	3.10098
7MO	5.33663	4.81750	4.31667	3.09850	0.41000	3.14153
8MO	5.35313	4.84625	4.32167	3.14000	0.44188	3.18361
9MO	5.37038	4.87500	4.33000	3.18088	0.47688	3.22506
10MO	5.38350	4.90313	4.34000	3.21138	0.50688	3.25598
11MO	5.39175	4.92500	4.34667	3.24513	0.53938	3.29020
12MO	5.40375	4.95000	4.35750	3.27525	0.57438	3.32074

Australia 61 2 9777 8600 Brazil 5511 3048 4500 Europe 44 20 7330 7500 Germany 49 69 920410
Hong Kong 852 2977 6000 Japan 81 3 3201 8900 Singapore 65 6212 1000 U.S. 1 212 318 2000
3 25-May-06 11:58:35

Figure 10.15 BBAM Libor fixing as at 25 May 2006

Figure 10.15 shows the Libor fix for the same day.

We see that the curve is essentially flat. The market expectations for 90-day money range from 5.275% in June 2006 to 5.235% in June 2007. This implies that fair value in a stable rate environment is roughly 22 basis points for US dollars.[4]

The scenario in the United Kingdom is slightly different. Figure 10.16, the short-sterling curve for 25 May 2006, shows an expectation of rising base rates in the following 12 months. We see that the expected 90-day Libor fix for June 2006 is 4.72%, compared to 5.070% for June 2007. In the case of sterling there is possibly greater uncertainty compared to the United States, which was approaching the end of an obvious rising rates cycle. In the United Kingdom, only a few months previously there was commentary that the next move in rates would be down (rates had been stable since the cut to 4.50% in August 2005). This uncertainty is perhaps reflected in the term premium of 20.5 basis points – we suggest that a greater level of certainty (of the next move being a rise in rates) would have translated into a greater term premium, as we saw with USD in May 2005. Notice also how the rest of the curve is very flat after that – the June 2008 forward rate is

[4] The curve was a reasonably accurate predictor: the Fed Funds rate was indeed raised to 5.25% at the June FOMC meeting, and maintained at this rate through the rest of 2006.

5.14%, a difference of only 7 basis points from the rate implied by the June 2007 contract. This is not really meaningful since rate changes these days are usually effected in 25 basis point clips.

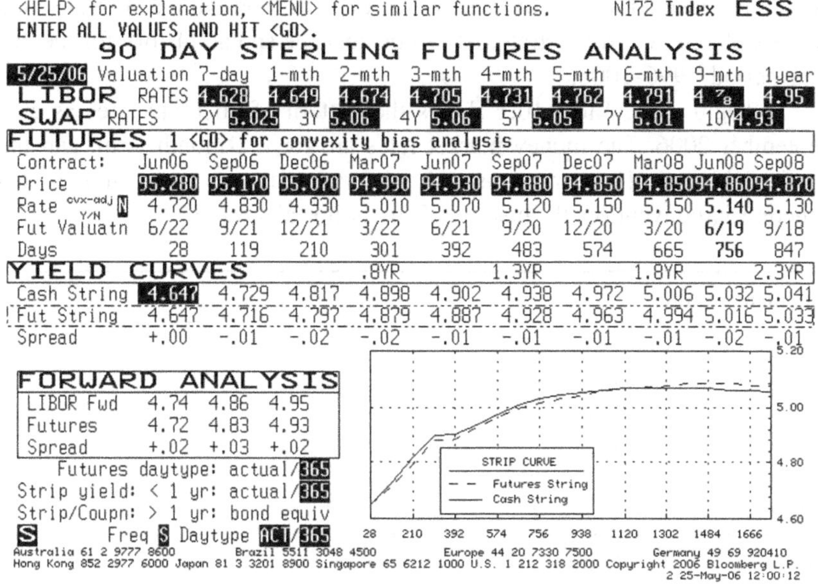

Figure 10.16 Short sterling futures curves as at 25 May 2006

In a stable interest rate environment then, we would suggest that the 90-day term premium would be between 15 and 20 basis points. This can be considered fair value. Considering the forward rates implied in Figures 10.14 and 10.16 (EDS and ESS), if we had a firm view in either direction, we would trade the contracts to reflect this. If we expect the base rate to be different at the time of the futures contract expiry, in our analysis we should logically build in a term premium to reflect this expected base rate, together with any further rate move expectations that we ourselves have.

The Fed Funds – Libor term premium[5]

We continue the discussion on the expected size of the term premium with a look at the USD Federal Funds rate ("Fed Funds") against the 1-month and

[5] With thanks to Nick Wallis, University of Nottingham Business School, for his assistance with preparing the charts in this section.

3-month USD Libor rate. Fed Funds is the US dollar base rate, and in a neutral interest-rate movement environment we would expect a spread of around 10-15 basis points for the 1-month rate and 20-25 basis points for the 3-month rate. That this is not always the case reflects the fact that the term premium is also a function of interest-rate expectations and the current shape of the yield curve. To illustrate, let us consider the spread history for the 10-year period 1996–2006.

To begin with, Table 10.1 shows the pattern of all USD rates as at 7 September 2006. The money market rates are for a 1-month term, and the bond yields are 10-year terms. We observe that the term (and credit) structure is conventionally positive. This is not always so.

One-month rates	
Treasury Bill	4.9469
CD	5.345
CP	5.24
Repo	5.22
10-year yields	
US Treasury	4.789
USD Swap	5.33
AAA	5.4387
A	5.6494
BBB	6.1196
B	8.2282

Table 10.1 USD rates as at 7 September 2006
Source: Bloomberg L.P.

That USD Libor rates are closely correlated to the Fed Funds rate would appear to be apparent from Figure 10.17, the rates spread history for the period 1996–2006. Figure 10.18 on page 470 shows high positive R^2 values for the 1-month and 3-month Libor rates when regressed against the Fed Funds rate.

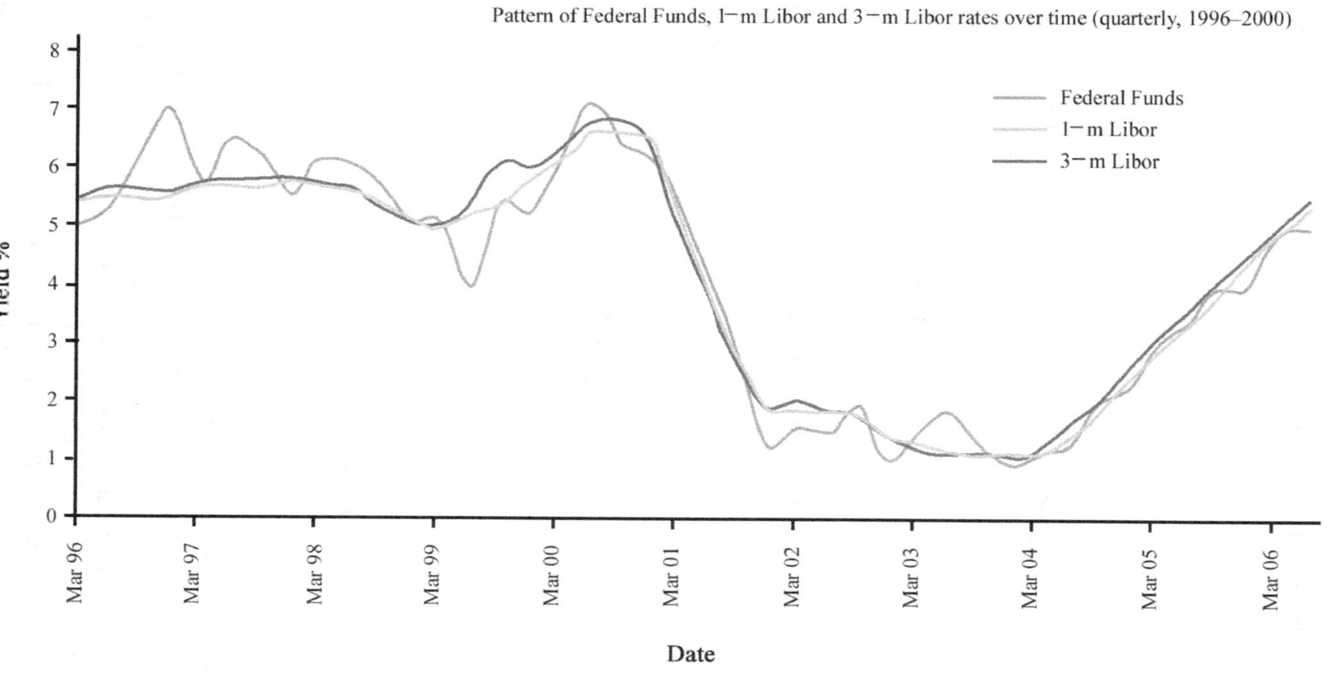

Figure 10.17 Fed Funds and USD Libor rates history, 1996–2006
Source: Bloomberg L.P.

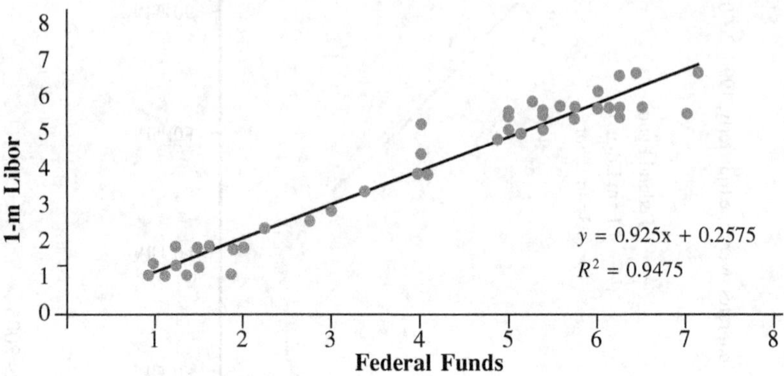

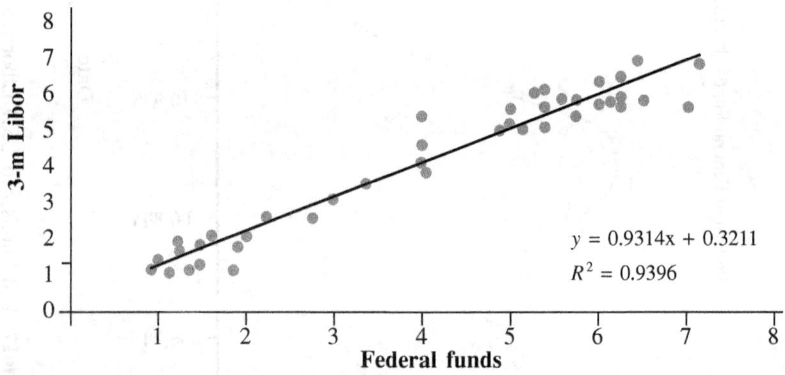

Figure 10.18 Relationship between 1-m and 3-m USD Libor to Fed Funds rate, 1996–2006

However, the term premium is not always the expected spread, and sometimes is very narrow, or even negative. The size of the premium fluctuates considerably during the period under observation, as shown at Figure 10.19. This reminds us of the importance of taking into consideration the current shape of the yield curve and the market's interest rate expectation when we analyse the term premium and our view on where this is likely to go in the near future. Incidentally, as Figure 10.19 might suggest, long-term predictions should always be taken with a pinch of salt!

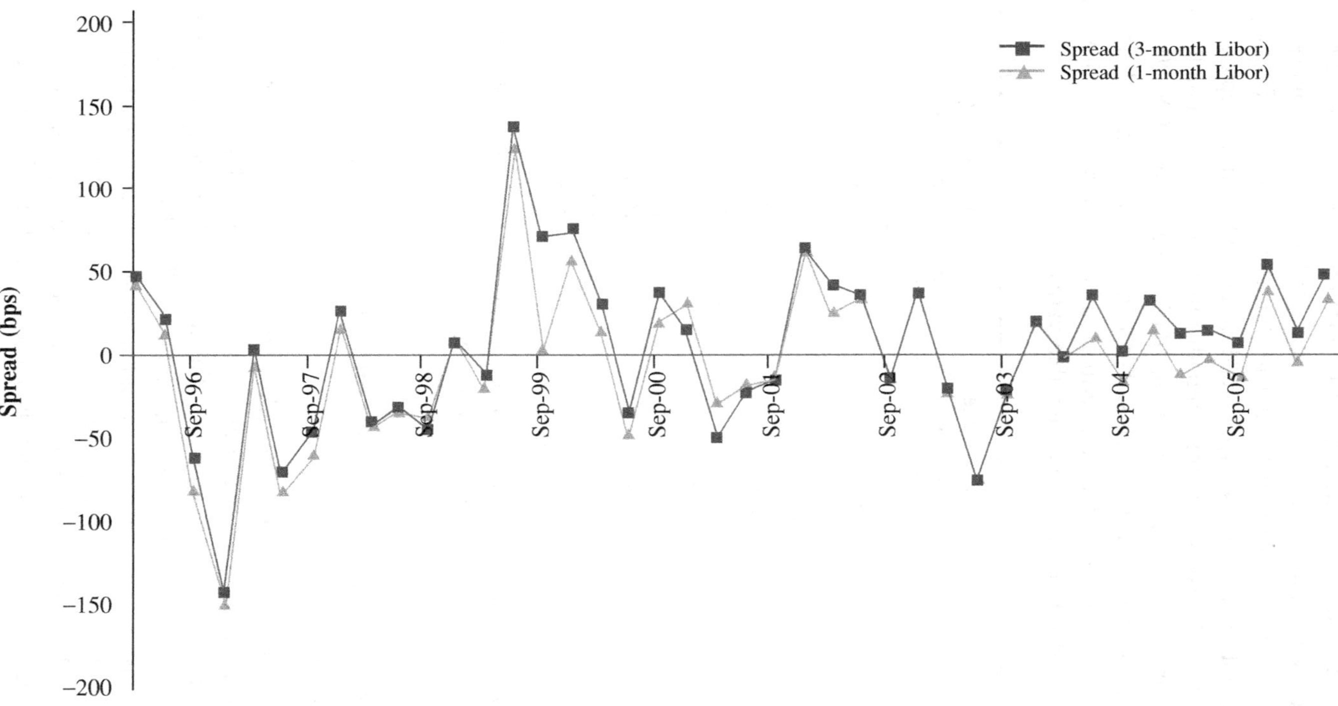

Figure 10.19 USD 1-month and 3-month Libor spread against Fed Funds, 1996–2006

Source: Bloomberg L.P.

The term premium during 2006 was within reasonable expectation, and this is not surprising as the market was still in a rising interest-rate environment, with the Fed continuing its "measured" pattern of steady 25 basis point rate rises. The average spread during 2006, up to September of that year, was 11 basis points for 1-month Libor and 32 basis points for 3-month Libor (see Table 10.2). However during the period 1996-2006 this average spread varied considerably. We conclude that while there is a reasonable expectation of what the term premium for funds should be, this expectation should allow for considerable variation.

Year	**Yearly average** (1-month Libor spread)	**Yearly average** (3-month Libor spread)
1996	–43.95	–34.57
1997	–32.81	–23.14
1998	–27.21	–27.46
1999	41.15	67.56
2000	3.52	11.42
2001	0.22	–6.28
2002	21.16	24.94
2003	–25.69	–24.52
2004	1.84	16.98
2005	2.22	21.56
2006	11.95	32.26

Table 10.2 1-month and 3-month USD Libor average yearly spread, 1996–2006
Source: Bloomberg L.P.

Impact of macro-level economic and political factors on swap spreads

Banks are an important part of the global economic system, if not the most important part. It goes without saying therefore that the efficient management of a bank's assets and liabilities feeds directly into overall economic development and national wellbeing. The Treasury or ALM desk of a bank must perforce have a keen understanding of macro-level economic factors, and the overall geo-political situation, because this drives swap spreads and the term premium. It is worth considering the impact of these factors, in general terms, on spreads and the overall level of interest rates because the ALM desk will need to take them into account as part of its strategy. Also, geo-political events often arrive unannounced – for example, the Iraqi invasion of Kuwait in 1990, the attack on the World Trade Centre in New York ("9/11"), and the conflict between Israel and Lebanese Hezbollah guerrillas in July 2006. An ability to work effectively under the circumstances prevailing in such occurrences is crucial to efficient ALM.

Events that impact the financial markets at a macro level are often termed market "shocks" or external geo-political events. Such events invariably result in higher market volatility. The immediate impact of this is a market sell-off and a "flight to quality", which is when investors move out of higher risk assets such as equities and emerging market sovereign bonds and into risk-free assets such as US Treasuries and UK gilts. This is an almost knee-jerk reaction as investors become more risk-averse.

Swap spreads, which we define as the spread between fixed-rate on a interest-rate swap over the yield of the government bond of similar maturity, reflect the market perception about the general health of the economy and its future prospects, as well as the overall macro-level geo-political situation. Because the swap curve is an indicator of interbank credit quality, the swap spread can be taken to be the market perception of the health and prospects of the interbank market specifically and the bank sector generally.

Speaking generally, swap spreads widen during periods of increased market volatility. By implication a flight-to-quality should be reflected in a widening of the spread. This is expected because investors' new risk aversion manifests itself in lower government bond yields, arising from higher demand for government bonds. However, on occasion this analysis might be overly simplistic, because other micro-level factors will still be in play and can be expected to influence market rates. How can we consider the interaction between government yields, swap rates and possible influences on the swap spread?

The research team at HBOS produced a report[6] that suggests a novel way for us to analyse this, and we summarise their findings here with permission. We require an indicator of market volatility; one measure of this for the US dollar market is the VIX index. The VIX index is produced by the Chicago Board Options Exchange (CBOE) and is a proxy measure of market volatility. It uses a weighted average of implied volatilities to calculate an estimate of future volatility. An increase in the level of the index indicates increased market volatility.

---

[6] "Geo-politics Returns to the Limelight", in *Economics Perspectives*, 8 August 2006 (HBOS Treasury Services). With thanks to Mark Miller at HBOS in London for his generous assistance.

We illustrate the relationship between geo-political events and the magnitude of the swap spread by looking at the correlation between the US dollar 10-year swap spread and the VIX index. Table 10.3 shows – as expected – a positive correlation between the VIX index and the swap spread during a period of both economic events, as well as macro-level geo-political events. For instance, the period covers the 9/11 events as well as the Ford and GM credit-rating downgrades of 2005. There is a notable exception for the period September 2001 to March 2002, when there is a negative correlation. This is our first indication that the relationship is not as simplistic as we might think. Although the geo-political situation was negative, with the events of 9/11 leading to the US war in Afghanistan, suggesting that swap spreads should widen, this was also a period of successive cuts in the US base interest rate (the "Fed rate"). During this time the swap rate fell by more than 100 basis points as the Fed rate was cut by 175 basis points. So here we observe that the impact of specific financial market factors was greater than macro-level geo-political issues. Generally though, we observe the strong positive correlation between the swap spread the volatility index.

Figure 10.20 is a chart of the spread to the level of the VIX index

Event	Correlation between VIX and 10-year swap spread	Correlation between VIX and 10-year US Treasury yield
Asian currency crisis (1997–1998)	0.71	−0.52
LTCM and Russian debt default (Jun.–Sept. 1998)	0.90	−0.78
9/11 to Afghan war (Sept. 2001–Mar. 2002)	−0.17	−0.67
Iraq War (Mar.–May 2003)	0.54	−0.08
Ford and GM credit rating downgrade (Mar.–May 2005)	0.38	−0.53

Table 10.3 Correlation between the USD 10-year swap spread and the CBOE VIX index and the 10-year US Treasury yield and the CBOE VIX index
Source: HBOS. Reproduced with permission.

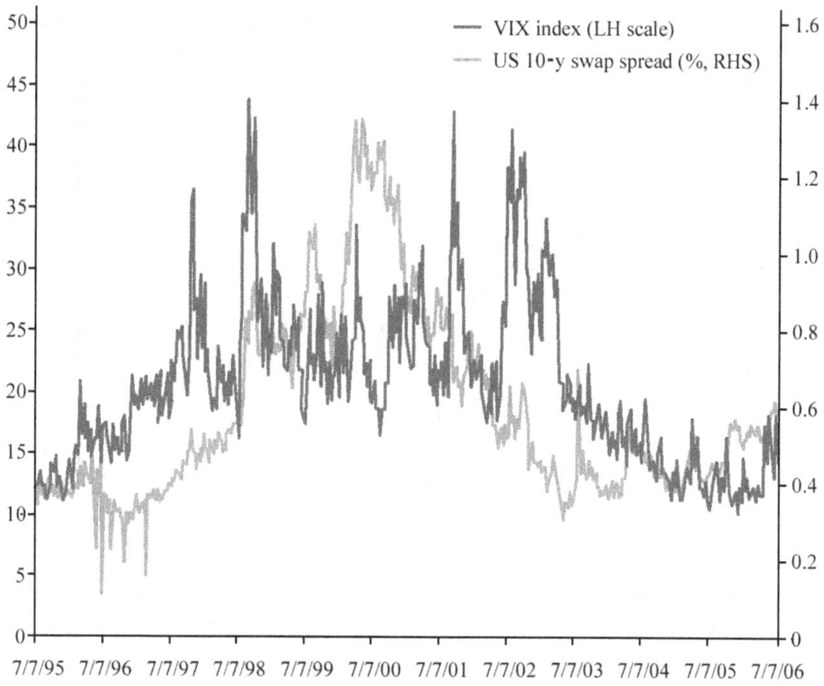

Figure 10.20 VIX index versus US 10-year swap spread
Source: HBOS. Reproduced with permission.

By the same analysis, we can expect a negative correlation between the US Treasury yield and the VIX index level. This is generally borne out in Table 10.3. However, as with the case of the swap spread correlation, we see an occasion when other factors impact the correlation value. The low negative value for the period in 2003 leading up to and after the second Iraq war shows other factors influencing the Treasury yield. The authors of the HBOS report suggest that the flight-to-quality had taken place before the war actually began and was fully priced-in to Treasury yields.

Figure 10.21 on page 476 illustrates the lower government bond yields that are observed at times of higher market volatility.

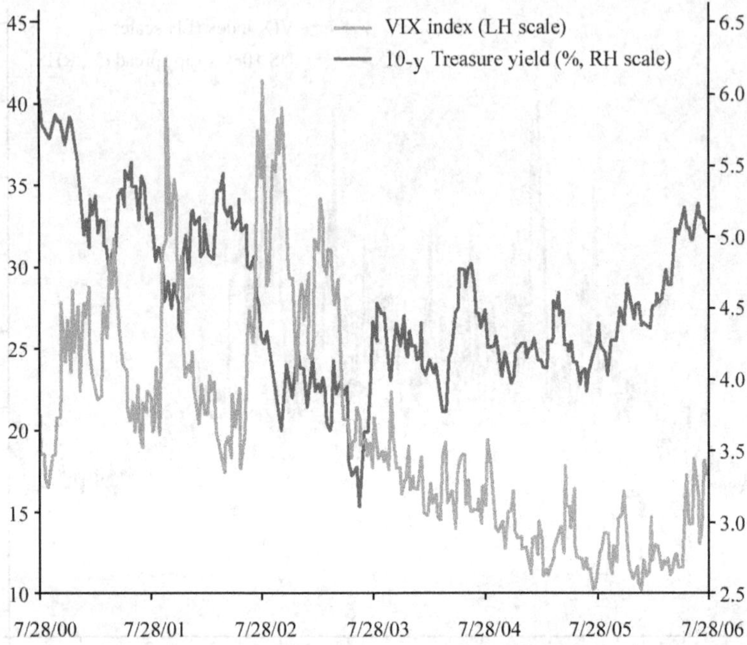

Figure 10.21 VIX index versus US 10-year Treasury
Source: HBOS. Reproduced with permission.

The purpose of the foregoing has been to illustrate how the swap spread interacts with macro-level geo-political factors. However, even during periods of high market tension, characterised by high levels of market volatility, the swap spread will respond also to more micro-level financial factors. ALM practitioners need to be aware of the nature of this interaction, and allow for this in their strategy and planning.

CHAPTER

11

Introduction to Relative Spread Analysis

We conclude Part II with a look at relative value analysis. This may seem slightly out of place in this book, especially in Part II, but we cover this subject here because actually we feel it is closely related to the previous two chapters. That makes an understanding of it vital to efficient ALM practice.

In Chapter 10 we discussed the determinants of the swap spread, as well as the expected magnitude of the money market term premium. The swap spread is a measure of the level of swap rates over and above risk-free rates. As such it is in essence the term Libor rate (beyond the 12-month term, the point at which formal Libor fixes end). This rate feeds into a bank's cost of funding, the rate at which it can hedge interest-rate exposure. To meet the target rate of return objectives, assets generally need to earn a spread over this cost of funding. For instance, it is common for bank Treasury desks to maintain a book of FRNs for liquidity purposes. In some cases a portion of the bank's capital may be invested in such bonds. The book will be required to meet a target rate of return, which might be x basis points above the cost of capital. This requires that the Treasury desk assess the relative spread earned by the FRN book (and individual FRNs) over the bank's funding costs. Hence, relative spreads analysis becomes important to the Treasury desk. This is only one example. There are many applications of this analysis; as a result, it is necessary to include an introduction to this subject here.

Relative value analysis: bond spreads

Investors measure the perceived market value, or relative value, of a corporate bond by measuring its yield spread relative to a designated benchmark. This is the spread over the benchmark that gives the yield of the corporate bond. A key measure of relative value of a corporate bond is its swap spread. This is the basis point spread over the interest-rate swap curve, and is a measure of the credit risk of the bond. In its simplest form, the swap spread can be measured as the difference between the YTM of the bond and the interest rate given by a straight-line interpolation of the swap curve. In practice traders use the asset-swap spread and the Z-spread as the main measures of relative value. The government bond spread is also used. In addition, now that the market in synthetic corporate credit is well established, using credit derivatives and credit default swaps (CDS), investors consider the cash-CDS spread as well, which is known as the *basis*.

Credit derivatives are introduced in Chapter 16 of this book; readers also may wish to read the author's book on credit derivatives (Choudhry 2004b) as well as his paper on the CDS basis (Choudhry 2004a).

The spread that is selected is an indication of the relative value of the bond, and a measure of its credit risk. The greater the perceived risk, the greater the spread should be. This is best illustrated by the credit structure of interest rates, which will (generally) show AAA– and AA-rated bonds trading at the lowest spreads, and BBB–, BB– and lower-rated bonds trading at the highest spreads. Bond spreads are the most commonly used indication of the risk-return profile of a bond.

In this section we consider the swap and Treasury spread, asset swap spread, Z-spread, and cash-CDS basis.

Swap spread and Treasury spread

A bond's swap spread is a measure of the credit risk of that bond, relative to the interest-rate swaps market. Because the swaps market is traded by banks, this risk is effectively the interbank market, so the credit risk of the bond over-and-above bank risk is given by its spread over swaps. This is a simple calculation to make, and is simply the yield of the bond minus the swap rate for the appropriate maturity swap. Figure 11.1 shows Bloomberg page IRSB for pounds sterling as at 10 August 2005. This shows the GBP swap curve on the left-hand side. The right-hand side of the screen shows the swap rates' spread over UK gilts. It is the spread over these swap rates that would provide the simplest relative value measure for corporate bonds denominated in GBP. If the bond has an odd maturity, say 5.5 years, we would interpolate between the five-year and six-year swap rates.

GRAB Govt IRSB

British Pound

Ticker	TIME	Bid	Ask	Change	Open	High	Low	Prev Cls
GBP Swap Rates								
2) 1 YR	11:22	4.4940	4.5020	--	4.4980	4.5005	4.4870	4.4980
3) 18 MO	11:22	4.3925	4.4225	-.0087	4.4150	4.4175	4.3950	4.4163
4) 2 YR	11:18	4.4070	4.4150	-.0055	4.4150	4.4225	4.3975	4.4175
5) 3 YR	11:23	4.4110	4.4350	-.0008	4.4225	4.4275	4.4000	4.4238
6) 4 YR	11:23	4.4150	4.4150	-.0118	4.4250	4.4515	4.4085	4.4263
7) 5 YR	11:23	4.4230	4.4240	-.0127	4.4350	4.4370	4.4125	4.4363
8) 6 YR	11:23	4.4340	4.4625	-.0030	4.4500	4.4550	4.4233	4.4513
9) 7 YR	11:23	4.4440	4.4520	-.0157	4.4600	4.4690	4.4355	4.4638
10) 8 YR	11:23	4.4520	4.4590	-.0158	4.4675	4.4750	4.4422	4.4713
11) 9 YR	11:23	4.4580	4.4630	-.0157	4.4725	4.4800	4.4478	4.4763
12) 10 YR	11:23	4.4610	4.4640	-.0138	4.4750	4.4840	4.4550	4.4763
13) 12 YR	11:23	4.4610	4.4640	-.0138	4.4750	4.4750	4.4585	4.4763
14) 15 YR	11:23	4.4520	4.4550	-.0128	4.4650	4.4735	4.4335	4.4663
15) 20 YR	11:23	4.4210	4.4230	-.0118	4.4325	4.5250	4.3912	4.4338
16) 25 YR	11:21	4.3175	4.4475	-.0125	4.3975	4.4367	4.3763	4.3963
17) 30 YR	11:21	4.3430	4.3550	-.0078	4.3550	4.4500	4.3225	4.3588

Page 1

Ticker	TIME	Bid	Ask	Change	Open	High	Low	Prev Cls
GBP Swap Spread								
19) 1 YR	11:22	33.80	39.80	+2.10	31.40	33.80	29.90	31.7000
20) 2 YR	11:21	29.50	33.50	+1.00	29.00	32.25	28.50	30.5000
21) 3 YR	11:21	31.00	35.00	+.75	30.75	33.25	30.00	32.2500
22) 4 YR	11:23	30.50	35.50	+.50	30.50	33.25	30.00	32.5000
23) 5 YR	11:14	26.50	36.00	-4.50	30.50	30.50	28.50	33.0000
24) 6 YR	11:23	32.75	37.75	+.50	32.50	35.50	32.50	34.7500
25) 7 YR	11:23	32.00	37.00	+.50	32.00	34.75	32.00	34.0000
26) 8 YR	11:21	31.00	36.00	+.50	30.75	33.75	30.75	33.0000
27) 9 YR	11:21	29.75	34.75	+.50	29.75	32.50	29.75	31.7500
28) 10 YR	8:05	29.75	34.75	+.25	32.25	32.50	32.25	32.0000
29) 15 YR	11:21	22.75	31.75	+.25	27.25	28.00	27.00	27.0000
30) 20 YR	11:21	19.00	32.00	+.13	25.50	26.00	25.25	25.3750
31) 30 YR	11:23	14.75	27.50	+.25	21.00	21.50	20.63	20.8750

For UK Govt Yield Curve, Click on any Tickers above & Select: IYC1 I22

For GBP Swap Curve, Click on any Tickers above & Select: IYC1 I55

Page 2

Australia 61 2 9777 8600 Brazil 5511 3048 4500 Europe 44 20 7330 7500 Germany 49 69 920410
Hong Kong 852 2977 6000 Japan 81 3 3201 8900 Singapore 65 6212 1000 U.S. 1 212 318 2000
2 22-Sep-05 11:23:44

Figure 11.1 Bloomberg page IRSB for pounds sterling, showing GBP swap rates and swap spread over UK gilts, 10 August 2005

The spread over swaps is sometimes called the *I-spread*. It has a simple relationship to swaps and Treasury yields, shown here in the equation for corporate bond yield:

$$Y = I + S + T$$

where

Y is the yield on the corporate bond
I is the I-spread or spread over swap
S is the swap spread
T is the yield on the Treasury security (or an interpolated yield).

In other words, the swap rate itself is given by $T + S$.

The I-spread is sometimes used to compare a cash bond with its equivalent CDS price, but for straightforward relative value analysis, it is usually dropped in favour of the asset-swap spread, which we look at later in this section.

Of course, the basic relative value measure is the Treasury spread or government bond spread. This is simply the spread of the bond yield over the yield of the appropriate government bond. Again, an interpolated yield may need to be used to obtain the right Treasury rate to use. The bond spread is given by:

$$BS = Y - T.$$

Using an interpolated yield is not strictly accurate because yield curves are smooth in shape and so straight-line interpolation will produce slight errors. The method is still commonly used though.

Asset-swap spread

An asset swap is a package that combines an interest-rate swap with a cash bond, the effect of the combined package being to transform the interest-rate basis of the bond. Typically, a fixed-rate bond will be combined with an interest-rate swap in which the bondholder pays fixed coupon and receives floating coupon. The floating-coupon will be a spread over Libor (see Choudhry et al. 2001). This spread is the asset-swap spread and is a function of the credit risk of the bond over and above interbank credit risk.[1] Asset swaps may be transacted at par or at the bond's market price, usually par. This means that the asset swap value is made up of the difference between the bond's market price and par, as well as the difference between the bond coupon and the swap fixed rate.

The zero-coupon curve is used in the asset swap valuation. This curve is derived from the swap curve, so it is the implied zero-coupon curve (see Chapter 9). The asset swap spread is the spread that equates the difference between the present value of the bond's cash flows, calculated using the swap zero rates, and the market price of the bond. This spread is a function of the bond's market price and yield, its cash flows and the implied zero-coupon interest rates.[2]

Figure 11.2 shows the Bloomberg screen ASW for a GBP-denominated bond, GKN Holdings 7% 2012, as at 10 August 2005. We see that the asset-swap spread is 121.5 basis points. This is the spread over Libor that will be

[1] This is because in the interbank market, two banks transacting an interest-rate swap will be paying/receiving the fixed rate and receiving/paying Libor-flat. See also the author's "Learning Curve" article on asset swaps available on www.yieldcurve.com

[2] Bloomberg refers to this spread as the Gross Spread.

received if the bond is purchased in an asset-swap package. In essence, the asset-swap spread measures the difference between the market price of the bond and the value of the bond when cash flows have been valued using zero-coupon rates. The asset-swap spread can therefore be regarded as the coupon of an annuity in the swap market that equals this difference.

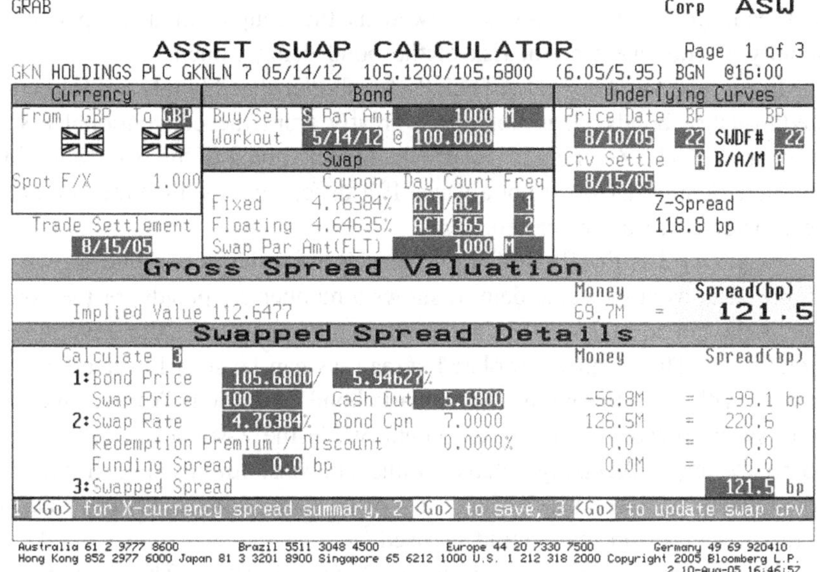

Figure 11.2 Bloomberg page ASW for GKN bond, 10 August 2005
© Bloomberg LP. Used with permission. Visit www.bloomberg.com

Z-spread

The conventional approach for analysing an asset swap uses the bond's YTM in calculating the spread. The assumptions implicit in the YTM calculation (see Chapter 4) make this spread problematic for relative value analysis, so market practitioners use what is termed the Z-spread instead. The Z-spread uses the zero-coupon yield curve to calculate spread, so it is a more realistic, and effective, spread to use. The zero-coupon curve used in the calculation is derived from the interest-rate swap curve.

Put simply, the Z-spread is the basis point spread that would need to be added to the implied spot yield curve such that the discounted cash flows of a bond are equal to its present value (its current market price). Each bond cash flow is discounted by the relevant spot rate for its maturity term. How does this differ from the conventional asset-swap spread? Essentially, in its use of zero-coupon rates when assigning a value to a bond. Each cash flow is discounted using its own particular zero-coupon rate. The price of a bond's price at any time can be taken to be the market's value of the bond's cash flows. Using the Z-spread we can quantify what the swap market thinks of this value; that is, by how much the conventional spread differs from the Z-spread. Both spreads can be viewed as the coupon of a swap market annuity of equivalent credit risk of the bond being valued.

In practice the Z-spread, especially for shorter-dated bonds and for better credit-quality bonds, does not differ greatly from the conventional asset-swap spread. The Z-spread is usually the higher spread of the two, following the logic of spot rates, but not always. If it differs greatly, then the bond can be considered to be mispriced.

Figure 11.3 is the Bloomberg screen YAS for the same bond shown in Figure 11.2, as at the same date. It shows a number of spreads for the bond. The main spread of 151.00 basis points is the spread over the government yield curve. This is an interpolated spread, as can be seen lower down the screen, with the appropriate benchmark bond identified. We see that the asset-swap spread is 121.6 basis points, while the Z-spread is 118.8 basis points. When undertaking relative value analysis, for instance if making comparisons against cash funding rates or the same company name CDS, it is this lower spread that should be used.[3]

The same screen can be used to check spread history. This is shown in Figure 11.4, the Z-spread graph for the GKN bond for the six months prior to our calculation date.

3 On the date in question the 10-year CDS for this reference entity was quoted as 96.8 basis points, which is an example of a negative basis, in this case of –22 basis points.

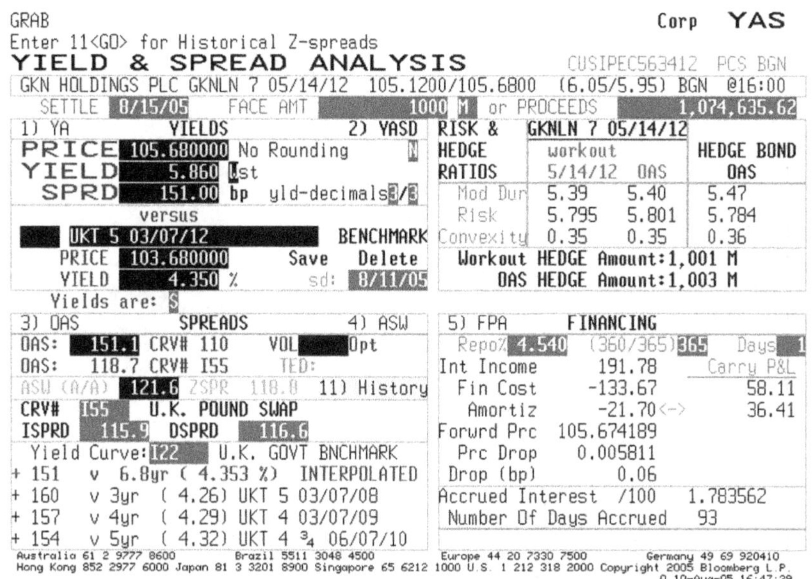

Figure 11.3 Bloomberg page YAS for GKN bond, 10 August 2005

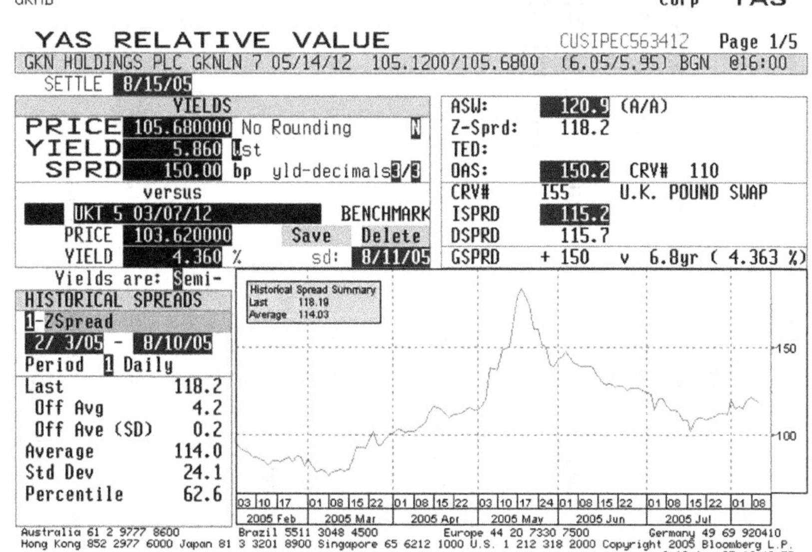

Figure 11.4 Bloomberg page YAS for GKN bond, 10 August 2005 showing Z-spread history

A1	B	C	D	E	F	G	H	I
2	**Issuer**		**XYZ plc**					
3	Settlement date		6/1/05					
4	Maturity date		6/1/08					
5	Coupon		5%	**YIELD**	**0.05635**			
6	Price		98.95	[Cell formula =YIELD(C4,C5,C6,C7,C8,C9,C10)]				
7	Par		100					
8	Semi-annual coupon		2	**PRICE**	**98.95000**			
9	act/act		1	[Cell formula =PRICE(C4,C5,C6,C6,C8,C9,C10)]				
10								
11	Bond yield		5.635%					
12	Sovereign bond yield		4.880%					
13	Swap rate (S)		5.200%					
14								
15	3-year CDS price		28 bps					
16								
17	**Treasury spread**							
18	5.635–4.88		55 bps					
19								
20	**I-spread**							
21	5.635–5.20		43.5 bps					
22								
23	**Z-spread (Z)**		19.4 bps	0.00194				
24	The Z-spread is found using iteration							

Continued from pp. 455

25								
26								**Sum of PVs**
27	Cash flow date	12/1/05	6/1/06	12/1/06	6/1/07	12/1/07	6/1/08	
28	Cash flow maturity (years)	0.50	1.00	1.50	2.00	2.50	3.00	
29	0.5-year swap rate (S)	4.31%	4.84%	4.99%	5.09%	5.18%	5.20%	
30	Cash flow (CF)	2.50	2.50	2.50	2.50	2.50	102.50	
31	Discount factor	0.97797598	0.951498751	0.926103469	0.900947692	0.875835752	0.852419659	
32	(DF calculation)	1/(1+(S+Z)/2)^1	1/(1+(S+Z)/2)^2	1/(1+(S+Z)/2)^3	1/(1+(S+Z)/2)^4	1/(1+(S+Z)/2)^5	1/(1+(S+Z)/2)^6	
33	CF present value (PV)	2.445	2.379	2.315	2.252	2.190	87.373	**98.95**
34								
35								
36								
37	A Z-spread of 19.4 basis points gives us the current bond price so is the correct one							
38	Using this value, the sum of all the discounted cash flows is equal to the market price							
39								
40	**CDS Basis**							
41	28–19.4	8.6 bps						
42	The basis is positive in this example							

Figure 11.5 Calculating the Z-spread, hypothetical 5% 2008 bond issued by XYZ plc

Z-spread is closely related to the bond price, as shown by equation (11.1),

$$P = \sum_{i=1}^{n}\left[\frac{C_i + M_i}{(1 + ((Z + S_i + T_i)/m))^i}\right] \quad (11.1)$$

where

n is the number of interest periods until maturity
P is the bond price
C is the coupon
M is the redemption payment (so bond cash flow is all C plus M)
Z is the Z-spread
m is the frequency of coupon payments.

In effect this is the standard bond price equation with the discount rate adjusted by whatever the Z-spread is; it is an iterative calculation. The appropriate maturity swap rate is used, which is the essential difference between the I-spread and the Z-spread. This is deemed to be more accurate, because the entire swap curve is taken into account rather than just one point on it. In practice though, as we have seen in the example above, there is often little difference between the two spreads.

To reiterate then, using the correct Z-spread, the sum of the bond's discounted cash flows will be equal to the current price of the bond.

We illustrate the Z-spread calculation at Figure 11.5. This is done using a hypothetical bond, the XYZ plc 5% of June 2008, a three-year bond at the time of the calculation. Market rates for swaps, Treasury and CDS are also shown. We require the spread over the swaps curve that equates the present values of the cash flows to the current market price. The cash flows are discounted using the appropriate swap rate for each cash flow maturity. With a bond yield of 5.635%, we see that the I-spread is 43.5 basis points, while the Z-spread is 19.4 basis points. In practice the difference between these two spreads is rarely this large.

For the readers' benefit we also show the Excel formula in Figure 11.5. This shows how the Z-spread is calculated; for ease of illustration we have assumed that the calculation takes place for value on a coupon date, so that we have precisely an even period to maturity.

Cash-CDS basis

The basis is the difference between a bond's asset-swap spread, or alternatively its Z-spread, and the CDS price for the same bond issuer. So the basis is given by:

$$B = D - I$$

where D is the CDS price. Where $D - I > 0$ it is a positive basis; the opposite is a negative basis.

Figure 11.6 shows page G <go> on Bloomberg, set up to show the Z-spread and CDS price history for the GKN 2012 bond, for the period March–September 2005. We can select the "Table" option to obtain the actual values, which can then be used to plot the basis. This is shown in Figure 11.7 on page 488, for the period 22 August to 22 September 2005. Notice how the basis was always negative during August–September; we see from Figure 11.7 that earlier in the year the basis had briefly been positive. Changes in the basis give rise to arbitrage opportunities between the cash and synthetic markets. This is discussed in greater detail in Choudhry (2004b).

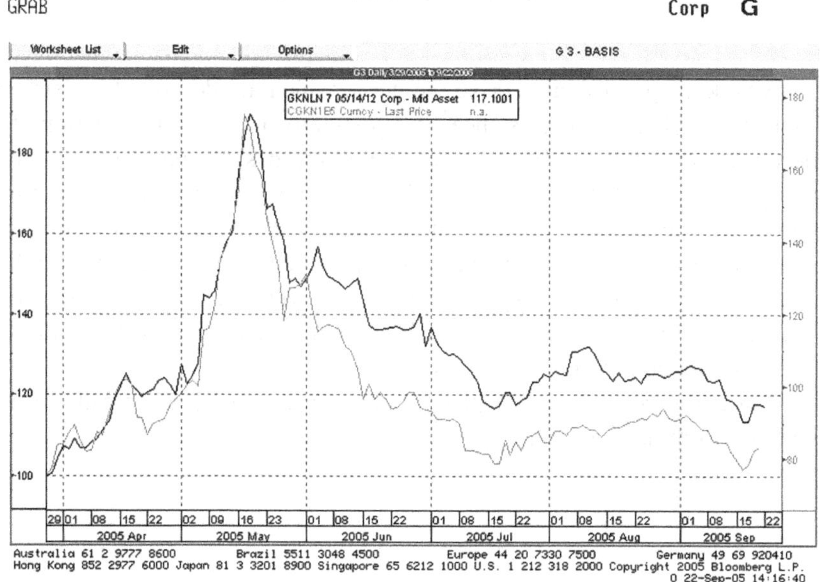

Figure 11.6 Bloomberg graph using screen G <go>, plot of asset-swap spread and CDS price for GKN bond, April–September 2005

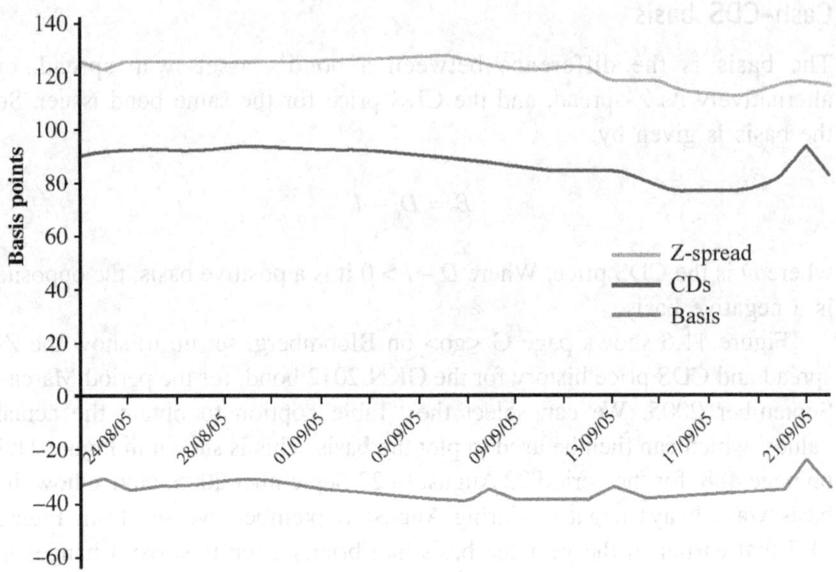

Figure 11.7 GKN bond, CDS basis during August–September 2005
Data source: Bloomberg L.P.

A wide range of factors drive the basis, which are described in detail in Choudhry (2004a). The existence of a non-zero basis has implications for the investment strategy. For instance, when the basis is negative investors may prefer to hold the cash bond, whereas if for liquidity, supply or other reasons, if the basis is positive the investor may wish to hold the asset synthetically, by selling protection using a credit default swap. Another approach is to arbitrage between the cash and synthetic markets, in the case of a negative basis by buying the cash bond and shorting it synthetically by buying protection in the CDS market.

Thus, we see that market practitioners have a range of spreads to use when performing their relative value analysis.

References and bibliography

Choudhry, M. 2004a, "The Credit Default Swap Basis: Analysing the Relationship Between Cash and Synthetic Credit Markets", *Journal of Derivatives Use, Trading and Regulation*, Vol. 10, No. 1, pp. 8–26.

Choudhry, M. 2004b, *Structured Credit Products: Credit Derivatives and Synthetic Securitisation*, John Wiley & Sons, Singapore.

Choudhry, M., Joannas, D., Pereira, R. and Pienaar, R. 2001, *Capital Market Instruments: Analysis and Valuation*, FT Prentice Hall, London.

Cohen, J., Zinbarg, E. and Zeikel, A. 1977, *Investment Analysis and Portfolio Management*, Richard D Irwin, New York.

S&P, *Credit Week*, 8 November 1993, Standard & Poor's.

S&P, *Credit Week*, 15 October 1999, Standard & Poor's.

Mills, R. 1994, *Strategic Value Analysis*, Mars Business Associates, Oxford.

Wilson, R. and Fabozzi F. 1996, *Corporate Bonds: Structures and Analysis*, FJF Associates, New Hope, PA.

Hi, Chaz. Moorad said I should sit here for a while to learn trading tips

He did, did he? Well, here's my number one tip..

DON'T SIT NEXT TO ME!

PART

III

Financial Instruments, Applications and Hedging

In Part III we drill down into the banking discipline, with a look at specific instruments. We look in detail at hedging instruments, both for interest-rate risk and credit risk. So we consider interest-rate derivatives such as futures, forward rate agreements (FRAs) and interest-rate swaps. We also look at credit derivatives, and introduce credit risk and credit value-at-risk. The use of these instruments for hedging applications is described and illustrated. Much ALM practice revolves around hedging risk exposure, making use of the instruments we discuss in the following chapters.

We begin, however, with a detailed look at repo, which warrants its own chapter separate to our earlier chapter on money market instruments.

PART III

Financial Instruments: Applications and Hedging

In Part III we drill down into the banking discipline, with a look at specific instruments. We look in detail at hedging instruments, both for interest-rate risk and credit risk, so we consider interest-rate derivatives such as futures, forward rate agreements (FRAs) and interest-rate swaps. We also look at credit derivatives, and introduce credit risk and credit value-at-risk. The use of these instruments for hedging applications is described and illustrated. Much of ALM practice revolves around hedging risk exposure, making use of the instruments we discuss in the following chapters.

We begin, however, with a detailed look at repo, which warrants its own chapter separate to our earlier chapter on money market instruments.

CHAPTER 12

Repo Instruments

One of the largest segments of the money markets worldwide is the market in repurchase agreements or *repo*. A most efficient mechanism by which to finance asset positions, repo transactions enable market-makers to take long and short positions in a flexible manner, buying and selling according to customer demand on a relatively small capital base. Repo is also a flexible and relatively safe investment opportunity for investors such as money market funds and corporate and local authority treasurers. The ability to execute repo is particularly important to overseas firms who might not have access to a domestic deposit base; where no repo market exists, funding is in the form of unsecured lines of credit from the banking system, which is restrictive for some market participants. An open market in repo, and its close cousin securities lending, is often cited as a key ingredient of a liquid equity and bond market. Repo is therefore a very important instrument.

In the United States, Europe and many countries in Asia repo is a well-established alternative money market instrument. By providing ready access to secured borrowing, and by enhancing liquidity in the securities markets, repo facilitates portfolio financing and the ability to run a short position in any bond. Banks can also use repo to extend credit to securities houses, who provide collateral in the form of government bonds and other high-quality bonds. In this chapter we review the main uses of repo and its structure.

Introduction to repo

A repo agreement is a transaction in which one party sells securities to another, and at the same time, and as part of the same transaction commits to repurchase identical securities on a specified date at a specified price. The seller delivers securities and receives cash from the buyer. The cash is supplied at a predetermined rate – the *repo rate* – that remains constant during the term of the trade. On maturity the original seller receives back collateral of equivalent type and quality, and returns the cash plus repo interest. One party to the repo requires either the cash or the securities and provides *collateral* to the other party, as well as some form of compensation for the temporary use of the desired asset. Although legal title to the securities is transferred, the seller/lender retains both the economic benefits and the market risk of owning them. The purpose of the transaction of course is to provide secured lending of cash.

There are two main repo types in operation in different markets, to begin with we shall consider the operation of a *classic* repo, the type prevalent in the UK and US bond markets.

Repo fundamentals

Repo is a short-term secured cash instrument that should always be labelled as part of the money markets. There is a wide range of uses to which repo might be put. Structured transactions that are very similar to repo include total return swaps, and other structured repo trades include floating-rate repo, which contains an option to switch to a fixed rate at a later date. In the equity market, repo is often conducted in a basket of stocks, which might be constituent stocks in an index such as the FTSE100 or CAC40, or user-specified baskets. Market-makers borrow and lend equities with differing terms to maturity, and generally the credit rating of the institution involved in the repo transaction is of more importance than the quality of the collateral. Central banks' use of repo also reflects its importance; it is a key instrument in the implementation of monetary policy in many countries. Essentially then, repo markets have vital links and relationships with global money markets, bond markets, futures markets, swap markets and OTC interest-rate derivatives.

Key features

Repo is essentially a secured loan. The term comes from *sale and repurchase agreement*; however, this is not necessarily the best way to look at it. Although in a *classic repo* transaction the legal title of an asset is transferred from the "seller" to the "buyer" during the term of the repo, in the author's opinion this detracts from the essence of the instrument: a secured loan of cash. It is therefore a money market instrument.

There are a number of benefits in using repo, which concurrently have been behind its rapid growth. These include the following:

- market-makers generally are able to finance their long bond and equity positions at a lower interest cost if they repo out the assets; equally they are able to cover short positions;
- there is greater liquidity in specific individual bond issues;
- greater market liquidity lowers the cost of raising funds for capital market borrowers;
- central banks are able to use repo in their open market operations;
- repo reduces *counterparty risk* in money market borrowing and lending, because of the security offered by the collateral given in the loan;
- investors have an added investment option when placing funds;
- institutional investors and other long-term holders of securities are able to enhance their returns by making their inventories available for repo trading.

The maturity of the majority of repo transactions are between overnight and three months, although trades of six months and one year are not uncommon. It is possible to transact in longer-term repo as well. Because of this, repo is best seen as a money market product.[1] However, because of the nature of the collateral, repo market participants must keep a close eye on the market of the asset collateral, whether this is the government bond market, Eurobonds, equity or another asset.[2] The counterparties to a repo transaction will have different requirements; for instance, to "borrow" a particular asset against an interest in lending cash. For this reason it is common to hear participants talk of trades being *stock-driven* or *cash-driven.* A corporate treasurer who invests cash while receiving some form of security is driving a cash-driven repo, whereas a market-maker who wishes to cover a short position in a particular stock, against which he or she lends cash, is entering into a stock-driven trade.

---

[1] The textbook definition of a "money market" instrument is of a debt product issued with between one day and one year to maturity, while debt instruments of greater than one-year maturity are known as capital market instruments. In practice, the money market desks of most banks will trade the yield curve to up to two years' maturity, so it makes sense to view a money market instrument as being of up to two years' maturity.

[2] This carries on to a bank's organisation structure. In most banks, the repo desk for bonds is situated in the money markets area, while in others it will be part of the bond division (the author has experience of banks employing each system). Equity repo is often situated as part of the back office settlement or Treasury function.

There is a close relationship between repo and both the bond and money markets. The use of repo has contributed greatly to the liquidity of government, Eurobond and emerging market bond markets. Although it is a separate and individual market itself, operationally repo is straightforward to handle, in that it generally settles through clearing mechanisms used for bonds.

Financial institutions will engage in both repo and reverse repo trades. Investors also, despite their generic name, will be involved in both repo and reverse repo. Their money market funds will be cash-rich and engage in investment trades; at the same time they will run large fixed-interest portfolios, the returns for which can be enhanced through trading in repo. Central banks are major players in repo markets and use repo as part of daily liquidity or *open market* operations, and as a tool of monetary policy.

Repo itself is an OTC market conducted over the telephone, with rates displayed on screens. These screens are supplied by both brokers and market-makers themselves. Increasingly, electronic dealing systems are being used, with live dealing rates displayed on screen and trades being conducted at the click of a mouse button.

There are three main basic types of repo: the *classic* repo, the *sell/buy-back* and *tri-party repo*. A sell/buy-back, referred to in some markets as a *buy–sell*, is a spot sale and the repurchase of assets are transacted simultaneously. It does not require a dealing and settlement system that can handle the concept of a classic repo and is often found in emerging markets. A classic repo is economically identical but the repo rate is explicit and the transaction is conducted under a legal agreement that defines the legal transfer of ownership of the asset during the term of the trade. Classic repo, the type of transaction that originated in the United States, is a sale and repurchase of an asset where the repurchase price is unchanged from the "sale" price. Hence, the transaction is better viewed as a loan and borrowing of cash. In a tri-party repo a third party acts as an agent on behalf of both seller and buyer of the asset, but otherwise the instrument is identical to classic repo.

Figure 12.1 illustrates the variety of assets used in repo transactions during 2002.

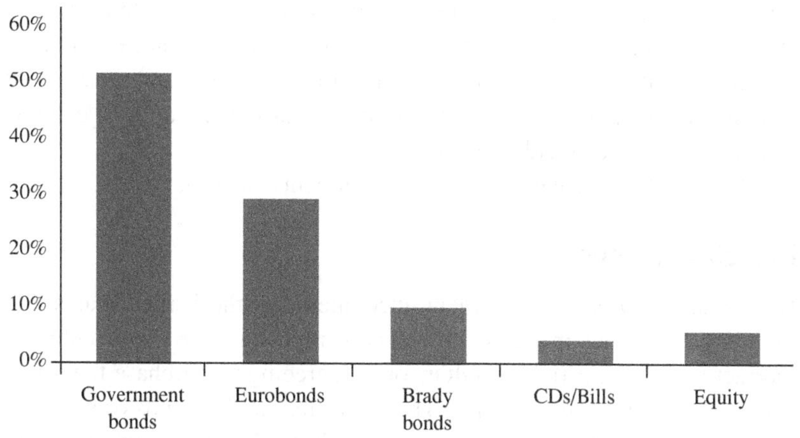

Figure 12.1 Assets used in repo transactions during 2002
Source: ISMA

Repo instruments

A repo agreement is a transaction in which one party sells securities to another, and at the same time and as part of the same transaction commits to repurchase identical securities on a specified date at a specified price. The seller delivers securities and receives cash from the buyer. The cash is supplied at a predetermined rate of interest – *the repo rate* – that remains constant during the term of the trade. On maturity the original seller receives back collateral of equivalent type and quality, and returns the cash plus repo interest. One party to the repo requires either the cash or the securities and provides *collateral* to the other party, as well as some form of compensation for the temporary use of the desired asset. Although legal title to the securities is transferred, the seller retains both the economic benefits and the market risk of owning them. This means that "sellers" will suffer losses if the market value of the collateral drops during the term of the repo, as they still retain beneficial ownership of the collateral. The "buyers" in a repo are not affected in profit/loss account terms if the value of the collateral drops, although as we shall see later, there will be other concerns for the buyer if this happens.

We have given here the legal definition of repo. However, the purpose of the transaction as we have described above is to borrow or lend cash, which is why we have used inverted commas when referring to sellers and buyers. The "sellers" of stock are really interested in borrowing cash, on which they will pay interest at a specified interest rate. The "buyers" require security or *collateral* against the loan they have advanced, and/or the specific security to borrow for a period of time. The first and most important thing to state is that repo is a secured loan of cash, and would be categorised as a money market yield instrument.[3]

We now look at the main repo instruments in turn.

The classic repo

The *classic repo* is the instrument encountered in the United States, United Kingdom and other markets. In a classic repo one party will enter into a contract to sell securities, simultaneously agreeing to purchase them back at a specified future date and price. The securities can be bonds or equities, but also money market instruments such as T-bills. The buyer of the securities is handing over cash, which on the termination of the trade will be returned to them, and on which they will receive interest.

The seller in a classic repo is selling or *offering* stock, and therefore receiving cash, whereas the buyer is buying or *bidding* for stock, and consequently paying cash. So if the one-week repo interest rate is quoted by a market-making bank as "$5^1/_2 - 5^1/_4$", this means that the market-maker will bid for stock – that is, lend the cash – at 5.50% and offer stock or pay interest on borrowed cash at 5.25%. In some markets the quote is reversed.

Illustration of classic repo

There will be two parties to a repo trade, let us say Bank A (the seller of securities) and Bank B (the buyer of securities). On the trade date the two banks enter into an agreement whereby on a set date, the *value* or *settlement* date Bank A will sell to Bank B a nominal amount of securities in exchange for cash.[4] The price received for the securities is the market price of the stock on the value date. The agreement also demands that on the termination date Bank B will sell identical stock back to Bank A at the previously agreed price; consequently, Bank B will have its cash returned with interest at the agreed repo rate.

---

[3] That is, a money market product quoted as a yield instrument, similar to a bank deposit or a CD. The other class of money market products are *discount* instruments such as a T-bill or CP.

[4] The two terms are not necessarily synonymous. The value date in a trade is the date on which the transaction acquires value; for example, the date from which accrued interest is calculated. Hence, it may fall on a non-business day such as a weekend or public holiday. The settlement date is the day on which the transaction settles or *clears*, and so can only fall on a business day.

In essence, a repo agreement is a secured loan (or *collateralised* loan) in which the repo rate reflects the interest charged on the cash being lent.

On the value date, stock and cash change hands. This is known as the start date, *on-side* date, *first leg* or *opening leg*, while the termination date is known as the *second leg*, *off-side leg* or *closing leg*. When the cash is returned to Bank B, it is accompanied by the interest charged on the cash during the term of the trade. This interest is calculated at a specified rate known as the *repo rate*. It is important to remember that although in legal terms the stock is initially "sold" to Bank B, the economic effects of ownership are retained with Bank A. This means that if the stock falls in price it is Bank A that will suffer a capital loss. Similarly, if the stock involved is a bond and there is a coupon payment during the term of the trade, this coupon is to the benefit of Bank A, and although Bank B will have received it on the coupon date, it must be handed over on the same day or immediately after to Bank A. This reflects the fact that although legal title to the collateral passes to the repo buyer, economic costs and benefits of the collateral remain with the seller.

A classic repo transaction is subject to a legal contract signed in advance by both parties. A standard document will suffice; it is not necessary to sign a legal agreement prior to each transaction.

Note that although we have called the two parties in this case "Bank A" and "Bank B", it is not only banks that get involved in repo transactions, and we have used these terms for the purposes of illustration only.

The basic mechanism is illustrated in Figure 12.2.

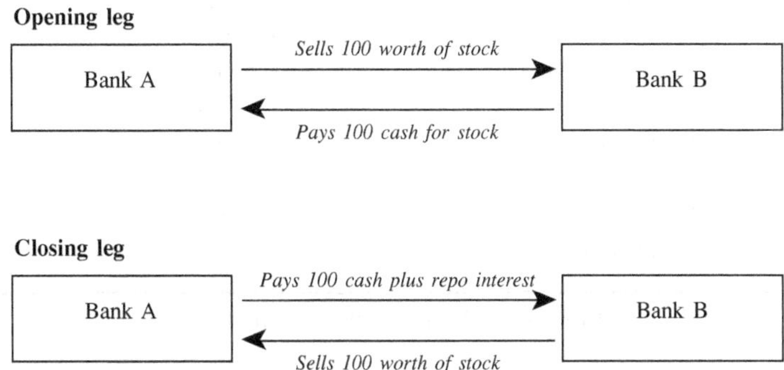

Figure 12.2 Classic repo transaction for 100-worth of collateral stock

A seller in a repo transaction is entering into a repo, whereas a buyer is entering into a *reverse repo*. In Figure 12.2 the repo counterparty is Bank A, while Bank B is entering into a reverse repo. That is, a reverse repo is a purchase of securities that are sold back on termination. As is evident from Figure 12.2 every repo is a reverse repo, and the name given to a deal is dependent on whose viewpoint one is looking at during the transaction.

Example of classic repo

The basic principle is illustrated with the following example. This considers a *specific* repo; that is, one in which the collateral supplied is specified as a particular stock, as opposed to a *general collateral* (GC) trade in which a basket of collateral can be supplied, of any particular issue, as long as it is of the required type and credit quality.

We consider first a classic repo in the United Kingdom gilt market between two market counterparties, in the 5.75% Treasury 2009 gilt stock. The terms of the trade are given in Table 12.1 and illustrated in Figure 12.3. Note that the terms of a classic repo trade are identical, irrespective of which market the deal is taking place in. So the basic trade, illustrated in Table 12.1, would be recognisable for bond repo in European and Asian markets.

Trade date	5 July 2000
Value date	6 July 2000
Repo term	1 week
Termination date	13 July 2000
Collateral (stock)	UKT 5.75% 2009
Nominal amount	£10,000,000
Price	104.60
Accrued interest (29 days)	0.4556011
Dirty price	105.055601
Settlement proceeds (*wired amount*)	£10,505,560.11
Repo rate	5.75%
Repo interest	£11,584.90
Termination proceeds	£10,517,145.01

Table 12.1 Terms of classic repo trade

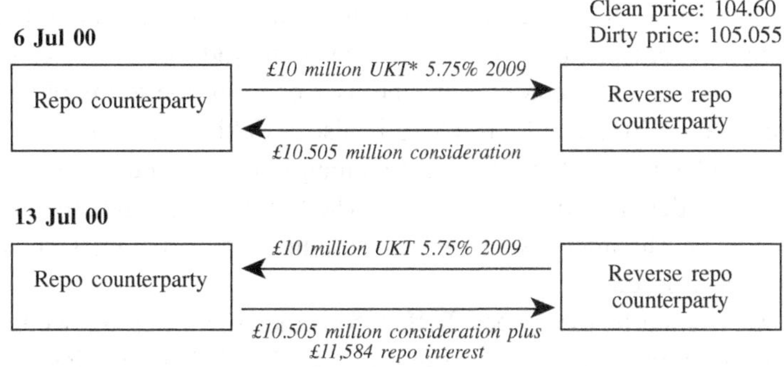

Figure 12.3 Diagram of a classic repo trade

The repo counterparty delivers to the reverse repo counterparty £10 million nominal of the stock, and in return receives the purchase proceeds. The clean market price of the stock is £104.60. In this example no *margin* (called haircut) has been taken so the start proceeds are equal to the market value of the stock, which is £10,505,560.11. It is common for a rounded sum to be transferred on the opening leg. The repo interest is 5.75%, so the repo interest charged for the trade is:

$$10{,}505{,}560 \times 5.75\% \times 7/365$$

or £11,584.90. The sterling market day-count basis is actual/365, and the repo interest is based on a seven-day repo rate of 5.75%. Repo rates are agreed at the time of the trade and are quoted, like all interest rates, on an annualised basis. The settlement price (dirty price) is used because it is the market value of the bonds on the particular trade date and therefore indicates the cash value of the gilts. By doing this the cash investor minimises credit exposure by equating the value of the cash and the collateral.

On termination the repo counterparty receives back its stock, for which it hands over the original proceeds plus the repo interest calculated above.

Market participants who are familiar with the Bloomberg trading system will use screen RRRA for a classic repo transaction. For this example the relevant screen entries are shown in Figure 12.4 on page 502. This screen is used in conjunction with a specific stock, so in this case it would be called up by entering:

UKT 5.75 09 <GOVT> RRRA <GO>

where "UKT" is the ticker for UK gilts. Note that the date format for Bloomberg screens is the US style, which is mm/dd/yy. The screen inputs are relatively self-explanatory, with the user entering the terms of the trade that are detailed in Table 12.1. There is also a field for calculating margin, labelled "collateral" on the screen. As no margin is involved in this example, it is left at its default value of 100.00%. The bottom of the screen shows the opening leg cash proceeds or "wired amount", the repo interest and the termination proceeds.

If we wanted to use screen RRRA for other securities we would enter the relevant bond ticker; for example, "T" for US Treasuries, "B" for German Bunds and so on. The principles are the same for classic repo trades whatever the jurisdiction, and the screen may be used for all markets that undertake classic repo.

```
<HELP> for explanation.                                    DL24 Corp   RRRA
Enter <1><GO> to send screen via <MESSAGE> System.
             REPO/REVERSE REPO ANALYSIS
TREASURY     UKT5 3/4 12/07/09   104.5800/104.6400  (5.13/5.12) BGN  @16:08
      *BOND IS CUM-DIVIDEND AT SETTLEMENT*                 CUSIP:  EC0113513
   SETTLEMENT DATE          7/ 6/00      RATE (365)     5.7500%
         <SETTLEMENT PRICE> <MARKET PRICE> COLLATERAL: 100.0000% OF MONEY
PRICE       104.6000000   104.600000   Y/N, HOLD COLLATERAL PERCENT CONSTANT? Y
YIELD         5.1275565    5.1275565   Y/N, BUMP ALL DATES FOR WEEKENDS/HOLIDAYS? Y
ACCRUED       0.4556011    0.4556011
   FOR  29 DAYS.                       ROUNDING 1  1 = NOT ROUNDED
TOTAL       105.0556011   105.055601               2 = ROUND TO NEAREST 1/8
      *BOND IS CUM-DIVIDEND AT TERMINATION*
  FACE AMT         10000000     <OR>   SETTLEMENT MONEY         10505560.11
<OR> To solve for PRICE: Enter NUMBER of BONDS, SETTLEMENT MONEY & COLLATERAL
  TERMINATION DATE  7/13/00     <OR>   TERM (IN DAYS)           7
  ACCRUED   0.565574 FOR  36 DAYS.
                 MONEY AT TERMINATION
WIRED AMOUNT                                  10,505,560.11
REPO INTEREST                                     11,584.90
TERMINATION MONEY                             10,517,145.01
NOTES:
Copyright 2000 BLOOMBERG L.P.   Frankfurt:69-920410  Hong Kong:2-977-6000  London:207-330-7500  New York:212-318-2000
Princeton:609-279-3000   Singapore:226-3000   Sydney:2-9777-8686   Tokyo:3-3201-8900   Sao Paulo:11-3048-4500
                                                                        1432-212-0 05-Jul-00 16:13:14
Bloomberg PROFESSIONAL
```

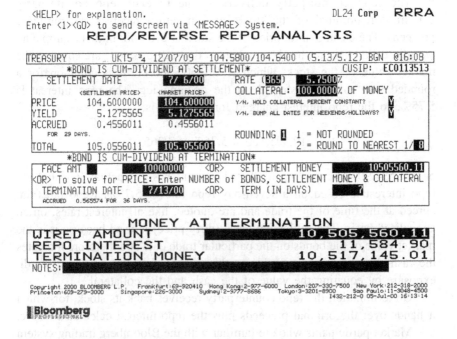

Figure 12.4 Bloomberg screen RRRA for classic repo transaction, trade date 5 July 2000

What if a counterparty is interested in investing £10 million against gilt collateral? Let us assume that a corporate treasury function with surplus cash wishes to invest this amount in repo for a one-week term. It invests this cash with a bank that deals in gilt repo. We can use Bloomberg screen RRRA to calculate the nominal amount of collateral required. Figure 12.5 shows the screen for this trade, again against the 5.75% Treasury 2009 stock as collateral. We see from Figure 12.5 that the terms of the trade are identical to that in Table 12.1, including the bond price and the repo rate; however, the opening leg wired amount is entered as £10 million, which is the cash being invested. Therefore the nominal value of the gilt collateral required will be different, as we now require a market value of this stock of £10 million. From the screen we see that this is £9,518,769. The cash amount is different from the example in Figure 12.4 so of course the repo interest charged is different, and is £11,027 for the seven-day term. Figure 12.6 on page 504 illustrates the transaction details.

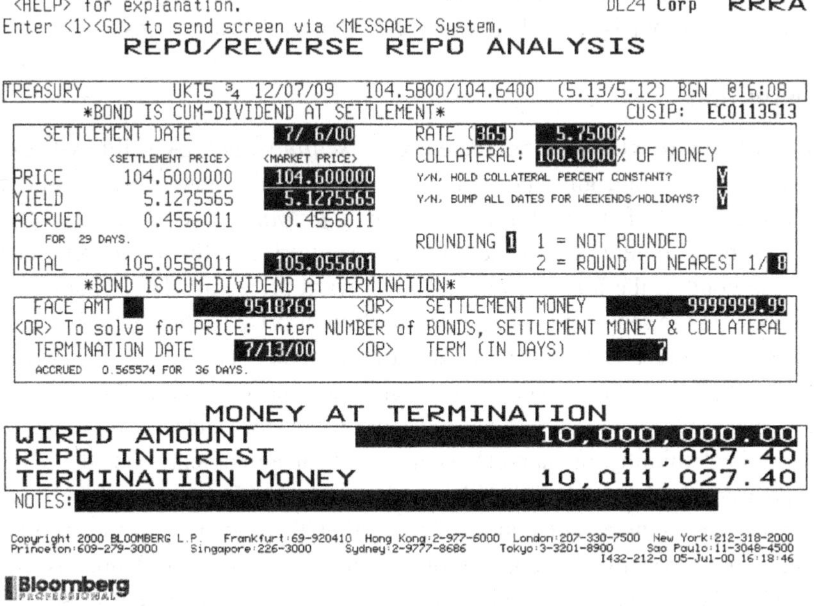

Figure 12.5 Bloomberg screen for the classic repo trade illustrated in Figure 12.6

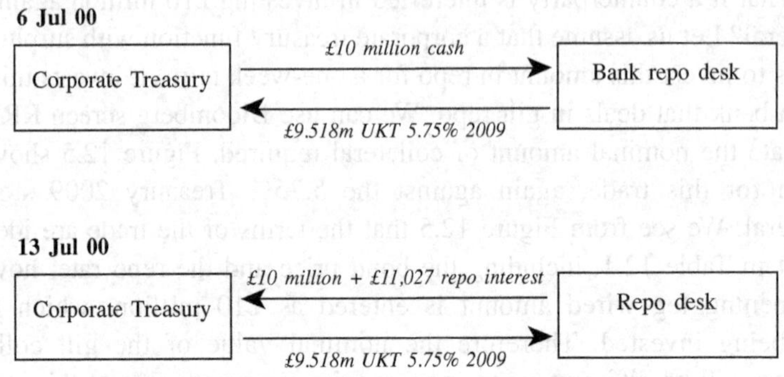

Figure 12.6 Corporate Treasury classic repo

The sell/buy-back

We next consider the sell/buy-back, which is economically identical to the classic repo, but is described under different cash flow terms.

Definition

In addition to classic repo there exists *sell/buy-back*. A sell/buy-back is defined as an outright sale of a bond on the value date, and an outright repurchase of that bond for value on a *forward* date. The cash flows therefore become a sale of the bond at a *spot* price, followed by repurchase of the bond at the *forward* price. The forward price calculated includes the interest on the repo, and is therefore a different price to the spot price.[5] That is, repo interest is realised as the difference between the spot price and forward price of the collateral at the start and termination of the trade. The sell/buy-back is entered into for the same reasons as a classic repo, but was developed initially in markets where no legal agreement existed to cover repo transactions, and where the settlement and IT systems of individual counterparties were not equipped to deal with repo. Over time, sell/buy-backs have become the convention in certain markets, most notably Italy, and so the mechanism is still used. In many markets therefore, sell/buy-

[5] The "forward price" is calculated only for the purpose of incorporating repo interest; it should not be confused with a forward interest rate, which is the interest rate for a term starting in the future and which is calculated from a spot interest rate. Nor should it be taken to be an indication of what the market price of the bond might be at the time of trade termination, the price of which could differ greatly from the sell/buy-back forward price.

backs are not covered by a legal agreement, although the standard legal agreement used in classic repo now includes a section that describes them.[6]

A sell/buy-back is a spot sale and forward repurchase of bonds transacted simultaneously, and the repo rate is not explicit, but is implied in the forward price. Any coupon payments during the term are paid to the seller; however, this is done through incorporation into the forward price, so the seller will not receive it immediately, but on termination. This is a disadvantage when compared to classic repo. However, there will be compensation payable if a coupon is not handed over straight away, usually at the repo rate used in the sell/buy-back. As sell/buy-backs are not subject to a legal agreement in most cases, in effect the seller has no legal right to any coupon, and there is no provision for marking-to-market and *variation margin*. This makes the sell/buy-back a higher risk transaction when compared to classic repo, even more so in volatile markets.

Note that in some markets the term "repo" is used to describe what are in fact sell/buy-backs. The Italian market is a good example of where this convention is followed.

A general diagram for the sell/buy-back is given in Figure 12.7.

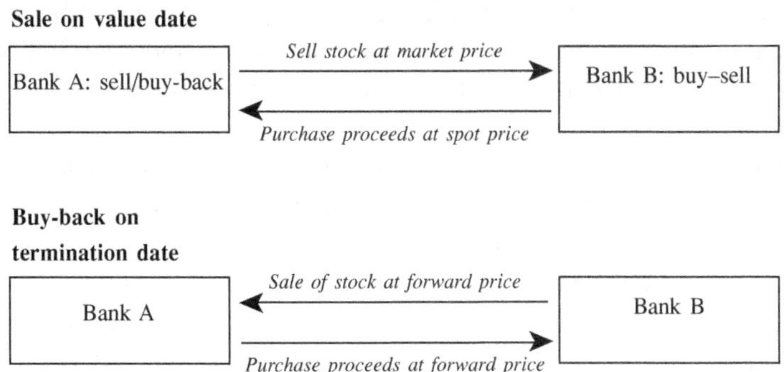

Figure 12.7 Sell/buy-back transaction

[6] This is the TBMA/ISMA Global Master Repurchase Agreement (GMPA). Note that in July 2006 the BMA merged with the Securities Industry Association, to create a new body known as the Securities Industry and Financial Markets Association, or SIFMA.

Example of sell/buy-back

We use the same terms of trade given in Figure 12.4 earlier but this time the trade is a sell/buy-back.[7] In a sell/buy-back we require the forward price on termination, and the difference between the spot and forward price incorporates the effects of repo interest. It is important to note that this forward price has nothing to with the actual market price of the collateral at the time of forward trade. It is simply a way of allowing for the repo interest that is the key factor in the trade. Thus in sell/buy-back the repo rate is not explicit (although it is the key consideration in the trade); rather, it is implicit in the forward price.

In this example, one counterparty sells £10 million nominal of the UKT 5.75% 2009 at the spot price of 104.60, this being the market price of the bond at the time. The consideration for this trade is the market value of the stock, which is £10,505,560 as before. Repo interest is calculated on this amount at the rate of 5.75% for one week, and from this the termination proceeds are calculated. The termination proceeds are divided by the nominal amount of stock to obtain the forward dirty price of the bond on the termination date. For various reasons, the main one being that settlement systems deal in clean prices, we require the forward clean price, which is obtained by subtracting from the forward dirty price the accrued interest on the bond on the termination date. At the start of the trade the 5.75% 2009 had 29 days' accrued interest, therefore on termination this figure will be 29 + 7 or 36 days.

Bloomberg users access a different screen for sell/buy-backs, which is BSR. This is shown in Figure 12.8. Entering in the terms of the trade, we see from Figure 12.8 that the forward price is 104.605876. However, the fundamental nature of this transaction is evident from the bottom part of the screen: the settlement amount ("wired amount"), repo interest and termination amount are identical for the classic repo trade described earlier. This is not surprising; the sell/buy-back is a loan of £10.505 million for one week at an interest rate of 5.75%. The mechanics of the trade do not differ on this key point.

---

[7] The Bank of England discourages sell/buy-backs in gilt repo and it is unusual, if not unheard of, to observe them in this market. However, we use these terms of trade for comparison purposes with the classic repo example given in the previous section. The procedure and the terms of the trade would be identical in other markets, such as Italy and Portugal, where sell/buy-back trades are the norm.

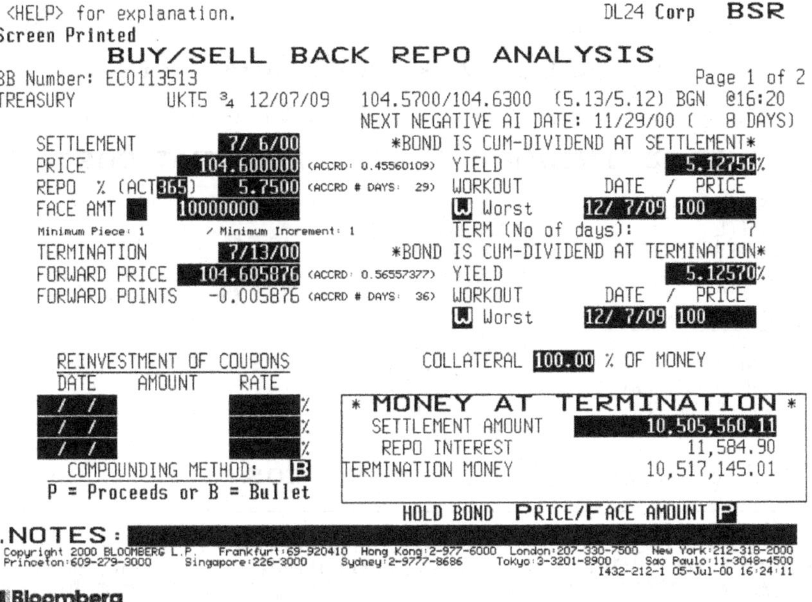

Figure 12.8 Bloomberg screen BSR for sell/buy-back trade in 5.75% 2009, trade date 5 July 2000.

Screen BSR on Bloomberg has a second page, which is shown in Figure 12.9 on page 508. This screen summarises the cash proceeds of the trade at start and termination. Note how the repo interest is termed "funding cost". This is because the trade is deemed to have been entered into by a bond trader who is funding his book. We can see from the screen details that during the one week of the trade the bond position has accrued interest of £10,997. This compares unfavourably with the repo funding cost of £11,584.

If there is a coupon payment during a sell/buy-back trade and it is not paid over to the seller until termination, a compensating amount is also payable on the coupon amount, usually at the trade's repo rate. When calculating the forward price on a sell/buy-back where a coupon will be paid during the trade, we must subtract the coupon amount from the forward price. Note also that sell/buy-backs are not possible on an open basis, as no forward price can be calculated unless a termination date is known.

<HELP> for explanation. DL24 Corp **BSR**

Screen Printed

BUY/SELL BACK REPO ANALYSIS

BB Number: EC0113513 Page 2 of 2

TREASURY UKT5 ¾ 12/07/09 104.5700/104.6300 (5.13/5.12) BGN @16:20

BOND INCOME		FUNDING COST
AT SETTLEMENT DATE:	7/ 6/00	
PRINCIPAL	10,460,000.00	
ACCRUED INTEREST	45,560.11	
TOTAL:	10,505,560.11	---> 10,505,560.11 @ 5.7500 for 7 day(s)
AT TERMINATION DATE:	7/13/00	
PRINCIPAL	10,460,000.00	
COUPON(S)	0.00	
ACCRUED INTEREST	56,557.38	
INTEREST ON CPNS	0.00	
TOTAL:	10,516,557.38	
NET INCOME:	10,997.27	COST: 11,584.90

DIFFERENCE -587.63 TERMINATION

PER 100 NOM: -0.00587633 AMOUNT 10,460,587.60

Bloomberg PROFESSIONAL

Figure 12.9 Bloomberg screen BSR page 2 for sell/buy-back trade in 5.75% 2009 gilt shown in Figure 12.8

Comparing classic repo and sell/buy-back

Fundamentally, both classic repo and sell/buy-backs are money market instruments that are a means by which one party may lend cash to another party, secured against collateral in the form of stocks and bonds. Both transactions are a contract for one party to sell securities, with a simultaneous agreement to repurchase them at a specified future date. They also involve:

- in economic terms, an exchange of assets, usually bonds, but also money market paper or equities as collateral against cash;
- the supplier of cash being compensated through the payment of interest, at an explicit (repo) or implicit (sell/buy-back) rate of interest;
- the short-covering of positions by market-makers or speculative sellers, when they are stock-driven trades.

In certain respects, however, there are significant differences between the two instruments. A classic repo trade is carried out under formal legal documentation, which sets out the formal position of each counterparty in the event of default. Sell/buy-backs have traditionally not been covered by this type of documentation, although this is no longer the case as standard documentation now exists to cater for them. There is no provision for *marking-to-market* and variation margining in sell/buy-backs, issues we shall look at shortly.

A summary of the main features of both types of trade is given in Table 12.2.

Classic repo	Sell/buy-back
"Sale" and repurchase	Outright sale; forward buy-back
Bid at repo rate: bid for stock, lend the cash (Offer at repo rate: offer the stock, take the cash)	Repo rate implicit in forward buy-back price
Sale and repurchase prices identical	Forward buy-back price different
Return to cash lender is repo interest on cash	Return to cash lender is the difference between sale price and forward buy-back price (the "repo" interest!)
Bond coupon received during trade is returned to seller	Coupon need not be returned to bond seller until termination (albeit with compensation)
Standard legal agreement (TBMA/ISMA GMRA)	No standard legal agreement (but incorporated in annexe under the GMRA)
Initial margin may be taken	Initial margin may be taken
Variation margin may be called	No variation margin unless transacted under a legal agreement
Specific repo dealing systems required	May be transacted using existing bond and equity dealing systems

Table 12.2 Summary of highlights of classic repo and sell/buy-back

Basket repo

Banks, securities houses and hedge funds often repo out entire portfolios of bonds with a repo market-maker. This is known as a *basket repo* and is operationally more convenient because it is treated as one repo trade rather than a large number of individual bond repo trades. The mechanics of a basket repo are identical to that for a single-name bond classic repo. In a basket repo the market-maker may set a margin level for each security or assign a uniform margin level for the whole basket.

Table 12.3 shows a portfolio of five structured finance bonds, a mix of ABS, MBS and CDO notes. Imagine that these are held by a securities house, ABC Securities Limited, that wishes to fund them using repo. It arranges a basket repo with an investment bank, with the following terms.

Basket repo trade terms

Trade date:	13 February 2004
Value date:	17 February 2004
Maturity date:	17 February 2005
Interest reset:	Three months
Wired proceeds:	USD 45,564,607.50
Rate:	1.18188
	[3-month Libor fix of 12 February 2004 plus 6 bps]
Interest:	USD 134,629.75
Maturity proceeds:	USD 45,699,237.25

These are quite favourable terms. The securities house has arranged funding of this portfolio at a rate of Libor plus 6 basis points. Given that most of the bonds are rated at A, this a good funding rate. In our example there are only five bonds; basket repo trades involving 50 or even 100 different securities are not uncommon. Each security in the basket will be delivered to the reverse repo counterparty, just like single-name classic repo trades.

Note that the investment bank that is entering into a basket reverse repo has applied a margin or haircut to each security, depending on what credit rating the security is assigned. The following margin levels can be assumed for haircut levels in this market:

AAA to AA:	3.5%
A:	5%
BBB:	7%
Sub-investment grade:	10%.

The repo is booked as one trade, even though the securities house is repo-ing out five different bonds. It has a one-year formal term, but its interest rate is reset every quarter. The first interest period rate is set as three-month Libor plus a spread of 6 basis points. The trade can be "broken" at

Bond	CUSIP	Type	Asset type	Original face amount	Pool factor	Current face	Credit rating	Price	Market value	Haircut	Loan value USD
ABCMT 2003-B B	00761HAU5	ABS	Credit card	10,000,000	1.0000	10,000,000	A	102.125	10,212,500	5.00%	9,701,875.00
ACAS 2002-2A B	00080AAL4	ABS	Small business loans	5,000,000	1.0000	5,000,000	A	102.25	5,112,500	5.00%	4,856,875.00
AMSI 2003-1 M2	03072SEZ4	MBS	Home equity	8,500,000	1.0000	8,500,000	A	102.25	8,691,250	5.00%	8,256,687.50
AMSI 2003-IA1 M2	03072SLH6	ABS	Residential B/C	4,000,000	0.99999	3,999,960	A	102.50	4,099,959	5.00%	3,894,961.05
Indosuez Capital Funding III	45578YAA0	CLO	Commercial bank loans	20,000,000	1.0000	20,000,000	AA	97.69	19,538,000	3.50%	18,854,170.00
									47,654,209		**45,564,568.55**
											Repo basket amount

Table 12.3 Hypothetical portfolio of ABS bonds, securities house basket repo trade
Price source: Bloomberg L.P. Prices as at 12 February 2004.

that date, or rolled for another three months. Table 12.4 shows the trade ticket.

During the term of the trade, the market-maker will make a margin call at pre-agreed intervals, say weekly or every fortnight. This is done by revaluing the entire basket and, if the portfolio has declined in value, a margin call will be made to restore the balance of the haircut. Table 12.5 shows a margin call statement for one week after the initial value date, we assume the portfolio has declined in value and hence a margin payment will need to be made by ABC Securities Limited.

As the trade is conducted under the GMRA agreement, the securities house will be able to substitute bonds out of the basket if it wishes, provided securities of equivalent quality are sent in the place of any bonds taken out of the basket. If a substitute is not available, the value of the loan can be reduced with the market-maker to reflect the lower value of the basket once a bond is taken out.

Reverse repo (RR)	**Contract**
Customer ID	123456789 ABC Securities Limited
Contract amount	$45,564,607.50
Rate (fixed)	1.18188%
Settle date	17-Feb-04
Lock-up date	17-May-04
Total repo principal	$45,564,607.50
Total repo interest	$134,629.75
Due at maturity	$45,699,237.25
Number of pieces	5

Table 12.4 Basket repo trade ticket, investment bank market-maker

Fixed-income financing margin call	
Date	24-Feb-04
Valuation date	23-Feb-04
Due date	24-Feb-04
Positive number =	Amount receivable
Negative number =	Amount payable
Exposure	(45,564,607.50)
Haircut amount	2,089,640.45
Portfolio revaluation	47,224,291.50
Margin call	429,917.50

Table 12.5 Margin call statement

Repo variations

In the earlier section we described the standard classic repo trade, which has a fixed term to maturity and a fixed repo rate. Generally, classic repo trades will range in maturity from overnight to one year; however, it is possible to transact longer maturities than this if required. The overwhelming majority of repo trades are between overnight and three months in maturity, although longer-term trades are not uncommon. A fixed-maturity repo is sometimes called a *term repo*. One could call this the "plain vanilla" repo. It is usually possible to terminate a vanilla repo before its stated maturity date if this is required by one or both of the counterparties.[8]

A repo that does not have a specified fixed-maturity date is known as an *open repo*. In an open repo the borrower of cash will confirm each morning that the repo is required for a further overnight term. The interest rate is also fixed at this point. If the borrower no longer requires the cash, or requires the return of his collateral, the trade will be terminated at one day's notice.

In the remainder of this section we present an overview of the most common variations on the vanilla repo transactions that are traded in the markets.

[8] The term *delivery repo* is sometimes used to refer to a vanilla classic repo transaction where the supplier of cash takes delivery of the collateral, whether in physical form or as a book-entry transfer to his or her account in the clearing system (or to the agent's account).

Tri-party repo

The tri-party repo mechanism is designed to make the repo arrangement accessible to a wider range of market counterparties. Essentially it introduces a third-party agent in between the two repo counterparties, who can fulfil a number of roles from security custodian to cash account manager. The tri-party mechanism allows bond and equity dealers full control over their inventory, and incurs minimal settlement cost to the cash investor, but gives investors independent confirmation that their cash is fully collateralised. Under a tri-party agreement, the securities dealer delivers collateral to an independent third-party custodian, such as Euroclear or Clearstream,[9] who will place it into a segregated tri-party account. The securities dealer maintains control over which precise securities are in this account (multiple substitutions are permitted), but the custodian undertakes to confirm each day to the investor that their cash remains fully collateralised by securities of suitable quality. A tri-party agreement needs to be in place with all three parties before trading can commence. This arrangement reduces the administrative burden for the cash investor, but is not, in theory, as secure as a conventional delivery-versus-payment structure. Consequently, the yield on the investor's cash (assuming collateral of identical credit quality) should be slightly higher. The structure is shown in Figure 12.10.

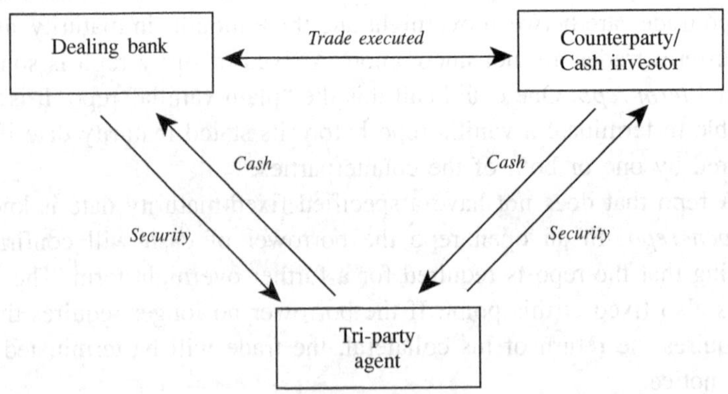

Figure 12.10 Tri-party repo structure

[9] Clearstream was previously known as Cedel Bank. Other tri-party providers include Deutsche Bank and Bank of New York.

The first tri-party repo deal took place in 1993 between the European Bank for Reconstruction and Development (EBRD) and the Swiss Bank Corporation.[10]

A tri-party arrangement is, in theory, more attractive to smaller market participants as it removes the expense of setting up in-house administration facilities that would be required for conventional repo. This is mainly because the delivery and collection of collateral is handled by the tri-party agent. Additional benefits to cash-rich investors include:

- no requirement to install repo settlement and monitoring systems;
- no requirement to take delivery of collateral, or to maintain an account at the clearing agency;
- independent monitoring of market movements and margin requirements;
- in the event of default, a third-party agent that can implement default measures.

Set against the benefits is of course the cost of tri-party repo, essentially the fee payable to the third-party agent. This fee will include a charge for setting up accounts and arrangements at the tri-party agent, and a custodian charge for holding securities in the clearing system.

As well as being attractive to smaller banks and cash-rich investors, the larger banks will also use tri-party repo, in order to be able to offer it as a service to their smaller size clients. The usual arrangement is that both dealer and cash investor will pay a fee to the tri-party agent based on the range of services that are required, and this will be detailed in the legal agreement in place between the market counterparty and the agent. This agreement will also specify, among other details, the specific types of security that are acceptable as collateral to the cash lender; the repo rate that is earned by the lender will reflect the nature of collateral that is supplied. In every other respect, however, the tri-party mechanism offers the same flexibility of conventional repo, and may be transacted from maturities ranging from overnight to one year.

The tri-party agent is an agent to both parties in the repo transaction. It provides a collateral management service overseeing the exchange of securities and cash, and managing collateral during the life of the repo. It

[10] Stated in Corrigan et al. 1999, *Repo: The Ultimate Guide*, Pearls of Wisdom Publishing, London, p. 27.

also carries out daily marking-to-market, and substitution of collateral as required. The responsibilities of the agent can include:

- the setting up of the repo account;
- monitoring of cash against purchased securities, both at inception and at maturity;
- initial and ongoing testing of *concentration* limits;
- the safekeeping of securities handed over as collateral;
- managing the substitution of securities, where this is required;
- monitoring the market value of the securities against the cash lent out in the repo;
- issuing margin calls to the borrower of cash.

The tri-party agent will issue close-of-business reports to both parties. The contents of the report can include some or all of the following:

- tri-party repo cash and securities valuation;
- corporate actions;
- pre-advice of expected income;
- exchange rates;
- collateral substitution.

The extent of the duties performed by the tri-party agent is dependent on the sophistication of an individual party's operation. Smaller market participants who do not wish to invest in extensive infrastructure may outsource all repo-related functions to the tri-party agent.

Tri-party repo was originally conceived as a mechanism through which repo would become accessible to smaller banks and non-bank counterparties. It is primarily targeted at cash-rich investors. However, users of the instrument range across the spectrum of market participants, and include, on the investing side, cash-rich financial institutions such as banks, fund managers, including life companies and pension funds, and savings institutions such as UK building societies. On the borrowing side, users include bond and equity market-makers, and banks with inventories of high-quality assets such as government bonds and highly rated corporate bonds.[11]

[11] Fabozzi (1997, p. 21) also refers to *four-party repos*. The difference between tri-party and four-party repo is given as follows: "in a four-party repo there is a sub-custodian that is the custodian for the lender". This might occur because of legal considerations; for instance, local regulations stating that the custodian in a repo transaction must be a financial institution or must be based in a particular location.

EXAMPLE 12.1 Tri-party repo: deal mechanics

The process of cash and collateral flow in a tri-party repo trade is illustrated in Figures 12.11 and 12.12.

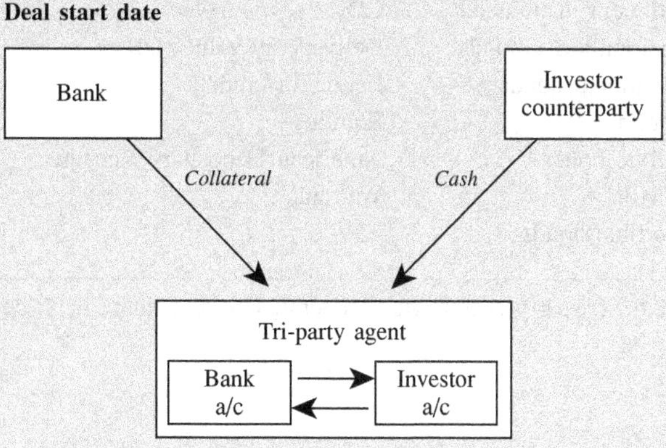

Figure 12.11 Tri-party repo flow: open leg

Cash is transferred to the bank's account and securities to the investor's account after the tri-party agent confirms the collateral quality and adequacy

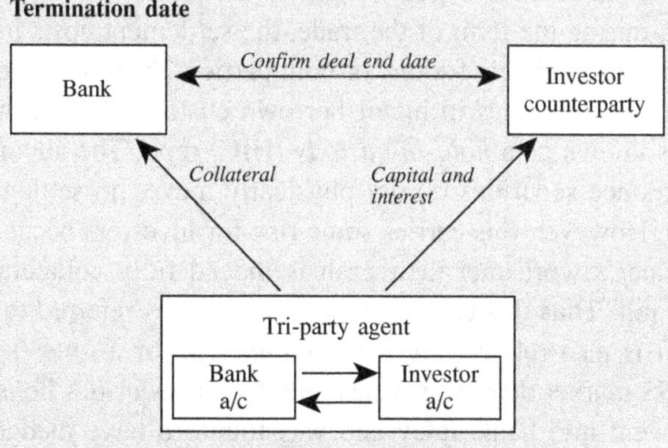

Figure 12.12 Tri-party repo flow: close leg

The tri-party agent effects a simultaneous transfer of cash (original capital plus repo interest) versus securities

Table 12.6 shows the acceptable collateral types as advised by the institutional trust arm of a US investment bank.

Government bonds	Cash
Government guaranteed/ local authority bonds	CDs
	Delivery by value (DBV)
Supranational bonds	Letters of credit
Eurobonds	Equities
Corporate bonds	American Depositary Receipts
ABS/MBS	Warrants
Convertible bonds	

Table 12.6 Tri-party acceptable collateral: US investment bank counterparty

Hold-in-custody repo

This is part of the GC market, and is more common in the United States than elsewhere. Consider the case of a cash-rich institution investing in GC as an alternative to deposits or CP. The better the quality of collateral, the lower the yield the institution can expect, while the mechanics of settlement may also affect the repo rate. The most secure procedure is to take physical possession of the collateral. However, if the dealer needs one or more substitutions during the term of the trade, the settlement costs involved may make the trade unworkable for one or both parties. Therefore, the dealer may offer to hold the securities in his or her own custody against the investor's cash. This is known as a *hold-in-custody* (HIC) repo. The advantage of this trade is that since securities do not physically move, no settlement charges are incurred. However, this carries some risk for investors because they only have the dealer's word that their cash is indeed fully collateralised in the event of default. Thus this type of trade is sometimes referred to as a "Trust Me" repo; it is also referred to as a *due-bill repo* or a *letter repo*.

In the US market there was a case in which a securities house (Drysdale Securities) went into bankruptcy and was found to have pledged the same collateral for multiple HIC repo trades. Investors dealing in HIC repo must ensure:

- they only invest with dealers of good credit quality, since an HIC repo may be perceived as an unsecured transaction;

- they receive a higher yield on their cash in order to compensate them for the higher credit risk involved.

A *safekeeping repo* is identical to an HIC repo, whereby the collateral from the repo seller is not delivered to the cash lender but held in "safe keeping" by the seller. This has advantages in that there is no administration and cost associated with the movement of stock. The risk is that the cash lender must entrust the safekeeping of collateral to the counterparty, and has no means of confirming that the security is indeed segregated, and only being used for one transaction.

Due to the counterparty risk inherent in an HIC repo, it is rare to see it transacted either in the US market or elsewhere. Certain securities are not suitable for delivery; for example, the class of mortgage securities known as *whole loans* in the United States, and these are often funded using HIC repo (termed *whole-loan repo*).

Borrow/loan vs cash

This is similar in almost all respects to a classic repo/reverse repo. A legal agreement between the two parties is necessary, and trades generally settle *delivery-versus-payment*. The key difference is that under a repo agreement legal title over the collateral changes hands. Under a securities lending agreement this is not necessarily the case. The UK standard securities lending agreement does involve transfer of title, but it is possible to construct a securities lending agreement where legal title does not move. This can be an advantage for customers who may have accounting or tax problems in doing a repo trade. Such institutions will opt to transact a *loan versus cash*. The UK standard lending agreement also covers items such as dividends and voting rights, and is therefore the preferred transaction structure in the equity repo market.

Bonds borrowed/collateral pledged

In the case of a bonds borrowed/collateral pledged trade, the institution lending the bonds does not want or need to receive cash against them, as it is already cash rich and would only have to reinvest any further cash generated. As such this transaction only occurs with *special collateral*. The dealer borrows the special bonds and pledges securities of similar quality and value (general collateral). The dealer builds in a fee payable to the lending institution as an incentive to do the trade.

EXAMPLE 12.2 Bonds borrowed/collateral pledged

ABC Bank plc wishes to borrow DKK 300 million of the Danish government bond 8% 2001. ABC owns the Danish government bond 7% 2007. ABC is prepared to pay a customer a 40 basis point fee in order to borrow the 8% 2001 for one month.

The market price of the 8% 2001 (including accrued interest) is 112.70. The total value of DKK 300 million nominal is therefore DKK 338,100,000.

The market price of the 7% 2007 (including accrued interest) is 102.55.

In order to fully collateralise the customer ABC needs to pledge (338,100,000/1.0255), which is 329,692,832.76. When rounded to the nearest DKK 1 million this becomes DKK 330 million nominal of the 7% 2007.

In a bonds borrowed/collateral pledged trade, both securities are delivered free of payment and ABC Bank plc would pay the customer a 40 basis points borrowing fee upon termination. In our example the fee payable would be:

$$338{,}100{,}000 \times (31/360) \times (0.4/100) = \text{DKK } 112{,}700.$$

Cross-currency repo

All of the examples of repo trades discussed so far have used cash and securities denominated in the same currency; for example, gilts trading versus sterling cash, and so on. In fact, there is no requirement to limit oneself to single-currency transactions. It is possible to trade, say, gilts versus US dollar cash (or any other currency), or pledge Spanish government bonds against borrowing Japanese government bonds. A cross-currency repo is essentially a plain vanilla transaction, but where collateral that is handed over is denominated in a different currency to that of the cash lent against it. Other features of cross-currency repo include:

- possible significant daylight credit exposure on the transaction if securities cannot settle versus payment;
- a requirement for the transaction to be covered by appropriate legal documentation;
- fluctuating foreign exchange rates, which mean that it is likely that the transaction will need to be marked-to-market frequently in order to ensure that cash or securities remain fully collateralised.

It is also necessary to take into account the fluctuations in the relevant exchange rate when marking securities used as collateral, which are obviously handed over against cash that is denominated in a different currency.

EXAMPLE 12.3 Cross-currency repo

On 4 January 2000 a hedge fund manager funds a long position in US Treasury securities against sterling, to value the following day. It is offered a bid of 4.90% in the one-week, and the market maker also requires a 2% margin. The one-week Libor rate is 4.95% and the exchange rate at the time of trade is £1/$1.63. The terms of the trade are given below.

Trade date:	4 January 2000
Settlement date:	5 January 2000
Stock (collateral):	US Treasury 6.125% 2001
Nominal amount:	$100 million
Repo rate:	4.90% (sterling)
Term:	7 days
Maturity date:	12 January 2001
Clean price:	99-19
Accrued interest:	5 days (0.0841346)
Dirty price:	99.6778846
Gross settlement amount:	$99,677,884.62
Net settlement amount (after 2% haircut):	$97,723,416.29
Net wired settlement amount in sterling:	£59,953,016.13
Repo interest:	£56,339.41
Sterling termination money:	£60,009,355.54

The repo market has allowed the hedge fund to borrow in sterling at a rate below the cost of unsecured borrowing in the money market (4.95%). The repo market-maker is "overcollateralised" by the difference between the value of the bonds (in £) and the loan proceeds (2%). A rise in USD yields or a fall in the USD exchange rate value will adversely affect the value of the bonds, causing the market-maker to be undercollateralised.

Repo-to-maturity

A *repo-to-maturity* is a classic repo where the termination date on the repo matches the maturity date of the bond in the repo. We can discuss this trade by considering the Bloomberg screen used to analyse repo-to-maturity, which is REM (see Figure 12.13). The screen used to analyse a reverse repo-to-maturity is RRM (see Figure 12.14).

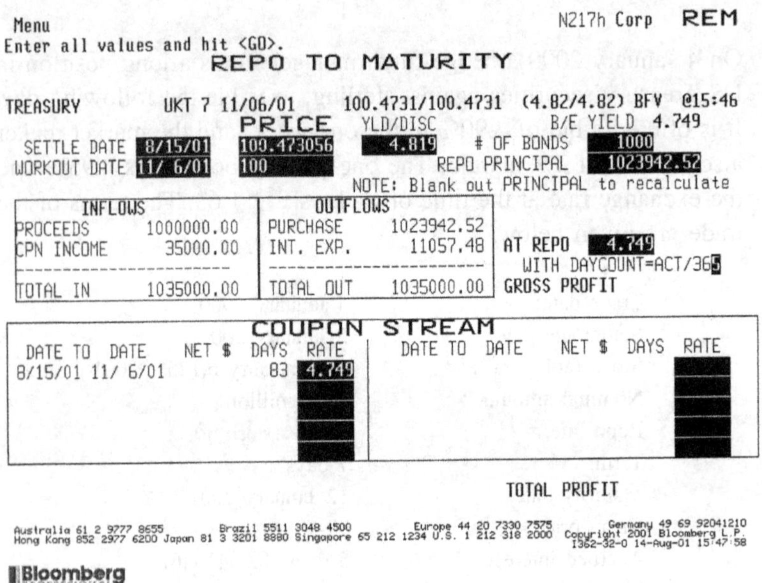

Figure 12.13 Bloomberg screen REM; used for repo-to-maturity analysis, for UK Treasury 7% 2001 on 14 August 2001

Screen REM is used to analyse the effect of borrowing funds in repo to purchase a bond, where the bond is the collateral security. This is conventional and we considered this earlier. In essence, the screen will compare the financing costs on the borrowed funds to the coupons received on the bond up to and including maturity. The key determining factor is the repo rate used to finance the borrowing. From Figure 12.13 we see that the screen calculates the breakeven rate, which is the rate at which the financing cost equals the bond return. The screen also works out cash flows at start and termination, and the borrowed amount is labelled as the "repo principal". This is the bond total consideration. Under "outflows" we see the repo interest at the selected repo rate, labelled as “Int. Exp”. Gross profit is the total inflow minus total outflow, which in our example is zero because the repo rate entered is the breakeven rate. The user will enter the actual repo rate payable to calculate the total profit.

A reverse repo-to-maturity is a reverse repo with matching repo termination and bond expiry dates. This is shown in Figure 12.14.

Repo-to-maturity is a low-risk trade as the financing profit on the bond position is known with certainty to the bond’s maturity. For financial institutions that operate on an accruals basis rather mark-to-market basis, the trade can guarantee a profit and not suffer any losses in the interim while they hold the bond.

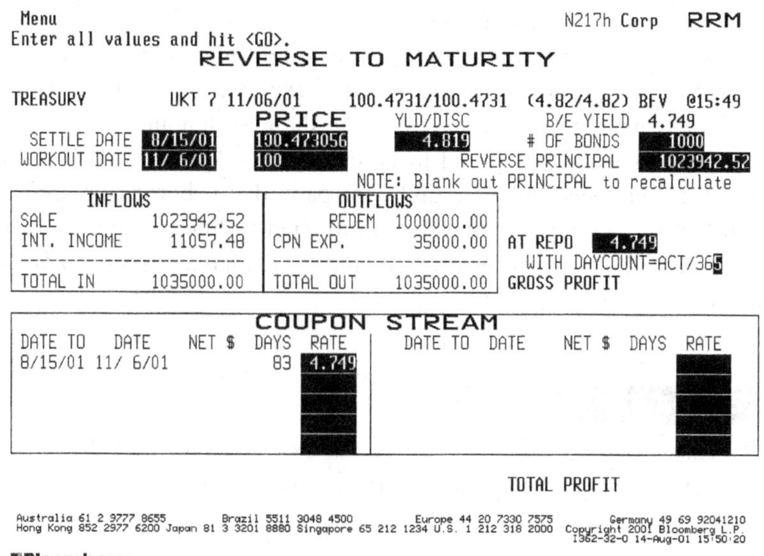

Figure 12.14 Bloomberg screen RRM, used for reverse repo-to-maturity analysis, for UK Treasury 7% 2001 on 14 August 2001

Stock lending

Institutional investors such as pension funds and insurance companies often prefer to enhance the income from their fixed-interest portfolios by lending their bonds, for a fee, rather than get involved in repo. A stock loan is a contract committing one party to lend, and the other to borrow, agreed securities for an agreed period. The borrower of stock is required to provide collateral to the lender in the form of cash, other securities or a letter of credit. The origins and history of the stock lending market are different from that of the repo market. The range of counterparties is also different, although of course a large number of counterparties are involved in both markets. Most stock loans are on an "open" basis, although term loans also occur. Initial margin is given to the lender of the securities.

Stock loan/borrow is also known as securities lending/borrowing. Stock loan has the same economic effect as repo, except a fee is charged for the loan rather than an interest rate quoted on the cash amount.

The loan is usually required to be collateralised; that is, cash or high-quality stock will need to be put up by the party that is borrowing securities. As with repo, if a coupon is payable on the bond while it is out on loan, is it will be passed on by the borrower of stock to the lender as a *manufactured dividend*.

EXAMPLE 12.4 Stock loan

A market-maker in convertible bonds borrows £100,000,000 of a convertible with the following terms:

Coupon:	7.25% (semi-annual, act/act)
Clean price:	107.84
Accrued:	29 days
	0.57 (from 7.25/2 x 29/183)
Dirty price:	108.41
Loan value:	£108,414,453
Loan term:	14 days
Stock loan fee:	40 basis points
	£16,633 (from 40 bps × loan value × 14/365).

The borrowed bond can be collateralised with cash or with another bond at margin (haircut) of 5%. Assume the following bond is supplied as collateral:

Coupon:	6.5%
Clean price:	100.42
Accrued:	29 days
	0.51 (from 6.5/2 × 29/183)
Dirty price:	100.93.

The borrower of stock will have to put up (£108,414,553 × 1.05) or £113,835,176 of market value of collateral stock. This is (113,835,176 / 1.0093) or £112,780,646 nominal of the collateral stock.

Margin

To reduce the level of risk exposure in a repo transaction it is common for the lender of cash to ask for a margin, which is where the market value of collateral is higher than the cash value of cash lent out in the repo. This is a form of protection should the cash-borrowing counterparty default on the loan. Another term for margin is *overcollateralisation* or *haircut*. There are two types of margin: an *initial margin* taken at the start of the trade, and *variation margin,* which is called if required during the term of the trade.

Initial margin

The cash proceeds in a repo are typically no more than the market value of the collateral. This minimises credit exposure by equating the value of the cash to that of the collateral. The market value of the collateral is calculated at its *dirty* price, not clean price; that is, including accrued interest. This is referred to as *accrual pricing*. To calculate the accrued interest on the (bond) collateral we require the day-count basis for the particular bond.

The start proceeds of a repo can be less than the market value of the collateral by an agreed amount or percentage. This is known as the *initial margin* or *haircut*. The initial margin protects the buyer against:

- a sudden fall in the market value of the collateral;
- illiquidity of collateral;

- other sources of volatility of value (for example, approaching maturity);
- counterparty risk.

The margin level of repo varies from 0–2% for collateral such as US treasuries or German bonds, to 5% for cross-currency and equity repo, to 10–35% for emerging market debt repo.

In both classic repo and sell/buy-back, any initial margin is given to the supplier of cash in the transaction. This remains true in the case of specific repo. For initial margin the market value of the bond collateral is reduced (or given a "*haircut*") by the percentage of the initial margin and the nominal value determined from this reduced amount. In a stock loan transaction the lender of stock will ask for margin.

There are two methods for calculating the margin; for example, for a 2% margin this could be one of the following:

- (dirty price of the bonds) × 0.98
- ((dirty price of the bonds)/1.02).

The two methods do not give the same value! The RRRA repo page on Bloomberg uses the second method for its calculations and this method is turning into something of a convention.

For a 2% margin level the BMA/ISMA GMRA defines a "margin ratio" as:

$$\text{collateral value/cash} = 102\%.$$

The size of margin required in any particular transaction is a function of the following:

- the credit quality of the counterparty supplying the collateral; for example, a central bank counterparty, interbank counterparty and corporate will all suggest different margin levels;
- the term of the repo; an overnight repo is inherently lower risk than a one-year risk;
- the duration (price volatility) of the collateral; for example, a T-bill compared to the long bond;
- the existence or absence of a legal agreement; repo traded under a standard agreement is considered lower risk.

Certain market practitioners, particularly those that work on bond research desks, believe that the level of margin is a function of the volatility of the collateral stock. This may be either, say, one-year historical volatility or the implied volatility given by option prices. Given a volatility level of, say, 10%, suggesting a maximum expected price movement of −10% to +10%, the margin level may be set at, say, 5% to cover expected movement in the market value of the collateral. This approach to setting initial margin is regarded as onerous by most repo traders, given the differing volatility levels of stocks within GC bands. The counterparty credit risk and terms of trade remain the most influential elements in setting margin, followed by quality of collateral.[12]

In the final analysis, margin is required to guard against market risk – the risk that the value of collateral will drop during the course of the repo. Therefore the margin call must reflect the risks prevalent in the market at the time; extremely volatile market conditions may call for large increases in initial margin.

Variation margin

The market value of the collateral is maintained through the use of *variation margin*. So if the market value of the collateral falls, the buyer calls for extra cash or collateral. If the market value of the collateral rises, the seller calls for extra cash or collateral. In order to reduce the administrative burden, margin calls can be limited to changes in the market value of the collateral in excess of an agreed amount or percentage, which is called a *margin maintenance limit*.

The standard market documentation that exists for the structures covered so far includes clauses that allow parties to a transaction to call for variation margin during the term of a repo. This can be in the form of extra collateral (if the value of the collateral has dropped in relation to the asset exchanged), or a return of collateral if the value has risen. If the cash-borrowing counterparty is unable to supply more collateral where required, it will have to return a portion of the cash loan. Both parties have an interest in making and meeting margin calls. The level at which variation margin is triggered is often agreed beforehand in the legal agreement put in place between individual counterparties. Although primarily viewed as an instrument used

[12] In his years of trading repo, during 1992–1997 and again in 2003–2006, the author never once came across a repo market-maker who set margin levels in line with collateral volatility levels. So much for certain bank research desks!

by the supplier of cash against a fall in the value of the collateral, variation margin can of course also be called by the repo seller if the value of the collateral has risen in value.

An illustration of variation margin being applied during the term of a trade is given in Example 12.5.

EXAMPLE 12.5 Variation margin

Figure 12.15 shows a 60-day repo in the 5% Treasury 2004, a UK gilt, where a margin of 2% is taken. The repo rate is 5%. The start of the trade is 5 January 2000. The clean price of the gilt is 95.25.

Nominal amount:	1,000,000
Principal:	£952,500.00
Accrued interest (29 days):	£3961.75
Total consideration:	£956,461.75

The consideration is divided by 1.02, the amount of margin, to give £937,707.60. Assume that this is rounded up to the nearest pound.

Loan amount:	£937,708.00
Repo interest at 5%:	£8,477.91
Termination proceeds:	£946,185.91

Assume that one month later there has been a catastrophic fall in the bond market and the 5% 2004 gilt is trading down at 92.75. Following this drop, the market value of the collateral is now:

Principal:	£927,500.00
Accrued interest (59 days):	£8,082.19
Market value:	£935,582.19.

However, the repo desk has lent £937,708 against this security, which exceeds its market value. Under a variation margin arrangement it can call margin from the counterparty in the form of general collateral securities or cash.

The formula used to calculate the amount required to restore the original margin of 2% is given by:

Margin adjustment =
((original consideration + repo interest charged to date) × (1 + initial margin)) – (new all-in price × nominal amount).

This therefore becomes:
((937,708 + 4238.96) × (1 + 0.02)) – (0.93558219 × 1,000,000) = £25,203.71.

The margin requirement can be taken as additional stock or cash. In practice, margin calls are made on what is known as a portfolio basis, based on the net position resulting from all repos and reverse repos in place between the two counterparties, so that a margin delivery may be made in a general collateral stock rather than more of the original repo stock. Figure 12.15 shows the relevant cash flows at the various dates.

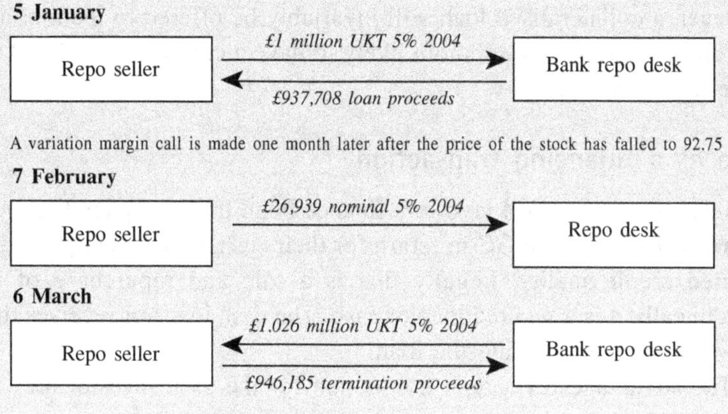

Figure 12.15 Margin call

Uses and economic functions of repo

The repo mechanism allows compensation for the use of a desired asset. If cash is the desired asset, the compensation for its use is simply the repo rate of interest paid on it. If bonds are the desired asset, the buyer (borrower) compensates the seller (lender) by accepting a repo interest rate that is below the market level.

Funding bond positions

In the normal course of business a bond trader or market-maker will need to finance his or her long and short positions. Figure 12.16 illustrates the basic principle for a bond trader running a bond market-making book.

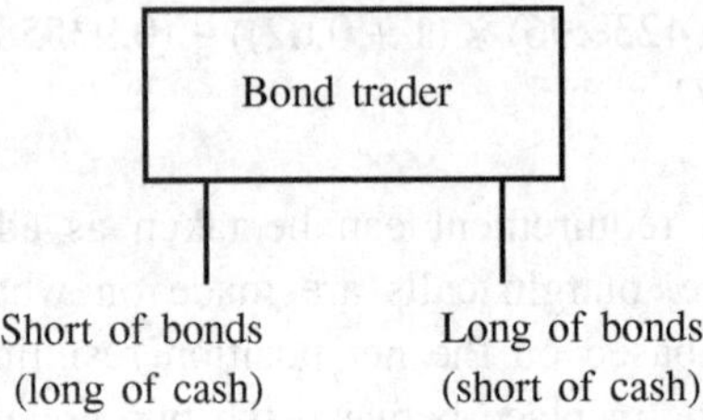

Figure 12.16 Financing bond positions

To finance a long position bond traders can borrow money unsecured in the interbank market, assuming that they have a credit line in this market. However, a collateralised loan will invariably be offered to them at a lower rate, and counterparties are more likely to have a credit line for bond traders if the loan is secured.

Repo as a financing transaction

Cash-rich money-market investors finance bond traders by lending out cash in a repo. They receive GC in return for their cash, which is any bond of the required credit quality. Legally this is a sale and repurchase of bonds; economically it is a secured loan of cash. The cash investor receives the repo rate of interest for making the loan.

The advantages of a repo transaction for the cash investor are:

- it is a secured investment;
- the returns are competitive with bank deposits and occasionally higher;
- this is a diversification from bank risk; that is, an extra form of investment outside a regular bank deposit.

Bond traders will enter into a *reverse repo* when they require a specific issue to deliver into a short sale. In this case the traders are effectively borrowing bonds and putting up cash as collateral. The bond traders receive the repo rate on their cash.

The position is shown in Figure 12.17.

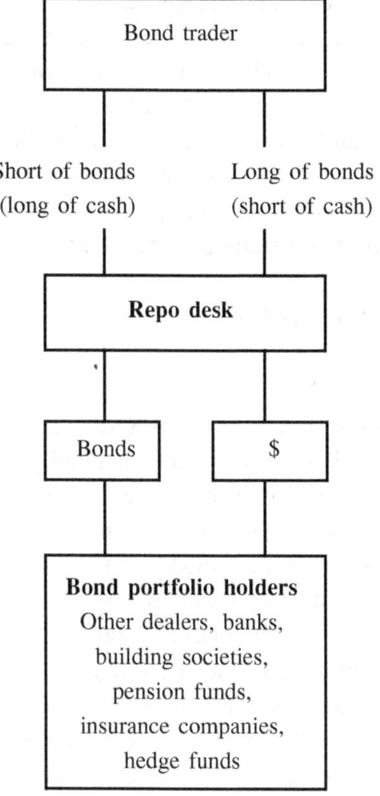

Figure 12.17 Financing a short position

In this transaction the bond lender's compensation is the difference between the repo rate paid on the dealer's cash and the market rate at which he or she can reinvest the cash. If the bond is particularly sought after – that is, it is *special* – the repo rate may be significantly below the GC rate. Special status in a bond will push the repo rate downwards. Zero rates and even negative rates are possible when dealing in specials. The repo rate will reflect supply and demand in the market. In a financing transaction, the dealer is paying the repo rate on the investor's cash. The GC rate tends to trade below the Libor rate, and also below the Libid rate, reflecting its status as a secured loan. In a positioning transaction, the dealer receives the repo rate on his or her cash. If the bond being borrowed (for this is, in effect what is happening) is special, the repo rate receivable will be lower to reflect the demand for the bond.

Active players in repo and interbank markets can enhance yield by lending bonds at the GC rate and then reinvesting the cash at a higher rate. This would of course introduce an element of credit risk. A market counterparty could also borrow bonds in the stock lending market, on-lend these bonds via repo and invest the cash proceeds in, say, CDs. Where the collateral is government bonds, the institution will usually be receiving a higher rate on the CD than the repo rate it is paying in the repo. The use of repo for arbitrage and basis trading is considered in Choudhry (2003).

Legal description of repo

PSA/ISMA GMRA Agreement

The Public Securities Association (PSA; renamed the Bond Market Association) is a US-based body that originally developed the market standard documentation for repo in the US domestic market, introduced in February 1986.[13] It developed in conjunction with the International Securities Market Association (ISMA) the Global Master Repurchase Agreement. This is the market standard repo document used as the legal basis for repo in non-US dollar markets, introduced in November 1992. It was updated three years later to include UK gilts, buy–sell transactions and relevant agency annexes. The latest update from September 2000 covered net-paying securities, equity repo and sell/buy-backs.

The agreement covers transactions between parties including repo, buy/sell–back and agency trades, and has adapted for securities paying net, as well as for equities.

The key features of the agreement are that:

- repo trades are structured as outright sales and repurchases;
- full ownership is conferred of securities transferred;
- there is an obligation to return "equivalent" securities;
- there is provision for initial and variation margin;
- coupon is paid over to the repo seller at the time of payment;
- legal title to collateral is confirmed in the event of default.

The main advantages of the agreement are (1) its allowance for close-out and netting are capital efficient for capital adequancy (CAD) purposes, (2) specifying action in the event of default and (3) its rules on margining.

A detailed look at the GMRA is contained in Choudhry (2006).

---

13 See Footnote 6: the BMA is now the SIFMA.

Gilt Repo Legal Agreement

The Gilt Repo Legal Agreement is an amended version of the revised (November 1995) PSA/ISMA agreement for the UK gilt repo market. The BMA/ISMA agreement was extended by supplemental terms and conditions for gilt repo forming Part 2 to Annex I of the BMA/ISMA agreement and modified by a side letter in connection with the upgrade to the Central Gilts Office service in November 1997. Participants in the gilt repo market are strongly recommended to adopt the Gilt Repo Legal Agreement for gilt repo transactions, as set out in the Gilt Repo Code of Best Practice. The Code was issued by the Bank of England. Use of the legal agreement is subject to legal confirmation of its effectiveness, if the specific circumstances in which it is to be used are not straightforward. The agreement is recommended as the umbrella documentation for all types of repo, including buy/sell-back.

The agreement provides for the following:

- the absolute transfer of title to securities;
- daily marking-to-market;
- appropriate initial margin and for maintenance of margin whenever the mark-to-market reveals a material change of value;
- clear events of default and the consequential rights and obligations of the counterparties;
- in the event of default, full set-off of claims between counterparties;
- clarification of rights of parties regarding substitution of collateral and the treatment of coupon payments;
- terms subject to English law.

These are essentially the same provisions as contained in the BMA/ISMA agreement.

The United Kingdom gilt repo market

Background

Trading in the UK gilt repo market began on 2 January 1996. Prior to this, stock borrowing and lending in the gilt market was available only to gilt-edged market-makers (GEMMs), dealing through approved intermediaries, the stock exchange money brokers (SEMBs). The introduction of gilt repo allowed all market participants to borrow and lend gilts. The market reforms also liberalised gilt stock lending by removing the restrictions on who could borrow and lend stock, thus ensuring a "level playing field" between the two types of transaction. The gilt-edged stock lending agreement (GESLA) was also updated to ensure that it dovetailed with the new gilt repo legal agreement; the revised GESLA was issued in December 1995, and repo and stock lending are inter-linked aspects of the new, open market. In the run-up to the start of repo trading, market practitioners and regulators drew up recommended market practices, set out in the Gilt Repo Code of Best Practice. The associated legal agreement is the BMA/ISMA Global Master Repurchase Agreement, with an addendum to cover special features of gilts such as the use of delivery by value (DBV) within the Central Gilts Office settlement mechanism.

The market grew to about £50 billion of repos and stock lending outstanding in the first two months, further growth took it to nearly £95 billion by February 1997, of which £70 billion was in repos. This figure fell to about £75 billion by November 1998, compared with £100 billion for sterling CDs. It had grown to over £90 billion at end-2004. Data collected on turnover in the market suggests that average daily turnover in gilt repo was around £17 billion through 2004. Figure 12.18 shows repo and stock lending volumes as at November 2003. Market volume growth is shown in Figure 12.19.

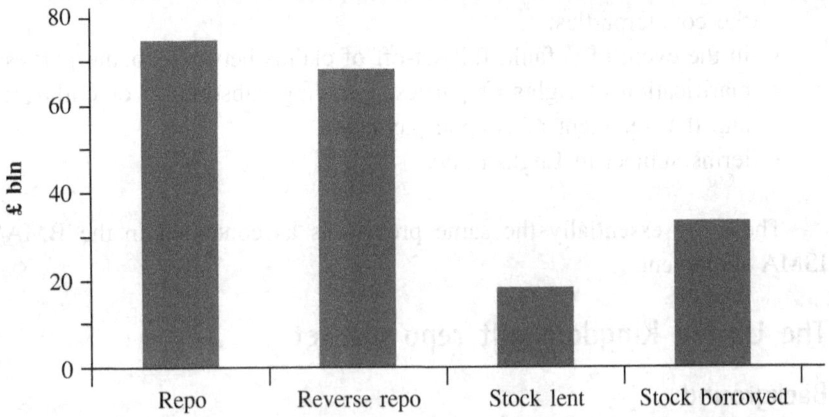

Figure 12.18 Gilt repo market volumes November 2003
Source: BoE.

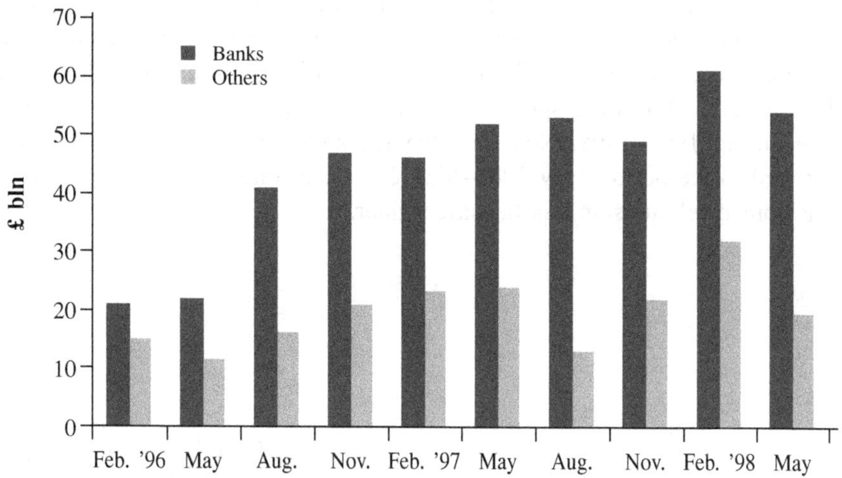

Figure 12.19 Gilt repo market growth, 1996–1998
Source: BoE.

Gilt repo and other sterling money markets

Because it was introduced as a "big bang" from one explicit start date, it is worth reviewing the input of the gilt repo market on the sterling money markets as a whole. This shows us that repo had a tremendously positive impact on the liquidity and transparency of the money market overall. Essentially, gilt repo developed alongside growth in the existing unsecured money markets. There has been a visible shift in short-term money market trading patterns from unsecured to secured money. According to the BoE, market participants estimate that gilt repo now accounts for about half of all overnight transactions in the sterling money markets. The repo GC rate tends to trade below the interbank rate, on average about 10–15 basis points below, reflecting its status as government credit. The gap is less obvious at very short maturities, due to the lower value of such credit over the short term and also reflecting the higher demand for short-term funding through repo by securities houses that may not have access to unsecured money.

The certificate of deposit (CD) market has grown substantially, partly because the growth of the gilt repo and stock lending market has contributed to demand for CDs for use as collateral in stock loans. One effect of gilt repo on the money market is a possible association with a reduction in the volatility of overnight unsecured rates. Fluctuations in the overnight unsecured market have been reduced since the start of an open repo market, although the evidence is not conclusive. This may be due to repo providing an alternative funding method for market participants, which may have reduced pressure on the unsecured market in overnight funds. It may also have enhanced the ability of financial intermediaries to distribute liquidity. Figure 12.20 shows the spread between the three-month sterling interbank rate during 1997–1998. Note that the spread is always positive. Moving forward to the period May 2005–May 2006, and Figure 12.21, we see that this spread relationship has become tighter.

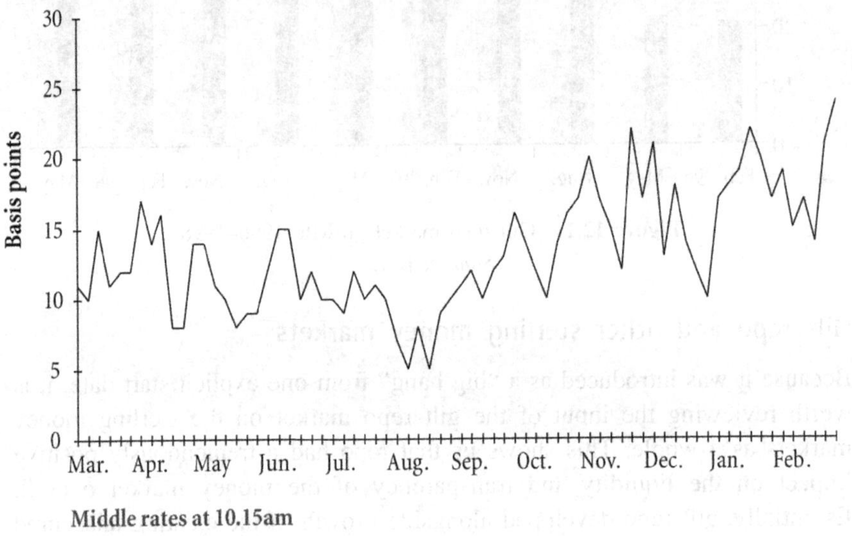

Figure 12.20 Three-month sterling interbank rate minus three-month Gilt Repo GC rate 1997/98
Sources: BoE, Bloomberg, Reuters

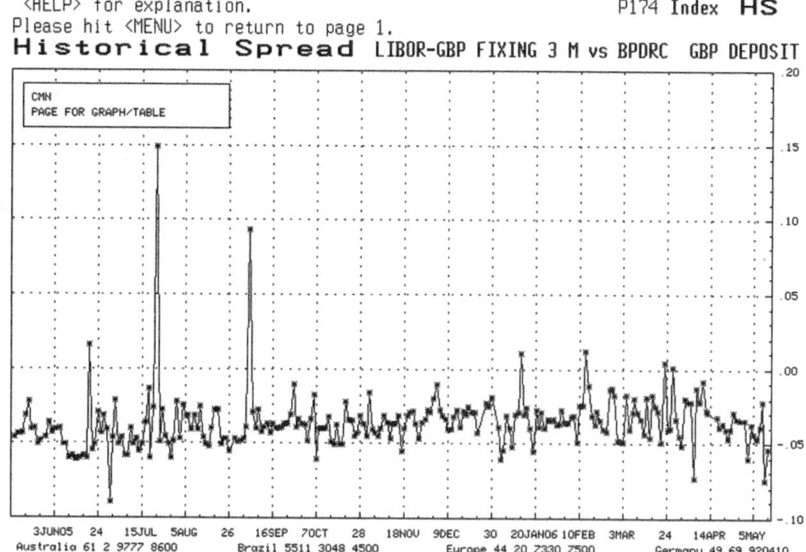

Figure 12.21 GBP 3-mo Libor and 3-mo GC rate spread

References and bibliography

Choudhry, M. 2003, *The Global Repo Market*, John Wiley & Sons, Singapore.

Choudhry, M. 2006, *An Introduction to Repo Markets,* 3rd Edition, John Wiley & Sons, Chichester.

Fabozzi, F. 1997, *Securities Lending and Repurchase Agreements*, FJF Associates, New Hope, PA.

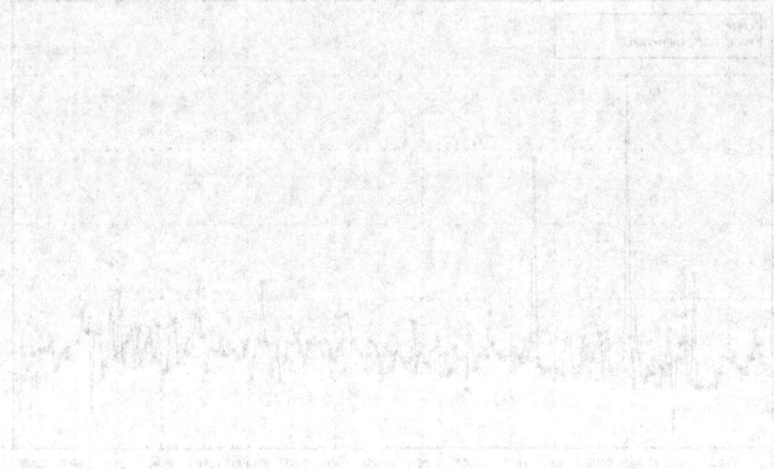

CHAPTER

13

Money Market Derivatives

ALM practitioners use a variety of derivative instruments for the purposes of trading and hedging. These are primarily interest-rate derivatives. In this chapter we review the two main contracts used in money markets trading, the short-term *interest-rate future* and the *forward rate agreement* (FRA). Money market derivatives are priced on the basis of the *forward rate*, and are flexible instruments for hedging against or speculating on forward interest rates. The FRA and the exchange-traded interest-rate future both date from around the same time, and although initially developed to hedge forward interest-rate exposure, they now have a variety of uses. In this chapter we review the instruments and their main uses.

Forward rate agreements

An FRA is an OTC derivative instrument that trades as part of the money markets. It is essentially a forward-starting loan, but with no exchange of principal, so that only the difference in interest rates is exchanged. Trading in FRAs began in the early 1980s and the market now is large and liquid; turnover in London exceeds $5 billion each day.[1] In effect, an FRA is a forward-dated loan, dealt at a fixed rate, but with no exchange of principal – only the interest applicable on the notional amount between the rate dealt at and the actual rate prevailing at the time of settlement changing hands. That is, FRAs are *off-balance sheet* (OBS) instruments. By trading today at an interest rate that is effective at some point in the future, FRAs enable banks and corporates to hedge forward interest-rate exposure. They are also used to speculate on the level of future interest rates.

---

[1] *Source*: British Bankers Association (BBA).

Definition of an FRA

An FRA is an agreement to borrow or lend a *notional* cash sum for a period of time lasting up to 12 months, starting at any point over the next 12 months, at an agreed rate of interest (the FRA rate). The "buyer" of an FRA is borrowing a notional sum of money while the "seller" is lending this cash sum. Note how this differs from all other money market instruments. In the cash market, the party buying a CD or Bill, or bidding for stock in the repo market, is the lender of funds. In the FRA market, to "buy" is to "borrow". Of course, we use the term "notional" because with an FRA no borrowing or lending of cash actually takes place, as it is an OBS product. The notional sum is simply the amount on which interest payment is calculated.

So when an FRA is traded, the buyer is borrowing (and the seller is lending) a specified notional sum at a fixed rate of interest for a specified period, the "loan" to commence at an agreed date in the future. The *buyer* is the notional borrower, and so if there is a rise in interest rates between the date that the FRA is traded and the date that the FRA comes into effect, he or she will be protected. If there is a fall in interest rates, the buyer must pay the difference between the rate at which the FRA was traded and the actual rate, as a percentage of the notional sum. The buyer may be using the FRA to hedge an actual exposure, that is an actual borrowing of money, or simply speculating on a rise in interest rates. The counterparty to the transaction, the *seller* of the FRA, is the notional lender of funds, and has fixed the rate for lending funds. If there is a fall in interest rates the seller will gain, and if there is a rise in rates the seller will pay. Again, the seller may have an actual loan of cash to hedge or be a speculator.

In FRA trading only the payment that arises as a result of the difference in interest rates changes hands. There is no exchange of cash at the time of the trade. The cash payment that does arise is the difference in interest rates between that at which the FRA was traded and the actual rate prevailing when the FRA matures, as a percentage of the notional amount. FRAs are traded by both banks and corporates, and between banks. The FRA market is very liquid in all major currencies, and rates are readily quoted on screens by both banks and brokers. Dealing is over the telephone or over a dealing system such as Reuters.

The terminology quoting FRAs refers to the borrowing time period and the time at which the FRA comes into effect (or matures). Hence, if a buyer of an FRA wished to hedge against a rise in rates to cover a three-month loan starting in three months' time, he or she would transact a "three-against-six-month" FRA, or more usually denoted as a 3x6 or 3-v-6 FRA. This is referred to in the market as a "threes-sixes" FRA, and means a three-month loan beginning in three months' time. So correspondingly a "ones-fours" FRA (1v4) is a three-month loan beginning in one month's time, and a "three-nines" FRA (3v9) is six-month money beginning in three month's time.

Note that when one buys an FRA one is "borrowing" funds. This differs from cash products such as CD or repo, as well as interest-rate futures, where to "buy" is to lend funds.

EXAMPLE 13.1 A forward-date interest-rate exposure

A company knows that it will need to borrow £1 million in three months' time for a 12-month period. It can borrow funds today at Libor + 50 basis points. Libor rates today are at 5%, but the company's treasurer expects rates to go up to about 6% over the next few weeks. So the company will be forced to borrow at higher rates unless some sort of hedge is transacted to protect the borrowing requirement. The treasurer decides to buy a 3v15 ("threes-fifteens") FRA to cover the 12-month period beginning three months from now. A bank quotes $5^1/_2$% for the FRA, which the company buys for a notional £1 million. Three months from now rates have indeed gone up to 6%, so the treasurer must borrow funds at $6^1/_2$% (the Libor rate plus spread). However, she will receive a settlement amount that will be the difference between the rate at which the FRA was bought and today's 12-month Libor rate (6%) as a percentage of £1 million, which will compensate for some of the increased borrowing costs.

FRA mechanics

In virtually every market FRAs trade under a set of terms and conventions that are identical. The British Bankers Association (BBA) has compiled standard legal documentation to cover FRA trading. The following standard terms are used in the market.

- *Notional sum*: the amount for which the FRA is traded.
- *Trade date*: the date on which the FRA is dealt.
- *Settlement date*: the date on which the notional loan or deposit of funds becomes effective; that is, is said to begin. This date is used, in conjunction with the notional sum, for calculation purposes only as no actual loan or deposit takes place.
- *Fixing date*: the date on which the *reference rate* is determined; that is, the rate to which the FRA dealing rate is compared.
- *Maturity date*: the date on which the notional loan or deposit expires.
- *Contract period*: the time between the settlement date and maturity date.
- *FRA rate*: the interest rate at which the FRA is traded.
- *Reference rate*: the rate used as part of the calculation of the settlement amount, usually the Libor rate on the fixing date for the contract period in question.
- *Settlement sum*: the amount calculated as the difference between the FRA rate and the reference rate as a percentage of the notional sum, paid by one party to the other on the settlement date.

These terms are illustrated in Figure 13.1.

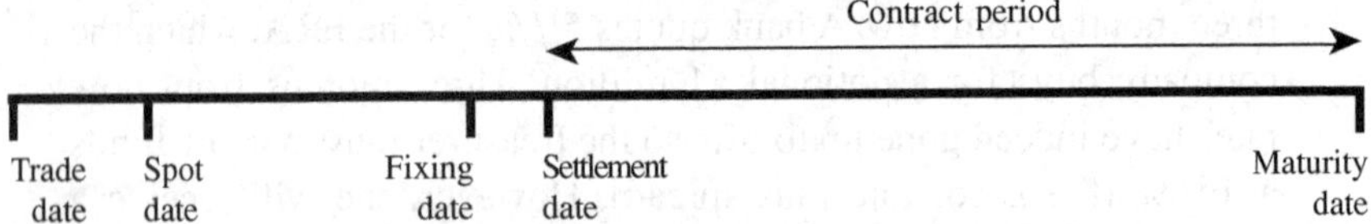

Figure 13.1 Key dates in an FRA trade

The spot date is usually two business days after the trade date; however, it can by agreement be sooner or later than this. The settlement date will be the time period after the spot date referred to by the FRA terms; for example, a 1x4 FRA will have a settlement date one calendar month after the spot date. The fixing date is usually two business days before the settlement date. The settlement sum is paid on the settlement date, and as it refers to an amount over a period of time that is paid up front, at the start of the contract period, the calculated sum is discounted present value. This is because a normal payment of interest on a loan/deposit is paid at the end of the time period to which it relates; because an FRA makes this payment at the *start* of the relevant period, the settlement amount is a discounted present value sum.

With most FRA trades the reference rate is the Libor setting on the fixing date.

The settlement sum is calculated after the fixing date, for payment on the settlement date. We may illustrate this with an hypothetical example. Consider a case where a corporate has bought £1 million notional of a 1v4 FRA, and dealt at 5.75%, and that the market rate is 6.50% on the fixing date. The contract period is 91 days. In the cash market the extra interest charge that the corporate would pay is a simple interest calculation, and is:

$$\frac{(6.50 - 5.75)}{100} \times 1{,}000{,}000 \times \frac{91}{365} = £1{,}869.86.$$

This extra interest that the corporate is facing would be payable with the interest payment for the loan, which (as it is a money market loan) is when the loan matures. Under an FRA then, the settlement sum payable should, if it were paid on the same day as the cash market interest charge, be exactly equal to this, which would make it a perfect hedge. As we noted above though, FRA settlement value is paid at the start of the contract period; that is, the beginning of the underlying loan and not the end. Therefore the settlement sum has to be adjusted to account for this, and the amount of the adjustment is the value of the interest that would be earned if the unadjusted cash value was invested for the contract period in the money market. The settlement value is given by (13.1):

$$\text{Settlement} = \frac{(r_{ref} - r_{FRA}) \times M \times {}^{n}/_{B}}{1 + (r_{ref} \times {}^{n}/_{B})} \tag{13.1}$$

where

r_{ref} is the reference interest-fixing rate
r_{FRA} is the FRA rate or *contract rate*
M is the notional value
n is the number of days in the contract period
B is the day-count base (360 or 365).

The expression in (13.1) simply calculates the extra interest payable in the cash market, resulting from the difference between the two interest rates, and then discounts the amount because it is payable at the start of the period and not, as would happen in the cash market, at the end of the period.

In our illustration, as the fixing rate is higher than the dealt rate, the corporate buyer of the FRA receives the settlement sum from the seller. This then compensates the corporate for the higher borrowing costs that he or she would have to pay in the cash market. If the fixing rate had been lower than 5.75%, the buyer would pay the difference to the seller, because the cash market rates will mean that he or she is subject to a lower interest rate in the cash market. What the FRA has done is hedge the interest rate, so that whatever happens in the market, it will pay 5.75% on its borrowing.

A market-maker in FRAs is trading short-term interest rates. The settlement sum is the value of the FRA. The concept is exactly as with trading short-term interest-rate futures; a trader who buys an FRA is running a long position, so that if on the fixing date $r_{ref} > r_{FRA}$, the settlement sum is positive and the trader realises a profit. What has happened is that the trader, by buying the FRA, "borrowed" money at an interest rate, which subsequently rose. This is a gain, exactly like a *short* position in an interest-rate future, where if the price goes down (that is, interest rates go up), the trader realises a gain. Equally, a "short" position in an FRA, put on by selling an FRA, realises a gain if on the fixing date $r_{ref} < r_{FRA}$.

FRA pricing

As their name informs us, FRAs are forward rate instruments and are priced using standard forward rate principles.[2] An introduction to the concept of spot and forward rates can be found. Consider an investor who has two alternatives, either a six-month investment at 5% or a one-year investment at 6%. If the investor wishes to invest for six months and then roll-over the investment for a further six months, what rate is required for the roll-over period such that the final return equals the 6% available from the one-year investment? If we view an FRA rate as the breakeven forward rate between the two periods, we simply solve for this forward rate and that is our approximate FRA rate. This rate is sometimes referred to as the interest-rate "gap" in the money markets (not to be confused with an interbank desk's

[2] An introduction to the basics of spot and forward rates can be found in any number of finance textbooks; the author particularly likes Windas (1993) and Fabozzi and Mann (2001) for their accessibility for beginners. His own treatment of the subject is in Chapter 9.

gap risk, the interest-rate exposure arising from the net maturity position of its assets and liabilities, and which was considered in Chapter 5.

We can use the standard forward-rate breakeven formula to solve for the required FRA rate; we established this relationship in Chapter 9 when discussing the calculation of forward rates that are arbitrage-free. The relationship given in (13.2) below connects simple (bullet) interest rates for periods of time up to one year, where no compounding of interest is required. As FRAs are money market instruments we are not required to calculate rates for periods in excess of one year,[3] where compounding would need to be built into the equation. The expression is given by (13.2):

$$(1 + r_2 t_2) = (1 + r_1 t_1)(1 + r_f t_f) \qquad (13.2)$$

where

r_2 is the cash market interest rate for the long period
r_1 is the cash market interest rate for the short period
r_f is the forward rate for the gap period
t_2 is the time period from today to the end of the long period
t_1 is the time period from today to the end of the short period
t_f is the forward gap time period, or the contract period for the FRA.

This is illustrated diagrammatically in Figure 13.2.

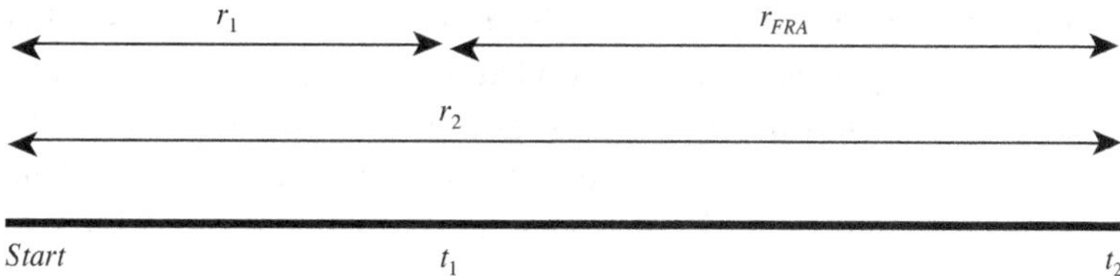

Figure 13.2 Rates used in FRA pricing

The time period t_1 is the time from the dealing date to the FRA settlement date, while t_2 is the time from the dealing date to the FRA maturity date. The time period for the FRA (contract period) is t_2 minus t_1. We can replace the symbol "t" for time period with "n" for the actual number of days in the time periods themselves. If we do this and then rearrange the equation to solve for r_{fra} the FRA rate, we obtain (13.3):

[3] Although it is of course possible to trade FRAs with contract periods greater than one year, for which a different pricing formula must be used.

$$r_{FRA} = \frac{r_2 n_2 - r_1 n_1}{n_{fra}\left(1 + r_1 \dfrac{n_1}{365}\right)} \tag{13.3}$$

where

n_1 is the number of days from the dealing date or spot date to the settlement date
n_2 is the number of days from dealing date or spot date to the maturity date
r_1 is the spot rate to the settlement date
r_2 is the spot rate from the spot date to the maturity date
n_{fra} is the number of days in the FRA contract period
r_{FRA} is the FRA rate.

If the formula is applied to, say, the US dollar money markets, the 365 in the equation is replaced by 360, the day-count base for that market.

In practice FRAs are priced off the exchange-traded short-term interest-rate future for that currency, so that sterling FRAs are priced off LIFFE short-sterling futures. Traders normally use a spreadsheet pricing model that has futures prices directly fed into it. FRA positions are also usually hedged with other FRAs or short-term interest-rate futures.

FRA prices in practice

The dealing rates for FRAs are possibly the most liquid and transparent of any non-exchange-traded derivative instrument. This is because they are calculated directly from exchange-traded interest-rate contracts. The key consideration for FRA market-makers, however, is how the rates behave in relation to other market interest rates. The forward rate calculated from two period spot rates must, as we have seen, be set such that it is arbitrage-free. If for example the six-month spot rate was 8.00% and the nine-month spot rate was 9.00%, the 6v9 FRA would have an approximate rate of 11%. What would be the effect of a change in one or both of the spot rates? The same arbitrage-free principle must apply. If there is an increase in the short-rate period, the FRA rate must decrease, to make the total return unchanged. The extent of the change in the FRA rate is a function of the ratio of the contract period to the long period. If the rate for the long period increases, the FRA rate will increase, by an amount related to the ratio between the total period to the contract period. The FRA rate for any term is generally a function of the three-month Libor rate generally, the rate traded under an interest-rate future. A general rise in this rate will see a rise in FRA rates.

The general relationship for FRA and money market rates can be shown by (13.4), which is obtained from a partial differentiation of r_{FRA} with respect to r_1 and r_2, the rates in the pricing equation in (13.3):

$$\frac{\partial r_{FRA}}{\partial r_1} \approx -\frac{n_1}{n_{FRA}}$$

$$\frac{\partial r_{FRA}}{\partial r_2} \approx -\frac{n_2}{n_{FRA}} \qquad (13.4)$$

$$\frac{\partial r_{FRA}}{\partial r_{ALL}} \approx 1.$$

EXAMPLE 13.2 Pricing FRAs from futures

The following are interest-rate futures prices for short-sterling contracts:

Jun 00 94.70 (implied three-month interest rate: 5.30%)
Sep 00 94.65 (implied three-month interest rate: 5.35%)
Dec 99 94.60 (implied three-month interest rate: 5.40%).

A trader is asked for the offer side of a 3v6 FRA in £5 million and also to advise on the hedge by futures. If we assume there are no bid–offer spreads, what should the rate on the FRA be?

The FRA dates are given below:

Contract period: 20 June to 20 September (92 days)
Settlement date: 18 June.

As the expiry date for the June futures contract is 18 June, the FRA rate will be the implied June futures rate of 5.30%. The settlement amount is:

$$\frac{5{,}000{,}000 \times (0.0530 - \text{Libor}) \times {}^{92}/_{365}}{1 + \text{Libor} \times {}^{92}/_{365}}.$$

The profit or loss on the futures contract, which is not discounted is calculated as:

No. of contracts × 500,000 × (0.0530 – Libor) × 90/365.

In a hedge the FRA buyer requires these two values to be equal, so we have:

$$\text{No. of contracts} = 10 \times \frac{92/90}{(1 + \text{Libor} \times 92/365)}.$$

The future Libor rate is of course not known at this point, but if we estimate it as 5.30%, we obtain:

$$\text{No. of contracts} = 10 \times \frac{92/90}{(1 + 0.0530 \times 92/365)} = 10.08746.$$

The hedge here is 10 contracts.

EXAMPLE 13.3 FRA hedging (1)

Using the same prices as in Example 13.2, what is the hedge and price for a sale of a 3v6 FRA against a 6v12 FRA?

The 3v6 FRA is priced at 5.30% as before. A 6v9 FRA, which is the 91 days from 20 September to 20 December, is also priced at the September futures price of 5.35%, and hedged with 10 futures contracts. This is only completely accurate if the futures contract delivery date is the same as the settlement date of the FRA, but it is close enough for our purposes. The 3v9 FRA is equivalent to a *strip* combining the 3v6 FRA and a 6v9 FRA, due to the principle of arbitrage-free pricing, so the 3v9 FRA price is calculated as:

$$((1 + 0.0530 \times 92/365) \times (1 + 0.0535 \times 91/365) - 1) \times 365/183$$

$$= 5.3604\%.$$

The price of the 6v12 FRA may be obtained from the price of a 6v9 FRA and a 9v12 FRA (90 days from 20 December to 20 March), because a strip of these two FRAs is the same as the 6v12 FRA. The price is calculated below.

$$((1 + 0.0535 \times 91/365) \times (1 + 0.0540 \times 90/365) - 1) \times 365/181$$

$$= 5.4107\%.$$

EXAMPLE 13.4 FRA hedging (2)

Again using the prices in Example 13.2, our trader now wishes to sell a 3v8 FRA (153 days from 20 June to 20 November) and a 6v11 FRA (153 days from 20 September to 20 February). How are these priced?

The 3v8 FRA is the implied rate for five-month money in three months' time. We do not have the spot or futures rates that allow us to calculate this rate exactly, so we must interpolate using the rates we do have. This then becomes:

$$3v6 + (3v9 - 3v6) \times \frac{\text{Days in 3v8} - \text{Days in 3v6}}{\text{Days in 3v8} - \text{Days in 3v6}}$$

$$= [5.30 + (5.3604 - 5.30) \times (153 - 92 / (183 - 92)]$$

$$= 5.3405\%.$$

EXAMPLE 13.5 Valuation of an existing FRA

In order to value an FRA, it must be decomposed into its constituent parts, which are equivalent to a loan and deposit. Both these parts are then present valued, and the value of the FRA is simply the net present value of both legs. For example, a 6v9 FRA is equivalent to a six-month asset and a nine-month liability. If we assume that the six-month rate is 5% and the nine-month rate is 6%, on a notional principal of £1 million, the value of the FRA is given by:

Value	Term (yr)	Rate (%)	PV
£1 million	0.4932	5.00	+£976,223
£1 million	0.7397	6.00	–£957,814

The value of the FRA is therefore £18,409.

EXAMPLE 13.6 Hedging an FRA position

An FRA market-maker sells an EUR100 million 3v6 FRA; that is, an agreement to make a notional deposit (without exchange of principal) for three months in three months' time, at a rate of 7.52%. He is exposed to the risk that interest rates will have risen by the FRA settlement date in three months' time.

Date:	14 December
3v6 FRA rate:	7.52%
March futures price:	92.50%
Current spot rate:	6.85%

Action

The dealer first needs to calculate a precise hedge ratio. This is a three stage process:

(1) Calculate the nominal value of a basis point move in Libor on the FRA settlement payment:

$$BPV = FRA_{nom} \times 0.01\% \times {}^{n}/360.$$

Therefore: EUR100,000,000 × 0.01% × 90/360 = EUR2,500

(2) Find the present value of (1) by discounting it back to the transaction date using the FRA and spot rates:

Present value of a basis point move =

$$\frac{\text{Nominal value of basis point}}{(1 + \text{Spot rate} \times \frac{\text{Days in hedge period}}{360})(1 + \text{FRA rate} \times \frac{\text{Days in hedge period}}{360})}$$

Therefore

$$\frac{\text{EUR2,500}}{(1 + 6.85\% \times {}^{90}/_{360})(1 + 7.52\% \times {}^{90}/_{360})}.$$

(3) Determine the correct hedge ratio by dividing (2) by the futures tick value:

Hedge ratio = 2,412/25 = 96.48.

The appropriate number of contracts for the hedge of an EUR 100,000,000 3v6 FRA would therefore be 96 or 97 – as the fraction is under one-half, 96 is correct. To hedge the risk of an increase in interest rates, the trader sells 96 EUR three months futures contracts at 92.50. Any increase in rates during the hedge period should be offset by a gain realised on the futures contracts through daily variation margin receipts.

Outcome

Date:	15 March
Three-month Libor:	7.625%
March exchange delivery settlement price (EDSP):	92.38

The hedge is lifted upon expiry of the March futures contracts. Three-month Libor on the FRA settlement date has risen to 7.625% so the trader incurs a loss of EUR25,759 on his FRA position (that is, EUR26,250 discounted back over the three-month FRA period at current Libor rate), calculated as follows:

$$\frac{(\text{Libor} - \text{FRA rate})(\text{Days in FRA period}/360) \times \text{Contract nominal amount}}{1 + \text{Libor rate} \times (\text{Days in FRA period}/360)}$$

Therefore:

$26{,}250^{*}/\ (1 + 7.625\% \times {}^{90}/_{360}) = \text{EUR}25{,}759$

*that is, $0.105\% \times {}^{90}/_{360} \times \text{EUR}10{,}000{,}000$

Futures P/L:
12 ticks (92.50 – 92.38) × EUR25 × 96 contracts = EUR28,800.

Conclusion

The EUR25,759 loss on the FRA position is more than offset by the EUR28,800 profit on the futures position when the hedge is lifted.

If the dealer has sold 100 contracts his futures profit would have been EUR30,000, and, accordingly, a less accurate hedge. The excess profit in the hedge position can mostly be attributed to the arbitrage profit realised by the market-maker (that is, the market-maker has sold the FRA for 7.52% and in effect bought it back in the futures market by selling futures at 92.50 or 7.50% for a 2 tick profit.)

Long-dated FRAs

There is a liquid market in FRAs that extend over periods longer than one year. For such instruments the calculation of the FRA rate is different because the pricing formula has to take into account the compounding effect that applies in the cash market. The correct approach is to calculate the zero-coupon discount factors for the relevant terms, and assume an equivalent cash loan over the contract period, and use these in an adjusted pricing formula. We illustrate this with an hypothetical example to calculate the price of a 15v18 FRA.

A sterling money market cash rate desk is given the following interest rates:

12 months: 6.75%
15 months: 6.875%
18 months: 6.9375%.

The 12-month discount factor is: $1/(1 + 0.0675) = 0.93677$.

An equivalent cash trade for the FRA would be a 15-month deposit and a simultaneous 12-month loan. The cash flows from such transactions would be:

Loan: $(-100) + (6.875 \times 0.93677) = -93.55971$
Deposit: $100 + (6.875 \times 91/365) = 101.71404$.

Therefore the 15-month discount factor is 93.55971/101.71404 or 0.919831. The cash flows from a deposit of 18 months and a loan of 12 months are:

Loan: $(-100) + (6.9375 \times 0.93677) = -93.50116$
Deposit: $100 + (6.9375 \times 183/365) = 103.47825$.

The 18-month discount factor may then be calculated, and is 93.55971/103.47825 or 0.9041486. Therefore, the 15v18 FRA rate is given by:

$$r_{FRA} = \left(\frac{1/0.9041486}{1/0.919831} - 1\right) \times \frac{365}{92} = 6.88140\%.$$

Bloomberg screens

FRA rates are available from a number of banks and brokers on the Bloomberg screens. Figure 13.3 on page 554 shows the rates page from BBVA as at 16 June 2004, with euro FRA rates alongside euro EONIA and EURIBOR swaps. The BBVA screen is available to all users, which is uncommon (and welcome!) since most banks make their screens available only to registered customers.

Broker screens are available to all users. Figure 13.4 on page 554 shows the USD FRA rates page from Tullett & Tokyo on the Bloomberg screens, as at 17 August 2004. Note that the longest date quoted is the 12x24 FRA.

The FRA valuation page on Bloomberg is BCFR. This is shown in Figure 13.5 on page 555. We see that the screen has been used to calculate the value of a 2x5 FRA with the following terms:

Trade date:	17 August 2004
Settlement date:	19 August 2004
Start date:	19 October 2004
End date:	19 January 2005
Amount:	USD1 million.

The FRA rate of 2.00106% has been input to obtain the valuation. When used the screen defaults with current cash and futures rates; the necessary futures contract prices to the equivalent maturity date are shown. In this case the Eurodollar contracts for Sep04, Dec04, Mar05 and Jun05 are shown.

2 P1P300 Govt **BBVC**

9:36 **BBVA** PAGE 1 / 1

EUR FWD EONIA (ACT/360) RATES	BID	ASK	TIME	EUR SWAPS vs EURIBOR (ACT/360) RATES	BID	ASK	TIME
1) 1X2	2.0450	2.0650	9:35	13) 1Y/3M	2.3700	2.3900	8:24
2) 2X3	2.0500	2.0700	9:32	14) 18M/3M	2.5900	2.6100	9:34
3) 1X4	2.0600	2.0800	9:30	15) 2Y/3M			
4) 2X5	2.0800	2.1000	9:31				
5) 3X6	2.1300	2.1500	9:32	16) 1Y/6M	2.3800	2.4000	8:00
6) 6X12	2.4450	2.4650	9:26	17) 18M/6M	2.6000	2.6200	9:34
				18) 2Y/6M			
3M EUR FRAS RATES	**BID**	**ASK**	**TIME**				
7) 1X4	2.1100	2.1300	7:05				
8) 2X5	2.1300	2.1500	7:10				
9) 3X6	2.2000	2.2200	7:16				
10) 4X7	2.2600	2.2800	8:23				
11) 5X8	2.3100	2.3300	9:27				
12) 6X9	2.3600	2.3800	8:23				

Australia 61 2 9777 8600 Brazil 5511 3048 4500 Europe 44 20 7330 7500 Germany 49 69 920410
Hong Kong 852 2977 6000 Japan 81 3 3201 8900 Singapore 65 6212 1000 U.S. 1 212 318 2000 Copyright 2004 Bloomberg L.P.
G657-802-2 02-Jul-04 9:36:01

Figure 13.3 BBVA euro FRA rates, as at 16 June 2004

1 N2N121 Govt **TTFR**

Screen Printed

11:21 **TULLETT & TOKYO** PAGE 1 / 1

USD FRAs	Bid	Ask	Time	USD FRAs	Bid	Ask	Time
1) 1 X 4	1.902	1.932	10:55	16) 12 X 18	3.189	3.219	11:16
2) 2 X 5	2.081	2.111	11:10	17) 1 X 10	2.231	2.261	11:16
3) 3 X 6	2.165	2.195	11:10	18) 2 X 11	2.339	2.369	11:16
4) 4 X 7	2.228	2.258	11:10	19) 3 X 12	2.444	2.474	11:16
5) 5 X 8	2.273	2.303	11:16	20) 6 X 18	2.913	2.943	11:16
6) 6 X 9	2.412	2.442	11:16	21) 12 X 24	3.467	3.497	11:09
7) 7 X 10	2.527	2.557	11:16				
8) 8 X 11	2.623	2.653	11:16				
9) 9 X 12	2.725	2.755	11:16				
10) 1 X 7	2.070	2.100	11:09				
11) 2 X 8	2.182	2.212	11:16				
12) 3 X 9	2.285	2.315	11:16				
13) 4 X 10	2.384	2.414	11:16				
14) 5 X 11	2.457	2.487	11:16				
15) 6 X 12	2.584	2.614	11:16				

Australia 61 2 9777 8600 Brazil 5511 3048 4500 Europe 44 20 7330 7500 Germany 49 69 920410
Hong Kong 852 2977 6000 Japan 81 3 3201 8900 Singapore 65 6212 1000 U.S. 1 212 318 2000 Copyright 2004 Bloomberg L.P.
2 17-Aug-04 11:21:35

Figure 13.4 Tullett and Tokyo USD FRA rates page, 17 August 2004

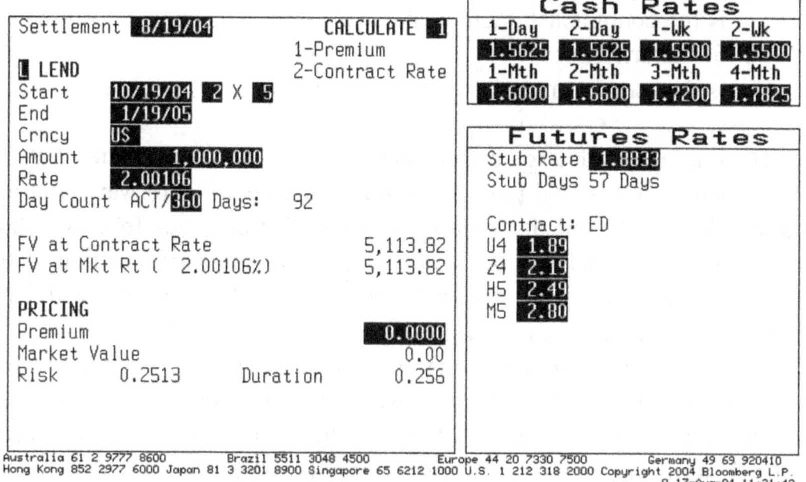

Figure 13.5 Bloomberg FRA valuation page BCFR

Forward contracts

A forward contract is an OTC instrument with terms set for delivery of an underlying asset at some point in the future. That is, a forward contract fixes the price and the conditions now for an asset that will be delivered in the future. As each contract is tailor-made to suit user requirements, a forward contract is not as liquid as an exchange-traded futures contract with standardised terms.

The theoretical textbook price of a forward contract is the spot price of the underlying asset plus the funding cost associated with holding the asset until forward expiry date, when the asset is delivered. More formally we may write the price of a forward contract (written on an underlying asset that pays no dividends, such as a zero-coupon bond), as (13.5):

$$P_{fwd} = P_{spot} e^{rn} \tag{13.5}$$

where

P_{spot} is the price of the underlying asset of the forward contract
r is the continuously compounded risk-free interest rate for a period of maturity n
n is the term to maturity of the forward contract in days.

The rule of no-arbitrage pricing states that (13.5) must be true. If $P_{fwd} < P_{und}e^{rn}$ then a trader could buy the cheaper instrument, the forward contract, and simultaneously sell the underlying asset. The proceeds from the short sale could be invested at r for n days; on expiry the short position in the asset is closed out at the forward price P_{fwd} and the trader will have generated a profit of $P_{und}e^{rn} - P_{fwd}$. In the opposite scenario, where $P_{fwd} > P_{und}e^{rn}$, a trader could put on a long position in the underlying asset, funded at the risk-free interest rate r for n days, and simultaneously sell the forward contract. On expiry the asset is sold under the terms of the forward contract at the forward price and the proceeds from the sale used to close out the funding initially taken on to buy the asset. Again a profit would be generated, which would be equal to the difference between the two prices.

The relationship described here is used by the market to assume that forward rates implied by the price of short-term interest-rate futures contracts are equal to forward rates given by a same-maturity forward contract. Although this assumption holds good for futures contracts with a maturity of up to three or four years, it breaks down for longer-dated futures and forwards. This is examined in the section on convexity bias in Choudhry (2004).

Short-term interest-rate futures

Description

A *futures* contract is a transaction that fixes the price today for a commodity that will be delivered at some point in the future. Financial futures fix the price for interest rates, bonds, equities and so on, and trade in the same manner as commodity futures. Contracts for futures are standardised and traded on recognised exchanges. In London the main futures exchange is LIFFE, although other futures are also traded on, for example, the International Petroleum Exchange and the London Metal Exchange. The money markets trade short-term interest-rate futures, which fix the rate of interest on a notional fixed-term deposit of money (usually for 90 days or three months) for a specified period in the future. The sum is notional because no actual sum of money is deposited when buying or selling futures; the instrument is off-balance sheet. Buying such a contract is equivalent to making a notional deposit, while selling a contract is equivalent to borrowing a notional sum.

The three-month interest-rate future is the most widely used instrument used for hedging interest-rate risk.

The LIFFE exchange in London trades short-term interest-rate futures for major currencies, including sterling, euros, yen and Swiss francs. Table 13.1 summarises the terms for the short sterling contract as traded on LIFFE.

Name:	90-day sterling Libor interest-rate future
Contract size:	£500,000
Delivery months:	March, June, September, December
Delivery date:	First business day after the last trading day
Last trading day:	Third Wednesday of delivery month
Price:	100 minus interest rate
Tick size:	0.005
Tick value:	£6.25
Trading hours:	LIFFE CONNECT™ 0805 – 1800 hours

Table 13.1 Description of LIFFE short sterling future contract
Source: LIFFE.

The original futures contracts related to physical commodities, which is why we speak of *delivery* when referring to the expiry of financial futures contracts. Exchange-traded futures such as those on LIFFE are set to expire every quarter during the year. The short sterling contract is a deposit of cash, so as its price refers to the rate of interest on this deposit, the price of the contract is set as $P = 100 - r$ where P is the price of the contract and r is the rate of interest at the time of expiry implied by the futures contract. This means that if the price of the contract rises, the rate of interest implied goes down, and vice versa. For example, the price of the June 1999 short sterling future (written as Jun99 or M99, from the futures identity letters of H, M, U and Z for contracts expiring in March, June, September and December respectively) at the start of trading on 13 March 1999 was 94.880, which implied a three-month Libor rate of 5.12% on expiry of the contract in June. If a trader bought 20 contracts at this price and then sold them just before the close of trading that day, when the price had risen to 94.96, an implied rate of 5.04%, she would have made 16 ticks profit or £2000. That is, a

16 tick upward price movement in a long position of 20 contracts is equal to £2000. This is calculated as follows:

Profit = Ticks gained × Tick value × Number of contracts
Loss = Ticks lost × Tick value × Number of contracts.

The tick value for the short sterling contract is straightforward to calculate, since we know that the contract size is £500,000. There is a minimum price movement (tick movement) of 0.005% and the contract has a three-month "maturity". So we have:

$$\text{Tick value} = 0.005\% \times £500{,}000 \times 3/12 = £6.25.$$

The profit made by the trader in our example is logical because if we buy short sterling futures we are depositing (notional) funds; if the price of the futures rises, it means the interest rate has fallen. We profit because we have "deposited" funds at a higher rate beforehand. If we expected sterling interest rates to rise, we would sell short sterling futures, which is equivalent to borrowing funds and locking in the loan rate at a lower level.

Note how the concept of buying and selling interest rate futures differs from FRAs: if we buy an FRA we are borrowing notional funds, whereas if we buy a futures contract we are depositing notional funds. If a position in an interest-rate futures contract is held to expiry, cash settlement will take place on the delivery day for that contract.

Short-term interest-rate contracts in other currencies are similar to the short sterling contract and trade on exchanges such as Eurex in Frankfurt and MATIF in Paris.

Pricing interest-rate futures

The price of a three-month interest-rate futures contract is the implied interest rate for that currency's three-month rate at the time of expiry of the contract. Therefore there is always a close relationship and correlation between futures prices, FRA rates (which are derived from futures prices) and cash market rates. On the day of expiry the price of the future will be equal to the Libor rate as fixed that day. This is known as the Exchange Delivery Settlement Price (EDSP) and is used in the calculation of the delivery amount. During the life of the contract its price will be less closely related to the actual three-month Libor rate *today*, but closely related to the *forward rate* for the time of expiry.

Equations (13.2) and (13.3) were our basic forward rate formulas for money market maturity forward rates, which we adapted to use as our FRA price equation. If we incorporate some extra terminology to cover the dealing dates involved it can also be used as our futures price formula. Let us say that:

T_0 is the trade date
T_M is the contract expiry date
T_{CASH} is the value date for cash market deposits traded on T_0
T_1 is the value date for cash market deposits traded on T_M
T_2 is the maturity date for a three-month cash market deposit traded on T_M.

We can then use Equation (13.3) as our futures price formula to obtain P_{fut}, the futures price for a contract up to the expiry date.

$$P_{fut} = 100 - \frac{r_2 n_2 - r_1 n_1}{n_f \left(1 + r_1 \dfrac{n_1}{365}\right)} \tag{13.6}$$

where

P_{fut} is the futures price
r_1 is the cash market interest rate to T_1
r_2 is the cash market interest rate to T_2
n_1 is the number of days from T_{CASH} to T_1
n_2 is the number of days from T_{CASH} to T_2
n_f is the number of days from T_1 to T_2.

The formula uses a 365-day count convention that applies in the sterling money markets; where the market convention is a 360-day base this is used in the equation instead.

In practice, the price of a contract at any one time will be close to the theoretical price that would be established by (13.6) above. Discrepancies will arise for supply and demand reasons in the market, as well as because Libor rates are often quoted only to the nearest sixteenth or 0.0625. The price between FRAs and futures are correlated very closely; in fact, banks will often price FRAs using futures, and use futures to hedge their FRA books. When hedging an FRA book with futures, the hedge is quite close to being exact, because the two prices track each other almost tick for tick.[4] However, the tick value of a futures contract is fixed, and uses (as we saw

[4] That is, the basis risk is minimised.

above) a 3/12 basis, while FRA settlement values use a 360- or 365-day base. FRA traders will be aware of this when putting on their hedge.

In any good discussion of forward rates it would be emphasised that they are the market's view on future rates using all information available today. As the available information is constantly updated, the forward rate will change. However, forward rates should not be taken to be the market's *prediction* of interest rates in the future; rather, they are the rate that a bank would write on a trade ticket for dealing today at value in the future, using all available information up to the minute the ticket is written. Of course, a futures price today is very unlikely to be in line with the actual three-month interest rate that is prevailing at the time of the contract's expiry. This explains why prices for futures and actual cash rates will differ on any particular day. Up until expiry the futures price is the implied forward rate; of course, there is always a discrepancy between this forward rate and the cash market rate *today*. The gap between the cash price and the futures price is known as the *basis*. This is defined as:

$$\text{Basis} = \text{Cash price} - \text{Futures price}.$$

At any point during the life of a futures contract prior to final settlement – at which point futures and cash rates converge – there is usually a difference between current cash market rates and the rates implied by the futures price. This is the difference we've just explained; in fact, the difference between the price implied by the current three-month interbank deposit and the futures price is known as *simple basis*, but it is what most market participants refer to as the basis. Simple basis consists of two separate components, *theoretical basis* and *value basis*. Theoretical basis is the difference between the price implied by the current three-month interbank deposit rate and that implied by the theoretical fair futures price based on cash market forward rates, given by (13.6) above. This basis may be either positive or negative, depending on the shape of the yield curve; this is illustrated in Example 13.7.

EXAMPLE 13.7 Theoretical basis

Let us examine the relationship between the shape of the yield curve and the basis. Assume that today is 14 March.

(1) Negative yield curve; negative theoretical basis:

3-month Libor:	6.50%
6-month Libor:	6.375%
9-month Libor:	6.25%
One-year Libor:	6.1875%.

Cash price (100 – Libor)	**Contract**	**Fair futures price**	**Theoretical basis**
93.5	Jun.	93.85	–0.35
	Sep.	94.19	–0.69
	Dec.	94.27	–0.77

(2) Flat yield curve; negative theoretical basis:

3-month Libor:	6.50%
6-month Libor:	6.50%
9-month Libor:	6.50%
One-year Libor:	6.50%.

Cash price (100 – Libor)	**Contract**	**Fair futures price**	**Theoretical basis**
93.50	Jun.	93.60	–0.10
	Sep.	93.70	–0.20
	Dec.	93.80	–0.30

(3) Positive yield curve; positive theoretical basis:

3-month Libor:	6.50%
6-month Libor:	6.75%
9-month Libor:	6.9375%
One-year Libor:	7.125%.

Cash price (100 – Libor)	**Contract**	**Fair futures price**	**Theoretical basis**
93.50	Jun.	93.11	0.39
	Sep.	92.93	0.57
	Dec.	92.69	0.81

The above is a very simple example and the steepness and shape of the yield curve will have an impact on the assumptions shown.

The value basis is the difference between the theoretical fair futures price and the actual futures price. It is a measure of how under- or over-valued the futures contract is relative to its fair value. Value basis reflects the fact that a futures contract does not always trade at its mathematically calculated theoretical price, due to the impact of market sentiment and demand and supply. The theoretical price and value can and do move independently of one another and in response to different influences. Both however converge to zero on the last trading day when final cash settlement of the futures contract is made.

Futures contracts do not in practice provide a precise tool for locking into cash market rates today for a transaction that takes place in the future, although this is what they are in theory designed to do. Futures do allow a bank to lock in a rate for a transaction to take place in the future, and this rate is the *forward rate*. The basis is the difference between today's cash market rate and the forward rate on a particular date in the future. As a futures contract approaches expiry, its price and the rate in the cash market will converge (the process is given the name *convergence*). As we noted earlier this is given by the EDSP and the two prices (rates) will be exactly in line at the exact moment of expiry.

Trading interest-rate futures

The term "trading" covers a wide range of activity. Market-makers who are quoting two-way prices to market participants may be tasked with providing a customer service, building up retail and institutional volume, or they may be tasked with purely running the book at a profit and trying to maximise return on capital. The nature of the market that is traded will also have an impact on their approach. In a highly transparent and liquid market such as the US Treasury or the UK gilt market the price spreads are fairly narrow, although increased demand has reduced this somewhat in both markets. However, this means that opportunities for profitable trading as a result of mispricing of individual securities, while not completely extinct, are rare. It is much more common for traders in such markets to take a view on relative-value trades, such as the yield spreads between individual securities or the expected future shape of the yield curve. This is also called spread trading.

A large volume of trading on derivatives exchanges is done for hedging purposes, but speculative trading is also prominent. Very often, bond and interest-rate traders will punt using futures or options contracts, based on their view of market direction. Ironically, market-makers who have a low level of customer business – perhaps because they are newcomers to the market, or for historical reasons or because they do not have the appetite for risk that is required to service the high-quality customers – tend to speculate on the futures exchanges to relieve tedium, often with unfortunate results.

Speculative trading is undertaken on the basis of the views of the trader, desk or head of the department. This view may be an "in-house" view; for example, the collective belief of the economics or research department, or the individual trader's view, which will be formulated as a result of fundamental analysis and technical analysis. The former is an assessment of macroeconomic and microeconomic factors affecting not just the specific bond market itself but the economy as a whole. Those running corporate-debt desks will also concentrate heavily on individual sectors and corporations and their wider environment, because the credit spread – and what drives the credit spread – of corporate bonds is of course key to the performance of the bonds. Technical analysis or charting is a discipline in its own right, and has its adherents. It is based on the belief that over time the patterns displayed by a continuous time series of asset prices will repeat themselves. Therefore, detecting patterns should give a reasonable expectation of how asset prices should behave in the future. Many traders use a combination of fundamental and technical analysis, although chartists often say that for technical analysis to work effectively, it must be the only method adopted by the trader.

A review of technical analysis or "charting" is presented in Chapter 63 of the author's book *The Bond and Money Markets: Strategy, Trading, Analysis* (Choudhry 2001).

In this section, we introduce some common methods and approaches, and some not so common, that might be employed on ALM desk.

Futures trading

Trading with derivatives is often preferred, for both speculative or hedging purposes, to trading in the cash markets mainly because of the liquidity of the market and the ease and low cost of undertaking transactions. The essential features of futures trading are volatility and leverage. To establish a futures position on an exchange, the level of margin required is very low proportional to the notional value of the contracts traded. For speculative purposes, traders often carry out open – that is, uncovered trading – which is a directional bet on the market. So, therefore, if traders believed that short-term sterling interest rates were going to fall, they could buy a short sterling contract on LIFFE. This may be held for under a day (in which case, if the price rises the traders will gain), or for a longer period, depending on their view. The 1 basis point tick value of a short sterling contract is £12.50; so, if they bought one lot at 92.75 (that is, 100 – 92.75 or 7.25%) and sold it at the end of the day for 92.85, they made a profit of £125 on their one lot, from which brokerage will be subtracted. The trade can be carried out with any futures contract. The same idea could be carried out with a cash-market product or an FRA, but the liquidity, narrow price spread and the low cost of dealing make such a trade easier on a futures exchange. It is much more interesting, however, to carry out a spread trade on the difference between the rates of two different contracts. Consider Figures 13.6 and 13.7, which relate to the prices for the LIFFE short-sterling futures contract on 25 March 2004.

<HELP> for explanation, <MENU> for similar functions. P174 Comdty SFR
n <Page> to scroll contracts, n <Go> for history, 98 <Go> to save defaults

LIF UK £ LIBOR SYNTHETIC FORWARD RATES

14:22	Date	Days		Last	Rate	6-Mo	1-Yr	18-Mo	2-Yr	3-Yr	4-Yr
Spot strip		84	Front	95.6805	4.3195	4.461	4.647	4.685	4.751	4.845	4.919
1)	6/17/04	91	L M4	95.4800	4.5200	4.611	4.763	4.776	4.827	4.900	4.971
2)	9/16/04	91	L U4	95.3500	4.6500	4.722	4.854	4.843	4.887	4.947	5.016
3)	12/16/04	91	L Z4	95.2600	4.7400	4.803	4.918	4.898	4.933	4.989	5.041
4)	3/17/05	91	L H5	95.1900	4.8100	4.866	4.963	4.941	4.969	5.025	5.062
5)	6/16/05	98	L M5	95.1400	4.8600	4.910	5.007	4.976	4.996	5.058	5.077
6)	9/22/05	91	L U5	95.1000	4.9000	4.943	5.043	5.005	5.024	5.091	
7)	12/22/05	84	L Z5	95.0700	4.9300	4.982	5.074	5.027	5.057	5.104	
8)	3/16/06	98	L H6	95.0300	4.9700	5.017	5.098	5.049	5.086	5.114	
9)	6/22/06	91	L M6	95.0000	5.0000	5.041	5.112	5.082	5.116		
10)	9/21/06	91	L U6	94.9800	5.0200	5.051	5.131	5.111			
11)	12/21/06	91	L Z6	94.9800	5.0200	5.056	5.167	5.141			
12)	3/22/07	90	L H7	94.9700	5.0300	5.082	5.206	5.177			
13)	6/20/07	92	L M7	94.9300b	5.0700	5.148	5.250	5.181			
14)	9/20/07	91	L U7	94.8400b	5.1600	5.198	5.292	5.180			

FRA and Bond yld:
Daytype ACT/365
Frequency S

Start	End	days	years	Front	stub	Back	stub	Bond yield	m-mkt yield ACT/365
3/25/04	3/25/05	365	1.00	4.32%	84 days	4.78%	8 days	4.594	4.647
3/25/04	3/25/05	365	1.00	4.32%	84 days	4.78%	8 days	4.594	4.647
3/25/04	3/25/05	365	1.00	4.32%	84 days	4.78%	8 days	4.594	4.647
3/25/04	3/25/05	365	1.00	4.32%	84 days	4.78%	8 days	4.594	4.647
3/25/04	3/25/05	365	1.00	4.32%	84 days	4.78%	8 days	4.594	4.647

Australia 61 2 9777 8600 Brazil 5511 3048 4500 Europe 44 20 7330 7500 Germany 49 69 920410
Hong Kong 852 2977 6000 Japan 81 3 3201 8900 Singapore 65 6212 1000 U.S. 1 212 318 2000
G657-802-0 25-Mar-04 14:22:26

Figure 13.6 LIFFE short-sterling contract analysis, 25 March 2004

Futures exchanges use the letters H, M, U and Z to refer to the contract months for March, June, September and December. So the June 2004 contract would be denoted by "M4". From Chapter 9 we know that forward rates can be calculated for any term, starting on any date. In Figure 13.6, we see the future prices on that day, and the interest rate that the prices imply. The "stub" is the term for the interest rate from today to the expiry of the first futures contract, which is called the front month contract (in this case the front month contract is the June 2004 contract) and is 84 days. Figure 13.7 lists the forward rates from the spot date to six months, one year and so on. It is possible to trade a strip of contracts to replicate any term, out to the maximum maturity of the contract. This can be done for hedging or speculative purposes. Note from Figure 13.7 that there is a spread between the cash curve and the futures curve. A trader can take positions on cash against futures, but it is easier to transact only on the futures exchange.

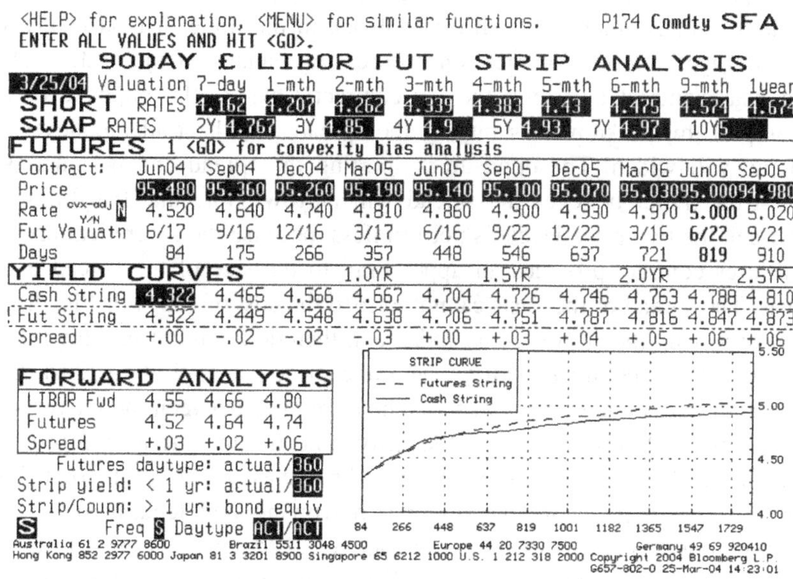

<HELP> for explanation, <MENU> for similar functions. P174 Comdty SFA
ENTER ALL VALUES AND HIT <GO>.

90DAY £ LIBOR FUT STRIP ANALYSIS

3/25/04 Valuation	7-day	1-mth	2-mth	3-mth	4-mth	5-mth	6-mth	9-mth	1year
SHORT RATES	4.162	4.207	4.262	4.339	4.383	4.43	4.475	4.574	4.674

SWAP RATES 2Y 4.767 3Y 4.85 4Y 4.9 5Y 4.93 7Y 4.97 10Y 5

FUTURES 1 <GO> for convexity bias analysis

Contract:	Jun04	Sep04	Dec04	Mar05	Jun05	Sep05	Dec05	Mar06	Jun06	Sep06
Price	95.480	95.360	95.260	95.190	95.140	95.100	95.070	95.030	95.000	94.980
Rate cvx-adj Y/N N	4.520	4.640	4.740	4.810	4.860	4.900	4.930	4.970	5.000	5.020
Fut Valuatn	6/17	9/16	12/16	3/17	6/16	9/22	12/22	3/16	6/22	9/21
Days	84	175	266	357	448	546	637	721	819	910

YIELD CURVES				1.0YR		1.5YR		2.0YR		2.5YR
Cash String	4.322	4.465	4.566	4.667	4.704	4.726	4.746	4.763	4.788	4.810
Fut String	4.322	4.449	4.548	4.638	4.706	4.751	4.787	4.816	4.847	4.873
Spread	+.00	-.02	-.02	-.03	+.00	+.03	+.04	+.05	+.06	+.06

FORWARD ANALYSIS

LIBOR Fwd	4.55	4.66	4.80
Futures	4.52	4.64	4.74
Spread	+.03	+.02	+.06

Futures daytype: actual/360
Strip yield: < 1 yr: actual/360
Strip/Coupn: > 1 yr: bond equiv
S Freq S Daytype ACT/ACT

Figure 13.7 LIFFE short-sterling forward rates analysis, 25 March 2004

Short-term money market interest rates often behave independently of the yield curve as a whole. A money markets trader may be aware of cash-market trends – for example, an increased frequency of borrowing at a certain point of the curve – as well as other market intelligence that suggests that one point of the curve will rise or fall relative to others. One way to exploit this view is to run a position in a cash instrument such as a CD against a futures contract, which is a *basis spread* trade.

However, the best way to trade on this view is to carry out a spread trade, shorting one contract against a long position in another trade. Consider Figure 13.6; if we feel that three-month interest rates in June 2004 will be lower than where they are implied by the futures price today, but that September 2004 rates will be higher, we will buy the M4 contract and short the U4 contract. This is not a market-directional trade; rather, it's a view on the relative spread between two contracts. The trade must be carried out in equal weights; for example, 100 lots of the June against 100 lots of the September. If the rates do move in the direction that the trader expects, the trade will generate a profit. There are similar possibilities available from an analysis of Figure 13.7, depending on our view of forward interest rates.

Spread trading carries a lower margin requirement than open position trading, because there is no directional risk in the trade. It is also possible to arbitrage between contracts on different exchanges. If the trade is short the near contract and long the far contract (that is, the opposite of our example) this is known as buying the spread and the trader believes the spread will widen. The opposite is shorting the spread and is undertaken when the trader believes the spread will narrow. Note that the difference between the two price levels is not limitless, because the theoretical price of a futures contract provides an upper limit to the size of the spread or the basis. The spread or the basis cannot exceed the cost of carry; that is, the net cost of buying the cash security today and then delivering it into the futures market on the contract expiry. The same principle applies to short-dated interest-rate contracts; the net cost is the difference between the interest cost of borrowing funds to buy the "security" and the income accruing on the security while it is held before delivery. The two associated costs for a short-sterling spread trade are the notional borrowing and lending rates from having bought one and sold another contract. If traders believe that the cost of carry will decrease, they could sell the spread to exercise this view.

Traders may have a longer time horizon and trade the spread between the short-term interest-rate contract and the long bond future. This is usually carried out only by the proprietary trading desk, because it is unlikely that one person would be trading both three-month and 10-year (or 20-year, depending on the contract specification) interest rates. A common example of such a spread trade is a yield-curve trade. If traders believe that the sterling yield curve will steepen or flatten between the three-month and the 10-year terms, they can buy or sell the spread by using the LIFFE short-sterling contract and the long gilt contract. To be first-order risk-neutral, however, the trade must be duration-weighted, as one short-sterling contract is not equivalent to one gilt contract. The tick value of the gilt contract is £10, however, although the gilt contract represents £100,000 of a notional gilt and the short-sterling contract represents a £500,000 time deposit. We use (13.7) to calculate the hedge ratio, with £1,000 being the value of a 1% change in the value of the gilt contract against £1,250 for the short sterling contract.

$$h = \frac{(100 \times Tick) \times P_b \times D}{(100 \times Tick) \times P_f} \tag{13.7}$$

where

Tick is the tick value of the contract
D is the duration of the bond represented by the long bond contract
P_b is the price of the bond futures contract
P_f is the price of the short-term deposit contract.

The notional maturity of a long bond contract is always given in terms of a spread; for example, for the long gilt it is $8^3/_4$–13 years. Therefore, in practice, one would use the duration of the cheapest-to-deliver bond.

A butterfly spread is a spread trade that involves three contracts, with the two spreads between all three contracts being traded. This is carried out when the middle contract appears to be mispriced relative to the two contracts either side of it. The trader may believe that one or both of the outer contracts will move in relation to the middle contract. If the belief is that only one of these two will shift relative to the middle contract, then a butterfly will be put on if the trader is not sure which of these will adjust. For example, consider Figure 13.6 again. The prices of the front three contracts are 95.48, 95.35 and 95.26. A trader may feel that the September contract is too low, having a spread of +13 basis points to the June contract, and +9 basis points to the December contract. The trader feels that the September contract will rise, but will that be because June and December prices fall or because the September price will rise? Instead of having to answer this question, all the trader need believe is that the June–September spread will widen and the September–December spread will narrow. To put this view into effect, the trader puts on a butterfly spread, which is equal to the September–December spread minus the June–September spread, which she expects to narrow. Therefore, she buys the June–September spread and sells the September–December spread, which is also known as *selling the butterfly spread.*

EXAMPLE 13.8 The Eurodollar futures contract

The Eurodollar futures contract is traded on the Chicago Mercantile Exchange, although it can be traded globally on a 24-hour basis on SIMEX and GLOBEX. The underlying asset is a deposit of US dollars in a bank outside the United States, and the contract is on the rate on dollar 90-day Libor. The Eurodollar future is cash settled on the second business day before the third Wednesday of the delivery month (London business day). The final settlement price is used to set the price of the contract, given by:

$$10{,}000(100 - 0.25r)$$

where r is the quoted Eurodollar rate at the time. This rate is the actual 90-day Eurodollar deposit rate.

The longest-dated Eurodollar contract has an expiry date of 10 years. The market assumes that futures prices and forward prices are equal; Appendix 13.1 shows that this is indeed the case under conditions where the risk-free interest rate is constant and the same for all maturities. In practice it is also holds for short-dated futures contracts, but is inaccurate for longer-dated futures contracts. Therefore using futures contracts with a maturity greater than five years to calculate zero-coupon rates or implied forward rates will produce errors in results, which need to be taken into account if the derived rates are used to price other instruments such as swaps.

Figure 13.8 shows the Bloomberg description page for the Eurodollar contract.

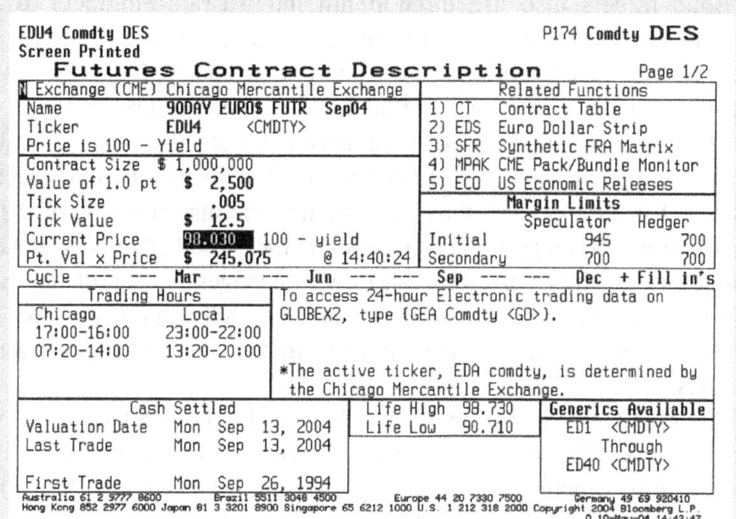

Figure 13.8 Bloomberg page DES for Eurodollar contract

Hedging using interest-rate futures

ALM desks use interest-rate futures to hedge interest rate risk exposure in cash and off-balance sheet instruments. Bond trading desks also often use futures to hedge positions in bonds of up to two or three years' maturity, as contracts are traded up to three years' maturity. The liquidity of such "far-month" contracts is considerably lower than for near-month contracts and the "front month" contract (the current contract, for the next maturity month). When hedging a bond with a maturity of say two years' maturity, the trader will put on a *strip* of futures contracts that matches as near as possible the expiry date of the bond.

The purpose of a hedge is to protect the value of a current or anticipated cash market or OBS position from adverse changes in interest rates. The hedgers will try to offset the effect of the change in interest rates on the value of their cash position with the change in value of their hedging instruments. If the hedge is an exact one the loss on the main position should be compensated by a profit on the hedge position. If traders are expecting a fall in interest rates and wish to protect against such a fall they will buy futures, known as a long hedge, and they will sell futures (a short hedge) if wishing to protect against a rise in rates.

Bond traders also use three-month interest-rate contracts to hedge positions in short-dated bonds; for instance, market-makers running a short-dated bond book would find it more appropriate to hedge their books using short-dated futures rather than the longer-dated bond futures contract. When this happens it is important to accurately calculate the correct number of contracts to use for the hedge. To construct a bond hedge it will be necessary to use a strip of contracts, thus ensuring that the maturity date of the bond is covered by the longest-dated futures contract. The hedge is calculated by finding the sensitivity of each cash flow to changes in each of the relevant forward rates. Each cash flow is considered individually and the hedge values are then aggregated and rounded to the nearest whole number of contracts.

Figure 13.9 is a reproduction of page TED on Bloomberg, which calculates the strip hedge for short-dated bonds. The example shown is for a short-sterling contract hedge for a position in the UK $8^1/_2$% 2005 gilt, for settlement on 11 November 2003. The screen shows the number of each contract that must be bought (or sold) to hedge the position, which in the example is a holding of £10 million of the bond. The "stub" requirement is met using the near-month contract. A total of 165 contracts are required.

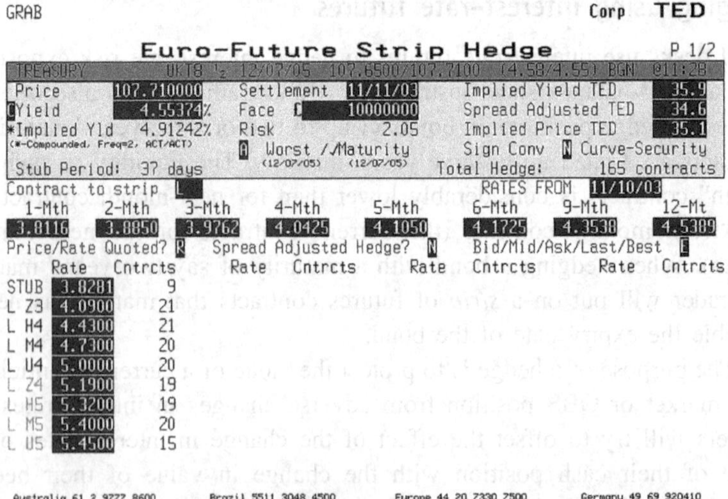

Figure 13.9 Bloomberg screen TED page, used to calculate hedge requirements for UK $8^1/_2$% 2005 gilt, 11 November 2003

The following examples illustrate hedging with short-term interest-rate contracts.

EXAMPLE 13.9 Hedging a forward three-month lending requirement

On 1 June a corporate treasurer is expecting a cash inflow of £10 million in three months' time (1 September), which will then be invested for three months. The treasurer expects that interest rates will fall over the next few weeks and wishes to protect the company against such a fall. This can be done using short sterling futures. Market rates on 1 June are as follows:

3-month Libor: $6^1/_2\%$
September futures price: 93.220.

The treasurer buys 20 September short sterling futures at 93.220, this number being exactly equivalent to a sum of £10 million. This allows the company to lock in a forward *lending* rate of 6.78%, if we assume there is no bid-offer quote spread.

Expected lending rate = rate implied by futures price
= 100 − 93.220
= 6.78%.

On 1 September market rates are as follows:

3-month Libor: 6.25%
September futures price: 93.705.

The treasurer unwinds the hedge at this price:

Futures p/l = + 97 ticks (93.705 − 93.22), or 0.485%
Effective lending rate = 3-mo Libor + futures profit
= 6.25% + 0.485%
= 6.735%.

The treasurer was quite close to achieving their target lending rate of 6.78% and the hedge has helped to protect against the drop in Libor rates from $6^1/_2\%$ to $6^1/_4\%$, due to the profit from the futures transaction.

In the real world the cash market bid–offer spread will impact the amount of profit/loss from the hedge transaction. Futures generally trade and settle near the offered side of the market rate (Libor) whereas lending, certainly by corporates, will be nearer the Libid rate.

EXAMPLE 13.10 Hedging a forward six-month borrowing requirement

A treasury dealer has a six-month borrowing requirement for EUR30 million in three months' time, on 16 September. She expects interest rates to rise by at least $^1/_2$% before that date and would like to lock in a future borrowing rate. The scenario is detailed below.

Date:	16 June
3-month Libor:	6.0625%
6-month Libor:	6.25
September futures contract:	93.66
December futures contract:	93.39

In order to hedge a six-month EUR30 million exposure the dealer needs to use a total of 60 futures contracts, as each has a nominal value of EUR1 million, and corresponds to a three-month notional deposit period. The dealer decides to sell 30 September futures contracts and 30 December futures contracts, which is referred to as a *strip* hedge. The expected forward borrowing rate that can be achieved by this strategy, where the expected borrowing rate is *rf*, is calculated as follows:

$$1 + rf \times \frac{\text{Days in period}}{360} = \left(1 + \text{Sep. implied rate} \times \frac{\text{Sep. days period}}{360}\right)$$
$$\times \left(1 + \text{Dec. implied rate} \times \frac{\text{Dec. days period}}{360}\right)$$

Therefore we have:

$$1 + rf \times \frac{180}{360} = \left(1 + 0.0634 \times \frac{90}{360}\right) \times \left(1 + 0.0661 \times \frac{90}{360}\right)$$

$rf = 6.53\%$.

The rate *rf* is sometimes referred to as the "strip rate". The hedge is unwound upon expiry of the September futures contract.

Assume the following rates now prevail:

3-month Libor:	6.4375%
6-month Libor:	6.8125
September futures contract:	93.56
December futures contract:	92.93.

The futures profit-and-loss is:

September contract:	+10 ticks
December contract:	+46 ticks.

This represents a 56 tick or 0.56% profit in three-month interest-rate terms, or 0.28% in six-month interest-rate terms. The effective borrowing rate is the six-month Libor rate minus the futures profit, that is:

$$6.8125\% - 0.28\% \text{ or } 6.5325\%.$$

In this case the hedge has proved effective because the dealer has realised a borrowing rate of 6.5325%, which is close to the target strip rate of 6.53%.

The dealer is still exposed to the basis risk when the December contracts are bought back from the market at the expiry date of the September contract. If, for example, the future was bought back at 92.73, the effective borrowing rate would be only 6.4325%, and the dealer would benefit. Of course, the other possibility is that the futures contract could be trading 20 ticks more expensive, which would give a borrowing rate of 6.6325%, which is 10 basis points above the target rate. If this happened, the dealer may elect to borrow in the cash market for three months, and maintain the December futures position until the December contract expiry date, and roll over the borrowing at that time. The profit (or loss) on the December futures position will compensate for any change in three-month rates at that time.

Refining the hedge ratio

A futures hedge ratio is calculated by dividing the amount to be hedged by the nominal value of the relevant futures contract and then adjusting for the duration of the hedge. When dealing with large exposures and/or a long hedge period, inaccuracy will result unless the hedge ratio is refined to compensate for the timing mismatch between the cash flows from the futures hedge and the underlying exposure. Any change in interest rates has an immediate effect on the hedge in the form of daily variation margin, but only affects the underlying cash position on maturity; that is, when the interest payment is due on the loan or deposit. In other words, hedging gains and losses in the futures position are realised over the hedge period while cash market gains and losses are deferred. Futures gains may be reinvested, and futures losses need to financed.

The basic hedge ratio is usually refined to counteract this timing mismatch, this process is sometimes called "tailing".

The TED Spread

From the inception of the Eurodollar contract in 1981, traders have frequently taken a view on the spread between the Eurodollar and US Treasury yields. This difference between the implied yield of the Eurodollar and Treasury yields is called the "TED spread". The TED spread is essentially a credit spread, because Treasury yields are risk-free while the Eurodollar is the implied forward fixing for three-month Libor. So the TED spread is a good indicator of interbank credit quality, and generally moves with the economic cycle. The main trades put on for the TED spread involve views on the change in the shape and slope of the two yield curves; for instance, a trader may go long the TED spread (buy the Eurodollar and sell the Treasury) if they expect the spread to widen, and go short the spread if they expected it to narrow.

As reported in Burghardt (2004) the most actively traded TED spread is that between the Eurodollar and the three-month T-bill. This spread is the difference between the market's expectations of three-month Libor and the three-month T-bill futures rate on expiration of the futures contract. Because the T-bill future (also traded on CBOT) and the Eurodollar contract both have a tick value of $25, there is no complicated hedge ratio calculation to make.

With term TED spreads, which is the spread between the Eurodollar and longer-term Treasury rates, it is necessary to weight the hedge ratio. This is not necessarily straightforward because while there is a standard way to calculate Treasury yields, there is more than one way to calculate the yield on the Eurodollar contract. Burghardt (2004) refers to two common ways of making this calculation:

- the unweighted Eurodollar strip yield, which uses a zero-coupon rate;
- the weighted Eurodollar strip yield, which translates futures rates into the yield on a coupon-bearing bond.

The unweighted form of the term TED spread requires us to calculate a Eurodollar bond-equivalent yield. This is given by the following, where the price of a \$1 zero-coupon bond P_{ED} is:

$$P_{ED} = \frac{1}{\left(1 + rs\left(\frac{T_{spot}}{360}\right)\right)\left(1 + rf_1\left(\frac{T_1}{360}\right)\right)\left(1 + rf_2\left(\frac{T_2}{360}\right)\right) \times \ldots \times \left(1 + rf_N\left(\frac{T_N}{360}\right)\right)} \tag{13.8}$$

where

rs is today's spot interest rate
rf_i is the Eurodollar futures rate
T_i is the days in each respective period.

Equation (13.8) weights each rate roughly equally because each futures contract has a 91-day term. (The exception to this is the period from the spot date (today) to the first contract, known as the "stub" period.[5]) This means it suffers from a term structure effect; that is, the term TED spread calculated is sensitive to changes in the slope of the yield curve.

To produce a TED spread value that is dependent only on changes in the credit spread and not on a term structure effect, we employ the weighted Eurodollar strip yield. There are two ways to do this.

Implied Eurodollar yield

To calculate this we determine what the yield of a Treasury Note would be if it were issued by a bank of Libor credit quality. This is the implied Eurodollar yield, and is calculated by finding the present value of the Note using discount factors given by the Libor and Eurodollar strip curve. The

[5] See pages 209–11 of Burghardt (2004) for a detailed account of the treatment of the stub period.

yield is then taken from this present value. The difference between this yield and the actual yield is the implied TED spread.

Fixed basis point spread to Eurodollar rates

This approach calculates how many basis points need to be subtracted from the Eurodollar futures rate to produce the current price of the Treasury note.

The three approaches of course produce different results. For example, following Burghardt we show the benchmark Treasury 2- and 5-year spreads using all three methods on 10 August 2004 in Table 13.2.

Term	Eurodollar strip	Implied Eurodollar	Fixed spread bps
2-year	18.9	17.4	18.2
5-year	39.7	36.8	36.0

Table 13.2 Term TED spreads, 10 August 2004

These differences arise from the weighted nature of the last two measures. The Eurodollar strip yield measure produces a higher spread than the implied Eurodollar yield; this is not unexpected because in a positive-sloping yield curve environment the higher rates at the further end of the yield curve produce a biased effect. This is similar to the effect one observes when constructing a zero-coupon yield curve from a positively sloping par yield curve (see Chapter 9).

Using Microsoft Excel to check the market forward rate[6]

Short-term interest-rate futures prices are a snapshot of the markets expectation of three-month Libor rates on contract expiry. As we demonstrated in Chapter 9, the forward rate can be calculated from market spot rates under the no-arbitrage argument. As such the price of the short sterling or Eurodollar contract at any one time (indeed, any 90-day futures contract) should reflect this no-arbitrage rate.

[6] This section was co-written with Stuart Turner of KBC Financial Products in London, who authored the accompanying Excel spreadsheets.

If we are calculating the forward rate from cash market rates we use:

$$r_f = \left\{ \frac{\left[1 + r_l \left(\frac{n_l}{360}\right)\right]}{\left[1 + r_s \left(\frac{n_s}{360}\right)\right]} - 1 \right\} \frac{360}{n_f} \qquad (13.9)$$

where

r_f is the forward rate
r_l is the long-term deposit rate
r_s is the short-term deposit rate
n_l is the number of days in the long term
n_s is the number of days in the short term
n_f is the number of days in the forward term.

In practice there will be some discrepancy in rates from what is suggested by the cash market Libor rates, for the following reasons:

- supply and demand;
- the futures market driving prices in the cash market, rather than vice-versa;
- differences in the term of actual periods under consideration.

If a market participant feels that the above do not adequately explain any rate discrepancies, it will trade according to its view.

Figure 13.10 on page 578 shows an Excel spreadsheet that has been used to check the market prices for the Eurodollar contract on 1 October 2004. The US dollar Libor fixings on that day are shown in Table 13.3 on page 579, while Figure 13.11 on page 579 shows the Eurodollar prices.

We see that the rates calculated from the Libor rates do not match the Eurdollar price-implied forward rates shown in Figure 13.11.

We obtain closer results if we input the precise terms that relate to each Eurodollar contract, and use interpolated Libor rates for these terms. This is shown on the second set of results in the spreadsheet. The last table shows the results obtained using extrapolated rates.

Figure 13.12 on page 580–1 is the Excel sheet with cell formulas shown so readers can replicate results for any interest-rate contract against its currency Libor fix.

$$rf_{3V6} = \left\{ \frac{\left[1 + 0.0235 \left(\frac{270}{360}\right)\right]}{\left[1 + 0.0220 \left(\frac{180}{360}\right)\right]} - 1 \right\} \frac{360}{90} = 2.62\%$$

3-month rate X months forward

Term	Days	Libor		Forward rate
3-month	90	2.02750%	3-month rate 3 months forward	2.360535038
6-month	180	2.20000%	3-month rate 6 months forward	2.621167161
9-month	270	2.35000%	3-month rate 9 months forward	2.854686156
12-month	360	2.48875%		

Using interpolated rates

Term	Days	Libor		Forward rate
3-month	75	1.97188%	3-month rate 3 months forward	2.344664706
6-month	166	2.16733%	3-month rate 6 months forward	2.624926233
9-month	257	2.32833%	3-month rate 9 months forward	3.087962132
12-month	355	2.48146%		

Using extrapolated rates

Term	Days	Libor		Forward rate
3-month	95	2.04604%	3-month rate 3 months forward	2.373676917
6-month	185	2.21167%	3-month rate 6 months forward	2.629924385
9-month	275	2.35833%	3-month rate 9 months forward	3.030861846
12-month	370	2.50333%		

Interpolation/Extrapolation term	355	
First known rate	2.44%	
Second known rate	2.49%	
First term	330	
Second term	360	2.48150%

Figure 13.10 Comparing cash-market no-arbitrage forward rates with the Eurodollar-implied forward rate

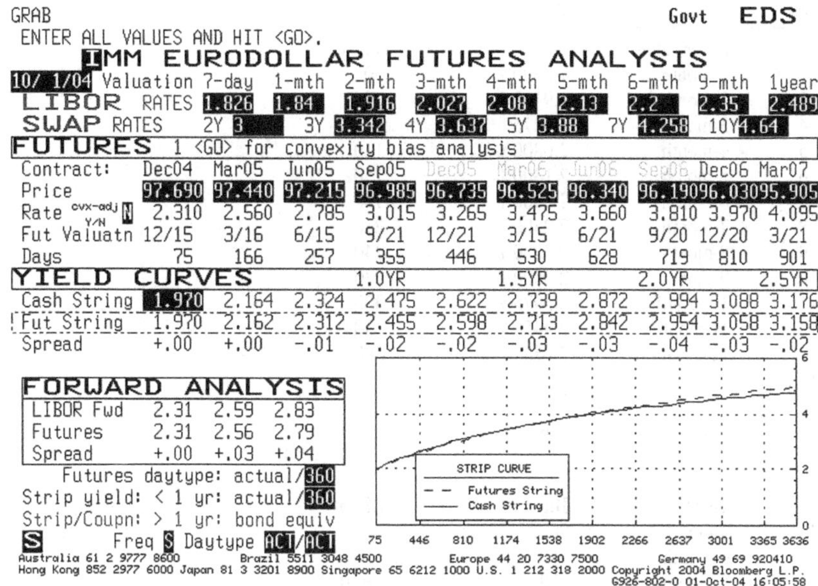

Figure 13.11 Bloomberg screen EDS showing Eurodollar futures prices as at 1 October 2004

	Libor rates	Term
1-month	1.8400%	30
2-month	1.9162%	60
3-month	2.0275%	90
4-month	2.0800%	120
5-month	2.1300%	150
6-month	2.2000%	180
7-month	2.2500%	210
8-month	2.3000%	240
9-month	2.3500%	270
10-month	2.3975%	300
11-month	2.4450%	330
12-month	2.4888%	360

Table 13.3 Libor fixes for US dollar on 1 October 2004

Cell	A	B	C
1	Libor rates		Term
2	1-month	1.8400%	30
3	2-month	1.9162%	60
4	3-month	2.0275%	90
5	4-month	2.0800%	120
6	5-month	2.1300%	150
7	6-month	2.2000%	180
8	7-month	2.2500%	210
9	8-month	2.3000%	240
10	9-month	2.3500%	270
11	10-month	2.3975%	300
12	11-month	2.4450%	330
13	12-month	2.4888%	360
14			
15			
16	3-month rate × months forward		
17			
18			
19	**Term**	**Days**	**Libor**
20	3-month	90	=B4
21	6-month	180	=B7
22	9-month	270	=B10
23	12-month	360	=B13
24			
25			
26			
27	Using interpolated rates		
28			
29	**Term**	**Days**	**Libor**
30	3-month	75	=$B3+(($B$4-$B$3)*(($B30-D$3)/($D$3-$D$2)))
31	6-month	166	=$B$6+(($B$7-$B$6)*(($B31-$D$6)/($D$7-$D$6)))
32	9-month	257	=$B$9+(($B$10-$B$9)*(($B32-$D$9)/($D$10-$D$9)))
33	12-month	355	=$B$12+(($B$13-$B$12)*(($B33-$D$12)/($D$13-$D$12)))
34			
35			
36			
37	Using extrapolated rates		
38			
39	**Term**	**Days**	**Libor**
40	3-month	95	=$C$4+(($C$5-$C$4)*(($C41-E$4)/($E$4-$E$3)))
41	6-month	185	=$C$7+(($C$8-$C$7)*(($C42-$E$7)/($E$8-$E$7)))
42	9-month	275	=$C$10+(($C$11-$C$10)*(($C43-$E$10)/($E$11-$E$10)))
43	12-month	370	=$C$13+(($C$14-$C$13)*(($C44-$E$13)/($E$14-$E$13)))
44			
45	Interpolation/Extrapolation term		355
46			
47	First known rate	2.44%	
48	Second known rate	2.49%	
49	First term	330	
50	Second term	360	
51			

Figure 13.12 Excel forward calculator showing cell formulas

D

	Forward rate
3-month rate 3 months forward	=(((1+$C$21*(B21/360))/(1+$C$20*(B20/360))-1)*(360/90))*100
3-month rate 6 months forward	=(((1+$C$22*(B22/360))/(1+$C$21*(B21/360))-1)*(360/90))*100
3-month rate 9 months forward	=(((1+$C$23*(B23/360))/(1+$C$22*(B22/360))-1)*(360/90))*100

	Forward rate
3-month rate 3 months forward	=(((1+$D32*(C32/360))/(1+$D31*(C31/360))-1)*(360/90))*100
3-month rate 6 months forward	=(((1+$D33*(C33/360))/(1+$D32*(C32/360))-1)*(360/90))*100
3-month rate 9 months forward	=(((1+$D34*(C34/360))/(1+$D33*(C33/360))-1)*(360/90))*100

	Forward rate
3-month rate 3 months forward	=(((1+$D42*(C42/360))/(1+$D41*(C41/360))-1)*(360/90))*100
3-month rate 6 months forward	=(((1+$D43*(C43/360))/(1+$D42*(C42/360))-1)*(360/90))*100
3-month rate 9 months forward	=(((1+$D44*(C44/360))/(1+$D43*(C43/360))-1)*(360/90))*100

=$C51+(($C52-$C51)*(($C49-$C53)/($C54-$C53)))

Options

The interest-rate risk management needs of a large number of banks can be met by the use of plain vanilla derivatives such as interest-rate swaps and exchange-traded futures. In some circumstances though, it may be more efficient and cost effective to use option products to effect the risk hedging. As such, ALM managers need to be familiar with the use and application of options, particularly interest-rate options such as caps and floors. For this reason we discuss options in this chapter.

As a risk management tool, option contracts allow banks to hedge market risk exposure but also to gain from upside moves in the market; thus they are unique among hedging instruments. Options have special characteristics that make them stand apart from other classes of derivatives. As they confer a right to conduct a certain transaction, but not an obligation, their payoff profile is different from other financial assets, both cash and off-balance sheet. This makes an option more of an insurance policy rather than a pure hedging instrument, as the person who has purchased the option for hedging purposes need only exercise it if required. The price of the option is in effect the insurance premium that has been paid for peace of mind. Options are also used for purposes other than hedging, as part of speculative and arbitrage trading. Many banks also act as option market-makers and generate returns from profitably managing the risk on their option books.

The subject of options is a large one, and there are a number of specialist texts devoted to them. In this chapter we introduce the basics of options, including a primer on option pricing. We also provide an example of the risk hedging application of an interest-rate option.

Introduction

An option is a contract in which the buyer has the right, but not the obligation, to buy or sell an underlying asset at a predetermined price during a specified period of time. The seller of the option, known as the writer, grants this right to the buyer in return for receiving the price of the option, known as the premium. An option that grants the right to buy an asset is a call option, while the corresponding right to sell an asset is a put option. The option buyer has a long position in the option and the option seller has a short position in the option.

Because options confer on a buyer the right to effect a transaction, but not the obligation (and correspondingly on a seller the obligation, if requested by the buyer, to effect a transaction), their risk/reward characteristics are different from other financial products. The payoff profile from holding an option is unlike that of any other instrument. Let us consider the payoff profiles for a vanilla call option and a gilt futures contract. Suppose that a trader buys one lot of the gilt futures contract at 114.00 and holds it for one month before selling it. On closing the position, the profit made will depend on the contract sale price. If it is above 114.00, the trader will have made a profit, and if below 114.00 a loss. On one lot, this represents a £1,000 gain for each point above 114.00. The same applies to someone who had a short position in the contract and closed it out – if the contract is bought back at any price below 114.00 the trader will realise a profit. The profile is shown in Figure 13.13.

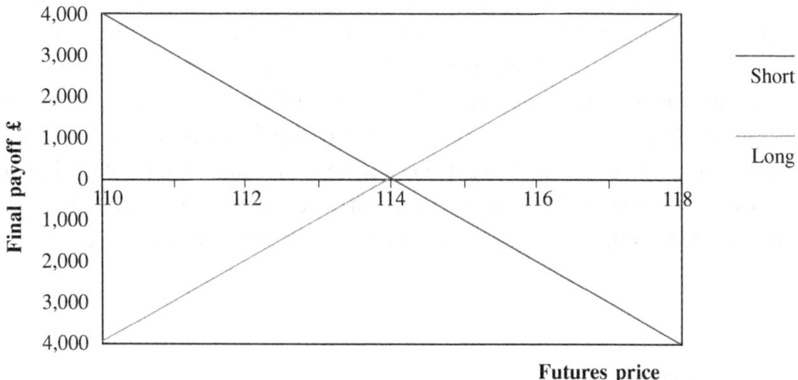

Figure 13.13 Payoff profile for a bond futures contract

This profile is the same for other derivative instruments such as FRAs and swaps, and, of course, for cash instruments such as bonds or equity. The payoff profile therefore has a linear characteristic, and it is linear whether one has bought or sold the contract.

The profile for an option contract differs from the conventional one. Because options confer a right, but not an obligation to one party (the buyer), and an obligation but not a right to the seller, the profile will differ according to whether one is the buyer or seller. Consider a trader who buys a call option that grants the right to buy a gilt futures contract at a price of 114.00 at some point during the life of the option, the resulting payoff profile will be like that shown in Figure 13.14 on page 584. If during the life of the option the price of the futures contract rises above 114.00, the trader will exercise the right to buy the future, under the terms of the option contract.

This is known as exercising the option. If, on the other hand, the price of the future falls below 114.00, the trader will not exercise the option and, unless there is a reversal in price of the future, it will eventually expire worthless on its maturity date. In this respect, it is exactly like an equity or bond warrant. The seller of this particular option has a very different payout profile. If the price of the future rises above 114.00 and the option is exercised, the seller will bear the loss equal to the profit that the buyer has made. The seller's payoff profile is also shown in Figure 13.14, as the dashed line. If the option is not exercised and expires, the trade will have generated premium income for the seller, which is revenue income that contributes to the p&l account.

So the holders of long and short positions in options do not have the same symmetrical payoff profile. The buyer of the call option will benefit if the price of the underlying asset rises, but will not lose if the price falls (except the funds paid for purchasing the rights under the option). The seller of the call option will suffer loss if the price of the underlying asset rises, but will not benefit if it falls (except realising the funds received for writing the option). The buyer has a right but not an obligation, while the seller has an obligation if the option is exercised. The premium charged for the option is the seller's compensation for granting such a right to the buyer.

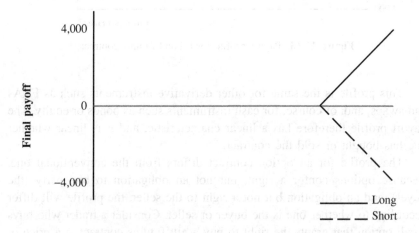

Figure 13.14 Payoff profile for call-option contract

Option terminology

Let us now consider some basic terminology used in the options markets.

A call option grants the buyer the right to buy the underlying asset, while a put option grants the buyer the right to sell the underlying asset. There are, therefore, four possible positions that an option trader may put on: long a call or put; and short a call or put. The payoff profiles for each type are shown at Figure 13.15.

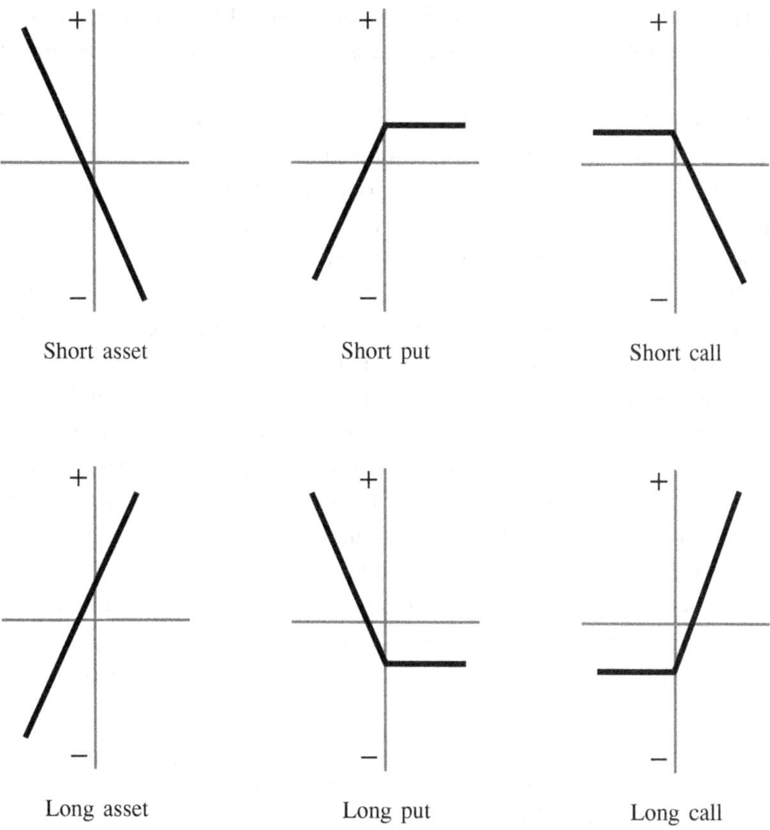

Figure 13.15 Basic option payoff profiles

The strike price describes the price at which an option is exercised. For example, a call option to buy ordinary shares of a listed company might have a strike price of £10.00. This means that if the option is exercised, the buyer will pay £10 per share. Options are generally either American- or European-style, which defines the times during the option's life when it can be exercised. There is no geographic relevance to these terms, as both styles trade can be traded in any market. It is very rare for an American option to be exercised ahead of its expiry date, so this distinction has little impact in practice, although of course the pricing model being used to value European options must be modified to handle American options. The holders of European options cannot exercise them prior to expiry. However, if they wish to realise their value, they will sell them in the market.

The premium of an option is the price at which the option is sold. Option premium is made up of two constituents: intrinsic value and time value.

The intrinsic value of an option is the value of the option if it is exercised immediately, and it represents the difference between the strike price and the current underlying asset price. If a call option on a bond futures contract has a strike price of 100.00 and the future is currently trading at 105.00, the intrinsic value of the option is 5.00, as this would be the immediate profit gain to the option holder if it were exercised. Since an option will only be exercised if there is benefit to the holder from so doing, its intrinsic value will never be less than zero. So, in our example, if the bond future was trading at 95.00, the intrinsic value of the call option would be zero, not –5.00. For a put option, the intrinsic value is the amount by which the current underlying price is below the strike price. When an option has intrinsic value, it is described as being *in-the-money*. When the strike price for a call option is higher than the underlying price (or for a put option is lower than the underlying price) and has no intrinsic value it is said to be *out-of-the-money*. An option for which the strike price is equal to the current underlying price is said to be *at-the-money*. This term is normally used at the time the option is first traded, in cases where the strike price is set to the current price of the underlying asset.

The time value of an option is the amount by which the option value exceeds the intrinsic value. An option writer will almost always demand a premium that is higher than the option's intrinsic value, because of the risk that the writer is taking on. This reflects the fact that over time the price of the underlying asset may change sufficiently to produce a much higher intrinsic value. During the life of an option, the option writer has nothing more to gain over the initial premium at which the option was sold. However, until expiry there is a chance that the writer will lose if the markets move against him or her, hence the inclusion of a time-value element. The value of an option that is out-of-the-money is composed entirely of time value.

Table 13.4 summarises the main option terminology that we have just been discussing.

Call	The right to buy the underlying asset
Put	The right to sell the underlying asset
Buyer	The person who has purchased the option and has the right to exercise it if he or she wishes
Writer	The person who has sold the option and has the obligation to perform if the option is exercised
Strike price	The price at which the option may be exercised, also known as the *exercise price*
Expiry date	The last date on which the option can be exercised, also known as the maturity date
American	The style of option; an American option can be exercised at any time up to the expiry date
European	An option which may be exercised on the maturity date only, and not before
Premium	The price of the option, paid by the buyer to the seller
Intrinsic value	The value of the option if it were exercised today, which is the difference between the strike price and the underlying asset price
Time value	The difference between the current price of the option and its intrinsic value
In-the-money	The term for an option that has intrinsic value
At-the-money	An option for which the strike price is identical to the underlying asset price
Out-of-the-money	An option that has no intrinsic value

Table 13.4 Basic option terminology

Option pricing

The price of an option is a function of six different factors, which are:

- the strike price of the option;
- the current price of the underlying;
- the time to expiry;
- the risk-free rate of interest that applies to the life of the option;
- the volatility of the underlying asset's price returns;

- the value of any dividends or cash flows paid by the underlying asset during the life of the option.

We review the basic parameters next.

Pricing inputs

Let us consider the parameters of option pricing. Possibly the two most important are the current price of the underlying and the strike price of the option. The intrinsic value of a call option is the amount by which the strike price is below the price of the underlying, as this is the payoff if the option is exercised. Therefore, the value of the call option will increase as the price of the underlying increases, and will fall as the underlying price falls. The value of a call will also decrease as the strike price increases. All this is reversed for a put option.

Generally, for bond options a higher time to maturity results in higher option value. All other parameters being equal, a longer-dated option will always be worth at least as much as one that had a shorter life. Intuitively we would expect this because the holder of a longer-dated option has the same benefits as someone holding a shorter-dated option, in addition to a longer time period in which the intrinsic value may increase. This rule is always true for American options, and usually true for European options. However, certain factors, such as the payment of a coupon during the option life, may cause a longer-dated option to have only a slightly higher value than a shorter-dated option.

The risk-free interest-rate is the rate applicable to the period of the option's life. So for our table of gilt options in the previous section, the option value reflected the three-month rate. The most common rate used is the T-bill rate, although for bond options it is more common to see the government-bond repo rate being used. A rise in interest rates will increase the value of a call option, although not always for bond options. A rise in rates lowers the price of a bond, because it decreases the present value of future cash flows. However, in the equity markets it is viewed as a sign that share price growth rates will increase. Generally, however, the relationship is the same for bond options as equity options. The effect of a rise in interest rates for put options is the reverse: they cause the value to drop.

A coupon payment made by the underlying asset during the life of the option will reduce the price of the underlying asset on the ex-dividend date. This will result in a fall in the price of a call option and a rise in the price of a put option.

Bounds in option pricing

The upper and lower limits on the price of an option are relatively straightforward to set because prices must follow the rule of no-arbitrage pricing. A call option grants the buyer the right to buy a specified quantity of the underlying asset, at the level of the strike price; so, therefore, it is clear that the option could not have a higher value than the underlying asset itself. Therefore, the upper limit or bound to the price of a call option is the price of the underlying asset. Therefore:

$$C \leq S$$

where C is the price of a call option and S is the current price of the underlying asset. A put option grants the buyer the right to sell a specified unit of the underlying asset at the strike price X. Therefore, the option can never have a value greater than the strike price X. So we may set:

$$P \leq X$$

where P is the price of the put option. This rule will still apply for a European put option on its expiry date. So, therefore, we may further set that the option cannot have a value greater than the present value of the strike price X on expiry. That is,

$$P \leq Xe^{-rT}$$

where r is the risk-free interest for the term of the option life and T is the maturity of the option in years.

The minimum limit or bound for an option is set according to whether the underlying asset is a dividend-paying security or not. For a call option written on a non-dividend paying security, the lower bound is given by:

$$C \geq S - Xe^{-rT}.$$

In fact, as we noted early in this chapter, a call option can only ever expire worthless, so its intrinsic value can never be worth less than zero. Therefore $C > 0$ and we then set the following:

$$C \geq \max[S - Xe^{-rT},0] .$$

This reflects the law of no-arbitrage pricing. For put options on a non-dividend paying stock, the lower limit is given by:

$$P \geq Xe^{-rT} - S$$

and again the value is never less than zero. So we may set:

$$P \geq \max[Xe^{-rT} - S, 0] .$$

As we noted above, payment of a dividend by the underlying asset affects the price of the option. In the case of dividend-paying stocks, the upper and lower bounds for options are as follows:

$$C \geq S - D - Xe^{rt}$$

and

$$P \geq D + Xe^{-rt} - \mathrm{S}$$

where D is the present value of the dividend payment made by the underlying asset during the life of the option.

We can now look at the option pricing methodology behind the Black–Scholes model.

Pricing methodology

The interest-rate products described in this book so far, both cash and derivatives, can be priced using rigid mathematical principles, because on maturity of the instrument there is a defined procedure that takes place such that one is able to calculate a fair value. This does not apply to options because there is uncertainty as to what the outcome will be on expiry; an option seller does not know whether the option will be exercised or not. This factor makes options more difficult to price than other financial-market instruments. In this section we review the parameters used in the pricing of an option, and introduce the Black–Scholes pricing model.

Pricing an option is a function of the probability that it will be exercised. Essentially, the premium paid for an option represents the buyer's expected profit on the option. Therefore, as with an insurance premium, the writer of an option will base his or her price on the assessment that the payout on the option will be equal to the premium, and this is a function on the probability that the option will be exercised. Option pricing, therefore, bases its calculation on the assessment of the probability of exercise and derives from this an expected outcome and, hence, a fair value for the option premium. The expected payout, as with an insurance company premium, should equal the premium received.

The following factors influence the price of an option.

- *the behaviour of financial prices*: one of the key assumptions made by the Black–Scholes model (B–S) is that asset prices follow a lognormal distribution. Although this is not strictly accurate, it is close enough of an approximation to allow its use in option pricing. In fact, observation shows that while prices themselves are not normally distributed, asset returns are, and we define returns as $\ln(\frac{P_{t+1}}{P_t})$ where P_t is the market price at time t and P_{t+1} is the price one period later. The distribution of prices is called a lognormal distribution because the logarithm of the prices is normally distributed. The asset returns are defined as the logarithm of the price relatives and are assumed to follow the normal distribution. The expected return as a result of assuming this distribution is given by $E\left[\ln\left(\frac{P_t}{P_0}\right)\right] = rt$ where $E[\ ]$ is the expectation operator and r is the annual rate of return. The derivation of this expression is given in Appendix 13.2;
- *the strike price*: the difference between the strike price and the underlying price of the asset at the time the option is struck will influence the size of the premium, as this will have an impact on the probability that the option will be exercised. An option that is deeply in-the-money has a greater probability of being exercised;
- *volatility*: the volatility of the underlying asset will influence the probability that an option is exercised, as a higher volatility indicates a higher probability of exercise. This is considered in detail below;
- *the term to maturity*: a longer-dated option has greater time value and a greater probability of eventually being exercised;
- *the level of interest rates*: the premium paid for an option in theory represents the expected gain to the buyer at the time the option is exercised. It is paid up-front so it is discounted to obtain a present value. The discount rate used, therefore, has an effect on the premium, although it is less influential than the other factors presented here.

The volatility of an asset measures the variability of its price returns. It is defined as the annualised standard deviation of returns, where variability refers to the variability of the returns that generate the asset's prices, rather than the prices directly. The standard deviation of returns is given by (13.10):

$$\sigma = \sqrt{\sum_{i=1}^{N} \frac{(x - \mu)^2}{N - 1}} \tag{13.10}$$

where x_i is the i'th price relative, μ the arithmetic mean of the observations and N is the total number of observations. The value is converted to an annualised figure by multiplying it by the square root of the number of days in a year, usually taken to be 250 working days. Using this formula from market observations it is possible to calculate the *historic volatility* of an asset. The volatility of an asset is one of the inputs to the B–S model. Of the inputs to the B–S model, the variability of the underlying asset, or its volatility is the most problematic. The distribution of asset prices is assumed to follow a lognormal distribution, because the logarithm of the prices is normally distributed (we assume lognormal rather than normal distribution to allow for the fact that prices cannot – as could be the case in a normal distribution – have negative values). The range of possible prices starts at zero and cannot assume a negative value.

Note that it is the asset price *returns* on which the standard deviation is calculated, and the not the actual prices themselves. This is because using prices would produce inconsistent results, as the actual standard deviation itself would change as price levels increased.

However, calculating volatility using the standard statistical method gives us a figure for historic volatility. What is required is a figure for *future* volatility, since this is relevant for pricing an option expiring in the future. Future volatility cannot be measured directly, by definition. Market-makers get around this by using an option-pricing model "backwards". An option-pricing model calculates the option price from volatility and other parameters. Used in reverse, the model can calculate the volatility implied by the option price. Volatility measured in this way is called implied volatility. Evaluating implied volatility is straightforward using this method and generally more appropriate than using historic volatility, as it provides a clearer measure of an option's fair value. Implied volatilities of deeply in-the-money or out-of-the-money options tend to be relatively high.

The Black–Scholes (B-S) option model

Most option-pricing models are based on one of two methodologies, although both types employ essentially identical assumptions. The first method is based on the resolution of the partial differentiation equation of the asset–price model, corresponding to the expected payoff of the option security. This is the foundation of the B–S model. The second type of model uses the martingale method, and was first introduced by Harrison and Kreps (1979) and Harrison and Pliska (1981), where the price of an asset at time 0 is given by its discounted expected future payoffs, under the appropriate probability measure, known as the risk-neutral probability. There is a third type that assumes lognormal distribution of asset returns but follows the two-step binomial process.

In order to employ the pricing models, we accept a state of the market that is known as a *complete market*,[7] one where there is a viable financial market. This is where the rule of no-arbitrage pricing exists, so that there is no opportunity to generate risk-free arbitrage due to the presence of, say, incorrect forward interest rates. The fact that there is no opportunity to generate risk-free arbitrage gains means that a zero-cost investment strategy that is initiated at time t will have a zero maturity value. The martingale property of the behavior of asset prices states that an accurate estimate of the future price of an asset may be obtained from current price information. Therefore, the relevant information used to calculate forward asset prices is the latest price information. This was also a property of the semi-strong and strong-form market-efficiency scenarios described by Fama (1970).

In this section, we describe the B–S option model in accessible fashion. More technical treatments are given in the relevant references listed in the bibliography.

Assumptions

The B–S model describes a process to calculate the fair value of a European call option under certain assumptions, and apart from the price of the underlying asset S and the time t, all the variables in the model are assumed to be constant, including – most crucially – the volatility. The following assumptions are made:

- there are no transaction costs, and the market allows short selling;
- trading is continuous;

[7] First proposed by Arrow and Debreu (1953, 1954), for reference details, see Choudhry (2001).

- underlying asset prices follow geometric Brownian motion, with the variance rate proportional to the square root of the asset price;
- the asset is a non-dividend-paying security;
- the interest rate during the life of the option is known and constant;
- the option can only be exercised on expiry.

The B–S model is neat and intuitively straightforward to explain, and one of its many attractions is that it can be readily modified to handle other types of options such as foreign-exchange or interest-rate options. The assumption of the behavior of the underlying asset price over time is described by (13.11), which is a generalised Weiner process, and where a is the expected return on the underlying asset and b is the standard deviation of its price returns.

$$\frac{\mathrm{d}S}{S} = a\mathrm{d}t + b\mathrm{d}W \tag{13.11}$$

The Black–Scholes model and pricing derivative instruments

We assume a financial asset is specified by its terminal payoff value. Therefore, when pricing an option we require the fair value of the option at the initial time when the option is struck, and this value is a function of the expected terminal payoff of the option, discounted to the day when the option is struck. In this section, we present an intuitive explanation of the B–S model, in terms of the normal distribution of asset–price returns. Background on the log-normal distribution of price returns is given in Appendix 13.2.

From the definition of a call option, we can set the expected value of the option at maturity T as:

$$E(C_T) = E[\max(S_T - X,0)] \tag{13.12}$$

where

S_T is the price of the underlying asset at maturity T
X is the strike price of the option.

From (13.12) we know that there are only two possible outcomes that can arise on maturity; either the option will expire in-the-money and the outcome is $S_T - X$, or the option will be out-of-the-money and the outcome will be 0. If we set the term p as the probability that on expiry $S_T > X$, equation (13.12) can be re-written as (13.13).

$$E(C_T) = p \times (E[S_T \mid S_T > X] - X) \tag{13.13}$$

where $E[S_T \mid S_T > X]$ is the expected value of S_T given that $S_T > X$. Equation (13.12) gives us an expression for the expected value of a call option on maturity. Therefore, to obtain the fair price of the option at the time it is struck, the value given by (13.13) must be discounted back to its present value, and this is shown as (13.14).

$$C = p \times e^{-rt} \times (E[S_T \mid S_T > X] - X) \tag{13.14}$$

where r is the continuously compounded risk-free rate of interest, and t is the time from today until maturity. Therefore, to price an option we require the probability p that the option expires in-the-money, and we require the expected value of the option given that it does expire in-the-money, which is the last term of (13.14). To calculate p we assume that asset prices follow a stochastic process, which enables us to model the probability function.

The B–S model is based on the resolution of the following partial differential equation,

$$\tfrac{1}{2}\sigma^2 S^2\left(\frac{\partial^2 C}{\partial S^2}\right) + rS\left(\frac{\partial C}{\partial S}\right) + \left(\frac{\partial C}{\partial t}\right) - rC = 0, \tag{13.15}$$

under the appropriate parameters. We do not demonstrate the process by which this equation is arrived at. The parameters refer to the payoff conditions corresponding to a European call option, which we considered above. We do not present a solution to the differential equation at (13.15), which is beyond the scope of the book, but we can consider now how the probability and expected-value functions can be solved. For a fuller treatment, readers may wish to refer to the original account by Black and Scholes. Other good accounts are given in Ingersoll (1987), Neftci (1996) and Nielsen (1999), among others.

We wish to find the probability p that the underlying asset price at maturity exceeds X is equal to the probability that the return over the time period the option is held exceeds a certain critical value. Remember that we assume normal distribution of asset–price returns. As asset returns are defined as the logarithm of price relatives, we require p such that:

$$p = prob[S_T > X] = prob\left[return > 1\text{n}\left(\frac{X}{S_0}\right)\right] \tag{13.16}$$

where S_0 is the price of the underlying asset at the time the option is struck. Generally, the probability that a normally distributed variable x will exceed a critical value x_c is given by (13.17):

$$p[x > x_c] = 1 - N\left(\frac{x_c - \mu}{\sigma}\right) \tag{13.17}$$

where μ and σ are the mean and standard deviation of x respectively and $N(\ )$ is the cumulative normal distribution. We know from our earlier discussion of the behaviour of asset prices that an expression for μ is the natural logarithm of the asset–price returns. We already know that the standard deviation of returns is $\sigma\sqrt{t}$. Therefore, with these assumptions, we may combine (13.16) and (13.17) to give us (13.18); that is,

$$p = prob.[S_T > X] = prob.\left[return > \ln\left(\frac{X}{S_0}\right)\right] = 1 - N\left[\frac{\ln\left(\frac{X}{S_0}\right) - \left(\frac{r - \sigma^2}{2}\right)t}{\sigma\sqrt{t}}\right]. \tag{13.18}$$

Under the conditions of the normal distribution, the symmetrical shape means that we can obtain the probability of an occurrence based on $1-N(d)$ being equal to $N(-d)$. Therefore, we are able to set the following relationship, as (13.19):

$$p = prob.[S_T > X] = N\left[\frac{\ln\left(\frac{S_0}{X}\right) + \left(r - \frac{\sigma^2}{2}\right)t}{\sigma\sqrt{t}}\right]. \tag{13.19}$$

Now we require a formula to calculate the expected value of the option on expiry, the second part of the expression in (13.14). This involves the integration of the normal distribution curve over the range from X to infinity. This is not shown here, but the result is given in (13.20):

$$E[S_T \mid S_T > X] = S_0 e^{rt}\frac{N(d_1)}{N(d_2)} \tag{13.20}$$

where

$$d_1 = \frac{\ln\left(\frac{S_0}{X}\right) + \left(r + \frac{\sigma^2}{2}\right)t}{\sigma\sqrt{t}}$$

and

$$d_2 = \frac{\ln\left(\frac{S_0}{X}\right) + \left(r - \frac{\sigma^2}{2}\right)t}{\sigma\sqrt{t}} = d_1 - \sigma\sqrt{t}.$$

We now have expressions for the probability that an option expires in-the-money as well as the expected value of the option on expiry, and we incorporate these into the expression at (13.14), which gives us (13.21):

$$C = N(d_2) \times e^{-rt} \times \left[S_0 e^{-rt}\frac{N(d_1)}{N(d_2)} - X\right]. \tag{13.21}$$

Equation (13.21) can be rearranged to give (13.22), which is the famous and well-known B–S option-pricing model for a European call option:

$$C = S_0 N(d_1) - Xe^{-rt}N(d_2) \tag{13.22}$$

where

S_0 is the price of the underlying asset at the time the option is struck
X is the strike price
r is the continuously compounded risk-free interest rate
t is the maturity of the option.

and d_1 and d_2 are as before.

What the expression in (13.22) states is that the fair value of a call option is the expected present value of the option on its expiry date, assuming that prices follow a lognormal distribution.

$N(d_1)$ and $N(d_2)$ are the cumulative probabilities from the normal distribution of obtaining the values d_1 and d_2, given above. $N(d_1)$ is the delta of the option. The term $N(d_2)$ represents the probability that the option will be exercised. The term e^{-rt} is the present value of one unit of cash received t periods from the time the option is struck. Where $N(d_1)$ and $N(d_2)$ are equal to 1, which is the equivalent of assuming complete certainty, the model is reduced to:

$$C = S - Xe^{-rt}$$

which is the expression for Merton's lower bound for continuously compounded interest rates, and which we introduced in intuitive fashion in the previous chapter. Therefore, under complete certainty, the B–S model reduces to Merton's bound.

The put-call parity relationship

Up to now we have concentrated on calculating the price of a call option. However, the previous section introduced the boundary condition for a put option, so it should be apparent that this can be solved as well. In fact, the price of a call option and a put option are related via what is known as the put-call parity theorem. This is an important relationship and obviates the need to develop a separate model for put options.

Consider a portfolio Y that consists of a call option with a maturity date T and a zero-coupon bond that pays X on the expiry date of the option. Consider also a second portfolio Z that consists of a put option also with maturity date T and one share. The value of portfolio A on the expiry date is given by (13.23):

$$MV_{Y,T} = \text{max.}[S_T - X,0] + X = \text{max}[X,S_T]. \tag{13.23}$$

The value of the second portfolio Z on the expiry date is:

$$MV_{Z,T} = \text{max.}[X - S_T,0] + S_T = \text{max}[X,S_T]. \tag{13.24}$$

Both portfolios have the same value at maturity. Therefore, they must also have the same initial value at start time t, otherwise there would be an arbitrage opportunity. Prices must be arbitrage-free; therefore, the following put-call relationship must hold:

$$C_t - P_t = S_t - Xe^{-r(T-t)}. \tag{13.25}$$

If the relationship in (13.24) did not hold, then arbitrage would be possible. So, using this relationship, the value of a European put option is given by the B–S model as shown below, in (13.26):

$$P(S,T) = -SN(-d_1) + Xe^{-rT}N(-d2). \tag{13.26}$$

EXAMPLE 13.11 The Black–Scholes model: Example

Here we illustrate a simple application of the B–S model. Consider an underlying asset, assumed to be a non-dividend-paying equity, with a current price of 25, and volatility of 23%. The short-term risk-free interest rate is 5%. An option is written with strike price 21 and a maturity of three months. Therefore, we have:

$S = 25$
$X = 21$
$r = 5\%$
$T = 0.25$
$\sigma = 23\%$.

To calculate the price of the option, we first calculate the discounted value of the strike price, as follows:

$$Xe^{-rT} = 21e^{-0.05(0.25)} = 20.73913.$$

We then calculate the values of d_1 and d_2:

$$d_1 = \frac{\ln(25 / 21) + [0.05 + (0.5)(0.23)^2]0.25}{0.23\sqrt{0.25}} = \frac{0.193466}{0.115}$$

$$= 1.682313$$

$$d_2 = d_1 - 0.23\sqrt{0.25} = 1.567313.$$

We now insert these values into the main price equation:

$$C = 25N(1.682313) - 21e^{-0.05(0.25)}N(1.567313).$$

Using the approximation of the cumulative normal distribution at the points 1.68 and 1.56, the price of the call option is:

$$C = 25(0.9535) - 20.73913(0.9406) = 4.3303$$

or 4.3303.

What would be the price of a put option on the same stock? The values of $N(d_1)$ and $N(d_2)$ are 0.9535 and 0.9406; therefore, the put price is calculated as:

$$P = 20.7391(1 - 0.9406) - 25(1 - 0.9535) = 0.06943.$$

If we use the call price and apply the put-call parity theorem, the price of the put option is given by:

$$P = C - S + Xe^{-rT}$$

$$= 4.3303 - 25 + 21e^{-0.05(0.25)}$$

$$= 0.069434.$$

This is exactly the same price that was obtained by the application of the put-option formula in the B-S model above.

As we noted early in this chapter, the premium payable for an option will increase if the time to expiry, the volatility or the interest rate is increased (or any combination is increased). Thus, if we keep all the parameters constant, but price a call option that has a maturity of six months or $T = 0.5$, we obtain the following values:

$d_1 = 1.3071$, giving $N(d_1) = 0.9049$

$d_2 = 1.1445$, giving $N(d_2) = 0.8740$.

The call price for the longer-dated option is 4.7217.

The B–S model as an Excel spreadsheet

In Appendix 13.3, we show the spreadsheet formulas required to build the B–S model into Microsoft® Excel. The user must ensure that the Analysis Tool-Pak add-in is available, otherwise some of the function references may not work. By setting up the cells in the way shown, the fair value of a vanilla call or put option may be calculated. The put-call parity is used to enable calculation of the put price.

B–S and the valuation of bond options

In this section, we illustrate the application of the B–S model to the pricing of an option on a zero-coupon bond and a plain vanilla fixed-coupon bond.

For a zero-coupon bond the theoretical price of a call option written on the bond is given by (13.27):

$$C = PN(d_1) - Xe^{-rT}N(d_2) \qquad (13.27)$$

where P is the price of the underlying bond and all other parameters remain the same. If the option is written on a coupon-paying bond, it is necessary to subtract the present value of all coupons paid during the life of the option from the bond's price. Coupons sometimes lower the price of a call option because a coupon makes it more attractive to hold a bond rather than an option on the bond. Call options on bonds are often priced at a lower level than similar options on zero-coupon bonds.

EXAMPLE 13.12 B–S model and bond option pricing

Consider a European call option written on a bond that has the following characteristics:

Price:	£98
Coupon:	8.00% (semi-annual)
Time to maturity:	Five years
Bond price volatility:	6.02%
Coupon payments:	£4 in three months and nine months
Three-month interest rate:	5.60%
Nine-month interest rate:	5.75%
One-year interest rate:	6.25%

The option is written with a strike price of £100 and has a maturity of one year. The present value of the coupon payments made during the life of the option is £7.78, as shown below:

$$4e^{-0.056\times0.25} + 4e^{-0.057\times0.25} = 3.9444 + 3.83117 = 7.77557.$$

This gives us $P = 98 - 7.78 = £90.22$.

Applying the B–S model we obtain:

$$d_1 = [\ln(90.22/100) + 0.0625 + 0.001812] / 0.0602 = -0.6413$$

$$d_2 = d_1 - (0.0602 \times 1) = -0.7015$$

$$\begin{aligned} C &= 90.22N(-0.6413) - 100e^{-0.0625}N(-0.7015) \\ &= 1.1514. \end{aligned}$$

Therefore, the call option has a value of £1.15, which will be composed entirely of time value. Note also that a key assumption of the model is constant interest rates, yet it is being applied to a bond price – which is essentially an interest rate – that is considered to follow a stochastic price process.

Interest-rate options and the Black model

The Black (76) model is used by banks to price instruments such as swaptions, in addition to bond and interest-rate options like caps and floors.

In this model, the spot price $S(t)$ of an asset or a commodity is the price payable for immediate delivery today (in practice, up to two days forward) at time t. This price is assumed to follow a geometric Brownian motion. The theoretical price for a futures contract on the asset, $F(t,T)$, is defined as the price agreed today for delivery of the asset at time T, with the price agreed today but payable on delivery. When $t = T$, the futures price is equal to the spot price. A futures contract is cash-settled every day via the clearing mechanism, whereas a forward contract is a contract to buy or sell the asset where there is no daily mark-to-market and no daily cash settlement.

Let us set f as the value of a forward contract, u as the value of a futures contract and C as the value of an option contract. Each of these contracts is a function of the futures price $F(t,T)$, as well as additional variables. So we may write at time t the values of all three contracts as $f(F,t)$, $u(F,t)$ and $C(F,t)$. The value of the forward contract is also a function of the price of the underlying asset S at time T and can be written $f(F,t,S,T)$. Note that the value of the forward contract f is not the same as the price of the forward contract. The forward price at any given time is the delivery price that would result in the contract having a zero value. At the time the contract is transacted, the forward value is zero. Over time, both the price and the value will fluctuate. The futures price, on the other hand, is the price at which a forward contract has a zero current value. Therefore, at the time of the trade the forward price is equal to the futures price F, which may be written as:

$$f(F,tF,T) = 0. \tag{13.28}$$

Equation (13.28) simply states that the value of the forward contract is zero when the contract is taken out and the contract price S is always equal to the current futures price, $F(t,T)$.[8]

---

[8] This assumption is held in the market but does not hold good over long periods, due chiefly to the difference in the way futures and forwards are marked-to-market, and because futures are cash-settled on a daily basis while forwards are not.

The principal difference between a futures contract and a forward contract is that a futures contract may be used to imply the price of forward contracts. This arises from the fact that futures contracts are repriced each day, with a new contract price that is equal to the new futures price. Hence, when F rises, such that $F>S$, the forward contract has a positive value, and when F falls, the forward contract has a negative value. When the transaction expires and delivery takes place, the futures price is equal to the spot price and the value of the forward contract is equal to the spot price minus the contract price or the spot price.

$$f(F,T,S,T) = F - S \tag{13.29}$$

On maturity, the value of a bond or commodity option is given by the maximum of zero, and the difference between the spot price and the contract price. Since at that date the futures price is equal to the spot price, we conclude that:

$$C(F,T) = \begin{cases} F - S & \text{if } F \geq S_T \\ 0 & \text{else} \end{cases}. \tag{13.30}$$

The assumptions made in the Black model are that the prices of futures contracts follow a lognormal distribution with a constant variance, and that the capital asset pricing model (CAPM) applies in the market. There is also an assumption of no transaction costs or taxes. Under these assumptions, we can create a risk-free hedged position that is composed of a long position in the option and a short position in the futures contract. Following the B–S model, the number of options put on against one futures contract is given by $[\partial C(F,t) / \partial F]$, which is the derivative of $C(F, t)$ with respect to F. The change in the hedged position resulting from a change in price of the underlying is given by (13.31) below:

$$\partial C(F,t) - [\partial C(F,t) / \partial F]\partial F. \tag{13.31}$$

Due to the principle of arbitrage-free pricing, the return generated by the hedged portfolio must be equal to the risk-free interest rate, and this together with an expansion of $\partial C(F,t)$ produces the following partial differential equation:

$$\left[\frac{\partial C(F,t)}{\partial t}\right] = rC(F,t) - \tfrac{1}{2}\sigma^2 F^2 \left[\frac{\partial^2 C(F,t)}{\partial F^2}\right] \tag{13.32}$$

which is solved by setting the following:

$$\tfrac{1}{2}\sigma^2 F^2\left[\frac{\partial^2 C(F,t)}{\partial F^2}\right] - rC(F,t) + \left[\frac{\partial C(F,t)}{\partial t}\right] = 0. \qquad (13.33)$$

The solution to the partial differential equation (13.32) is not presented here.

The result, by denoting $T = t - T$ and using (13.19) and (13.32), gives the fair value of a commodity option or option on a forward contract as shown in (13.34):

$$C(F,t) = e^{-rT}[FN(d_1) - S_T N(d_2)] \qquad (13.34)$$

where

$$d_1 = \frac{1}{\sigma\sqrt{t}}\left[\ln\left(\frac{F}{S_T}\right) + \tfrac{1}{2}\sigma^2)T\right]$$

$$d_2 = d_1 - \sigma\sqrt{t}.$$

There are a number of other models that have been developed for specific contracts; for example, the Garman and Kohlhagen (1983) and Grabbe (1983) models, used for currency options, and the Merton, Barone-Adesi and Whaley or BAW model (1987) used for commodity options. For the valuation of American options, on dividend-paying assets, another model has been developed by Roll, Geske and Whaley. More recently the Black–Derman–Toy model (1990) has been used to price exotic options. A survey of these, though very interesting, is outside the scope of this book.

Comment on the B–S model

The introduction of the B–S model was one of the great milestones in the development of the global capital markets, and it remains an important pricing model today. Many of the models introduced later for application to specific products are still based essentially on the B–S model. Subsequently, academics have presented some weaknesses in the model that stem from the nature of the main assumptions behind the model itself, which we will summarise here. The main critique of the B–S model appears to centre on:

- its assumption of frictionless markets. This is at best only approximately true for large market counterparties;
- the assumption of a constant interest rate. This is possibly the most unrealistic assumption. Interest rates over even the shortest time frame (the overnight rate) fluctuate considerably. In addition to a

dynamic short rate, the short-end of the yield curve often moves in the opposite direction to moves in underlying asset prices, particularly so with bonds and bond options;

- the assumption of lognormal distribution. This is accepted by the market as a reasonable approximation but not completely accurate, and also misses out most extreme moves or market shocks;
- it being a European option only. Although it is rare for US options to be exercised early, there are situations when it is optimal to do so, and the B–S model does not price these situations.
- for stock options, the assumption of a continuous constant dividend yield is clearly not realistic, although the trend in the US markets is for ordinary shares to cease paying dividends altogether.

These points notwithstanding, the B–S model paved the way for the rapid development of options as liquid tradeable products and is widely used today.

Stochastic volatility

The B–S model assumes a constant volatility and for this reason, and because it is based on mathematics, often fails to pick up on market "sentiment" when there is a large downward move or shock. This is not a failing limited to the B–S model, however. For this reason, though, it undervalues out-of-the-money options, and to compensate for this market-makers push up the price of deep in- or out-of-the-money options, giving rise to the volatility *smile*.

The effect of stochastic volatility not being catered for then is to introduce mispricing, specifically the undervaluation of out-of-the-money options and the overvaluation of deeply in-the-money options. This is because when the price of the underlying asset rises, its volatility level also increases. The effect of this is that assets priced at relatively high levels do not tend to follow the process described by geometric Brownian motion. The same is true for relatively low asset prices and price volatility, but in the opposite direction. To compensate for this, stochastic volatility models have been developed, such as the Hull–White model (1987).

Implied volatility

The volatility parameter in the B–S model, by definition, cannot be observed directly in the market as it refers to volatility going forward. It is different from historic volatility which can be measured directly, and this value is sometimes used to estimate implied volatility of an asset price. Banks therefore use the value for implied volatility, which is the volatility obtained using the prices of exchange-traded options. Given the price of an option and all the other parameters, it is possible to use the price of the option to determine the volatility of the underlying asset implied by the option price. The B–S model, however, cannot be rearranged into a form that expresses the volatility measure σ as a function of the other parameters. Generally, therefore, a numerical iteration process is used to arrive at the value for σ, given the price of the option; this is usually the Newton–Raphson method.

The market uses implied volatilities to gauge the volatility of individual assets relative to the market. Volatility levels are not constant, and fluctuate with the overall level of the market, as well as for stock-specific factors. When assessing volatilities with reference to exchange-traded options, market-makers will use more than one value, because an asset will have different implied volatilities depending on how in-the-money the option itself is. The price of an at-the-money option will exhibit greater sensitivity to volatility than the price of a deeply in- or out-of-the-money option. Therefore, market-makers will take a combination of volatility values when assessing the volatility of a particular asset.

Collars, caps and floors

An option combination that is very important in money markets is the cap and floor, which is used to hedge interest-rate exposure. Caps and floors are combinations of the same types of options with identical strike prices but arranged to run over a range of time periods.

We have reviewed the main types of instruments used to hedge interest-rate risk, and short-dated interest-rate futures and FRAs are usually used. For example, a bank that wished to protect against a rise in funding costs in the future could buy FRAs or sell futures, which would lock in the forward interest rate available today. Such an arrangement does not allow the hedgers to gain if market rates actually go their way. They would have prevented loss, but also any extra gain. To overcome this the hedgers might choose to construct the hedge-using options. Note that the term *cap* and *floor* is not to be confused with FRN products that have caps and/or floors set into their coupon reset terms

Description

A cap is essentially a strip of options. A borrower with an existing interest-rate liability can protect against a rise in interest rates by purchasing a cap.

If rates rise above the cap, the borrower will be compensated by the cap payout; however, if rates fall the borrower gains from lower funding costs, and does not have an equivalent loss on the other side that would have to be taken out of a conventional hedge.

A cap is composed of a series of individual options or *caplets*. The price of a cap is obtained by pricing each of the caplets individually. Each caplet has a strike interest rate that is the rate of the cap. For example, a borrower might purchase a 7.0% cap, which means that if rates rise above 7% the cap will pay out the difference between the cap rate and the actual Libor rate. A five-year cap might be composed of a strip of nine individual caplets, each providing protection for successive six-month periods. The first six-month period in the five-year term is usually not covered, because the interest rate for that period, as it begins straight away, will be known already. A caplet runs over two periods of time, the exposure period and the protection period. The exposure period runs from the date the cap is purchased to the interest reset date for the next borrowing period. At this point the protection period begins and runs to the expiry of the caplet. The protection period is usually three months, six months or one year, and will be set to the interest-rate reset liability that the borrower wishes to hedge. Therefore the protection period is usually identical for all the caplets in a cap. This is illustrated for a two-year cap in Figure 13.16.

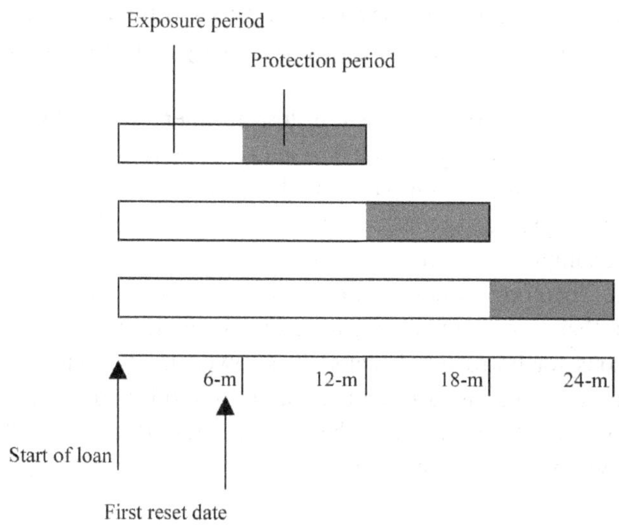

Figure 13.16 Two-year cap and caplets

Caps and floors are options on interest rates. They are commonly written on Libor or another interest rate such as Euribor, the US prime rate or a CP rate. In this section, we review caps, which are essentially calls on an interest rate, while a floor is a put on an interest rate.

A cap is an option contract in which an upper limit is placed on the interest rate payable by the borrower on a cash loan. The limit is known as the cap level. The seller of the cap, who is the market-making bank, agrees to pay to the buyer the difference between the cap rate and the higher rate should interest rates rise above the cap level. The buyer of the cap is long the option and will have paid the cap premium to the seller. Hence, a cap is a call option on interest rates. The cash loan may have been taken out before the cap, or indeed with another counterparty, or the cap may have been set up alongside the loan as a form of interest-rate risk management. If a cap is set up in conjunction with a cash loan, the notional amount of the cap will be equal to the amount of the loan. Caps can be fairly long-dated options; for example, 10-year caps are not uncommon.

In a typical cap, the cap rate is measured alongside the indexed interest rate at the specified fixing dates. So during its life a cap may be fixed semi-annually with the six-month Libor rate. At the fixing date, if the index interest rate is below the cap level, no payment changes hands and if there is a cash loan involved, the borrower will pay the market interest rate on the loan. If the index rate is fixed above the cap level, the cap seller will pay the difference between the index interest rate and the cap level, calculated for the period of the fix (quarterly, semi-annually and so on) on the notional amount of the cap.

It is possible to protect against a drop in interest rates by purchasing a *floor*. This is conceptually identical to a cap, but with the interest rate set as one below, which the option pays out. This would be used by an institution that wished to protect against a fall in income caused by a fall in interest rates; for example, a commercial bank with a large proportion of floating-rate assets. The combination of a call and a floor creates a *collar*, which is a corridor that fixes interest payment or receipt levels. This is sometime advantageous for borrowers because it is lower in cost than a straight cap. A collar protects against a rise in rates, and provides some gain if there is a fall down to the floor rate. The cheapest structure is a collar with a narrow spread between cap and floor rates.

Pricing

Individual contracts – that is, each fixing – during the life of the cap are known as caplets. The interest payment on each caplet is given by (13.35):

$$Int = \frac{\max.[r - rX,0] \times (N / B) \times M}{1 + r(N / B)} \tag{13.35}$$

where

r is the interest-rate fixing for the specified index
rX is the cap level
M is the notional amount of the cap
B is the day-base (360 or 365)
N is the number of days in the interest period (days to the next rate fix).

In the UK, settlement is an upfront payment for the period covered, and so is discounted at the index-rate level.

Most banks use a modified version of the standard B–S model to price caps and floors. We described this model in this chapter. The price of the underlying and the strike price that are input to the model, which we denoted with S and X, are replaced by interest rates. This is shown in 13.36.

$$S = \frac{MfTe^{-rt}}{(1 + fT)} \tag{13.36}$$

$$X = \frac{MxT}{(1 + fT)}$$

where

M is the notional value of the cap (and principal amount of borrowing)
f is the forward rate over the protection period
T is the length of the protection period
x is the cap rate
r is the continuously compounded zero-coupon rate over the exposure period.

Substituting these expressions into the basic B–S equation results in the pricing formula for caplets given in 13.37:

$$Caplet = \frac{Te^{-rt}}{(1 + fT)} \left[fN(d_1) = xN(d_2) \right] \tag{13.37}$$

where

$$d_1 = \frac{1\text{n}\left(\frac{f}{x}\right) + \left(\frac{\sigma^2}{2}\right)t}{\sigma\sqrt{t}}$$

$$d_2 = d_1 - \sigma\sqrt{t}$$

where

t is the length of the exposure period
σ is the volatility of the forward interest rate.

A caplet is normally quoted as the percentage of the principal rather than an actual amount. The term r is the zero-coupon rate, used as a substitute for the risk-free rate.

Each caplet can be priced individually and the total premium payable on the cap is the sum of the caplet prices. The Black model assumes constant volatility, and so banks use later models to price products when this assumption is considered to be materially unrealistic.

A vanilla cap-pricing calculator is part of the rate application software, included in this book.

In the same way as caps and caplets, a floorlet is essentially a put option on an interest rate, with a sequence of floorlets being known as a floor. This might be used, for example, by a lender of funds to limit the loss of income should interest-rate levels fall. If a firm buys a call and sells a floor, this is known as buying a collar because the interest rate payable is bound on the upside at the cap level and on the downside at the floor level. It is possible to purchase a zero-cost collar where the premium of the cap and floor elements are identical. This form of interest-rate risk management is very popular with corporates rather than bonds.

Interest-rate risk exposure and option hedging

Managing interest-rate risk exposure is a significant responsibility of the bank ALM practitioner. We have seen how FRAs, futures and swaps can be used to hedge such exposure, and the flexibility and liquidity offered by these instruments means that in most cases they are all that is needed when hedging interest-rate risk. However, in certain cases a bank ALM desk may want to use option products. We illustrate such use here.

A bank that made extensive use of floating-rate liabilities in its funding is exposed to the risk of lower net interest income (NII) in the event that interest rates rise. It would be described as a "liability-sensitive" bank, because as interest rates rose its funding cost would increase, while its asset returns may not.[9] This would cause the NII margin to reduce. This risk exposure can be hedged by using an interest-rate cap, essentially a put option on interest rates, to reduce the extent of the risk exposure.

EXAMPLE 13.13 Using options to hedge interest-rate risk exposure

Let us consider a hypothetical small-sized retail bank with a USD200 million balance sheet. Its simplified gap report is shown at Table 13.5 on page 614. This shows that the majority of the bank's assets are fixed rate, while a majority of its funding (liabilities) are floating-rate. This liability sensitivity is indicated by the "instant" gap of −80.00, as shown in the Table.[10] In other words, the bank exhibits an earnings stream that is at risk from a rise in interest rates. We illustrate this in Table 13.6 on page 615, which shows the impact of a 100 basis point parallel shift in market interest rates (we assume that all the floating-rate assets and liabilities would reprice immediately following the change in market rates). We observe that if there is a 1% upward parallel shift in rates, NII is reduced by USD800,000.00. Thus the bank is carrying currently approximately 7.8% of earnings-at-risk exposure (EAR). Put another way, the risk represents a 40 basis point reduction in the net interest margin (NIM).[11] It may be that this is acceptable to ALCO, although typically ALCO will set a ±5% or ±10% limit on EAR. For our hypothetical bank under the current scenario the latter would not present a problem, however the former would. The ALM desk would want to reduce the EAR to within the formal limit, and this can be undertaken in a number of ways. If derivatives are not available, the ALM desk could reduce the amount of floating-rate

---

[9] Even if all the assets are not fixed-rate, as indeed many would not be, they may still re-price on a less frequent basis than the liabilities and this also creates interest-rate risk in a rising rate environment.

[10] This gap report is simplified because we do not take into account the tenor of the assets and liabilities. Rather, we view this as a snapshot gap report of interest-rate sensitivity to a change in rates today.

[11] We define NIM as the dollar difference between interest income and interest expenses, expressed as a percentage of average earning assets. In our example, all USD200 million of assets are earning a return – there are no non-earning assets on the balance sheet.

funding and increase fixed-rate funding; equally it could increase the amount of floating-rate assets.[12] The problem with using cash assets to reduce EAR exposure is that they cannot be effected right away.

By using derivatives the risk exposure can be adjusted immediately. An FRA can be used to cover the funding risk; or, the ALM desk can use an interest-rate cap. If it believes rates are going up, it can buy a cap. In this case, the bank can buy a cap of notional USD80 million (the amount of the funding gap at risk), which would remove the EAR completely. A lower notional would leave some exposure, and a higher notional would change the interest-rate sensitivity of the bank to one that benefited from a rise in rates. The tenor of the option would be set to match the risk horizon of the bank; if for example the ALM desk believes rates will change in the next six to 12 months, it would buy a one-year cap. Generally, the strike price of the option would be set at the prevailing interest rate (at-the-market), so if the current three-month Libor rate is 3% then the cap strike would be set at 3%. This removes any downside risk. For a lower option premium, the ALM desk may want to set a higher strike rate, say 4%, which is "out-of-the-money" and leaves some residual EAR. This would be done to reduce the cost of the hedge, and also if the bank feels that it can live with a small increase in rates.

By buying a 3% strike USD80 million one-year cap, the bank is hedged if rates rise above the strike rate. If on option maturity rates are indeed higher, the seller of the cap (usually a bank that is a market-maker in options) will pay to the buyer the difference between the current rate and the strike rate, multiplied by the notional. If rates have not risen or if they have fallen, the option expires worthless (the buyer would have paid the option premium on purchase and this remains income for the market-maker). Table 13.7 on page 616 shows the effect on EAR if the bank buys the cap to hedge its interest-rate risk. The cap is an off-balance sheet instrument, but its cash flows on execution and expiry impact the

[12] The ALM desk might consider this if it firmly believed that the next move in interest rates was upward.

bank's balance sheet position, in this case altering its risk profile. The risk exposure has been reduced such that if rates do increase, there is no negative impact for the bank.[13] The NII and NIM are unchanged even when rates have moved upward, and the EAR has been eliminated completely, so on paper this hedge looks very effective. The option premium is key to the analysis; of course, in our example it is sufficiently low to be not material, but this may not necessarily be the case in practice.

The illustration in Table 13.7 shows one advantage of using options to hedge rather than other derivatives: the ability to gain from an upside move and yet not pay – option premium excepted – on a downside move. In a falling interest-rate environment the NIM increases, but the option hedge is unused. If the hedge was constructed with an interest-rate swap or FRA, the bank would have to pay out on either of these instruments if rates moved lower. This is not the case with the option, and when the hedge is in place the only cost is the one-off premium. In other words, a swap removes earnings volatility in both a rising and a falling interest-rate environment, so while the risk protection is complete there is no chance of upside gain. With an option the bank has a chance to benefit from an upward move in rates. The cost of the hedge is the premium, which is of course paid irrespective of whether the option expires in-the-money or not. In our example, this hedge cost amounted to 5 basis points in NIM terms.

Note that a bank that was "asset sensitive" would do the opposite to what is described here, it would purchase a floor option that would pay out if the Libor rate on expiry was below the strike rate.

[13] We have set a premium price of 0.1 to make the illustration clear. The payout on the option is shown in Table 13.7.

Asset–liability gap

Assets	(million)	Fixed rate or current floating-rate
Loans: fixed rate	140	8%
Bonds: fixed rate	40	7%
Bonds: floating-rate	20	5%
Total assets	200	
Risk-sensitive assets (RSA)	20	
Liabilities		
Deposits: floating-rate	100	3%
Deposits: fixed rate	60	3%
NIBLs	20	0%
Capital	20	0%
	200	
Risk-sensitive liabilities (RSL)	100	
Gap	–80.0	
RSA/RSL	20%	

Table 13.5 Bank simplified gap report

	No rate change		−1% parallel shift		+1% parallel shift	
Interest income						
Loans: fixed rate	11.2	[140 * 0.08]	11.2	[140 * 0.08]	11.2	[140 * 0.08]
Bonds: fixed rate	2.8	[40 * 0.07]	2.8	[40 * 0.07]	2.8	[40 * 0.07]
Bonds: floating-rate	1.0	[20 * 0.05]	0.8	[20 * 0.04]	1.2	[20 * 0.06]
Total	15.0		14.8		15.2	
Interest cost						
Deposits: floating-rate	3.0	[100 * 0.03]	2.0	[100 * 0.02]	4.0	[100 * 0.04]
Deposits: fixed rate	1.8	[60 * 0.03]	1.8	[60 * 0.03]	1.8	[60 * 0.03]
Total	4.8		3.8		5.8	
Net interest income (NII)	**10.2**		**11**		**9.4**	
Net interest margin (NIM)	5.10%		5.50%		4.70%	
Earnings at risk					7.84%	

Table 13.6 Net interest income scenarios

	No rate change		–1% parallel shift		+1% parallel shift	
Interest income						
Loans: fixed rate	11.2	[140 * 0.08]	11.2	[140 * 0.08]	11.2	[140 * 0.08]
Bonds: fixed rate	2.8	[40 * 0.07]	2.8	[40 * 0.07]	2.8	[40 * 0.07]
Bonds: floating-rate	1	[20 * 0.05]	0.8	[20 * 0.04]	1.2	[20 * 0.06]
Payments from Cap	0		0		0.8	[80mm * (5% - 4%)]
Total	15		14.8		16	
Interest cost						
Deposits: floating-rate	3	[100 * 0.03]	2	[100 * 0.02]	4	[100 * 0.04]
Deposits: fixed rate	1.8	[60 * 0.03]	1.8	[60 * 0.03]	1.8	[60 * 0.03]
Cap premium	0.1		0.1		0.1	
Total	4.9		3.9		5.9	
Net interest income (NII)	**10.1**		**10.9**		**10.1**	
Net interest margin (NIM)	5.05%		5.45%		5.05%	
Earnings at risk					0.00%	

Table 13.7 Net interest income and option hedge

Hedging considerations when using options

The simple example above serves to illustrate how an ALM desk can reduce or eliminate interest-rate risk through the use of options. The desk should also be aware of other issues when using options to construct the hedge.

Basis risk

Basis risk exists for all hedging instruments, not just options. If all the cash assets on the bank's balance sheet were referenced to Libor, then basis risk would be zero because the option fix on expiry is also with reference to Libor. However, some assets will be linked to other reference rates such as the Prime rate or the T-bill rate. Risk hedging needs to be aware of any divergence between the hedge index and the reference index, and rebalance the hedge accordingly.

Counterparty risk

When buying options for hedging purposes, a bank will need to monitor the credit quality of the option seller, as it will have an exposure to it should the option expire in-the-money. This can be carried out as part of the standard credit analysis carried out by the bank for its own customers. Generally, option market-makers are of interbank quality and this is considered more than acceptable credit risk.

Option pricing

Interest-rate options are generally priced using the Black model or a binomial or trinomial pricing model. However, different banks may use slightly different parameter values for implied volatility, when pricing the same option. A bank looking to use options can ensure that it is paying fair value for the hedge by asking more than one market-maker for a price quote. A more efficient method would be for the bank to implement its own option pricing model, which it can then use to compare prices and also to mark-to-market.

Appendices

APPENDIX 13.1 The forward interest rate: Arbitrage proof of the futures price being equal to the forward price

The markets assume that the forward rate implied by the price of a futures contract is the same as the futures price itself for a contract with the same expiry date. This assumption is the basis on which futures contracts are used to price swaps and other forward-rate instruments such as FRAs. Here we summarise a strategy first described by Cox, Ingersoll and Ross (1981)[14] to show that under certain assumptions, namely that when the risk-free interest rate is constant and identical for all maturities (that is, in a flat term structure environment), this assumption holds true. However, in practice, because the assumptions are not realistic under actual market conditions, this relationship does not hold for longer-dated futures contracts and forward rates. In the first place, term structures are rarely flat or constant. The main reason however is because of the way futures contracts are settled, compared to forward contracts. Market participants who deal in exchange-traded futures must deposit daily margin with the exchange clearing house, reflecting their profit and loss on futures trading. Therefore a profit on a futures position will be received immediately, and in a positive-sloping yield curve environment this profit will be invested at a higher-than-average rate of interest. In the same way a loss on futures trading would have to be funded straight away, and the funding cost would be at a lower-than-average rate of interest. However, the profit on a forward contract is not realised until the maturity of the contract, and so a position in a forward is not affected by daily profit or loss cash flows. Therefore, a long-dated futures contract will have more value to an investor than a long-dated forward contract, because of the opportunity to invest mark-to-market gains made during the life of the futures contract.

When the price of the underlying asset represented by a futures contract is positively correlated with interest rates, the price of futures contracts will be higher than the price of the same-maturity forward contract. When the price of the underlying asset is negatively correlated with interest rates, which is the case with three-month interest-rate futures like short sterling, forward prices are higher than futures prices. That is, the forward interest rate is lower than the interest rate implied by the futures contract price. This difference is not pronounced for short-dated contracts, and so is ignored by

[14] See their article, "A Re-examination of Traditional Hypotheses about the Term Structure of Interest Rates", 1981 *Journal of Finance*, 36, pp. 769–99.

the market. There are also other factors that will cause a difference in forward and futures prices, the most significant of these being transaction costs and liquidity: it is generally cheaper to trade exchange-traded futures and they tend to more liquid instruments. However, for longer-dated instruments, the difference in treatment between forwards and futures means that their rates will not be the same, and this difference needs to be taken into account when pricing long-dated forward instruments. This is discussed in Choudhry (2004), in the section on convexity bias.

Under certain assumptions it can be shown that the price of same-maturity futures and forward contracts are equal. The primary assumption is that interest rates are constant. The strategy used to prove this was first described by Cox, Ingersoll and Ross.

Consider a futures contract with maturity of n days and with a price of P_i at the end of day i. Set r as the constant risk-free interest rate per day. Assume a trading strategy that consists of:

- establishing a long position in the futures of e^r at the start of day 0;
- adding to the long position to make a total of e^{2r} at the end of day 1;
- adding to the long position to make a total of e^{3r} at the end of day 2;
- increasing the size of the position daily by the amount shown.

At the start of day i the long position is e^{ir}. The profit or loss from the position is given by (A13.1.1):

$$P/L = (P_i - P_{i-1})e^{ir}. \tag{A13.1.1}$$

If this amount is compounded on a daily basis using r, the final value on the expiry of the contract is given by:

$$(P_i - P_{i-1})e^{ir}\, e^{(n-i)r} = (P_i - P_{i-1})e^{nr}$$

so that the value of the position on the expiry of the contract at the end of day n is given by (A13.1.2):

$$FV = \sum_{i=1}^{n} (P_i - P_{i-1})e^{nr}. \tag{A13.1.2}$$

The expression in (A13.1.2) may also be written as (A13.1.3):

$$FV = [(P_n - P_{n-1}) + (P_{n-1} - P_{n-2}) + \ldots + (P_1 - P_0)]e^{nr} \quad \text{(A13.1.3)}$$
$$= [(P_n - P_0)]e^{nr}.$$

In theory the price of a futures contract on expiry must equal the price of the underlying asset on that day. If we set the price of the underlying asset on expiry as $P_{n\text{-}underlying}$, as P_n is equal to the final price of the contract on expiry, the final value of the trading strategy may be written as (A13.1.4) below.

$$FV = (P_{n-underlying} - P_0)e^{nr} \quad \text{(A13.1.4)}$$

Investing P_0 in a risk-free bond and using the same strategy as that described above will therefore return:

$$P_0 e^{nr} + (P_{n-underlying} - P_0)e^{nr}$$

or an amount equal to $P_{n\text{-}underlying}e^{nr}$ at the expiry of the contract at the close of day n. Therefore this states that an amount P_0 may be invested to return a final amount of $P_{n\text{-}underlying}e^{nr}$ at the end of day n.

Assume that the forward contract price at the end of day 0 is $P_{0-forward}$. By investing this amount in a risk-free bond, and simultaneously establishing a long forward position of e^{nr} forward contracts, we are guaranteed an amount $P_{n-underlying}e^{nr}$ at the end of day n. We therefore we have two investment strategies that both return a value of $P_{n-underlying}e^{nr}$ at the end of the same time period; one strategy requires an investment of P_0 while the other requires an investment of $P_{0-forward}$. Under the rule of no-arbitrage pricing, the price of both contracts must be equal, that is:

$$P_0 = P_{0-fwd}\,.$$

That is, the price of the futures contract and the price of the forward contract at the end of day 0 are equal.

APPENDIX 13.2 Lognormal distribution of returns

In the distribution of asset–price returns, returns are defined as the logarithm of price relatives and are assumed to follow the normal distribution, given by:

$$\ln\left(\frac{P_t}{P_0}\right) \sim N\left(rt, \sigma\sqrt{t}\right) \tag{A13.2.1}$$

where

P_t	is the price at time t
P_0	is the price at time 0
$N(m,s)$	is a random normal distribution with mean m and standard deviation s
r	is the annual rate of return
σ	is the annualised standard deviation of returns.

From (A13.2.1) we conclude that the logarithm of the prices is normally distributed, due to (A13.2.2) where P_0 is a constant:

$$\ln(P_t) \sim \ln(P_0) + N\left(rt, \sigma\sqrt{t}\right). \tag{A13.2.2}$$

We conclude that prices are normally distributed and are described by the relationship:

$$\frac{P_1}{P_0} \sim e^{N(rt,\sigma\sqrt{t})}$$

and from this relationship we may set the expected return as rt.

APPENDIX 13.3 B–S model in Microsoft® Excel

To value a vanilla option under the following parameters, we can use Microsoft Excel to carry out the calculation as shown in Figure A13.3.1.

Price of underlying:	100
Volatility:	0.0691
Maturity of option:	3 months
Strike price:	99.5
Risk-free rate:	5%

Cell	C	D	
8	**Underlying price**, *S*	100	
9		Volatility %	0.0691
10	Option maturity years	0.25	
11	**Strike price**, *X*	99.50	
12	Risk-free interest rate %	0.05	
13			
14			
15			Cell formulas:
16	ln (S/X)	0.005012542	=LN (D8/D11)
17	Adjusted return	0.0000456012500	=((D12-D9)^2/ 2)*D10
18	Time-adjusted volatility	0.131434394	=(D9*D10)^0.5
19	d_2	0.038484166	=(D16+D17)/D18
20	$N(d_2)$	0.515349233	=NORMSDIST(D19)
21			
22	d_1	0.16991856	=D19+D18
23	$N(d_1)$	0.56746291	=NORMSDIST(D22)
24	e^{-rt}	0.9875778	=EXP(-D10*D12)
25			
26	**CALL**	6.106018498	=D8*D23-D11*D20*D24
27	**PUT**	4.370009648	* =D26-D8+D11*D24

*By put-call parity, $P = C - S + Xe^{-rt}$

Figure A13.3.1 Microsoft Excel calculation of vanilla option price

References and bibliography

Black, F. and Scholes, M. 1973, "The Pricing of Options and Corporate Liabilities", *Journal of Political Economy*, 81, May-June, pp. 637–59.

Black, F., Derman, E. and Toy, W. 1996, "A One-factor Model of Interest Rates and its Application to Treasury Bond Options", in Hughston, L. (ed), *Vasicek and Beyond*, Risk Publications, London.

Brace, A., Gatarek, D. and Musiela, M. 1996, "The Market Model of Interest Rate Dynamics", in Hughston, L. (ed), *Vasicek and Beyond*, Risk Publications, London.

Briys, E. et al. 1998, *Options, Futures and Exotic Derivatives*, John Wiley & Sons, Chichester.

Burghardt, G. 1994, *The Treasury Bond Futures Basis*, McGraw Hill, New York.

Burghardt, G. 2004, *The EuroDollar Futures and Options Handbook*, McGraw Hill, New York.

Choudhry, M. 2001, *The Bond and Money Markets: Strategy, Trading, Analysis*, Butterworth-Heinemann, Oxford, chapters 42–49.

Choudhry, M. 2004, *Fixed Income Markets*, John Wiley & Sons, Singapore.

Cox, D. and Miller, H. 1965, *The Theory of Stochastic Processes*, Chapman & Hall, Oxford.

Cox, J. and Ross, S. 1976, "The Valuation of Options for Alternative Stochastic Processes", *Journal of Financial Economics*, 3, pp. 145–66.

Cox, J., Ross, S. and Rubinstein, M. 1979, "Option Pricing: A Simplified Approach", *Journal of Financial Economics*, 7, October, pp. 229–64.

Debreu, G. 1954, "Representation of a Preference Ordering by a Numerical Function", in Thrall, R., Coombs, C. and Davis, R. (eds) *Decision Processes*, John Wiley & Sons, Chichester.

Fabozzi, F. and Mann, S. 2001, *Introduction to Fixed Income Analysis*, FTJ Associates, New Hope, PA.

Fama, E. 1965, "The Behaviour of Stock Prices", *Journal of Business*, 38, January, pp. 34–105.

Fama, E.F. 1970, "Efficient Capital Markets: A Review of Theory and Empirical Work", *Journal of Finance*, Vol. 25, pp. 383–417.

Harrison, J. and Kreps, D. 1979, "Martingales and Arbitrage in Multi-period Securities markets", *Journal of Economic Theory*, 20, pp. 381–408.

Harrison, J. and Pliska, S. 1981, "Martingales and Stochastic Integrals in the Theory of Continuous Trading", *Stochastic Processes and Their Applications*, 11, pp. 216–60.

Haug, E.G. 1998, *The Complete Guide to Option Pricing Formulas*, McGraw-Hill, New York.

Heston, S. 1993, "A Closed Form Solution for Options with Stochastic Volatility with Application to Bond and Currency Options", *Review of Financial Studies*, 6, pp. 327–43.

Heston, S. 1993, "Invisible Parameters in Option Prices", *Journal of Finance*, 48(3), pp. 933–47.

Hull, J. 2000, *Options, Futures and Other Derivatives* (4th edition), Prentice Hall, New Jersey.

Hull, J. and White, A. 1987, "The Pricing of Options on Assets with Stochastic Volatilities", *Journal of Finance,* 42, pp. 281–300.

Hull, J. and White, A. 1988, "An Analysis of the Bias Caused by a Stochastic Volatility in Option Pricing", *Advances in Futures and Options Research,* 3, pp. 29–61.

Ingersoll, J. 1987, *Theory of Financial Decision Making*, Rowman & Littlefield, Princeton, Chapter 18, Savage, MA.

Ito, K. 1951, "On Stochastic Differential Equations", *American Mathematical Society,* 4, pp. 1–51.

Joshi, M. 2004, *The Concepts and Practice of Mathematical Finance*, Cambridge University Press, Cambridge.

Klemkosky, R. and Resnick, B. 1979, "Put-Call Parity and Market Efficiency", *Journal of Financial Economics*, 34, December, pp. 1141–55.

Kolb, R. 2003, *Futures, Options and Swaps* (4th edition), Blackwell, Oxford.

Marshall, J. and Bansal, V. 1992, *Financial Engineering*, New York Institute of Finance, New York.

Merton, R. 1973, "Theory of Rational Option Pricing", *Bell Journal of Economics and Management Science* 4, Spring, pp. 141–83.

Merton, R. 1976, "Option Pricing When Underlying Stock Returns are Discontinuous", *Journal of Financial Economics,* 3, Jan.–March, pp. 125–44.

Neftci, S. 1996, *An Introduction to the Mathematics of Financial Derivatives*, Academic Press, San Francisco.

Nielsen, L.T. 1999, *Pricing and Hedging of Derivative Securities*, OUP, Oxford.

Rendleman, R. and Barter, B. 1979, "Two State Option Pricing", *Journal of Finance,* 34, pp. 1092–110.

Rubinstein, M. 1985, "Nonparametric Tests of Alternative Option Pricing Models", *Journal of Financial Economics,* 40, pp. 455–80.

Scott, L. 1987, "Option Pricing When the Variance Changes Randomly", *Journal of Financial and Quantitative Analysis,* 22, pp. 419–38.

Stein, E. and Stein, J. 1991, "Stock Price Distributions with Stochastic Volatility: An Analytic Approach", *Review of Financial Studies,* 4, pp. 113–35.

Whaley, R. 1981, "On the Valuation of American Call Options on Stocks with Known Dividends", *Journal of Financial Economics*, 9, pp. 207–11.

Windas, T. 1993, *An Introduction to Option-adjusted Spread Analysis*, Bloomberg Publishing, Princeton.

CHAPTER

14

Interest-rate Swaps and Overnight-index Swaps

Swaps are important tools for use in asset–liability management. They are off-balance sheet instruments involving combinations of two or more basic building blocks. Most swaps currently traded in the market involve combinations of cash-market securities; for example, a fixed interest-rate security combined with a floating interest-rate security, possibly also combined with a currency transaction. However, the market has also seen swaps that involve a futures or forward component, as well as swaps that involve an option component. The market in, say, dollar, euro and sterling interest-rate swaps is very large and very liquid. The main types of swap are interest-rate swaps, asset swaps, basis swaps, fixed-rate currency swaps and currency-coupon swaps. The market for swaps is organised by the International Swaps and Derivatives Association (ISDA).

Swaps are now one of the most important and useful instruments in the money markets. They are used by a wide range of institutions, including banks, mortgage banks and building societies, corporates and local authorities. As the market has matured, the instrument has gained wider acceptance, and is regarded as a "plain vanilla" product in the debt capital markets. Virtually all commercial and investment banks will quote swap prices for their customers, and as they are OTC instruments, dealt over the telephone, it is possible for banks to tailor swaps to match the precise requirements of individual customers. There is also a close relationship between the money market and the swap market, and the interplay between both markets is keenly observed by ALM practitioners. Their use as hedging tools is the focus of this chapter.

Basic characteristics of swaps

In this section we review vanilla interest-rate swaps as well as swaps that have one leg linked to the overnight interest rate, either the pay or receive leg, known as overnight-index swaps or OIS. These have maturities of up to two years and are often traded by money market desks for hedging and speculative purposes. Longer-dated conventional interest-rate swaps are a vital part of the debt capital markets, and not part of the money markets, but we present an introduction to interest-rate swaps here for background purposes.

Interest-rate swaps

Swaps are derivative instruments involving combinations of two or more interest-rate bases or other building blocks. They are used to transform the interest-rate basis of a particular cash flow, and as such, important instruments for use in interest-rate risk hedging.

EXAMPLE 14.1 Comparative advantage and interest-rate swap structure

When entering into a swap, either for hedging purposes or to alter the basis of an interest-rate liability, the opposite to the current cash flow profile is required. Consider a homeowner with a variable rate mortgage. The homeowner is at risk from an upward move in interest rates, which will result in her being charged higher interest payments. She wishes to protect against such a move and as she is *paying floating*, must *receive floating* in a swap. Therefore she will pay fixed in the swap. The floating interest payments cancel each other out, and the homeowner now has a fixed rate liability. The same applies in a hedging transaction: a bondholder *receiving fixed* coupons from the bond issuer (that is, the bondholder is a *lender* of funds) can hedge against a rise in interest rates that lowers the price of the bond by *paying fixed* in a swap with the same basis point value as the bond position; the bondholder receives floating interest. *Paying fixed* in a swap is conceptually the same as being a *borrower of funds*; this borrowing is the opposite of the loan of funds to the bond issuer and therefore the position is hedged.

Consider two companies borrowing costs for a five-year loan of £50 million.

- **Company A**: can pay fixed at 8.75% or floating at Libor. Its desired basis is floating.
- **Company B**: can pay fixed at 10% or floating at Libor + 100 basis points. Its desired basis is fixed.

Without a swap:

- Company A borrows fixed and pays 8.75%.
- Company B borrows floating and pays Libor + 100 basis points.

Let us say that the two companies decide to enter into a swap, whereby company A borrows floating-rate interest and therefore receives fixed from company B at the five-year swap rate of 8.90%. Company B, who has borrowed at Libor + 100 basis points, pays fixed and receives Libor in the swap. Company A ends up paying floating-rate interest, and company B ends up paying fixed. This is shown in Figure 14.1.

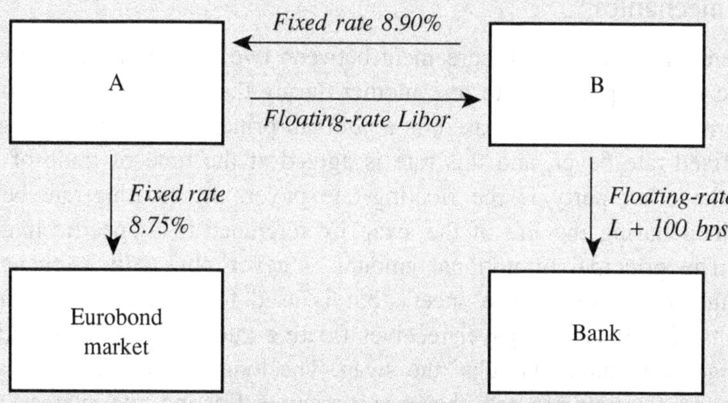

Figure 14.1 Interest-rate swap

Results after the swap:

A pays 8.75% + Libor – 8.90% = Libor – 15 bps
B pays Libor + 100 bps + 8.90% – Libor = 9.90%.

Company A saves 15 basis points (pays L – 15 basis points rather than L flat) and B saves 10 basis points (pays 9.90% rather than 10%).

Both parties benefit from a *comparative advantage* of A in the fixed-rate market and B in the floating-rate market (spread of B over A is 125 basis points in the fixed-rate market, but 100 basis points in the floating-rate market). Initially, swap banks were simply brokers, and charged a fee to both counterparties for bringing them together. In the example, company A deals direct with company B, although it is more likely that an intermediary bank would have been involved. As the market developed, banks would become principals and deal direct with counterparties, eliminating the need to find someone who had requirements that could be met by the other side of an existing requirement.

Swap mechanics

An interest rate swap is an agreement between two counterparties to make periodic interest payments to one another during the life of the swap, on a predetermined set of dates, based on a *notional* principal amount. One party is the fixed-rate payer, and this rate is agreed at the time of trade of the swap; the other party is the floating-rate payer, the floating-rate being determined during the life of the swap by reference to a specific market index. The principal or notional amount is never physically exchanged, hence the term "off-balance sheet", but is used to calculate the interest payments. The fixed-rate payer receives floating-rate interest and is said to be "long" or to have "bought" the swap. The long side has conceptually purchased a floating-rate note (because it receives floating-rate interest) and issued a fixed coupon bond (because it pays out fixed interest at intervals); that is, it has in principle borrowed funds. The floating-rate payer is said to be "short" or to have "sold" the swap. The short side has conceptually purchased a coupon bond (because it receives fixed-rate interest) and issued a floating-rate note (because it pays floating-rate interest).

So an interest rate swap is:

- an agreement between two parties, to exchange a stream of cash flows;
- calculated as a percentage of a *notional* sum;
- calculated on different interest bases.

For example, in a trade between Bank A and Bank B, Bank A may agree to pay fixed semi-annual coupons of 10% on a notional principal sum of £1 million, in return for receiving from Bank B the prevailing six-month sterling Libor rate on the same amount. The known cash flow is the fixed payment of £50,000 every six months by Bank A to Bank B.

The value of a swap moves in line with market interest rates, in exactly the same fashion as bonds. If a five-year interest-rate swap is transacted today at a rate of 5%, and five-year interest rates fall to 4.75% shortly thereafter, the swap will have decreased in value to the fixed-rate payer, and correspondingly increased in value to the floating-rate payer, who has now seen the level of interest payments fall. The opposite would be true if five-year rates moved to 5.25%. Why is this? Consider the fixed-rate payer in an interest-rate (IR) swap to be a borrower of funds; if he or she fixes the interest rate payable on a loan for five years, and then this interest rate decreases shortly afterwards, is that person better off? No, because he or she is now paying above the market rate for the funds borrowed. For this reason a swap contract decreases in value to the fixed-rate payer if there is a fall in rates. Equally, a floating-rate payer gains if there is a fall in rates, as that person can take advantage of the new rates and pay a lower level of interest; hence the value of a swap increases to the floating-rate payer if there is a fall in rates.

The profit/loss profile of a swap position is shown in Table 14.1.

	Fall in rates	**Rise in rates**
Fixed-rate payer	Loss	Profit
Floating-rate payer	Profit	Loss

Table 14.1 Swap p&l profile

A bank swaps desk will have an overall net interest-rate position arising from all the swaps it has traded that are currently on the book. This position is an interest rate exposure at all points along the term structure, out to the maturity of the longest-dated swap. At the close of business each day all the swaps on the book will be *marked-to-market* at the interest-rate quote for that day, and the resulting p/l for the book will be in line with the profile shown in Table 14.1.

A swap can be viewed in two ways: either as a bundle of forward or futures contracts, or as a bundle of cash flows arising from the "sale" and "purchase" of cash market instruments. If we imagine a strip of futures contracts, maturing every three or six months out to three years, we can see how this is conceptually similar to a three-year interest-rate swap. However, in the author's view it is better to visualise a swap as being a bundle of cash flows arising from cash instruments.

Let us imagine we have only two positions on our book:

- a long position in £100 million of a three-year FRN that pays six-month Libor semi-annually, and is trading at par;
- a short position in £100 million of a three-year gilt with coupon of 6% that is also trading at par.

Being short a bond is the equivalent to being a borrower of funds. Assuming this position is kept to maturity, the resulting cash flows are shown in Table 14.2.

Cash flows resulting from long position in FRN and short position in gilt

Period (6-mo)	FRN	Gilt	Net cash flow
0	–£100m	+£100m	£0
1	+(Libor × 100)/2	–3	+(Libor × 100)/2 – 3.0
2	+(Libor × 100)/2	–3	+(Libor × 100)/2 – 3.0
3	+(Libor × 100)/2	–3	+(Libor × 100)/2 – 3.0
4	+(Libor × 100)/2	–3	+(Libor × 100)/2 – 3.0
5	+(Libor × 100)/2	–3	+(Libor × 100)/2 – 3.0
6	+[(Libor × 100)/2] + 100	–103	+(Libor × 100)/2 – 3.0

The Libor rate is the six-month rate prevailing at the time of the setting; for instance, the Libor rate in period 4 will be the rate actually prevailing in period 4.

Table 14.2 Three-year fixed and floating cash flows

There is no net outflow or inflow at the start of these trades, as the £100 million purchase of the FRN is netted with receipt of £100 million from the sale of the gilt. The resulting cash flows over the three-year period are shown in the last column of Table 14.2. This net position is exactly the same as that of a fixed-rate payer in an IR swap. As we had at the start of the trade, there is no cash inflow or outflow on maturity. For a floating-rate payer, the cash flow would mirror exactly a long position in a fixed-rate bond and a short position in an FRN. Therefore the fixed-rate payer in a swap is said to be short in the bond market, or a borrower of funds; the floating-rate payer in a swap is said to be long the bond market.

Market terminology

Virtually all swaps are traded under the legal terms and conditions stipulated in the ISDA standard documentation.

The trade date for a swap is not surprisingly the date on which the swap is transacted. The terms of the trade include the fixed interest rate, the maturity and notional amount of the swap, and the payment bases of both legs of the swap. The date from which floating interest payments are determined is the *setting date*, which may also be the trade date. Most swaps fix the floating-rate payments to Libor, although other reference rates that are used include the US prime rate, Euribor, the T-bill rate and the CP rate. In the same way as for FRA and eurocurrency deposits, the rate is fixed two business days before the interest period begins. The second (and subsequent) setting date will be two business days before the beginning of the second (and subsequent) swap periods. The *effective date* is the date from which interest on the swap is calculated, and this is typically two business days after the trade date. In a *forward*–start swap the effective date will be at some point in the future, specified in the swap terms. The floating interest rate for each period is fixed at the start of the period, so that the interest payment amount is known in advance by both parties (the fixed rate is known, of course, throughout the swap by both parties).

Although for the purposes of explaining swap structures, both parties are said to pay interest payments (and receive them), in practice only the net difference between both payments changes hands at the end of each interest payment. This eases the administration associated with swaps and reduces the number of cash flows for each swap. The counterparty that is the net payer at the end of each period will make a payment to the counterparty. The first payment date will occur at the end of the first interest period, and subsequent payment dates will fall at the end of successive interest periods.

The final payment date falls on the maturity date of the swap. The calculation of interest is given by (14.1):

$$I = m \times r \times \frac{n}{B} \qquad (14.1)$$

where I is the interest amount, m is the nominal amount of the swap and B is the day-base for the swap. Dollar and euro-denominated swaps use an actual/360 day-count, similar to other money market instruments in those currencies, while sterling swaps use an actual/365 day-count basis.

The cash flows resulting from a vanilla IR swap are illustrated in Figure 14.2, using the normal convention where cash inflows are shown as an arrow pointing up, while cash outflows are shown as an arrow pointing down. The counterparties in a swap transaction only pay across net cash flows, however, so at each interest payment date only one actual cash transfer will be made, by the net payer. This is shown as Figure 14.2 (iii).

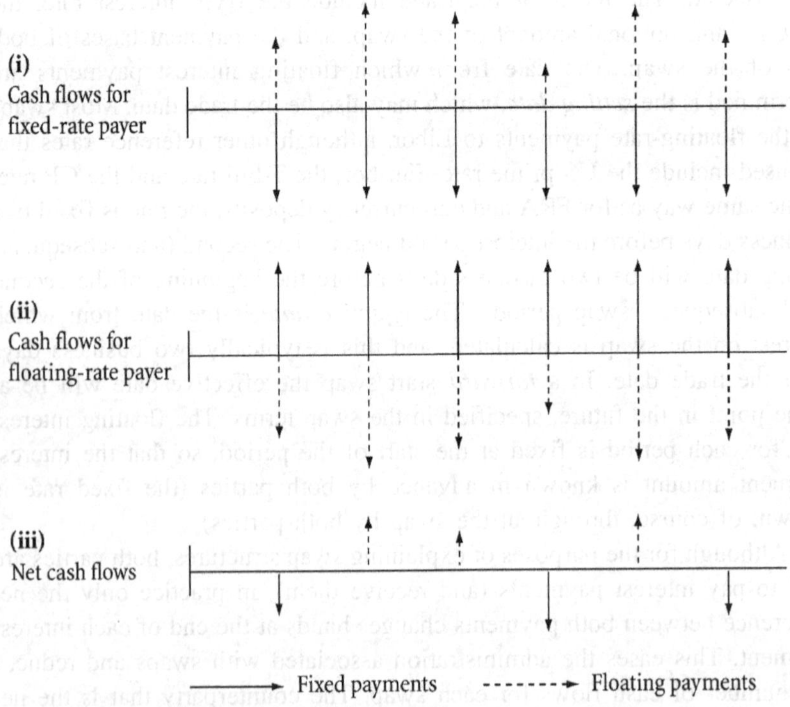

Figure 14.2 Cash flows for typical interest rate swap

Example of a vanilla interest-rate swap

The following swap cash flows are for a "pay fixed, receive floating" interest-rate swap with the following terms:

Trade date:	3 December 1999
Effective date:	7 December 1999
Maturity date:	7 December 2004
Interpolation method:	Linear interpolation
Day-count (fixed):	Semi-annual, act/365
Day-count (floating):	Semi-annual, act/365
Nominal amount:	£10 million
Term:	Five years
Fixed rate:	6.73%.

To calculate the cash flows, we construct a zero-coupon curve and value the swap with this curve (zero-coupon pricing is discussed later in this chapter). Using a conventional swap calculator, we obtain the following cash flows for the pay and receive legs of the swap, shown in Table 14.3 on page 634. The summary details for the swap, valued as at 20 January 2000, are shown in Table 14.4 on page 635.

The interest payment dates of the swap fall on 7 June and 7 December; the coupon dates of benchmark gilts also fall on these dates, so even though the swap has been traded for conventional dates, it is safe to surmise that it was put on as a hedge against a long gilt position. The fixed-rate payments are not always the same, because the actual/ 365 basis will calculate slightly different amounts. The net payments for the fixed-rate payer are also shown. Note also that the present value of each cash flow is also shown; the net difference of the cash, present valued, is the current value of the swap. This is shown in Table 14.4. The present values are calculated using a spot rate yield curve, which has been calculated using money market and government bond yields. The integrated discount function that is used to value the swap is not shown.

Cash flow table

Pay leg

Start date	End date	Interest period (days)	Interest rate	Nominal	Interest (£)	Discount factor	Interest present value (£)
07-Dec-99	07-Jun-00	183	6.73%	10,000,000	337,421.92	0.970787	327,564.98
07-Jun-00	07-Dec-00	183	6.73%	10,000,000	337,421.92	0.934890	315,452.27
07-Dec-00	07-Jun-01	182	6.73%	10,000,000	335,578.08	0.903668	303,251.27
07-Jun-01	07-Dec-01	183	6.73%	10,000,000	337,421.92	0.873975	294,898.27
07-Dec-01	07-Jun-02	182	6.73%	10,000,000	335,578.08	0.843748	283,143.40
07-Jun-02	09-Dec-02	185	6.73%	10,000,000	341,109.59	0.814353	277,783.70
09-Dec-02	09-Jun-03	182	6.73%	10,000,000	335,578.08	0.787777	264,360.77
09-Jun-03	08-Dec-03	182	6.73%	10,000,000	335,578.08	0.762992	256,043.24
08-Dec-03	07-Jun-04	182	6.73%	10,000,000	335,578.08	0.739486	248,155.28
07-Jun-04	07-Dec-04	183	6.73%	10,000,000	337,421.92	0.717683	242,161.99
Receive leg							
07-Dec-99	07-Jun-00	183	5.87%	10,000,000	294,554.79	0.970787	285,950.11
07-Jun-00	07-Dec-00	183	7.66%	10,000,000	383,979.03	0.934890	358,978.04
07-Dec-00	07-Jun-01	182	6.93%	10,000,000	345,496.21	0.903668	312,213.97
07-Jun-01	07-Dec-01	183	6.78%	10,000,000	339,751.52	0.873975	296,934.29
07-Dec-01	07-Jun-02	182	7.18%	10,000,000	358,242.71	0.843748	302,266.64
07-Jun-02	09-Dec-02	185	7.12%	10,000,000	360,960.68	0.814353	293,949.50
09-Dec-02	09-Jun-03	182	6.77%	10,000,000	337,354.53	0.787777	265,760.22
09-Jun-03	08-Dec-03	182	6.51%	10,000,000	324,848.55	0.762992	247,856.70
08-Dec-03	07-Jun-04	182	6.37%	10,000,000	317,864.09	0.739486	235,056.03
07-Jun-04	07-Dec-04	183	6.06%	10,000,000	303,795.95	0.717683	218,029.20
					Net payments:		42,867.13
							46,557.11
							−9,918.13
							−2,329.60
							−22,664.63
							−19,851.09
							−1,776.45
							10,729.53
							17,713.99
							33,625.97

Table 14.3 Interest-rate swap cash flows

Trade date:	03-Dec-99
Effective date:	07-Dec-99
Maturity date:	07-Dec-04
Margin:	0.00%
Fixed rate:	6.73%
Nominal:	£10 million
Present value (£):	4179.52
Duration:	2.6259
Modified duration:	2.5395
Convexity:	9.5991

Table 14.4 Summary of swap terms

If the five-year swap rate changes, the present value of the swap will change. The swap has a fixed rate of 6.73%, therefore a fall in market interest rates will result in the swap being marked-to-market at a loss to the fixed-rate payer, and a profit to the floating-rate payer. The opposite applies if there is a rise in market rates. Table 14.5 shows the valuation of the swap where the five-year interest rate has risen to 7.00%. The present value of the swap has risen to £144,103, which is a mark-to-market profit.

Trade date:	03-Dec-99
Effective date:	07-Dec-99
Maturity date:	07-Dec-04
Margin:	0.00%
Market rate:	7.00%
Fixed rate:	6.73%
Nominal:	£10 million
Present value (£):	144,103.67
Duration:	2.4917
Modified duration:	2.4081
Convexity:	9.5089

Table 14.5 Revaluation of interest-rate swap

The swap we have described is a plain vanilla swap, which means it has one fixed-rate and one floating-rate leg. The floating interest rate is set just before the relevant interest period and is paid at the end of the period. Note that both legs have identical interest dates and day-count bases, and the term to maturity of the swap is exactly five years. It is of course possible to ask for a swap quote where any of these terms has been set to customer requirements; so, for example, both legs may be floating-rate, or the notional principal may vary during the life of the swap. Non-vanilla interest-rate swaps are very common, and banks will readily price swaps where the terms have been set to meet specific requirements. The most common variations are different interest payment dates for the fixed- and floating-rate legs, on different day-count bases, as well as terms to maturity that are not whole years.

Swap spreads and the swap yield curve

In the market, banks will quote two-way swap rates: on screens and on the telephone or via a dealing system such as Reuters. Brokers will also be active in relaying prices in the market. The convention in the market is for the swap market-maker to set the floating leg at Libor and then quote the fixed rate that is payable for that maturity. So for a five-year swap a bank's swap desk might be willing to quote the following:

Floating-rate payer:	pay 6-mo Libor
	receive fixed rate of 5.19%
Fixed-rate payer:	pay fixed rate of 5.25%
	receive 6-mo Libor.

In this case the bank is quoting an offer rate of 5.25%, which the fixed-rate payer will pay, in return for receiving Libor flat. The bid price quote is 5.19%, which is what a floating-rate payer will receive fixed. The bid–offer spread in this case is therefore 6 basis points, which is actually quite wide for a GBP, USD or EUR swap. The fixed-rate quotes are always at a spread above the government bond yield curve. Let us assume that the five-year gilt is yielding 4.88%; in this case then the five-year swap bid rate is 31 basis points above this yield. So the bank's swap trader could quote the swap rates as a spread above the benchmark bond yield curve, say 37–31, which is his or her swap spread quote. This means that the bank is happy to enter into a swap, paying fixed 31 basis points above the benchmark yield and receiving Libor, and receiving fixed 37 basis points above the yield curve and paying Libor. The bank's screen on, say, Bloomberg or Reuters might look something like Table 14.6, which quotes the swap rates as well as the current spread over the government bond benchmark.

1-yr	4.50	4.45	+17
2-yr	4.69	4.62	+25
3-yr	4.88	4.80	+23
4-yr	5.15	5.05	+29
5-yr	5.25	5.19	+31
10-yr	5.50	5.40	+35

Table 14.6 Swap quotes

An actual interest-rate swap screen is shown in Figure 14.3, which is the US dollar swaps page from Garban ICAP (a money market and bond broker) distributed via the Bloomberg on 10 November 2003.

GRAB Corp **ICAP**

11:33 **Intercapital** PAGE 1 / 2

USD Swap Rates vs 3 Month Libor vs. LIBOR	Ask	Bid	Time	USD Swap Spreads	Ask	Bid	Time
1) 1 Year	1.576	1.546	10:35	16) 1 Year			
2) 2 Year	2.367	2.338	10:35	17) 2 Year	37.2	34.2	8:02
3) 3 Year	3.000	2.971	10:35	18) 3 Year	55.8	52.8	10:12
4) 4 Year	3.480	3.451	10:43	19) 4 Year	55.0	52.0	8:02
5) 5 Year	3.850	3.821	10:43	20) 5 Year	44.2	41.2	8:02
6) 6 Year	4.137	4.108	10:43	21) 6 Year	52.8	49.8	8:02
7) 7 Year	4.372	4.343	10:43	22) 7 Year	56.0	53.0	8:02
8) 8 Year	4.565	4.536	10:43	23) 8 Year	54.8	51.8	8:02
9) 9 Year	4.725	4.696	10:43	24) 9 Year	50.8	47.8	8:06
10) 10 Year	4.862	4.833	10:43	25) 10 Year	44.0	41.0	8:02
11) 12 Year	5.072	5.043	10:43	26) 12 Year	65.8	62.8	8:02
12) 15 Year	5.305	5.276	10:43	27) 15 Year	68.2	65.2	8:02
13) 20 Year	5.500	5.471	10:43	28) 20 Year	67.2	64.2	8:02
14) 25 Year	5.552	5.523	10:43	29) 25 Year	52.2	49.2	8:02
15) 30 Year	5.558	5.529	10:44	30) 30 Year	32.8	29.8	8:02

Page Forward for USD IRS vs 1Mth LIBOR

Day Count: ANN ACT/360
EDU2↑ 93.125 --
TYU2 0-00 --
USU2 0-00 --

Australia 61 2 9777 8600 Brazil 5511 3048 4500 Europe 44 20 7330 7500 Germany 49 69 920410
Hong Kong 852 2977 6000 Japan 81 3 3201 8900 Singapore 65 6212 1000 U.S. 1 212 318 2000 Copyright 2003 Bloomberg L.P.
G657-802-0 10-Nov-03 11:33:35

Figure 14.3 Garban ICAP brokers US dollar swaps page, 10 November 2003

The page shows the swap bid and offer rates for swaps of maturities from one year to 30 years. The bid–offer quotes are on the left-hand side, the swap spread over the yield of the benchmark government bond is shown on the right-hand side.

We can summarise by saying that swap spreads over government bonds reflect the supply and demand conditions of both swaps and government bonds, as well as the market's view on the credit quality of swap counterparties. This subject was discussed in Chapter 10. There is considerable information content in the swap yield curve, much like that in the government-bond yield curve. During times of credit concerns in the market, such as the corrections in the Asian and Latin American markets in summer 1998, and the possibility of default by the Russian government regarding its long-dated US-dollar bonds, the swap spread will increase, more so at higher maturities. To illustrate this, let us consider the sterling swap spread in 1998/99. The UK swap spread widened from the second half of 1998 onwards, a reaction to bond market volatility around the world. At such times, investors embark on a "flight to quality" that results in yield spreads widening. In the swap market, the spread between two-year and 10-year swaps also increased, reflecting market concern with credit and counterparty risk. The spreads narrowed in the first quarter 1999, as credit concerns brought about by market corrections in 1998 declined. The change in swap spreads is shown in Figure 14.4.

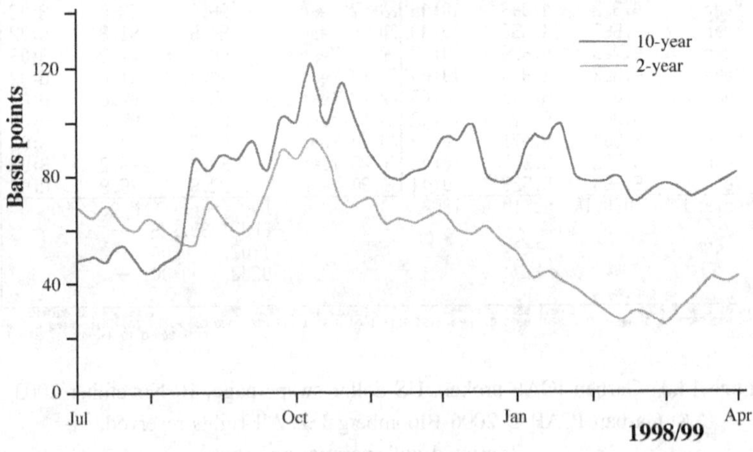

Figure 14.4 Sterling two-year and 10-year swap spreads during 1998/99

The relationship between interest-rate swaps and FRAs

A strip of FRAs is conceptually similar to an interest-rate swap. This is because one FRA fixes the interest rate for a period starting in the future, so that a strip of continuous FRAs will fix the interest rate for a continuous period. The rates implied by the FRA strip will equate to that payable on a swap, to avoid arbitrage opportunities arising. To consider this, a borrowing arranged on a rolling three-month basis at Libor, while simultaneously transacting a swap to receive quarterly three-month Libor against a fixed payment, is the same as borrowing on the three-month basis and fixing the interest cost with a series of rolling FRAs, starting with a 3v6 FRA, then followed by a 6v9 FRA and so on. If the swap and FRA rates were out of line, then it would be possible to put on opposing positions in both and pocket the difference as an arbitrage profit. For example, if the two-year swap rate is too low, it would be possible to trade the swap to pay fixed and receive floating, simultaneously selling a strip of FRAs to offset this.

EXAMPLE 14.2 Calculating the one-year swap rate

Assume the following sterling FRA rates:

Three-month cash:	7.625%
3v6 FRA:	6.875%
6v9 FRA:	6.125%
9v12 FRA:	5.75%.

If we assume the cash period is 92 days and the FRA periods are 91 days, with FRA settlement made at the end of the period rather than at the beginning, we may use the cash and FRA rates to calculate the one-year swap rate, which is given as:

$$(1 + 0.07625 \times 92/365) \times (1 + 0.06875 \times 91/365)$$
$$\times (1 + 0.0615 \times 91/365) \times (1 + 0.0575 \times 91/365)$$
$$= 6.761\%.$$

This means that the fixed cost of a borrowing of cash over the one-year period is 6.6761%, which is the theoretical price of a one-year swap transacted today. As the swap would pay on a quarterly basis we convert the rate to a quarterly equivalent, which is:

$$\left((1 + 0.0761)^{1/4} - 1\right) = 6.596\%.$$

In practice a slightly different procedure is used, which we discuss in the section on pricing.

In this example we used FRAs with final maturity periods extending to one year from now. The existence of a forward rate, which is what FRA rates are, enables us to calculate a swap rate. The result is known as a *zero-coupon swap rate*, which is examined next. As FRA rates, which are calculated from interest-rate futures prices, are only available out to two or three years, we use bond yields to calculate longer-dated swaps. The convention is to calculate zero-coupon bond yields and use these to price swaps. Swap rates that have been calculated in this way are known as *par swap rates* and are the fixed-rates payable on a swap for which the floating-rate is Libor.

Generic swap valuation

Banks generally use par-swap (zero-coupon) swap pricing. We will look at this method in the next section. First, however, we will introduce an intuitive swap valuation method.

Intuitive swap pricing

Assume we have a vanilla interest-rate swap with a notional principal of N that pays n payments during its life, to a maturity date of T. The date of each payment is on t_i with $i = 1, \ldots n$. The present value today of a future payment is denoted by $PV(0, t)$. If the swap rate is r, the value of the fixed-leg payments is given by (14.2) below.

$$PV_{fixed} = N\sum_{i=1}^{n} PV(0,t_i) \times \left[r \times \left(\frac{t_i - t_{i-1}}{B}\right)\right] \tag{14.2}$$

where B is the money market day base. The term Σ is simply the number of days between the ith and the i–1th payments.

The value of the floating-leg payments at the date t_1 for an existing swap is given by:

$$PV_{float} = N \times \left[rl \times \frac{t_1}{B}\right] + N - [N \times PV(t_1,t_n)] \tag{14.3}$$

where rl is the Libor rate that has been set for the next interest payment. We set the present value of the floating-rate payment at time 0 as follows:

$$PV(0,t_1) = \frac{1}{1 + rl(t_1)(\frac{t_1}{B})} . \quad (14.4)$$

For a new swap, the value of the floating payments is given by:

$$PV_{float} = N\left[rl \times \frac{t_1}{B} + 1\right] \times PV(0,t_1) - PV(0,t_n). \quad (14.5)$$

The swap valuation is then given by $PV_{fixed} - PV_{float}$. The swap rate quoted by a market-making bank is that which sets $PV_{fixed} = PV_{float}$ and is known as the par or zero-coupon swap rate. We consider this next.

Zero-coupon swap pricing

So far, we have discussed how vanilla swap prices are often quoted as a spread over the benchmark government-bond yield in that currency, and how this swap spread is mainly a function of the credit spread required by the market over the government (risk-free) rate. This method is convenient and also logical because banks use government bonds as the main instrument when hedging their swap books. However, because much bank swap trading is now conducted in non-standard, tailor-made swaps, this method can sometimes be unwieldy, as each swap needs to have its spread calculated to suit its particular characteristics. Therefore, banks use a standard pricing method for all swaps known as zero-coupon swap pricing.

In Chapter 9, we referred to zero-coupon bonds and zero-coupon interest rates. Zero-coupon or spot rates, are true interest rates for their particular term to maturity. In zero-coupon swap pricing, a bank will view all swaps, even the most complex, as a series of cash flows. The zero-coupon rates that apply now for each of the cash flows in a swap can be used to value these cash flows. Therefore, to value and price a swap, each of the swap's cash flows are present-valued using known spot rates; the sum of these present values is the value of the swap.

In a swap, the fixed-rate payments are known in advance and so it is straightforward to present-value them. The present value of the floating-rate payments is usually estimated in two stages. First, the implied forward rates can be calculated using (14.6). We are quite familiar with this relationship from our reading of Chapter 9.

$$rf_i = \left(\frac{df_i}{df_{i+1}} - 1\right)N \quad (14.6)$$

where

rf_i is the one-period forward rate starting at time i
df_i is the discount factor for the maturity period i
df_{i+1} is the discount factor for the period $i + 1$
N is the number of times per year that coupons are paid.

By definition, the floating-payment interest rates are not known in advance, so the swap bank will predict what these will be, using the forward rates applicable to each payment date. The forward rates are those that are currently implied from spot rates. Once the size of the floating-rate payments have been estimated, these can also be valued by using the spot rates. The total value of the fixed and floating legs is the sum of all the present values, so the value of the total swap is the net of the present values of the fixed and floating legs.

While the term "zero-coupon" refers to an interest rate that applies to a discount instrument that pays no coupon and has one cash flow (at maturity), it is not necessary to have a functioning zero-coupon bond market in order to construct a zero-coupon yield curve. In practice, most financial pricing models use a combination of the following instruments to construct zero-coupon yield curves:

- money market deposits;
- interest-rate futures;
- FRAs;
- government bonds.

For best results, an overlap in the maturity period of all instruments must be used. FRA rates are usually calculated from interest-rate futures so it is only necessary to use one of either FRA or futures rates.

Once a zero-coupon yield curve (term structure) is derived, this may be used to value a future cash flow maturing at any time along the term structure. This includes swaps: to price an interest-rate swap, we calculate the present value of each of the cash flows using the zero-coupon rates and then sum all the cash flows. As we noted above, while the fixed-rate payments are known in advance, the floating-rate payments must be estimated, using the forward rates implied by the zero-coupon yield curve. The net present value of the swap is the net difference between the present values of the fixed- and floating-rate legs.

Calculating the forward rate from spot-rate discount factors

Remember that one way to view a swap is as a long position in a fixed-coupon bond that was funded at Libor, or against a short position in a floating-rate bond. The cash flows from such an arrangement would be paying floating-rate and receiving fixed-rate. In the former arrangement, where a long position in a fixed-rate bond is funded with a floating-rate loan, the cash flows from the principals will cancel out, as they are equal and opposite (assuming the price of the bond on purchase was par), leaving a collection of cash flows that mirror an interest-rate swap that pays floating and receives fixed. Therefore, as the fixed-rate on an interest-rate swap is the same as the coupon (and yield) on a bond priced at par, calculating the fixed-rate on an interest-rate swap is the same as calculating the coupon for a bond that we wish to issue at par.

The price of a bond paying semi-annual coupons is given by (14.7), which may be rearranged for the coupon rate r to provide an equation that enables us to determine the par yield, and hence the swap rate r, given by (14.8).

$$\mathrm{P} = \frac{r_n}{2}df_1 + \frac{r_n}{2}df_2 + \ldots + \frac{r_n}{2}df_n + Mdf_n \tag{14.7}$$

where r_n is the coupon on an n-period bond with n coupons and M is the maturity payment. It can be shown that:

$$\begin{aligned} r_n &= \frac{1 - df_n}{\frac{df_1}{2} + \frac{df_2}{2} + \ldots + \frac{df_n}{2}} \\ &= \frac{1 - df_n}{\sum_{i=1}^{n} \frac{df_i}{2}}. \end{aligned} \tag{14.8}$$

For annual coupon bonds there is no denominator for the discount factor, while for bonds paying coupons on a frequency of N we replace the denominator 2 with N.[1] The expression in (14.8) may be rearranged again, using F for the coupon frequency, to obtain an equation that may be used to calculate the nth discount factor for an n-period swap rate, given in (14.9).

[1] The expression also assumes an actual/365 day-count basis. If any other day-count convention is used, the $1/N$ factor must be replaced by a fraction made up of the actual number of days as the numerator and the appropriate year base as the denominator.

$$df_n = \frac{1 - r_n \sum_{i=1}^{n-1} \frac{df_i}{N}}{1 + \frac{r_n}{N}} \tag{14.9}$$

The expression in (14.9) is the general expression for the *bootstrapping* process that we first encountered in Chapter 9. Essentially, to calculate the n-year discount factor we use the discount factors for the years 1 to n-1, and the n-year swap rate or zero-coupon rate. If we have the discount factor for any period, we may use (14.9) to determine the same period zero-coupon rate, after rearranging it, shown at (14.10):

$$rs_n = \sqrt[t_n]{\frac{1}{df_n}} - 1 \ . \tag{14.10}$$

Discount factors for spot rates may also be used to calculate forward rates. We know that:

$$df_1 = \frac{1}{\left(1 + \frac{rs_1}{N}\right)} \tag{14.11}$$

where rs is the zero-coupon rate. If we know the forward rate we may use this to calculate a second discount rate, shown by (14.12):

$$df_2 = \frac{df_1}{\left(1 + \frac{rf_1}{N}\right)} \tag{14.12}$$

where rf_1 is the forward rate. This is of no use in itself; however, we may derive from it an expression to enable us to calculate the discount factor at any point in time between the previous discount rate and the given forward rate for the period n to $n + 1$, shown in (14.13), which may then be rearranged to give us the general expression to calculate a forward rate, given in (14.14):

$$df_{n+1} = \frac{df_n}{\left(1 + \frac{rf_n}{N}\right)} \tag{14.13}$$

$$rf_n = \left(\frac{df_n}{df_{n+1}} - 1\right)N. \tag{14.14}$$

The general expression for an n-period discount rate at time n from the previous period forward rates is given by (14.15).

$$df_n = \frac{1}{\left(1 + \frac{rf_{n-1}}{N}\right)} \times \frac{1}{\left(1 + \frac{rf_{n-2}}{N}\right)} \times \ldots \times \frac{1}{\left(1 + \frac{rf_n}{N}\right)}$$

$$df_n = \prod_{i=0}^{n-1}\left[\frac{1}{\left(1 + \frac{rf_i}{N}\right)}\right]. \qquad (14.15)$$

From the above, we may combine equations (14.8) and (14.14) to obtain the general expression for an n-period swap rate and zero-coupon rate, given by (14.16) and (14.17), respectively.

$$r_n = \frac{\sum_{i=1}^{n}\frac{rf_{i-1}df_i}{N}}{\sum_{i=1}^{n}\frac{df_i}{F}} \qquad (14.16)$$

$$1 + rs_n = \sqrt[t_n]{\prod_{i=0}^{n-1}\left(1 + \frac{rf_i}{N}\right)} \qquad (14.17)$$

The two expressions do not tell us anything new, as we have already encountered their results in Chapter 9. The swap rate, which we have denoted as r_n is shown by (14.16) to be the weighted average of the forward rates. If we consider that a strip of FRAs constitutes an interest-rate swap, then a swap rate for a continuous period could be covered by a strip of FRAs. Therefore, an average of the FRA rates would be the correct swap rate. As FRA rates are forward rates, we may be comfortable with (14.16), which states that the n-period swap rate is the average of the forward rates from rf_0 to $rf_{n.}$. To be accurate, we must weight the forward rates, and these are weighted by the discount factors for each period.

Note that although swap rates are derived from forward rates, interest payments under a swap are paid in the normal way at the end of an interest period, while payments for an FRA are made at the beginning of the period and must be discounted.

Equation (14.17) states that the zero-coupon rate is calculated from the geometric average of (one plus) the forward rates. The n-period forward rate is obtained using the discount factors for periods n and n–1. The discount factor for the complete period is obtained by multiplying the individual discount factors together, and exactly the same result would be obtained by using the zero-coupon interest-rate for the whole period to obtain the discount factor.

Illustrating interest-rate swap pricing

The rate charged on a newly transacted interest-rate swap is the one that gives its net present value as zero. The term "valuation" of a swap is used to denote the process of calculating the net present value of an existing swap, when marking-to-market the swap against current market interest rates. Therefore, when we *price* a swap, we set its net present value to zero; while, when we *value* a swap, we set its fixed rate at the market rate and calculate the net present value.

To illustrate the basic principle, we price a plain vanilla interest-rate swap with the terms set out below; for simplicity we assume that the annual fixed-rate payments are the same amount each year, although in practice there would be slight differences. Also, assume we already have our zero-coupon yields as shown in Table 14.7 on page 647.

We use the zero-coupon rates to calculate the discount factors, and then use the discount factors to calculate the forward rates. This is done using equation (14.14). These forward rates are then used to predict what the floating-rate payments will be at each interest period. Both fixed-rate and floating-rate payments are then present-valued at the appropriate zero-coupon rate, which enables us to calculate the net present value.

The fixed-rate for the swap is calculated using equation (14.8) to give us:

$$\frac{1 - 0.71298618}{4.16187950}$$

or 6.8963%.

The swap terms are:

Nominal principal:	£10 million
Fixed rate:	6.8963%
Day-count fixed:	Actual/365
Day-count floating:	Actual/365
Payment frequency fixed:	Annual
Payment frequency floating:	Annual
Trade date:	31 January 2000
Effective date:	2 February 2000
Maturity date:	2 February 2005
Term:	Five years.

Period	Zero-coupon rate %	Discount factor	Forward rate %	Fixed payment	Floating payment	PV fixed payment	PV floating payment
1	5.50	0.94	5.50	689,625	550,000.00	653,672.98	521,327.01
2	6.00	0.88	6.50	689,625	650,236.96	613,763.79	578,708.58
3	6.25	0.83	6.75	689,625	675,177.02	574,944.84	562,899.47
4	6.50	0.77	7.25	689,625	725,353.49	536,061.43	563,834.02
5	7.00	0.71	9.02	689,625	902,358.47	491,693.09	643,369.11
		4.16				2,870,137.00	2,870,137.00

Table 14.7 Generic interest-rate swap

CELL	C	D	E	F	G	H	I	J
21			10000000					
22								
23	**Period**	**Zero-coupon rate %**	**Discount factor**	**Forward rate %**	**Fixed payment**	**Floating payment**	**PV fixed payment**	**PV floating payment**
24	1	5.50	0.94	5.50	689,625	“(F24*10000000)/100	“G24/1.055	“H24/(1.055)
25	2	6.00	0.88	“((E24/E25)-1)*100	689,625	“(F25*10000000)/100	“G24/(1.06)^2	“H25/(1.06)^2
26	3	6.25	0.83	“((E25/E26)-1)*100	689,625	“(F26*10000000)/100	“G24/(1.0625)^3	“H26/(1.0625^3)
27	4	6.50	0.77	“((E26/E27)-1)*100	689,625	“(F27*10000000)/100	“G24/(1.065)^4	“H27/(1.065)^4
28	5	7.00	0.71	“((E27/E28)-1)*100	689,625	“(F28*10000000)/100	“G24/(1.07)^5	“H28/(1.07)^5
			“SUM(E24:E28)				2,870,137.00	2,870,137.00

Table 14.8 Generic interest-rate swap (Excel formulas)

This swap is shown in Table 14.7. For reference, the Microsoft Excel® formulas are shown in Table 14.8. It is not surprising that the NPV is zero, because the zero-coupon curve is used to derive the discount factors that are then used to derive the forward rates, which are used to value the swap. As with any financial instrument, the fair value is its breakeven price or hedge cost, and in this case the bank that is pricing the five-year swap shown in Table 14.7 could hedge the swap with a series of FRAs transacted at the forward rates shown. If the bank is paying fixed and receiving floating, the value of the swap will rise if there is a rise in market rates, and fall if there is a fall in market rates. Conversely, if the bank were receiving fixed and paying floating, the swap value would fall if there were a rise in rates, and vice versa.

This method is used to price any interest-rate swap, even an exotic one.

Valuation using final-maturity discount factor

A short-cut to valuing the floating-leg payments of an interest-rate swap involves using the discount factor for the final maturity period. This is possible because, for the purposes of valuation, an exchange of principal at the beginning and end of the swap is conceptually the same as the floating-leg interest payments. So this holds because, in an exchange of principal, the interest payments earned on investing the initial principal would be uncertain, as they are floating-rate, while on maturity the original principal would be returned. The net result is a floating-rate level of receipts, exactly similar to the floating-leg payments in a swap. To value the principals, then, we need only the final maturity discount rate.

To illustrate, consider Table 14.7, where the present value of both legs was found to be £2,870,137. The same result is obtained if we use the five-year discount factor, as shown below.

$$PV_{floating} = (10{,}000{,}000 \times 1) - (10{,}000{,}000 \times 0.71298618) = 2{,}870{,}137$$

The first term is the principal multiplied by the discount factor 1; this is because the present value of an amount valued immediately is unchanged (or rather, it is multiplied by the immediate payment discount factor, which is 1.0000).

Therefore, we may use the principal amount of a swap if we wish to value the swap. This is, of course, for valuation only, as there is no actual exchange of principal in a swap.

Period	Zero-coupon rate %	Discount factor	Forward rate %	Principal	Margin	Fixed payment	Floating payment	PV fixed payment	PV floating payment
1	5.50	0.94786730	5.500000	5,000,000	Libor + 25	323,728	287,500	306,851	272,512
2	6.00	0.88999644	6.502370	8,000,000	Libor + 25	517,965	540,192	460,987	480,769
3	6.25	0.83370649	6.751770	10,000,000	Libor + 25	647,456	700,180	539,788	583,745
		2.67157023						1,337,626	1,337,025
	Swap rate	0.062245606							
		6.2246	6.4746						

Table 14.9 Accreting interest-rate swap

This method is used to price any interest-rate swap, even exotic ones. To illustrate, consider the three-year accreting swap shown in Table 14.9, which pays fixed against floating plus 25 basis points. The fixed rate must be adjusted accordingly and is shown to be 6.475%, calculated under the same zero-coupon rate environment as the previous example.

To calculate the present value of the fixed-rate leg of an interest-rate swap we use (14.18), while the present value of the floating leg is given by (14.19):

$$PV_{fixed} = r_n \sum_{i=1}^{n} M_i \frac{d_i}{B} v_i \tag{14.18}$$

$$PV_{floating} = \sum_{i=1}^{n} rf_{i-1} M_i \frac{d_i}{B} v_i \tag{14.19}$$

where

r_n is the swap fixed rate
M_i is the notional principal from time i–1 to time i
rf_i is the forward rate applicable to the period i–1 to i
d_i is the number of days in the interest period (time i–1 to time i)
v_i is the discount factor at time i
B is the year day-count, either 360 or 365.

Summary of pricing principles

To recap, we have stated that the first step in swap pricing is to derive the spot rates up to the maturity required. These spot rates are then used to value all the cash flows in a swap; the floating-leg cash flows are estimated using the forward rates that have been derived from the spot rates. The fixed-rate for the swap may be obtained from the discount factors for all the spot rates from the current date to the final maturity period. The technique we have described is used for both pricing and valuing the swap. The market convention is to use the term *pricing* when trying to find the correct fixed rate for a new swap such that its NPV is zero. *Valuing* is the term used to describe the process of finding the NPV of an existing swap for which the fixed rate has already been set. A description of the process used to calculate implied swap rates from future prices is given in Appendix 14.1.

EXAMPLE 14.3 Mark-to-market valuation

The following receive fixed, pay floating interest-rate swap is marked-to-market on 26 February 1999.

Nominal amount:	$10 million
Effective date:	21 June 1998
Maturity:	21 June 2001
Fixed rate:	7.40%
Basis:	Annual, act/360
Floating-rate:	Libor
Basis:	Semi-annual, act/360
Previous fixing:	9.30%
	from 21 December 1998 to 21 June 1999

The discount factors as at the valuation date are:

21 June 1999:	0.970312
21 December 1999:	0.924923
21 June 2000:	0.882531
21 December 2000:	0.841539
21 June 2001:	0.801009.

The discount factors are used to calculate the forward rates, which are used to estimate the floating-rate payments. The forward rates are:

21 December 1999:	9.604%
21 June 2000:	9.556%
21 December 2000:	9.691%
21 June 2001:	10.001%.

The cash flows for the swap are therefore:

Date	Net cash flows	Present value
21 June 1999	+272 417	+264 326
21 December 1999	–490 866	–454 002
21 June 2000	+259 546	+229 049

21 December 2000	–487 227	–410 002
21 June 2001	+234 384	+187 742

The net present value of the swap, and hence its mark-to-market valuation, is –$182,887.

Non-vanilla interest-rate swaps

Swap instruments can be tailor-made to fit the requirements of individual customers. A wide variety of swap contracts have been traded in the market. Although the most common reference rate for the floating-leg of a swap is six-month Libor, for a semi-annual paying floating leg, other reference rates that have been used include three-month Libor, the prime rate (for dollar swaps), the one-month CP rate, the T-bill rate and the municipal bond rate (again, for dollar swaps). The term of a swap need not be fixed; swaps may be extendable or put-able. In an extendable swap, one of the parties has the right, but not the obligation to extend the life of the swap beyond the fixed maturity date, while in a put-able swap one party has the right to terminate the swap ahead of the specified maturity date. It is also possible to transact options on swaps, known as swaptions, which we consider later in this chapter.

Currency swaps

A *cross-currency* swap or *currency swap* is similar to an interest-rate swap, except that the currencies of the two legs are different. The legs are usually fixed- and floating-rate, although it is common to come across both fixed-rate or both floating-rate legs. On maturity of the swap there is an exchange of principals, and usually (but not always) there is an exchange of principals at the start of the swap. Where currencies are exchanged at the start of the swap, at the prevailing spot exchange rate for the two currencies, the exact same amounts are exchanged back on maturity. During the time of the swap, the parties make interest payments in the currency that they have *received* where principals are exchanged. It may seem that exchanging the same amount on maturity gives rise to some sort of currency risk, in fact it is this feature that removes any element of currency risk from the swap transaction.

Currency swaps are widely used in association with bond issues by borrowers who seek to tap opportunities in different markets but have no requirement for that market's currency. By means of a currency swap, a company can raise funds in a foreign currency market and swap the proceeds into the currency that it requires.

With regard to currency swap pricing, the principles we established for the pricing and valuation of interest-rate swaps may be applied to currency swaps. A generic currency swap with fixed-rate payment legs would be valued at the fair value swap rate for each currency, which would give a net present value of zero. So the swap rates for a fixed-fixed five-year sterling/dollar currency swap would be the five-year sterling swap rate and the five-year dollar swap rate. A floating-floating currency swap may be valued in the same way, and for valuation purposes the floating-leg payments are replaced with an exchange of principals, as we observed for the floating leg of an interest-rate swap. A fixed-floating currency swap is therefore valued at the fixed-rate swap rate for that currency for the fixed leg, and at Libor or the relevant reference rate for the floating leg.

Example 14.4 Currency swap hedge for bond issue

The client of a bank's convertible bond market-making desk would like exposure to a particular bond, but it is denominated in an illiquid currency (ILC) that the client cannot settle. The bank's solution is to purchase the bond, and then issue a bond to the client denominated in USD with a return linked to the ILC bond. This provides the client with the credit exposure to the bond's issuer that he or she desires, without any of the settlement issues associated with the ILC bond. The market-making desk is long the ILC bond and short the USD note that it has sold to the client. It asks the Treasury desk to hedge its currency exposures.

The Treasury desk enters into currency swap with a swap market-maker, exchanging USD for ILC, that matches the term of the ILC bond. During the life of the swap, Treasury pays ILC-Libor plus a spread, and receives USD Libor. This hedges the currency and interest-rate risk exposure. Note that the bank may also want to hedge the credit risk of the ILC bond it is holding via a credit default swap (CDS).

The transaction is illustrated in Figure 14.5 on page 654, which shows the hedge structure and the main terms of the currency swap (see box inside the figure). Note that ILCBOR refers to the local fixed market rate (in the illiquid currency or ILC).

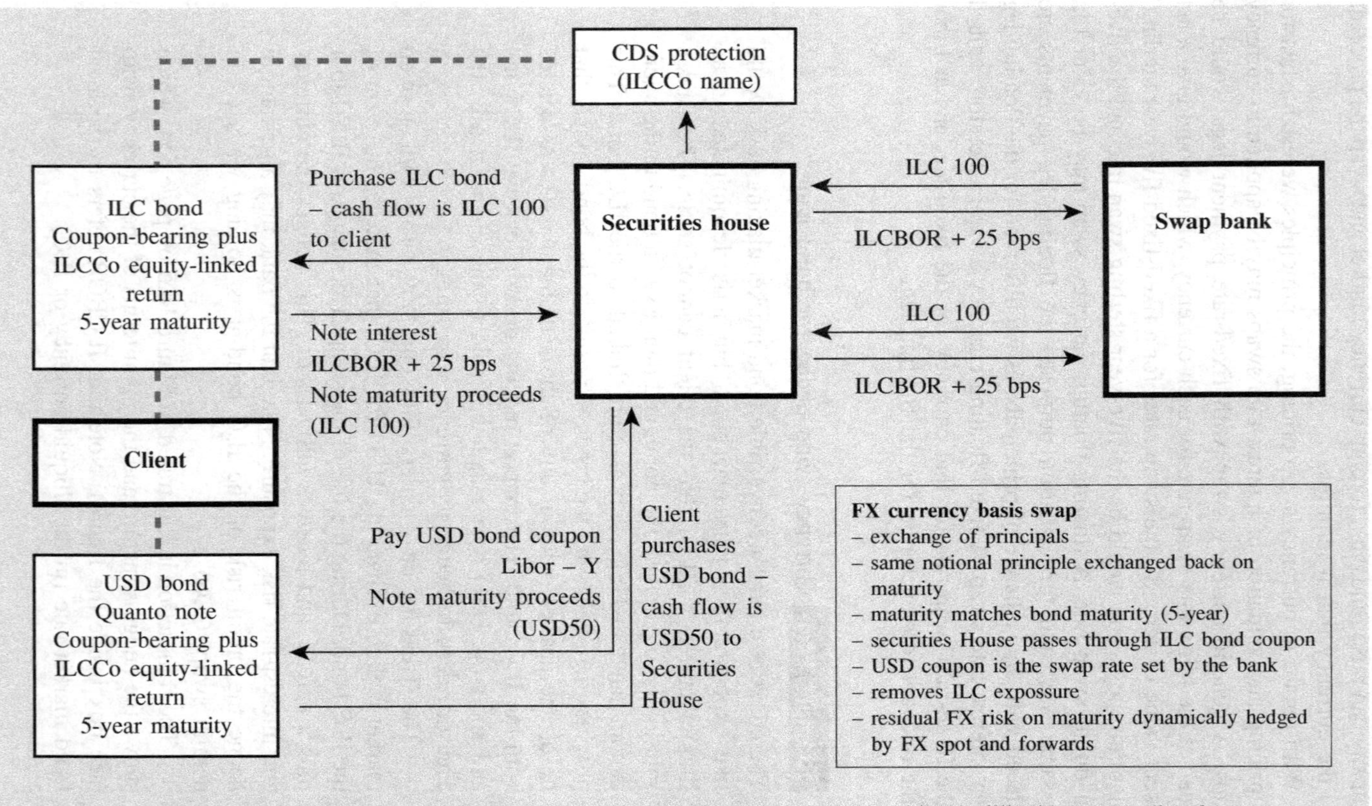

Figure 14.5 Illiquid currency/USD currency swap structure to hedge position in illiquid currency bond

Constant-maturity swap

A constant-maturity swap is a swap in which the parties exchange a Libor rate for a fixed swap rate. For example, the terms of the swap might state that six-month Libor is exchanged for the five-year swap rate on a semi-annual basis for the next five years, or for the five-year government bond rate. In the US market, the second type of constant-maturity swap is known as a constant-maturity Treasury swap.

Accreting or amortising swap

In a plain vanilla swap the notional principal remains unchanged during the life of the swap. However, it is possible to trade a swap where the notional principal varies during its life. An accreting (or step-up) swap is one in which the principal starts off at one level and then increases in amount over time. The opposite, an amortising swap, is one in which the notional reduces in size over time. An accreting swap would be useful where, for instance, a funding liability that is being hedged increases over time. The amortising swap might be employed by a borrower hedging a bond issue that featured sinking-fund payments, where a part of the notional amount outstanding is paid off at set points during the life of the bond. If the principal fluctuates in amount – for example, increasing in one year and then reducing in another – the swap is known as a roller-coaster swap. Another application for an amortising swap is as a hedge for a loan that is itself an amortising one. Frequently, this is combined with a forward-starting swap, to tie in with the cash flows payable on the loan. The pricing and valuation of an amortising swap is no different in principle from a vanilla interest-rate swap; a single swap rate is calculated using the relevant discount factors, and at this rate the NPV of the swap cash flows will equal zero at the start of the swap.

An example of an accrediting interest-rate swap and its cash flows is shown in Table 14.9 on page 649.

Libor-in-arrears swap

In a Libor-in-arrears swap (also known as a back-set swap), the setting date is just before the end of the accrual period for the floating-rate setting and not just before the start. Such a swap would be attractive to a counterparty who had a different view on interest rates from the market consensus. For instance, in a rising yield-curve environment, forward rates will be higher than current market rates, and this will be reflected in the pricing of a swap. A Libor-in-arrears swap would be priced higher than a conventional swap.

If floating-rate payers believed that interest rates would, in fact, rise more slowly than forward rates (and the market) were suggesting, they may wish to enter into an arrears swap as opposed to a conventional swap.

Basis swap

In a conventional swap, one leg comprises fixed-rate payments and the other floating-rate payments. In a basis swap, both legs are floating-rate but linked to different money market indices. One leg is normally linked to Libor, while the other might be linked to the CD rate, say, or to the CP rate. This type of swap would be used by a bank in the United States that had made loans which paid at the prime rate, and financed its loans at Libor. A basis swap would eliminate the basis risk between the bank's income and expense cash flows. Other basis swaps have been traded where both legs are linked to Libor, but at different maturities; for instance, one leg might be at three-month Libor and the other at six-month Libor. In such a swap, the basis is different and so is the payment frequency: one leg pays out semi-annually while the other would be paying on a quarterly basis. Note that where the payment frequencies differ, there is a higher level of counterparty risk for one of the parties. For instance, if one party is paying out on a monthly basis but receiving semi-annual cash flows, it would have made five interest payments before receiving one in return.

Differential swap

A differential swap is a basis swap, but with one of the legs calculated in a different currency. Typically, one leg is floating-rate, while the other is floating-rate, and with the reference index rate for another currency, but denominated in the domestic currency. For example, a differential swap may have one party paying six-month sterling Libor, in sterling, on a notional principal of £10 million, and receiving euro-Libor, minus a margin, payable in sterling and on the same notional principal. Differential swaps are not very common and are the most difficult for a bank to hedge. The hedging is usually carried out using what is known as a quanto option.

Margin swap

It is common to encounter swaps where there is a margin above or below Libor on the floating leg, as opposed to a floating leg of Libor flat. If a bank's borrowing is financed at Libor + 25 basis points, it may wish to receive Libor + 25 basis points in the swap so that its cash flows match exactly. The fixed-rate quote for a swap must be adjusted correspondingly to allow for the margin on the floating side. This is known as a margin swap. In our example, if the fixed-rate quote is, say, 6.00%, it would be adjusted to around 6.25%; differences in the margin quoted on the fixed leg might arise if the day-count convention or payment frequency were to differ between fixed and floating legs. Another reason why there may be a margin is if the credit quality of the counterparty demanded it, so that highly rated counterparties may pay slightly below Libor, for instance.

When a swap is transacted, its fixed rate is quoted at the current market rate for that maturity. Where the fixed rate is different from the market rate, this is an off-market swap, and a compensating payment is made by one party to the other. An off-market rate may be used for particular hedging requirements, for example, or when a bond issuer wishes to use the swap to hedge the bond as well as to cover the bond's issue costs.

Forward-start swap

A forward-start swap is one where the effective date is not the usual one or two days after the trade date but a considerable time afterwards; for instance, say, six months after trade date. Such a swap might be entered into where one counterparty wanted to fix a hedge or cost of borrowing now, but for a point some time in the future. Typically, this would be because the party considered that interest rates would rise or the cost of hedging would rise. The swap rate for a forward-starting swap is calculated in the same way as that for a vanilla swap.

Overnight interest-rate swaps and Eonia/SONIA swaps

This section could also have been placed in Chapter 13, our chapter on money market derivatives. OIS are interest-rate swaps that are traded in the money markets. This is sometimes called a *basis* swap, but this term should be used really for swaps whose legs have different bases such as different currencies to them.

We saw earlier in the chapter that an interest-rate swap contract, which is generally regarded as a capital market instrument, is an agreement between two counterparties to exchange a fixed interest-rate payment in return for a floating interest-rate payment, calculated on a notional swap amount, at regular intervals during the life of the swap. A swap may be viewed as being equivalent to a series of successive FRA contracts, with each FRA starting as the previous one matures. The basis of the floating interest rate is agreed as part of the contract terms at the inception of the trade. Conventional swaps index the floating interest rate to Libor; however, an exciting recent development in the money markets has been the OIS. In the sterling market they are known as sterling overnight interest rate average swaps, or SONIA, while euro-currency OIS are known as Eonia. In this section we review OIS swaps, which are used extensively by commercial and investment banks. (The USD market name for an OIS swap is, I believe, the DORIS).

SONIA swaps

SONIA is the average interest rate of interbank (unsecured) overnight sterling deposit trades undertaken before 1530 hours each day between members of the London Wholesale Money Brokers' Association. Recorded interest rates are weighted by volume. A SONIA swap is a swap contract that exchanges a fixed interest rate (the swap rate) against the geometric average of the overnight interest rates that have been recorded during the life of the contract. Exchange of interest takes place on maturity of the swap. SONIA swaps are used to speculate on or to hedge against interest rates at the very short end of the sterling yield curve; in other words, they can be used to hedge an exposure to overnight interest rates.[2] The swaps themselves are traded in maturities of one week to one year, although two-year SONIA swaps have also been traded.

Conventional swap rates are calculated off the government bond yield curve and represent the credit premium over government yields of interbank default risk. Essentially they represent an average of the forward rates derived from the government spot (zero-coupon) yield curve. The fixed rate quoted on a SONIA swap represents the average level of the overnight interest rates expected by market participants over the life of the swap. In practice, the rate is calculated as a function of the BoE's repo rate. This is the two-week rate at which the BoE conducts reverse repo trades with banking counterparties as part of its open market operations. In other words, this is the BoE's base rate. In theory one would expect the SONIA rate to follow the repo rate fairly closely, since the credit risk on an overnight deposit is low. However, in practice the spread between the SONIA rate and the BoE repo rate is very volatile, and for this reason the swaps are used to hedge overnight exposures.

---

2 Traditionally, overnight rates fluctuate in a very wide range during the day, depending on the day's funds shortage, and although volatility has reduced since the introduction of gilt repo, it is still unpredictable on occasions.

The daily turnover in SONIA swaps is considerably lower than cash instruments such as gilt repo (£20 billion) or more established derivative instruments such as short sterling (£45 billion); however, it is now a key part of the sterling market. Most trades are between one-week and three-month maturity, and the bid–offer spread has been reported by the BoE as around 2 basis points, which compares favourably with the 1 basis point spread of short sterling.

Figure 14.6 illustrates the monthly average of the SONIA index minus the BoE's repo rate during 1999 and 2000, with the exaggerated spread in December 1999 reflecting millenium bug concerns.

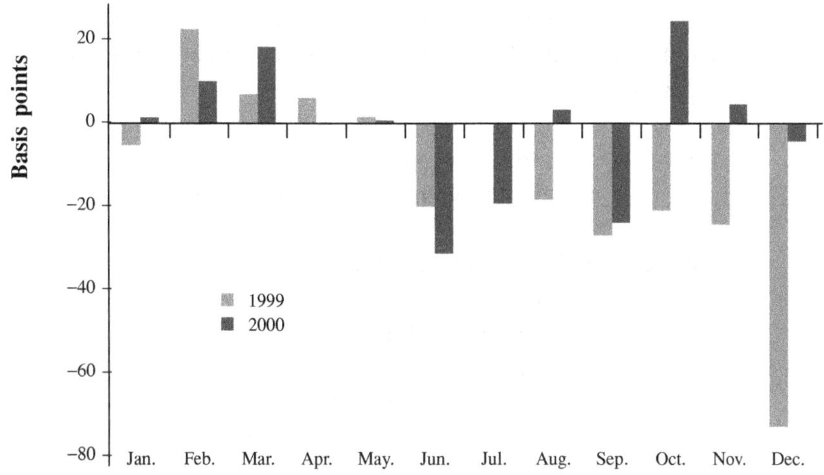

Figure 14.6 SONIA average rate minus BoE repo rate
Source: BoE.

EXAMPLE 14.5 Using an OIS swap to hedge a funding requirement

A structured hedge fund derivatives desk at an investment bank offers a leveraged investment product to a client in the form of a participating interest share in a fund of hedge funds. The client's investment is leveraged up by funds lent to it by the investment bank, for which the interest rate charged is overnight Libor plus a spread. (In other words, for instance, for each $25 invested by the client, the investment bank puts up $75 to make a total investment of $100. This gives the investor a leveraged investment in the hedge fund of funds. In most cases, the client would also bear the first $25 of loss of the $100 share of the investment).

Assume that this investment product has an expected life of at least two years, and possibly longer. As part of its routine ALM operations, the bank's Treasury desk has been funding this requirement by borrowing overnight each day. It now wishes to match the funding requirement raised by this product by matching asset term structure to the liability term structure. Let us assume that this product creates a USD1 billion funding requirement for the bank.

The current market deposit rates are shown in Figure 14.7 on page 661. The Treasury desk therefore funds this requirement in the following way:

Assets:	$1 billion, > 1-year term
	Receiving overnight Libor + 130 bps
Liabilities:	$350 million, six-month loan
	Pay 1.22%
	$350 million, 12-month loan
	Pay 1.50%
	$300 million, 15-month loan
	Pay 1.70% (not shown in Figure 14.6).

This matches the asset structure more closely to the term structure of the assets; however, it opens up an interest-rate basis mismatch in that the bank is now receiving an overnight Libor-based income, but paying a term-based liability. To remove this basis mismatch, the Treasury desk transacts an OIS swap to match the amount and term of each of the loan deals, paying overnight floating-rate interest and receiving fixed-rate interest. The rates for OIS swaps of varying terms are shown in Figure 14.8, which show two-way prices for OIS swaps up to two years in maturity. So for the six-month OIS the hedger is receiving fixed-interest at a rate of 1.085% and for the 12-month OIS he or she is receiving 1.40%. The difference between what it is receiving in the swap and what it is paying in the term loans is the cost of removing the basis mismatch, but more fundamentally reflects a key feature of OIS swaps versus deposit rates: deposit rates are Libor-related, whereas US dollar OIS rates are driven by the Fed Funds rate. On average, the Fed Funds rate lies approximately 8–10 basis points below the dollar deposit rate, and sometimes as much as 15 basis points below cash levels. Note that at the time of this trade, the Fed Funds rate was 1% and the market was not expecting a rise in this rate until at least the second half of 2004. This sentiment would have influenced the shape of the USD OIS curve.

The action taken above hedges out the basis mismatch and also enables the Treasury desk to match its asset profile with its liability profile. The net cost to the Treasury desk represents its hedging costs.

Figure 14.9 illustrates the transaction.

GRAB M-Mkt TTDE

11:37 TULLETT & TOKYO PAGE 1 / 1

USD Cash Deposits	Non-Japanese Bid	Ask	Time	USD Cash Deposits	Japanese Bid	Ask	Time
1) Spot	1.0000	1.0200	9:33	18) T/N	1.0000	1.0300	11/07
2) T/N	1.0100	1.0300	11/07	19) 1 Week	1.0400	1.0600	9:33
3) 1 Week	1.0300	1.0500	9:33	20) 2 Week	1.0500	1.0700	9:33
4) 2 Week	1.0300	1.0500	9:33	21) 3 Week	1.0600	1.0800	9:33
5) 3 Week	1.0300	1.0500	9:33	22) 1 Month	1.0800	1.1000	9:33
6) 1 Month	1.0400	1.0500	9:33	23) 2 Month	1.1800	1.2100	9:33
7) 2 Month	1.1200	1.1400	9:33	24) 3 Month	1.1900	1.2200	9:33
8) 3 Month	1.1300	1.1500	9:33	25) 4 Month	1.2000	1.2300	9:33
9) 4 Month	1.1400	1.1700	9:33	26) 5 Month	1.2100	1.2400	9:33
10) 5 Month	1.1600	1.1900	9:33	27) 6 Month	1.2300	1.2600	9:33
11) 6 Month	1.2000	1.2200	9:33	28) 7 Month	1.2700	1.3000	9:33
12) 7 Month	1.2300	1.2500	9:33	29) 8 Month	1.3100	1.3400	9:33
13) 8 Month	1.2700	1.2900	9:33	30) 9 Month	1.3800	1.4100	9:33
14) 9 Month	1.3300	1.3600	9:33	31) 10 Month	1.4600	1.4900	9:33
15) 10 Month	1.3800	1.4100	9:33	32) 11 Month	1.5300	1.5600	9:33
16) 11 Month	1.4500	1.4800	9:33	33) 12 Month	1.5500	1.5800	9:33
17) 12 Month	1.5000	1.5300	9:33				

Australia 61 2 9777 8600 Brazil 5511 3048 4500 Europe 44 20 7330 7500 Germany 49 69 920410
Hong Kong 852 2977 6000 Japan 81 3 3201 8900 Singapore 65 6212 1000 U.S. 1 212 318 2000
G657-802-0 10-Nov-03 11:37:50

Figure 14.7 Tullet US dollar deposit rates, 10 November 2003

GRAB Corp ICAU

11:34 USD OIS – ICAU PAGE 1 / 1

	USD OIS	Ask	Bid	Time
1)	1 Month	1.0190	0.9990	9:30
2)	2 Month	1.0240	1.0040	9:30
3)	3 Month	1.0310	1.0110	9:30
4)	4 Month	1.0440	1.0240	10:59
5)	5 Month	1.0710	1.0510	10:59
6)	6 Month	1.1050	1.0850	11:04
7)	7 Month	1.1420	1.1220	10:59
8)	8 Month	1.1920	1.1720	11:00
9)	9 Month	1.2420	1.2220	11:05
10)	10 Month	1.2930	1.2730	11:00
11)	11 Month	1.3580	1.3380	11:00
12)	12 Month	1.4210	1.4000	11:06
13)	15 Month	1.6250	1.6040	11:00
14)	18 Month	1.8090	1.7890	11:00
15)	21 Month	2.0080	1.9880	11:00
16)	24 Month	2.2030	2.1820	11:00

Figure 14.8 Garban ICAP US dollar OIS rates, 10 November 2003

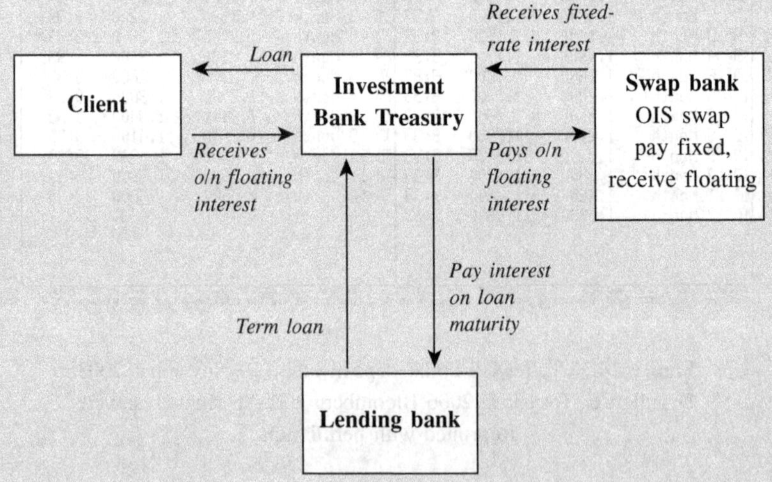

Figure 14.9 Illustration of interest basis mismatch hedging using OIS instrument

OIS swap terms

To illustrate OISs further, we give here the terms of one of the OIS executed in Example 14.6, the six-month swap. The counterparties to the trade are as labelled in Figure 14.8:

Notional:	\$350 million
Trade date:	10 November 2003
Effective date:	12 November 2003
Termination date:	12 May 2004
Payment terms:	The net interest payment is paid as a bullet amount on maturity.

Fixed Amounts

Fixed-rate payer:	OIS swap bank
Fixed-rate period end-date:	12 May 2004
Fixed-rate:	1.085%
Fixed-rate day-count fraction:	Act/360

Floating Amounts

Floating-rate payer:	Treasury desk
Floating-rate period end date:	12 May 2004
Floating-rate option:	USD–FedFunds

The floating-rate is calculated as follows:

$$F_{OIS} = \left[\prod\left(1 + \frac{FedFunds_i \times n_i}{360}\right) - 1\right] \times \frac{360}{d} \tag{14.20}$$

where

i	is a series of whole numbers from 1 to d_0, each representing a New York banking day
$FedFunds_i$	is a reference rate equal to the overnight USD Federal Funds interest rate, as displayed on Telerate page 118 and Bloomberg page BTMM
n_i	is the number of calendar days in the calculation period on which the rate is $FedFunds_i$
d	is the number of days in the calculation period.

Floating-rate day-count:	Act/360
Reset dates:	The last day of each calculation period
Compounding:	Inapplicable
Business day convention:	Modified following business day
Calculation agent:	OIS swap bank

EXAMPLE 14.6 Cash flows on OIS

Table 14.10 shows the daily rate fixes on a six-month OIS that was traded for effective date 17 October 2003, at a fixed rate of 1.03%. The swap notional is USD200 million.

From Table 14.10 we see that the average rate for Fed Funds during this period was 0.99952%. Hence on settlement the fixed-rate payer would have passed over a net settlement amount of USD 30,480.

Overnight-index swap

Effective date	17-Oct-03
Maturity	19-Apr-04
Notional	USD200 million
Fixed-leg pay	1.030%
Floating-leg receive	Fed Funds overnight act/360
Fixed-leg pay	USD1,030,000
Floating-leg receive	USD999,520
Settlement amount	USD30,480

Fix date	Maturity	Rate fix
10/17/2003	10/20/2003	0.98
10/20/2003	10/21/2003	1.02
10/21/2003	10/22/2003	1.02
10/22/2003	10/23/2003	0.99
10/23/2003	10/24/2003	0.99
10/24/2003	10/27/2003	1.02
10/27/2003	10/28/2003	1.01

10/28/2003	10/29/2003	0.98
10/29/2003	10/30/2003	0.98
10/30/2003	10/31/2003	0.97
10/31/2003	11/3/2003	1.02
11/3/2003	11/4/2003	1.02
11/4/2003	11/5/2003	1.02
11/5/2003	11/6/2003	0.98
11/6/2003	11/7/2003	0.98
11/7/2003	11/10/2003	0.98
11/10/2003	11/12/2003	0.98
11/12/2003	11/13/2003	0.99
11/13/2003	11/14/2003	1
11/14/2003	11/17/2003	0.99
11/17/2003	11/18/2003	1.04
11/18/2003	11/19/2003	1.04
11/19/2003	11/20/2003	0.98
11/20/2003	11/21/2003	1
11/21/2003	11/24/2003	1
11/24/2003	11/25/2003	0.98
11/25/2003	11/26/2003	0.98
11/26/2003	11/28/2003	1.02
11/28/2003	12/1/2003	1.01
12/1/2003	12/2/2003	1.03
12/2/2003	12/3/2003	0.97
12/3/2003	12/4/2003	0.97
12/4/2003	12/5/2003	0.98
12/5/2003	12/8/2003	0.98
12/8/2003	12/9/2003	0.98
12/9/2003	12/10/2003	0.99
12/10/2003	12/11/2003	0.97
12/11/2003	12/12/2003	0.99
12/12/2003	12/15/2003	0.99
12/15/2003	12/16/2003	0.99
12/16/2003	12/17/2003	1.04
12/17/2003	12/18/2003	0.99
12/18/2003	12/19/2003	0.99
12/19/2003	12/22/2003	0.98
12/22/2003	12/23/2003	0.98
12/23/2003	12/24/2003	1.02
12/24/2003	12/26/2003	1
12/26/2003	12/29/2003	0.97
12/29/2003	12/30/2003	0.97

12/30/2003	12/31/2003	0.98
12/31/2003	1/2/2004	0.93
1/2/2004	1/5/2004	0.94
1/5/2004	1/6/2004	1.01
1/6/2004	1/7/2004	0.97
1/7/2004	1/8/2004	0.94
1/8/2004	1/9/2004	0.94
1/9/2004	1/12/2004	0.99
1/12/2004	1/13/2004	0.99
1/13/2004	1/14/2004	1
1/14/2004	1/15/2004	0.99
1/15/2004	1/16/2004	1.04
1/16/2004	1/20/2004	0.98
1/20/2004	1/21/2004	1.02
1/21/2004	1/22/2004	1
1/22/2004	1/23/2004	1.02
1/23/2004	1/26/2004	1
1/26/2004	1/27/2004	1
1/27/2004	1/28/2004	1.08
1/28/2004	1/29/2004	1.02
1/29/2004	1/30/2004	0.99
1/30/2004	2/2/2004	1.03
2/2/2004	2/3/2004	1.01
2/3/2004	2/4/2004	1.01
2/4/2004	2/5/2004	0.97
2/5/2004	2/6/2004	1
2/6/2004	2/9/2004	1.01
2/9/2004	2/10/2004	0.99
2/10/2004	2/11/2004	1
2/11/2004	2/12/2004	1
2/12/2004	2/13/2004	1.02
2/13/2004	2/17/2004	1.02
2/17/2004	2/18/2004	1.02
2/18/2004	2/19/2004	1
2/19/2004	2/20/2004	1
2/20/2004	2/23/2004	0.99
2/23/2004	2/24/2004	0.99
2/24/2004	2/25/2004	1
2/25/2004	2/26/2004	0.99
2/26/2004	2/27/2004	1.02

2/27/2004	3/1/2004	1.04
3/1/2004	3/2/2004	1.04
3/2/2004	3/3/2004	1.04
3/3/2004	3/4/2004	1
3/4/2004	3/5/2004	0.99
3/5/2004	3/8/2004	0.99
3/8/2004	3/9/2004	1
3/9/2004	3/10/2004	0.99
3/10/2004	3/11/2004	0.99
3/11/2004	3/12/2004	1
3/12/2004	3/15/2004	0.99
3/15/2004	3/16/2004	1.05
3/16/2004	3/17/2004	1.05
3/17/2004	3/18/2004	1
3/18/2004	3/19/2004	1
3/19/2004	3/22/2004	0.99
3/22/2004	3/23/2004	1.01
3/23/2004	3/24/2004	1.01
3/24/2004	3/25/2004	0.99
3/25/2004	3/26/2004	0.99
3/26/2004	3/29/2004	1.02
3/29/2004	3/30/2004	1
3/30/2004	3/31/2004	1
3/31/2004	4/1/2004	0.98
4/1/2004	4/2/2004	1.05
4/2/2004	4/5/2004	1.03
4/5/2004	4/6/2004	1.01
4/6/2004	4/7/2004	1.01
4/7/2004	4/8/2004	1
4/8/2004	4/9/2004	1
4/9/2004	4/12/2004	1.02
4/12/2004	4/13/2004	1.01
4/13/2004	4/14/2004	1
4/14/2004	4/15/2004	1
4/15/2004	4/16/2004	1.01
4/16/2004	4/19/2004	0.99
	Average rate	**0.99952**

Table 14.10 OIS swap pay schedule, swap traded 17 October 2003

Basic interest-rate swap hedging applications

In this section, we review some of the principal uses of swaps as a hedging tool, and also how to hedge a swap book.

Corporate applications

Swaps are part of the OTC market and so they can be tailored to suit the particular requirements of the user. It is common for swaps to be structured so that they match particular payment dates, payment frequencies and Libor margins, which may characterise the underlying exposure of the customer. As the market in interest-rate swaps is so large, liquid and competitive, banks are willing to quote rates and structure swaps for virtually all customers, although it may be difficult for smaller customers to obtain competitive piece quotes as notional values below $10 million or $5 million.

Swap applications can be viewed as being one of two main types; asset-linked swaps and liability-linked swaps. Asset-linked swaps are created when the swap is linked to an asset such as a bond in order to change the characteristics of the income stream for investors. Liability-linked swaps are traded when borrowers of funds wish to change the pattern of their cash flows. Of course, just as with repo transactions, the designation of a swap in such terms depends on from whose point of view one is looking at the swap. An asset-linked swap hedge is a liability-linked hedge for the counterparty, except in the case of swap market-making banks who make two-way quotes in the instruments.

A straightforward application of an interest-rate swap is when a borrower wishes to convert a floating-rate liability into a fixed-rate one, usually in order to remove the exposure to upward moves in interest rates. For instance, a company may wish to fix its financing costs. Let us assume a company currently borrowing money at a floating-rate, say six-month Libor + 100 basis points, fears that interest rates may rise in the remaining three years of its loan. It enters into a three-year semi-annual interest-rate swap with a bank, as the fixed-rate payer, paying say 6.75% against receiving six-month Libor. This fixes the company's borrowing costs for three years at 7.75% (7.99% effective annual rate). This is shown in Figure 14.10.

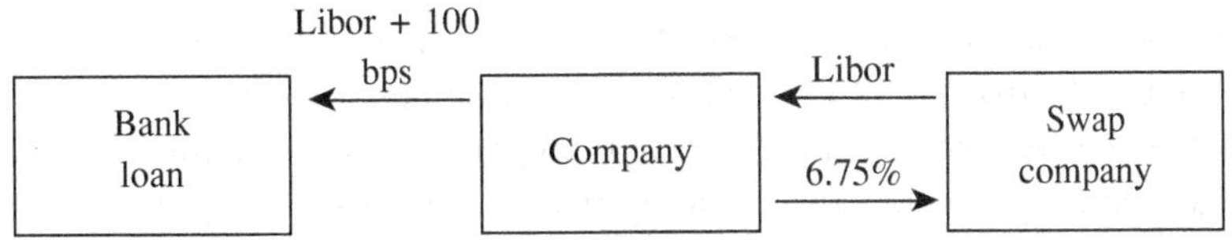

Figure 14.10 Changing liability from floating- to fixed-rate

EXAMPLE 14.7 Liability-linked swap, fixed- to floating- to fixed-rate exposure

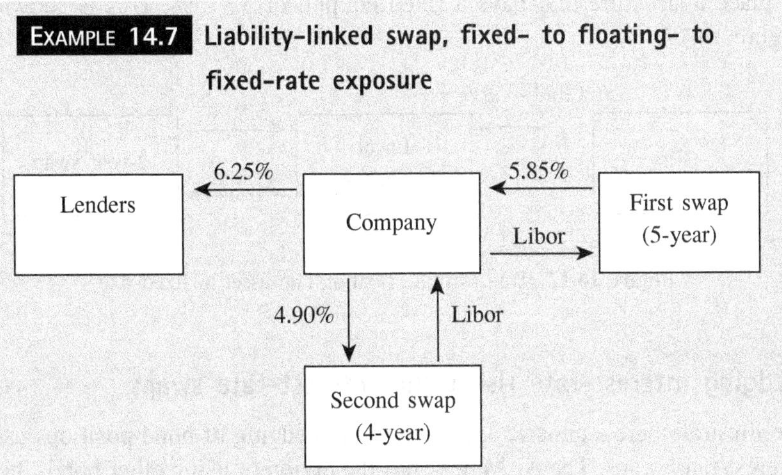

Figure 14.11 Liability-linked swap

A corporate borrows for five years at a rate of $6^1/_4$% and shortly after enters into a swap paying floating-rate, so that its net borrowing cost is Libor + 40 basis points. After one year, swap rates have fallen such that the company is quoted four-year swap rates as 4.90%–4.84%. The company decides to switch back into fixed-rate liability in order to take advantage of the lower interest rate environment. It enters into a second swap paying fixed at 4.90% and receiving Libor. The net borrowing cost is now 5.30%. The arrangement is illustrated in Figure 14.11. The company has saved 95 basis points on its original borrowing cost, which is the difference between the two swap rates.

Asset-linked swap structures might be required when, for example, investors require a fixed-interest security when floating-rate assets are available. Borrowers often issue FRNs, the holders of which may prefer to switch the income stream into fixed coupons. As an example, consider a local authority pension fund holding two-year floating-rate gilts. This is an asset of the highest quality, paying Libid minus 12.5 basis points. The pension fund wishes to swap the cash flows to create a fixed-interest asset. It obtains a quote for a tailor-made swap where the floating leg pays Libid, the quote being 5.55–50%. By entering into this swap, the pension fund has in place a structure that pays a fixed coupon of 5.375%. This is shown in Figure 14.12.

Figure 14.12 Transforming floating-rate asset to fixed-rate

Hedging interest-rate risk using interest-rate swaps

We illustrate here a generic approach to the hedging of bond positions using interest-rate swaps. The ALM desk has the option of using other bonds, bond futures or bond options, as well as swaps, when hedging the interest-rate risk exposure of a bond position. However, swaps are particularly efficient instruments to use because they display positive convexity characteristics; that is, the increase in value of a swap for a fall in interest rates exceeds the loss in value with a similar magnitude rise in rates. This is exactly the price/yield profile of vanilla bonds.

The primary risk measure we require when hedging using a swap is its present value of a basis point or PVBP.[3] This measures the price sensitivity of the swap for a basis-point change in interest rates. The PVBP measure is used to calculate the hedge ratio when hedging a bond position. The PVBP can be given by:

$$PVBP = \frac{\text{Change in swap value}}{\text{Rate change in basis points}}. \tag{14.21}$$

[3] This is also known as DVBP, or dollar value of a basis point or DV01.

which can be written as:

$$PVBP = \frac{dS}{dr}. \tag{14.22}$$

Using the basic relationship for the value of a swap, which is viewed as the difference between the values of a fixed-coupon bond and equivalent-maturity floating-rate bond (see Table 14.2) we can also write:

$$PVBP = \frac{d\text{Fixed bond}}{dr} - \frac{d\text{Floating bond}}{dr}, \tag{14.23}$$

which essentially states that the basis-point value of the swap is the difference in the basis-point values of the fixed-coupon and floating-rate bonds. The value is usually calculated for a notional £1 million of swap. The calculation is based the duration and modified-duration calculations used for bonds[4] and assumes that there is a parallel shift in the yield curve.

Table 14.11 illustrates how equations (14.23) and (14.24) can be used to obtain the PVBP of a swap. Hypothetical five-year bonds are used in the example. The PVBP for a bond can be calculated using Bloomberg or the MDURATION function on Microsoft Excel. Using either of the two equations above we see that the PVBP of the swap is £425.00. This is shown below.

Interest-rate swap			
	Term to maturity:	5 years	
	Fixed leg:	6.50%	
	Basis:	Semi-annual, act/365	
	Floating leg:	6-month Libor	
	Basis:	Semi-annual, act/365	
	Nominal amount:	£1,000,000	
		Present value £	
	Rate change −10 bps	0 bps	Rate change +10 bps
Fixed-coupon bond	1,004,940	1,000,000	995,171
Floating-rate bond	1,000,640	1,000,000	999,371
Swap	4,264	0	4,236

Table 14.11 PVBP for interest-rate swap

[4] See Chapter 4.

Calculating the PVBP using (14.23), we have:

$$PVBP_{swap} = \frac{dS}{dr} = \frac{4264 - (-4236)}{20} = 425$$

while we obtain the same result using the bond values:

$$PVBP_{swap} = PVBP_{fixed} - PVBP_{floating}$$

$$= \frac{1{,}004{,}940 - 995{,}171}{20} - \frac{1{,}000{,}640 - 999{,}371}{20}$$

$$= 488.45 - 63.45$$

$$= 425.00.$$

The swap basis-point value is lower than that of the five-year fixed-coupon bond; that is, £425 compared to £488.45. This is because of the impact of the floating-rate bond risk measure, which reduces the risk exposure of the swap as a whole by £63.45. As a rough rule of thumb, the PVBP of a swap is approximately equal to that of a fixed-rate bond that has a maturity similar to the period from the next coupon reset date of the swap through to the maturity date of the swap. This means that a 10-year semi-annual paying swap would have a PVBP close to that of a 9.5-year fixed-rate bond, and a 5.5-year swap would have a PVBP similar to that of a five-year bond.

When using swaps as hedge tools, we bear in mind that over time the PVBP of swaps behaves differently from that of bonds. Immediately preceding an interest reset date, the PVBP of a swap will be near-identical to that of the same-maturity fixed-rate bond, because the PVBP of a floating-rate bond at this time has essentially nil value. Immediately after the reset date, the swap PVBP will be near-identical to that of a bond that matures at the next reset date. This means that at the point (and this point only) right after the reset the swap PVBP will decrease by the amount of the floating-rate PVBP. In between reset dates, the swap PVBP is quite stable, as the effects of the fixed- and floating-rate PVBP changes cancel each other out. Contrast this with the fixed-rate PVBP, which decreases in value over time in stable fashion.[5] This feature is illustrated in Figure 14.13. A slight anomaly is that the PVBP of a swap actually increases by a small amount between reset dates; this is because the PVBP of a floating-rate bond decreases at a slightly faster rate than that of the fixed-rate bond during this time.

[5] This assumes no sudden large-scale yield movements.

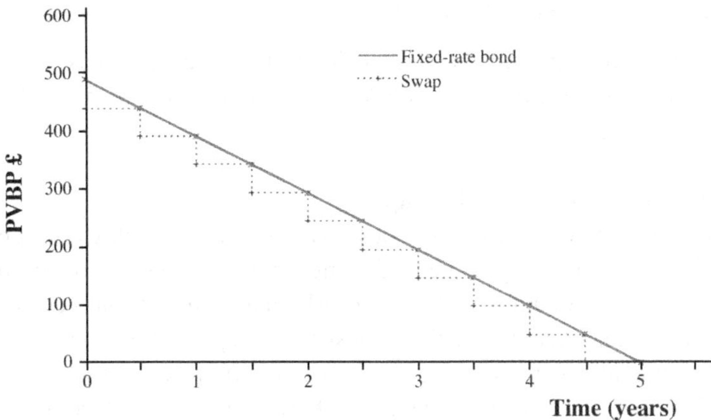

Figure 14.13 The PVBP of a five-year swap and fixed-rate bond

Hedging bond instruments with interest-rate swaps is conceptually similar to hedging with another bond or with bond futures contracts. If one is holding a long position in a vanilla bond, the hedge requires a long position in the swap: remember that a long position in a swap is to be paying fixed (and receiving floating). This hedges the receipt of fixed from the bond position. The change in the value of the swap will match the change in value of the bond, only in the opposite direction.[6] The maturity of the swap should match that of the bond as closely as possible. As swaps are OTC contracts, it should be possible to match interest dates as well as maturity dates. If one is short the bond, the hedge is to be short the swap, so the receipt of fixed matches the pay-fixed liability of the short bond position.

The correct nominal amount of the swap to put on is established using the PVBP hedge ratio. This is given as:

$$\text{Hedge ratio} = \frac{PVBP_{bond}}{PVBP_{swap}}. \tag{14.24}$$

This technique is still used in the market but suffers from the assumption of parallel yield-curve shifts and can therefore lead to significant hedging error at times. More advanced techniques are used by banks when hedging books using swaps, which space does not permit any discussion of here. Nevertheless, the technique described is widely used in banks.

[6] The change will not be an exact mirror. It is very difficult to establish a precise hedge for a number of reasons, which include differences in day-count bases, maturity mismatches and basis risk.

Hedging an interest-rate swap

A swap position is usually hedged with another swap that has offsetting characteristics, or with futures or FRAs. Less often it may be hedged using government bonds.

Hedging using bonds and swaps

A swap book can be hedged using other swaps, futures contracts or bonds. A bond book can similarly be hedged using futures, swaps and other bonds. In some of the larger banks an integrated risk management technique is used, whereby the bank's overall net risk exposure, arising from its entire position in all instruments including swaps, FRAs and futures, is managed as a whole. This results in cheaper hedging. However, it is still common for individual books to be hedged separately. If an integrated method is used, the bank must identify all the points along the term structure where it has an interest rate exposure, and then calculate the present value of a basis point (PVBP) at each of these points. That is, it must calculate the change in value of its positions along each maturity bucket that would result from a 1 basis point change in that maturity's interest rate. The bank's daily risk report will also list the bank's aggregate risk along the entire yield curve.

When hedging a position, we will want to put on another position of the same basis point value (BPV) and in the opposite direction. Assume we have only one position on the book, a five-year sterling swap of £5 million notional, in which we pay fixed- and receive floating-rate interest. This is conceptually similar to borrowing money. As the maturity of the swap is longer than that of the longest interest-rate futures contract, which is three years, we decide to hedge the position using a UK government bond, or gilt. As we have "borrowed" funds, the hedge action must be to "lend" funds. Therefore we need to buy a gilt to hedge the swap. In summary:

Swap position	*Hedge*
Pay fixed	Receive fixed (buy bond)
Receive fixed	Pay fixed (sell bond).

In normal situations we will probably wish to put on the hedge using the five-year benchmark gilt. We need to establish the hedge ratio to enable us to decide how much nominal of the gilt to buy, which is done using each instrument's BPV. To establish the nominal amount of the gilt required, the basic calculation is:

$$(\text{BPV swap} \ / \ \text{BPV gilt}) \times 10{,}000.$$

In our example we would need to calculate the BPV for the five-year swap. One way to do this is to view the swap as a strip of futures contracts, whose BPV is known with certainty. The short sterling future traded on LIFFE is a standardised contract with a BPV or "tick value" of £12.50 (in fact short sterling futures move in minimum units of 0.005, so that a tick value is actually £6.25. However, this is exactly half of a basis point). As our swap is a sterling swap it will pay semi-annually, while short sterling futures mature every quarter. The calculations are:

Convert swap nominal to futures:	5m × 2	= £10m
Futures periods:	4 × 5 years	= 20 contracts
Less "fixing" of first period of swap:	–2	= 18 contracts
(if a quarterly paying swap, this is –1)		
BPV:	18 × 12.5 × 10	= £2250.

The illustration we have used is a "rough-and-ready" hedge.

Hedging a swap transaction using futures contracts

In this section we use a worked example to illustrate how a swaps trader hedges a short-dated swap with derivative instruments.

Consider a Eurocurrency swaps trader who enters into a one-year swap transaction, paying fixed against three-month Libor. The first swap receipt is set at 3.27%, which is the current three-month Libor. As a receiver of floating-rate Libor, the dealer is exposed to a fall in interest rates over the period of the swap, and wishes to hedge this exposure. The terms of the trade are:

Date:	17 March
Swap principal:	EUR100 million
Fixed rate:	3.50%
Floating-rate:	Three-month Libor
First fixing:	3.26953%

The current prices for interest-rate futures contracts are:

June futures price:	96.67 (implied rate 3.33%)
September futures price:	96.55 (implied rate 3.45%)
December futures price:	96.37 (implied rate 3.63%)

To hedge the exposure, the trader buys a strip of June, September and December three-month Euribor futures contracts. The one-year strip rate is derived from calculating the returns on a three-month deposit reinvested along the futures implied forward rate curve for one year. This is shown below, with the strip rate given as *rf*, where:

$$\left[1 + rf \times \frac{d}{360}\right] = \left[1 + \text{fixing rate} \times \frac{d_1}{360}\right] \times \left[1 + rf_{fut1} \times \frac{d_2}{360}\right] \times \left[1 + rf_{fut2} \times \frac{d_3}{360}\right] \times \left[1 + rf_{fut3} \times \frac{d_4}{360}\right].$$

Substituting the values into the above expression, we obtain:

$$\left[1 + rf \times \frac{364}{360}\right] = \left[1 + 0.0326953 \times \frac{91}{360}\right] \times \left[1 + 0.0333 \times \frac{91}{360}\right] \times \left[1 + 0.0345 \times \frac{91}{360}\right] \times \left[1 + 0.0363 \times \frac{91}{360}\right].$$

This is solved to give *rf* equal to 3.46%. If we assume that the price of the futures contracts closed at the levels shown, the outcome of the hedge is shown in Table 14.12.

June contract	
Date:	16 June
Settlement price;	96.35
3-month Libor:	3.6500%
June contract P/L:	–32 ticks, or 96.35 – 96.67
Effective rate:	0.0365 + (-0.0032) or 3.3300%
September contract	
Date:	15 September
Settlement price:	96.32
3-month Libor:	3.6875%
September contract P/L:	–23 ticks, or 96.32 – 96.55
Effective rate:	0.036875 + (–0.0023) or 3.4485%
December contract	
Date:	15 December
Settlement price:	96.19
3-month Libor:	3.8125%
December contract P/L:	–18 ticks, or 96.19 – 96.37
Effective rate:	0.038125 + (–0.0018) or 3.6325%

Table 14.12 Swap hedge using interest-rate futures contracts

From Table 14.12. we see that as the trader has locked into the swap rate implied by each of the futures contracts at the time the hedge was put on, she achieved the anticipated 3.46% strip rate over the one-year hedge period. This example also illustrates how a trader can hedge a swap using a strip of futures, and also how the futures rates can be used to price the swap. Notice however that we did not calculate the actual number of futures contracts to put on against the 100 million swap position; this is a theoretical approach only. In practice this method will not provide a hedge of sufficient accuracy, due to convexity bias between futures prices and swap rates in the markets. To overcome this a slightly modified hedge calculation is employed.

To determine the correct number of futures contracts with which to construct the strip, the trader must carry out the following:

- calculate all the cash flows and their present values, using implied futures forward rates;
- calculate the basis point value (BPV) of the present value of the cash flows for a one tick change in each of the futures contracts;
- calculate the futures hedge ratio for each period in the strip using the BPV of the cash flow and the BPV of the future.

This procedure is shown in Tables 14.13 to 14.15, with the expected strip rate calculated as 3.57%.

Date	Days	Contract	Price	Implied rate %	Fixed cash flow	Floating cash flow	PV fixed cash flow	PV floating cash flow
17 Mar.	91	Stub		3.69		932,750		924,130
16 June	91	Jun.	96.67	3.33		841,750		827,010
15 Sep.	91	Sep.	96.55	3.45		872,083		849,404
15 Dec.	91	Dec.	96.37	3.63		917,583		885,595
16 Mar.	364							
		Fixed strip		3.57	(3,612,061)		(3,486,139)	3,486,139

Table 14.13 Futures hedging: strip calculation (i)

The change in the present value of each cash flow is calculated for a 1 basis point fall in each futures price. A new strip rate is calculated to each futures maturity date and is used to discount each cash flow to its new present value. In this way it is possible to observe how a 1 basis point change in any of the futures contracts will impact the overall position of the swap.

Contract	June future less 1 tick; PV of cash flow	Change	Sep. future less 1 tick; PV of cash flow	Change	Dec. future less 1 tick; PV of cash flow	Change
Stub	924,130	0	924,130	0	924,130	0
Jun.	829,473	2,463	827,010	0	827,010	0
Sep.	849,383	(21)	851,845	2,441	849,404	0
Dec.	885,573	(22)	885,573	(22)	888,013	2,417
Strip rate	(3,486,052)	87	(3,486,052)	87	(3,486,052)	87
		2,507		**2,506**		**2,504**

Table 14.14 Futures hedging: strip calculation (ii)

We are now in a position to calculate the number of contracts to put against the swap, based on the BPV of the two instruments. The hedge ratio is given by:

$$\text{Hedge} = \frac{BPV_{cash\ flow}}{BPV_{fut}}$$

so for the June contract it is 2,507/25 or 100.28, for the September contract it is 2,506/25 or 100.24, and for the December contract it is 2,504/25 or 100.16. In fact it is only possible to transact futures contracts in round lots, so the strip put on by the trader is comprised of 100 lots each of June, September and December contracts.

The outcome of the hedge, assuming the closing prices in the previous illustration, is shown in Table 14.15.

June contract	
Date:	16 June
Settlement price:	96.35
Three-month Libor:	3.6500%
June contract P/L:	–32 ticks, or 96.35 – 96.67
	32 × 100 × EUR25 = –EUR80,000
Effective rate:	0.0365 + (–0.0032) or 3.3300%
September contract	
Date:	15 September
Settlement price:	96.32
Three-month Libor:	3.6875%
September contract P/L:	–23 ticks, or 96.32 – 96.55
	23 × 100 × EUR25 = –EUR57500
Effective rate:	0.036875 + (–0.0023) or 3.4485%
December contract	
Date:	15 December
Settlement price:	96.19
Three-month Libor:	3.8125%
December contract P/L:	–18 ticks, or 96.19 – 96.37
	18 × 100 × EUR25 = –EUR45,000
Effective rate:	0.038125 + (–0.0018) or 3.6325%

Table 14.15 Futures hedging: strip calculation (iii)

The example above illustrates how the trader was able, by locking into the swap rate implied by the futures contracts at the time the hedge was initiated, to achieve the anticipated 3.57% strip rate during the one-year swap period.

While corporates tend to use FRAs and swaps to hedge interest-rate exposure, thus creating a large demand for them among banks, banks themselves tend to use futures contracts to hedge both FRAs and swaps. The advantages of using futures contracts are that:

- the bid–offer spread in the futures market is usually very close, and invariably tighter than in the swap market;
- in practice there is no credit risk associated with trading futures contracts, because the clearing house assumes the credit risk (as it is the central counterparty to everyone that transacts exchange-traded futures), while swap contracts carry associated credit risk;

- in the system of depositing *variation margin* at the clearing house to cover losses in daily trading, where there is a positive variation margin as a result of profitable trading, this is paid "up front", thus offering the additional benefit of allowing reinvestment of realised profits;
- there is no regulatory capital requirement for futures positions, so from a capital point of view they are cheaper than swaps.

Hence it is most common to see swap books hedged using futures contracts.

Swaptions

Description

Swaptions are options on swaps. The buyers of swaption have the right but not the obligation to enter into an interest-rate swap agreement during the life of the option. The terms of the swaption will specify whether the buyers are the fixed- or floating-rate payers; the sellers of the options (the *writers*) become the counterparty to the swaps if the options are exercised. The convention is that if the buyers have the right to exercise the option as the fixed-rate payers, they have traded a *call swaption*, also known as a *payer swaption*. If, upon exercising, the buyers of the swaption become the floating-rate payers then they have bought a *put swaption* (also known as a *receiver swaption*). The writer of the swaption are the parties to the other leg. In the sterling market, swaption are referred to in terms similar to FRA terminology, so that a 3/6 or 3–6 payer's swaption is a three-year option to pay fixed on a three-year interest-rate swap.

Swaptions are similar to forward start swaps up to a point, but the buyers have the *option* of whether or not to commence payments on the effective date. A bank may purchase a call swaption if it expects interest rates to rise, and will exercise the option if indeed rates do rise as the bank has expected.

As with conventional put and call options, swaption turn in-the-money under opposite circumstances. A call swaption increases in value as interest rates rise, and a put swaption becomes more valuable as interest rates fall. Consider a one-year European call swaption on a five-year semi-annual interest-rate swap, purchased by a bank counterparty. The notional value is £10 million and the "strike price" is 6%, against Libor. Assume that the price (premium) of the swaption is 25 basis points, or £25,000. On expiry of the swaption, the buyers will either exercise it, in which case they will enter into a five-year swap paying 6% and receiving floating-rate interest, or elect to let the swaption expire with no value. If the five-year swap rate for counterparty of similar credit quality to the bank is above 6%, the swaption holders will exercise the swaption, while if the rate is below 6% the buyers will not exercise. The principle is the same for a put swaption, only in reverse.

A company will use swaption as part of an interest-rate hedge for a future exposure. For example, assume that a company will be entering into a five-year bank loan in three months' time. Interest on the loan is charged on a floating-rate basis, but the company intends to swap this to a fixed-rate liability after it has entered into the loan. As an added hedge, the company may choose to purchase a swaption that gives it the right to receive Libor and pay a fixed rate, say 10%, for a five-year period beginning in three months' time. When the time comes for the company to take out a swap and exchange its interest-rate liability in three months' time (having entered into the loan), if the five-year swap rate is below 10%, the company will transact the swap in the normal way and the swaption will expire worthless. However, if the five-year swap rate is above 10%, the company will instead exercise the swaption, giving it the right to enter into a five-year swap and pay a fixed rate of 10%. Essentially the company has taken out protection to ensure that it does not have to pay a fixed rate of more than 10%. Hence, swaption can be used to guarantee a maximum swap rate liability. They are similar to forward-starting swaps, but do not commit a party to enter into a swap on fixed terms. The swaption enables a company to hedge against unfavourable movements in interest rates, but also to gain from favourable movements, although there is of course a cost associated with this, which is the premium paid for the swaption.

Valuation

Swaptions are typically priced using the B–S or Black 76 option pricing models. These are used to value a European option on a swap, assuming that the appropriate swap rate at the expiry date of the option is lognormal. Consider a swaption with the following terms:

Swap rate on expiry: rs
Swaption strike rate: rX
Maturity: T
Start date: t
Pay basis: F (say, quarterly, semi-annual or annual)
Notional principal: M

If the actual swap rate on the maturity of the swaption is rs, the pay off from the swaption is given by:

$$\frac{M}{F}\max.(r-r_n,0)\ .$$

The value of a swaption is essentially the difference between the strike rate and the swap rate at the time it is being valued. If a swaption is exercised, the payoff at each interest date is given by $(rs - rX) \times M \times F$. As a call swaption is only exercised when the swap rate is higher than the strike rate (that is, $rs > rX$), the option payoff on any interest payment in the swap is given by:

$$Swaption_{Interest\ payment} = \max.[0,(rs - rX)] \times M \times F \tag{14.25}$$

It can then be shown that the value of a call swaption on expiry is given by:

$$PV_{Swaption} = \sum_{n=1}^{N} Df_{(0,n)}(rs - rX) \times M \times F \tag{14.26}$$

where $Df_{(0,n)}$ is the spot rate discount factor for the term beginning now and ending at time t. By the same logic the value of a put swaption is given by the same expression except that $(rX - rs)$ is substituted at the relevant point above.

Consider then, that a swaption can be viewed as a collection of calls or puts on interest deposits or Libor, enabling us to use the Black model when valuing it. This means that we value each call or put on for a single payment in the swap, and then sum these payments to obtain the value of the swaption. The main assumption made when using this model is that the Libor rate follows a lognormal distribution over time, with constant volatility.

Consider a call swaption being valued at time t that matures at time T. We begin by valuing a single payment under the swap (assuming the option is exercised) made at time T_n. The point at time T_n is into the life of the swap, so that we have $T_n > T > t$. At the time of valuation, the option time to expiry is $T - t$ and there is $T_n - t$ until the nth payment. The value of this payment is given by:

$$C_t = MFe^{-r(T_n-t)}[rsN(d1) - rXN(d2)] \tag{14.27}$$

where

C_t is the price of the call option on a single payment in the swap
r is the risk-free instantaneous interest rate
$N(.)$ is the cumulative normal distribution
σ is the interest-rate volatility

and where

$$d_1 = \frac{\ln(rs_t / rX) + \frac{\sigma^2}{2}(T - t)}{\sigma\sqrt{T - t}}$$

$$d2 = d1 - \sigma\sqrt{T - t}\,.$$

The remaining life of the swaption $(T - t)$ governs the probability that it will expire in-the-money, determined using the lognormal distribution. On the other hand the interest payment itself is discounted (using $e^{-r(T_n-t)}$) over the period $T_n - t$ as it is not paid until time T_n.

Having valued a single interest payment, viewing the swap as a collection of interest payments, we value the call swaption as a collection of calls. Its value is given therefore by:

$$PVSwaption_t = \sum_{n=1}^{N} MFe^{-r(T_n-t)}[rsN(d_1) - rXN(d_2)] \tag{14.28}$$

where t, T and n are as before.

If we substitute discrete spot rate discount factors instead of the continuous form given by (14.28) the expression becomes:

$$PVSwaption_t = MF[rsN(d_1) - rXN(d_2)] \sum_{n=1}^{N} Df_{t,T_n}\,. \tag{14.29}$$

Note that vanilla caps and floors are also priced using the Black 76 model, as are European swaptions. This leads to some interesting results.[7] For instance, given our basic assumption that a forward-starting swap is a linear function of forward interest rates, using the Black 76 model for caps or floors assumes that forward *interest rates* follow a lognormal distribution. Using the same model for swaptions means we are assuming that forward *swap* rates are lognormally distributed. This is a contradictory set of assumptions; nevertheless, the market uses the same model to price both products.

If we consider a payer's swaption with strike rX and value of PV_F and PV_L for fixed and floating sides respectively, the swaption payoff is given by:

$$\max.[0, PV_L - PV_F].$$

As the level of interest rates fluctuates during the life of the swaption, the values PV_F and PV_L will also move. This produces a payoff that does not follow the general form for the Black 76 model, which is a stochastic pattern in relation to the fixed level of rX. To counter this the market also uses a "spread option model",[8] which is given below.

$$PV_{Swaption} = PV_L \times N(d_1) - PV_F \times N(d_2) \qquad (14.30)$$

where

$d1 = [\ln(PV_L / PV_F) + {}^1/_2\sigma^2 t] / (\sigma\sqrt{t})$, and so on

$\sigma^2 = (\sigma_L)^2 + (\sigma_F)^2 - 2\sigma_L\sigma_F\rho_{LF}$

and

σ_L and σ_F are the volatilities of the floating and fixed sides
ρ_{LF} is the correlation between the two sides.

7 See, for example, Flavell, R. (2002), *Swaps and Other Derivatives*, John Wiley & Sons, Singapore, Chapter 7.

8 See Flavell, Chapter 7.

Example 14.8 Swaption pricing[9]

We present a hypothetical term structure environment in this example to illustrate the basic concept. This is shown in Table 14.16. We wish to price a forward-starting annual interest swap starting in two years for a term of three years. The swap has a notional of £10 million.

Date	Term (years)	Discount factor	Par yield	Zero-coupon rate	Forward rate
2/18/2001	0	1	5	5	5
2/18/2002	1	0.95238095	5.00	5	6.03015
2/18/2003	2	0.89821711	5.50	5.51382	7.10333
2/18/2004	3	0.83864539	6.00	6.04102	6.66173
2/18/2005	4	0.78613195	6.15	6.19602	6.71967
2/20/2006	5	0.73637858	6.25	6.30071	8.05230
2/19/2007	6	0.68165163	6.50	6.58946	8.70869
2/18/2008	7	0.62719194	6.75	6.88862	9.40246
2/18/2009	8	0.57315372	7.00	7.20016	10.1805
2/18/2010	9	0.52019523	7.25	7.52709	5.80396
2/18/2011	10	0.49165950	7.15	7.35361	6.16366

Table 14.16 Interest-rate data for swaption valuation

The swap rate is given by:

$$rs = \frac{\sum_{n=1}^{N} rf_{(t-1),t} \times Df_{0,t}}{\sum_{n=1}^{N} Df_{0,t}}$$

where rf is the forward rate.

[9] This example follows an approach described in a number of other texts; for example, Kolb, R. (2000), *Futures, Options and Swaps*, Blackwell, Oxford; although here we use discount factors in the calculation, whereas in Kolb (2000), for example, the illustration uses zero-coupon factors which are (1 + spot rate).

Using the above expression, the numerator in this example is (0.0666 × 0.8386) + (0.0672 × 0.7861) + (0.0805 × 0.7634) or 0.1701.

The denominator is:

$$0.8386 + 0.7861 + 0.7634 \text{ or } 2.3881.$$

Therefore the forward-starting swap rate is 0.1701/2.3881 or 0.071228 (7.123%).

We now turn to the call swaption on this swap, the buyer of which acquires the right to enter into a three-year swap paying the fixed-rate swap rate of 7.00%. If the volatility of the forward swap rate is 0.20, the d_1 and d_2 terms are:

$$d_1 = \frac{\ln\left(\frac{rs}{rX}\right) + \frac{\sigma^2}{2}(T-t)}{\sigma\sqrt{T-t}} = \frac{\ln\left(\frac{0.071228}{0.07}\right) + \left(\frac{0.2^2}{2} \times 2\right)}{0.2\sqrt{2}}$$

or 0.2029068

$$d^2 = d^1 - \sigma\sqrt{T-t} = 0.20290618 - 0.2(1.4142)$$

or −0.079934.

The cumulative normal values are:

$N(d_1) = N(0.2029)$ which is 0.580397
$N(d_2) = N(-0.079934)$ which is 0.468145.[10]

From above we know that $\sum Df_{t,T_n}$ is 2.3881. So using (14.28) we calculate the value of the call swaption to be:

$$PVSwaption_t = MF[rsN(d_1) - rXN(d_2)] \sum_{n=1}^{N} Df_{t,T_n}$$

$$= 10{,}000{,}000 \times 1 \times [0.07228 \times 0.580397 - 0.07 \times 0.468145] \times 2.3881$$

$$= 219{,}250.$$

[10] These values may be found from standard normal distribution tables or by using the Microsoft Excel formula =NORMSDIST().

or £219,250. Option premiums are frequently quoted as basis points of the notional amount, so in this case the premium is (219,250/10,000,000) or 219.25 basis points.

Swaptions and interest-rate risk management

A swaption is another instrument that may be used for interest-rate risk management purposes. Hence, they are an alternative to swaps, caps and floors. In some cases, an institution will have the option of using any of these products. For instance, consider a situation where a corporate entity is aware that it must borrow funds at a future date, for a fixed period of time. The funds are only available at a floating-rate. This requirement presents an interest-rate risk in that rates may rise between now and the start date of the loan, and then rise during the loan. If the Treasury desk of the entity wishes to remove uncertainty and nullify this risk, it may consider the following:

- trade in a forward-start swap, for the term of the loan, paying fixed and receiving floating. The swap will come into effect at the start of the loan. This removes uncertainty in that the company knows what it will be paying for the term of the loan, thus it's interest-rate exposure is known. The downside is that the company cannot benefit if interest rates fall;
- enter into a forward-start cap: the company can buy a cap, with start date for the start of the loan, and this fixes its upper borrowing rate. It also enables the company to gain if rates fall;
- buy a swaption. The company can purchase a payers' swaption, with expiry date matching the start date of the loan, which if exercised kicks in a pay-fixed swap for the term of the loan. If rates were above the strike rate of the swaption on expiry, the swaption will be exercised, otherwise it would expire worthless.

Alternatively, the company could leave the exposure intact and do nothing. It will suffer if rates rise, but it will benefit if rates fall, and it wouldn't have paid any money for the privilege! Shareholders prefer certainty over risk exposure, however, so this strategy is rarely followed.

The choice between a cap and a swaption will be influenced by their relative cost. Cap premiums are significantly higher than swaption premiums, both at-the-money or out-of-the-money. This is not unexpected, because a cap provides a greater level of protection for its buyer. It lasts for the entire period of the exposure, and also enables its buyer to benefit from downward movements in rates. The swaption only provides protection for the period leading up the start of the loan, and then can be exercised only on expiry. If rates have fallen, it will expire un-exercised. The cap can be exercised at fixed times during the term of the loan (as each caplet approaches its exercise date). It therefore incorporates more time value than a swaption. So it is a straightforward choice the company is faced with: the higher priced cap that offers more insurance, or the lower cost swaption. This is illustrated further in Example 14.9.

EXAMPLE 14.9 Swaption and cap premiums

A bank will need to enter into a two-year sterling loan in one year's time. The loan rate will be a spread over three-month Libor. To hedge the future risk exposure, the bank can purchase a forward-start vanilla cap for the term of the loan, a mid-curve cap or a 1/3 payer's swaption. We have the following terms:

Trade date:	8 January 2001
Start date:	9 January 2002
Terms:	3-month Libor from 9 Jan 02 to 9 Jan 04
Strike:	5.50%
Volatility:	12% p.a.

In the sterling market as at January 2001 we observed the following premiums:

Two-year vanilla cap:	44.7 bps
Two-year mid-curve cap:	36.5 bps
1/3 payer swaption:	32.9 bps.

If the bank exercises the swaption, it will be paying a fixed rate on its loan. This, being the swap rate, is in effect the average of the implied forward rates given by the zero-coupon curve as at January 2001. If Libor falls after the exercise date, the company will not benefit. The vanilla cap is the expensive approach, but it has eight exercise dates – every quarter for the two-year period of the loan. The mid-curve cap has one exercise date, but is made up of eight separate options. The swaption is the cheapest instrument because it is a single option on one exercise date.

Bloomberg screens

A number of screens on Bloomberg are of value to swaps users and traders. We highlight a selection of some of them here.

Broker rates screens

Swap rates can be viewed on a number of brokers' pages. We show those from Tullett as at 9 February 2004.

Figure 14.14 is the USD swaps page SMKR. Rates for semi-annual and annual swaps are shown. This page also shows benchmark Treasury yields for selected maturities, and the swap spread over the benchmark. Figure 14.15 shows USD OIS and FRA rates.

GRAB Govt **SMKR**
(c) 2003 Tullett Financial Information Page 1 of 1
09-Feb-04 12:27 GMT

------------------ Tullett plc USD Medium Term Swaps ------------------

	Price Bid	Price Ask	Mid Yield	Swap Spread Bid	Swap Spread Ask	IRS Semi-Bond	IRS Ann-Actual	When Issued	
2Y	100.070	100.076	1.756	32.50	36.50	2.081-121	2.062-102	2Y	
3Y	101.06+	101.076	2.165	49.75	53.75	2.662-702	2.643-683	3Y	2.304
4Y			2.624	49.25	53.25	3.117-157	3.098-139	5Y	3.107
5Y	100.230	100.240	3.087	39.50	43.50	3.482-522	3.463-503	10Y	4.102
6Y			3.287	47.75	51.75	3.765-805	3.748-788	30Y	
7Y			3.488	50.25	54.25	3.990-030	3.975-015		
8Y			3.690	48.75	52.75	4.177-217	4.162-202		
9Y			3.890	44.75	48.75	4.337-377	4.323-363	Spread to 10Y	
10Y	101.080	101.09+	4.090	38.50	42.50	4.475-515	4.462-502	Bid	Ask
11Y			4.132	46.00	50.00	4.592-632	4.580-620	50.18	54.18
12Y			4.174	52.25	56.25	4.696-736	4.685-726	60.61	64.61
13Y			4.216	57.50	61.50	4.791-831	4.780-820	70.07	74.07
14Y			4.257	62.00	66.00	4.877-917	4.868-908	78.74	82.74
15Y			4.299	63.75	67.75	4.937-977	4.928-968	84.66	88.66
20Y			4.508	63.25	67.25	5.141-181	5.134-174	105.08	109.0
25Y			4.717	49.25	53.25	5.210-250	5.203-244	111.99	115.99
30Y	106.200	106.220	4.927	30.25	34.25	5.229-269	5.222-263		

Australia 61 2 9777 8600 Brazil 5511 3048 4500 Europe 44 20 7330 7500 Germany 49 69 920410
Hong Kong 852 2977 6000 Japan 81 3 3201 8900 Singapore 65 6212 1000 U.S. 1 212 318 2000
G926-802-2 09-Feb-04 12:27:41

Figure 14.14 Screen SMKR on Bloomberg, Tullet USD swaps page, 9 February 2004

```
GRAB                                                              Govt  SMKP
(c) 2003 Tullett Financial Information                            Page 1 of 1
                                                         09-Feb-04 12:27 GMT
                       USD Overnight Index Swaps Composite
     OIS                FWD OIS              3M FRA              SHORT SWAPS
1M  0.994 1.024  1X2 0.992 1.022 | 1X4  1.141 1.171 | IRS Vs 3 MONTH LIBOR
2M  0.993 1.023  2X3 1.007 1.037 | 3X6  1.229 1.259 |     6M 1.174 1.204
3M  0.998 1.028  3x4 1.050 1.080 | 6X9  1.446 1.476 |     9M 1.269 1.299
4M  1.012 1.042  4x5 1.091 1.121 |      6M FRA      |    12M 1.403 1.433
5M  1.029 1.059  1x4 1.017 1.047 | 1X7  1.217 1.247 |    18M 1.721 1.751
6M  1.040 1.070  2x5 1.051 1.081 | 3X9  1.340 1.370 | IRS Vs 1MONTH LIBOR
7M  1.081 1.111  3x6 1.078 1.108 | 6X12 1.617 1.647 |     3M
8M  1.108 1.138  4x7 1.165 1.195 |                  |     4M
9M  1.130 1.160  1x7 1.093 1.123 | ---------------- |     5M
10M 1.182 1.212  2x8 1.144 1.174 |    IMM SWAPS     |     6M
11M 1.221 1.251  3x9 1.191 1.221 |      1 YEAR      |     7M
12M 1.257 1.287 4x10 1.288 1.318 | Mar04 1.483-513  |     8M
-------------------------------- | Jun04 1.779-809  |     9M
USD LIBOR FIX     ON FED FUNDS   | Sep04 2.153-183  |    10M
 Mon 09-Feb       Bid    Ask     | Dec04 2.536-566  |    11M
1M   1.10000      0.9700 0.9800  |      2 YEAR      |    12M
2M   1.11625      High   Low     | Mar04 2.181-211  | -----------------------
3M   1.13000      0.9900 0.9700  | Jun04 2.511-541  | BASIS SWAPS (1M) / (3M)
6M   1.20000      Last   Close   | Sep04 2.840-870  |  1Y  1M+ -0.250 3.750
9M   1.29250      0.9800 1.0000  | Dec04 3.163-193  |  2Y  1M+ -0.500 3.500
Australia 61 2 9777 8600         Brazil 5511 3048 4500          Europe 44 20 7330 7500          Germany 49 69 920410
Hong Kong 852 2977 6000 Japan 81 3 3201 8900 Singapore 65 6212 1000 U.S. 1 212 318 2000 Copyright 2004 Bloomberg L.P.
                                                                                   G926-802-2 09-Feb-04 12:28:30
```

Figure 14.15 Screen SMKP on Bloomberg, Tullet USD OIS and FRA rates page, 9 February 2004

Figures 14.16-14.18 show the same broker's composite pages for AUD, SGD and TWD currencies. A composite page shows both cash and derivative rates.

GRAB Govt SMKP
(c) 2003 Tullett Financial Information Page 1 of 1
09-Feb-04 12:29 GMT

AUSTRALIAN DOLLAR COMPOSITE

IR SWAPS			BASIS SWAPS			FRA			CASH DEPOSITS			SPOT FX
1Y3	5.58	5.62	1Y	7.00	9.00	1X4	5.55	5.57	TN	5.1900	5.2600	AUD
2Y3	5.68	5.72	2Y	8.00	10.00	2X5	5.55	5.57	1W	5.2300	5.2800	0.7776/80
3Y3	5.75	5.79	3Y	9.00	11.00	3X6	5.58	5.60	1M	5.3700	5.4000	JPY
4Y6	5.87	5.91	4Y	9.50	11.50	4X7	5.58	5.60	2M	5.4300	5.4700	105.65/69
5Y6	5.92	5.96	5Y	11.00	13.00	5X8	5.60	5.62	3M	5.4600	5.5000	EUR
7Y6	5.97	6.01	6Y	11.00	13.00	6X9	5.61	5.63	4M	5.4900	5.5400	1.2741/43
10Y6	6.04	6.08	7Y	11.00	13.00	7X10	5.63	5.65	5M	5.5000	5.5700	GBP
			8Y	11.00	13.00	8X11	5.64	5.66	6M	5.5500	5.6000	1.8617/19
			9Y	11.00	13.00	9X12	5.65	5.67	9M	5.5900	5.6500	HKD
			10Y	11.00	13.00				1Y	5.6600	5.7000	7.7680/82

INTEREST RATE OPTIONS

SWAPTIONS

Ex	1Y	2Y	3Y	4Y	5Y	7Y	10Y
1M	15.50	16.60	17.60	17.50	17.40	17.20	17.00
2M	15.70	17.00	17.70	17.60	17.50	17.40	17.10
3M	15.70	17.40	17.80	17.70	17.60	17.50	17.30
6M	16.10	17.30	17.80	17.70	17.50	17.40	17.20
1Y	16.40	17.00	17.40	17.20	17.10	17.00	16.90
2Y	15.80	16.10	16.90	16.70	16.60	16.60	16.60
3Y	15.20	15.60	16.40	16.40	16.40	16.30	16.20

CAPS			FLOORS		
1Y	13.50	15.50	1Y	13.50	15.50
2Y	14.90	16.90	2Y	14.90	16.90
3Y	15.20	17.20	3Y	15.20	17.20
4Y	14.90	16.90	4Y	14.90	16.90
5Y	14.70	16.70	5Y	14.70	16.70
7Y	14.10	16.10	7Y	14.10	16.10
10Y	13.80	15.80	10Y	13.80	15.80

Australia 61 2 9777 8600 Brazil 5511 3048 4500 Europe 44 20 7330 7500 Germany 49 69 920410
Hong Kong 852 2977 6000 Japan 81 3 3201 8900 Singapore 65 6212 1000 U.S. 1 212 318 2000 Copyright 2004 Bloomberg L.P.
G926-802-2 09-Feb-04 12:29:59

Figure 14.16 Tullett Australian dollar composite page

GRAB Govt SMKP
(c) 2003 Tullett Financial Information Page 1 of 4
09-Feb-04 12:29 GMT

SINGAPORE DOLLAR COMPOSITE

IR SWAPS			OIS			SGD/USD SWAPS			CASH DEPOSITS			SPOT FX
1Y	0.98	1.00	1M	0.70	0.74	Sem Bnd/6M (L)			TN	0.6250	0.6250	SGD
2Y	1.49	1.52	2M	0.70	0.74	1Y	-3.00	0.00	SW	0.6250	0.6250	1.6842/58
3Y	1.90	1.93	3M	0.70	0.74	2Y	-3.00	0.00	1M	0.6250	0.6250	
4Y	2.21	2.24	6M	0.78	0.82	3Y	-3.00	0.00	2M	0.6250	0.6250	JPY
5Y	2.51	2.54	9M	0.85	0.89	4Y	-3.00	0.00	3M	0.6250	0.6250	105.65/69
6Y	2.77	3.81	1Y	0.95	0.99	5Y	-3.00	0.00	4M	0.6875	0.6875	
7Y	3.05	3.08				7Y	-3.00	-1.00	5M	0.6875	0.6875	EUR
10Y	3.55	3.59				10Y	-3.00	-1.00	6M	0.6875	0.6875	1.2741/43
12Y	3.61	3.71							9M	0.7500	0.7500	
15Y	3.72	3.82							1Y	0.8750	0.8750	

SIBOR FIX		CAPS & FLOORS		
Mon 09-Feb		1Y	56.00	63.50
1M	0.75000	2Y	54.50	58.00
2M	0.75000	3Y	49.00	52.50
3M	0.75000	4Y	44.50	47.50
6M	0.81250	5Y	40.00	43.50
12M	1.00000	7Y	33.50	37.50
		10Y	28.00	32.00

SWAPTIONS (MID)

Ex	1Y	2Y	3Y	5Y	10Y
3M	#	#	#	44.00	34.50
6M	#	#	#	41.50	32.50
1Y	56.00	47.50	43.00	37.50	#
2Y	41.00	38.50	35.50	31.00	#
3Y	35.50	32.50	30.50	27.00	#
5Y	26.00	24.50	24.00	23.25	#

Australia 61 2 9777 8600 Brazil 5511 3048 4500 Europe 44 20 7330 7500 Germany 49 69 920410
Hong Kong 852 2977 6000 Japan 81 3 3201 8900 Singapore 65 6212 1000 U.S. 1 212 318 2000 Copyright 2004 Bloomberg L.P.
G926-802-2 09-Feb-04 12:30:33

Figure 14.17 Tullett Singapore dollar composite page

```
GRAB                                                          Govt  SMKP
(c) 2003 Tullett Financial Information                        Page 3 of 4
                                                      09-Feb-04 12:29 GMT
                     TAIWAN DOLLAR COMPOSITE

IR SWAPS      TWD/USD SWAPS      SPOT FX
 Act/365      Sem Mny/6M (L)      TWD
1.15 1.19  1Y  0.73  0.83       | 33.17/27
1.49 1.53  2Y  1.05  1.15       |
1.82 1.86  3Y  1.35  1.45       |  JPY
2.02 2.06  4Y  1.55  1.65       | 105.65/69
2.22 2.26  5Y  1.68  1.78       |
2.45 2.55  7Y  1.81  1.91       |  EUR
2.73 2.83  10Y 1.96  2.06       | 1.2741/43

Australia 61 2 9777 8600         Brazil 5511 3048 4500         Europe 44 20 7330 7500         Germany 49 69 920410
Hong Kong 852 2977 6000 Japan 81 3 3201 8900 Singapore 65 6212 1000 U.S. 1 212 318 2000 Copyright 2004 Bloomberg L.P.
                                                                          G926-802-2 09-Feb-04 12:31:10
```

Figure 14.18 Tullett Taiwan dollar composite page

Calculation screens

A number of analytics pages are also used by swap traders and analysts. Figure 14.19 on page 694 shows the vanilla swap calculator page, BCSW. We illustrate its use to price a five-year Singapore dollar swap where there the floating leg has a spread below Libor of 15 basis points. As there is a spread, the fixed rate will differ from the standard interbank quote for five-year SGD swaps, which was 2.317% on the calculation date of 22 March 2004. The terms of the swap are:

Trade date:	22 March 2004
Effective date:	24 March 2004
Nominal:	SGD 10,000,000
Floating-rate:	Libor minus 15 bps
Curve:	Singapore government benchmark (Bloomberg number 44)
Floating pay:	Semi-annual, act/365
Fixed pay:	Semi-annual, act/365.

Figure 14.19(a) shows the calculation and that the fixed rate for the swap was 2.16750%. This differs from the swap rate because of the spread under Libor on the floating side. The standard swap rate of 2.317% can be seen on the swap rate curve on the right-hand side of the screen. As the swap is being calculated as at its start date, the market value and accrued is zero. Figure 14.19(b) shows the cash flows for the swap; this is page 2 of the screen.

This screen can also be used to obtain the present-value of an existing swap, used when swaps are terminated ahead of maturity (and a one-off cash payment is made to close out the swap). The user selects the yield curve against which the swap is valued, usually the generic benchmark curve. For this particular swap the curve selected was number 44 on the Bloomberg menu, the Singapore government bond yield curve.

Screen SWPM, shown in Figure 14.20(a) on page 695, allows greater flexibility as more of the swap terms can be set by the user themselves. For comparison we have used the terms for the same Singapore dollar swap calculated using screen BCSW in Figure 14.19. The one difference is that we have elected for the floating leg to pay quarterly, rather than semi-annual, payments; the fixed leg still pays semi-annually. We can see the difference this causes to the DV01 measure, which was SGD4,738 in the first swap against SGD4,507 in this one. The "Index" is also different, which is expected: the first swap seen in Figure 14.19(a) shows the six-month SGD fix, whereas the rate shown on Figure 14.20(a) is the three-month rate, since this swap pays floating-rate quarterly. All this can be observed on the screen.

Figure 14.20(b) is from the same screen, with the user selecting

2 <Go>

to view the swap curve.

Figure 14.21 on page 696 is the swaption valuation page OVSW. We have input details for a one-year option on the same SGD swap analysed in Figure 14.19. The user must select the pricing model as well as other parameters such as the volatility level. We show the same swaption valuation using first the Black 76 model in Figure 14.21(a) and the Black–Derman–Toy model in Figure 14.21(b). As expected the option premium differs according to the model selected. The zero-yield volatilities are listed on the bottom right-hand of the screen.

Note how the fixed rate calculated for the swap is the five-year forward rate in one year's time.

```
<HELP> for explanation.                                    N219 Govt  BCSW
CMPN
        SWAP VALUATION                                  Swap Curve
Settlement  3/24/04   Calculate 1               M Bid/Ask/Mid  SD Curve # 44
R Receive  Currency SD   1-Fixed Coupon            BGN CURVE DATED  3/22/04
Maturity    3/24/09   2-Spread                        Rates as of  3/22/04
Effective Date 3/24/04  3-Premium                 Cash Rates      Swap Rates
Notional     10,000,000                           1 Wk  0.605     2 Yr  1.325
             FIXED         FLOATING               1 Mo  0.646     3 Yr  1.697
Coupon              2.16750%  Index  0.72854%     2 Mo  0.679     4 Yr  2.020
Nominal Payment Date 3/24  +  Spread -15.00 bp    3 Mo  0.684      Mty  2.317
First Cpn Date      9/24/04         9/24/04       4 Mo  0.699     7 Yr  2.825
Next to Last Cpn Dt 9/24/08         9/24/08       5 Mo  0.713     10Yr  3.325
Freq/DayCount  S  ACT/365     S/S   ACT/365       Reset 0.729     15Yr  3.540
Business Day Adjustment:  3                       9 Mo  0.790
Swap Premium                        0.0000        1 Yr  0.890
Prin. Value                          0.00
Accrued                              0.00
Market Value                         0.00
                                                  Enter:
  10 DV01 (Equv)            4 Mod. Dur. (Equv)    1 <Go> Update Swap Curve
                                                  2 <Go> View Cashflows
FIXED        4738.51               4.77           3 <Go> Horizon Analysis
FLOATING     -482.99              -0.49           4 <Go> To Save Swap
NET          4255.52               4.29
Australia 61 2 9777 8600      Brazil 5511 3048 4500      Europe 44 20 7330 7500      Germany 49 69 920410
Hong Kong 852 2977 6000 Japan 81 3 3201 8900 Singapore 65 6212 1000 U.S. 1 212 318 2000 Copyright 2004 Bloomberg L.P.
                                                                        G926-802-0 22-Mar-04 11:13:11
```

Figure 14.19(a) Bloomberg screen BCSW, swap valuation page, calculation on 22 March 2004


```
<HELP> for explanation.                                    N219 Govt  BCSW
                    SWAP VALIDATION SCREEN
                                                              Page  1/ 1
Pay/Rec   R       Maturity          Effective Date       Settlement
                  3/24/2009           3/24/2004           3/24/2004
         Coupon     Spread       Pay   Reset    Day Cnt          Notional
Fixed  2.16750%                   S             ACT/365          10000000
Float  0.72854% + -15.0bp         S     S       ACT/365          10000000

Currency SD      Payments                          Present       3         5
Date         Fixed        Float          Net        Value     FltIndex  SpotRate
9/24/04    109265.75     29164.76     80101.00     79807.89             0.728540
3/24/05    107484.25     44877.82     62606.42     62052.70   1.054995  0.892347
9/26/05    110453.42     71533.26     38920.16     38272.90   1.553744  1.120294
3/24/06    106296.58     90242.06     16054.51     15634.92   1.990131  1.341836
9/25/06    109859.59    108138.58      1721.00      1656.85   2.283545  1.544626
3/26/07    108078.08    124393.95    -16315.86    -15503.20   2.644714  1.744129
9/24/07    108078.08    136617.05    -28538.97    -26732.28   2.889847  1.928719
3/24/08    108078.08    151813.25    -43735.17    -40324.14   3.194606  2.113309
9/24/08    109265.75    167036.01    -57770.25    -52350.56   3.463486  2.297103
3/24/09    107484.25    177748.87    -70264.63    -62515.08   3.734439  2.477900

                                             Total        0.00
Australia 61 2 9777 8600      Brazil 5511 3048 4500      Europe 44 20 7330 7500      Germany 49 69 920410
Hong Kong 852 2977 6000 Japan 81 3 3201 8900 Singapore 65 6212 1000 U.S. 1 212 318 2000 Copyright 2004 Bloomberg L.P.
                                                                        G926-802-0 22-Mar-04 11:13:18
```

Figure 14.19(b) Bloomberg screen BCSW, page forward to show swap cash flows

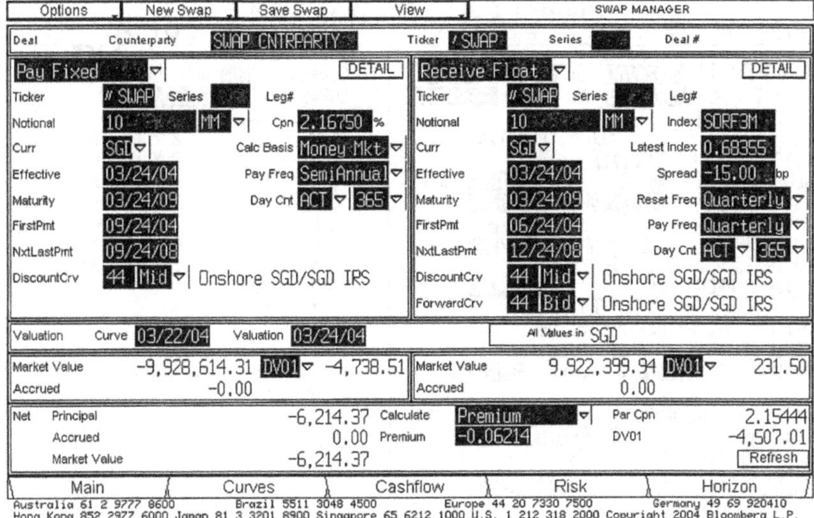

Figure 14.20(a) Bloomberg screen SWPM, user-selected swap calculator on 22 March 2004 to analyse same swap shown in Figure 14.19

<HELP> for explanation. N219 Govt SWPM

Options | New Swap | Save Swap | View | SWAP MANAGER

Deal Counterparty SWAP CNTRPARTY Ticker / SWAP Series Deal #

Curve # 44 Mid Onshore SGD/SGD IRS EXPORT TO EXCEL Mty Par Cpn 2.31750 Stub Reset 0.68355

#	TERM	RATE	DISCNT	#	TERM	RATE	DISCNT	#	TERM	RATE	DISCNT
1	1 DY	0.47995	0.999987	13	5 YR	2.31750	0.889709				
2	1 WK	0.60470	0.999884	14	7 YR	2.82500	0.817791				
3	1 MO	0.64634	0.999416	15	10 YR	3.32500	0.710153				
4	2 MO	0.67933	0.998866	16	12 YR	3.42000	0.655584				
5	3 MO	0.68355	0.998280	17	15 YR	3.54000	0.578655				
6	6 MO	0.72854	0.996341								
7	9 MO	0.79007	0.994083								
8	1 YR	0.89000	0.991155								
9	18 MO	1.11250	0.983369								
10	2 YR	1.32500	0.973885								
11	3 YR	1.69750	0.950192								
12	4 YR	2.02000	0.922007								

DAYTYPE/FREQ CONVENTIONS: ACT/365; ACT/365 (S; Standard

INTERPOLATION METHOD: Piecewise Linear (Simple)

GLOBAL CHANGE FIELDS: From 1 To 17 Shift 0.00

Valuation Curve 03/22/04 Valuation 03/24/04 All Values in SGD

Market Value -9,928,614.31 DV01 -4,738.51 | Market Value 9,922,399.94 DV01 231.50

Accrued -0.00 | Accrued 0.00

Net Principal -6,214.37 Par Cpn 2.15444

Accrued 0.00 Premium -0.06214 DV01 -4,507.01

Market Value -6,214.37 Refresh

Main | Curves | Cashflow | Risk | Horizon

Australia 61 2 9777 8600 Brazil 5511 3048 4500 Europe 44 20 7330 7500 Germany 49 69 920410
Hong Kong 852 2977 6000 Japan 81 3 3201 8900 Singapore 65 6212 1000 U.S. 1 212 318 2000 Copyright 2004 Bloomberg L.P.
G926-802-2 22-Mar-04 12:08:49

Figure 14.20(b) Bloomberg screen SWPM, page forward to show swap curve

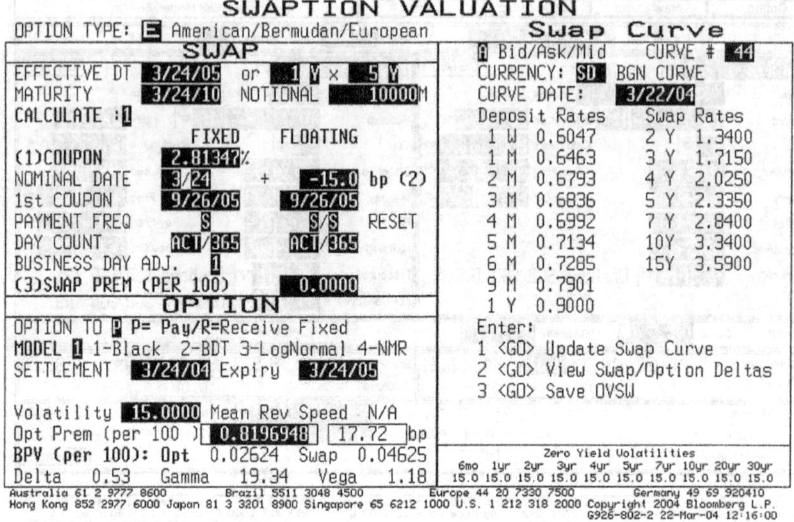

Figure 14.21(a) Bloomberg screen OVSW, swaption valuation screen for SGD swap on 22 March 2004, using Black 76 model

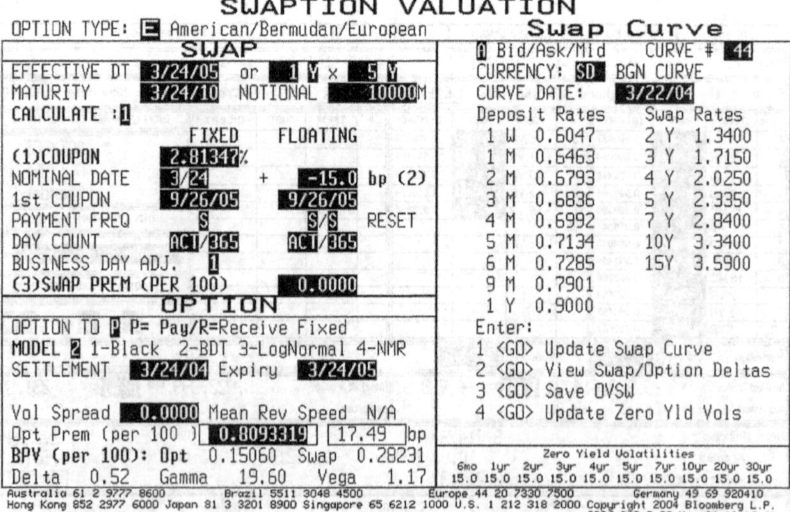

Figure 14.21(b) Bloomberg screen OVSW, swaption valuation screen using Black–Derman–Toy model

Swap rates and the convexity bias

It is common for swaps traders to calculate swaps prices from the prices of interest-rate futures contracts. The price of a futures contract is the implied three-month forward rate on the expiry date of the contract. However, there are differences in the way that futures contracts and swaps behave that means swap rates derived from futures prices, or a zero-coupon yield curve constructed from futures contracts and swap rates, will not be completely accurate. The main difference between the two instruments is that futures contracts move in minimum increments of a tick, which applies to the number of months covered by the contract. Swaps on the other hand have less discrete rate movements and accrue interest on a daily basis. These differences lead to swap rates exhibiting lower convexity than futures prices, which can lead to inaccuracies in pricing. In this section we review the impact of the *convexity bias* and how it should be accounted for in futures and swaps analysis. The convexity bias in interest rate futures contracts was first highlighted by Galen Burghardt in a research paper for Dean Witter Futures in 1994. This paper was later published in Burghardt (2003). The original paper was a ground-breaking piece of research and led to changes in the way futures are used to price swaps.

The convexity bias in futures contracts

Although in practice the rates implied by futures contracts are assumed to be equal to actual forward rates, for longer-dated futures contracts, differences in the way that forwards and exchange-traded futures are handled will result in futures rates not being equal to forward rates. In this section we review how the difference between rates implied by futures contracts and forward rates in practice must be taken into account when pricing long-dated forward instruments.

The convexity bias is the term used to explain the observation that the price of futures contracts such as the Eurodollar contract (traded on the Chicago Mercantile Exchange) should in fact be lower than their fair value; that is, the three-month interest rates implied by the contract should be higher than the three-month forward rates to which they are tied. The bias becomes more prominent for longer-dated contracts, but is negligible for contracts that have an expiry date of under two years. The presence of this bias will however influence the fair value for a swap; for example, a five-year swap rate should be lower than the yield implied by the first five years of the Eurodollar contract. Where swap rates do not take the convexity bias into account, there would be an advantage to being short of the swap, against a hedge with futures contracts. Let us consider the main issues.

Interest-rate swaps and futures contracts such as Eurodollar futures are both priced under the same type of forward interest-rate environment. The two instruments are fundamentally different in one key respect; however, with an interest-rate swap, cash flows are exchanged (in fact a net cash payment) only once for each leg of a swap, and then only in arrears. With an exchange-traded futures contract though, profits and losses are settled every day. The difference in the way profit and loss are settled affects the values of swap and futures relative to each other. The resulting bias acts in favour of a short swap (paying floating, receiving fixed) against a long futures contract. It is therefore important to measure the extent of this bias when calculating swap rates. As first reported by Burghardt (2003), the bias is worth about 6 basis points for a five-year swap, when compared to the price implied by the Eurodollar futures contract. For a 10-year swap the bias is about 18 basis points.

Interest-rate swaps and futures

From our reading of the chapter to now, we are familiar with the structure of an interest-rate swap as being an exchange of fixed- versus floating-rate interest payments on a specified notional principal. The floating-leg may be on any required basis but is usually reset on a semi-annual or quarterly basis. A five-year swap that paid fixed and received quarterly floating payments would require the floating-rate to be reset 20 times during its life, once when the swap was transacted and then every three months thereafter. We may therefore view the swap as being conceptually the same as the sum of 20 separate segments, with the value of each segment being dependent on the fixed rate of the swap and on the market's expectation of what the floating-rate will be on the quarterly reset date.

The basis point value (BPV) of a swap is given by (14.31) and is the amount by which the swap changes value for every basis point that the closing day's same-maturity swap rate fixes above or below the swap fixed rate. A change in value given by a change in market rates is not realised on the day however,[11] but is realised on the maturity of the swap.

$$BPV = 0.00001 \times \frac{d}{B} \times M \tag{14.31}$$

where

[11] The mark-to-market is unrealised p&l.

d is the number of days in the floating period
B is the year day-base (360 or 365)
M is the notional principal of the swap.

The BPV of a futures contract is fixed, however, irrespective of the maturity of the contract, and is the "tick value" of the contract itself. For example, the Eurodollar futures contract has a BPV of $25, while the short-sterling contract on LIFFE has a tick value of £6.25. In a combined position therefore, consisting of an interest-rate swap hedged with futures contracts, both instruments are sensitive to the same change in interest rates. If we wish to compare the effects of a change in the value of both instruments, the most straightforward way to do this is to use the present value for both price changes. As futures contracts are settled on a daily basis, the present value of its basis point value is unchanged, so this is $25 in the case of the Eurodollar contract. The present value of the BPV of an interest-rate swap can be determined using a set of futures rates from a strip of similar maturity. How could we obtain the discount rate used?

In his illustration, Burghardt (2003) assumed a hypothetical $100 million five-year swap, with quarterly floating coupons, with a BPV of $2,500, but with a forward start date five years away. We require a means of calculating the present value of the BPV. Ordinarily we would require the five-year discount rate. However, the simplest way to calculate the present value is to first calculate what $1 would grow to if we invested it at the successive rates given by the futures strip, out to five years (that is, invest for the first 91 days at the front month futures rate, then the next 91 days for the following contract's futures rate and so on). Let us say that this resulted in a future value of $1.55 at the end of the five-year period. This would give us a present value of: $1/$1.55 = 0.645161. That is, $0.645161 is the present value of $1 to be received in five years' time. We may use this value to calculate the present value of our hypothetical five-year swap. We said that this had a BPV of $2,500, so the present value of this sum is obtained as follows:

$$\$2,500 \times 0.645161 = \$1,612.90.$$

Given these values, we can determine the number of Eurodollar futures contracts that would be required to hedge our hypothetical swap, which is 1 612.90/25 = 64.516 or 65 contracts. That is, 65 Eurodollar futures would have the same exposure to a change in the five-year three-month forward rate, as would the $100 million five-year swap. If a bank is short the swap, that is receiving fixed-rate and paying floating-rate, it could hedge the interest-rate exposure arising from a rise in the forward rate by selling 65 Eurodollar futures. Therefore we may set the hedge calculation for any leg of a swap whose floating-rate is three-month Libor as (14.32):

$$Hedge\ ratio = \frac{M \times (0.00001 \times \frac{d}{B}) \times P_{zero\text{-}coupon}}{PV(BPV_{fut})} \qquad (14.32)$$

where $P_{zero\text{-}coupon}$ is the price today of a bond that pays $1 on the same day when the swap settlement is paid. In the hypothetical example we discussed, the swap settlement is five years away, and the price of such a bond was given as 0.645161. The denominator of (14.32) requires the present value of the BPV of the futures contract; however, this is for a cash flow that is received on the same day so it is unchanged from the BPV itself.

The BPV of the future and the swap is a measure of their interest-rate risk. A swap contract has another type of interest-rate risk, however. Since any gain or loss on a swap contract in unrealised, and realised only at the end of the term, a swap may have unrealised asset value. In particular, the present value of a short position in the hypothetical swap we described may be calculated using (14.33):

$$PV_{swap} = M \times ((r_{swap} - rf) \times \frac{d}{B}) \times P_{zero\text{-}coupon} \qquad (14.33)$$

where

r_{swap} is the swap fixed rate
rf is the current market same-maturity forward rate.

Equation (14.33) tells us that the unrealised asset value of a swap depends both on the difference between the swap fixed rate and the market swap rate, as well as on the present value of one dollar (or pound or euro) to be received on the swap's maturity date. In effect, (14.33) states that there are in fact two sources of interest-rate risk in a forward-starting swap. The first is the uncertainty surrounding the forward rate *rf*. The other concerns uncertainty about the zero-coupon bond price, which is a reflection of the term structure of forward rates from today to the swap cash settlement date. If the forward rate turns out to be below the fixed rate, then this would present a loss to the swap holder if he or she is receiving fixed and paying floating; thus this swap is an asset whose value is reduced in the event of a general rise in interest rates. To protect against interest-rate risk then, the person hedging the swap must not only offset the exposure to changes in the forward rate, but also the exposure to changes in the term structure of the zero-coupon yield curve as well. This may be done by buying or selling an appropriate quantity of zero-coupon bonds whose maturity matches that of the swap.

This is the key difference between an interest-rate swap and a futures contract. With contracts such as Eurodollar futures the only source of market risk is the forward or futures rate. When the futures rate changes, the holder of a futures contract experiences a profit or loss, and collects the profit or pays out the loss the next day. The holder of a swap however faces two types of risk, arising from a change in the forward rate and a change in the term rate. What is the impact of this?

The effect on the change in value of the swap contract will differ from interest-rate moves in different directions, because of the convexity effect, while the futures will experience the same change whatever direction rates move in. Put another way, and alluding to our hypothetical example again, if the prices of all futures contracts from the front month out the five-year contract moved up or down by 10 basis points, the effect on the p&l of our 65 contracts would be the same. However, the swap would behave differently. If there were a parallel shift upwards of 10 basis points, the present value of the loss on the five-year swap would be lower than the present value of the profit if there were a parallel shift downwards of the same magnitude. The precise amounts will depend on the maturity and BPV of the swap; however, for the purposes of our discussion, the hedge position of futures contracts makes a net gain if there is a rise in forward rates and loss if forward rates fall. Remember this is from the point of view of someone who is short the swap. The opposite will apply for someone long the swap.

This relationship is illustrated graphically in Figure 14.22.

As a result of the difference in convexities of the two instruments, a short swap hedged with a short position in Eurodollar futures benefits from changes in the level of interest rates. The difference in the performance of a swap and a futures contract is a function of the:

- magnitude of the change in the forward rate;
- magnitude of the change in the term rate (or zero-coupon bond price);
- correlation between the two rates.

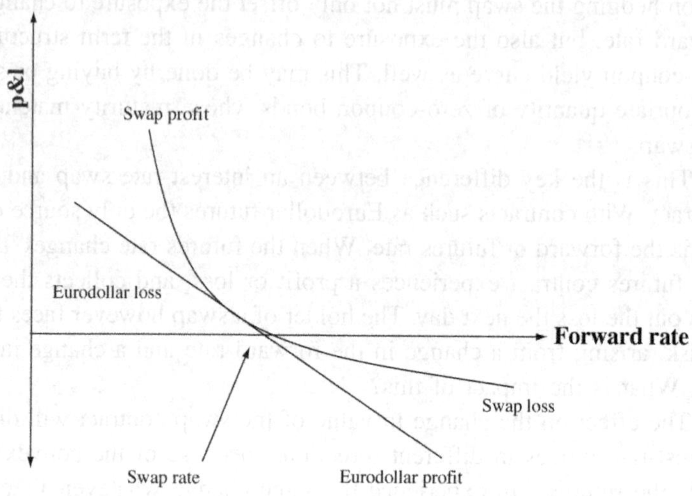

Figure 14.22 The convexity difference between swaps and futures

As we might expect, there is a very close positive correlation between forward interest rates and zero-coupon rates, verging on unity. With virtually no exceptions, increases in the forward rate are accompanied by increases in the term rate, and vice-versa.

Calculating the convexity bias

Banks often calculate the value of the convexity bias by empirical analysis of their futures and swaps p&l history. There is a more systematic approach that may be used, however, and this involves estimating the bias using three parameters: the volatility of the forward rate, the volatility of the corresponding term rate and the correlation between the two rates – the three factors we noted above. The extent of the bias can be measured using (14.34), first demonstrated by Burghardt (2003), which calculates the *drift* in the spread between the futures rates and the forward rates. This drift is the amount of bias that must be accounted for when, say, pricing swaps or arranging a hedge.

$$CVbias = s_{rf} \times s_{rs} \times r_{rf/rs} \tag{14.34}$$

where

$CVbias$ is the amount of drift
s_{rf} is the standard deviation of changes in the forward rate
s_{rs} is the standard deviation of changes in the zero-coupon rate
$r_{rf/rs}$ is the correlation coefficient between changes in the two rates.

The drift is the number of ticks that the swap rate spread has to fall during any given period to compensate for the convexity bias. The derivation of this expression is given in Appendix 14.2.

The value of the convexity bias is a function of the convexity of the forward swap that is associated with the futures contract. This depends in turn on the price sensitivity of the zero-coupon bond that corresponds to the swap maturity. Since the price of a zero-coupon bond with, say, five years to maturity is more interest-rate sensitive than the price of a bond with less than five years to maturity (measured by the modified duration of the bond), the value of the bias is higher the longer the maturity of the futures contract. This is why the convexity bias effect is greatest for long-dated futures and swaps positions. The highlighting of the convexity bias is a relatively recent phenomenon for this reason; as the longest-dated futures contracts have extended out to 10 years, and very long-dated swaps are now fairly common, the impact of the convexity bias has been more pronounced.

Impact of the convexity bias

It is common practice for swaps traders to price forward-starting dollar swaps against Eurodollar futures contracts, and this is not surprising given the liquidity and transparency of the contract, as well as its narrow bid–offer spread. However, the convexity bias that results from the inherent differences between the two instruments makes it important for traders to price in the effect of the bias for long-dated forward swaps. By adjusting the prices of futures contracts by the amount of the convexity bias before using them to calculate the implied swap rate, we will obtain a more accurate reflection of the forward rates implied by the futures prices. The extent of the bias is indicated in Table 14.17, which was calculated as the convexity bias to be applied for Eurodollar contracts used to price forward swaps during 1994 and is reproduced with kind permission of McGraw-Hill from Burghardt (2003).

Swap term (years)

Years forward	1	2	3	4	5	6	7	8	9	10
Spot	0.23	1.08	2.32	3.83	5.58	7.57	9.77	12.189	14.79	17.58
1	1.99	3.49	5.23	7.21	9.44	11.88	14.55	17.42	20.48	
2	5.11	7.05	9.25	11.71	14.39	17.32	20.46	23.78		
3	9.16	11.58	14.31	17.24	20.43	23.85	27.47			
4	14.22	17.22	20.42	23.91	27.61	31.52				
5	20.48	23.94	27.71	31.73	35.95					
6	27.71	31.81	36.14	40.69						
7	36.28	40.91	45.77							
8	45.93	51.13								
9	56.76									

Table 14.17 Convexity bias in forward swaps (basis points)
Reproduced with permission from Burghardt, G. (2003),
The Eurodollar Futures and Options Handbook, McGraw-Hill, New York.

Any calculation of convexity bias is based on an assumption about the volatility of market interest rates. This assumption must be advertised before the values may be used. From Table 14.17 we see that the bias effect is greatest for long-dated long forward swaps. The effect is least for "spot swaps" or swaps that have an immediate effective date. Therefore at the time that these rates were effective, if we were pricing a five-year swap with a one-year forward start date, we would adjust the one-year futures contract by 9.44 basis points before using it to calculate the swap rate.

The other effect of the convexity bias concerns the marking-to-market of the swap book. The common practice is for the mark to be based on the closing prices of the futures contracts, and for dollar swaps this may go out to long-dated swaps. However, the convexity bias means that Eurodollar futures prices produce forward rates that are higher than the forward rates that should ideally be used to value swaps. Therefore some banks make an allowance for the value of the bias, which enables a more accurate picture of the value of the swap book to be drawn. However, such an adjustment is based on assumptions of interest-rate volatilities, which is one reason why many banks do not make the convexity adjustment.

Example 14.10 Using Bloomberg to observe convexity bias in the Eurodollar contract

Figure 14.23 shows the Eurodollar futures analysis, page EDS on Bloomberg, as at 2 June 2004. This shows the implied three-month USD Libor rates from the futures prices, starting with the Jun04 contract, as well as the actual cash rates as at that date. Exchange-traded futures contracts, including the Eurodollar, trade at a fixed value per basis point, and hence have zero convexity. However, the market uses these contracts to hedge other instruments that do possess a convexity effect, hence the impact on this when undertaking hedging, especially for longer-dated assets, which needs to be known as well. Hitting

1 <Go>

at page EDS will bring up the convexity bias analysis for this contract. We see from Figure 14.24 that this is calculated as the:

futures rate – the adjusted rate

and is shown under column 7 of Figure 14.24.

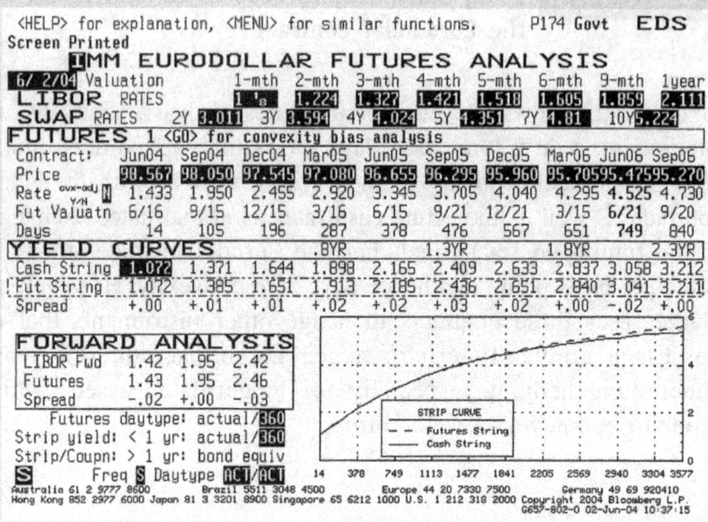

Figure 14.23 Eurodollar futures analysis, Bloomberg page EDS, as at 2 June 2004

<HELP> for explanation. P174 Comdty EDS
Screen Printed

IMM EURODOLLAR FUTURES ANALYSIS

6/ 2/04 Valuation Mean Rev Speed 0.030 Rate Volatility 1.145%

(1) Valuation Date	(2) #of Days	(3) Futures Price	(4) Future Rate	(5) Adjust Rate	(6) Cash Forwrd	(7) Convexi Bias bp	(8) Future Strip	(9) Adj Fu Strip	(10) Cash Strip	(11) = 8-9
6/16/04	14	98.5675	1.4325	1.4324	1.4163	0.01	1.0723	1.0723	1.0723	0.00bp
9/15/04	105	98.0500	1.9500	1.9485	1.9514	0.15	1.3850	1.3849	1.3709	0.01
12/15/04	196	97.5450	2.4550	2.4513	2.4220	0.37	1.6510	1.6502	1.6440	0.08
3/16/05	287	97.0800	2.9200	2.9133	2.9616	0.67	1.9129	1.9112	1.8976	0.17
6/15/05	378	96.6550	3.3450	3.3343	3.2784	1.07	2.1849	2.1820	2.1645	0.29
9/21/05	476	96.2950	3.7050	3.6897	3.6872	1.53	2.4359	2.4314	2.4092	0.46
12/21/05	567	95.9600	4.0400	4.0198	4.0439	2.02	2.6505	2.6442	2.6332	0.63
3/15/06	651	95.7050	4.2950	4.2684	4.3064	2.66	2.8397	2.8316	2.8368	0.82
6/21/06	749	95.4750	4.5250	4.4916	4.2123	3.34	3.0406	3.0299	3.0580	1.07
9/20/06	840	95.2700	4.7300	4.6892		4.08	3.2108	3.1976	3.2121	1.32

(4)-(5)=(7)

Futures daytype: ACT/360
Strip yield (<1 yr): ACT/360
Strip/Coupn (>1 yr): bond equiv
S Freq S Daytype ACT/ACT

Hit <MENU> to return main page

Australia 61 2 9777 8600 Brazil 5511 3048 4500 Europe 44 20 7330 7500 Germany 49 69 920410
Hong Kong 852 2977 6000 Japan 81 3 3201 8900 Singapore 65 6212 1000 U.S. 1 212 318 2000 Copyright 2004 Bloomberg L.P.
G657-802-2 02-Jun-04 10:37:21

Figure 14.24 Convexity bias calculation

Appendices

APPENDIX 14.1 Calculating futures strip rates and implied swap rates

A futures strip is a position that contains one each of the futures contracts in a sequence of contract months. For example, the one-year short sterling strip in August 2004 would consist of one each of the Sep04, Dec04, Mar05 and Jun05 contracts. The two-year strip would contain these but be followed by one each of the Sep05, Dec05, Mar06 and Jun06 contracts. The three-month forward rates that are implied by the prices of these contracts, together with the initial cash market deposit rate for the *stub* period, may be used to obtain the future value of an investment made today. The expression to calculate this is given in (A14.1.1):

$$FV_N = \left(1 + r_0 \times \left(\frac{d_0}{B}\right)\right) \times \left(1 + rf_1 \times \left(\frac{d_0}{B}\right)\right) \times \text{L} \times \left(1 + rf_n \times \left(\frac{d_n}{\text{B}}\right)\right) \tag{A14.1.1}$$

where

FV_N is the future value of £1 invested today for N years
r_0 is the cash market deposit rate (Libor) for the period from today to the expiry date of the first futures contract
rf_1 is the forward rate implied by the price of the front-month futures contract
rf_n is the forward rate implied by the price of the last futures contract in the strip
d_n is the number of days in each futures period, where $i = 0, 1, \ldots n$
B is the year day-base (360 or 365).

The future value of an investment made at futures rates can then be used to calculate implied zero-coupon bond yields. The continuously compounded yield r_{CC} is given by (A14.1.2) while the price $P_{zero\text{-}coupon}$ of a zero-coupon bond of maturity N years is given by (A14.1.3):

$$r_{CC} = ln\left(\frac{FV_N}{N}\right) \tag{A14.1.2}$$

$$P_{zero\text{-}coupon} = \frac{1}{FV_N}. \tag{A14.2.3}$$

The forward rates implied by a strip of futures contracts may be used to calculate implied swap rates. As we saw in this chapter, a plain vanilla interest-rate swap is priced on the basis that it consists of conceptually a short position in a fixed-coupon bond and a long position in a floating-rate bond; that is, a pay fixed- and receive floating-rate swap. The theoretical swap rate is therefore the average of the forward rates given by the futures strip from rf_1 to rf_N where N is the maturity of the swap. The most straightforward way to calculate this is using the discount factors of each spot rate, rather than the forward rates, and this was described in the main body of the text in this chapter.

APPENDIX 14.2 Calculating the convexity bias

Appendix 14.2 is reproduced with kind permission of McGraw-Hill from Burghardt (2003).

A method that is used to calculate the convexity bias in Eurodollar rates, the rate of *drift* relative to forward rates, involves calculating the expected gain when a forward swap is hedged with Eurodollar futures, and assuming specified volatility levels for the change in forward rates and zero-coupon rates.

Swap value

The NPV of a forward swap that receives fixed and pays quarterly floating is given by (A14.2.1):

$$PV_{swap} = M \times (r_{swap} - rf) \times \frac{d}{B} \times P_{zero\text{-}coupon} \qquad \text{(A14.2.1)}$$

where r_{swap} and rf are expressed in basis points. Multiplying the expression by \$1 million and dividing by 90, and them rearranging gives us an expression setting the new present value in terms of the \$25 tick value of a Eurodollar futures contract, shown as (A14.2.2):

$$PV_{swap} = (\frac{M}{\$1m}) \times (r^{¢}_{swap} - rf¢) \times \frac{d}{90} \times \$25 \times P_{zero\text{-}coupon} \qquad \text{(A14.2.2)}$$

At the time the forward swap is transacted the difference between the two rates is zero as the NPV of the swap is zero. As interest rates change, the rate rf and the value of $P_{zero\text{-}coupon}$ both change, which affects the present value of the swap.

Swap p&l and hedge ratio

For a change of Δrf in the forward rate and $\Delta P_{zero\text{-}coupon}$ in the price of the zero-coupon bond, the mark-to-market profit on a forward swap is given by (A14.2.3):

$$\Delta PV = -\left(\frac{M}{\$1m}\right) \times \left(\frac{d}{90}\right) \times \$25 \times \Delta rf \times (P_{zero\text{-}coupon} + \Delta P_{zero\text{-}coupon}). \tag{A14.2.3}$$

The change in the value of one Eurodollar futures contract is equal to the tick value multiplied by the change in the forward rate, therefore the number of contracts required to hedge against \$1 million notional of the swap is given by (A14.2.4):

$$HedgeRatio = -\left(\frac{M}{\$1m}\right) \times \left(\frac{d}{90}\right) \times P_{zero\text{-}coupon}. \tag{A14.2.4}$$

The negative sign in (A14.2.4) indicates that the hedge against the short swap position (receive fixed, pay floating) is a short sale of Eurodollar futures. Given this hedge ratio the profit on the short Eurodollar futures position is expressed as (A14.2.5):

$$\text{Profit or loss} = \left(\frac{M}{\$1m}\right) \times \left(\frac{d}{90}\right) \times P_{zero\text{-}coupon} \times (\Delta rf + drift) \times \$25 \tag{A14.2.5}$$

where *drift* is the systematic change in the Eurodollar futures rate relative to the forward rate required to compensate for the convexity difference between the swap contract and the futures contract.

To preserve no-arbitrage pricing, the expected profit from such a hedge must be zero. That is, the expected profit on the swap must offset precisely the expected profit on the Eurodollar position. This principle enables us to calculate the drift. The expression $(M/\$1m) \times (d/90) \times \$25$ is used to calculate the profit for both swaps and futures, therefore it cancels out. Thus we may set the following expression, which recognises that there is no profit advantage (in theory) between the short swap and futures hedge, so if we arrange the profit expressions as equal to zero, we may rearrange to solve for drift. This is shown as (A14.2.6):

$$E[\Delta rf \times (P_{zero\text{-}coupon} + \Delta P_{zero\text{-}coupon})] = E[P_{zero\text{-}coupon} \times (\Delta rf + drift)] \tag{A14.2.6}$$

where $E[\ ]$ represents the market's expectation today of the value of profit. As $P_{zero\text{-}coupon}$ is known, we may solve for drift by dividing the expression by it, which gives us (A14.2.7):

$$E(drift) = E\left(\Delta rf \times \left(\frac{\Delta P_{zero\text{-}coupon}}{P_{zero\text{-}coupon}}\right)\right). \tag{A14.2.7}$$

This is the expression for the calculation of the convexity bias. Assuming that the average change in forward rates and zero-coupon rates is zero, we may combine the expression with the standard formula for correlation to give us an expression that may be used to approximate the amount of the convexity bias, shown as (A14.2.8):

$$E(drift) = \sigma(\Delta rf) \times \sigma\left(\frac{\Delta P_{zero\text{-}coupon}}{P_{zero\text{-}coupon}}\right) \times \rho\left(\Delta rf, \frac{\Delta P_{zero\text{-}coupon}}{P_{zero\text{-}coupon}}\right). \tag{A14.2.8}$$

No assumption is made about the distribution of rate changes. The drift is expressed in basis points per period.

References and bibliography

Bicksler, J. and Chen, A. 1986, "An Economic Analysis of Interest Rate Swaps", *Journal of Finance,* 41, 3, pp. 645–55.

Block, T. 1994, *Pricing and Hedging Interest-rate Swaps*, Mars Business Associates, Oxford.

Brotherton-Ratcliffe, R. and Iben, B. 1993, "Yield Curve Applications of Swap Products", in Schwartz, R. and Smith, C. (eds), *Advanced Strategies in Financial Risk Management*, New York Institute of Finance, New York.

Burghardt, G. 2003, *The Eurodollar Futures and Options Handbook*, McGraw-Hill New York.

Das, S. 1994, *Swaps and Financial Derivatives*, 2nd edition, IFR Publishing, London.

Decovny, S. 1998, *Swaps* (2nd edition), FT Prentice Hall, London.

Dunbar, N. 2000, "Swaps Volumes See Euro Wane", *Risk*, September London.

Eales, B. 1995, *Financial Risk Management*, McGraw Hill, London, Chapter 3.

Fabozzi, F. (ed.) 1998, *Perspectives on Interest Rate Risk Management for Money Managers and Traders*, FJF Associates, New Hope, PA.

Flavell, R. 2003, *Swaps and Other Derivatives*, John Wiley & Sons, Singapore.

French, K. 1983, "A Comparison of Futures and Forwards Prices", *Journal of Financial Economics*, 12, November, pp. 311–42.

Gup, B. and Brooks, R. 1993, *Interest Rate Risk Management*, Irwin, New York.

Henna, P. 1991, *Interest-rate Risk Management Using Futures and Swaps*, Probus, London.

International Swaps and Derivatives Association 1991, *Code of Standard Working, Assumptions and Provisions for Swaps*, New York.

Jarrow, R. and Turnbul, S. 2000, *Derivative Securities*, 2nd edition, South-Western Publishing, South-Western University, Cincinnati, OH.

Jarrow, R. and Oldfield, G. 1981, "Forward Contracts and Futures Contracts", *Journal of Financial Economics*, 9, December, pp. 373–82.

Khan, M. 2000, "Online Platforms Battle for Business", *Risk*, September.

Kolb, R. 2004, *Futures, Options and Swaps*, 4th edition, Blackwell, Oxford.

Li, A. and Raghavan, V.R. 1996, "LIBOR-In-Arrears Swaps", *Journal of Derivatives,* 3, Spring, pp.44-8.

Lindsay, R. 2000, "High Wire Act", *Risk*, August.

Marshall, J. and Kapner, K. 1990, *Understanding Swap Finance*, South-Western Publishing, South-Western University, Cincinnati, OH.

Park, H. and Chen, A. 1985, "Differences between Futures and Forward Prices: A Further Investigation of Marking to Market Effects", *Journal of Futures Markets,* 5, February, pp. 77–88.

Turnbull, S. 1987, "Swaps: A Zero Sum Game", *Financial Management,* 16, Spring, pp. 15–21.

CHAPTER 15

Hedging using Bond Futures Contracts

A widely used risk-management instrument on ALM desks is the government-bond futures contract. This is an exchange-traded standardised contract that fixes the price today at which a specified quantity and quality of a bond will be delivered at a date during the expiry month of the futures contract. Unlike short-term interest-rate futures, which only require cash settlement, and which we encountered in the section on money markets, bond futures require the actual physical delivery of a bond when they are settled. They are used to hedge longer-dated risk exposures, such as a portfolio of government bonds.

In this chapter we review bond futures contracts and their use for hedging purposes.

Introduction

A bond futures contract represents an underlying physical asset, the bond itself, and a bond must be delivered on expiry of the contract. In this way, bond futures are similar to commodity futures, which also require physical delivery of the underlying commodity.

A futures contract is an agreement between two counterparties that fix the terms of an exchange that will take place between them at some future date. They are standardised agreements as opposed to OTC ones, when traded on an exchange, so they are also referred to as exchange-traded futures. In the United Kingdom, financial futures are traded on LIFFE, which opened in 1982. There are four classes of contract traded on LIFFE: short-term interest-rate contracts; long-term interest-rate contracts (bond futures); currency contracts; and stock-index contracts. We discussed interest-rate futures contracts, which generally trade as part of the money markets, in Chapter 13. In this chapter we will look at bond futures contracts, which are an important part of the banking markets; they are used for hedging and speculative purposes. Most futures contracts on exchanges around the world trade at three-month maturity intervals, with maturity dates fixed in March, June, September and December each year. Therefore, at preset times during the year a contract for each of these months will expire, and a final settlement price is determined for it. The further out one goes, the less liquid the trading is in that contract. It is normal to see liquid trading only in the front month contract (the current contract; for example, if we are trading in April 2006 the front month is the June 2006 future), and possibly one or two of the next contracts, for most bond futures contracts. The liquidity of contracts diminishes the further one trades out in the maturity range.

When a party establishes a position in a futures contract, it can either run this position to maturity or close out the position between trade date and maturity. If a position is closed out, the party will have either a profit or loss to book. If a position is held until maturity, the party who is long the future will take delivery of the underlying asset (bond) at the settlement price; the party who is short futures will deliver the underlying asset. This is referred to as physical settlement or sometimes, confusingly, as cash settlement.

There is no counterparty risk associated with trading exchange-traded futures, because of the role of the clearing house, such as the London Clearing House (LCH). This is the body through which contracts are settled. A clearing house acts as the buyer for all contracts sold on the exchange, and the seller for all contracts that are bought. So in the London market, the LCH acts as the counterparty to all transactions, so that settlement is effectively guaranteed. The clearing house requires all exchange participants to deposit margin with it, a cash sum that is the cost of conducting business (plus broker's commissions). The size of the margin depends on the size of a party's net open position in contracts (an open position is a position in a contract that is held overnight and not closed out). There are two types of margin, maintenance margin and variation margin. Maintenance margin is the minimum level required to be held at the clearing house; the level is set by the exchange. Variation margin is the additional amount that must be deposited to cover any trading losses as the size of the net open positions increases. Note that this is not like margin in, say, a repo transaction. Margin in repo is a safeguard against a drop in value of collateral that has been supplied against a loan of cash. The margin deposited at a futures exchange clearing house acts essentially as "good faith" funds, required to provide comfort to the exchange that the futures trader is able to satisfy the obligations of the futures contract that are being traded.

Figure 15.1 shows the Bloomberg page for US Treasury long bond futures prices.

GRAB Govt CTM
<PAGE> now scrolls 17 contracts. Enter # <GO> to scroll contracts.
Session: D Contract Table
US LONG BOND(CBT)
Exchange Web Page Pricing Date: 3/19/04 Price Display: 2
Chicago Board of Trade --AS REPORTED 3/19 -- 2
Grey date = options trading

	Last	Pct Chg	Time	High	Low	OpenInt 556509	TotVol 18187	Previous Close
1)USH4 Mar04	116-12s	-.35%	Close	116-23	113-21	23157	2274	116-25
2)USM4 Jun04	114-29s	-.35%	Close	115-10	114-25	520921	15753	115-10
3)USU4 Sep04	113-16s	-.36%	Close	113-27b	113-13	12056	159	113-29
4)USZ4 Dec04	112-04s	-.36%	Close			194	0	112-17
5)USH5 Mar05	110-27s	-.37%	Close			181	1	111-08

Australia 61 2 9777 8600 Brazil 5511 3048 4500 Europe 44 20 7330 7500 Germany 49 69 920410
Hong Kong 852 2977 6000 Japan 81 3 3201 8900 Singapore 65 6212 1000 U.S. 1 212 318 2000 Copyright 2004 Bloomberg L.P.
G926-802-0 22-Mar-04 8:45:33

Figure 15.1 Bond futures price quotes, Bloomberg page CTM, 22 March 2004

Bond futures contracts

We have noted that futures contracts traded on an exchange are standardised. This means that each contract represents exactly the same commodity, and it cannot be tailored to meet individual customer requirements. In this section, we describe two very liquid and commonly traded contracts, starting with the US T-bond contract traded on the Chicago Board of Trade (CBOT). The details of this contract are given in Table 15.1.

Unit of trading:	US Treasury bond with notional value of $100,000 and a coupon of 6%
Deliverable grades:	US T-bonds with a minimum maturity of 15 years from first day of delivery month
Delivery months:	March, June, September, December
Delivery date:	Any business day during the delivery month
Last trading day:	12:00 noon, seventh business day before last business day of delivery month
Quotation:	Percent of par expressed as points and thirty seconds of a point; for example, 108–16 is 108 16/32 or 108.50
Minimum price movement:	1/32
Tick value:	$31.25
Trading hours:	07.20 – 14.00 (trading pit) 17.20 – 20.05 22.30 – 06.00 hours (screen trading)

Table 15.1 CBOT US T-Bond futures contract specifications

The terms of this contract relate to a US Treasury bond with a minimum maturity of 15 years and a notional coupon of 6%. A futures contract specifies a notional coupon to prevent delivery and liquidity problems that would arise if there was a shortage of bonds with exactly the coupon required, or if one market participant purchased a large proportion of all the bonds in issue with the required coupon. For exchange-traded futures, a short future can deliver any bond that fits the maturity criteria specified in the contract terms. Of course, a long future would like to be delivered a high-coupon bond with significant accrued interest, while the short future would want to deliver a low-coupon bond with low interest accrued. In fact, this issue does not arise because of the way the invoice amount (the amount paid by the long future to purchase the bond) is calculated. The invoice amount on the expiry date is given in (15.1) below:

$$Inv_{\text{amt}} = P_{fut} \times CF + AI \tag{15.1}$$

where

Inv_{amt}	is the invoice amount
P_{fut}	is the price of the futures contract
CF	is the conversion factor
AI	is the bond accrued interest.

Any bond that meets the maturity specifications of the futures contract is said to be in the delivery basket, the group of bonds that are eligible to be delivered into the futures contract. Every bond in the delivery basket will have its own *conversion factor*, which is used to equalise coupon and accrued interest differences of all the delivery bonds. The exchange will announce the conversion factor for each bond before trading in a contract begins; the conversion factor for a bond will change over time, but remains fixed for one individual contract. That is, if a bond has a conversion factor of 1.091252, this will remain fixed for the life of the contract. If a contract specifies a bond with a notional coupon of 7%, like the long gilt future on LIFFE, then the conversion factor will be less than 1.0 for bonds with a coupon lower than 7% and higher than 1.0 for bonds with a coupon higher than 7%. A formal definition of conversion factor is given below.

Conversion factor

The conversion factor (or price factor) gives the price of an individual cash bond such that its YTM on the delivery day of the futures contract is equal to the notional coupon of the contract. The product of the conversion factor and the futures price is the forward price available in the futures market for that cash bond (plus the cost of funding, referred to as the gross basis).

Although conversion factors equalise the yield on bonds, bonds in the delivery basket will trade at different yields and, for this reason, they are not "equal" at the time of delivery. Certain bonds will be cheaper than others, and one bond will be the cheapest-to-deliver bond. The cheapest-to-deliver bond is the one that gives the greatest return from a strategy of buying a bond and simultaneously selling the futures contract, and then closing out positions on the expiry of the contract. This so-called cash-and-carry trading is actively pursued by proprietary trading desks in banks. If a contract is purchased and then held to maturity the buyer will receive, via the exchange's clearing house, the cheapest-to-deliver gilt. Traders sometimes try to exploit arbitrage price differentials between the future and the cheapest-to-deliver gilt, known as basis trading. This is discussed in the author's book *The REPO Handbook*, Butterworth-Heinemann, Oxford (2002). The mathematical calculation of the conversion factor for the gilt future is given in Appendix 14.1 of Choudhry (2004).

We summarise the contract specification of the long gilt futures contract traded on LIFFE in Table 15.2. There is also a medium gilt contract on

LIFFE, which was introduced in 1998 (having been discontinued in the early 1990s). This trades a notional five-year gilt, with eligible gilts being those of four to seven years maturity.

Unit of trading:	UK gilt bond having a face value of £100,000, a notional coupon of 6% and a notional maturity of 10 years, changed from contract value of £50,000 from the September 1998 contract
Deliverable grades:	UK gilts with a maturity ranging from $8^3/_4$ to 13 years from the first day of the delivery month (changed from 10–15 years from the December 1998 contract)
Delivery months:	March, June, September, December
Delivery date:	Any business day during the delivery month
Last trading day:	11:00 hours two business days before last business day of delivery month
Quotation:	Percent of par expressed as points and hundredths of a point; for example, 114.56 (changed from points and 1/32nds of a point, as in 11,717 meaning 114 17/32 or 114.53125, from the June 1998 contract)
Minimum price movement:	0.01 of one point (one tick)
Tick value:	£10
Trading hours:	08:00–16:15 hours 16:22–18:00 hours All trading conducted electronically on LIFFE Connect

Table 15.2 LIFFE Long gilt future contract specifications

Futures pricing

The theoretical principle

In essence, because a futures contract represents an underlying asset, albeit a synthetic one, its price cannot differ from the actual cash-market price of the asset itself. This is because the market sets futures prices such that they are arbitrage-free. We can illustrate this with a hypothetical example.

Let us say that the benchmark 10-year bond, with a coupon of 8%, is trading at par. This bond is the underlying asset represented by the long bond futures contract; the front month contract expires in precisely three months.

If we also say that the three-month Libor rate (the repo rate) is 6%, what is fair value for the front month futures contract?

For the purpose of illustration, let us start by assuming the futures price to be 105. We could carry out the following arbitrage-type trade:

- buy the bond for £100;
- simultaneously sell the future at £105;
- borrow £100 for three months at the repo rate of 6%.

As this is a leveraged trade, we have borrowed the funds with which to buy the bond, and the loan is fixed at three months because we will hold the position to the futures contract expiry, which is in exactly three months' time. At expiry, as we are short futures we will deliver the underlying bond to the futures clearing house and close out the loan. This strategy will result in cash flows for us as shown below.

Futures settlement cash flows

Price received for bond =	105.00
Bond accrued =	2.00 (8% coupon for three months)
Total proceeds =	107.00

Loan cash flows

Repayment of principal =	100.00
Loan interest =	1.500 (6% repo rate for three months)
Total outlay =	101.50

The trade has resulted in a profit of £5.50, and this profit is guaranteed as we have traded the two positions simultaneously and held them both to maturity. We are not affected by subsequent market movements. The trade is an example of a pure arbitrage, which is risk-free. There is no cash outflow at the start of the trade because we borrowed the funds used to buy the bond. In essence, we have locked in the forward price of the bond by trading the future today, so that the final settlement price of the futures contract is irrelevant. If the situation described above were to occur in practice it would be very short-lived, precisely because arbitrageurs would buy the bond and sell the future to make this profit. This activity would force changes in the prices of both bond and future until the profit opportunity was removed.

So in our illustration, the price of the future was too high (and possibly the price of the bond was too low as well) and not reflecting fair value because the price of the synthetic asset was out of line with the cash asset. What if the price of the future was too low? Let us imagine that the futures contract is trading at 95.00. We could then carry out the following trade:

- sell the bond at 100;
- simultaneously buy the future for 95;
- lend the proceeds of the short sale (100) for three months at 6%.

This trade has the same procedure as the first one, with no initial cash outflow, except that we have to cover the short position in the repo market, through which we invest the sale proceeds at the repo rate of 6%. After three months, we are delivered a bond as part of the futures settlement, and this is used to close out our short position. How has our strategy performed?

Futures settlement cash flows

Clean price of bond =	95.00
Bond accrued =	2.00
Total cash outflow =	97.00

Loan cash flows

Principal on loan maturity =	100.00
Interest from loan =	1.500
Total cash inflow =	101.500

The profit of £4.50 is again a risk-free arbitrage profit. Of course, our hypothetical world has ignored considerations such as bid–offer spreads for the bond, future and repo rates, which would apply in the real world and impact on any trading strategy. Yet again, however, the futures price is out of line with the cash market and has provided opportunity for arbitrage profit.

Given the terms and conditions that apply in our example, there is one price for the futures contract at which no arbitrage–profit opportunity is available. If we set the future price at 99.5, we would see that both trading strategies, buying the bond and selling the future or selling the bond and buying the future, yield a net cash flow of zero. There is no profit to be made from either strategy. So at 99.5 the futures price is in line with the cash market, and it will only move as the cash market price moves; any other price will result in an arbitrage–profit opportunity.

Arbitrage-free futures pricing

The previous section demonstrated how we can arrive at the fair value for a bond futures contract provided we have certain market information. The market mechanism and continuous trading will ensure that the fair price *is* achieved, as arbitrage–profit opportunities are eliminated. We can determine the bond future's price given:

- the coupon of the underlying bond, and its price in the cash market;
- the interest rate for borrowing or lending funds, from the trade date to the maturity date of the futures contract. This is known as the repo rate.

For the purpose of deriving this pricing model we can ignore bid–offer spreads and borrowing and lending spreads. If we set the following:

r	is the repo rate
rc	is the bond's running yield
P_{bond}	is the price of the cash bond
P_{fut}	is the price of the futures contract
t	is the time to the expiry of the futures contract.

We can substitute these symbols into the cash flow profile for our earlier trade strategy, that of buying the bond and selling the future. This gives us:

Futures settlement cash flows

Clean price for bond = P_{fut}

Bond accrued = $rc.t.P_{bond}$

Total proceeds = $P_{fut} + (rc.t.P_{bond})$

Loan cash flows

Repayment of loan principal = P_{bond}

Loan interest = $r.t.P_{bond}$

Total outlay = $P_{bond} + (r.t.P_{bond})$

The profit from the trade would be the difference between the proceeds and outlay, which we can set as follows:

$$\text{Profit} = P_{fut} + rc.t.P_{bond} \quad (P_{bond} + r.t.P_{bond}).$$

We have seen how the futures price is at fair value when there is no profit to be gained from carrying out this trade, so if we set profit at zero, we obtain the following:

$$0 = P_{\text{fut}} + rc.t.P_{\text{bond}} - (P_{\text{bond}} + r.t.P_{\text{bond}}).$$

Solving this expression for the futures price P_{fut} gives us:

$$P_{fut} = P_{\text{bond}} + P_{\text{bond}}\, t(r - rc).$$

Rearranging this we get:

$$P_{fut} = P_{\text{bond}} + (1 + t[r - rc]). \qquad (15.2)$$

If we repeat the procedure for the other strategy, that of selling the bond and simultaneously buying the future, and set the profit to zero, we will obtain the same expression for the futures price as given in (15.2) above.

It is the level of the repo rate in the market, compared to the running yield on the underlying bond, that sets the price for the futures contract. From the examples used at the start of this section we can see that it is the cost of funding compared to the repo rate that determines if the trade strategy results in a profit. The expression $[r - rc]$ from (15.2) is the net financing cost in the arbitrage trade, and is known as the *cost of carry*. If the running yield on the bond is higher than the funding cost (the repo rate) this is positive funding or *positive carry*. Negative funding (*negative carry*) is when the repo rate is higher than the running yield. The level of $[r - rc]$ will determine whether the futures price is trading above the cash market price or below it. If we have positive carry (when $rc > r$) then the futures price will trade below the cash market price, known as trading at a *discount*. Where $r > rc$ and we have negative carry, then the futures price will be at a premium over the cash market price. If the net funding cost was zero, such that we had neither positive or negative carry, then the futures price would be equal to the underlying bond price.

The cost of carry related to a bond futures contract is a function of the yield curve. In a positive yield-curve environment, the three-month repo rate is likely to be lower than the running yield on a bond so that the cost of carry is likely to be positive. As there is generally only a liquid market in long bond futures out to contracts that mature up to one year from the trade date, with a positive yield curve it would be unusual to have a short-term repo rate higher than the running yield on the long bond. So, in such an environment, we would have the future trading at a discount to the underlying cash bond. If there is a negative-sloping yield curve, the futures price will trade at a premium to the cash price. It is in circumstances of changes in the shape of the yield curve that opportunities for relative value and arbitrage trading arise, especially as the bond that is cheapest-to-deliver for the futures contract may change with large changes in the curve.

A trading strategy that involved simultaneous and opposite positions in the cheapest-to-deliver bond (CTD) and the futures contract is known as cash-and-carry trading or basis trading. However, by the law of no-arbitrage pricing, the payoff from such a trading strategy should be zero. If we set the profit from such a trading strategy as zero, we can obtain a pricing formula for the fair value of a futures contract, which summarises the discussion above, and states that the fair-value futures price is a function of the cost of carry on the underlying bond. This is given in (15.3):

$$P_{fut} = \frac{(P_{bond} + AI_0) \times (1 + rt) - \sum_{i=1}^{N} C_i(1 + rt_{i.del}) - AI_{del}}{CF} \qquad (15.3)$$

where

AI_0 is the accrued interest on the underlying bond today

AI_{del} is the accrued interest on the underlying bond on the expiry or delivery date (assuming the bond is delivered on the final day, which will be the case if the running yield on the bond is above the money market rate)

C_i is the i'th coupon

N is the number of coupons paid from today to the expiry or delivery date.

Hedging using futures

The theoretical position

Bond futures are used for a variety of purposes. Much of one day's trading in futures will be speculative; that is, a punt on the direction of the market. Another main use of futures is to hedge bond positions. In theory, when hedging a cash bond position with a bond futures contract, if cash and futures prices move together, then any loss from one position will be offset by a gain from the other. When prices move exactly in lock-step with each other, the hedge is considered perfect. In practice, the price of even the CTD bond (which one can view as being the bond being traded – implicitly –

when one is trading the bond future) and the bond future will not move exactly in line with each other over a period of time. The difference between the cash price and the futures price is called the basis. The risk that the basis will change in an unpredictable way is known as *basis risk.*

The futures basis

The term "basis" is also used to describe the difference in price between the future and the deliverable cash bond. The basis is of considerable significance. It is often used to establish the fair value of a futures contract, as it is a function of the cost of carry. The gross basis is defined (for deliverable bonds only) as follows:

Gross basis = Clean bond price − (Futures price × Conversion factor).

Futures are a liquid and straightforward way of hedging a bond position. By hedging a bond position, the trader or fund manager is hoping to balance the loss on the cash position by the profit gained from the hedge. However, the hedge will not be exact for all bonds except the CTD bond, which we can assume is the futures contract underlying bond. The basis risk in a hedge position arises because the bond being hedged is not identical to the CTD bond. The basic principle is that if the trader is long (or net long, where the desk is running long and short positions in different bonds) in the cash market, an equivalent number of futures contracts will be sold to set up the hedge. If the cash position is short, the trader will buy futures. The hedging requirement can arise for different reasons. A market-maker will wish to hedge positions arising out of client business, when she is unsure when the resulting bond positions will be unwound. A fund manager may, for example, know that he needs to realise a cash sum at a specific time in the future to meet fund liabilities, and sell bonds at that time. The market-maker will want to hedge against a drop in the value of positions during the time the bonds are held. The fund manager will want to hedge against a rise in interest rates between now and the bond sale date, to protect the value of the portfolio.

When putting on the hedge position, the key is to trade the correct number of futures contracts. This is determined by using the hedge ratio of the bond and the future, which is a function of the volatilities of the two instruments. The number of contracts to trade is calculated using the hedge ratio, which is given by:

$$\text{Hedge ratio} = \frac{\text{Volatility of bond to be hedged}}{\text{Volatility of hedging instrument}}.$$

Therefore one needs to use the volatility values of each instrument. We can see from the calculation that if the bond is more volatile than the hedging instrument, then a greater amount of the hedging instrument will be required. Let us now look in greater detail at the hedge ratio.

There are different methods available to calculate hedge ratios. The most common ones are the conversion factor method, which can be used for deliverable bonds (also known as the price factor method) and the modified-duration method (also known as the BPV method).

Where a hedge is put on against a bond that is in the futures delivery basket it is common for the conversion factor to be used to calculate the hedge ratio. A conversion factor hedge ratio is more useful as it is transparent and remains constant, irrespective of any changes in the price of the cash bond or the futures contract. The number of futures contracts required to hedge a deliverable bond using the conversion factor hedge ratio is determined using the following equation:

$$Number\ of\ contracts = \frac{M_{bond} \times CF}{M_{fut}} \tag{15.4}$$

where M is the nominal value of the bond or futures contract.

The conversion factor method may be used only for bonds in the delivery basket. It is important to ensure that this method is only used for one bond. It is an erroneous procedure to use the ratio of conversion factors of two different bonds when calculating a hedge ratio.

Unlike the conversion factor method, the modified-duration hedge ratio may be used for all bonds, both deliverable and non-deliverable. In calculating this hedge ratio the modified duration is multiplied by the dirty price of the cash bond to obtain the BPV. As we discovered in Chapter 4, the BPV represents the actual impact of a change in the yield on the price of a specific bond. The BPV allows the trader to calculate the hedge ratio to reflect the different price sensitivity of the chosen bond (compared to the CTD bond) to interest-rate movements. The hedge ratio calculated using BPVs must be constantly updated, because it will change if the price of the bond and/or the futures contract changes. This may necessitate periodic adjustments to the number of lots used in the hedge. The number of futures contracts required to hedge a bond using the BPV method is calculated using the following:

$$Number\ of\ contracts = \frac{M_{bond}}{M_{fut}} \times \frac{BPV_{bond}}{BPV_{fut}} \tag{15.5}$$

where the BPV of a futures contract is defined with respect to the BPV of its CTD bond, as given by (15.6):

$$BPV_{fut} = \frac{BPV_{CTDbond}}{CF_{CTDbond}}. \tag{15.6}$$

The simplest hedge procedure to undertake is one for a position consisting of only one bond, the CTD bond. The relationship between the futures price and the price of the CTD given by (15.3) indicates that the price of the future will move for moves in the price of the CTD bond; therefore, we may set:

$$\Delta P_{fut} \cong \frac{\Delta P_{bond}}{CF} \tag{15.7}$$

where CF is the CTD conversion factor.

The price of the futures contract, over time, does not move tick-for-tick (although it may on an intra-day basis), but rather by the amount of the change divided by the conversion factor. It is apparent, therefore, that to hedge a position in the CTD bond we must hold the number of futures contracts equivalent to the value of bonds held multiplied by the conversion factor. Obviously, if a conversion factor is less than one, the number of futures contracts will be less than the equivalent nominal value of the cash position; the opposite is true for bonds that have a conversion factor greater than one. However, the hedge is not as simple as dividing the nominal value of the bond position by the nominal value represented by one futures contract (!); this error is frequently made by those new to the desk.

To measure the effectiveness of the hedge position, it is necessary to compare the performance of the futures position with that of the cash bond position, and to see how much the hedge instrument mirrored the performance of the cash instrument. A simple calculation is made to measure the effectiveness of the hedge, given by (15.8), which is the percentage value of the hedge effectiveness.

$$Hedge\ effectiveness = -\left[\frac{Fut\ p/l}{Bond\ p/l}\right] \times 100 \tag{15.8}$$

Hedging a bond portfolio

The principles established above may be applied when hedging a portfolio containing a number of bonds. It is more realistic to consider a portfolio as holding not just bonds that are outside the delivery basket, but are also non-government bonds. In this case, we need to calculate the number of futures contracts to put on as a hedge based on the volatility of each bond in the portfolio compared to the volatility of the CTD bond. Note that, in practice, there is usually more than one futures contract that may be used as the hedge instrument. For example, in the sterling market it would be more sensible to use LIFFE's medium gilt contract, whose underlying bond has a notional maturity of four to seven years, if hedging a portfolio of short- to medium-dated bonds. However, for the purposes of illustration we will assume that only one contract, the long gilt, is available.

To calculate the number of futures contracts required to hold as a hedge against any specific bond, we use the expression in (15.9):

$$Hedge = \frac{M_{bond}}{M_{fut}} \times Vol_{bond/CTD} \times Vol_{CTD/fut} \tag{15.9}$$

where

M is the nominal value of the bond or future

$Vol_{bond/CTD}$ is the relative volatility of the bond being hedged compared to that of the CTD bond

$Vol_{CTD/fut}$ is the relative volatility of the CTD bond compared to that of the future.

It is not necessarily straightforward to determine the relative volatility of a bond vis-à-vis the CTD bond. If the bond being hedged is a government bond, we can calculate the relative volatility using the two bonds' modified duration. This is because the yields of both may be safely assumed to be strongly positively correlated. If, however, the bond being hedged is a corporate bond and/or a non-vanilla bond, we must obtain the relative volatility using regression analysis, as the yields between the two bonds may not be strongly positively correlated. This is apparent when one remembers that the yield spread of corporate bonds over government bonds is not constant, and will fluctuate with changes in government bond yields. To use regression analysis to determine relative volatilities, historical price data on the bond is required. The daily price moves in the target bond and the CTD bond are then analysed to assess the slope of the regression line. In this section, we will restrict the discussion to a portfolio of government bonds.

If we are hedging a portfolio of government bonds, we can use (15.10) to determine relative volatility values, which are based on the modified duration of each of the bonds in the portfolio.

$$Vol_{bond/CTD} = \frac{\Delta P_{bond}}{\Delta P_{CTD}} = \frac{MD_{bond} \times P_{bond}}{MD_{CTD} \times P_{CTD}} \tag{15.10}$$

where MD is the modified duration of the bond being hedged or the CTD bond, as appropriate. This preserves the terminology we introduced in Chapter 4.[1]

Once we have calculated the relative volatility of the bond being hedged, equation (15.11) (obtained by rearranging (15.7)) tells us that the relative volatility of the CTD bond to that of the futures contract is approximately the same as its conversion factor. We are then in a position to calculate the futures hedge for each bond in a portfolio.

$$Vol_{CTD/fut} = \frac{\Delta P_{CTD}}{\Delta P_{fut}} \approx CF_{CTD} \tag{15.11}$$

Table 15.3 shows a portfolio of five UK gilts on 20 October 1999. The nominal value of the bonds in the portfolio is £200 million, and the bonds have a market value, excluding accrued interest, of £206.84 million. Only one of the bonds is a deliverable bond, the 5.75% 2009 gilt, which is in fact the CTD bond. For the Dec99 futures contract the bond had a conversion factor of 0.9124950. The fact that this bond is the CTD explains why it has a relative volatility of 1. We calculate the number of futures contracts required to hedge each position, using the equations listed above. For example, the hedge requirement for the position in the 7% 2002 gilt was calculated as follows:

$$\frac{5{,}000{,}000}{100{,}000} \times \frac{2.245 \times 101.50}{7.235 \times 99.84} \times 0.9124950 = 14.39.$$

[1] In certain textbooks and research documents, it is suggested that the ratio of the conversion factors of the bond being hedged (if it is in the delivery basket) and the CTD bond can be used to determine the relative volatility of the target bond. This is a fallacious argument. The conversion factor of a deliverable bond is the price factor that will set the yield of the bond equal to the notional coupon of the futures contract on the delivery date, and it is a function mainly of the coupon of the deliverable bond. The price volatility of a bond, on the other hand, is a measure of its modified duration, which is a function of the bond's duration (that is, the term to maturity). Therefore, using conversion factors to measure volatility levels will produce erroneous results. It is important not to misuse conversion factors when arranging hedge ratios.

The volatility of all the bonds is calculated relative to the CTD bond, and the number of futures contracts is determined using the conversion factor for the CTD bond. The bond with the highest volatility is, not surprisingly, the 6% 2028, which has the longest maturity of all the bonds and hence the highest modified duration. We note from Table 15.3 that the portfolio requires a hedge position of 2,091 futures contracts. This illustrates how a "rough-and-ready" estimate of the hedging requirement, based on nominal values, would be insufficient as that would suggest a hedge position of only 2000 contracts.

CTD:	5.75% 2009
Modified duration:	7.2345656
Conversion factor:	0.9124950
Price:	99.84

Bond	**Nominal amount (£m)**	**Price**	**Yield %**	**Duration**	**Modified duration**	**Relative volatility**	**Number of contracts**
UKT 8% 2000	12	102.17	5.972	1.072	1.01158797	0.143090242	15.67
UKT 7% 2002	5	101.50	6.367	2.388	2.24505721	0.315483336	14.39
UKT 5% 2004	38	94.74	6.327	4.104	3.85979102	0.50626761	175.55
UKT 5.75% 2009	100	99.84	5.770	7.652	7.23456557	1	912.50
UKT 6% 2028	45	119.25	4.770	15.031	14.3466641	2.368603078	972.60
Total	200						2,090.71

Table 15.3 Bond futures hedge for hypothetical gilt portfolio, 20 October 1999

The effectiveness of the hedge must be monitored over time. No hedge will be completely perfect, however, and the calculation illustrated above, as it uses modified-duration value, does not take into account the convexity effect of the bonds. The reason why a futures hedge will not be perfect is because, in practice, the price of the futures contract will not move tick-for-tick with the CTD bond, at least not over a period of time. This is the basis risk that is inherent in hedging cash bonds with futures. In addition, the calculation of the hedge is only completely accurate for a parallel shift in yields, as it is based on modified duration, so as the yield curve changes around pivots, the hedge will move out of line. Finally, the long gilt future is not the appropriate contract to use to hedge three of the bonds in the portfolio, or over 25% of the portfolio by nominal value. This is because these bonds are short- or medium-dated, and so their price movements will not track the futures price as closely as longer-dated bonds. In this case, the more appropriate futures contract to use would have been the medium gilt contract, or (for the first bond, the 8% 2000) a strip of short sterling contracts. Using shorter-dated instruments would reduce some of the basis risk contained in the portfolio hedge.

The primary hedge measure: bond modified duration and PV01[2]

The main risk sensitivity measure used in calculating hedges is modified duration, or minor variations of this. We observed this earlier in the chapter when we described how to hedge a bond position using futures. The market uses variations of modified duration including the following:

- PV01: the present value of 1 basis point, also referred to as PVBP or DV01 ("dollar value of an 01"). This is the change in the bond's value for a 1 basis point change in market yields.
- Dollar duration: this is the change in bond value for a 1 basis point change in the bond's yield.

In fact both measures are essentially the same thing, and, strictly speaking, only the first one is totally correct if one is following modified duration principles. In any case, once we know an instrument's risk sensitivity, we can construct the hedge, because the futures contract DV01 is fixed and known. Here we use Excel spreadsheets to calculate PV01 for a plain vanilla bond.

[2] Very big, big thanks to Professor Carol Alexander at the ICMA Centre, University of Reading, who let me use her spreadsheets in this section! It is a privilege to work with her.

Table 15.4 on pages 732–3 shows an hypothetical four-year 5% annual coupon bond, valued given an assumed zero-coupon curve. Table 15.5 on pages 734–5 is the same spreadsheet but with the Excel formulas shown in the cells. The PV01 value shows the change in the value of the bond for a 1 basis point parallel shift in the curve; the second calculation shows dollar durations which is the change in the bond price for a 1 basis point change in the bond's yield. The difference between the two calculations is minor.

Table 15.6 on pages 736 shows a three-year bond, with additional calculations of convexity and the change in bond value for a 1 point change in the yield curve. Table 15.7 on pages 737 shows the spreadsheet formulas.

A1	B	C	D	E
2				
3	Time	Cash flow	PV	Time*PV
4	1	4	3.8095	3.8095
5	2	4	3.6281	7.2562
6	3	104	89.8391	269.5173
7	Price		97.2768	
8	Macaulay duration			2.8844
9	Modified duration			2.7470
10	Dollar duration			0.0267
11	Yield	5.00%		
12				

13 Example 4-year bond: assuming zero-coupon curve given, calculation of bond price,

	Years to maturity	Interest rate	Cash flow
15	1	4.5%	5
16	2	4.75%	5
17	3	4.85%	5
18	4	5%	105
19		Macaulay duration	3.72
20			
21			
22			

	Years to maturity	Cash flow	Interest rate
24	1	5	4.5%
25	2	5	4.75%
26	3	5	4.85%
27	4	105	5.0%
28			
29			

	Years to maturity	Cash flow	Yield
31	1	5	4.97%
32	2	5	4.97%
33	3	5	4.97%
34	4	105	4.97%
35			
36			
37		Solver objective:	0.002479757
38			

Table 15.4 Calculation of interest-rate risk sensitivities for a 4-year bond, given a zero-coupon curve

F	G	H	I

yield and interest-rate risk sensitivities

	PV	PV × Maturity
	4.78	4.78
	4.56	9.11
	4.34	13.01
	86.38	345.54
	100.0630	372.45

	PV	Yield –1bp	PV	PV01
	4.7847	4.49%	4.7851	0.00046
	4.5568	4.74%	4.5577	0.00087
	4.3378	4.84%	4.3390	0.00124
	86.3838	4.99%	86.4167	0.03292
	100.0630		100.0985	0.03549
	PV	Yield –1bp	PV	Dollar duration
	4.7633	4.96%	4.7638	0.00045
	4.5379	4.96%	4.5388	0.00086
	4.3231	4.96%	4.3243	0.00124
	86.4885	4.96%	86.5214	0.03297
	100.1128		100.1483	0.03552

A1	B	C	D	E
2				
3	Time	Cash flow	PV	Time*PV
4	1	4	=C4/(1+$C$11)	=B4*D4
5	2	4	=C5/(1+$C$11)^2	=B5*D5
6	3	104	=C6/(1+$C$11)^3	=B6*D6
7	Price		=SUM(D4:D6)	
8	Macaulay duration			=SUM(E4:E6)/D7
9	Modified duration			=E8/(1+C11)
10	Dollar duration			=D7*E9*0.0001
11	Yield	5.00%		
12				
13	Example 4-year bond: assuming zero-coupon curve given, calculation of bond price,			
14		Years to maturity	Interest rate	Cash flow
15		1	4.5%	5
16		2	4.75%	5
17		3	4.85%	5
18		4	5%	105
19			Macaulay duration	=G20/F20
20				
21				
22				
23		Years to maturity	Cash flow	Interest rate
24		1	5	=D16
25		2	5	=D17
26		3	5	=D18
27		4	105	=D19
28				
29				
30		Years to maturity	Cash flow	Yield
31		1	5	4.97%
32		2	5	4.97%
33		3	5	4.97%
34		4	105	4.97%
35				
36				
37			Solver objective:	=(F36–F29)^2
38				

Table 15.5 Table showing Excel formulas

F	G	H	I

yield and interest-rate risk sensitivities

	PV	PV × Maturity
	=E16/(1+D16)	=F16*C16
	=E17/(1+D17)^C17	9.11
	=E18/(1+D18)^C18	13.01
	=E19/(1+D19)^C19	345.54
	=SUM(F16:19)	=SUM(G16:G19)

PV	Yield –1bp	PV	**PV01**
=D25/(1+E25)	=E25–0.0001	=D25/(1+G25)	=H25–F25
=D26/(1+E26)^C26	=E26–0.0001	=D26/(1+G26)^C26	=H26–F26
=D27/(1+E27)^C27	=E27–0.0001	=D27/(1+G27)^C27	=H27–F27
=D28/(1+E28)^C28	=E28–0.0001	=D28/(1+G28)^C28	=H28–F28
=SUM(F25:F28)		=SUM(H25:H28)	=SUM(125:128)
PV	Yield –1bp	PV	**Dollar duration**
=D32/(1+E32)	=E32–0.0001	=D32/(1+G32)	=H32–F32
=D33/(1+E33)^C33	=E33–0.0001	=D33/(1+G33)^C33	=H32–F32
=D34/(1+E34)^C34	=E34–0.0001	=D34/(1+G34)^C34	=H32–F32
=D35/(1+E35)^C35	=E35–0.0001	=D35/(1+G35)^C35	=H32–F32
=SUM(F32:F35)		=SUM(H325:H35)	=SUM(132:135)

A1	B	C	D	E	F	G	H	I	J
2	**Market interest rates**		Coupon =	**5%**	Face value =	**100**			
3	**4%**								
4	**4.25%**		Maturity	Interest rate	Cash flow	PV			
5	**4.50%**		1	4.00%	5	4.81		MaCaulay duration	**2.86**
6	**4.25%**		2	4.25%	5	4.60		Modified duration	**2.74**
7			3	4.50%	105	92.01		Convexity	**10.31**
8			Bond 1		**Price**	**101.419**		Duration–convexity approximation	
9								Yield change	**1%**
10			Maturity	**Yield**	Cash flow	PV	PV*maturity	Percentage price change	**−2.686%**
11			1	4.48%	5	4.79	4.79	Actual percentage price change	**−2.687%**
12			2	4.48%	5	4.58	9.16		
13			3	4.48%	105	92.05	276.16		
14			Bond 1	**4.48%**	0.00	101.42			
15									
16			Maturity	Yield	Cash flow	PV			
17			1	5.48%	5	4.74			
18			2	5.48%	5	4.49			
19			3	5.48%	105	89.46			
20			Bond 1	5.48%	7.43	**98.69**			
21									
22									
23									
24									

Table 15.6 Bond convexity calculation

A1	B	C	D	E	F	G	H
2	**Market interest rates**		Coupon =	**5%**	Face value =	**100**	
3	4%						
4	4.25%		Maturity	Interest Rate	Cash flow	PV	
5	4.50%		1	=B3	=$E$2*$G$2	=F5/(1+E5)	
6	4.25%		2	=B4	=$E$2*$G$2	=F6/(1+E6)^D6	
7			3	=B5	=$E$2*$G$2+G2	=F7/(1+E7)^D7	
8			Bond 1		**Price**	**=SUM(G5:G7)**	
9							
10			Maturity	**Yield**	Cash flow	PV	PV*Maturity
11			1	=E14	=F5	=F11/(1+E11)	=G11*D11
12			2	=E14	=F6	=F12/(1+E12)^D12	=G12*D12
13			3	=E14	=F7	=F13/(1+E13)^D13	=G13*D13
14			Bond 1	**4.48%**	=(G8-G14)^2	=SUM(G11:G13)	
15							
16			Maturity	Yield	Cash flow	PV	
17			1	=E20	=F5	=F17/(1+E17)	
18			2	=E20	=F6	=F18/(1+E18)^D18	
19			3	=E20	=F7	=F19/(1+E19)^D19	
20			Bond 1	=E14+1%	=(G14-G20)^2	**=SUM(G17:G19)**	
21							
22							
23							
24							

Macaulay dauration	**=SUM(H11:H13)/G8**
Modified duration	**=J5/(1+E14)**
Convexity	**=(2*F5/(1+E14)^3+6*F6/(1+E14)^4+12*F7/(1+E14)^5)/G8**
Duration–convexity approximation	
Yield change	1%
Percentage price change	**=-J6*J9+0.5*J7*J9^2**
Actual percentage price change	**=(G20-G8)/G8**

Table 15.7 Convexity calculation spreadsheet formula

Hedging the bond element in a credit basis trade

Credit traders and investors now undertake basis-type trades using cash bonds, or asset swaps, and credit derivative contracts such as credit default swaps. While this is not the preserve of the ALM or Treasury desk, well not usually anyway, we do not need to consider these types of trades here (although credit derivatives themselves, which are important credit risk management tools, are covered in detail in Chapter 16). However, we briefly describe a basis-type trade here so that we can then illustrate the interest-rate risk hedge put on for the cash bond element of the trade, which may be undertaken by the Treasury desk in some banks.

In a "positive basis" trade, the CDS trades above the cash spread, which can be measured using the asset-swap spread (ASW) or the z-spread.[3] The potential arbitrage trade is to sell the basis; that is, sell the cash bond and sell protection on the same reference name. We would do this if we expected the basis to converge or narrow.

---

[3] See Chapter 11 for a description of the different ways to measure the basis and an example of a z-spread calculation.

To illustrate this we describe an example of a basis trade in France Telecom credit. The cash side of the trade is an EUR-denominated bond issued by it, the 3.625% 2015, rated A3/A– and which is trading on 8 December 2005 as follows:[4]

Bond:	France Telecom 3.625% 2015
ISIN:	FR0010245555
Maturity:	14 October 2015
Price:	97.52–97.62 clean
ASW:	42.9 bps
z-spread:	45.2 bps
CDS price:	77–87 bps (10-year CDS)
Repo rate:	2.06 – 2.02 (Libor minus 35 bps).

The asset-swap spreads can be seen in Figure 15.2 (they are slightly different to the levels quoted above because the screens were printed the next day and the market had moved). This is Bloomberg screen ASW for the bond. The basis for this bond is positive, as shown in Figure 15.3, which is Bloomberg screen CRVD.

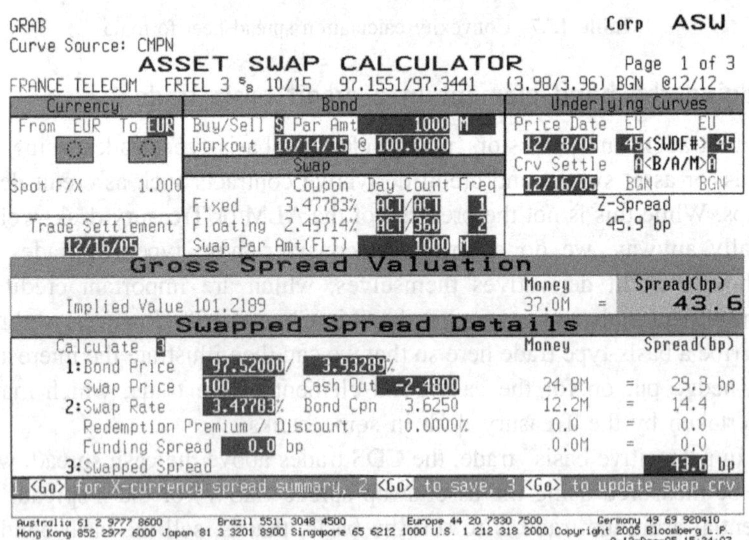

Figure 15.2 Asset-swap spread on screen ASW,
France Telecom 3.625% 2015 bond, 9 December 2005

[4] Prices are taken from Bloomberg L.P. (bond and repo) and market-makers (CDS).

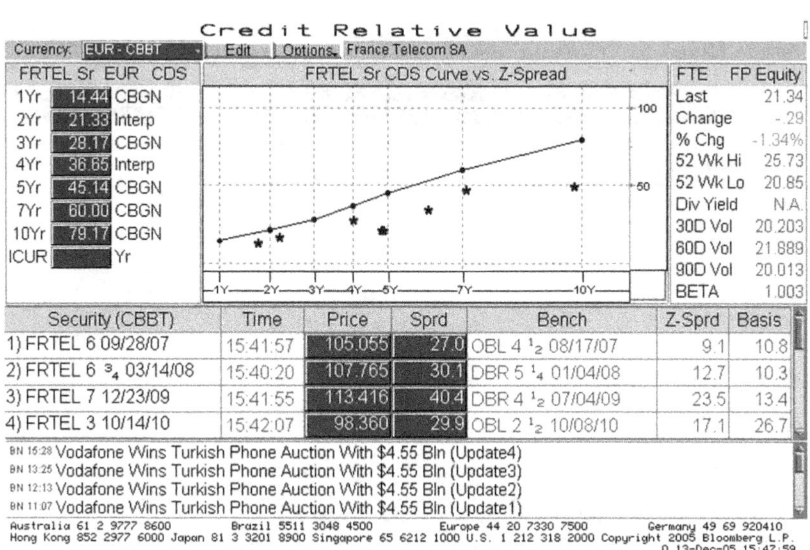

Figure 15.3 Cash–CDS basis for France Telecom, 9 December 2005

Above we see that the basis is (77 – 45.2) or +31.8 basis points. If we have the view that the bond will underperfom, or the basis will otherwise narrow and go towards zero and/or negative, we will sell the basis. We consider historical data on the basis during our analysis, as shown in Figure 15.4 on page 740 which is from screen BQ and shows the one-year historical ASW spread against the five-year CDS spread.[5]

[5] Our view on where the basis is going may be based on any combination of factors; these can include speculation about future direction based on historical trade patterns, specific company intelligence such as expectations of a takeover or other buy-out, views on credit quality, and so on. We do not discuss the rationale behind the trades in this article, merely the trade mechanics!

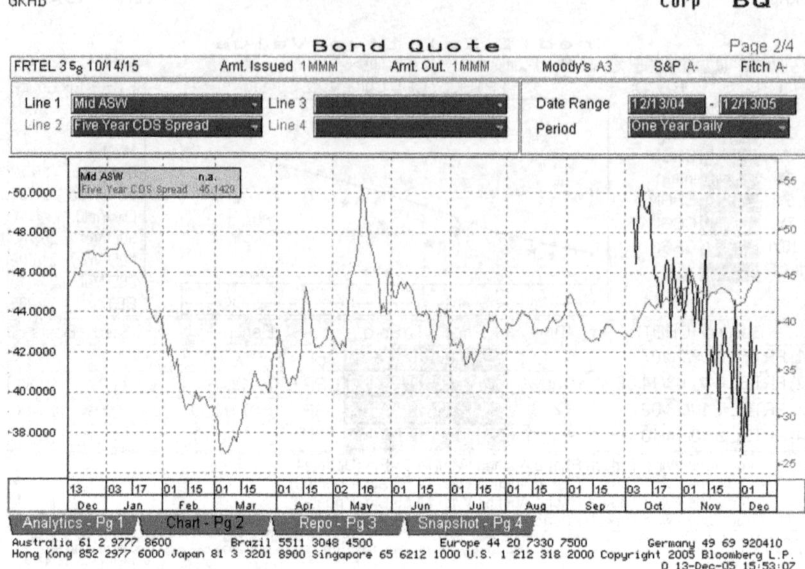

Figure 15.4 One-year historical CDS–ASW spread, France Telecom, December 2005

The trade is put on in the following terms:

- sell EUR6 million nominal of the bond at 97.52 clean price, 98.1158 dirty price;
- sell protection EUR5.85 million CDS at 77 basis points.

As we are shorting the bond we fund it in reverse repo, which is done at 2.02 basis points, or Libor minus 35 basis points.

The credit risk on the bond position is hedged using the CDS. The interest-rate risk ("DV01") is hedged using Bund futures contracts. The hedge calculation is a straightforward one and uses the ratio of the respective DV01 of the bond and futures contract; see earlier in this chapter for the hedge calculation mechanics.[6] From this we determine that we need to buy 52 lots of the Bund future to hedge the bond position.

[6] The hedge calculation is based on a ratio of BPV ("DV01") of the bond to be hedged and the futures contract. See Table 15.8 and Table 15.9 for the calculation spreadsheet.

We show the DV01 hedge calculation in Table 15.8, which is the Excel spreadsheet used to determine the futures hedge. Note that the example shown is for an hypothetical hedge, not our example – we show it here for instructional purposes. Table 15.9 on page 742 shows the Excel formulas used in the spreadsheet.

A1	B	C
2	**Hedging bonds with futures**	
3		
4		
5	$Number\ of\ contracts = \frac{M_{bond}}{M_{fut}} \times \frac{BPV_{bond}}{BPV_{fut}}$	
6		
7		
8		
9		
10	**Inputs**	
11		
12	**Nominal value of the bond ($\mathbf{M_{bond}}$)**	10,000,000.00
13		
14	**Nominal value of futures contract ($\mathbf{M_{fut}}$)**	100,000.00
15		
16	**BPV of the futures CTD bond**	7.484
17		
18	**Conversion factor of CTD**	0.852
19		
20	**BPV of the Bond ($\mathbf{BPV_{bond}}$)**	7.558
21		
22	**BPV of the future ($\mathbf{BPV_{fut}}$)**	8.780
23		
24		
25	**Number of contracts to hedge**	**86.083**
26		
27		
28		

Table 15.8 Futures hedge calculation spreadsheet

A1	B	C
2	**Hedging bonds with futures**	
3		
4		
5	$$Number\ of\ contracts = \frac{M_{bond}}{M_{fut}} \times \frac{BPV_{bond}}{BPV_{fut}}$$	
6		
7		
8		
9		
10	**Inputs**	
11		
12	**Nominal value of the bond (M_{bond})**	10,000,000.00
13		
14	**Nominal value of futures contract (M_{fut})**	100,000.00
15		
16	**BPV of the futures CTD bond**	7.484
17		
18	**Conversion factor of CTD**	0.852
19		
20	**BPV of the bond (BPV_{bond})**	7.558
21		
22	**BPV of the future (BPV_{fut})**	=C16/C18
23		
24		
25	**Number of contracts to hedge**	**=((C12/C14)*(C20/C22))**
26		
27		
28		

Table 15.9 Table 15.8 with Microsoft Excel formulas shown

The analysis is undertaken with reference to Libor, not absolute levels such as the YTM. The cash flows are:

Sell bond: pay 42.9 bps
Sell protection: receive 62 bps.

In addition, the reverse repo position is 35 basis points below Libor; as it represents interest income we consider this spread a funding loss so we incorporate this into the funding calculation; that is, we also pay 35 basis points. We ignore the futures position for funding purposes. This is a net carry of:

$$62 - (42.9 + 35)$$

or −15.9 basis points. In other words, the net carry for this position is negative. Funding cost must form part of the trade analysis. Funding has a greater impact on the trade net p&l the longer it is kept on. If the trade is maintained over one month, the funding impact will not be significant if we generated, say, a 5 basis points gain in the basis, because that is 5 basis points over a 10-year horizon (the maturity of the bond and CDS), the present value of which will exceed the 15.9 basis points loss on one month's funding. If the position is maintained over a year, the impact of the funding cost will be greater.

Position after one month

On 10 January 2006 we recorded the following prices for the France Telecom bond and reference name:

Bond:	France Telecom 3.625% 2015
Price:	98.35–98.45
ASW:	42.0 bps
z-spread:	43.8 bps
CDS price:	76–80 bps.

Spreads are shown in Figure 15.5.

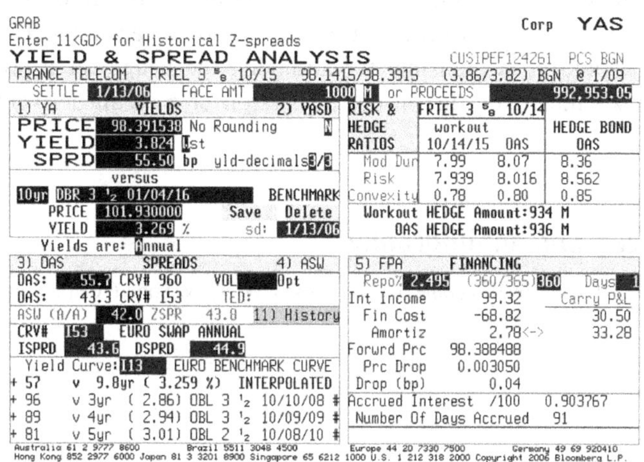

Figure 15.5 France Telecom bond YAS page for asset-swap and z-spreads, 10 January 2006

To unwind this position we would take the other side of the CDS quote, so the basis is now at (80 – 43.8) or 36.2 basis points. In other words, it has not gone the way we expected but has widened. As we sold the basis, the position has lost money if we unwind it now. The decision to unwind would be based on the original trade strategy: if the trader's time horizon was six months or longer, then the decision may be made to continue holding the position. If the trader's time horizon was shorter, it is probably sensible to cut one's losses now. Note that this trade is running at negative net carry so it incurs a carry loss if maintained irrespective of where the basis is going.

Conclusions

Exchange-traded bond futures contracts are very important as interest-rate risk hedging tools, and as such are widely used by bank ALM desks. Because ALM desks frequently maintain a portfolio of short-dated (on average, about three-year) government bonds for capital and liquidity purposes, they sometimes use bond futures to hedge the portfolio interest-rate risk. In this chapter we have described the contracts in the USD and GBP markets, the Treasury bond and long gilt future. We also illustrated the calculation of the hedge, which uses the relative basis point values of the cash instrument and the futures contract.

The modified duration method is still commonly used in risk hedging. We showed the calculation of "PV01" as well as "Dollar Duration" for an hypothetical bond. A Treasury desk would use this approach to calculate the hedge for a portfolio of government bonds.[7] In some banks, the Treasury or repo desk would be responsible for arranging the hedge for a proprietary trade, and we illustrated this in our discussion of a credit derivative basis trade.

References and bibliography

Choudhry, M. 2004, *Fixed Income Markets*, John Wiley & Sons (Asia), Singapore.

[7] It is by no means the case that a liquidity portfolio of government bonds would be hedged against interest-rate risk exposure. In many case the bonds held in such a portfolio are purchased on a "buy-to-hold" basis and held to maturity, so hedging may be considered unnecessary. However an ALM desk sometimes will hedge against anticipated yield curve shifts on a short-term basis.

CHAPTER

16

Credit Risk and Credit Derivatives

At a strategy level, credit risk management is partly the responsibility of the ALCO. Individual business lines will manage their respective credit risks, under the overall direction of the Credit Risk Committee, which sets policy on credit risk. However, under its remit of managing the balance sheet for ALM purposes, certain aspects of credit risk management will also be undertaken by ALCO. This may sound deliberately confusing, but in practice it is not. The distinction lies in the stage of the business cycle. The direction for originating credit risk exposure will be set by a credit committee; once it is on board, subsequent management of credit exposure – at the balance sheet level – is frequently undertaken by a Treasury or ALM desk. So for example a business line that is seeking to enter into new business will need to have this signed off at the credit committee level, as the credit committee sets policy on the type of credit risk that is acceptable to the bank. Subsequently, the assets of this specific business may be securitised, in cash or synthetic form, and this securitisation is often undertaken by the ALM desk.

Before the advent of credit derivatives, there was no instrument available that could be used to hedge credit risk in isolation. This changed during the 1990s. Credit derivatives, and structured credit products that incorporate credit derivatives in their construction, have transformed the way that credit risk can be managed, and are a significant development in banking. Therefore ALM practitioners must be familiar with such instruments, and more importantly, how they can be used as part of ALM and balance sheet development.

Credit derivatives are set to make the same impact on global capital markets as interest-rate derivatives did when the latter were first introduced in the early 1980s. Then, as now, market participants benefited from improved liquidity, transparency and accessibility in the cash market directly as a result of developments in the derivative market. The increasingly wide use of credit derivatives suggests that we are in the process of a transformation in credit markets in the same way that use of derivatives transformed interest-rate markets a generation earlier.

An editorial article in the 15 March 2003 issue of *The Economist* reported that credit derivatives were used by just 0.2% of American banks. This implies that they are not vital or important instruments in the financial markets. In a way, this would be a reasonable conclusion to make. However, while this figure is undoubtedly higher now, its absolute value is not really relevant. The importance of credit derivatives lies in the potential they generate for greater transparency and disintermediation for the market *as a whole*; transparency with regard to asset valuation, liquidity and accessibility. Greater transparency and liquidity for just a small percentage of the market – typically the largest banks and securities houses that take on and manage credit risk – works through into better trading conditions for all market participants. This then is the new paradigm shift currently taking place in credit markets, brought about by the isolation of credit as an asset class: greater transparency in evaluating fair value, and increased opportunity to speculate and hedge in credit.

The universe of credit derivatives includes credit default swaps (CDS), total return swaps (TRS), credit-linked notes (CLNs) and structured credit products such as synthetic structured finance securities. Market notional volumes as a whole, of which the CDS is the most frequently traded, are shown at Figure in 16.1 on page 747. This illustrates the steady rise in use of these products.

Recent occurrences would seem to imply a growing maturity in the credit derivatives market. High-profile credit events such as the Parmalat default in 2003 or the Ford and GM downgrades in 2005 have not seen market liquidity dry up; rather the opposite, as dealers sought to make two-way prices continuously available. The revised ISDA definitions from 2003 mean we have a standard legal agreement to cover all trades, significantly reducing translation risk. And widely available pricing platforms such as those from CreditTrade and Mark-It provide an independent third-party price for investors. All this serves to make the synthetic market more of a driver of the cash market than the other way around; in other words, the "tail wagging the dog" scenario that exists now in interest-rate markets after the introduction of derivatives there.

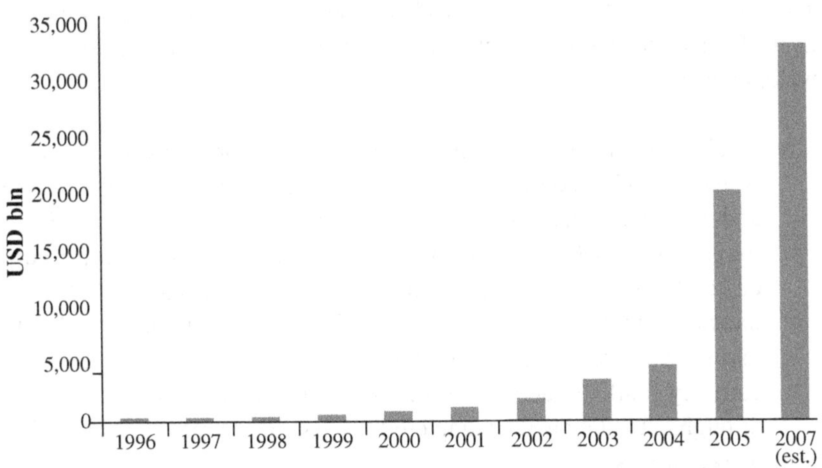

Figure 16.1 Credit derivatives volumes, $bln notional
Source: British Bankers Association.

In this chapter we provide an overview of the main elements of the market. We describe credit derivatives, instruments that are used both to invest in and trade credit synthetically, and to manage credit risk in banking and portfolio management. Credit derivatives exist in a number of forms. We classify these into two main types, *funded* and *unfunded* credit derivatives, and give a description of each type. We then discuss the main uses of these instruments by banks and portfolio managers. We also consider the main credit events that act as triggering events under which payouts are made on credit derivative contracts.

Credit derivative pricing is covered at the end of the chapter.

ALM and credit risk

Credit risk emerged as a significant risk management issue during the 1990s. In increasingly competitive markets, banks and securities houses began taking on greater credit risk from this period onwards. While the concept of "credit risk" is as old as banking itself, it is only recently that the nature and extent of it has increased dramatically. For example, consider the following developments:

- credit spreads tightened during the late 1990s onwards, to the point where blue-chip companies such as General Electric, British Telecom and Shell were being offered syndicated loans for as little as 10–12 basis points over Libor. To maintain margin, or the increased return on capital, banks increased lending to lower-rated corporates, thereby increasing their credit risk both overall and as a share of overall risk;
- investors were finding fewer opportunities in interest rate and currency markets, and therefore moved towards yield enhancement through extending and trading credit across lower-rated and emerging market assets;
- the rapid expansion of high-yield and emerging market sectors, again lower-rated assets, increased the magnitude of credit risk for investors and the banks that held and traded such assets.

The growth in credit risk exposure would naturally be expected to lead to more sophisticated risk management techniques than those employed hitherto. It was accompanied, however, by a rise in the level of corporate defaults and consequently higher losses due to credit deterioration, which led to a rigorous test of banks' risk management systems and procedures. It also led to a demand for the type of product that resulted in the credit derivative market.

The development of the credit derivatives market, and hence the subsequent introduction of structured credit products, was a response to the rising importance attached to credit risk management. For this reason, it is worthwhile beginning this chapter with a look at credit risk, credit ratings, default and credit risk measurement. So we will look at the concept of credit risk, before considering the main way that it is measured in banks and financial institutions, using the technique known as credit VaR. We also introduce two credit risk measurement methodologies. First, though, we look at the incidence of corporate defaults during the 1990s.

Corporate default

During the second half of the 1990s and into the new century, credit risk and credit risk management have been topical issues in the financial markets industry. Viewed statistically, 1999 onwards appear to be years of excessive corporate default, when compared with the market experience in the previous two decades. This is vividly illustrated in Figure 16.2, which shows the monetary value of corporate defaults for the period 1980–2002. The average size of corporate bond defaults also rose significantly, as we show in Figure 16.3. Adjusted for inflation, the average size of default in 2002 was over five times that for the entire period 1980–2002.

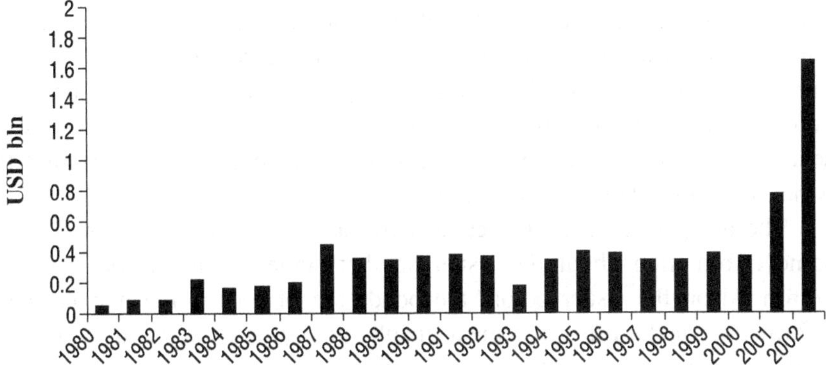

Figure 16.2 Global corporate defaults, 1980–2002
Sources: S&P, CFSB. Used with permission.

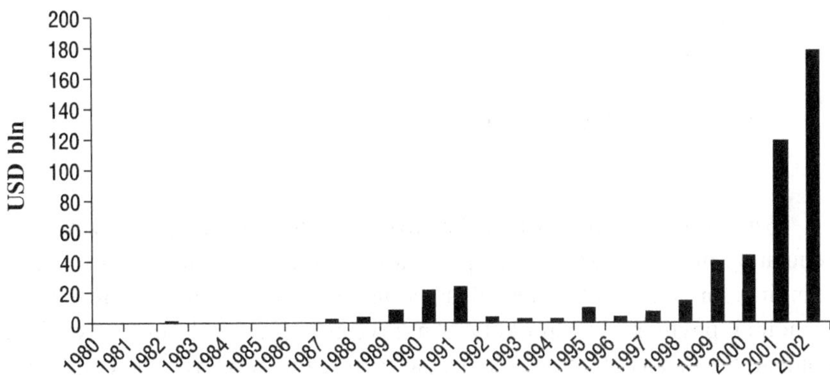

Figure 16.3 Average size of corporate bond defaults
Sources: Moody's, CSFB. Used with permission.

The excessive levels of corporate defaults provided confirmation that banks needed to focus closely on credit risk management. They did this using a two-pronged approach, by concentrating on risk measurement and risk hedging. The former used so-called VaR techniques, introduced earlier in the 1990s for market risk measurement, while the latter was accomplished with credit derivatives.

Credit risk

Investors in securities accept the risk that the issuer may default on coupon payments or fail to repay the principal in full on the maturity date. Generally, credit risk is greater for securities with a long maturity, as there is a longer period for the issuer potentially to default. For example, if a company issues ten-year bonds, investors cannot be certain that the company will still exist in ten years' time. It may have failed and gone into liquidation some time before that. That said, there is also risk attached to short-dated debt securities; indeed, there have been instances of default by issuers of CP, which is a very short-term instrument.

The prospectus or offer document for an issue provides investors with some information about the issuer so that some credit analysis can be performed on the issuer before the bonds are placed on the market. The information in the offer document enables investors to perform their own credit analysis by studying this information before deciding whether or not to invest in the bonds. Credit assessments take up time, however, and also require the specialist skills of credit analysts. Large institutional investors employ specialists to carry out credit analysis; however, often it is too costly and time-consuming to assess every issuer in every debt market. Therefore investors commonly employ two other methods when making a decision on the credit risk of debt securities:

- name recognition;
- formal credit ratings.

Name recognition is when the investor relies on the good name and reputation of the issuer and accepts that the issuer is of such good financial standing, or sufficient financial standing, that a default on interest and principal payments is unlikely. An investor may feel this way about companies such as Microsoft or British Petroleum. However, the collapse of Barings Bank in 1995 suggested to many investors that it may not be wise to rely on name recognition alone in today's marketplace. The tradition and reputation behind the Barings name allowed the bank to borrow at Libor or occasionally at sub-Libor interest rates in the money markets, which put it on a par with the highest quality clearing banks in terms of credit rating. The Barings case illustrated that name recognition needs to be augmented by other methods to reduce the risk of loss due to unforeseen events. Credit ratings are increasingly used to make investment decisions about corporate or lesser developed government debt.

There are two main types of credit risk that a portfolio of assets, or a position in a single asset, is exposed to. These are credit default risk and credit spread risk.

Credit default risk

This is the risk that an issuer of debt (obligor) is unable to meet its financial obligations. This is known as *default*. There is also the case of technical default, which is used to describe a company that has not honoured its interest payments on a loan for (typically) three months or more, but has not reached a stage of bankruptcy or administration. Where an obligor defaults, a lender generally incurs a loss equal to the amount owed by the obligor less any recovery amount that the firm recovers as a result of foreclosure, liquidation or restructuring of the defaulted obligor. This recovery amount is usually expressed as a percentage of the total amount and is known as the *recovery rate*. All portfolios with credit exposure exhibit credit default risk.

The measure of a firm's credit default risk is given by its *credit rating*. The three largest credit rating agencies are Moody's, Standard & Poor's (S&P) and Fitch Ratings. These institutions undertake qualitative and quantitative analysis of borrowers and formally rate the borrower after their analysis. The issues considered in the analysis include:

- the financial position of the firm itself; for example, its balance sheet position and anticipated cash flows and revenues;
- other firm-specific issues such as the quality of management and succession planning;
- an assessment of the firm's ability to meet scheduled interest and principal payments, both in its domestic and in foreign currencies;
- the outlook for the industry as a whole, and competition within it, together with general assessments of the domestic economy.

We discuss credit ratings again shortly. The range of credit ratings awarded by the three largest rating agencies is shown in Table 16.1 on page 752. Ratings can be seen on the Bloomberg page RATD, shown in Figure 16.4 on page 753.

Fitch	Moody's	S&P	Summary description
Investment grade – High creditworthiness			
AAA	Aaa	AAA	Gilt-edged, prime, maximum safety, lowest risk
AA+	Aa1	AA+	
AA	Aa2	AA	High-grade, high credit quality
AA–	Aa3	AA–	
A+	A1	A+	
A	A2	A	Upper medium grade
A–	A3	A–	
BBB+	Baa1	BBB+	
BBB	Baa2	BBB	Lower medium grade
BBB–	Baa3	BBB–	
Speculative – Lower creditworthiness			
BB+	Ba1	BB+	
BB	Ba2	BB	Lower grade; speculative
BB–	Ba3	BB–	
B+	B+		
B	B	B	Highly speculative
B–	B–		
Predominantly speculative, substantial risk or in default			
		CCC+	
CCC	Caa	CCC	Considerable risk, in poor standing
		CCC–	
CC	Ca	CC	May be in default, very speculative
C	C	C	Extremely speculative
		CI	Income bonds – no interest being paid
DDD			
DD			Default
D		D	

Table 16.1 Long-term bond credit ratings

GRAB Govt **RATD**

LONG-TERM RATING SCALES COMPARISON Page 1/2

MOODY'S	Aaa	Aa1	Aa2	Aa3	A1	A2	A3	Baa1	Baa2	Baa3
S&P	AAA	AA+	AA	AA-	A+	A	A-	BBB+	BBB	BBB-
COMP	AAA	AA1	AA2	AA3	A1	A2	A3	BBB1	BBB2	BBB3
TBW	AAA	AA+	AA	AA-	A+	A	A-	BBB+	BBB	BBB-
FITCH	AAA	AA+	AA	AA-	A+	A	A-	BBB+	BBB	BBB-
CBRS	AAA	AA+	AA	AA-	A+	A	A-	BBB+	BBB	BBB-
DOMINION	AAA	AAH	AA	AAL	AH	A	AL	BBBH	BBB	BBBL
R&I	AAA	AA+	AA	AA-	A+	A	A-	BBB+	BBB	BBB-
JCR	AAA	AA+	AA	AA-	A+	A	A-	BBB+	BBB	BBB-
MI	AAA		AA			A			BBB	

Note: white = investment grade, yellow = non-investment grade

Figure 16.4 Bloomberg screen RATD, long-term credit ratings

Credit spread risk

Credit spread is the excess premium, over and above government or risk-free risk, required by the market for taking on a certain assumed credit exposure. For example, Figure 16.5 on page 754 shows the credit spreads in January 2003 for US dollar corporate bonds with different credit ratings (AAA, A and BBB). The benchmark is the on-the-run or *active* US Treasury issue for the given maturity. Note that the higher the credit rating, the smaller the credit spread. Credit spread risk is the risk of financial loss resulting from changes in the level of credit spreads used in the marking-to-market of a product. It is exhibited by a portfolio for which the credit spread is traded and marked-to-market. Changes in observed credit spreads affect the value of the portfolio and can lead to losses for investors.

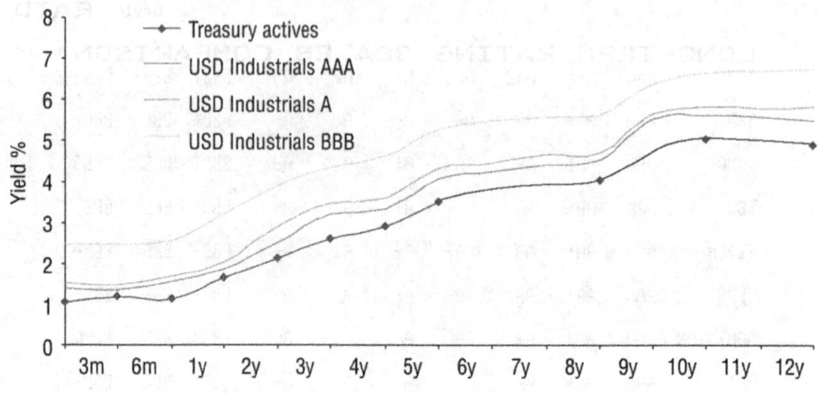

Figure 16.5 USD bond yield curves, January 2004

Credit ratings

Only the highest quality government debt, and a small amount of supranational and corporate debt are considered to be entirely free of credit risk. Therefore at any time the yield on a bond reflects investors' views on the ability of the issuer to meet its liabilities as set out in the bond's terms and conditions. A delay in paying a cash liability as it becomes due is known as technical default and is a cause for extreme concern for investors – failure to pay will result in the matter going to court as investors seek to recover their funds. In order to determine the ability of an issuer to meet its obligations for a particular debt issue, judgmental analysis of the issuer's financial strength and business prospects is required for the entire life of the issue. There are a number of factors that must be considered, and larger banks, fund managers and corporates carry out their own *credit analysis* of individual borrowers' bond issues. The market also makes considerable use of formal credit ratings that are assigned to individual bond issues by a formal credit rating agency. In the international markets the two most influential ratings agencies are Standard & Poor's Corporation (S&Ps) and Moody's Investors Service, Inc (Moody's), based in the United States. Fitch Investors Service, Inc (Fitch) also has a high profile.

The specific factors that are considered by a ratings agency, and the methodology used in conducting the analysis, differ slightly among the individual ratings agencies. Although in many cases the ratings assigned to a particular issue by different agencies are the same, they occasionally differ and in these instances investors usually seek to determine what aspect of an issuer is given more weight in an analysis by which individual agency. Note that a credit rating is not a recommendation to buy (or equally, sell) a particular bond, nor is it a comment on market expectations. Credit analysis does take into account general market and economic conditions, but the overall point of credit analysis is to consider the financial health of the issuer and its ability to meet the obligations of the specific issue being rated. Credit ratings play a large part in the decision-making of investors, and also have a significant impact on the interest rates payable by borrowers.

A credit rating is a formal opinion given by a rating agency of the credit risk for investors holding a particular issue of debt securities. Ratings are given to public issues of debt securities by any type of entity, including governments, banks and corporates. They are also given to short-term debt such as CP, as well as medium-term notes and long-term debt such as bonds.

On receipt of a formal request, the credit rating agencies carry out a rating exercise on a specific issue of debt capital. The request for a rating comes from the organisation planning the issue of bonds. Although ratings are provided for the benefit of investors, the issuer must bear the cost. However, it is in the issuer's interest to request a rating as it raises the profile of the bonds, and investors may refuse to buy paper that is not accompanied with a recognised rating. Although the rating exercise involves a credit analysis of the issuer, the rating is applied to a specific debt issue. This means that, in theory, the credit rating is applied not to an organisation itself, but to specific debt securities that the organisation has issued or is planning to issue. In practice, it is common for the market to refer to the creditworthiness of organisations in terms of the rating of their debt. A highly rated company such as Rabobank is therefore referred to as a "triple-A rated" company, although it is the banks' debt issues that are rated as triple-A.

The rating for an issue is kept constantly under review and if the credit quality of the issuer declines or improves, the rating will be changed accordingly. An agency may announce in advance that it is reviewing a particular credit rating, and may go further and state that the review is a precursor to a possible downgrade or upgrade. This announcement is referred to as putting the issue under *credit watch*. The outcome of a credit watch is, in most cases, likely to be a rating downgrade; however, the review may reaffirm the current rating or possibly upgrade it. During the credit watch phase the agency will advise investors to use the current rating with caution. When an agency announces that an issue is under credit watch, the price of the bonds will fall in the market as investors look to sell out of their holdings. This upward movement in yield will be more pronounced if an actual downgrade results.

Ratings changes over time

We have noted that the rating agencies constantly review the credit quality of firms they have rated. The credit rating of many companies will fluctuate over time as they experience changes in their corporate wellbeing. As a guide to the change in credit rating that might be expected over a one-year period, Moody's and S&P publish historical transition matrices, which provide average rating transition probabilities for each class of rating. An example is shown in Table 16.2, which is Moody's one-year ratings transition matrix for 2002. These results are obtained from a sample of a large number of firms over many years. In Table 16.2, the first column shows the initial rating and the first row the final rating. For instance, the probability of an A-rated company being downgraded to Baa in one year is 4.63%. The probability of the A-rated company defaulting in this year is 0.00%.

There are some inconsistencies in the ratings transition table and this is explained by Moody's as resulting from scarcity of data for some ratings categories. For instance, an Aa-rated company has a 0.02% probability of being in default at year-end, which is higher than the supposedly lower-rated A-rated company. Such results must be treated with caution. The conclusion from Table 16.2 is that the most likely outcome at year-end is that the company rating remains the same. It may be that a one-year time horizon provides little real value, hence the rating agencies also publish transition matrices for longer periods, such as five and ten years.

	Aaa	Aa	A	Baa	Ba	B	Caa	Default
Aaa	93.40%	5.94%	0.64%	0.00%	0.02%	0.00%	0.00%	0.00%
Aa	1.61%	90.55%	7.46%	0.26%	0.09%	0.01%	0.00%	0.02%
A	0.07%	2.28%	92.44%	4.63%	0.45%	0.12%	0.01%	0.00%
Baa	0.05%	0.26%	5.51%	88.48%	4.76%	0.71%	0.08%	0.15%
Ba	0.02%	0.05%	0.42%	5.16%	86.91%	5.91%	0.24%	1.29%
B	0.00%	0.04%	0.13%	0.54%	6.35%	84.22%	1.91%	6.81%
Caa	0.00%	0.00%	0.00%	0.62%	2.05%	4.08%	69.20%	24.06%

Table 16.2 Moody's one-year rating transition matrix for 2002

We might expect an increased level of default as we move lower down the credit ratings scale. This is borne out in Figure 16.6, which is a reproduction of data published by Moody's. It shows average one-year default rates by credit rating category, for the period 1985–2000. We see that the average one-year default rate rises from zero for the highest rated Aaa, to 15.7% for the B3 rating category. However, investors generally attach little value to one-year results. Figure 16.7 shows average cumulative default rates for five- and 10-year time horizons, for the same period covered in Figure 16.6. This repeats the results shown in Figure 16.6, with higher default rates associated with lower credit ratings.

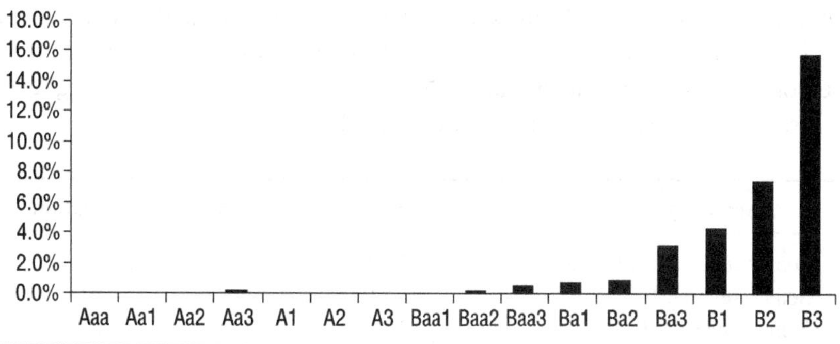

Figure 16.6 One-year default rates, 1985–2000
Source: Moody's. Reproduced with permission.

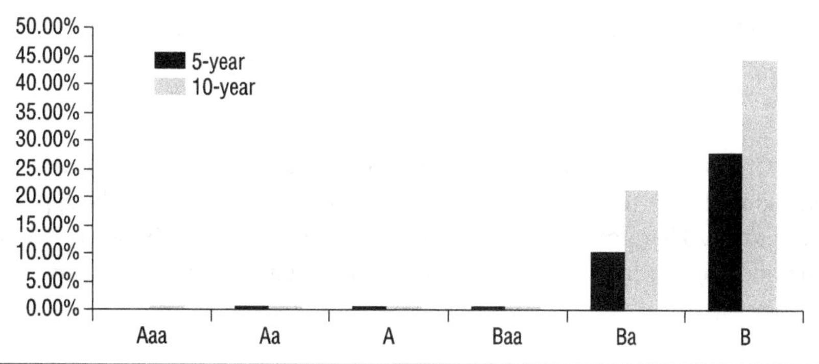

Figure 16.7 Five- and 10-year average cumulative default rates, 1985–2000
Source: Moody's. Reproduced with permission.

Corporate recovery rates

When a corporate obligor experiences bankruptcy or enters into liquidation or administration, it defaults on its loans. However, this does not mean that all the firm's creditors will lose everything. At the end of the administration process, the firm's creditors will typically receive a portion of their outstanding loans, a *recovery* amount.[1] The percentage of the original loan that is received back is known as the *recovery rate*, which is defined as the percentage of par value that is returned to the creditor.

The seniority of a loan strongly influences the level of the recovery rate. Table 16.3 shows recovery rates for varying levels of loan seniority in 2002 as published by Moody's. The standard deviation for each recovery rate reported is high, which illustrates the dispersion around the mean and reflects widely varying recovery rates even within the same level of seniority. It is clear that the more senior a loan or a bond is, the higher the recovery rate it will have in the event of default.

Seniority	Mean	Standard deviation
Senior secured bank loans	60.70%	26.31%
Senior secured	55.83%	25.41%
Senior unsecured	52.13%	25.12%
Senior subordinated	39.45%	24.79%
Subordinated	33.81%	21.25%
Junior subordinated	18.51%	11.26%
Preference shares	8.26%	10.45%

Table 16.3 Moody's recovery rates for varying levels of loan seniority, 2002

Credit risk is measured using the VaR technique. This was first introduced as a market risk measurement tool, and subsequently applied to credit risk. Therefore in the next chapter we introduce the basics of the VaR methodology, which we require for an understanding of credit VaR.

[1] This recovery may be received in the form of other assets, such as securities or physical plant, instead of cash.

Credit derivatives: An introduction

Credit derivatives are financial contracts designed to enable traders and investors to access specific credit-risky investments in synthetic (that is, non-cash) form. They can also be used to hedge credit risk exposure by providing insurance against losses suffered due to credit events. Credit derivatives allow investors to manage the credit risk exposure of their portfolios or asset holdings, essentially by providing insurance against deterioration in credit quality of the borrowing entity. The simplest credit derivative works exactly like an insurance policy, with regular premiums paid by the protection buyer to the protection seller, and a payout in the event of a specified credit event.

The principle behind credit derivatives is straightforward. Investors desire exposure to debt that has a risk of defaulting because of the higher returns this offers. However, such exposure brings with it concomitant credit risk. This can be managed with credit derivatives. At the same time, the exposure itself can be taken on synthetically if, for instance, there are compelling reasons why a cash market position cannot be established. The flexibility of credit derivatives provides users a number of advantages, and as they are OTC products they can be designed to meet specific user requirements.

What constitutes a credit event is defined specifically in the legal documents that describe the credit derivative contract. A number of events may be defined as credit events that fall short of full bankruptcy, administration or liquidation of a company. For instance, credit derivatives contracts may be required to pay out under both technical as well as actual default.

A *technical default* is a delay in the timely payment of an obligation, or a non-payment altogether. If an obligor misses a payment, by even one day, it is said to be in technical default. This delay may be for operational reasons (and so not really a great worry) or it may reflect a short-term cash flow crisis, such as the Argentina debt default for three months. But if the obligor states it intends to pay the obligation as soon as it can, and specifies a time-span that is within, say, one to three months, then while it is in technical default it is not in actual default. If an obligor is in *actual default*, it is in default and declared as being in default. This does not mean a mere delay of payment. If an obligor does not pay, and does not declare an intention to pay an obligation, it may then be classified by the ratings agencies as being in 'default'; such assets are rated 'D' by S&P.

If there is a technical or actual default by the borrower so that, for instance, a bond is marked down in price, the losses suffered by the investor can be recouped in part or in full through the payout made by the credit derivative. A payout under a credit derivative is triggered by a *credit event*. As banks define default in different ways, the terms under which a credit derivative is executed usually include a specification of what constitutes a credit event.

We provide background here on credit derivatives, prior to discussing specific instruments.

Why use credit derivatives?

Credit derivative instruments enable participants in the financial market to trade in credit as an asset, as they isolate and transfer credit risk. They also enable the market to separate funding considerations from credit risk.

For ALM practitioners, credit derivatives have the principle application of reducing credit exposure. A bank can reduce credit exposure either for an individual loan or for a sectoral concentration by buying a credit default swap. This may be desirable for assets that cannot be sold for client relationship or tax reasons. For fixed-income managers a particular asset or collection of assets may be viewed as an attractive holding in the long term, but at risk from a short-term downward price movement. In this instance a sale would not fit in with long-term objectives; however, short-term credit protection can be obtained via a credit swap. For instance, a bank can buy credit protection on a BB-rated entity from a AA-rated bank. It then has eliminated its credit risk to the BB entity, and substituted it for AA-rated counterparty risk. Notice that as the bank retains a counterparty risk to the credit default swap issuer, one could argue that its credit risk exposure is never completely removed. In practice this is not a serious problem since the bank can manage counterparty risk through careful selection and diversification of counterparties. In fact, in the interest-rate swap market, AA (interbank) quality is now considered a proxy for the government benchmark.

The intense competition among commercial banks, combined with rapid disintermediation, has meant that banks have been forced to evaluate their lending policy with a view to improving profitability and return on capital. The use of credit derivatives assists banks with restructuring their businesses, because they allow banks to repackage and parcel out credit risk, while retaining assets on the balance sheet (when required) and thus maintaining client relationships. As the instruments isolate certain aspects of credit risk from the underlying loan or bond, and transfer them to another entity, it becomes possible to separate the ownership and management of credit risk from the other features of ownership of the assets in question. This means that illiquid assets such as bank loans and illiquid bonds can have their credit risk exposures transferred; the bank owning the assets can protect against credit loss even if it cannot transfer the assets themselves.

Thus credit derivatives can be an important instrument for bond portfolio managers, as well as commercial banks wishing to increase the liquidity of their portfolios, gain from the relative value arising from credit pricing anomalies, and enhance portfolio returns.

Classification of credit derivative instruments

A number of instruments come under the category of credit derivatives. Irrespective of the particular instrument under consideration, all credit derivatives can be described with respect to the following characteristics:

- the *reference entity*, which is the asset or name on which credit protection is being bought and sold;
- the *credit event*, or events, which indicate that the reference entity is experiencing or about to experience financial difficulty, and which act as trigger events for payments under the credit derivative contract;
- the *settlement mechanism* for the contract, whether cash settled or physically settled;
- the *deliverable obligation* that the protection buyer delivers (under physical settlement) to the protection seller on the occurrence of a trigger event.

Credit derivatives are grouped into *funded* and *unfunded* instruments. In a funded credit derivative, typified by a CLN, the investor in the note is the credit-protection seller and is making an upfront payment to the protection buyer when it buys the note. Thus, the protection buyer is the issuer. If no credit event occurs during the life of the note, its redemption value is paid to the investor on maturity. If a credit event does occur, then on maturity a value less than par will be paid out to the investor. This value will be reduced by the nominal value of the reference asset that the CLN is linked to. The exact process will differ according to whether *cash settlement* or *physical settlement* has been specified for the note. We will consider this later.

In an unfunded credit derivative, typified by a CDS, the protection seller does not make an upfront payment to the protection buyer. Instead, the protection seller will pay the nominal value of the contract (the amount insured, in effect), on occurrence of a credit event, minus the current market value of the asset or its recovery value.

Definition of a credit event

The occurrence of a specified credit event will trigger the default payment by the protection seller to the protection buyer. Contracts specify physical or cash settlement. In physical settlement, the protection buyer transfers to the protection seller the deliverable obligation (usually the reference asset or assets), with the total principal outstanding equal to the nominal value specified in the default swap contract. The protection seller simultaneously pays to the buyer 100% of the nominal value. In cash settlement, the protection seller hands to the buyer the difference between the nominal amount of the default swap and the final value for the same nominal amount of the reference asset. This final value is usually determined by means of a poll of dealer banks.

The following may be specified as credit events in the legal documentation between counterparties:

- a downgrade in S&P and/or Moody's credit rating below a specified minimum level;
- financial or debt restructuring; for example, occasioned under administration or as required under US bankruptcy protection;
- bankruptcy or insolvency of the reference asset obligor;
- default on payment obligations such as bond coupon and continued non-payment after a specified time period;
- technical default; for example, the non-payment of interest or coupon when it falls due;
- a change in credit spread payable by the obligor above a specified maximum level.

The 1999 ISDA documentation specifies bankruptcy, failure to pay, obligation default, debt moratorium and "restructuring" to be credit events. Note that it does not specify a rating downgrade to be a credit event.[2]

---

[2] The ISDA definitions from 1999, restructuring supplement from 2001 and updated definitions from 2003 are available at www.ISDA.org.

The precise definition of "restructuring" is open to debate and has resulted in legal disputes between protection buyers and sellers. Prior to issuing its 1999 definitions, ISDA had specified restructuring as an event or events that resulted in making the terms of the reference obligation "materially less favourable" to the creditor (or protection seller) from an economic perspective. This definition is open to more than one interpretation and caused controversy when determining if a credit event had occurred. The 2001 definitions specified more precise conditions, including any action that resulted in a reduction in the amount of principal. In the European market restructuring is generally retained as a credit event in contract documentation, but in the US market it is less common to see it included. Instead, US contract documentation tends to include as a credit event a form of modified restructuring, the impact of which is to limit the options available to the protection buyer as to the type of assets it could deliver in a physically settled contract.

EXAMPLE 16.1 Restructuring, modified restructuring and modified–modified restructuring

The original 1999 ISDA credit definitions defined restructuring among the standard credit events. The five specified definitions included events such as a reduction in the rate of interest payable, a reduction in the amount of principal outstanding and a postponement or deferral of payment. Following a number of high-profile cases where there was disagreement or dispute between protection buyers and sellers on what precisely constituted a restructuring, the supplement to the 1999 ISDA limited the term to maturity of deliverable obligations. This was modified restructuring or Mod-R, which was intended to reduce the difference between the loss suffered by a holder of the actual restructured obligation and the writer of a CDS on that reference name. In practice this has placed a maturity limit on deliverable obligations of 30 months.

The 2003 definitions presented further clarification and stated that the restructuring event had to be binding on all holders of the restructured debt. The modified–modified restructuring definition, or Mod–Mod-R, described in the 2003 ISDA, defines the modified restructuring term to maturity date as the later of:

- the scheduled termination date;
- 60 months following the restructuring date

in the event that a restructured bond or loan is delivered to the protection seller. If another obligation is delivered, the limitation on maturity is the scheduled maturity date and 30 months following the restructuring date.

Asset swaps

Asset swaps pre-date the introduction of the other instruments we discuss in this chapter and so strictly speaking are not credit derivatives. However, they are used for similar purposes and there is considerable interplay between the cash and synthetic markets using asset swaps, hence the need to discuss them here.

Asset swaps are used to alter the cash flow profile of a bond. The asset swap market is an important segment of the credit derivatives market since it explicitly sets out the price of credit as a spread over Libor. Pricing a bond by reference to Libor is commonly used and the spread over Libor is a measure of credit risk in the cash flow of the underlying bond. Asset swaps can be used to transform the cash flow characteristics of reference assets, so that investors can hedge the currency, credit and interest-rate risks to create synthetic investments with more suitable cash flow characteristics. An asset-swap package involves transactions in which investors acquire a bond position and then enter into an interest-rate swap with the bank that sold them the bond. The investors pay fixed and receive floating. This transforms the fixed coupon of the bond into a Libor-based floating coupon.

One example would be where the protection buyer holds a risky bond and wishes to hedge the credit risk of this position. By means of an asset swap the protection seller will agree to pay the protection buyer Libor +/– a spread in return for the cash flows of the risky bond (there is no exchange of notional at any point). In the event of default the protection buyer will continue to receive the Libor +/– a spread from the protection seller. In this way the protection buyer has transformed its original risk profile by changing both its interest rate and credit risk exposure.

The generic structure is shown in Figure 16.8.

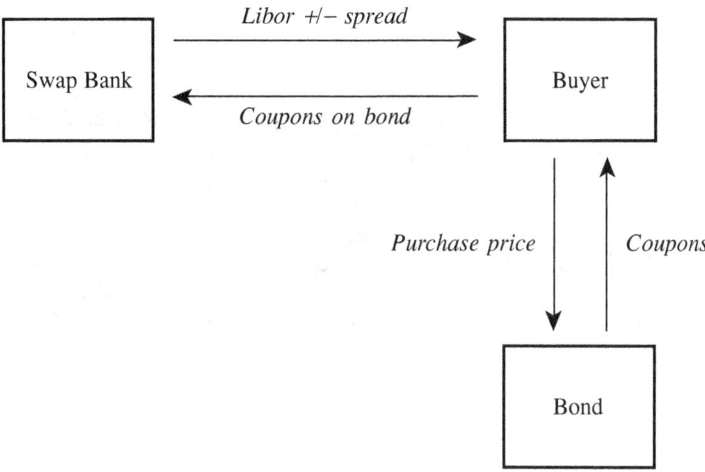

Figure 16.8 Asset swap

EXAMPLE 16.2 Asset swap

Assume that an investor holds a bond and enters into an asset swap with a bank. Then the value of an asset swap is the spread the bank pays over or under Libor. This is based on the following components:

(a) value of the coupons of the underlying asset compared to the market swap rate;
(b) the accrued interest and the clean price premium or discount compared to par value.

Thus when pricing the asset swap it is necessary to compare the par value to the underlying bond price. The spread above or below Libor reflects the credit spread difference between the bond and the swap rate.

The Bloomberg asset swap calculator pricing screen in Figure 16.9 on page 766 shows these components in the analysis of the swapped spread details.

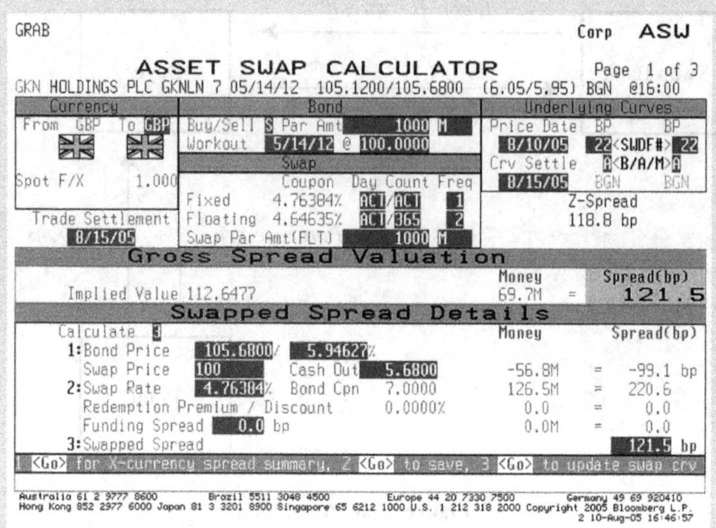

Figure 16.9 Bloomberg example of asset swap calculator screen

EXAMPLE 16.3 Asset swap terms

Let us assume that we have a credit risky bond with the following details:

Currency:	EUR
Issue date:	31 March 2000
Maturity:	31 March 2007
Coupon:	5.5% per annum
Price (dirty):	105.3%
Price (clean):	101.2%
Yield:	5%
Accrued interest:	4.1%
Rating:	A1

To buy this bond the investor would pay 105.3% of par value. The investor would receive the fixed coupons of 5.5% of par value. Let us assume that the swap rate is 5%. The investor in this bond enters into an asset swap with a bank in which the investor pays the fixed coupon and receives Libor +/– spread.

The asset swap price (that is, spread) on this bond has the following components:

(a) the value of the excess value of the fixed coupons over the market swap rate is paid to the investor. Let us assume that in this case it is approximately 0.5% when spread into payments over the life of the asset swap;

(b) the difference between the bond price and par value is another factor in the pricing of an asset swap. In this case the price premium, which is expressed in present value terms, should be spread over the term of the swap and treated as a payment by the investor to the bank (if a dirty price is at a discount to the par value then the payment is made from the bank to the investor). For example, in this case let us assume that this results in a payment from the investor to the bank of approximately 0.23% when spread over the term of the swap.

These two elements result in a net spread of 0.5% – 0.23% = 0.27%. Therefore the asset swap would be quoted as Libor + 0.27% (or Libor plus 27 basis points).

Credit default swaps

The most common credit derivative is the *credit default swap* (CDS). This is sometimes abbreviated to *credit swap* or *default swap*. A CDS is a bilateral contract in which a periodic fixed fee or a one-off premium is paid to a protection seller, in return for which the seller will make a payment on the occurrence of a specified credit event. The fee is quoted as a basis point multiplier of the nominal value. It is usually paid quarterly in arrears.

The swap can refer to a single asset, known as the *reference asset* or *underlying asset*, or a basket of assets. The default payment can be paid in whatever way suits the protection buyer or both counterparties. For example, it may be linked to the change in price of the reference asset or another specified asset, it may be fixed at a predetermined recovery rate, or it may be in the form of actual delivery of the reference asset at a specified price. The basic structure is illustrated in Figure 16.10 on page 768.

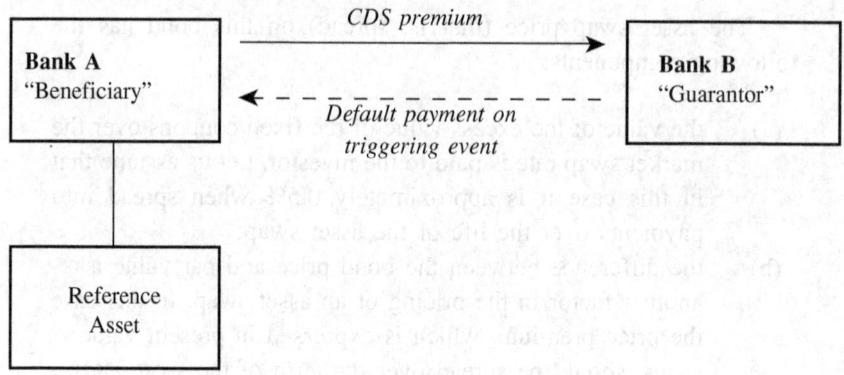

Figure 16.10 Credit default swap

The maturity of the credit swap does not have to match the maturity of the reference asset and often does not. On occurrence of a credit event, the swap contract is terminated and a settlement payment made by the protection seller or guarantor to the protection buyer. This termination value is calculated at the time of the credit event, and the exact procedure that is followed to calculate the termination value will depend on the settlement terms specified in the contract. This will be either a cash settlement or physical settlement:

- Cash settlement: The contract may specify a pre-determined payout value on occurrence of a credit event. This may be the nominal value of the swap contract. Such a swap is known in some markets as a *digital credit derivative*. Alternatively, the termination payment is calculated as the difference between the nominal value of the reference asset and its market value at the time of the credit event. This arrangement is more common with cash-settled contracts.[3]
- Physical settlement: On the occurrence of a credit event the buyer delivers the reference asset to the seller, in return for which the seller pays the face value of the delivered asset to the buyer. The contract may specify a number of alternative assets that the buyer can deliver; these are known as *deliverable obligations*. This may apply when a

[3] Determining the market value of the reference asset at the time of the credit event may be a little problematic as the issuer of the asset may well be in default or administration. An independent third-party *calculation agent* is usually employed to make the termination payment calculation.

swap has been entered into on a reference name rather than a specific obligation (such as a particular bond) issued by that name. Where more than one deliverable obligation is specified, the protection buyer will invariably deliver the asset that is the cheapest on the list of eligible assets. This gives rise to the concept of the *cheapest to deliver*, as encountered with government bond futures contracts, and is in effect an embedded option afforded the protection buyer.

In theory, the value of protection is identical irrespective of which settlement option is selected. However, under physical settlement the protection seller can gain if there is a recovery value that can be extracted from the defaulted asset; or its value may rise as the fortunes of the issuer improve. Despite this, swap market-making banks often prefer cash settlement as there is less administration associated with it. It is also more suitable when the swap is used as part of a synthetic structured product, because such vehicles may not be set up to take delivery of physical assets. Another advantage of cash settlement is that it does not expose the protection buyer to any risks should there not be any deliverable assets in the market; for instance, due to shortage of liquidity in the market. Were this to happen, the buyer may find the value of its settlement payment reduced. Nevertheless, physical settlement is widely used because counterparties wish to avoid the difficulties associated with determining the market value of the reference asset under cash settlement. Physical settlement also permits the protection seller to take part in the creditor negotiations with the reference entity's administrators, which may result in improved terms for them as holders of the asset.

Example 16.4 Physically-settled contracts and the delivery option

Many CDS contracts that are physically settled name a reference *entity* rather than a specific reference asset. On occurrence of a credit event, the protection buyer often has a choice of deliverable assets with which to effect settlement. The looser the definition of deliverable asset is in the CDS contract documents, the larger the potential delivery basket: as long as the bond meets pre-specified requirements for seniority and maturity, it may be delivered. Contrast this with the position of the bondholder in the cash market, who is aware of the exact issue that he or she is holding in the event of default. Credit default swap sellers, on the other hand, may receive potentially any bond from the basket of deliverable instruments that rank *pari passu* with the cash asset – this is the delivery option afforded the long swap holder.

In practice therefore, the protection buyer will deliver the *cheapest-to-deliver* bond from the delivery basket, exactly as it would for an exchange-traded futures contract. This delivery option has debateable value in theory, but significant value in practice. For instance, the bonds of a specific obligor that might be trading cheaper in the market include:

- the bond with the lowest coupon;
- a convertible bond;
- an illiquid bond;
- an ABS bond compared to a conventional fixed coupon bond;
- a very-long-dated bond.

Following experience in the US market (see Tolk 2001), the US adopted "modified restructuring" as one of the definitions of a credit event, which specifically restricts the delivery of long-dated bonds where restructuring is the credit event that triggers a contract payout. Nevertheless the last-named item is still relevant in the European market.

We see then that the delivery option therefore does carry value in the market. Similarly for an option contract, this value increases the closer the contract holder gets to the "strike price", which for a CDS is a credit event. Market sentiment on the particular reference name will drive the basis more or less positive, depending on how favourable the name is viewed. As the credit quality of the reference name worsens, protection sellers will quote higher CDS premiums; the basis will also widen as the probability of a credit event increases.

EXAMPLE 16.5 CDS hedge

XYZ plc credit spreads are currently trading at 120 basis points relative to government-issued securities for five-year maturities and 195 basis points for 10-year maturities. A portfolio manager hedges a $10 million holding of 10-year paper by purchasing the following CDS, written on the five-year bond. This hedge protects for the first five years of the holding, and in the event of XYZ's credit spread widening, it will increase in value and may be sold before expiry at profit. The 10-year bond holding also earns 75 basis points over the shorter-term paper for the portfolio manager.

Term:	Five years
Reference credit:	XYZ plc five-year bond
Credit event payout date:	The business day following occurrence of specified credit event
Default payment:	Nominal value of bond × [100 – price of bond after credit event]
Swap premium:	3.35%

Assume now that midway into the life of the swap there is a technical default on the XYZ plc five-year bond, such that its price now stands at $28. Under the terms of the swap the protection buyer delivers the bond to the seller, who pays out $7.2 million to the buyer.

The CDS enables one party to transfer its credit risk exposure to another party. Banks may use default swaps to trade sovereign and corporate credit spreads without trading the actual assets themselves; for example, someone who has gone long a default swap (the protection buyer) will gain if the reference asset obligor suffers a rating downgrade or defaults, and can sell the default swap at a profit if he or she can find a buyer counterparty.[4] This is because the cost of protection on the reference asset will have

[4] Be careful with terminology here. To "go long" of an instrument generally is to purchase it. In the cash market, going long of the bond means one is buying the bond and so receiving coupon; the buyer has therefore taken on credit risk exposure to the issuer. In a CDS, to go long is to buy the swap, but the buyer is purchasing protection and therefore paying premium; the buyer has no credit exposure on the name and has in effect "gone short" on the reference name (the equivalent of shorting a bond in the cash market and paying coupon). So buying a CDS is frequently referred to in the market as "shorting" the reference entity.

increased as a result of the credit event. The original buyer of the default swap need never have owned a bond issued by the reference asset obligor. CDS are used extensively for flow trading (that is, the daily customer buys and sells business) of single reference name credit risks or, in *portfolio swap* form, for trading a basket of reference credits. CDSs and CLNs are also used in structured products, in various combinations, and their flexibility has been behind the growth and wide application of the synthetic collateralised debt obligation and other credit hybrid products.

Figure 16.11 shows US dollar CDS price levels (in basis points) during 2003 and 2004 for BBB-rated reference entities, for three- and five-year CDS contracts. The graph shows the level of fluctuation in CDS prices, it also shows clearly the term structure of credit rates, as the five-year CDS price lies above the three-year rate at all times.

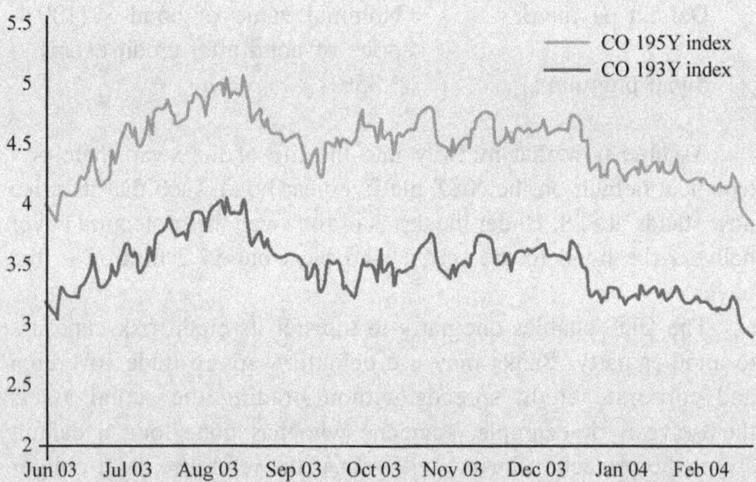

Figure 16.11 Investment-grade credit default swap levels, 2003–2004
Source: Bloomberg.

Figure 16.12 shows the Bloomberg screen WCDS, which contains CDS prices for a wide range of reference names, grouped according to industry category. Our example, from 1 December 2005, shows a selection of industrial corporate names.

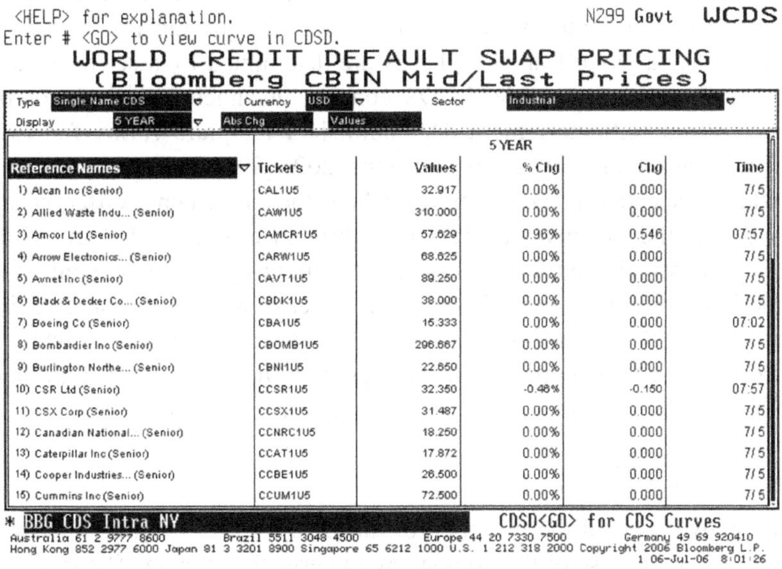

<HELP> for explanation. N299 Govt **WCDS**
Enter # <GO> to view curve in CDSD.

WORLD CREDIT DEFAULT SWAP PRICING
(Bloomberg CBIN Mid/Last Prices)

Type: Single Name CDS | Currency: USD | Sector: Industrial
Display: 5 YEAR | Abs Chg | Values

Reference Names	Tickers	5 YEAR Values	% Chg	Chg	Time
1) Alcan Inc (Senior)	CAL1U5	32.917	0.00%	0.000	7/5
2) Allied Waste Indu... (Senior)	CAW1U5	310.000	0.00%	0.000	7/5
3) Amcor Ltd (Senior)	CAMCR1U5	57.629	0.96%	0.546	07:57
4) Arrow Electronics... (Senior)	CARW1U5	68.625	0.00%	0.000	7/5
5) Avnet Inc (Senior)	CAVT1U5	89.250	0.00%	0.000	7/5
6) Black & Decker Co... (Senior)	CBDK1U5	38.000	0.00%	0.000	7/5
7) Boeing Co (Senior)	CBA1U5	15.333	0.00%	0.000	07:02
8) Bombardier Inc (Senior)	CBOMB1U5	296.667	0.00%	0.000	7/5
9) Burlington Northe... (Senior)	CBNI1U5	22.650	0.00%	0.000	7/5
10) CSR Ltd (Senior)	CCSR1U5	32.350	-0.46%	-0.150	07:57
11) CSX Corp (Senior)	CCSX1U5	31.487	0.00%	0.000	7/5
12) Canadian National... (Senior)	CCNRC1U5	18.250	0.00%	0.000	7/5
13) Caterpillar Inc (Senior)	CCAT1U5	17.872	0.00%	0.000	7/5
14) Cooper Industries... (Senior)	CCBE1U5	26.500	0.00%	0.000	7/5
15) Cummins Inc (Senior)	CCUM1U5	72.500	0.00%	0.000	7/5

* BBG CDS Intra NY CDSD<GO> for CDS Curves
Australia 61 2 9777 8600 Brazil 5511 3048 4500 Europe 44 20 7330 7500 Germany 49 69 920410
Hong Kong 852 2977 6000 Japan 81 3 3201 8900 Singapore 65 6212 1000 U.S. 1 212 318 2000 Copyright 2006 Bloomberg L.P.
1 06-Jul-06 8:01:26

Figure 16.12 Bloomberg screen WCDS showing extract of world CDS prices, as at 6 July 2006

Loan-only credit default swaps

A development in the CDS market from 2006 is the loan-only credit default swap (LCDS). This is a CDS that references specifically a syndicated secured loan and not any other type of asset.[5] The main motive for the creation of a specific loan-only CDS is that syndicated loans rank above bonds in a corporate winding-up (where loans are secured), so are slightly different assets compared to bonds. As such, there are times when only this specific asset class, as opposed to loans and bonds together, needs to be hedged or accessed by investors. Written on the same reference name an LCDS would, all else being equal, trade tighter than a CDS, because there is a higher expected recovery rate on the former. LCDS has potential to be a very popular hedging tool for banks.

A CDS is sometimes described as analogous to an insurance contract, but actually this is not quite correct. The protection buyer does not need to

[5] A vanilla CDS would reference bonds and unsecured loans, ABS-CDS would reference asset-backed securities.

own the asset on which the CDS is written, nor to have suffered a loss on occurrence of a credit event. Also different from insurance is that a CDS contract has a pay-off amount that is pre-determined by a set formula.

At the time of writing, LCDS contract documentation had not been standardised, although the ISDA published template forms for LCDS documentation in May 2006 and June 2006 for the European and US markets respectively. This highlights how the instruments differ in some respects in the two markets. The main difference is that a US LCDS does not automatically expire following the maturity or repayment of the underlying reference loan. This is not the case with European LCDS. In effect the US instrument is more of an investment product, while the European LCDS is more of a hedging product. It is possible that ultimately both forms of product will be available in either market.

Growth of LCDS

The motives behind the inception of the LCDS are essentially the same as those behind the rise of the original credit derivative market. The instrument is used for the same reasons as vanilla CDS, including credit risk management, as an alternative to the cash market; its principal use in the European market is as a risk management tool by banks that originate syndicated secured loans. The implementation of Basel II has been a trade driver, as the new regulatory regime will result in higher capital charges for certain types of syndicated loans. The growth in collateralised loan obligation (CLO) business has also lead to the demand for LCDS, in two ways: as a hedging tool, and also as an investment tool for synthetic CLOs that source their assets in the LCDS market. The advantages of LCDS to a synthetic CLO manager mirror those of CDS with regard to synthetic CDOs: they provide access to assets that might not otherwise be available in the cash loan market.

LCDS have the same flexibility as vanilla CDS and have the same application for bank ALM purposes. These include:

- credit risk management: managing exposure of syndicated loan books without having to impact on client relationships;
- regulatory capital management: reducing Basel capital charge (connected with the above).

For investors, LCDS enable access to the syndicated loan market, which might not otherwise be available; other advantages include:

- ability to transact tax-efficient deals that might not be possible in the cash market, where loans are subject to withholding tax and other tax consequences;
- capital structure arbitrage: relative-value type trades involving loans spread against bonds, or senior loans against mezzanine or junior loans, and so on.

At the time of writing, in the European market LCDS were trading at a negative basis to cash loans, making them unattractive for investment purposes when compared to cash.[6] The negative basis appeared to be driven by an excess of demand over supply, driving spreads down; this demand was driven by banks hedging their syndicated loan books.

Characteristics of LCDS[7]

LCDS features the following characteristics which are worth considering when making a comparison to vanilla CDS contracts:

- *Reference obligation*: in the European market the reference obligation for an LCDS is all the tranches of a syndicated loan in the name of the obligor, including any un-drawn tranches or an un-drawn credit facility. It can be a 2nd-line or 3rd-line tranche as well as a 1st-line one. In a US LCDS the reference obligation is similar except it must be specifically designated as a reference obligation. In theory this is more restrictive. The deliverable obligation on occurrence of a credit event is (i) for European LCDS, the reference obligations and (ii) for US LCDS a loan as defined in the contract definitions;
- *Cancellability*: in the cash market in Europe, syndicated loans may be paid off ahead of the stated maturity date (in some cases there is a period of one year after the start of the loan when they cannot be repaid). Consequently, European LCDS terminate on paydown of the underlying reference loan. However, there is no feature for adjusting notional on the LCDS, which one might have expected given that many syndicated loans are amortising. US LCDS are not cancellable upon repayment of the reference asset, and instead allow for substitution of the reference asset with an equivalent one;

---

6 See Choudhry (2006a) and chapters 7 and 8 of Choudhry (2004a) for details on the CDS basis.

7 The source for background and technical data in this section is the pamphlet *Loan-Only Credit Default Swaps*, written by Martin Bartlam and Karin Artman (Orrick, Herrington & Sutcliffe 2006). Cited with permission.

- *Restructuring*: European LCDS include loan restructuring as a credit event. Such occurrences are fairly frequent in the syndicated loan market and hence banks would wish to be able to buy protection on the loans that covered for this risk. Restructuring is not a credit event for US LCDS.

  Note that under Basel II, full regulatory capital relief on a syndicated loan asset is granted only if credit derivative protection written on that asset includes restructuring as a credit event. Otherwise, only partial capital relief can be obtained, to a maximum of 60% of the LCDS notional value.
- *Pricing*: LCDS premiums, like vanilla CDS, are fixed. This contrasts with the underlying syndicated loan, which is invariably floating-rate. In addition there will be a basis difference between the swap and loan, arising from a number of different factors;
- *Settlement*: the settlement mechanism for both European and US LCDS is predominantly physical settlement. This has the potential to create delivery issues in future, if there is a shortage of deliverable assets. A Notice of Physical Settlement (NOPS) must be delivered within 30 days of the credit event determination date, upon which the protection seller must pay over the protection payment to the protection buyer. This is:
  - ➤ for physical settlement, an amount equal to the notional amount multiplied by the reference price. The protection buyer delivers the deliverable obligation in return;
  - ➤ for cash settlement, an amount equal to the reference price minus the recovery rate on the reference obligation, multiplied by the notional amount.

  Note how the protection payment formulas for settlement of LCDS differ from those of vanilla CDS.

  Partly as a means to avoid such problems, in a European LCDS the protection seller can request cash settlement. If no market price is available for any of the deliverable obligations, then physical settlement will have to apply.

  The protection buyer cannot select cash settlement.

It is unlikely that the differences between European and US LCDS will remain in place, and we would expect some convergence between the two forms. Possibly both versions may be available in either market at some stage, but market demand will ultimately demand which structure is most popular and thus retained.

Total return swaps

A *total return swap* (TRS), sometimes known as a *total rate of return swap* or *TR swap*, is an agreement between two parties to exchange the total returns from financial assets. This is designed to transfer the credit risk from one party to the other. It is one of the principal instruments used by banks and other financial institutions to manage their credit risk exposure, and as such is a credit derivative. One definition of a TRS is given in Francis et al. (1999), which states that a TRS is a swap agreement in which the *total return* of a bank loan or credit-sensitive security is exchanged for some other cash flow, usually tied to Libor or some other loan or credit-sensitive security.

In some versions of a TRS the actual underlying asset is actually sold to the counterparty, with a corresponding swap transaction agreed alongside; in other versions there is no physical change of ownership of the underlying asset. The TRS trade itself can be to any maturity term; that is, it need not match the maturity of the underlying security. In a TRS the total return from the underlying asset is paid over to the counterparty in return for a fixed or floating cash flow. This makes it slightly different from other credit derivatives, as the payments between counterparties to a TRS are connected to changes in the market value of the underlying asset, as well as changes resulting from the occurrence of a credit event.

Figure 16.13 on page 778 illustrates a generic TR swap. The two counterparties are labelled as banks, but the party termed "Bank A" can be another financial institution, including insurance companies and hedge funds that often hold fixed income portfolios. In Figure 16.13 Bank A has contracted to pay the "total return" on a specified reference asset, while simultaneously receiving a Libor-based return from Bank B. The reference or underlying asset can be a bank loan such as a corporate loan or a sovereign or corporate bond. The total return payments from Bank A include the interest payments on the underlying loan, as well as any appreciation in the market value of the asset. Bank B will pay the Libor-based return; it will also pay any difference if there is a depreciation in the price of the asset. The economic effect is as if Bank B owned the underlying asset, as such TRS are synthetic loans or securities. A significant feature is that Bank A will usually hold the underlying asset on its balance sheet, so that if this asset was originally on Bank B's balance sheet, this is a means by which the latter can have the asset removed from its balance sheet for the term of the TRS.[8] If

[8] Although it is common for the receiver of the Libor-based payments to have the reference asset on its balance sheet, this is not always the case.

we assume Bank A has access to Libor funding, it will receive a spread on this from Bank B. Under the terms of the swap, Bank B will pay the difference between the initial market value and any depreciation, so it is sometimes termed the "guarantor", while Bank A is the "beneficiary".

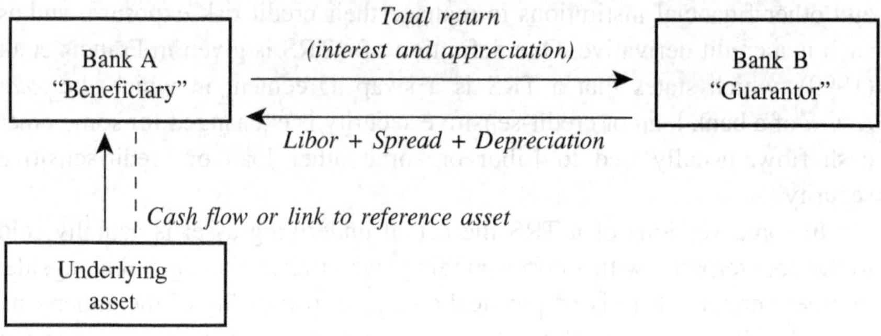

Figure 16.13 Total return swap

The total return on the underlying asset is the interest payments and any change in the market value if there is capital appreciation. The value of an appreciation may be cash settled, or alternatively there may be physical delivery of the reference asset on maturity of the swap, in return for a payment of the initial asset value by the total return "receiver". The maturity of the TRS need not be identical to that of the reference asset, and in fact it is rare for it to be so.

The swap element of the trade will usually pay on a quarterly or semi-annual basis, with the underlying asset being revalued or marked-to-market on the refixing dates. The asset price is usually obtained from an independent third-party source such as Bloomberg or Reuters, or as the average of a range of market quotes. If the obligor of the reference asset defaults, the swap may be terminated immediately, with an NPV payment changing hands according to what this value is, or it may be continued with each party making appreciation or depreciation payments as appropriate. This second option is only available if there is a market for the asset, which is unlikely in the case of a bank loan. If the swap is terminated, each counterparty will be liable to the other for accrued interest plus any appreciation or depreciation of the asset. Commonly under the terms of the trade, the guarantor bank has the option to purchase the underlying asset from the beneficiary bank, then dealing directly with the loan defaulter.

With a TRS the basic concept is that one party "funds" an underlying asset and transfers the total return of the asset to another party, in return for a (usually) floating return that is a spread to Libor. This spread is a function of:

- the credit rating of the swap counterparty;
- the amount and value of the reference asset;
- the credit quality of the reference asset;
- the funding costs of the beneficiary bank;
- any required profit margin;
- the capital charge associated with the TRS.

The TRS counterparties must therefore consider a number of risk factors associated with the transaction, which include:

- the probability that the TR beneficiary may default while the reference asset has increased in value;
- the reference asset obligor defaults, followed by default of the TRS receiver before payment of the depreciation has been made to the payer or "provider".

The first risk measure is a function of the probability of default by the TRS receiver and the market volatility of the reference asset, while the second risk is related to the joint probability of default of both factors as well as the recovery probability of the asset.

TRS contracts are used in a variety of applications by banks. They can be written as pure exchanges of cash flow differences – rather like an interest-rate swap – or the reference asset can be actually transferred to the total return payer, which would then make the TRS akin to a "synthetic repo" contract.[9] Some of the most common applications of TRS contracts include:

- *As pure exchanges of cash flow differences*: Using TRSs as a credit derivative instrument, a party can remove exposure to an asset without having to sell it. This is conceptually similar to interest-rate

[9] When a bank sells stock short, it must borrow the stock to deliver it to its customer, in return for a fee (called a stock loan), or it may lend cash against the stock which it then delivers to the customer (called a "sale and repurchase agreement" or *repo*). The counterparty is "selling and buying back" while the bank that is short the stock is "buying and selling back". A TRS is a synthetic form of repo, as the bond is sold to the TRS payer.

swaps, which enable banks and other financial institutions to trade interest-rate risk without borrowing or lending cash funds. A TRS agreement entered into as a credit derivative is a means by which banks can take on unfunded off-balance sheet credit exposure. Higher rated banks that have access to Libid funding can benefit by funding on-balance-sheet assets that are credit protected through a credit derivative such as a TRS, assuming the net spread of asset income over credit protection premium is positive.

- *Reference asset transferred to the total return payer*: In a vanilla TRS the total return payer retains rights to the reference asset, although in some cases servicing and voting rights may be transferred. The total return receiver gains an exposure to the reference asset without having to pay out the cash proceeds that would be required to purchase it. As the maturity of the swap rarely matches that of the asset, the swap receiver may gain from the positive funding or *carry* that derives from being able to roll over the short-term funding of a longer-term asset.[10] The total return payer, on the other hand, benefits from protection against market and credit risk for a specified period of time, without having to liquidate the asset itself. On maturity of the swap the total return payer may reinvest the asset if it continues to own it, or it may sell the asset in the open market. Thus the instrument may be considered a *synthetic repo*.

The economic effect of the two applications may be the same, but they are considered different instruments:

- The TRS as a credit derivative instrument actually takes the assets off the balance sheet, whereas the tax and accounting authorities treat repo as if the assets remain on the balance sheet.
- A TRS trade is conducted under the ISDA standard legal agreement, while repo is conducted under a standard legal agreement called the Global Master Repurchase Agreement (GMRA).

It is these differences that, under certain circumstances, make the TRS funding route a more favourable one.

We now explain in more detail the main uses of TRSs.

[10] This assumes a positively sloping yield curve.

Synthetic repo

A portfolio manager believes that a particular bond (which she does not hold) is about to decline in price. To reflect this view she may do one of the following.

- *Sell the bond in the market and cover the resulting short position in repo.* The cash flow out is the coupon on the bond, with capital gain if the bond falls in price. Assume that the repo rate is floating, say Libor plus a spread. The manager must be aware of the funding costs of the trade, so that unless the bond can be covered in repo at *general collateral* rates,[11] the funding will be at a loss. The yield on the bond must also be lower than the Libor plus spread received in the repo.
- *As an alternative, enter into a TRS.* The portfolio manager pays the total return on the bond and receives Libor plus a spread. If the bond yield exceeds the Libor spread, the funding will be negative; however, the trade will gain if the trader's view is proved correct and the bond falls in price by a sufficient amount. If the breakeven funding cost (which the bond must exceed as it falls in value) is lower in the TRS, this method will be used rather than the repo approach. This is more likely if the bond is special.

Reduction in credit risk

A TRS conducted as a synthetic repo is usually undertaken to effect the temporary removal of assets from the balance sheet. This can be done by entering into a short-term TRS with, say, a two-week term that straddles the reporting date. Bonds are removed from the balance sheet if they are part of a sale plus TRS transaction. This is because legally the bank selling the asset is not required to repurchase bonds from the swap counterparty, nor is the total return payer obliged to sell the bonds back to the counterparty (or indeed sell the bonds at all on maturity of the TRS).

Hence, under a TRS an asset such as a bond position may be removed from the balance sheet. This may be desired for a number of reasons; for example, if the institution is due to be analysed by credit rating agencies or if the annual external audit is due shortly. Another reason why a bank may wish to temporarily remove lower credit-quality assets from its balance sheet

[11] That is, the bond cannot be *special*. A bond is special when the repo rate payable on it is significantly (say, 20–30 basis points or more) below the *general collateral* repo rate, so that covering a short position in the bond entails paying a substantial funding premium.

is if it is in danger of breaching capital limits in between the quarterly return periods. In this case, as the return period approaches, lower quality assets may be removed from the balance sheet by means of a TRS, which is set to mature after the return period has passed. In summary, to avoid adverse impact on regular internal and external capital and credit exposure reporting a bank may use TRSs to reduce the amount of lower quality assets on the balance sheet.

The TRS as a funding instrument

The TRS is often used as a funding instrument; in other words, as an alternative to a repo trade. There may be legal, administrative, operational or other reasons why a repo trade is not entered into to begin with. In these cases, provided that a counterparty can be found and the funding rate is not prohibitive, a TRS may be just as suitable.

Consider a financial institution such as a regulated broker-dealer that has a portfolio of assets on its balance sheet that it needs to obtain funding for. These assets are investment-grade structured finance bonds such as credit card asset-backed securities, residential mortgage-backed securities and collateralised debt obligation notes, and investment-grade convertible bonds. In the repo market, it is able to fund these at Libor plus 6 basis points. That is, it can repo the bonds out to a bank counterparty, and will pay Libor plus 6 basis points on the funds it receives.

Assume that for operational reasons the bank can no longer fund these assets using repo. It can fund them using a basket TRS instead, provided that a suitable counterparty can be found. Under this contract, the portfolio of assets is swapped out to the TRS counterparty, and cash received from the counterparty. The assets are therefore sold off the balance sheet to the counterparty, an investment bank. The investment bank will need to fund this itself, it may have a line of credit from a parent bank or it may swap the bonds out itself. The funding rate it charges the broker-dealer will depend on the rate in which it can fund the assets itself. Assume this is Libor plus 12 basis points – the higher rate reflects the lower liquidity in the basket TRS market for non-vanilla bonds.

The broker-dealer enters into a three-month TRS with the investment bank counterparty, with a one-week interest-rate reset. This means that at each week interval the basket is revalued. The difference in value from the last valuation is paid (if higher) or received (if lower) by the investment bank to the broker-dealer; in return, the broker-dealer also pays one-week interest on the funds it received at the start of the trade. In practice these two cash flows are netted off and only one payment changes hands, just as in an interest-rate swap. The terms of the trade are shown below.

Trade date:	22 December 2003
Value date:	24 December 2003
Maturity date:	24 March 2004
Rate reset:	31 December 2003
Interest rate:	1.19875% (this is the one-week USD Libor fix of 1.07875 plus 12 bps)

The swap is a three-month TRS with one-week reset, which means that the swap can be broken at one-week intervals and bonds in the reference basket can be returned, added to or substituted.

Assume that the portfolio basket contains five bonds, all US dollar denominated. Assume further that these are all investment-grade credit card asset-backed securities with prices available on Bloomberg. The combined market value of the entire portfolio is taken to be $151,080,951.00.

At the start of the trade, the five bonds are swapped out to the investment bank, which pays the portfolio value for them. On the first reset date, the portfolio is revalued and the following calculations confirmed:

Old portfolio value:	$151,080,951.00
Interest rate:	1.19875%
Interest payable by broker-dealer:	$35,215.50
New portfolio value:	$152,156,228.00
Portfolio performance:	+ $1,075,277
Net payment – broker-dealer receives:	$1,040,061.50.

The rate is reset for value 31 December 2003 for the period to 7 January 2004. The rate is 12 basis points over the one-week USD Libor fix on 29 December 2003, which is 1.15750 + 0.12 or 1.2775%. This interest rate is payable on the new "loan" amount of $152,156,228.00.

The TRS trade has become a means by which the broker-dealer can obtain collateralised funding for its portfolio. Like a repo, the bonds are taken off the broker-dealer's balance sheet, but unlike a repo the tax and accounting treatment also assumes they have been permanently taken off the balance sheet. In addition, the TRS is traded under the ISDA legal definitions, compared to a repo that is traded under the GMRA standard repo legal agreement.

Credit-linked notes

A standard credit-linked note (CLN) is a security, usually issued by an investment-grade entity, that has an interest payment and fixed maturity structure similar to a vanilla bond. The performance of the note, however, including the maturity value, is linked to the performance of a specified underlying asset or assets, as well as to that of the issuing entity. Notes are usually issued at par. The notes are often used by borrowers to hedge against credit risk, and by investors to enhance the yield received on their holdings. Hence, the issuer of the note is the protection buyer and the buyer of the note is the protection seller.

CLNs are essentially credit derivatives but in the shape of a vanilla bond. The CLN pays regular coupons; however, the credit derivative element is usually set to allow the issuer to decrease the principal amount if a credit event occurs. For example, consider an issuer of credit cards that wants to fund its (credit card) loan portfolio via an issue of debt. In order to hedge the credit risk of the portfolio, it issues a two-year CLN. The principal amount of the bond is 100% as usual, and it pays a coupon of 7.50%, which is 200 basis points above the two-year benchmark. If, however, the incidence of bad debt among credit card holders exceeds 10%, then the terms state that note holders will only receive back £85 per £100 nominal. The credit card issuer has in effect purchased a credit option that lowers its liability in the event that it suffers from a specified credit event, which in this case is an above-expected incidence of bad debts. The credit card bank has issued the CLN to reduce its credit exposure, in the form of this particular type of credit insurance. If the incidence of bad debts is low, the note is redeemed at par. However, if there is a high incidence of such debt, the bank will only have to repay a part of its loan liability.

Figure 16.14 depicts the cash flows associated with a CLN. CLNs exist in a number of forms, but all of them contain a link between the return they pay and the credit-related performance of the underlying asset. Investors may wish to purchase the CLN because the coupon paid on it will be above what the same bank would pay on a vanilla bond it issued, and higher than other comparable investments in the market. In addition, such notes are usually priced below par on issue. Assuming the notes are eventually redeemed at par, investors will also have realised a substantial capital gain.

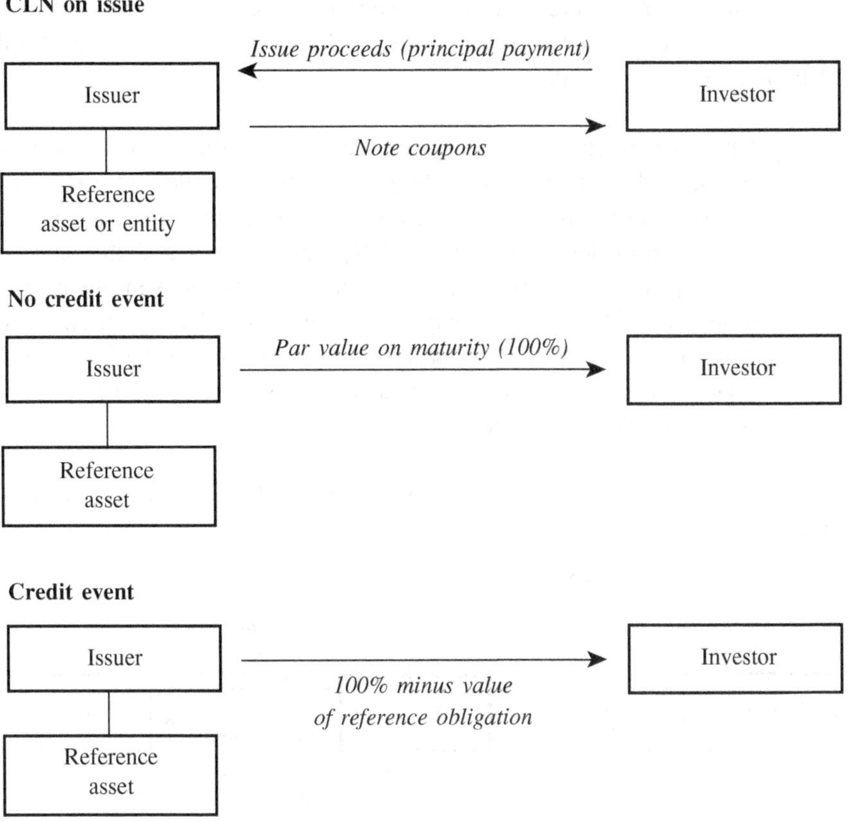

Figure 16.14 Cash-settled CLN

As with CDS, CLNs may be specified under cash or physical settlement; however, there are differences associated with the funded nature of CLNs and also with the specific type of CLN that is being considered.

The true credit derivative CLN is a note issued by one party that references another party as the credit reference name. However, certain bonds have been labelled as "CLNs" despite being issued by the same company that is the credit reference. For these bonds, the occurrence of a credit event signifies immediate termination of the bond; however, there is no settlement process as such because the protection seller is already holding the bond. In this respect such CLNs are more akin to vanilla cash bonds of the same issuer.[12]

[12] The reason such bonds are termed "CLNs" is because their pay-off is linked to a credit-related performance of the issuer; for example, a change in the credit rating.

For true CLNs, there is a similar settlement process to that for CDS contracts. Consider a CLN issued by ABC Securities that references XYZ Automotive plc. Specifically:

- Under cash settlement, on occurrence of a credit event the note is terminated. The protection buyer will pay the default value, or recovery value (RR), of the reference name to the protection seller. This is equivalent to the [100 – RR] payout under a CDS contract;
- Under physical settlement, on occurrence of a credit event the note is terminated. The protection buyer will deliver an XYZ Automotive plc bond, out of a deliverable basket of XYZ bonds, to the protection seller. The protection seller of course retains the original CLN bond, issued by ABC Securities.

Note that the protection buyer may well be ABC Securities, but it does not have to be.

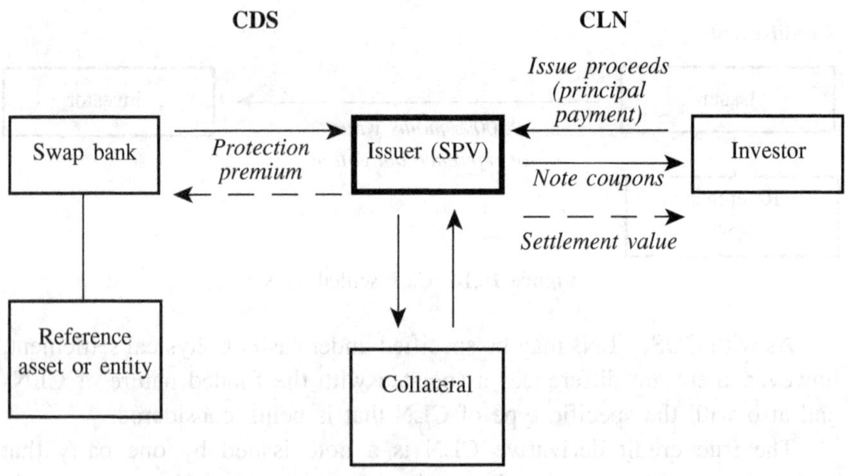

Figure 16.15 CDS and CLN structure on single reference name

Structured products may combine both CLNs and CDSs to meet issuer and investor requirements. For instance, Figure 16.15 shows a credit structure designed to provide a higher return for an investor on comparable risk to the cash market. An issuing entity is set up in the form of an SPV which issues CLNs to the market. The structure is engineered so that the SPV has a neutral position on a reference asset. It has bought protection on a single reference name by issuing a funded credit derivative, the CLN, and simultaneously sold protection on this name by selling a CDS on this name.

The proceeds of the CLN are invested in risk-free collateral such as T-bills or a Treasury bank account. The coupon on the CLN will be a spread over Libor. It is backed by the collateral account and the fee generated by the SPV in selling protection with the CDS. Investors in the CLN will have exposure to the reference asset or entity, and the repayment of the note is linked to the performance of the reference entity. If a credit event occurs, the maturity date of the CLN is brought forward and the note is settled at par minus the value of the reference asset or entity.

Credit options

Credit options are bilateral OTC financial contracts. A credit option is a contract designed to meet specific hedging or speculative requirements of an entity, which may purchase or sell the option to meet its objectives. A credit call option gives the buyer the right – without the obligation – to purchase the underlying credit-sensitive asset, or a credit spread, at a specified price and specified time (or period of time). A credit put option gives the buyer the right – without the obligation – to sell the underlying credit-sensitive asset or credit spread. By purchasing credit options, banks and other institutions can take a view on credit spread movements for the cost of the option premium only, without recourse to actual loans issued by an obligor. The writer of credit options seeks to earn premium income.

Credit option terms are similar to those used for conventional equity options. A *call* option written on a stock grants the purchaser the right but not the obligation to purchase a specified amount of the stock at a set price and time. A credit option can be used by bond investors to hedge against a decline in the price of specified bonds, in the event of a credit event such as a ratings downgrade. The investor would purchase an option whose payoff profile is a function of the credit quality of the bond, so that a loss on the bond position is offset by the payout from the option.

As with conventional options, there are both vanilla credit options and exotic credit options. The vanilla credit option grants the purchaser the right, but not the obligation, to buy (or sell if a *put* option) an asset or credit spread at a specified price (the *strike* price) for a specified period of time up to the maturity of the option. A credit option allows a market participant to take a view on credit only, and no other exposure such as interest rates. As an example, consider investors who believe that a particular credit spread, which can be that of a specific entity or the average for a sector (such as "all

AA-rated sterling corporates"), will widen over the next six months. They can buy a six-month call option on the relevant credit spread, for which a one-off premium (the price of the option) is paid. If the credit spread indeed does widen beyond the strike during the six months, the option will be in-the-money and the investors will gain. If not, the investors' loss is limited to the premium paid. Depending on whether the option is American or European, the option may be exercised before its expiry date or on its expiry date only.

Exotic credit options are options that have one or more of their parameters changed from the vanilla norm; the same terms are used as in other option markets. Examples include the barrier credit option, which specifies a credit event that would trigger (activate) the option or inactivate it. A digital credit option would have a payout profile that would be fixed, irrespective of how much in-the-money it was on expiry, and a zero payout if out of the money.

Index credit derivatives

The iTraxx series is a set of credit indices that enable market participants to trade funded and unfunded credit derivatives linked to a credit benchmark. There are a number of different indices covering different sectors; for example, iTraxx Europe, iTraxx Japan, iTraxx Korea and so on. The equivalent index in the North American market is known as CD-X. The iTraxx exhibits relatively high liquidity and for this reason is viewed as a credit benchmark, and its bid–offer spread is very narrow at 1–2 basis points. This contrasts with spreads generally between 10 and 30 basis points for single-name CDS contracts. Because of its liquidity and benchmark status, the iTraxx is increasingly viewed as a leading indicator of the credit market overall, and the CDS index basis is important in this regard as an indicator of relative value.

The iTraxx series is a basket of reference credits that is reviewed on a regular basis. For example, the iTraxx Europe index consists of 125 corporate reference names, so that each name represents 0.8% of the basket. Figure 16.16 on page 790 shows the an extract from a Bloomberg screen for the June 2011 iTraxx Europe index, with the first page of reference names. The menu for this screen shows additional terms for the contract.[13]

The index rolls every six months (in March and September), when reference names are reviewed and the premium is set. Hence there is a rolling series of contracts with the "front contract" being the most recent.

[13] The screens for the iTraxx are found by typing ITRX CDS <Corp> <go>.

There are two standard maturities, which are 5.25 years and 10.25 years. Figure 16.17 on page 791 shows a list of iTraxx indices as at June 2006; the second-listed contract is the current one, with a June 2011 maturity and a premium of 40 basis points (see Figure 16.16). All existing indices can be traded although the most liquid index is the current one. Reference names are all investment-grade rated and are the highest traded names by CDS volume in the past six months.

A bank buying protection in EUR10 million notional of the index has in effect bought protection on EUR80,000 each of 125 single-name CDS. The premium payable on a CDS written on the index is set at the start of the contract and remains fixed for its entire term; the premium is paid quarterly in arrears in the same way as a single-name CDS. The premium remains fixed but of course the market value fluctuates on a daily basis. This works as follows:

- the constituents of the index are set about one week before it goes live, with the fixed premium being set two days before. The premium is calculated as an average of all the premiums payable on the reference names making up the index. In June 2006 the current 5-year index for Europe was the iTraxx Europe June 2011 contract. The reference names in the index were set on 13 March 2006, with the premium fixed on 18 March 2006. The index went live on 20 March 2006. The index is renewed every six months in the same way;
- after the roll date, a trade in the iTraxx is entered into at the current market price;
- because this is different to the fixed premium, an up-front payment is made between the protection seller and protection buyer, which is the difference between the present values of the fixed premium and the current market premium.

So, for example, on 21 June 2006 the market price of the June 2011 iTraxx Europe was 34 basis points. An investor selling protection on this contract would receive 40 basis points quarterly in arrears for the five years from June 2006 to June 2011. The difference is made up front: the investor receives 40 basis points although the market level at the time of trade is 34 basis points. Therefore the protection seller pays a one-off payment of the difference between the two values, discounted. The present value of the contract is calculated assuming a flat spread curve and a 40% recovery rate. We can use Bloomberg screen CDSW to work this out, and Figure 16.18 on page 791 shows such a calculation using this screen. This shows a trade for

EUR10 million notional of the current iTraxx Europe index on 19 June 2006. We see the deal spread is 40 basis points; we enter the current market price of 34 basis points, and assume a flat credit term structure.

From Figure 16.18 we see that the one-off payment for this deal is EUR 27,280. The protection seller, who will receive 40 basis points quarterly in arrears for the life of the deal, pays this amount at trade inception to the protection buyer.[14]

If a credit event occurs on one of the reference entities in the iTraxx, the contract is physically settled, for that name, for 0.8% of the notional value of the contract. This is similar to the way that a single-name CDS would be settled. Unlike a single-name CDS, the contract continues to maturity at a reduced notional amount. Note that European iTraxx indices trade under modified–modified restructuring (MMR) terms, which are prevalent in the European market. Under MMR, a debt restructuring is named as a credit event.[15]

<HELP> for explanation, <MENU> for similar functions. P174 **Corp**

CREDIT DEFAULT SWAPS for ticker ITRX CDS Page 1/ 11
Found 194

	ISSUER	SPREAD	MATURITY	SERS	RTNG	FREQ	TYPE	CNTRY/CURR
1)	ITRX EUR	25	6/20/09	5EU	N.A.	Qtr	iTRAXX	EU /EUR
2)	ITRX EUR	40	6/20/11	5EU2	N.A.	Qtr	iTRAXX	EU /EUR
3)	ITRX EUR	50	6/20/13	5EU3	N.A.	Qtr	iTRAXX	EU /EUR
4)	ITRX EUR	60	6/20/16	5EU4	N.A.	Qtr	iTRAXX	EU /EUR
5)	ITRX SDI	45	6/20/16	2SD	N.A.	Qtr	iTRAXX	GB /GBP
6)	ITRX INDS	40	6/20/11	5IND	N.A.	Qtr	iTRAXX	EU /EUR
7)	ITRX INDS	60	6/20/16	5IN2	N.A.	Qtr	iTRAXX	EU /EUR
8)	ITRX SUB	25	6/20/11	5SUB	N.A.	Qtr	iTRAXX	EU /EUR
9)	ITRX SUB	45	6/20/16	5SU2	N.A.	Qtr	iTRAXX	EU /EUR
10)	ITRX SNR FIN	15	6/20/11	5SNR	N.A.	Qtr	iTRAXX	EU /EUR
11)	ITRX SNR FIN	25	6/20/16	5SN2	N.A.	Qtr	iTRAXX	EU /EUR
12)	ITRX CROSS	290	6/20/11	5XOV	N.A.	Qtr	iTRAXX	EU /EUR
13)	ITRX CROSS	350	6/20/16	5XO2	N.A.	Qtr	iTRAXX	EU /EUR
14)	ITRX NON-FINL	40	6/20/11	5NF1	N.A.	Qtr	iTRAXX	EU /EUR
15)	ITRX NON-FINL	60	6/20/16	5NF2	N.A.	Qtr	iTRAXX	EU /EUR
16)	ITRX TMT	40	6/20/11	5TMT	N.A.	Qtr	iTRAXX	EU /EUR
17)	ITRX TMT	60	6/20/16	5TM2	N.A.	Qtr	iTRAXX	EU /EUR
18)	ITRX HVOL	40	6/20/09	5HI	N.A.	Qtr	iTRAXX	EU /EUR
19)	ITRX HVOL	70	6/20/11	5HI2	N.A.	Qtr	iTRAXX	EU /EUR

Australia 61 2 9777 8600 Brazil 5511 3048 4500 Europe 44 20 7330 7500 Germany 49 69 920410
Hong Kong 852 2977 6000 Japan 81 3 3201 8900 Singapore 65 6212 1000 U.S. 1 212 318 2000
0 19-Jun-06 15:35:31

Figure 16.16 List of iTraxx indices as shown on Bloomberg, 19 June 2006

[14] The one-off payment reflects the difference between the prevailing market rate and the fixed rate. If the market rate was above 40 basis points at the time of this trade, the protection buyer would pay the protection seller the one-off payment reflecting this difference.

[15] This contrasts with the North American market, which includes the CDX family of indices, where CDSs trade under no-restructuring terms; this describes only bankruptcy and liquidation as credit events.

<HELP> for explanation. P174 **Corp** **CDSW**
1<GO> to sort by name. 3<Go> to sort by weight. 4<Go> to download to Excel.
Page 1/7

REFERENCE ENTITY LIST

Reference Entity Legal Name	Weight (%)
ABN AMRO Bank N.V.	0.800
ACCOR	0.800
Adecco S.A.	0.800
Aegon N.V.	0.800
Aktiebolaget Electrolux	0.800
Aktiebolaget Volvo	0.800
AKZO Nobel N.V.	0.800
Allianz Aktiengesellschaft	0.800
ALTADIS, S.A.	0.800
ARCELOR FINANCE	0.800
ASSICURAZIONI GENERALI - SOCIETA PER A	0.800
AVIVA PLC	0.800
AXA	0.800
BAA PLC	0.800
BAE SYSTEMS PLC	0.800
BANCA INTESA S.P.A.	0.800
BANCA MONTE DEI PASCHI DI SIENA S.P.A.	0.800
BANCA POPOLARE ITALIANA - BANCA POPOLA	0.800
BANCO BILBAO VIZCAYA ARGENTARIA, SOCIE	0.800
Banco Comercial Portugues, S.A.	0.800

Australia 61 2 9777 8600 Brazil 5511 3048 4500 Europe 44 20 7330 7500 Germany 49 69 920410
Hong Kong 852 2977 6000 Japan 81 3 3201 8900 Singapore 65 6212 1000 U.S. 1 212 318 2000 Copyright 2006 Bloomberg L.P.
0 19-Jun-06 15:39:20

Figure 16.17 Page 1 of list of reference names in iTraxx Europe June 2011 index © Bloomberg L.P. Used with permission. All rights reserved.

<HELP> for explanation. P174 **Corp** **CDSW**
2<GO> to save curve source

CREDIT DEFAULT SWAP CPU:121

Deal | Curves | View

Deal Information

Reference: **ITRAXX EUROPE**
Counterparty: ITRX EUR Deal#: SPN5ZTGM
Ticker: ITRX CDS Series: 5EU2
Business Days: EUR Settlement Code: EUR
Business Day Adj: 1 Following Currency: EUR
B BUY **Notional:** 10.00 MM **Factor:**1
Effective Date: 3/20/06 Knock Out: N
Maturity Date: 6/20/11 Day Count: ACT/360
Payment Freq: Q Quarterly Month End: N
Pay Accrued: T True First Cpn: 6/20/06
Curve Recovery: T True Next to Last Cpn: 3/21/11
Recovery Rate: 0.40 Date Gen Method: B Backward
Deal Spread: 40.000 bps

Calculator **Mode:** 1 Calc Price

Settlement Date: 6/20/06 Model: J JPMorgan
Cash Settled On: 6/22/06
Price: 100.27280594 **Repl Sprd:**34.000 bps
Market Val: -27,280.59 **Days:** 0
Accrued: 0.00 **Sprd DV01:**4,557.82
Total Val: -27,280.59 **IR DV01:** 6.71

Spreads 1 Term

Curve Date: 6/19/06
Benchmark: S 45 A Ask
EU BGN Swap Curve
Sprds: U User A Ask
CDSD SPN5ZTGM IMM N

Par Cds Spreads Default
Flat: Y

	(bps)	Prob
6 mo	34.000	0.0029
1 yr	34.000	0.0057
2 yr	34.000	0.0114
3 yr	34.000	0.0171
4 yr	34.000	0.0226
5 yr	34.000	0.0282
7 yr	34.000	0.0393
10 yr	34.000	0.0556

Frequency: Q Quarterly
Day Count: ACT/360
Recovery Rate: 0.40

Australia 61 2 9777 8600 Brazil 5511 3048 4500 Europe 44 20 7330 7500 Germany 49 69 920410
Hong Kong 852 2977 6000 Japan 81 3 3201 8900 Singapore 65 6212 1000 U.S. 1 212 318 2000 Copyright 2006 Bloomberg L.P.
0 19-Jun-06 15:37:06

Figure 16.18 Screen CDSW used to calculate up-front present value payment for trade in EUR10 million notional iTraxx Europe index CDS contract, 19 June 2006 © Bloomberg L.P. Used with permission. All rights reserved.

Bank ALM applications of credit derivatives

Credit derivatives have allowed market participants to separate and disaggregate credit risk, and hence to trade this risk in a secondary market (see, for example, Das 2004). Initially, portfolio managers used them to reduce credit exposure; subsequently they have been used in the management of portfolios, to enhance portfolio yields and in the structuring of synthetic CDOs. Banks use credit derivatives to transfer credit risk of their loan and other asset portfolios, and to take on credit exposure based on their views on the credit market. In connection with this some of them act as credit derivatives market-makers, running mismatched books in long- and short-position CDSs and TRSs. This is exactly how they operate in the interest-rate market, using interest-rate swaps.

We consider below some general bank applications of credit derivatives.

Credit risk management

Banks were the first users of credit derivatives. The market developed as banks sought to protect themselves from loss due to default on portfolios of mainly illiquid assets, such as corporate loans and emerging-market syndicated loans. While securitisation was a well-used technique to move credit risk off the balance sheet, often this caused relationship problems with obligors, who would feel that their close relationship with their banker was being compromised if the loans were sold off the bank's balance sheet. Banks would therefore buy protection on the loan book using CDSs, enabling them to hedge their credit exposure while maintaining banking relationships. The loan would be maintained on the balance sheet but would be fully protected by the CDSs.

To illustrate, consider Figure 16.19 which is a Bloomberg description page for a loan in the name of Haarman & Reimer, a chemicals company rated A3 by Moody's. We see that this loan pays 225 basis points over Libor. Figure 16.20 shows the BBVA CDS prices page for A3-rated chemicals entities: Akzo Nobel is trading at 28 basis points (to buy protection) as at 9 March 2004. A bank holding this loan can protect against default by purchasing this credit protection, and the relationship manager does not need to divulge this to the obligor. (In fact, we may check the current price of this loan in the secondary market on the page BOAL, the Bank of America loan trading page on Bloomberg.)

GRAB Corp **DES**

Enter 99<GO> for options. <HELP> for Disclaimer

TRANCHE LOAN DESCRIPTION Page 1 of 1

Tranche# LN085232 Tranche A IVSXF Maturity 10/01/09 Country DE
Cusip# Type TERM Mkt Type EURO
Facility# LN085249 Amend N.A. Issue Status SIGNED

Issue Information

Borrower HAARMANN & REIMER
Industry Chemicals - Diversified
Calc Type (99) *NO CALCULATIONS*
Fac/Trnch Amts EUR 880MM /400MM
Purpose LBO
Signing Date 11/28/02
Effective Date 08/22/02
Outstanding 400MM

Sub Limit Borrowings

Not Applicable

Bank Group

Ld Arranger COBA,JPM
Agent
Participants 55<GO>

Assignment Info

Min Pc
Increment
Fee
Retain

Tranche Ratings

S&P NR
Moody's NR
FI NR

Senior Debt Ratings

S & P A+
MOODY A3

Info @ Close

EURIBOR +225.000BP

Current Sprd & Fees

Interest Typ FLOATER
Current Base EURIBOR
Spread 225.0BP

SR RTGS REFLECT: BAYER AG. TOTAL FAC INCLUDES AN ADDL €240MM MEZZANINE LOAN

Australia 61 2 9777 8600 Brazil 5511 3048 4500 Europe 44 20 7330 7500 Germany 49 69 920410
Hong Kong 852 2977 6000 Japan 81 3 3201 8900 Singapore 65 6212 1000 U.S. 1 212 318 2000 Copyright 2004 Bloomberg L.P.
G657-802-1 09-Mar-04 14:09:34

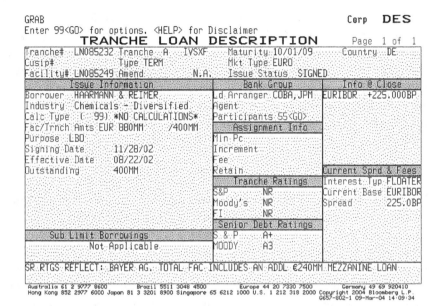

Figure 16.19 Haarman & Reimer loan description

GRAB Curncy **BBCS**

14:11 **CHEMICALS/PHARMACEUTICALS** PAGE 1 / 1

CHEMICALS/ PHARMACEUTICALS		3 Y - CDS Quotes BID	/	ASK	CHG		5 Y - CDS Quotes BID	/	ASK	CHG	TIME
AKZO NOBEL	1)	20	/	28	7:29	15)	43	/	53		7:29
AVENTIS	2)	13	/	23	7:29	16)	24	/	34		7:29
BASF	3)	10	/	17	7:29	17)	10	/	20		7:29
BAYER	4)	30	/	42	7:29	18)	43	/	53		7:29
DEGUSSA	5)	10	/	23	7:29	19)	24	/	31		7:29
DSM	6)	10	/	23	7:29	20)	27	/	37		7:29
GSK	7)	2	/	12	7:29	21)	8	/	18		7:29
HENKEL KGAA	8)	23	/	33	7:29	22)	35	/	45	+2	12:28
ICI	9)	55	/	75	7:29	23)	80	/	90		7:29
LINDE	10)	25	/	35	7:29	24)	40	/	50		7:29
NOVARTIS	11)	2	/	12	7:29	25)	6	/	16		7:29
SOLVAY	12)		/			26)	25	/	32		7:29
SVENSKA AB	13)		/			27)	25	/	32		7:29
SYNGENTA AG	14)		/			28)	24	/	34		7:29

Tel: +34 91 537 6087
INDICATIVE PRICES FOR CREDIT DEFAULT SWAPS ON STANDARD
ISDA 2003 DOCUMENTATION WITH 3 CREDIT EVENTS
MATURITIES ARE ON QUARTERLY BASIS

BBVA

Australia 61 2 9777 8600 Brazil 5511 3048 4500 Europe 44 20 7330 7500 Germany 49 69 920410
Hong Kong 852 2977 6000 Japan 81 3 3201 8900 Singapore 65 6212 1000 U.S. 1 212 318 2000 Copyright 2004 Bloomberg L.P.
G657-802-3 09-Mar-04 14:11:38

Figure 16.20 Chemicals sector CDS prices for Banco Bilbao Vizcaya, 9 March 2004

The other major use by banks of credit derivatives is as a product offering for clients. The CDS market has developed exactly as the market did in interest-rate swaps, with banks offering two-way prices to customers and other banks as part of their product portfolio. Most commercial banks now offer this service, as they do in interest-rate swaps. In this role banks are both buyers and sellers of credit protection. Their net position will reflect their overall view on the market as well the other side of their customer business.

Enhancing portfolio returns

Banks can derive premium income by trading credit exposures in the form of derivatives issued with synthetic structured notes. This would be part of a structured credit product. A pool of risky assets can be split into specific tranches of risk, with the most risky portion given the lowest credit rating in the structure. This is known as "multi-tranching". The multi-tranching aspect of structured products enables specific credit exposures (credit spreads and outright default), and their expectations, to be sold to meet specific areas of demand. By using structured notes such as CLNs, tied to the assets in the reference pool of the portfolio manager, the trading of credit exposures is crystallised as added yield on the asset manager's fixed-income portfolio. In this way the portfolio manager enables other market participants to gain an exposure to the credit risk of a pool of assets but not to any other aspects of the portfolio, and without the need to hold the assets themselves.

Reducing credit exposure

Consider a bank that holds a large portfolio of bonds issued by a particular sector (say, utilities) and believes that spreads in this sector will widen in the short term. Previously, in order to reduce the credit exposure the bank would have to sell bonds; however, this may crystallise a mark-to-market loss and may conflict with any long-term liquidity strategy. An alternative approach would be to enter into a CDS, purchasing protection for the short term; if spreads do widen these swaps will increase in value and may be sold at a profit in the secondary market. Alternatively, the bank may enter into TRS on the desired credits. It pays the counterparty the total return on the reference assets, in return for Libor. This transfers the credit exposure of the bonds to the counterparty for the term of the swap, in return for the credit exposure of the counterparty.

Consider the case of a bank wishing to mitigate credit risk from a growing loan book. Figure 16.21 shows an example of an unhedged credit exposure to a hypothetical credit-risky portfolio. It illustrates the bank's expectation of credit risk building up to $250 million as assets are acquired, and then reducing to a more stable level as the credits become more established.[16] A three-year CDS entered into shortly after provides protection on half of the notional exposure, shown as the broken line. The net exposure to credit events has been reduced by a significant margin.

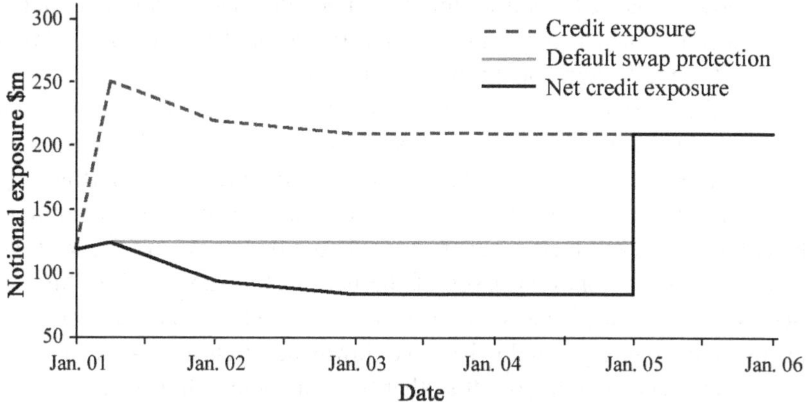

Figure 16.21 Reducing credit exposure

Credit switches and zero-cost credit exposure

Protection buyers utilising CDSs must pay premium in return for laying off their credit risk exposure. An alternative approach for a bank involves the use of credit switches for specific sectors of the loan book. In a credit switch the bank purchases credit protection on one reference asset or pool of assets, and simultaneously sells protection on another asset or pool of assets.[17] So, for example, it would purchase protection for a particular pool and sell protection on another. Typically, the entire transaction would be undertaken with one counterparty, which would price the structure so that the net cash flows would be zero. This has the effect of synthetically diversifying the credit exposure of the bank, enabling a gain and/or reduced exposure to sectors as desired.

[16] For instance, the fund may be invested in new companies. As the names become more familiar to the market the credits become more "established" because the perception of how much credit risk they represent falls.

[17] A pool of assets would be concentrated on one sector, such as utility company bonds.

Exposure to market sectors

Investors can use credit derivatives to gain exposure to sectors for which they do not wish a cash market exposure. This can be achieved with an *index* swap, which is similar to a TRS, with one counterparty paying a total return that is linked to an external reference index. The other party pays a Libor-linked coupon or the total return of another index. Indices that are used might include the government bond index, a high-yield index or an ABS index. Assume investors believe that the bank loan market will outperform the mortgage-backed bond sector; to reflect this view they enter into an index swap in which they pay the total return of the mortgage index and receive the total return of the bank loan index.

Another possibility is synthetic exposure to foreign currency and money markets. Again we assume that investors have a particular view on an emerging market currency. If they wish they can purchase a short-term (say one-year) domestic coupon-bearing note, whose principal redemption is linked to a currency factor. This factor is based on the ratio of the spot value of the foreign currency on issue of the note to the spot value on maturity. Such currency-linked notes can also be structured so that they provide an exposure to sovereign credit risk. The downside of currency-linked notes is that if the exchange rate goes the other way, the note will have a zero return, in effect a negative return once the investor's funding costs have been taken into account.

Trading credit spreads

Assume that a bank has negative views on a certain emerging-market government bond credit spread relative to UK gilts. The simplest way to reflect this view would be to go long a CDS on the sovereign, paying X basis points. Assuming that the investor's view is correct and the sovereign bonds decrease in price as their credit spread widens, the premium payable on the credit swap will increase. The investor's swap can then be sold into the market at this higher premium.

Credit derivatives and ABS markets

Credit derivatives markets have expanded rapidly since the first instruments were introduced in 1994. They have been extended into the asset-backed and mortgage-backed markets, partly due to the shortage of paper in the cash market. The standardisation of CDS contracts and trading terminology also facilitated the expansion of credit derivatives into structured finance markets.

There are a number of detail differences between ABS credit risk and corporate credit risk. A single-name corporate CDS transacted under the standard 2003 ISDA Credit Derivatives definitions[18] will be based on clearly defined trigger events ("credit events") and a transparent process of settlement, either physical or cash settlement. A CDS written on an ABS issue can present problematic issues with regard to both these items. Corporate CDS-triggered events are, following some initial problems with definitions, straightforward to describe. They include bankruptcy, failure to pay, debt restructuring and in some cases ratings downgrade. Such occurrences can be identified easily in most cases. Also, the outstanding debt of a corporate entity can be expected to trade at roughly the same level in the event of issuer default, irrespective of coupon or maturity.

Structured finance securities such as ABS and MBS differ in both these respects. The key difference is that unlike corporate bonds, most ABS are issued by SPVs, bankruptcy-remote legal entities created solely for the purpose of facilitating the bond issue. Bankruptcy and restructuring rarely, if ever, apply to SPVs. Also, it may be less clear in the case of an SPV that there has been a failure to pay. Unlike corporate entities, credit ratings of SPVs are based essentially on the quality of the underlying assets. The repayment of these assets is not known with certainty, which is why ABS bonds are given long legal final maturities. Other issues that complicate the matter of CDS on ABS include the following:

- ABS structures with an element of uncertain cash flow patterns include the provision for the write-down of principal in the event of losses. This does not always constitute a "default" as the write-down can be reversed and made good later;
- many ABS structures allow for a delay in interest payment; for example, during a time when the excess spread in the vehicle has been reduced. Again this may not constitute default and may not necessarily lead instantly to a ratings downgrade as the interest coverage may be expected to become sufficient again;
- the structure represents a distinct pool of assets, ring-fenced within the SPV. This contrasts with the general pool of assets represented in a corporate entity;
- it is quite possible for the more junior tranches of an ABS issue to be in default while the senior tranches are not, again representing the way the asset pool is performing.

[18] See www.isda.org

The significant difference therefore, between an ABS CDS and a single-name corporate CDS is that the former is written against a specific security, while the latter is written at an entity level on a corporate name. However, writing a contract on a specific security means that physical settlement on occurrence of a credit event is impractical. For this reason physical settlement is not used. Cash settlement may also be problematic because of the difficulty with ascertaining the market value of the ABS tranche. A new type of CDS, the pay-as-you-go CDS (PAUG CDS) has been developed for this market.

PAUG CDS

PAUG CDS has been developed to meet the distinct requirements of synthetic investment in ABS issues. A PAUG CDS acts like a standard CDS, with provision for termination on occurrence of specified credit events. The protection buyer pays a fixed basis point fee to the protection seller, which is also standard. However, the PAUG contract also permits the

- payment of an additional floating payment from the protection seller to the protection buyer in event of principal write-down;
- payment of a fixed payment from the protection buyer to the protection seller in event of write-up;
- provision for altering cash flows in event of an interest shortfall of the ABS vehicle.

To illustrate, consider the case where the performance of the underlying asset pool in an ABS, due to underperformance or default, means that the principal amount of one or more of the overlying note tranches must be reduced.[19] The protection seller would make a floating payment to the protection buyer to cover this written-down amount. The CDS itself would not terminate. If at a later date the principal balance is reinstated, for example because the portfolio performance has improved, the protection buyer would then make a fixed payment to the seller.

Figure 16.22 illustrates the mechanics of a PAUG CDS in the event of write-down.

[19] This would normally be decided by the Trustee or the Servicer to the transaction.

(a) Start of contract

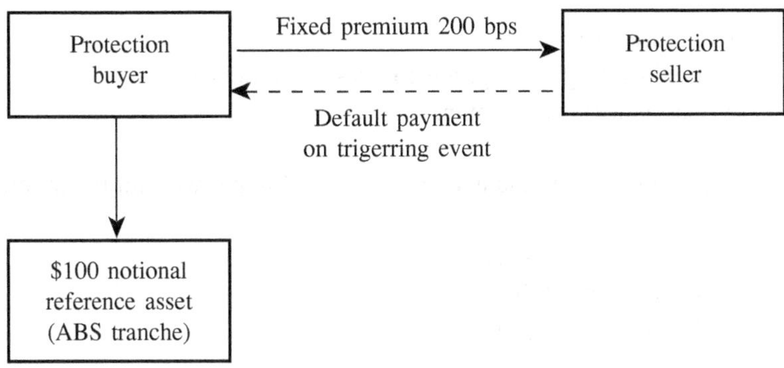

(b) ABS tranche $10 principal write-down

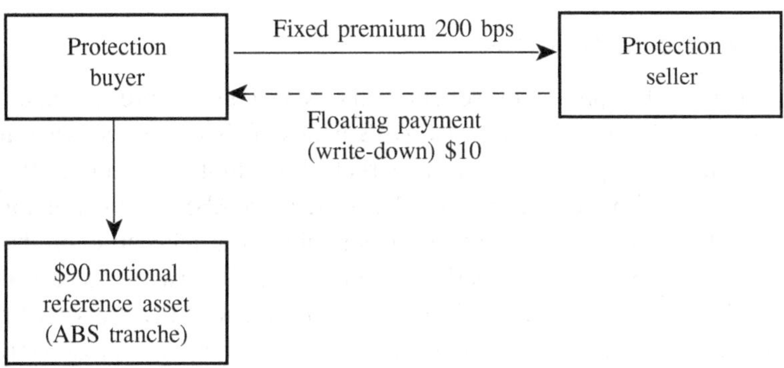

(c) ABS tranche $10 principal write-up

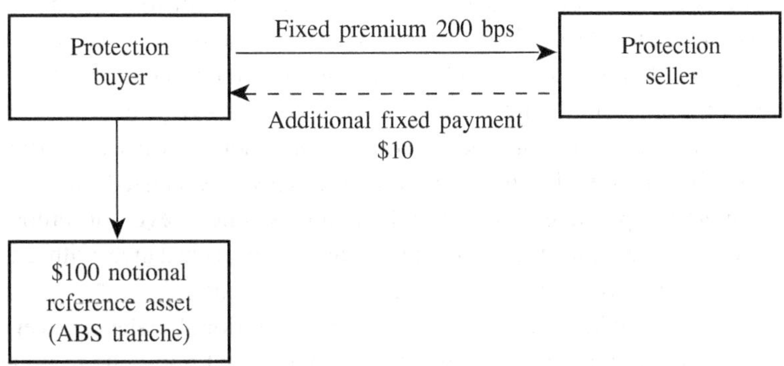

Figure 16.22 PAUG CDS cash flow mechanics in event of an ABS note principal write-down

A standard CDS would generally cover the following credit events:

- failure to pay;
- credit-rating downgrade to sub-investment grade;
- permanent write-down.

A PAUG CDS would also cover the following without being terminated:

- principal write-down;
- interest shortfall;
- failure to pay principal.

By incorporating this flexibility, investors are better able to gain a realistic exposure to the ABS market, albeit synthetically.

Market considerations

Generally, the protection sellers in the ABS CDS market include investors who would normally hold cash ABS bonds. This is marked when there is a shortage of paper in the cash market. The ability to short ABS tranches means that investors can also take a view on ABS credit; previously, this would not necessarily have been straightforward because of the illiquid nature of the ABS repo market. The differences between the corporate and ABS markets are mirrored in the synthetic market. Investors will be aware that corporate entities are dynamic corporations that are proactively able to avoid credit events, which is not the case with SPVs. Synthetic ABS investors must therefore still be concerned primarily with the quality of the underlying collateral and the specific risk/return profile of the individual ABS tranche. Also, there is the issue of prepayment uncertainty. Most corporate bonds have a bullet maturity or fixed redemption date. Non-redemption would constitute a credit event. ABS securities, however, amortise over time, with the redemption date not known with certainty. (For analysis purposes the *average life* of the ABS note is used, this figure is an estimated repayment term based on an assumed level of prepayments.) However, the non-redemption of a tranche in accordance with an average life estimate would not be deemed a credit event.

ABS tranches experience a declining notional balance over time as principal is repaid in stages in the underlying asset pool, due to prepayments and other factors. The outstanding notional value of ABS tranches therefore reduces over time; investors would observe this also occurring with ABS CDS contract notionals as they mirror the behaviour of the cash bond.

ABS CDS and cash bond valuation

In theory the basis between a PAUG CDS and its reference cash bond should be small because the contract mirrors the profile and behaviour of the cash bond closely.[20] In practice, a number of market and structural factors cause the cash and synthetic markets to trade at a negative or positive basis. These include the following:

- in the synthetic market, the investor is exposed additionally to counterparty risk, as it is the counterparty who is paying the coupon (CDS premium). The cash investor is exposed to the quality of the reference collateral only;
- the ABS CDS is an unfunded instrument and so carries no funding cost; this is an additional factor in relative value analysis;
- supply and demand factors may be more prevalent in the synthetic market, as the availability of protection buyers may be limited (unlike ABS transaction originators in the cash market, there is no natural market for protection buyers in the ABS CDS market outside market-makers).

As a relatively new market, the depth and transparency of the ABS CDS market may be limited for certain sectors. This should not be a problem once the market develops.

Supply and demand: CDS of ABS

For many reference names there is greater liquidity in the synthetic market than in the cash market, which would tend to influence the basis into negative territory, but other factors push the basis the other way (see Choudhry 2004a). With structured finance assets such as asset-backed securities (ABS) though, supply in the cash market is a key factor, and has been responsible for a negative cash-CDS basis over a longer time period than observed in conventional bond markets.

---

[20] See the author's paper, "The Credit Default Swap Basis: Analysing the Relationship Between Cash and Synthetic Markets", in the *Journal of Derivatives Use, Trading and Regulation*, Vol. 10, Issue 1, June 2004, for more detail on the CDS basis.

Supply and demand

The bonds we will consider in this illustration are all examples of residential mortgage-backed securities (RMBS), in fact a special class of RMBS known as Home Equity.[21] We show three of these bonds in Table 16.4.

Bond	Amount issued $m	CDS spread	Libor spread on note	CUSIP number	Interest frequency
ACCR 2004-3 2M7	7.665	335	350	004375BX8	Monthly on 25th
CWL 2004-6 B	46.0	340	375	126673BL5	Monthly on 25th
NCHET 2004-2 M9	19.374	345	400	64352VGJ4	Monthly on 25th

Table 16.4 Securities used in illustration, showing CDS and cash market prices, 21 September 2004
Sources: Bloomberg L.P. (bond terms), KBC Financial Products (CDS prices).

All three bonds were part of new issues, for first settlement in September 2004. The mezzanine tranches were in high demand at the time of issue. Under conventional circumstances the CDS price for these securities would be expected to lie above the note yield. But in fact the opposite is true, as the market quotes shown in Table 16.4 indicate. This reflects the lack of supply of these bonds in the market, such that investors are forced to access them in the synthetic market.

The small size of these note tranches is a key reason behind the low availability of paper. We see that only $7.6 million of the ACCR bond is available, a very low figure in any securitisation. The entire securitisation itself is a large issue, as we see from Figure 16.23. This shows the Bloomberg DES page for the transaction, which is called Accredited Mortgage Loan Trust. From this we see that a total of $766.43 million of notes was issued as part of this deal, but the tranche in question – the Baa3 / BBB-rated 2M7 piece – made up less than 1% of this total. Given this paucity of supply, the bond can be sourced more easily in the CDS market, but this carries with it a reduction in yield spread, associated with the greater demand over supply.[22]

[21] For further information on Home Equity securities see Fabozzi (2004).

[22] In effect, the cash market note yield of 350 basis points for this bond is a theoretical construct. As the bond in practice cannot be purchased, as no paper is available, the cash market yield for this name cannot actually be earned by any investor.

Mtge DES

50<Go> for alternate group.

Bloomberg ABS

GROUP DESCRIPTION

ACCR 2004-3 Group-4: 30YR/MIX/G2G3

Page 2 of 3 last 8/31/04

Issuer: ACCREDITED MORTGAGE LOAN TRUST

8) Prospectus

Series 2004-3

Assumed: HOMEEQ 6.36 N

ACTUAL COLLATERAL NOT AVAILABLE

GROUP - ASSUMED		
USD		766,436,984
Net		6.357%
WAC		6.859%
WAM	29:8	356 mo
AGE	0:1	1 mo
1st paymt		9/25/04
1st settle		8/26/04
px3.00 PPS		8/17/04
PAC 0%	SUP	0%
Dated		8/26/04

PSA-GROUP-CPR HOMEEQ 6.25 N				
1mo	-	-	-	-
3mo	-	-	-	-
6mo	-	-	-	-
12mo	-	-	-	-
Life	-	-	-	-

Monthly PAYMENT
pays 25th day
0 day delay
accrues ACT/360

6) Lead Mgr: LB

7) Trustee: DBT

See Page 3 For Comments.

Australia 61 2 9777 8600 Brazil 5511 3048 4500 Europe 44 20 7330 7500 Germany 49 69 920410
Hong Kong 852 2977 6000 Japan 81 3 3201 8900 Singapore 65 6212 1000 U.S. 1 212 318 2000 Copyright 2004 Bloomberg L.P.
G657-802-2 21-Sep-04 11:40:01

Figure 16.23 Bloomberg screen DES for ACCR Home Equity securitisation transaction

We observe similar characteristics for the two other bonds in our sample. The Countrywide Asset-Backed Certificates transaction is made up of a total of $4.426 billion in 12 different tranches; the mezzanine tranche rated Baa3 / BBB was issued in a size of only $46 million. The total size of the New Century Home Equity Loan Trust deal was $1.937 billion, while the particular mezzanine tranche we are interested in was issued in the size of only 1% of this total. This bond exhibits the widest spread in our small group, with the CDS trading at a premium of 55 basis points to the theoretical cash price.

CDS of ABS mechanics

The CDS contracts written on these structured finance securities have minor differences in their terms compared to vanilla single-name CDS instruments. These include the following:

- a premium payment set to match the payment date of the cash bond, in this case a monthly payment on the 25th of each month. The standard CDS payment terms are quarterly in arrears;

- in practice, an un-fixed maturity date. The CDS written on these bonds is set to match their maturity. From Figure 16.24, we see that the ACCR 2M7 tranche has a weighted-average life of 5.4 years. This is of course an estimate based on a specified prepayment rate, which is standard practice for all RMBS bonds. In reality, the bond may well pay off before or after 5.4 years. The CDS contract language specifies that the contract expires when the cash bond itself is fully paid off;
- the transaction undertaken by the investor for the CDS that references the ACCR 2M7 tranche was for a notional of $10 million. This is more than the actual amount in existence of the physical bond. Hence, it is standard practice for all structured finance CDS contracts to always be cash-settled instruments.

By setting the terms in this way, banks and other investors are able to access these types of names and asset classes where the cash market bond is no longer available to them, by selling protection on the bond tranches using a CDS.

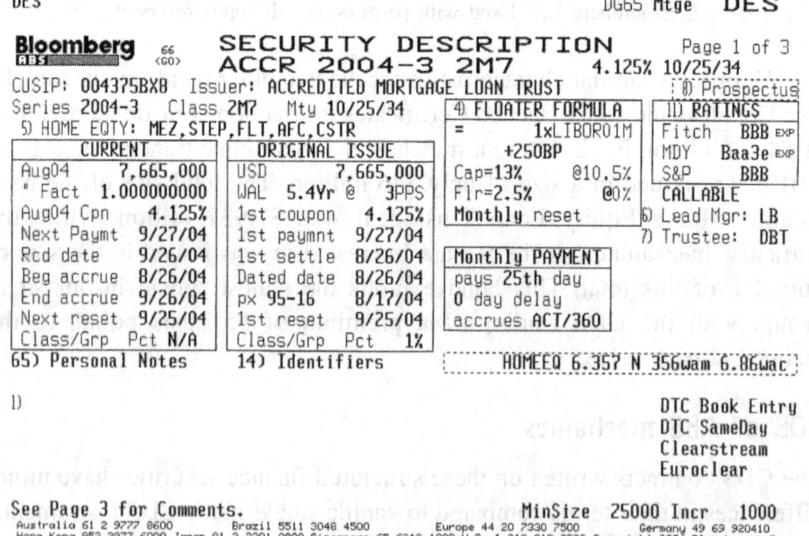

Figure 16.24 Bloomberg screen DES for 2M7 tranche of ACCR transaction, 21 September 2004

The CDS market-maker that is the counterparty to the CDS investor may gain from acting in this business in the following ways:

- buying protection on this class of assets releases economic capital that can be invested in higher yielding assets elsewhere;
- it may be able to find similar assets in the cash market that yield a higher spread than the CDS protection it is paying for;
- it can treat this business as trading activity – CDS market-making – and seek to gain a trading profit.

Irrespective of the motivation of the investor and the CDS counterparty to these trades, this business illustrates the contribution to market liquidity of credit derivatives, as well as the impact of supply and demand on reversing the market convention of a positive basis.

Contract documentation

In recognition of the different nature of ABS CDS, ISDA published a template CDS confirmation in June 2005.[23] This described the contract as physically settled for a specific reference obligation (not a basket of same-name obligations that one would have with a corporate CDS) or as a "pay-as-you-go" (PAUG) contract. The PAUG is the most common type of ABS CDS contract. The documentation does not specify credit events of the type described in conventional CDS, instead it specifies cash PAUG settlement events. PAUG settlement enables the contract to mirror synthetically the risk and cash flow profile of the underlying ABS security; it enables this by allowing ongoing multiple settlements throughout the life of the contract. In other words, a PAUG event does not terminate the contract. PAUG settlement requires the protection seller to pay the protection buyer on occurrence of any of the "floating" events with the underlying bond. These include (i) a delay in paying principal; (ii) a write-down of notional; (iii) a shortfall of cash to pay ABS note interest. Under PAUG there is a payment of cash to reflect these events but the contract does not terminate; instead, the notional value is adjusted downwards.

---

[23] See *Journal of Structured Finance*, Spring 2006, page 9.

Risks in CDS positions

As credit derivatives can be tailored to specific requirements in terms of reference exposure, term to maturity, currency and cash flows, they have enabled market participants to establish exposure to specific entities without the need for them to hold the bond or loan of that entity. This has raised issues of the different risk exposure that this entails compared to the cash equivalent. A recent Moody's special report highlights the unintended risks of holding credit exposures in the form of default swaps and credit-linked notes.[24] Under certain circumstances it is possible for CDSs to create unintended risk exposure for holders, by exposing them to greater frequency and magnitude of losses compared to that suffered by a holder of the underlying reference credit.

In a CDS, the payout to a buyer of protection is determined by the occurrence of credit events. The definition of a credit event sets the level of credit-risk exposure of the protection seller. A wide definition of "credit event" results in a higher level of risk. To reduce the likelihood of disputes, counterparties can adopt the ISDA Credit Derivatives definitions to govern their dealings. The Moody's paper states that the current ISDA definitions do not unequivocally separate and isolate credit risk and, in certain circumstances, credit derivatives can expose holders to additional risks. A reading of the paper would appear to suggest that differences in definitions can lead to unintended risks being taken on by protection sellers. Two examples from the paper are cited below as illustration.

Extending loan maturity

The bank debt of Conseco, a corporate entity, was restructured in August 2000. The restructuring provisions included deferment of the loan maturity by three months, higher coupon, corporate guarantee and additional covenants. Under the Moody's definition, as lenders received compensation in return for an extension of the debt, the restructuring was not considered to be a "diminished financial obligation", although Conseco's credit rating was downgraded one notch. However, under the ISDA definition, the extension of the loan maturity meant that the restructuring was considered to be a credit event, and thus triggered payments on default swaps written on Conseco's bank debt. Hence, this was an example of a loss event under ISDA definitions that was not considered by Moody's to be a default.

[24] Jeffrey Tolk (2001), "Understanding the Risks in Credit Default Swaps", *Moody's Investors Service Special Report*, 16 March.

Risks of synthetic positions and cash positions compared

Consider two investors in XYZ, one of whom owns bonds issued by XYZ while the other holds a credit-linked note (CLN) referenced to XYZ. Following a deterioration in its debt situation, XYZ violates a number of covenants on its bank loans, but its bonds are unaffected. XYZ's bank accelerates the bank loan, but the bonds continue to trade at 85 cents on the dollar, coupons are paid and the bond is redeemed in full at maturity. However, the default swap underlying the CLN cites "obligation acceleration" (of either bond or loan) as a credit event, so the holder of the CLN receives 85% of par in cash settlement and the CLN is terminated. However, the cash investor receives all the coupons and the par value of the bonds on maturity.

These two examples illustrate how, as CDSs are defined to pay out in the event of a very broad range of definitions of a "credit event", banks may suffer losses as a result of occurrences that are not captured by one or more of the ratings agencies' rating of the reference asset. This results in a potentially greater risk for the bank compared to the position were it to actually hold the underlying reference asset. Essentially, therefore, it is important for the range of definitions of a "credit event" to be fully understood by counterparties, so that holders of default swaps are not taking on greater risk than is intended.

Issues in reference name succession

Just as the Conseco affair of 2000 highlighted problems associated with CDS contract documentation with regard to reference name restructuring, so events in 2005 and 2006 raised potential issues that arise after corporate activity. The area of concern is corporate name succession, or what happens to a CDS after the reference entity has been taken over by another entity and it no longer exists as a legal entity. Where the succession is clear-cut, then generally there is no issue as the successor entity is the new reference entity in CDS contracts that previously were linked to the entity that was taken over.

A problem may arise when it is not clear-cut, in legal terms, if there has been a take-over. New corporate financing techniques used by companies as part of their restructuring or as part of the takeover of another company are not always explicitly described in a CDS contract terms. When this happens, it may lead to confusion as to whether a succession event has occurred, or what the successor reference entity is. Generally, the successor language in a CDS contract will follow that for a cash loan, and describe the circumstances under which the CDS protection will migrate to the successor entity. A new entity would be required to take on the debt of the existing entity through a succession event. Under this event the new entity will assume the debt that is the underlying reference in the CDS. So the new entity would assume directly the existing debt of the old company, or issue new debt in exchange for the old debt that was the reference debt in the CDS. During 2006 a proposed leveraged buy-out raised concerns if neither of these two conditions were satisfied, in which case what would happen to CDS contracts referencing the takeover target?[25] Under the LBO, the bid was going to be financed by a specially created acquisition company that would raise equity at the target company level, as well as pay off all existing debt, again at the target company level. This would mean that the successor entity would not transfer any old debt into its name, nor would there be a debt exchange. This may then have resulted in CDS contracts written on the target company becoming worthless because the reference name no longer existed, and nor did its debt. In the United Kingdom another acquisition[26] raised questions of whether the target debt would be deliverable into the target reference-name CDS once the acquisition was complete. If a CDS is left without a deliverable obligation, it becomes effectively worthless.

At the time of writing this issue was still a live one, with one solution being additional wording to the standard ISDA CDS contract documentation to cover succession events. This may lead to ISDA updating the language in the 2003 definitions.

Credit default swap pricing[27]

Bank ALM practitioners need be familiar only with the basic principles of credit derivative pricing. To this end we illustrate these here, first with a look at the theoretical approach based on Hull-White (2000) and then with an application of market pricing techniques for a credit default swap.

---

[25] The case was the proposed leveraged buy-out (LBO) of ProSieben, a television company, by Axel Springer in Germany. This was described in *RISK*, May 2006, pp. 26–27.

[26] Pilkington Glass, takeover by Nippon Sheet Glass, a Japanese entity (*RISK* 2006).

[27] This section is co-authored with Abukar M Ali, Bloomberg L.P., London. The views and opinions expressed herein represent those of the authors in their individual private capacity.

Theoretical Pricing approach

The present value (PV) of a credit default swap can be viewed as the algebraic sum of the present values of its two legs. The market premium is similar to an interest-rate swap in that the premium makes the current aggregate PV equal to zero. That is, for a par interest-rate swap, the theoretical net present value of the two legs must equal zero; the same principle applies for the two cash flow legs of a CDS.

The cash flows of a CDS are shown in Figure 16.25.

a) No default

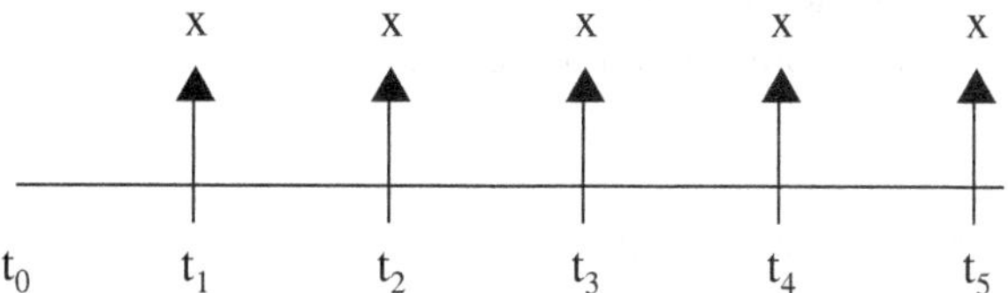

b) Default

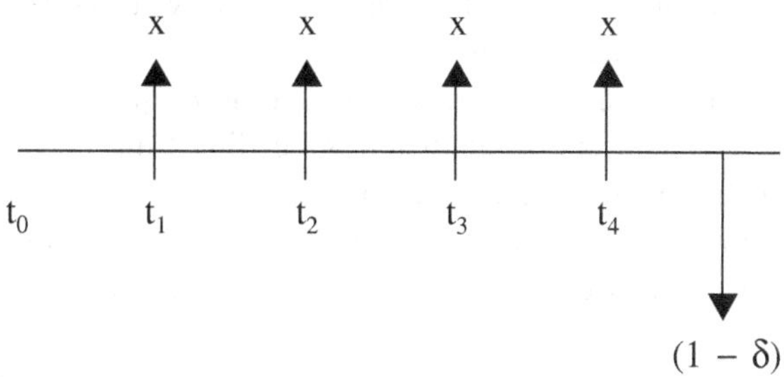

Figure 16.25 Illustration of cash flows in a default swap

Normally, the default payment on a credit default swap will be $(1 - \delta)$ times its notional amount, where δ is defined as the recovery rate of the reference security. The reason for this payout is clear – it allows a risky asset to be transformed into a risk-free asset by purchasing default protection referenced to this credit. For example, if the expected recovery rate for a given reference asset is 30% of its face value, upon default the remaining 70% will be paid by the protection seller. Credit agencies such as Moody's provide recovery rate estimates for corporate bonds with different credit ratings using historical data.

The valuation of each leg of the cash flows is considered below. As these cash flows may terminate at an unknown time during the life of the deal, their values are computed in a probabilistic sense, using the discounted expected value as calculated under the risk-neutral method and assumptions. A commonly cited approach to pricing is a reduced-form type model developed by Hull and White (2000). Their approach was to calibrate the model based on the traded bonds of the underlying reference name on a time series of credit default swap prices. This model assumes that there is no counterparty default risk. Default probabilities, interest rates and recovery rates are independent. It also assumes that the claim in the event of default is the face value plus accrued interest.

We introduce first some notation below.

- T: Life of credit default swap in years.
- $q(t)$: Risk neutral probability density at time t.
- R: Expected recovery rate on the reference obligation in a risk-neutral world (independent of the time of default).
- $u(t)$: Present value of payments at the rate of \$1 per year on payment dates between time zero and time t.
- $e(t)$: Present value of an accrual payment at time t equal to $t - t^*$ where t^* is the payment date immediately preceding time t.
- $v(t)$: Present value of \$1 received at time t.
- w: Total payment per year made by credit default swap buyer.
- s: Value of w that causes the value of credit default swap to have a value of zero.
- π: The risk-neutral probability of no credit event during the life of the swap.
- $A(t)$: Accrued interest on the reference obligation at time t as a per cent of face value.

Consider the valuation of a plain vanilla credit default swap with \$1 notional principal. The value π is one minus the probability that a credit event will occur by time T.

This is also referred to as the survival probability and can be calculated from $q(t)$:

$$\pi = 1 - \int_0^T q(t)dt. \tag{16.1}$$

The payments last until a credit event or until time T, whichever is sooner. If default occurs at $t\,(t < T)$, the present value of the payment is $w[u(t) + e(t)]$. If there is no default prior to time T, the present value of the payment is $wu(T)$. The expected present value of the payment is, therefore:

$$w\int_0^T q(t)\ [u(t) + e(t)]dt + wpu(T). \tag{16.2}$$

Given the assumption about the claim amount, the risk-neutral expected payoff from the credit default swap (CDS) contract is derived as follows:

$1 - R\,[1 + A(t)]$
multiplying $-R$ by $[1 + A(t)]$
$1 - R\,[1 + A(t)] = \ 1 - R\ - A(t)R.$

The present value of the expected payoff from the CDS is given as

$$\int_0^T [1 - R - A(t)R]q(t)v(t)dt. \tag{16.3}$$

The value of the CDS to the buyer is the present value of the expected payoff minus the present value of the payments made by the buyer, or:

$$\int_0^T [1 - R - A(t)R]q(t)v(t)dt - w\int_0^T q(t)[u(t) + e(t)]dt + w\pi u(T). \tag{16.4}$$

In equilibrium, the present value of each leg of the above equation should be equal. We can now calculate the CDS spread s, which is the value of w that makes the equation equal to zero by simply rearranging the equation, as shown below.

$$s = \frac{\int_0^T [1 - R - A(t)R]q(t)v(t)dt}{\int_0^T q(t)[u(t) + e(t)]dt + \pi u(T)} \tag{16.5}$$

The variable s is referred to as the CDS spread.

The formula in (16.5) is simple and intuitive for developing an analytical approach for pricing CDS because of the assumptions used. For example, the model assumes that interest rates and defaults events are independent; also, the possibility of counterparty default is ignored. The spread s is the payment per year, as a per cent of notional principal, for a newly issued CDS.

Market approach

We now present a discrete form pricing approach that is used in the market, using market-observed parameter inputs.

At the inception of the credit market, some banks adopted the no-arbitrage principle that stated that CDS prices must equal the asset swap (ASW) price for a bond in the same reference name, as the ASW spread is a measure of the credit risk of a bond. For a number of reasons this is not the case and the two prices always differ, so asset swap pricing is not a reliable way to price a CDS contract. This price difference is known as the *CDS basis* and is discussed in Choudhry (2004a) and Choudhry (2006a).

We stated earlier that a CDS has two cash flow legs, the fee premium leg and the contingent cash flow leg. We wish to determine the par spread or premium of the CDS, remembering that for a par spread valuation, in accordance with no-arbitrage principles the net present value of both legs must be equal to zero. The market approach to CDS pricing adopts the same no-arbitrage concept as used in interest-rate swap pricing. This states that, at inception:

$$PV\ fixed\ leg = PV\ floating\ leg.$$

Therefore for a CDS we set:

$$PV\ premium\ leg = PV\ contingent\ leg.$$

The PV of the premium leg is straightforward to calculate, especially if there is no credit event during the life of the CDS. However, the contingent leg is just that – contingent on occurrence of a credit event. Hence we need to determine the value of the premium leg at the time of the credit event. This requires us to use default probabilities. We can use historical default rates to determine default probabilities, or back them out using market CDS prices. The latter approach is in fact *implied default probabilities.*

The valuation of the fee leg is given by the following relationship:

$$PV\ of\ no\text{-}default\ fee\ payments = s_N \times Annuity_N$$

which is given by

$$PV = s_N \sum_{i=1}^{N} DF_i \bullet PND_i \bullet A_i \tag{16.6}$$

where

s_N is the par spread (CDS premium) for maturity N
DF_i is the risk-free discount factor from time T_0 to time T_i
PND_i is the no-default probability from T_0 to T_i
A_i is the accrual period from T_{i-1} to T_i.

Note that the value for *PND* is for the specific reference entity for which a CDS is being priced.

If the accrual fee for the CDS is paid upon default and termination, then the valuation of the fee leg is given by the relationship:

PV of No-default fee payments + PV of default accruals =
$s_N \times Annuity_N + s_N \times Default\ accrual_N$

which is given by:

$$PV_{NoDefault+DefaultAccrual} = S_N \sum_{i=1}^{N} DF_i \bullet PND_i \bullet A_i + S_N \sum_{i=1}^{N} DF_i \bullet (PND_{i-1} - PND_i) \bullet \frac{A_i}{2} \qquad (16.7)$$

where

$(PND_{i-1} + PND_i)$ is the probability of a credit event occurring during period T_{i-1} to T_i
$A_i/2$ is the average accrual amount from T_{i-1} to T_i.

The valuation of the contingent leg is approximated by:

$$PV\ of\ contingent = Contingent_N$$

which is given by:

$$PVContingent = (1 - R) \sum_{i=1}^{N} DF_i \bullet (PND_{i-1} - PND_i) \qquad (16.8)$$

where

R is the recovery rate of the reference obligation.

For a par CDS, we know that:

Valuation of fee leg = Valuation of Contingent leg.

Therefore we can set:

$$S_N \sum_{i=1}^{N} DF_i \bullet PND_i \bullet A_i + S_N \sum_{i=1}^{N} DF_i \bullet (PND_{i-1} - PND_i) \bullet \frac{A_i}{2}$$

$$= (1 - R) \sum_{i=1}^{N} DF_i \bullet (PND_{i-1} - PND_i), \qquad (16.9)$$

which may be rearranged to give us the formula for the CDS premium s as follows:

$$S_N = \frac{(1 - R) \sum_{i=1}^{N} DF_i \bullet (PND_{i-1} - PND_i)}{\sum_{i=1}^{N} DF_i \bullet PND_i \bullet A_i + DF_i \bullet (PND_{i-1} - PND_i) \bullet \frac{A_i}{2}}. \qquad (16.10)$$

The market approach to CDS pricing as described above is based on default probabilities. As this approach notes, to price a credit derivative we consider two basic questions:

- What is the probability of a credit event?
- If a credit event occurs, how much is the protection seller likely to pay?

We may also need to know:

- If a credit event occurs, when does this happen?

Probability of default is an important statistic; one way to obtain default probabilities is to observe credit spreads in the cash corporate bond market. From Figure 9.9 in Chapter 9 we observed that risky corporate bonds trade at a spread to government bonds, the credit spread, and this varies with credit quality (best described by the bond's credit rating) and term-to-maturity. From Figure 9.9 on pages 357–59 we can determine that:

- credit spreads depend on maturity;
- lower quality credits trade at a wider spread than higher-quality credits;
- longer-dated obligations normally have higher spreads than shorter-dated ones.

The yield curves in Figure 9.9 are known as the term structure of credit spreads.

Of these factors, one of the most significant is the term to maturity. The *term structure of credit spreads* exhibits a number of features. For instance, lower quality credits trade at a wider spread than higher quality credits, and longer-dated obligations normally have higher spreads than shorter-dated ones. For example, for a particular sector they may look like this:

- 2-yr AA: 20 bps
- 5-yr AA: 30 bps
- 10-yr AA: 37 bps

An exception to this is at the very low end of the credit spectrum; for example, we may observe the following yields for CCC-rated assets:

- 2-yr CCC: 11%
- 5-yr CCC: 7.75%
- 10-yr CCC: 7%.

In the case of the CCC rating this reflects the belief that there is a higher probability of default risk right now rather than five years from now, because if the company survives the first few years, the risk of later default is much lower later on. This gives rise to lower spreads the further along the term structure for very lower-rated assets.

Suppose that the corporate bonds of a particular issuer trade at the yields shown in Table 16.5.

Maturity t	Risk-free yield r	Corporate bond yield $r + y$	Risk spread y
0.5	3.57%	3.67%	0.10%
1.0	3.70%	3.82%	0.12%
1.5	3.81%	3.94%	0.13%
2.0	3.95%	4.10%	0.15%
2.5	4.06%	4.22%	0.16%
3.0	4.16%	4.32%	0.16%
3.5	4.24%	4.44%	0.20%
4.0	4.33%	4.53%	0.20%
4.5	4.42%	4.64%	0.22%
5.0	4.45%	4.67%	0.22%

Table 16.5 Hypothetical corporate bond yields and risk spread

We calculate the continuously compounded rate of return on the risk-free asset to be:

$$e^{rt}.$$

The rate of return on the risky asset is therefore given by:

$$e^{(r+y)t}.$$

We now calculate the default probability assuming zero recovery of the asset value following default. On this assumption, if the probability of default is p, then an investor should be indifferent between an expected return of

$$(1 - p)e^{(r+y)t}$$

on the risky corporate bond, and

$$e^{rt}.$$

Setting these two expressions equal we have:

$$(1 - p)e^{(r+y)t} = e^{rt}. \tag{16.11}$$

Solving for p gives:

$$p = 1 - e^{-yt}. \tag{16.12}$$

Using $p = 1 - e^{-yt}$ we can calculate therefore the probabilities of default from credit spreads that were shown in Table 16.5. These are shown in Table 16.6.

Maturity t	Risk-free yield r	Corporate bond yield $r + y$	Risk spread y	Cumulative probability of default	Annual probability of default
0.5	3.57%	3.67%	0.10%	0.050%	0.050%
1.0	3.70%	3.82%	0.12%	0.120%	0.070%
1.5	3.81%	3.94%	0.13%	0.195%	0.075%
2.0	3.95%	4.10%	0.15%	0.299%	0.104%
2.5	4.06%	4.22%	0.16%	0.399%	0.100%
3.0	4.16%	4.32%	0.16%	0.479%	0.080%
3.5	4.24%	4.44%	0.20%	0.698%	0.219%
4.0	4.33%	4.53%	0.20%	0.797%	0.099%
4.5	4.42%	4.64%	0.22%	0.985%	0.188%
5.0	4.45%	4.67%	0.22%	1.094%	0.109%

Table 16.6 Default probabilities

For example,

$$p_{0,5} = 1 - e^{-0.0110} = 1.094\%$$

(where $yt = 0.0022 \times 5$) is the cumulative probability of default over the complete five-year period, while

$$p_{4,5} = p_{0,5} - p_{0,4.5} = 1.094 - 0.985 = 0.109\%$$

is the probability of default in year 5.

We then extend the analysis to an assumption of a specified recovery rate following default. If the probability of default is p, and the recovery rate is R, then an investor should now be indifferent between an expected return of:

$$(1 - p)e^{(r+y)t} + Rpe^{(r+y)t} \tag{16.13}$$

on the risky corporate bond, and e^{rt} on the (risk-free) government bond.

Again, setting these two expressions equal, and solving for p gives:[28]

$$(1-p)e^{(r+y)t} + Rpe^{(r+y)t} = e^{rt}$$

$$p = \frac{1-e^{-yt}}{1-R}. \tag{16.14}$$

Using this formula and assuming a recovery rate of 30% we calculate the cumulative default probabilities shown in Table 16.7.

Maturity t	Risk-free yield r	Corporate bond yield $r + y$	Risk spread y	Cumulative probability of default
0.5	3.57%	3.67%	0.10%	0.071%
1.0	3.70%	3.82%	0.12%	0.171%
1.5	3.81%	3.94%	0.13%	0.279%
2.0	3.95%	4.10%	0.15%	0.427%
2.5	4.06%	4.22%	0.16%	0.570%
3.0	4.16%	4.32%	0.16%	0.684%
3.5	4.24%	4.44%	0.20%	0.997%
4.0	4.33%	4.53%	0.20%	1.139%
4.5	4.42%	4.64%	0.22%	1.407%
5.0	4.45%	4.67%	0.22%	1.563%

Table 16.7 Cumulative default probabilities

For example,

$$p_{0,5} = \frac{1 - e^{-0.0110}}{1 - 0.30} = 1.563\%$$

is the cumulative probability of default over the five-year period.

[28] The steps in between are:

$$(1-p)e^{(r+y)t} = e^{rt}$$
$$(1-p)e^{rt}.e^{yt} = e^{rt}$$
$$(1-p)e^{-yt} = 1$$
$$1-p = e^{-yt}$$
$$p = 1 - e^{-yt}$$

Incorporating the recovery rate R we have the following steps:

$$1 - p + pR = e^{-yt}$$
$$-p + pR = e^{-yt} - 1$$
$$-p(1-R) = e^{-yt} - 1$$
$$-p = \frac{e^{-yt} - 1}{1-R}$$
$$p = \frac{1 - e^{-yt}}{1-R}$$

We now expand the analysis to default and survival probabilities. Consider what happens to a risky asset over a specific period of time. There are just two possibilities, which are:

- there is a credit event, and the asset defaults;
- there is no credit event, and the asset survives.

Let us call these outcomes D (for default), having a probability q, and S (for survival) having probability of $(1-q)$. We can represent this as a binary process, shown as Figure 16.26.

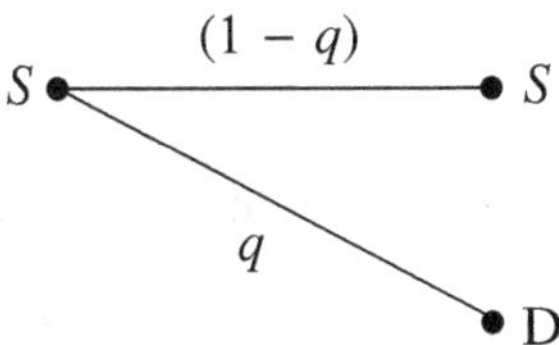

Figure 16.26 Binary process of survival or default

Over multiple periods this binary process can be illustrated as shown in Figure 16.27.

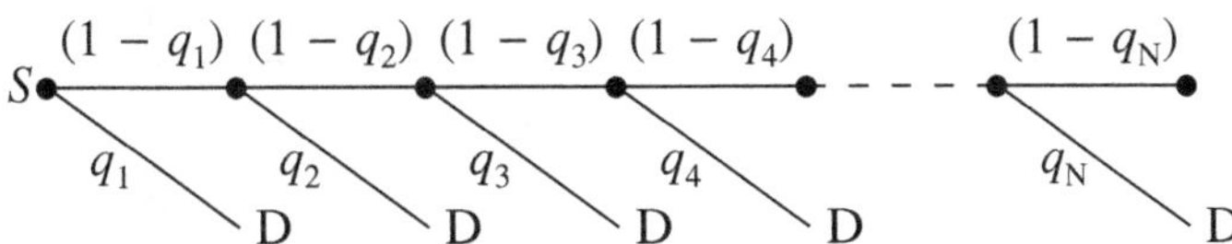

Figure 16.27 Binary process of survival or default over multiple periods

As shown in Figure 16.27, the probability of survival to period N is then:

$$PS_N = (1 - q_1) \times (1 - q_2) \times (1 - q_3) \times (1 - q_4) \times \ldots \times (1 - q_N) \quad (16.15)$$

while the probability of default in any period N is:

$$PS_{N-1} \times q_N = PS_{N-1} - PS_N. \quad (16.16)$$

Given these formulas, we can now price a CDS contract.

Pricing CDS contract

Given a set of default probabilities, we can calculate the fair premium for a CDS contract. To do this, consider a CDS as a series of contingent cash flows, the cash flows depending upon whether a credit event occurs. This is shown in Figure 16.28. The symbols are:

s is the CDS premium
k is the day count fraction when default occurred
R is the recovery rate.

a) No default

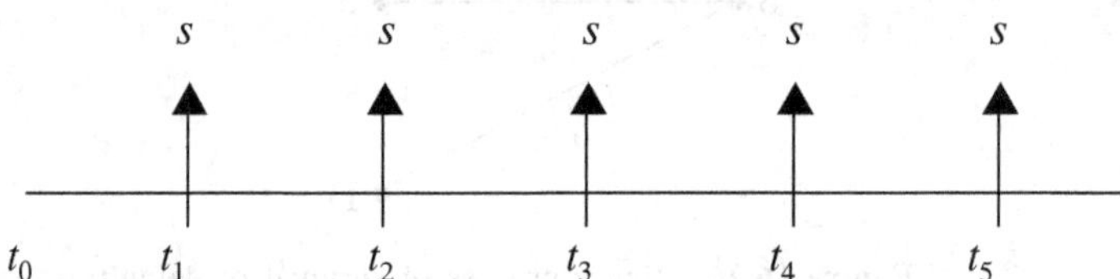

b) Default

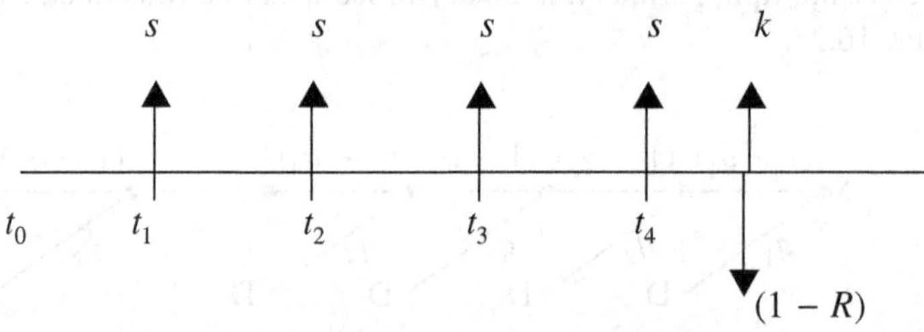

Figure 16.28 CDS contingent cash flows

We wish first to value the premium stream given no default, shown in Figure 16.28(a). The expected PV of the stream of CDS premiums over time can be calculated as:

$$PVS_{nd} = s\sum_{j=1}^{N} DF_j PS_j T_{j-1,j} \qquad (16.17)$$

where

PVS_{nd} is the expected present value of the stream of CDS premiums if there is no default
s is the CDS spread (fee or premium)
DF_j is the discount factor for period j
PS_j is the probability of survival through period j
$T_{j-1,j}$ is the length of time of period j (expressed as a fraction of a year).

We now require an expression for the value of the premium stream given default, which are the cash flows shown in Figure 16.28(b). If a default occurs half-way through period C, and the CDS makes the default payment at the end of that period, the expected present value of the fees received is:

$$PVS_d = s\sum_{j=1}^{C} DF_j PS_j T_{j-1,j} + s.DF_C PD_C \frac{T_{C-1,C}}{2} \tag{16.18}$$

while the value of the default payment is:

$$(1 - R)DF_C PD_C \tag{16.19}$$

where:

PVS_d is the expected present value of the stream of CDS premiums if there is default in period C
PD_C is the probability of default in period C
R is the recovery rate

and the other terms are as before.

On the no-arbitrage principle, which is the same approach used to price interest-rate swaps, for a CDS to be fairly priced the expected value of the premium stream must equal the expected value of the default payment.

As default can occur in any period j, we can therefore write:

$$s\sum_{j=1}^{N} DF_j PS_j T_{j-1,j} + s\sum_{j=1}^{N} DF_j PD_j \frac{T_{j-1,j}}{2} = (1 - R)\sum_{j=1}^{N} DF_j PD_j \tag{16.20}$$

In equation (16.20) the first part of the left-hand side (LHS) is the expected present value of the stream of premium payments if no default occurs, and the second part of the LHS is the expected present value of the accrued premium payment in the period when default occurs. The right-hand side of (16.20) is the expected present value of the default payment in the period when default occurs.

Rearranging this expression gives the fair premium s for the CDS shown as (16.21).

$$s = \frac{(1-R)\sum_{j=1}^{N} DF_j PD_j}{\sum_{j=1}^{N} DF_j PS_j T_{j-1,j} + \sum_{j=1}^{N} DF_j PD_j \frac{T_{j-1,j}}{2}} \tag{16.21}$$

Example calculation

We have shown then that the price of a CDS contract can be calculated from the spot rates and default probability values given earlier. In this example we assume that the credit event (default) occurs halfway through the premium period, thus enabling us to illustrate the calculation of the present value of the receipt in the event of default (the second part of the left-hand side of the original no-arbitrage equation (16.20), the accrual factor) in a more straightforward fashion.

Table 16.8 illustrates the pricing of a CDS contract written on the reference entity whose credit spread premium over the risk-free rate was introduced earlier. The default probabilities were calculated as shown in Table 16.7.

Table 16.9 on pages 824–5 shows the Microsoft Excel formula used in the calculation spreadsheet.

Consider the one-year CDS premium. From Table 16.8 the one-year CDS premium is 0.17%. To check this calculation, we observe the expected present value of the premium for the six-month and one-year dates, which is:

Survival probability × Discount factor × Premium × Day count fraction

For the six-month period this is 0.9993 × 0.9826 × 0.0017 × 0.5 or

0.0008346.

For the one-year period this is 0.9983 × 0.9643 × 0.1017 × 0.5 or

0.00081826.

The expected present-value of the accrued premium if default occurs halfway through a period is:

Default probability × Discount factor × Premium × Day count fraction.

Cell	B	C	D	E	F	G	H	I	J
3									
4						Probability-weighted PVs			
5	**Maturity** t	**Spot rates**	**Discount factors** DFj	**Survival probability** PSj	**Default** ***probability*** PDj	**PV of receipt if no default**	**PV of Receipt if default**	**Default payment if default**	**CDS premiums**
6	0.5	3.57%	0.9826	0.9993	0.0007	0.4910	0.0002	0.0005	0.10%
7	1.0	3.70%	0.9643	0.9983	0.0017	0.9723	0.0006	0.0016	0.17%
8	1.5	3.81%	0.9455	0.9972	0.0028	1.4437	0.0012	0.0035	0.24%
9	2.0	3.95%	0.9254	0.9957	0.0043	1.9044	0.0022	0.0063	0.33%
10	2.5	4.06%	0.9053	0.9943	0.0057	2.3545	0.0035	0.0099	0.42%
11	3.0	4.16%	0.8849	0.9932	0.0068	2.7939	0.0050	0.0141	0.50%
12	3.5	4.24%	0.8647	0.9900	0.0100	3.2220	0.0072	0.0201	0.62%
13	4.0	4.33%	0.8440	0.9886	0.0114	3.6392	0.0096	0.0269	0.74%
14	4.5	4.42%	0.8231	0.9859	0.0141	4.0450	0.0125	0.0350	0.86%
15	5.0	4.45%	0.8044	0.9844	0.0156	4.4409	0.0156	0.0438	0.98%
16									
17	Recovery rate								
18	0.3								

Table 16.8 Calculation of CDS prices

Cell	B	C	D	E	F	G
3						
4						—— Probability-weighted PVs ——
5	**Maturity** *t*	**Spot rate**	**Discount factors**	**Survival probability**	**Default probability**	**PV of receipts if no default**
6	0.5	3.57%	=1/(1+C6)^0.5	=1-F6	0.0007	=SUMPRODUCT($D$6:D6,$E$6:E6)*0.5
7	1.0	3.70%	=1/(1+C7)^1	=1-F7	0.0017	=SUMPRODUCT($D$6:D7,$E$6:E7)*0.5
8	1.5	3.81%	=1/(1+C8)^1.5	=1-F8	0.0028	=SUMPRODUCT($D$6:D8,$E$6:E8)*0.5
9	2.0	3.95%	=1/(1+C9)^2	=1-F9	0.0043	=SUMPRODUCT($D$6:D9,$E$6:E9)*0.5
10	2.5	4.06%	=1/(1+C10)^2.5	=1-F10	0.0057	=SUMPRODUCT($D$6:D10,$E$6:E10)*0.5
11	3.0	4.16%	=1/(1+C11)^3	=1-F11	0.0068	=SUMPRODUCT($D$6:D11,$E$6:E11)*0.5
12	3.5	4.24%	=1/(1+C12)^3.5	=1-F12	0.0100	=SUMPRODUCT($D$6:D12,$E$6:E12)*0.5
13	4.0	4.33%	=1/(1+C13)^4	=1-F13	0.0114	=SUMPRODUCT($D$6:D13,$E$6:E13)*0.5
14	4.5	4.42%	=1/(1+C14)^4.5	=1-F14	0.0141	=SUMPRODUCT($D$6:D14,$E$6:E14)*0.5
15	5.0	4.45%	=1/(1+C15)^5	=1-F15	0.0156	=SUMPRODUCT($D$6:D15,$E$6:E15)*0.5
16						
17	Recovery rate					
18	0.3					

Table 16.9 CDS price calculation: Excel spreadsheet formula

H	I	J
PV of receipt if default	Default payment if default	CDS premiums
=SUMPRODUCT($D$6:D6,$F$6:F6)*0.5/2	=(1-$B$18)*SUMPRODUCT($D$6:D6,$F$6:F6)	=I6/(G6+H6)
=SUMPRODUCT($D$6:D7,$F$6:F7)*0.5/2	=(1-$B$18)*SUMPRODUCT($D$6:D7,$F$6:F7)	=I7/(G7+H7)
=SUMPRODUCT($D$6:D8,$F$6:F8)*0.5/2	=(1-$B$18)*SUMPRODUCT($D$6:D8,$F$6:F8)	=I8/(G8+H8)
=SUMPRODUCT($D$6:D9,$F$6:F9)*0.5/2	=(1-$B$18)*SUMPRODUCT($D$6:D9,$F$6:F9)	=I9/(G9+H9)
=SUMPRODUCT($D$6:D10,$F$6:F10)*0.5/2	=(1-$B$18)*SUMPRODUCT($D$6:D10,$F$6:F10)	=I10/(G10+H10)
=SUMPRODUCT($D$6:D11,$F$6:F11)*0.5/2	=(1-$B$18)*SUMPRODUCT($D$6:D11,$F$6:F11)	=I11/(G11+H11)
=SUMPRODUCT($D$6:D12,$F$6:F12)*0.5/2	=(1-$B$18)*SUMPRODUCT($D$6:D12,$F$6:F12)	=I12/(G12+H12)
=SUMPRODUCT($D$6:D13,$F$6:F13)*0.5/2	=(1-$B$18)*SUMPRODUCT($D$6:D13,$F$6:F13)	=I13/(G13+H13)
=SUMPRODUCT($D$6:D14,$F$6:F14)*0.5/2	=(1-$B$18)*SUMPRODUCT($D$6:D14,$F$6:F14)	=I14/(G14+H14)
=SUMPRODUCT($D$6:D15,$F$6:F15)*0.5/2	=(1-$B$18)*SUMPRODUCT($D$6:D15,$F$6:F15)	=I15/(G15+H15)

For the six-month period this is 0.0007 × 0.9826 × 0.0017 × 0.25, which actually comes out to a negligible value. For the one-year period the amount is 0.0017 × 0.9643 × 0.0017 × 0.25, which is also negligible. The total expected value of premium income is **0.00166.**

The expected present-value of the default payment if payment is made at end of the period is:

Default probability × Discount factor × (1 – Recovery rate)

which for the two periods is:

- 6 months: 0.0007 × 0.9826 × (1 – 30%) = 0.000482
- 12 months: 0.0017 × 0.9643 × (1 – 30%) = 0.001148

So the total expected value of the default payment is **0.00166**, which is equal to the earlier calculation. Our present values for both fixed leg and contingent legs are identical, which means we have the correct no-arbitrage value for the CDS contract.

From the CDS premium values we can construct a term structure of credit rates for this particular reference credit (or reference sector), which is shown in Figure 16.29. We can also construct a term structure of default probabilities, and this shown in Figure 16.30.

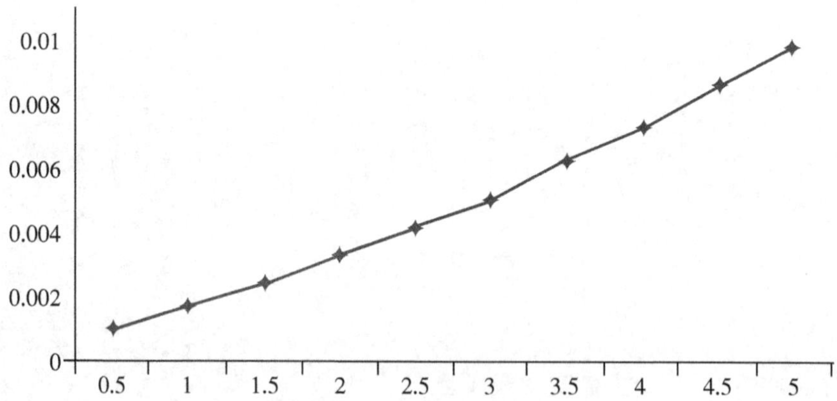

Figure 16.29 Term structure of credit rates

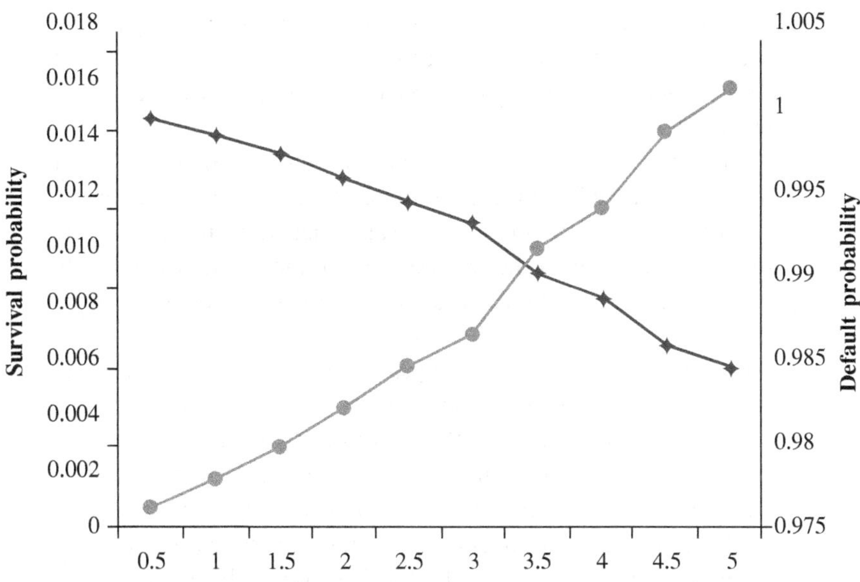

Figure 16.30 Term structure of default probabilities

The foregoing discussion shows the solution to pricing CDS premiums given the default probabilities. This assumes that we obtain the default probability first and then work out CDS premiums, and so further assumes that we can obtain reliable default probabilities, either from cash market corporate bond spreads or from the credit-rating agencies which publish cumulative default probability tables. In practice, for many reference names it is the CDS market that is the most liquid and so, in effect, we have the CDS premiums first! We would then imply default probabilities from CDS prices.

Example 16.6(i) Calculating the notional amount of the credit risk hedge[29]

It is intuitively easy to view a credit hedge as a straight par-for-par trade of notionals. That is, we would buy (or sell) USD10 million nominal of a bond against buying (or selling) USD10 million of notional in the CDS. This is still quite common due to its simplicity.

[29] With special thanks to Niall Considine and Suraj Gohil for their assistance with the technical details in this section.

However, unless the cash bond in question is priced at par, this approach is not correct and the analysis will not be accurate. The biggest errors will arise when the bond is trading significantly away from par.

To avoid the risk of being over- or under-hedged we must assess how much CDS protection to put on against a set amount of the bond. There is no one way to approach this; the key is the assumption made about the recovery rate in the event of default. In practice traders will adopt one of the following methods:

- par/par: this is a common approach. In such a trade, identical par amounts of the bond and the CDS are traded. The advantage of this method is that the position is straightforward to maintain. The disadvantage is that the trader is not accurately credit-risk hedged if the bond is priced away from par. The CDS pays out par (minus the deliverable asset or cash value on default) on default, but if the bond is priced above par greater cash value is at risk. Therefore this approach is recommended for bonds priced near to par or for trades with a long-term horizon. It is not recommended for use with bonds at higher risk of default (for instance, sub-investment-grade bonds) as default events will expose this approach to be under-hedged;
- delta-neutral: this is a similar approach used to duration-weighted bond spread trades such as butterfly/barbell trades (see Choudhry 2004). It is appropriate when the maturity of the bond does not match precisely the maturity of the CDS;
- DV01: this approach sets the CDS notional relative to the actual price of the bond. For example, if the bond is trading at 120 then we would buy 120% notional of the CDS. This is a logical approach and recommended if the bond is trading away from par.

An assumption of the recovery rate will influence the choice of hedging approach and the notional amount of CDS protection to buy.

A key risk factor is the recovery rate assumed for the bond. The rate of recovery cannot be hedged and the actual recovery after event of default will impact the final profit/loss position. The impact is greatest for bonds that are priced significantly away from par. To illustrate this, consider a bond priced at \$110.00. To hedge a long position of \$10 million of this bond, assume we buy protection in \$11 million nominal of the CDS. We do not use a par/par approach because otherwise we would be under-hedged. Now consider, in the event of default, the following recovery rates:

- 0% recovery: we receive \$11 million on the CDS, and lose \$11 million (1.10 × 10,000,000) on the bond, so net we are flat;
- 50% recovery: we receive \$5.5 million on the CDS, and lose \$6 million on the bond (the bond loss is \$5 million nominal and so we receive back \$5 million, having paid out \$11 million), so net we are down \$500,000.

So in other words, under a 50% recovery rate scenario we are under-hedged still and would need more notional of CDS to cover the loss on the bond. If the recovery rate is 30%, we still lose on the position, while at 50% or more we will lose progressively more. Note that the reverse analysis applies when the bond is priced below par. Overall then we conclude that the assumption of the recovery rate must influence the notional size of the CDS position.

Generally, the market assumes the following recovery rates:

- investment-grade 40%;
- insurance companies and corporates 30%;
- sub-investment grade 20%.

Some banks assume a 50% recovery rate in their pricing models. While a more robust approach might be to use historical data of actual defaults and ultimate recovery rates, at the current time some markets, notably those in Europe and Asia, suffer from a paucity of data and so for the time being market participants use assumed recovery rates.

To construct the correct hedge, we use the following formula for a bond priced over par:

$$\text{Hedge} = N + \left[\left(\frac{P - 100}{1 - R}\right) \times N\right] \qquad (16.22)$$

where

N is the bond notional
P is the bond price
R is the (assumed) recovery rate.

In the earlier example of a bond priced at 110.00, a CDS notional of USD11,428,571 would provide an adequate hedge if the recovery rate was at 30%.

For a bond priced below par, we subtract the adjustment from the bond notional.

EXAMPLE 16.6 (ii) Comparing cash and synthetic bond price

The existence of a liquid market in credit derivatives allows banks and fund managers to calculate a theoretical cash market bond price from the CDS curve. By comparing the actual market price to the theoretical price, investors can determine relative value and any mispricing in one market vis-à-vis the other. The cash market price is observed in the market. The CDS curve implies the theoretical bond price: we can use the CDS curve and an assumed recovery rate to calculate the default probability of the reference name for any point along the CDS term structure. With a term structure of default probabilities, we can imply the likelihood of default or that all the bond's coupons and redemption payments will be made. If no default occurs, the bondholder receives the expected cash flows; if default occurs, the investor's payout is determined by the recovery rate. The theoretical bond price is the net present value of all probability-weighted payments, in the event of default or no default.

In other words, using prices observed in the CDS market we can calculate the theoretical value of a bond's cash flows, given the value of the same name as implied in the CDS market. We can then consider whether the bond is cheap or dear relative to the synthetic credit market.

Bloomberg screen HG can be used to make the calculation.[30] It is used with a single bond position, and we illustrate this here.

[30] This screen has more than one application, and can also be used for a number of interest-rate risk ("DV01") and credit risk hedge calculations.

Figure 16.31 shows the page selected for use with a bond issued by British Airways plc, the $10\frac{7}{8}\%$ June 2008. The analysis was conducted on 11 December 2006. This page uses the CDS spreads for British Airways plc plus an assumed recovery rate of 30% to determine future default probability. The model price (shown in the bottom left-hand corner, beneath the market price) is the net present value of the bond's probability-weighted cash flows. We see that the model price of 107.232 differs from the observed market offer price of 107.103, a matter of 13 pence or so.

The "Default Adj Spread" field shows the number of basis points by which the CDS curve would need to be moved in order to equate the theoretical price to the market price. In this case we see that this adjustment is around 8.5 basis points.

Warning: Function is under test - Not formally released. NN120 Corp **HGBD**

Save | Send | Copy | Single Bond Hedge

Bond Information			
BAB 10.875 06/15/2008		Bloomberg ID	TT2008429
Reference Name			British Airways PLC
Workout Date			06/15/2008
Maturity Date			06/15/2008
Notional			10.00 MM
Currency			GBP
Coupon			10.875
Recovery Rate			0.30
Collateral			Notes
Calculations			
Valuation Date	12/14/2006	Model	JPMorgan
Market Price	107.103	Market Yield	5.753
Model Price	107.232	Model Yield	5.667
Default Adj Sprd (bp)	8.493	Z-Spread	31.53
Accrued	540,729.17		
Market Value	11,251,005.49		
IR DV01	1,516.23		
Sprd DV01	-1,613.96		

Spread		
Curve Date		12/11/2006
Benchmark	S 22	Ask
BP BGN Swap Curve		
Spreads	Contributor	Ask
100226 EUR Senior	IMM	N
		23) CDSD Dflts
Par Cds Spreads (bps)		Default Prob
Flat	N	
6 mo	23.500	0.0017
1 yr	23.500	0.0034
2 yr	33.000	0.0095
3 yr	47.000	0.0206
4 yr	66.339	0.0391
5 yr	83.000	0.0612
7 yr	109.500	0.1123
10 yr	132.000	0.1886
Frequency		Quarterly
Day Count		ACT / 360
Recovery Rate		0.30

11) Strategy | 12) Structures | 13) Valuation | 14) Cashflows

Australia 61 2 9777 8600 Brazil 5511 3048 4500 Europe 44 20 7330 7500 Germany 49 69 920410
Hong Kong 852 2977 6000 Japan 81 3 3201 8900 Singapore 65 6212 1000 U.S. 1 212 318 2000 Copyright 2006 Bloomberg L.P.
G364-793-2 11-Dec-2006 14:44:17

Figure 16.31 Bloomberg screen HG showing implied price and market price for British Airways 10.875% 2008 bond, as at 11 December 2006

References and bibliography

Ames, C. 1997, "Collateralised Mortgage Obligation", in Fabozzi, F. (ed.), *The Handbook of Fixed Income Securities*, 5th edition, McGraw-Hill, New York.

Bhattacharya, A. and Fabozzi, F. (eds) 1996, *Asset-backed Securities*, FJF Associates New Hope, PA.

Choudhry, M. 2001, *The Bond and Money Markets: Strategy, Trading, Analysis*, Butterworth-Heinemann, Oxford.

Choudhry, M. 2001, "Some Issues in the Asset-swap Pricing of Credit Default Swaps", *Derivatives Week,* Euromoney Publications, 2 December.

Choudhry, M. 2003, "Some Issues in the Asset-swap Pricing of Credit Default Swaps," in Fabozzi, F. (editor), *Professional Perspectives on Fixed Income Portfolio Management*, volume 4, John Wiley & Sons, New York.

Choudhry, M. 2004a, *Structured Credit Products: Credit Derivatives and Synthetic Securitisation*, Singapore: John Wiley & Sons, Singapore.

Choudhry, M. 2004b, "The Credit Default Swap Basis: Analysing the Relationship Between Cash and Synthetic Markets", *Journal of Derivatives Use, Trading and Regulation,* June, pp. 9–26.

Choudhry, M. 2006a, *The Credit Default Swap Basis*, Bloomberg Press, Princeton, NJ.

Choudhry, M. 2006b, "Further Observations on the CDS Basis", *Journal of Structured Finance,* Winter, pp. 21–32.

Das S. 2004, *Credit Derivatives and Credit Linked Notes*, 2nd edition. John Wiley & Sons, Singapore, chapters 2–4.

Duffie, D. and M. Huang 1996, "Swap Rates and Credit Quality," *Journal of Finance*, 51, No. 3, July, pp. 609–31.

Fabozzi, F. 1998, *Handbook of Structured Financial Products*, FJF Associates.

Fabozzi, F. and Jacob, D. 1996, *The Handbook of Commercial Mortgage-backed Securities*, FJF Associates.

Fabozzi, F. 2004. *The Handbook of European Structured Financial Products*, John Wiley & Sons, New York.

Fabozzi, F., Ramsey, C. and Ramirez, F. 1994, *Collateralised Mortgage Obligations*, FJF Associates.

Francis, J., Frost, J. and Whittaker, G. 1999, *Handbook of Credit Derivatives*, Irwin, NY.

Hogg, R. and Craig A. 1970, *Introduction to Mathematical Statistics*, 3rd edition, Macmillan, New York.

Hull, J. and White, A. 2000, "Valuing Credit Default Swaps I: No Counter-party Default Risk," *Journal of Derivatives*, 8 (1), Fall, pp. 71–9.

Jarrow, R.A. and Turnbull S.M. 1995, "Pricing Options on Derivative Securities Subject to Credit Risk," *Journal of Finance*, 50, pp. 53–8.

Oppenheimer & Co. 1994, "Qualitatively Assessing Prepayments of Current- and Discount-coupon Passthroughs", *Mortgage Research*, Oppenheimer & Co. Inc., 20 October.

Tolk, J. 2001 'Understanding the Risks in Credit Default Swaps', *Moody's Investors Service Special Report*, 16 March.

CHAPTER

17

Value-at-Risk (VaR) and Credit VaR

In this chapter, we review the main risk-measurement tool used in banking, known as Value-at-Risk (VaR). ALM managers up to ALCO level consider the bank's interest-rate risk exposure, and to a certain extent its credit risk exposure, on a regular basis. Their review takes into account both the business lines' adherence to the set exposure limits, as well as whether the limits themselves are at the correct level to enable the bank to achieve its objectives. Although many smaller banks employ the modified duration method to measure interest-rate risk exposure, more and more banks are moving to a VaR-based calculation of risk exposure. Hence it is important for ALM managers to be aware of the VaR measure.

This chapter looks at the three main methodologies used to calculate VaR, as well as some of the key assumptions used in the calculations, including those on the normal distribution of returns, volatility levels and correlations. We also discuss the use of the VaR methodology with respect to credit risk.

Introducing Value-at-Risk

The introduction of VaR as an accepted methodology for quantifying market risk and its adoption by bank regulators is part of the evolution of risk management. The application of VaR has been extended from its initial use in securities houses to commercial banks and corporates, following its introduction in October 1994 when JPMorgan launched RiskMetrics™.

VaR is a measure of the worst expected loss that a firm may suffer over a period of time that has been specified by the user, under normal market conditions and a specified level of confidence. This measure may be obtained in a number of ways, using a statistical model or by computer simulation. We can define VaR as follows:

VaR is a measure of market risk. It is the maximum loss that can occur with X% confidence over a holding period of n *days.*

VaR is the expected loss of a portfolio over a specified time period for a set level of probability. For example, if a daily VaR is stated as £100,000 to a 95% level of confidence, this means that during the day there is a only a 5% chance that the loss the next day will be *greater* than £100,000. VaR measures the potential loss in market value of a portfolio using estimated volatility and correlation. The "correlation" referred to is the correlation that exists between the market prices of different instruments in a bank's portfolio. VaR is calculated within a given confidence interval, typically 95% or 99%; it seeks to measure the possible losses from a position or portfolio under "normal" circumstances. The definition of normality is critical and is essentially a statistical concept that varies by firm and by risk-management system. Put simply, however, the most commonly used VaR models assume that the prices of assets in the financial markets follow a normal distribution. To implement VaR, all of a firm's positions data must be gathered into one centralised database. Once this is complete, the overall risk has to be calculated by aggregating the risks from individual instruments across the entire portfolio. The potential move in each instrument (that is, each risk factor) has to be inferred from past daily price movements over a given observation period. For regulatory purposes, this period is at least one year. Hence, the data on which VaR estimates are based should capture all relevant daily market moves over the previous year.

The main assumption underpinning VaR – and which in turn may be seen as its major weakness – is that the distribution of future price and rate changes will follow past variations. Therefore, the potential portfolio loss calculations for VaR are worked out using distributions from historic price data in the observation period.

VaR is a measure of the volatility of a firm's banking or trading book. A portfolio containing assets that have a high level of volatility has a higher risk than one containing assets with a lower level of volatility. The VaR measure seeks to quantify in a single measure the potential losses that may be suffered by a portfolio.

VaR is therefore a measure of a bank's risk exposure; it is a tool for measuring market risk exposure. There is no one VaR number for a single portfolio, because different methodologies used for calculating VaR produce different results. The VaR number captures only those risks that can be measured in quantitative terms. It does not capture risk exposures such as operational risk, liquidity risk, regulatory risk or sovereign risk. It is important to be aware of what precisely VaR attempts to capture and what it clearly makes no attempt to capture. Also, VaR is not "risk management". A risk-management department may choose to use a VaR-measurement system in an effort to quantify a bank's risk exposure; however, the application itself is merely a tool. Implementing such a tool in no way compensates for inadequate procedures and rules in the management of a trading book.

Assumption of normality

A distribution is described as normal if there is a high probability that any observation from the population sample will have a value that is close to the mean, and a low probability of having a value that is far from the mean. The normal distribution curve is used by many VaR models, which assume that asset returns follow a normal pattern. A VaR model uses the normal curve to estimate the losses that an institution may suffer over a given time period. Normal distribution tables show the probability of a particular observation moving a certain distance from the mean.

If we look along a normal distribution table we see that at −1.645 standard deviations, the probability is 5%. This means that there is a 5% probability that an observation will be at least 1.645 standard deviations below the mean. This level is used in many VaR models.

Further discussion on characteristics of the normal distribution is given in Appendix 17.1.

Calculation methods

The three traditional methods for calculating VaR are:

- the variance–covariance (or *correlation* or *parametric* method);
- historical simulation;
- Monte Carlo simulation.

We consider each of these in turn.

Variance–covariance method

This method assumes the returns on risk factors are normally distributed, the correlations between risk factors are constant and the delta (or price sensitivity to changes in a risk factor) of each portfolio constituent is constant. Using the correlation method, the volatility of each risk factor is extracted from the historical observation period. Historical data on investment returns is therefore required. The potential effect of each component of the portfolio on the overall portfolio value is then worked out from the component's delta (with respect to a particular risk factor) and that risk factor's volatility.

There are different methods of calculating the relevant risk factor volatilities and correlations. Two alternatives are:

- simple *historic volatility*: this is the most straightforward method but the effects of a large one-off market move can significantly distort volatilities over the required forecasting period. For example, if using 30-day historic volatility, a market shock will stay in the volatility figure for 30 days until it drops out of the sample range and correspondingly causes a sharp drop in (historic) volatility 30 days *after* the event. This is because each past observation is equally weighted in the volatility calculation;
- to weight past observations unequally: this is done to give more weight to recent observations so that large jumps in volatility are not caused by events that occurred some time ago. One method is to use exponentially weighted moving averages.

Historical simulation method

The historical simulation method for calculating VaR is arguably the simplest. The three main assumptions behind correlation (normally distributed returns, constant correlations and constant deltas) are not needed in this case. For historical simulation, the model calculates potential losses using actual historical returns in the risk factors and so captures the non-normal distribution of risk-factor returns. This means rare events and crashes can be included in the results. As the risk-factor returns used for revaluing the portfolio are actual past movements, the correlations in the calculation are also actual past correlations. They capture the dynamic nature of correlation as well as scenarios when the usual correlation relationships break down.

Monte Carlo simulation method

The third method, Monte Carlo simulation, is more flexible than the previous two. As with historical simulation, Monte Carlo simulation allows the risk manager to use actual historical distributions for risk-factor returns rather than having to assume normal returns. A large number of randomly generated simulations are run forward in time using volatility and correlation estimates chosen by the risk manager. Each simulation will be different but, in total, the simulations will aggregate to the chosen statistical parameters (that is, historical distributions and volatility and correlation estimates). This method is more realistic than the previous two models and therefore is more likely to estimate VaR more accurately. However, its implementation requires powerful computers and there is also a trade-off in that the time required to perform calculations is longer.

The level of confidence in the VaR estimation process is selected by the number of standard deviations of variance applied to the probability distribution. A standard deviation selection of 1.645 provides a 95% confidence level (in a one-tailed test) that the potential estimated price movement will not be more than a given amount based on the correlation of market factors to the position's price sensitivity.

Correlation

Measures of correlation between variables are important to banks that are interested in reducing their risk exposure through diversifying their portfolio. Correlation is a measure of the degree to which a value of one variable is related to the value of another. The correlation coefficient is a single number that compares the strengths and directions of the movements in two instruments' values. The sign of the coefficient determines the relative directions that the instruments move in, while its value determines the strength of the relative movements. The value of the coefficient ranges from −1 to +1, depending on the nature of the relationship. So if, for example, the value of the correlation is 0.5, this means that one instrument moves in the same direction by half of the amount that the other instrument moves. A value of zero means that the instruments are uncorrelated, and their movements are independent of each other.

Correlation is a key element of many VaR models, including parametric models. It is particularly important in the measurement of the variance (hence, volatility) of a portfolio. If we take the simplest example, a portfolio containing just two assets, (17.1) below gives the volatility of the portfolio based on the volatility of each instrument in the portfolio (x and y) and their correlation with one another.

$$V_{port} = \sqrt{x^2 + y^2 + 2xy \cdot \rho(xy)} \tag{17.1}$$

where

x is the volatility of asset x
y is the volatility of asset y
ρ is the correlation between assets x and y.

The correlation coefficient between two assets uses the covariance between the assets in its calculation. The standard formula for covariance is shown in (17.2):

$$Cov = \frac{\sum_{i=1}^{n} (xi - \overline{x})(yi - \overline{y})}{(n - 1)} \tag{17.2}$$

where the sum of the distance of each value x and y from the mean is divided by the number of observations minus one. The covariance calculation enables us to calculate the correlation coefficient, shown in (17.3):

$$\rho = Cov \frac{(1,2)}{\sigma_1 \times \sigma_2} \tag{17.3}$$

where σ is the standard deviation of each asset.

Equation (17.1) may be modified to cover more than two instruments. In practice, correlations are usually estimated on the basis of past historical observations. This is an important consideration in the construction and analysis of a portfolio, as the associated risks will depend to an extent on the correlation between its constituents.

It should be apparent that from a portfolio perspective a positive correlation increases risk. If the returns on two or more instruments in a portfolio are positively correlated, strong movements in either direction are likely to occur at the same time. The overall distribution of returns will be wider and flatter, as there will be higher joint probabilities associated with extreme values (both gains and losses). A negative correlation indicates that the assets are likely to move in opposite directions, thus reducing risk.

It has been argued that in extreme situations, such as market crashes or large-scale market corrections, correlations cease to have any relevance, because all assets will be moving in the same direction. However, under most market scenarios, using correlations to reduce the risk of a portfolio is considered satisfactory practice, and the VaR number for a diversified portfolio will be lower than that for an undiversified portfolio.

Simple VaR calculation

To calculate the VaR for a single asset, we would calculate the standard deviation of its returns, using either its historical volatility or implied volatility. If a 95% confidence level is required, meaning we wish to have 5% of the observations in the left-hand tail of the normal distribution, this means that the observations in that area are 1.645 standard deviations away from the mean. This can be checked from standard normal tables. Consider the following statistical data for a government bond, calculated using one year's historical observations.

Nominal:	£10 million
Price:	£100
Average return:	7.35%
Standard deviation:	1.99%

The VaR at the 95% confidence level is 1.645 × 0.0199 or 0.032736. The portfolio has a market value of £10 million, so the VaR of the portfolio is 0.032736 × 10,000,000 or £327,360. So this figure is the maximum loss the portfolio may sustain over one year for 95% of the time.

We may extend this analysis to a two-stock portfolio. In a two-asset portfolio, we stated in (17.1) that there is a relationship that enables us to calculate the volatility of such a portfolio; this expression is used to calculate the VaR, and is shown in (17.4):

$$VaR_{port} = \sqrt{w_1^2\sigma_1^2 + w_2^2\sigma_2^2 + 2w_1w_2\sigma_1\sigma_2\rho_{1,2}} \tag{17.4}$$

where

w_1 is the weighting of the first asset
w_2 is the weighting of the second asset
σ_1 is the standard deviation or volatility of the first asset
σ_2 is the standard deviation or volatility of the second asset
$\rho_{1,2}$ is the correlation coefficient between the two assets.

In a two-asset portfolio, the undiversified VaR is the weighted average of the individual standard deviations; the diversified VaR, which takes into account the correlation between the assets, is the square root of the variance of the portfolio. In practice, banks will calculate both diversified and undiversified VaR. The diversified VaR measure is used to set trading limits, while the larger undiversified VaR measure is used to gauge an idea of the bank's risk exposure in the event of a significant correction or market crash. This is because in a crash situation, liquidity dries up as market participants all attempt to sell off their assets. This means that the correlation relationship between assets ceases to have any impact on a book, as all assets move in the same direction. Under this scenario, then, it is more logical to use an undiversified VaR measure.

Although the description given here is very simple, it nevertheless explains what is the essence of the VaR measure. VaR is essentially the calculation of the standard deviation of a portfolio, which is used as an indicator of the volatility of that portfolio. A portfolio exhibiting high volatility will have a high VaR number. An observer may then conclude that the portfolio has a high probability of making losses. Risk managers and traders may use the VaR measure to help them to allocate capital to more efficient sectors of the bank, as return on capital can now be measured in terms of return on risk capital. Regulators may use the VaR number as a guide to the capital-adequacy levels that they feel the bank requires.

Matrix calculation of variance–covariance VaR

Consider the following hypothetical portfolio, invested in two assets, as shown in Table 17.1(i). The standard deviation of each asset has been calculated on historical observation of asset returns. Note that returns are returns of asset prices, rather than the prices themselves; they are calculated from the actual prices by taking the ratio of closing prices. The returns are then calculated as the logarithm of the price relatives. The mean and standard deviation of the returns are then calculated using standard statistical formulas. This would then give the standard deviation of daily price relatives, which is converted to an annual figure by multiplying it by the square root of the number of days in a year, usually taken to be 250.

The standard equation (shown in (17.4)) is used to calculate the variance of the portfolio, using the standard deviations of the individual assets and the asset weightings. The VaR of the book is the square root of the variance. Multiplying this figure by the current value of the portfolio gives us the portfolio VaR, which is £2,113,300.72. The Excel formulas are shown in Table 17.1(ii).

D	E	F	G	H
		Asset		
8		Bond 1	Bond 2	
9	Standard deviation	11.83%	17.65%	
10	Portfolio weighting	60%	40%	
11	Correlation coefficient			0.647
12	Portfolio value			$10,000,000.00
13	Confidence level			95%
14				
15	Portfolio variance			0.016506998
16	Standard deviation			12.848%
17				
18	95% c.i. standard deviations			1.644853627
19				
20	Value-at-Risk			0.211330072
21	Value-at-Risk £			$2,113,300.72
22				

Table 17.1(i) Two-asset portfolio VaR

D	E	F	G	H
		Asset		
8		Bond 1	Bond 2	
9	Standard deviation	11.83%	17.65%	
10	Portfolio weighting	60%	40%	
11	Correlation coefficient			0.647
12	Portfolio value			$10,000,000.00
13	Confidence level			95%
14				
15	Portfolio variance			=F9^2*F10^2+G9^2*G10^2 +2*F9*F10*G9*G10
16	Standard deviation			=H15^0.5
17				
18	95% c.i. standard deviations			=NORMSINV(H13)
19				
20	Value-at-Risk			=H18*H16
21	Value-at-Risk £			=H20*H12
22				

Table 17.1(ii) Spreadsheet formulas for Table 17.1(i)

The RiskMetrics™ VaR methodology uses matrices to obtain the same results that we have shown here. This is because once a portfolio starts to contain many assets, the method we described above becomes unwieldy. Matrices allow us to calculate VaR for a portfolio containing many hundreds of assets, which would require assessment of the volatility of each asset and correlations of each asset to all the others in the portfolio. We can demonstrate how the parametric methodology uses variance and correlation matrices to calculate the variance, and hence standard deviation, of a portfolio. The matrices are shown in Figure 17.1. Note that the multiplication of matrices carries with it some unique rules; readers who are unfamiliar with matrices should refer to a standard mathematics textbook.

As shown in Figure 17.1, using the same two-asset portfolio described, we can set a 2x2 matrix with the individual standard deviations inside; this is labelled the "variance" matrix. The standard deviations are placed on the horizontal axis of the matrix, and a zero entered in the other cells. The second matrix is the correlation matrix, and the correlation of the two assets is placed in cells corresponding to the other asset. That is why a "1" is placed in the other cells, as an asset is said to have a correlation of 1 with itself. The two matrices are then multiplied to produce another matrix, labelled "VC" in Figure 17.1.[1]

The VC matrix is then multiplied with the V matrix to obtain the variance–covariance matrix or VCV matrix. This shows the variance of each asset; for Bond 1 this is 0.01399, which is expected, as that is the square of its standard deviation, which we were given at the start. The matrix also tells us that Bond 1 has a covariance of 0.0135 with Bond 2. We then set up a matrix of the portfolio weighting of the two assets, and this is multiplied by the VCV matrix. This produces a 1x2 matrix, which we need to change to a single number, so this is multiplied by the W matrix, reset as a 2x1 matrix, which produces the portfolio variance. This is 0.016507. The standard deviation is the square root of the variance, and is 0.1284795 or 12.848%, which is what we obtained before. In our illustration it is important to note the order in which the matrices were multiplied, as this will obviously affect the result. The volatility matrix contains the standard deviations along the diagonal, and zeros are entered in all the other cells. So if the portfolio we were calculating has 50 assets in it, we would require a 50x50 matrix and enter the standard deviations for each asset along the diagonal line. All the other cells would have a zero in them. Similarly for the weighting matrix;

[1] Microsoft Excel has a function for multiplying matrices that may be used for any type of matrix. The function is "=MMULT()" typed in all the cells of the product matrix.

this is always one row, and all the weights are entered along the row. To take the example just given, the result would be a 1x50 weighting matrix.

	Variance matrix		**Correlation matrix**		**VC matrix**	
			Bond 1	Bond 2		
Bond 1	11.83%	0	1	0.647	0.1183	0.07654
Bond 2	0	17.65%	0.647	1	0.114196	0.1765

VC matrix		**Variance matrix**		**VCV matrix**	
0.1183	0.07654	11.83%	0	0.013995	0.013509
0.114196	0.1765	0	17.65%	0.013509	0.031152

Weighting matrix		VCV matrix		WVCV	
60%	40%	0.013995	0.013509	0.013801	0.020566
		0.013509	0.031152		

WVCV		W	WVCVW
0.013801	0.020566	60%	0.016507
		40%	
		Standard deviation	0.12848

Figure 17.1 Matrix variance–covariance calculation for a two-asset portfolio shown in Table 17.1

The matrix method for calculating the standard deviation is more effective than the first method we described, because it can be used for a portfolio containing a large number of assets. In fact, this is exactly the methodology used by RiskMetrics™ and the computer model used for the calculation will be set up with matrices containing the data for hundreds, if not thousands, of different assets.

The variance–covariance method captures the diversification benefits of a multi-product portfolio because of the correlation coefficient matrix used in the calculation. For instance, if the two bonds in our hypothetical portfolio had a negative correlation, the VaR number produced would be lower. To apply it, a bank would require data on volatility and correlation for the assets in its portfolio. These data are actually available from the RiskMetrics™ website (and other sources), so a bank does not necessarily need its own data. It may wish to use its own datasets, however, should it have them, to tailor the application to its own use. The advantages of the variance–covariance methodology are that:

- it is simple to apply, and fairly straightforward to explain;
- datasets for its use are immediately available.

The drawbacks of the variance–covariance are that it assumes stable correlations and measures only linear risk; it also places excessive reliance on the normal distribution, and returns in the market are widely believed to have "fatter tails" than a true-to-normal distribution. This phenomenon is known as leptokurtosis; that is, the non-normal distribution of outcomes. Another disadvantage is that the process requires mapping. To construct a weighting portfolio for the RiskMetrics™ tool, cash flows from financial instruments are mapped into precise maturity points, known as grid points. We will review this later in the chapter. However, in most cases, assets do not fit into neat grid points, and complex instruments cannot be broken down accurately into cash flows. The mapping process makes assumptions that frequently do not hold in practice.

Nevertheless, the variance–covariance method is still popular in the market, and is frequently the first VaR method installed in a bank.

Mapping

The cornerstone of the variance–covariance methodology is the requirement for data on volatilities and correlations for assets in the portfolio. The RiskMetrics™ dataset does not contain volatilities for every maturity possible, as that would require a value for very period from one day to over 10,950 days (30 years) and longer, and correlations between each of these days. This would result in an excessive amount of calculation. Rather, volatilities are available for set maturity periods, and these are shown in Table 17.2.

If a bond is maturing in six years' time, its redemption cash flow will not match the data in the RiskMetrics™ dataset, so it must be mapped to two periods; in this case, being split to the five-year and seven-year grid point. This is done in proportions so that the original value of the bond is maintained once it has been mapped. More importantly, when a cash flow is mapped, it must split in a manner that preserves the volatility characteristic of the original cash flow. Therefore, when mapping cash flows, if one cash flow is apportioned to two grid points, the share of the two new cash flows must equal the present value of the original cash flows, and the combined volatility of the two new assets must be equal to that of the original asset. A simple demonstration is given in Example 17.1.

RiskMetrics grid points
1 month
3 months
6 months
1 year
2 years
3 years
4 years
5 years
7 years
9 years
10 years
15 years
20 years
30 years

Table 17.2 RiskMetrics™ grid points

EXAMPLE 17.1 Cash flow mapping

A bond trading book holds £1 million nominal of a gilt strip that is due to mature in precisely six years' time. To correctly capture the volatility of this position in the bank's RiskMetrics™ VaR estimate, the cash flow represented by this bond must be mapped to the grid points for five years and seven years, the closest maturity buckets for which the RiskMetrics™ dataset holds volatility and correlation data. The present value of the strip is calculated using the six-year zero-coupon rate, which RiskMetrics™ obtains by interpolating between the five-year rate and the seven-year rate. The details are shown in Table 17.3.

Note that the correlation between the two interest rates is very close to 1. This is expected because five-year interest rates generally move very closely in line with seven-year rates.

We wish to assign the single cash flow to the five-year and seven-year grid points (also referred to as vertices). The present value of the bond, using the six-year interpolated yield, is £728,347. This is shown in Table 17.4, which also uses an interpolated volatility to calculate the volatility of the six-year cash flow. However, we wish to calculate a portfolio volatility based on the apportionment of the cash flow to the five-year and seven-year grid points. To do this, we need to use a weighting to allocate the cash flow between the two vertices. In the hypothetical situation used here, this presents no problem because six years falls precisely between five years and seven years. Therefore, the weightings are 0.5 for year 5 and 0.5 for year 7. If the cash flow had fallen in a less obvious maturity point, we would have to calculate the weightings using the formula for portfolio variance. Using these weightings, we calculate the variance for the new "portfolio", containing the two new cash flows, and then the standard deviation for the portfolio. This gives us a VaR for the strip of £265,853.

Gilt strip nominal (£):	1,000,000
Maturity (years):	6
5-year zero-coupon rate:	5.35%
7-year zero-coupon rate:	5.50%
5-year volatility:	24.50%
7-year volatility:	28.95%
Correlation coefficient:	0.979
Lower period:	5
Upper period:	7

Table 17.3 Bond position to be mapped to grid points

Interpolated yield:	0.05425
Interpolated volatility:	0.26725
Present value:	728,347.0103
Weighting 5-year grid point:	0.5
Weighting 7-year grid point:	0.5
Variance of portfolio:	0.070677824
Standard deviation:	0.265853012
VaR £:	265,853

Table 17.4 Cash flow mapping and portfolio variance

Confidence intervals

Many models estimate VaR at a given confidence interval, under normal market conditions. This assumes that market returns generally follow a random pattern but one that approximates over time to a normal distribution. The level of confidence at which the VaR is calculated will depend on the nature of the trading book's activity and what the VaR number is being used for. The market risk amendment to the Basel capital accord stipulates a 99% confidence interval and a 10-day holding period if the VaR measure is to be used to calculate the regulatory capital requirement. However, certain banks prefer to use other confidence levels and holding periods; the decision on which level to use is a function of the asset types in the portfolio, the quality of market data available and the accuracy of the model itself, which will have been tested over time by the bank.

For example, a bank may view a 99% confidence interval as providing no useful information, as it implies that there should only be two or three breaches of the VaR measure over the course of one year. That would leave no opportunity to test the accuracy of the model until a longer period of time had elapsed and, in the meantime, the bank would be unaware if the model were generating inaccurate numbers. A 95% confidence level implies that the VaR level is being exceeded around one day each month, if a year is assumed to contain 250 days.[2] If a VaR calculation is made using 95% confidence, and a 99% confidence level is required for, say, regulatory purposes, we need to adjust the measure to take account of the change in standard deviations required. For example, a 99% confidence interval corresponds to 2.32 standard deviations, while a 95% level is equivalent to 1.645 standard deviations. Thus, to convert from 95% confidence to 99% confidence, the VaR figure is divided by 1.645 and multiplied by 2.32.

In the same way, there may be occasions when a firm will wish to calculate VaR over a different holding period to that recommended by the Basel rules. The holding period of a portfolio's VaR calculation should represent the period of time required to unwind the portfolio; that is, sell off the assets on the book. A 10-day holding period is recommended but would be unnecessary for a highly liquid portfolio; for example, one holding government bonds.

To adjust the VaR number to fit it to a new holding period we simply scale it upwards or downwards by the square root of the time period

---

[2] For the 99% confidence level, $250 \times 1\% = 2.5$ days in one year, while 95% confidence is $250 \times 5\%$ or 12.5 days.

required. For example, a VaR calculation measured for a 10-day holding period will be $\sqrt{10}$ times larger than the corresponding 1-day measure.

Historical VaR methodology

The historical approach to VaR is a relatively simple calculation, and it is also easy to implement and explain. To implement it, a bank requires a database record of its past profit/loss figures for the total portfolio. The required confidence interval is then applied to this record, to obtain a cut-off of the worst-case scenario. For example, to calculate the VaR at a 95% confidence level, the fifth percentile value for the historical data is taken, and this is the VaR number. For a 99% confidence level measure, the 1% percentile is taken. The advantage of the historical method is that it uses the actual market data that a bank has recorded (unlike RiskMetrics™, for example, for which the volatility and correlations are not actual values, but estimated values calculated from average figures over a period of time, usually the last five years), and so produces a reasonably accurate figure. Its main weakness is that as it is reliant on actual historical data built up over a period of time, generally at least one year's data is required to make the calculation meaningful. Therefore, it is not suitable for portfolios whose asset weightings frequently change, as another set of data would be necessary before a VaR number could be calculated.

To overcome this drawback banks use a method known as historical simulation. This calculates VaR for the current portfolio weighting, using the historical data for the securities in the current portfolio. To calculate historical simulation VaR for our hypothetical portfolio considered earlier, comprising 60% of bond 1 and 40% of bond 2, we require the closing prices for both assets over the specified previous period (usually three or five years). We then calculate the value of the portfolio for each day in the period assuming constant weightings.

Simulation methodology

The most complex calculations use computer simulations to estimate VaR. The most common of these is the Monte Carlo method. To calculate VaR using a Monte Carlo approach, a computer simulation is run to generate a number of random scenarios, which are then used to estimate the portfolio VaR. The method is probably the most realistic, if we accept that market returns follow a similar "random walk" pattern. However, Monte Carlo simulation is best suited to trading books containing large option portfolios, whose price behavior is not captured very well with the RiskMetrics™

methodology. The main disadvantage of the simulation methodology is that it is time-consuming and uses a substantial amount of computer resources.

A Monte Carlo simulation generates simulated future prices, and it may be used to value an option as well as for VaR applications. When used for valuation, a range of possible asset prices are generated and these are used to assess what intrinsic value the option will have at those asset prices. The present value of the option is then calculated from these possible intrinsic values. Generating simulated prices, although designed to mimic a "random walk", cannot be completely random because asset prices, although not a pure normal distribution, are not completely random either. The simulation model is usually set to generate very few extreme prices. Strictly speaking, it is asset price *returns* that follow a normal distribution, or rather a lognormal distribution. Monte Carlo simulation may also be used to simulate other scenarios; for example, the effect on option "Greeks" for a given change in volatility, or any other parameters. The scenario concept may be applied to calculating VaR as well. For example, if 50,000 simulations of an option price are generated, the 95th lowest value in the simulation will be the VaR at the 95% confidence level. The correlation between assets is accounted for by altering the random selection program to reflect relationships.

EXAMPLE 17.2 Portfolio volatilty using variance–covariance and simulation methods

A simple two-asset portfolio is composed of the following instruments:

	Gilt strip	FTSE100 stock
Number of units	£100 million	£5 million
Market value	£54.39 million	£54 million
Daily volatility	£0.18 million	£0.24 million

The correlation between the two assets is 20%. Using (17.4) we calculate the portfolio VaR as follows:

$$\text{Vol.} = \sqrt{s_{bond}^2 + s_{stock}^2 + 2s_{bond}s_{stock}r_{bond,stock}}$$

$$\text{Vol.} = \sqrt{0.18^2 + 0.24^2 + (2 \times 0.18 \times 0.24 \times 0.2)}$$

$$= 0.327.$$

We have ignored the weighting element for each asset because the market values are roughly equal. The calculation gives a portfolio volatility of £0.327 million. For a 95% confidence level VaR measure, which corresponds to 1.645 standard deviations (in a one-tailed test), we multiply the portfolio volatility by 1.645, which gives us a portfolio VaR of £0.538 million.

In a Monte Carlo simulation, we also calculate the correlation and volatilities of the portfolio. These values are used as parameters in a random-number simulation to throw out changes in the underlying portfolio value. These values are used to reprice the portfolio, and this value will be either a gain or loss on the actual mark-to-market value. This process is repeated for each random number that is generated. In Table 17.5 we show the results for 15 simulations of our two-asset portfolio. From the results we read off the loss level that corresponds to the required confidence interval.

Simulation	Market value: bond	Market value: stock	Portfolio value	Profit/Loss
1	54.35	54.9	109.25	0.86
2	54.64	54.02	108.66	0.27
3	54.4	53.86	108.26	−0.13
4	54.25	54.15	108.4	0.01
5	54.4	54.17	108.57	0.18
6	54.4	54.03	108.43	0.04
7	54.31	53.84	108.15	−0.24
8	54.3	53.96	108.26	−0.13
9	54.46	54.11	108.57	0.18
10	54.32	53.92	108.24	−0.15
11	54.31	53.97	108.28	−0.11
12	54.47	54.08	108.55	0.16
13	54.38	54.03	108.41	0.02
14	54.71	53.89	108.6	0.21
15	54.29	54.05	108.34	−0.05

Table 17.5 Monte Carlo simulation results

As the number of trials is increased, the results from a Monte Carlo simulation approach those of the variance–covariance measure. This is shown in Figure 17.2.

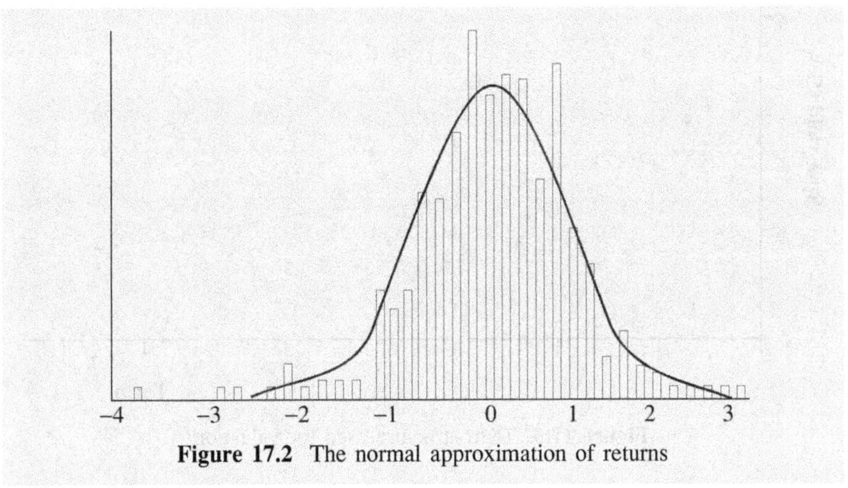

Figure 17.2 The normal approximation of returns

VaR for fixed-income instruments

Perhaps the most straightforward instruments to which VaR can be applied are foreign-exchange and interest-rate instruments such as money market products, bonds, forward-rate agreements and swaps. In this section, we review the calculation of VaR for a simple portfolio of bonds.

Sample bond portfolio

Table 17.6 details the bonds that are in our portfolio. For simplicity, we assume that all the bonds pay an annual coupon and have full years left to maturity. In order to calculate the VaR, we first need to value the bond portfolio itself. The bonds are valued by breaking them down into their constituent cash flows; the present value of each cash flow is then calculated, using the appropriate zero-coupon interest rate. Note from Figure 17.3 on page 852 that the term structure is inverted.

Table 17.7 on page 852 shows the present values for each of the cash flows. The total portfolio value is also shown.

	Bond 1	**Bond 2**	**Bond 3**
Nominal value	10,000,000	3,800,000	9,700,000
Coupon	5%	7.25%	6%
Maturity	5	7	2

Table 17.6 Sample three-bond portfolio

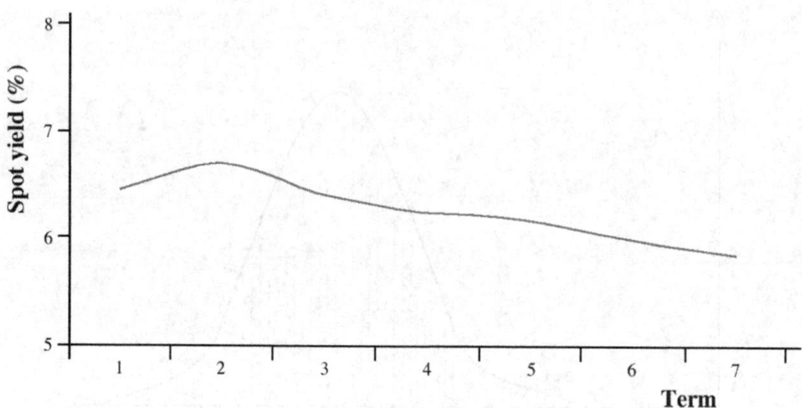

Figure 17.3 Term structure used for valuation

Period	Cash flows: Bond 1	Bond 2	Bond 3	Zero-coupon rates	Discount factor	Present values		
1	500,000	275,500	582,000	6.45	0.939408173	469,704	258,807	546,736
2	500,000	275,500	10,282,000	6.7	0.878357191	439,179	241,987	9,031,269
3	500,000	275,500		6.4	0.830185447	415,093	228,716	
4	500,000	275,500		6.25	0.784664935	392,332	216,175	
5	10,500,000	275,500		6.18	0.740945722	7,779,930	204,131	
6		275,500		5.98	0.705759136		194,437	
7		4,075,500		5.87	0.670794678		2,733,824	
					Totals	9,496,238	4,078,077	9,578,004
				Portfolio value		23,152,319		

Table 17.7 Bond portfolio valuation

We then use the volatility for each period rate to calculate the VaR. The volatility levels for our hypothetical currency are relatively low in this example. The VaR for each maturity period is then obtained by multiplying the total present value of the cash flows for that period by its volatility level. This is shown in Table 17.8. By adding together all the individual values, we obtain an undiversified VaR for the portfolio. The total VaR is £1.77 million, for a portfolio with a market value of £23.1 million.

Period	Cash flows	Present value	Volatility	VaR
1	1,357,500.00	1,275,246.59	0.0687	87,609.44
2	11,057,500.00	9,712,434.64	0.0695	675,014.21
3	775,500.00	643,808.81	0.07128	45,890.69
4	775,500.00	608,507.66	0.0705	42,899.79
5	10,775,500.00	7,984,060.63	0.08501	678,724.99
6	275,500.00	194,436.64	0.08345	16,225.74
7	4,075,500.00	2,733,823.71	0.08129	222,232.53
			Undiversified VaR	1,768,597.39

Table 17.8 Bond portfolio undiversified VaR

The figure just calculated is the undiversified VaR for the bond portfolio. To obtain the diversified VaR for the book, we require the correlation coefficient of each interest rate with the other interest rates (the correlation will be very close to unity, although the shorter-dated rates will be closer in line with each other than they will be with long-dated rates). We may then use the standard variance–covariance approach, using a matrix of the undiversified VaR values and a matrix with the correlation values. However, the diversification benefit of a portfolio of bonds will be small, mainly because their volatilities will be closely correlated.

Forward-rate agreements

The VaR calculation for a FRA follows the principles reviewed in the previous section. An FRA is a notional loan or deposit for a period starting at some point in the future; in effect, it is used to fix a borrowing or lending rate. The derivation of an FRA rate is based on the principle of what it would cost for a bank that traded one to hedge it; this is known as the "breakeven" rate. So a bank that has bought 3v6 FRA (referred to as a "threes-sixes FRA") has effectively borrowed funds for three months and placed the funds on deposit for six months. Therefore, an FRA is best viewed as a combination of an asset and a liability, and that is how one is valued. So a long position in a 3v6 FRA is valued as the present value of a three-month cash flow asset and the present value of a six-month cash flow liability, using the three-month and six-month deposit rates. The net present value is taken, of course, because one cash flow is an asset and the other a liability.

Consider a 3v6 FRA that has been dealt at 5.797%, the three-month forward–forward rate. The value of its constituent (notional) cash flows is shown in Table 17.9. The three-month and six-month rates are cash rates in the market, while the interest-rate volatilities have been obtained from RiskMetrics™. The details are summarised in Table 17.9.

Cash flow	Term (days)	Cash rate	Interest-rate volatilities	Present value	Undiversified VaR
10,000,000	91	5.38%	0.14%	9,867,765	13,815
–10,144,536	182	5.63%	0.21%	–9,867,765	20,722

Table 17.9 Undiversified VaR for a 3v6 FRA contract

The undiversified VaR is the sum of the individual VaR values, and is £34,537. It has little value in the case of an FRA, however, and would overstate the true VaR, because an FRA is made up of a notional asset and liability, so a fall in the value of one would see a rise in the value of the other. Unless a practitioner was expecting three-month rates to go in an opposite direction to six-month rates, there is an element of diversification benefit. There is a high correlation between the two rates, so the more logical approach is to calculate a diversified VaR measure.

For an instrument such as an FRA, the fact that the two rates used in calculating the FRA rate are closely positively correlated will mean that the diversification effect will be to reduce the VaR estimate, because the FRA is composed notionally of an asset and a liability. From the values in Table 17.9, therefore, the six-month VaR is actually a negative value (if the bank had sold the FRA, the three-month VaR would have the negative value). To calculate the diversified VaR, then, requires the correlation between the two interest rates, which may be obtained from the RiskMetrics™ dataset. This is observed to be 0.87. This value is entered into a 2x2 correlation matrix and used to calculate the diversified VaR in the normal way. The procedure is:

- transpose the weighting VaR matrix, to turn it into a 2x1 matrix;
- multiply this by the correlation matrix;
- multiply the result by the original 1x2 weighting matrix;
- this gives us the variance; the VaR is the square root of this value.

The result is a diversified VaR of £11,051.

Interest-rate swaps

To calculate a variance–covariance VaR for an interest-rate swap, we use the process described earlier for an FRA. There are more cash flows that go to make up the undiversified VaR, because a swap is essentially a strip of FRAs. In a plain vanilla interest-rate swap, one party pays on a fixed-rate basis on an annual or semi-annual basis, and receives floating-rate interest, while the other party pays floating-rate interest payments and receives fixed-rate interest. Interest payments are calculated on a notional sum, which does not change hands, and only interest payments are exchanged. In practice, it is the net difference between the two payments that is transferred.

The fixed rate on an interest-rate swap is the breakeven rate that equates the present value of the fixed-rate payments to the present value of the floating-rate payments. As the floating-rate payments are linked to a reference rate such as Libor, we do not know what they will be, but we use the forward rate applicable to each future floating payment date to calculate what it would be if we were to fix it today. The forward rate is calculated from zero-coupon rates today. A "long" position in a swap is to pay fixed and receive floating, and is conceptually the same as being short in a fixed-coupon bond and being long in a floating-rate bond. In effect, the long is "borrowing" money, so a rise in the fixed rate will result in a rise in the value of the swap. A "short" position is receiving fixed and paying floating, so a rise in interest rates results in a fall in the value of the swap. This is conceptually similar to a long position in a fixed-rate bond and a short position in a floating-rate bond.

Describing an interest-rate swap in conceptual terms of fixed- and floating-rate bonds gives some idea as to how it is treated for VaR purposes. The coupon on a floating-rate bond is reset periodically in line with the stated reference rate, usually Libor. Therefore, the duration of a floating-rate bond is very low, and conceptually the bond may be viewed as being the equivalent of a bank deposit, which receives interest payable at a variable rate. For market-risk purposes,[3] the risk exposure of a bank deposit is nil, because its present value is not affected by changes in market interest rates. Similarly, the risk exposure of a floating-rate bond is very low and to all intents and purposes its VaR may be regarded as zero. This leaves only the fixed-rate leg of a swap to measure for VaR purposes.

---

[3] We emphasise for *market*-risk purposes; the credit-risk exposure for a floating-rate bond position is a function of the credit quality of the issuer.

Pay date	Swap rate	Principal (£)	Coupon (£)	Coupon present value (£)	Volatility	Undiversified VaR
7-Jun-00	6.73%	10,000,000	337,421	327,564	0.05%	164
7-Dec-00	6.73%	10,000,000	337,421	315,452	0.05%	158
7-Jun-01	6.73%	10,000,000	335,578	303,251	0.10%	303
7-Dec-01	6.73%	10,000,000	337,421	294,898	0.11%	324
7-Jun-02	6.73%	10,000,000	335,578	283,143	0.20%	566
9-Dec-02	6.73%	10,000,000	341,109	277,783	0.35%	972
9-Jun-03	6.73%	10,000,000	335,578	264,360	0.33%	872
8-Dec-03	6.73%	10,000,000	335,578	256,043	0.45%	1,152
7-Jun-04	6.73%	10,000,000	335,578	248,155	0.57%	1,414
7-Dec-04	6.73%	10,000,000	337,421	242,161	1.90%	4,601
					Total	**10,528**

Table 17.10 Fixed-rate leg of five-year interest-rate swap and undiversified VaR

Table 17.10 shows the fixed-rate leg of a five-year interest-rate swap. To calculate the undiversified VaR, we use the volatility rate for each term interest rate; this may be obtained from RiskMetrics™. Note that the RiskMetrics™ dataset supports only liquid currencies; for example, data on volatility and correlation is not available for certain emerging-market economies. We show the VaR for each payment; the sum of all the payments constitutes the undiversified VaR. We then require the correlation matrix for the interest rates, and this is used to calculate the diversified VaR. The weighting matrix contains the individual term VaR values, which must be transposed before being multiplied by the correlation matrix.

Using the volatilities and correlations supplied by RiskMetrics™, the diversified VaR is shown to be £10,325. This is very close to the undiversified VaR of £10,528. This is not unexpected because the different interest rates are very closely correlated.

Using VaR to measure market-risk exposure for interest-rate products enables a risk manager to capture non-parallel shifts in the yield curve, which is an advantage over the traditional duration measure and interest-rate gap measure. Therefore, estimating a book's VaR measure is useful not only for the trader and risk manager, but also for senior management, who by using VaR will have a more accurate idea of the risk-market exposure of the bank. VaR methodology captures pivotal shifts in the yield curve by using the correlations between different maturity interest rates. This reflects the fact that short-term interest rates and long-term interest rates are not perfectly positively correlated.

Derivative products and VaR

The variance–covariance methodology for calculating VaR is considered adequate for trading books that contain mostly products that have a linear payoff profile. This covers money market interest-rate instruments; however, the price/yield relationship for bonds exhibits a curved relationship, which gives rise to the convexity property. A trading book with convex instruments will have an added convexity risk exposure, and while most VaR methodologies are able to capture convexity risks adequately, an adjustment to the basic calculation has to be made. Such an adjusted measure is known as the *delta–gamma VaR*. Option products, however, have a non-linear payoff profile, and it is more difficult to capture risks associated with option trading books using the variance–covariance approach. In this section we review the delta–gamma approach and its application to bonds and options.

Option gamma

The gamma measurement for an option is conceptually similar to convexity for a bond. Convexity is a measure of the error made in using modified duration; that is, the curvature of the price/yield relationship. Gamma is the second derivative of an option's delta, so in effect it measures the same thing as convexity. As with convexity, it is important for traders to be aware of the gamma exposure of their books, as at a high gamma level, even very small changes in the price of the underlying asset may lead to substantial mark-to-market losses. A trader who writes options, whether put or call options, is effectively short gamma.

The gamma effect on an option book cannot be captured accurately by most VaR models. This is because the relationship between gamma and the price of the underlying asset is non-linear. To approximate the VaR measure for an option book, a *delta–gamma* calculation is made, and although it is still not completely accurate, it is a better estimate than the conventional delta-normal approach. However, although intuitively delta–gamma is similar to the convexity adjustment for a bond portfolio, it is not as good an approximation as the convexity measure. This is because behaviour of an option is more unpredictable than that of a bond. A bond instrument may be broken down into a series of zero-coupon bonds, so that volatility and other data maybe adjusted for convexity with relative ease. This is not as easy for options, and becomes particularly acute as an option approaches maturity. For example, an at-the-money option will experience extreme movement in its gamma as it approaches maturity, in a way that is unpredictable. It is difficult to capture this effect in a VaR model. Nevertheless, the delta–gamma measure is recognised as a close approximation of option book risk, short of using simulation-type VaR models.

The gamma effect has an impact on the distribution of returns from an option book. This transforms the distribution from normal to one with slightly skewed tails, as illustrated by Figure 17.4.

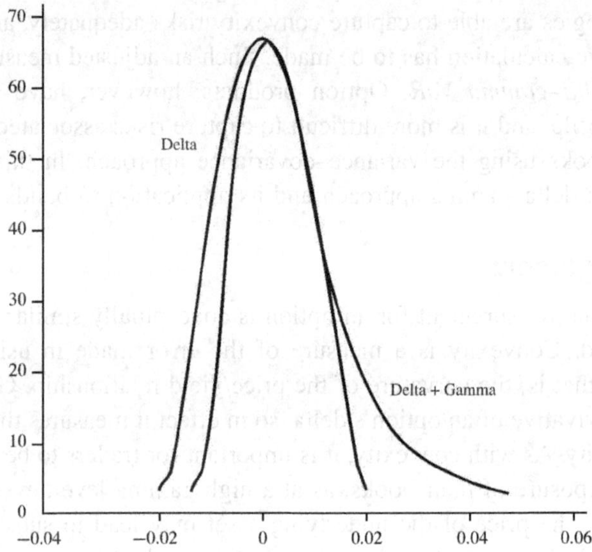

Figure 17.4 Delta + gamma effect

To illustrate the gamma adjustment, consider a position in a bond instrument and a put option on foreign exchange. The details are set out in Table 17.11. The interest-rate and FX volatility and correlation data may be obtained from RiskMetrics™. Using these, we calculate the undiversified VaR in the normal manner, multiplying the market value of the instrument by the volatility value to obtain VaR. For the option, we also multiply the value and the volatility by the delta (that is, 1,507,000 × 0.54 × 6.10%). The delta adjustment is required because the price of the option does not move "tick-for-tick" with the underlying asset, but by 0.54 for each unit change in the underlying asset. The undiversified VaR is 49,641.

Bond nominal:	2,000,000
Maturity (years):	2
Market value:	1,507,000
Volatility:	1.60%
Undiversified VaR:	24,112
Nominal value FX option:	1,507,000
Delta:	0.54
Gamma:	3.9
FX volatility:	6.10%
Undiversified VaR:	49,641
Correlation coefficient:	–0.31

Table 17.11 Hypothetical portfolio and undiversified VaR

To calculate the undiversified VaR we require the portfolio variance, which would normally be done in the conventional way using matrices; here there are only two assets so we may use the standard variance equation. The square root of this is the VaR, which is calculated as:

$$Var_{port} = \sqrt{24{,}112^2 + 49{,}641^2 + (2 \times -0.31 \times 24{,}112 \times 49{,}641)}$$

$$= 41{,}498.$$

Although the undiversified VaR is more realistic a measure, it will not take into account the gamma effect of the option. Previously we allowed for the delta of the option, which was used to modify the volatility level, which changed from 6.10% to 3.294%. The gamma adjustment is made by using Equation (36.5) in Choudhry (2001), which in this case gives a gamma adjustment of 0.7256%. The delta–gamma approximation for the volatility is therefore 2.568%. Multiplying this by the weighting (the option value) we have a new diversified VaR for the option of 38,700. If we use the same portfolio variance equation we obtain a delta–gamma adjusted diversified VaR of 27,488.

The delta–gamma adjustment is only an approximation of an option book's gamma risk exposure, and it is not as close as a convexity adjustment. This is due mainly to the unpredictable behaviour of gamma as an option approaches maturity, more so if it is at-the-money.

Stress testing

Risk-measurement models and their associated assumptions are not without limitation. It is important to understand what will happen should some of the model's underlying assumptions break down. Stress testing is a process whereby a series of scenario analyses or simulations are carried out to investigate the effect of extreme market conditions on the VaR estimates calculated by a model. It is also an analysis of the effect of violating any of the basic assumptions behind a risk model. If carried out efficiently, stress testing will provide clearer information on the potential exposures at risk due to significant market corrections, which is why the Basel Committee recommends that it be carried out.

Simulating stress

There is no standard way to undertake stress testing. It is a means of experimenting with the limits of a model. It is also a means to measure the residual risk which is not effectively captured by the formal risk model, thus complementing the VaR framework. If a bank uses a confidence interval of 99% when calculating its VaR, the losses on its trading portfolio due to market movements should not exceed the VaR number on more than one day in 100. For a 95% confidence level the corresponding frequency is one day in 20, or roughly one trading day each month. The question to ask is "What are the expected losses on those days?" Also, what can an institution do to protect itself against these losses? Assuming that returns are normally distributed provides a workable daily approximation for estimating risk, but when market moves are more extreme these assumptions no longer add value. The 1% of market moves that are not used for VaR calculations include events such as the October 1987 crash, the bond market collapse of February 1994 and the Mexican peso crisis at the end of 1994. In these cases, market moves were much larger than any VaR model could account for; in fact, the October 1987 crash was a 20-standard deviation move. Under these circumstances, correlations between markets also increase well above levels normally assumed in models.

An approach used by risk managers is to simulate extreme market moves over a range of different scenarios. One method is to use Monte Carlo simulation. This allows dealers to push the risk factors to greater limits. For example, a 99% confidence interval captures events up to 2.33 standard deviations from the mean asset-return level. A risk manager can calculate the effect on the trading portfolio of a 10-standard deviation move. Similarly, risk managers may want to change the correlation assumptions under which they normally work. For instance, if markets all move down together, something that happened in Asian markets from the end of 1997 and emerging markets generally from July 1998 after the Russian bond technical default, losses will be greater than if some markets are offset by other negatively correlated markets.

Only by pushing the bounds of the range of market moves that are covered in the stress-testing process can financial institutions have an improved chance of identifying where losses might occur and, therefore, a better chance of managing their risk effectively.

Stress testing in practice

For effective stress testing, a bank has to consider non-standard situations. The Basel policy group has recommended certain minimum standards in respect of specified market movements. The parameters chosen are considered large moves to overnight marks, and include:

- parallel yield-curve shifts of 100 basis points up and down;
- steepening and flattening of the yield curve (two-year to 10-year) by 25 basis points;
- increase and decrease in three-month yield volatilities by 20%;
- increase and decrease in equity index vales by 10%;
- increase and decrease in the swap spread by 20 basis points.

These scenarios represent a starting point for a framework for routine stress testing.

Banks agree that stress testing must be used to supplement VaR models. The main problem appears to be difficulty in designing appropriate tests. The main issues are:

- difficulty in "anticipating the unanticipated";
- adopting a systematic approach, with stress testing carried out by looking at past extremes and analysing the effect on the VaR number under these circumstances;
- selecting 10 scenarios based on past extreme events and generating portfolio VaRs based on reruns of these scenarios.

The latest practice is to adapt stress tests to suit the particular operations of a bank itself. On the basis that one of the main purposes of stress testing is to provide senior management with accurate information concerning the extent of a bank's potential risk exposure, more valuable data will be gained if the stress test is particularly relevant to the bank. For example, an institution such as Standard Chartered Bank, which has a relatively high level of exposure to exotic currencies, may design stress tests that take into account extreme movements in, say, regional Asian currencies. A mortgage book holding option positions only to hedge its cash book – say, one of the former UK building societies that subsequently converted to banks – may have no need for excessive stress testing on, perhaps, the effect of extreme moves in derivatives liquidity levels.

Issues in stress testing

It is to be expected that extreme market moves will not be captured in VaR measurements. The calculations will always assume that the probability of events such as the Mexican peso devaluation are extremely low when analysing historical or expected movements of the currency. Stress tests need to be designed to model for such occurrences. Back-testing a firm's qualitative and quantitative risk-management approach for actual extreme events often reveals the need to adjust reserves, increase the VaR factor, adopt additional limits and controls, and expand risk calculations. With back-testing, a firm will take, say, its daily VaR number, which we will assume is computed to 95% degree of confidence. The estimate will be compared to the actual trading losses suffered by the book over a 20-day period and, if there is a significant discrepancy, the firm will need to go back to its model and make adjustments to parameters. Frequent and regular back-testing of the VaR model's output with actual trading losses is an important part of stress testing. To conduct back-testing efficiently, a firm would need to be able to strip out its intra-day profit-and-loss figures, so it could compare the actual change in p&l to what was forecast by the VaR model.

The procedure for stress testing in banks usually involves:

- creating hypothetical extreme scenarios;
- computing corresponding hypothetical p&ls.

One method is to imagine *global* scenarios. If one hypothesis is that the euro appreciates sharply against the dollar, the scenario needs to consider any related areas, such as the effect, if any, on the Swiss franc and Norwegian krone rate, or the effect on the yen and on interest rates. Another method is to generate many *local* scenarios and so consider a few risk factors at a time. For example, given an FX option portfolio a bank might compute the hypothetical p&l for each currency pair under a variety of exchange rate and implied volatility scenarios. There is then the issue of amalgamating the results: one way would be to add the worst-case results for each of the sub-portfolios, but this ignores any portfolio effect and cross-hedging. This may result in an over-estimate that is of little use in practice.

Nevertheless, stress testing is one method to account for the effect of extreme events that occur more frequently than would be expected were asset returns to follow a true normal distribution. For example, five standard-deviation moves in a market in one day have been observed to occur twice every 10 years or so, which is considerably more frequent than given by a normal distribution. Testing for the effects of such a move gives a bank an idea of its exposure under these conditions.

VaR methodology for credit risk

Credit risk emerged as a significant risk-management issue during the 1990s. In increasingly competitive markets, banks and securities houses began taking on greater credit risk in this period. The growth in credit exposures and the rise of complex instruments have led to a need for more sophisticated risk-management techniques to measure credit risk.

Modelling credit risk

Credit-risk VaR methodologies take a portfolio approach to credit-risk analysis. This means that:

- credit risks to each obligor across the portfolio are restated on an equivalent basis and aggregated in order to be treated consistently, regardless of the underlying asset class;
- correlations of credit-quality moves across obligors are taken into account.

This allows portfolio effects – the benefits of diversification and risks of concentration – to be quantified.

The portfolio risk of an exposure is determined by four factors:

- size of the exposure;
- maturity of the exposure;
- probability of default of the obligor;
- systematic or concentration risk of the obligor.

Credit VaR, like market-risk VaR, considers (credit) risk in a mark-to-market framework. It arises from changes in value due to credit events; that is, changes in obligor credit quality including defaults, upgrades and downgrades.

Nevertheless, credit risk is different in nature from market risk. Typically, market-return distributions are assumed to be relatively symmetrical and approximated by normal distributions. In credit portfolios, value changes will be relatively small upon minor up/downgrades, but can be substantial upon default. This remote probability of large losses produces skewed distributions, with heavy downside tails that differ from the more normally distributed returns assumed for market VaR models. This is shown in Figure 17.5.

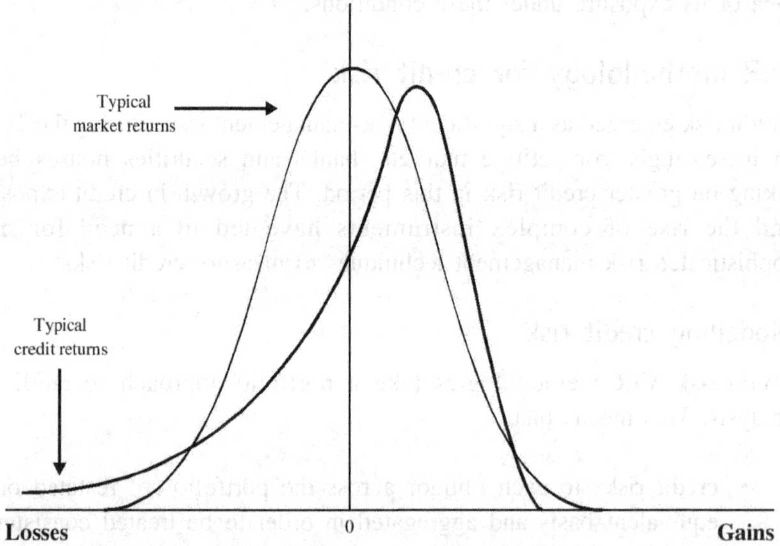

Figure 17.5 Comparison of distribution of market returns and credit returns

This difference in risk profiles does not prevent us from assessing risk on a comparable basis. Analytical market VaR models consider a time horizon and estimate VaR across a distribution of estimated market outcomes. Credit VaR models similarly look to a horizon and construct a distribution of value given different estimated credit outcomes.

When modelling credit risk the two main measures of risk are:

- distribution of loss: obtaining such distributions that may arise from the current portfolio. This considers the question of what the expected loss is for a given confidence level;
- identifying extreme or catastrophic outcomes; this is addressed through the use of scenario analysis and concentration limits.

To simplify modelling, no assumptions are made about the causes of default. Mathematical techniques used in the insurance industry are used to model the event of an obligor default.

Time horizon

The choice of time horizon will not be shorter than the timeframe over which risk-mitigating actions can be taken. There are two approaches:

- a constant time horizon such as one year;
- a hold-to-maturity time horizon.

The constant time horizon is similar to the CreditMetrics™ approach developed by JPMorgan and also to that used for market-risk measures. It is more suitable for trading desks. The hold-to-maturity approach is used by institutions such as portfolio managers.

Data inputs

Modelling credit risk requires certain data inputs. These include:

- credit exposures;
- obligor default rates;
- obligor default-rate volatilities;
- recovery rates.

These data requirements present some difficulties. There is a lack of comprehensive default and correlation data, and assumptions need to be made at certain times. The most accessible data are compiled by the credit ratings agencies such as Moody's.

We now consider two methodologies used for measuring credit VaR, the CreditMetrics™ model and the CreditRisk+ model.

CreditMetrics™

CreditMetrics™ is JPMorgan's portfolio model for analysing credit risk, and provides an estimate of VaR due to credit events caused by upgrades, downgrades and default.

Methodology

There are two main frameworks in use for quantifying credit risk. One approach considers only two states: default and no default. This model constructs a binomial tree of default versus no default outcomes until maturity. This approach is shown in Figure 17.6.

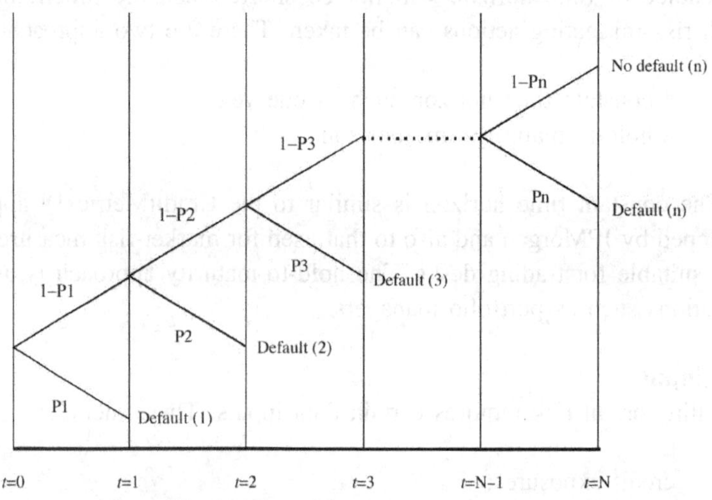

Figure 17.6 A binomial model of credit risk

The other approach, sometimes called the RAROC (Risk-Adjusted Return on Capital) approach holds that risk is the observed volatility of corporate-bond values within each credit-rating category, maturity band and industry grouping. The idea is to track a benchmark corporate bond (or index) that has observable pricing. The resulting estimate of volatility of value is then used to proxy the volatility of the exposure (or portfolio) under analysis.

The CreditMetrics™ methodology sits between these two approaches. The model estimates portfolio VaR at the risk horizon due to credit events that include upgrades and downgrades, rather than just defaults. Thus, it adopts a mark-to-market framework. As shown in Figure 17.7, bonds within each credit rating category have volatility of value due to day-to-day credit-spread fluctuations. The figure shows the loss distributions for bonds of varying credit quality. CreditMetrics™ assumes that all credit migrations have been realised, weighting each by a migration likelihood.

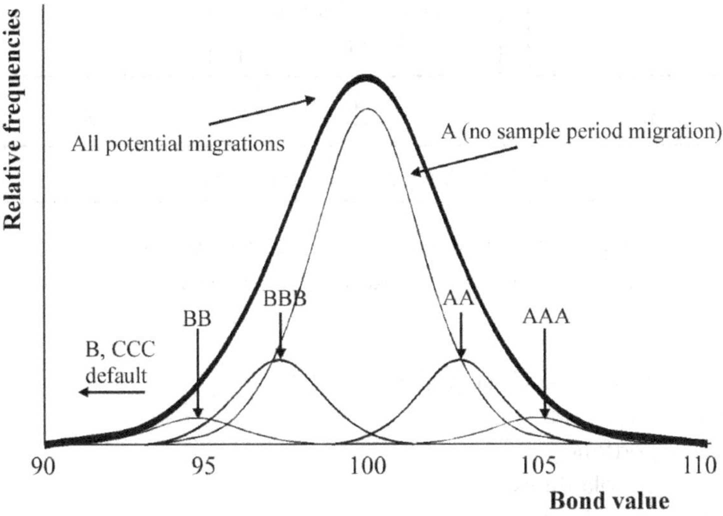

Figure 17.7 Distribution of credit returns by rating

Time horizon

CreditMetrics™ adopts a one-year risk horizon. The justification given in its technical document[4] is that this is because much academic and credit agency data are stated on an annual basis. This is a convenient convention similar to the use of annualised interest rates in the money markets. The risk horizon is adequate as long as it is not shorter than the time required to perform risk-mitigating actions. Users must therefore adopt their risk-management and risk-adjustment procedures with this in mind.

The steps involved in CreditMetrics™ measurement methodology are shown in Figure 17.8 on page 868.

[4] JPMorgan (1997), *Introduction to CreditMetrics™*, JPMorgan & Co.

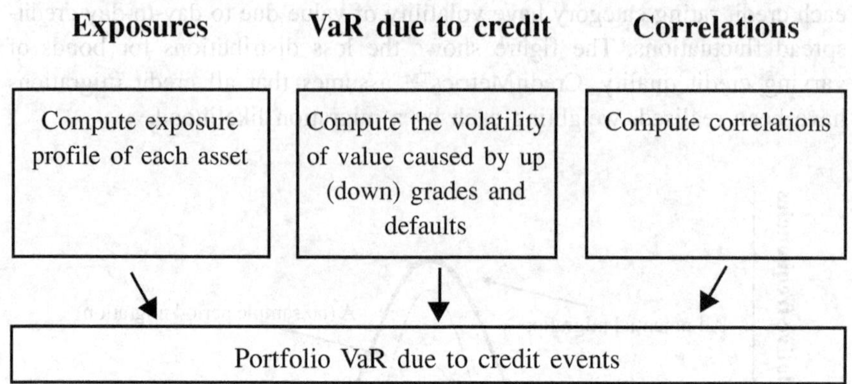

Figure 17.8 Analytics road map for CreditMetrics™
Source: JPMorgan 1997. Reproduced with permission.

The elements in each step are:
Exposures
- user portfolio
- market volatilities
- exposure distributions

VaR due to credit events
- credit rating
- credit spreads
- rating change likelihood
- recovery rate in default
- present-value bond revaluation
- standard deviation of value due to credit-quality changes

Correlations
- ratings series
- models (for example, correlations)
- joint credit-rating changes

Calculating the credit VaR

The CreditMetrics™ methodology assesses individual and portfolio VaR due to credit in three steps:

- Step 1: it establishes the exposure profile of each obligor in a portfolio.
- Step 2: it computes the volatility in value of each instrument caused by possible upgrade, downgrade and default.
- Step 3: taking into account correlations between each of these events, it combines the volatility of the individual instruments to give an aggregate portfolio risk.

Step 1 – Exposure Profiles

CreditMetrics™ incorporates the exposure of instruments such as bonds (fixed- or floating-rate), as well as other loan commitments and market-driven instruments such as swaps. The exposure is stated on an equivalent basis for all products. Products covered include:

- receivables (or trade credit);
- bonds and loans;
- loan commitments;
- letters of credit;
- market-driven instruments.

Step 2 – Volatility of each exposure from up(down)grades and defaults

The levels of likelihood are attributed to each possible credit event of upgrade, downgrade and default. The probability that an obligor will change over a given time horizon to another rating is calculated. Each change (migration) results in an estimated change in value (derived from credit-spread data and – in default – recovery rates). Each value outcome is weighted by its likelihood to create a distribution of value across each credit state, from which each asset's expected value and volatility (standard deviation) of value are calculated.

There are three steps to calculating the volatility of value in a credit exposure:

- the senior unsecured credit rating of the issuer determines the chance of either defaulting or migrating to any other possible credit-quality state in the risk horizon;
- revaluation at the risk horizon can be by either (i) the seniority of the exposure, which determines its recovery rate in case of default, or (ii) the forward zero-coupon curve (spot curve) for each credit-rating category that determines the revaluation upon up(down)grade;

- the probabilities from the two steps above are combined to calculate volatility of value due to credit-quality changes.

Step 3 – Correlations

Individual value distributions for each exposure are combined to give a portfolio result. To calculate the portfolio value from the volatility of individual asset values requires estimates of correlation in credit-quality changes. CreditMetrics™ itself allows for different approaches to estimating correlations, including a simple constant correlation. This is because of frequent difficulty in obtaining directly observed credit-quality correlations from historical data.

EXAMPLE 17.3 Credit-rating migration: Illustration of a probability-step calculation

An example of calculating the probability step is illustrated in Figure 17.9. The probabilities of all possible credit events on an instrument's value must be established first. Given this data, the volatility of value due to credit-quality changes for this one position can be calculated. The process is shown in Figure 17.9.

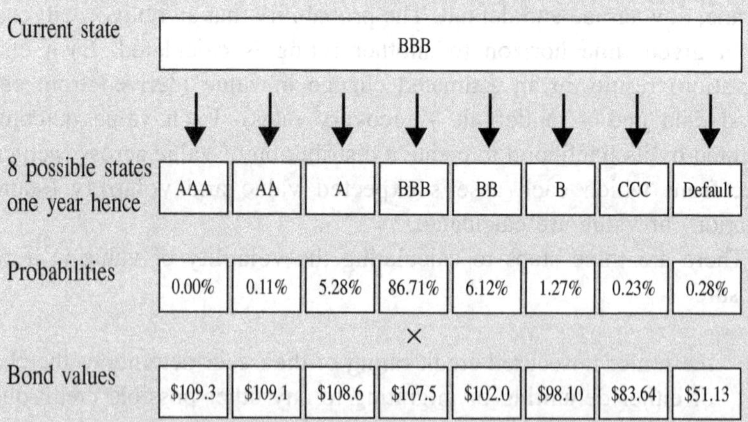

Figure 17.9 Constructing the distribution value for a BBB-rated bond
Source: JPMorgan 1997. Reproduced with permission.

CreditRisk+

CreditRisk+ was developed by Credit Suisse First Boston and can, in theory, handle all instruments that give rise to credit exposure including bonds, loans commitments, letters of credit and derivative instruments. We provide a brief description of its methodology here.

Modelling process

CreditRisk+ uses a two-stage modelling process as illustrated in Figure 17.10.

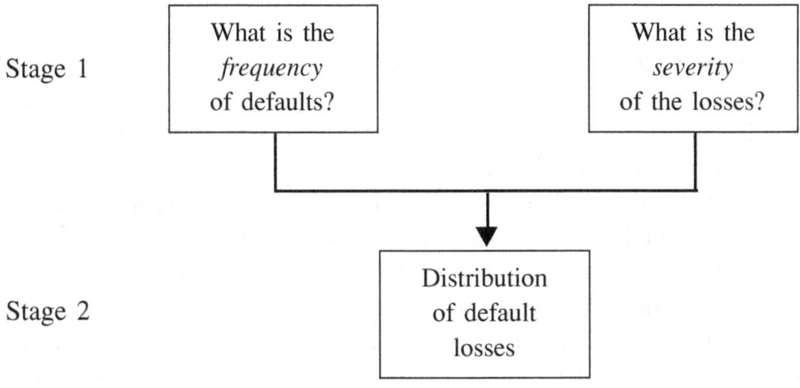

Figure 17.10 CreditRisk+ modelling process

CreditRisk+ considers the distribution of the number of default events in a time period such as one year, within a portfolio of obligors having a range of different annual probabilities of default.

The annual probability of default of each obligor can be determined by its credit rating and then mapping between default rates and credit ratings. A default rate can then be assigned to each obligor (an example of what this would look like is shown in Table 17.12 on page 872). Default rate volatilities can be observed from historic volatilities.

Credit rating	One-year default rate (%)
Aaa	0.00
Aa	0.03
A	0.01
Baa	0.12
Ba	1.36
B	7.27

Table 17.12 One-year default rates (%)

Correlation and background factors

Default correlation affects the variability of default losses from a portfolio of credit exposures. CreditRisk+ incorporates the effects of default correlations by using default-rate volatilities and sector analysis.

Unsurprisingly enough, it is not possible to forecast the exact occurrence of any one default or the total number of defaults. Often there are background factors that may cause the incidence of default events to be correlated, even though there is no causal link between them. For example, an economy in recession may give rise to an unusually large number of defaults in one particular month, which would increase the default rates above their average level. CreditRisk+ models the effect of background factors by using default-rate volatilities rather than by using default correlations as a direct input. Both distributions give rise to loss distributions with fat tails.

There are background factors that affect the level of default rates. For this reason, it is useful to capture the effect of concentration in particular countries or sectors. CreditRisk+ uses a sector analysis to allow for concentration. Exposures are broken down into an obligor-specific element independent of other exposures, as well as non-specific elements that are sensitive to particular factors such as countries or sectors.

Distribution of the number of default events

CreditRisk+ models the underlying default rates by specifying a default and a default-rate volatility. This aims to take account of the variation in default rates. The effect of using volatility is illustrated in Figure 17.11, which shows the distribution of default rates generated by the model when rate volatility is varied. The distribution becomes skewed to the right when volatility is increased.

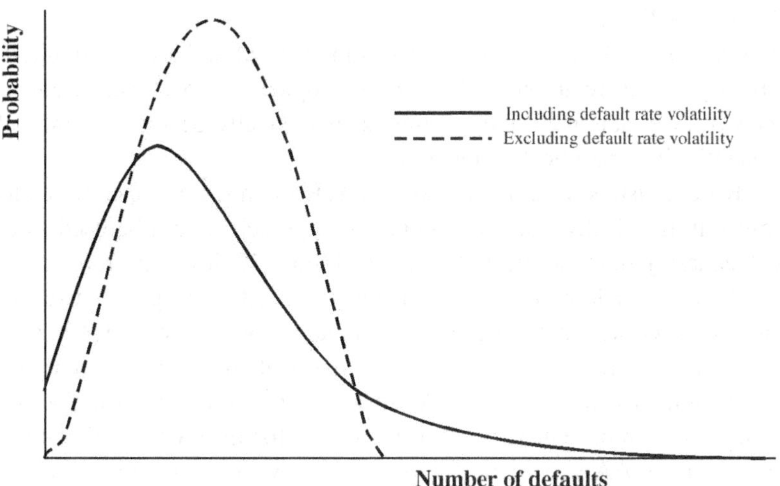

Figure 17.11 CreditRisk+ distribution of default events

This is an important result and demonstrates the increased risk represented by an extreme number of default events. By varying the volatility in this way, CreditRisk+ is attempting to model for real-world shock in much the same way that market-risk VaR models aim to allow for the fact that market returns do not follow exact normal distributions, as shown by the incidence of market crashes.

Applications of Credit VaR

One purpose of a risk-management system is to direct and prioritise actions. When considering risk-mitigating actions, there are various features of risk worth targeting, including obligors having:

- the largest absolute exposure;
- the largest percentage level of risk (volatility);
- the largest absolute amount of risk.

A CreditMetrics™-type methodology helps to identify these areas and allows the risk manager to prioritise risk-mitigating action.

Exposure limits

Within bank trading desks, credit-risk limits are often based on intuitive, but arbitrary, exposure amounts. This is not a logical approach because resulting decisions are not risk-driven. Limits should ideally be set with the help of a quantitative analytical framework.

Risk statistics used as the basis of VaR methodology can be applied to limit setting. Ideally, such a quantitative approach should be used as an aid to business judgment and not as a stand-alone limit-setting tool.

A credit-risk committee considering limit setting can use several statistics such as marginal risk and standard deviation or percentile levels. Figure 17.12 illustrates how marginal risk statistics can be used to make credit limits sensitive to the trade-off between risk and return. The lines in Figure 17.12 represent risk/return trade-offs for different credit ratings, all the way from AAA to BBB. The diagram shows how marginal contribution to portfolio risk increases geometrically with the exposure size of an individual obligor, noticeably so for weaker credits. To maintain a constant balance between risk and return, proportionately more return is required with each increment of exposure to an individual obligor.

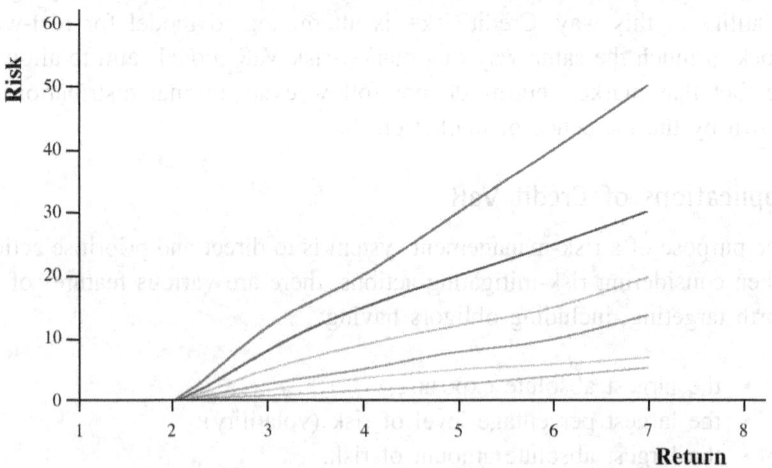

Figure 17.12 Size of total exposure to obligor – risk/return profile

Standard credit-limit setting

In order to equalise a firm's risk appetite between obligors as a means of diversifying its portfolio, a credit-limit system could aim to have a large number of exposures with equal expected losses. The expected loss for each obligor can be calculated as default rate × (exposure amount – expected recovery).

This means that individual credit limits should be set at levels that are inversely proportional to the default rate corresponding to the obligor rating.

Concentration limits

Concentration limits identified by CreditRisk+-type methodologies have the effect of trying to limit the loss from identified scenarios and are used for managing "tail" risk.

Integrating credit-risk and market-risk functions

It is logical for banks to integrate credit-risk and market-risk management for the following reasons:

- the need for comparability between returns on market and credit risk;
- the convergence of risk-measurement methodologies;
- the transactional interaction between credit and market risk;
- the emergence of hybrid-credit and market-risk product structures.

The objective is for returns on capital to be comparable for businesses involved in credit and market risk, to aid strategic allocation of capital.

EXAMPLE 17.4 Firm-wide integrated risk management

Assume that at the time of annual planning a bank's lending manager says his department can make £5 million over the year if they can increase their loan book by £300 million, while the trading manager says they can also make £5 million if the position limits are increased by £20 million.

Assuming that capital restrictions will allow only one option to be chosen, which should it be? The ideal choice is the one giving the higher return on capital, but the bank needs to work out how much capital is required for each alternative. This is a quantitative issue that calls for the application of similar statistical and analytical methods to measure both credit and market risk, if one is compare like with like.

With regard to the loan issue, the expected return is the mean of the distribution of possible returns. Since the revenue side of a loan – that is, the spread – is known with certainty, the area of concern is the expected credit-loss rate. This is the mean of the distribution of possible loss rates, estimated from historical data based on losses experienced with similar quality credits.

In the context of market-price risk, the common-denominator measure of risk is volatility (the statistical standard deviation of the distribution of possible future price movements). To apply this to credit risk, the decision-maker therefore needs to take into account the standard deviation of the distribution of possible future credit-loss rates, thereby comparing like with like.

We have shown that as VaR was being adopted as a market-risk measurement tool, the methodologies behind it were steadily applied to the next step along the risk continuum, that of credit risk. Market events, such as bank trading losses in emerging markets and the meltdown of the LTCM hedge fund in summer 1998, have illustrated the interplay between credit risk and market risk. The ability to measure market and credit risk in an integrated model would allow for a more complete picture of the underlying risk exposure. (We would add that adequate senior management understanding and awareness of a third type of risk – liquidity risk – would almost complete the risk-measurement picture).

Market-risk VaR measures can adopt one of the different methodologies available; in all of them there is a requirement for the estimation of the distribution of portfolio returns at the end of a holding period. This distribution can be assumed to be normal, which allows for analytical solutions to be developed. The distribution may also be estimated using historical returns. Finally, a Monte Carlo simulation can be used to create a distribution based on the assumption of certain stochastic processes for the underlying variables. The choice of methodology is often dependent on the characteristics of the underlying portfolio, plus other factors. For example, risk managers may wish to consider the degree of leptokurtosis in the underlying asset-returns distribution, the availability of historical data or the need to specify a more sophisticated stochastic process for the underlying assets. The general consensus is that Monte Carlo simulation, while the most IT-intensive methodology, is the most flexible in terms of specifying an integrated market and credit model.

The preceding paragraphs in this section have shown that credit-risk measurement models generally fall into two categories. The first category includes models that specify an underlying process for the default process.

In these models, firms are assumed to move from one credit rating to another with specified probabilities. Default is one of the potential states that a firm could move to. The CreditMetrics™ model is of this type. The second type of model requires the specification of a stochastic process for firm value. Here, default occurs when the value of the firm reaches an externally specified barrier. In both models, when the firm reaches default, the credit exposure is impacted by the recovery rate. Again market consensus would seem to indicate that the second type of methodology, the firm value model, most easily allows for development of an integrated model that is linked not only through correlation but also the impact of common stochastic variables.

Appendix

APPENDIX 17.1 Assumption of normality

The RiskMetrics™ assumption of conditional multivariate normality is open to criticism that financial series tend to produce "fat tails" (leptokurtosis). That is, in reality there is a greater occurrence of non-normal returns than would be expected for a purely normal distribution. This is shown in Figure A17.1. There is evidence that fat tails are a problem for calculations. The RiskMetrics™ technical document defends its assumptions by pointing out that if volatility changes over time there is a greater likelihood of incorrectly concluding that the data are not normal when in fact they are. In fact, conditional distribution models can generate data that possess fat tails.

Higher moments of the normal distribution

The skewness of a price data series is measured in terms of the third moment about the mean of the distribution. If the distribution is symmetric, the skewness is zero. The measure of skewness is given by:

$$\frac{\frac{1}{n}\sum_{i=1}^{n}(x_i - \bar{x})^3}{S^3}. \qquad \text{(A17.1)}$$

The kurtosis describes the extent of the peak of a distribution; that is, how peaked it is. It is measured by the fourth moment about the mean. A normal distribution has a kurtosis of three. The kurtosis is given by:

$$\frac{\frac{1}{n}\sum_{i=1}^{n}(x_i-\bar{x})^4}{S^4}. \tag{A17.2}$$

Distributions with a kurtosis higher than three are commonly observed in asset-market prices and are called leptokurtic. A leptokurtic distribution has higher peaks and fatter tails than the normal distribution. A distribution with a kurtosis lower than three is known as platykurtic.

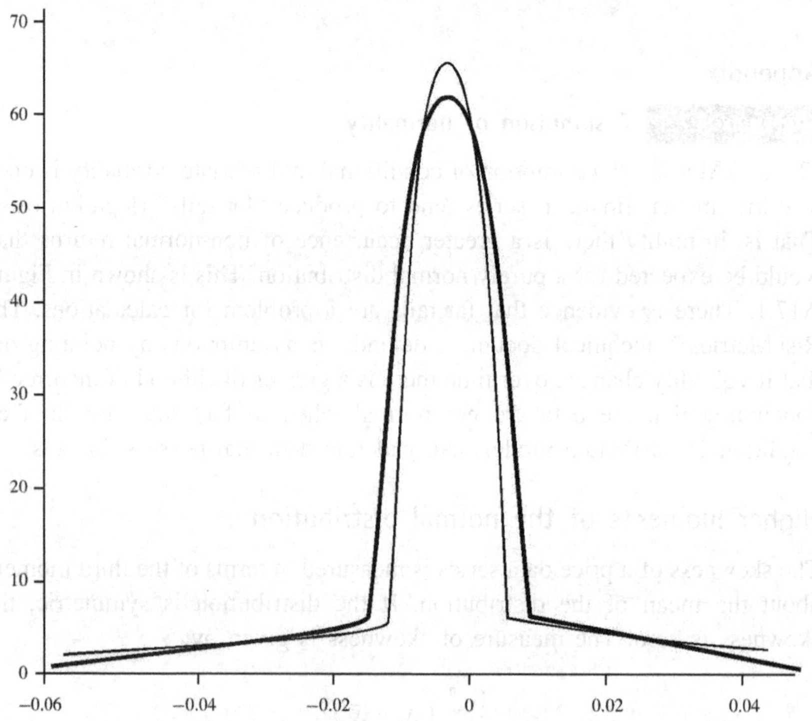

Figure A17.1 Leptokurtosis

References and bibliography

Alexander, C. 1996, *Risk Management and Analysis*, John Wiley & Sons, Chichester.

Beckstrom, R. and Campbell, A. (eds) 1995, *An Introduction to VAR*, CATS Software, London.

Beder, T. 1995, "VAR: Seductive but Dangerous", *Financial Analysts Journal*, 51, pp. 12–24.

Bollerslev, T. 1986, "Generalised Autoregressive Conditional Heteroscedasticity", *Journal of Econometrics*, 31, pp. 307–27.

Chew, L. 1996, *Managing Derivatives Risks*, John Wiley & Sons, New Jersey, NJ.

Choudhry, M. 2001, *The Bond and Money Markets*, Butterworth-Heinemann, Oxford.

Engle, R. 1982, "Autoregressive Conditional Heteroscedasticity with Estimates of the Variance of UK Inflation", *Econometrica*, 50, pp. 987–1008.

Holton, G. 2003, "Value-at-Risk: Theory and Practice", Academic Press, San Francisco.

Jorion, P. 1997, *Value-at-Risk*, Irwin, New York, NY.

Jorion, P. 2007, "Value-at-Risk: The Benchmark for Controlling Market Risk", 3rd Edition, McGraw-Hill, New York.

JPMorgan. 1995, *RiskMetrics Technical Manual*, JPMorgan Bank.

JPMorgan & Co. Inc. 1997, *CreditMetrics®* – Technical Document.

Schwartz, R. and Clifford, W. 1993, *Advanced Strategies in Financial Risk Management*, New York Institute of Finance, New York.

... HOW DARE YOU!
DO YOU KNOW WHO
I AM?
TIN
TIN
Olga Mears

YES, I DO.
DO YOU KNOW WHO
I AM?

NO? GOOD!
LET'S KEEP IT THAT WAY.
CLICK!
TIN
TIN

PART

IV

Funding and Balance Sheet Management using Securitisation and Structured Credit Vehicles

Securitisation is an important and well-established technique employed by banks for ALM purposes. By using securitisation, banks have been able to grow their businesses much more quickly than would otherwise have been possible. In Part IV we consider the subject as well as look in detail at the securities and structures that result from the technique, which include asset-backed commercial paper conduits (ABCP), asset-backed securities (ABS), mortgage-backed securities (MBS), collateralised debt obligations (CDO) and structured investment vehicles (SIV). There are separate chapters for these products, as well as a chapter on different types of structured funding vehicles, which are often used by non-bank financial institutions as well as banks.

For beginners we introduce here the main concepts, from the point of view of the bank ALM practitioner.

Introduction

Securitisation is when an institution's loans (assets) are removed from its balance sheet and packaged together as one large loan, and then "sold" on to an investor, or series of investors, who then receive the interest payments due on the assets until they are redeemed. The purchasers of the

securitised assets often have no recourse to the original borrowers; in fact, the original borrowers are not usually involved in the transaction or any of its processes.

Securitisation was introduced in the US market in 1970 and this market remains the largest for asset-backed bonds. The earliest examples of such bonds were in the US mortgage market, where residential mortgage loans made by a *thrift* (building society) were packaged together and sold on to investors who received the interest and principal payments made by the borrowers of the original loans. The process benefited the original lender in a number of ways. One key benefit was that removing assets from the balance sheet reduced risk exposure for the bank and enhanced its liquidity position.

The effects of these benefits are increased with the maturity of the original loans. For example, in the case of mortgage loans, the term to maturity can be up to 25 years, perhaps longer. The bulk of these loans are financed out of deposits that can be withdrawn on demand, or at relatively short notice. In addition it is often the case that as a result of securitisation, the packaged loans are funded at a lower rate than that charged by the original lending institution. This implies that the bundled loans can be sold off at a higher value than the level at which the lending institution valued them. Put another way, securitising loans adds value to the loan book and it is the original lender that receives this value. Another benefit is that as a result of securitisation, the total funding available to the lending institution may well increase due to its access to capital markets; in other words, the firm becomes less dependent on its traditional deposit base. And finally, by reducing the level of debt on the lending institution's balance sheet, securitisation can improve the firm's gearing ratio.

Securitisation was introduced in the UK market in 1985. A number of institutions were established for the purpose of securitising mortgages and other assets such as car loans and credit card debt. These included the National Home Loans Corporation, Mortgage Funding Corporation and First Mortgage Securities. Since then the technique has been widely used by banks as a standard tool in balance sheet capital management and asset–liability management.

Asset-backed securities

Asset-backed securities (ABS) are the bonds that are created by securitisation. The ABS notes are sold to a diverse group of investors, and are rated by the credit rating agencies on the basis of a number of factors. These factors include the quality of the collateral pool, as well as any other features, known as credit enhancements, that are part of the securitisation. However, the credit rating is independent of the credit quality of the originating institution.

Note tranching

The notes issued in a securitisation represent the liability side of the transaction, against the underlying assets. More than one class of securities is issued, a process known as *tranching*. Tranched notes exhibit different risk-reward features because they rank in order of seniority. Hence they have different credit ratings as well as different coupons. The most junior note is usually not rated, and is also known as the *equity piece*. This note is usually retained by the originator, and is the first to suffer loss if the asset collateral pool experiences loss. A good analogy for the equity note is the excess payable by the insured party for an insurance policy. By accepting this excess, the insured party reduces his premium; likewise, the equity holder is able to lower the rate payable by the issuer.

Underlying assets

Virtually any asset that carries a present and/or future cash flow can be securitised, and a very wide variety of assets can be securitised. Assets that have been securitised in the past include:

- residential and commercial mortgages;
- real-estate investment trusts;
- consumer debt including credit card receivables, auto-loans and student loans;
- bank assets such as corporate loans, non-performing loans, and small- and medium-sized enterprise (SME) loans;
- commercial lease receivables, such as office equipment leases and aircraft leases;
- trade receivables;

- cash flow revenue from public houses, nursing homes, airports, hospitals and museums;
- whole businesses, which is the securitisation of an entire company's operating assets and cash flow.

In theory any asset that generates cash is one that can be securitised. One-off transactions of esoteric assets that fall outside the above categories are not uncommon.

Administrator and servicer

ABS transactions require the services of third parties in a way that plain vanilla bonds do not. Servicing is the process of administering the underlying assets, including collecting interest and redemption payments, following up late payments and passing funds on to the SPV. The servicer in a deal is usually the originator.

Structural features

A wide variety of structural features are employed in the ABS market. These include:

- pass-through: this is when redemption payments on underlying assets are passed straight through to noteholders. Most asset classes are amortising; that is, the principal amount is paid down over a period of time. Also, assets such as mortgages are usually paid down some time ahead of their legal maturity date. When this happens the redemption payments are used to pay down note principal values, as and when they come in. It is not possible to know with certainty when these pay-downs will happen, as it depends on the speed of repayment of the assets. Models are used to estimate the time of this prepayment;
- over-collateralisation: this is the process of issuing notes to a lower nominal value than the value of the underlying assets. For example, a USD500 million pool of bank loans being securitised to back an issue of USD475 million of notes;

- subordination: in the ABS market, this is the level of debt that is junior to any particular tranche of note. For example, if an ABS transaction consists of A, B, C and D notes, the subordination of the B note is the amount of debt in the C and D notes. Subordinated debt is paid down only after the due amount on senior notes has been paid;
- revolving structures: this is an arrangement often used in the securitisation of short-dated asset classes, such as credit card debt or equipment receivables. In such structures, assets are purchased on a rolling basis, with note issue proceeds being used to purchase new assets, the cash flows from which are used to pay note interest. When the revolving period is over, the principal is used to pay down notes on an amortising basis;
- credit enhancement: this is the provision of various facilities designed to provide investor comfort with regard to the notes' credit risk. These include a bank liquidity line and overcollateralisation, as well as a cash reserve account and the excess interest spread generated by the difference in interest rates on assets and liabilities.

From the point of view of a bank originator, it is important to understand how securitisation can be used as part of balance sheet management and as a funding tool. It is also necessary to be aware of the features of a transaction that would make it attractive to investors, such that the deal can be placed at the rate of interest that makes it worthwhile to the bank.

Part IV of this book begins with an introduction to the key concepts of securitisation, and the motivations behind it. It then looks at specific deal types, including ABS, MBS, CDOs and SIVs. We also look at structured funding vehicles, which are transactions used to raise funding as well as diversify funding sources.

CHAPTER

18

Introduction to Securitisation[1]

Securitisation is an important ALM tool for banks. In this chapter we introduce the basic concepts of securitisation and look at the motivation behind their use, as well as their economic impact. We also illustrate the process with an hypothetical case study.

The concept of securitisation

Securitisation is a well-established practice in the global debt capital markets. It refers to the sale of assets, which generate cash flows from the institution that owns the assets, to another company that has been specifically set up for the purpose of acquiring them, and the issuing of notes by this second company. These notes are backed by the cash flows from the original assets. The technique was introduced initially as a means of funding for US mortgage banks. Subsequently, the technique was applied to other assets such as credit card payments and equipment leasing receivables. It has also been employed as part of ALM, as a means of managing balance sheet risk.

Securitisation allows institutions such as banks and corporations to convert assets that are not readily marketable – such as residential mortgages or car loans – into rated securities that are tradeable in the secondary market. The investors that buy these securities gain exposure to these types of

[1] This chapter was co-authored with Anuk Teasdale.

original assets that they would not otherwise have access to. The technique is well established and was first introduced by mortgage banks in the United States during the 1970s. The synthetic securitisation market was established much more recently, dating from 1997. The key difference between cash and synthetic securitisation is that in the former the assets in question are actually sold to a separate legal company, known as a special purpose vehicle (SPV).[2] This does not occur in a synthetic transaction, as we shall see.

Sundaresan (1997, p. 359) defines securitisation as:

> ... a framework in which some illiquid assets of a corporation or a financial institution are transformed into a package of securities backed by these assets, through careful packaging, credit enhancements, liquidity enhancements and structuring.

The process of securitisation creates a*sset-backed bonds*. These are debt instruments that have been created from a package of loan assets on which interest is payable, usually on a floating basis. The asset-backed market is a large, diverse market containing a wide range of instruments. Techniques employed by investment banks today enable an entity to create a bond structure from any type of cash flow. Assets that have been securitised include loans such as residential mortgages, car loans and credit card loans. The loans form assets on a bank or finance house balance sheet, which are packaged together and used as backing for an issue of bonds. The interest payments on the original loans form the cash flows used to service the new bond issue. Traditionally, mortgage-backed bonds are grouped in their own right as mortgage-backed securities (MBS), while all other securitisation issues are known as asset-backed bonds or ABS.

Figure 18.1 shows the growth in securitisation markets during the 1990s.

---

[2] An SPV is also referred to as a special purpose entity (SPE) or a special purpose company (SPC). See Example 18.1 on page 890 for more information on SPVs.

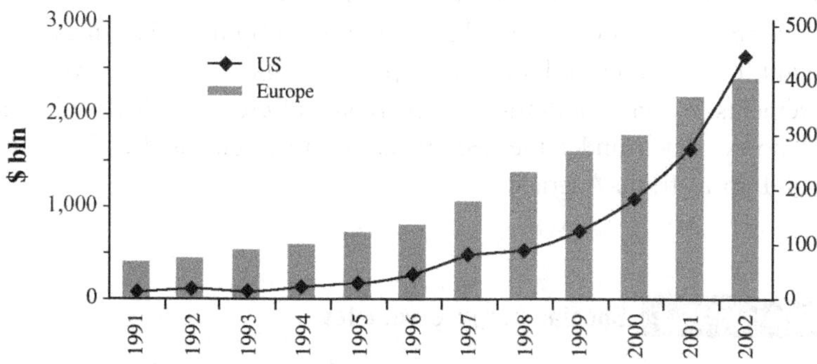

Figure 18.1 Asset-backed securities, notional amounts outstanding
Sources: BBA, ISMA, Federal Reserve.

Market participants

The securitisation process involves a number of participants. In the first instance there is the originator, the firm whose assets are being securitised. The most common process involves an issuer acquiring the assets from the originator. The issuer is usually a company that has been specially set up for the purpose of the securitisation and is the SPV, and is usually domiciled offshore. The creation of an SPV ensures that the underlying asset pool is held separate from the other assets of the originator. This is done so that in the event that the originator is declared bankrupt or insolvent, the impact on the original assets is minimised.

This last is often the responsibility of a trustee. The issuer trustee is responsible for looking after the interests of bondholders. Its roles include:

- representing the interests of investors (noteholders);
- monitoring the transaction and issuer to see if any violation of the deal covenants has occurred;
- enforcing the rights of the noteholders in the event of bankruptcy.

The security trustee is responsible for undertaking the following duties:

- holding the security interest in the underlying collateral pool;
- liaising with the manager of the underlying collateral;
- acting under the direction of the note trustee in the event of default.

By holding the assets within an SPV framework, defined in formal legal terms, the financial status and credit rating of the originator becomes almost irrelevant to the bondholders. The process may also involve credit enhancements, in which a third-party guarantee of credit quality is obtained, so that notes issued under the securitisation are often rated at investment grade and up to triple-A grade.

EXAMPLE 18.1 Special purpose vehicles

The key to undertaking securitisation is the special purpose vehicle or SPV. They are also known as special purpose entities (SPE) or special purpose companies (SPC). They are distinct legal entities that act as the "company" through which a securitisation is undertaken. They act as a form of repackaging vehicle, used to transform, convert or create risk structures that can be accessed by a wider range of investors. Essentially they are a legal entity to which assets such as mortgages, credit card debt or synthetic assets such as credit derivatives are transferred, and from which the original credit risk/reward profile is transformed and made available to investors. An originator will use SPVs to increase liquidity and to make liquid risks that cannot otherwise be traded in any secondary market.

An SPV is a legal trust or company that is not, for legal purposes, linked in any way to the originator of the securitisation. As such it is *bankruptcy-remote* from the sponsor. If the sponsor suffers financial difficulty or is declared bankrupt, this will have no impact on the SPV, and hence no impact on the liabilities of the SPV with respect to the notes it has issued in the market. Investors have credit risk exposure only to the underlying assets of the SPV.[3]

To secure favourable tax treatment, SPVs are frequently incorporated in offshore business centres such as Jersey or the Cayman Islands, or in jurisdictions that have set up SPV-friendly business legislation such as Ireland or The Netherlands. The choice of location for an SPV is dependant on a number of factors as well

[3] In some securitisations, the currency or interest-payment basis of the underlying assets differs from that of the overlying notes, and so the SPV will enter into currency and/or interest-rate swaps with a (bank) counterparty. The SPV would then have counterparty risk exposure.

as taxation concerns, such as operating costs, legal requirements and investor considerations.[4] The key issue is taxation however; the sponsor will want all cash flows both received and paid out by the SPV to attract low or no tax. This includes withholding tax on coupons paid on notes issued by the SPV. In other words, the SPV must be set up as a tax-neutral entity.

SPVs are used in a wide variety of applications and are an important element of the market in structured credit products. An established application is in conjunction with an asset swap, when an SPV is used to securitise the asset swap so that it becomes available to investors who cannot otherwise access it. Essentially, the SPV will purchase the asset swap and then issue notes to the investor, who gains an exposure to the original asset swap albeit indirectly. This is illustrated in Figure 18.2.

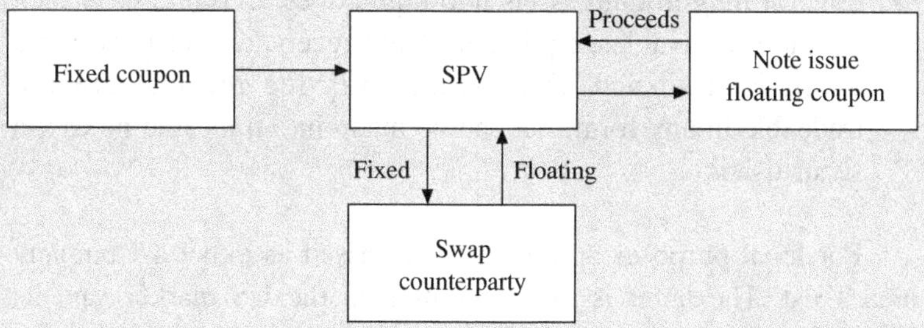

Figure 18.2 Asset swap package securitised and economic effect sold on by SPV

The most common purpose for which an SPV is set up is a cash flow securitisation, in which the sponsoring company sells assets off its balance sheet to the SPV, which funds the purchase of these assets by issuing notes. The revenues received by the assets are used to pay the liability of the issued overlying notes. Of course, the process itself has transformed previously untradeable assets such as residential mortgages into tradeable ones, and freed up the balance sheet of the originator.

SPVs are also used for the following applications:

[4] For instance, investors in some European Union countries will only consider notes issued by an SPV based in the EU, so that would exclude many offshore centres.

- converting the currency of underlying assets into another currency more acceptable to investors, by means of a currency swap;
- issuing credit-linked notes. Unlike CLNs issued by originators direct, CLNs issue by SPVs do not have any credit-linkage to the sponsoring entity. The note is linked instead to assets that have been sold to the SPV, and its performance is dependent on the performance of these assets. Another type of credit-linked SPV is when investors select the assets that (effectively) collateralise the CLN and are held by the SPV. The SPV then sells credit protection to a swap counterparty, and on occurrence of a credit event the underlying securities are sold and used to pay the SPV liabilities. Yet another type of SPV-issued CLN references a third-party bond or bonds that are not used by the SPV, but to which its returns are linked;
- transforming illiquid assets into liquid ones. Certain assets such as trade receivables, equipment lease receivables or even more exotic assets such as museum entry-fee receipts are not tradeable in any form, but can be made into tradeable notes via securitisation.

For legal purposes an SPV is categorised as either a Company or a Trust. The latter is more common in the US market, and its interests are represented by a Trustee, which is usually the Agency services department of a bank such as the Bank of New York or Citibank, or a specialist Trust company such as Wilmington Trust. In the euromarkets, SPVs are often incorporated as companies instead of Trusts.

After the Enron episode, when SPVs were seen to be used to assist fraudulent activity, accounting rules were changed to the extent that banking groups must now consolidate all legal entities into one set of accounts. Under the US accounting rule, Fin 46 R, banks that report their result under US GAAP are required to consolidate SPVs, including ABCP and other securitisation SPVs. However, it is possible to avoid the consolidation requirement if the originator can show that the first-loss piece in a transaction has been sold or otherwise transferred to a genuine third-party. This is an incentive for banks to not retain the equity tranche in a securitisation; there are also advantages to so doing under the Basel II regime (see Chapter 27).

The SPV-consolidation issue is also relevant in Europe, where it is required under International Accounting Standards (ISA) rules. Again, in some cases consolidation of an SPV into the group accounts may be avoidable if the first-loss piece in the deal is held by a third party.

Reasons for undertaking securitisation

The driving force behind securitisation has been the need for banks to realise value from the assets on their balance sheet. Typically, these assets are residential mortgages, corporate loans, and retail loans such as credit card debt. Let us consider the factors that might lead a financial institution to securitise part of its balance sheet. These might be the following:

- if revenues received from assets remain roughly unchanged but the size of assets has decreased, there will be an increase in the return on equity ratio;
- where the level of capital required to support the balance sheet will be reduced, which again can lead to cost savings or allow the institution to allocate the capital to other, perhaps more profitable, business;
- to obtain cheaper funding: frequently the interest payable on asset-backed securities is considerably below the level receivable on the underlying loans. This creates a cash surplus for the originating entity.

In other words, the main reasons that a bank securitises part of its balance sheet is for one or all of the following reasons, all of which form part of bank ALM to one degree or another:

- funding the assets it owns;
- balance sheet capital management;
- risk management and credit-risk transfer.

We shall now consider each of these in turn.

Funding

Banks can use securitisation to: (i) support rapid asset growth; (ii) diversify their funding mix, and reduce the cost of funding, and (iii) reduce maturity mismatches.

The market for asset-backed securities is large, with an estimated size of USD1,000 billion invested in ABS issues worldwide annually, of which USD150 billion is in the European market alone.[5] Access to this source of funding enables a bank to grow its loan books at a faster pace than if they were reliant on traditional funding sources alone. For example, in the United Kingdom a former building society turned bank, Northern Rock plc, has taken advantage of securitisation to back its growing share of the UK residential mortgage market. Securitising assets also allows a bank to diversify its funding mix. Banks generally do not wish to be reliant on a single or just a few sources of funding, as this can be high risk in times of market difficulty. Banks aim to optimise their funding between a mix of retail, interbank and wholesale sources. Securitisation has a key role to play in this mix. It also enables a bank to reduce its funding costs. This is because the securitisation process de-links the credit rating of the originating institution from the credit rating of the issued notes. Typically, most of the notes issued by SPVs will be higher rated than the bonds issued directly by the originating bank itself. While the liquidity of the secondary market in ABS is frequently lower than that of the corporate bond market, and this adds to the yield payable by an ABS, it is frequently the case that the cost to the originating institution of issuing debt is still lower in the ABS market because of the latter's higher rating. Finally, there is the issue of maturity mismatches. The business of bank ALM is inherently one of maturity mismatch, since a bank often funds long-term assets such as residential mortgages, with short-term asset liabilities such as bank account deposits or interbank funding. This can be reduced via securitisation, as the originating bank receives funding from the sale of the assets, and the economic maturity of the issued notes frequently matches that of the assets.

Balance sheet capital management

Banks use securitisation to improve balance sheet capital management. This provides: (i) regulatory capital relief; (ii) economic capital relief; and (iii) diversified sources of capital.

---

[5] *Source*: CSFB, *Credit Risk Transfer*, 2 May 2003.

As stipulated in the Bank for International Settlements (BIS) capital rules,[6] also known as the Basel rules, banks must maintain a minimum capital level for their assets, in relation to the risk of these assets. Under Basel I, for every $100 of risk-weighted assets, a bank must hold at least $8 of capital; however, the designation of each asset's risk-weighting is restrictive. For example, with the exception of mortgages, customer loans are 100% risk-weighted regardless of the underlying rating of the borrower or the quality of the security held. The anomalies that this raises, which need not concern us here, are being addressed by the Basel II rules that become effective from 2007 or 2008 (depending on jurisdiction). However, the Basel I rules, which have been in place since 1988 (and effective from 1992), have been a driving force behind securitisation. As an SPV is not a bank, it is not subject to Basel rules and it therefore only needs such capital that is economically required by the nature of the assets they contain. This is not a set amount, but is significantly below the 8% level required by banks in all cases. Although an originating bank does not obtain 100% regulatory capital relief when it sells assets off its balance sheet to an SPV, because it will have retained a "first-loss" piece out of the issued notes, its regulatory capital charge will be significantly reduced after the securitisation.[7]

To the extent that securitisation provides regulatory capital relief, it can be thought of as an alternative to capital raising, compared with the traditional sources of Tier 1 (equity), preferred shares, and perpetual loan notes with step-up coupon features. By reducing the amount of capital that has to be used to support the asset pool, a bank can also improve its return-on-equity (ROE) value. This is received favourably by shareholders.

Risk management

Once assets have been securitised, the credit risk exposure on these assets for the originating bank is reduced considerably and, if the bank does not retain a first-loss capital piece (the most junior of the issued notes), it is removed entirely. This is because assets have been sold to the SPV. Securitisation can also be used to remove non-performing assets from banks' balance sheets. This has the dual advantage of removing credit risk and removing a potentially negative sentiment from the balance sheet, as well as freeing up regulatory capital. Further, there is a potential upside from securitising such assets, if any of them start performing again, or there is a

[6] For further information on this see Chapter 26.

[7] We discuss first-loss later on.

recovery value obtained from defaulted assets, the originator will receive any surplus profit made by the SPV.

Benefits of securitisation to investors

Investor interest in the ABS market has been considerable from the market's inception. This is because investors perceive asset-backed securities as possessing a number of benefits. Investors can:

- diversify sectors of interest;
- access different (and sometimes superior) risk-reward profiles;
- access sectors that are otherwise not open to them.

A key benefit of securitisation notes is the ability to tailor risk-return profiles. For example, if there is a lack of assets of any specific credit rating, these can be created via securitisation. Securitised notes frequently offer better risk-reward performance than corporate bonds of the same rating and maturity. While this might seem peculiar (why should one AA-rated bond perform better in terms of credit performance than another just because it is asset-backed?), this often occurs because the originator holds the first-loss piece in the structure.

A holding in an ABS also diversifies the risk exposure. For example, rather than invest \$100 million in a AA-rated corporate bond and be exposed to "event risk" associated with the issuer, investors can gain exposure to, say, 100 pooled assets with a collective AA rating. These pooled assets will clearly have lower concentration risk.

Investors also benefit from the superior ratings migration of structured finance securities over vanilla Eurobonds. This is shown in Figure 18.3, which is Moody's annual ratings transition matrix for June 2006.

Structured Finance securities

	Aaa	Aa	A	Baa	Ba	B	Caa or below
Aaa	99.82%	0.15%	0.03%	0.00%	0.00%	0.00%	0.00%
Aa	6.07%	93.31%	0.48%	0.07%	0.05%	0.02%	0.00%
A	1.60%	4.75%	92.56%	0.88%	0.16%	0.03%	0.02%
Baa	0.20%	0.71%	3.69%	93.79%	0.98%	0.54%	0.09%
Ba	0.09%	0.04%	0.35%	3.44%	93.44%	1.76%	0.88%
B	0.18%	0.28%	0.09%	0.46%	3.04%	90.41%	5.54%
Caa or below	0.00%	0.00%	0.00%	0.00%	0.10%	0.41%	99.49%

Corporate bonds

	Aaa	Aa	A	Baa	Ba	B	Caa or below
Aaa	97.92%	1.04%	1.04%	0.00%	0.00%	0.00%	0.00%
Aa	0.12%	98.00%	1.88%	0.00%	0.00%	0.00%	0.00%
A	0.14%	2.67%	92.69%	4.15%	0.35%	0.00%	0.00%
Baa	0.00%	0.34%	5.19%	89.10%	4.00%	1.02%	0.34%
Ba	0.00%	0.18%	0.18%	7.49%	84.49%	6.95%	0.71%
B	0.00%	0.00%	0.26%	0.00%	11.67%	82.50%	5.57%
Caa or below	0.00%	0.00%	0.00%	0.36%	0.36%	27.65%	71.63%

Figure 18.3 Moody's annual ratings transition matrix, June 2006
Source: Moody's. Reproduced with permission.

EXAMPLE 18.2 (i) Summary of motivations for undertaking securitisation

A summary of reasons why banks undertake securitisation is given below; many transactions fulfil a number of these objectives simultaneously:

- reducing and releasing regulatory capital;
- increasing RoE and RoA;
- increasing mortgage lending capacity, and growing asset books quicker than would be possible through the normal course of business;
- improving the bank's cost-to-income ratio;
- diversifying funding sources;
- increasing market share;
- preserving customer relationships with obligor clients whose assets are securitised;
- with regard to non-performing loan (NPL) assets:
  - ➤ transferring the risk associated with NPL assets
  - ➤ freeing up capital for employment elsewhere;
- providing positive research material for equity analysts.

EXAMPLE 18.2 (ii) Parties to the deal

Rating agencies
Rating agencies undertake due diligence on the transaction and assign the rating to the issued liabilities.

Lawyers
The originator, arranger and Trustee will assign external counsel to draft and review the legal documents that describe the deal.

Servicer/Administrator
The servicer administers the underlying assets in the portfolio. This includes monitoring of loans/bonds, collection of interest, enforcing late payments and producing statements. This role is often retained by the administrator, although third-party servicing firms also exist.

The quality and reputation of the servicer is considered by the rating agencies when they assign the transaction rating.

Monoline insurer

A specialist class of investor, known as a monoline insurer, is available to provide a "wrap" or guarantee of the ABS notes, in return for a fee. This acts as a credit enhancement to the transaction, particularly if a AAA rating for the senior note is dependent on availability of a monoline insurance wrap.

Bank counterparty services

A transaction may require one, more or all of the following in its structure:

- interest-rate swap and/or FX swap, to hedge interest-rate and FX risk where there is a mismatch between the assets and liabilities of the vehicle;
- committed liquidity line, to be drawn on to cover principal and interest payments in the event that the SPV cannot make them;
- GIC, to act as a reserve in which the proceeds of note issuance are invested.

These services are provided by a bank or banks, which act as counterparty to the SPV.

Depositary

The depositary for a Eurobond issue is responsible for the safekeeping of securities. The common depositary is responsible for:

- representing Euroclear and Clearstream, and facilitating delivery-versus-payment of the primary market issue by collecting funds from the investors, taking possession of the temporary global note (which allows securities to be released to investors), and making a single payment of funds to the issuer;
- holding the temporary global note in safe custody, until it is exchanged for definitive notes or a permanent global note.

Trustee
An issuer may appoint a trustee to represent the interests of investors. In the event of default, the trustee is required to discharge its duties on behalf of bondholders. A trustee has a variety of powers and discretion, which are stated formally in the issue trust deed, and these include its duties in relation to the monitoring of covenants, and duties to bondholders.

Custodian
A custodian provides safekeeping services for securities belonging to a client. The client may be an institutional investor such as a pension fund, that requires a portfolio of securities in many locations to be kept in secure custody on their behalf. As well as holding securities, the custodian usually manages corporate actions such as dividend payments.

EXAMPLE 18.2 (iii) ABS terminology

Master Trust
A legal structure that allows for repeat issuances of notes from the same vehicle, usually where the underlying asset pool that is being securitised is a revolving pool. Common for credit card ABS and residential MBS transactions.

Static pool
A pool of assets that does not change; that is, the assets in the pool at deal inception remain there to the end of the deal's life. There is no removal or addition of assets.

Soft bullet
A bond that has an expected redemption date, but this date is not its formal legal maturity. If the bond does not redeem on this date, it is not an event of default.

Pass-through
Where the repayments of underlying assets are used to redeem overlying bonds as and when they occurr. This creates uncertainty when determining weighted-average life (WAL) of the notes.

Sequential pay
A term referring to the process whereby senior bonds in the liability structure are redeemed fully, before amortisation of the junior note classes can begin.

Pro-rata
Senior and junior bonds are redeemed at the same time pro-rata. However, triggers are in place that kick in to revert to a sequential pay structure should the collateral pool performance deteriorate, such that it cannot support the liabilities in full.

The process of securitisation

We now look at the process of securitisation, the nature of the SPV structure and issues such as credit enhancements and the cash flow "waterfall".

The securitisation process involves a number of participants. In the first instance there is the *originator*, the firm whose assets are being securitised. The most common process involves an *issuer* acquiring the assets from the originator. The issuer is usually a company that has been specially set up for the purpose of the securitisation, which is the SPV and is usually domiciled offshore. The creation of an SPV ensures that the underlying asset pool is held separate from the other assets of the originator. This is done so that in the event that the originator is declared bankrupt or insolvent, the assets that have been transferred to the SPV will not be affected. This is known as being bankruptcy-remote. Conversely, if the underlying assets begin to deteriorate in quality and are subject to a ratings downgrade, investors have no recourse to the originator.

By holding the assets within an SPV framework, defined in formal legal terms, the financial status and credit rating of the originator becomes almost irrelevant to the bondholders. The process of securitisation often involves *credit enhancements*, in which a third-party guarantee of credit quality is obtained, so that notes issued under the securitisation are often rated at investment grade and up to AAA-grade.

The process of structuring a securitisation deal ensures that the liability side of the SPV – the issued notes – carries a lower cost than the asset side of the SPV. This enables the originator to secure lower cost funding that it would not otherwise be able to obtain in the unsecured market. This is a tremendous benefit for institutions with lower credit ratings.

Figure 18.4 illustrates the process of securitisation in simple fashion.

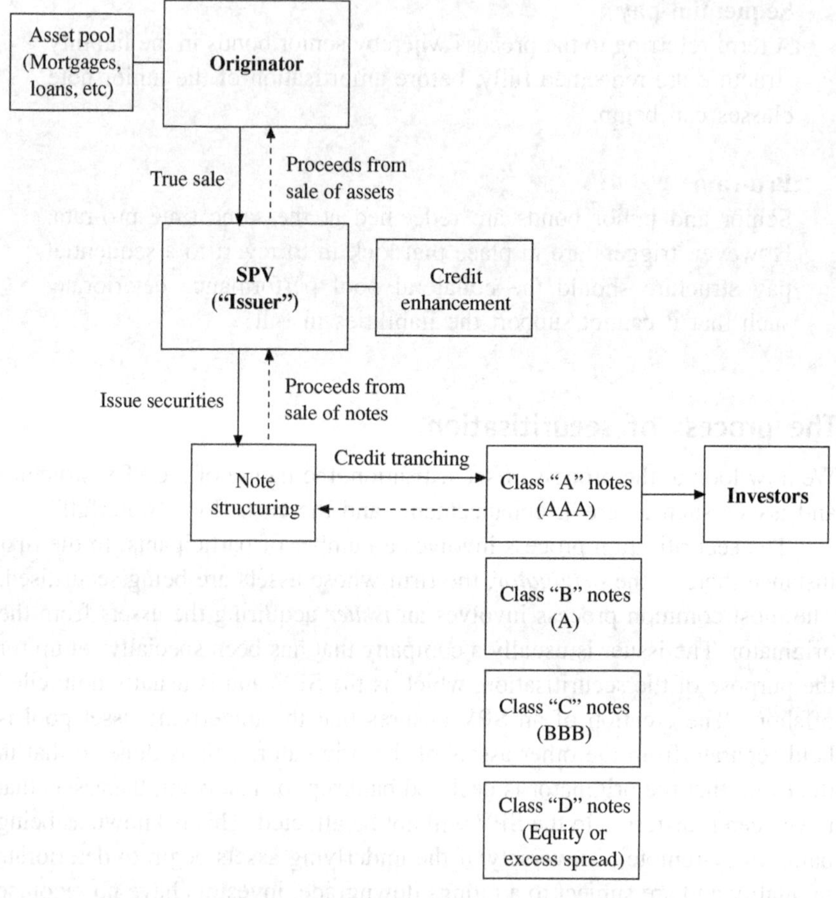

Figure 18.4 The securitisation process

Mechanics of securitisation

Securitisation involves a "true sale" of the underlying assets from the balance sheet of the originator. This is why a separate legal entity, the SPV, is created to act as the issuer of the notes. The assets being securitised are sold on to the balance sheet of the SPV. The process involves:

- undertaking "due diligence" on the quality and future prospects of the assets;
- setting up the SPV and then effecting the transfer of assets to it;

- underwriting of loans for credit quality and servicing;
- determining the structure of the notes, including how many tranches are to be issued, in accordance with originator and investor requirements;
- the rating of notes by one or more credit-rating agencies;
- placing of notes in the capital markets.

The sale of assets to the SPV needs to be undertaken so that it is recognised as a true legal transfer. The originator obtains legal counsel to advise it in such matters. The credit rating process considers the character and quality of the assets, and also whether any enhancements have been made to the assets that will raise their credit quality. This can include *over-collateralisation,* which is when the principal value of notes issued is lower than the principal value of assets and a liquidity facility is provided by a bank.

A key consideration for the originator is the choice of the underwriting bank, which structures the deal and places the notes. The originator awards the mandate for its deal to an investment bank on the basis of fee levels, marketing ability and track record with assets being securitised.

SPV structures

There are essentially two main securitisation structures: amortising (pass-through) and revolving. A third type, the master trust, is used by frequent issuers.

Amortising structures

Amortising structures pay principal and interest to investors on a coupon-by-coupon basis throughout the life of the security, as illustrated in Figure 18.5. They are priced and traded based on expected maturity and weighted-average life (WAL), which is the time-weighted period during which principal is outstanding. A WAL approach incorporates various prepayment assumptions, and any change in this prepayment speed will increase or decrease the rate at which principal is repaid to investors. Pass-through structures are commonly used in residential and commercial MBSs, and consumer loan ABS.

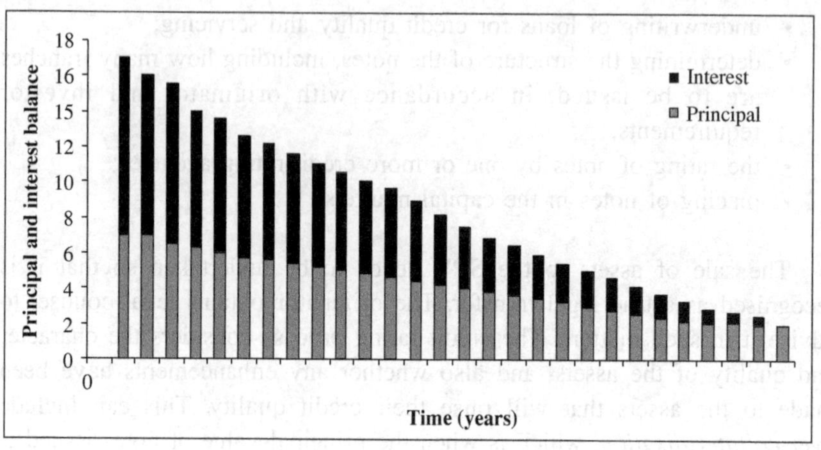

Figure 18.5 Amortising cash flow structure

Revolving structures

Revolving structures revolve the principal of the assets; that is, during the revolving period, principal collections are used to purchase new receivables which fulfill the necessary criteria. The structure is used for short-dated assets with a relatively high prepayment speed, such as credit card debt and auto-loans. During the amortisation period, principal payments are paid to investors either in a series of equal installments (*controlled amortisation*) or principal is "trapped" in a separate account until the expected maturity date and is then paid in a single lump sum to investors (*soft bullet*).

Master trust

Frequent issuers under US and UK law use *master trust* structures, which allow multiple securitisations to be issued from the same SPV. Under such schemes, the originator transfers assets to the master trust SPV. Notes are then issued out of the asset pool based on investor demand. Master trusts are used by MBS and credit card ABS originators.

Securitisation note tranching

As illustrated in Figure 18.2, in a securitisation the issued notes are structured to reflect specified risk areas of the asset pool, and thus are rated differently. The senior tranche is usually rated AAA. The lower-rated notes usually have an element of *over-collateralisation* and are thus capable of absorbing losses. The most junior note is the lowest rated or non-rated. It is often referred to as the *first-loss piece*, because it is impacted by losses in the underlying asset pool first. The first-loss piece is sometimes called the *equity piece* or equity note (even though it is in effect a bond) and is usually held by the originator.

Credit enhancement

Credit enhancement refers to the group of measures that can be instituted as part of the securitisation process for ABS and MBS issues so that the credit rating of the issued notes meets investor requirements. The lower the quality of the assets being securitised, the greater the need for credit enhancement. This is usually by some or all of the following methods:

- *Over-collateralisation*: where the nominal value of the assets in the pool are in excess of the nominal value of issued securities.
- *Pool insurance*: an insurance policy provided for a fee by a composite insurance company to cover the risk of principal loss in the collateral pool. The claims paying rating of the insurance company is important in determining the overall rating of the issue.
- *Senior/Junior note classes*: credit enhancement is provided for a fee by subordinating a class of notes ("class B" notes) to the senior class notes ("class A" notes). The class B note's right to its proportional share of cash flows is subordinated to the rights of the senior noteholders. Class B notes do not receive payments of principal until certain rating agency requirements have been met, specifically satisfactory performance of the collateral pool over a pre-determined period, or in many cases until all of the senior note classes have been redeemed in full.
- *Margin step-up*: a number of ABS issues incorporate a step-up feature in the coupon structure, which typically coincides with a call date. Although the issuer is usually under no obligation to redeem the notes at this point, the step-up feature was introduced as an added incentive for investors, to convince them from the outset that the economic cost of paying a higher coupon is unacceptable and that the issuer would seek to refinance by exercising its call option.
- *Excess spread*: this is the difference between the return on the underlying assets and the interest rate payable on the issued notes (liabilities). The monthly excess spread is used to cover expenses and any losses. If any surplus is left over, it is held in a reserve account to cover against future losses or (if not required for that), as a benefit to the originator. In the meantime the reserve account is a credit enhancement for investors.

Cash flow waterfall

All securitisation structures incorporate a *cash waterfall* process, whereby all the cash that is generated by the asset pool is paid in order of payment priority. Only when senior obligations have been met can more junior obligations be paid. An independent third-party agent is usually employed to run "tests" on the vehicle to confirm that there is sufficient cash available to pay all obligations. If a test is failed, then the vehicle will start to pay off the notes, starting from the senior notes. The waterfall process is illustrated in Figure 18.6.

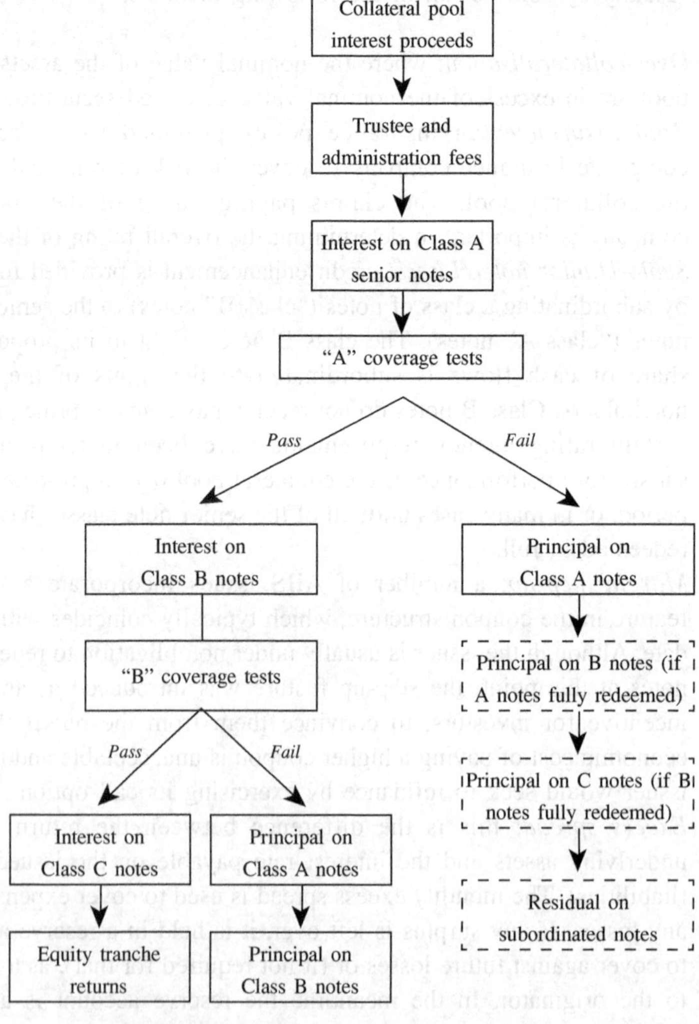

Figure 18.6 Cash flow waterfall (priority of payments)

Impact on balance sheet

Figure 18.7 illustrates, by way of an hypothetical example, the effect of a securitisation transaction on the liability side of an originating bank's balance sheet. Following the process, selected assets have been removed from the balance sheet, although the originating bank will usually have retained the first-loss piece. With regard to the regulatory capital impact, this first-loss amount is deducted from the bank's total capital position. For example, assume a bank has $100 million of risk-weighted assets and a target Basel ratio of 12%,[8] and it securitises all $100 million of these assets. It retains the first-loss tranche that forms 1.5% of the total issue. The remaining 98.5% will be sold on to the market. The bank will still have to set aside 1.5% of capital as a buffer against future losses, but it has been able to free itself of the remaining 10.5% of capital.

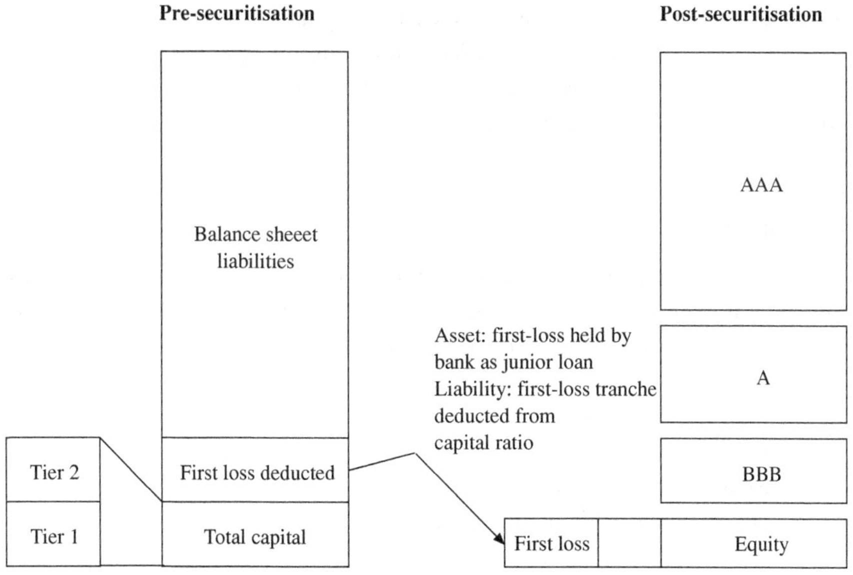

Figure 18.7 Regulatory capital impact of securitisation

[8] The minimum is 8%, but many banks prefer to set aside an amount well in excess of this minimum required level.

Illustrating the process of securitisation: Airways No. 1 Limited

To illustrate the process of securitisation, we consider an hypothetical airline ticket receivables transaction, originated by a fictitious company called ABC Airways plc and arranged by the equally fictitious XYZ Securities Limited. The following illustrates the kind of issues that are considered by the investment bank that is structuring the deal.

Originator:	ABC Airways plc
Issuer:	"Airways No. 1 Ltd"
Transaction:	Ticket receivables airline future flow securitisation bonds, €200m three-tranche floating-rate notes, legal maturity 2010
	Average life 4.1 years
Tranches:	Class "A" note (AA), Libor plus [ ] bps[9]
	Class "B" note (A), Libor plus [ ] bps
	Class "E" note (BBB), Libor plus [ ] bps
Arranger:	XYZ Securities plc

Due diligence

XYZ Securities undertakes due diligence on the assets to be securitised. In this case, it examines the airline performance figures over the last five years, as well as modelling future projected figures, including:

- total passenger sales;
- total ticket sales;
- total credit card receivables;
- geographical split of ticket sales.

It is the future flow of receivables, in this case credit card purchases of airline tickets, that is being securitised. This is a higher risk asset class than, say, residential mortgages, because the airline industry has a tradition of greater volatility of earnings than mortgage banks.

[9] The price spread is determined during the marketing stage, when the notes are offered to investors during a "roadshow".

Marketing approach

The investment bank's syndication desk seeks to place the notes with institutional investors across Europe. The notes are first given an indicative pricing ahead of the issue, to gauge investor sentiment. Given the nature of the asset class, let us assume the notes are marketed at around three-month Libor plus 70–80 basis points (AA note), 120–130 basis points (A note) and 260–270 basis points (BBB note). The notes are "benchmarked" against recent issues with similar underlying asset classes, as well as the spread level in the unsecured market of comparable issuer names.

Deal structure

The deal structure is shown in Figure 18.8.

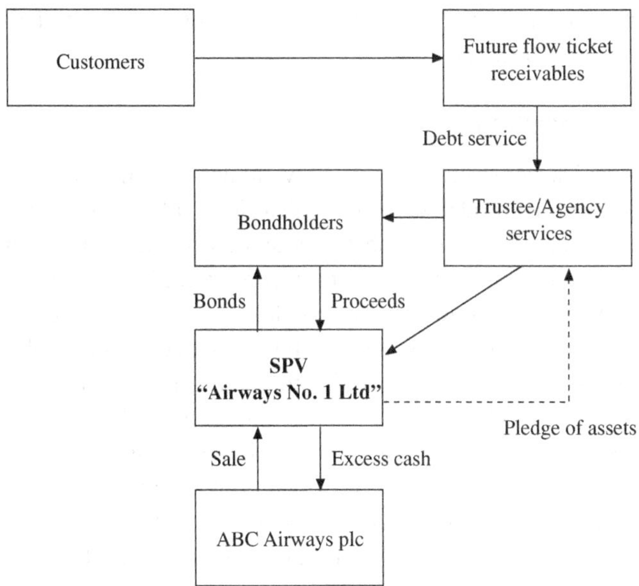

Figure 18.8 Airways No. 1 Limited deal structure

The process leading to the issue of notes is as follows:

- ABC Airways plc sells its present and all future flow credit card ticket receivables to an offshore SPV set up for this deal, incorporated as Airways No. 1 Ltd;

- the SPV issues notes in order to fund its purchase of the receivables;
- the SPV pledges its right to the receivables to a fiduciary agent, the Security Trustee, for the benefit of the bondholders;
- the Trustee accumulates funds as they are received by the SPV;
- the bondholders receive interest and principal payments, in the order of priority of the notes, on a quarterly basis.

In the event of default, the Trustee will act on behalf of the bondholders to safeguard their interests.

Financial guarantors

The investment bank decides whether or not an insurance company, known as a monoline insurer, should be approached to "wrap" the deal by providing a guarantee of backing for the SPV in the event of default. This insurance is provided in return for a fee.

Financial modelling

XYZ Securities constructs a cash flow model to estimate the size of the issued notes. The model considers historical sales values, any seasonal factors in sales, credit card cash flows and so on. Certain assumptions are made when constructing the model; for example, growth projections, inflation levels and tax levels. The model considers a number of different scenarios, and also calculates the minimum asset coverage levels required to service the issued debt. A key indicator in the model is the debt service coverage ratio (DSCR). The more conservative the DSCR, the more comfort there is for investors in the notes. For a residential mortgage deal, this ratio may be approximately 2.5–3.0; however, for an airline ticket receivables deal, the DSCR is unlikely to be lower than 4.0. The model therefore calculates the amount of notes that can be issued against the assets, while maintaining the minimum DSCR.

Credit rating

It is common for securitisation deals to be rated by one or more of the formal credit ratings agencies such as Moody's, Fitch or Standard & Poor's. A formal credit rating makes it easier for XYZ Securities to place the notes with investors. The methodology employed by the ratings agencies takes into account both qualitative and quantitative factors, and differs according to the asset class being securitised. The main issues in a deal such as our hypothetical Airways No. 1 deal would be expected to include:

- corporate credit quality: these are risks associated with the originator, and are factors that affect its ability to continue operations, meet its financial obligations, and provide a stable foundation for generating future receivables. This might be analysed according to the following:
  (1) ABC Airways' historical financial performance, including its liquidity and debt structure;
  (2) its status within its domicile country; for example, whether or not it is state-owned;
  (3) the general economic conditions for industry and for airlines;
  (4) the historical record and current state of the airline; for instance, its safety record and age of its aeroplanes;
- the competition and industry trends: ABC Airways' market share, the competition on its network;
- regulatory issues, such as the need for ABC Airways to comply with forthcoming legislation that will impact its cash flows;
- legal structure of the SPV and transfer of assets;
- cash flow analysis.

Based on the findings of the ratings agency, the arranger may redesign some aspect of the deal structure so that the issued notes are rated at the required level.

This is a selection of the key issues involved in the process of securitisation. Depending on investor sentiment, market conditions and legal issues, the process from inception to closure of the deal may take anything from three to 12 months or more. After the notes have been issued, the arranging bank no longer has anything to do with the issue; however, the bonds themselves require a number of agency services for their remaining life until they mature or are paid off (see Procter and Leedham 2004). These agency services include paying the agent, cash manager and custodian.

Credit rating considerations

The originator in a securitisation will take a keen interest in the various factors that are of importance to the credit-rating agencies.[10] These factors must be met if the transaction is to be rated at the required level, otherwise it will be difficult to place the liabilities. We consider some of the key issues here.

True sale and ownership of assets

A prime consideration is that, in the event of default, the underlying assets are able to be liquidated and the proceeds used to repay noteholders. The true sale of the assets to the SPV, which then ring-fences them, ensures this. However, it also means that the assets must be able to be sold to the SPV and transferred into its ownership. If the assets cannot be sold easily in the traditional manner, such as hedge fund assets, then a synthetic securitisation may be more appropriate. In such a deal, typically the assets are referenced synthetically and cash flows from them transferred via means of a swap such as a total return swap.

Asset quality and loss rate

As part of the process of assigning a rating, the agencies will undertake due diligence on the asset pool. This includes reviewing the nature of the cash flows, the state of interest servicing payments to date, the status and ability to pay of the obligors. In their modelling process they will calculate probabilities of default for the assets. This includes looking at historical default rates and recovery rates. These two values are used to calculate a potential loss rate, which is of interest to investors.

The loss rate is calculated as follows: if the historical default rate is 1% and the recovery rate (RR) is 30%, then the loss rate is 0.7%. This rate states that for every $100 of assets, $1 will default. If $0.30 of this is recovered, then the ultimate loss is $0.70. Hence the loss rate is 0.7%.

Agencies will also be interested in the diversity of the asset pool, and its concentration among one borrower or one type of borrower.

[10] These are Standard & Poor's, Moody's and FitchRatings. There are other agencies but in the capital markets it is invariably that at least one, and often all three, of these agencies will be retained to provide the rating. Their dominance is illustrated by the fact that many fund managers, especially money market funds, will not invest in a security unless it has an S&P rating.

Asset servicing

We noted earlier that in many, if not most, securitisation transactions the servicing function is retained by the originator. This is logical because the originator will be familiar with the obligors and the industry, and should be best placed to administer the assets. From the point of view of the credit rating agency, this is the best arrangement. If the servicing function is transferred to a third party, the rating agency will review this entity and assess its ability to undertake the servicing function. The assessment will consider the servicer's experience in the industry and other facets of its expertise. In some transactions, a back-up servicer is assigned to the deal, who is on stand-by to take over the role if necessary, for any reason.

Cash flow modelling[11]

The rating process will project cash flows for the deal, and hence determine the likelihood of the vehicle to meet its payment obligations. The obligations include not only the principal and interest payments on the notes, but also fees for third parties such as the Trustee, the sub-administrator, and the servicer – not to mention the fees of the rating agencies! Cash flow projections are based on assumptions about default and recovery rates.

The arranging bank will also undertake modelling for the deal, as they work towards putting together the final structure of the deal. There is a distinct difference in the objective of their modelling, in that they seek to structure to meet the rating agency requirements and so be assigned the rating they need. The rating agencies on the other hand run the deal mechanics through their model, which then produces a result based on these inputs. From the point of view of the arranging bank, there is further distinction between the two main types of structure: ABS/MBS and collateralised debt obligation (CDO). The models differ as follows:

- In a CDO model, cash flows are less of a concern. Instead the model is used to determine the final form of the underlying portfolio. The model runs various permutations on a subset of a pool of securities (bonds and/or loans) to achieve the necessary diversity and note spread. The diversity requirement is a rating agency consideration. The key objective is to construct the most efficient portfolio in order

[11] The author thanks Suleman Baig at Deutsche Bank AG in London for his generous help and input with this section.

to enable the CDO to achieve the rating agency requirements at the lowest funding costs;

- In an ABS transaction, the originator is not concerned over-much with the portfolio: the portfolio is given and there is little quantifiable diversity. For example, the entire portfolio will be residential mortgages or credit card. The arrangers will be concerned with the cash flows to ensure they have the mechanics right, but the focus is on structuring around the mechanical obstacles that the portfolio brings. For example, if the deal is concerned with residential mortgages in a certain jurisdiction, then that jurisdiction may state that there is set-off risk (that is, customers can offset mortgage balances that belong to the SPV against current account deposits that do not).

Of these two deal types, probably the static balance sheet CDO is the closest to the ABS type in terms of modelling aspect.

Loan-to-value ratio

The loan-to-value (LTV) ratio is the ratio of the amount of the loan to the market value of the asset. The value of the asset is a market value, which can be estimated from secondary market trading of similar assets, or independently valued when it is sold to the SPV. An LTV ratio of 0.8 indicates that the value of the loan is 80% of the market value of the asset. The difference between the value of an asset and the loan amount is known as the "borrower's equity". If the LTV is below 1, this means that the borrower has positive equity in the asset and so is less likely to default. If the LTV is higher than 1 it means that the amount borrowed is above the market value of the asset and it may be advantageous to default. Rating agencies view LTV as an important indicator of the likelihood of default.

$$\text{Loan to value ratio} = \frac{\text{Loan amount}}{\text{Market value of the asset}}$$

Payment-to-income ratio

The payment-to-income ratio (PTI) is the ratio of the amount of the monthly loan interest payment to the income available each month to make the loan interest payment. A higher PTI means that a higher amount of a borrower's income needs to be set aside to meet the interest servicing.

A related ratio is the "debt service coverage ratio" (DSCR). This is the mortgaged property's net operating income as a percentage of the debt service cost. A low ratio is indicative of potential default as the income may not be sufficient to cover interest costs.

CASE STUDY 18.1 Shipshape Residential Mortgages No. 1

Bristol & West plc is a former UK building society that is now part of the Bank of Ireland group. In October 2000, it issued £300 million of residential MBS through ING Barings. It was the third time that Bristol & West had undertaken a securitisation of part of its mortgage book. The Shipshape Residential Mortgages No. 1 was structured in the following way:

- a £285 million tranche senior note, rated Aaa by Moody's and Fitch IBCA, with an average life of 3.8 years and paying 25 basis points over three-month Libor;
- a Class "B" note of £9 million, rated A1 by Moody's and paying a coupon on 80 basis points over three-month Libor. These notes had an average life of 6.1 years;
- a junior note of £6 million nominal, rated triple-B by Moody's and with an average life of 6.8 years. These notes paid a coupon of 140 basis points over Libor.

CASE STUDY 18.2 Fosse Securities No. 1 plc

This was the first securitisation undertaken by Alliance & Leicester plc, a former UK building society that converted into a commercial bank in 1997. The underlying portfolio was approximately 6,700 loans secured by first mortgages on property in the United Kingdom. The transaction was a £250 million securitisation via the SPV, named Fosse Securities No. 1 plc. The underwriter was Morgan Stanley Dean Witter, which placed the notes in November 2000. The transaction structure was:

- a senior Class "A" note with AAA/Aaa rating by Standard & Poor's and Moody's, which represented £235 million of the issue, with a legal maturity of November 2032;
- a Class "B" note rated Aa/Aa3 of nominal £5 million;
- a Class "C" note rated BBB/Baa2 of nominal £10 million.

The ratings agencies cited the strengths of the issue as:[12] the loans were *prime* quality; there was a high level of *seasoning* in the underlying asset pool, with an average age of 35 months; the average level of the loan-to-value ratio (LTV) was considered low, at 73.5%; and there were low average loan-to-income multiples among underlying borrowers.

CASE STUDY 18.3 SRM Investment No. 1 Limited

Sveriges Bostadsfinansieringsaktiebolag (SBAB) is the Swedish state-owned national housing finance corporation. Its second-ever securitisation issue was the EUR1 billion SRM Investment No. 1 Limited, issued in October 2000. The underlying asset backing was Swedish residential mortgage loans, with properties being mainly detached and semi-detached single-family properties. The issue was structured and underwritten by Nomura International.

The underlying motives behind the deal were that it allowed SBAB to:

- reduce capital allocation, thereby releasing capital for further lending;
- remove part of its mortgage loan-book off the balance sheet;
- obtain a more diversified source for its funding.

The transaction was structured into the following notes:

- senior Class "A1" floating-rate note rated AAA/Aaa by S&P and Moody's, issue size EUR755 million, with a legal maturity date in 2057;
- senior Class "A2" fixed coupon note, rated AAA/Aaa and

[12] *Source*: *International Securitisation Review*, London, November 2000.

denominated in Japanese yen, incorporating a step-up facility, legal maturity 2057; issue size JPY20 billion;

- Class "M" floating-rate note rated A/A2, due 2057; issue size EUR20 million;
- Class "B" floating-rate note, rated BBB/Baa2, issue size EUR10 million.

The yen tranche reflects the targeting of a Japanese domestic investor base. On issue, the Class A1 notes paid 26 basis points over Euribor. The structure is illustrated in Figure 18.9.

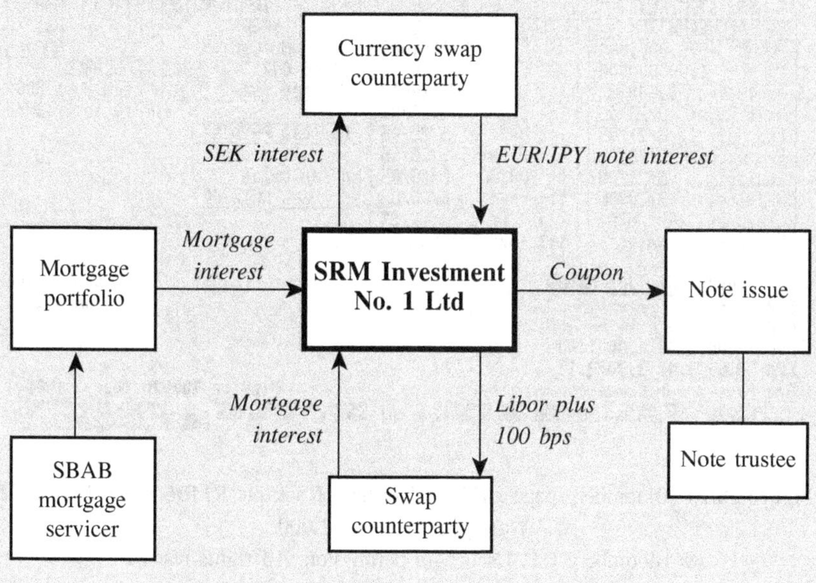

Figure 18.9 SRM Investment No. 1 Limited

Structured finance securities such as RMBS issues have a different description page on the Bloomberg system compared to vanilla conventional bonds. This page details additional information of use to investors, such as pool factors. The pool factor is a value assigned to an ABS tranche that indicates how much of its original notional amount has been reduced since issue, due to pre-payments of the underlying assets. If the pool factor, often referred to simply as the factor, of a note tranche is 0.9135, then one would multiply the notional amount of the note with the pool factor and the note dirty price to obtain the market value. On first issue, a note factor will be

1.0000, and this can be expected to reduce over time as early repayments of the underlying assets start to reduce the overlying note notional amounts. Figure 18.10 shows Bloomberg page DES for an issue in May 2005, Granite Master Issuer plc 2005-2 A1. The originator is Northern Rock plc. As it is the very early stages of the bond issue, the pool factor is still 1.0000. This issue pays USD coupon on a monthly basis.

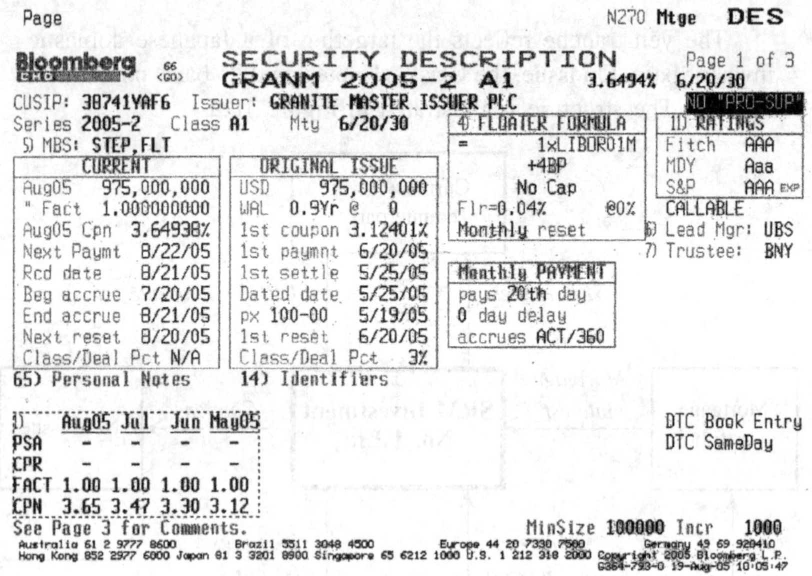

Figure 18.10 Bloomberg page DES for Northern Rock plc RMBS issue, May 2005. Note pool factor of 1.000

References and bibliography

Bhattacharya, A. and Fabozzi, F. (eds.) 1996, *Asset-backed Securities*, FJF Associates, New Hope, PA.

Choudhry, M. 2001, *The Bond and Money Markets: Strategy, Trading, Analysis*, Butterworth-Heinemann, Oxford.

Fabozzi, F. and Choudhry, M. 2004, *The Handbook of European Structured Financial Products*, John Wiley & Sons, New Jersey.

Hayre, L. (ed) 2001, *The Salomon Smith Barney Guide to Mortgage-backed and Asset-backed Securities*, John Wiley & Sons, New Jersey.

Martellini, L., Priaulet P. and Priaulet S. 2003, *Fixed Income Securities*, John Wiley & Sons, Chichester.

Procter, N. and Leedham, E. 2004, "Trust and Agency Services in the Debt Capital Market", in Fabozzi, F. and Choudhry, M. 2004, *The Handbook of European Fixed Income Securities*, John Wiley & Sons, New Jersey.

Sundaresan, S. 1997, *Fixed Income Markets and Their Derivatives*, South-Western Publishing, Cincinnatti, Chapter 9.

CHAPTER

19

Structured, Synthetic and Repackaged Funding Vehicles

Banks and financial institutions have an interest in setting up alternative funding arrangements, outside of normal bank lines or vanilla conduit structures such as commercial paper (CP) programmes, wherever these offer additional funding capacity, cheaper interest rates, funding source diversity or any combination of these. Another reason for setting up such alternatives is where an illiquid asset pool requires funding and cannot be repo'ed in the normal manner, either because it is low-rated or not easily transferable. Securitisation, and more recently synthetic securitisation, techniques allow banks to access funding sources outside the conventional avenues.

In this chapter we describe a number of different funding structures, the motivation behind all of which is to widen the opportunities for raising funds and assisting liquidity management. In some cases they also enable the funding of illiquid asset pools. We also introduce here the concept of synthetic securitisation, which does not involve the "true sale" of assets into an SPV. We will look at this again in subsequent chapters. We begin with a look at the application of securitisation to vanilla conduit structures, the asset-backed CP structure.

Asset-backed commercial paper

During the 1980s and 1990s the rise in popularity in the use of securitisation as a means of diversifying bank liquidity led to the introduction of short-term money market paper backed by the cash flows from other assets, known as *asset-backed commercial paper* (ABCP). Vehicles through which ABCP is issued are usually called *conduits*. These issue paper backed by the cash flows from specified assets, such as residential mortgages, car loans or commercial bank loans, as backing for an issue of short-term paper. The assets themselves are transferred from the original owner (the *originator*) to a specially created legal entity, the SPV.

Generally, securitisation is used as a funding instrument by companies for three main reasons: it offers lower cost funding compared to traditional bank loan or bond financing; it is a mechanism by which assets such as corporate loans or mortgages can be removed from the balance sheet, thus improving the lenders' return on assets or return on equity ratios; and it increases a borrowers' funding options.

Entities usually access the CP market in order to secure permanent financing, rolling over individual issues as part of a longer-term programme and using interest-rate swaps to arrange a fixed rate if required. Conventional CP issues are typically supported by a line of credit from a commercial bank, and so this form of financing is in effect a form of bank funding. Issuing ABCP enables an originator to benefit from money market financing that it might otherwise not have access to because its credit rating is not sufficiently strong. A bank may also issue ABCP for balance sheet or funding reasons. ABCP trades exactly as conventional CP. The administration and legal treatment is more onerous, however, because of the need to establish the CP trust structure and issuing SPV. The servicing of an ABCP programme follows that of conventional CP and is carried out by the same type of entities, such as the Trust arms of banks such as Deutsche Bank and Bank of New York.

ABCP was discussed in detail in Chapter 3.

Evolution of ABCP programmes

As with conventional CP programmes, as ABCP paper matures it is redeemed with the proceeds of a roll-over issue. If for any reason a roll-over issue cannot be placed in the market (for example, there is a market correction and investor confidence disappears, or the issuer suffers a credit rating downgrade), the issuer will need to call on a bank loan of credit to repay investors. This line of credit is known as a *liquidity facility*. The liquidity facility acts as a form of credit enhancement to investors, providing comfort that in the last resort there will be sufficient funds available to repay them.

ABCP conduits have followed an evolutionary path thus:

First generation: A fully supported programme backed by 100% letters-of-credit (LOC) from sponsor banks.

Second generation:	Partially supported programmes with multi-asset backing, with 100% bank LOC and 10–15% credit enhancement.
Third generation:	Security arbitrage vehicles that are unsupported by bank LOCs and have minimal credit enhancement. These conduits issue both CP and MTNs, and are also known as structured investment vehicles (SIVs).
Fourth generation:	Multi-asset conduits also viewed as finance companies in their own right, with credit ratings based on quality of underlying assets. There is no bank LOC and the companies invest in high-quality assets and project finance programmes. Credit enhancement in SIV-type structures may take the form of subordinated notes and capital notes or "equity".

Figure 19.1 on page 924 shows a single-seller ABCP structure.

A single-seller conduit is established for the sale of assets originated by one entity. Typically it is 100% supported by a bank liquidity facility and by 10% credit enhancement. The liquidity provider is usually required by the credit ratings agencies to have a short-term rating of A–1/P–1/F–1.

A multi-seller conduit would have more than one seller into the conduit SPV.

Liquidity and credit enhancement

ABCP conduits require liquidity support to cover 100% of their outstanding CP for 364 days. A liquidity facility will guarantee a timely repayment of CP as it matures, and is vital because most conduits do not match the term structure of their assets and liabilities. Facilities are typically required to purchase assets, in accordance with a pre-specified formula. Generally, the facility will be called upon in the event of bankruptcy occurring with respect to the conduit, if it is otherwise unable to honour its liabilities as they fall due, or if the underlying assets become rated at Caa1 or lower by Moody's, and CCC+ or lower by Standard & Poor's and Fitch.

Liquidity support can be in the form of either a Liquidity Asset Purchase agreement (LAPA) or a Liquidity Loan agreement (LLA), which differ as follows:

- LAPA: the liquidity provider(s) purchase non-defaulted assets when called upon;

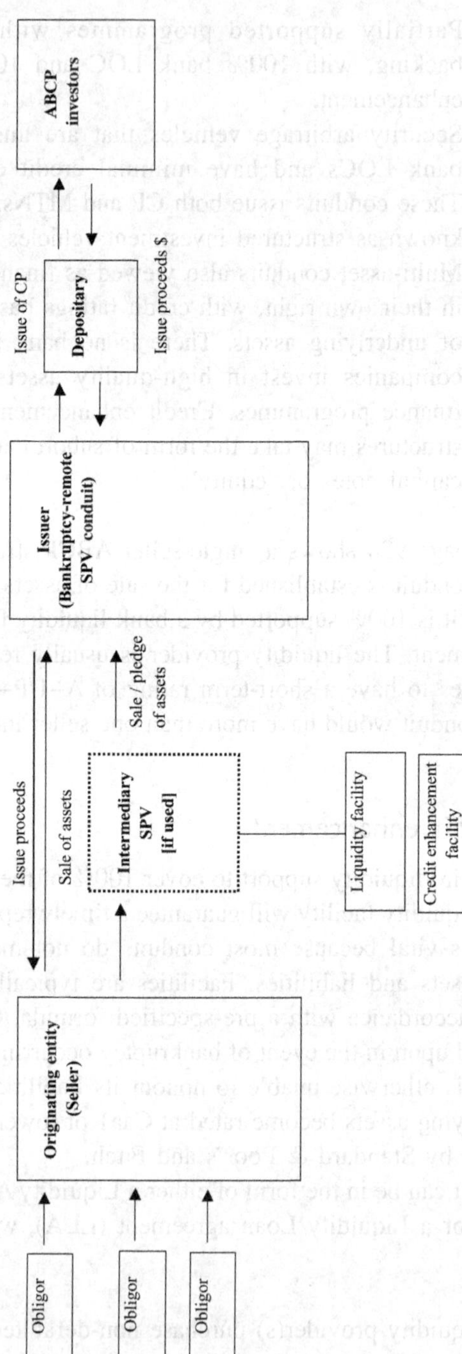

Figure 19.1 Single-seller ABCP conduit structure

- LLA: the liquidity provider(s) lend money to the conduit in return for a security pledge over the underlying asset cash flows.

A liquidity facility also covers other risks such as dilution, hedging and legal issues.

Other forms of credit enhancement are also set in place. If it is transaction-specific, credit enhancement provides the first layer of protection against shortfalls from the underlying collateral on specific asset pools, typically in the form of over-collateralisation, excess spread, a bank LOC or surety bond. The main features are that they are maintained as protection against delinquencies, losses or dilution, and that reserves are generally based on a multiple of the seller's historical delinquency, net losses and dilutions of the pool of assets.

If it is programme-wide, credit enhancement provides the second layer of protection coverage for repurchase of cash receivables or guarantee of losses on the receivables. It supplements the seller's reserves, and will be used only after the seller's reserves are depleted. Its main features are:

- it is calculated as a percentage of the entire ABCP conduit;
- it is mainly in the form of a LOC, surety bond, subordinated notes, cash collateral bank account, or a total return swap;
- traditional receivables and loan programmes sized at a minimum 5% of the total size and which fluctuate in accordance with the credit quality of the asset pool.

Note that the enhancement for security arbitrage conduits and SIVs is usually at 0%, provided that the underlying assets are rated at AA–/Aa3/ AA– or better.

Structural development

During 2001 and 2002 new structures were observed in the market that built on the first- and second-generation conduits first introduced. These focused on arrangements that reduced the need for bank liquidity support, and set up alternative sources of liquidity and credit enhancement. This was a response to the increasing difficulty in arranging traditional liquidity; for instance, the number of banks rated A–1/P–1 was in decline, banks were conserving their liquidity lines, investors were demanding higher return to reflect the true level of risk involved in these vehicles, and the growing popularity of conduits themselves made liquidity more expensive.

The newer generation of conduits featured alternative sources of liquidity including:

- capturing liquidity from the underlying assets, through matching asset–liability profiles, and capturing the excess spread between assets and liabilities;
- using non-bank liquidity providers, such as highly rated entities;
- using investors as proxy liquidity providers, through the issue of extendible notes and structured liquidity notes, and through the issue of long-dated MTNs;
- use of derivative structures, such as TRSs, CDSs and CLNs;
- using monoline insurance firms to provide support backing to the conduit.

Vehicles such as arbitrage conduits and SIVs have much lower levels of credit enhancement, typically ranging from 0%–4% rather than 10%–15%.

Another development in the United States and ECP market is floating-rate CP. Unlike traditional CP, which is discount paper, this is issued as interest-bearing CP at par. The paper is rolled typically at one-month or three-month Libor reset dates. Interest is paid to investors at each Libor reset date. Floating-rate paper is preferred by issuers to discount CP if they are expecting short-term interest rates to fall.

The newer vehicles securitise a wider range of assets, including equities and synthetic structures. We consider the synthetic ABCP conduit later in this chapter.

Committed liquidity line funding

This section could comfortably sit in a number of other chapters, including Chapter 3 and Chapter 12. We have placed it here however because it combines a plain vanilla instrument – the bank liquidity facility – with an element of repo, and is frequently attached to structured funding vehicles such as ABCP conduits and SIVs.

The standard bank liquidity line is a standing credit facility set up for a borrower that may be drawn on at any time. A commitment fee is charged annually on the entire line size, irrespective of whether any or all of the line is used. If the line is drawn on, this borrowing is then charged at the agreed rate. Lines are usually reviewed on an annual basis, so they represent a maximum 364-day facility. Longer-dated facilities can be agreed, but these attract a higher capital charge so the commitment fee will be higher. A structure offered by banks to clients that desire longer-term funding is the *evergreen* committed line, which is in theory a 364-day tenor, but which is formally "renewed" on a daily basis. This enables the borrower to view the line as longer-dated funding, because it is always 364 days away from maturity.

Under Basel I the capital charge for liquidity lines in the interbank market was nil provided the line had a maximum 364-day maturity. For lines of greater than 1-year maturity, the capital charge would be [50% × 20% × 8%] for the unused portion. Essentially, liquidity credit facilities attract 0% weighting if they have a tenor of one year or less. For credit lines with a tenor of more than one year, there is a 50% product weighting on the unused portion of the line. This product weighting is then to be combined with the counterparty risk, which is 20% for banking and credit institutions under Basel I. Under Basel II the counterparty risk weighting changes; for example, under the standardised approach it would depend on the counterparty's credit rating (see Chapter 27).

For structured finance counterparties such as ABCP conduits and SIV SPVs, it is common for any borrowings on the line to be collateralised. This turns the liquidity into a committed repo line. The repo is usually transacted under a GMRA agreement that is executed between the bank lender and the SPV.

Figure 19.2 on page 928 is a sample term sheet for a committed repo liquidity line between two interbank counterparties. We see that this facility has been set up to provide funding for real-estate assets, which we presume is a line of business that the borrower ("Global Bank") is involved in. The fact that a long-term facility has been offered enables ABC Securities Limited to lend at a relatively high rate, as interbank repo funding rates in 2006 would be considerably below Libor plus 18–20 basis points. However, we presume that as Global Bank is seeking long fixed-term committed funding, it is willing to pay above-market rates for this facility. If the line is drawn on, Global Bank will provide collateral in the form of real-estate assets, at minimum loan-to-value (LTV) levels stated, and also with a haircut.

Committed Repo Liquidity Line
USD 2 billion standing collateralised loan facility
Indicative Terms and Conditions
[11 October 2006]

Line provider:	ABC Securities Limited.
Obligor:	Global Bank International Limited Global Bank Funding.
Instrument:	A standing liquidity facility, drawn down in the form of a collateralised loan as and when required by the borrower. The number of drawdowns outstanding at any time is unlimited on condition the aggregate outstanding balance is at or below the Principal Amount.
Maturity:	Two-year final maturity, to be reviewed on an annual basis at anniversary of execution date OR One-year evergreen facility renewed on rolling one-day basis
Loan tenor:	Between 7-day and 364-day, up to the date of the Maturity Date.
Status:	Ranks *parri passu*
Principal amount:	USD 2 billion
Commitment fee:	[6-7] basis points p.a.
Drawdown:	The facility drawdown will be in the form of a repo transaction executed under GMRA on a T+2 settlement basis.
Loan rate:	Libor plus [18-20] basis points.
Interest basis:	Fixed- or floating-rate.
Denominations:	The facility may be drawn down in USD, EUR, GBP, CHF, HKD, JPY, AUD, NZD, SGD, CAD, SEK, NOK, DKK and ZAR. For currencies for which no Libor fix is quoted, the official local market interbank fixing rate will be taken.
Collateral:	All drawdowns from the facility will be collateralised under the GMRA repo. Collateral will be in the form of commercial loans, real-estate loans, B Notes and Mezzanine notes. Underlying loans to be collateralised with commercial property or other real-estate, with maximum accepted LTV ratio of 80%.
Collateral report:	Asset summary to be provided for each pool of collateral at time of each drawdown.
Execution Date:	[ ] 2006.
Maturity Date:	[ ] 2008.
Haircut:	7% [Collateral LTV 50%-75%] 10% [Collateral LTV 75%-90%].

Security charge:	Repo will be executed via a Tri-Party Agent that will be responsible for settling cash and collateral on behalf of the lender and obligor.
Tri-Party Agent:	Trust Bank, New York.
Business Days:	London, New York, TARGET.
Redemption:	100% of the drawndown Principal Amount payable on the Maturity Date.
Guarantee:	Payment of the maturity value of all repo trades is guaranteed by Global Bank [A1/A].
Governing Law:	English.

Figure 19.2 Committed repo liquidity line, term sheet

The synthetic ABCP conduit

The latest development in conduits is the synthetic structure. Exactly as with synthetic structured credit products, this uses credit derivatives to make an economic transfer of risk and exposure between the originator and the issuer, so that there is not necessarily a sale of assets from the originator to the Issuer. We describe synthetic conduits by means of an hypothetical transaction, "Golden Claw Funding", which is a TRS-backed ABCP structure.

EXAMPLE 19.1 Hypothetical case study: Golden Claw Funding

Figure 19.3 is a structure diagram for a synthetic ABCP vehicle that uses a TRS in its structure. It illustrates an hypothetical conduit, Golden Claw Funding Ltd, which issues paper into both the US CP market and the EuroCP market. It has been set up as a funding vehicle, with the originator accessing the CP market to fund assets that it holds on its balance sheet. The originator can be a bank, non-bank financial institution such as a hedge fund, or a corporate. In our case study the originator is a hedge fund called ABC Fund Limited.

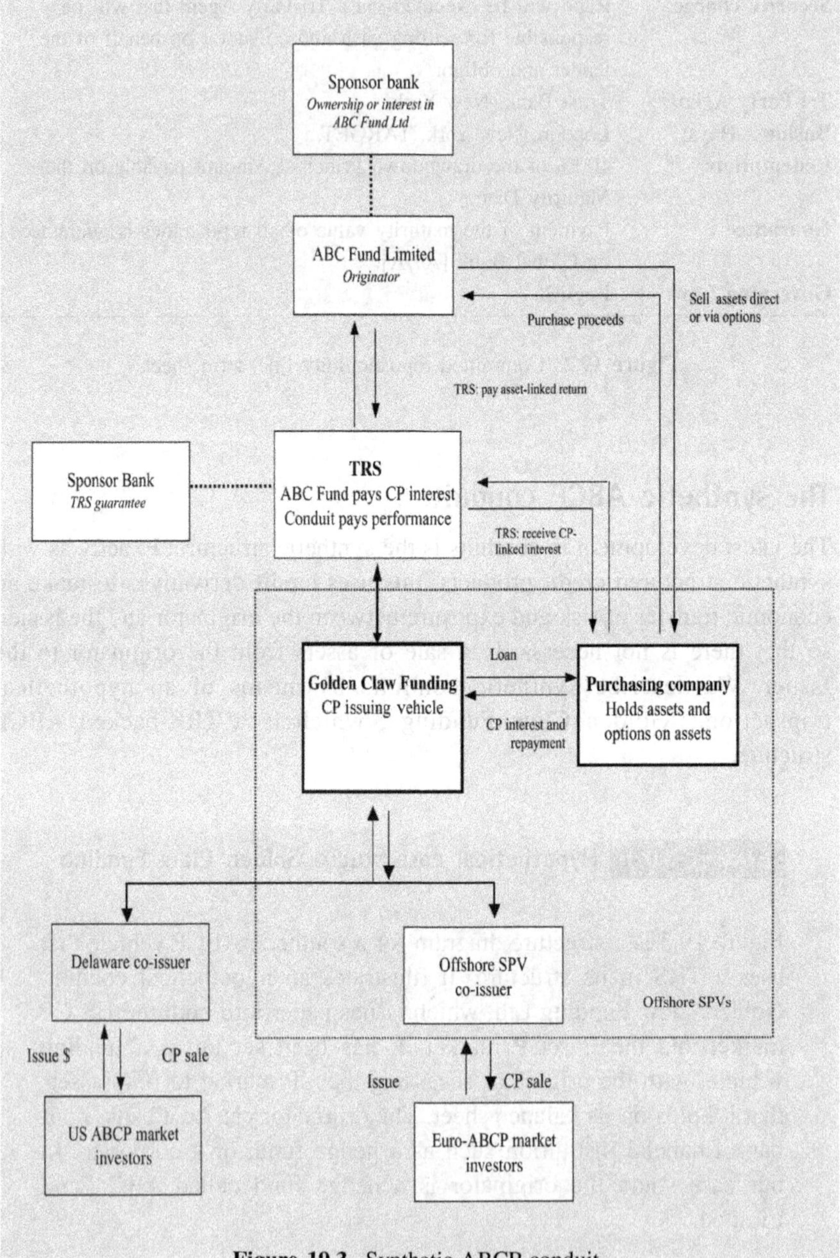

Figure 19.3 Synthetic ABCP conduit, hypothetical deal "Golden Claw Funding"

The structure shown in Figure 19.3 has the following features:

- the CP issuance vehicle and the purchase company (PC) are based off-shore at a location such as Jersey, Ireland or Cayman Islands;
- the conduit issues CP in the USD market via a co-issuer based in Delaware. It also issues ECP via an offshore SPV;
- proceeds of the CP issue are loaned to the PC, which uses these funds to purchase assets from the originator. As well as purchasing assets directly, the vehicle may also acquire an "interest" in assets that are held by ABC Fund Limited via an option called a zero-strike call (ZSC). (We describe ZSCs in Example 19.3.) If assets are purchased directly on to the balance sheet of the PC, this is akin to what happens in a conventional ABCP structure. If interests in the assets are acquired via a ZSC then they are not actually sold to the PC, and remain on the balance sheet of ABC Fund Limited. Assets can be bonds, structured finance bonds, equities, mutual funds, hedge fund shares, convertible bonds, synthetic products and private equity;
- simultaneously as it purchases assets or ZSCs on assets, the PC enters into a TRS contract with ABC Fund Limited, under which it pays the performance on the assets and receives interest on the CP proceeds it has used to purchase assets and ZSCs. The TRS is the means by which ABC Fund retains the economic interest in the assets it is funding, and the means by which PC receives the interest it needs to pay back to Golden Claw as CP matures;
- the issue vehicle itself may also purchase assets and ZSCs, so we show in Figure 19.3 that it also has a TRS between itself and ABC Fund Limited.

We reproduce the term sheet for the TRS contract below. This states that the notional value and maturity of the TRS matches those of the CP issue.

The Golden Claw structure is a means by which funds can be raised without a true sale structure. The TRS is guaranteed by the sponsor bank, so will ensure that the conduit is rated at the short-term rating of the sponsor bank. As CP matures, it will be repaid with a roll-over issue of CP, with interest received via the TRS contract. If CP cannot be rolled over, then the PC or the issuer will need to sell assets or exercise ZSCs in assets to repay principal, or otherwise the TRS guarantor will need to cover the repayment.

EXAMPLE 19.2 Zero-strike calls

A zero-strike call (ZSC) is a call option with strike price set at zero. It is written on an underlying asset such as a bond or shares in a hedge fund, and is sold at par. It is essentially a means by which an interest in illiquid assets can be transferred to a customer. Consider the two following examples showing how ZSCs might be used:

- Buying a ZSC: a hedge fund of funds wishes to acquire an interest in assets that are not on its balance sheet. It buys a ZSC from a hedge fund that holds the assets, who writes the ZSC. If the asset appreciates in value, the gain is realised by the hedge fund of funds.
- Selling a ZSC: a hedge fund of funds holds assets on its books, which a client (investor) wishes to acquire an interest in. The fund of funds writes a ZSC to the investor, enabling the investor to acquire an interest in the assets.

These examples are illustrated in Figure 19.4.

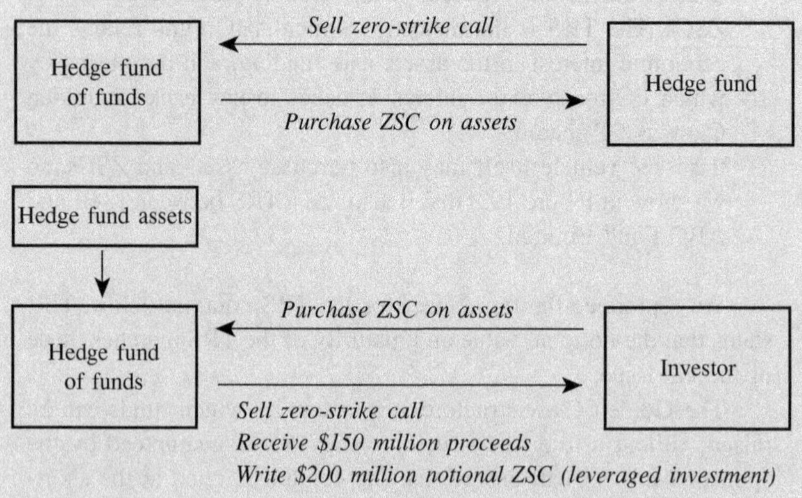

Figure 19.4 ZSC options

Frequently the ZSC is transacted as part of a leveraged investment play, so that in the example above described as "selling a ZSC", the fund of funds will invest its own funds in a leveraged proportion to those of the client. For example, for every $25 invested by the client, the fund of funds will invest $75, as part of a notional $100 investment in a ZSC option.

Synthetic ABCP conduit: Example TRS term sheet

To illustrate the terms of the TRS used in the Golden Claw Funding Limited hypothetical case study, we produce below an example of what the term sheet for the TRS contract might look like. This describes the terms of the TRS used in the structure and has been produced for the Sponsoring Bank that is the guarantor to the TRS.

ABC Fund Limited
Golden Claw Funding Limited
Total Return Swap Term Sheet

Programme summary

Golden Claw will raise money in the US CP and Euro CP market. It will lend this money to Golden Claw Purchase Company (PC). PC will buy assets such as bonds or equity from ABC Fund Limited. Golden Claw PC simultaneously enters into a TRS contract with ABC Fund Limited. The TRS contract is the means by which ABC Fund Limited retains the price risk of the assets. Via the TRS, Golden Claw PC will transfer the return on the assets to ABC Fund Limited, and receive sufficient interest from ABC Fund Limited to pay Golden Claw the interest on maturing CP. The mark-to-market on the TRS will be set in line with CP repayment dates, and is guaranteed by the Sponsor Bank.

General terms	A TRS is entered into between Golden Claw PC and ABC Fund Limited. One leg of the TRS pays the performance of the underlying assets, while the other leg will pay the maturing CP interest. These payments are made two days after the TRS reset dates, which coincide with the CP issue maturity date.

	A TRS is entered into simultaneously each time CP is issued. The notional value of each TRS will be equivalent to the outstanding nominal value of each CP issue. The maturity of the TRS will match the maturity of the CP issue.
Assets	Each issuer and each PC will own a portfolio of assets of a particular type. Initially, the types of assets will include debt securities; equity securities; and hedge fund investments (including zero strike calls relating to such investments).
TRSs	The issuer and the PC will enter into a TRS ("Swap") with the swap counterparty (as defined below). The aggregate amount paid to the issuer or PC under the swap shall be sufficient to pay: (1) the interest payable on the CP issued to fund the related assets through maturity and (2) expenses of the issuer or the PC, including the fees of the issuer's or PC's agents, taxes, rating agency and legal fees. All payments received in relation to the assets held by the Issuer or the PC will be paid to the related swap counterparty. Each swap agreement may also provide for periodic transfer (1) by the Issuer or the PC to the swap counterparty of market value increases of the related Assets and (2) by the swap counterparty to the issuer or the PC, of market value decreases of the related assets.
Swap counterparty	[tbc]
TRS bookings	The issuer or PC will enter into a TRS with ABC Fund Limited under which the issuer or PC will (1) pay the performance on the TRS reference asset to ABC Fund Limited and (2) receive proceeds equivalent to maturing CP interest and costs. ABC Fund Limited will enter into a TRS with the issuer or PC under which it will (1) pay proceeds equivalent to maturing CP interest and other costs, and (2) receive the performance on the TRS reference assets. The notional value of the swap will

be equal to the nominal value of outstanding CP. A swap will be written each time there is an issue of CP. Net payments will be exchanged on swap payment dates (value two days after the swap reset date), which will coincide with CP maturity payment date and swap maturity.

Issue mechanics

Golden Claw will issue CP on the trade date for settlement on T+2. Simultaneously, on T+0 PC will (1) enter into a loan with Golden Claw for the CP settlement proceeds, value date T+2, loan to expire on CP maturity date; (2) will transact to purchase assets to the value of the loan from ABC Fund Limited, or ZSCs written on assets held by ABC Fund Limited, for asset delivery to PC on T+2; and (3) will enter into a TRS agreement with ABC Fund Limited, for value date T+2, for the nominal value of the CP issue. The TRS reset date will be two days prior to CP maturity. ABC Fund Limited will pay CP interest and receive asset performance on this Swap. On T+0 ABC Fund Limited will enter into a TRS with PC for nominal value of CP issue, for value T+2. PC will pay asset performance and receive CP maturing interest on this swap.

The term sheet describes the mechanics of the swap arrangement for the synthetic ABCP structure.

This type of structure is a means by which funds can be raised without a true sale structure. The TRS is guaranteed by the sponsor bank, so will ensure that the conduit is rated at the short-term rating of the sponsor bank. As CP matures, it will be repaid with a roll-over issue of CP, with interest received via the TRS contract. If CP cannot be rolled over, then the PC or the issuer will need to sell assets or referenced notes to repay principal, or otherwise the TRS guarantor will need to cover the repayment.

Essentially, the TRS is the means by which the conduit can be used to secure Libor-flat based funding for the originator, as long as payments under it are guaranteed by a sponsor or guarantor bank. Alternatively, the originator can arrange for a banking institution to provide a stand-by liquidity back-up for the TRS in the event that it cannot roll over maturing CP. This service would be provided for a fee.

EXAMPLE 19.3 "Golden Claw" synthetic ABCP conduit cash-flow mechanics

Assume the first issue of CP by the Golden Claw structure. The vehicle issues $100 nominal of one-month CP at an all-in price of $99.50. These funds are lent by the vehicle to its purchase company, which uses these funds to buy $99.50 worth of assets synthetically from ABC Fund, in the form of par-priced options referenced to these assets. Simultaneously it enters into a TRS with ABC Fund, for a nominal amount of $100.

On CP maturity, assume that the reference assets are valued at $103. This represents an increase in value of $3. ABC Fund will pay this increase in value to the purchase company, which would then pay this, under the terms of the TRS, back to ABC Fund (in practice, this cash flow nets to zero so money actually moves). Also, under the terms of the TRS, ABC Fund pays the maturing CP interest of $0.50, plus any expenses and costs of Golden Claw itself, to the purchase company, which in turn pays this to Golden Claw, enabling it to repay CP interest to investors. The actual nominal amount of the CP issue is repaid by rolling it over (re-issuing it).

If for any reason CP cannot be rolled over on maturity, the full nominal value of the CP must be paid under the terms of the TRS by ABC Fund to the purchase company.

The basket total return swap

Simpler and more straightforward than the structure described in the previous section, a vanilla total return swap (TRS) may be used as a funding tool, but only where the reference assets are transferable and also able to be priced independently. Typically, this instrument is used as a means of securing off-balance sheet financing for assets held (for example) on a market making book. It is most commonly used in this capacity by broker-dealers and securities houses that have little or no access to unsecured or Libor-flat funding. When used for this purpose the TRS is similar to a repo transaction, although there are detail differences. Often a TRS approach is used instead of classic repo when the assets that require funding are less liquid or indeed not really tradeable. These can include lower rated bonds, illiquid bonds such as certain ABS, MBS and CDO securities, and assets such as hedge fund shares.

Bonds that are taken on by the TRS provider must be acceptable to it in terms of credit quality. If no independent price source is available the TRS provider may insist on pricing the assets itself.

As a funding tool the TRS is transacted as follows:

- the broker-dealer swaps out a bond or basket of bonds that it holds to the TRS counterparty (usually a bank), who pays the market price for the security or securities;
- the maturity of the TRS can be for anything from one week to one year or even longer. For longer-dated contracts, a weekly or monthly reset is usually employed, so that the TRS is repriced and cash flows exchanged each week or month;
- the funds that are passed over by the TRS counterparty to the broker-dealer have the economic effect of being a loan to cover the financing of the underlying bonds. This loan is charged at Libor plus a spread;
- at the maturity of the TRS, the broker-dealer will owe interest on funds to the swap counterparty, while the swap counterparty will owe the market performance of the bonds to the broker-dealer if they have increased in price. The two cash flows are netted out;
- for a longer-dated TRS that is reset at weekly or monthly intervals, the broker-dealer will owe the loan interest plus any decrease in basket value to the swap counterparty at the reset date. The swap counterparty will owe any increase in value.

By entering into this transaction the broker-dealer obtains Libor-based funding for a pool of assets it already owns, while the swap counterparty earns Libor plus a spread on funds that are in effect secured by a pool of assets. This transaction takes the original assets off the balance sheet of the broker-dealer during the term of the trade, which may also be desirable.

The broker-dealer can add or remove bonds from or to the basket at each reset date. When this happens the swap counterparty revalues the basket and will hand over more funds or receive back funds as required. Bonds are removed from the basket if they have been sold by the broker-dealer, while new acquisitions can be funded by being placed in the TRS basket.

We illustrate a funding TRS trade using an example. Figure 19.5 on pages 938–9 shows a portfolio of five hypothetical convertible bonds on the balance sheet of a broker-dealer. The spreadsheet also shows market prices. This portfolio has been swapped out to a TRS provider in a six-month, weekly reset TRS contract. The TRS bank has paid over the combined market value of the portfolio at a lending rate of 1.14125%. This represents

Market rates	
EUR/USD FX Rate	1.266550
US$ 1-w Libor	1.4055

Name	Currency	Nominal value	Price	Accrued
ABC Telecom	EUR	16,000,000	111.671%	0.8169%
XYZ Bank	USD	17,000,000	128.113%	1.7472%
XTC Utility	EUR	45,000,000	102.334%	0.3135%
SPG Corporation	EUR	30,000,000	100.32500	
Watty Exploited	USD	15,000,000	114.997%	0.7594%

Payments		
Interest ($)		
Rate	0.000000%	
Principle	151,080,000.00	
Interest payable	+0.00	
Performance ($)		
New portfolio value	151,080,621.72	
Old portfolio value	n/a	
Performance payment	n/a	
Net payment ($)		
Broker-dealer receives from swap counterparty	+0.00	
New loan		
Portfolio additions ($)	0.00	
New loan amount ($)	151,080,621.72	
New interest rate	1.141250%	1-w Libor + 7 bps

Figure 19.5 Spreadsheet showing basket of bonds used in TRS funding trade

Amount	FX rate	ISIN / CUSIP code	Market price	Accrued interest
22,795,534.57	1.2666		111.6713875	0.81693989
22,076,259.03	1.0000		128.113125	1.74722222
58,845,000.00	1.2666		102.3337875	0.31352459
30,000,325.00	1.2666		100.325	0
17,363,503.12	1.0000		114.9973125	0.759375
151,080,621.72				

EUR/USD	**1.2431**			
Bond	**Curr**	**Nominal value**	**Price**	**Accrued**
ABC Telecom	EUR	16,000,000	111.5000%	0.78%
XYZ Bank	USD	17,000,000	125.0000%	1.58%
XTC Utility	EUR	45,000,000	113.0000%	0.28%
SPG Corporation	EUR	30,000,000	100.75	
Watty Exploited	USD	15,000,000	113.0620%	0.63%

Payments		
Interest		
Rate	1.14125%	1-w Libor + 7 bps
Amount	151,080,000.00	151,113,526.12
Interest payable	33,526.12	
Performance		
Old portfolio value	151,080,000.00	
New portfolio value	154,498,511.95	
Performance payment	**(3,418,511.95)**	
Swap ctpy pays	**(3,384,985.83)**	[if negative, swap counterparty pays; if positive, broker-dealer pays
New loan		
Additions	0.00	← Net payment
New loan amount	**154,498,511.95**	
New interest rate	1.14875%	

Figure 19.6 Spreadsheet showing basket of bonds at TRS reset date plus performance and interest payments due from each TRS counterparty

Amount	FX	ISIN/CUSIP	Market price	Accrued
22,331,239	1.2431		111.5	0.77595628
21,518,931	1		125	1.58194444
63,369,825	1.2431		113	0.28278689
30,225,000	1.2431		100.75	
17,053,518.2	1		113.0619965	0.628125
154,498,511.95				

Old portfolio value: +151,080,951.67 US$
Interest rate: 1.14125%
Interest payable by broker-dealer +33,526.33 US$

New portfolio value: +154,498,511 US$
Performance: 3,418,511 US$

EUR/USD 1.228

Name	Curr	Nominal	Price	Accrued	Amount	FX	Isin	Price	Accrued
ABC Telecom	EUR	16,000,000	111.5000%	0.78%	22,331,239	1.2431		111.5	0.77595628
XYZ Bank	USD	17,000,000	125.0000%	1.58%	21,518,931	1		125	1.58194444
XTC Utility	EUR	45,000,000	113.0000%	0.28%	63,369,825	1.2431		113	0.28278689
SPG Corporation	EUR	30,000,000	100.75		30,225,000	1.2431		100.75	
Watty Exploited	USD	15,000,000	113.0620%	0.00628125	17,053,518	1		113.061996	0.628125
Lloyd Cole Funding	USD	15,000,000	112.0923%	0.57%	16,899,628	1		112.092313	0.571875
			171,398,140.07						

Payments		
Interest		
Rate	1.14875%	1W Libor + 7bps
Amount	154,498,511.95	
Interest payable	34,510.03	
Performance		
Old portfolio value	154,498,511.95	
New portfolio value	171,398,140.07	
Performance payment	(16,899,628.12)	
Swap ctpy pays	(16,865,118.09)	
New loan		
Additions	16,899,628.12	
New loan amount	171,398,140.07	
New interest rate	1.22750%	

Figure 19.7 TRS basket value after addition of new bond

one-week Libor plus 7 basis points. We assume the broker-dealer usually funds at above this level, and that this rate is an improvement on its normal funding. It is not unusual for this type of trade to be undertaken even if the funding rate is not an improvement, however, for diversification reasons.

We see from Figure 19.5 that the portfolio has a current market value of approximately USD151,080,000. This value is lent to the broker-dealer in return for the bonds.

One week later the TRS is reset. We see from Figure 19.6 on pages 940–1, that the portfolio has increased in market value since the last reset. Therefore the swap counterparty pays this difference over to the broker-dealer. This payment is netted out with the interest payment due from the broker-dealer to the swap counterparty. The interest payment is shown as USD33,526.

Figure 19.7 shows the basket after the addition of new bond, and the resultant change in portfolio value.

Structured funding vehicles: Repo conduit

As a result of their requirements for greater funding diversity, banks and financial institutions now make increasing use of cash structured vehicles to raise funds and generate liquidity. In this section we describe one of the latest structures worked on by the author in the US dollar and euro markets.

Securities repo conduit

There are various forms of a repo-based structured funding vehicle that provide efficient funding of a securities portfolio, known as a securities repo conduit. This is used to provide funding for a wide range of assets, including residential mortgages, commercial mortgages, structured finance securities such as student loan ABS, and existing conduit vehicles.[1] It is an on-balance sheet funding mechanism, and is similar to a CP conduit, but with added flexibility both on its asset and liability side. It provides access to the CP market but without the requirement of a back-up bank liquidity facility, because the conduit is supported by the pool of assets that are being financed. As such it enables the originator to reduce its reliance on CP and repo dealers, while also guaranteeing access to the market during times of market disruption.

---

[1] See Chapter 3 for background on CP conduits.

Structure

The securities repo conduit is essentially a means by which an investment bank, via a separate legal entity or via its own balance sheet, will provide a "warehouse" funding vehicle for a client that wishes to finance a pool of assets.

The structure is designed as follows: a separate legal entity (the SPV) is set up as a bankruptcy-remote funding vehicle, which is the issuer. Thereafter:

- the issuer issues short-term notes, termed loan notes or asset-backed loan notes (ABNs) that are issued at A–1/P–1/F–1 or better,[2] which are backed by repo agreements between it and the client entity;
- the client will repo securities out to the issuer, which act as the collateral for the ABNs. The amount of collateral will be equal to the value of notes issues plus an additional amount as credit enhancement;
- the repo provides sufficient funds to pay off the ABNs on maturity, with the repo and ABNs being set with identical maturities;
- the repo between the issuer and the client will allow for the repo securities (collateral) to be bankruptcy-remote from the fortunes of the client.

In effect the ABNs are a repo-backed funding issue rather than a pure asset-backed note issue. It is the repo that provides the security for the ABNs, rather than the underlying securities themselves. So the cash-flow patterns of the underlying securities, whatever type they are, are not strictly relevant to the security-backing of the ABN issue.

Figure 19.8 shows the structure diagram.

[2] The top S&P and Fitch short-term credit ratings are A-1+ and F-1+.

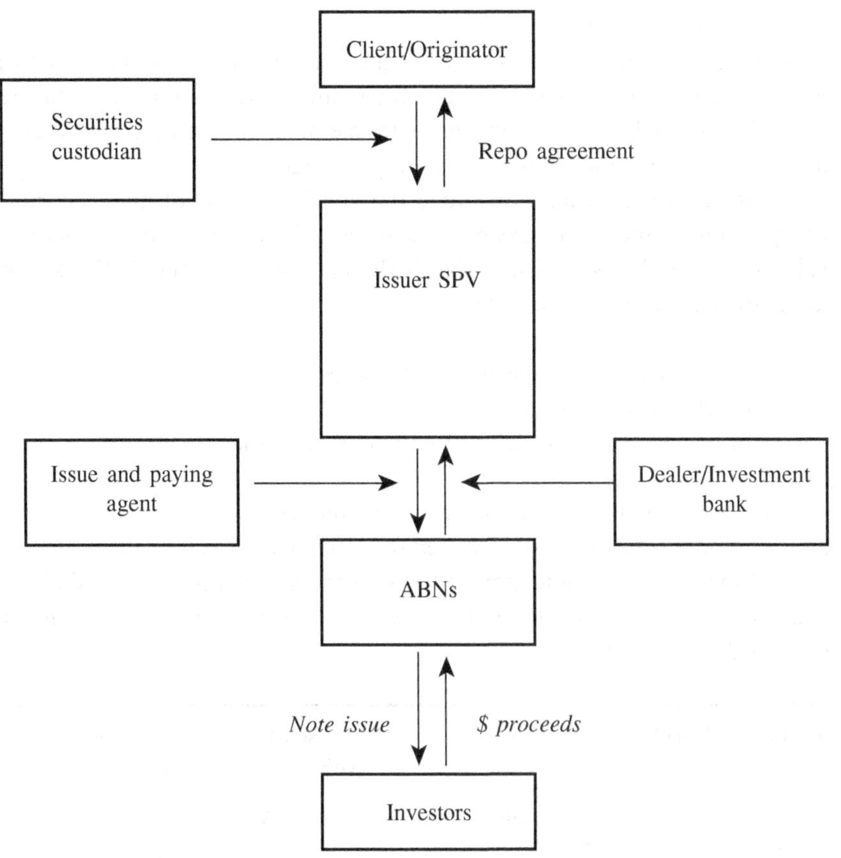

Figure 19.8 Securities repo conduit structure

The terms of an ABN issue might look something like this:

Instrument type:	Discount paper
Maturity:	30–270 days (USD); 364 days (EUR, GBP)
Legal final maturity:	[30] days after expected final maturity
Rate:	Libor minus [5–7] basis points (excluding dealer fee)
Repo terms:	Equal nominal value plus haircut Identical maturity date

The repo agreement is entered into simultaneously with any ABN issue, and is the security backing for the ABN.

Credit enhancement

A key element of securitisation technology is the concept of credit enhancement, which is set to achieve the required credit rating. A securities repo conduit will employ one or both methods of credit enhancement, namely over-collateralisation and a swap arrangement.

Through over-collateralisation, the market value of the securities assigned under the repo agreement is set at a higher level of the nominal value of the ABN issue. This value is the margin or "haircut". The size of the haircut is based on the following:

- credit quality of securities being repoed;
- overall market liquidity;
- historical price volatility of collateral securities.

The repo side of the transaction is marked-to-market on a regular basis and additional collateral will be called for if the haircut value falls during the term of the trade. An indication of the size of expected haircut for different classes of security is shown in Table 19.1, which outlines the levels described by Moody's.

Maturity	RMBS		CMBS		Credit card ABS		Manufactured housing	
	Aaa	Aa2	Aaa	Aa2	Aaa	Aa2	Aaa	Aa2
1 year	3.4%	3.9%	3.4%	4.1%	3.1%	3.7%	4.8%	5.6%
5 years	15.5%	16.3%	15.7%	17.8%	13.7%	15.5%	17.0%	22.1%
10 years	19.1%	21.2%	21.4%	24.3%	17.4%	19.6%	21.0%	26.5%

Table 19.1 Example of haircut value for security type
Source: Moody's. Reproduced with permission.

The other method of credit enhancement is a swap arrangement. Under this, a swap counterparty that is rated at least A–1+/P–1/F–1+ and AA–/AA–/Aa3 will be contracted to cover the market risk of the collateral. The swap is set for a fixed term, say three or five years; at all times the notional value of the swap will be equal to the total value of outstanding collateral in the repo facility. The maximum such size is the total issuance under the conduit.

The swap payment profile under a regular-setting market value swap is:

- the issuer pays to the swap counterparty any upside performance received from sale of securities;
- the swap counterparty pays to the issuer any shortfall in the market value of the securities incurred by the sale of said securities.

A mirror arrangement is put in place between the swap counterparty and both the originator and the issue.

The swap cash flows are shown in Figure 19.9.

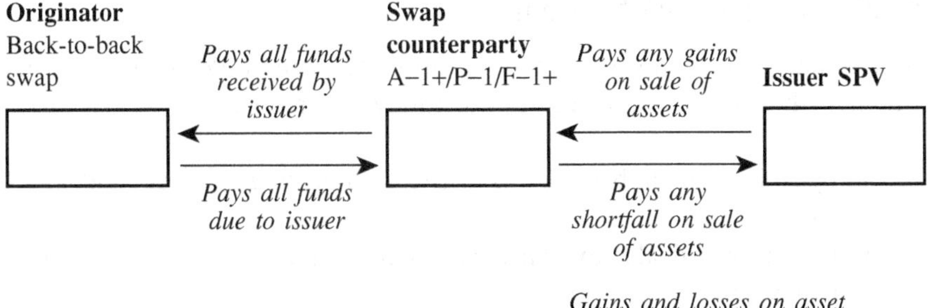

Figure 19.9 Securities repo conduit, swap arrangement: structure of cash flows

Synthetic repackaging structures

Repackaging structures or "repacks" were introduced in the cash securitisation market first, before also becoming a feature of the synthetic markets. In its simplest form, a repack is an underlying security or group of securities that have been packaged-up and transformed into a new note or class of notes that are more attractive to investors than the original securities. This may have been done because the original security has become illiquid or otherwise not tradeable.[3] Repacks were originally classed as "single-asset" or "multi-asset" repacks according to how many underlying securities they represented. A single-asset repack would be a repackaging of just one security. Multi-asset repacks contained a pool of securities and may be considered prototype CDOs. They are not strictly speaking securitisations in the true sense because there is no sale of the underlying securities into a bankruptcy-remote SPV.

[3] For instance, one of the first repacks was of Japanese convertible bonds. With the bear market in Japanese equities during the 1990s, these became illiquid as they no longer were attractive to investors. Individual convertibles or groups of convertibles were packaged up, often with an enhanced coupon or additional new features of attraction added on, and sold on to new investors.

In the synthetic market, investment banks have also structured repacks using credit derivatives. Often this will be done to transform a particular feature of an existing bond (or bonds) in ways other than to make it more attractive to new investors; for example, to transfer an existing credit exposure or to reduce balance sheet capital requirements. In other words, synthetic market repacks make use of the credit derivatives market to hedge out risk exposure on other bonds, which are frequently also structured products.

Synthetic repack motivations

A synthetic repack uses funded or unfunded credit derivatives in its structure. It may be originated for the following reasons:

- by an investment bank that is tasked with making an asset "tradeable" again;
- by a broker-dealer to transform a current interest-rate or credit risk exposure;
- by a portfolio manager looking to extract value from assets currently held on the balance sheet or assets in the market that are trading below fair value.

The assets in question are often existing structured finance securities, such as CDO notes or CLNs. Hence, if the repack vehicle SPV issues securities, this will be a repack of securities issued by another SPV. Hence, a repack structure is usually similar in certain respects to a synthetic CDO and often targeted at the same class of investors.

Example deal structure

To illustrate the mechanics of a synthetic repack, we present an hypothetical transaction that is a repack of a synthetic CDO. The repack has been structured by an investment bank, ABC Securities Limited, to hedge a position it holds in the junior tranche of a CDO. Through this transaction the bank hedges the credit risk exposure in its existing holding, while also meeting the needs of client investors who seek an exposure to the risk-reward profile the repack represents.

It is necessary to describe first the original synthetic CDO deal. We then consider the motivation behind and structure of the repack.

All names and situations quoted are of course fictitious.

CASE STUDY 19.1 Synthetic CDO: Black Island Finance Ltd

The underlying CDO is a fully unfunded synthetic CDO ("Black Island Finance Ltd"). This is a CDO originated on a pool of 100% risk-weighted bank assets, with the credit risk and regulatory capital requirements of the assets transferred via a tranched series of credit default swaps to investors. Figure 19.10 shows the structure of Black Island Finance Ltd.

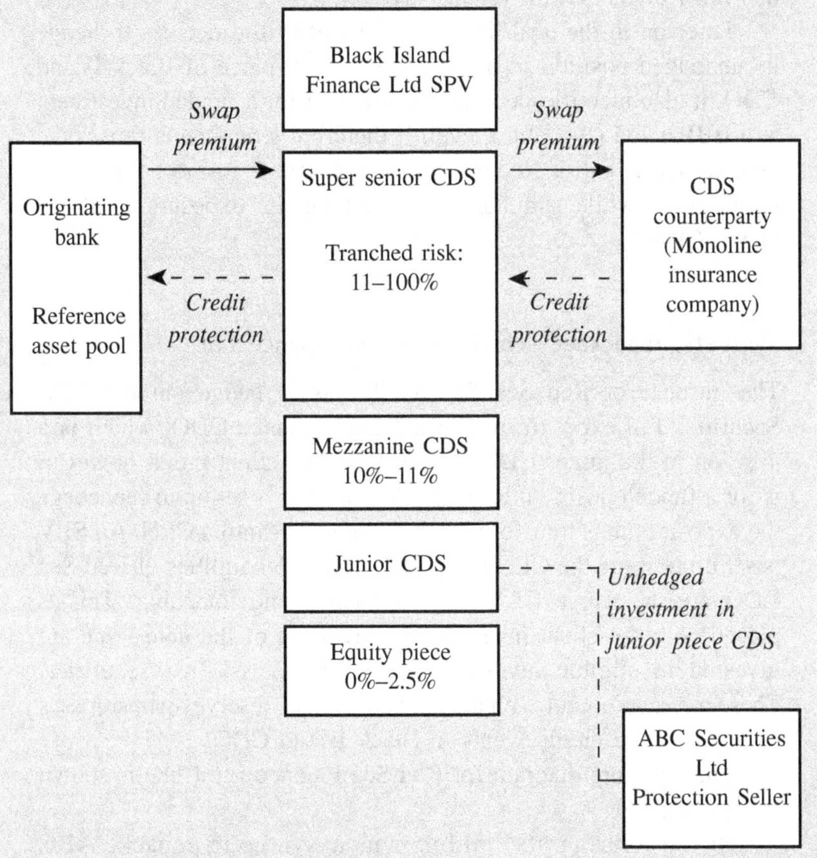

Figure 19.10 Black Island Finance Ltd, hypothetical unfunded synthetic CDO

The liabilities of the CDO are split into a series of credit default swaps (CDS), which pay a premium based on their seniority. If there are any credit events among reference assets then the nominal amounts of the CDS contracts is reduced (thereby reducing the interest receivable by protection sellers) in order of priority. On issue, ABC Securities invests in the junior tranche of Black Island CDO. This represents the 2.5% to 10% tranche of risk in the reference pool. Assume it is at BBB level and so would represent this level of risk-return for the investor.

Later on in the deal life, ABC Securities Ltd decides to hedge its unhedged position in the 2.5%–10% risk piece of Black Island CDO. It also identifies a client requirement for a funded investment at a BBB-rated risk-return level. It therefore structures a repackage vehicle, let us call it Red Sea Finance Limited, to meet this client requirement while simultaneously hedging its exposure in Black Island CDO.[4]

Synthetic repackage vehicle: Red Sea Finance Ltd

The purpose of Red Sea Finance Ltd is to hedge out the ABC Securities Ltd exposure in Black Island Finance CDO, which is a position in the junior CDS of that deal. The client order, however, is for a funded position. Red Sea Finance Ltd is set up to repackage the exposure, thus transforming it from a CDS into a CLN. An SPV is set up to issue the CLN to the investor. The liabilities of Red Sea CDO are the single CLN; that is, there is no tranching. This is placed with the client investor. The proceeds of the note issue are invested in eligible investments, which are risk-free securities. These are repo'ed out with a bank and act as a reserve against losses suffered due to credit events in Black Island CDO.

The structure diagram for Red Sea Finance Ltd CDO is shown at Figure 19.11.

By structuring its holding via a synthetic repack, ABC Securities has transferred its credit risk exposure in its initial investment, while also meeting the needs of its client.

---

4 The author has no qualms in admitting that he is a keen fan of the works of Georges Remi, specifically the adventures of *Tintin*.

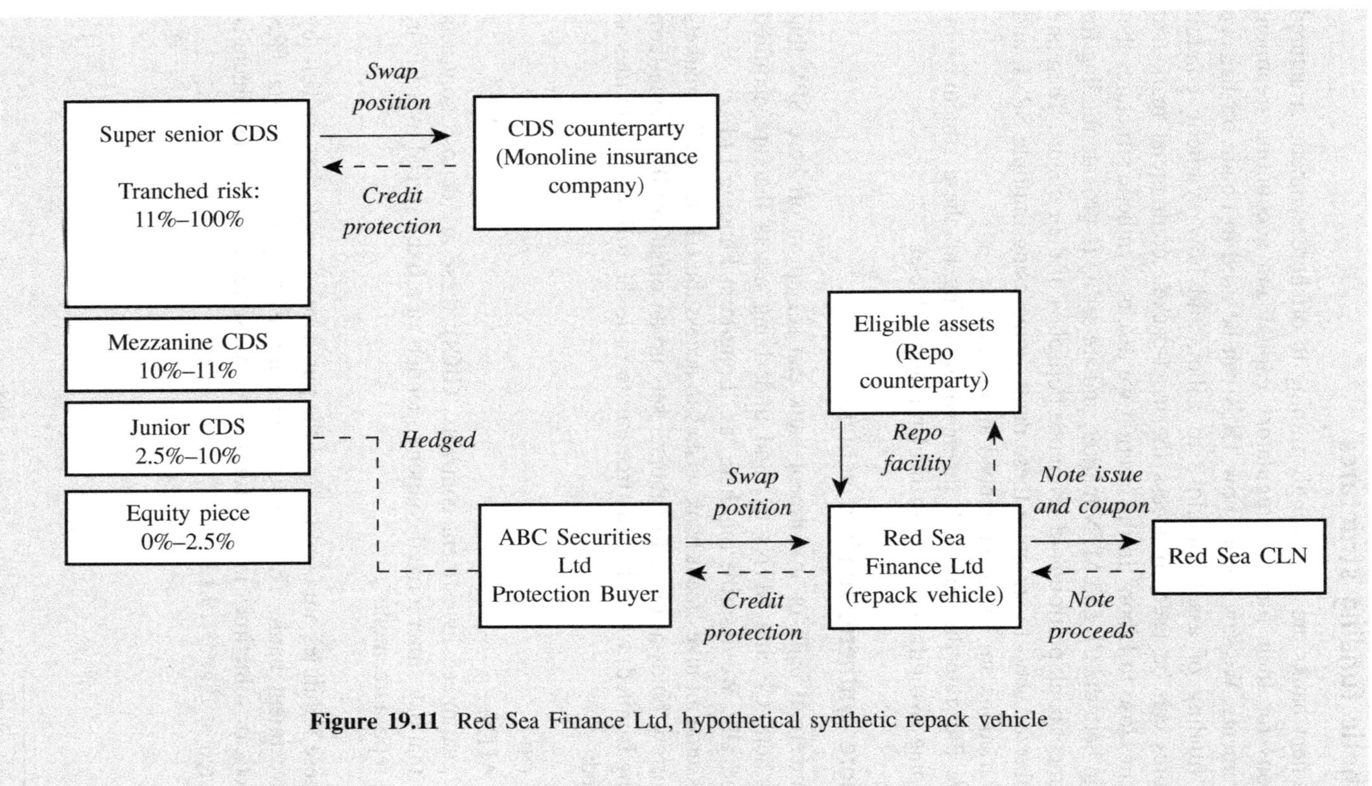

Figure 19.11 Red Sea Finance Ltd, hypothetical synthetic repack vehicle

Synthetic funding structures

Investment banks are increasingly turning to offshore synthetic structured solutions for their funding, regulatory capital and accounting treatment requirements. We saw earlier how TRSs can be used to obtain off-balance sheet funding of assets at close to Libor, and how synthetic conduit structures can be used to access the asset-backed commercial market at Libor or close to Libor.[5] In this section we discuss synthetic structures that issue in both the CP and MTN market, and are set up to provide funding for investment bank portfolios or reference portfolios of their clients. There are a number of ways to structure these deals, some using multiple SPVs, and new variations are being introduced all the time.

We illustrate the approach taken when setting up these structures by describing two different hypothetical funding vehicles.

Offshore synthetic funding vehicle

A commercial bank or investment bank can set up an offshore SPV that issues both CP and MTNs to fund underlying assets that are acquired synthetically. We describe this here, as "Long-term Funding Ltd".

Assume an investment bank wishes to access the CP and MTN markets and borrow funds at close to Libor. It sets up an offshore SPV, Long-term Funding Limited, which has the freedom to issue the following liabilities as required:

- CP;
- MTNs;
- guaranteed investment contracts (GICs): these are deposit contracts that pay either a fixed coupon to lenders or a fixed spread over Libor;
- repo agreements.

These liabilities are used to fund the purchase of assets that are held by the investment bank. These assets are purchased synthetically via TRS contracts, or sometimes in cash form as a reverse repo trade. The vehicle is illustrated at Figure 19.12.

[5] For more information on ABCP, see Choudhry (2004c)

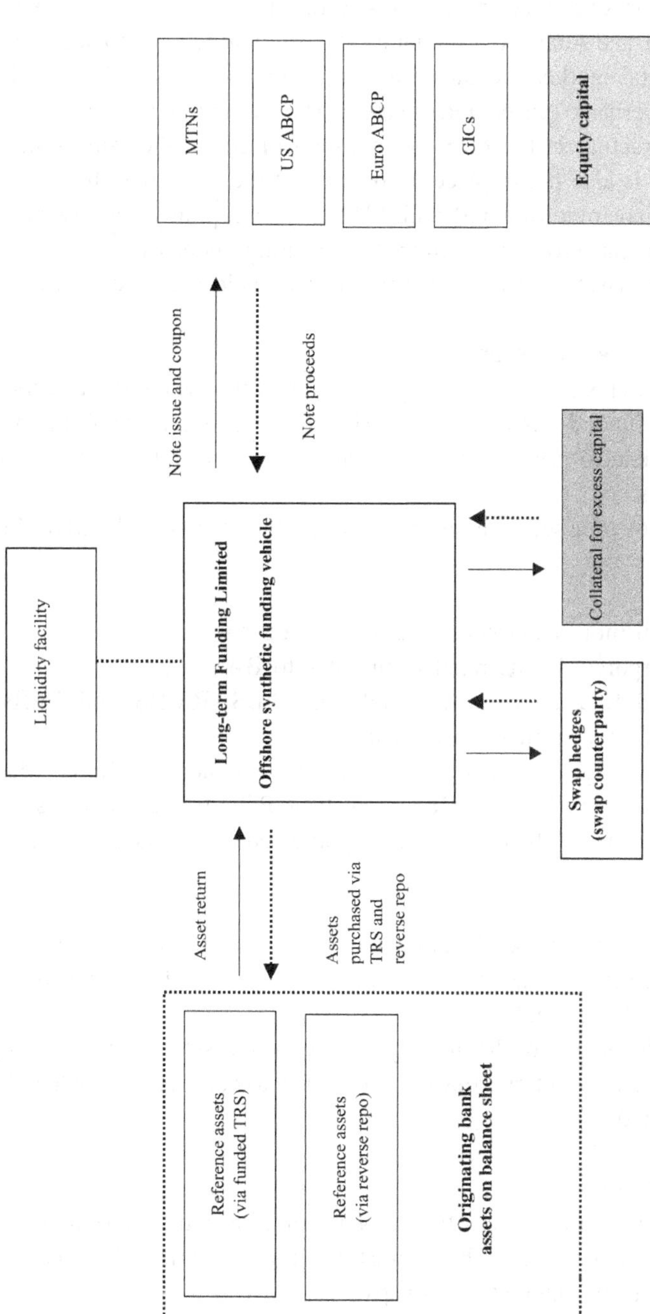

Vehicle capital structure
MTNs maximum $5,000 million (Aaa/AAA)
USCP maximum $4,000 million (A–1/F–1)
ECP maximum $1,000 million (A–1/F–1)

Figure 19.12 Long-term Funding Ltd, offshore synthetic funding vehicle

The vehicle is structured in such a way that the liabilities it issues are rated at A–1/F–1 and Aaa/AAA. It enables the originating bank to access the money and capital markets at rates that are lower than it would otherwise obtain in the interbank (unsecured) market. The originator invests its own capital in the structure in the form of an equity piece. At the same time, a liquidity facility is also put in place, to be used in the event that the vehicle is not able to pay maturing CP and MTNs. The liquidity facility is an additional factor that provides comfort to the rating agencies.

The types of assets and liabilities that can be held are described next.

Underlying reference assets

The vehicle's asset structure is composed of mainly synthetic securities, accessed using funded TRS contracts. However, to retain flexibility the vehicle is also able to bring in assets in cash form in the shape of reverse repo transactions.

Possible types of assets that can be acquired by Long-term Funding Ltd include:

- short-term money market instruments rated AAA;
- bullet corporate bonds rated from AAA to BB;
- structured finance securities including ABS, RMBS and CMBS securities rated from AAA to BB;
- government agency securities such as those issued by Ginnie Mae, Fannie Mae and Freddie Mac, as well as Pfandbriefe securities;
- secondary market bank loans and syndicated loans rated at AAA to BBB.

Reference assets can be denominated in any currency, and currency swaps are entered into hedge currency mismatch, as the vehicle only issues liabilities in US dollars and euros.

As well as the quality of the underlying reference assets, the credit rating of the TRS and repo counterparties is also taken into consideration when the liabilities are rated.

Liability transactions

Long-term Funding Ltd finances the purchase of TRS and reverse repos by issuing CP, MTNs and GICs. The interest-rate risk that arises from issuing GICs is hedged using interest-rate swaps.

The ability of Long-term Funding Ltd to issue different types of liabilities means that the originating bank can access funding at any maturity from one-month to very long term, and across a variety of sources. For instance, CP may be bought by banks, corporates, money market funds and super-national institutions such as the World Bank; GIC contracts are frequently purchased by insurance companies and CDO vehicles.

Multi-SPV synthetic conduit funding structure

One of the main drivers behind the growth of synthetic funding structures has been the need for banks to reduce regulatory capital charges. While this has been achieved by setting up an offshore SPV that issues liabilities and references assets synthetically, recent changes in accounting treatment for SPVs means that this approach may not be sufficient for some institutions.[6] The structure we describe here can reference an entire existing SPV synthetically, in effect a synthetic transfer of assets that have already been synthetically transferred. The vehicle would be used by banks or fund managers to obtain funding and capital relief for an entire existing portfolio without having to move any of the assets themselves.

The key to the synthetic multi-SPV conduit is the CP and MTN issuance vehicle, which is a stand-alone vehicle established by a commercial or investment bank. This provides funding to an existing SPV or SPVs, and acquires the assets of the assets synthetically. The assets are deemed as being held within the structure and as such attract a 0% risk-weighting under Basel I.

The structure is illustrated in Figure 19.13 on page 956.

[6] We refer to new US accounting rules on consolidating SPVs that are not deemed truly arms-length, part of FASB 142. This was partly a response to the Enron affair, which uncovered the use of SPVs for less-than-savoury purposes. While we discuss a new synthetic structure that would enable banks to maintain separate accounting treatment for offshore companies, the subject of accounting treatment is outside the scope of this book.

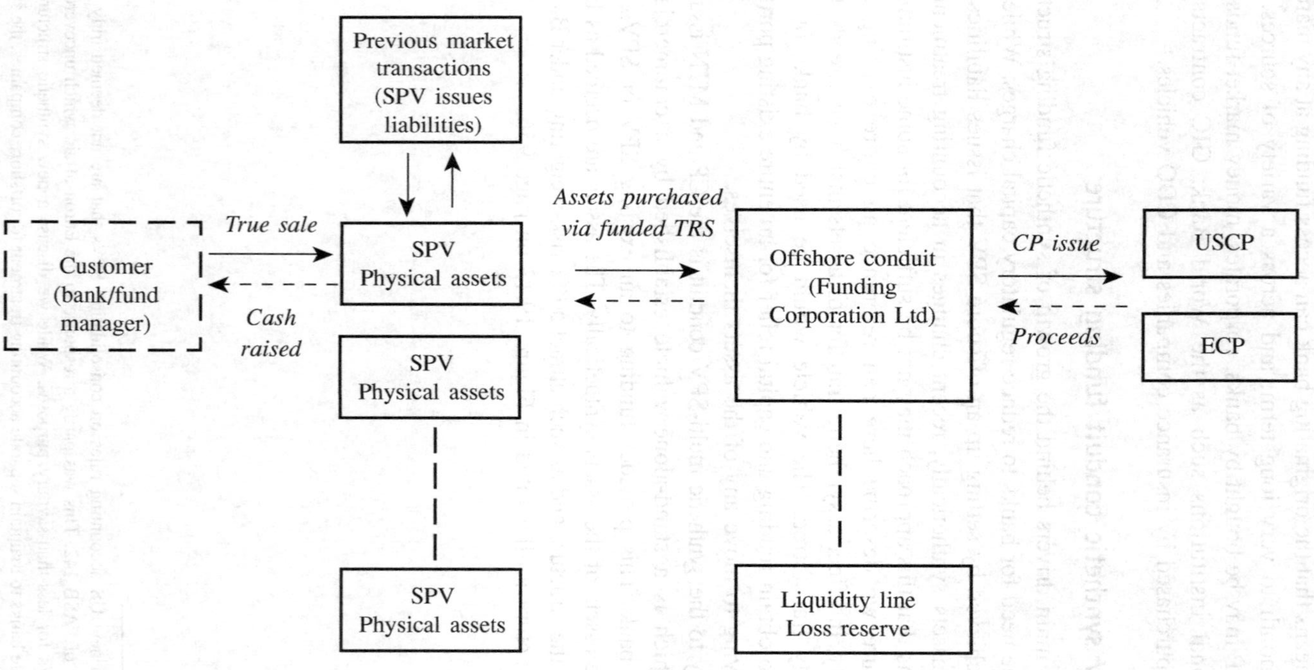

Figure 19.13 Multi-SPV offshore synthetic conduit funding structure

This structure has the following features:

- an offshore SPV that issues CP into the US and Euro markets;
- a synthetic purchase of the entire balance sheet of an existing SPV; the funds issued in the CP market are used to provide a funded TRS contract to the SPV whose assets are being funded;
- the customer realises funds and also retains the return on the assets; however, it benefits from reduced capital charge and there is no more necessity to mark-to-market the assets;
- the investment bank originator, and CP investors (in that order), offers to wear any losses on the reference portfolio due to credit events or default, and earns a fee income for setting up this facility;
- assets and additional SPVs can be added at any time;
- a liquidity facility is in place in the event that CP cannot be issued.

This structure is yet another illustration of the flexibility of credit derivatives, and structured credit products created from credit derivatives, in the debt capital markets today.

Combined referenced note and TRS funding structure

For a number of reasons, entities such as hedge funds or other investment companies, whether they are independent entities or part of a banking or bancassurance conglomerate, are not able to obtain funding from mainstream banks directly. Hedge funds, for example, are commonly funded via a prime brokerage facility set up with banks. Put simply, under a prime brokerage the provider of the facility holds the assets of the hedge fund in custody, and these assets act as security collateral against which funds are advanced. These funds are used by the hedge fund to pay for the assets it has purchased, and are lent by the prime broker at a spread over Libor, typically 50–70 basis points. The prime broker also lends assets to cover short positions. In both cases margin is required by the prime broker.

Many investment companies hold positions in illiquid assets, such as hedge fund of funds shares, or other difficult-to-trade assets. It is more difficult to raise funds in the wholesale markets using such assets as collateral, because of the problem associated with transferring them to the custody of the cash lender. The advent of credit derivatives and financial engineering has enabled companies to get around this problem by setting up tailor-made structures for funding purposes. Here we describe an example of a funding or liquidity structure that raises cash in the wholesale market via a note and TRS structure that references a basket of illiquid assets.

Assume two entities that are part of a bancassurance group: a regulated broker-dealer ("Smith Securities") and a hedge fund derivative investment house ("Smith Investments Company"). The investment house raises funds primarily from its parent banking group; however, for diversity purposes it also wishes to raise funds from other sources. One such source is the wholesale markets, via a note and TRS structure, illustrated in Figure 19.14.

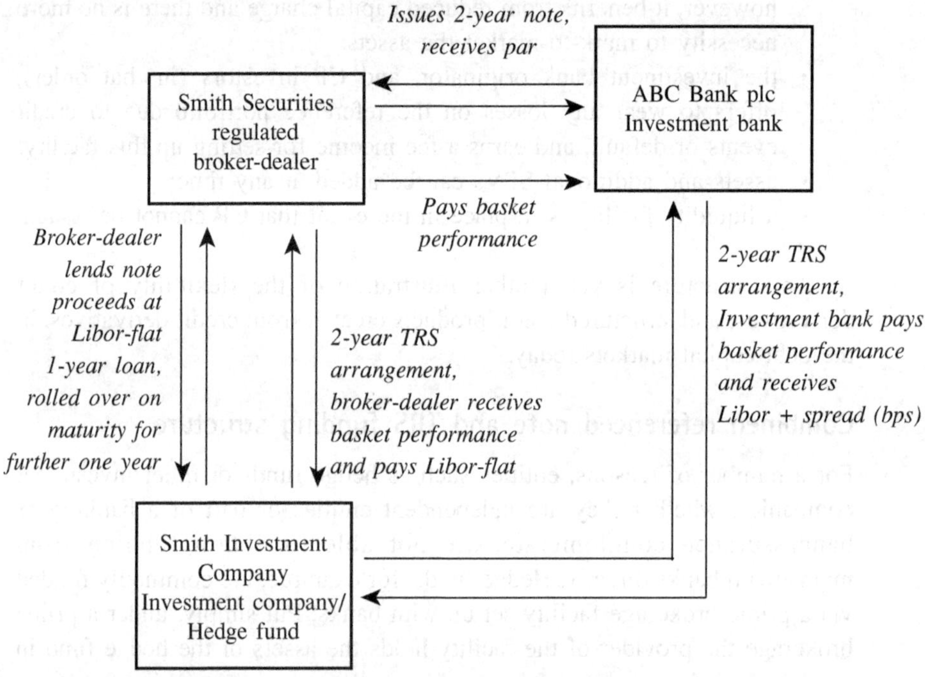

Figure 19.14 Combined note and TRS funding structure

The lender is an investment bank ("ABC Bank plc"). It is willing to advance funds to the investment company, secured by its assets, at a rate of Libor plus 20 basis points. This is a considerable saving on the investment company's cost of funds with a prime broker, and comparable with its parent group funding rate. However, its assets cannot be transferred as they are untradeable assets, and so cannot act as collateral in the normal way one observes in, say, repo trades.

Instead we structure the following in order to enable the funding to be raised:

- ABC Bank plc does not lend funds directly, instead it purchases a two-year note at a price of par. The return on this note is linked to the performance of a basket of assets held by Smith Investment Company. As Smith Investment Company is an unregulated entity, it cannot issue a note into the wholesale markets. Therefore the note is issued by its sister company, Smith Securities;
- the funds raised by the sale of the note are transferred, in the form of a loan, from Smith Securities to Smith Investment Company at Libor-flat;
- simultaneously the two companies enter into a TRS arrangement, with start and maturity dates matching that of the note. Under this TRS, Smith Securities receives the performance of the basket of assets and pays Libor-flat;
- also simultaneously, Smith Investment Company and ABC Bank plc enter into a TRS arrangement whereby the bank pays the performance of the basket of assets, and receives Libor plus 20 basis points.

The net cash flow of this structure is that Smith Investment Company pays ABC Bank plc Libor plus 20 basis points, and raises funds via the proceeds of the note issue by Smith Securities. The economic effect is that of a two-year loan from ABC Bank to Smith Investment Company, but because of legal, regulatory, operational and administrative restrictions we need to have the structure described above to effect this.

Note that under some jurisdictions, it is not possible for group companies to make inter-company loans, particularly if the two companies are incorporated in different countries, without attracting withholding tax on the loan. For example, it may be that inter-company loans must be of under one-year maturity. To get around this, in Figure 19.14 we have shown the loan from Smith Securities to be a one-year loan, which is then rolled over for another year on maturity.

References and bibliography

Choudhry, M. 2004a, *Fixed Income Markets: Instruments, Applications, Mathematics*, John Wiley & Sons, Singapore.

Choudhry, M. 2004b, *Structured Credit Products: Credit Derivatives and Synthetic Securitisation*, John Wiley & Sons, Singapore.

Choudhry, M. 2004c, *The Money Markets: A Practitioner's Guide*, John Wiley & Sons, Singapore.

CHAPTER

20

Mortgage-backed Securities and Covered Bonds

In this chapter we consider mortgage-backed securities, the largest of the asset-backed bond markets. They are very important instruments for use in the undertaking of bank ALM.[1]

Mortgage-backed securities

A mortgage is a loan made for the purpose of purchasing property, which in turn is used as the security for the loan itself. It is defined as a debt instrument giving conditional ownership of an asset, and secured by the asset that is being financed. The borrower provides the lender a mortgage in exchange for the right to use the property during the term of the mortgage, and agrees to make regular payments of both principal and interest. The mortgage lien is the security for the lender, and is removed when the debt is paid off. A mortgage may involve residential property or commercial property and is a long-term debt, normally 25 to 30 years; however, it can be drawn up for shorter periods if required by the borrower. If the borrower or *mortgagor* defaults on the interest payments, the lender or *mortgagee* has the right to take over the property and recover the debt from the proceeds of selling the property. Mortgages can be either fixed-rate or floating-rate interest. Although in the United States mortgages are generally amortising loans, known as *repayment* mortgages, in the United Kingdom there are also *interest-only* mortgages where the borrower only pays the interest on the loan; on maturity the original loan amount is paid off by the proceeds of a

[1] Many texts place MBS in a separate category, distinct from asset-backed bonds (for example, see the highly recommended Fabozzi [1998]). Market practitioners also tend to make this distinction. Generally, the market is viewed as being composed of MBS and ABS (which encompass all other asset types).

maturing investment contract taken out at the same time as the mortgage. These are known as *endowment* mortgages and are popular in the UK market, although their popularity has been waning in recent years.

A lending institution may have many hundreds of thousands of individual residential and commercial mortgages on its book. If the total loan book is pooled together and used as collateral for the issue of a bond, the resulting instrument is a mortgage-backed security (MBS). This process is known as *securitisation*, which is the pooling of loan assets in order to use them as collateral for a bond issue. An SPV is set up specifically to serve as the entity representing the pooled assets. This is done for administrative reasons and also sometimes to enhance the credit rating that may be assigned to the bonds. In the United Kingdom some SPVs have a triple-A credit rating, although the majority of SPVs are below this rating, while retaining investment grade status. In the US market, certain MBSs are backed, either implicitly or explicitly, by the government, in which case they trade essentially as risk-free instruments and are not rated by the credit agencies. In the United States a government agency, the Government National Mortgage Association (GNMA, known as "Ginnie Mae") and two government-sponsored agencies, the Federal Home Loan Corporation and the Federal National Mortgage Association ("Freddie Mac" and "Fannie Mae" respectively), purchase mortgages for the purpose of pooling them and holding them in their portfolios; they may then be securitised. Bonds that are not issued by government agencies are rated in the same way as other corporate bonds. On the other hand, non-government agencies sometimes obtain mortgage insurance for their issue, in order to boost its credit quality. When this happens the credit rating of the mortgage insurer becomes an important factor in the credit standing of the bond issue.

Mortgages

In the US market, the terms of a conventional mortgage, known as a *level-payment fixed-rate mortgage*, will state the interest rate payable on the loan, the term of the loan and the frequency of payment. Most mortgages specify monthly payment of interest. These are in fact the characteristics of a level-payment mortgage, which has a fixed interest rate and fixed term to maturity. This means that the monthly interest payments are fixed, hence the term "level-pay".

The singular feature of a mortgage is that, even if it charges interest at a fixed rate, its cash flows are not known with absolute certainty. This is because the borrower can elect to repay any or all of the principal before the final maturity date. This is a characteristic of all mortgages, and although some lending institutions impose a penalty on borrowers who retire the loan early, this is a risk for the lender, known as *prepayment risk*. The uncertainty of the cash-flow patterns is similar to that of a callable bond, and as we shall see later this feature means that we may value mortgage-backed bonds using a pricing model similar to that employed for callable bonds.

The monthly interest payment on a conventional fixed-rate mortgage is given by (20.3), which is derived from the conventional present value analysis used for an annuity. Essentially, the primary relationship is:

$$M_{m0} = I\left(\frac{1 - [1/(1+r)^n]}{r}\right) \tag{20.1}$$

from which we can derive:

$$I = \frac{M_{m0}}{\dfrac{1 - [\,1/(1+r)^n\,]}{r}}\,. \tag{20.2}$$

This is simplified to:

$$I = M_{m0}\,\frac{r(1+r)^n}{(1+r)^n - 1} \tag{20.3}$$

where

M_{m0} is the original mortgage balance (the cash amount of loan)
I is the monthly cash mortgage payment
r is the simple monthly interest rate, given by (annual interest rate/12)
n is the term of the mortgage in months.

The monthly repayment includes both the interest servicing and a repayment of part of the principal. In Example 20.1, after the 264th interest payment, the balance will be zero and the mortgage will have been paid off. Since a portion of the original balance is paid off every month, the interest payment reduces by a small amount each month; that is, the proportion of the monthly payment dedicated to repaying the principal steadily increases. The remaining mortgage balance for any particular month during the term of the mortgage may be calculated using (20.4):

$$M_{mt} = M_{m0}\,\frac{(1+r)^n - (1+r)^t}{(1+r)^n - 1} \tag{20.4}$$

where M_{mt} is the mortgage cash balance after t months and n remains the original maturity of the mortgage in months.

The level of interest payment and principal repayment in any one month during the mortgage term can be calculated using the equations below. If we wish to calculate the value of the principal repayment in a particular month during the mortgage term, we may use (20.5):

$$p_t = M_{m0} \frac{r(1+r)^{t-1}}{(1+r)^n - 1} \tag{20.5}$$

where p_t is the scheduled principal repayment amount for month t, while the level of interest payment in any month is given by (20.6):

$$i_t = M_{m0} \frac{r(1+r)^n - (1+r)^{t-1}}{(1+r)^n - 1} \tag{20.6}$$

where i_t is the interest payment only in month t.

EXAMPLE 20.1 Mortgage contract calculations

A mortgage borrower enters into a conventional mortgage contract, in which he borrows £72,200 for 22 years at a rate of 7.99%. What is the monthly mortgage payment?

This gives us n equal to 264 and r equal to (0.0799/12) or 0.0066583. Inserting the above terms into (20.3) we have:

$$I = 72{,}200 \left(\frac{0.0066583\ (1.0066583)^{264}}{[(1.0066583)^{264} - 1]} \right)$$

or I equal to £581.60.

The mortgage balance after ten years is given below, where t is 120:

$$M_{m120} = 72{,}200 \left(\frac{[(1.0066583)^{264} - (1.0066583)^{120}]}{(1.0066583)^{264} - 1} \right)$$

or a remaining balance of £53,756.93.

In the same month the scheduled principal repayment amount is:

$$P_{120} = 72{,}200 \left(\frac{[0.0066583\ (1.0066583)^{120-1}]}{[(1.0066583)^{264} - 1]} \right)$$

or £222.19.

The interest only payable in month 120 is shown below:

$$i_{120} = 72{,}200\left(\frac{0.0066583\ [(1.0066583)^{264} - (1.0066583)^{120-1}]}{[(1.0066583)^{264} - 1]}\right)$$

and is equal to £359.41.

The combined mortgage payment is £581.60, as calculated before.

Some mortgage contracts incorporate a *servicing fee*. This is payable to the mortgage provider to cover the administrative costs associated with collecting interest payments, sending regular statements and other information to borrowers, chasing overdue payments, maintaining the records and processing systems and other activities. Mortgage providers also incur costs when repossessing properties after mortgagors have fallen into default. Mortgages may be serviced by the original lender or another third-party institution that has acquired the right to service it, in return for collecting the fee. When a servicing charge is payable by a borrower, the monthly mortgage payment is comprised of the interest costs, the principal repayment and the servicing fee. The fee incorporated into the monthly payment is usually stated as a percentage, say 0.25%. This is added to the mortgage rate.

Another type of mortgage in the US market is the *adjustable-rate mortgage* or ARM, which is a loan in which the interest rate payable is set in line with an external reference rate. The resets are at periodic intervals depending on the terms of the loan, and can be on a monthly, six-monthly or annual basis, or even longer. The interest rate is usually fixed at a spread over the reference rate. The reference rate that is used can be a market-determined rate such as the prime rate, or a calculated rate based on the funding costs for US savings and loan institutions or *thrifts*. The cost of funds for thrifts is calculated using the monthly average funding cost on the thrifts' activities, and there are "thrift indexes" that are used to indicate the cost of funding. The two most common indices are the Eleventh Federal Home Loan Bank Board District Cost of Funds Index (COFI) and the National Cost of Funds Index. Generally, borrowers prefer to fix the rate they pay on their loans to reduce uncertainty, and this makes fixed-rate mortgages more popular than variable rate mortgages. A common incentive used to entice borrowers away from fixed-rate mortgages is to offer a below-market interest rate on an ARM mortgage, usually for an introductory period. This comfort period may be from two to five years or even longer.

Mortgages in the United Kingdom are predominantly *variable rate mortgages*, in which the interest rate is moved in line with the clearing bank base rate. It is rare to observe fixed-rate mortgages in the UK market, although short-term fixed-rate mortgages are more common (the rate reverts to a variable basis at the termination of the fixed-rate period).

A *balloon mortgage* entitles a borrower to long-term funding, but under its terms, at a specified future date the interest rate payable is renegotiated. This effectively transforms a long-dated loan into a short-term borrowing. The balloon payment is the original amount of the loan, minus the amount that is amortised. In a balloon mortgage therefore the actual maturity of the bonds is below that of the stated maturity.

A *graduated payment mortgage* (GPM) is aimed at lower earning borrowers, as the mortgage payments for a fixed initial period, say the first five years, are set at a lower level than would be applicable for a level-paying mortgage with an identical interest rate. The later mortgage payments are higher as a result. Hence, a GPM mortgage will have a fixed term and a mortgage rate, but the offer letter will also contain details on the number of years over which the monthly mortgage payments will increase and the point at which level payments will take over. There will also be information on the annual increase in the mortgage payments. As the initial payments in a GPM are below the market rate, there will be little or no repayment of principal at this time. This means that the outstanding balance may actually increase during the early stages, a process known as *negative amortisation*. The higher payments in the remainder of the mortgage term are designed to pay off the entire balance in maturity. The opposite to the GPM is the *growing equity mortgage* or GEM. This mortgage charges fixed-rate interest but the payments increase over its life; this means that a greater proportion of the principal is paid off over time, so that the mortgage itself is repaid in a shorter period than the level-pay mortgage.

In the UK market it is more common to encounter hybrid mortgages, which charge a combination of fixed-rate and variable-rate interest. For example, the rate may be fixed for the first five years, after which it will vary with changes in the lender's base rate. Such a mortgage is known as a *fixed/adjustable hybrid mortgage*.

Mortgage risk

Although mortgage contracts are typically long-term loan contracts, running for 20 to 30 years or even longer, there is no limitation on the amount of the principal that may be repaid at any one time. In the US market there is no penalty for repaying the mortgage ahead of its term, known as a mortgage prepayment. In the United Kingdom some lenders impose a penalty if a mortgage is prepaid early, although this is more common for contracts that have been offered at special terms, such as a discounted loan rate for the start of the mortgage's life. The penalty is often set as extra interest; for example, six months' worth of mortgage payments at the time when the contract is paid off. As borrowers are free to prepay a mortgage at a time of their choosing, the lender is not certain of the cash flows that will be paid after the contract is taken out. This is known as *prepayment risk.*

A borrower may pay off the principal ahead of the final termination date for a number of reasons. The most common reason is when the property on which the mortgage is secured is subsequently sold by the borrower; this results in the entire mortgage being paid off at once. The average life of a mortgage in the UK market is eight years, and mortgages are most frequently prepaid because the property has been sold.[2] Other actions that result in the prepayment of a mortgage are when a property is repossessed after the borrower has fallen into default, if there is a change in interest rates making it attractive to refinance the mortgage (usually with another lender), or if the property is destroyed due to accident or natural disaster.

An investor acquiring a pool of mortgages from a lender will be concerned at the level of prepayment risk, which is usually measured by projecting the level of expected future payments using a financial model. Although it would not be possible to evaluate meaningfully the potential of an individual mortgage to be paid off early, it is tenable to conduct such analysis for a large number of loans pooled together. A similar activity is performed by actuaries when they assess the future liability of an insurance provider who has written personal pension contracts. Essentially, the level of prepayment risk for a pool of loans is lower than that of an individual mortgage. Prepayment risk has the same type of impact on a mortgage pool's performance and valuation as a call feature does on a callable bond. This is understandable because a mortgage is essentially a callable contract, with the "call" at the option of the borrower of funds.

---

[2] *Source*: Halifax plc.

The other significant risk of a mortgage book is the risk that the borrower will fall into arrears, or be unable to repay the loan on maturity (in the United Kingdom). This is known as *default risk*. Lenders take steps to minimise the level of default risk by assessing the credit quality of each borrower, as well as the quality of the property itself. A study has also found that the higher the deposit paid by the borrower, the lower the level of default.[3] Therefore lenders prefer to advance funds against a borrower's *equity* that is deemed sufficient to protect against falls in the value of the property. In the United Kingdom the typical deposit required is 25%, although certain lenders will advance funds against smaller deposits such as 10% or 5%.

Securities

MBSs are bonds created from a pool of mortgages. They are formed from mortgages that are for residential or commercial property, or a mixture of both. Bonds created from commercial mortgages are known as *commercial mortgage-backed securities*. There are a range of different securities in the market, known in the United States as *mortgage pass-though securities*. There also exist two related securities known as *collateralised mortgage securities* and *stripped mortgage-backed securities*. Bonds that are created from mortgage pools that have been purchased by government agencies are known as *agency mortgage-backed securities*, and are regarded as risk-free in the same way as Treasury securities.

A mortgage-backed bond is created by an entity out of its mortgage book or a book that it has purchased from the original lender (there is very often no connection between a mortgage-backed security and the firm that made the original loans). The mortgage book will have a total nominal value comprised of the total value of all the individual loans. The loans will generate cash flows, consisting of the interest and principal payments, and any prepayments. The regular cash flows are received on the same day each month, so the pool resembles a bond instrument. Therefore bonds may be issued against the mortgage pool. Example 20.2 is a simple illustration of a type of mortgage-backed bond known as a *mortgage pass-through security* in the US market.

[3] Brown, S. et al. 1990, *Analysis of Mortgage Servicing Portfolios*, Financial Strategies Group, Prudential-Bache Capital Funding.

EXAMPLE 20.2 Mortgage pass-through security

An investor purchases a book consisting of 5,000 individual mortgages, with a total repayable value of $500,000,000. The loans are used as collateral against the issue of a new bond, and the cash flows payable on the bond are the cash flows that are received from the mortgages. The issuer sells 1,000 bonds, with a face value of $500,000. Each bond is therefore entitled to 1/1,000 or 0.02% of the cash flows received from the mortgages.

The prepayment risk associated with the original mortgages is unchanged, but any investor can now purchase a bond with a much lower value than the mortgage pool, but with the same level of prepayment risk, which is lower than the risk of an individual loan. This would have been possible if an investor were buying all 100 mortgages, but by buying a bond that represents the pool of mortgages, a smaller cash value is needed to achieve the same performance. The bonds will also be more liquid than the loans, and the investor will be able to realise his investment ahead of the maturity date if he wishes. For these reasons the bonds will trade at higher prices than would an individual loan. A mortgage pass-through security therefore is a way for mortgage lenders to realise additional value from their loan book, and if it is sold to another investor (who issues the bonds), the loans will be taken off the original lender's balance sheet, thus freeing up lending lines for other activities.

A *collateralised mortgage obligation* (CMO) differs from a pass-through security in that the cash flows from the mortgage pool are distributed on a prioritised basis, based on the class of security held by the investor. In Example 20.2 this might mean that three different securities are formed, with a total nominal value of $100 million each entitled to a pro-rata amount of the interest payments, but with different priorities for the repayment of principal. For instance, $60 million of the issue might consist of a bond known as "Class A", which may be entitled to receipt of all the principal repayment cash flows, after which the next class of bonds is entitled to all the repayment cash flow; this bond would be "Class B" bonds, of which, say, $25 million was created and so on. If 300 Class A bonds are created, they will have a nominal value of $200,000 and each will receive 0.33% of the total cash flows received by the Class A bonds. Note that all classes of bonds receive an equal share of the interest payments; it is the principal repayment cash flows received that differ. What is the main effect of this security structure? The most significant factor is that, in our illustration, the Class A bonds will be repaid earlier than any other class of bond that is formed from the securitisation. It therefore has the shortest maturity. The last class of bonds will have the longest maturity. There is still a level of uncertainty associated with the maturity of each bond, but this is less than the uncertainty associated with a pass-through security.

Another type of mortgage bond is the *stripped mortgage-backed security*. As its name suggests, this is created by separating the interest and principal payments into individually distinct cash flows. This allows an issuer to create two very interesting securities: the IO-bond and the PO-bond. In a stripped mortgage-backed bond the interest and principal are divided into two classes, and two bonds are issued that are each entitled to receive one class of cash flow only. The bond class that receives the interest payment cash flows is known as an *interest-only* or IO class, while the bond receiving the principal repayments is known as a *principal-only* or PO class. The PO-bond is similar to a zero-coupon bond in that it is issued at a discount to par value. The return achieved by a PO-bondholder is a function of the rapidity at which prepayments are made; if prepayments are received in a relatively short time the investor will realise a higher return. This would be akin to the buyer of a zero-coupon bond receiving the maturity payment ahead of the redemption date, and the highest possible return that a PO-bond holder could receive would occur if all the mortgages were prepaid the instant after the PO-bond was bought! A low return will be achieved if all the mortgages are held until maturity, so that there are no prepayments. Stripped mortgage-backed bonds present potentially less advantage to an issuer compared to a pass-through security or a CMO; however, they are liquid instruments and are often traded to hedge a conventional mortgage bond book.

The price of a PO-bond fluctuates as mortgage interest rates change. As we noted earlier, in the US market the majority of mortgages are fixed-rate loans, so that if mortgage rates fall below the coupon rate on the bond, the holder will expect the volume of prepayments to increase as individuals refinance loans in order to gain from lower borrowing rates. This will result in a faster stream of payments to the PO-bondholder as cash flows are received earlier than expected. The price of the PO rises to reflect this, and also because cash flows in the mortgage will now be discounted at a lower rate. The opposite happens when mortgage rates rise and the rate of prepayment is expected to fall, which causes a PO-bond to fall in price. An IO-bond is essentially a stream of cash flows and has no par value. The cash flows represent interest on the mortgage principal outstanding, therefore a higher rate of prepayment leads to a fall in the IO price. This is because the cash flows cease once the principal is redeemed. The risk for the IO-bondholder is that prepayments occur so quickly that interest payments cease before the investor has recovered the amount originally paid for the IO-bond. The price of an IO is also a function of mortgage rates in the market, but exhibits more peculiar responses. If rates fall below the bond coupon, again the rate of prepayment is expected to increase. This would cause the cash flows for the IO to decline, as mortgages were paid off more quickly. This would cause the price of the IO to fall as well, even though the cash flows themselves would be discounted at a lower interest rate. If mortgage rates rise, the outlook for future cash flows will improve as the prepayment rate falls; however, there is also a higher discounting rate for the cash flows themselves, so the price of an IO may move in either direction. Thus IO-bonds exhibit a curious characteristic for a bond instrument, in that their price moves in the same direction as market rates. Both versions of the stripped mortgage bond are interesting instruments, and they have high volatilities during times of market rate changes. Note that PO- and IO-bonds could be created from the hypothetical mortgage pool described above; therefore the combined modified duration of both instruments must equal the modified duration of the original pass-through security.

Covered bonds

Covered bonds are similar in most economic aspects to residential MBS instruments, but have detail differences in their structure and legal definition. The longest established covered bond market is that in German *Pfandbriefe*; there are also covered bond markets in other European markets such as the Netherlands, Ireland, Spain and the United Kingdom. In this section we describe UK covered bonds, which represent a new market for issuers and investors alike.

Covered bond markets and securitisation

The low profile of covered bonds in the financial literature is surprising, given that some of the earliest bond market instruments were in the form of covered bonds, including German *Pfandbriefe*, Danish *Realkreditobligationer* and French *Obligations Foncieres*. More recently, covered bonds have been introduced in Spain (*Cedulas Hipotecarias*) and

Ireland. At the end of 2003 it was estimated that over €1.5 trillion of covered bonds was in issue in Europe.[4]

A covered bond may be defined as a full recourse debt issue secured against a pool of mortgages or public-sector assets. In certain countries, such as Germany, the central authorities have enacted specific legislation that govern covered bonds. In countries where no specific legislation exists, such as the United Kingdom, originators have used traditional securitisation structuring techniques to create an identical instrument, the *structured covered bond*. With a covered bond, investors continue to have recourse to the originator, but it is only upon default that the assigned underlying collateral pool is used to repay the principal. Otherwise, the cash flows from the collateral are not used to service the debt. In a traditional securitisation, investors would have only the cash flows from the assigned collateral pool to repay their amount owed on the debt.

Hence, the key difference between a residential mortgage-backed security (RMBS) and a mortgage-backed covered bond is that an SPV is not created and assets are not transferred to an SPV. Instead, a wholly owned subsidiary is created within the originating bank or financial institution and assets are transferred to this legal entity. Hence, these assets are not taken off the originating entity's balance sheet, as they remain part of the group structure's assets.

Issuer and investor factors

Covered bonds in the euro and sterling markets present new attractions for investors. For instance, they:

- offer a diversified alternative for investors' funds, away from traditional issuers;
- offer access to the residential mortgage market, but outside of RMBS securities;
- present a structure that provides potentially a greater ability to repay liabilities on a stand-alone basis;
- are rated AAA/Aaa;
- are issued in large size and hence offer liquidity;
- are risk-weighted at 20% for Basel I capital purposes.

[4] *Source*: HBOS plc.

Covered bonds also present certain advantages for originators, these include:

- a potential new investor base that may not have been tapped previously;
- due to rating and collateral security, a lower cost of funds than a traditional (unsecured) MTN program, as well as more longer-term funding;[5] also a lower cost and longer-term funding than securitised securities;
- potential ease of reissue under the program structure.

These points illustrate the value of covered bonds as part of bank ALM, and would suggest strong future growth potential in this market.

HBOS plc covered bond

As an example, consider the mortgage covered bond issued by Halifax plc (a former UK building society and part of the HBOS group). It is illustrated in Figure 20.1 on page 975. This was created as follows:

- the arm of HBOS responsible for funding activity, HBOS Treasury, issued covered bonds to investors. It is legally obliged to pay the interest and principal on the bonds;
- funds raised by this issue were loaned to a new group company, Halifax LLP, a wholly owned subsidiary of the HBOS group. The LLP guarantees the covered bonds;
- the group sold a pool of residential mortgages to Halifax LLP, at an over-collateralisation of 15%;
- Halifax LLP placed these assets under a security trust and guarantee that was placed in favour of the investors.

Unlike a traditional securitisation, the liabilities on the issues notes were held by HBOS Treasury, not the new legal entity. It funded the liabilities out of its normal activities, not out of the cash flows represented by the mortgages transferred to Halifax LLP. Only in the event of default on the issued notes would investors have recourse to the assets held by Halifax

[5] During January 2004 the covered bond yield in the United Kingdom ranged around 5–10 basis points lower, compared to MTN yields from the same issuer.

LLP. This structure presented certain advantages over traditional RMBS issues, as it was operated as a program of rolling issues and also appealed to a wider investor base.

The bonds were rated at AAA/Aaa/AAA. The initial pool was comprised entirely of Halifax plc, although there is freedom to include any mortgage (provided certain criteria are met) from within the HBOS group.

The covered bonds are part of a €14 billion MTN program set up by HBOS plc. For investor comfort, various tests are performed on the portfolio to ensure that it maintains minimum quality levels during the bonds' lives. This process is similar to the quality tests performed on CDO structures. The Halifax bond test is called the Asset Coverage Test; it is designed to protect investors and aims to ensure that the value of the underlying assets (mortgages, substitute assets and cash reserves) is equal to the outstanding principal. It includes:

- portfolio revaluation: the value of the portfolio is updated every quarter and is over-collateralised by 15% (that is, its value is calculated using 85% of the Halifax house price index);
- defaulted mortgages: any mortgage in the collateral pool that is over 90 days in arrears is designated a defaulted mortgage and for asset valuation purposes is assigned a zero value;
- repurchase and substitution: to satisfy the asset coverage test, Halifax must repurchase defaulted mortgages from the LLP company at principal value, and either assign replacement mortgages or supply cash collateral until the asset coverage test is passed.

The asset coverage test is:

$$AALA \geq \sum PAO$$

where

AALA is the adjusted aggregate loan amount; it is comprised as follows:

$$AALA = \text{Outstanding loan value} + \text{Cash} + \text{Substitute assets} - (\text{Set-off risk} + \text{Redraws} + \text{Negative carry})$$

and where

PAO is the principal amount outstanding.

Other tests and triggers in the structure include the following:

- if the issuer's rating falls below a certain level, then Halifax must repurchase sufficient mortgages and/or inject cash into the LLP to cover the next maturing bond;
- if the issuer short-term rating falls below A–1+/P–1/F1+ then the LLP must establish a reserve fund, which will then accumulate interest to cover the coupon on the covered bond as it falls due;
- the LLP bank accounts must be maintained at an A–1+/P–1/F1+ rated bank.

The HBOS-covered bond was a ground-breaking deal in the UK-covered bond market. It established a precedent that subsequently attracted interest from other UK mortgage banks.

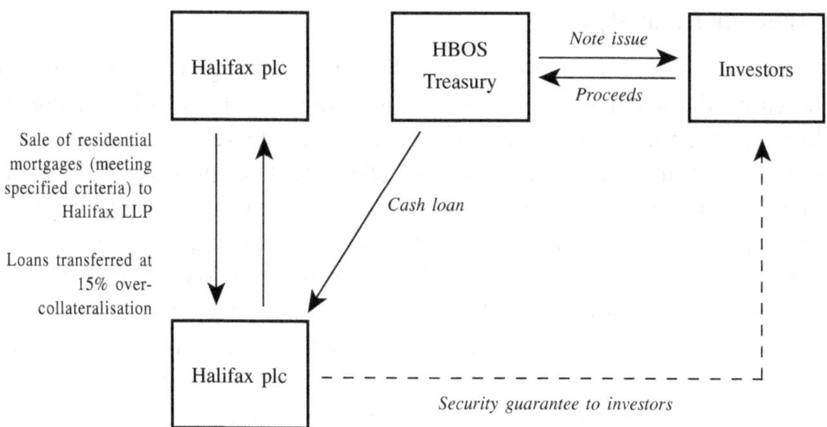

Figure 20.1 Halifax mortgage covered bond, July 2003
© HBOS. Reproduced with permission.

Evaluation and analysis of mortgage-backed bonds

Cash-flow patterns

We stated that the exact term of MBSs cannot be stated with accuracy at the time of issue, because of the uncertain frequency of mortgage prepayments. This uncertainty means that it is not possible to analyse the bonds using the conventional methods used for fixed-coupon bonds. The most common approach used by the market is to assume a fixed prepayment rate at the time of issue and use this to project the cash flows, and hence the life span, of the bond. The choice of prepayment selected therefore is significant, although it is recognised also that prepayment rates are not stable and will fluctuate with changes in mortgage rates and the economic cycle. In this section we consider some of the approaches used in evaluating the prepayment pattern of a mortgage-backed bond.

Prepayment analysis

Some market analysts assume a fixed life for a mortgage pass-through bond based on the average life of a mortgage. Traditionally, a "12-year prepaid life" has been used to evaluate the securities, as market data suggested that the average mortgage was paid off after the twelfth year. This is not generally favoured because it does not take into account the effect of mortgage rates and other factors. A more common approach is to use a *constant prepayment rate* (CPR). This measure is based on the expected number of mortgages in a pool that will be prepaid in a selected period, and it is an annualised figure. The measure for the monthly level of prepayment is known as the *constant monthly repayment*, and measures the expected amount of the outstanding balance, minus the scheduled principal, that will be prepaid in each month. Another name for the constant monthly repayment is the *single monthly mortality rate* or SMM. In Fabozzi (1997) the SMM is given by (20.7) and is an expected value for the percentage of the remaining mortgage balance that will be prepaid in that month.

$$SMM = 1 - (1 - CPR)^{1/12}. \tag{20.7}$$

EXAMPLE 20.3 Constant prepayment rate

The constant prepayment rate for a pool of mortgages is 2% each month. The outstanding principal balance at the start of the month is £72,200, while the scheduled principal payment is £223. This means that 2% of £71,977, or £1,439, will be prepaid in that month. To approximate the amount of principal prepayment, the constant monthly prepayment is multiplied by the outstanding balance.

In the US market the convention is to use the prepayment standard developed by the Public Securities Association (PSA), which is the domestic bond market trade association.[6] The PSA benchmark, known as 100% PSA, assumes a steadily increasing constant prepayment rate each month until the thirtieth month, when a constant rate of 6% is assumed. The starting prepayment rate is 0.2%, increasing at 0.2% each month until the rate levels off at 6%.

For the 100% PSA benchmark we may set, if t is the number of months from the start of the mortgage, that if $t < 30$, the CPR = 6% × $t/30$, while if $t > 30$, then CPR is equal to 6%.

This benchmark can be altered if required to suit changing market conditions, so for example the 200% PSA has a starting prepayment rate and an increase that is double the 100% PSA model, so the initial rate is 0.4%, increasing by 0.4% each month until it reaches 12% in the thirtieth month, at which point the rate remains constant. The 50% PSA has a starting (and increases by a) rate of 0.1%, remaining constant after it reaches 3%.

The prepayment level of a mortgage pool will have an impact on its cash flows. As we saw in Example 20.1 if the amount of prepayment is nil, the cash flows will remain constant during the life of the mortgage. In a fixed-rate mortgage the proportion of principal and interest payment will change each month as more and more of the mortgage amortises. That is, as the principal amount falls each month, the amount of interest decreases. If we assume that a pass-through security has been issued today, so that its coupon reflects the current market level, the payment pattern will resemble the bar chart shown in Figure 20.2.

---

[6] Since renamed the Bond Market Association, which subsequently merged with the Securities Industry Association in July 2006, to form the Securities Industry and Financial Markets Association (SIFMA).

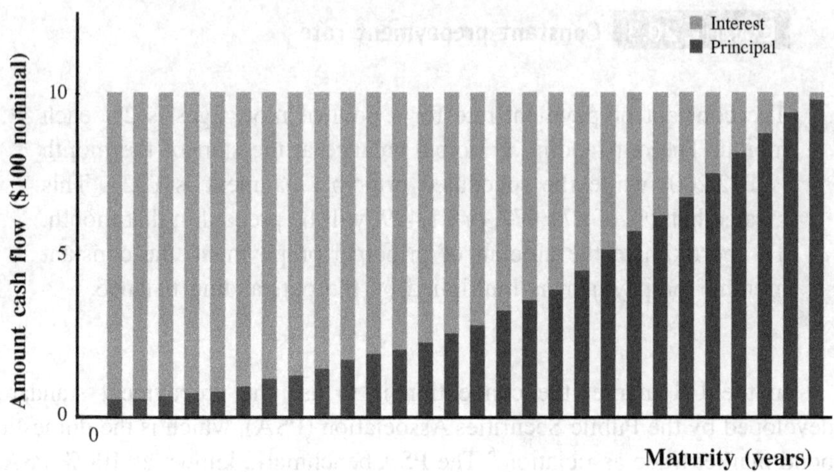

Figure 20.2 Mortgage pass-through security with 0% constant prepayment rate

When there is an element of prepayment in a mortgage pool, for example as in the 100% PSA or 200% PSA model, the amount of principal payment will increase during the early years of the mortgages and then it becomes more steady, before declining for the remainder of the term. This is because the principal balance has declined to such an extent that the scheduled principal payments become less significant. The two examples are shown in Figures 20.3 and 20.4 below.

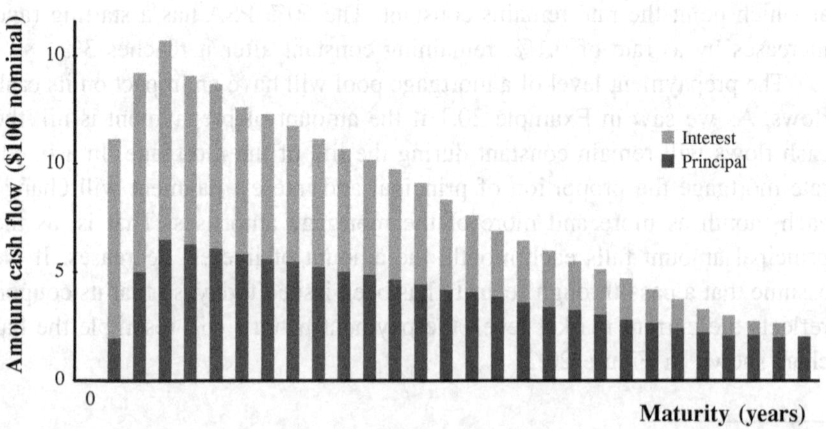

Figure 20.3 100% PSA model

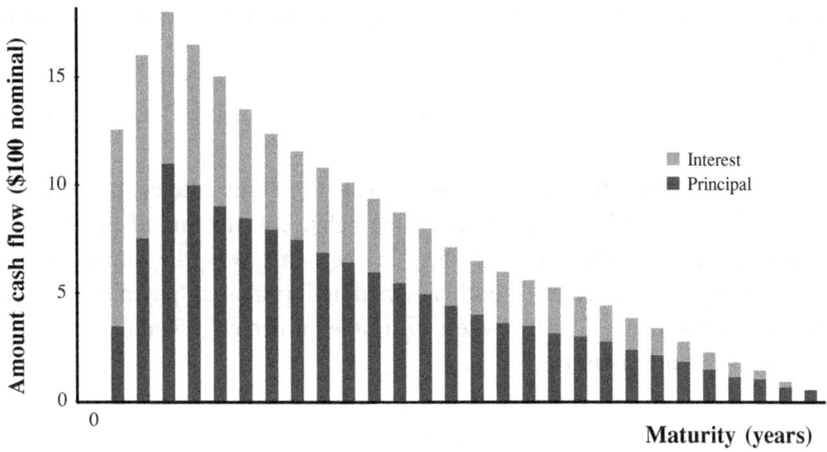

Figure 20.4 200% PSA model

The prepayment volatility of a mortgage-backed bond will vary according to the interest rate of the underlying mortgages. It has been observed that where the mortgages have interest rates of between 100 and 300 basis points above current mortgage rates, the prepayment volatility is the highest. At the bottom of the range, any fall in interest rates often leads to a sudden increase in the refinancing of mortgages, while at the top of the range, an increase in rates will lead to a decrease in the prepayment rate.

The actual cash flow of a mortgage pass-through of course is dependent on the cash-flow patterns of the mortgages in the pool. The relationships described in Example 20.1 can be used to derive further expressions to construct a cash-flow schedule for a pass-through security, using a constant or adjustable assumed prepayment rate. Fabozzi (1997) describes the projected monthly mortgage payment for a level-paying fixed rate mortgage in any month as:

$$\bar{I}_t = \bar{M}_{mt-1} \frac{r(1+r)^{n-t+1}}{(1+r)^{n-t+1} - 1} \tag{20.8}$$

where

$\bar{I}_t$ is the projected monthly mortgage payment for month t

$\bar{M}_{mt-1}$ is the projected mortgage balance at the end of month t assuming that prepayments have occurred in the past.

To calculate the interest proportion of the projected monthly mortgage payment we use (20.9) where $\overline{i}_t$ is the projected monthly interest payment for month t.

$$\overline{i}_t = M_{mt-1} \times i \tag{20.9}$$

Expression (20.9) states that the projected monthly interest payment can be obtained by multiplying the mortgage balance at the end of the previous month by the monthly interest rate. In the same way the expression for calculating the projected monthly scheduled principal payment for any month is given by (20.10), where $\overline{p}_t$ is the projected scheduled principal payment for the month t.

$$\overline{p}_t = \overline{I}_t - \overline{i}_t \tag{20.10}$$

The projected monthly principal prepayment, which is an expected rate only and not a model forecast, is given by (20.11):

$$\overline{pp}_t = SMM_t\,(\overline{M}_{mt-1} - \overline{p}_t) \tag{20.11}$$

where $\overline{pp}_t$ is the projected monthly principal prepayment for month t.

The above relationships enable us to calculate values for the projected monthly:

- interest payment;
- scheduled principal payment; and
- principal prepayment.

These values may be used to calculate the total cash flow in any month that a holder of a mortgage-backed bond receives, which is given by (20.12) below, where cf_t is the cash flow receipt in month t.

$$cf_t = \overline{i}_t + \overline{p}_t + \overline{pp}_t \tag{20.12}$$

The practice of using a prepayment rate is a market convention that enables analysts to evaluate mortgage-backed bonds. The original PSA prepayment rates were arbitrarily selected, based on the observation that prepayment rates tended to stabilise after the first 30 months of the life of a mortgage. A linear increase in the prepayment rate is also assumed.

However, this is a market convention only, adopted by the market as a standard benchmark. The levels do not reflect seasonal variations in prepayment patterns, or the different behaviour patterns of different types of mortgages.

The PSA benchmarks can be (and are) applied to default assumptions to produce a default benchmark. This is used for non-agency mortgage-backed bonds only, as agency securities are guaranteed by one of the three government or government-sponsored agencies. Accordingly, the PSA *standard default assumption* (SDA) benchmark is used to assess the potential default rate for a mortgage pool. For example, the standard benchmark, 100SDA, assumes that the default rate in the first month is 0.02% and increases in a linear fashion by 0.02% each month until the 30th month, at which point the default rate remains at 0.60%. In month 60 the default rate begins to fall from 0.60% to 0.03% and continues to fall linearly until month 120. From that point the default rate remains constant at 0.03%. The other benchmarks have similar patterns.

Prepayment models

The PSA standard benchmark reviewed in the previous section uses an assumption of prepayment rates and can be used to calculate the prepayment proceeds of a mortgage. It is not, strictly speaking, a prepayment *model* because it cannot be used to estimate actual prepayments. A prepayment model on the other hand does attempt to predict the prepayment cash flows of a mortgage pool, by modelling the statistical relationships between the various factors that have an impact on the level of prepayment. These factors are the current mortgage rate, the characteristics of the mortgages in the pool, seasonal factors and the general business cycle.

The prevailing mortgage interest rate is probably the most important factor in the level of prepayment. The level of the current mortgage rate and its spread above or below the original contract rate will influence the decision to refinance a mortgage; if the rate is materially below the original rate, the borrower will prepay the mortgage. As the mortgage rate at any time reflects the general bank base rate, the level of market interest rates has the greatest effect on mortgage prepayment levels. The current mortgage rate also has an effect on housing prices, since if mortgages are seen as "cheap" the general perception will be that now is the right time to purchase: this affects housing market turnover. The pattern followed by mortgage rates since the original loan also has an impact, a phenomenon known as *refinancing burnout*.

Observation of the mortgage market has suggested that housing market and mortgage activity follows a strong seasonal pattern. The strongest period of activity is during the spring and summer, while the market is at its quietest in the winter. The various factors may be used to derive an expression that can be used to calculate expected prepayment levels. For example, a US investment bank uses the following model to calculate expected prepayments:[7]

$$\text{Monthly prepayment rate} = (\text{Refinance incentive}) \times (\text{Season multiplier}) \times (\text{Month multiplier}) \times (\text{Burnout}).$$

Term to maturity

The term to maturity cannot be given for certain for a mortgage pass-through security, since the cash flows and prepayment patterns cannot be predicted. To evaluate such a bond therefore it is necessary to estimate the term for the bond, and use this measure for any analysis. The maturity measure for any bond is important, as without it, it is not possible to assess over what period of time a return is being generated; also, it will not be possible to compare the asset to any other bond. The term to maturity of a bond also gives an indication of its sensitivity to changes in market interest rates. If comparisons with other securities such as government bonds are made, we cannot use the stated maturity of the mortgage-backed bond because prepayments will reduce this figure. The convention in the market is to use other estimated values, which are *average life* and the more traditional duration measure.

The *average life* of a mortgage pass-through security is the weighted-average time to return of a unit of principal payment, made up of projected scheduled principal payments and principal prepayments. It is also known as the *weighted-average life*. It is given by (20.13):

$$\text{Average life} = \frac{1}{12}\sum_{t=1}^{n} \frac{(\text{Principal received at } t)}{\text{Total principal received}} \tag{20.13}$$

where n is the number of months remaining. The time from the term measured by the average life to the final scheduled principal payment is the bond's *tail*.

[7] Fabozzi (1997).

In Chapter 4 we saw that, to calculate duration (or Macaulay's duration) for a bond we required the weighted present values of all its cash flows. To apply this for a mortgage-backed bond therefore it is necessary to project the bond's cash flows, using an assumed prepayment rate. The projected cash flows, together with the bond price and the periodic interest rate, may then be used to arrive at a duration value. The periodic interest rate is derived from the yield. This calculation for a mortgage-backed bond produces a periodic duration figure, which must be divided by 12 to arrive at a duration value in years (or by 4 in the case of a quarterly paying bond).

EXAMPLE 20.4 Macaulay duration

A 25-year mortgage security with a mortgage rate of 8.49% and monthly coupon is quoted at a price of $98.50, a bond-equivalent yield of 9.127%. To calculate the Macaulay duration we require the present value of the expected cash flows using the interest rate that will make this present value, assuming a constant prepayment rate, equate to the price of 98.50. Using the expression below,

$$rm = 2\ [(1 + r)^n - 1]$$

where rm is 9.127% and $n = 5$, this is shown to be 9.018%.

For the bond above this present value is 6,120.79. Therefore the mortgage security Macaulay duration is given by:

$$Dm = \frac{6{,}120.79}{98.50} = 62.14.$$

Therefore the bond-equivalent Macaulay duration in years is given by:

$$D = \frac{62.14}{12} = 5.178.$$

Calculating yield and price: static cash flow model

There are a number of ways that the yield on a mortgage-backed bond can be calculated. One of the most common methods employs the *static cash-flow model.* This assumes a single prepayment rate to estimate the cash flows for the bond, and does not take into account how changes in market conditions might impact on the prepayment pattern.

The conventional yield measure for a bond is the discount rate at which the sum of the present values of all the bond's expected cash flows will be equal to the price of the bond. The convention is usually to compute the yield from the *clean* price; that is, excluding any accrued interest. This yield measure is known as the bond's *redemption yield* or *yield-to-maturity* (YTM). However, for mortgage-backed bonds it is known as a *cash flow yield* or *mortgage yield*. The cash flow for a mortgage-backed bond is not known with certainty, due to the effect of prepayments, and so must be derived using an assumed prepayment rate. Once the projected cash flows have been calculated, it is possible to calculate the cash flow yield. The formula is given by (20.14):

$$P = \sum_{n=1}^{N} \frac{C\ (t)}{(1 + ri/1200)^{t-1}}. \tag{20.14}$$

Note however that a yield so computed will be for a bond with monthly coupon payments,[8] so it is necessary to convert the yield to an annualised equivalent before any comparisons are made with conventional bond yields. In the US and UK markets, the bond-equivalent yield is calculated for mortgage-backed bonds and measured against the relevant government bond yield, which (in both cases) is a semi-annual yield. Although it is reasonably accurate to simply double the yield of a semi-annual coupon bond to arrive at the annualised equivalent,[9] to obtain the bond equivalent yield for a monthly paying mortgage-backed bond we use (20.15):

$$rm = 2[(1 + ri_M)^6 - 1] \tag{20.15}$$

where rm is the bond equivalent yield (we retain the designation that was used to denote YTM in Chapter 4) and ri_M is the interest rate that will equate the present value of the projected monthly cash flows for the mortgage-backed bond to its current price. The equivalent semi-annual yield is given by (20.16):

$$rm_{s/a} = (1 + ri_M)^6 - 1. \tag{20.16}$$

[8] The majority of mortgage-backed bonds pay interest on a monthly basis, since individual mortgages usually do as well; certain mortgage-backed bonds pay on a quarterly basis.

[9] See Chapter 4 for the formulas used to convert yields from one convention basis to another.

The cash-flow yield calculated for a mortgage-backed bond in this way is essentially the redemption yield, using an assumption to derive the cash flows. As such, the measure suffers from the same drawbacks as it does when used to measure the return of a plain vanilla bond, which are that the calculation assumes a uniform reinvestment rate for all the bond's cash flows and that the bond will be held to maturity. The same weakness will apply to the cash-flow yield measure for a mortgage-backed bond. In fact, the potential inaccuracy of the redemption yield measure is even greater with a mortgage-backed bond because the frequency of interest payments is higher, which makes the reinvestment risk greater. The final yield that is returned by a mortgage-backed bond will depend on the performance of the mortgages in the pool, specifically the prepayment pattern.

Given the nature of a mortgage-backed bond's cash flows, the exact yield cannot be calculated; however, it is common for market practitioners to use the cash flow yield measure and compare this to the redemption yield of the equivalent government bond. The usual convention is to quote the spread over the government bond as the main measure of value. When measuring the spread, the mortgage-backed bond is compared to the government security that has a similar duration, or a term to maturity similar to its average life.

It is possible to calculate the price of a mortgage-backed bond once its yield is known (or vice-versa). As with a plain vanilla bond, the price is the sum of the present values of all the projected cash flows. It is necessary to convert the bond-equivalent yield to a monthly yield, which is then used to calculate the present value of each cash flow. The cash flows of IO- and PO-bonds are dependent on the cash flows of the underlying pass-through security, which is itself dependent on the cash flows of the underlying mortgage pool. Again, to calculate the price of an IO- or PO-bond, a prepayment rate must be assumed. This enables us to determine the projected level of the monthly cash flows of the IO and the principal payments of the PO. The price of an IO is the present value of the projected interest payments, while the price of the PO is the present value of the projected principal payments, comprising the scheduled principal payments and the projected principal prepayments.

Bond price and option-adjusted spread

The option-adjusted spread (OAS) and its use in the analysis and valuation of bonds with embedded options was covered in Chapter 4. The behaviour of mortgage securities often resembles that of callable bonds, because effectively there is a call feature attached to them, in the shape of the prepayment option of the underlying mortgage holders. This option feature is the principal reason why it is necessary to use average life as the term to maturity for a mortgage security. It is frequently the case that the optionality of a mortgage-backed bond and the volatility of its yield have a negative impact on the bondholders. This is for two reasons: the actual yield realised during the holding period has a high probability of being lower than the anticipated yield, which was calculated on the basis of an assumed prepayment level, and mortgages are frequently prepaid at the time when the bondholder will suffer the most; that is, prepayments occur most often when rates have fallen, leaving the bondholder to reinvest repaid principal at a lower market interest rate.

These features combined represent the biggest risk to an investor of holding a mortgage security, and market analysts attempt to measure and quantify this risk. This is usually done using a form of OAS analysis. Under this approach the value of the mortgagor's prepayment option is calculated in terms of a basis point penalty that must be subtracted from the expected yield spread on the bond. This basis point value is calculated using a binomial model or a simulation model to generate a range of future interest rate paths, only some of which will cause a mortgagor to prepay his or her mortgage. The interest rate paths that would result in a prepayment are evaluated for their impact on the mortgage bond's expected yield spread over a government bond.[10] As OAS analysis takes account of the option feature of a mortgage-backed bond, it will be less affected by a yield change than the bond's yield spread. Assuming a flat yield curve environment, the relationship between the OAS and the yield spread is given by:

$$\text{OAS} = \text{Yield spread} - \text{Cost of option feature.}$$

This relationship can be observed occasionally when yield spreads on current coupon mortgages widen during upward moves in the market. As interest rates fall, the cost of the option feature on a current coupon mortgage will rise, as the possibility of prepayment increases. Put another way, the option feature begins to approach being in-the-money. To adjust for

[10] The yield spread from OAS analysis is based on the discounted value of the expected cash flow using the government bond-derived forward rate. The yield spread of the cash-flow yield to the government bond is based on YTM. For this reason, the two spreads are not strictly comparable. The OAS spread is added to the entire yield curve, whereas a yield spread is a spread over a single point on the government bond yield curve.

the increased value of the option, traders will price in higher spreads on the bond, which will result in the OAS remaining more or less unchanged.

Effective duration and convexity

The modified duration of a bond measures its price sensitivity to a change in yield; the calculation is effectively a snapshot of one point in time. It also assumes that there is no change in expected cash flows as a result of the change in market interest rates. Therefore it is an inappropriate interest rate risk for a mortgage-backed bond, whose cash flows would be expected to change after a change in rates, due to the prepayment effect. Hence, mortgage-backed bonds react differently to interest rate changes compared to conventional bonds, because when rates fall, the level of prepayments is expected to rise (and vice-versa). Therefore when interest rates fall, the duration of the bond may also fall, which is opposite to the behaviour of a conventional bond. This feature is known as *negative convexity* and is similar to the effect displayed by a callable bond. The prices of both these types of security react to interest rate changes differently compared to the price of conventional bonds.

For this reason the more accurate measure of interest rate sensitivity to use is *effective duration* described by Fabozzi (1997). As described in the text, effective duration is the approximate duration of a bond as given by (20.17):

$$\Delta_{app} = \frac{P_- - P_+}{2P_0\ (\Delta rm)} \tag{20.17}$$

where

P_0 is the initial price of the bond
P_- is the estimated price of the bond if the yield decreases by Δrm
P_+ is the estimated price of the bond if the yield increases by Δrm
Δrm is the change in the yield of the bond.

The approximate duration is the effective duration of a bond when the two values P_- and P_+ are obtained from a valuation model that incorporates the effect of a change in the expected cash flows (from prepayment effects) when there is a change in interest rates. The values are obtained from a pricing model such as the static cash flow model, binomial model or simulation model. The calculation of effective duration uses higher and lower prices that are dependent on the prepayment rate that is assumed.

Generally, analysts will assume a higher prepayment rate when the interest rate is at the lower level of the two.

Figure 20.5 illustrates the difference between modified duration and effective duration for a range of agency mortgage pass-through securities, where the effective duration for each bond is calculated using a 20 basis point change in rates. This indicates that the modified duration measure effectively over-estimates the price sensitivity of lower coupon bonds. This factor is significant when hedging a mortgage-backed bond position, because using the modified duration figure to calculate the nominal value of the hedging instrument will not prove effective for anything other than very small changes in yield.

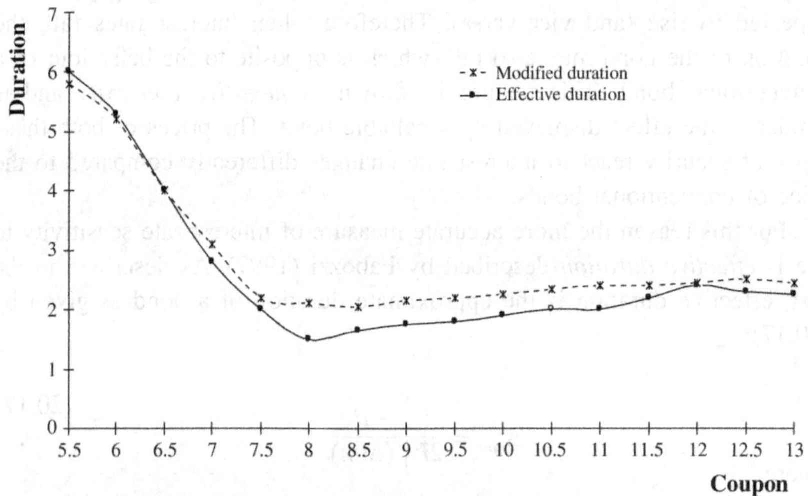

Figure 20.5 Modified duration and effective duration for agency mortgage-backed bonds

The formula to calculate approximate convexity (or *effective convexity*) is given below as (20.18); again if the values used in the formula allow for the cash flow to change, the convexity value may be taken to be the effective convexity. The effective convexity value of a mortgage pass-through security is invariably negative.

$$CV_{app} = \frac{P_+ + P_- - 2P_0}{P_0\,(\Delta rm)^2}. \tag{20.18}$$

Total return

To assess the value of a mortgage-backed bond over a given investment horizon it is necessary to measure the return generated during the holding period from the bond's cash flows. This is done using what is known as the *total return* framework. The cash flows from a mortgage-backed bond are comprised of (i) the projected cash flows of the bond (which are the projected interest payments and principal repayments and prepayments), (ii) the interest earned on the reinvestment of all the payments, and (iii) the projected price of the bond at the end of the holding period. The first sum can be estimated using an assumed prepayment rate during the period the bond is held, while the second cash flow requires an assumed reinvestment rate. To obtain (iii) the bondholder must assume first, what the bond equivalent yield of the mortgage bond will be at the end of the holding period; and second, what prepayment rate the market will assume at this point. The second rate is a function of the projected yield at the time. The total return during the time the bond is held, on a monthly basis, is then given by (20.19),

$$TR = \left[\frac{\text{Total future cash flow amount}}{P_m}\right]^{1/n} - 1 \qquad (20.19)$$

which can be converted to an annualised bond-equivalent yield using (20.15) or (20.16).

Note that the return calculated using (20.19) is based on a range of assumptions, which render it almost academic. The best approach to use is to calculate a yield for a range of different assumptions, which then give some idea of the likely yield that may be generated over the holding period, in the form of a range of yields (that is, an upper and lower limit).

EXAMPLE 20.5 Mortgage-backed bond issue

Bradford & Bingley Building Society £1 billion three-tranche MBS due 2031

Bradford & Bingley is a UK building society that planned to list on the London Stock Exchange (and convert to a bank) during 2000/2001. In August 2000 it issued a mortgage-backed security that was underwritten by UBS Warburg, via Aire Valley Finance (No. 2), an SPV. The transaction structure diagram is shown in Figure 20.6.

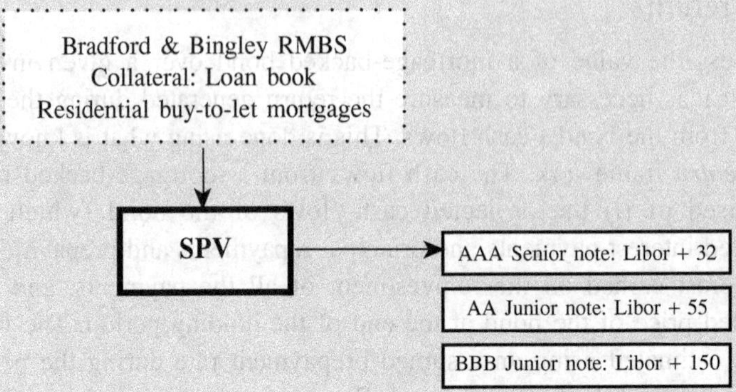

Figure 20.6 Bradford Bingley RMBS transaction

Loan portfolio

The underlying collateral consists of approximately 14,000 residential mortgages with an average loan balance of £74,000. Around two-thirds of the mortgages are on properties located in London and the south-east of England. An interesting feature of the mortgages is that they are *buy-to-let* loans; the issuer had previously undertaken a securitisation of its owner-occupier mortgage portfolio. These buy-to-let mortgages allow overpayment of the principal without penalty; consequently, early prepayment is more likely with this type of collateral.

Bond structure

The issue is callable, with the structure composed of the following notes:

- £892.5 million senior note with AAA-rating, offered at a yield of three-month Libor plus 32 basis points;
- £57.5 million junior note with AA-rating, offered at three-month Libor plus 55 basis points;
- £50 million junior note with BBB-rating, offered at Libor plus 150 basis points.

Although the issue has a legal maturity to 2031, it is callable and the senior note has a feature that raises its coupon to Libor plus 80 basis points if it is not called after September 2008. This makes it likely that the bond will be called at that time.

Investor profile
The issue was placed with around 50 institutional investors, with other UK banks and large building societies and European banks being the largest buyers of the senior notes; fund managers were purchasers of the junior notes.

Price-yield curves of mortgage pass-through, PO and IO securities

This section is an introduction to the yield behaviour of selected mortgage-backed securities under conditions of changing interest rates. To recap, in an environment of high interest rates the holders of mortgage-backed bonds prefer prepayments to occur. This is because the mortgage will be paying at a low interest rate relative to market conditions, and the likelihood of mortgage prepayment at par results in a higher value for the bond. In the same way, when interest rates are low, noteholders would prefer that there not be any prepayment, as the bond will be paying interest at a relatively high rate and will therefore be price-valuable.

Figure 20.7 illustrates the price behaviour of pass-through securities, with nominal coupon of 7%.

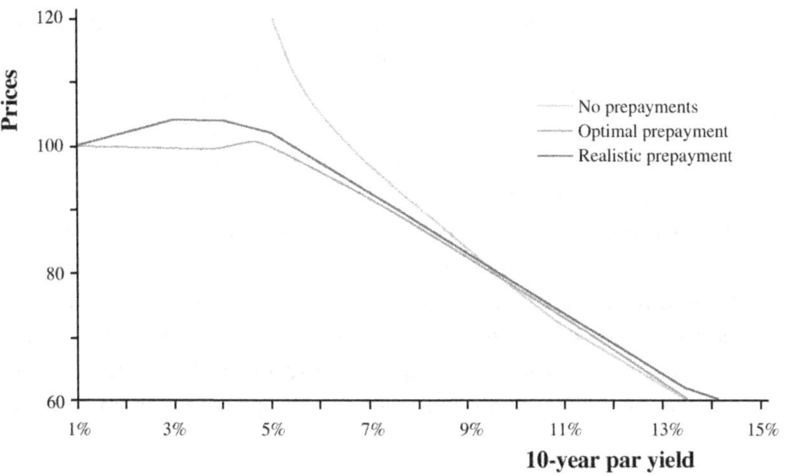

Figure 20.7 Price behaviour of pass-through security

Under conditions of no prepayments, the bond cash flows are certain and the price–yield behaviour resembles that of a conventional bond. Under optimal prepayment, the bond will behave similarly to a callable bond: in a high interest-rate environment the bond behaves much like a vanilla bond, while under lower rates the price of the bond is capped at par. However, under what Tuckman (1996) calls "realistic payment" conditions the price behaviour is somewhat different, as illustrated in Figure 20.7. In an environment of very low rates, bond value is higher with the realistic payments assumption than the other two scenarios. This is because there are always a number of mortgage borrowers who will repay their loans irrespective of the level of interest rates, whether rates are low or high. Remember that noteholders desire prepayments when interest rates are high, and the bond value under the realistic payments model is higher than those of the other two, which predict no prepayments under high interest-rate conditions.

As interest rates decline, certain mortgage borrowers will prepay their loans, but by no means all. As prepayment decreases the value of a mortgage under low interest rates, the fact that not all borrowers prepay under the "optimal" scenario results in an increase in the value of a mortgage to a level greater than its optimal prepaid value. This non-prepayment behaviour can lead to an increase in bond value above par. This is something of an anomaly, as the bond is then priced above the level at which it can theoretically be called. The scenario concludes when eventually all borrowers redeem their mortgages as rates have fallen far enough. This is why the realistic prepayments curve moves down to par at very low levels of rates. The graph shows the existence of negative convexity as bond prices fall as interest rates decline, which reflects the behaviour of mortgage borrowers after a long enough period of very low rates. However, this does not mean that investors should not buy mortgage-backed bonds at that range of yields when negative convexity applies: as Tuckman notes, the mortgages will be earning rates at above-market levels. It is the total return of the bond over the holding period that is relevant, rather than its price behaviour.[11]

It is also worth commenting on the behavior of IO and PO securities, which we described earlier. To recap, an IO receives the interest payments of the underlying collateral while the PO receives principal payments. Figure

[11] This is especially true when compared to the performance of other debt-market investments. Investment reasoning on price behaviour alone is "as bad as concluding that premium Treasuries should never be purchased because they will eventually decline in price to par"! (author's exclamation mark; Tuckman 1996, pp. 256).

20.8 illustrates the price behaviour of these instruments, based on a $100 nominal amount for both the underlying mortgage and the IO/PO.

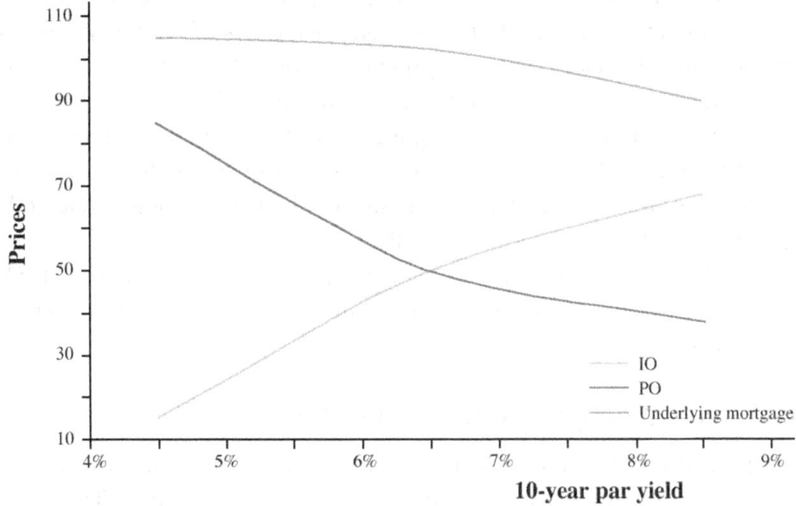

Figure 20.8 Price behaviour of IO and PO securities

Under very high interest rates and where prepayments are unlikely, a PO will behave in a similar way to a zero-coupon bond, repayable at par on maturity, similar to a zero-coupon bond. As interest rates decline and the level of prepayments increases, the value of the PO will increase. However, other forces are at work that, as rates change further, make PO securities more interesting than vanilla strips. These are:

- the conventional price/yield effect, as lower interest rates cause higher prices;
- that the PO, again similarly to vanilla strips, is very sensitive to the price/yield effect;
- as the level of prepayments increases, with the expectation of higher levels still, the effective maturity of the PO declines. The effect of this lower maturity is to raise the price of the PO even higher.

The impact of these factors is that PO securities are highly volatile.

The price/yield relationship of the IO is a function of that for the PO, and is obtained by subtracting the value of the latter from that of the underlying mortgage. A significant feature is the high price volatility of the IO under conditions of lower and falling interest rates. This is explained as follows: in a high interest-rate environment, with very low prepayment levels, IOs act as vanilla bonds, with cash flows known with certainty. This changes as interest rates start to fall, and the cash flows of the IO effectively disappear. This is because as more principal is repaid, the nominal amount of the mortgage on which interest is charged decreases in amount. However, unlike pass-through or other mortgage securities, which receive some principal payment when interest payments decline or cease, IOs receive no cash flow. The impact of a vanishing cash flow is that, as interest rates fall, the price of the IO declines dramatically.

As well as purchases by investors, this negative duration property of IOs makes them of use as interest-rate hedging instruments by market-makers in mortgage-backed securities.

Commercial mortgage-backed securities

The mortgage-backed bond market includes a sector of securities that are backed by commercial, as opposed to residential, mortgages. These are known as *commercial mortgage-backed securities* (CMBS). They trade essentially as other mortgage securities, but there are detail differences in their structure, which are summarised in this section.

Issuing a CMBS

As with a residential mortgage security, a CMBS is created from a pool or "trust" of commercial mortgages, with the cash flows of the bond backed by the interest and principal payments of the underlying mortgages. A commercial mortgage is a loan made to finance or refinance the purchase of a commercial (business) property. There is a market in the direct purchase of a commercial loan book in addition to the more structured CMBS transaction. An issue of CMBS is rated in the same way as a residential mortgage security and usually has a credit-enhancement arrangement to raise its credit rating. The credit rating of a CMBS takes into account the size of the issue as well as the level of credit-enhancement support.

Classes of bonds in a CMBS structure are usually arranged in a sequential pay series, and bonds are retired in line with their rating in the structure; the highest-rated bonds are paid off first.

Commercial mortgages impose a penalty on borrowers if they are redeemed early, usually in the form of an interest charge on the final principal. There is no such penalty in the US residential mortgage market, although early retirement fees are still a feature of residential loans in the United Kingdom. The early payment protection in a commercial loan can have other forms as well, such as a prepayment "lockout", which is a contractual arrangement that prevents early retirement. This early prepayment protection is repeated in a CMBS structure, and may be in the form of call protection of the bonds themselves. There is already a form of protection in the ratings of individual issues in the structure, because the highest-rated bonds are paid off first. That is, the triple-A-rated bonds will be retired ahead of the double-A-rated bonds and so on. The highest-rated bonds in a CMBS structure also have the highest protection from default of any of the underlying mortgages, which means that losses of principal arising from default will affect the lowest-rated bond first.

As well as the early retirement protection, commercial mortgages differ from residential loans in that many of them are *balloon* mortgages. A balloon loan is one on which only the interest is paid, or only a small amount of the principal is paid as well as the interest, so that all or a large part of the loan remains to be paid off on the maturity date. This makes CMBSs potentially similar to conventional vanilla bonds (which are also sometimes called "bullet" bonds) and so attractive to investors who prefer less uncertainty on term to maturity of a bond.

Types of CMBS structures

In the US market there are currently five types of CMBS structures. They are:

- liquidating trusts;
- multi-property single borrower;
- multi-property conduit;
- multi-property non-conduit;
- single-property single-borrower.

We briefly describe the three most common structures here.

- *Liquidating trusts.* This sector of the market is relatively small by value and represents bonds issued against non-performing loans, hence the other name of *non-performing CMBS*. The market is structured in a slightly different way to regular commercial mortgage securities. The features include a *fast-pay structure*, which states that all cash flows from the mortgage pool be used to redeem the most senior bond first, and *over-collateralisation*, which is when the value of bonds created is significantly lower than the value of the underlying loans. This over-collateralisation results in bonds being paid off sooner. Due to the nature of the asset backing for liquidating CMBSs, bonds are usually issued with relatively short average lives, and will receive cash flows on only a portion of the loans. A target date for paying off is set and in the event that the target is not met, the bonds usually have a provision to raise the coupon rate. This acts as an incentive for the borrower to meet the retirement target.

- *Multi-property single borrower*. The single borrower/multi-property structure is an important and large-size part of the CMBS market. The special features of these bonds include *cross-collateralisation*, which is when properties that are used as collateral for individual loans are pledged against each loan. Another feature, known as *cross-default,* allows the lender to call each loan in the pool if any one of them defaults. Since cross-collateralisation and cross-default links all the properties together, sufficient cash flow is available to meet the collective debt on all of the loans. This influences the grade of credit rating that is received for the issue. A *property release provision* in the structure is set up to protect the investor against the lender removing or prepaying the stronger loans in the book. Another common protection against this risk is a clause in the structure terms that prevents the issuer from substituting one property for another.
- *Multi-borrower/conduit*. A *conduit* is a commercial lending entity that has been set up solely to generate collateral to be used in securitisation deals. The major investment banks have all established conduit arms. Conduits are responsible for originating collateral that meet requirements on loan type (whether amortising or balloon, and so on), loan term, geographic spread of the properties and the time that the loans were struck. Generally, a conduit will want to have a diversified range of underlying loans, known as *pool diversification*, with a wide spread of location and size. A diversified pool reduces the default risk for the investor. After it has generated the collateral, the conduit then structures the deal, on terms similar to CMOs, but with the additional features described in this section.

CMBS trade in the US market on a yield, as opposed to a price, basis and are usually quoted as a spread over the Treasury benchmark. The underlying asset pool can be comprised of as few as five or 10 loans.

References and bibliography

Fabozzi, F., Ramsey, C. and Ramirez, F. 1994, *Collateralised Mortgage Obligations: Structures and Analysis*, FJF Associates, New Hope, PA, Chapter 3.

Fabozzi, F. 1997, *Fixed Income Mathematics*, McGraw-Hill, New York.

Fabozzi, F. (ed.) 1998, *Handbook of Structured Financial Products*, FJF Associates, New Hope, PA.

Hayre, L. and Mohebbi, C. 1989, "Mortgage Pass-through Securities", in Fabozzi, F. (ed.), *Advances and Innovations in the Bond and Mortgage Markets*, Probus Publishing, New York, pp. 259–304.

Pinkus, S. and Chandoha, M. 1987, "The Relative Price Volatility of Mortgage Securities", in Fabozzi, F. (ed.), *Mortgage-backed Securities: New Strategies, Applications and Research*, Probus Publishing, New York, pp. 121–38.

Tuckman, B. 1996, *Fixed Income Securities*, John Wiley & Sons, New Jersey.

CHAPTER

21

Asset-backed Securities

The market in asset-backed securities contains instruments that have widely varying payment terms and conditions, and different collateral bases. The subject matter is a large one and so in this chapter we present only a summary of the main instruments. Interested readers may wish to consult the texts listed under the references and bibliography. Here we review the characteristics of the main asset-backed instruments, which were introduced in the US market, but are also now issued in other markets including those in the United Kingdom and Europe. They are an important part of the ALM toolkit. The instruments we will consider are:

- auto-loan-backed securities;
- credit card-backed securities;
- net interest margins (NIM) structures.

We also present some further issues connected with the analysis of these securities. Table 21.1 shows US market ABS issuance during 1999–2006.

Year	1999	2000	2001	2002	2003	2004	2005	2006
Type								
Credit card	43	56	71	71	67	54	65	46
Auto-loan	63	87	97	107	95	82	115	56
Home equity	60	49	101	147	206	245	274	193
Manufactured housing	16	11	7	5	1	1	1	0
Student loan	10	18	11	22	33	45	64	38
Other	78	70	83	89	118	314	477	387
Total	270	291	370	441	520	741	996	720

Table 21.1 ABS Issuance volume, US market 1999–2006 $billion
Sources: Bloomberg, Internet.

Auto-loan-backed securities

Description

Bonds issued against car loan finance are known as *auto-loan-backed securities* (auto-ABS) in the United States or simply as *car-loans* in the United Kingdom. The auto-loan-backed market in the United States is one of the largest in the asset-backed market. It is also one of the oldest sectors, with the first deal being issued in May 1985. Auto-loans are amortising private loans in the manner of residential mortgages, but are typically of much shorter duration than mortgages and carry no prepayment risk. This makes bonds that are issued against them attractive instruments for investors who are seeking more stable, shorter-dated paper of high credit quality but yielding more than Treasury bonds. As their cash flows are more straightforward, their analysis presents fewer problems than other asset-backed securities. Up to the middle of 2004, approximately $230 billion of auto-loan bonds had been issued in the United States, and the sector is a liquid and fairly transparent one.

Car loans in the United States are short-term amortising deals, ranging from three to six years in maturity. The average maturity is four years. Loans are made either direct at the dealership, in which case finance is supplied by an arm of the car manufacturer, or at a commercial (retail) bank. In the United Kingdom, car loans are of two types: the amortising loan from a bank, or a bullet loan usually taken from a finance house, known as leasing. Both types of loans are used as collateral in a car-loan bond issue. The US car loan market is dominated by the "Big Three" car manufacturers: General Motors, Ford Motor Corporation and Chrysler Corporation, who issued over 33% of all auto-ABS in 2004. The large commercial banks are also big issuers of auto-ABS bonds, and include Capital One, NationsBank and Bank of America. Independent finance companies make up the third category of issuers, companies such as Western Financial and Union Acceptance Corporation. The independent houses are much more reliant on the auto-ABS market and can fund their books at lower rates directly as a result, since they create AAA securities out of securitised car loans that pay a lower yield than their individual credit standings would allow. To achieve a high credit rating most auto-ABS issues are structured with a form of credit enhancement. The most common form of enhancement is a senior/subordinated structure, similar to mortgage-backed bonds, although letters of credit and over-collateralisation are also used.

The underlying assets in an auto-ABS issue are bank or finance house car loans, which may be purchased or originated by an SPV called a *special purpose corporation* (SPC). Interest payments from the original borrowers are passed to investors via the SPC. There are two main types of auto-ABS bonds: pass-through securities and *pay-through* securities. The majority of issues are pass-throughs.

The prepayment risk on auto-ABS bonds is low. Car loans have a very low response to changes in market interest rates, and loans are rarely repaid ahead of the maturity date. Auto-ABS bonds therefore do not exhibit the negative convexity of mortgage-backed bonds. There are non-interest-rate reasons why prepayment might occur, however, such as customers "trading up" to another car, or theft or destruction of the vehicle.

Yield spreads

The structure of auto-ABS bonds is relatively straightforward compared to other asset-backed securities, and possibly simpler than credit card-backed securities. They are amortising bonds (in the United States), but because they have little prepayment risk they do not exhibit negative convexity. They are also shorter-dated securities compared to other ABS issues; most auto pass-throughs have average lives of 1.8 to 2.2 years, which is considerably lower than mortgage bonds. The yield spread over Treasury securities for auto-ABS issues is tighter than mortgage securities, but slightly over that for credit card securities. During 2004 they typically yielded around 15–20 basis points over credit card securities, and on average 10–20 basis points below manufactured housing mortgage securities. The market places a premium on auto-ABS bonds issued by the independent finance companies, which trade at around 5–10 basis points above issues made by the Big Three manufacturers and the commercial banks.

Issue and tranche	Close date	Amount $m	Average life (years)	Spread (bps)
First Finance 2004-1	21-Jan-04	1100	2.1	36
Alliance 2004-A	19-Mar-04	650	1.9	33
Pacific Finance 2004-A	31-Mar-04	500	2.0	34
Banc One 2004-1	4-Apr-04	800	2.1	28

Table 21.2 US market auto-ABS issues during 2004
Source: Asset-Banked News, January 2005.

This is illustrated in Table 21.2. The First Finance and Alliance transactions were issued by independent finance houses. These notes traded at a yield that was 5–8 basis points higher than the one issued by Banc One, a commercial bank; their relatively small size will also impact liquidity and add to their yield premium.

Auto-ABS bonds have a wider range of payment windows than comparable securities and this makes their relative value more closely related to the shape of the yield curve. Securities such as credit card ABS bonds provide a higher return in an environment with a steeply positive short-date yield curve, due to their "roll down" effect, so that in a steepening yield curve scenario auto-ABS bonds will be outperformed by credit card securities. This reflects that in a stable yield curve environment auto-ABS bonds will achieve a higher total return, compared to their spread, than credit card securities.

Credit card-backed securities

Another large sector in the asset-backed market is the credit card market. It experienced steady growth during the 1990s, with over $390 billion nominal outstanding in June 2004.[1] The rise in credit card securitisation reflects the increasing use of credit cards by consumers, such that is now a significant national economic indicator. The public are now able to pay for a large number of goods and services using credit cards, and as a payment medium they are increasingly used for regular, "day-to-day" purchases as well as larger-size one-off transactions. The first example of a credit card securitisation was in 1987 in the US domestic market, as banks sought to move credit card assets off their balance sheets, thus freeing up lending lines, and diversify their funding sources. The first banks to securitise their

[1] The source of the statistical data in this section is *Asset-Backed Alert, www.asset-backedalert.com*

credit card books were Capital One, MBNA and Advanta, among others. They were able to benefit from funding at triple-A rates, due to the credit enhancement used on the bond structures and consequently low charges on their capital. The largest issuers of credit card-backed bonds in the US market are shown in Table 21.3.

Securitising banks	$ billion
Citibank	44.6
MBNA America	29.3
Discover	15.1
First USA	14.8
First Chicago	12.8
HFC	11.2
Capital One	10.9
JPMorgan	9.8
Advanta	6.6

Table 21.3 Largest issuers of credit card-backed bonds, US domestic market, June 2004
Source: ABS News.

Credit card ABS bonds, along with auto-ABS issues, remain the most accessible instruments for investors who are interested in having an exposure to the asset-backed market. As they have maturities that are shorter than the average lives of mortgage-backed securities, as well as cash-flow patterns that are more akin to conventional bonds, they are attractive investments to institutions such as banks and money market funds. In the United States, and increasingly in the United Kingdom and Europe, the combination of credit card, auto-loan and mortgage-backed securities means that there are highly rated asset-backed instruments, paying reasonable spreads over government securities, available along the entire yield curve.

Issuing structures

In the US market there are two different structures under which credit card debt is securitised. The *stand-alone trust* is a pool of credit card accounts that have been sold to a trust, and then used as collateral for a single security. As with CMOs there are usually several classes of bonds within a single issue. If a subsequent class of bonds is issued, the issuer must designate a new pool of *receivables* and sell these card accounts to a separate trust. This structure was used at the start of the market, but has been all but replaced by the *master trust*, which is a structure that allows the securitising bank to issue successive securities from the same trust, which are all backed by the same pool of credit card loan collateral. Under this arrangement the issuer retains greater flexibility for issuing securities, and without the cost associated with setting up a new trust each time a new issue is required.

EXAMPLE 21.1 Credit Card ABS master trust structure

An issuing bank transfers the cash flows represented by 100,000 credit card accounts, with a nominal value of $200 million, to a separate trust. It then issues different classes of securities, with different coupons, maturities and nominal values, all backed by the same collateral. At a later date the issuer requires further funding. It transfers the receivables from more card accounts to the same trust and issues more securities. The different tranches of receivables, transferred at two different times, are not differentiated from one another and are not segregated; that is, the combined receivables in the trust back all the bond issues made against the trust.

As a master trust will comprise receivables transferred to it over time, it will contain cash flows that have different payment terms and interest rates (or *annual payment rate* [APR], used in quoting credit card interest rates), reflecting the terms and conditions of cards issued at different times. For instance, a bank may issue cards under a special low interest rate as part of a special promotion designed to attract new customers. New cardholders will have accounts with different terms and cash flows to existing cardholders. Investors in credit card ABS must be aware therefore that the composition of accounts in a master trust pool are liable to alter over time, sometimes significantly, as existing cardholder accounts are closed or fall dormant, and as new accounts are added, with or without different terms and conditions.

Issuers of credit card ABS in the US market are required to retain ownership, or a shared ownership, in the trust. This is so the issuer can ensure that fluctuations in the balance of the receivables due to seasonal factors, as well as factors such as returned goods and credit card fraud, can be handled. It is also an incentive for the issuer to maintain the credit quality of the pool. The participation level is set at the minimum level of the receivables balance in the trust, which is 7% in the US market. This minimum level is set at 10% in the UK market and for sterling credit card ABS. If the level of its participation falls below the minimum required, the issuer must add further credit card accounts to the trust.

The issuing structure for credit card ABS is similar irrespective of the type of trust that is used. Generally, there are three types of cash flow periods: *revolving, amortisation* (or otherwise *accumulation*) and *early amortisation*. Each period generates a different cash flow. This structure essentially replicates a conventional plain vanilla bond, with regular coupon payments and a single redemption amount on maturity, sometimes called the *bullet* payment. The main difference however is that credit card ABS pay monthly interest, instead of the traditional semi-annual interest basis. Credit card bonds also differ from other asset-backed securities because they do not have an amortising payment structure. Such an arrangement would not be appropriate for credit card bonds, since the average life of a receivable is shorter, ranging from between five to ten months. Under the amortising structure, which is used for mortgage-backed bonds and some auto-ABS bonds, payments of principal and interest are passed directly to investors each month. This would lead to an uncertain and volatile payment structure for credit card bonds. Therefore a revolving structure is used instead, with all cash flows being split into interest payments and principal payments. The monthly interest payment is used to cover the coupon on the bond. Also, cash flow that remains after this liability has been discharged, known as *excess spread*, is passed to the issuer or seller. The collection of principal differs according to the payment period, which is reviewed below.

- *Revolving period*. The revolving period in the structure is not fixed, and has ranged from two to 11 years. During the period, bondholders receive only interest payments, when monthly payments of principal are used to purchase new receivables in accounts held in the trust; if there are no new receivables, the cash flows are used to purchase a share of the issuer's participation. If there are insufficient receivables available, this effects an early amortisation, as the issuer's participation would have fallen to below the minimum level. This is an incentive to the issuer to maintain a participation above the minimum.
- *Amortisation/accumulation*. This period starts after the revolving period has ceased. With amortisation or *controlled amortisation*, principal payments are no longer used for reinvestment in more receivables, but instead are used to pay off bondholders in a series of

amortisation payments. The size of these payments depends on how long the amortisation period runs for; the usual length is one year, so that investors receive 12 equal amortisation periods over the year. Excess principal payments received during this period are used to purchase new receivables, similar to the process followed in the revolving period. Accumulation is similar to controlled amortisation, but for investors the results of the process are akin to a conventional bond. The monthly principal payments are deposited in a trust account or *principal funding account* over the 12-month period, and then paid out to bondholders as one lump sum on the maturity date. During this time, interest payments are made each month on the balance of the total invested amount. Accumulation is therefore attractive to investors who wish the redemption payment to be a single bullet payment, and during the process they will not notice any change as the bond moves from the revolving period to the accumulation period.

- *Early amortisation*. An early amortisation is not a planned event, and is triggered if there is decline in asset quality, or the issuer is found to be in financial trouble. The bonds enter into an early amortisation so that investors start to receive their principal immediately, and not be subject to delays in repayment that might otherwise occur. The terms under which credit card ABS deals are issued specify a range of events that, if they occur, will cause the issue to enter early amortisation. These include failure to make required interest payments, failure to transfer receivables to the trust when required, and certain events of bankruptcy and default connected with the issuer. Other triggering events include if the excess spread falls to zero, and if the issuer's participation level falls below the minimum level. The occurrence of early amortisation is a rare event.

Credit enhancement

Bonds issued against credit card receivables are unsecured in that the receivables provide no collateral if cardholders default. Credit card bonds require therefore some form of credit enhancement if they are to receive investment-grade credit ratings, and the majority of them are highly rated once the enhancement has been set up. In this section we briefly describe the main types of credit enhancement that are arranged for credit card issues; many structures have two or more of these enhancements.

- *Excess spread*. The excess spread payment is the amount of cash flow over and above the amount required to discharge the bond's interest obligations. There is usually a significant excess spread due to the interest rate charged on credit cards being substantially higher than money market and bond market interest rates. For example, the average credit card APR in the United Kingdom market during 1998 was over 19%, and sometimes as high as 23%. This means that once the coupon on the bond has been issued and service and other charges paid, there is usually a substantial excess spread, often as high as 5%. The excess spread is used in one or more ways, including to pay the fees of credit-enhancement institutions, being deposited in a trust reserve account or being released to the issuer.

- *Senior/subordinated notes.* Issues are often split into different classes of bonds, to suit investor taste. A common credit enhancement is the senior/subordinated structure, with bonds split into higher and lower rated issues. The subordinated notes absorb the losses in the structure ahead of the senior notes, if any other credit-enhancement features have not proved sufficient. On maturity or early amortisation, the senior notes will be repaid ahead of the subordinated notes. The latter trade at a higher yield as a result.
- *Letter of credit.* As with other asset-backed markets, a bank letter of credit is a common form of credit enhancement used in the credit card market. This is a guarantee from a bank to provide payment in the event that the trust is unable to meet the commitments of the bond issue. The bank guarantee is up to an amount stipulated in the letter of credit. A fee is payable to the bank for providing the letter. This type of enhancement has proved less popular in recent years, after some issuers were themselves downgraded, leading to a downgrading of assets that they had provided letters of credit against.
- *Cash collateral account.* This is a segregated bank account for the benefit of the trust. It is set up and funded at the time of the issue, and funds in it may be used to cover occasions when there is insufficient payments received to cover required interest and principal payments. The funds in the account are borrowed from a third-party bank, and the terms of the issue usually provide for repayment of the cash collateral account only after all the bonds in the issue have been repaid. The excess spread may also be used to fund or top-up the account.
- *Collateral invested amount.* The collateral invested amount, also known as *collateral interest* or *enhancement invested amount*, is a share of ownership in the trust and works in the same way as the cash

collateral account. It is usually placed with a third-party bank, and is also funded by part of the excess spread.

Credit analysis

Credit card ABS are rated by the major credit ratings agencies, in the same way as other asset-backed bonds. The variables in the credit card market mean that there are a larger number of scenarios that the agencies must consider. For example, the quality of a pool of credit card receivables is a function of (among other issues) the:

- type of credit cards in the pool, whether standard, low-rate, affinity cards, store cards and so on;
- credit scoring model used by the card issuer;
- interest rates charged on the cards, whether fixed or floating, and the frequency with which rates are changed or reset;
- amount of dormant cards in the pool;
- behaviour of cardholders in the pool;
- yield on the portfolio;
- monthly payment rate, which will fluctuate as the number of accounts changes, or as cardholders pay a smaller amount of their balance each month or pay off balances entirely;
- coupon on the bonds: a floating coupon on the bond is more at risk if it is backed with card receivables that are fixed rate, and vice-versa.

The credit rating a bond issue receives will also consider the possibility that it will be forced into early amortisation. This is separate to the issue of credit enhancement, and unaffected by it. The rating of a credit card issue indicates the likelihood that the issue will be able to redeem in full all the bonds in the structure under any possible scenario. A triple-A rating indicates that investors should receive all their principal.

Securitisation net interest margin (NIM) structures

The third type of ABS we consider in this chapter is less common but nevertheless a useful tool for ALM purposes. A net interest margin (NIM) securitisation enables a bank to further benefit from an existing MBS or ABS transaction, which would itself have been originated to meet balance sheet management objectives. We describe the basic concept here and also illustrate the deal type with a case study.

NIM ABS origin and structure

A NIM transaction is in effect a securitisation of an existing securitisation.[2] It is a securitisation structure that is backed by the excess cash flow generated from an existing asset-backed or mortgage-backed deal. The liabilities payable on overlying notes created in an NIM deal can only be paid after all the interest, principal, fees and expenses payable on the original transaction have been discharged. In other words, the NIM notes are subordinated entirely to the underlying deal. This results in a potentially more volatile cash-flow profile than that for vanilla ABS notes. Figure 21.1 shows where the NIM class of notes would sit in the waterfall structure.

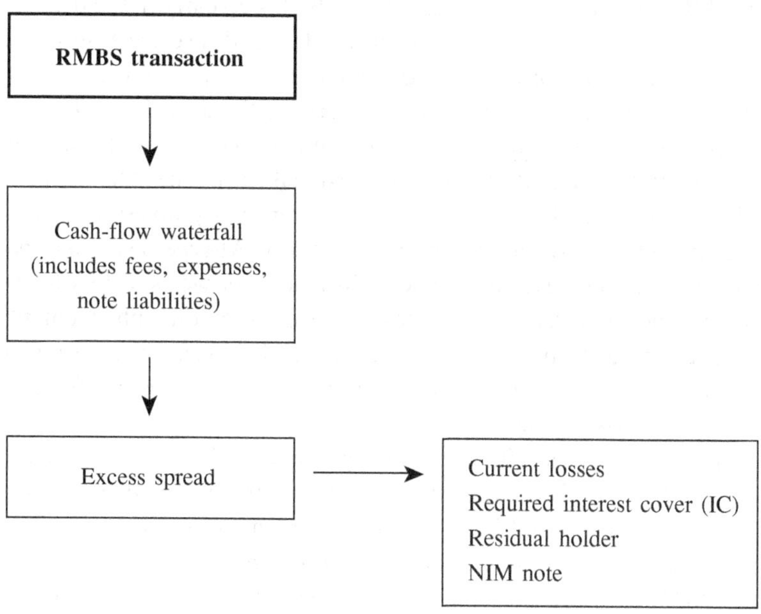

Figure 21.1 NIM structure cash flow waterfall process

[2] The use of this term in a securitisation context should not be confused with the more general banking meaning of "net interest margin", which is defined as the net margin across all maturities between assets and liabilities. It is a measure of the net interest income received by a bank once funding costs are taken into account.

NIM structures are not uncommon in the US market and have also been observed in Europe. Typically, they are created from underlying RMBS and home-equity transactions, which often exhibit a significant amount of excess spread. The level of excess spread will vary, but generally needs to be around 3% or more for it to be considered for an NIM deal. The level of excess spread varies with market conditions; for example, in a mortgage deal the level of prepayment of the underlying collateral is directly related to the level of market interest rates (when rates are high, prepayment levels are higher). For this reason, NIM notes trade in similar fashion to MBS interest-only (IO) notes.

The driver of an NIM deal may be originator- or investor-focused. In many ABS and MBS deals, excess spread builds up early in the deal because any losses incurred occur later on in the deal and also because of elapsed time taken for loan originators to foreclose on non-performing loans. As such, excess spread becomes available early in the deal. It can be collected in a reserve account, which acts as a credit enhancement in the structure, or flow through to a liability known as a residual certificate. This is often held by the originator or issuer. If sold on to a third-party investor, it is usually called an NIM certificate. A further driver of NIM-type deals may become apparent once the Basel II regime is in place. As we note in Chapter 27, Basel II does not recognise excess spread as credit enhancement in a securitisation transaction. This may provide added incentive to originators to undertake NIM repackagings to continue to derive benefit from excess spread in an existing deal.

An NIM note is in effect a repackaged interest in the residual cash pool of a securitisation. The basic structure of an NIM deal is that of a separate Trust (often incorporated in an SPV) into which the residual cash-flow of a previous securitisation transaction, or transactions, is placed. The Trust then issues NIM notes backed by these cash-flows. NIM notes are only repaid if sufficient cash is available in the Trust to effect redemption, if not they cannot be repaid. This cash is what is left over after all the liabilities of the underlying ABS deal(s) have been discharged. This is the most important factor that affects NIM note performance; other issues include:

- the speed of repayment of underlying assets;
- the occurrence of credit losses in the portfolio;
- the reduction in excess spread due to liability charges increasing;
- the position and standing of the transaction originator, and its strength as loans servicer.

NIMs may be created to meet an investor demand or simply to try to realise further value from an existing transaction. They exhibit a higher risk-reward profile than standard ABS notes of equivalent rating quality.

A typical transaction structure is shown in Figure 21.2.

Master Trust series 2007-1
$1 billion sub-prime residential mortgage-backed securities

Capital structure

Tranche	**Nominal**	**Over-collateralisation**
Senior A1, A2, A3	800mm	20mm
Mezz M1, M2, M3	180mm	
Equity		
Residual certificate	[20mm]	

NIM balance sheet

Assets	
Series 2007-1 residual certificate	[20mm]
Liabilities	
NIM	[20mm]
Residual cash flow	

Figure 21.2 Hypothetical NIM securitisation capital structure

Illustration of an NIM repackaging deal

We use a very interesting structure to illustrate both a variation on the concept of the NIM securitisation, as well as a synthetic transaction (see Chapter 23). Dovedale Finance No. 1 plc is classed as an RMBS transaction, but is also a synthetic securitisation, using credit default swaps (CDS) to effect the risk transfer. This risk transfer involves an existing securitisation, Leek Finance plc.

Underlying transaction[3]

Britannia Building Society is the 2nd largest building society in the United Kingdom, its principal business is the provision of mortgage and savings products to retail customers.[4] It is the originator of a long-standing RMBS programme, Leek Finance plc. Figure 21.3 shows the Bloomberg header page for this transaction, and we see that the first multi-tranche issue in this series took place in 1996; Leek series 18 was an issue ten years later. The underlying assets are referred to as "whole loans" and are sub-prime residential mortgages; "ARM" refers to adjustable-rate mortgage.

<HELP> for explanation, <MENU> for similar functions. N120 **Mtge**

CMO/ABS SECURITIES Pg 1 of 2

All Series for **LEEK** LEEK FINANCE PLC

~ = preliminary cashflows

	Series	Pricing Date	Collateral	Net Cpn	WAC	WAM	Orig Bal at Iss (000s)
Pd 1)	1	12/13/96	Whole Loan				794,600
Pd 2)	2	5/10/99	Whole Loan				173,200
Pd 3)	3	7/19/01	Whole ARM				312,300
Pd 4)	7	4/11/02	Whole Loan		3.870		389,100
* 5)	10	4/25/03	Whole Loan		3.720	22Y 10M	0
* 6)	11A	10/16/03	Whole Loan			17Y 7M	0
* 7)	11X	10/16/03	Whole Loan			17Y 7M	0
* 8)	12A	3/19/04	Whole Loan				0
* 9)	12X	3/19/04	Whole Loan				0
*10)	14A	10/19/04	Whole Loan				528,000
*11)	14X	10/19/04	Whole Loan				0
*12)	15A	4/13/05	Whole Loan			22Y 4M	310,000
*13)	15X	4/14/05	Whole Loan			22Y 4M	0
*14)	16A	10/13/05	Whole Loan				0
*15)	16X	10/13/05	Whole Loan				0
*16)	17A	3/31/06	Whole Loan			21Y 10M	697,000
*17)	17X	3/31/06	Whole Loan			21Y 10M	1,200,000
~*18)	18A	10/19/06	Whole Loan			21Y 10M	1,000,000

Australia 61 2 9777 8600 Brazil 5511 3048 4500 Europe 44 20 7330 7500 Germany 49 69 920410
Hong Kong 852 2977 6000 Japan 81 3 3201 8900 Singapore 65 6212 1000 U.S. 1 212 318 2000
G364-793-0 11-Dec-2006 14:51:44

Figure 21.3 Britannia Building Society deal "Leek Finance plc" showing series issuance

---

3 Special thanks to Nick Bourne at GMAC RFC, Bracknell, Berkshire, England, for assistance with preparing this section. Any errors or omissions remain the responsibility of the author.

4 Building societies are similar in concept to the "thrifts" or Savings & Loan institutions in the United States.

The Leek deals are structured with a Reserve Fund that traps excess spread. According to Moody's, the deals have exhibited very low loss performance to date, no more than 5 basis points on a handful of the series, and all losses have been covered by the excess spread in each deal; hence, no noteholder has suffered a loss.[5]

Dovedale Finance No. 1 plc

The Dovedale transaction is a synthetic securitisation of the reserve accounts in the Leek transaction, closed in June 2006. In effect it is akin to an NIM transaction, but in a synthetic form. Figure 21.4 shows the note structure for Dovedale, which we observe comprises six tranches. The deal size is GBP 138 million. The coupon on each note appears to be fixed; in fact, the notes pay 3-month Libor plus a spread, and what we see in Figure 21.4 is the latest fixing (as at 11 December 2006). Figure 21.5 on page 1014 shows the Bloomberg page DES for the senior tranche in the deal, which we see has a pool factor of 1.00000. From Figure 21.6 we see that the coupon on this tranche is 3-month Libor plus 58 basis points. If the note is not redeemed at its first optional maturity date in December 2008, this spread will increase to 116 basis points.

<HELP> for explanation. N120 **Mtge**

CMO/ABS SECURITIES

All Classes for **DOVE 2006-1** DOVEDALE FINANCE NO. 1 PLC

Class	Orig Amt (000s)	Coupon	Orig WAL	Orig Maturity	x = Non-CUSIP	GRADE	Description
* 1) A1	2,500	5.631	2.24	12/21/38	xBCCOQXPL6	-	FLT,STEP
* 2) A2	14,000	3.929	2.24	12/21/38	xBCCOQXPM4	-	FLT,STEP
* 3) B1	4,000	6.051	3.28	12/21/38	xBCCOQXPN2	-	MEZ,FLT,STEP
* 4) B2	47,500	4.349	3.28	12/21/38	xBCCOQXPP7	-	MEZ,FLT,STEP
* 5) C1	14,500	8.301	4.54	12/21/38	xBCCOQXPQ5	-	MEZ,FLT,STEP
* 6) C2	55,500	6.599	4.54	12/21/38	xBCCOQXPR3	-	MEZ,FLT,STEP

Figure 21.4 Dovedale transaction note structure

[5] Moody's Pre-Sale report, *Dovedale Finance No. 1 plc*, Moody's Investor Service, 26 May 2006.

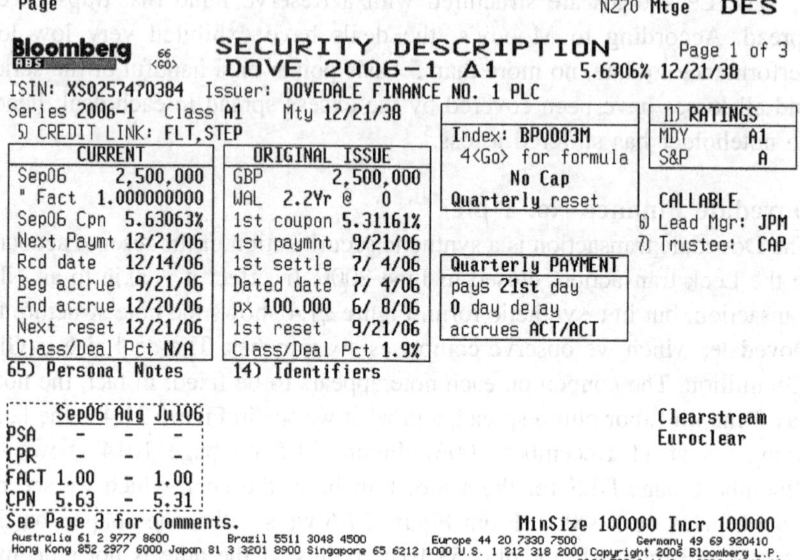

Figure 21.5 Dovedale A1 senior tranche, note description

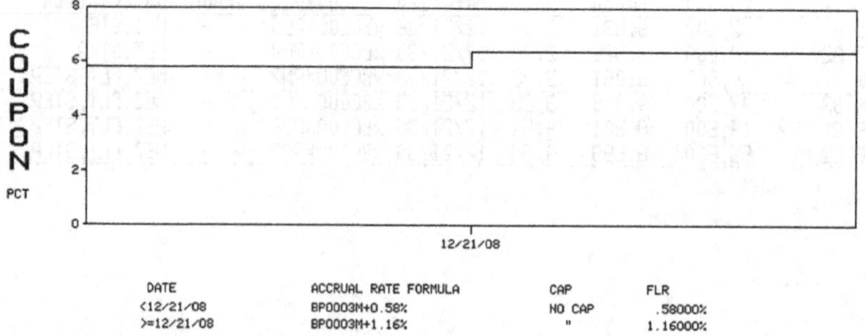

Figure 21.6 Dovedale A1 note coupon spread

The Dovedale securitisation references its underlying assets by means of a CDS between it and the originator, Britannia Building Society. The proceeds from the issue of notes are deposited in an Issuer account at the originator. Investors suffer a loss on occurrence of a credit event, which is defined as one of three types of credit event (failure to pay, bankruptcy and restructuring) in any of the referenced Leek deals. There is no excess spread in the Dovedale deal; credit enhancement in the transaction consists of:

- excess spread in the Leek deals;
- threshold amount in the Leek deals, that must be eaten into first;
- subordination of the overlying note classes.

This transaction illustrates how Britannia has transferred the credit risk of the Leek excess spread (which form, in effect, its first-loss piece) to investors; at the same time, investors gain access to an asset class (sub-prime RMBS) paying a higher return than prime RMBS.

Figure 21.7 shows the deal structure diagram.

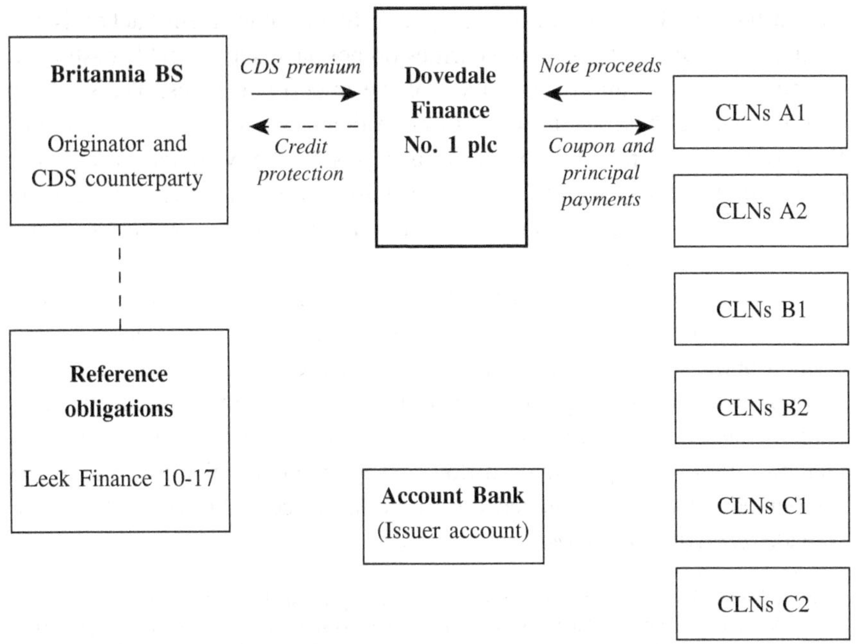

Figure 21.7 Dovedale Finance No. 1 plc structure diagram
Source: Moody's. Used with permission.

Static spread analysis of asset-backed bonds

It is apparent that the traditional gross redemption yield or YTM method for measuring the return available from a particular instrument, and its relative value compared to the government yield curve, is not appropriate in the case of asset-backed bonds. In order to calculate a meaningful redemption yield measure, the cash flows for a particular instrument must be known with a degree of certainty. This is not the case for many asset-backed securities. The inaccuracy of the redemption yield measure also must take into account the fact that, even for conventional bonds, it ignores the reinvestment and dispersion of coupon payments, discounting them all at the same rate. This is, to all intents and purposes, glossed over for conventional bonds because the calculation treats all bonds the same, creating in effect a level- playing field.

Asset-backed bonds have subtle differences in cash flow profiles and prepayment rates, making it more difficult to analyse them all in the same way. The exception to this is most credit card–ABS issues, which have a single bullet payment on maturity and (usually, but not always) a fixed-coupon payment every month. It would be in order to compare the yield on such a bond with a conventional corporate bond. Other asset-backed issues such as mortgage and car loan securities do not have such a stable cash flow, mainly due to the amortising nature of the underlying loans. The simplest way to analyse these securities is to price them as a spread to the yield of the government bond whose maturity is closest to the weighted average life of the bonds being analysed. This is still an approximate measure and can be inaccurate under certain circumstances, and the convention now is to use the *static spread* measure.

Static spread analysis assumes that a particular bond itself represents a portfolio of individual securities, so that each cash flow is viewed as a zero-coupon bond. Under the static spread method each of these individual cash flows is discounted using a rate made up of the relevant government zero-coupon rate plus a spread. The spot rate used is the one whose duration matches that of the specific cash flow.[6] The spread at which the sum of the discounted cash flows equalled their nominal price is known as the static spread, *zero-volatility spread,* or *Z-spread.*

[6] In the United States, United Kingdom and certain European markets there is a market in zero-coupon government bonds, known as strips. Therefore it is straightforward to find the appropriate spot rate to use in discounting the asset-backed bond cash flows, although banks frequently use an implied spot-rate curve because of liquidity effects of the observed zero-coupon curve. In the absence of an actual strip market, the implied spot rate calculated from the benchmark government bond yield curve is used.

This is illustrated with the following example, which uses three hypothetical securities. The first bond (Bond A) has a maturity of one year (12 months), while the remaining bonds B and C have average maturities of 12 months. Bond A has a single bullet redemption payment in exactly 12 months' time, exemplified by a conventional corporate bond or certain credit card-backed bonds. Bond B repays its principal over a 12-month period beginning six months from now, similar to a credit card-backed bond that has a controlled amortisation process. Bond C has an amortising principal repayment pattern, so that the amount of repayment declines gradually starting in the next month and finishing 24 months from now. This bond resembles an auto-ABS bond and certain mortgage pass-through securities. The principal payment cash flows are shown as Figures 21.8 (a), (b) and (c).

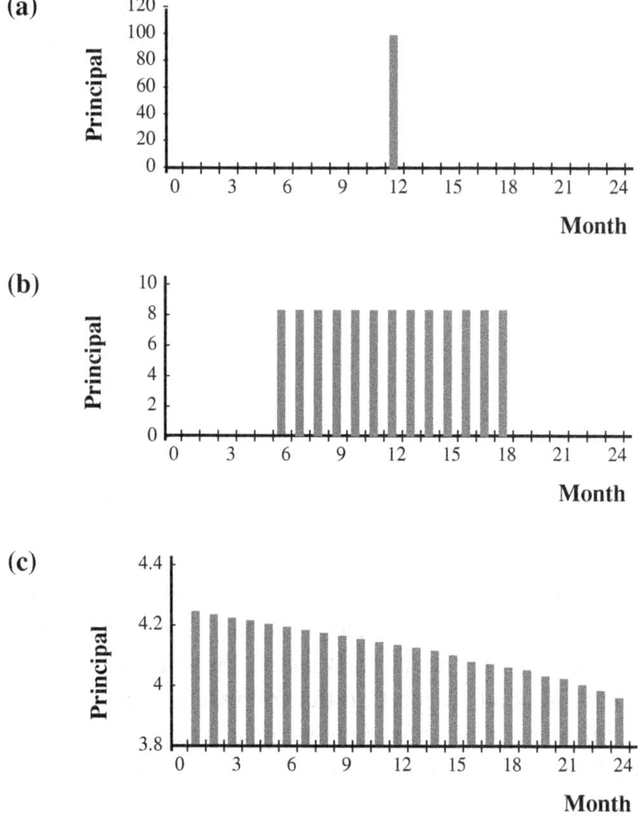

Figure 21.8 Cash flow profiles for bullet, controlled amortisation and amortised principal bonds (a), (b), (c).

Assume that all bonds are trading at a yield to maturity of 6.33%. The one-year government bond is trading at a yield of 5.98%, therefore the yield spread on the three bonds is 35 basis points.[7] This spread is also called the *nominal spread.*

We know that the redemption yield calculation discounts each cash flow at the internal rate of return, here 6.33%, which has been based on the average maturity of 12 months for receipt of the principal. In a positively sloping short-term yield curve environment, cash flows received early on would be discounted at a rate that was above the actual rate for that term, while cash flows received later would be discounted at a rate that was below the actual rate. This is an accepted drawback of the redemption yield method, and is accepted on the belief that the two effects will cancel each other out.

The static spread gives a more accurate picture yield. Assume that the short-term zero-coupon yield curve is as follows, as shown in Figure 21.9:

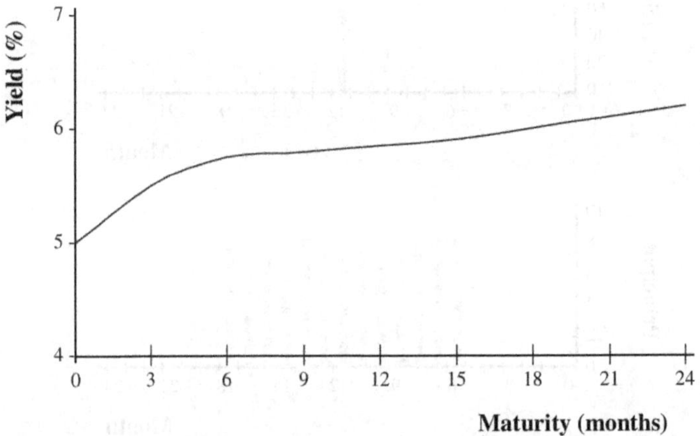

Figure 21.9 Short-term yield curve

This is obtained by observing the yield of government discount instruments in the market. If we use the relevant yields from this curve to discount each of the principal cash flows for bonds A, B and C, the static spreads that are obtained, in the case of bonds B and C, differ from the nominal spread. This is because using this method more accurately captures the value of each cash flow over the period that they are received. The static spreads are shown in Table 21.4.

[7] The yields are based on market conditions for sterling asset-backed bonds in October 1999, against the gilt yield curve at that time.

	Bond A	Bond B	Bond C
Nominal spread	35	35	35
Static spread	35	30	28

Table 21.4 Static and nominal spreads of hypothetical bonds A, B and C

What is behind the difference in spreads for the two bonds with non-bullet principal repayment? Essentially, these bonds, when based on an average maturity yield level plus spread, are over-valued. This is because cash flows received after the average maturity date are more sensitive to the discount rate which, using the 12-month yield, is below the actual rate in a positive yield curve environment. To allow for the lower present value of the individual cash flows to equate the higher price of the cash flows obtained using the single average maturity yield, the spread used to discount each cash flow must be lower. This is the static spread. Bond C has the greatest difference between the nominal spread and the static spread, because the cash flows are dispersed over a longer period, making each cash flow more sensitive to the discount rate used to obtain its present value. There is no difference in the two spreads for bond A, because the cash flow has been discounted at the correct rate.

In a positively sloped yield curve environment, the static spread on an amortising security will be lower than the nominal yield spread, while it will be higher than the nominal yield spread in a negative yield curve environment. The extent of the difference between the static spread and the nominal spread is a function of the slope of the yield curve and the dispersion of the bond's cash flows.

Yield analysis of asset-backed securities must take into account their uncertain cash flows. We have demonstrated that the traditional redemption yield measure, calculated using the security's average life maturity, is inappropriate, because it does not allow for the dispersed nature of the bond's cash. A mortgage or auto-loan-backed bond has a principal repayment structure that disperses the payments over a length of time, so the more accurate yield measure to use is static spread. As well as accounting for dispersion, this approach also overcomes the traditional drawback of YTM as it discounts each cash flow at the correct rate for that cash flow's maturity.

References and bibliography

Ames, C. 1997, "Collaterialised Mortgage Obligation", in Fabozzi, F. (ed.), *The Handbook of Fixed Income Securities*, 5th edition, McGraw-Hill, New York, pp. 569–97.

Bear Stearns 1994, *Asset-backed Securities Special Report*, 5 December, New York.

Bhattacharya, A. and Fabozzi, F. (eds) 1996, *Asset-backed Securities*, FJF Associates.

Fabozzi, F. 1998, *Handbook of Structured Financial Products*, FJF Associates, New Hope, PA.

Fabozzi, F. and Jacob, D. 1996, *The Handbook of Commercial Mortgage-backed Securities*, FJF Associates, New Hope, PA.

Fabozzi, F., Ramsey, C. and Ramirez, F. 1994, *Collateralised Mortgage Obligations*, FJF Associates, New Hope, PA.

CHAPTER

22

Collateralised Debt Obligations[1]

Collateralised debt obligations (CDOs) are structured finance products that are related to asset-backed securities. They are important tools in bank ALM, first employed for asset management purposes as vehicles to reduce balance sheet risk. Subsequently, they became an asset class in their own right and later developed into mini-investment funds. In this chapter we look at different types of CDO structures and how they are used as ALM tools.

Collateralised bond obligations (CBOs) and collateralised loan obligations (CLOs), which together make up collateralised debt obligations (CDOs), are natural developments in securitisation. The origins of the market are generally held to be the repackaging of high-yield debt or loans into higher-rated bonds, which began in the late 1980s. Today, there is great diversity in CDO transactions, and the market has expanded into Europe and Asia from its origin in the United States. Both CBOs and CDOs are notes or securities issued against an underlying collateral of assets, almost invariably a diverse pool of corporate bonds or loans, or a combination of both. A transaction with a corporate- or sovereign-bond asset pool is a CBO, while a CLO is backed by a portfolio of secured and/or unsecured corporate and commercial bank loans. Cash flow CBOs/CDOs fall into two types; these are arbitrage and balance sheet CDOs.

A typical CDO structure involves the transfer of credit risk from an underlying asset pool to an SPV and this credit risk is then transferred to investors via the issue of credit-linked notes by the SPV. The objectives behind CDO transactions undertaken by banks include:

- optimisation of returns on regulatory capital by reducing the need for capital to support assets on the balance sheet;

[1] This chapter was co-authored with Richard Pereira.

- improvement of return on economic capital by managing risk effectively;
- management of risk (for example, purchasing or transferring credit risk) and balance sheet capital;
- issue of securities as a means of raising funding;
- provision of funding for the acquisition of assets;
- increasing funds under management.

Figure 22.1 shows CDO issue volumes in the years to 2004, while Figure 22.2 shows the country of origin of underlying assets during 2004. The "family tree" of CDOs is shown in Figure 22.3. A typical conventional CDO structure is shown in Figure 22.4 and Figure 22.5 on page 1025.

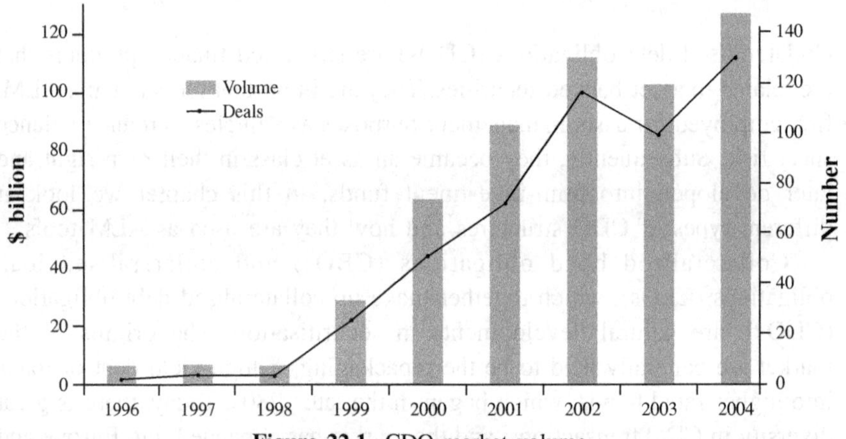

Figure 22.1 CDO market volume
Source: Moody's.

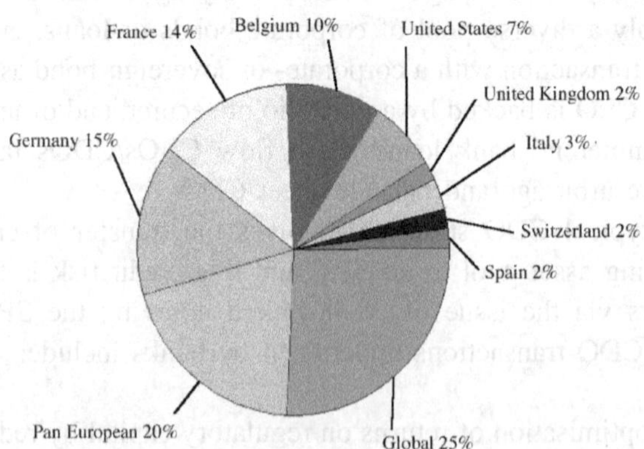

Figure 22.2 Origin of assets, 2004
Source: Moody's

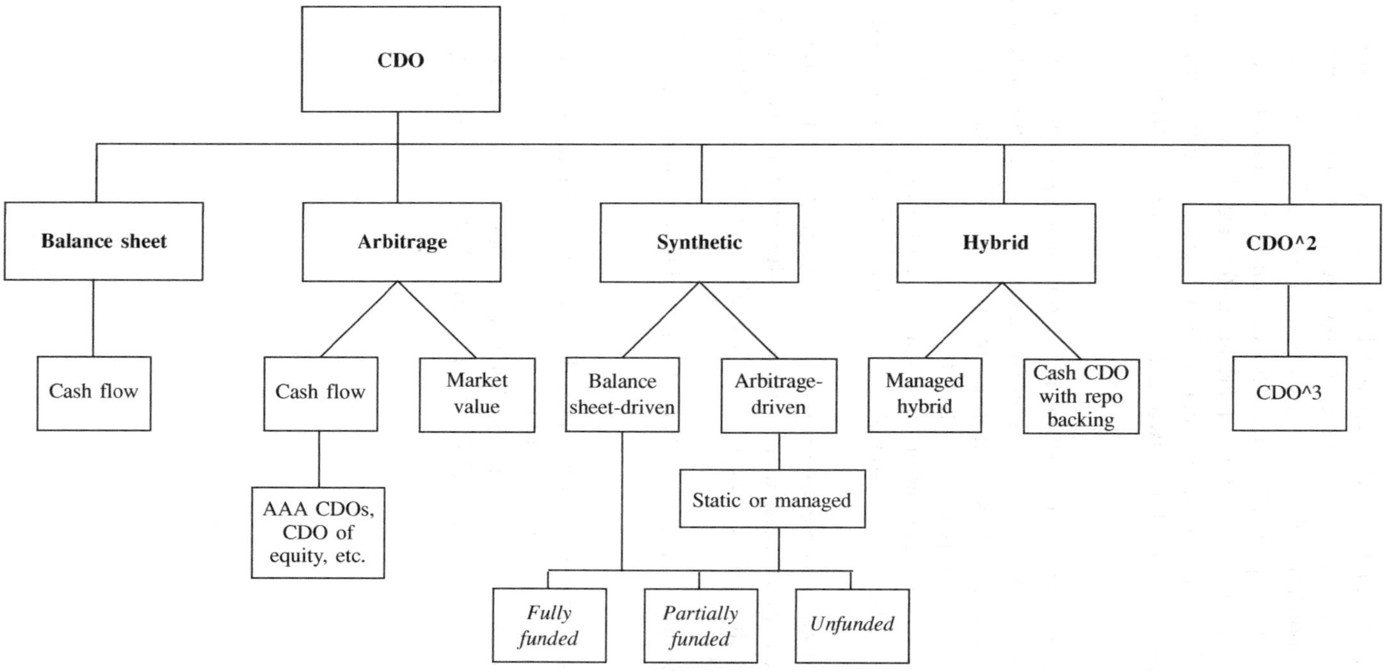

Figure 22.3 The CDO family

The main distinction between a CLO and CBO is the dominant investment class in the underlying asset pool. With a CLO, the underlying asset pool is a portfolio of bank loans, while a CBO series is issued against an underlying asset pool of a portfolio of bonds. So although they are grouped into a single generic form, there are differences between CBOs and CLOs. In the first instance, assets such as bank loans have different features to bonds; the analysis of the two will therefore differ. Note also the following:

- loans are less uniform instruments, and their terms vary widely. This includes terms such as interest dates, amortisation schedules, reference rate indices, reset dates, terms to maturity and so on, which affect the analysis of cash flows;
- the legal documentation for loans is less standardised, in part reflecting the observation above, and this calls for more in-depth legal review;
- it is often possible to restructure a loan portfolio to reflect the changed or changing status of borrowers (for example, their ability to service the debt), a flexibility not usually afforded to participants in a CBO;
- the secondary market in bank loans is far less liquid than that in bonds.

These issues, among others, mean the analysis of CBOs often presents differences from that used for CLOs.

This chapter briefly introduces CDOs, describes the motivation for an originator such as a commercial bank, and some of the issues relating to the CDO structures.

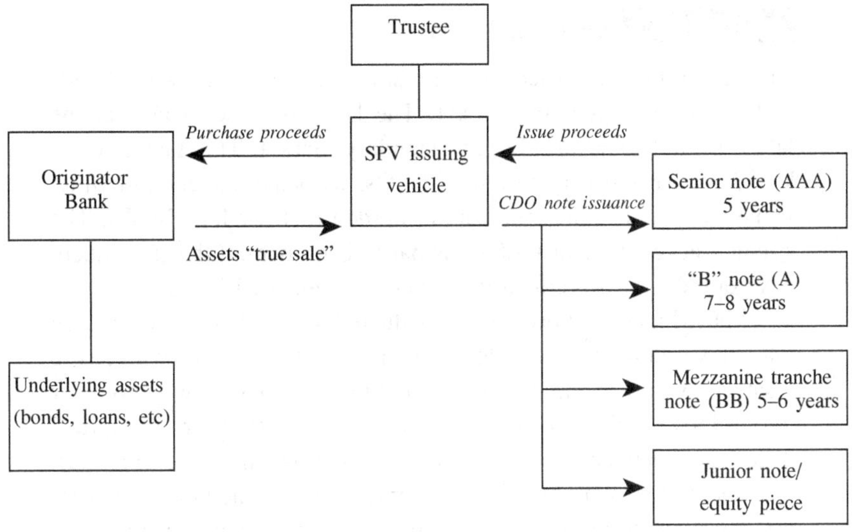

Figure 22.4 Generic cash flow CDO

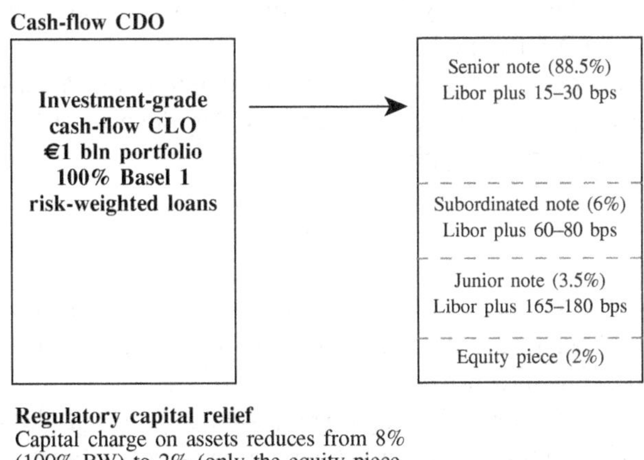

Figure 22.5 Conventional CDO hypothetical mechanics

Example 22.1 Bonds and loans

Until the mid-1990s there was a distinct separation between bonds and loans in the capital market. The key difference was that the latter did not trade in a liquid secondary market. This factor was a key driver in the origination of CLOs, as banks sought to extract value from and reduce the capital burden of their loan books. The rise and acceptance of CLOs has partly been behind the subsequent development of a secondary market in syndicated loans.

Many loans are now priced, evaluated and traded in a secondary market. Certain syndicated loans can be sold to investors who desire a safer haven than the corporate bond market, or who wish to enter into relative value positions by taking advantage of the spread differential between loans and bonds issued by the same borrower. Syndicated loans are classified as senior debt, so they have a higher priority over corporate bonds in the event of a winding-up of the issuer.

It can be problematic to value a syndicated loan, as it may have a repayment schedule, as well as a floating interest rate that may step up or down, depending on changes in (say) the credit rating of the issuer. This is a key issued addressed whenever loans are evaluated for a CLO portfolio.

Bloomberg's YA page, which we encountered in Chapter 4, can also be used for syndicated loan analysis. Any loan must be found on the system first by typing

LOAN <Go>

which brings up the syndicated bank loan menu function. This includes a loan finder function. Once the loan is found, it can be evaluated using screen YA.

Figure 22.6 shows the page being used to assess a USD loan issued by Singapore Aircraft Leasing, which is part of the Singapore Airlines group. At the time it was evaluated the loan had approximately six years left to maturity, having been issued originally in 1998 at a spread of 70 basis points over Libor.

GRAB Corp DES
Enter 99<GO> for options. <HELP> for Disclaimer
TRANCHE LOAN DESCRIPTION Page 1 of 1

Tranche# LN008473 Tranche SIASP Maturity 07/30/10 Country SG
Cusip# Type TERM Mkt Type ASIA/PAC RIM
Facility# Amend N.A. Issue Status SIGNED

Issue Information
Borrower SINGAPORE AIRCRAFT LEASING
Industry Finance - Leasing Compan
Calc Type (533) TERM-TYPE:COM LOAN
Fac/Trnch Amts USD 98MM /98MM
Purpose WORKING CAPITAL
Effective Date 07/30/98
Outstanding 98MM
Secured Yes

Sub Limit Borrowings
Not Applicable

Bank Group
Ld Arranger
Agent WESTLB
Participants 55<GO>

Assignment Info
Min Pc
Increment
Fee
Retain

Tranche Ratings
S&P NR
Moody's NR
FI NR

Senior Debt Ratings
S & P NA
MOODY NA

Info @ Close
Not Applicable

Current Sprd & Fees
Interest Typ FLOATER
Int Freqncy SEMI-AN
Current Base LIBOR
Spread 70.00BP
Reset Freq SEMI-AN

Australia 61 2 9777 8600 Brazil 5511 3048 4500 Europe 44 20 7330 7500 Germany 49 69 920410
Hong Kong 852 2977 6000 Japan 81 3 3201 8900 Singapore 65 6212 1000 U.S. 1 212 318 2000 Copyright 2004 Bloomberg L.P.
G926-802-2 17-Mar-04 8:48:32

Figure 22.6 Loan information data on Bloomberg for a loan issued by Singapore Aircraft Leasing

Figure 22.7 shows the yield analysis function for the same loan, as at 17 March 2004. The screen is split into four parts that include:

- loan information data;
- curve information about the yield curve selected to analyse this loan;
- the calculator that shows the IRR and the current spread over the Libor forward curve (zero-discount margin or Z-DM field).

The Z-DM field is the main measure of return on the loan. It shows the current spread on the loan over the Libor forward curve, in this case 71.341 basis points. The evaluation is carried out against the USD swap curve, on a 30/360 and semi-annual basis (the same terms as the loan). The IRR of the loan is shown to be 1.87%.

The discount margin assumes that this day's Libor is unchanged for the life of the loan (a necessary, but unrealistic, assumption).

This spread can be used to compare the return on the loan compared to that on a bond. If there is a similar maturity floating-rate bond available from the same issuer, then the comparison is easily made. Otherwise we can compare the asset swap spread for a fixed-coupon bond. To do that we can call up a similar maturity bond for the same issuer on page ASW on Bloomberg. The ASW page calculates the swap market's value of a fixed-rate bond as a spread over Libor. This spread can be compared to the spread for the loan to assess relative value. At any time that the loan pays a higher spread, it might be deemed an attractive investment compared to the bond, especially since it has a repayment priority on default over the bond.

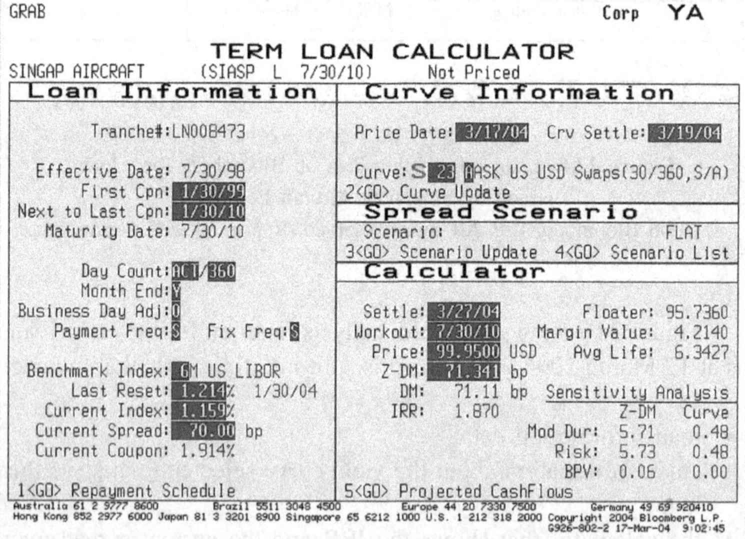

Figure 22.7 Bloomberg page YA used to evaluate the Singapore Aircraft Leasing syndicated loan, as at 17 March 2004

An overview of CDOs

CDO is the generic term for two distinct products, so-called balance sheet transactions and arbitrage transactions. The common thread between these structures is that they are both backed by some form of commercial or corporate debt or loan receivable. The primary differences between the two types are the type of collateral backing the newly created securities in the CDO structure, and the motivations behind the transaction. The growth of the market has been in response to two key requirements: the desire of investors for higher yield investments in higher risk markets, managed by portfolio managers skilled at extracting value out of poorly performing or distressed debt, and the need for banks to extract greater value out of assets on their balance sheet, almost invariably because they are generating a below-market rate of return. By securitising bond or loan portfolios, banks can lower their capital charge by removing them off their balance sheet and funding them at a lower rate. Figure 22.8 is a summary of the key differences between balance sheet and arbitrage CDOs.

Collateralised debt obligations (CDOs)

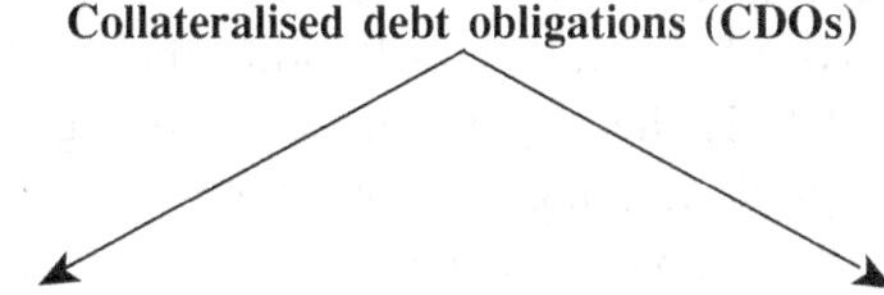

Balance sheet CDOs	**Arbitrage CDOs**
Collateral: high-grade, bank-oriented commercial and corporate loans	**Collateral**: high-yield corporate bonds or corporate loans
Key motivations: reducing balance sheet to improve capital ratios; obtain off-balance sheet treatments; obtain lower funding rates	**Key motivations**: arbitrage opportunity; increasing assets under management; assets purchased in secondary market
Typical issuers: domestic and international banks	**Typical issuers**: insurance companies; mutual funds; private equity funds
Market liquidity: generally lower than investor-driven trades	

Figure 22.8 Collateralised debt obligations

Balance sheet CDOs are structured securities developed because banks wished to securitise part of their loan portfolios, in order to improve their capital adequacy position. Securitising a bank's loans reduces the size of its balance sheet, thereby improving its capital ratio and lowering its capital charge. The first domestic balance sheet CLO in the US market was the NationsBank Commercial Loan Master Trust, series 1997–91 and 1997–92, issued in September 1997, which employed what is known as a Master Trust structure to target investors who had previously purchased asset-backed securities.[2]

As balance sheet CLOs are originated mainly by commercial banks, the underlying collateral is usually part of their own commercial loan portfolios, and can be fixed-term, revolving, secured and unsecured, syndicated and other loans. Although most CLOs have been issued by banks that are domiciled in the main developed economies, the geographical nature of the underlying collateral often has little connection with the home country of the originating bank. Most bank CLOs are floating-rate loans with average lives of five years or less. They are targeted mainly at bank sector Libor-based investors, and are structured with an amortising payoff schedule.

Arbitrage CDOs are backed with high-yield corporate bonds or loans. As the collateral can take either form, arbitrage CDOs can be either CLOs or CBOs. Market practitioners often refer to all arbitrage deals as CDOs for simplicity, irrespective of the collateral backing them. The key motivation behind arbitrage CDOs is the opportunity for arbitrage, or the difference between investment-grade funding rates and high-yield investment rates. In an arbitrage CDO, the income generated by the high-yield assets should exceed the cost of funding, as long as no credit event or market event takes place.

Although CDOs are not a recent innovation, the market only experienced high growth rates from 1995 onwards, and certain investors are still prone to regard it as an "emerging" asset class. However, in terms of volume in the US market, CDOs are comparable to credit card and automobile loan asset-backed securities.

CDO structures are classified into conventional CDO structures and synthetic CDO structures. The difference between these structures lies in the method of risk transfer from the originator to the SPV. In conventional CDO structures, the transfer of assets, known as a true sale, is how credit risk is transferred to the SPV. In synthetic CDO structures, credit-derivative instruments are used to transfer credit risk.

---

[2] The Master Trust structure is a generic set-up that allows originators to issue subsequent asset-backed deals under the same legal arrangement, thus enabling such issues to be made quicker than they otherwise might be. Investors also welcome such a structure, as they indicate a commitment to liquidity by implying further issues into the market.

In practice, the two structures are categorised by the motivation behind their issue. There are two main motivations: issuer- or balance sheet-driven transactions and investor-driven or market-value arbitrage transactions. To date, balance sheet-driven transactions have been the main reason for structuring the majority of CDOs in Europe. However, investor-driven arbitrage CDO transactions have experienced strong growth as investment managers increase funds under management and release value through management expertise of the underlying asset portfolio.

Synthetic structures are described in the next chapter.

CDOs issue notes from an SPV to investors. SPVs are created to enable the effective transfer of risk from the originator. Most SPVs are set up so that they are bankruptcy-remote and isolated from the originator's credit risk. The creation of an SPV usually involves a nominal amount of equity and the main funding comes from the issue of notes. SPVs may be set up and registered in a tax haven. The funds from the issue of the notes are used to "acquire" the pool of underlying assets (the bonds or loans) from the originator. This will result in the "true sale" of the assets to the SPV. In this way, the SPV has an asset-and-liability profile which must be managed during the term of the CDO.

The ownership of the assets is transferred into the SPV. This asset transfer, if performed and structured properly, removes assets from the balance sheet of a bank originator. As a result, the securitised assets would not be included in the calculation of capital ratios. This provides regulatory-capital relief and is the main motivation for some of the CDO structures in the market today.

The typical liability structure would include a senior tranche rated in the Aaa/Aa category, a junior tranche rated in the Ba category and an un-rated equity tranche. The equity tranche is the most risky, as first losses in the underlying portfolio are absorbed by the equity tranche. For this reason, the equity tranche is often referred to as the "first-loss" tranche. The losses on the notes are said to "indemnify" the SPV.

In the case of bank CLOs, the bank will continue to service the loans in the portfolio and usually also retains the first-loss interest.

Structuring a conventional CDO may give rise to significant other issues. The transfer of assets into the SPV in practice may have adverse tax, legal and regulatory implications. The impact will depend on the jurisdiction in which the transfer of assets takes place and the detailed legislation of that jurisdiction. Another practical issue is that the conventional CDO is a funded transaction as the originator receives cash. However, if the originator's main intention is to transfer credit risk or to acquire protection for credit risk, then the conventional CDO structure introduces reinvestment risk, as the cash received would need to be reinvested in other assets.

The SPV which issues the notes is generally an offshore bankruptcy-remote entity to isolate the underlying assets from the default risk of the originator. In most structures, the transfer of credit risk to the investors is via the notes issued by the SPV. The return to investors in the issued notes will be dependent on the performance of the underlying asset pool.

Credit enhancement is provided via subordination (prioritisation of cash-flow payments to investors) of the tranches issued by the SPV. However, in addition to a multi-tranche structure, the bank may also use other mechanisms to credit-enhance the senior notes. An example might include credit insurance on the underlying portfolio, known as a credit wrap, and the use of reserve accounts that assume a loss before the equity tranche.

Comparisons with other asset-backed securities

The CDO asset class has similarities in its fundamental structure with other securities in the ABS market. Like other asset-backed securities, a CDO is a debt obligation issued by an SPV, secured by a form of receivable. In this case though, the collateral concerned is high-yield loans or bonds, rather than, say, mortgage or credit card receivables. Again, similar to other ABS, CDO securities typically consist of different credit tranches within a single structure, and the credit ratings range from AAA to B or unrated. The rating of each CDO class is determined by the amount of credit enhancement in the structure, the ongoing performance of the collateral, and the priority of interest in the cash flows generated by the pool of assets. The credit enhancement in a structure is among items scrutinised by investors, who will determine the cash-flow waterfalls for the interest and principal, the prepayment conditions, and the methods of allocation for default and recovery. Note that the term "waterfall" is used in the context of asset-backed securitisations that are structured with more than one tranche, to refer to the allocation of principal and interest to each tranche in a series. If there is excess cash and this can be shared with other series, the cash flows are allocated back through the waterfall, running over the successive tranches in the order of priority determined at issue.

A significant difference between CDOs and other ABS is the relationship to the servicer. In a traditional ABS the servicing function is usually performed by the same entity that sources and underwrites the original loans. These roles are different in a CDO transaction; for instance, there is no servicer that can collect on non-performing loans. Instead, the portfolio manager for the issuer must actively manage the portfolio. This might include sourcing higher quality credits, selling positions before they deteriorate and purchasing investments that are expected to appreciate. In essence, portfolio managers assume the responsibility of a servicer. Therefore investors in CDOs must focus their analysis on the portfolio manager as well as on the credit quality of the collateral pool. CDO structures also differ from other ABS in that they frequently hold non-investment-grade collateral in the pool, which is not a common occurrence in traditional ABS structures.

CDO asset types

The arbitrage CDO market can be broken down into two main asset types: *cash flow* and *market value* CDOs. Balance sheet CDOs are all cash-flow CDOs.

Cash-flow CDOs share more similarities to traditional ABS than market value transactions. Collateral is usually a self-amortising pool of high-yield bonds and loans, expected to make principal and interest payments on a regular basis. Most cash-flow CDO structures allow for a reinvestment period, and while this is common in other types of ABS, the period length tends to be longer in cash-flow CDOs, typically with a minimum of four years. The cash-flow structure relies upon the collateral's ability to generate sufficient cash to pay principal and interest on the rated classes of securities. This is similar to an automobile ABS, in which the auto loan-backed securities rely upon the cash flows from the fixed pool of automobile loans to make principal and interest payments on the liabilities. Trading of the CDO collateral is usually limited – for instance, in the event of a change in credit situation – and so the value of the portfolio is based on the par amount of the collateral securities.

A portfolio of bonds could be traded more often than a portfolio of loans, although with the growing secondary market in loans this distinction is being blurred. A simplified diagram of the liability structure for a portfolio of cash bonds is given in Figure 22.9 on page 1036. The diagram for a market value CBO is shown in Figure 22.10 also on page 1036.

Market value CDOs, which were first introduced in 1995, resemble hedge funds more than traditional ABS. The main difference between a cash-flow CDO and a market value CDO is that the portfolio manager has the ability to freely trade the collateral. This means investors focus on expected appreciation in the portfolio, and the portfolio itself may be quite different in, say, 12 months' time compared to its composition today. This leads to the analogy with the hedge fund. Investors in market value CDOs are as concerned with the management and credit skills of the portfolio manager as they are with the credit quality of the collateral pool. Market value CDOs rely upon the portfolio manager's ability to generate total returns and to liquidate the collateral in a timely fashion, if necessary, in order to meet the cash-flow obligations (principal and interest) of the CDO structure.

Different portfolio objectives result in distinct investment characteristics. Cash-flow CDO assets consist mainly of rated, high-yield debt or loans that are *current* in their principal and interest payments; that is, they are not in default. In a market value CDO the asset composition is more diversified. The collateral pool might consist of, say, a 75 : 25 percentage split between assets to support liability payments and investments to produce increased equity returns. In this case, the first 75% of assets of a market value CDO asset will resemble those of a conventional cash-flow CDO, with, say, 25% invested in high-yield bonds and 50% in high-yield loans. These assets should be sufficient to support payments on 100% of the liabilities. The remaining 25% of the portfolio might be invested in "special situations" such as distressed debt, foreign bank loans, hybrid capital instruments and other investments. The higher yielding investments are required to produce the higher yields that are marketed to equity investors in market value CDOs.

We have described in general terms the asset side of a CDO. The liability side of a CDO structure is similar to other ABS structures, and encompasses several investment-grade and non-investment-grade classes with an accompanying equity tranche that serves as the first loss position. In, say, a mortgage-backed transaction the equity class is not usually offered but instead held by the issuer. Typically, in the US market-rated CDO, liabilities have a 10–12-year legal final maturity. The three main rating agencies all actively rate cash flow CDOs, although commonly transactions carry ratings from only one or two of the agencies.

Liabilities for market value CDOs differ in some ways from cash-flow CDOs. In most cases senior bank facilities provide more than half of the capital structure, with a 6–7-year final maturity. When a market value transaction is issued, cash generated by the issuance is usually not fully invested at the start. There is a *ramp-up* period to allow the portfolio manager time to make investment decisions and effect collateral purchases. Ramp-up periods result in a risk that cash flows on the portfolio's assets will not be sufficient to cover liability obligations at the start. Rating agencies consider this ramp-up risk when evaluating the transaction's credit enhancement. Ramp-up periods are in fact common to both cash-flow and market value CDOs, but the period is longer with the latter transactions, resulting in more significant risk.

Although CDOs were created only shortly after the first ABS issues, with the first structure appearing in 1988, it was only in the latter half of the 1990s that the product evolved sufficiently and in enough volume to be regarded as a distinct investment instrument and hence, bank ALM tool. The US market has witnessed the most innovative structures, but interesting developments have also taken place in the United Kingdom and Germany. Table 22.1 summarises the evolution in the CDO product in the US market from its first appearance to present arrangements. In particular, collateral types backing the securities have grown considerably, with increasing sophistication in structure and cash-flow mechanics. By 2000, CDOs covered a wide spectrum of credit risk and investment returns, from a diverse pool of high-yielding assets. Investors analyse CDOs as investment instruments in their own right and also with regard to the relative value offered by them vis-à-vis other ABS products.

Early CDO balance sheet

Assets	*Liabilities*
US domestic high-yield bonds	Fixed-rate private securities
	Equity

Present-day CDO balance sheet

Assets	*Liabilities*
US domestic high-yield bonds	AAA to BBB fixed-rate securities
US domestic high-yield loans	AAA to BBB floating-rate securities
Emerging market debt	BB mezzanine securities
Special situation/distressed debt	Contingent interest securities
Foreign bank loan	Credit-linked notes
	Equity

Table 22.1 CDO product evolution

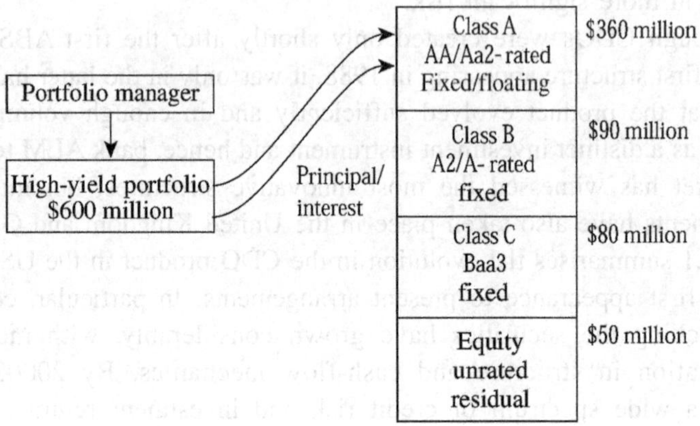

Figure 22.9 Hypothetical cash-flow CBO structure

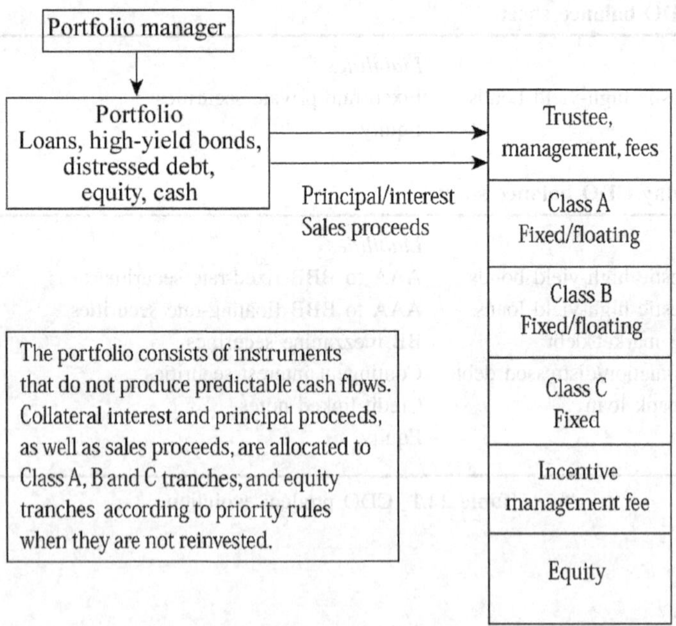

Figure 22.10 Hypothetical market value CBO structure

Motivation behind CDO issue

Bank balance sheet-driven transactions

In a balance sheet CDO, the motivation for the originator is to obtain capital relief through the transfer of credit risk on the pool of underlying assets. The transaction is intended to obtain off-balance sheet treatment for existing on-balance sheet assets to which bank capital has been allocated. The regulatory off-balance sheet treatment enables an originator bank to manage capital constraints and to improve the return on capital for the bank.

The originators of bank balance sheet CLOs are mainly commercial banks. The underlying asset pool may include commercial loans, both secured and unsecured, guarantees and revolving credits. The originator of the underlying assets usually acts as an investment advisor so as to maintain the quality of the underlying asset pool. Although there is usually no trading intention for the underlying asset pool, over the life of the structure there may be changes, such as substitutions or replenishments to the underlying asset pool. A form of protection to the noteholders from these changes is usually that the quality of the underlying pool of assets does not significantly deteriorate. This may be via the maintenance of an average credit quality of the asset pool. Such a restriction is often required by the rating agencies.

The equity tranche in a CDO structure is commonly held by the originator for the following reasons:

- the bank has detailed information on the loans, which will allow it to effectively manage the risk it retains;
- the bank retains economic interest in the performance of the loan portfolio and remains motivated to service the asset pool;
- the return required by a potential purchaser of the equity tranche may be too high, and this tranche may therefore be difficult to place if the overall risk/reward profile is not attractive to investors.

In some cases, the lowest-rated debt tranche is also held by the originator.

Investor-driven arbitrage transactions

In an arbitrage CDO, the underlying asset pool is more actively managed. The investment advisor is usually the manager of the CDO. The type of structure is driven by the opportunity to actively manage the portfolio with the intention of generating arbitrage profits from the spread differential between the investment- and sub-investment-grade markets. The underlying asset pool includes investments which not only provide investment income, but may provide the opportunity to generate value from active trading strategies. The opportunity to generate arbitrage profits is often dependent on the quality and expertise of the manager of the CDO.

The underlying assets may be existing positions that are being managed or may be acquired for the CDO. In practice, when structuring the transaction the profitability of the transaction will depend on factors such as:

- the required return to the noteholders of the issued tranches;
- the portfolio return of the underlying asset pool;
- the expenses (for example, management fee) of managing the SPV.

If the underlying portfolio performs well and the loss-in-the-event-of-default profile is lower than expected, due to lower-than-expected default levels and higher levels of recovery, the required return to investors in the tranches of the CDO will be achieved and the return to the equity holder will be higher than expected. However, if the underlying portfolio performs poorly and the loss in the event of default is higher than expected (due to higher-than-expected default levels and lower levels of recovery rate, perhaps due to adverse economic conditions), then the return on the tranches issued will be lower than expected. Poor investment-management performance will also have an adverse impact on the return to investors.

Fund managers use arbitrage CDOs in higher yielding markets since the CDO structure may allow the manager to achieve a large size of funds under management for a comparatively small level of equity. This has been used effectively in the United States in the past few years. The objective is to set up the CDO so that the returns produced by the underlying pool of high-yielding assets will be enough to pay off investors and provide the originator/fund manager with a profit from the management fee and the return on the equity tranche.

Market convergence: money and debt capital markets

The CDO is a product that was introduced, initially, as a capital-market instrument aimed at medium- and longer-dated investors. But that feature is being blurred. In Chapter 19 we described Treasury and the ALM desk application of synthetic structured products that are used for funding purposes. These are instruments that are utilised at the short-end of the market; that is, they are originated for use by money market desks and the liabilities are bought by short-dated money market investors. In recent years money market investors have also become buyers of shorter-dated CDO paper, thus leading to the concept of the money market CDO.

From an ALM point of view, a securitisation originated for funding and balance sheet management purposes, such as a balance sheet CLO of bank loans, will have a similar structure to a money market CDO. The only difference is that the liability structure will consist of short-dated notes; perhaps only the most junior note will have a maturity of five years or more.

Money market CDO

Reviewing the CDO from first principles, we can point out similarities between a CDO balance sheet and a commercial bank balance sheet. A conventional cash CDO will parcel up its balance sheet into different pieces of risk, with each piece exhibiting different risk-reward profiles. CDOs rely on subordination and diversification, in the same way that a bank does.

Figure 22.11 on page 1040 illustrates this concept. It shows the capital structure of a CDO (or synthetic CDO, the point is the same[3]) alongside the asset structure of a bank. Note the sample liability charges depending on the risk associated with each piece; these rates would be reasonable expectation during the first half of 2006. The lowest risk piece carries the lowest return, around 10–12 basis points. The equity piece is unrated and expected to return 18–22%. With the CDO, its "balance sheet" is in effect made up as follows:

- the vehicle borrows money of varying cost and maturity (the liabilities);
- it invests in collateral, which is given or one that the CDO manager selects. This is a pool of credits or assets.

The bank's balance sheet, on the asset side, is similarly composed of loans made by it to corporates and consumers. The Equity tranche in the CDO receives the residual cash flows from the asset pool; the bank retains its surplus earnings, after discharging liabilities, for its equity holders.[4] So in these respects the capital structure of a commercial bank is similar to that of a CDO.

---

[3] Synthetic CDOs are discussed in the next chapter.

[4] To make another analogy, consider the equity piece in a CDO to be like the "excess" in a car or home insurance policy. By retaining the "first loss" piece in an insurance policy, the customer is charged a lower premium by the insurance company. If there is no excess, the cost of insurance (or, by analogy, bank funding costs) would be much higher.

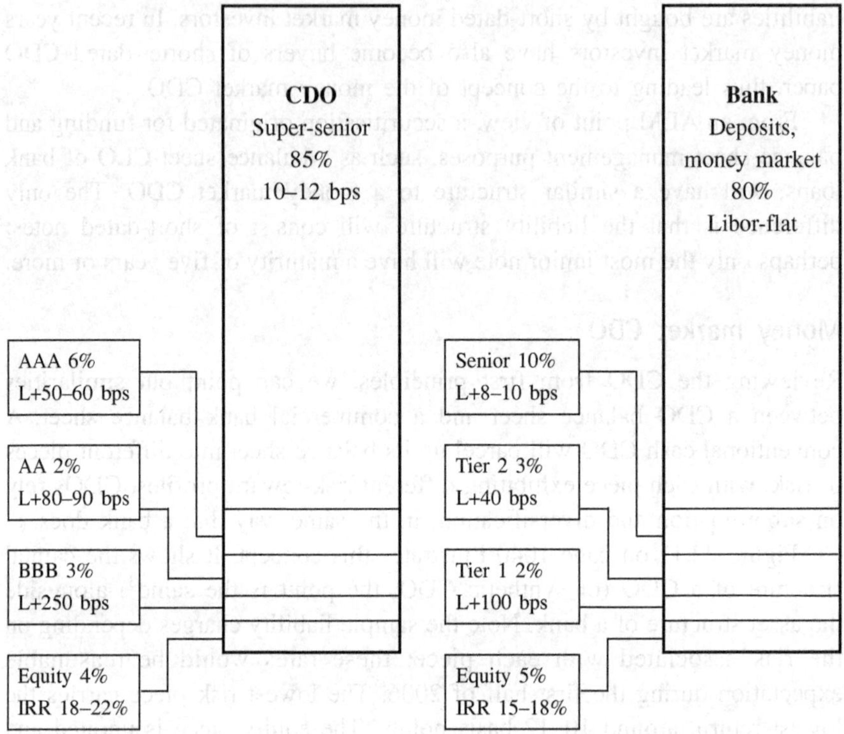

Figure 22.11 Bank and CDO "balance sheets" and capital costs

With a conventional CDO, the average life of notes, both senior and junior, is invariably five years or longer. A prime reason why this maturity is necessary is because it is important to lock-in term funding if, at the time the deal is being closed, market levels are such that the liability cost is sufficiently low that the structure creates value from the assets. If market levels are not attractive when the debt is priced, the deal will probably be delayed or shelved. Given this average maturity, money market investors and bank ALM desks would not be natural holders of CDO paper. A typical structure is shown in Figure 22.12; as money market funds seldom look beyond a three-year investment horizon, and more usually a two-year horizon, such a structure will present no attraction to them.

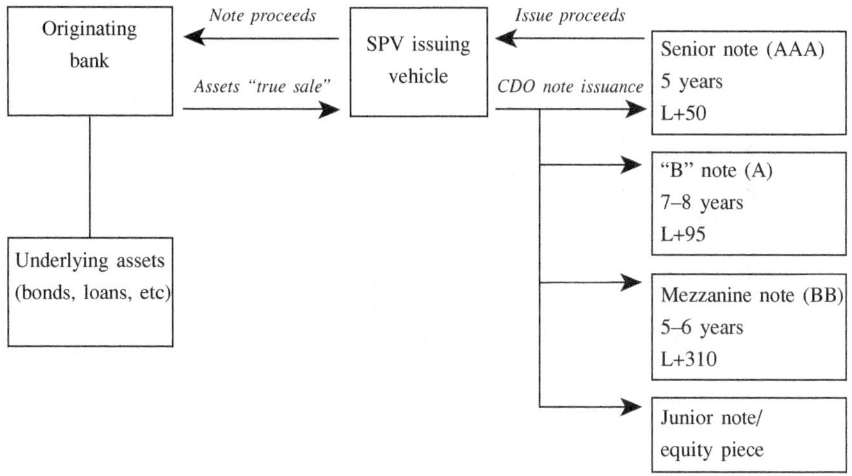

Figure 22.12 Typical liability maturity strucure, cash CDO

Money market CDO return and structure

At the start of 2005, yield spreads across the credit curve had tightened considerably, such that even relatively risk-averse investors such as bank ALM desks were receiving around Libor plus 9–11 basis points for repoing in assets down to a BBB credit rating. Sub-investment grade assets were being funded at Fed Funds plus 15–20 basis points.[5] Given this situation, money market investors have become buyers of CDO paper, which simultaneously, as this interest was appearing, have been structured to meet this new demand. There is also an attraction for the CDO originator: by structuring the liabilities with a money market piece, the vehicle is able to secure lower cost funding at the short end of the yield curve (the money market curve), which in a positive yield curve environment will be below the capital market curve.

To structure a transaction such that its liabilities will be considered by short-term investors, CDOs have been introduced that incorporate an element of money market funding. This is in the form of a short-dated tranche or a series of short- and medium-term tranches. This appeals to money market investors and also enables the issuer to benefit from lower-cost funding at the short-end of the credit curve. This is illustrated in Figure

[5] *Sources*: Market counterparties.

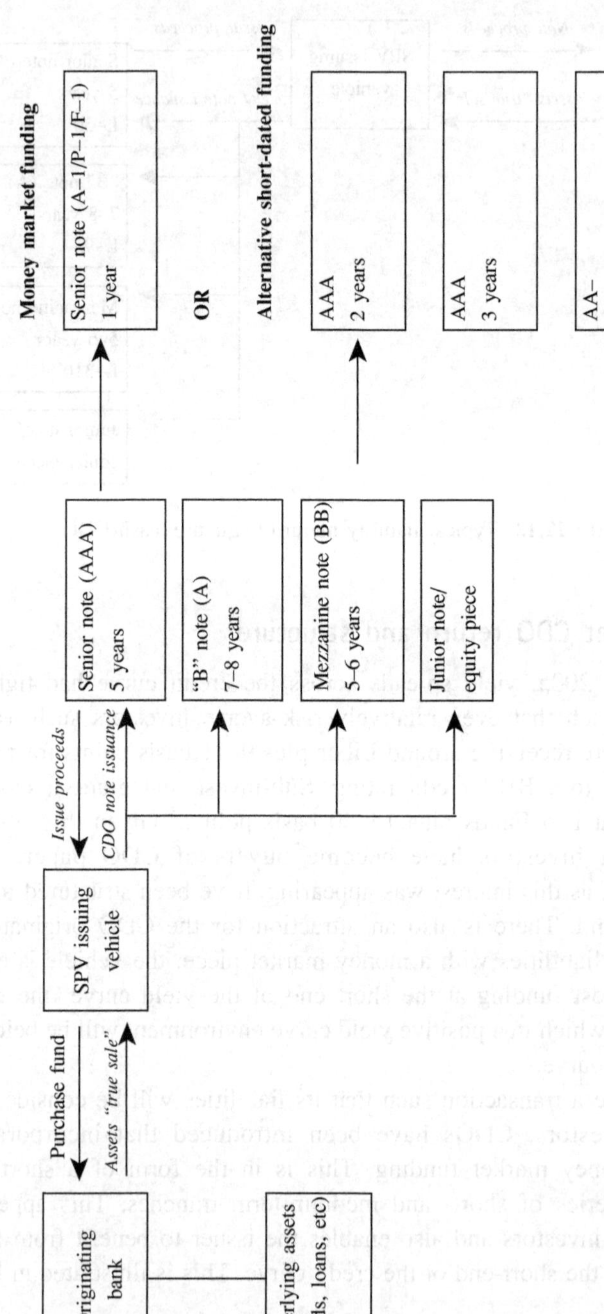

Figure 22.13 Short-dated CDO structure

22.13, a short-term CDO. This "short-dated CDO" is structurally identical to the regular CDO, except that the senior note tranche is now much shorter-dated. The issuer can roll the senior note each maturity, presenting an element of gap risk, or can structure a series of rolling note tranches at one-year maturities. Alternatively, the issuer can have a multi-tranche senior note arrangement. The short-dated notes are just like a regular capital market note or CDO note, the only difference being that they have an average life below five years.

Money market investors can therefore gain from a yield pick-up compared to bank FRNs or other senior bank paper, but at the same or better credit rating. The short maturity of the CDO note means that its price carries relatively low DV01 risk. Compared to alternative short-dated asset classes, given their higher credit-risk nature, money market CDOs present a yield pick-up compared to bank FRNs. This is illustrated in Figure 22.14, which shows the spread between Residential MBS paper and three different assets, bank senior subordinated FRNs, bank CLOs and synthetic CDOs during 2004–2005. The rates are taken from a sample of European transactions and are averaged, with the notes being in the 1–3 year range maturity.

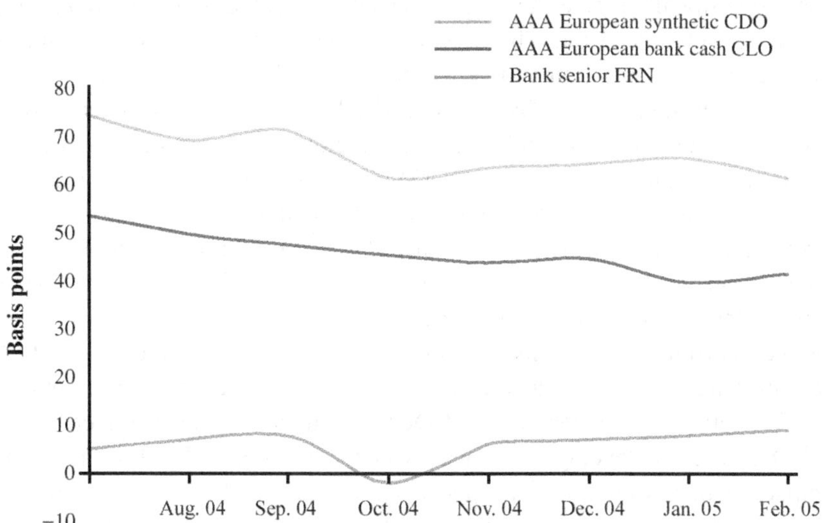

Figure 22.14 RMBS spread minus three different asset classes including CLO/synthetic CDO
Source: Bloomberg L.P.

CDO-squared

The CDO-squared (CDO^2) is a more recent product in CDO development, and the market has witnessed also the CDO-cubed or CDO^3. A CDO^2 provides investors with greater leverage compared to a standard CDO, with more exposure to credit risk and less so to event risk. It also increases the choice of risk/reward profiles for investors. CDO^2 was developed as an alternative investment product and its use is not associated with bank ALM.

In a CDO^2, the liability notes are linked to an underlying portfolio of CDO notes and sometimes ABS notes. As a result the structure may reference as many as 1,000 names or more, with some names repeated in underlying note tranches. Figure 22.15 shows a representation of the structure, with six CDO tranches, although in practice this number has ranged from five to 20.

The rationale behind CDO^2 is appealing for certain investors. If the underlying notes include ABS as well as CDO notes, investors can potentially benefit from exposure to a diversified portfolio that might not be readily accessible otherwise. Because CDO^2 notes have lower exposure to event risk than in a standard synthetic CDO, they are able to withstand a higher number of reference entity defaults before suffering loss. However, the proportionally greater leverage means that as defaults start to mount, the level of losses is faster. This risk means that investors receive a higher spread, for the same ratings risk, compared to CDO noteholders.

As with standard CDOs, the CDO^2 liability side can be unfunded, partially funded or fully funded. The key factor for investors to be aware of is the double subordination in a CDO^2 note. In a standard CDO, losses in the underlying portfolio feed through immediately to overlying notes, in order of subordination. This would only affect CDO^2 notes when the losses in an underlying CDO reached the specific level to affect the tranche being held in the portfolio. Thus CDO^2 investors benefit from an extra level of protection from credit events. This double subordination enables the CDO^2 to withstand a higher frequency of default of the ultimate reference entities.

The other key factor behind CDO^2 is higher leverage. Given that a CDO is itself a leveraged product, CDO^2 leverages this leverage. The impact of this is that, although the notes themselves begin to be impacted after a higher number of defaults, the effect is magnified once notes do start to suffer loss.

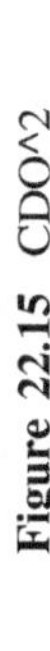

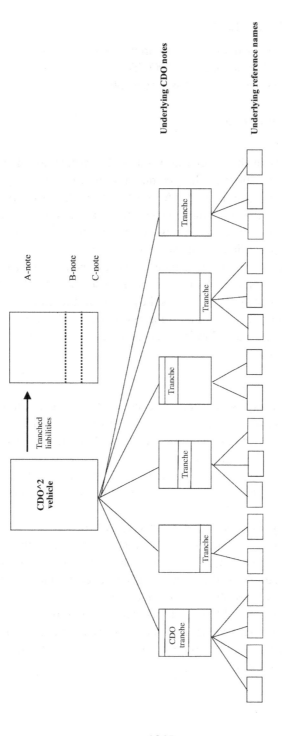

Figure 22.15 CDO^2

Analysis and evaluation

Here, we introduce a number of important factors that are relevant when analysing, evaluating or rating a CDO. The list is not an exhaustive one; rather, we address some of the basic concepts.

Portfolio characteristics

Credit quality

The credit quality of the underlying asset pool is critical as this is a source of credit risk in the structure. It is common to allocate an average rating to the initial reference asset pool. A constraint in the structuring of the transaction may be that any future changes to the asset pool that the structure allows should not reduce the average rating below the initial rating. The analysis of the portfolio's credit and the possible variability of the credit quality is used to determine the default frequency and the loss rates that may be experienced by the underlying asset pool. In some cases, the originator's internal credit-scoring system is a key part of the rating process. In particular, for unrated assets the rating process should involve a mapping process between the internal rating system and the agency's rating system to determine accuracy.

Diversity

The level of diversity within the reference portfolio directly influences the level of credit risk in the portfolio. Broadly, we would expect that the greater the level of diversification, the lower the level of credit risk. Diversity may be determined by considering concentrations by industry group, obligor and sovereign country. The level of diversity in the portfolio may be quantified by attributing a single diversity score to reflect the level of diversification of the underlying asset pool.

The diversity score is a weighted-average credit score for a portfolio of credit exposures. The marginal score allocated to each marginal credit exposure in the underlying asset pool depends on the existing credit portfolio. For example, if the portfolio has a concentration in a category – for example, in an industry group – the marginal score attributed to the marginal credit is reduced to reflect this concentration (or lack of diversity). This has the effect that a higher diversity score is attributed to an asset pool where the range of credit exposure is wide. The higher the score, the better the level of diversification.

A constraint may be placed on the level of change in the diversity as a result of a change to the underlying asset pool. For example, a minimum required diversity score for a transaction may need to be maintained.

Cash-flow analysis

The cash-flow profile of a CDO structure depends on the following issues:

- the spread between the interest earned on the loans/collateral and the coupon paid on the securities issued by the CDO;
- the impact of default events – for example, default frequency and severity (level of recovery rates) in the underlying asset pool – and the impact of losses on the principal of investors;
- the principal repayment profile/expected amortisation;
- the contingent payments in the event of default under any credit-default swap which may be used to transfer credit risk from the originator to another party (such as the SPV or an OECD bank);
- contingent cash flows on any credit wrap or credit insurance on the underlying asset pool;
- cash flows receivable/payable with the hedge counterparty; for example, under swap agreements or derivative contracts;
- fees and expenses.

The sensitivity of these cash flows is tested to obtain an understanding of the impact on the cash-flow profile under stressed and normal scenarios. The relevant stress scenarios that are tested are dependent on the underlying asset pool.

Originator's credit quality

The impact of the credit quality of the originator on the rating of the notes issued is dependent upon the structure. For example, where the underlying assets are transferred to the SPV (which is bankruptcy-remote) from the originator, the credit quality of the CDO notes is only dependent on the portfolio performance and the credit enhancement. The credit performance of the CDO notes can be said to be "de-linked" from the credit quality of the originator.

However, in some structures the underlying asset pool remains on the balance sheet of the originator; for instance, as with credit-linked CDOs, as shown in Figure 22.16 on page 1048. In this case, the notes issued by the SPV remain "linked" to the credit of the originator.

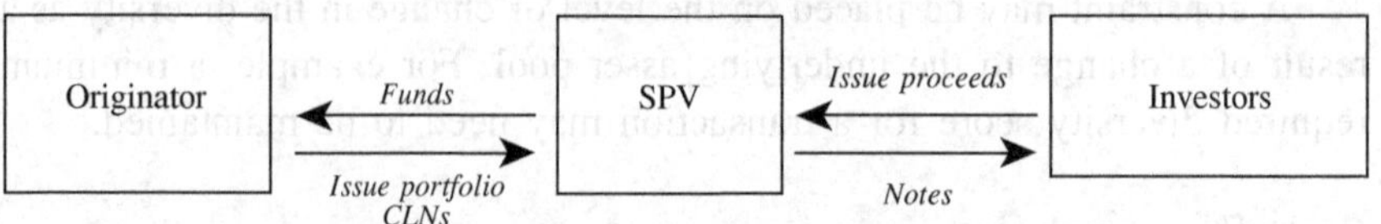

Figure 22.16 Credit-linked CDO

Here, an investor in the CDO has exposure to both the credit quality of the bank and the portfolio performance. The rating of the credit-linked CDO is capped by the rating of the originator, because payment of interest and principal depends on the originator's ability to pay.

However, for the senior tranches of a synthetic de-linked CDO, the portfolio may remain on the originator's balance sheet, but the senior tranches may be collateralised and de-linked from the bank's rating by using AAA-rated collateral and default swaps. The final rating is influenced by the credit rating of the default-swap provider, the extent to which the cash flows to investors are exposed to the risk of default by the originator.

Operational aspects

In market value transactions, the abilities of the manager are a key aspect to consider, since the performance of the underlying portfolio is critical to the success of the structure. The review of the credit-approval and monitoring process of the originator is another factor that may provide further comfort on the integrity and quality of the underlying asset portfolio. Better credit assessment and monitoring processes will lead to higher levels of comfort.

Review of credit-enhancement mechanisms

Credit enhancement may include the use of reserve accounts, subordinated tranches, credit wraps and liquidity facilities. These are briefly defined below. The impact of any credit-enhancement methods should be considered and understood. This will usually be observed via stress scenarios, which are developed to determine the impact on the cash flows.

Subordination

The rights and priority of each tranche to interest and principal is set out in the offering circular for the issue. This is a detailed description of the notes, together with the legal structure. The cash flows are allocated according to priority of the notes. Typically, fees and expenses are paid first. The most senior tranches are then serviced, followed by the junior tranches and, finally, the equity tranche. The method by which excess cash flows can be allocated to remaining subordinated tranches is referred to as a cash-flow *waterfall*. This was illustrated in Figure 18.6.

Credit wrap

This is a credit protection of a debt instrument by an insurer or bank to improve the credit quality of the portfolio, guaranteeing the note nominal value. The wrap is provided in return for a fee.

Reserve accounts

Reserve accounts are cash reserves set up at the outset from note proceeds, which provide first-loss protection to investors. Such surplus funds are usually invested by the servicing agent or specialised cash-management provider.

Liquidity facility

A liquidity facility may exist to ensure that short-term funding is available to pay any interest or principal obligations on the notes if there is a temporary cash shortfall.

Legal structure of the transaction

A typical CDO structure is described in a number of legal agreements. For example, the offering circular is the legal document that presents the transaction in detail to investors.

The various legal agreements formalise the roles played in the CDO structure by the various counterparties to the deal. The documentation includes:

- trustee agreements: the provision of administrative duties and maintenance of books and records;
- manager/servicer agreement: describes management of the underlying portfolio and provides market expertise;
- sale agreement or CDS agreements used to transfer credit risk;
- hedging agreements: for example, interest-rate or cross-currency swaps and other derivative contracts;
- guarantees or insurance: for example, credit wraps on the underlying asset pool.

Prior to the closure of the deal, the SPV incorporation documents are also reviewed to ensure that it is bankruptcy-remote and that it is established in a tax-neutral jurisdiction.

Expected loss

The rating process for each transaction involves a detailed analysis of the CDO structure, including the points noted above. However, the actual process of assigning a rating to the notes issued in the CDO will include a quantitative assessment. Often this is based on the expected loss (EL) to noteholders, which is an important statistic when deciding on the quality of a tranche.

The EL may be defined as:

$$EL = \sum_x P_x * L_x \tag{22.1}$$

where

L_x is the loss on the notes under scenario 'x'
P_x is the probability of the scenario 'x' occurring.

The calculated EL statistic will be mapped to a table of ratings and their corresponding expected losses. In this way, the rating can be allocated to each tranche.

The loss to noteholders is determined by considering the impact of credit losses on the cash flows to noteholders, which would occur under the various possible scenarios. This would involve the allocation of any credit loss to the various tranches in issue.

The cash flows to the noteholders depend on whether or not a default has occurred, and the size of the loss in the event of default. The severity of the loss will depend on the par value of the note less the recovery rate. The calculated probability of default may be inferred from the rating of the underlying credit exposures. In practice, the calculation of the expected loss may be based on Monte Carlo simulation techniques in which thousands of scenarios and cash flows are simulated. This requires sophisticated computational models.

The expected losses on the tranches should be in line with the level of subordination. The expected losses on the tranche will be a key factor in the process of assigning a credit rating to the tranche. The credit rating of the tranche is a key determinant in the ultimate pricing and marketability of the tranche.

Investor analysis

Investors have a number of motivations when considering the CDO market both in their domestic market and abroad. These include:

- the opportunity to gain exposure to a high-yield market on a diversified basis, without committing significant resources;
- the ability to choose from a number of portfolio managers that manage the CDO;
- CDOs acting as an initial entry point into the high-yield market;
- with respect to lower-rated (BBB and below) tranches, achieving leveraged returns while gaining benefit from a diversified portfolio;
- the appeal of a wide investor base, with ratings ranging from AAA to B, and maturities from four years to as long as 20 years;
- a wide variety of collateral.

CDOs offer investors a variety of risk/return profiles, as well as market volatilities, and their appeal has widened as broader macroeconomic developments in the global capital markets have resulted in lower yields on more traditional investments.

Investors analysing CDO instruments will focus on particular aspects of the market. For instance, those with a low appetite for risk will concentrate in the higher-rated classes of cash-flow transactions. Investors that are satisfied with greater volatility of earnings, but who still wish to hold AA- or AAA-rated instruments, may consider market value deals. The "arbitrage" that exists in the transaction may be a result of:

- industry diversification;
- differences between investment grade and high-yield spreads;
- the difference between implied default rates in the high-yield market and expected default rates;
- the liquidity premium embedded in high-yield investments;
- the Libor rate versus the Treasury spread.

The CDO asset class cannot be compared in a straightforward fashion to other ABS classes, which makes relative value analysis difficult. Although a CDO is a structured finance product, it does not have sufficient common characteristics with other such products. The structure and cash flow of a CDO are perhaps most similar to a commercial MBS; the collateral backing of the two types share comparable characteristics. Commercial mortgage pools and high-yield bonds and loans both have fewer obligors and larger balances than other ABS collateral, and each credit is rated. On the other hand, CDOs often pay floating-rate interest and are private securities,[6] whereas commercial MBS (in the US market) pay a fixed rate and are often public securities.

EXAMPLE 22.2 Guaranteed investment contracts

A part of the cash raised from the liability side of a CDO is often invested in AAA bonds or other such high-quality assets, to act as a reserve for investors. The collateral reserve in a CDO can be invested in a number of ways. One option is a guaranteed investment contract or GIC. GICs are offered by certain insurance companies, and (less frequently) by banks.

A GIC can be interpreted in a number of ways. In trust banks, it is often no more than a bank account that pays a fixed spread below Libor for the term of the account. The payment frequency is tied in to match that of the coupon on the CDO note liabilities. Strictly speaking, this is not a GIC. Formally defined, a GIC is an obligation from the GIC provider to pay a guaranteed principal and interest rate on an invested premium. The investor places a lump-sum amount (the premium) in a GIC, and the GIC provider guarantees a specified cash amount that will be paid to the investor on the maturity date.

As an example, an investor places \$10 million in a five-year GIC that pays an annual rate of 5.00%. The GIC maturity value is therefore:

$$10{,}000{,}000 \times (1.05)^5 = \$12{,}762{,}815.62.$$

[6] In the US market, they are also filed under Rule 144A, as opposed to public securities which must be registered with the Securities and Exchange Commission. Rule 144A securities may only be sold to investors classified as professional investors under specified criteria. Rule 144A provides an exemption from the registration requirements of the Securities Act (1933) for resale of privately placed securities to qualified institutional buyers. Such buyers are deemed to be established and experienced institutions, and so the SEC does not regulate or approve disclosure requirements.

There are variations on GICs, but the standard version pays a fixed rate of interest so the investors know their final return with certainty. In some cases, a floating rate may apply, with a fixed spread to the floating-rate index. This is what is usually offered by banks that do not offer the fixed-rate version. GIC maturities can range from one to 20 years. There can be a one-off lump-sum premium or regular premium payments by the investor. Also, some GICs pay interest on a periodic basis to the investor.

GICs therefore make suitable cash reserves for a CDO, but of course this is not risk-free like an investment in US Treasuries would be; rather, its risk is the credit quality of the GIC provider. However, one advantage it has over of a bond is that its value is always postive, unlike that of a bond that suffers marked-to-market fluctuations, and compared to a standard bank account it offers a known return.

CASE STUDY 22.1 H2 Finance Ltd[7]

To conclude this discussion of CDOs we describe a structure that incorporates elements of previous transactions. H2 Finance Limited is an arbitrage CDO of ABS; that is, a cash CDO with underlying assets of asset-backed securities. The underlying securities are purchased through the issuance of both long-dated notes and short-term liabilities. As such it combines elements of a cash CDO, as well as investment entities known as SIVs.[8] H2 Finance is the name of the SPV, a private company with limited liability incorporated in the Cayman Islands. As with other CDO SPVs, it was incorporated on behalf of the sponsor, Wharton Asset Management, for the sole purpose of acquiring the portfolio and issuing notes and short-term liabilities.

An innovative aspect of this transaction is the repo feature. The majority of the portfolio is financed via a short-term repo arrangement with a number of counterparties, with the portfolio itself acting as collateral for the repo. As such, H2 issues two types of liabilities:

[7] The author thanks Serj Walia at KBC Financial Products in London for assistance with providing information for this section.

[8] SIVs are covered in Chapter 25. They are essentially CDOs that issue both AB-CP and MTNs.

- medium-term tranched notes;
- repo agreements using eligible collateral.

The terms of the structure are shown below.

Name:	H2 Finance Ltd €105 million senior secured floating-rate notes
Sponsor and manager:	Wharton Asset Management Bermuda Ltd
Arranger and underwriter:	Nomura International
Trustee:	Deutsche Trustee Co. Ltd
Pay agent, account bank, and administrator:	Deutsche Bank AG, London
Custodian:	HSBC Bank plc
Repo counterparties:	Multiple counterparties rated at A–1 or above by S&P
Closing date:	March 2004

The structure is shown in Figure 22.17 on page 1056, while Table 22.2 on page 1057 shows the note tranching.

H2 Finance is a CDO of high-rated ABS securities. It is fully funded; that is, the complete value of the portfolio is purchased through the issue of notes and via the repo facility. The underlying portfolio has an average maturity of 3.5 years and weighted-average rating of AAA from S&P, so it is a high-quality portfolio.

Repo arrangement

The repo facility in H2 Finance is one of more unusual features of the transaction. The majority of securities purchased by H2 Finance is repo'ed out to repo counterparties. Counterparties pay the market value of the securities to H2 Finance minus the haircut, which is around 1% of the purchase price.[9] Repo trades are put on for a one-year maturity, at a rate of Libor flat.

[9] This is a very low level of haircut and reflects the quality of the collateral. Usual haircut levels for repo of ABS assets range from 3% to 15%, depending on collateral quality; see the author's book *The Global Repo Markets*, John Wiley & Sons, Singapore, 2004.

During the term of the trade, variation margin will be called if the value of the securities plus the margin level drops outside the 1% threshold. Margin payments are paid out of the cash reserve account that is held by the CDO account bank on behalf of the vehicle. On repo maturity date, the securities are rolled over in a new repo, at the prevailing market price for the securities.

Repo securities are ABS bonds, made up of credit card, consumer loans, auto loans, trade receivables, whole business, sovereign and public-sector ABS, RMBS and CMBS bonds. A minimum of 95% of the securities must be rated at AAA. The portfolio must also meet other specified requirements, laid out by S&P as part of its criteria for rating the vehicle liabilities. Among these are:

- a maximum portfolio amount of €1.5 billion;
- only a maximum of 10% of securities that have coupon frequencies of greater than quarterly.

In addition, no CDO notes or aviation securities (aircraft leasing ABS and so on) are allowed in the portfolio.

Portfolio management

The portfolio is actively managed by the manager, Wharton Asset Management Bermuda Ltd. The manager is permitted to sell and repurchase portfolio securities, in accordance with specified criteria, during the reinvestment period for the deal. It is also permitted to sell and substitute portfolio securities under the following conditions:

- if the security is in default;
- if the security is deemed a credit risk;
- if the security is rated below AA– and the amount of securities below AAA exceeds the 5% level;
- if the security is rated A or below.

Under these circumstances the manager may bring in replacement assets of acceptable quality.

The ability of the asset manager to manage the CDO is what will attract investors to the notes. The D noteholder, in particular, is expecting the vehicle to generate excess spread on its portfolio, after allowing for vehicle liabilities, that will be an attractive return for its investment. The rated note investors are attracted to the risk/return profile of the notes, which, given the high quality of the underlying assets, presents a high return for comparatively low risk.

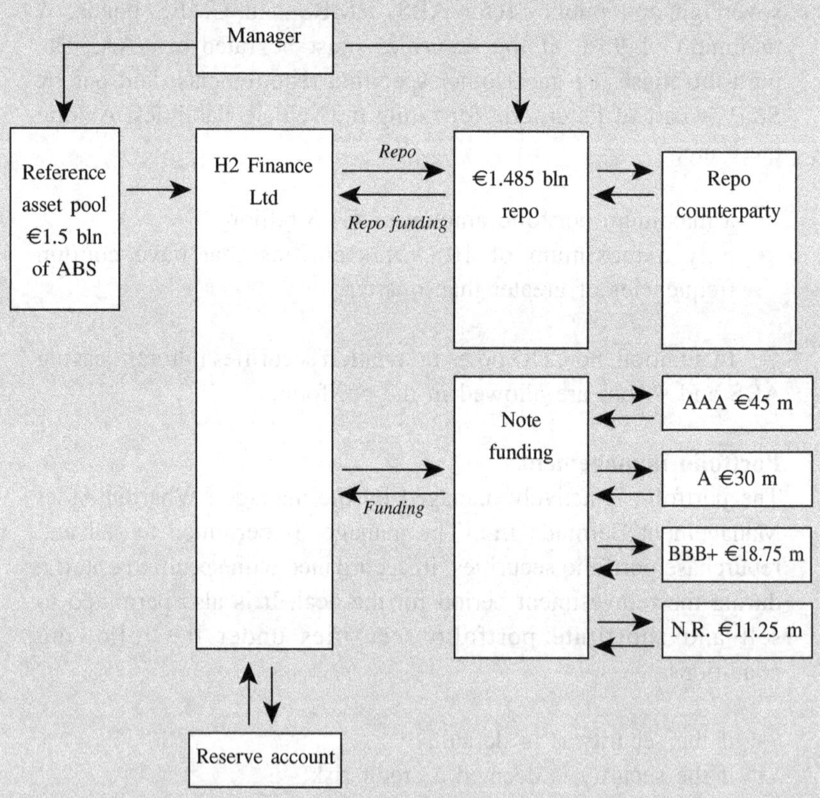

Figure 22.17 H2 Finance Ltd structure diagram
Source: Standard & Poor's. Reproduced with permission.

Class	Rating	Nominal amount (m)	Weighted-average life (years)	Libor spread (bps)	Legal final maturity
Senior repo programme	A–1+	1,485.00	n/a	0	2052
A	AAA	45.00	5.4	22	2052
B	AA	30.00	6.7	40	2052
C	BBB+	18.75	7.1	120	2052
D	NR	22.25	n/a	Excess	2052

Table 22.2 H2 Finance Ltd note tranching
Source: Standard & Poor's. Reproduced with permission.

CHAPTER

23

Synthetic Collateralised Debt Obligations

In the previous chapter we looked at cash-flow CDO securitisation, an important bank balance sheet management and ALM tool. Combining certain aspects of this technique with credit derivatives technology gives rise to so-called *synthetic securitisation*, also known as unfunded securitisation. In a synthetic transaction, the credit risk of a pool of assets is transferred from an originator to investors, but the assets themselves are not sold.[1] In certain jurisdictions, it may not be possible to undertake a cash securitisation due to legal, regulatory, cross-border or other restrictions. Or, it may be that the process simply takes too long under the prevailing market conditions. In such cases, originators use synthetic transactions, which employ some part of the traditional process allied with credit derivatives. However, if the main motivation of the originator remains funding concerns, then the cash-flow approach must still be used. Synthetic transactions are mainly used for credit risk and regulatory capital reasons, and not funding purposes. They were first developed as a bank balance sheet management technique, used to transfer credit risk but without recourse to a true-sale cash securitisation. Although subsequent applications of the technique saw synthetic CDOs structured for credit arbitrage reasons and as pseudo-fund management vehicles, they remain important bank ALM instruments. It is not uncommon to see them originated and structured by bank Treasury desks.

---

[1] Although the first synthetic transactions were "balance sheet" deals, in which the originating bank transferred the credit risk of a pool of assets it held without actually selling them off its balance sheet, the fact that assets are not actually transferred means that the originator does not actually have to own them in the first place. It may wish to transfer the credit risk for portfolio trading reasons. We look at this development of collateralised synthetic obligations (CSOs) in this chapter too.

This chapter is an analysis of the synthetic collateralised debt obligation, or CSO. We focus on the key drivers of this type of instrument, from an issuer and investor point of view, before assessing the mechanics of the structures themselves. This includes a case study-type review of selected innovative transactions.

The synthetic CDO

Synthetic CDOs were introduced to meet differing needs of originators, where credit risk transfer is of more importance than funding considerations. Compared with conventional cash-flow deals, which feature an actual transfer of ownership or *true sale* of the underlying assets to a separately incorporated legal entity, a synthetic securitisation structure is engineered so that the credit risk of the assets is transferred by the sponsor or originator of the transaction, from itself, to the investors by means of credit derivative instruments. The originator is therefore the credit protection buyer and investors are the credit protection sellers. This credit risk transfer may be undertaken either directly or via an SPV. Using this approach, underlying or *reference* assets are not moved off the originator's balance sheet, so it is adopted whenever the primary objective is to achieve risk transfer rather than balance sheet funding. The synthetic structure enables removal of credit exposure without asset transfer, so may be preferred for risk management and regulatory capital relief purposes. For banking institutions it also enables loan risk to be transferred without selling the loans themselves, thereby allowing customer relationships to remain unaffected.

The first synthetic deals were observed in the US and Europe in 1997. Figure 23.1 illustrates market growth in Europe. Figure 23.2 shows growth for selected deal types.

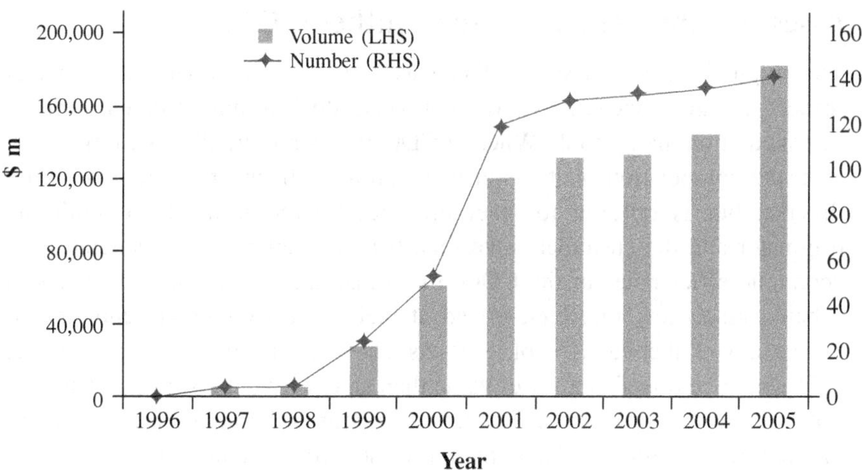

Figure 23.1 Synthetic CDO market growth in Europe
Source: Moody's. Reproduced with permission.

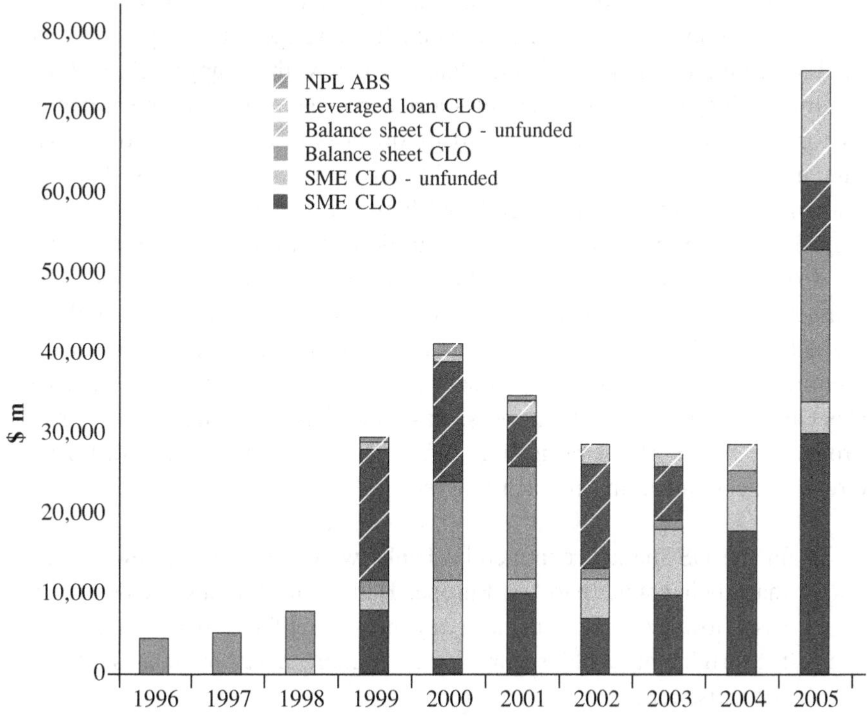

Figure 23.2 European CLO volumes, funded and unfunded amount (USD million)
Source: HSBC

Assessing the genesis of the synthetic CDO

The original cash flow-style CDO was a tool for intermediation. In this respect, it can be viewed as a (mini-) bank, albeit a more efficient tool for intermediation than a bank. Where a CDO-type structure differs from a bank is in the composition of its asset pool: unlike a bank, its asset pool is not diverse, but is tailored to meet the specific requirements of both the originator and the customer (investor). It is this tailoring that generates the economic efficiencies of the CDO. In an institutional scenario, as exists in a bank, assets are, in effect, priced at their lowest common denominator. Hence, a bank that has 10% of its assets held in the form of emerging market debt would be priced at a lower value than an equivalent institution that does not hold such risky assets. The CDO-structure's liabilities are also more tailored to specific needs, with a precise mix of equity holders, AAA liabilities and so on.

We may view the CDO-type entity as similar to a banking institution and a tool for the intermediation of risk. A synthetic CDO may be viewed in similar terms, but in its case the analogy is more akin to that of an insurance company rather than a bank. This reflects the separation of funding from credit risk that is facilitated by the synthetic approach, and the resulting ability to price pure credit – a risk management mechanism that is analogous to how an insurance company operates in comparison to a bank. The investors in a synthetic CDO do not purchase the assets that are referenced in a vehicle, they merely wish an economic exposure to it. This is made possible through the use of credit derivatives in the CDO structure.

Combining securitisation technology with credit derivatives, into synthetic structures, was particularly suited to the European market, with its myriad of legal and securitisation jurisdictions. The traditional method of securitisation, involving selling assets into an SPV and used for balance sheet and risk management purposes, was viewed as less efficient than it had proved in the North American market. This was due to the differing circumstances prevailing in each market:

- In the US market, commercial banks were traditionally lower-rated than their counterparts in Europe. Hence, the funding element of a cash-flow securitisation was a key motivating factor behind a deal, as the originator could secure lower funding costs by means of the securitisation;
- European banks, being on average higher-rated than US banks, had less need of the funding side in a securitisation deal – compared to

US banks, they obtained a greater share of their funding from their retail customer base. A significant portion of their funding was obtained at Libor-minus, compared to the Libor-flat funding of US banks.

So although European banks had an interest in transferring risk from their balance sheet, they had less need of the funding associated with traditional securitisation. A cash-flow CDO was not as economic for originators in the European market because they did not have such a great need for funding, and so this approach had less benefit for them. However, banks still needed to reduce regulatory capital requirements and transfer credit risk. This led to the first static balance sheet synthetic CDO, known as BISTRO, which was originated by JPMorgan in 1997.[2]

The first synthetic CDOs were balance sheet driven; banks structured deals for regulatory capital management purposes. These deals reflected a desire by banks to shift their credit risk and by so doing, manage capital more efficiently. In other words, the deals had an ALM objective. Later deals followed an arbitrage model: they were originated by fund managers, who were perceived by investors as being efficient at managing risk. Hence, the "second generation" of CDO structures, which reflected the comparative advantage generated as insurance fund management companies were able to split up an overall "pool" of risk and break this into separate pieces. These pieces were tailored to specific investor preferences. Compared to cash-flow structures, synthetic structures separate the risk transfer element from the funding element. This mirrors what occurred in the early 1980s with interest-rate swaps, shortly after these were introduced. Interest-rate swaps also split the interest-rate risk from the funding risk, as they were off-balance sheet instruments with no exchange of principal. This is the same case with credit derivatives and is precisely what has happened in the credit derivatives market.

Deal motivations

Differences between synthetic and cash CDOs are perhaps best reflected in the different cost–benefit economics of issuing each type. The motivations behind the issue of each type may also differ.

The originators of the first synthetic deals were banks that wished to manage the credit risk exposure of their loan books, without having to resort to the administrative burden of true sale cash securitisation. They are a

[2] This deal is discussed later in this chapter.

natural progression in the development of credit derivative structures, with single-name CDSs being replaced by portfolio default swaps. Synthetic CDOs can be "de-linked" from the sponsoring institution, so that investors do not have any credit exposure to the sponsor itself. The first deals were introduced at a time when widening credit spreads and the worsening of credit quality among originating firms meant that investors were sellers of those cash CDOs that had retained a credit linkage to the sponsor. A synthetic arrangement also means that the credit risk of assets that are otherwise not suited to conventional securitisation may be transferred, while assets are retained on the balance sheet. Such assets include bank guarantees, letters of credit or cash loans that have some legal or other restriction on being securitised. For this reason, synthetic deals are more appropriate for assets that are described under multiple legal jurisdictions.

The economic advantage of issuing a synthetic versus a cash CDO can be significant. Put simply, the net benefit to the originator is the gain in regulatory capital cost, minus the cost of paying for credit protection on the CDS side. In a partially funded structure, which combines cash notes and credit derivatives, a sponsoring bank obtains full capital relief when note proceeds are invested in 0% risk-weighted collateral such as Treasuries or gilts. The "super-senior" swap portion carries a 20% risk weighting.[3] A synthetic deal would be cheaper – where CDSs are used, the sponsor pays a basis point fee, which for a AAA-rated security might be in the range of 10–30 basis points, depending on the stage of the credit cycle. In a cash structure where bonds are issued, the cost to the sponsor is the benchmark yield plus the credit spread, which is often higher when compared to the default swap premium. This is illustrated in Figure 23.3 on page 1066, where we assume certain spreads and premiums in comparing a partially funded synthetic deal with a cash deal. The assumptions are:

- that the super-senior credit swap cost is 15 basis points, and carries a 20% risk weight;
- the equity piece retains a 100% risk-weighting;
- the synthetic CDO invests note proceeds in sovereign collateral that pays sub-Libor.

[3] This is under Basel I, and as long as the counterparty is an OECD bank, which is invariably the case. It is called "super-senior" because the swap is ahead of the most senior of any funded (note) portion.

Synthetic deals can be *unfunded*, *partially funded* or *fully funded*. An unfunded CDO is comprised wholly of CDSs, while fully funded structures are arranged so that the entire credit risk of the reference portfolio is transferred through the issue of CLNs. A managed or partially managed underlying pool is now more usual with bank CLOs. Issues that determine whether a fully funded or partially funded deal is adopted include:

- the cost of CDS protection (that is, the premiums each quarter) versus issuing CLNs (and their coupon payments);
- the level of capital relief that can be achieved – under Basel I, the level of the CDS counterparty risk weighting versus 0% for cash collateral.

Within the European market, static synthetic balance sheet CDOs are the most common structure. The reasons that banks originate them are twofold:

- *capital relief*: banks can obtain regulatory capital relief by transferring lower yield corporate credit risk such as corporate bank loans off their balance sheet. Under Basel I rules, all corporate debt carries an identical 100% risk-weighting; therefore, with banks having to assign a minimum 8% of capital for such loans, higher-rated (and hence lower yielding) corporate assets require the same amount of capital, but generate a lower return on that capital. A bank may wish to transfer such higher-rated, lower yield assets from its balance sheet, and this can be achieved via a CDO transaction. The capital requirements for a synthetic CDO are lower than for a pool of corporate assets. For example, the funded segment of the deal is supported by high-quality collateral such as government bonds, and via a repo arrangement with an OECD bank, it carries a 20% risk weighting, as does the super-senior element;

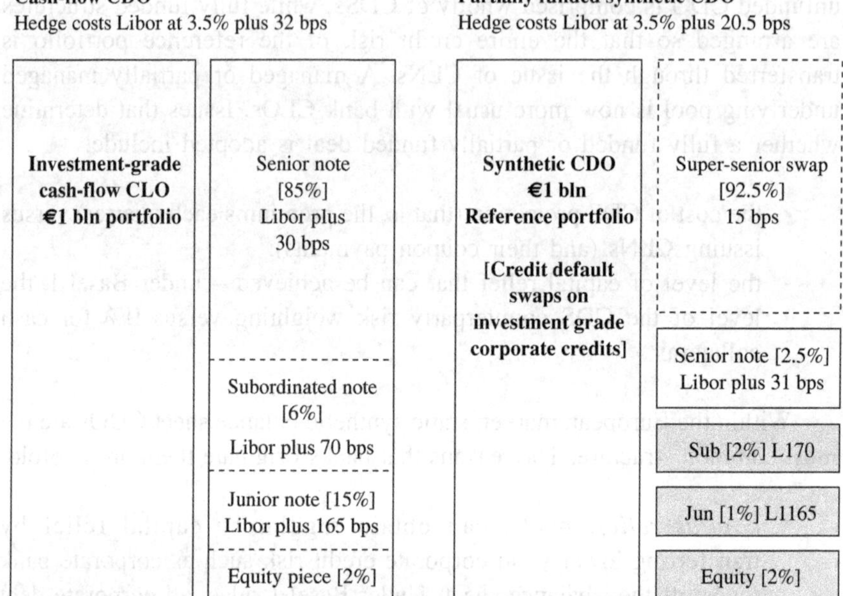

Regulatory capital relief

Cash CDO

Capital charge on assets reduces from 8% (100% risk-weighted or RW) to 2% (equity piece only now 100% RW)

Regulatory capital relief is 6%

Synthetic CDO

Capital charge on assets reduces from 8% (100% RW) to 3.48% (equity piece plus super-senior swap at 20% RW)

Regulatory capital relief is 4.52%

Figure 23.3 Hypothetical generic cash flow and synthetic CDO comparative deal economics.

- *transfer of credit risk*: the cost of servicing a fully funded CDO, and the premium payable on the associated CDS, can be prohibitive. With a partially funded structure, the issue amount is typically a relatively small share of the asset portfolio. This substantially lowers the default swap premium. Also, as the CDO investors suffer the first loss element of the portfolio, the super-senior default swap can be entered into at a considerably lower cost than that on a fully funded CDO.

Deal mechanics

A synthetic CDO is so-called because the transfer of credit risk is achieved "synthetically" via a credit derivative, rather than by a "true sale" to an SPV. Thus in a synthetic CDO, the credit risk of the underlying loans or bonds is transferred to the SPV using credit default swaps (CDSs) and/or total return swaps (TRSs). However, the assets themselves are not legally transferred to the SPV, and they remain on the originator's balance sheet. Using a synthetic CDO, the originator can obtain regulatory capital relief[4] and manage the credit risk on its balance sheet, but it will not receive any funding. In other words, a synthetic CDO structure enables originators to separate credit risk exposure and asset-funding requirements. The credit risk of the asset portfolio, now known as the reference portfolio, is transferred, directly or to an SPV, through credit derivatives. The most common contracts used are CDSs. A portion of the credit risk may be sold on as CLNs. Typically, a large majority of the credit risk is transferred via a super-senior CDS,[5] which is dealt with a swap counterparty, but usually sold to monoline insurance companies at a significantly lower spread over Libor compared with the senior AAA-rated tranche of cash-flow CDOs. This is a key attraction of synthetic deals for originators. Most deals are structured with mezzanine notes sold to a wider set of investors, the proceeds of which are invested in risk-free collateral such as Treasury bonds or Pfandbriefe securities. The most junior note, known as the "first-loss" piece, may be retained by the originator. On occurrence of a credit event among the reference assets, the originating bank receives funds remaining from the collateral after they have been used to pay the principal on the issued notes, less the value of the junior note.

A generic synthetic CDO structure is shown in Figure 23.4 on page 1068. In this generic structure, the credit risk of the reference assets is transferred to the issuer SPV and ultimately the investors, by means of the CDS and an issue of CLNs. In the default swap arrangement, the risk transfer is undertaken in return for the swap premium, which is then paid to investors by the issuer. The note issue is invested in risk-free collateral rather than passed on to the originator, in order to de-link the credit ratings of the notes from the rating of the originator. If the collateral pool is not established, a downgrade of the sponsor may result in a downgrade of the

---

[4] This is because reference assets that are protected by credit derivative contracts, and which remain on the balance sheet, attract a lower regulatory capital charge under Basel I rules.

[5] So called because the swap is ahead of the most senior of any funded (note) portion, the latter being "senior" means the swap must be "super-senior".

issued notes. Investors in the notes expose themselves to the credit risk of the reference assets, and if there are no credit events they will earn returns to at least equal the collateral assets and the default swap premium. If the notes are credit-linked, they will also earn excess returns based on the performance of the reference portfolio. If there are credit events, the issuer will deliver the assets to the swap counterparty and will pay the nominal value of the assets to the originator out of the collateral pool. CDSs are unfunded credit derivatives, while CLNs are funded credit derivatives where the protection seller (the investors) funds the value of the reference assets up-front, and receives a reduced return on the occurrence of a credit event.

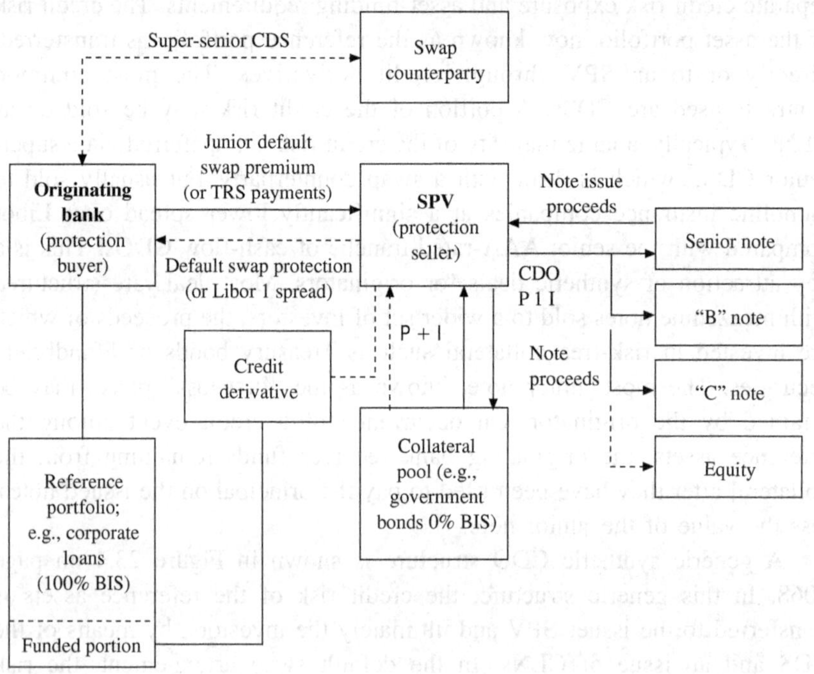

Figure 23.4 Generic synthetic CDO structure

Funding mechanics

As the super-senior piece in a synthetic CDO does not need to be funded, there is a potential advantage of the synthetic mechanism compared to a cash-flow CDO. During the first half of 2002, the yield spread for the AAA note piece averaged 45–50 basis points over Libor,[6] while the cost of the super-senior swap was around 10–12 basis points. This means that the CDO manager can reinvest in the collateral pool risk-free assets at Libor minus 5 basis points, and it is able to gain from a saving of 28–35 basis points on each nominal $100 of the structure that is not funded. This is a considerable gain. If we assume that a synthetic CDO is 95% unfunded and 5% funded, this is equivalent to the reference assets trading at approximately 26–33 basis points cheaper in the market. There is also an improvement to the return on capital measure for the CDO manager. Since typically the manager retains the equity piece, if this is 2% of the structure and the gain is 33 basis points, the return on equity is improved by [0.36/0.02] or 16.5%.

Another benefit of structuring CDOs as synthetic deals is their potentially greater attraction for investors (protection sellers). Often, selling CDS protection on a particular reference credit generates a higher return than "going long" the underlying cash bond. In general this is because the CDS price is greater than the asset swap price for the same name; this is the so-called CDS basis and is discussed fully in Choudhry (2006). For example, during 2001 the average spread of the synthetic price over the cash price was 15 basis points in the five-year maturity area for BBB-rated credits.[7] The reasons why credit default swap spreads tend to be above cash spreads are discussed in Choudhry (2006).

EXAMPLE 23.1 Credit risk transfer

In simple terms, the protection buyer, which is usually the originating bank or collateral manager of the CDO, enters into a CDS with the SPV, which is the junior default swap labelled in Figure 23.4. By buying protection on the reference entities, the CDO manager transfers the credit risk on these entities to the CDO investors, who are protection sellers. In return for taking on this risk, investors receive a premium from the protection buyer. Therefore, as shown in Figure 23.3, the return for investors is the coupon on the collateral securities together with the CDS premium.

The super-senior piece is unfunded and typically sold to a swap counterparty or monoline insurer as a basket CDS, called the super-

6 Averaged from the yield spread on seven synthetic deals closed during January–June 2002, yield spread at issue, rates data from Bloomberg.

7 Source: JPMorgan, *CDO Research*, September 2002.

senior CDS. The credit risk on this piece is statistically very low, because it represents the most senior piece of the portfolio and is usually comprised of high-quality investment-grade credits. There is thus a very low probability that loss due to default will exceed the portion of the CDO that is funded, thereby eating into the super-senior piece, so this represents a very low risk, termed "catastrophe risk" in an insurance company. Because the senior note is often AAA-rated, and the super-senior piece ranks above this, it is a higher quality risk than AAA risk.

Advantages of synthetic structures

The introduction of synthetic securitisation vehicles was in response to specific demands of sponsoring institutions, and they present certain advantages over traditional cash-flow structures. These include:

- speed of implementation: a synthetic transaction can, in theory, be placed in the market sooner than a cash deal, and the time from inception to closure can be as low as four weeks, with an average execution time of 6–8 weeks compared to 3–4 months for the equivalent cash deal. This reflects the shorter ramp-up period noted above;
- banking relationships, which can be maintained with clients whose loans need not be sold off of the sponsoring entity's balance sheet;
- no requirement to fund the super-senior element;
- for many reference names the CDS price is frequently cheaper than the same name underlying cash bond;
- transaction costs such as legal fees can be lower, as often there is no necessity to set up an SPV;
- the range of reference assets that can be covered is wider, and includes undrawn lines of credit, bank guarantees and derivative instruments that give rise to legal and true sale issues in a cash transaction;
- the use of credit derivatives, which introduces greater flexibility to provide tailor-made solutions for credit risk requirements;
- the cost of buying protection, which is usually lower as there is little or no funding element and the credit protection price is frequently below the equivalent-rate note liability;

- the flexibility retained in determining credit event definitions (bankruptcy, failure to pay, restructuring) and methods of calculating losses (accrued interest, foreclosure costs and so on).

This does not mean that the cash transaction is now an endangered species. It retains certain advantages of its own over synthetic deals, which include:

- no requirements for an OECD bank (the 20% BIS risk-weighted entity) to act as the swap counterparty to meet capital relief requirements;
- lower amounts of capital relief available compared to the 20% risk-weighting on the OECD bank counterparty;
- larger potential investor bases, as the number of counterparties is potentially greater (certain financial and investing institutions have limitations on the degree of usage of credit derivatives);
- lower degrees of counterparty exposure for the originating entity. In a synthetic deal the default of a swap counterparty means the cessation of premium payments, or more critically a credit event protection payment and termination of the CDS.

Banks will structure the arrangement that best meets their ALM requirements. Depending on the nature of these, this can be either a synthetic or cash deal.

Synthetic CDO deal structures

We now look in further detail at the various types of synthetic CDO structures.

Generic concept

Synthetic CDOs have been issued in a variety of forms, labelled in generic form as arbitrage CDOs or balance sheet CDOs. Structures can differ to a considerable degree from one another, having only the basics in common with each other. A later development is the *managed synthetic* CDO.

A synthetic arbitrage CDO is originated generally by collateral managers who wish to exploit the difference in yield between that obtained on the reference assets and that payable on the CDO, both in liabilities and servicing fees. The generic structure is as follows: a specifically created SPV enters into a CDS with the originating bank or financial institution, referencing the bank's underlying portfolio (the reference portfolio). The SPV sells protection on the portfolio, which can be static, partially managed or actively managed by the bank. The portfolio can be synthetic or cash (if the latter, it may be funded on the bank's balance sheet). The SPV receives the protection premium from the bank, and in return it pays the swap premium and note interest on the liability side. The liabilities can be all notes, all basket CDS or a mixture of both. If it issues notes, the proceeds from these are invested in AAA collateral such as sovereign debt, senior tranche of credit card ABS or RMBS, or a GIC contract. A typical structure is shown in Figure 23.5.

A balance sheet synthetic CDO is employed by banks that wish to manage regulatory capital. As before, the underlying assets are bonds, loans and credit facilities originated by the issuing bank. In a balance sheet CDO, the SPV enters into a CDS agreement with the originator, with the specific collateral pool designated as the reference portfolio. The SPV receives the premium payable on the default swap, and thereby provides credit protection on the reference portfolio. There are three types of CDO within this structure. A fully synthetic CDO is a completely *unfunded* structure, which uses CDSs to transfer the entire credit risk of the reference assets to investors who are protection sellers. In a *partially funded* CDO, only the highest credit risk segment of the portfolio is transferred. The cash flow that is needed to service the synthetic CDO overlying liability is received from the AAA-rated collateral that is purchased by the SPV with the proceeds of an overlying note issue. An originating bank obtains maximum regulatory capital relief by means of a partially funded structure, through a combination of the synthetic CDO and a super-senior swap arrangement with an OECD banking counterparty. A super-senior swap provides additional protection to that part of the portfolio, the senior segment, which is already protected by the funded portion of the transaction. The sponsor may retain the super-senior element or may sell it to a monoline insurance firm or CDS provider.

Some commentators categorise synthetic deals using slightly different terms. For instance Boggiano, Waterson and Stein (2002) define the following types:

- balance sheet static synthetic CDO;
- managed static synthetic CDO;
- balance sheet variable synthetic CDO;
- managed variable synthetic CDO.

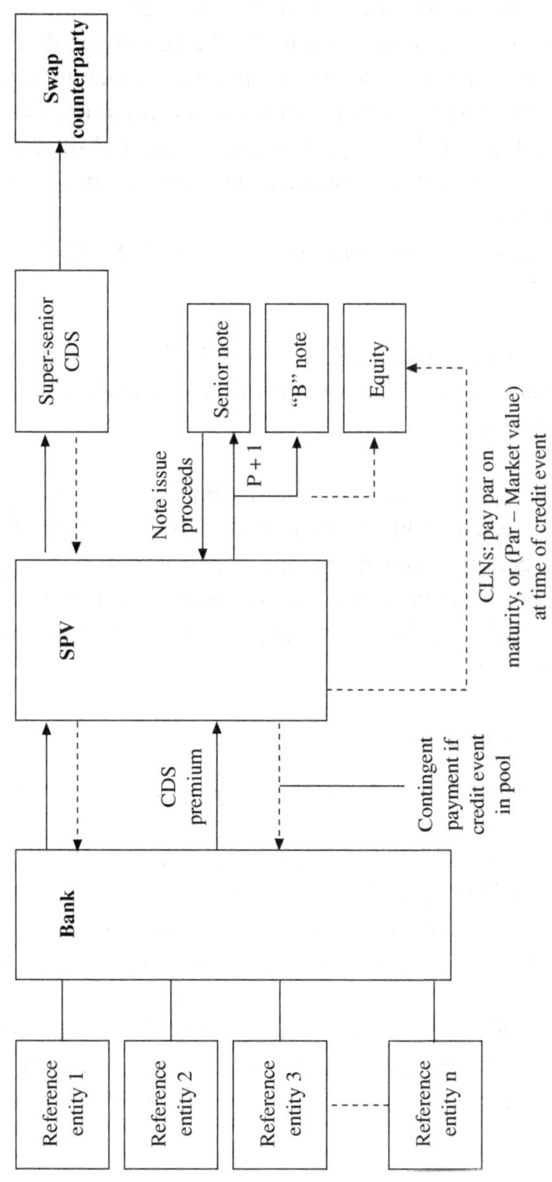

Figure 23.5 Generic synthetic arbitrage CDO structure

As described by Boggiano et al. (2002), the basic structure is similar to that for a partially funded synthetic CDO. In fact there is essentially little difference between the first two types of deal, in the latter an investment manager rather than the credit swap counterparty selects the portfolio. However, the reference assets remain static for the life of the deal in both cases. For the last two deal types, the main difference is that an investment manager, rather than the originator bank, trades the portfolio of credit swaps under specified guidelines. This is arguably not a structural difference and so for the purposes of this book we consider them both as managed CDOs, which are described later.

Synthetic deals may be either static or managed. Static deals have the following advantages:

- there are no ongoing management fees to be borne by the vehicle;
- the investor can review and grant approval to credits that are to make up the reference portfolio.

The disadvantage is that if there is a deterioration in credit quality of one or more names, there is no ability to remove or offset this name from the pool and the vehicle continues to suffer from its performance. During 2001, a number of high-profile defaults in the market meant that static pool CDOs performed below expectation. This explains partly the rise in popularity of the managed synthetic deal.

Funded and unfunded deals

Synthetic deal structures are arranged with funded or unfunded elements to meet investor and market demand. A generic partially funded synthetic transaction is shown in Figure 23.6. It shows an arrangement whereby the issuer enters into two CDSs – the first with an SPV that provides protection for losses up to a specified amount of the reference pool,[8] while the second swap is set up with the OECD bank or, occasionally, an insurance company.[9]

A *fully funded* CDO is a structure where the credit risk of the entire portfolio is transferred to the SPV via CLNs. In a fully funded (or just "funded") synthetic CDO, the issuer enters into the CDS with the SPV,

[8] In practice, to date this portion has been between 5% and 15% of the reference pool.

[9] An "OECD" bank, thus guaranteeing a 20% risk-weighting for capital ratio purposes, under Basel I rules.

which itself issues CLNs to the value of the assets on which the risk has been transferred. The proceeds from the notes are invested in risk-free government or agency debt such as gilts, bunds or *Pfandbriefe*, or in senior unsecured bank debt. Should there be a default on one or more of the underlying assets, the required amount of the collateral is sold and the proceeds from the sale are paid to the issuer to recompense for the losses. The premium paid on the CDS must be sufficiently high to ensure that it covers the difference in yield between that on the collateral and that on the notes issued by the SPV. The generic structure is illustrated in Figure 23.7 on page 1076.

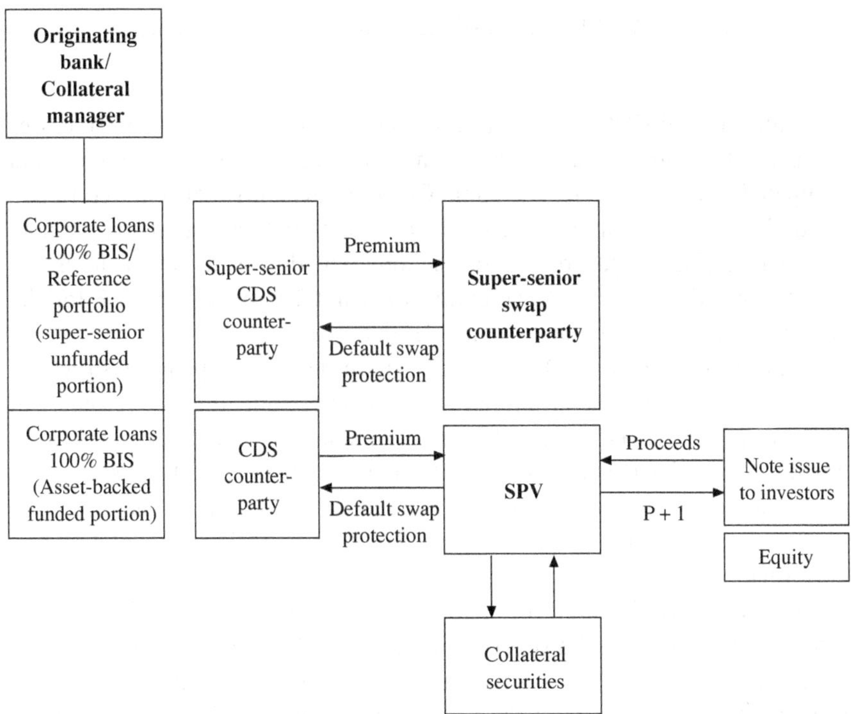

Figure 23.6 Partially funded synthetic CDO structure

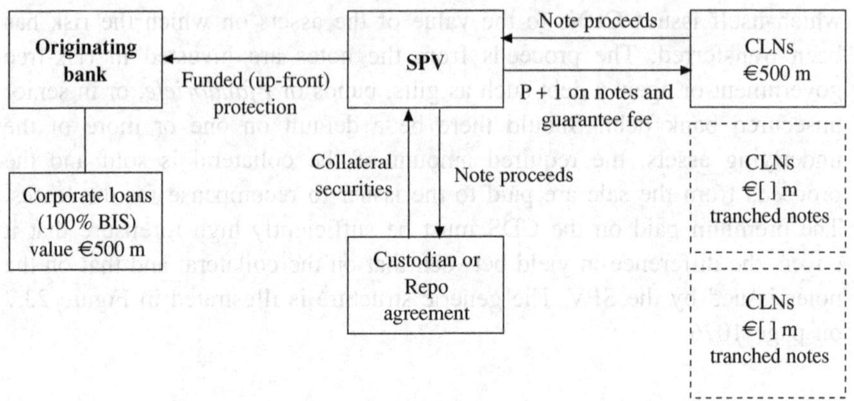

Figure 23.7 Fully funded synthetic balance sheet CDO structure

Fully funded CDOs are relatively uncommon. One of the advantages of the partially funded arrangement is that the issuer pays a lower premium compared to a fully funded synthetic CDO, because it is not required to pay the difference between the yield on the collateral and the coupon on the note issue (the unfunded part of the transaction). The downside is that the issuer receives a reduction in risk-weighting for capital purposes to 20% for the risk transferred via the super-senior default swap.

The fully *unfunded* CDO uses only credit default swaps in its structure. The swaps are rated in a similar way to notes, and there is usually an "equity" piece that is retained by the originator. The reference portfolio is again commercial loans, usually 100% risk-weighted, or other assets. The credit rating of the swap tranches is based on the rating of the reference assets, as well as other factors such as the diversity of the assets and ratings performance correlation. The typical structure is illustrated in Figure 23.8. As well as the equity tranche, there is one or more junior tranches, one or more senior tranches and a super-senior tranche. The senior tranches are sold on to AAA-rated banks as a portfolio CDS, while the junior tranche is usually sold to an OECD bank. The ratings of the tranches are typically:

- super-senior: AAA;
- senior: AA to AAA;
- junior: BB to A;
- equity: unrated.

The CDSs are not single-name swaps, but are written on a class of debt. The advantage for the originator is that it can name the reference asset class to investors without having to disclose the name of specific loans. Default swaps are usually cash settled and not physically settled, so that the reference assets can be replaced with other assets if desired by the sponsor.

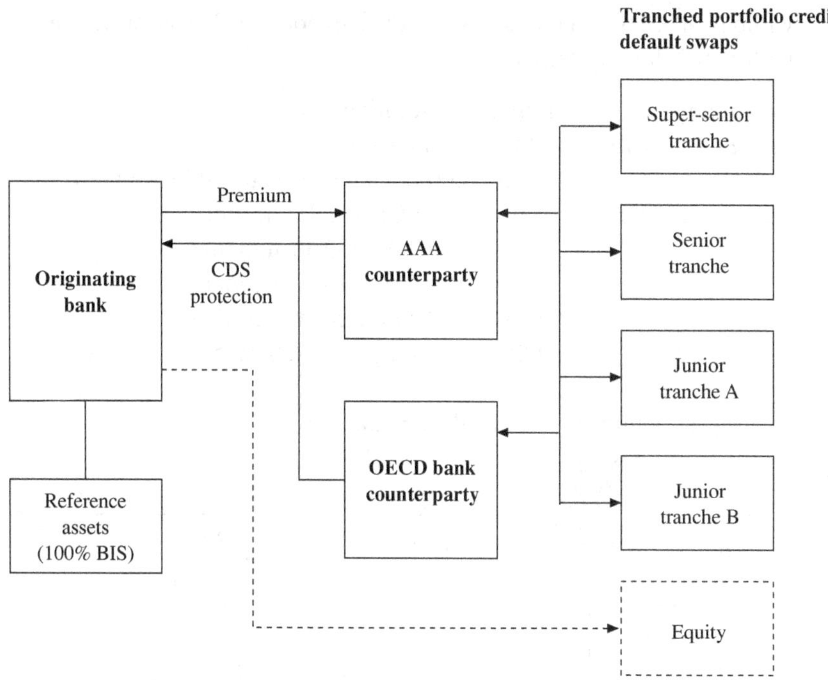

Figure 23.8 The fully unfunded synthetic CDO

Deal term sheet

In the markets, the first description of a transaction is usually provided in the deal term sheet, produced by the arranging bank. For illustrative purposes, we show in Appendix 23.1, a sample term sheet for a hypothetical deal, which we have called Scarab CSO Limited. This term sheet is representative of what may be encountered in the market, although there is a wide discrepancy among these, with some being just one side of an A4 paper, while others may be 40 or 50 pages long. The full legal description of the deal is given in the deal offering circular (OC). For full details of the legal and documentation aspects of a securitisation, see Garcia and Patel (2004).

EXAMPLE 23.2 The fully unfunded synthetic CDO

This example illustrates a fully unfunded deal, which can be either on the balance sheet or it can source reference assets externally. Because it is fully unfunded, the liabilities of the deal structure are comprised purely of CDS, and so it can also be structured with or without an SPV. Our example is of a hypothetical deal structure with the following terms:

Originator:	Banking institution
Reference portfolio:	€900 m notional
	80–100 corporate names sourced in the market
CDS tranching:	Super-senior CDS €815 m notional
	"Class A" CDS €35 m notional
	"Class B" CDS €15 m notional
	"Class C" CDS €20 m notional
	"Class D" or equity CDS €15 m notional

The structure is illustrated in Figure 23.9.

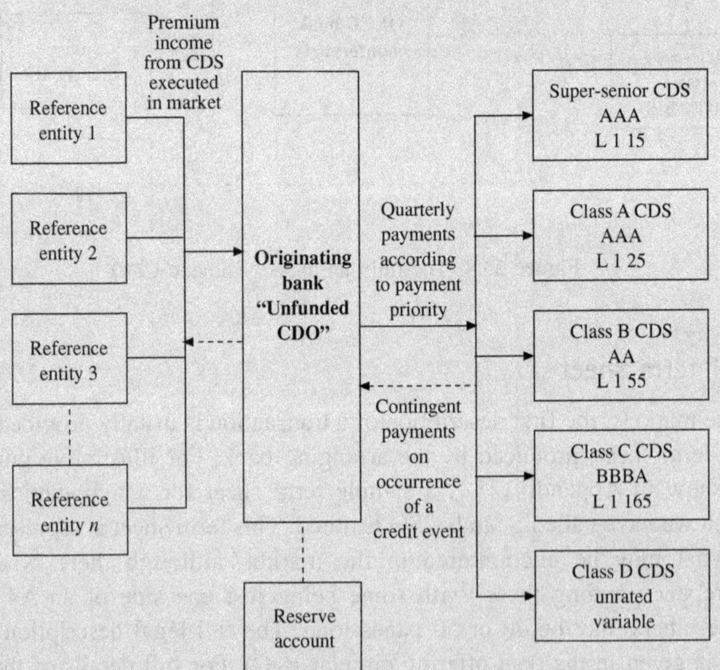

Figure 23.9 Fully unfunded synthetic CDO, structure diagram

The key difference with this structure is that it can be arranged directly by the originating institution. There is no need to set up an SPV. In fact, this is also an on-balance sheet deal. The rating of the tranches is based on the loss allocation, with credit events among reference assets being set up so that the junior note suffers losses first. This follows traditional structured finance technology. However, unlike traditional structures, the interest payments on the liability side are not subject to a waterfall; instead, they are guaranteed to investors. This increases the attraction of the deal. Thus, on occurrence of a credit event, interest payments are still received by investors. It is the notional amount, on which interest is calculated, that is reduced, thereby reducing the interest received. Losses of notional value above the Class D threshold eat into the Class C swap notional amount.

This is a version of an arbitrage deal, with the originating bank taking the role of a fund manager. It features the following:

- the bank selects the initial portfolio, using its credit skills to select credits in the market, which are referenced via CDSs. The bank sells protection on these assets; the premium received exceeds the premium paid on the liability side, which creates the arbitrage gain for the bank. The reduced premium payable on the liability side reflects the tranches arrangement of the liabilities;
- the reference assets are sourced by the bank on its own balance sheet, before the CDO itself is closed in the market;
- the bank has freedom to dynamically manage the portfolio during the life of the deal, taking a view on credits in line with its fundamental analysis of the market;
- trading profits are trapped in a "reserve account", which is also available to cover trading losses and losses suffered due to credit events.

As part of the rating requirements for the deal, the originating bank follows certain eligibility constraints concerning which exposures it can take on. This can include restrictions on:

- reference entities being rated at investment grade by the ratings agencies;
- there being no single reference credit to have a total exposure of more than €10 million;
- where the reference entity can be incorporated in a specified list of countries;
- geographical and industrial concentration;
- a trading turnover limit of 20% of notional value per annum;
- a Moody's diversity score of at least 45 on closing and no lower than 42 during life of deal.[10]

In addition to the "guaranteed" nature of interest payments for investors (subject to level of credit events), the principal advantage of this structure is that it may be brought to market very quickly. There is no requirement for the originator to set up an SPV, and no need to issue and settle notes. The originator can therefore take advantage of market conditions and respond quickly to investor demands for return enhancement and diversification.

The managed synthetic CDO

Managed synthetic CDOs are the latest variant of the synthetic CDO structure.[11] They are similar to the partially funded deals we described earlier, except that the reference asset pool of credit derivatives is actively traded by the sponsoring investment manager. It is the maturing market in CDSs, resulting in high liquidity in a large number of synthetic corporate credits, which has facilitated the introduction of the managed synthetic CDO. With this structure, originators can use credit derivatives to arbitrage cash and synthetic liabilities, as well as leverage off their expertise in credit trading to generate profit. The advantages for investors are the same as the advantages of earlier generations of CDOs, except that with active trading they are gaining a larger exposure to the skills of the investment manager. The underlying asset pool is again a portfolio of CDSs. However, these are now dynamically managed and actively traded, under specified guidelines.

[11] See Appendix 23.2 for an introduction to the concept of the diversity score.

[12] These are also commonly known as CSOs within the market. *RISK* magazine has called them collateralised swap obligations, which handily also shortens to CSOs. Boggiano et al. (2002) refer to these structures as managed variable synthetic CDOs, although the author has not come across this term in other literature.

Thus, there is greater flexibility afforded to the sponsor, and the vehicle records trading gains or losses as a result of credit derivative trading. In most structures, the investment manager can only buy protection (short credit) in order to offset an existing sold protection default swap. For some deals, this restriction is removed and the investment manager can buy or sell credit derivatives to reflect its view.

Note that this structure is a credit trading vehicle. It is not really a tool for use in bank ALM.

Structure

The structure of the managed synthetic is similar to the partially funded synthetic CDO, with a separate legally incorporated SPV.[12] On the liability side, there is an issue of notes, with note proceeds invested in collateral or *eligible investments* that are made up of one or a combination of the following:

- a bank deposit account or guaranteed investment contract (*GIC*) which pays a pre-specified rate of interest;[13]
- risk-free bonds such as US Treasury securities, German *Pfandbriefe* or AAA-rated bonds such as credit-card ABS securities;
- a repo agreement with risk-free collateral;
- a liquidity facility with a AA-rated bank;
- a market-sensitive debt instrument, often enhanced with the repo or liquidity arrangement described above.

On the asset side, the SPV enters into CDSs and/or total return swaps, selling protection to the sponsor. The investment manager (or "collateral manager") can trade in and out of CDSs after the transaction has closed in the market.[14] The SPV enters into credit derivatives via a single basket CDS to one swap counterparty, written on a portfolio of reference assets, or via multiple single-name credit swaps with a number of swap counterparties.

---

[12] We use the term SPV for *special purpose vehicle*. This is also referred to as a special purpose entity (SPE) or special purpose corporation (SPC).

[13] A GIC has been defined either as an account that pays a fixed-rate of interest for its term, or more usually an account that pays a fixed spread below Libor or Euribor, usually three-month floating rolled over each interest period.

[14] This term is shared with other securitisation structures. When notes have been priced, and placed in the market, and all legal documentation signed by all named participants, the transaction has *closed*. In effect, this is the start of the transaction, and the noteholders should receive interest payments during the life of the deal and principal repayment on maturity.

The latter arrangement is more common and is referred to as a *multiple dealer* CDO. A percentage of the reference portfolio is identified at the start of work on the transaction, with the remainder of the entities being selected during the ramp-up period ahead of closing. The SPV enters into the other side of the CDSs by selling protection to one of the swap counterparties on specific reference entities. Thereafter, the investment manager can trade out of this exposure in the following ways:

- buying credit protection from another swap counterparty on the same reference entity. This offsets the existing exposure, but there may be residual risk exposure unless premium dates are matched exactly or if there is a default in both the reference entity and the swap counterparty;
- unwinding or terminating the swap with the counterparty;
- buying credit protection on a reference asset that is outside the portfolio. This is uncommon as it leaves residual exposures and may affect premium spread gains.

The SPV actively manages the portfolio within specified guidelines, the decisions being made by the investment manager. Initially, the manager's opportunity to trade may be extensive, but this will be curtailed if there are losses. The trading guidelines will extend to both individual CDSs and at the portfolio level. They may include:

- parameters under which the investment manager (in the guise of the SPV) may actively close out, hedge or substitute reference assets using credit derivatives;
- guidelines under which the investment manager can trade credit derivatives to maximise gains or minimise losses on reference assets that have improved or worsened in credit quality or outlook.

CDSs may be cash settled or physically settled, with physical settlement being more common in a managed synthetic deal. In a multiple dealer CDO, the legal documentation must be in place with all names on the counterparty dealer list, which may add to legal costs as standardisation may be difficult.

Investors who are interested in this structure are seeking to benefit from the following advantages compared to vanilla synthetic deals:

- active management of the reference portfolio and the trading expertise of the investment manager in the corporate credit market;

- a multiple-dealer arrangement, so that the investment manager can obtain the most competitive prices for CDSs;
- under physical settlement, the investment manager (via the SPV) has the ability to obtain the highest recovery value for the reference asset.

A generic managed synthetic CDO is illustrated in Figure 23.10.

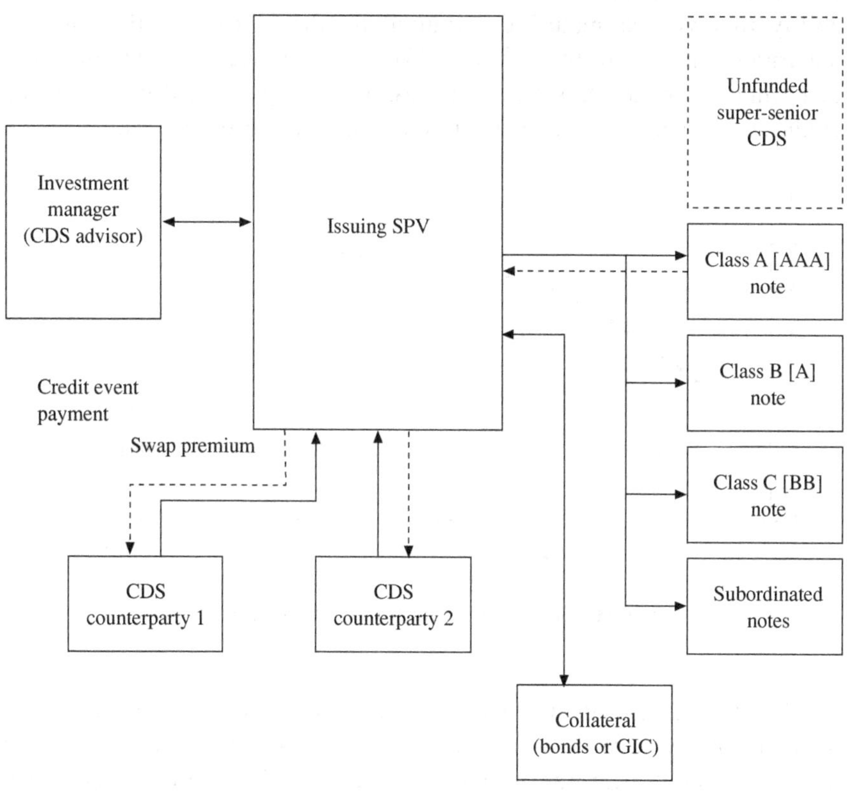

Figure 23.10 Generic managed synthetic CDO

Originators generally appoint third-party portfolio administrators for managed synthetic CDOs to look after the deal during its life, because they are the most complex CSOs. The portfolio administrator is responsible for running (among other things) the rating agency compliance tests, such as the waterfall tests, and reporting on the quality of the reference portfolio to investors.

A schematic diagram of the roles performed by the portfolio administrator on a hypothetical managed CSO is shown in Appendix 23.3.

A detailed case study of an innovative managed synthetic deal, Robeco CSO BV, is provided in Chapter 20 of Choudhry (2005).

The single-tranche synthetic CDO

One of the advantages offered to investors in the synthetic market is the ability to invest at maturities required by the investor, rather than at maturities selected by bond issuers. For example, Figure 23.11 illustrates that while the bond market provides assets at only selected points on the credit curve, synthetic products allow investors to access the full curve.

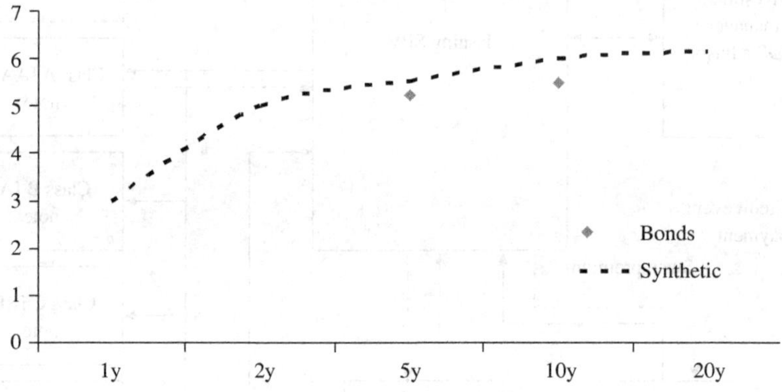

Figure 23.11 Hypothetical credit term structure

The flexibility of the CSO, enabling deal types to be structured to meet the needs of a wide range of investors and issuers, is well illustrated with the tailor-made or "single-tranche CDO" structure.[15] This structure has been developed in response to investor demand for exposure to a specific part of a pool of reference credits. With this structure an arranging bank creates a tailored portfolio that meets specific investor requirements with regard to:

[15] These deals have been arranged by a number of investment banks, including JPMorgan Chase, Bank of America, UBS Warburg and Credit Agricole Indosuez. They are known variously as *mono-tranche CDOs*, *tailor-made CDOs*, *tranche-only CDOs*, *on-demand CDOs*, *iCDOs* and *investor-driven CDOs,* as well as single-tranche CDOs. The author prefers the last one!

- portfolio size and asset class;
- portfolio concentration, geographical and industry variation;
- portfolio diversity and rating;
- investment term-to-maturity.

At the same time, the single-tranche CDO is also a means by which a bank can transfer credit risk to the market, similarly to a basket CDS. Hence they are used as part of credit risk management.

The structure is illustrated in Figures 23.12 and 23.13 on page 1086, respectively with and without an SPV issuer. Under this arrangement, there is only one note tranche. The reference portfolio, made up of CDSs, is dynamically hedged by the originating bank itself. The deal has been arranged to create a risk/reward profile for one investor only (or possibly multiple investors with identical requirements), who buys the single tranche note. This also creates an added advantage that the deal can be brought to market very quickly. The key difference with traditional CSOs is that the arranging bank does not transfer the remainder of the credit risk of the reference pool. Instead, this risk is dynamically managed, and hedged in the market using derivatives.

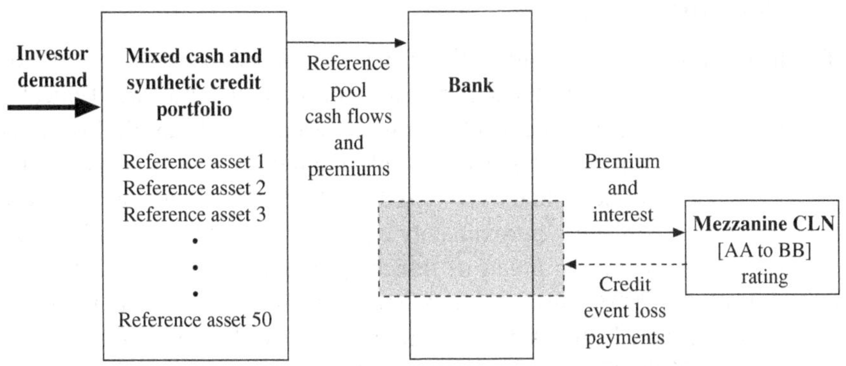

Figure 23.12 Single-tranche CDO I: issue direct from arranging bank

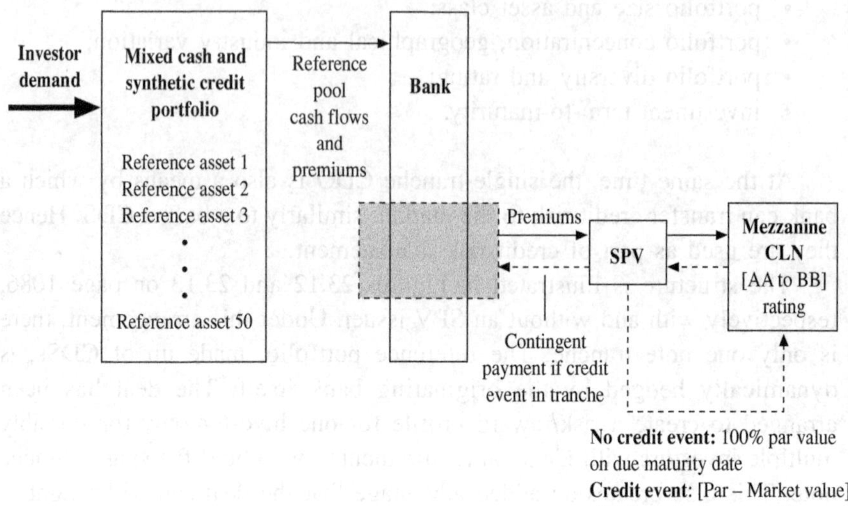

Figure 23.13 Single tranche CDO II: issue via SPV

Deal structure

The investor in a single-tranche CDO makes a decision on the criteria of assets in the portfolio, and the subordination of the issued tranche. Typically this will be at the mezzanine level; that is, covering the 4% to 9% loss level in the portfolio. This enables a favourable risk/return profile to be set up because a CDO tranche that is exposed to 4–9% losses has a very low historical risk of default (approximately equivalent to a Moody's A2 rating) and a high relative return given its tranching, around Libor plus 200 basis points as at May 2003. This is the risk/return profile of the mezzanine piece.

Figure 23.14 illustrates the default probability distribution for credit events in a CDO. Figure 23.15 shows the more specific distribution as applicable to the mezzanine tranche. We clarify this further with some hypothetical values for a capital structure and default distribution in Figure 23.16 on page 1088.

Unlike a traditional CDO, a single-tranche CDO has a very simple cash-flow "waterfall". Compared with Figure 18.6, which showed the waterfall for a vanilla cash securitisation transaction, a single-tranche waterfall will consist of only agency service and hedge costs, and the coupon of the single tranche itself.

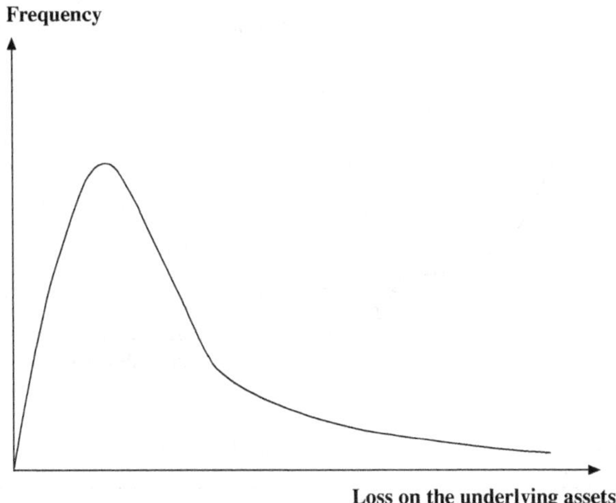

Figure 23.14 Credit loss distribution

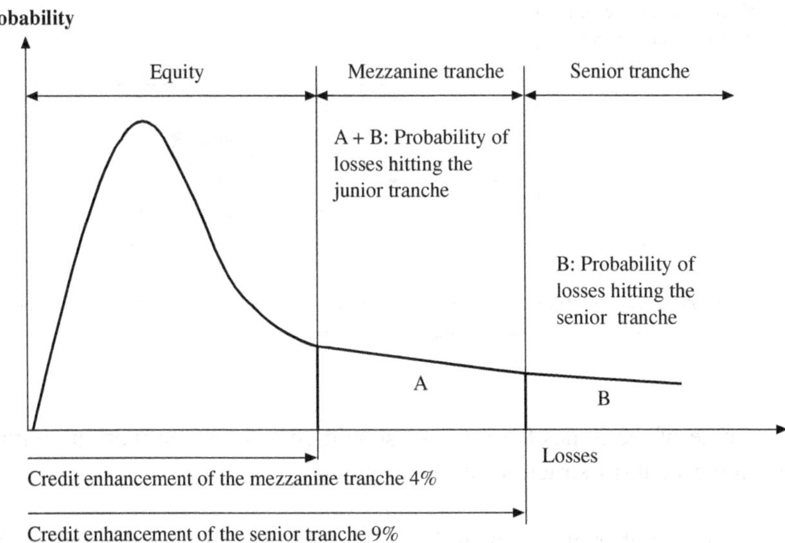

Figure 23.15 Expected loss distribution for tranched notes

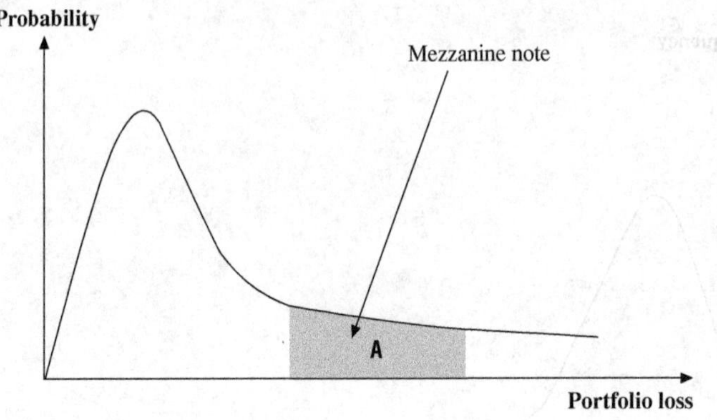

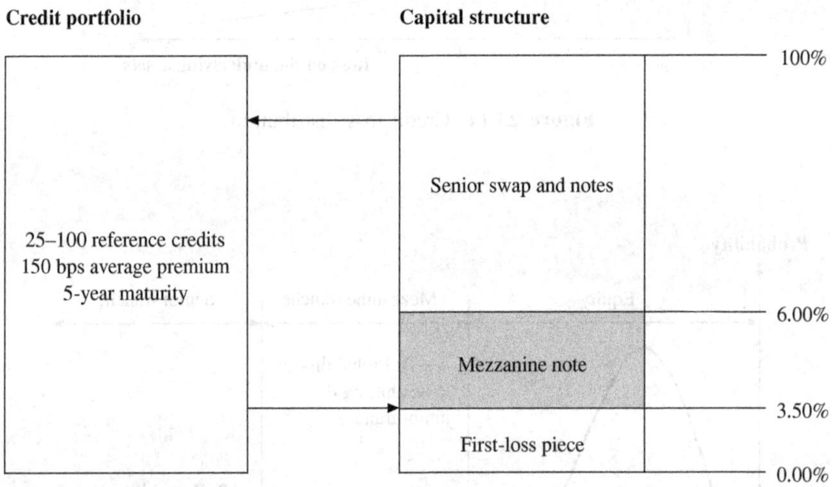

Figure 23.16 Capital structure and default distribution for a single-tranche (mezzanine note) synthetic CDO

Some of the issues the investor should consider when working with the arranging bank to structure the deal include:

- the number of names in the credit portfolio, usually this ranges from 50 to 100 names;
- the geographical split of the reference names;
- the required average credit rating and average interest spread of the portfolio;
- the minimum credit rating required in the portfolio.

If the deal is being rated, as with any CDO type, the mix of assets needs to meet ratings agency criteria for diversity and average rating. The *diversity score* of a portfolio is a measure of the diversity of a portfolio based on qualities such as industrial and geographical concentration. It can be defined as the number of equivalent uncorrelated assets in the pool.[16] We illustrate an hypothetical portfolio in Figure 23.17, which shows the composition of a generic portfolio for a single-tranche CDO.

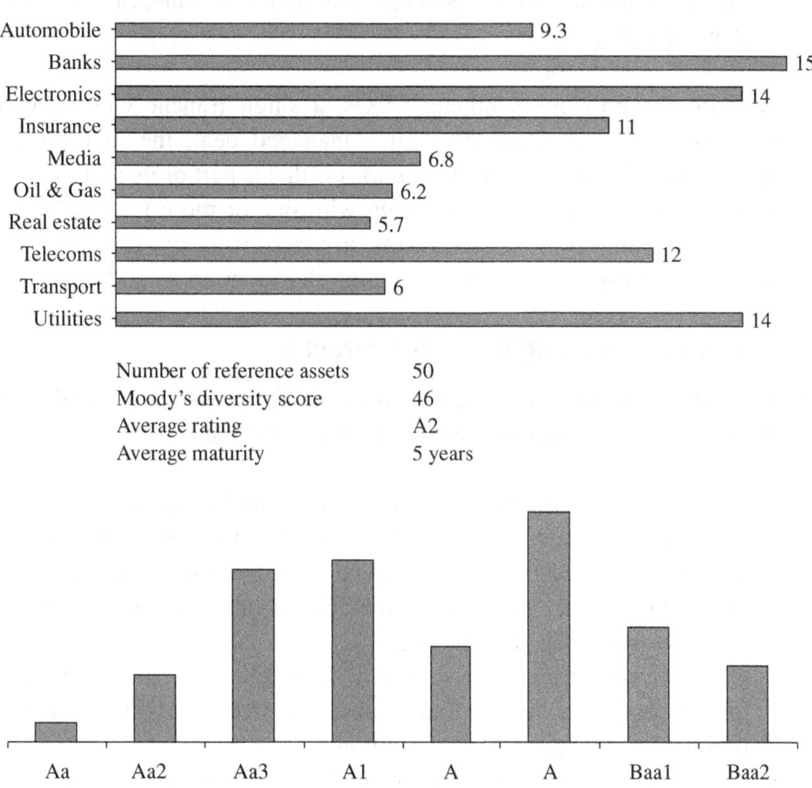

Figure 23.17 Hypothetical portfolio composition for a generic single-tranche CDO

The position and rating of the issued single-tranche is as required by the investor. The subordination of the note follows from the required rating of the investor. For instance, the investor may require an A2 rating for the note. The process followed involves:

[16] Further background on Moody's diversity score is given at Appendix 23.2.

- targeting the required rating on the issued tranche;
- setting the required return on the note, and hence determining where the tranche will lie;
- defining the percentage of first loss that must occur before the issued tranche is impacted by further losses;
- setting the size of the note issue, in line with investor requirements. For instance, if the investor wishes to place $20 million in the note, and the reference pool is $800 million nominal value, this implies a 2.5% tranche.

As with the previous synthetic CDOs, a single-tranche CDO can be either a static or a managed deal. In a managed deal, the investor can manage the portfolio and effect substitutions if this is part of its requirement. To facilitate this, the deal may be set up with one or more fund managers in place to deal when substitutions are required by the investor. Alternatively, an investor may leave trading decisions to a fund manager.

Advantages of the single-tranche structure

For certain investors, the single-tranche CDO presents a number of advantages over the traditional structure. These include:

- flexibility: the features of the investment can be tailor-made to suit the investor's needs. The investor can select the composition of the portfolio, the size of the tranche and its subordination level;
- note terms exactly as required: the coupon and maturity of the note are tailor-made for the investor;
- a shorter time frame: the deal can be brought to market relatively quickly, and in as little as four weeks compared to anything from two months to one year for a conventional CSO;
- lower cost of issue: including lower legal costs because of the short time to issue and no protracted marketing effort by the arranger.

For a bank, a single-tranche CDO can be used as part of its asset pool credit risk management process.

The market has seen both "static" and "managed" single-tranche CDOs, following experience with traditional CSOs. Table 23.1 is a summary of the differences between traditional and single-tranche synthetic CDOs.

Characteristic	Single-tranche	Traditional synthetic CDO
Type	Static, substitution, managed	Static, substitution, managed
Structure	A portfolio of reference credits, for which protection sold via a basket CDS	A portfolio of reference credits, for which protection sold via a basket CDS
	A specific tranche of the portfolio credit risk is transferred to a sole investor. Remaining risk stays with originator, and is delta-hedged	The portfolio risk is transferred in its entirety, through a tranched CDS and/or CLN arrangement, to market investors
	A bilateral arrangement	A syndicated securitisation arrangement
Portfolio	Between 20–100 reference credits diversified across geography, industry	Between 100–150 reference credits, diversified across geography, industry
	Typically investment-grade	Can include investment-grade, high-yield, emerging market, special situations (sole AAA-rated, etc.)
	Can be customised to meet specific credit rating, foreign-exchange and interest-rate requirements of the investor	Can be customised at structuring stage but to meet needs of a wider group of investors. Will be marketed once the general structure is known
Deal economies	Shorter time scale, increased deal volume	Longer time-scale to bring to market
	Greater opportunity to react to specific market conditions and capture arbitrage	Decreased ability to capture arbitrage opportunities as they arise

Table 23.1 Differences between traditional and single-tranche synthetic CDOs

Hypothetical pricing example

Figure 23.18 is a simplified illustration of a pricing example for a single-tranche CDO, with market rates as observed on Bloomberg during April 2003. We assume the portfolio is constituted in the following way:

Number of credits:	100
Size:	€8 million each
Nominal size:	€800 million
Diversity score:	48
Average rating:	BBB1/Baa1
Minimum rating:	BBB2/Baa3
Maturity:	5 years.

The originating bank structures a single-tranche CDO following investor interest with the following terms:

Subordination level:	3.90% (this means that five defaults are supported, assuming a 35% recovery rate)
Calculation of attachment point:	6th name default [6 × 8 million = 48 million; 35% recovery rate = €31.2 million loss; 31.2/800 = 3.90%]
Attachment/detachment points:	3.90%–5.85%
Tranche size:	€25 million
Expected rating:	A/A2
Spread:	Euribor + 1,220 basis points.

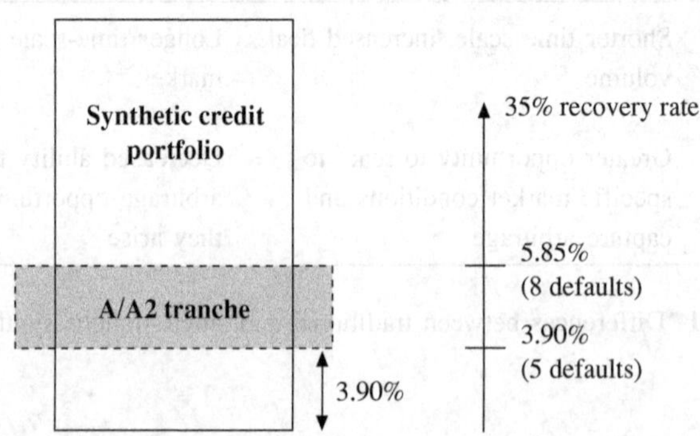

Figure 23.18 Single-tranche CDO illustrative pricing example

EXAMPLE 23.3 CDO equity note

Equity is the most junior note in the capital structure of a CDO. For this reason it is also known as the "first-loss" piece of the CDO, carrying the highest risk of payment delays and losses due to credit events or default. The equity, which is actually issued as a "bond" with an international security number (known as an ISIN), receives any cash that is left over after all other liabilities and claims have been paid from the asset cash flows. These include management and servicing fees plus the senior debt liabilities. In a cash-flow structure, the return to the equity holder is a function of defaults and payment delays of assets in the collateral portfolio. The level of trading or credit rating downgrades does not have an impact on the equity unless they affect the cash flows of the structure. The equity piece receives the residual cash flows generated by the structure, but there is a distinction between coupon cash flows and principal cash flows. The residual coupon is paid out as it is received, while the residual principal cash flows are not paid out until after all debt notes are paid off.

Given all this, we can see that CDO equity is a "leveraged" exposure to credit risk, taken on by the equity investor. The holder of CDO equity, which is frequently the collateral manager or sponsor of the deal, will have a view that the cash flows generated by the underlying assets will be sufficient to bear expected credit losses and provide enough surplus to pay on the equity note. When assessing the expected returns therefore, the investor considers the expected level of defaults and how this will impact on the structure. This assessment must also take into account the leveraged nature of the structure, because of the large amount of the debt in the vehicle.

The timing, as well as extent, of defaults is critical to equity return. With a cash-flow CDO the initial size of the excess net spread of assets over liabilities means that there is a "front-loaded" pattern to equity cash receipts. Equity holders receive a significant part of return early in the deal, because the initial excess spreads are high, since defaults are unlikely to occur at the start of the deal and will not peak until later on in the deal's life. The later in life that defaults do occur, the greater will be the return to the equity holder.

CDO equity is not a straightforward bond and must be assessed carefully by investors due to their complexity. The structure of the

CDO and the quality of the collateral pool are very important issues for consideration, as is the extent of secondary market trading of the note (which will be low to start with). In addition, potential investors must consider what benchmark should be used as a comparison when assessing the return on the note, and what product can be used to hedge the equity note if needed.

Risk and return on CDOs

The return analysis for CDOs performed by potential investors is necessarily different to that undertaken for other securitised asset classes. For CDOs the three key factors to consider are:

- default probabilities and cumulative default rates;
- default correlations;
- recovery rates.

Default probability rates

The level of default probability rates will vary with each deal. Analysts such as the rating agencies will use a number of methods to estimate default probabilities, such as individual reference credit ratings and historical probability rates. Since there may be as many as 150 or more reference names in the CDO, a common approach is to use the average rating of the reference portfolio. Rating agencies such as Moody's provide data on the default rates for different ratings as an "average" class, which can be used in the analysis.

Correlation

The correlation between assets in the reference portfolio of a CDO is an important factor in CDO returns analysis. A problem arises with what precise correlation value to use; these can be correlation between default probabilities, correlation between timing of default and correlation between spreads. The *diversity score* value of the CDO plays a part in this: it represents the number of uncorrelated bonds with identical par value and the same default probability.

Recovery rates

Recovery rates for individual obligors differ by issuer and industry classification. Rating agencies such as Moody's publish data on the average prices of all defaulted bonds, and generally analysts will construct a database of recovery rates by industry and credit rating for use in modelling the expected recovery rates of assets in the collateral pool. Note that for synthetic CDOs with CDSs as assets in the portfolio, this factor is not relevant.

Analysts undertake simulation modelling to generate scenarios of default and expected return. For instance, they may model the number of defaults up to maturity, the recovery rates of these defaults and the timing of defaults. All these variables are viewed as random variables, so they are modelled using a stochastic process.

CDO yield spreads

Fund managers consider investing in CDO-type products as they represent a diversification in the European bond markets, with yields that are comparable to credit-card or auto-loan ABS assets. A cash CDO also gives investors exposure to sectors in the market that may not otherwise be accessible to most investors; for example, credits such as small- or medium-sized corporate entities that rely entirely on bank financing. Also, the extent of credit enhancement and note tranching in a CDO means that they may show better risk/reward profiles than straight conventional debt, with a higher yield but incorporating asset backing and insurance backing. In cash and synthetic CDOs the issues notes are often bullet bonds, with fixed term to maturity, whereas other ABS and MBS products are amortising securities with only average (expected life) maturities. This may suit certain longer-dated investors.

An incidentally perceived advantage of cash CDOs is that they are typically issued by financial institutions such as higher-rated banks. This usually provides comfort on the credit side, but also on the underlying administration and servicing side with regard to underlying assets, compared to consumer receivables securitisations.

Figure 23.19 is a comparison of balance sheet CLO deals in 2005–2006.

To illustrate yields, Figure 23.20 on page 1098 shows the spreads on a selected range of notes during February 2003 over the credit spectrum. Figure 23.21 on page 1098 shows a comparison of different asset classes in European structured products during this time.

	Metrix Funding No. 1	Lambda Finance	Start II CLO
Originator	HSBC	Barclays plc	Standard Chartered Bank
Closing date	15 Nov. 2005	29 Nov. 2005	22 Jun. 2006
Structure	Cash	Fully funded Synthetic	Partially funded synthetic
Notional size (EUR mm)	2,962	7,293	1,272
Funded amount (EUR mm)	2,962	7,293	191
Asset pool origin	Multinational	UK	Multinational (Asia)
No. of assets (obligors) in pool	99	577	174
AAA subordination (cash tranche)	15.00%	11.80%	8.25%
Pool rating equivalent	BBB–	BB/Ba2	Baa2
Credit event (synthetic deals)	–	Bankruptcy Failure to pay Restructuring	Bankruptcy Failure to pay Restructuring
Pricing (basis points over Libor) and tenor			
– AAA tranche	21 (4.8 yr)	24 (4.5 yr)	33 (5.0 yr)
– AA tranche	31 (6.3 yr)	37 (6.0 yr)	40 (5.0 yr)
– A tranche	60 (6.6 yr)	62 (6.0 yr)	75 (5.0 yr)
– BBB tranche	95 (6.7 yr)	92 (6.0 yr)	185 (5.0 yr)
– BB tranche	310 (6.7 yr)	275 (6.0 yr)	400 (5.0 yr)
– B tranche	–	450 (6.0 yr)	–
Other notes (non-rated)	Class F +550 bps	Class G +900 bps (7.5 yr)	Class F
Equity / First loss	Reserve account of GBP 34 mm, target size GBP 48 mm (2.4%)	0.5% available quarterly as excess spread to cover for losses	Class F

Figure 23.19 Balance sheet CLOs – comparison of sample deals in 2005–2006
Sources: Deal documents, Bloomberg L.P.

Arran Corporate Loans No. 1	**SEA FORT Securities**	**Amstel Corporate 2006-1**
Royal Bank of Scotland	Sampo Bank	ABN Amro Bank N.V.
26 Jun. 2006	28 Jun. 2006	17 Nov. 2006
Fully funded synthetic	Partially funded synthetic	Partially funded cash
5,071	1,000	10,000
5,071	145	1,130
UK	Finland	Multinational
126	608	531 (minimum 400)
17.60%	10.35%	6.80%
BB+/Ba2	BBB–	BBB–/Baa3
Bankruptcy Failure to pay Restructuring	Bankruptcy Failure to pay	–
17 (2.87 yr)	16 (4.95 yr WAL)	20 (4.1 yr)
33 (6.5 yr)	26 (5.26 yr WAL)	30 (4.1 yr)
60 (7.32 yr)	38 (5.50 yr WAL)	48 (4.1 yr)
100 (7.68 yr)	70 (5.50 yr WAL)	100 (4.1 yr)
325 (7.72 yr)	250 (5.50 yr WAL)	305 (4.1 yr)
550 (7.72 yr)	–	–
Class G	Class F	Class F
Credit enhancement available from synthetic excess spread (0.30% pa). Excess spread is trapped in reserve account up to GBP35 mm when notional balance of defaulted reference assets exceeds initial balance of Class G.	Synthetic excess spread 10 bps per year available as first-loss reserve, although not trapped in a reserve account	Unrated equity piece is 2.3% of reference amount. If OC test is breached, excess spread placed in reserve account, which acts as buffer if F note suffers total loss

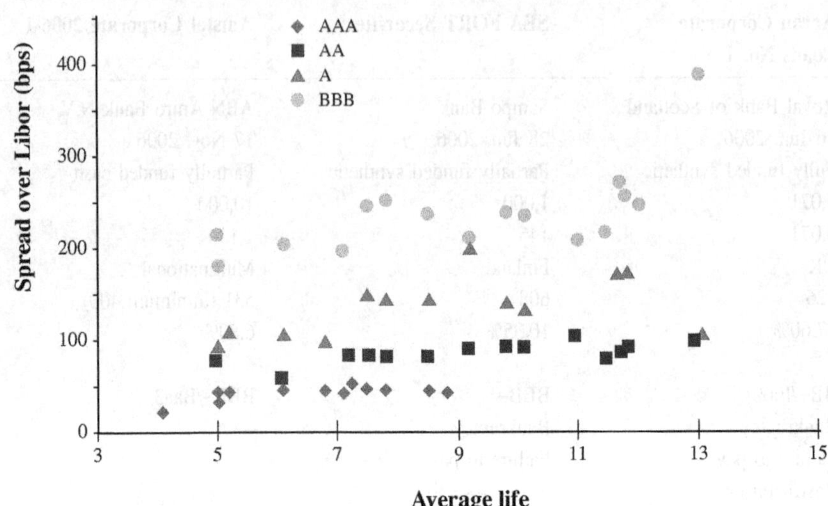

Figure 23.20 Rating spreads, February 2003
Source: JPMorgan.

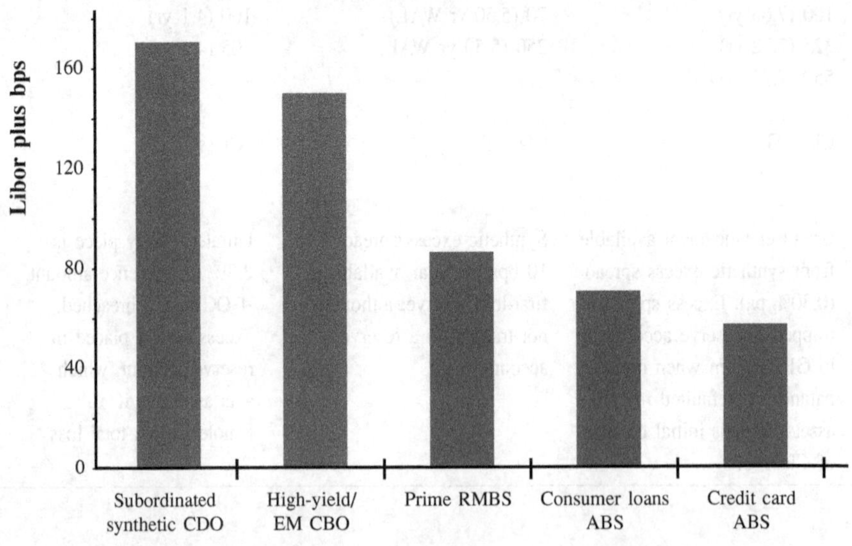

Figure 23.21 Comparing CDO yields to other securitisation asset classes, February 2004
Source: JPMorgan.

Pricing methodology for synthetic CDO notes[17]

A synthetic CDO is made up of a portfolio of credit default swaps. The arranger of a synthetic CDO distributes the credit risk of the portfolio by creating and selling tranches to investors. Every tranche has an attachment and detachment point that determines the amount of loss, and correspondingly the number of defaults that the tranche can absorb. For example, the first tranche, known as the equity tranche, might be responsible for portfolio credit losses between 0% and 3%, the next tranche would then be responsible for portfolio losses that exceed 3% up to the size of the tranche, and so on. The least risky tranche of a CDO is known as the senior tranche, or super-senior tranche. Tranches between the equity tranche and the most senior tranche are known as mezzanine tranches.

The challenge in pricing a synthetic CDO lies in the difficult task of formulating a model for the joint default behaviour of the underlying reference assets. Understanding and modelling the joint default dynamics of the reference assets are important in order to compute the expected losses for each tranche. The expected losses, in turn, determine the fair spread of the tranche. In fact, once the joint default distribution of the reference assets has been specified, we can price any tranche that references these assets.

In this section we present an approach to computing the joint default distribution of a reference portfolio. The approach is based on a one-factor recursive procedure and requires no Monte Carlo simulations. We compare the results of this recursive approach with the results obtained using a Monte Carlo procedure that simulates the default times of the reference assets and the corresponding losses in the portfolio. The Monte Carlo approach is computationally time-consuming as it requires a large number of simulations in order to produce enough defaults that can impact the most senior tranches of a CDO.

Computing the distribution of default losses

Pricing a synthetic CDO boils down to computing the joint distribution of defaults of the reference portfolio. Computing the default distribution, in

[17] This section was written by Jaffar Hussain. The author is writing in his individual private capacity.

Jaffar Hussain is Head of Investment Analytics in the Capital Markets Division of the Saudi National Commercial Bank, Bahrain. Before joining NCB, he worked as a Credit Risk Manager at Gulf International Bank. Jaffar has an MBA from Rollins College, Florida and a BSc in Accounting from the University of Iowa. He holds the FRM designation of the Global Association of Risk Professionals.

turn, depends crucially on the default probabilities of the reference credits and the pairwise correlation between every pair of credits. The correlation among the assets will drive the joint default behaviour of the assets. The model we use here is a one-factor model whereby the defaults are driven by one factor which we take to represent a common economic driver of credit events. Default losses are then calculated conditional on the state of this economic factor. This procedure will result in computing the conditional default distribution. The next step is to integrate the conditional default distribution over the common factor to arrive at the unconditional distribution of default losses. This modelling framework has an appealing and easy interpretation. Conditional on the state of the common economic factor, credits will default when their asset values fall below a pre-specified threshold. This default threshold usually represents the level of debt of a company. If we further assume that the variables driving the returns process follow a normal distribution, then this modelling framework is also known as the Gaussian copula.

We assume that the reference portfolio contains n credits and each credit is described by its notional amount, probability of default, and recovery rate. For any credit "i" we then have a notional $A(i)$, a default probability $p(i)$ and a recovery rate $r(i)$. The return process of each credit is driven by a common factor M, and a noise factor $\varepsilon(i)$ that is specific to the i-th credit according to the following equation:

$$Z(i) = \beta(i).M + \varepsilon(\mathrm{i}).\sqrt{(1 - \beta(i)^2)} \qquad (23.1)$$

where the $Z(i)$ represents the returns of credit i. The market factor M, and the idiosyncratic factor $\varepsilon(i)$ are independent standard normals with zero means and unit variances. The asset returns, $Z(i)$, follow a standard normal distribution as well. Within this specification of the returns dynamics, the correlation between any two credits, i and j, is simply given by the product of $\beta(i)$ and $\beta(j)$, where $\beta(i)$ and $\beta(j)$ are taken to represent the betas of credits i and j respectively. That is, they represent the sensitivities of credits i and j to changes in the common factor, as shown below.

$$p[Z(i), Z(j)] = \beta(i).\beta(j) \qquad (23.2)$$

Conditional on the realisations of the common factor, defaults are only driven by the noise factors $\varepsilon(i)$ and are thus independent. A credit, i, is assumed to default if its asset return, $Z(i)$, falls below a pre-specified level or default threshold given by the $\Phi^{-1}[p(i)]$ where Φ^{-1} denotes the inverse of the cumulative standard normal distribution. If we denote the default threshold of credit i by $D(i)$, then a credit i defaults when:

$$Z(i) < D(i), \text{ where } D(i) = \Phi^{-1}[p(i)]. \tag{23.3}$$

Equivalently by rearranging equation (23.1), default occurs when:

$$\varepsilon(i) < [D(i) - \beta(i).M] \,/\, \sqrt{(1 - \beta(i)^2)}. \tag{23.4}$$

Finally, since $\varepsilon(i)$ are standard normals and we assume a flat correlation across all credits, the default probability of credit i conditional on the realisations of the common factor M is given by:

$$\text{Prob}[Z(i) < D(i)| \, M] = \Phi \left([D(i) - \text{M}.\sqrt{\text{p}}] \,/\, \sqrt{[1 - p]}\right). \tag{23.5}$$

This last equation demonstrates that only a single correlation parameter and a single common factor M are needed to calculate the joint distribution of default losses.

There are two ways to move on from here. One approach involves a Monte Carlo simulation of M and $\varepsilon(i)$ in equation (23.1) to generate realisations of the asset returns $Z(i)$. Defaults will then be triggered whenever $Z(i)$ falls below a threshold as described by equation (23.3). The term structure of default probabilities for each credit can be calibrated to market spreads or implied from the credit ratings. A second approach takes advantage of the fact that defaults are independent, conditional on the common market factor. It then uses a recursive method to construct the conditional default distribution. The details of this recursion method are discussed in Gibson (2004); Hull and White (2003); and Andersen, Sidenius and Basu (2003); and an alternative approach using generating functions is discussed in Mina and Stern (2003). We can calculate the conditional probability that a portfolio of n credits will lose exactly k credits by time t with the following recursion:

$$\begin{aligned} P^n(k, t| \, M) = {} & P^{n-1}(k, t| \, M).(1 - P(Z(i) < D(i)| \, M)) \\ & + P^{\,n-1}(k - 1, t| \, M).P(Z(i) < D(i)| \, M) \end{aligned} \tag{23.6}$$

where the superscript n in P^n refers to the size of the portfolio and should not be understood as P to the power of n. By starting with a portfolio of size 0 and successively adding credits according to the recursion equation we can construct the conditional default distribution. Finally, by weighting the conditional probabilities by the probability distribution of the common factor we arrive at the unconditional default distribution.

For the results here we use the Monte Carlo and the recursion methods to generate the default loss distribution. The Monte Carlo method, though slower, allows more flexibility in modelling the correlation and default parameters. If we run both models using the same correlation and default assumptions, we will obtain the same results.

Pricing synthetic CDO tranches

Pricing a CDO tranche is a function of the tranche's notional, spread and expected default losses. The expected losses on a tranche can be estimated from the default distribution of the reference portfolio. Thus, for each payment date we need to estimate the credit losses sustained by the portfolio and distribute these losses to each tranche based on the relative position of the tranche in the capital structure: the protection leg. Also, each tranche receives a premium that is a function of the remaining notional amount of the tranche on the payment date: the premium leg. Thus, both the premium leg and the protection leg are a function of a common denominator: the portfolio credit losses sustained by the payment date. To compute the fair spread on a tranche we need to equate its premium leg to its protection leg, which reduces the pricing of a synthetic tranche to the more familiar analytics of a single-name default swap. If we denote the expected loss of a tranche at payment date t_i by $E(L_i)$, then:

$$\text{Total expected losses on the tranche} = \textstyle\sum_i DF_i \,.\, [E(L_i) - E(L_{i-1})] \qquad (23.7)$$

$$\text{Total expected premium payments} = s.\textstyle\sum_i DF_i \,.\, E(N_i) \qquad (23.8)$$

where DF_i is the discount factor at payment date i, s is the tranche spread, $E(N_i)$ is the tranche expected remaining notional by payment date i, and the summation is taken over all payment dates. We also note that the remaining notional is a function of the expected losses on the tranche, which is driven by the portfolio credit losses. That is:

$$E(N_i) = N_0 - E(L_i) \qquad (23.9)$$

where N_0 is the original notional of the tranche.

Based on standard swap pricing that both legs must have net present value equal, we can then calculate the fair spread of the tranche as:

$$s_{fair} = \Sigma_i DF_i \, . \, [E(L_i) - E(L_{i-1})] \; / \; \Sigma_i DF_i \, . \, E(N_i) \qquad (23.10)$$

Once again, the pricing equations show that all one needs in order to compute the price of any synthetic CDO tranche is the default distribution of the reference credits.

Example illustration: pricing the tranche

To illustrate the results of the modelling approach described above, we work with the following transaction: \$1 billion reference portfolio for a 5-year hypothetical CDO consisting of 100 reference credits. All credits have the same spread of 100 basis points and an average recovery rate of 40%. The flat asset correlation is assumed to be 25%, and the risk-free discount rate is a constant 5%. In addition, all credits have the same notional amount: \$10 million. Table 23.2 shows the tranches of this hypothetical CDO, along with their fair spreads as calculated using the one-factor pricing model.

Tranches	Attachment point	Detachment point	Expected loss %	Fair spread (bps)	Implied rating
Equity	0%	3%	65.05	2557	Un-rated
Class D	3%	6%	34.27	923	Caa3
Class C	6%	9%	19.15	465	Caa1
Class B	9%	12%	10.99	255	B2
Class A	12%	22%	3.81	86	Ba2
Senior	22%	100%	0.08	1.8	Aa3
Portfolio	0.00%	100%	4.80%	100	Ba2

Table 23.2 Pricing of a hypothetical CDO

As Table 23.2 shows, the equity and more junior tranches bear the majority of the portfolio credit risk, although they represent a small portion of the capital structure of the CDO. In addition, we can use the expected losses to infer the implied rating of each tranche. The implied ratings show how the credit risk of a Ba2-rated reference portfolio can be distributed as to create buckets of lower and higher quality tranches suitable for various investors. Figure 23.22 on page 1104 shows the unconditional default probability distribution of the reference credits.

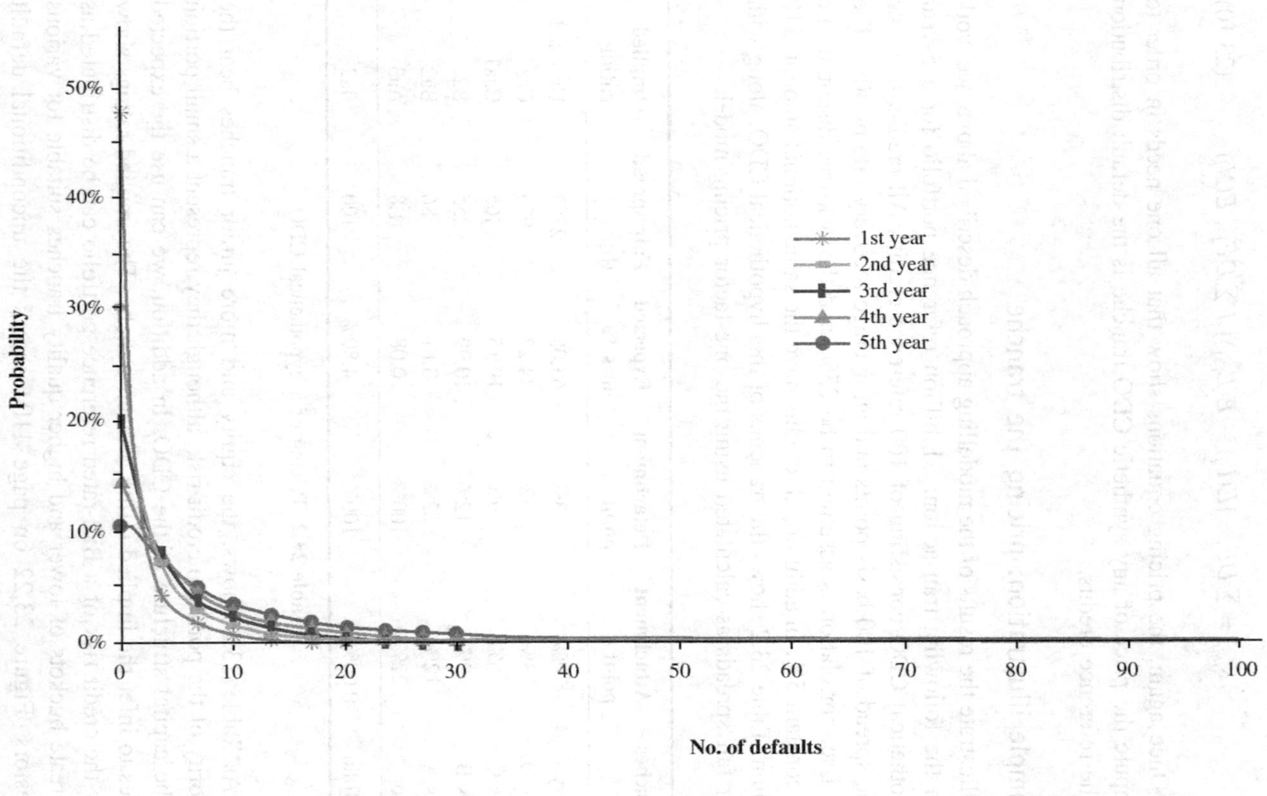

Figure 23.22 Unconditional default probability distributions of a hypothetical CDO

Figure 23.23 on page 1106 shows the total expected losses on the reference credits conditional on the realisations of the common economic factor. In this graph, the common factor takes values in the interval [–5, 5] where the negative realisations represent progressively deteriorating market conditions. For example, a value of –5 for the common factor represents a 5-sigma market event. This graph has an intuitive interpretation: lower values of the common economic factor correspond to lower economic growth and higher probabilities of economic recession. Therefore, the expected losses of the portfolio conditional on the economic factor will be higher for lower values of the common factor. The graph can therefore serve as a "scenario" or "what-if" analysis.

Similar graphs can also be produced for each tranche. To illustrate this analysis further, I take the 37th, 50th, and 63rd percentiles of the common factor realisations and calculate the portfolio expected losses at these points. The 37th percentile corresponds to a value of –1.3 for the common factor and represents a market downturn, the 50th corresponds to a value of 0 for the common factor and represents a stable market, and the 63rd percentile corresponds to a value of 1.3 for the common factor and represents an expanding market. Table 23.3 shows the results of this scenario analysis. For the sake of completion, Figure 23.24 on page 1106 and Table 23.4 on page 1107 show the conditional expected losses for the equity tranche, class A tranche, and the senior tranche.

Figure 23.24 clearly shows that the most senior tranche is not totally immune to losses, while the equity tranche bears a substantial risk of default losses even under relatively positive market conditions. In interpreting these results, the reader should bear in mind that we are starting with a Ba2-rated reference portfolio.

Scenario analysis of expected losses	**The states of the economy**		
	Downturn	Stability	Growth
Expected losses of the portfolio	11.63%	3.20%	0.54%

Table 23.3 Scenario analysis of conditional expected losses over five years

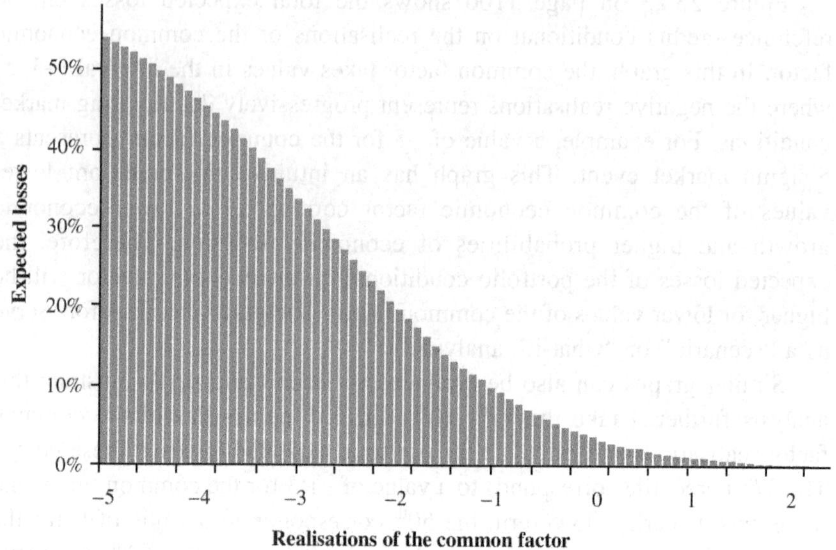

Figure 23.23 Conditional distribution of expected losses for the reference credits over 5 years

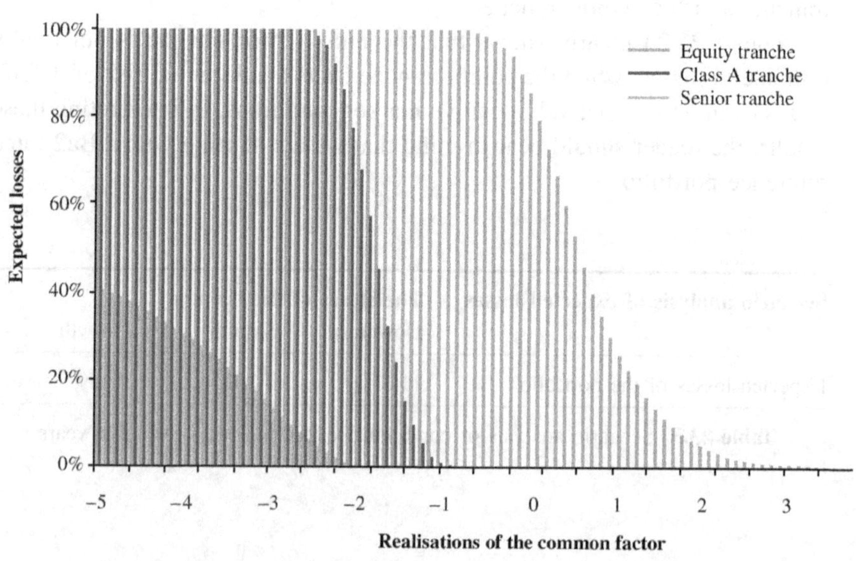

Figure 23.24 Conditional distribution expected losses for selected tranches over 5 years

Scenario analysis of expected losses	The states of the economy		
	Downturn	Stability	Growth
Expected losses of equity tranche	100%	85.6%	18.0%
Expected losses of Class A	7.74%	0.00%	0.00%
Expected losses of senior tranche	0.00%	0.00%	0.00%

Table 23.4 Scenario analysis of conditional expected losses for selected tranches over five years

As discussed in Gibson (2004), Table 23.4 illustrates how the mezzanine tranches can be thought of as leveraged bets on business cycle risk. Investors in mezzanine tranches receive spreads ranging from 923 to 86 bps according to Table 23.2; however, they have to absorb the majority of credit risk in difficult and recessionary market conditions.

Parameter sensitivities of synthetic CDO tranches

In addition to calculating the conditional and unconditional expected losses of the tranches, we can also extend the risk analysis of a synthetic CDO tranche to include:

- computing the tranche sensitivity to changes in correlation;
- computing the tranche sensitivity to broad changes in credit spreads;
- computing the change in subordination necessary to maintain the base value of a tranche as a function of the average credit quality of the reference portfolio; and
- computing the standard deviation of losses.

We consider these issues next.

Correlation Sensitivity

Figure 23.25 on page 1109 shows the correlation sensitivity of the equity and mezzanine tranches. The graph shows the fair spread of each tranche at different correlation assumptions as a multiple of the base spread 25% correlation. The equity tranche is clearly long correlation as its value increases with higher correlations: the spread falls as correlation increases. This is typical for an equity tranche because higher correlation increases the probability of fewer defaults as well as the probability of more defaults. Since equity investors are sensitive to any default it makes sense that they would prefer higher probabilities of fewer defaults – hence higher correlation. In contrast, Class A investors, the 12–22% tranche, are short correlation. For Class A investors, higher correlation reduces the value of the tranche and increases its spread.

Tranches in the middle of the capital structure share similar behaviour with either the equity tranche or the more senior tranches, but with much less sensitivity to correlation assumptions. For example, Class C, the 6–9% tranche, shows very little sensitivity to changes in correlations far beyond the initial assumption of 25% correlation. Figure 23.26 completes the picture by showing the high sensitivity of the most senior tranche to changes in correlation. More senior tranches of a CDO transaction are only susceptible to extreme market shocks that cause higher market correlations and multiple defaults to occur.

These observations are consistent with the scenario analysis shown in Table 23.4 and Figure 23.25, which illustrate the conditional impact of wide economic downturns on the value of senior tranches. In fact, although not shown in Table 23.4, at the 24th percentile value of the common default driver, Class A is expected to lose all its notional and the most senior tranche is expected to suffer a 7% loss. Economic shocks of such a magnitude are not unheard of.

The correlation sensitivity analysis illustrates two important features of CDO investing:

- Investors with different correlation assumptions will attach different values to the same tranche. This creates both model risk and an opportunity for correlation and/or model arbitrage. Correlation is a very difficult parameter to measure and estimates of correlation are susceptible to estimation errors, personal judgments and correlation breakdowns among many others.
- Mezzanine tranches are the least sensitive to changes in the correlation parameter. Therefore, these tranches are also the least sensitive to modelling errors. For example, Class C investors will notice very little change to the value of their tranche even if correlation doubles. Investors who wish to minimise parameter risk will therefore prefer the middle tranches of a CDO transaction.

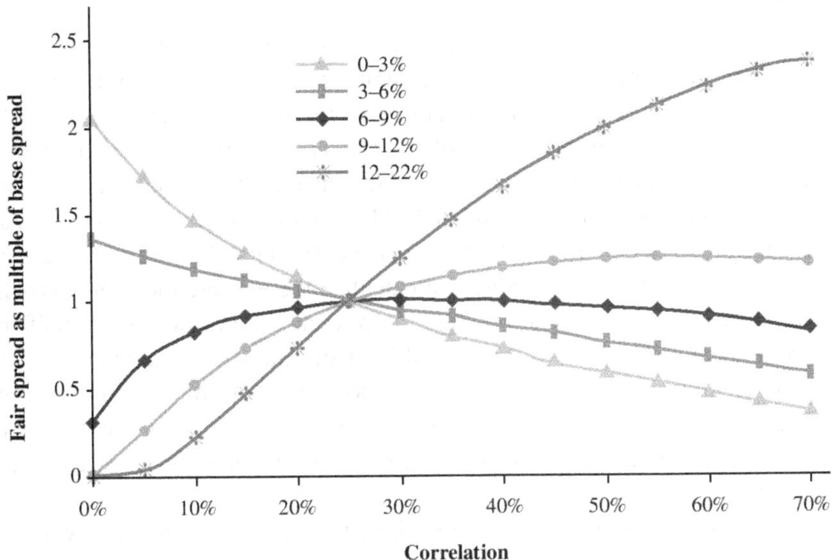

Figure 23.25 Correlation sensitivity of CDO tranches: base spread is calculated at 25% correlation

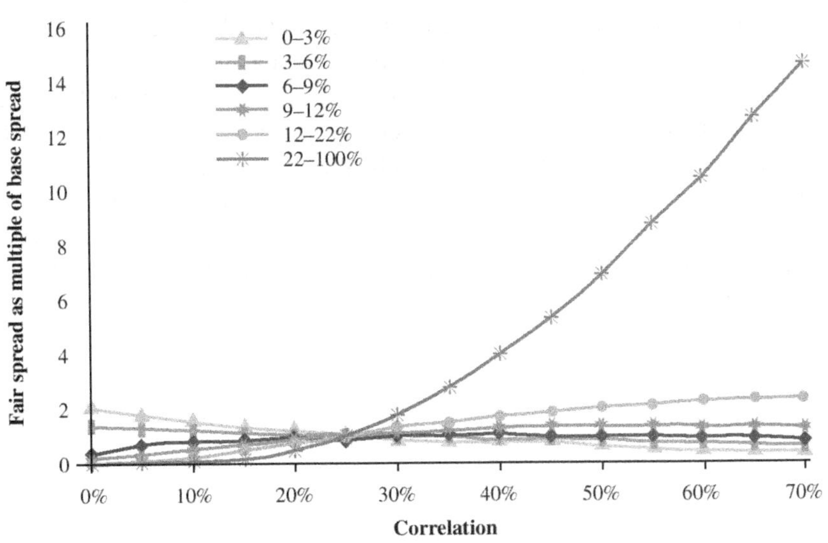

Figure 23.26 Correlation sensitivity of CDO tranches, including senior tranche: base spread is calculated at 25% correlation

The subordination effect

The expected loss of a tranche is driven not only by the credit spreads of the reference assets but also by the credit enhancement available to the tranche. To illustrate the effect of subordination, or location of a tranche within the capital structure, consider the following analysis: the original reference portfolio is divided into two equal groups. In the first group, the reference credits retain their initial spreads of 100 bps, while the second group's credit spreads are varied to 120, 130, 140, 150 and 160 bps. Starting with the base case of a 100 bps for all credits, we calculate the expected loss on Class D, the 3–6% tranche. Then we change the reference portfolio so that half the credits have a spread of 120 bps, and back out the subordination necessary to bring about a similar expected loss for Class D. We repeat the same analysis with 130, 140, 150, 160 and 180 bps to obtain the levels of subordination that will maintain the expected loss of Class D at the same base level in each case.

The graph in Figure 23.27 shows how the subordination varies with the average spread on the reference portfolio. As we progressively decrease the quality of the reference portfolio, we need higher levels of subordination to maintain the expected loss of Class D at a level similar to its base level of 34.27%. This analysis illustrates another subtle feature of CDO structuring: practically any desirable rating can be attained for a tranche provided the right amount of credit enhancement can be provided to that tranche. The lower the credit quality of the reference portfolio, the more subordination the tranche will require to achieve the same rating. Figure 23.27 also shows the effect of higher subordination on tranche leverage. Leverage is defined as the expected loss of the tranche divided by the expected loss of the reference portfolio. As Figure 23.27 shows, higher subordination leads to lower leverage. In other words, the lower the credit quality of the reference portfolio, the lower the leverage a tranche will require to achieve a particular rating. These are important results.

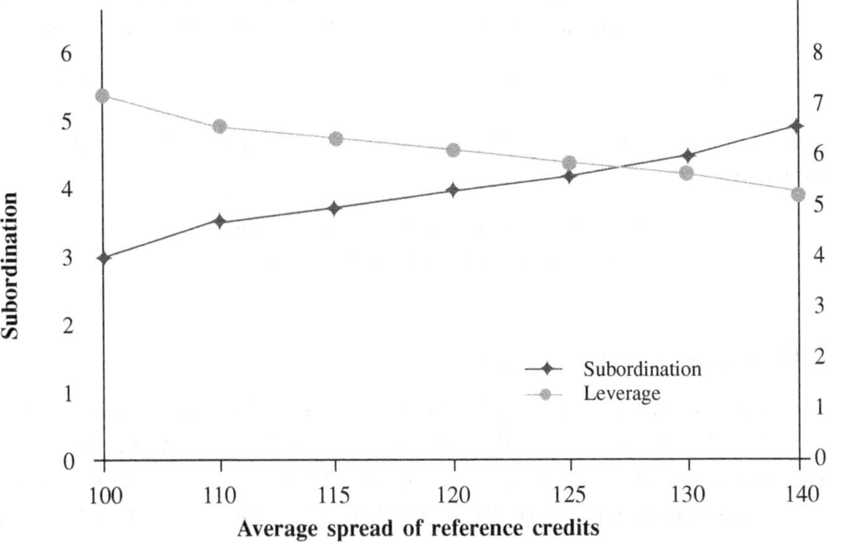

Figure 23.27 Subordination effect on expected losses and leverage

Monte Carlo simulation of losses

The Monte Carlo approach, described in Li (2000), generates the loss distribution by simulating the default times of the reference credits using the Gaussian copula. This approach is flexible in that it allows for stochastic modelling of the recovery and default parameters. The Monte Carlo approach can easily incorporate more than one economic factor, it allows for sampling losses from fat-tailed distributions, and it is capable of capturing a more complex correlation structure. However, it is time-consuming as it requires a large number of simulations in order to reduce estimation error and capture extreme losses that will only affect the most senior tranches. The recursive approach, on the other hand, is simpler and faster, but lacks the flexibility of the Monte Carlo approach.

Using the same modelling assumptions, the Monte Carlo approach should produce similar results to those obtained from the recursion method. That is, if we set the recovery rates, credit spreads and correlation parameter in the Monte Carlo model to those used for the recursion method, the results of both approaches ought to be similar. Table 23.5 on page 1112 shows Monte Carlo results using one million simulations. As evident from Table 23.5, the recursion approach provides a robust and accurate estimation of expected losses and standard deviations.

	Portfolio	0–3%	3–6%	6–9%	9–12%	12–22%	22–100%
Expected losses (%)	4.8	66.8	35	19.1	10.6	3.5	0.076
Standard deviations(%)	5.0	37.8	44	37	29.3	15.5	0.009

Table 23.5 Expected losses and standard deviations with one million Monte Carlo simulations

CDO note pricing: summary

We have demonstrated a simple, yet accessible technique to calculate the default distribution of a credit portfolio. Using this technique, we have shown how the fair spreads and risk parameters of synthetic CDO tranches can be calculated. The important highlights can be summarised as follows:

- The equity and most junior tranches of a synthetic CDO bear the majority of credit risk of the reference portfolio;
- The most senior tranche is not completely immune to credit losses;
- The value of the equity and most junior tranches increases as correlation across the credits rises. On the other hand, the value of the senior tranches decreases with higher correlation;
- The mezzanine tranche has the least sensitivity to the correlation parameter and to correlation model risk;
- The senior tranches are more sensitive to broad changes in credit spreads;
- There is a trade-off between the quality of the reference credits and the subordination required to attain a particular rating for a tranche. The lower the quality of the reference credits, the higher the required subordination.

Both ALM originators and investors will need to be aware of the main issues associated with CDO structuring and pricing, most especially with regard to tranche correlation sensitivity.

Case studies

Let us now consider a number of specific deals to illustrate the progressive development of synthetic CDOs and their use in bank ALM since inception. These are:

- BISTRO: the first static synthetic balance sheet CDO;
- ALCO1: a balance sheet deal arranged for credit risk management and regulatory capital purposes;
- Jazz I CDO: a managed synthetic "hybrid" CDO;
- Dynaso 2002-1 Limited: a dynamic synthetic CSO;
- Leonardo Synthetic Plc: a synthetic aviation securities CDO.

With the exception of Jazz CDO, all these deals were originated by banks as part of their credit risk management process. As such, they can be seen to be an important tool in bank ALM. The Jazz CDO was a managed synthetic deal.

BISTRO: The first synthetic securitisation

Generally viewed as the first synthetic securitisation, BISTRO was a JPMorgan vehicle brought to the market in December 1997. The transaction was designed to remove the credit risk on a portfolio of corporate credits held on JPMorgan's books, with no funding or balance sheet impact. The overall portfolio was $9.7 billion, with $700 million of notes issued, in two tranches, by the BISTRO SPV. The proceeds of the note issue were invested in US Treasury securities, which in turn were used as collateral for the CDS entered into between JPMorgan and the vehicle. This was a five-year swap written on the whole portfolio, with JPMorgan as the protection buyer. BISTRO, the protection seller, paid for the coupons on the issued notes from funds received from the collateral pool and the premiums on the CDS. Payments on occurrence of credit events were paid out from the collateral pool.

Under this structure, JPMorgan transferred the credit risk on $700 million of its portfolio to investors, and retained the risk on a first-loss piece and the residual piece. The first-loss piece was not a note issue, but a $32 million reserve cash account held for the five-year life of the deal. First losses were funded out of this cash reserve, which was held by JPMorgan. This is shown in Figure 23.28 on page 1114.

The asset pool is static for the life of the deal. The attraction of the deal for investors included a higher return on the notes compared to bonds of the same credit rating and a bullet-maturity structure, compared to the amortising arrangement of other ABS asset classes.

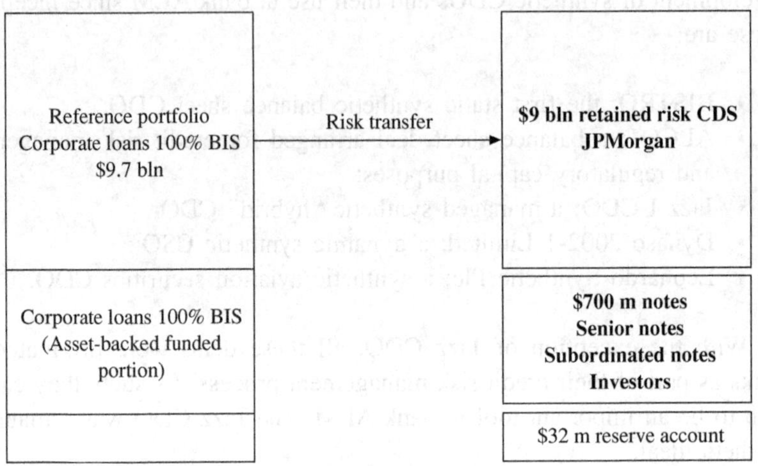

Figure 23.28 BISTRO deal structure
Source: JPMorgan. Used with permission.

The BISTRO deal featured:

- the credit risk exposure of a pool of assets being transferred without moving the assets themselves from the balance sheet;
- a resultant reduction of the credit exposure for the originator;
- no funding element for the originator: in other words, a securitisation deal that separated the liquidity feature from the risk transfer;
- the application of structured finance rating technology;
- unfunded liabilities which were nevertheless tranched, as in a traditional cash-flow securitisation, so that these liabilities could be rated.

Investors in the deal, who were effectively taking on the credit risk of the assets on the originator's balance sheet, were attracted to the deal because:

- the deal provided exposure to particular credits and a credit risk/return profile, but without a requirement for this exposure to be funded;

- the deal economics were aimed at a precise transfer of specifically packaged segments of risk, enabling the investor to realise greater value;
- the equity holder gained from a leveraged exposure, which meant the cost of this exposure was lowered.

The originating bank retained a comparative advantage on the funding, while the investor gained the required exposure to the credit risk. The investor, in effect, provided the comparative advantage because it is not subject to regulatory capital requirements. In summary, the deal was a "win–win" transaction for both the bank and the investor. The investor – here typically a fund manager or insurance company – can price the risk very efficiently because it is an expert in the market. It also benefits from the cheap(er) funding that the bank is able to source.

ALCO 1 Limited

The ALCO 1 CDO is described as the first Asian market-rated synthetic balance sheet CDO from a non-Japanese bank.[18] It is a S$2.8 billion structure sponsored and managed by the Development Bank of Singapore (DBS). The structure diagram is shown in Figure 23.29 on page 1116.

The structure allowed DBS to transfer the credit risk on a S$2.8 billion reference portfolio of mainly Singapore corporate loans to an SPV, ALCO 1, using CDSs. As a result, DBS was able to reduce the risk capital it had to hold on the reference loans, without physically moving the assets from its balance sheet. The structure is a S$2.45 billion super-senior tranche – unfunded CDS – with a S$224 million notes issue and S$126 million first-loss piece retained by DBS. The notes are issued in six classes, collateralised by Singapore government T-bills and a reserve bank account, the "GIC" account. There is also a currency and interest-rate swap structure in place for risk hedging, and a put option that covers the purchase of assets by the arranger if the deal terminates before expected maturity date. The issuer enters into CDSs with a specified list of counterparties. The default swap pool is static, but there is a substitution facility for up to 10% of the portfolio. This means that under certain specified conditions, up to 10% of the reference loan portfolio may be replaced by loans from outside the vehicle. Other than this, though, the reference portfolio is static. The liability structure is shown in Table 23.6 on page 1116.

[18] Source: Moody's.

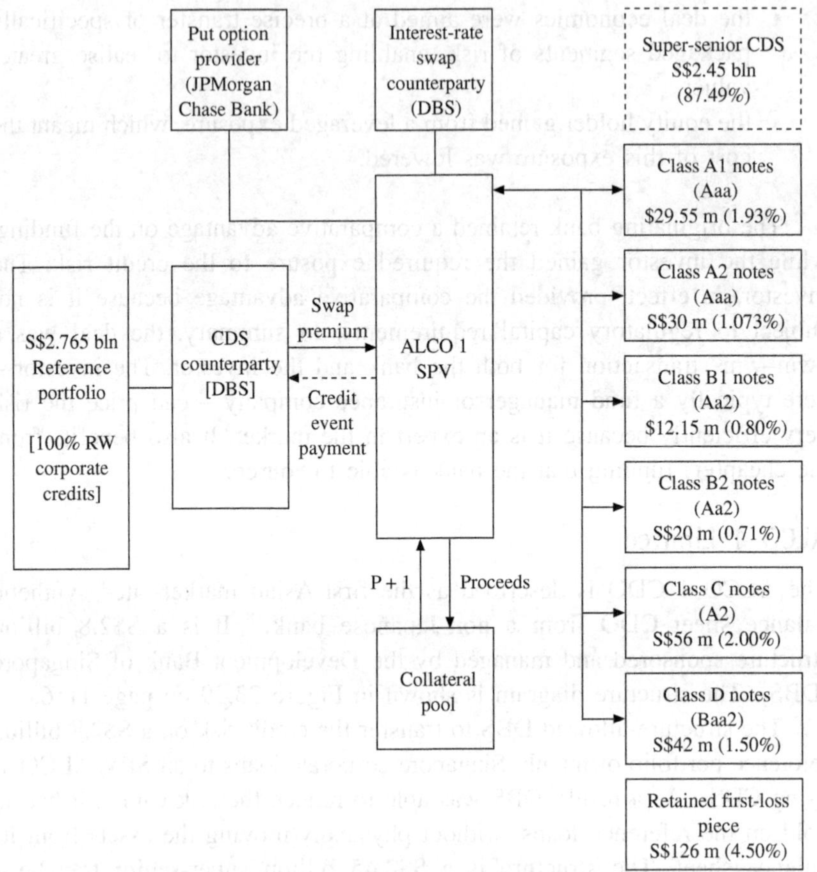

Figure 23.29 ALCO 1 deal structure
Source: Moody's. Used with permission.

Class	Amount	Per cent	Rating	Interest rate
Super-senior swap	S$2.450 m	87.49%	NR	14 bps
Class A1	US$29.55 m	1.93%	AAA	3 m USD Libor + 50 bps
Class A2	S$30 m	1.07%	Aaa	3 m SOR + 45 bps
Class B1	US$12.15 m	0.80%	Aa2	3 m USD Libor + 85 bps
Class B2	S$20 m	0.71%	Aa2	3 m SOR + 80 bps
Class C	S$56 m	2.00%	A2	5.20%
Class D	S$42 m	1.50%	Baa2	6.70%

Table 23.6 ALCO 1 note tranching
Source: Moody's. Used with permission.

Name:	ALCO 1 Limited
Originator:	Development Bank of Singapore Ltd
Arrangers:	JPMorgan Chase Bank
	DBS Ltd
Trustee:	Bank of New York
Closing date:	15 December 2001
Maturity:	March 2009
Portfolio:	S$2.8 billion of credit default swaps
Reference assets:	199 reference obligations (136 obligors)
Portfolio administrator:	JPMorgan Chase Bank Institutional Trust Services

As the first rated synthetic balance sheet deal in Asia, ALCO 1-type structures have subsequently been adopted by other commercial banks in the region. The principal innovation of the vehicle is the method by which the reference credits are selected. The choice of reference credits on which swaps are written must, as expected with a CDO, follow a number of criteria set by the ratings agency, including diversity score, rating factor, weighted average spread, geographical and industry concentration, among others.

Structure and mechanics

The issuer enters into a portfolio CDS with DBS as the CDS counterparty to provide credit protection against losses in the reference portfolio. The CDSs are cash-settled. In return for protection premium payments, after aggregate losses exceeding the S$126 million "threshold" amount, the issuer is obliged to make protection payments to DBS. The maximum obligation is the S$224 million note proceeds value. As per market convention with securitised notes, further losses above the threshold amount are allocated to overlying notes in their reverse order of seniority. The note proceeds are invested in a collateral pool comprised initially of Singapore T-bills.

During the term of the transaction, DBS, as the CDS counterparty, is permitted to remove any eliminated reference obligations that are fully paid, terminated early or otherwise no longer eligible. In addition, DBS has the option to remove up to 10% of the initial aggregate amount of the reference portfolio, and substitute new or existing reference names.

For this structure, credit events are defined specifically as:

- failure to pay,
- bankruptcy.

Note how this differs from European market CDOs where the list of defined credit events is invariably longer, frequently including restructuring and credit rating downgrades.

The reference portfolio is an Asian corporate portfolio, but with a small percentage of loans originated in Australia. The portfolio is concentrated in Singapore (80%). The weighted average credit quality is Baa3/Ba1, with an average life of three years. The Moody's diversity score is low (20), reflecting the concentration of loans in Singapore. There is a high industrial concentration. The total portfolio at inception was 199 reference obligations among 136 reference entities (obligors). By structuring the deal in this way, DBS obtains capital relief on the funded portion of the assets, but at a lower cost and with less administrative burden than a traditional cash-flow securitisation, and without having to undertake a true sale of the assets.

Jazz CDO I BV

Jazz CDO I BV is an innovative CDO structure and one of the first *hybrid* CDOs introduced in the European market. A hybrid CDO combines elements of a cash-flow arbitrage CDO and a managed synthetic CDO. Therefore, the underlying assets are investment-grade bonds and loans, and synthetic assets such as CDSs and TRSs. The Jazz vehicle comprises a total of €1.5 billion of referenced assets, of which €210 million is made up of a note issue. Its hybrid arrangement enables the portfolio manager to take a view on corporate and bank credits in both cash and synthetic markets. Therefore a structure like Jazz bestows the greatest flexibility for credit trading on CDO originators. The vehicle is illustrated in Figure 23.30 on page 1120.

The main innovation of the structure is a design that incorporates both funded and unfunded assets, as well as funded and unfunded liabilities. This arrangement means that the portfolio manager is free to trade both cash and derivative instruments, thereby exploiting its experience and knowledge across the markets. At a time of increasing defaults in CDOs, during 2001 and 2002, static pool deals began to be viewed unfavorably by certain investors, because of the inability to offload deteriorating or defaulted assets. Jazz CDO I is an actively managed deal, and its attraction reflects to a great extent the perception with which the portfolio manager is viewed by investors. So the role of the portfolio manager is critical to the ratings analysis of the deal. This covered:

- experience in managing cash and synthetic assets;
- its perceived strength in credit research;

- previous experience in managing CDO vehicles;
- infrastructure arrangements, such as settlement and processing capability.

These factors, together with the traditional analysis used for static pool cash CDOs, were used by the ratings agencies when assessing the transaction.

Name:	Jazz CDO I B.V.
Manager:	Axa Investment Managers SA
Arranger:	Deutsche Bank AG
Closing date:	8 March 2002
Maturity:	February 2011
Portfolio:	€1.488 billion
Reference assets:	Investment-grade synthetic and cash securities
Portfolio administrator:	JPMorgan Chase Bank

Structure

The assets in Jazz CDO I may be comprised of CDSs, TRSs, bonds and loans, at the manager's discretion. The asset mix is set up by:

- purchase of cash assets, funded by the proceeds of the note issue and the liquidity facility;
- selling protection via CDSs;
- buying protection via CDSs;
- entering into TRSs, whereby the total return of the reference assets is received by the vehicle in return for a payment of Libor plus spread (on the notional amount). This is funded via the liquidity facility.

The liability side of the structure is a combination of:

- the super-senior CDS;
- issued notes and equity piece (see Figure 23.30).

However, the asset and liability mix can be varied by the portfolio manager at its discretion, and can be expected to change over time. In theory the asset pool can comprise 100% cash bonds or 100% CDSs; in practice, we should expect to see a mixture as shown in Figure 23.30.

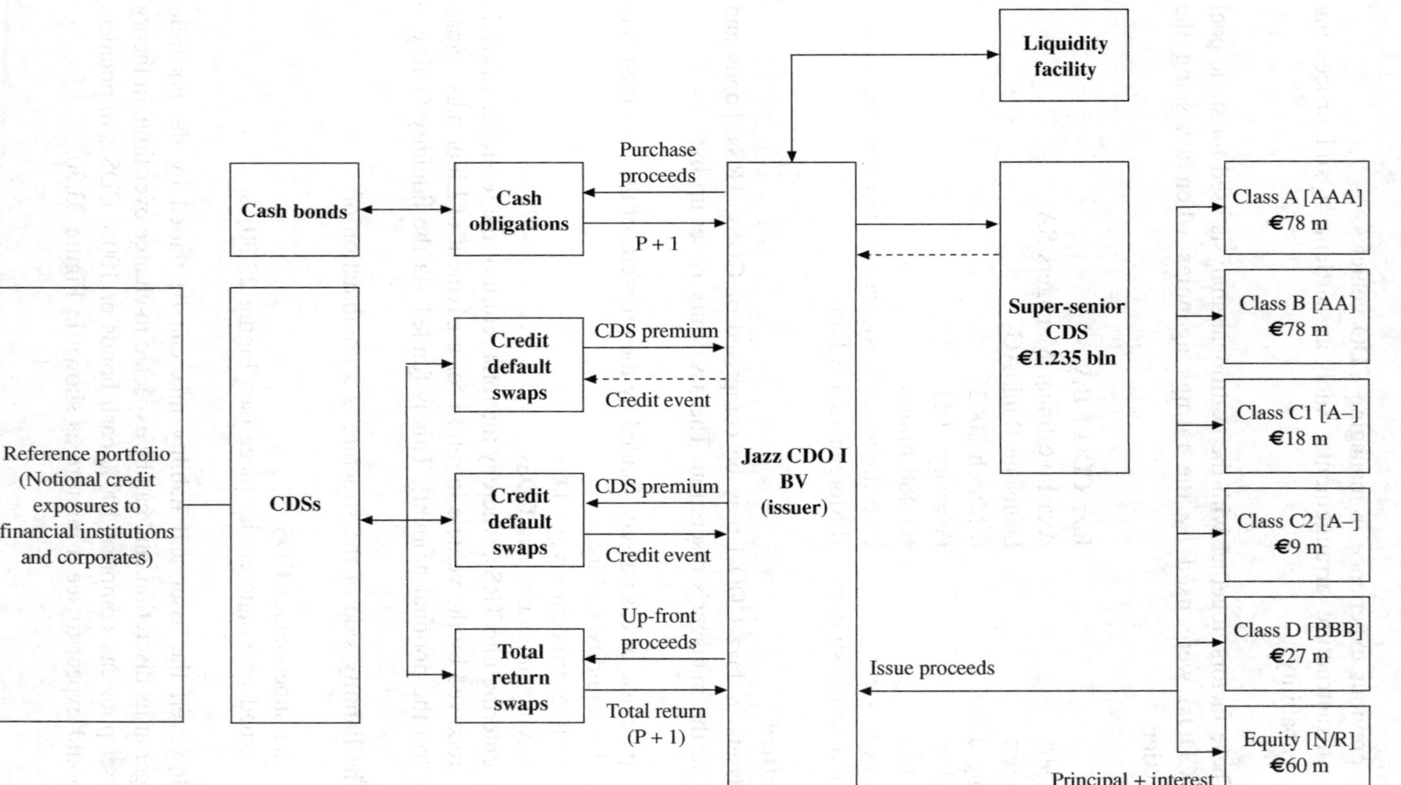

Figure 23.30 Jazz CDO I BV structure diagram
Source: S&P. Used with permission.

The total return swap and the Jazz I CDO

The TRS used as part of the Jazz I CDO structure is a funded TRS. The generic TRS is an unfunded credit derivative. The TRS arrangement is shown in Figure 23.31.

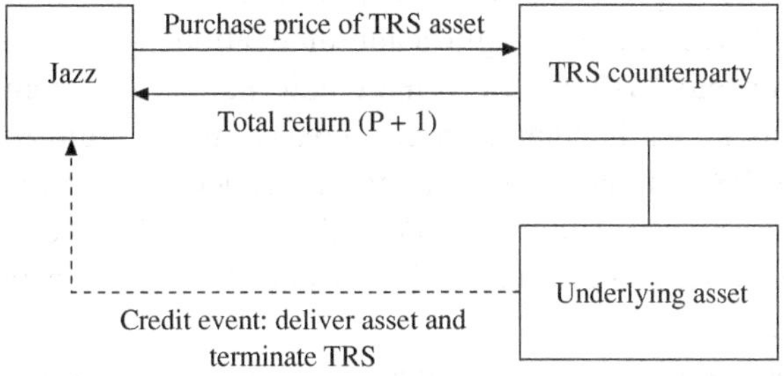

Figure 23.31 TRS as used in Jazz I CDO BV

Liquidity facility

A liquidity facility of €1.7 billion is an integral part of the structure. It is used as a reserve to cover losses arising from CDS trading, occurrence of credit events, and to fund any purchases when the mix of cash versus synthetic assets is altered by the manager. This includes the purchase of bonds and the funding of TRSs. The facility is similar to a revolving credit facility and is provided by the arrangers of the transaction.

If the manager draws on the liquidity facility, this is viewed as a funded liability, similar to an issue of notes, and is in fact senior in the priority of payments to the overlying notes and the super-senior CDS.

Trading arrangements

The Jazz CDO structure enables the portfolio manager to administer credit risk across cash and synthetic markets. The cash market instruments that may be traded include investment-grade corporate bonds, structured finance securities such as ABS or MBS, and corporate loans. The portfolio manager may buy and sell both types of assets; that is, it may short credit in accordance with its view. In other words, the restriction that exists with other managed synthetic deals is removed in Jazz CDO. Therefore, the portfolio manager can buy protection in the credit derivative market as it wishes, and not only to offset an existing long credit position (sold protection). The only rules that must be followed when buying protection are that:

- the counterparty risk is of an acceptable level;
- there are sufficient funds in the vehicle to pay the credit derivative premiums.

The manager may trade where existing assets go into default, or where assets have either improved or worsened in credit outlook (to take or cut a trading profit/loss). Another significant innovation is the ability of the vehicle to enter into *basis trades* in the credit market. An example of such a trade is to buy a cash bond and simultaneously purchase protection on that bond in the CDS market. Similar to trades undertaken in the exchange-traded government bond futures market, this is an arbitrage-type strategy where the trader seeks to exploit price mismatches between the cash and synthetic markets.

The various combinations of trades that may be entered into are treated in different ways for counterparty risk and regulatory capital. For an offsetting position in a single name, the options are to use:

- only CDSs to cancel out an exposure, when both CDSs are traded with the same counterparty: this is netted out for risk purposes;
- CDSs only, but with different counterparties: there will be a set-aside for counterparty risk requirement exposure;
- a CDS and cash bond: regarded as a AAA-rated asset for capital purposes.

The Offering Circular for the deal lists a number of trading guidelines that must be followed by the manager. These include a limit of 20% by volume annual turnover level.

Dynaso 2002-1 Limited

The Dynaso CSO is a managed synthetic CDO that presents features of interest because of the way the excess spread in the vehicle impacts the way the note tranches are rated. It also has other distinguishing structural features. The originator of the deal is DZ Bank in Germany. The terms of the deal are:

Issuer:	Dynaso 2002-1 Limited, Jersey SPV
Effective date:	6 November 2002
Schedule maturity:	6 November 2007
Arranger:	DZ Bank
Co-arranger:	The Bank of Nova Scotia, London branch
Trustee:	JPMorgan Chase Bank
Reference portfolio:	Notional credit exposure on 100 corporate credits
Amount:	€1 billion
Minimum diversity score:	55
Weighted average rating:	A3.

The transaction structure is shown in Figure 23.32 and the note tranching in Table 23.7 both on page 1124.

This deal was originated to provide investors with exposure to corporate credits. Investors were among DZ Bank's network of cooperative banks in Germany. The key feature of interest in this structure concerns the Class E note (see Table 23.7). Any excess spread that remains in the vehicle after the senior liabilities have been paid is paid into an excess spread account. The Class E note differs from the Class A, B and C notes in that on maturity, the balance of the excess spread account may be used to restore the Class E note to par value. The remaining residual balance is then available to pay Class D noteholders. This structure has resulted in the Class E note being rated Aaa by Moody's, which is a unique arrangement. The E note also has a fixed coupon, a rare feature in European deals.

The deal structure is based around the super-senior CDS, which forms 85% of the liabilities. The remaining 15% is split into the five classes of notes. The note proceeds are held in a cash deposit account. In the event of any defaults in the reference portfolio, the notes are written off in order of priority. The portfolio CDS does not amortise. The reference pool is managed dynamically by DZ Bank as portfolio advisor, although as the substitution is limited to 10% of the pool in any one year, this is not a fully "managed" synthetic CDO.

Credit events are defined as (i) bankruptcy (ii) failure to pay and (iii) restructuring, with "modified restructuring" applying to US reference credits and "old restructuring" to any other reference credits.

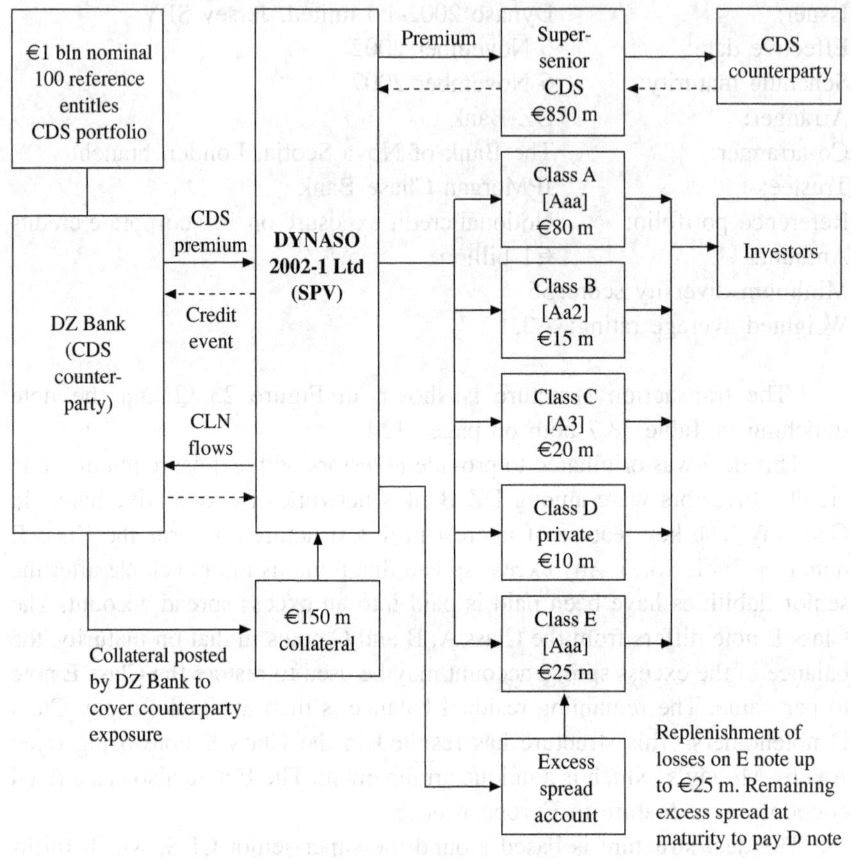

Figure 23.32 Dynaso 2002–1 CSO structure diagram
Source: Moody's. Used with permission.

Class	Nominal size €m	Per cent	Rating	Coupon
Senior CDS	850	85.00%	NR	n/a
Class A	80	8.00%	Aaa	3-m Euribor + 100 bps
Class B	15	1.50%	Aa2	3-m Euribor + 125 bps
Class C	20	2.00%	A3	3-m Euribor + 250 bps
Class D	10	1.00%	Private	n/a
Class E	25	2.50%	Aaa	5.00%

Table 23.7 Dynaso 2002–1 CSO note tranching
Source: Moody's. Used with permission.

Leonardo Synthetic CDO

The Italian capital market witnessed a number of innovative transactions early in the development of synthetic structured products. The Leonardo Synthetic plc deal is one such transaction. Closing in June 2001, it was an early example of a balance sheet synthetic CDO, as well as the first synthetic securitisation of aircraft financing and aviation industry loans and letters of credit. The originator, IntesaBCI, sought to transfer the credit risk on a revolving pool of loans made to clients in connection with aircraft purchases and leases. This transfer was effected partly by a CDS between the originator and a swap counterparty (Merrill Lynch), and partly by a combination of funded and unfunded credit derivatives issued by the SPV for the transaction.

The terms of the deal are summarised below:

Originator (and Servicer):	IntesaBCI
Issuer:	Leonardo Synthetic plc
Structure:	CDSs and CLNs
Trustee:	Deutsche Bankers Trust
Reference portfolio:	Aviation industry loans and letters of credit
Notional value:	USD1 billion
Secured liability proportion:	97%
Unsecured liability proportion:	3%
Collateral (Classes "A" and "B"):	Italian government bonds
Collateral (Class "C"):	Cash deposit at account bank.

The transaction structure is shown in Figure 23.33 on page 1126, while the note tranching is shown in Table 23.8 on page 1126.

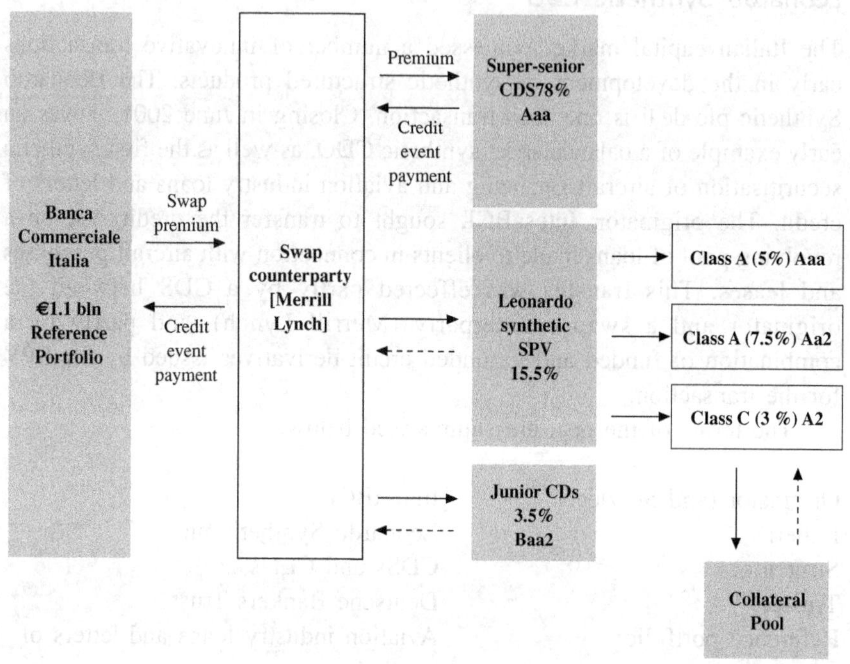

Figure 23.33 Leonardo synthetic CDO

Class	Amount USD m	Per cent	Issue price	Rating	Coupon Euribor 3-month
Senior swap	[780]	78	n/a	Aaa	Premium 12 bps
A	55	5.0	100	Aaa	[26]
B	82.5	7.5	100	Aa2	[35]
C	33	3.0	100	A2	[67]
Junior CDS	[35]	3.5	n/a	Baa2	Premium 124 bps
[First loss]	33	3.0	100	NR	Excess

Table 23.8 Leonardo synthetic CDO tranche summary
Source: Moody's. *Yields source*: Bloomberg.

The proceeds of the CLN issue were invested in Italian government bonds, which act as collateral to support the Class “A” and “B” notes. The junior Class “C” notes are collateralised by a bank account deposit.

A feature of the structure is that a credit event is described as being related specifically to the reference obligations of the named corporates. Investors therefore acquire an exposure only to the corporate obligors themselves, mainly airlines, and not to the issuer SPV. They do not have an exposure to the issuer itself. Credit events are defined as bankruptcy of a reference entity, and failure to pay, only. There is a five-year revolving period during which loans can be replaced, as they drop out of the reference portfolio for redemption, prepayment and other reasons. Substitute loans must meet pre-specified criteria. The first 3% of losses in the portfolio are covered by the equity holder, losses beyond this threshold level are allocated first to the junior CDS, and then to the Class “C” CLN and so on.

The transaction was designed to remove the credit risk of an initial pool of 127 reference loans and letters of credit, made to 32 borrowers by IntesaBCI. It also resulted in the lowering of the bank’s regulatory capital requirement.

Appendices

APPENDIX 23.1 Hypothetical deal term sheet

Scarab CSO Limited

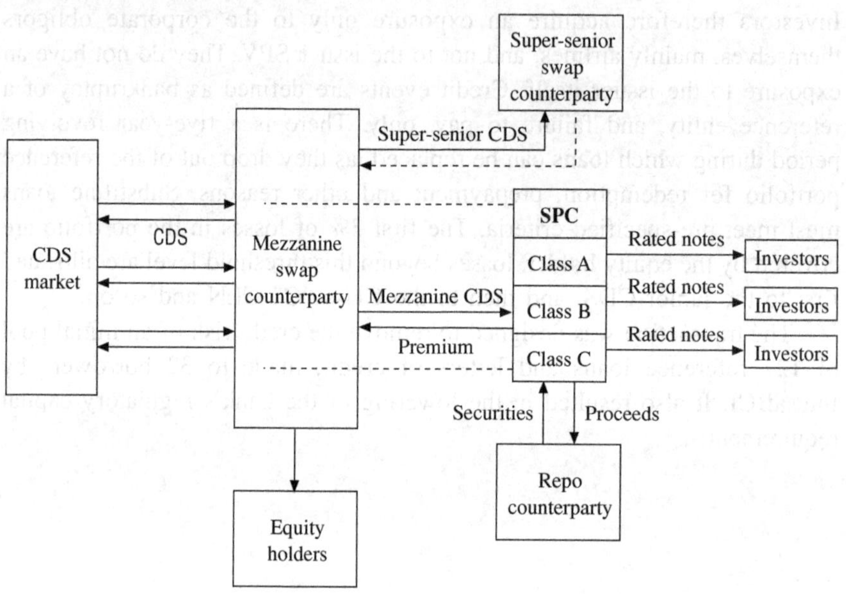

Transaction indicative terms and conditions

The Issuer [Scarab CSO Ltd] is a special purpose, bankruptcy remote, company (SPV). The company will be registered in [Jersey/Ireland/Luxembourg]. It is set up in order to acquiring securities through a **Repurchase Agreement**, selling credit protection through a **Mezzanine CDS Agreement,** refinancing through the issuance of **CDOs** ("the Notes"), and charging its assets as security for its obligations under the Mezzanine CDS Agreement and the Notes

The Issuer is required to produce annual audited accounts and annual management reports.

The SPV shares will be held on trust (or equivalent in Netherlands/Luxembourg) under a Charitable Trust Agreement

Trustee [Trust Bank of London plc]

Auditors [ ]

SPV Administrator [ ]

The Mezzanine Credit The Issuer will enter into a Mezzanine Credit Swap Agreement with the Mezzanine Swap Counterparty under which the Issuer agrees to provide up to [ ] of credit protection in respect of the Portfolio, provided aggregated losses on such Portfolio exceed [ ]

Premium**:** on each Interest Payment Date, the Mezzanine Swap Counterparty will pay to the Issuer a premium defined as follow:

[A*Ma + B*Mb + C*Mc + Spd*(A + B + C)]*(Nd/360) + OpEx

where

A: average daily principal amount outstanding on Class A Notes

B: average daily principal amount outstanding on Class B Notes

C: average daily principal amount outstanding on Class C Notes

Ma: [ ]% per annum (Class A Notes spread over Euribor)

Mb: [ ]% per annum (Class B Notes spread over Euribor)

Mc: [ ]% per annum (Class C Notes spread over Euribor)

Spd: [ ]%

Nd: Actual number of days of the Interest Period

OpEx: the Operating Expenses payable by the Issuer on the Interest Payment Date

Credit events: means the occurrence of any of the following, each of which has the meaning given to it by the 2003 ISDA Credit Derivatives Definitions:

- Failure to pay
- Modified restructuring
- Obligation acceleration
- Bankruptcy
- Repudiation/Moratorium

The Mezzanine Swap Counterpart

XYZ Bank plc

The Repurchase

On the Issue Date, the Issuer will enter into the Repurchase Agreement with the Repo Counterpart pursuant to which, both parties agree to enter into a series of repurchase transactions in respect of Collateral Securities. Each transaction will begin on an Interest Payment Date (Issue Date for the first transaction) and end on the following Interest Payment Date. The Issuer receives the Collateral Securities against the payment of the **Purchase Price** by the Repo Counterpart in the beginning and receives the **Repurchase Price** against delivery of the Collateral Securities at the end of the repurchase transaction.

Collateral Securities to be chosen by the Repo Counterpart, they must be Government Securities or ABS Securities as described thereafter:

Government Securities: bonds issued by a government of a country of European Union with a maturity below 10 years and a rating of at least AA1 by S&P's/Aa1 by Moody's and denominated in Euro.

ABS Securities: floating rate asset-backed securities and fixed-rate covered bonds (*Pfandbriefe*) with an expected maturity below 10 years, rated AAA S&P's/Aaa Moody's and denominated in Euro (or any former currency of the member states of the European Union that have adopted the Euro).

Price differential: the difference between the Repurchase Price and the Purchase Price on each Repurchase transaction will be the following: (3M Euribor–Spd)*(Nd/360)*N

where
Spd: [ ]% per annum
Nd: the actual number of days of the Repo Transaction
N: the average principal outstanding amount of the Notes during that Transaction

Haircut and Margin call
Haircut: Agreed Collateralisation Level: [to be checked with the rating agencies]
Margin call: bilateral
Frequency: daily
Threshold Amount: €100,000
Delivery: within 3 Business Days

Credit Settlement Amounts
Notice: within 6 Business Days
Collateral Securities concerned: the highest bid price

Substitution
Option for the Repo Counterpart to make any substitution in the composition of the Collateral

	Securities within the agreed constraints without any prior consent from the Issuer. Downgrade • In case of downgrade of any ABS Securities, the Repo Counterpart will have to replace the affected ABS Securities by eligible Collateral Securities (within 10 Business Days) • If the short-term senior unsecured debt of the Repo Counterpart ceased to be rated at least A211/P21, the Repo Counterpart should switch all ABS Securities for Government Securities • If the short-term senior unsecured debt of the Repo Counterpart ceased to be rated at least A211/P21, the Repo Counterpart should within 10 Business Days (a) procure credit support under conditions satisfactory to Rating Agencies in order to avoid the current rating of the Notes, or (b) procure that a third party having such rating substitutes itself to the Repo Counterpart in the Repurchase Agreement
The Repo Counterparty	XYZ Bank plc
The Security Trustee	[Trust Bank of London plc]
The Arranger	XYZ Bank plc
The Lead Manager	XYZ Bank plc
The Principal Paying Agent	[ ]
The Agent Bank and Listing Agent	[ ]

The Class A Notes

The Class B Notes	
The Class C Notes	
Use of Proceeds	The Issuer will use the net proceeds of the Notes to purchase the Collateral Securities under the Repurchase Agreement.
Status of the Notes	
Interest on the Notes	
Mandatory Redemption	In case of termination of the Repurchase Agreement or the Mezzanine CDS Agreement for any reason.
Optional Redemption	For tax reasons.
Final Redemption	The Notes will be redeemed on the **Scheduled Maturity Date**, unless a Credit Event Notice is served to the Issuer less than [ ] Business Days before the Scheduled Maturity Date, in which case the redemption may be postponed until at most [ ] Business Days after the Schedule Maturity Date, which is expected to be [ ] (the "**Final Maturity Date**").
Cash Management	On each Interest Payment Date, the Cash Manager will use the Price Differential received under the Repurchase Agreement and the Premium received under the Mezzanine CDS to pay in order • The Operating Expenses due to the Trustee • The Operating Expenses due to the other creditors • The termination payment under the Mezzanine Swap Agreement (provided that credit event has been verified …)

- Any interest due on Class A Notes
- Any interest due on Class B Notes
- Any interest due on Class C Notes

Security for the Notes The notes will be secured by first ranking fixed security interest over the Issuer rights against its counterparts and the balance standing to the credit of the Issuer's Account. The Issuer will also pledge in favor of the Trustee its securities and bank account.

In case of enforcement of the security, the Trustee will use the proceeds to make payment in the following order of priority:

1. The Repurchase Price due to the Repo Counterpart
2. Any Operating Expense due to the Trustee
3. Operating Expenses due to the Operating Creditors
4. The aggregate amounts in respect of the Cash Settlement Amounts due to the Mezzanine Swap Counterpart
5. Accrued and unpaid interest to Class A Notes
6. Unpaid principal due to Class A Notes
7. Accrued and unpaid interest to Class B Notes
8. Unpaid principal due to Class B Notes
9. Accrued and unpaid interest to Class C Notes
10. Unpaid principal due to Class C Notes
11. Termination payment to the Mezzanine Swap Counterpart

Limited Recourse The Notes will be limited recourse obligations of the Issuer. If the net proceeds of the Security after it has been enforced or liquidated are not sufficient to cover all payments due under the Notes, no other assets of the Issuer will be

	available to pay any shortfall, and all the liabilities of the Issuer will be extinguished.
Rating	AAA/Aaa for class A Notes A/A1 for Class B Notes BBB/Baa1 for Class C Notes
Listing	[Luxembourg Stock Exchange]

Further documentation for review:

The Offering Circular
The Deed of Charge
The Articles of Incorporation
The List of Relevant Agreements
The Investor Reports
The Subscription Agreement
The Agency Agreement
The Trust Deed
The Repurchase Agreement
The Mezzanine CDS Agreement
The Pledge Agreement
The Cash Management Agreement
The Domiciliation Agreement
The Bank Agreement

APPENDIX 23.2 The Moody's Diversity Score

The diversity score for a CDO is Moody's measure for the number of uncorrelated assets in a portfolio. A CDO portfolio must meet a minimum diversity score to obtain its required credit rating. The strict definition of diversity score is the number of independent assets with identical nominal amounts which as a portfolio have the same total notional amount, expected loss and variance as the portfolio itself. Moody's divides assets in accordance with their industry sector and assigns a default correlation among assets in each industry.

The diversity score D is given by:

$$D=\frac{\left\{\sum_{j=1}^{T}(N_j * P_j)\right\} * \left\{\sum_{j=1}^{T}(N_j\,(1 - P_j)\right\}}{\sum_{j=1}^{T}\left[\left(\sum_{k=1}^{T}(r_{jk} * N_k * \sqrt{(p_k * (1 - P_j))}\right) * N_j * \sqrt{(p_j * (1 - P_j))}\right]}$$

where

N_j is the outstanding principal balance of collateral debt security j
N_k is the outstanding principal balance of collateral debt security k
p_j is the default probability of security j
p_k is the default probability of security k
T is the total number of collateral debt securities in the portfolio
r_{jk} is the correlation of security j with security k.

The default correlations are assigned by Moody's to each industry sector that it classifies. The default probability is the cumulative probability that a collateral debt security defaults during its life. It is given by:

$$P_j = \frac{E}{(1 - R)}$$

where

E is the expected loss
R is the Moody's recovery rate.

The expected loss is assigned to a security based as shown on a standard table supplied by Moody's, and is based on its credit rating and term to maturity. The recovery rate is assigned to each class of security by Moody's, in accordance with its credit rating.

APPENDIX 23.3 The roles of the Trustee and portfolio administrator on a CSO.

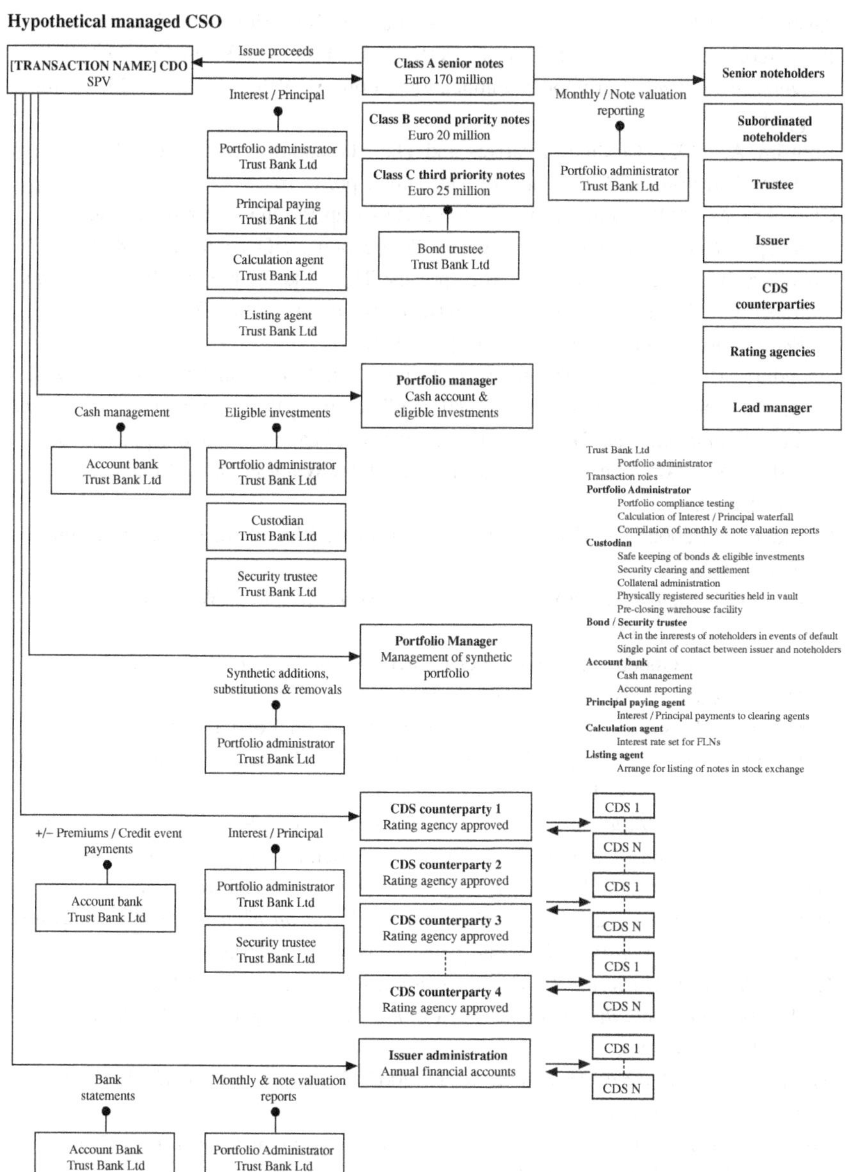

References and bibligraphy

Andersen, L., Sidenius, J. and Basu, S. 2003. "*All Your Hedges in One Basket*", *Risk*, November, pp. 67-72

Anson M. 1999, *Credit Derivatives*, FJF Associates, New Hope, PA, Chapter 3.

Boggiano, K., Waterson, and Stein, C. 2002, "Four Forms of Synthetic CDOs", *Derivatives Week*, Euromoney Publications, London, Volume XI, No. 23, 10 June, pp. 8–9.

Bomfim, A. 2002, "Credit Derivatives and Their Potential to Synthesize Riskless Assets", *Journal of Fixed Income*, December, pp. 6–16.

Choudhry, M. 2001, "Some Issues in the Asset-swap Pricing of Credit Default Swaps", *Derivatives Week*, Euromoney Publications, 2 December, pp. 8–9.

Choudhry, M. 2002a, "Trading Credit Spreads: The Case for a Specialised Exchange-traded Credit Futures Contract", *Journal of Derivatives Use, Trading and Regulation*, Volume 8, No. 1, June, pp. 33–58.

Choudhry, M. 2002b, "Combining Securitisation and Trading in Credit Derivatives: An Analysis of the Managed Synthetic Collateralised Debt Obligation", *Euromoney Debt Capital Markets Yearbook*, Euromoney Publications, London, pp. 64–79.

Choudhry, M. 2005, *Corporate Bond Markets*, John Wiley & Sons, Singapore, Chapter 20.

Choudhry, M. 2006, *The Credit Default Swap Basis*, Bloomberg Press, Princeton, New Jersey.

Das, S. 2001, *Structured Products and Hybrid Securities*, John Wiley & Sons, Singapore, chapter 12.

Fabozzi, F. and Goodman, L. (eds) 2001, *Investing in Collateralised Debt Obligations*, FJF Associates, New Hope, PA.

Garcia, L. and Patel, T. 2004, "Legal Documentation on Bond Issuances," in Fabozzi, F. and Choudhry, M. (eds), *Handbook of European Fixed Income Securities*, John Wiley & Sons, New Jersey.

Gibson, M. 2004, *Understanding the Risk of Synthetic CDOs*. Trading Risk Analysis Section, Division of Research and Statistics, Federal Reserve Board.

Gregory, J. 2003, *Credit Derivatives: The Definitive Guide*, RISK Books, London.

Hull, J., and White, A. 2004, *Valuation of a CDO and an nth to Default CDS without Monte Carlo Simulation*, Working paper, University of Toronto.

Kasapi, A. 1999, *Mastering Credit Derivatives*, FT Prentice Hall, London.

Li, D. 2000, *On Default Correlation: A Copula Function Approach*, Working paper, RiskMetrics Group.

McPherson, N., Remeza, H. and Kung, D. 2002, *Synthetic CDOs and Credit Default Swaps*, CSFB, London.

Mina, J. and Stern, E. 2003, "Examples and Applications of Closed-form CDO Pricing", *RiskMetrics Journal*, Fall, pp. 5-24.

CHAPTER

24

Synthetic Mortgage-backed Securities

In this chapter, we look at synthetic mortgage-backed securitisation, which was introduced in the European market. We can see that it is based on exactly the same principles as the CSO market, and that deals are originated for similar reasons to balance sheet static synthetic CDOs.[1] The deals have been arranged by banks as part of the balance sheet management of their residential and commercial mortgage pools.

Transaction description

As has been observed in the CSO market, the European CMBS and RMBS markets have witnessed a range of different synthetic deal structures. The first deal was issued in 1998. As with CSOs, synthetic MBS deal structures involve the removal of the credit risk associated with a pool of mortgages by means of credit derivatives, rather than by recourse to a true sale to an SPV. The originator, typically a mortgage bank, is the credit protection buyer and retains ownership, as well as the economic benefit, of the assets. The credit risk is transferred to the investors, who are the protection sellers. As with synthetic CDOs, there exist funded and unfunded synthetic MBS deals, as well as partially funded deals. The type of structure adopted by the originator depends on the legal jurisdiction, the regulatory environment, capital requirements and also the preferences of investors.

---

[1] Residential MBS and commercial MBS (RMBS and CMBS) follow the same principles that we discussed in Chapter 18. For more detail on MBS structures, see Hayre (2001), referenced in Chapter 18, or the author's own *Bond Market Securities* (FT Prentice Hall, London, 2001), Chapter 8.

The main market for synthetic MBS to date has been Germany, although deals have also involved UK, Swedish and Dutch originators.

Deal structures

Unfunded synthetic MBS

An unfunded synthetic MBS deal uses CDS to transfer the credit risk of a pool of mortgages from the originator to a swap counterparty. There is no note issue and frequently no SPV involved. The investor receives the CDS premium during the life of the transaction, in return for which they agree to pay out on any losses incurred by the originator on the pool of assets. The CDS references the pool of mortgages, which remain on the originator's balance sheet.

The CDS protection seller pays out on the occurrence of a credit event. The precise definition and range of credit events differs by transaction and jurisdiction, but generally there are fewer credit events associated with a synthetic MBS compared to a synthetic CDO deal. This reflects the nature of the reference assets. The common credit events described in a synthetic MBS are:

- failure to pay;
- bankruptcy.

Credit events are defined in the deal documentation and their occurrence triggers a payment from the protection seller.

As with vanilla CDS, in an unfunded synthetic MBS, the investor is exposed to counterparty risk if the originator is unable to continue paying its premium. To overcome this, some shorter maturity deals are arranged with a one-off premium aid at the start of the deal, that covers the credit protection for the life of the deal. Conversely, the risk for the protection buyer is if the protection seller becomes bankrupt, upon which the former will no longer be receiving any credit protection.

As there is no SPV involved, unfunded deals can be brought to market relatively quickly, and this is a key advantage over funded deals. Because the CDS counterparty must be rated equivalently to an OECD bank, the investor base is narrower than for funded deals.

Funded synthetic MBS

In a funded synthetic MBS structure, an SPV is set up that issues a tranched series of CLNs. These CLNs are referenced to the credit performance and risk exposure of a portfolio of reference assets, which may be residential mortgages, real-estate loans or commercial mortgages. The proceeds of the CLNs are either:

- invested in eligible collateral, such as a GIC account or AAA-rated government securities; or
- passed to the originator or a third party.

If the note issue proceeds are invested in collateral, this is known as a collateralised funded synthetic MBS, otherwise the deal is uncollateralised.

Although fully funded synthetic MBS deals have been observed, it is more common to see partially funded transactions, in which a portion of the reference pool credit risk is transferred via a CDS. This achieves a credit risk transfer from the SPV to investors without any funding issues.

Figure 24.1 on page 1142 shows a typical funded synthetic MBS structure. Figure 24.2 on page 1142 shows a simplified structure for a synthetic CMBS where the originator is transferring credit risk on assets spread across more than one legal jurisdiction.

Generally, the structure is initially brought to market by the originator entering into a credit protection agreement with the SPV, which requires it to pay the protection premium (or interest on par value) to the SPV, and secondly by the SPV ("issuer") transferring this risk exposure to investors by means of the note issue. These investors ultimately pay out on occurrence of a triggering event. The credit risk of the CLNs is, in effect, linked to the aggregated credit performance for the relevant tranche of risk of the reference pool. It is also linked to the risk profile of the collateral assets, but this is not significant because only high-quality investments are eligible for the collateral pool.

If the CLN note(s) is (are) to be collateralised, the cash raised from the issue is used to purchase eligible securities or placed in a reserve cash account. The note collateral is used to back the coupon payments on the CLNs; it is also a reserve fund that can be used to cover losses in the reference asset pool and to pay expenses associated with the vehicle. If the losses suffered by the reference assets are greater than the reserve account balance, or the nominal value of the junior note, the note collateral is available to cover the originator for the loss. This is the loss borne by the investors who purchased the CLNs. This arrangement, because it is funded, eliminates the counterparty risk (for the protection buyer) associated with unfunded structures, because investors have covered the credit risk exposure with an up-front payment. If the CLN notes are not to be collateralised, the

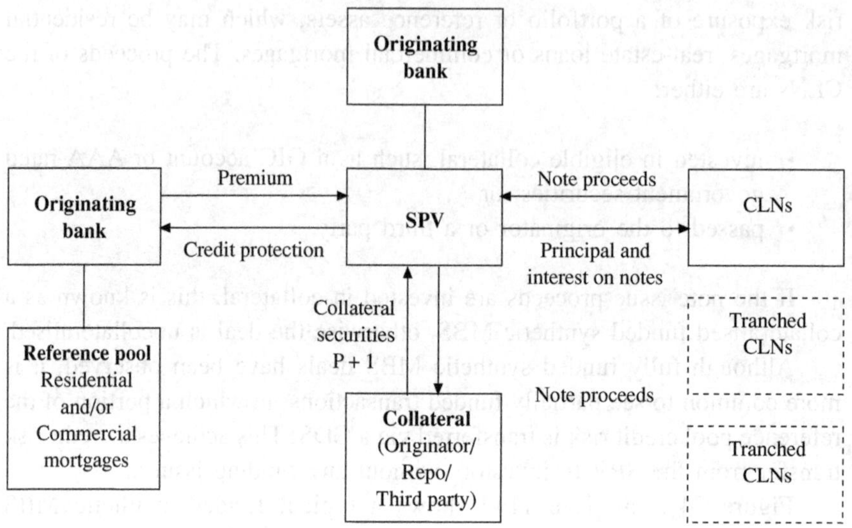

Figure 24.1 Funded synthetic MBS generic structure

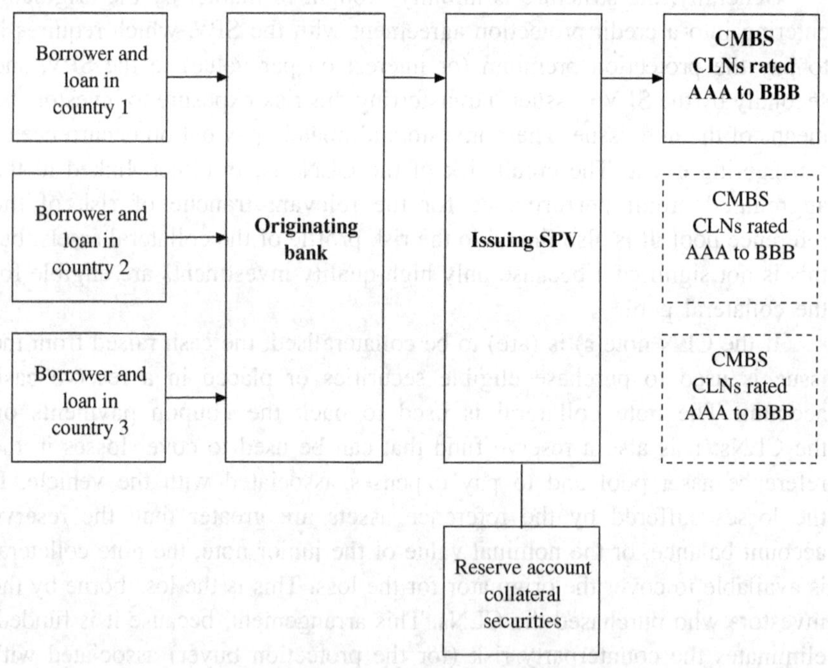

Figure 24.2 Pan-European synthetic CMBS generic structure

note proceeds are passed to the originator directly or to a third-party agent. The originator or third party is obliged to repay principal on the CLNs on maturity, but only if no triggering events have occurred.

On occurrence of losses in the reference pool, the effect follows established synthetic deal procedures. Each loss is applied only to the most junior CLN (or CDS in an unfunded or partially funded deal) outstanding. More senior noteholders should not see their cash flows effected until the note below them is fully absorbed by continuing losses.

Partially funded synthetic MBS

In a partially funded deal, the issue of CLNs is combined with a CDS which transfers part of the credit risk on an unfunded basis. Frequently this is a basket or portfolio CDS that is ranked above the CLNs, so it becomes a super-senior CDS.

A selection of synthetic RMBS deals in Europe is listed in Table 24.1 on page 1144.

Investor considerations

Traditional cash MBS and synthetic MBS deals have several features in common, and both aim to achieve several common objectives. The main one of these is the transfer of the credit risk associated with a pool of mortgage assets away from the originating bank, usually via an SPV. Key to the attraction of a synthetic deal is the fact that it can be customised to investors' requirements more closely. In a synthetic deal, the credit risk exposure that is transferred is (in theory) defined precisely, compared to a cash deal where any and all risks associated with the assets are transferred. Thus a synthetic deal can be structured and documented to transfer precisely the risk exposures that the investors are looking for.

In this section we highlight those areas of difference between the two products.

Close date	Name	Origin of assets	Size of reference pool m	Funded portion m	Unfunded portion m	Loss definition
Jun-00	Eurohypo 2000–1	Germany	500	500		Principal plus accrued interest
Nov-00	Haus 200–2	Germany	2,885	159	2,726	Principal only
Dec-00	Neuschwanstein 2000–1	Germany	279		273	Principal only
Sep-01	Residence 2001–1	Germany	1,541		1,404	Principal only
Oct-01	HVB Real Estate 2001–1	Germany	1,311	44	1,232	Principal only
Oct-01	Provide-A-2001–1	Germany	1,000	145	855	Principal plus external enforcement costs plus accrued interest of 4% p.a.
Nov-01	FARMS Securitisation Ltd	Sweden	1,535	203	1,332	Principal
Mar-02	Provide-Gems-2002–1	Germany	1,052	159	873	Principal plus external enforcement costs plus accrued interest of 4% p.a.
Jun-02	Bouwfonds 2002	Netherlands	1,000		1,000	Principal losses plus 3-month interest accrual plus enforcement costs
Jul-02	Provide Resident 2002–1	Germany	1,508	210	1,267	Principal losses plus enforcement costs

Table 24.1 Selected European synthetic MBS deals, 2000–2002
Source: Moody's. Used with permission.

Originator issues

As a synthetic MBS does not involve a true sale of assets, investors' fortunes are still connected with those of the originator. Therefore, if the originator becomes insolvent, the deal can be expected to terminate. Should this happen, an estimated loss is calculated, which is then applied to the most junior note in the structure.[2] The collateral assets are then realised and the proceeds are used to pay off the outstanding CLNs.

Cash-flow liquidity risk

In a traditional cash MBS, a shortfall in cash in the vehicle may lead to disruption of cash receipts by investors. Typically, cash MBS deals are structured with a *liquidity provider* or *liquidity facility* to cover such temporary shortfalls, which may be the arranging bank for the deal. With such an arrangement, the credit rating of the deal is linked to some extent to that of the liquidity provider. With a synthetic MBS this does not apply. Losses in the reference pool are applied to the note structure in priority order, not when a credit event has been verified, but when the loss has been realised. In these circumstances, investors should continue to receive cash flows during the time interval up to the loss realisation, and so a liquidity provider is not required.

Loss severity

In a customised structure aimed at transferring credit risk, the probability of default is an important factor, but not the sole factor. The severity of loss is also significant, and the impact of this differs according to whether it is a cash or synthetic deal. Under a cash structure, if an event occurs which results in potential loss to investors, any outstanding principal, together with accrued interest and recovery costs, needs to be recovered from the securities. So the performance of a cash deal is dependent on the recovery time and costs incurred during the process (such as legal costs of administration).

---

[2] Under this approach, an expected loss is calculated on non-performing loans, but which may not have become a credit event.

With a synthetic deal, the originator may customise the type and level of risk protection that it pays for. So it may, if it wishes, purchase protection for one or a combination of the following:

- principal outstanding;
- interest costs, capped or uncapped;
- recovery costs.

Table 24.1 shows the type of protection adopted by the various deals. We can see that for two of the deals, where accrued interest was covered, the cost was capped at 4%.

CDS of ABS

A recent development in the credit derivatives market has been credit default swaps (CDS) that reference specific tranches of ABS and MBS notes. These are sometimes referred to as synthetic MBS securities. The first such contracts were written on Home Equity ABS (a type of Residential MBS) in the US market. These products are offered by banks to their investor clients, and as such they are not a tool of bank ALM. They were considered in Chapter 18.

CHAPTER

25

Structured Investment Vehicles

Structured investment vehicles (SIVs) are investment management funds that operate almost as mini-banks. The first SIV was launched in 1988.[1] They have similarities with managed CDOs, but feature detailed differences, the most significant of which is that they are perpetual. Originally developed as highly rated credit arbitrage vehicles, SIVs are not set up to achieve ALM objectives but their objectives can include freeing up the balance sheet, reducing regulatory capital requirements and improving return on capital. SIVs are stand-alone investment companies in their own right, but have been originated by banks seeking to leverage off their credit and funding expertise. Because they are operationally intensive, they require greater effort to bring to market and partly for this reason a much lower number of transactions have been closed compared to, say, CDOs.

Banking groups that set up SIVs will seek to generate returns based on their high credit rating and funding advantage. Changes to regulatory capital requirements under Basel II mean that SIVs may present further advantages, so they may become more common. In this chapter we provide an overview of SIVs, their structure and mechanics.

Overview and structure

Unlike CDOs there is more uniformity to SIV structures, although different versions variously characterised as hybrid SIVs also exist. We look first at the SIV structure and mechanics.

---

[1] This was Citigroup's Alpha Corporation. The same bank then followed with Beta, Centauri, Dorada and Five. Other high-profile early SIVs include Sigma Finance Corporation in 1995, managed by Gordian Knot, and K2 (Dresdner Bank), Links Finance Corporation (Bank of Montreal) and Abacas Investments (Quadrant Capital), all in 1999.

SIV rationale

SIVs are capitalised as mini-bank structures, and must maintain sufficient capital to back their liabilities. They are large-size entities, often of USD 5 billion or more. The main objective of a SIV is to generate return for its investors by means of efficient management of a credit portfolio and active ALM. The return is created by the spread differential between the yield on the assets and that payable on the liabilities. This is supplemented by the positive gain between the return on the long-dated assets and that payable on the short-dated liabilities. A simplified structure diagram is shown in Figure 25.1.

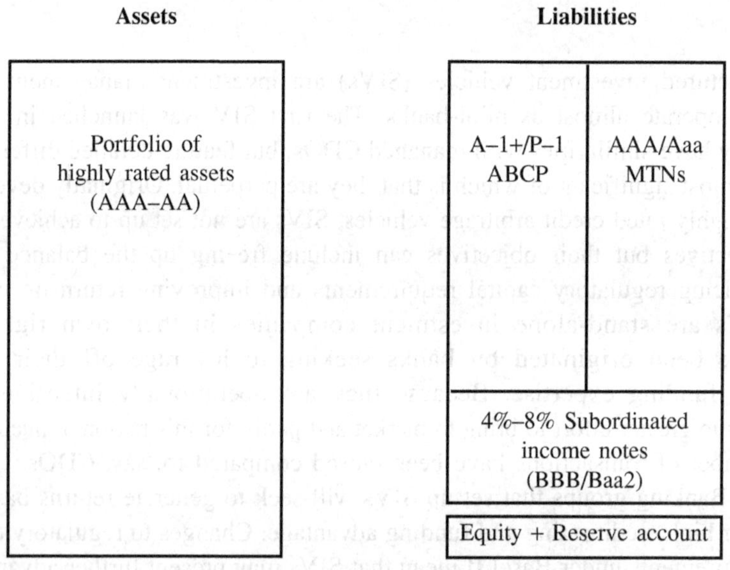

Figure 25.1 SIV structure

The basic structure of a SIV is of an entity that is a perpetual finance company that actively manages a portfolio of investment-grade rates assets. These assets are financed by the issue of debt, both short- and long-dated, in the capital markets. As shown in Figure 25.1, the simplest liability structure is one in which the debt is composed of two tranches, senior debt rated AAA (A–1+/P–1 in the money markets) and subordinated debt. The subordinated debt is usually rated at BBB. Senior debt is issued as both CP and MTNs. There is also a tranche of equity capital and/or a cash reserve account, usually supplied by the originator.

The portfolio is generally diversified across geography and sector. The SIV is structured such that excess spread can, in theory, be generated because:

- the weighted-average rating of the portfolio tends to be around AA– or A, whereas the senior debt is rated AAA; this means the asset side benefits from the term structure of credit rates;
- the weighted-average duration of the asset portfolio will be in the region of 5–7 years, whereas that of the liabilities will be much lower, around 2–3 years; the asset side benefits from the term structure of interest rates.

Furthermore, unlike CDOs and virtually all ABCP vehicles, SIVs are usually multi-currency vehicles that fund in both the US CP and MTN markets, as well as the EuroCP and MTN markets, thus benefiting from reduced funding cost opportunities as they arise in different markets.

Thus, SIVs combine the features of an asset-backed CP (ABCP) vehicle as well as an actively managed CDO. Their main business is akin to a credit arbitrage ABCP conduit, but one that can also secure a proportion of its funding in the longer-dated capital markets. To maintain the AAA and A–1+ ratings of its debt, an SIV must comply with strict rating agency rules on the composition of its asset portfolio and the structure of its assets and liabilities. It also needs to ensure that sufficient liquidity is guaranteed to cover expected cash-flow liabilities, as well as hedge the interest-rate and currency risks that arise due to its mismatched asset and funding profile.

The asset portfolio is diversified but in many cases concentrates on specific asset classes. For example, the Harrier and Kestrel SIVs focus on asset-backed securities, while Centauri and Dorada specialise in financial institutions' credit and on bonds wrapped by monoline insurance companies.[2] The value of assets is reduced by a haircut for the purposes of establishing collateral levels, so in effect SIVs are permanently over-collateralised.

[2] Harrier and Kestrel are managed by Brightwater Capital Management, a UK-incorporated entity, while Centauri and Dorada are managed by Citigroup.

Structure

All SIVs are incorporated as stand-alone, bankruptcy-remote entities, often in tax-beneficial jurisdictions such as Jersey, Cayman Islands and Ireland. Often, both a US-incorporated and an offshore entity are established as part of the structure, to enable the SIV to issue debt in both the domestic USCP as well as the ECP markets. Both debt and equity can be issued. The SIV manager is an important element in the set-up because it is its skills as a credit portfolio manager that is being invested in. The manager will report monthly on the operating performance of the vehicle, to investors and the rating agencies.

To maintain its status as a perpetual company, the SIV capital structure must have similar features. The lower tier debt is usually issued as long-dated income notes, which are MTNs with an initial maturity of 10 years or longer. The notes carry an option on behalf of the issuer to have their final maturity date extended. This feature means the notes can be treated as pseudo-undated subordinated debt. For investor comfort, the notes may carry punitive rates if their life is extended beyond an initial maturity date, and there are often put option features incorporated. Income notes feature hybrid debt and equity characteristics, as often they pay both a fixed spread over Libor or Euribor, as well as a share of the vehicle performance profits. The vehicle is required to maintain capital to support its debt – a key difference between a SIV and a CDO. With the changes to regulatory capital rules being implemented under Basel II, more favourable capital treatment is expected for income notes, which may make SIVs more attractive for bank originators using them for ALM purposes, especially when compared to CDOs.

To maintain rating agency ratings a SIV will need to adhere to detailed investment guidelines. These guidelines will set limits, such as concentration and diversity limits, on the type and quantity of each type of asset that is purchased by the vehicle. Individual assets are required to meet credit rating criteria; for example, a minimum investment-grade rating. The development of a liquid CDS market has led to SIVs using these instruments both to gain exposure (synthetically) on the asset side as well as to hedge credit risk exposure on the liability side.

Liquidity

Liquidity requirements for a SIV are also subject to rating agency scrutiny. A key feature of the vehicle is the dynamic, and mixed, approach taken to structure its funding arrangements. The ability to continuously roll the vehicle's funding liabilities is important; an inability to roll funding would mean that the asset portfolio would have to start to be liquidated so that maturing liabilities could be paid. The liquidity exposure is estimated on a daily basis and projected forward by the SIVs cash-flow model. The portfolio manager must monitor the payment liabilities on this daily basis, and ensure that cash outflow requirements can be met.

As added investor comfort, a bank liquidity line is sometimes set up with the vehicle, to be drawn in the event that funding cannot be rolled. The line is provided by an A–1/P–1-rated bank, and of sufficient size to meet a five-day forward liability.[3] A ratings agency test on the portfolio composition will also specify that a proportion of it be held in highly liquid assets.

Note that synthetic assets, held in CDS form, do not require funding because they are unfunded instruments. These assets reduce the liquidity risk exposure because they do not add to the funding requirement.

Investor considerations

The basic rationale behind a SIV – that of generating excess spread by means of credit and funding arbitrage – together with the application of securitisation technology to produce highly rated tranched liabilities results in attractive alternative investment opportunities. Investors in the senior and subordinated notes of a SIV will consider the following factors:

- stable cash flows and returns: both senior and income notes generate fixed-spread floating returns that are considered stable. The income notes, in particular, pay a generous return, commensurate with their rating, when set against the high credit quality asset portfolio risk exposure that they represent. Most SIVs are structured with a cash reserve account, which provides cover against portfolio credit losses and also can be dipped into to pay note interest in the event of portfolio losses. This is an added investor comfort;
- low leveraged exposure to highly rated asset portfolios: the leverage in a SIV is low, typically 10–12 times, and on high-quality assets. The mezzanine notes of CDOs and other structured finance securities are usually structured at higher leverage and to lower-rated assets, for the same return levels. Another objective of SIVs is to generate stable returns, and as such they are often structured as pass-through

[3] This is a Moody's requirement, for example.

vehicles: investors have direct exposure to the assets. Once net cash flow is calculated (capital and interest income minus costs), the proceeds are passed to investors, with excess accruing to the manager;
- accessible exposure to alternative asset classes, managed by expert fund managers: SIVs are often an accessible route to alternative asset types, one that is managed by a fund manager with expertise in that area. In effect, the investor is buying into the credit skills of the portfolio manager, for a better risk-reward profile than CDO or ABS notes;
- reporting: the SIV manager will provide a detailed monthly report to investors and rating agencies. The level of detail usually matches that provided to the vehicle's auditors. This transparency is similar to that observed with CDOs, but usually higher than with other structured finance securities. In addition, portfolio assets are marked-to-market on a daily basis, so investors can observe the market value of the portfolio closely.

SIVs are, essentially, straightforward and simple structures. The senior debt represents AAA-rated risk, but paying a higher return than sovereign or multilateral bank risk, while the income notes usually compare favourably to CDO mezzanine paper.

The SIV market was estimated to stand at over USD200 billion as at the end of 2005,[4] and is expected to grow further after the introduction of Basel II from 2007 onwards. For instance, a more recent development, sometimes dubbed "SIV-Lite",[5] is a hybrid structure that is a cross between a CDO and an SIV, capitalised like a CDO but managed like a SIV portfolio, with dynamic hedging and daily marking-to-market.

The number of vehicles is relatively low compared to CDO and ABS transaction numbers, reflecting their operationally intensive nature and high start-up costs. Nevertheless, SIVs remain flexible vehicles with wide application for credit and funding arbitrage, and hence can be expected to be originated for bank ALM purposes, as well as to meet fund manager objectives.

---

[4] *Source*: *AsiaMoney*, May 2006.

[5] *RISK*, May 2006, news report.

SIVs and credit arbitrage conduits

SIVs exhibit some commonality with ABCP conduits that have been originated for credit arbitrage purposes. Both vehicles exist to fund a pool of highly-rated assets that are intended to be held to maturity, and both seek to generate funding arbitrage between assets and liabilities. They also leverage off the credit and portfolio management expertise of their originators. The key differences between the two vehicles arise in the areas of liability structure, credit enhancement, liquidity and risk exposure hedging. SIVs are also generally more operationally intensive, and hence take longer to bring to market. Banks wishing to structure a credit arbitrage funding vehicle for ALM purposes will assess both vehicles and adopt the type that is most appropriate given their objectives.

Table 25.1 is a summary comparison of the two vehicles. For comparison we also show in Figure 25.2 on page 1154 a comparison of the SIV structure against the CDO and Conduit structures, as well as against the capital structure of a monoline insurance investor company.

	SIV	ABCP conduit
Funding structure	CP (1-270 days) ECP (1-364 days) MTN (2-30 years)	CP (1–270 days) ECP (1–364 days)
Credit enhancement	Capital intensive Reserve account Equity tranche	Less capital intensive Excess spread account
Leverage	Up to 12–15× levered	
Hedging	Follows rating agency requirements on hedging, SIV must be market-neutral IR, FX and CDS swap hedging	FX swap if multi-currency
Liquidity support	Can feature: – Liquidity line – Committed repo line – Liquidity asset purchase agreement (LAPA)	Liquidity line

Table 25.1 SIVs and ABCP credit arbitrage conduits compared

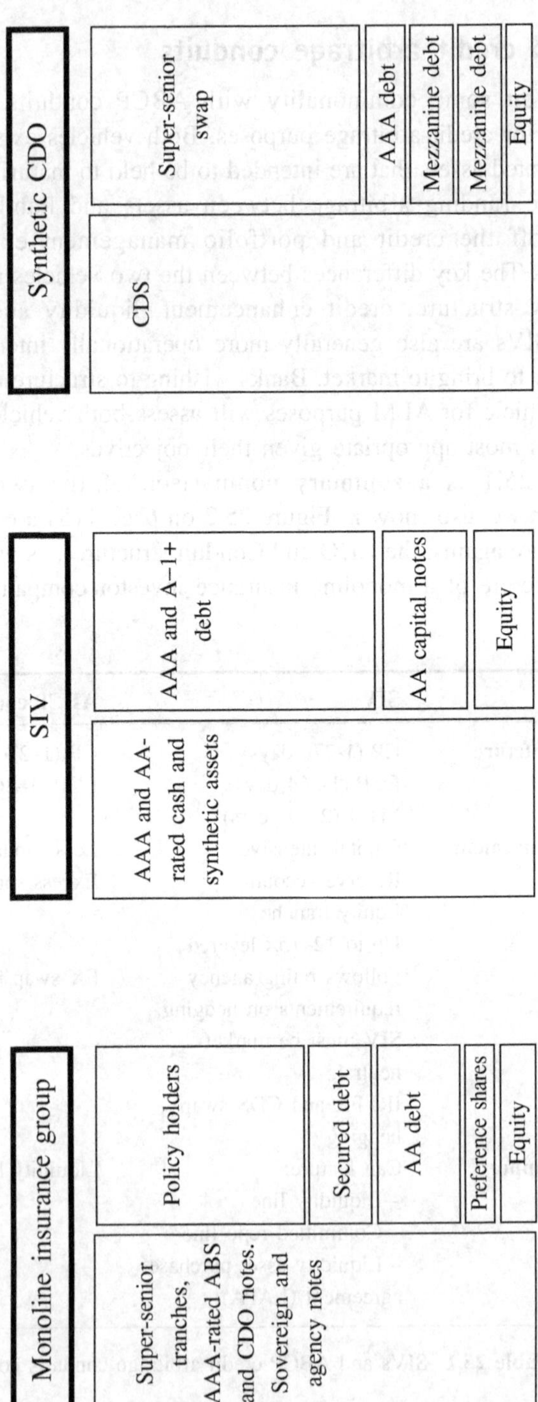

Figure 25.2 Structured credit vehicle comparison

Both structures exist to facilitate credit arbitrage, generating above-Libor returns for noteholders. The arbitrage is really a funding arbitrage, and comprises two elements:

- credit spread: the underlying portfolio will have an average credit rating of AAA/Aaa to AA/Aa, generating higher return than the cost of the vehicle's liabilties;
- average life spread: in a positive yield curve environment longer-dated assets will carry higher yields than shorter-dated liabilities. For SIVs and ABCP conduits the asset portfolio typically exhibits a weighted-average life (WAL) of around 4.5–5.5 years, but fund at around the 3–4 year (SIVs) or 0.5-year (ABCP) segment of the term structure.

Figure 25.3 illustrates the credit and funding arbitrage.

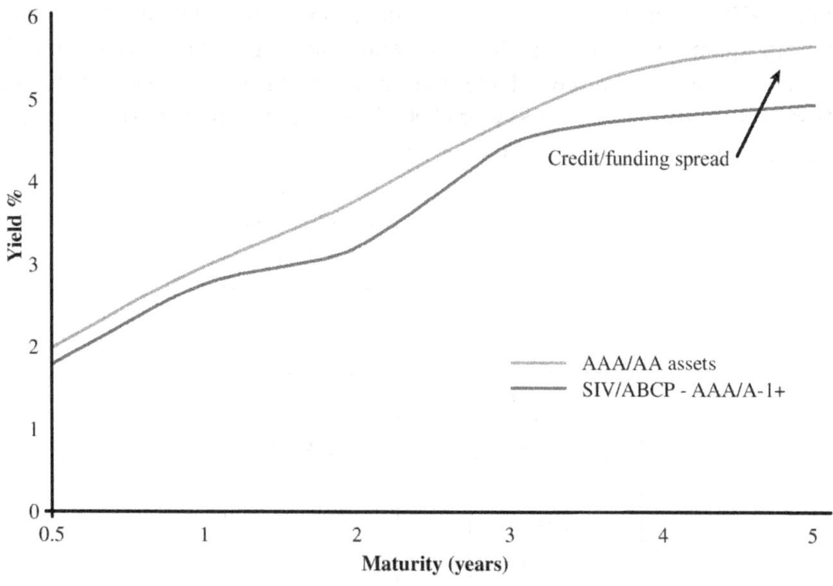

Figure 25.3 The SIV and ABCP credit and funding spread

The ABCP conduit structure is more flexible and typically quicker to close, so may be favoured because there are fewer constraints for the fund manager when selecting assets for the portfolio. Conduits can also be used as asset warehouses for third-party vehicles and also offer liquidity to other entities, both services of which can be offered to the market for a fee. None of these features are available with a SIV. Because of their flexibility, they are much more common than SIVs.

Conduit structure

We describe a hypothetical credit arbitrage ABCP conduit that has been set up to incorporate SIV-like aspects. In fact it can be considered an SIV in all but name, except that it does not issue capital market notes. It is shown here to give a flavour of the structure and objectives of such a vehicle. Often they are managed by a bank's Treasury desk because they can be used to fulfil ALM-related objectives. This calls for portfolio and credit expertise within the Treasury area, which is not necessarily overly common in banks.

Our structure is an ABCP conduit that holds a portfolio of AAA and AA-rated ABS securities. It also has a repo conduit line that means it lends money against very high quality collateral. The originator – assume this is a bank – also sets up the vehicle with an injection of cash, equivalent to a first-loss equity piece in an SIV or CDO. The main features are shown below and the basic structure is in Figure 25.4.

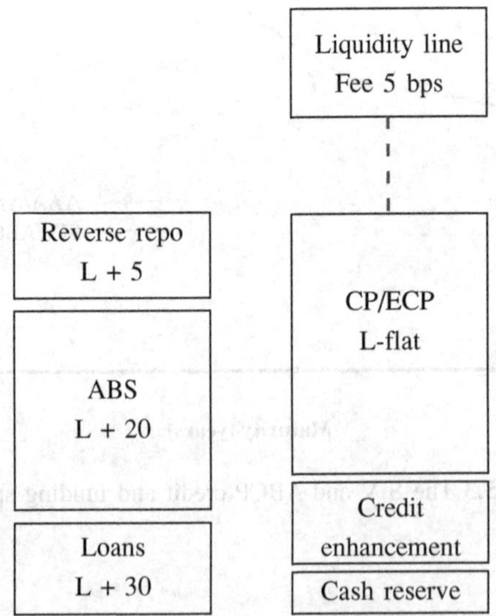

Figure 25.4 Structured finance conduit

ABS-backed credit arbitrage conduit
[Jersey/Ireland/Netherlands] SPV
USD5 billion
Rated A–1+/P–1/F–1+
Initial reserve cash $0.5 million
Account to trap excess spread
Collateral

- Structured finance securities (MBS, ABS, CDO, whole-loan ABS, SIV notes)
- Investment-grade loans
- Reverse repo (AAA collateral)

Credit enhancement: cash reserve, bank back-stop liquidity line

The vehicle is able to secure A–1+/P–1/F–1+ rating because of the quality of the assets and their low probability of default when one considers the average tenor of the liabilities. It is essentially these two factors that drive the rating:

- CP and ECP have a maximum maturity of 270 and 364 days respectively; in practice the weighted-average tenor at any one time will be around 180 days. Within this relatively short time span, the risk of investment grade assets migrating to default is very low, implying a low probability that the vehicle would need to draw on its liquidity line or default on its liabilities;
- rating agency statistics show that AAA/AA– rated ABS paper has a very low default probability over a one-year time horizon. This enables a conduit to acquire an A–1+/P–1 rating on the overlying notes. Figures 25.5 and 25.6 on page 1158 are reproduced with permission from an S&P report and demonstrate this low default probability and ratings migration probability.[6] Figure 25.5, which is the S&P chart on cumulative average default rates per ratings grade, shows the very low default levels for a one-year time horizon. Figure 25.6 illustrates how for all but the very low end of the ratings scale, the actual default experience of institutions is very low for up to a one-year time horizon.

[6] *Structured Finance: Request for Comment*, Standard & Poor's, 13 November 2006. With thanks to Andrea Quirk and Andrew Aston at S&P for their assistance with securing the charts and the permission.

At the same time other factors, such as diversity of the portfolio and credit-enhancement facilities, help to secure the rating.

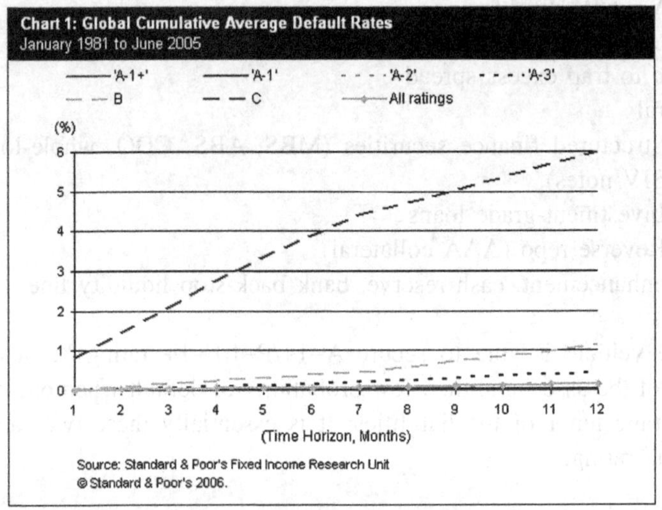

Figure 25.5 Global cumulative average default rates 1981–2005
© Standard & Poor's 2006. Reproduced with permission.

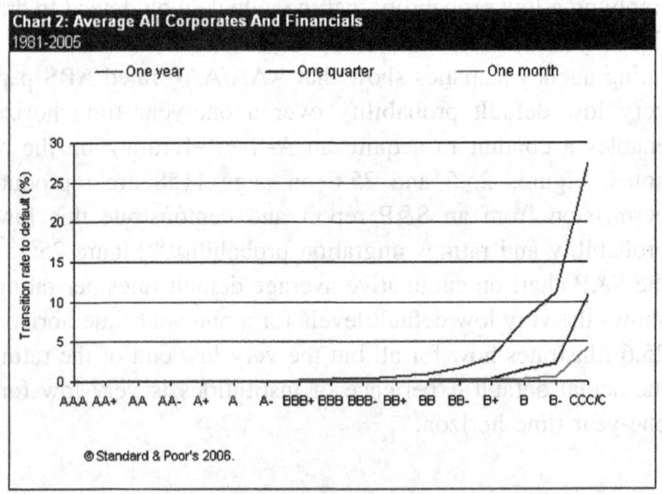

Figure 25.6 Average default rates 1981–2005
© Standard & Poor's 2006. Reproduced with permission.

Sample portfolio

We suggest in Table 25.2 the shape of a sample portfolio for the structured finance conduit, which would also be relevant for a SIV portfolio.

WAL	2.8–3.2 years
WAS	24 bps
Portfolio composition	AAA 70%
	AA 30%
Geographic spread	USA 50%
	UK 35%
	Asia-Pacific 15%
Asset pool	RMBS 10%
	CMBS 10%
	CBO 20%
	CLO 20%
	HEQ 5%
	SIV 5%
	Credit card 5%
	Whole business 5%
	Other 20%

Table 25.2 Indicative asset portfolio

This structure would be a means by which a bank could exploit its credit and portfolio management skills to generate off-balance sheet profit. It could also use the vehicle to offer facilities such as liquidity lines to produce fee-based income. Because the technology behind it is not new, it can be brought to market relatively quickly. As such they are useful tools for use in ALM and balance sheet management.

I think the other important issue with the band's sound was that we really put our hearts into our performances. At the end of the day there is really no substitute for passion. We were not particularly good musicians, but no one really seemed bothered because we put all our energy into our live performances. Also, and maybe most importantly, it was obvious to people who came to see the band that we actually meant the things we were talking about.

– Martin Hewes,
interviewed on www.redskins.co.uk
October 2003

PART V

Bank Regulatory Capital

In Part V we review a topic of fundamental importance to bank ALM, that of regulatory capital and the Basel capital ratios. The cost of capital is the driver behind return on capital calculations, and the prime objective of banking operations is to meet return on capital targets. Hence, regulatory capital issues play an important part in bank strategy. The next two chapters consider the Basel I and Basel II rules.

The need for adequate regulation of the banking industry is widely recognised, and a string of banking failures in the 1990s have possibly emphasised this. The most spectacular instances of failure, for example the collapse of Barings Bank in 1995, were found to have resulted from dishonest actions and a lack of internal management control, as were other large-scale trading losses such as those at Kidder Peabody and Daiwa Securities, which allegedly resulted from individual traders mis-marking their books to cover up losses. The closure of Yamaichi Securities was an instance of large-scale bad loans no longer being tenable, although other issues were involved as well. Although such cases raise the importance of a strong system and culture of risk management and internal controls in commercial and investment banking, they do not in themselves necessarily strengthen the need for excessive capital levels. By the nature of their activities, bank trading and lending desks are risk-takers, and the reward culture in many banks provides strong incentives for perhaps excessive risk-taking. However, the regulators are more concerned with *systemic risk*, the risk that, as a result of the failure of one bank, the whole banking system is put in danger, due to knock-on effects. This did not arise in 1995 in the United Kingdom when Barings collapsed, because the bank was not a large enough part of the monetary system. However, the integrated nature of the global financial industry means that banks are closely entwined, and the failure of one bank generates a risk of failure for all those banks that have lent funds to the failed bank. So systemic risk management is a major challenge for regulators. While a bank will be concerned with risk management of its own operations, regulators are concerned with the risk to the whole financial system. The interrelationships between banks means that they have exposures to one another, while the profit motive encourages risk-taking. The systemic risk inherent in the banking system means that it is important to have sufficiently adequate financial regulation, of which the capital requirements rules are one example.

The Basel rules

The Basel rules that came into effect in 1992 are popularly referred to as *Basel I*. Additional guidelines were published in final form in June 2004 with implementation set for 2007 or 2008, depending on the specific jurisdiction. These new guidelines are popularly referred to as Basel II. Part V of the book is concerned with a discussion of both frameworks.

Basel I

The Basel I rules set a minimum ratio of capital to assets of 8% of the value of the assets. The shortcoming of Basel I is that it makes no allowance for the credit risk ratings of different corporate borrowers, and that does not align risk-based capital with the economic risk. That these were valid issues was recognised when, on 3 June 1999, the BIS published proposals to update the capital requirements rules. These were finalised as Basel II in June 2004.

Basel II

Basel I was based on very broad counterparty credit requirements, and despite an amendment introduced in 1996 (covering trading book requirements), remained open to the criticism of inflexibility. The Basel II rules have three pillars, designed to be more closely related to the risk levels of particular credit exposures.

Under Pillar 1, the capital requirements are stated using two approaches – the standardised approach and the internal ratings based (IRB) approach. In the standardised approach banks will risk-weight assets in accordance with a set matrix, which splits assets according to their formal credit rating. Within the IRB approach there is a foundation approach and an advanced approach, the latter of which gives banks more scope to set elements of the capital charges themselves. In the IRB approach banks' assets are categorised in accordance with their own internal risk assessment. To undertake this approach a bank must have its internal systems recognised by its relevant supervisory body, and systems and procedures must have been in place for at least three years previously. This includes a system that enables the bank to assess the default probability of borrowers.

Compared to the Basel I rules, general market opinion holds that the Basel II rules are an improved benchmark for assessing capital adequacy relative to true economic risk.

CHAPTER

26

Bank Regulatory Capital and the Basel Rules

The capital allocation requirements of a bank are behind its overall strategy. Asset allocation decisions are influenced to a great extent by the capital considerations that such allocation implies. Lower capital requirements for derivatives explain to a great extent why derivatives are used by banks and corporates instead of cash products. This is as true of the retail markets as it is of the debt capital and wholesale banking markets. For that reason, a book on bank ALM must cover capital itself, otherwise it will be incomplete. So an understanding of banking is not possible without an understanding of one of its key aspects: regulatory capital.

For instance, a large part of the money markets involves securitised products; for example, ABCP. One of the key motivations behind securitisation is the requirement to obtain capital relief. This leads to mortgages, trade receivables and other assets being securitised. We can see that it is vital to understand the implications of capital costs. Additionally, the issue of the cost of capital that we introduced in Part I must also take into account the regulatory capital implications of any asset allocation taken by a trading desk. Money and capital market participants must know about regulatory capital issues – whether they trade CDs, bills, repo, FRNs, ABCP or structured products – or they will not fully understand the cost of their own capital and hence their return on capital.

Background

Banking activity and the return it generates reflects the asset allocation policies of a bank and the capital costs incurred. The cost of capital itself is a function of the amount of capital that a bank must set aside to cover its lending activity, whether this lending is via short-term loans, repurchase agreements, CDs, Banker's bills or more long-term instruments. The rules defining what constitutes *capital* and how much of it to allocate are laid out in the Bank for International Settlements (BIS) guidelines, known as the *Basel rules*. The BIS is not a regulatory body in itself, and its pronouncements carry no legislative weight; however, national authorities are keen to demonstrate that they follow the Basel rules at a minimum, to maintain investor and public confidence.

In this chapter we review the main elements of the Basel rules, which were replaced by a new set of guidelines termed Basel II. Money market participants are keenly aware of the basic tenets of the rules, so as to optimise their asset allocation and hedging policy. Derivatives, for instance, require a significantly lower level of capital allocation than cash products, which (along with their liquidity) is a primary reason for their use as hedge instruments instead of cash, despite the existence of basis risk. In addition, the credit quality of a bank's counterparty also affects significantly the level of capital charge, and regulatory rules influence a bank's lending policy and counterparty limit settings. All bank's have internal rules dictating the extent of lending, across all money market products, to their counterparties. Capital allocation, targeted rates of return (which are a function of capital costs) and the extent of counterparty risk aversion all dictate the extent to which funds may be lent to counterparties of various credit ratings. For this reason the bank ALM desk needs to be keenly aware of the approximate extent of capital allocation that results from its operations.

This chapter considers the main aspects of the capital rules and also introduces the Basel II proposals, and how credit risk exposure determines the extent of capital allocation. It also indicates the interplay between the money market desk and longer term traders, whose capital allocation requirements are greater. This will enable the money market participant to place his or her operations in the context of banking specifically and capital markets business generally.

Banking regulatory capital requirements

Banks and financial institutions are subject to a range of regulations and controls; the primary one is concerned with the level of capital that a bank holds, and that this level is sufficient to provide a cushion underpinning the activities that the bank enters into. Typically, an institution is subject to regulatory requirements of its domestic regulator, but may also be subject to cross-border requirements such as the European Union's Capital Adequacy

Directive.[1] A capital requirements scheme proposed by a committee of central banks acting under the auspices of the BIS in 1988 has been adopted universally by banks around the world. These are known as the BIS regulatory requirements or the Basel capital ratios, from the town in Switzerland where the BIS is based.[2] Under the Basel requirements all cash and off-balance sheet instruments in a bank's portfolio are assigned a risk weighting, based on their perceived credit risk, that determines the minimum level of capital that must be set against them.

A bank's *capital* is, put simply, the difference between assets and liabilities on its balance sheet, and is the property of the bank's owners. It may be used to meet any operating losses incurred by the bank, and if such losses exceeded the amount of available capital then the bank would have difficulty in repaying liabilities, which may lead to bankruptcy. However, for regulatory purposes capital is defined differently; again in its simplest form regulatory capital is comprised of those elements in a bank's balance sheet that are eligible for inclusion in the calculation of capital ratios. The ratio required by a regulator will be that level deemed sufficient to protect the bank's depositors. Regulatory capital includes equity, preference shares and subordinated debt, as well as the general reserves. The common element of these items is that they are all *loss-absorbing*, whether this is on an ongoing basis or in the event of liquidation. This is crucial to regulators, who are concerned that depositors and senior creditors are repaid in full in the event of bankruptcy.

The Basel rules on regulatory capital originated in the 1980s, when there were widespread concerns that a number of large banks with cross-border business were operating with insufficient capital. The regulatory authorities of the G-10 group of countries established the Basel Committee on Banking Supervision. The Basel Committee on Banking Supervision's 1988 paper, *International Convergence of Capital Measurement and Capital Standards*, set proposals that were adopted by regulators around the world as the "Basel rules". The Basel Accord was a methodology for calculating risk, weighting assets according to the type of borrower and its domicile. The Basel ratio[3] set a minimum capital requirement of 8% of risk-weighted assets.

The Basel rules came into effect in 1992.

---

[1] In the United Kingdom, banking regulation is now the responsibility of the Financial Services Authority, which took over responsibility for this area from the Bank of England in 1998. In the United States, banking supervision is conducted by the Federal Reserve; it is common for the central bank to be a country's domestic banking regulator.

[2] Bank for International Settlements, Basle Committee on Banking Regulations and Supervisory Practice, *International Convergence of Capital Measurement and Capital Standards*, July 1988.

[3] Also known as the "Cooke ratio" after the Chairman of the Basel Committee at the time, Peter Cooke.

Regulatory capital requirements

The origin of the current capital adequacy rules was a desire by banking regulators to strengthen the stability of the global banking system as well as harmonise international regulations. The 1988 Basel accord was a significant advancement in banking regulation, setting a formal standard for capitalisation worldwide. It was subsequently adopted by the national regulators in over 100 countries. The Basel rules have no regulatory force as such; rather, individual country regulatory regimes adopt them as a minimum required standard. This means that there are slight variations on the basic Basel requirements around the world, of which the European Union's Capital Adequacy Directives are the best example.

The Basel I rules

The BIS rules set a minimum ratio of capital to assets of 8% of the value of the assets. Assets are defined in terms of their risk, and it is the *weighted risk assets* that are multiplied by the 8% figure. Each asset is assigned a risk-weighting, which is 0% for risk-free assets such as certain country government bonds, to 20% for interbank lending, and up to 100% for the highest risk assets such as certain corporate loans. So while a loan in the interbank market would be assigned a 20% weighting, a loan of exactly the same size to a corporate would receive the highest weighting of 100%. The risk weights are given at Table 26.1 on page 1170.

Formally, the BIS requirements are set in terms of the type of capital that is being set aside against assets. International regulation (and UK practice) defines the following types of capital for a bank:

- *Tier 1*: perpetual capital, capable of absorbing loss through the non-payment of a dividend. This is shareholders' equity and also non-cumulative preference shares;
- *Upper Tier 2*: this is also perpetual capital, subordinated in repayment to other creditors; this may include, for example, undated bonds such as building society PIBS, and other irredeemable subordinated debt;
- *Lower Tier 2*: this is capital that is subordinated in repayment to other creditors, such as long-dated subordinated bonds.

Further detail on the composition of capital for UK-regulated institutions is given in Appendix 26.1.

The level of capital requirement is given by (26.1):

$$\frac{\text{Tier 1 capital}}{\text{Risk-adjusted exposure}} > 4\% \qquad \frac{\text{Tier 1 + Tier 2 capital}}{\text{Risk-adjusted exposure}} > 8\%. \tag{26.1}$$

The ratios in (26.1) therefore set minimum levels. A bank's *risk-adjusted exposure* is the cash risk-adjusted exposure, together with the total risk-adjusted off-balance sheet exposure. For cash products on the banking book the capital charge calculations (risk-adjusted exposure) is given by:

$$\text{Principal value} \times \text{Risk weighting} \times \text{Capital charge [8\%]}$$

calculated for each instrument.

The sum of the exposures is taken. Firms may use netting or portfolio modelling to reduce the total principal value.

The capital requirements for off-balance sheet instruments are lower because for these instruments the *principal* is rarely at risk. Interest-rate derivatives such as FRAs of less than one year's maturity have no capital requirement at all, while a long-term currency swap requires capital of between 0.08% and 0.2% of the nominal principal.

The BIS makes a distinction between *banking book* transactions as carried out by retail and commercial banks (primarily deposits and lending) and *trading book* transactions as carried out by investment banks and securities houses. Capital treatment sometimes differs between banking and trading books. A repo transaction, for example, attracts a charge on the *trading book*. The formula for calculating the capital allocation is:

$$CA = max.\ (((C_{mv} - S_{mv}) \times 8\% \times RW), 0) \tag{26.2}$$

where

C_{mv} is the value of cash proceeds
S_{mv} is the market value of securities
RW is the counterparty risk-weighting (as a percentage).

EXAMPLE 26.1 Basel I capital charge illustration

Calculate the CAD charge for a repo transaction with the following terms:

Clean price of collateral:	100
Accrued interest:	0
Cash proceeds on £50 m nominal:	£50,000,000
Counterparty:	OECD bank
Counterparty risk-weighting:	20%

CA = (((50,000,000 − 50,000,000) × 8% × 20%), 0)
= 0.

The CAD charge for a loan/deposit transaction of the same size is as follows:

Unsecured loan:	£50,000,000
Counterparty:	OECD bank
Counterparty risk weighting:	20%

CA = max((50,000,000 × 8% × 20%), 0)
= £800,000.

The detailed risk weights for market instruments are given in Table 26.1.

Weighting	Asset type	Remarks
0%	■ Cash ■ Claims on own sovereign and Zone A sovereigns and central banks ■ Claims on Zone B sovereign issuers denominated in that country's domestic currency	Zone A countries are members of the OECD and countries that have concluded special lending arrangements with the IMF. Zone B consists of all other countries. Under certain regulatory regimes, holdings of other Zone A government bonds are given 10% or 20% weightings,

		and Zone B government bonds must be funded in that country's currency to qualify for 0% weighting, otherwise 100% weighting applies.
20%	■ Claims on multilateral development banks ■ Claims on regional governments or local authorities in own or Zone A countries ■ Senior claims on own country or guaranteed by Zone A banking institutions ■ Senior claims on Zone B banking institutions with an original maturity of under one year	Under certain regulatory regimes, claims on Zone B banking institutions with residual maturity of less than one year also qualify for 20% weighting.
50%	■ Claims secured on residential property ■ Mortgage-backed securities	
100%	■ All other claims	

Table 26.1 Risk weightings of typical banking book assets, Basel I

Under the original Basel rules, assets are defined as belonging to a bank's banking book or its trading book. The banking book essentially comprises the traditional activities of deposit taking and lending, with assets booked at cost and not revalued. Trading book assets, which include derivatives, are marked-to-market on a daily basis, with a daily unrealised profit or loss recorded. Such assets are risk-weighted on a different basis to that shown in Table 26.1, on a scale made up of market risk and credit risk. Market risk is estimated using techniques such as VaR, while credit risk is a function of the type of asset. The calculation of capital requirements for trading book assets is more complex than that for banking book assets.

The process of determining the capital requirement of a banking institution involves calculating the quantitative risk exposure of its existing operations and comparing this amount to the level of regulatory capital of the bank. The different asset classes are assigned into the risk buckets of 0%, 20%, 50% and 100%. Not surprisingly, this somewhat rigid classification has led to distortions in the pricing of assets, as any movement between the risk buckets has a significant impact on the capital required and the return on capital calculation. Over time the impact of the Basel rules has led to the modified rules now proposed as Basel II, which are coming into force during 2007–2009, depending on jurisdiction.

Table 26.2 summarises the elements that comprise the different types of capital that make up regulatory capital as set out in the EU's Capital Adequacy Directive. Tier 1 capital supplementary capital is usually issued in the form of non-cumulative preference shares, known in the US as preferred stock. Banks generally build Tier 1 reserves as a means of boosting capital ratios, as well as to support a reduced pure equity ratio. Tier 1 capital now includes certain securities that have similar characteristics to debt, as they are structured to allow interest payments to be made on a pre-tax basis rather than after tax; this means they behave like preference shares or equity, and improve the financial efficiency of the bank's regulatory capital. Such securities, along with those classified as Upper Tier 2 capital, contain interest deferral clauses so that they may be classified similar to preference shares or equity.

The UK capital regulations are summarised in Appendix 26.1.

	Limits	Capital type	Deductions
Tier 1	▮ No limit to Tier 1 ▮ "Esoteric" instruments such as trust-preferred securities are restricted to 15% of total Tier 1	▮ Equity share capital, including share premium account ▮ Retained profits ▮ Non-cumulative preference shares and other hybrid capital securities	▮ Bank holdings of its own Tier 1 instruments ▮ Goodwill and other intangible assets ▮ Current-year unpublished losses
Tier 2	▮ Total Tier 2 may not exceed 100% of Tier 1		
Upper Tier 2		▮ Perpetual subordinated, loss-absorbing debt ▮ Cumulative preference shares ▮ General reserves ▮ Revaluation reserves	▮ Holdings of other banks' own fund instruments in excess of 10% of the value of own capital ▮ Holding of more than 10% of another credit institution's own funds ▮ Specified investments in non-consolidated subsidiaries

			▮ Qualified investments, defined as a holding of more than 10% of a company
Lower Tier 2	▮ Cannot exceed 50% of Tier 1 ▮ Amount qualifying as capital amortises on a straight-line basis in the last five years	▮ Fixed maturity subordinated debt ▮ Perpetual subordinated non-loss absorbing debt	
Tier 3	▮ Minimum 28.5% of capital covering market risk must be Tier 1 ▮ Tier 3 capital can only cover market risk on trading books. All credit risk must be covered by Tier 1 and Tier 2 capital	▮ Trading book profits ▮ Short-term subordinated debt with a minimum maturity of two years, plus a feature enabling regulator to block payment of interest or principal in the event of financial weakness	▮ Trading book losses
Other	▮ Capital to only include fully paid-up amounts ▮ Issues of capital cannot include cross-default or negative pledge clauses ▮ Default of Lower Tier 2 capital is defined as non-payment of interest or a winding-up of the bank ▮ No rights of set-off to be included in capital issues documentation ▮ Early repayment of debt must be approved by the bank's regulator ▮ Interim profits must be audited accounts, and net of expected losses, tax and dividends		

Table 26.2 European Union regulatory capital rules

Example 26.2 illustrates a simple capital adequacy calculation for a hypothetical bank. To illustrate, consider a bank with a loan book made up of the following assets:

- £100 million gilts;
- £315 million corporate loans;
- £600 million residential mortgages.

The risk-adjusted exposure of the bank's portfolio is (0.0 × 100) + (1.0 × 315) + (0.5 × 600) or £615 million. Therefore the bank would require a minimum Tier 1 capital level of £24.6 million (that is, 4% × 615 million). If the capital available to support the loan book comprised both Tier 1 and Tier 2 capital, the minimum amount required would be higher, at £49.2 million.

There is of course a cost associated with maintaining capital levels, which is one of the main reasons for the growth in the use of derivative (off-balance sheet) instruments, as well as the rise in securitisation. Derivative instruments attract a lower capital charge than cash instruments, because the principal in a derivative instrument does not change hands and so is not at risk, while the process of securitisation removes assets from a bank's balance sheet, thereby reducing its capital requirements.

The capital rules for off-balance sheet instruments are slightly more involved. Certain instruments, such as FRAs and swaps with a maturity of less than one year, have no capital requirement at all, while longer-dated interest-rate swaps and currency swaps are assigned a risk-weighting of between 0.08% ands 0.20% of the nominal value. This is a significantly lower level than for cash instruments. For example, a £50 million 10-year interest-rate swap conducted between two banking counterparties would attract a capital charge of only £40,000, compared to the £800,000 capital an interbank loan of this value would require; a corporate loan of this value would require a higher capital level still, of £4 million.

The capital calculation for derivatives have detail differences between them, depending on the instrument that is being traded. For example, for interest-rate swaps the exposure includes an "add-on factor" to what is termed the instrument's "current exposure". This add-on factor is a percentage of the nominal value, and is shown in Table 26.3.

Maturity	Plain vanilla	Floating/Floating swaps	Currency swaps
Up to 1 year	0.0	0.0	1.0
Over 1 year	0.5	0.0	5.0

Table 26.3 Add-on risk adjustment for interest-rate swaps, percentage of nominal value

EXAMPLE 26.2 Simple illustration of calculation of capital adequacy, Basel I rules

ABC Bank plc Balance Sheet

Assets	**Weighting (%)**	**Value (£m)**	**Capital risk-weighting (£m)**
T-Bills	0	250	0
Cash	0	30	0
Interbank loans	20	790	158
Mortgage book	50	652	326
Commercial loan book	100	814	814
TOTAL		**2536**	**1298**
Capital charge (8%)			103.84
Liabilities			
Shareholders' funds	100		
Reserves	356	456	
Long-term debt	500		
Deposits	1580	2080	
		2536	

Table 26.4 Example of capital adequacy calculation

The assets of ABC Bank plc are £2.536 billion, which are balanced by shareholders' funds and long-term borrowings, as well as the deposit base of the bank. The Basel risk-weighting assigns the various types of assets a certain risk-weighting, and using the rules we calculate a capital at risk value of £1.298 billion. The capital required is 8% of this sum, or just over £103 million. The Basel rule states that at least 50% of this amount must be sourced from Tier 1 capital. We see from Table 26.4 that the level of Tier 1 capital is well above the sum required. The combination of Tier 1 and Tier 2 capital is also well above the minimum required.

Action in the event of failure

The existence of a regulatory capital system is designed to protect the financial system, and therefore by definition the free market economy, by attempting to ensure that credit institutions carry adequate reserves to allow for counterparty risk. However, domestic regulators are also faced with a dilemma should a banking institution find itself in an insolvency situation; namely, to what extent should the bank be "rescued" by the authorities. If the bank is sufficiently large, its failure could have a significant negative impact on the national and global economy, as other banks, businesses and ultimately individuals also suffered losses. The large "high street" banks[4] are obvious examples of the type of firm that is considered too important to be allowed to fail. It is not desirable though for regulators or national governments to present explicit guarantees against failure, however, as this introduces the risk of moral hazard as risk of loss is reduced.[5] There would also be an element of subsidy as a bank that was perceived as benefiting from an explicit or implicit guarantee would be able to raise finance at below-market cost. This introduces an anti-competitive element in one of the most important sectors of the economy.

Observation would appear to indicate that domestic regulators do not treat all banks as equal, however, notwithstanding the reluctance of regulators to provide even implicit guarantees. The desire to avoid knock-on effects and safeguard the financial system means that large banks may be rescued while smaller banks are allowed to fail. This has the effect of maintaining an orderly market but also emphasising the need for discipline and effective risk management. For example, in the United Kingdom both BCCI and Barings were allowed to fail, as their operations were deemed to affect relatively few depositors and their failure did not threaten the banking system. In the United States Continental Illinois was saved, as was Den Norske Bank in Norway, while two smaller banks in that country were allowed to fail, these being Norian Bank and Oslobanken. In Japan many small banks have been allowed to fail, as was Yamaichi Securities, while Long Term Credit Bank and Nippon Credit Bank both were rescued.

4 Known as "money centre" banks in the United States.

5 This is the risk that, given that a guarantee against loss is available, a firm ceases to act prudently and enters into high-risk transactions, in the expectation that it can always call on the authorities should its risk strategy land it in financial trouble.

The original Basel II proposals

The perceived shortcomings of the 1988 Basel capital accord attracted much comment from academics and practitioners alike, almost as soon as they were adopted. The main criticisms were that the requirements made no allowance for the credit risk ratings of different corporate borrowers, and that they were too rigid in their application of the risk-weightings. That these were valid issues was recognised when, on 3 June 1999, the BIS published proposals to update the capital requirements rules. The new guidelines are designed "to promote safety and soundness in the financial system, to provide a more comprehensive approach for addressing risks, and to enhance competitive equality". The proposals are also intended to apply to all banks worldwide, and not simply those that are active across international borders.

The 1988 accord was based on very broad counterparty credit requirements, and despite an amendment introduced in 1996 to cover trading book requirements, it remained open to the criticism of inflexibility. The new Basel II rules have three pillars, and are designed to be more closely related to the risk levels of particular credit exposures. These are:

- **Pillar 1**: a new capital requirement for credit risk, as well as a charge for the new category of *operational risk*;
- **Pillar 2**: the requirement for supervisors to take action if a bank's risk profile is high compared to the level of capital held;
- **Pillar 3**: the requirement for greater disclosure from banks than before, to enhance market discipline.

The markets have developed to a much greater level of sophistication since the original rules were drafted, and the Committee has considered a wide range of issues related to the determinants of credit risk. In this section we consider the main points of the Basel II rules published in June 2004 and also assess market reaction to them during the discussion phase.

Elements of the new Basel II rules

The new Basel accord is split into three approaches or pillars, which we consider in this section.

Pillar 1 – the minimum capital requirements

(1) Credit risk

The capital requirements are stated under two approaches:

- the standardised approach;
- the internal ratings-based (IRB) approach. Within IRB there is a foundation approach and an advanced approach, the latter of which gives banks more scope to set elements of the capital charges themselves.

Standardised approach

In the standardised approach banks will risk-weight assets in accordance with a set matrix, which splits assets according to their formal credit ratings. The matrix is detailed in Table 26.5, which shows the new risk weights as percentages of the standard 8% ratio.

	Credit rating						
Asset	**AAA to AA**	**A+ to A–**	**BBB+ to BBB-**	**BB+ to B–**	**B+ to B–**	**Below B–**	**Unrated**
Sovereign	0%	20%	50%	100%	100%	150%	100%
Banks –							
option 1[(1)]	0%	20%	50%	100%	100%	150%	100%
option 2[(2)]							
< 3 months	20%	20%	20%	50%	50%	150%	20%
> 3 months	20%	50%	50%	100%	100%	150%	50%
Corporates	20%	50%	100%	100%	150%	150%	100%

(1) Based on the risk-weighting of the sovereign in which the bank is incorporated.
(2) Based on the assessment of the individual bank.

Table 26.5 Basel II capital requirement risk weights, percentage weightings
Source: BIS.

The greatest change is to the four risk weight buckets of the current regime. The revised ruling redistributes the capital required for different types of lending and also adds an additional category for very low-rated assets. For sovereign lending there is a smooth scale from 0% to 150%, while the scale is more staggered for corporates. An unusual feature is that low-rated companies attract a higher charge than non-rated borrowers. For lending to other banks there are two options; in the first, the sovereign risk of the home country of the bank is used, and the bank is placed in the next lower category. In the second option, the credit rating of a bank itself is used. Whatever option is selected, the main effect will be that the capital charge for interbank lending will increase significantly, to virtually double the current level.

National regulators will select which of the two approaches to use for interbank exposures. Under option 1, loans will be categorised in accordance with the rating of their sovereign domicile, while under option 2 loans would be slotted according to the bank's own rating. If using the latter approach, assets of below three months will receive preferential treatment.

Loans made to unrated borrowers will be placed in a separate band that carries the full risk weighting of 100%, although the BIS has stated that regulators should review the historical default experience of the relevant market and assess whether this weighting is sufficient. Short-term credit facilities with corporates that remain undrawn, which under Basel I attract a zero weighting, would be weighted at 20% under Basel II.

Compared to Basel I, under Basel II there is a greater allowance for credit risk reduction, principally in the form of recognition of securities as collateral. The following assets would be recognised as collateral:

- cash and government securities (as currently recognised under Basel I);
- securities rated BB– and above issued by a sovereign or public-sector entity;
- securities rated BBB– and above;
- equities that are constituents of a main index, or listed on a recognised investment exchange;
- gold.

Securities placed as collateral will be given a "haircut" to their market value to reflect their price volatility.

Internal ratings-based (IRB) approach

In the IRB approach, banks' assets are categorised in accordance with their own internal risk assessment. To undertake this approach a bank must have its internal systems recognised by its relevant supervisory body, and systems and procedures must have been in place for at least three years previously. This includes a system that enables the bank to assess the default probability of borrowers. If using an IRB approach a bank will use its own internal ratings to categorise loans in *probability-to-default* or PD bands. The number of PD bands set up is at the discretion of the bank. The BIS has compiled a formula that enables the bank to calculate the capital allocation requirement in accordance with its PD bands. Table 26.6 sets out the capital requirements under Basel I and both the standard and IRB approaches under Basel II.

	%			
	PD band	**Basel I**	**Standard approach**	**IRB foundation approach**
AAA	0.03	8.0	1.6	1.13
AA	0.03	8.0	1.6	1.13
A	0.03	8.0	4.0	1.13
BBB	0.20	8.0	8.0	3.61
BB	1.40	8.0	8.0	12.35
B	6.60	8.0	12.0	30.96
CCC	15.00	8.0	12.0	47.04

Table 26.6 Capital requirements under specified PD bands

If using the advanced approach, banks may recognise any form of collateral and set their own parameters when using the BIS formula for calculating capital, following approval from their banking supervisory body. For the first two years after such approval, the credit risk element of capital allocation cannot be lower than 90% of the allocation calculated under the foundation approach; after two years the BIS propose to review the advanced approach and comment.

(2) Operational risk

One of the most controverisal elements of the Basel II is the new capital charge to cover banks' operational risk. The Committee proposed three different approaches for calculating the operational risk capital charge. These were:

- the basic indicator approach, under which 20% of total capital would be allocated;
- a standardised approach, under which different risk indicators will be allocated to different lines of business within a bank; this would be the level of average assets for a retail bank and assets under management for a fund manager. The Committee would set the

capital charge level for each business line, in accordance with its perceived level of risk in each national jurisdiction, and the total operational risk would be the sum of the exposures of all business lines;

- an internal estimation by a bank of the expected losses due to operational risk for each business line. Operational risk here would be risk of loss as a result of fraud, IT failures, legal risk and so on.

(3) Total minimum capital
The sum of the capital calculation for credit risk exposure, operational risk and the bank's trading book will be the total minimum capital requirement. This capital requirement will be expressed as a 8% risk-asset ratio, identical to the rules under Basel I.

Pillar 2 – Supervisory approach

A new element of the Basel II accord is the requirement for a supervision approach to capital allocation. This is based on three principles. First, banks must have a procedure for calculating their capital requirements in accordance with their individual risk profile. This means they are required to look beyond the minimum capital requirement as provided for under Pillar 1, and assess specific risk areas that reflect their own business activities. This would consider, for instance, interest-rate risk exposure within the banking book, or prepayment risk as part of mortgage business. This process will be reviewed constantly by banking supervisory authorities. Second, the risk-weighted capital requirement calculated under Pillar 1 is viewed as a minimum only, and banks are expected to set aside capital above this minimum level to provide an element of reserve. Supervisors will be empowered to require a bank to raise its capital level above the stipulated minimum. Finally, supervisors are instructed to constantly review the capital levels of banks under their authority, and act accordingly in good time so that such levels do not fall below a level deemed sufficient to support an individual bank's business activity.

Pillar 3 – Disclosure

The Basel II accord sets out rules on core disclosure that banks are required to meet, and which supervisors must enforce. In addition there are supplementary disclosure rules; these differ from core rules in that banks have more flexibility on reporting them if they are deemed not relevant to their specific operating activities, or of they are deemed non-material. The disclosures include:

- ***capital:*** the elements that make up the bank's capital, such as the types of instruments that make up the Tier 1 and Tier 2 capital;
- ***capital adequacy:*** this covers the amount of capital required against credit, market and operational risk, as well as capital requirements as a percentage of the total capital of the bank;
- ***risk exposure:*** the overall risk exposure of a bank, as measured by credit risk, market risk, operational risk and so on. Hence this would include a profile of the ALM book, including maturity profile of the loan book, interest-rate risk, other market risk, essentially the sum of the exposures measured and monitored by a bank's risk management department.

As part of Pillar 3, banks using an IRB approach when calculating their capital requirement are required to disclose their internal policies and procedures used as part of the approach.

In compiling the new Accord, the Basel committee wished to expand capital requirements to cover other areas of risk, such as market risk and operational risk. It recognised that a bank's capital should reflect the level of risk of its own portfolio, but also that this may best be estimated by a bank's own internal model rather than any standard ruling provided by a body such as the BIS. In any event the proposed rule changes attracted considerable comment, although the final form of the rules that were eventually adopted are very similar to the proposals listed above. There is a growing consensus among practitioners that perhaps the markets themselves should carry more of the supervisory burden rather than regulators; for example narrowing the scope of deposit insurance,[6] or by requiring banks to issue specific kinds of uninsured debt, similar to the PIBS issued by UK building societies. Holders of such subordinated debt are more concerned with the financial health of a bank, because their investment is not guaranteed, and at the same time they are not interested in high-risk strategies because their return is the same every year irrespective of the profit performance of the bank; that is, the fixed coupon of their subordinated bond. Therefore the yield on this subordinated debt is in effect the market's assessment of the risk exposure of the bank. An academic at Columbia University[7] has suggested that regulators should place a cap on

[6] Many countries operate a deposit insurance scheme that guarantees the level of a private customer's deposits in a bank should that bank fail. In the United Kingdom for example, the arrangement is that if a bank or building society is declared bankrupt, individuals are entitled to compensation of 90% of their savings with that institution, up to a maximum of £18,000 per individual.

[7] Charles Calomiris, as described in "Better than Basle", *The Economist*, 19 June 1999.

this yield, which would force the bank to cap the level of its risk exposure, but this level would have been evaluated by the market, and not the regulatory authority.

One improvement of Basel II over Basel I is that it acknowledges that "one size" does not fit all banks, and that greater flexibility is required in the capital allocation process. The IRB approach should result in a lower capital charge than the standardised approach, and as such should encourage the development of risk management systems in banks which are incentivised to adopt this approach. Depending on the nature of their activities, some banks will have higher risk profiles compared to others, and as such need more risk management than would be provided simply by a minimum capital level. This is the reasoning behind the three-Pillar approach, and principally Pillar 2, which empowers supervisors to intervene if they feel steps taken by an individual bank are not adequate. This is meant to extend beyond a requirement to increase capital levels. Pillar 3 is also crucial to this overall process, as it is designed to ensure that there is adequate disclosure, not just of risk exposure, but also of the procedures used to calculate capital under the IRB approach.

Reaction and critique

The weight of market reaction and comment to the Basel proposals initially led to a second draft of the proposals being introduced, in January 2000, following the first draft in June 1999. The consultative period was also extended by three more years, so that final implementation of the Accord was not possible until 2007 in the European Union.

The general market opinion has been that Basel II does at least attempt to focus on the economic substance and risk characteristics of new market instruments, as opposed to their structural form. With one or two notable exceptions, banks should find that their overall level of capital allocation remains broadly similar to that under the previous regime. The IRB approach, by being split into a foundation and advanced options,[8] enables a larger range of banks to opt to adopt it, rather than just the larger ones that might be expected to have the requisite internal systems.

The most contentious element of the proposals was the charge for operational risk. The Accord allows three approaches for determining this charge. The first, the "basic indicator", uses a simple one-level indicator, while the second is a standardised approach that specifies different levels of

[8] This was introduced at the time of the second draft proposals.

charge for different business lines. The third option is an internal measurement mechanism that enables banks to use their own internal loss data to estimate the charge. The overwhelming market response to these proposals was that they resulted in too high a charge for an element of risk that is still vaguely defined. However, the three different options will produce different results, and this flexibility was introduced in the second draft after the market's negative reaction to the blanket 20% operational risk charge stated in the first draft. For instance, a senior vice-president of a middle-tier investment bank has stated that using the third approach produces a capital charge that is $500 million lower than that produced by the flat 20% charge.[9] Therefore banks will probably wish to ensure that their internal systems and procedures are developed such that they can employ the internal method.

Under the proposals, capital relief can be obtained by the use of collateral, bank guarantees and credit derivatives. This is expected to see a rise in the use of synthetic securitisations such as synthetic CDO transactions, to reduce capital exposure of bank balance sheets. The Accord stipulates a haircut to be applied to collateral, in accordance with its credit quality, as a protection against market risk. This is not controversial. Collateral, non-bank and non-soveriegn guarantees and credit derivatives also will be subject to a charge of 0.15 of the original charge on the exposure, known as *w*. This charge is designed to reflect risks associated with these instruments, such as legal and documentation risks. However, the credit derivatives market has reacted negatively to this proposal, suggesting that *w* is not required and will have an impact on the liquidity of the default swap market.

The Accord has greatest impact in emerging markets, and has been welcomed, for instance, by non-sovereign issuers in these markets. This is because under the new Accord banks may rate other banks and corporate borrowers at a higher level than the sovereign rating of the home country. Under Basel I no institution could be rated higher than its domicile country rating. As a result, banks may target stronger corporate borrowers in lower-rated emerging market economies. In the standardised approach, extra risk buckets of 50% and 150% for corporate exposures have been added to the existing 20% and 100% buckets. This makes the new Accord more risk-sensitive. The impact on bank risk-weightings of the new proposals for certain sovereign credits is given in Table 26.7. Higher-rated banks will

9 *RISK*, February 2001, p. 27.

probably wish to adopt the IRB approach, while smaller banks are likely to adopt the standardised approach until they have developed their internal risk management systems.

	Sovereign rating	Current risk weight (%)	Basel II risk weight
Australia	Aa2 / AA+	20	20
China	A3 / BBB	100	100
India	Ba2 / BB	100	100
South Korea	Baa2 / BBB	20	100
Malaysia	Baa2 / BBB	100	100
Pakistan	Caa1 / B-	100	150
Philippines	Ba1 / BB+	100	100
Singapore	Aa1 / AAA	100	20
Taiwan	Aa3 / AA+	100	20
Thailand	Baa3 / BBB-	100	100

Table 26.7 Bank risk weightings under Basel II: selected Asian economies
Ratings source: Moody's/S&P

Basel II framework

Following over six years of debate and consultation on its proposals, the BIS published the final version of the Basel II regulatory capital framework in June 2004.[10] This represented a significant milestone in risk management development. By enabling the use of advanced risk measurement techniques and internal bank credit ratings, the Basel II IRB framework should result in the adoption of stronger risk management policies, procedures and controls for banks worldwide. Although its adoption will not be required by all banks, the credit-rating agencies will generally view as a positive factor its adoption by any particular bank. Compared to the Basel I regime, general market opinion holds that the Basel I rules are a much improved benchmark for assessing capital adequacy relative to true economic risk.

The broad objectives of Basel II remain as they were at the start of the formulation process, and are:

[10] *International Convergence of Capital Measurement and Capital Standards, a Revised Framework*, Bank for International Settlements, June 2004.

- to maintain generally the same level of capital in the banking system as currently;
- to improve on the safety and rigour of financial systems worldwide;
- to allow for a more flexible approach to the measurement of risk, and to align more closely the regulatory capital framework with what is calculated by bank's own internal risk measurement systems;
- to set up an environment that would result in improvement to bank internal risk management methodologies.

The three-pillar structure described earlier in the chapter has remained in place in the final draft. The published final rules have made revisions to the earlier proposals, for all pillars. The most significant changes are to the methodology to calculate the IRB and the treatment of expected and unexpected losses.

With regard to implementation, for European Union countries this took place in January 2007 (with parallel running for up to two years after that). In the US, the regulatory authorities have determined that only the top 20 or so large banks with significant overseas operations need to adopt Basel II, from January 2008 onwards.

The final IRB approach

The basic IRB framework that was in the first proposals has remained in place. However, a significant change was the decision to base the capital charges for all asset classes on *unexpected loss* (UL) only, and not on both UL and *expected loss* (EL). In other words, banks must hold sufficient reserves to cover EL, or otherwise face a capital penalty. This move to an UL-only risk-weight arrangement should result in the alignment of regulatory capital more closely with banks' actual economic capital requirement levels.[11] A UL-only framework should result in banks regarding their capital base in a different light, but should leave overall capital levels the same. The EL portion of risk-weighted assets is part of total eligible capital provision; and shortage in eligible provisions will be deducted in a proportion of 50% from Tier 1 capital and 50% from Tier 2 capital. So the definition of Tier 1 and Tier 2 capital has changed under Basel II; the final framework withdraws the inclusion of general loan loss reserves in Tier 2 capital and excludes expected credit losses from required capital.

[11] For instance, as suggested in "An Overview and Impact Assessment of the Revised Basel II Framework", *Basel Alert* (Incisive Media) 2004, and *Demystifying Basel II* (Fitch special report), 25 August 2004.

Note that the BIS's desire to leave the general level of capital in the system at current levels means that a "scaling factor" can be applied to adjust the level of capital. This scaling factor has not been determined, but will be assessed based on data collected by the BIS during the parallel running period. It will then be applied to risk-weighted assets' value for credit risk.

The building blocks of the IRB approach remain as when first described; namely, the statistical measures of individual asset credit risk levels. This incorporates:

- probability of default (PD); that is, the measure of probability that the obligor defaults over a specified time horizon;
- loss-given-default (LGD); that is, the amount that a bank expects to incur in the event of default. A cash amount measure per asset, showing VaR in the event of default;
- exposure-at-default (EAD); that is, bank guarantees, credit lines and liquidity lines, which are the forecast amount of how much a borrower will draw upon in the event of default;
- remaining maturity (M) of an asset; that is, on the basis that an asset with a longer remaining term-to-maturity will have a higher probability of experiencing defaut or other such credit event compared to an asset of shorter maturity.

Under the advanced IRB approach a bank is allowed to calculate their own capital requirement using its own internal measures of PD, LGD, EAD and M. These will be calculated by the bank's internal model using historical data on each asset, plus asset-specific data. The calculation method itself is described in Basel II; however, a bank will supply its own internal data on the assets. This includes the confidence level: the IRB formula is calculated based on a 99.9% confidence level and a one-year time horizon. This means there is a 99.9% probability that the minimum amount of regulatory capital held by a bank will cover its economic losses over the next 12 months. Put simply, that means that statistically there is only a one in 1,000 chance that a bank's losses would erode completely its capital base, assuming that this was kept at the regulatory minimum level.

The economic losses covered by the IRB-calculated amount represent, in effect, a bank's UL. That is, they do not represent what a bank would expect to lose, which is what EL is. The EL amount, where it is calculated by a bank, must be covered by reserves.

Basel II recognises that different types of assets behave differently, and is much more flexible than Basel I in this respect. The level of economic loss of an asset will differ by asset type, notwithstanding that credit ratings might be identical. For example, for each of the following assets:

- loan to large corporate;
- loan to individual;
- loan secured by collateral;
- cash flows expected by the obligor to service and repay the loan;
- term of loan;
- loan value sensitivity to market movements;

we would expect quite different types of behaviour. Basel II provides specific capital calculation formulas for the following four asset types in a banking book: corporates, commercial real estate and retail. Different asset classes will see different capital requirements under Basel II: Figure 26.1 shows the BIS's own estimate of the change in requirements for Basel II compared to Basel I.

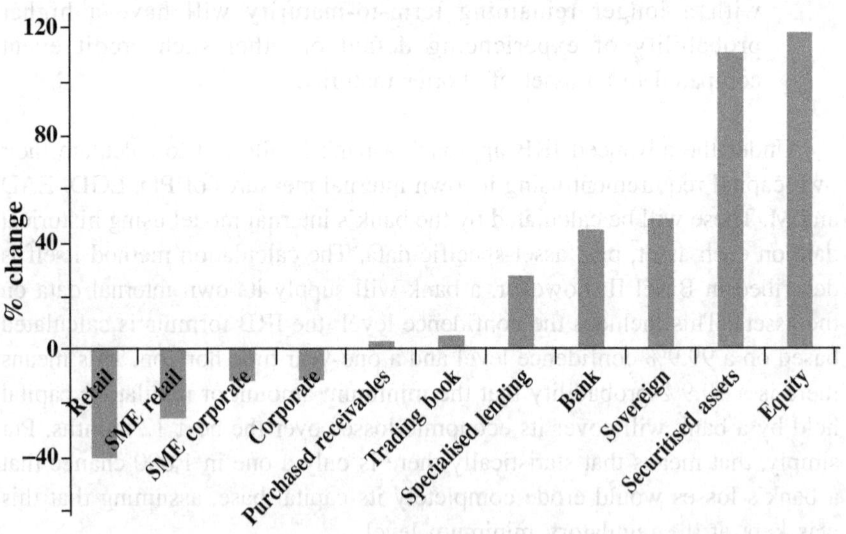

Figure 26.1 Basel II capital requirements for different asset classes: expected % change versus Basel I
Source: BIS.

Asset correlation and diversity

To allow for asset pool diversity, the Basel II capital calculation formulas assume values for the correlation between different types of assets. In this regard banks do not have a free hand: they must use the BIS correlation values and may not use ones they have calculated. Under the framework, a single risk factor is used to account for asset correlation. The BIS makes a number of assumptions about asset behaviour to allow this single factor to be used.

A downside of this is that the Basel II framework does not account for, or cover, concentration risk. For instance, if a bank had a particularly high proportion of its asset book held in a single type of asset, across a single industry or in a single geographic location, it is reasonable to assume that its asset behaviour correlation would be higher than what is stated in the Basel II framework. This opens up the risk that the bank may be putting up insufficient capital to cover its credit risk.

Securitisation

When first aired, the Basel II proposals were expected to have a significant impact on the securitisation market, but this is not so evident on final publication. There is now a common hierarchical approach to the calculation methodology that is applied under the IRB approach to determine risk-weighting for a securitisation transaction. This applies irrespective of whether a bank is the originator or an investor in the transaction. For ABCP conduits, an internal assessment approach (IAA) has been set up, to be used to calculate internal ratings. To use the IAA, a bank will need to meet certain requirements laid down in the rules.

Essentially, however, there is a uniform treatment of securitisation transactions. For use with the ratings-based approach, there is a set of appropriate risk-weights to use to calculate the weightings in a securitisation deal.

The next chapter covers the essential elements of Basel II in greater detail.

Appendix

APPENDIX 26.1 UK capital regulations

	Tier 1	Upper Tier 2	Lower Tier 2	Tier 3
Description	* Ordinary shares	* Revaluation reserves	* Dated cumulative preference shares	* Term subordinated debt
	* Preference shares (perpetual non-cumulative)	* General provisions (to maximum of 1.25% of the sum of risk-weighted assets for the regulated bank)	* Subordinated term debt	* Minority interests arising from consolidation of Tier 3 capital instruments
	* Reserves created by appropriations of retained earnings, share premium and other surpluses	* Minority interests arising from consolidation of interests in Tier 2 capital items	* Dated convertible bonds	
	* Audited retained profit from previous year	* Hybrid capital instruments (if perpetual and cumulative)		
	* Minority interests	* Capitalisation of property reserves		
Deductions	* Bank's holdings of own Tier 1 paper	* See Lower Tier 2	* Selected investments in subsidiaries and associates	
	* Goodwill and other intangible assets		* Connected lending of a capital nature and qualifying holdings	
	* Current year's unpublished losses		* All holdings of capital instruments issued by other credit institutions and financial entities	

	* Capitalisation of property revaluation reserves		* Holdings of own capital	
Innovative Tier 1 capital	* Permitted			
Maturity	* Undated	* Undated; no repayment without regulator's permission	* Minimum five years and one day from draw-down date	* Minimum initial maturity of two years
Call characteristics	* Only after five years	* Generally after five years and one day	* No early repayment without consent of the Financial Services Authority (FSA)	* No early repayment without regulator's consent
	* Call option at discretion of issuer (five-year intervals between calls)		* Not before five years and one day	
	* Must have no other provisions which require future redemption			
Step-up	* Only after ten years	* Yes, a maximum of 50 bps in the first 10 years of issue and a maximum of 100 bps over the whole life of the issue	* See Upper Tier 2	* Yes, see Upper Tier 2, but not before five years
	* Maximum of 100 bps, less swap spread between the initial and stepped-up indices, or 50% of the initial credit spread less the swap spread between the initial and	* Subordinated debt issues with set-ups in the first five years are inelgible for inclusion in the capital base		

	stepped-up indices			
Interest accrual	* Non-cumulative (but may be paid in scrip)	* Cumulative, deferred interest may bear interest, but not at penal rates	* Non-payment constitutes default	* Cumulative blocking clause: neither interest nor principal may be paid if, as a result, own funds will fall below minimum requirement. Must notify FSA if capital ratio falls below 10%
Interest deferral	* Yes	* Yes, at option of issuer	* N/A	* Yes, see Upper Tier 2, but not before five years
Loss absorption	* Yes	* Yes, conversion into common equity either initial or deemed	* N/A	* No
Subordination	* Junior to Tier 2 capital except for dated preference shares with which it ranks *pari passu*	* Generally subordinated to Lower Tier 2	* Subordinated to all senior creditors * Generally subordinated to Tier 3 in a winding-up	* Generally senior to Lower Tier 2 in a winding-up
Amortisation			* Amortised over the last five years at a rate of 20% per annum	* No

Source: Financial Services Authority.

References and bibliography

Basel Committee on Banking Supervision 1995, *An Internal Model-based Approach to Market Risk Capital Requirements*, Bank for International Settlements, Basel.

Bhattacharya, S. and Thakor, R. 1993, "Contemporary Banking Theory", *Journal of Financial Intermediation*, 3–1, October, pp. 2–50.

Cass, D. 2001, "Basel Part One: The New Accord", *RISK*, February, pp. 24–9.

Dimson, E. and Marsh, P. 1995, "Capital Requirements for Securities Firms", *Journal of Finance*, 50, pp. 821–51.

Moir, C. 1999, "Basle or Bust?", *Securities and Investment Review*, September, London, pp. 6–7.

PriceWaterhouse 1991, *Bank Capital Adequacy and Capital Convergence*, PriceWaterhouseCoopers.

Van Deventer, D. and Imai, K. 2003, *Credit Risk Models and the Basel Accords*, John Wiley & Sons, New Jersey.

Wall, L., Pringle, J. and McNulty, J. 1990, "Capital Requirements for Interest-rate and Foreign Exchange Hedges", Federal Reserve Bank of Atlanta, *Economic Review*, 75, May–June, pp. 14–29.

CHAPTER

27

A Primer on Basel II

The Basel II rules were published in final form in June 2004.[1] Although they replace the Basel I framework on the calculation of bank capital requirements, they are not being implemented in every jurisdiction. However, most banks worldwide will be required to adopt the rules, including all banks in the European Union.[2] This chapter follows on from Chapter 26 and considers the main tenets of the new rules, and the likely impact of the rules on specific sectors and asset classes. We also present some example calculations.

A proper assessment of the impact of Basel II will have to wait until it has been implemented across most jurisdictions for at least one year; one conclusion that can be reached right away is that the new rules will result in a realignment of capital into sectors that require a lower regulatory charge. This will result in a rebalancing of bank asset portfolios, which is very relevant for ALM strategy. However, the issue of which asset classes should be targeted under the new regime, and which ones should be divested, is outside the scope of this book. This chapter concentrates instead on the essentials behind the main rulings contained in the BIS document, and which are important from an ALM strategist's point of view.

---

1 The actual title of the document, published by the Basel Committee on Banking Supervision of the Bank for International Settlements on 26 June 2004, is *International Convergence of Capital Measurements and Capital Standards*.

2 At the time of writing, the European Union was implementing the rules from January 2007, while the United States was implementing them from January 2008. See the case study on page 1203.

Introduction

The aim of Basel II is to align economic and regulatory capital more closely than was the case under Basel I. It introduces three different approaches that a bank can adopt to achieve this: the standardised approach, which is not far removed from the current Basel I framework, but which applies more risk-weighting categories and uses formal credit ratings; and the foundation and advanced internal ratings-based (IRB) approaches, which are more complex and allow for a bank to use its own risk models and risk exposure data in line with the Basel II framework. The implementation of the new rules should result in changes in specic areas of bank and ALM activity, with certain products and sectors seeing greater activity and other areas less, as capital is realigned and banks seek to meet adjusted required target rates of return.

Overview

We now have the final form of the new rules, so we can suggest some likely impacts upon implementation. Of course, the full effects can only be accurately gauged a few years after full implementation. But a preliminary analysis would suggest a number of developments.

Given that the primary objective behind Basel II is to better align economic with regulatory capital, we can conclude that banking activity exhibiting low economic risk will attract a low capital charge. Such activity might include residential mortgages and high-grade corporate lending. By the same token, business that previously was of interest to banks because the regulatory treatment seemed less onerous compared to the perceived economic risk, such as low-rated securitisation tranches and non-OECD country lending, should become less attractive. Following this logic, banks that have a high proportion of lower risk business, such as commercial and retail banks, will find that their capital charge has reduced. The model-based approaches, foundation and advanced IRB, require less capital to be held, compared to the standardised approach. Implementing these approaches will call for a large investment in risk management models and internal data systems – something only the larger banks can afford. Thus an advantage is presented to large banks over small banks straight away.

Figures 27.2 and 27.3 on pages 1235 and 1236, which form part of the discussion on the new operational risk capital charge, show the results of a BIS study on the expected change in capital levels compared to the Basel I regime.

Three-pillar approach

The cornerstone of the Basel II rules is the three-pillar approach. These are the minimum capital requirements, the supervisory review and market discipline. A general description of these follows.

- *Minimum capital requirements*: the objective of these is to produce a closer link between economic and regulatory capital. The idea here is to remove any possibility of regulatory capital arbitrage, which was common under Basel I. There is a more tailored regime, with more specific targeting of individual credits rather the broad-brush approach of Basel I, which targeted whole asset classes. An example of this was the 20% risk-weighting to OECD-country banks, which meant some low-rated banks required the same capital put aside against them as very highly rated banks. The 100% risk-weighting for all corporates, regardless of their credit quality or country of incorporation, was another example of this. Also within this pillar is a more contentious issue, a new capital charge for operational risk. This is designed to cover the risk of IT breakdown, as well as risks such as fraud and trading irregularity.

  The definition of bank capital remains as it is under Basel I, and the minimum capital ratios of 4% for Tier 1 and 8% for total capital also remain in place. So Pillar 1, and Basel II as a whole, is concerned only with the denominator of the capital ratio calculation as established under Basel I, and not the numerator, which stays unchanged.[3]
- *Supervisory review process*: this is the focus of Pillar 2 and covers the national regulator's review of bank capital assessment models. It describes the process by which the regulator sets minimum capital requirements that exceed those outlined in Pillar 1, with the exact requirements being a function of the risk profile of each bank. Banks also must assess their credit concentration risks, and stress-test these under various conditions.
- *Enhanced public disclosure*: this Pillar 3 strand requires banks to publish their risk-weighting calculations, capital breakdown and capital adequacy requirements.

[3] There is a slight change to the numerator in the ratio under Basel II in circumstances where deductions of capital for certain asset classes must be made, but this will not apply to all banks.

Approaches to credit risk

Basel II rules can be implemented under three alternative approaches: the standardised, foundation IRB and advanced IRB approaches. Briefly, these can be described as follows:

- *standardised approach*: the most straightforward to apply, with risk-weights being assigned according to asset class or formal credit ratings. The assets are described as residential mortgages, corporate loans and so on;
- *foundation IRB*: under foundation IRB, the capital calculation is made after the bank itself sets default probabilities for each class of assets. The bank assigns probabilities of default (PD) to each asset class, or each asset in accordance with credit rating; using Basel II guidelines it then sets the loss-given-default (LGD), exposure-at-default (EAD) and maturity (M) parameters. These inputs are then used to calculate risk-weights for each asset class using the Basel II capital calculation formula. Foundation IRB may be used as a stepping-stone before implementation of the advanced IRB methodology, or retained as a calculation method in its own right;
- *advanced IRB*: under advanced IRB, a bank will calculate risk-weights using its own parameters, which are arrived at from its own default data and internal models.

Under the IRB approach the banks may use their own data, significantly including data for PD, LGD and EAD. Their own model can be used to calculate risk-weights, which is then adjusted by a scaling factor. In practice this means a scaling factor of 1.06 will be applied. Note that a bank must adopt the same approach for both its banking book and its trading book.

The majority of banks, especially those outside Europe, are expected to employ the standardised approach. Smaller banks with extensive retail and mortgage business are also expected to adopt the standardised approach. Only the largest banks are expected to adopt the advanced IRB approach, which requires significant investment in internal systems. Banks that do wish to implement the advanced IRB approach must seek supervisory approval of their systems and models from their national regulator.

Operational risk

Basel II introduces a capital set-aside to cover operational risk, which was a contentious departure from the requirements of Basel I. Banks are required to calculate a capital charge for operational risk, separate to the capital charge for credit risk. Each approach has its own calculation method. The general calculation is that a bank must apply 15% of its average revenue over the last three years; revenue is defined as net interest income (NII) plus non-interest income.[4] Under the standardised approach a bank may calculate its own level of operational risk, per business line, and apply the capital charge based on this risk exposure. The charge itself can then lie within a 12%–18% range, rather than the uniform 15% level.

Under the advanced IRB approach a bank will calculate its own operational risk level and then apply its own capital charge, under BIS guidelines. This enables a bank to set lower operational risk charges for certain business lines, where it can show that the risk exposure is lower.

Overall expected impact

Table 27.1 on pages 1199–200 is a summary of the main differences between Basel I and II by asset class. Certain sectors, such as residential mortgages and high-credit-rated corporate lending, gain substantially under the new regime, whereas some businesses, such as fund management, which previously attracted no charge, now carry the operational risk charge.

It is safe to say that the full impact of Basel II on banking business will only be completely apparent a few years after implementation. However, we can gauge some general expected effects by making a broad-brush comparison, as shown in Table 27.1. As regulatory capital is realigned in banks, as they seek to minimise their capital charge, we would expect the following:

- *corporate lending*: this is perhaps the most significant impact area. The uniform 100% risk-weighting under Basel I has been removed, with charges now varying according to credit rating. This will impact in a number of ways. Lower-rated borrowers can expect higher lending rates, as banks turn away from this sector, while paradoxically they may increase lending to unrated corporate entities. Highly rated entities may return to straight bank lending from capital market borrowing, as this will be a capital-charge-friendly sector for banks. The standardised approach favours lower-rated and unrated

[4] Some national regulators have specified that a bank may take average volume of business, such as volume of assets, over the last three years rather than revenues.

Asset class	Risk-weights Basel I	Basel II		Notes
		Standardised	IRB (⊗)	
Sovereign	0% OECD	0–150%(*)	0–400%	New regime is essentially rating-based. 100% risk-weighting for unrated sovereigns. Lower-rated OECD sovereigns attract a higher charge, whereas high-rated non-OECD sovereigns now attract lower charges.
	100% non-OECD			
Bank sector	20% OECD	20–150%*	6–400%	There are two approaches, either (i) one rank lower than sovereign rating or (ii) based on the bank's own credit rating.
	100% non-OECD			Unrated banks carry 50% weighting. Banks rated A to BBB attract a higher charge of 50% from 20% under the old regime.
Retail				
– mortgages	50%	35%	13–227%	Banks with large and/or high-quality mortgage books will have an incentive to move to IRB.
– credit card, etc.	100%	75%	10–227%	Overdue unsecured loans are weighted at 100–150% under the standardised approach.
Corporate loans	100%	20–150%	14–400%	Under IRB there is more favourable treatment for investment-grade-rated loans. Under the standardised approach there is a gain for certain sub-investment grade loans and also, paradoxically, for unrated lending. The latter attract 100% under the standardised approach.

Small/Medium enterprises (SME)	100%	100%	11–198%	Certain lending to small corporates (<EUR50m annual sales) gains advantages under Basel II.
Structured finance (ABS, etc.)	100% 50% AAA/ AA-rated RMBS	20–1250%	7–1250%	There is a deduction from capital for tranches rated below B+. There is favourable treatment for senior tranches, which attract a lower charge compared to Basel I. This may result in increased demand for senior tranches of ABS/MBS/CDO/SIV. There is a higher charge for sub-investment-grade tranches.
Operational risk	0%	15%	12–18%	A new charge, the effect is to increase overall capital charge for most banks. Biggest impact on business lines in banking that attract no regulatory capital charge under Basel I (e.g., fund management, advisory services, etc.).

⊗ Ranges given under assumptions of worst case scenarios including 50% LGD and 10% PD.

* There is a reduced risk-weighting if the exposure is denominated, and funded, in the bank's domestic currency.

Table 27.1 Comparison of regime change from Basel I to Basel II
Sources: BIS, EU CRD.

lending, while the IRB approach will favour high-rated lending. It may be then that banks adopting the standardised approach conduct more lower-rated corporate lending than IRB-based banks;

- *bank lending*: the uniform 20%/100% split between OECD and non-OECD banks has been removed, so the interbank market will experience significant impact. Higher-rated banks domiciled in non-OECD countries such as Malaysia will benefit as they should be able to access more lending lines. Conversely, low-rated banks in OECD countries such as Italy will find their borrowing rates increase;
- *retail business*: residential mortgage business will attract a lower charge and so mortgage banks, or banks with a high percentage of residential mortgage business, will benefit. Some retail business, particularly unsecured retail lending, will attract higher charges so this may be to customers' detriment;
- *subsidiary business*: large integrated banking groups may hive off business lines that previously attracted no regulatory capital charge, but now attract 15% operational risk charge.

Investment banks may find that commercial banks that undertake more traditional-style business are now a good strategic fit for their business, leading to merger or acquisition, as these banks will attract low capital charges under Basel II.

Implementation

The BIS has timetabled a period of parallel running of Basel I and II in the first year after Basel II is introduced. Initial implementation in the European Union and Asia is set for January 2007, so there will be parallel running for banks adopting the foundation IRB approach for one year after this date. Parallel running for banks adopting the advanced IRB approach will continue for another year after this, to January 2009. The United States has delayed implementation of Basel II until January 2008, and only for a specified handful of the largest banks.

The European Union has published its own interpretation of the BIS rules, known as the Capital Requirements Directive (CRD). This is essentially identical to Basel II, except for a different treatment of the capital deductibility for a bank group insurance subsidiary. Under CRD, the standard deduction of 50% from Tier 1 capital and 50% from Tier 2 capital has been left out, with the European Union leaving this issue to national regulators.

At the time of writing over 60 countries had shown an intention to adopt Basel II, compared with the over 100 countries that would have been operating under Basel I as at June 2006.[5]

CASE STUDY 27.1 The Basel II implementation timetable

The Basel II framework is not being implemented worldwide in one step. Banks in the European Union will adopt the rules, in accordance with the CAD directive, from January 2007 for the standardised and foundation IRB approach, and from January 2008 for the advanced IRB approach. The latter will allow an extra year of parallel running. Most Asian countries – including Japan, Hong Kong, Singapore and India – have set up the same timetable. The United States will implement the standardised and foundation approach from January 2008 and the advanced IRB approach in January 2009, one year later than the European Union, with the opportunity to conduct parallel running also delayed by one year, from January 2008. Only nine of the country's largest banks, its globally integrated banking houses such as Citigroup and JPMorgan Chase, will be required to adopt the new framework. The remainder of the country's banks will continue to follow the Basel I rules, with Basel II being only a voluntary requirement for these banks.

Impact on specific sectors

To illustrate Basel II further, we consider it with regard to specific selected asset classes. One can gain some idea of the objectives of the new rules by looking at the impact on different business lines. We review sovereigns first, followed by bank assets, structured finance securities, corporate and retail lending, and credit derivatives.

Sovereign assets

As was the case with all asset classes, the treatment of sovereign debt under Basel I was very simple. Sovereigns were divided into OECD and non-

[5] *Source*: BIS.

OECD debt.[6] OECD sovereign debt was risk-weighted at 0%, while non-OECD sovereigns were weighted at 100%. Under Basel II there is a deeper distinction, with the risk-weighting assigned by credit rating (under the standardised approach). This is shown at Table 27.2.

Basel I		Basel II	
OECD	0%	AA– and above	0%
Non-OECD	100%	A	20%
		BBB	50%
		BB+ to B–	100%
		Below B–	150%
		Unrated	100%

Table 27.2 Basel II sovereign debt risk weightings (standardised approach)
Source: BIS.

Both IRB approaches use banks' own internal measures of risk. Under the standardised approach, formal credit ratings from the "external credit assessment institutions" (ECAIs) assume a high importance. The BIS document describing Basel II states that if a country carries a rating each from S&P, Moody's and Fitch, and one of these is lower than the other two, then the higher one can be assumed. For a bank holding the debt of a country like China, which is rated A/A2/A– this rule has no impact; however, for a bank holding the debt of Hungary, which is rated A1/BBB+/A, this is significant. It means that the bank can take the two higher ratings, which enable it to apply a 20% risk-weighting. This is a considerable saving compared to the Basel I weighting of 100%.

An effective, if simple, illustration of the new regime can be given as follows: consider a bank holding two bonds, each of USD10 million nominal, issued by Korea and South Africa respectively. Under Basel I, and taking the minimum 8% capital requirement, the capital charges for each are:

[6] The Organisation for Economic Cooperation and Development (OECD) member countries are Australia, Austria, Belgium, Canada, Czech Republic, Denmark, Finland, France, Germany, Greece, Hungary, Iceland, Ireland, Italy, Japan, Korea, Luxembourg, Mexico, the Netherlands, New Zealand, Norway, Poland, Portugal, Slovakia, Spain, Sweden, Switzerland, Turkey, United Kingdom and the United States.

Korea government bond capital:
USD 0.00
South Africa government bond capital:
[10,000,000 × 100% × 8%] or USD800,000

Under the Basel II standardised approach the charges are:

Korea
[10,000,000 × 50% × 8%] or USD400,000
South Africa
[10,000,000 × 50% × 8%] or USD400,000.

So in this stylised example the impact is quite significant. The make-up and composition of government bond portfolios in banks will be reviewed and heavily influenced by each sovereign credit ECAI. As capital charges rise for certain borrowers compared to others, those sovereigns that suffer an adverse impact in terms of the capital that a bank investor is required to hold against them may find their issuance yields rise. It is not necessarily emerging-market sovereigns that will be so impacted. Italy is currently rated at A by S&P (although it is rated Aa2 by Moody's and AA by Fitch). If one of the other agencies also effects a downgrade to Italian sovereign debt, then such debt will lose its 0% risk-weighting under Basel II standardised approach rules. This point also highlights an advantage of adopting the IRB rules. Under foundation IRB, countries such as Italy and Greece that will, or may, attract a 20% weighting under a standardised approach will probably be weighted at 0% under a bank's own PD values for sovereign debt. However, there is no doubt that higher-rated non-OECD sovereigns will gain under Basel II, and may well see their bond yield spreads narrow. Less clear-cut, but still a strong possibility, is that lower-rated OECD members will see their debt attract a higher charge.

Description of calculation

Although we describe the calculation for sovereign assets here, note that much of the calculation framework for Basel II is the same for corporates as well as sovereign assets. Under Basel II the standardised approach applies risk-weights in accordance with asset credit rating, as shown in Table 27.2. Under the IRB approach, banks that meet minimum specified requirements, and have obtained their regulator's approval, can use their internal estimates of risk parameters to determine their capital requirements. These parameters are:

- probability-of-default (*PD*): this is key to the IRB approach, and is the one-year probability that an obligor will default;
- loss-given-default (*LGD*): this is a measure of the expected average loss that a bank will suffer per unit of asset or exposure, in the event of counterparty default. Whereas a borrower can only have one credit rating and hence only one PD, different sets of exposure to the same borrower may have different LGDs; for example, if one exposure is collateralised and another is not;
- exposure-at-default (*EAD*): this is a measure of the extent to which a bank is exposed to a counterparty in the event of the latter's default. For cash transactions, this amount is the nominal amount of the exposure. For derivative transactions and transactions with variable drawdown options, a credit conversion factor is applied to convert notional amounts to nominal values;
- maturity (*M*): generally speaking, longer-dated loans represent higher credit risk. Up to a point, the longer the maturity of an exposure the higher the probability of decrease in its credit quality; hence, the higher the PD. Somewhat counter-intuitively, this effect is higher for better-rated entities, because the higher the credit rating the more downward categories, short of default, there are for the entity to migrate to. Hence the risk-weight, in terms of M, is actually higher.

Foundation IRB: a bank adopting this approach may use its internal credit risk-scoring model to estimate PD,[7] but must use BIS-prescribed LGD, EAD and M values. Senior unsecured claims on corporates, sovereigns and banks are assigned a 45% LGD; subordinated unsecured borrowings are assigned a 75% LGD. There is an assigned value of 2.5 for M. For EAD a credit conversion factor of 75% is applied for undrawn liquidity facilities and unused credit lines.

Advanced IRB: banks that implement the advanced IRB approach will use their own values for PD, EAD and LGD, and calculate their own M value. Because national regulatory authorities will also be setting their own prescribed levels for these parameters, adopting the advanced approach will be beneficial for banks that believe their own estimates will be lower than those of the regulator. The calculation of M is dependent on the cash flows of the actual assets on the book. Generally, if the M value is below 2.5, then the risk-weight will be lower under the advanced approach compared to the

[7] There is a minimum level of 0.03% specified by BIS for corporates and banks.

foundation approach. If M lies above 2.5, then the opposite is true. The maximum value for M is 5.0.

Formulas: for all assets not in default, the formulas for calculating the risk-weights and capital requirements under both foundation and advanced approaches are as follows:

Correlation (R) =

$$0.12 \times \frac{[1 - \exp(-50 \times PD)]}{[1 - \exp(-50)]} + 0.24 \times \left[1 - \frac{[1 - \exp(-50 \times PD)]}{[1 - \exp(-50)]}\right]. \tag{27.1}$$

Maturity adjustment (b) =

$$(0.11852 - 0.05478 \times 1\text{n}(PD))^2. \tag{27.2}$$

Capital requirement (K) =

$$\left[LGD \times N\left((1 - R)^{0.5} \times G(PD) + \left[\frac{R}{(1 - R)}\right]^{0.5} \times G(0.999)\right) - (PD \times LGD)\right]$$

$$\times \left(\frac{1}{1 - 1.5 \times b}\right) \times [1 + (M - 2.5) \times b] \tag{27.3}$$

where

$N(\ )$ is the cumulative distribution function for a standard normal variable with $N(0, 1)$

$G(z)$ is the inverse cumulative distribution function for a standard normal variable (that is, the value of x is such that $N(x) = z$).

Risk-weighted assets (RWA) =

$$K \times 12.5 \times EAD.$$

The formula for K says that, ignoring the correlation and maturity factors, the capital requirement represents the difference between the loss under the worst case scenario (assumed to be an event with a probability less than 0.1%) and the expected loss (given by $PD \times LGD$).

Of course, the correlation parameter is key, because the defaults of different obligors are not independent of each other. General macroeconomic factors impact all obligors, more so for higher-rated entities (on the assumption that lower-rated firms are more likely to experience difficulty due to firm-specific issues rather than the general state of the economy). The correlation parameter value in the formula lies between 0.12 and 0.24; the value increases from 0.12 for entities with a higher credit rating. The maturity adjustment factor *b* is a correction to allow for the fact that the tenor of the exposure will be shorter or longer than the benchmark value of 2.5.

The standard formula given here is not used for assets in default. For such exposures the capital requirement is given by:

$$Max\,[0, LGD - (PD \times LGD)]$$

where the expected loss $(PD \times LGD)$ is the bank's best estimate. This estimate is used to calculate loan loss provision and set-off charges for each asset in default.

Example illustration[8]

To help illustrate the new calculation rules, and as an indication of how capital requirements can be significantly different under Basel II when compared to Basel I, we present a stylised example using two sovereign assets. Imagine that a bank holds the following two sovereign bonds:

- USD100 million, Republic of Turkey ten-year, rated BB–;
- USD100 million, Malaysia ten-year, rated A–.

Under Basel I the regulatory capital requirement for this portfolio is zero for the Turkey bond, because the country is an OECD member, and USD8 million for the Malaysia bond, which is 100% risk-weighted.

Under Basel II this requirement changes, with the exact calculation being dependent on the approach being adopted.

[8] The author thanks Rameez Saboowala for his assistance with gathering data for use in this section.

Standardised approach
Under the standardised approach, the ratings of each sovereign determine its risk-weighting.[9] So the capital calculation is:

- Turkey: USD4 million;
- Malaysia: USD1.6 million.

This illustrates a general comment on the impact of Basel II compared to Basel I: under the simple standardised approach, asset portfolios that gain include those of highly rated non-OECD obligations such as China, Chile, Hong Kong and South Africa, while portfolios that would suffer higher capital charges would include OECD-member countries that are lower-rated, such as Mexico, Poland, Slovakia, South Korea and, as shown here, Turkey. In our example, the holding of the Turkey sovereign bond suffers a significant increase in capital charge, while the Malaysia bond benefits from a much-reduced requirement.

Foundation IRB
For this example we extract statistical data from debt market prices in January 2006. This is given in Table 27.3 on page 1210. For the PD values these are unnecessarily severe, and rating agency PD would for both countries be nearer to zero.[10] However, the illustration works better using our unrealistic estimates, which produce the risk-weights shown in Table 27.3. The M and LGD values are those prescribed in the BIS document for the foundation approach.

With the calculated risk-weights, we produce a capital requirement of:

- Turkey: USD5.1 million;
- Malaysia: USD3.3 million.

So under foundation IRB we have a still higher capital charge for Turkey, and a lower requirement for Malaysia. Note that our calculation, using market data from 2006, produced different results to the BIS example calculation released at the time of the final draft.

---

9 In our example there is one uniform rating for each exposure. Very broadly speaking, if a sovereign or other entity is rated differently across different agencies, the lower rating applies.

10 And this is significant: at a zero PD there would be a zero capital requirement, because there is no minimum level of PD for sovereign exposures. For corporate exposures, a minimum floor PD applies irrespective of rating.

	PD	Correlation factor	M	LGD[(1)]
Turkey	0.34	0.2	2.5	45%
Malaysia	0.15	0.2	2.5	45%

(1) Senior-level debt

	Risk-weights
Turkey	66%
Malaysia	41%

Table 27.3 Calculation parameters

Advanced IRB

Under the advanced IRB, as sovereign Malaysia has a lower PD value its impact is, somewhat counter-intuitively, greater over a longer period compared to Turkey. This produces a greater increase in capital charge for a ten-year exposure for Malaysia compared to Turkey. The risk-weight for Malaysia rises from 41% to 66%, while that for Turkey rises from 66% to 100%.

Note that the values arrived under advanced IRB are heavily influenced by the PD, M and LGD parameters used. Significant differences in results can emerge based on what values are assigned for these inputs. For example, rating-agency PDs often differ greatly from CDS-implied PD values. In the case of sovereign exposures, because PDs can assume zero value, the choice of which number to use is significant.

Basel I and Basel II comparison

The hypothetical example above illustrated in obvious terms the impact of the new capital regime. This impact is best viewed in terms of risk-weights, and how specific single-exposure risk-weights change from the early regime to the new one. It is apparent though that Basel II results in a less "scatter-gun" approach when assigning risk-weights.

Table 27.4 shows an example of calculated IRB risk-weights for an arbitrary set of country exposures, compared to the Basel I risk-weights. These values were presented by the BIS in June 2004, and are a good illustration of the impact of the new rules.

Country	Basel I	Standardised Basel II	Foundation IRB	Advanced IRB
Australia	0%	20%	0%	0%
Chile	100%	20%	30%	47%
China	100%	20%	44%	68%
Czech Republic	0%	20%	0%	0%
Hong Kong	100%	20%	0%	0%
Indonesia	100%	100%	143%	153%
Malaysia	100%	50%	0%	0%
Poland	0%	50%	44%	68%
Portugal	0%	50%	44%	47%
Slovakia	0%	50%	0%	0%
South Africa	100%	50%	57%	86%
South Korea	0%	20%	57%	86%

Table 27.4 Comparison of Basel I and Basel II risk-weights: selected countries
Sources: BIS based on S&P rating agency data.

Bank assets

For bank ALM strategy purposes this is perhaps the most important asset class to assess with respect to the impact of Basel II. Banks are significant holders of short- and medium-term bank-issued debt, and will look to rebalance liquidity portfolios for any types of asset that are adversely affected under the new rules.[11]

Note that Basel II does not redefine (or seek to redefine) bank "capital". The definition of Tier 1 and Tier 2 capital remains the same as under Basel I. So a bank holding another bank's capital instruments must continue to observe specific rules, although in practice there might be a possibility of more favourable treatment in practice under the IRB approach. Essentially, a holding of bank capital in the form of equity or subordinated debt by another bank, that is greater than the equivalent of 10% of the holding bank's own capital, is deducted from the holding bank's capital base or risk-weighted at 100%. In other words, a minimum of 8% capital would have to be held against an asset comprised of bank capital, whether this is Tier 1 equity, upper Tier 2 or lower Tier 2 subordinated debt. Under the IRB

[11] Banks hold a large part of their liquidity book in short-term bank debt such as CDs, CP and FRNs.

approach in Basel II, there is no specific new treatment for bank capital, but applying the IRB rules may result in some bank capital being risk-weighted at lower than 100%. We can see how this may well be the case where the instrument is issued by a highly-rated bank.

Short-term debt

The new rules for short-term bank debt can be summarised as follows:

- debt of one-year maturity or less is assigned 20% risk-weighting, assuming it is rated at A–1/P–1.[12] Short-term bank debt rated at A–2/P–2 is assigned a 50% weighting, while A–3/P–3 paper is weighted at 100%;
- very short-term debt of three-month maturity or less that is unrated, but whose issuer has a long-term rating equivalent to A–3/P–3, will be rated at 20%.

Essentially, it is apparent that virtually all short-term bank paper will continue to be rated at 20%, which is unchanged from the Basel I regime. The preferential treatment of very short-term debt, which enables even low-rated (A–3/P–3) assets to be weighted at 20% is prescribed in Option 2 of the standardised approach to bank debt (see Example 27.2). It is not available under Option 1, so banks that are required to adopt the latter by their national regulator will not have this flexibility. Under Option 1 short-term assets will be rated at 20%, 50% and 100% for A–1/P–1, A–2/P–2 and A–3/P–3 ratings respectively. In the event that a sovereign or bank has three ratings, the two highest ratings will apply.

Table 27.5 summarises the Option 1 and Option 2 risk-weights.

We can identify certain anomalies that may arise under this two-alternative ruling. For all assets of over three-month maturity, there is a clear difference at the BBB+ to BBB– rating band. Under Option 1 a bank in that rating range would be 100% risk-weighted, whereas under Option 2 it would carry only a 50% risk-weighting. Another potential anomaly is a BBB-rated bank incorporated in an A-rated country: under Option 1 it would carry a 50% weighting, compared to a 100% weighting under Option 2. Note also the preferential treatment for very short-term bank debt under Option 2.

From Table 27.5 we would conclude that banks of lower credit rating, but which are incorporated in a highly rated country, would benefit from the

[12] Note that the highest S&P short-term rating is A–1+, while the highest Moody's short-term rating is P–1.

Option 1: Central government risk-weight-based method

Rating of sovereign	AAA to AA–	A+ to A–	BBB+ to BBB–	BB+ to B–	Below B–	Unrated
Risk-weight for senior bank debt	20%	50%	100%	100%	150%	100%

Option 2: Credit assessment-based method

Rating of bank	AAA to AA–	A+ to A–	BBB+ to BBB–	BB+ to B–	Below B–	Unrated
Risk-weight for senior bank debt	20%	50%	50%	100%	150%	50%
Risk-weight for very short-term senior debt (< 3-month maturity)	20%	20%	20%	50%	150%	20%

Table 27.5 Basel II bank debt capital charge, Option 1 and Option 2
Source: BIS.

adoption of Option 1, while in the case of the converse Option 2 would be advantageous.[13] Note that the United Kingdom's regulatory agency, the Financial Services Authority, has stated that Option 2 is the more risk-sensitive of the two approaches and should be the one that is used.[14]

EXAMPLE 27.1 Bank debt risk-weight options

Under Basel I bank debt was risk-weighted at 20% if the bank was incorporated in an OECD country and 100% if incorporated in a non-OECD country. Under the Basel II standardised approach the risk-weights are a function of the bank's credit rating. National regulators have two options: Option 1, where the risk-weighting is assigned based on the credit rating of the country of incorporation, and Option 2, under which the risk-weights are based on the actual bank's own external credit rating. The weights differ according to which option is selected (see Table 27.5).

IRB approach

The procedure for applying the IRB rules in both foundation and advanced form for bank assets is virtually identical to that used for sovereign assets. The only significant difference is that a minimum value of 0.03% for the PD parameter must be applied for bank assets when calculating the risk weighting. If applying foundation IRB, a bank may use its own internal credit analysis results when estimating the PD parameter (subject to the 0.03% minimum), while the values for the EAD, LGD and M parameters are set in the BIS guidelines. Senior unsecured bank debt is assigned a 45% LGD value, with subordinated unsecured debt given a 75% LGD level. The value for M is 2.5. If applying advanced IRB, a bank may use its own internally calculated values for PD, EAD, LGD and M.

As we may have guessed by now, the change from the Basel I regime will be felt mainly with regard to lower-rated bank assets. Under Option 2 of Basel II, risk-weighting for bank assets that are rated at A or BBB will rise to 50% from the previous level of 20%. The capital required to be held

[13] Note that the rating agencies do not rate a corporate entity, including a bank, at a higher rating than the rating of its country of incorporation (although an equivalent rating is possible). Hence, such banks are rare beasts.

[14] Consultation Paper 189, FSA.

against instruments issued by weaker-rated banks will therefore be substantially higher under Basel II, which implies that the yield payable on such instruments will rise to compensate. Until Basel II has been in place for at least one year or more; however, it is difficult to describe further what its likely impact should be. In particular, banks that implement the advanced IRB approach may see substantial reductions in their capital charge, with all the implications that carries for such banks vis-à-vis banks that do not employ the advanced approach.

Covered bonds[15]

Under Basel I covered bonds were risk-weighted at 10%, which made them particularly attractive for both issuers and bank investors.[16] In the Basel II standardised approach regime, covered bonds will be assigned the same weighting as senior subordinated debt, which places them at 10% risk-weight for banks rated AA and above, and 20% for other banks. From Table 27.6 on page 1216 we see a wide range of ratings for just a small sample of banks.[17] However, if a bank applies foundation or advanced IRB this weighting is likely to fall to below 10%. Therefore these assets could become more attractive for banks employing the IRB approach, with the attendant implications for both yield spreads and further issuance.

A consideration for banks with large residential mortgage portfolios is the choice of whether to concentrate on issuing covered bonds or RMBS. Securitising mortgage books not only achieves capital relief for banks under Basel I, it is also an important liquidity and funding mechanism for many banks. In the United Kingdom, banks such as Northern Rock plc and Bradford & Bingley plc followed the example of credit card banks in the United States and were able to significantly grow their mortgage books after employing securitisation techniques. This makes RMBS generally more attractive as a balance sheet management tool than covered bonds. Under Basel II though, for many banks there will no longer be a capital advantage in securitising residential mortgages – it will be cheaper, in capital charge terms, to keep them on their balance sheet. Therefore covered bonds may become more attractive for these banks, rather than RMBS.

[15] Covered bonds are described in Chapter 20.

[16] Covered bonds issued by banks in Italy, Portugal, Sweden and the United Kingdom were assigned 20% risk-weighting by their respective national regulators, thus making them equal in capital charge terms to other bank debt instruments in these jurisdictions.

[17] *Pfandbriefe* are a particular type of MBS issued by banks in Germany, which are very similar to covered bonds. For more detail on Pfandbriefe securities see the chapter by Harry Cross in Fabozzi and Choudhry (2004).

	S&P	Moody's
Pfandbriefe issues		
Depfa	A+	Aa3
EuroHypo	A	A2
HypoBank AG	BBB	Baa1
Covered bonds		
Banco Santander	A+	Aa3
Bayerische Landesbank	AAA	Aaa
Bradford & Bingley	–	A1
HBOS	AA	Aa2
Lloyds TSB	Aa2	AA–
Northern Rock	A	A1
West LB	AA–	Aa3

Table 27.6 Covered bond ratings sample
Sources: Moody's/S&P.

Repo agreements and securities lending

A 0% risk-weight is applied to an exposure that is collateralised under a repo agreement if the counterparty is a "core market participant". Otherwise, the risk-weight is 10%. This assumes that (i) the loan and the collateral are denominated in the same currency, (ii) the position is marked-to-market on a daily basis and margin taken where necessary, and (iii) the transaction takes place under a standard legal agreement such as the GMRA.[18]

Any other collateralised exposure is also risk-weighted at 0%, provided that the collateral is in the form of cash or sovereign debt issued by a country also risk-weighted at 0% under the standardised approach, and there is a haircut of at least 20%.[19]

Derivative positions

Banks are the largest users of off-balance sheet derivatives such as swaps. Under Basel I, banks calculated the credit exposure arising from derivatives trading using the "current exposure" method, which entailed taking the mark-to-market value of each position and basing the exposure on that.

[18] See Chapter 12 on repo for detail on the GMRA.

[19] This is a substantial haircut. The haircut for A-rated assets would seldom exceed 10% in a repo under GMRA,

Basel II continues essentially with this approach. The counterparty charge for derivatives transactions is given by:

$$Counterparty\ charge = [(RC + Add\text{-}on) - CA] \times r \times 0.08 \quad (27.4)$$

where

RC	is the replacement cost
add-on	is the potential future exposure
CA	is the collateral value
r	is the counterparty risk-weight.

Note that this applies to OTC derivative contracts only, not exchange-traded ones, for which no counterparty charge is required. Formula (27.4) shows that a bank will obtain capital relief for any of its derivative trades that are collateralised by the counterparty.

Structured finance assets

We discuss the impact of Basel II on securitisation in detail in the next section of this chapter. Here we introduce the main issues in the context of the impact on bank capital.

Basel I applied a very simple regime to structured finance securities. There was a 100% risk-weight for all ABS securities, with the exception of AAA-rated senior tranche RMBS bonds, which were weighted at 50%.[20] Under Basel II different risk weights are applied according to the rating of the individual tranche. As such, Basel II is expected to have a significant impact on structured finance securities, from the point of view of both originator and investor (if the latter is also a bank). The key areas of impact arise from the following:

- the capital charge requirement against assets such as residential mortgages and credit card debt will reduce under Basel II;
- banks that invest in ABS (certain tranches) will be required to hold less capital against these assets under Basel II.

As such, we would reasonably expect to see reduced issuance of RMBS and credit card ABS from certain classes of banks, as well as a decreased yield on high-rated ABS notes. However, lower-rated banks may continue to

[20] Junior tranches rated below BB– are deducted from capital under Basel I.

originate ABS, and the lower interest payable on it because of their lower risk-weighting may mean that this instrument remains an attractive funding mechanism for many banks. So overall issuance levels may remain stable. From an ALM point of view, banks will have a continuing incentive to securitise lower-rated mortgage books such as commercial mortgages.

Approach under Basel II

The standardised approach for ABS follows a similar procedure as that for sovereign and bank assets. Risk-weights that are assigned to ABS tranches, depending on whether the bank is originating the instrument or investing in it, are shown in Table 27.7. These weights are prescribed by the BIS. Note that all unrated tranches require that a deduction be made from capital, unless the tranche concerned is the most senior in a securitisation, when in such cases the tranche is assigned the average risk-weight of the underlying assets.

ABS tranches risk-weighting	**%**	
	Investor	**Originator**
Long-term		
AAA to AA–	20	20
A+ to A–	50	50
BBB+ to BBB–	100	100
BB+ to BB–	350	Deduction
B+ to below/unrated	Deduction	Deduction
Short-term		
A–1/P–1	20	20
A–2/P–2	50	50
A–3/P–3	100	100
Unrated	350	350

Table 27.7 Basel II standardised approach for ABS tranches
Source: BIS.

The procedure for the IRB method is slightly more complex, with three different methods depending on the rating of the ABS tranche. These are the:

- ratings-based approach (RBA);
- supervisory formula (SF);
- internal assessment approach (IAA).

These are considered further below.

Ratings-based approach (RBA)

The RBA is applied where a structured finance security is rated, or where a rating can be implied from the formal rating of a reference entity. The tranche rating governs the risk-weight applicable, as does three other parameters, which are:

- the seniority of the tranche;
- the long-term or short-term rating;
- the granularity of the underlying asset pool.

Granularity in this case refers to how many individual assets are in the underlying asset pool.[21] For Basel II purposes, a pool is said to be granular if it holds six or more assets.

The risk-weights applied under RBA to the most senior tranche of a securitisation transaction, which are governed by the tranche's rating, are shown in Table 27.8(b). Note that these apply to originating as well investing banks. Table 27.8(a) shows the risk weight for a non-granular pool, as well as the base case.

<table>
<tr><th>Rating</th><th>Tranches and eligible senior notes</th><th>Base case</th><th>Non-granular pool</th></tr>
<tr><td>Aaa</td><td>7</td><td>12</td><td>20</td></tr>
<tr><td>Aa</td><td>8</td><td>15</td><td>25</td></tr>
<tr><td>A1</td><td>10</td><td>18</td><td rowspan="3">35</td></tr>
<tr><td>A2</td><td>12</td><td>20</td></tr>
<tr><td>A3</td><td>20</td><td>35</td></tr>
<tr><td>Baa1</td><td>35</td><td colspan="2">50</td></tr>
<tr><td>Baa2</td><td>60</td><td colspan="2">75</td></tr>
<tr><td>Baa3</td><td colspan="3">100</td></tr>
<tr><td>Ba1</td><td colspan="3">250</td></tr>
<tr><td>Ba2</td><td colspan="3">425</td></tr>
<tr><td>Ba3</td><td colspan="3">650</td></tr>
<tr><td>Below Ba3</td><td colspan="3">Deduction</td></tr>
</table>

Table 27.8(a) RBA risk-weights (%)
Source: BIS.

[21] While a large RMBS transaction may contain many hundreds, if not thousands, of individual assets in the asset pool, other securitisations such as CMBS may contain only a handful of assets. Esoteric asset securitisations may contain only one asset (for example, a museum entry fee receivables securitisation).

Long-term	RW %
AAA	7
AA	8
A+	10
A	12
A–	20
BBB+	35
BBB	60
BBB–	100
BB+	250
BB	425
BB–	650
Below BB–/Unrated	Deduction from capital

Short-term	RW %
A–1/P–1	7
A–2/P–2	12
A–3/P–3	60
Unrated	Deduction from capital

Table 27.8(b) Structured finance securities: senior tranche risk-weightings %
Source: BIS.

For all tranches ranked below the senior note in a structured finance transaction, the risk-weightings are as listed in Table 27.9 (a) for granular pools and Table 27.9 (b) for non-granular pools.

(a) Granular asset pool

Long-term	RW %
AAA	12
AA	15
A+	18
A	20
A–	35
BBB+	50
BBB	75
BBB-	100
BB+	250

BB	425
BB–	650
Below BB–/Unrated	Deduction from capital

Short-term	**RW %**
A–1/P–1	12
A–2/P–2	20
A–3/P–3	75
Unrated	Deduction from capital

(b) Non-granular asset pool

Long-term	**RW %**
AAA	20
AA	25
A+	35
A	35
A–	35
BBB+	50
BBB	75
BBB-	100
BB+	250
BB	425
BB–	650
Below BB– / Unrated	Deduction from capital

Short-term	**RW %**
A–1/P–1	20
A–2/P–2	35
A-3/P–3	75
Unrated	Deduction from capital

Table 27.9 Structured finance securities: all tranches (except senior tranche) risk-weightings %
Source: BIS.

Supervisory formula (SF)

The SF is applied where no external formal rating is available for a structured finance security. The calculation of the capital charge using the SF, which is given in the BIS document, is quite involved. Note that an ALM desk will rarely, if ever need to apply the SF because unrated ABS tranches outside the first-loss ("equity") piece are invariably rated. Therefore we do not reproduce the SF here.[22]

Internal assessment approach (IAA)

The IAA is an approach applicable in the case of asset-backed commercial paper (ABCP) programmes, specifically where credit enhancements, including liquidity facilities, are unrated. Note that the ABCP programme itself must be rated. When calculating the risk-weighting for unrated liquidity and other credit enhancements, a bank can apply its own internal assessment of the exposures. The BIS prescribes that the internal assessment approach must be similar to the methodology employed by the rating agencies.

Liquidity facilities

Liquidity facilities are a key credit-enhancement mechanism in the securitisation market, and are particularly important in the ABCP market. The providers of such facilities are usually banking groups. Under Basel I not all liquidity lines were subject to capital rules, but this changes under Basel II when all such facilities become subject to regulation.[23] All banks will be required to hold capital against liquidity facilities; as such, ALM strategy may need to be modified to reduce the extent of these that are made available to customers, at least in their traditional form. The treatment of liquidity facilities differs according to whether the standardised or IRB approach is adopted. Banks that adopt the IRB should see a smaller capital charge compared to the charge calculated under the standardised method.

The standardised approach states that the risk-weight of an unrated facility is given by:

$$100\% \times RW$$

[22] The SF calculation assumes five drivers of credit risk. These are: (i) K, the capital charge if the assets were not securitised; (ii) L, any credit enhancement; (iii) T, thickness of the exposure (which is the ratio of the nominal size of the ABS tranche to the total size of the underlying pool); (iv) N, the effective number of exposures, which is the ratio of the square of the sum of the individual exposures to the sum of squares of individual exposures; and (v) LGD, the loss-given-default.

[23] Note that this impacts the providers of the liquidity lines only (that is, the banks), not the issuing vehicle that has a line in place.

where *RW* is the risk-weight of the lowest rating category for which the facility is granted.

The risk-weight for a rated facility of less than one-year maturity is 20%, while if the maturity is greater than one year it is 50%. If a facility is only made available in the event of severe market correction or other market disturbance, the risk-weight is 0%.

The IRB approach is summarised in Figure 27.1.

Unrated facility

100% × SF risk-weight

Rated facility

100% × RBA risk-weight

For < 1-year maturity:

50% × risk-weight determined by rating

For > 1-year maturity:

100% × risk-weight determined by rating

For facility only available in market correction:

20% × SF risk-weight

Figure 27.1 Liquidity facility risk-weighting: IRB approach
Source: BIS.

From the ALM strategy point of view, given that liquidity facilities are a traditional asset in a bank asset portfolio, we would expect that banks will seek to offer alternatives to the traditional liquidity line. For instance, we may observe greater use of extendible CP and callable CP in ABCP programmes, which reduce the liquidity facility requirement under rating agency methodologies.

Corporate and retail lending

The area of corporate and retail lending should see some of the biggest impacts under Basel II. This is important for ALM practitioners to be aware of because corporate lending is, in many cases, the largest proportion of a bank's balance sheet. Many commentators have remarked that stronger-rated corporates will seek greater disintermediation, while banks may find it attractive to lend to unrated or low-rated corporates compared to middle-rated corporates. Although as we have noted elsewhere a full assessment should wait until at least one year after implementation, we present here some basic considerations for the ALM strategist.

Corporate assets

The simple 100% risk-weight for corporate lending that applied under Basel I is discarded. In its place is the ratings-based methodology for the standardised approach shown in Table 27.10. Under the foundation IRB approach the capital charge reduces for higher-rated corporates, so that AA-rated companies, previously rated 100% under Basel I would now be at around 15%. The class of assets termed "small- and medium-sized enterprises" (SMEs) will also gain under Basel II when compared to non-SME corporates; under the IRB approach it is expected that the weighting will be approximately 20% lower for small SMEs.[24]

Rating	Risk-weight %
AAA to AA–	20
A+ to A–	50
BBB+ to BB–	100
Below BB–	150
Unrated	100

Table 27.10 Basel II standardised approach: corporate risk-weights
Source: BIS.

Retail assets risk-weighting under Basel II will be at 75% in the standardised approach, compared to 100% under Basel I. Residential mortgages risk-weighting decreases from 50% to 35%; under the IRB method they are expected to fall to lower than this, around 15%. Thus banks with large pools of residential mortgages will gain in capital charge terms compared to non-mortgage banks.

Corporate assets: Standardised approach

Under the blanket 100% risk-weighting of Basel I, banks had a greater incentive, somewhat perversely, to lend to lower-rated corporates because this resulted in higher return on capital. This anomaly is better addressed

[24] An SME is defined for Basel II purposes as a corporate with annual sales of €50 million or less.

under Basel II. In the standardised approach the obligor's formal credit rating determines the capital charge risk-weighting. Broadly, the only unchanged case is corporates rated from BBB+ to BB– that remain at 100%. All other corporates have changed risk-weights. Banks that adopt the standardised approach then have little incentive to lend to entities in this rating category, whereas they have an incentive to lend to un-rated corporates compared to those rated below BB–. An un-rated corporate will have no incentive to apply for a credit rating unless this is likely to be better than BBB+, as the lending rate to it may be prohibitive.

Corporate assets: IRB approaches

Banks implementing the foundation IRB methodology are allowed to use their internal credit-risk models to estimate the PD values for each obligor;[25] the values for the LGD, EAD and M parameters are prescribed by the BIS. Under the advanced IRB a bank may use its own estimates of all four parameters.

Impact on corporate lending

Higher-rated corporates might be expected to reduce their use of the capital markets and increase straight bank borrowing, because this business will become more attractive. Low-rated corporate lending (BBB+ and below) will become less attractive in comparison, and BB-rated corporate lending will become almost prohibitive. Under the standardised approach higher-rated corporate lending will be the most attractive, while under advanced IRB most corporate lending below AA-rated will become expensive. However, SME assets become more attractive compared to Basel I, so this sector would be expected to grow as an asset class. These holdings will be a cheaper asset for capital purposes compared to BB-rated corporates, because SMEs are invariably unrated. Under the IRB approach SMEs are expected to be better capital value than all corporates rated A or below.

Illustration using hypothetical example

We use a simple example to illustrate the impact of Basel II. Consider a bank lending to two entities:

- a utility company rated AA;
- an industrial company rated BB–.

[25] There is a BIS-imposed minimum PD of 0.03%.

Under Basel I a loan of $10 million to each company would each attract a minimum capital charge of $800,000.00. Under the standardised approach of Basel II the charge for the loan to the utility company would be $160,000, while the requirement for the industrial company would be unchanged at $800,000.

Under the foundation approach, the bank would use its PD value to calculate the risk-weighting; assuming the calculation came to 15% for the utility company the capital charge would now be $120,000. Again, we assume the risk-weight for the industrial company was worked out as 95%; this leads to a capital charge of $760,000. The risk-weight values under the advanced IRB would use the bank's internal data for all the calculation parameters, but may well be higher for the industrial company, making this asset an even more expensive one when compared to the Basel I regime.

Retail assets

Under Basel I there was a blanket 100% risk-weight for all retail assets, except for residential mortgages, which were weighted at 50%. Under Basel II more types of retail assets are specifically defined, as residential mortgages were under the earlier regime, so that there is less blanket coverage. A retail asset is defined as:

- an exposure to an individual person, or to an SME;
- an exposure that is one of a "significant number" of similar such assets;
- comprising a total exposure to an individual exposure that does not exceed €1 million.

Standardised approach

Under the standardised approach the risk-weighting for retail assets falls to 75%, which is a substantial reduction from the Basel I 100% risk-weight. For residential mortgages the risk-weight is 35% (down from 50%) and for commercial mortgages the risk-weight is 50%, which is reduced from 100%.[26] Non-performing loans (NPLs) are risk-weighted at (i) 150% if the value adjustment is less than 20% of the unsecured portion of the exposure; (ii) 100% if the value adjustment is above 20% of the unsecured portion of the exposure; or (iii) 50% if the value adjustment is above 50%.[27] The value

[26] Note that this assumes that the Loan-to-Value (LTV) does not exceed 50%. This level is by no means common. If the LTV exceeds this, the risk-weight assumes the standard 75% value for retail assets.

[27] NPLs are defined for Basel II purposes as being (interest and/or principal) past due for over 90 days.

adjustment is the amount of loss transferred to the profit-and-loss (p&l) account for that loan. Non-performing residential mortgages are risk-weighted at 100%.

IRB approach

Retail assets are described somewhat differently under the IRB approaches compared to sovereign or corporate assets. There is only one IRB approach; that is, we do not have separate foundation and advanced approaches. A bank adopting the IRB method for retail assets may use its own internal PD, LGD and EAD values. Unlike for large corporates and sovereigns, where there is a wealth of historical and other published data, this may prove problematic for retail assets. A bank would need sufficient statistical data for each retail borrower, which may not be available.

Credit derivatives

Credit derivatives are classed as a "credit risk mitigation" tool. Basel I allowed for such instruments, but only explicitly named collateral and bank guarantees. Exposures backed by collateral are risk-weighted at the risk-weight of the collateral, be it cash, sovereign bonds or other suitable securities. Exposures backed by a bank guarantee are risk-weighted at 20% if the bank is an OECD bank. Credit derivatives are treated as implicit guarantees under Basel I, so an exposure backed by a CDS is risk-weighted at the level of the entity that is selling protection. This would be 20% for an OECD bank. If there is a currency mismatch between the exposure and the denomination of swap, this is taken to be an 8% reduction in protection. Exposures protected by a basket CDS are risk-weighted according to the type of instrument it is; for example, in a first-to-default (FtD) CDS, only one asset in the basket is recognised as being under protection, and the bank can nominate which one this is and which receives the 20% weighting. The remaining assets would be weighted as if they had no credit risk mitigation treatment.

Basel II explicitly identifies a larger number of credit risk mitigation instruments, and these include credit derivatives. In addition to collateral and guarantees, they include:

- netting agreements;
- third-party guarantees;
- buying credit protection using credit derivatives.

An instrument is recognised as a credit risk mitigation tool if it is transacted under standard documentation that can be enforced in all legal jurisdictions. The procedure is slightly different, depending on what type of risk mitigation tool is used; however, certain factors are common to all three types. The most important of these is the maturity mismatch. A hedging tool of different maturity to the exposure is only considered if the maturity of the latter is one year or more. The BIS prescribes an adjustment factor that reduces the amount considered to be under protection for all hedges that do not match the exposure maturity.

We consider only credit derivatives in this section.

Standardised and IRB approach

Under the standardised approach of Basel II, if an asset is protected with a credit derivative its risk-weight is deemed to be equal to the risk-weight of the credit protection seller. This is identical treatment to that under Basel I. For capital charge purposes then, there is an advantage to obtaining credit protection only from counterparties whose risk-weight is lower than the asset being protected; this may well be a majority of cases with regard to corporate and developing economy sovereign assets. The BIS document states that the credit events protected under the credit derivative must include failure to pay, bankruptcy and restructuring. These are all included under standard ISDA credit derivative documentation. If the contract excludes restructuring, then the level of capital charge relief is reduced.

The foundation IRB approach to treating credit derivatives is similar to the standardised approach. The PD value that is used in the calculation will be that of the entity that is providing the credit risk protection. Under the advanced IRB approach, a bank's own PD and LGD values can be adjusted to account for the CDS protection.

Selling protection via CDS

The Basel II capital treatment of a CDS contract used to sell protection assumes it is a cash instrument. Thus, capital must be allocated to the position as if it were a cash asset in the name of the reference entity. This is the same principle as Basel I, although now of course the reference entity rating is the key factor. For example, under Basel I selling protection on an A-rated corporate entity would attract a 100% risk-weighting, whereas under standardised Basel II the risk-weight would be 50%. Under the foundation IRB this weighting would be lower still. In the new regime we predict therefore an increased usage of CDS as investment instruments for higher-rated names.

Credit derivatives and synthetic securitisation

As we saw in Part IV, the use of credit derivatives in a structured finance transaction produces a so-called synthetic securitisation, in which the credit risk transfer of a pool of assets is achieved via the credit derivatives rather than a 'true sale' of the assets to a specially incorporated legal entity. For a synthetic CDO (see Chapter 23) the Basel II rules prescribe separate approaches for originators and investors.

Standardised approach: Synthetic CDO

The risk-weights to use for synthetic CDO note tranches are shown in Table 27.11.

	Risk-weight %	
Tranche rating	**Investing banks**	**Originating banks**
AAA to AA–	20	20
A+ to A–	50	50
BBB+ to BBB-	100	100
BB+ to BB–	350	Deduction from capital
B+ and below	Deduction from capital	Deduction from capital
Unrated	Deduction from capital	Deduction from capital

Table 27.11 Standardised approach for synthetic CDO tranches: risk-weights %
Source: BIS.

IRB approach

When calculating the capital charge for CDO note assets, banks have less freedom to use their own internal data, even under the IRB approach. This stands it apart from other asset classes. An originating bank must nevertheless apply the IRB approach if it is using this same approach to assign risk-weights for the underlying assets of the CDO. If the tranche is rated, then the bank must apply the RBA approach; if not, then the SF calculation method will apply. If neither of these methods can be used, then the CDO asset must be deducted from capital. The RBA approach is essentially identical to that described earlier for ABS assets.

Basel II and securitisation

In Part IV we discussed securitisation and its importance as a tool and technique in ALM. It is also one of the sectors in banking where the Basel II rules are expected to make the greatest impact. Given that so much securitisation business is driven by regulatory capital issues, a bank will regard it as imperative to assess the economic effects of the rule changes and position itself accordingly. In the previous section we introduced the Basel II rules for structured finance assets; in this section we discuss further the likely impact of the new rules on securitisation, and the relevance of this for ALM strategists and practitioners.

From a reading of the previous section we can suggest a number of actions that banks can be expected to take with regard to both originating and investing in securitisation notes. For instance, the different treatment of assets such as residential mortgages and credit cards compared to Basel I means that there is less incentive to securitise them, compared with, say, lower-rated corporate loans. From an ALM strategy perspective, the way securitisation deals are structured can also be expected to change, as the cost of investing in the junior notes and sub-investment-graded notes in an ABS deal will be higher in many cases. So we may observe that for many ABS deals the capital structure on the liability side will change to reflect this. The capital calculation approach adopted will also influence securitisation. Larger banks with more sophisticated or diverse asset portfolios are expected to adopt the IRB approach, which produces more favourable treatment for higher-rated assets. Banks using the IRB method may have less incentive to securitise high-quality assets or invest in anything other than the senior tranche in an ABS deal. Smaller banks would be expected to adopt the standardised approach, which paradoxically creates a greater incentive to hold lower-rated ABS tranches in some cases.

We now discuss some scenarios of likely interest to ALM strategists.

Change from Basel I to Basel II

A direct result of the original Basel accord, albeit an unplanned one, was the widespread adoption of securitisation as a balance sheet management tool among banks. This reflected the blanket coverage of the rules to a wide range of assets held on bank balance sheets, of widely varying credit quality. Basel I created a strong incentive to reduce regulatory capital charges by removing exposures, particularly higher quality ones, from balance sheets by securitising them. In order to help place the deal in the market, originators often retained the "first-loss" or equity tranche of the structure, which meant that the highest risk part of the asset pool was retained by the bank. The somewhat ironic result of such a procedure is that, while the regulatory capital requirement would have been reduced, the economic risk to the bank would not have been. This was one of the main areas of complaint on the original accord, that it did not align closely enough the regulatory capital requirement to actual economic risk exposure of a bank's asset pool.

Basel II has addressed this issue, and even in the standardised approach it manages to produce less of a "shotgun" approach to risk capital calculations compared to Basel I. The IRB approach attempts to align regulatory capital with economic risk closer still. The main impact of this should be to reduce the incentive to securitise assets, especially higher quality ones. In addition, Basel II carries a high capital charge for securitised assets where the junior tranche is retained by the bank, so the deal economics in a securitisation will no longer be as attractive as before if the first-loss piece is retained. As we noted above, though, a significant influence on whether securitisation should be undertaken will be whether the standardised or IRB approach is adopted. For instance, the capital charge against investment in an AA-rated ABS tranche is higher for a standardised bank than an IRB bank. Table 27.12, which is reproduced with the kind permission of FitchRatings Ltd, shows the difference in capital charges between the two approaches in a securitisation issue. The figures are for banks that invest in ABS tranches.

External rating	Standardised securitisation charges (1)	Basel II IRB securitised (2)	IRB vs standardised securitisation charges
AAA	1.60	0.56	(65)
AA	1.60	0.64	(60)
A	4	0.96	(76)
BBB+	8	2.80	(65)
BBB	8	4.80	(40)
BBB–	8	8	0
BB+	28	20	(29)
BB	28	34	21
BB–	28	52	86
B	Full deduction	Full deduction	NA
CCC+	Full deduction	Full deduction	NA

(1) Applies to investing standardised banks only; originating standardised banks are required to deduct non-investment-grade tranches. Rated BB+ and below out of capital.
(2) For positions rated BBB and above, the most favourable ratings-based approach (RBA) charges available for granular and senior positions are used in this comparison, given the severe stress scenarios and conservative enhancement levels needed to achieve an investment-grade rating.

IRB – internal ratings based

NA – not applicable

Table 27.12 Basel II risk-weights under securitisation: Standardised versus IRB approach (%)

One further significant impact of Basel II is the new distinction it introduces between investment-grade and sub-investment-grade assets. The increased capital charge that results once one moves into a sub-investment-grade rating is pronounced. This has the effect of creating a wall of higher charges across just one notch in rating; for example, from Table 27.12 we observe that under the RBA method a BBB– note tranche attracts a 8% charge, whereas a note rated one notch lower at BB+ requires more than double this amount of capital (20%). This sudden steep increase will have an impact on the amount of lower-rated assets held on the balance sheet; at the same time, it gives banks an incentive to minimise the number and size of un-rated tranches. In practice usually only the equity tranche is un-rated, so to reduce the regulatory capital charge to the lowest possible amount this note piece will need to be as small as possible. Balanced against this is the need for the equity piece to be of sufficient size such that it provides sufficient credit enhancement and protection for the tranches lying above it, as required by the rating agencies.

Under Basel II not only will banks be penalised if they retain an un-rated securitisation note and/or the equity notes, other banks have no incentive to hold these as investments. Hence, banks can be expected to market such notes to non-bank investors not subject to Basel II regulation, such as hedge funds.

Securitised versus unsecuritised assets

We now consider the likely impact of the new Basel rules on securitisation markets, from the point of view of both bank originator and investor. In this section we summarise findings stated in a report published in 2005 by the credit rating agency Fitch, Inc, with their kind permission.[28]

ALM strategists may wish to consider the following after the implementation of Basel II:

- rated versus un-rated securitisation: while noting that un-rated notes in a securitisation transaction are very rare, excepting the first-loss or equity piece, in general IRB banks will have a lower capital charge

[28] The report is entitled *Basel II: Bottom-line Impact on Securitization Markets*, and is a special report from FitchRatings, dated 12 September 2005. The report is available at www.fitchratings.com. Special thanks to Frances Xavier at FitchRatings for her assistance with the permissions.

for rated tranches compared to un-rated ones. This is because the RBA method is expected to result in a lower charge compared to the SF formula. The impact of this should be to incentivise banks to hold rated notes only. However, the effect differs across asset classes: according to Fitch the RBA approach results in a lower charge for all except credit card and commercial mortgage asset pools;
- the impact of the RBA calculation should differ across securitisation tranches. The difference between the capital charge under RBA and under SF is expected to be largest in the BBB-ratings area.

Thus IRB banks will want to hold the rated tranches of an ABS issue because of the benefit from lower capital charges.

One of the most anticipated impacts of Basel II has been which asset classes it will provide greatest incentive to securitise, and which it will not. The expectation stated in the Fitch report is that credit card ABS and CMBS remain attractive investments for IRB banks. It suggests that the unsecuritised capital charge is several multiples higher for these two asset classes than the securitised capital charge. In other words, if an IRB bank is targeting this asset class for holding on its balance sheet, it gains more in capital charge terms by holding a bond securitised from these asset types rather than the underlying assets themselves. As a result then, we would expect banks with large holdings of these assets to securitise them, as the demand for such notes should increase. This should produce lower funding costs for such banks. The case of credit card ABS reflects the role that excess spread – the surplus on the receivables over what is paid out on the liability side of the structure – plays as a credit enhancement mechanism. Basel II does not recognise excess spread as an enhancement mechanism, so where a structure incorporates an un-rated note, it does not feed into the SF formula. Hence, this creates a higher charge than might otherwise be the case, thus creating an incentive to securitise such assets.

There should be a similar effect on RMBS, according to the Fitch report, although in the author's opinion this is less clear cut as the treatment for residential mortgages on the balance sheet is very favourable under Basel II.

Other asset classes are not expected to experience this phenomenon; for example, there is expected to be no difference in capital charge whether one is holding securitised or unsecuritised CDO assets. In other words, Basel II seems to have aligned fairly closely the capital charge under IRB for a pool of corporate debt (bonds or loans) and the RBA charge for a CDO note securitised on such assets.

Transaction structuring

Another pertinent comment in the Fitch report is the likely impact of Basel II on deal structuring. The expectation is that a bank originator will wish to minimise the size and number of sub-investment-grade tranches in the liability structure of a deal, given the unfavourable treatment that such exposures are given under Basel II.

We saw from Chapter 18 that regulatory capital management is one of three main strategic motivations behind the origination of a securitisation deal. The final structure of a deal reflects tactical issues including:

- market conditions such as supply and demand for specific assets, and interest-rate spreads;
- rating agency requirements;
- legal, tax and administrative considerations.

Basel II will introduce another element in the structuring decision; namely, the lower attraction of sub-investment-grade tranches. Therefore from a capital charge perspective, and also the viewpoint of potential bank investors in the issued notes, the liability structure of an ABS deal would be expected to minimise the size, or eliminate entirely, all tranches rated below BBB–. There will always be a junior piece to an ABS deal, the first-loss piece, but under Basel II its size should be as small as possible.

Operational risk

The operational risk capital charge introduced in Basel II is the most significant departure in regulatory capital rules when compared to the previous regime. It is also the most controversial element of the new capital accord.[29] We will leave aside the controversy in this account and instead focus on the methodology behind the new rules, which are of relevance to ALM practitioners. As there was no explicit capital charge for operational risk under Basel I, we cannot make any comparisons with the old regime; the operational risk charge is a new capital requirement. The primary objective of the new charge is to cover for the possibility of catastrophic loss situations *à la* Barings or Kidder Peabody.

[29] Some commentators have suggested that the operational risk capital charge is nothing more than a tax on bank income.

It is expected that the new charge will be significant in terms of magnitude, particularly for large banking groups. A study conducted by the BIS itself concluded as much: the operational risk charge was a sizeable additional capital segment.[30] Figure 27.2 shows the expected percentage change in capital for different business lines as reported in the BIS study. Calculations are shown for two sets of banks, large banking groups and smaller specialised banks, and for the standardised and IRB approach. Figure 27.3 on page 1236 is from the same report, and shows clearly the significant contribution to overall capital levels made by the operational risk charge.[31]

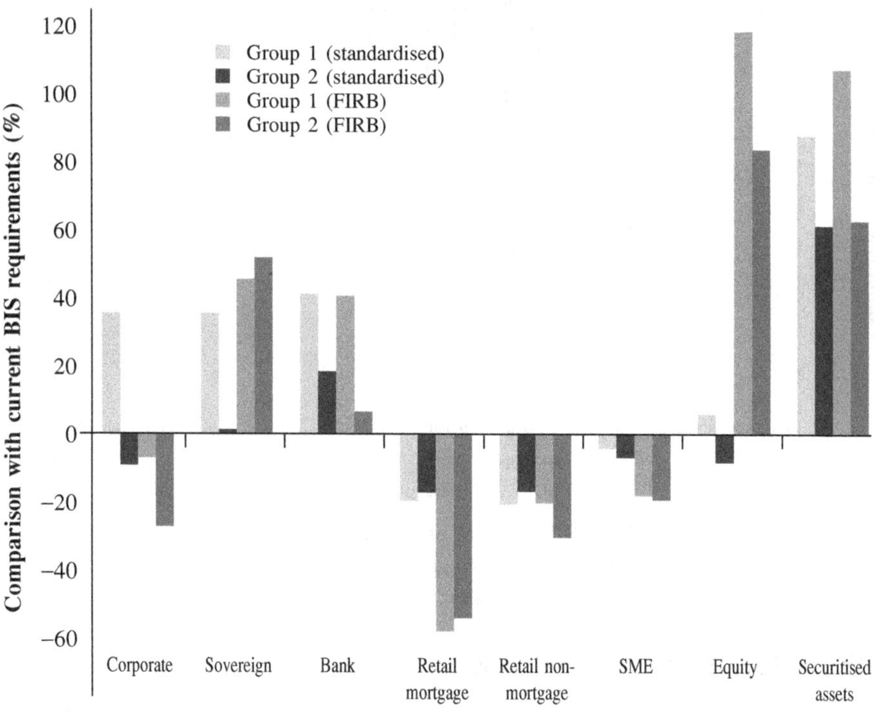

Figure 27.2 BIS estimate of percentage change in capital per business line
Source: BIS.

[30] BIS, *Quantitative Impact Survey 3*, 2003.

[31] In the BIS study the operational risk charge was estimated using the standardised approach only. "Group 1" banks were defined as large, diversified and internationally active banks with Tier 1 capital exceeding €3 billion. "Group 2" banks were defined as smaller, and more specialised, banks.

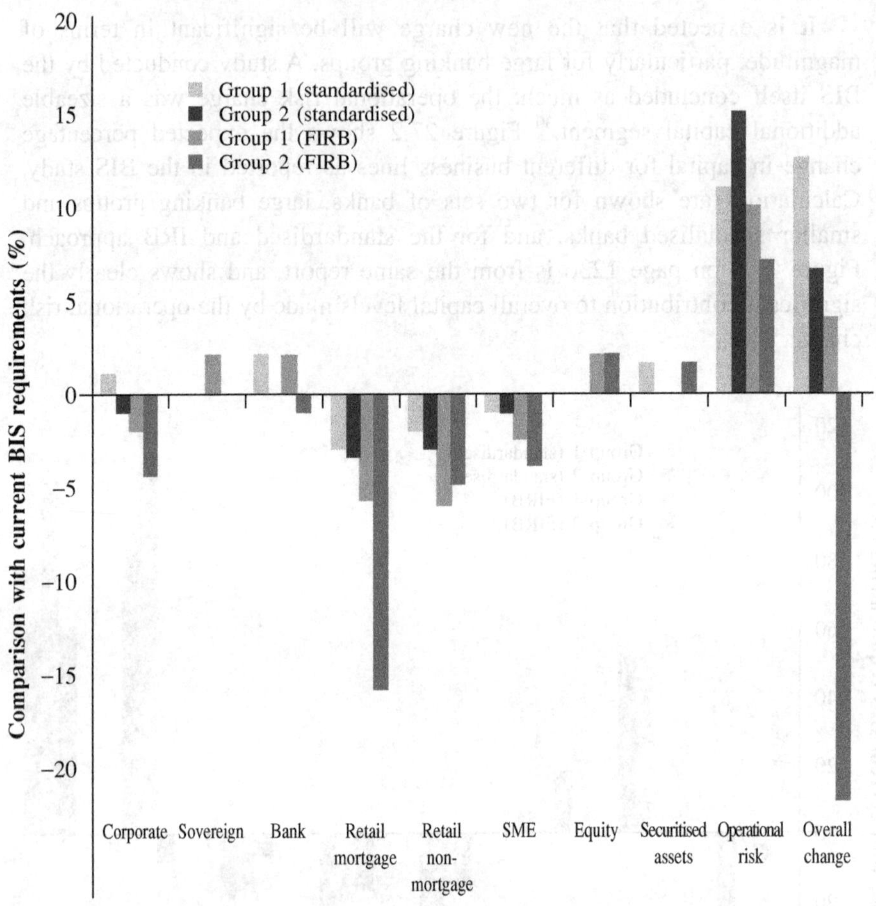

Figure 27.3 BIS estimate of elements contributing to overall capital levels expected under Basel II
Source: BIS.

The nature of operational risk

The BIS defines operational risk as "the risk of loss resulting from inadequate or failed internal processes, people and systems or from external events".[32] Put in this way, operational risk covers a very wide range of risk exposures; some of these include the following:

- *fraud*: the risk of loss arising from fraudulent activity, both internal to the bank undertaken by employees and external to the bank and

[32] BIS document of 26 June 2004 (see Footnote 1 at the start of this chapter).

undertaken by a third party. This would cover trading fraud of the type perpetrated by Nick Leeson at Barings;
- *system failures*: the risk of loss arising from a breakdown of systems and processes;
- *employment practice and workplace safety*: risk of loss due to litigation for personal or other injury, including sexual harassment claims;
- *physical plant and assets*: risk of loss arising from damage to office property and buildings, say from natural disaster or other such events.

The above is only a small sample. We observe then that the operational risk category is a wide one, and in fact can be taken to be a catch-all for all unforeseen risks and losses that are not market risks. Essentially, the operational risk capital charge is designed to protect against low-frequency, but large-impact, rare events.

Calculation methodology

The BIS specifies three methods by which the operational risk charge may be calculated. These are the:

- basic indicator approach (BIA);
- standardised approach (SA);
- advanced measurement approach (AMA).

The BIS has suggested that banks adopt the more sophisticated SA or AMA methods over the BIA approach. Banks are allowed to select more than one method if they wish to apply different approaches for different parts of their business.

Basic indicator approach (BIA)

This is fairly simple calculation which states that the operational risk charge is the average over the bank's last three years of 15% of its positive annual gross income. It is given by:

$$BIA = \frac{\left(15\% \times \sum \text{Years 1–3 Annual gross income}\right)}{3}. \qquad (27.5)$$

The definition of gross income is given as net interest income plus net non-interest income: a fairly wide coverage. However, it would exclude the insurance income of bancassurance groups.

Standardised approach (SA)

The SA method is slightly more sophisticated. It divides a bank's activities into eight different business lines, which are:

- corporate finance;
- trading and sales;
- retail banking
- commercial banking;
- payment and settlements;
- agency services;
- asset management;
- retail brokerage.

Gross income is taken for each business line; the capital charge is the product of the gross income and a factor termed the *beta* for that business line. Beta is prescribed by the BIS, and is meant to denote the relationship between the level of operational risk for that business line and the aggregate level of gross income for that line. The formula for the capital charge is:

$$SA = \frac{\left(\sum \text{Years 1–3 max.}\left[\sum(\text{Annual gross income}_{1\text{–}8} \times \beta_{1\text{–}8}),\ 0\right]\right)}{3}. \tag{27.6}$$

The business line beta factors are:

Corporate finance:	18%
Trading and sales:	18%
Retail banking:	12%
Commercial banking:	15%
Payment and settlements:	18%
Agency services:	15%
Asset management:	12%
Retail brokerage:	12%.

The beta factors are lower for more "traditional" banking factors, which suggests that the SA method would be favoured by retail and commercial banks; conversely, investment banks may retain the BIA approach, or adopt the AMA approach.

Advanced measurement approach (AMA)

The AMA might be said to be the advanced IRB approach for operational risk, as it uses a bank's internal operational risk measurements and requires the approval of the national supervisor. A five-year database (three years when the method is first adopted) of internal operational risk measurement data is required to implement AMA. This includes five years of historical observation.

To calculate the capital charge requires that the bank maps the historical loss data for each of the eight business lines from its internal measures, for each of the risk types that are defined to be "operational risk". This requires complex and sophisticated systems, which not all banks will have in place.

Insurance policy mitigation

Under Basel II a bank can make use of insurance policies to offset a maximum of 20% of its operational risk capital charge. The BIS prescribes the circumstances in which a bank can use insurance to achieve this. These include terms such as: (i) the insurance policy must have a minimum initial term of one year with a minimum 90-day cancellation notice period; (ii) the policy must contain no exclusions for events triggered by supervisory action; and (iii) the policy must be provided by a third-party institution. The maximum relief that can be granted is 20% of a bank's operational risk capital charge. The insurance policy cannot cover any fines levied by bank regulatory authorities.

Concluding remarks

Basel II is sure to prove to be a milestone in international banking supervision and regulation. It is designed to better align bank capital with bank economic risk, which is a positive development for the global economy. In the process of this taking place, certain asset classes will benefit and other, generally lower credit-quality classes, will lose out. As a result, we should observe divestment of certain asset classes and growth in others. Banks will reallocate capital to sectors that provide the best return on capital. The process will not be an instant one, and a proper assessment of the impact of Basel II on the banking sectors, and the benefits it has delivered, will have to wait until implementation is at least one year old.

References and bibliography

Fabozzi, F. and Choudhry, M. (eds) 2004, *The Handbook of European Fixed Income Securities*, John Wiley & Sons, New Jersey.

Gup, B. 2004, *The New Basel Capital Accord*, Thomson Corporation, New York, NY.

LIFT
GREAT! IT'S FRIDAY AGAIN
Olga Mears

YOU CAN ALWAYS TELL IT'S DRESS-DOWN DAY BY OUR CHAZ'S CLOTHES
OH, YES?

.....MMM..... HE WEARS HIS THOMAS PINK SHIRT WITH THE FRAYED COLLAR
MORNING, LADIES

PART

VI

Treasury Middle Office Operations

Part VI consists of one chapter and covers a range of topics of importance in ALM operations. Generally, issues such as internal cost allocation, p&l reporting, and allocation and transfer pricing are increasingly managed within the Treasury middle office function. These topics, together with other essential aspects of the Treasury operation, are described in the following chapter.

CHAPTER

28

Funding and Treasury Procedures for Banking Corporations[1]

The purpose of this chapter is to address the issues specifically faced by a bank Middle Office in their support of the ALM function. While the Treasury front office has primary responsibility for managing transactions facing the external market, Middle Office (MO) plays an important role in *controlling* the ALM function, and the corresponding internal allocations of those transactions across the various internal business units.

This chapter describes what is meant by the term "funding cost" and the various methods of their internal allocation, as well as the logistical issues faced by many banking corporations in effecting this allocation.

Funding

In today's increasingly complex financial markets where focus is often placed on the development of new and innovative structures designed to unlock financial value, practitioners will do well to remember the age-old banking maxim that "Cash is King". Regardless of the simplicity or complexity of a transaction, invariably there is either a payment or receipt of cash at some stage throughout its life. In fact, that is ultimately all that banking corporations are – payers and receivers of cash today made in consideration for commitments to paying or receiving cash in the future.

The term "funding cost" in banking refers to the financial cost in the form of interest that is incurred when cash is borrowed to finance other

---

[1] This chapter was written by Andrew Oliver, KBC Financial Products, London. The views, thoughts and opinions contained herein remain those of the author in his individual private capacity.

trading assets. Traditionally, investment banks are net borrowers of cash, but the same principles apply to net lenders of cash.

Accordingly, regardless of its size and nature, there are some fundamental questions that an organisation which manages its cash well must address, including:

- Where is cash being borrowed from?
- What is the financial cost (interest) of borrowing this cash?
- Where is the cash being used within the organisation?
- How is the financial cost of borrowing this cash being internally allocated to the areas of the organisation that are using it?

These costs can be real costs or they can be opportunity costs, and the larger and more complex the organisation, so too are the issues around attributing those costs to individual business areas.

Internal funding cost allocation

Banking corporations are often structured with a dedicated Treasury department that is responsible for managing the cash flow of the business, and for arranging the cash borrowings required to finance trading assets. In that respect, the external funding trades are often booked in Treasury's book, which initially bears the funding cost of those borrowings. Those funding costs are then allocated internally to the areas of the business that have generated the funding requirement by internally lending the cash to whoever needs it. Treasury is therefore acting as a conduit between the external sources of funding and the internal businesses requiring it.

There are two broadly different approaches to determining the amount of cash Treasury is required to internally lend to each business:

(1) Funding "Cash";
(2) Funding "Balance sheet".

These are linked by the principles of double-entry accounting (see Figure 28.1), and differ in their treatment of funding profit and loss generated by each business.

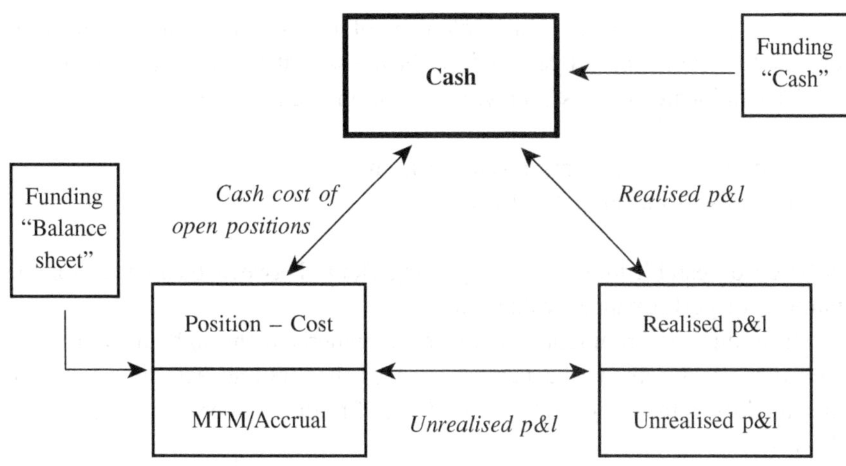

Figure 28.1 Double-entry accounting and funding cash allocation

Funding "Cash"

This approach is both the simplest in theory and the simplest to apply, in that each individual business is deemed to own a portion of the overall entity's cash balance.

This portion represents that business' overall contribution since inception to the entity's cash balance, not only includes the amount required to fund that business' current open positions, but incorporates previously generated realised p&l as well. The amount that each business is therefore required to borrow from Treasury is simply the amount that would flatten that business' own cash balance.

Funding "Balance sheet"

This approach treats Treasury as the owner of all cash, which then lends to businesses to fund the *value* of their current trading portfolio. Figure 28.1 illustrates the difference between the cash balance of the first approach and the balance sheet value of this second approach as being the *realised* and *unrealised p&l*.

It can be less common in some organisations for there to be a clear and effective policy surrounding the funding benefit/detriment of profits earned / losses incurred.

However, particularly in trading environments, it is good practice to dictate that the funding cost/benefit of profits and losses are the property of

Treasury (or some other central element of the organisation structure), as opposed to being the property of the business that has generated them.

The rationale for this policy, which applies equally to:

- current year and prior year p&l, and
- realised and unrealised p&l

is based on establishing a "level playing field" between businesses for the purpose of performance evaluation.

In trading environments where p&l is generated throughout the trading day, the assessment of the performance of that trading activity should be insulated from the ongoing funding effect of trading undertaken on previous days.

Where historical profits have been *realised*, under "Cash funding" these act to increase the business' cash balance, and therefore decrease its ongoing funding requirement and associated interest cost. This funding benefit attaches itself to the businesses in perpetuity, and may have the effect of distorting the performance assessment of future trading.

Under "Balance sheet funding", however, the ongoing funding benefit of these realised profits remains with Treasury, since it continues to fund the business according to its current open trading portfolio value, but the aggregate external funding requirement of the whole entity on which Treasury pays the interest has been reduced.

Additionally, there is an opportunity cost/benefit to the entity of *unrealised p&l*, since by merely realising that p&l, there would be an immediate impact on the entity's cash borrowing cost. By funding each business based on its current open trading portfolio value, then the business is effectively paying Treasury for this opportunity cost.

By applying "Balance sheet funding", the Treasury p&l should therefore reflect the funding benefit of the entity's p&l as if it was all realised, with the businesses reflecting the opportunity cost of unrealised p&l. Businesses are therefore incentivised not to carry unrealised p&l unnecessarily. As a result, the recognition by a business of a non-cash asset/liability on the entity's balance sheet should incentivise the business concerned to use that asset/liability in a manner that generates a benefit to the entity over and above that which could be generated by Treasury just lending/borrowing the cash equivalent of that asset/liability in the overnight money market.

In practice, for logistical reasons, some organisations set up their cash management operations to adopt the cash funding basis where the amount of internal funding booked to each business flattens their cash balance, which is supplemented by an additional balance sheet charge that transfers funding p&l back to Treasury to capture the funding benefit of historic profits/losses. This method has the added benefit of capturing errors by cash management operations in assigning cash funding to each business, as illustrated in Appendix 28.1.

Transfer pricing

A sometimes contentious issue in banking corporations is often the determination of the rate at which internal businesses borrow their funding requirement from Treasury. This is often impacted by the mandate of the Treasury department, in terms of whether it is set-up as:

(1) a cost centre whose purpose is to act as a service provider to the organisation that provides a central coordination point for funding;
(2) a profit centre whose purpose is not only to arrange funding, but is also to make p&l from trading the interest-rate risk often produced as a by-product of funding activities at the shorter end of the yield curve.

The transfer pricing rate is usually representative of the rate that Treasury pays on the external borrowings. In some organisations a spread is applied to this rate to compensate Treasury for the operational costs involved in acting as the centralised funding provider.

However, further complications arise when the term structure of funding is taken into consideration, since different rates are payable on borrowings of different maturity, as determined by the ALM profile.

Again there are at least two approaches to addressing this issue.

Weighted average rate (WAR)

In order for the businesses to incur a funding cost that incorporates the term structure of funding, Treasury may calculate a daily weighted average rate (WAR) that is then applied to each daily internal borrowing. The advantage to this is that Treasury is compensated by the businesses for the additional funding cost incurred in the borrowing term as required by the ALM profile.

The disadvantage of this transfer pricing approach is that businesses often have different maturity profiles of their assets, and therefore contribute in different amounts to the term funding cost incurred by Treasury, but ultimately all pay the same WAR. Some businesses can therefore end up effectively subsidising other businesses.

"Marginal rate" with term premium allocation

ALM generates the requirement to borrow cash for committed periods longer than overnight.

Incorporated into the cost of borrowing term cash is a market "*term premium*". This is the spread between borrowing term cash, and the equivalent OIS for swapping that term cash down to overnight floating.

Where the size and tenor of an individual business' portfolio warrants it, term funding may be allocated directly to that individual business' book, or passed on to that book "back-to-back" through the Treasury book. Note: The by-product of this is the generation of interest-rate risk in the business' book.

However, if the term funding is booked into the Treasury book, this term premium will become part of the Treasury p&l, requiring reallocation.

The "marginal rate" transfer pricing approach is to initially charge each business using the incremental overnight funding rate, and to then allocate the term premium back to those businesses with the longer term assets that are being liquidity risk managed.

Allocation methodology

The Treasury book can be split between term funding portfolios and an overnight funding "pool". The term funding book would then internally lend the cash raised from term borrowings to the overnight pool at the overnight rate, with the resultant term premium p&l being captured within the term funding portfolio, along with any other gap p&l generated by Treasury electing not to swap down the term funding to OIS.

The reallocation method of the term premium p&l is to use:

(1) the asset liquidation profile from the ALM process as the basis for the amounts to be charged (the rationale being that it is this profile which the term funding is being benchmarked against to ensure satisfactory management of liquidity gaps),

in combination with:

(2) a published term premium matrix maintained by Treasury that reflects the current premium of term cash rates by maturity bucket over and above the equivalent OIS rate.

The ALM asset value per bucket is to be multiplied by the term premium for that bucket, for whatever period of time the allocation is being made (possibly in conjunction with ALM reporting), with buckets per business summed together to provide a business total.

This total allocation will not match the actual term premium p&l (since actual term funding will not perfectly match the asset liquidation profile, and the term premium matrix is only indicative), so the actual term premium p&l can then be allocated in the same proportion per business as the theoretical results calculated above.

Depending on the currency mix of the term funding, this methodology may need to be applied at a currency level.

For example, consider Table 28.1 on page 1250–1. Note how "Business F" has 25% of the total asset value, but incurs 50% of the total term premium. This reflects the disproportionate impact that Business F has on the term funding requirement under prudent ALM management.

Capital structure

The funding cost of an entity is also impacted by its capital structure. The relative contributions of debt and share capital, including various different forms and hybrids of each, all have a bearing on the amount of interest-bearing funding required, and the rates of interest payable on that funding.

To demonstrate how the impact of the capital structure on an entity's funding cost is treated, we will address share capital and subordinated debt as examples.

Share capital

The share capital of a legal entity represents a source of funding like any other, except it has one main defining characteristic: it bears no real interest cost. Again, there are different approaches as to where the share capital is booked and where the benefit of this free source of funding is assigned.

Since the share capital is a specific type of external funding source, it is often booked in the Treasury books of the entity in which the capital resides, with the cash forming part of the general cash funding pool of the entity that is then managed by Treasury.

The net interest benefit of the utilisation of this "free" cash is subject to the same transfer pricing issues as those discussed in the Transfer Pricing section above. It can either be:

Asset liquidation profile ($M)

Business	o/n	o/n–1m	1m–6m	6m–12m	12m–2yr
Business A	42	268	150	78	43
Business B	14	113	199		
Business C	32	88	266	512	478
Business D	16	503	168		
Business E	9	20	20		
Business F	7	19	23	150	220
Business G	44	448	213		
Totals	**164**	**1,459**	**1,038**	**740**	**741**

Term premium matrix (bps)

Premium		o/n	o/n–1m	1m–6m	6m–12m
Term premium (bp)	0	0	3	5	7

Annual term premium p&l allocation ($)

Business	o/n	o/n–1m	1m–6m	6m–12m	12m–2yr	2yr–5yr
Business A		80,318	75,000	54,600	43,000	
Business B		34,045	99,500			
Business C		26,398	133,000	358,400	478,000	
Business D		150,750	83,750			
Business E		5,959	9,932			
Business F		5,700	11,500	105,000	220,000	240,000
Business G		134,400	106,500			
Totals		**437,569**	**519,182**	**518,000**	**741,000**	**240,000**

Table 28.1 Asset liquidation profile and term premium allocation

2yr–5yr	5yr–10yr	10yr–15yr	15yr+	TOTAL	%
				581	12%
				326	7%
				1,376	28%
				686	14%
				49	1%
200	185	300	170	1,274	25%
				705	14%
200	**185**	**300**	**170**	**4,997**	

12m–2yr	2yr–5yr	5yr–10yr	10yr–15yr	15yr+
10	12	15	20	25

5yr–10yr	10yr–15yr	15yr+	Theoretical allocation	Actual allocation	%
			252,918	235,538	7%
			133,545	124,368	4%
			995,798	927,371	26%
			234,500	218,386	6%
			15,891	14,799	0%
277,500	600,000	425,000	1,884,700	1,755,191	50%
			240,900	224,346	6%
277,500	**600,000**	**425,000**	**3,758,251**	**3,500,000**	
		Actual term premium p&l:	**3,500,000**		

- factored into the WAR calculation, such that the net interest benefit is distributed across the businesses. The rationale behind this approach is that the benefit is a product of conducting business from a legal entity, and therefore each business operating from that legal entity is entitled to benefit from it;
- it can be retained within Treasury, such that it forms part of the overall Treasury p&l. The rationale behind this approach is that each business should be assessed on its incremental contribution to the profitability of the entity, and should not reflect entity-level share capital that has already been injected.

Either way, the treatment should be consistent with the treatment of retained earnings discussed in the Internal Funding Cost Allocation section above. Since retained earnings and share capital are both similar sources of funding in that neither have a real interest cost, it makes sense that under cash funding, where the business benefits from retained earnings, that share capital is factored into the WAR. Alternatively, under balance sheet funding, where the benefit of retained earnings is retained within Treasury, it makes sense for Treasury also to retain the benefit of share capital.

Subordinated debt

As a mechanism of capital structure management, subordinated debt can sometimes be issued by an entity. This type of debt has characteristics of both share capital and term funding.

It has characteristics of share capital: in ranks below senior debt-holders in the pecking order of net asset distribution in the event of the entity being liquidated. In order to compensate the subordinated debt-holder for this perceived increase in credit risk relative to senior debt-holders, the entity must pay an interest premium on the subordinated debt.

Additionally, subordinated debt has characteristics of term funding in that it is generally of a longer maturity term.

Therefore, the rate paid on the subordinated issue will have three elements:

- the base short-term Libor rate for short-term *senior* debt;
- the *term premium*: this will initially be captured within the Treasury p&l, and possibly reallocated as per the Transfer Pricing section above.
- the *subordinated premium*: this will also initially be captured within the Treasury p&l, and should be treated consistently with the return on initial share capital per the Share Capital section above.

Bid–offer spread

When funding larger organisations with potentially multiple legal entities, there is generally a requirement to consider the bid–offer spread. We consider the approaches in this section.

Entity netting

Where the banking corporation is a *price-taker* in the money markets, and the funding position of multiple entities are "swept" together to generate one central funding requirement, then there is often a netting benefit across the entities within the Group in determining which side of the bid–offer spread it will pay/receive.

If the Group is a *net borrower* of cash, then all entities pay/receive the higher "*offer*" rate on their funding position.

- Individual entities that are net *borrowers* pay the *same side* of the spread as what they would pay if funded separately in an external market.
- Individual entities that are net *lenders* receive the *more beneficial side* of the spread than what they would receive if funded separately in an external market.

If the Group is a *net lender* of cash, then all entities pay/receive the lower "*bid*" rate on their funding position.

- Individual entities that are net *borrowers* pay the *more beneficial side* of the spread than what they would pay if funded separately in an external market.
- Individual entities that are net *lenders* receive the *same side* of the spread as what they would receive if funded separately in an external market.

Individual entities may therefore receive a "subsidy" from other entities in the Group by having an opposite cash position to the combined Group.

Business netting

The same relationship as the above applies to businesses operating within an entity; that is, there is a *funding rate benefit* available to businesses whose cash position is *opposite* to that of the combined entity.

Under these circumstances, there are two policy options available:

(1) Apply the same side of the bid–offer spread to all internal funding tickets, thereby feeding any funding rate netting benefit down to the entities and businesses that are creating the netting benefit.

Factors to consider include the implications on the tax status of an entity obtaining a benefit from other group entities, as well as the "benefit at risk" to each entity/business of the existing funding relationships with existing funding sources.

(2) Treat each entity and each business within an entity as a discrete price-taking funding unit that borrows at "offer" and lends at "bid". The funding rate netting benefit would then accumulate centrally in the Treasury book, both at an entity level and at a group level, and may then be available for some form of reallocation, although the possible allocation bases for this are numerous.

Example ticket booking structure

Figure 28.2 is an example ticket booking structure which incorporates many of the above concepts. It shows the individual books within Treasury, each capturing a particular facet of the entity's funding, providing highly desired transparency of the funding p&l.

As an alternative to actually booking this multitude of internal transactions, which do provide transparency but also require a degree of operational effort to capture and control (especially in larger and more complex organisations), there are systems in the market whose objective is to achieve the same funding p&l allocation as the above without actually capturing the internal funding as ticketed transactions per se.

When implemented correctly, these can achieve the same granularity of management information without the same degree of operational effort, although these function by applying a cost of carry to open trading positions and therefore are inextricably linked to the balance sheet funding method discussed above.

Organisation of reporting line

To support effective asset and liability management (ALM), it is essential that the appropriate corporate structure is in place with associated internal reporting lines, to ensure that the goals of the organisation are best served. All matters regarding ALM are dealt with by a specific committee which has responsibility for ALM decision-making. This committee is labelled the

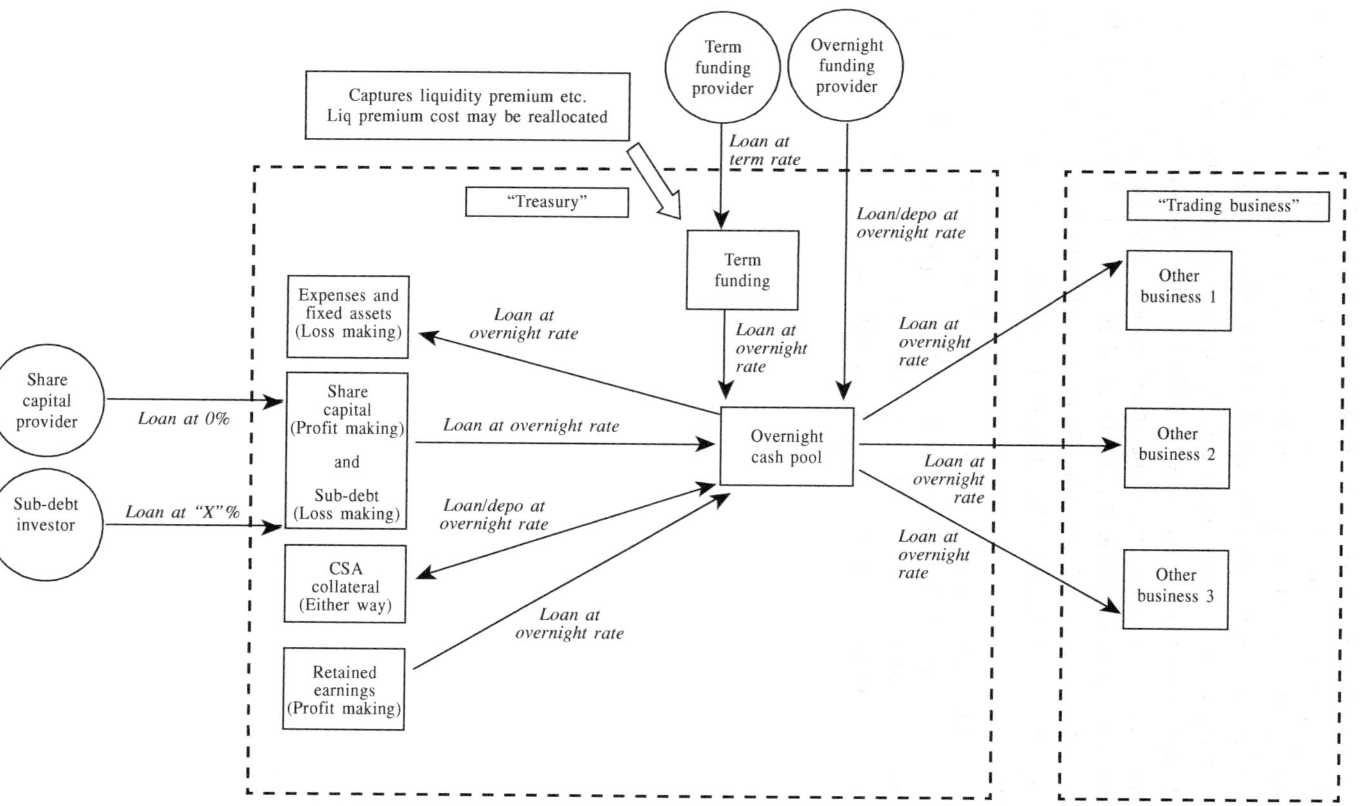

Figure 28.2 Ticket booking structure

asset and liability committee, otherwise known as "ALCO".

The chairman of ALCO reports to the Board, and the committee members of the ALCO always include the heads of the key departments, these being the Finance Director, Head of Risk, Head of Front Office, and Head of Operations. Other supporting departmental heads may also have direct representation on the ALCO, although this is not essential and depends on the size and nature of the organisation. For example, the Finance Director may also be flanked by the Head of Finance, the Head of Middle Office and the Head of Regulatory Reporting. The Head of Middle Office may report to the firm Chief Operating Officer (COO) or direct to an ALCO member.

The ALCO determines the remit of the head of ALM, who is therefore also a member of ALCO. The head of ALM is responsible for the day-to-day implementation of the policies and procedures determined by ALCO. The head of ALM is therefore a key direct report of the head of Treasury.

Appendix

APPENDIX 28.1

Example A: Balance sheet funding capturing daily profit remittance

Business A has:

- current-year profits of $500 (realised $350, unrealised $150);
- prior year losses of $200 (realised $170, unrealised $30);
- balance sheet trading assets purchased with cash for $2,000 consideration, now worth $2,120 (thus the net unrealised profit of $150 – $30 = $120 above);
- no physical remittance of cash to Treasury;
- The net cash position of the above has been accurately funded with Treasury via inter-book lending (*ticketed funding*); that is, + $350 – $170 – $2,000 = –$1,820.

Business A's Balance sheet therefore looks like:

{+ve = Debit, -ve = Credit}

Trading assets	$2,120
Ticketed funding liability	($1,820)
Net non-cash assets	**$300**
Cash	$0
p&l/Retained earnings	($300)
Cash and p&l	($300)
	$0

In this example, a charge on the net positional assets of $300 at the overnight rate is payable to Treasury, which represents:

- a transfer from the business to Treasury of the real benefit to the entity of reinvesting the $180 *realised* p&l;
- a transfer from the business to Treasury of the notional opportunity cost of being unable to reinvest the $120 *unrealised* p&l.

Applying this charge creates the effect of daily profit remittance to Treasury without the need to actually book the remittance in systems. Note that from Treasury's perspective, the p&l on its external borrowing of $1,820 is offset with that of the ticketed internal lending of $1,820 to Business A, so the Treasury p&l is just left with the unticketed net asset charge from Business A.

Example B: Balance sheet charge capturing daily profit remittance and incorrectly ticketed funding

Business B has:

- current-year profits of $1,000 (realised $600, unrealised $400);
- no prior year p&l;
- balance sheet trading assets purchased with cash for $3,000 consideration, now worth $3,400 (thus the net unrealised profit of $400 above);
- no physical remittance of cash to Treasury;
- the net cash position of the above has been *accurately* funded externally by Treasury, but has been *inaccurately* allocated to Business B due to errors in the cash management funding allocation processes. The funding ticket in Business B has been booked for $2,100 (as opposed to +$600 – $3,000 = –$2,400).

Business B's Balance sheet therefore looks like:

{+ve = Debit, -ve = Credit}

Trading assets	$3,400
Funding liability	($2,100)
Net non-cash assets	**$1,300**
Cash	($300)
p&l/Retained earnings	($1,000)
Cash and p&l	($1,300)
	$0

In this example, a charge on the net positional assets of $1,300 at the overnight rate is payable to Treasury, which represents:

- a transfer from the business to Treasury of the real benefit to the entity of reinvesting the $600 *realised* p&l;
- a transfer from the business to Treasury of the notional opportunity cost of being unable to reinvest the $400 *unrealised* p&l;
- a transfer from the business to Treasury of the mis-allocated cash funding of $300. Note: The business with the opposite side to the funding mis-allocation will have the opposite impact on the Treasury p&l, and will therefore net to zero across the entity.

Andrew Oliver is a Director of Treasury Middle Office at KBC Financial Products, London. He was previously the vice-president of Money Market Trading and Treasury Middle Office at Deutsche Bank. Andrew is a member of the Institute of Chartered Accountants of Australia, and the Securities Institute of Australia. He obtained his Economics degree at Sydney University where he is a member of the Golden Key Society.

This is a process that just about all of us go through: a realisation, a reluctant acceptance of the fact that life is difficult and that our wildest dream will always be both wild and dreamy. No shame attaches to this adjustment: it is a common experience.

– Simon Barnes,
The Meaning of Sport,
Short Books 2006, p. 138

Falling in love is also something that gives you a very high chance of disappointment. Having children brings you a certainty of anxiety. A lifelong marriage gives you 50-50 chance of bereavement. It seems to me that the human condition is based around things that give you a very high chance of pain, misery, distress, anxiety. We do not seek to avoid them at all: on the contrary. We seek them out, avidly, voraciously, incontinently.

– Simon Barnes, *Ibid.*, p. 171

Humans are contradictory creatures. This matter is familiar to us all: we want at the same time to be married, to be free; to be wildly promiscuous, to be forever faithful; to travel, to stay at home; to seek adventures, to remain in safety; to be idle, to be rewardingly busy; to revel in company, to be contentedly alone.

– Simon Barnes, *Ibid.*, p. 237

PART

VII

Applications software enclosed with the book

Part VII consists of one chapter, which describes the software and applications available on the CD-R accompanying this book. The software and spreadsheets can be used to undertake a number of the calculations and analyses that have been described in the book.

CHAPTER

29

Applications Software and Spreadsheet Models

In this chapter we describe the software and applications that are available on the CD-ROM that accompanies this book. All the methods and techniques that are available with these applications are relevant to material that has been covered in various parts of the main text.

The software files that are available are:

- YCF 2.0, a cubic B-spline yield curve model;
- RATE^{TM}; a yield curve and spot and forward rate calculator, and interest-rate swap and vanilla cap/floor pricing model;
- ABS and CDO cash-flow waterfall models;
- Excel spreadsheets that can be used for pricing, hedging and funding calculations.

For each application described below we also identify for the reader the relevant chapter in the book that is related to it, shown in square brackets. After loading the CD-ROM to your PC or laptop, please select the required application from within the relevant directory in Windows Explorer or relevant file manager. Further details are given in the descriptive text below.

YCF Cubic B-Spline yield curve application

YCF 2.0 is a Cubic B-Spline yield curve fitting application, written by Kevin Zhuoshi Liu and Moorad Choudhry. It has a Microsoft Excel front-end for accessibility and user-friendliness. The model enables users to fit the current discount function as well as zero-coupon rate and forward rate yield curves from bond yields and swap rates. Users can also calculate forward rates for any required term and any required starting date. The application uses the cubic B-spline methodology to fit the yield curve.

To access and load this application, load the CD-R onto your PC or laptop and in Windows Explorer open the directory named "YCF Cubic B-Spline". First open the .txt file named "password", which gives the password for the application. Note this password. Then click on the "Setup" file and the application will take you through the set-up instructions. When set-up is complete, go to the "All Programmes" entry on the PC main menu and select "YCF 2.0 xls". This will launch the programme.

There is also a User Manual in the same directory (the .pdf file, which is read in Adobe Acrobat) that describes the application in full and complete detail. We recommend that readers review this document before using the application.

[Chapter 9]

RATE yield curve and swap/vanilla option pricing application

RATE is a model designed to demonstrate a selection of interest-rate products and fixed-income market concepts. It was written by Rod Pienaar and Moorad Choudhry. It has components for modelling the zero-coupon curve using either bond yields or a combination of cash money market and interest-rate derivative rates, which we have called the "standard" yield curve. RATE also contains interest-rate swap and option cap valuation tools.

[Chapter 9]

Getting started: installing the application[1]

To access and load this application, load the CD-R to your PC or laptop, and in Windows Explorer open the directory named "RATE". Then open the sub-directory named RATEv3_Setup, and within that double-click on the file named "RateSetup". This is an Application file. Opening this file takes the user through the set-up process. After set-up is complete, go to the "All

[1] These instructions must be followed precisely. Only click on the file named "RateSetup", which is an Application file. When installing the application, do not open any other file in either directory. Some PCs, especially those in corporate offices, may not open these files because of a firewall. In this case, please request your IT department to install the application. Note that the RATE source code is also available for inspection and modification by programmers.

Programmes" menu item on the PC or laptop main menu and RATE will be located within the list of programmes. Click on this and the application will load.

RATE is designed for use on Windows operating systems and will function in Windows 95/98, Windows 2000, Windows NT and Windows XP environments. During the application process, select all of the default installation options. If the user prefers to customise the installation location of RATE and its data tables, then the data engine path may need to be modified after RATE has been installed.

Once RATE has been successfully installed and launched, the user will be presented with an opening screen that introduces the application. This is shown in Figure 29.1.

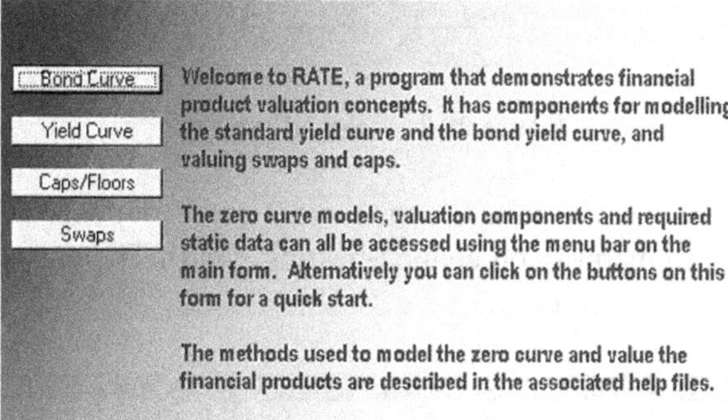

Figure 29.1 Introduction screen

RATE allows the user to construct zero-coupon curves using either a standard yield curve model or a bond yield model. Select a preferred method and click on the "bond curve" or "yield curve" quick start button. The user will need to capture curve data before a swap or cap can be valued. Ignore the cap and swap options for now!

Using the zero curve models

RATE's yield curve model constructs a zero-coupon curve using a combination of short-term money market, exchange-traded futures and OTC swap instruments. The yield curve screen will initially contain no market data. The basic template is shown in Figure 29.2 on page 1266.

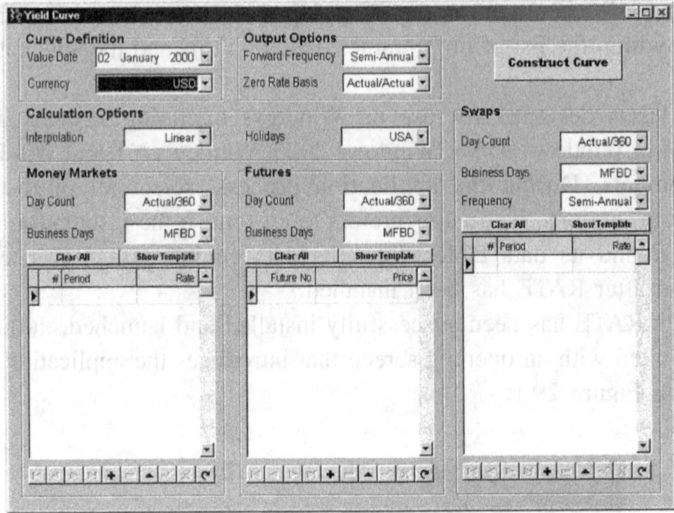

Figure 29.2 Yield curve screen

RATE's bond curve model constructs a zero-coupon curve using the effective yield to maturity on coupon-bearing bonds. The empty bond curve screen is given in Figure 29.3.

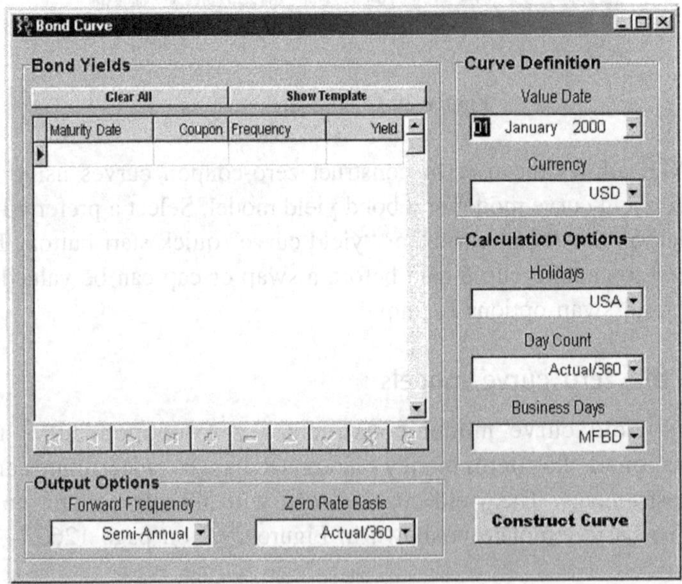

Figure 29.3 Bond curve screen

A RATE zero curve is defined by the value date and currency. These two input parameters are used to filter the underlying input data and therefore determine which market quotes are used to construct a zero curve. It is important to set the value date and currency before attempting to capture any market data.

RATE places no limitation on the number of yield curve or bond curve forms that can be opened. Each form can have its own curve definition. However, where two forms define the same curve (that is, the same currency and value date), but use different calculation parameters, RATE will only display the most recently calculated zero curve. Remember that each new screen utilises computer memory and will place an extra burden on the operating system. It is therefore advisable to limit the number of forms that are kept open at any one time.

Selecting your calculation parameters

In order to construct the zero curve, RATE requires calculation parameters. The parameters required are holiday country and, in respect of the standard yield curve, interpolation method. Holiday country selects the set of holidays that will be used to identify whether settlement dates are business days or public holidays. A list of holidays can be created, edited or deleted on the holiday form. The holiday form is accessed from the "Static Data" menu.

Two types of standard yield curve interpolation are supported by RATE: linear and exponential. The interpolation methods are discussed in Choudhry et al. (2005).

To calculate the zero curve, RATE needs to know what output options to apply. It is common practice to display the zero curve after applying the Actual/Actual method to calculate the zero rate. RATE also allows the user to convert discount factors into zero rates using the 360/Actual and 365/Actual methods. These day-count methods were covered in more detail in Chapter 4.

In addition to calculating the zero curve, RATE also calculates and displays the forward rates derived from the zero curve. RATE can align its forward rate periods with the zero curve tenors, but also allows the user to select the length of the forward rate period. Quarterly, semi-annual and annual options can be applied to the forward rate period. It is common market practice to calculate each forward period using the curves' tenor points.

Capturing your market inputs

When the user is ready to construct a curve for a value date and currency, then RATE will need the user to populate the market grid with quoted rates. To simplify this process an input template can be created using the "show template" button. A template creates a matrix of dates so that only the market rates need to be captured. An example data set where the money markets are populated by the template method is shown in Figure 29.4. The user may of course select her own dates without recourse to the template.

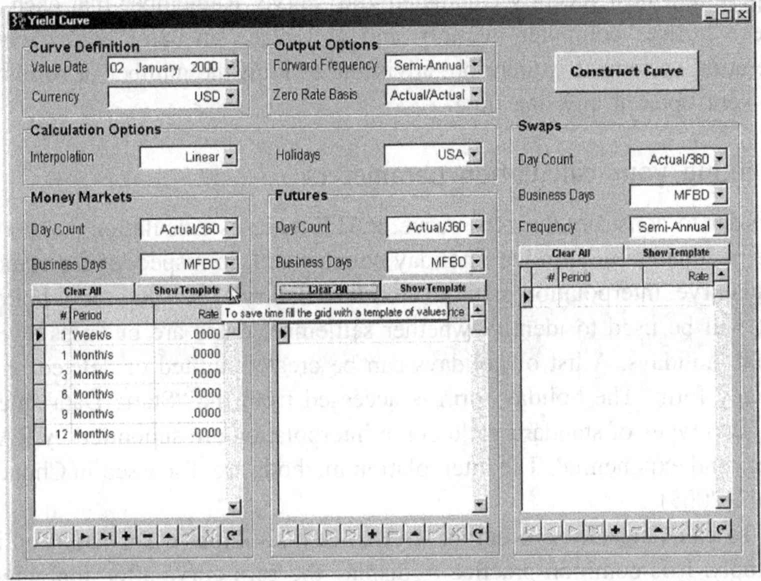

Figure 29.4 Populated data set

RATE automatically saves market data in underlying data tables. The data grid on the yield curve and bond curve screens provides a method of capturing and editing this market data. Once data has been captured it is automatically saved to the underlying tables. This auto save feature works each time the cursor moves from one record to the next. The most recent data item to be input or edited will not be saved until the cursor is moved to the next record, or the "Post" button on the data editor is pressed. The user should generally change the day-count basis, business day basis and, where applicable, the coupon payment frequency to match the market's standards. When using the bond model a coupon frequency, generally annual or semi-annual, is required for each bond.

To return to previous input data, simply change the currency and value date to the relevant curve definition and the input data will be displayed. Be careful to ensure that the curve value date and currency are correctly defined before market data is captured. Data captured to the incorrect value date or currency can only be corrected by recapturing this information to the properly defined curve.

For any particular value date and currency, market inputs should have only one quoted rate for each maturity date. RATE prevents duplicate maturity dates and will highlight this with a "key error" when there has been an attempt to create a duplicate entry. A "key error" is explained in more detail in the application's help file.

The TAB and arrow keys can be used to move through the input grids. If the cursor is positioned in the last cell in the data grid then the TAB key will create a new record.

Below each market data grid is a data navigator and editor. This data editor provides assistance with capturing and editing market data. The data navigator is presented in Figure 29.5.

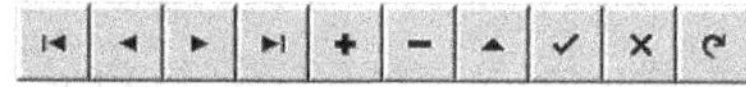

Figure 29.5 Data navigator

Each button on the editor performs the following functions:

First	Moves to the first record.
Prior	Moves to the previous record.
Next	Moves to the next record.
Last	Moves to the last record.
Insert	Inserts a new record before the current record.
Delete	Deletes the current record and prompts for confirmation before deleting.
Edit	Puts the record in Edit mode so that it can be modified.
Post	Saves changes to the data.
Cancel	Cancels any edits to the current record.
Refresh	Refreshes the data grid from the underlying data.

The zero curve output display

The calculation output is shown in Figure 29.6.

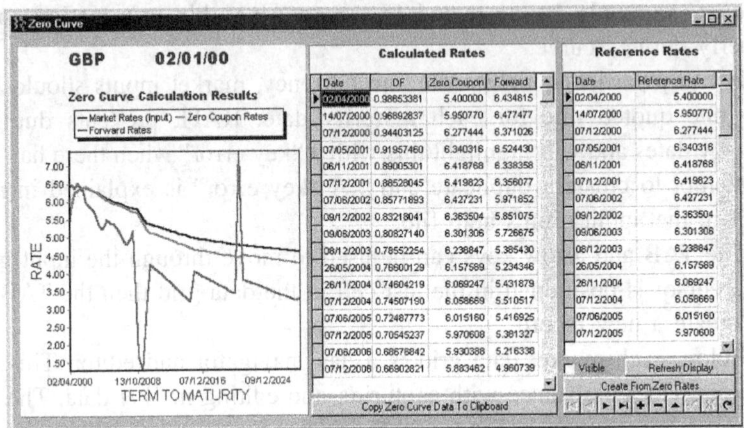

Date	DF	Zero Coupon	Forward
02/04/2000	0.98653381	5.400000	6.434815
14/07/2000	0.96892837	5.950770	6.477477
07/12/2000	0.94403125	6.277444	6.371026
07/05/2001	0.91957460	6.340316	6.524430
06/11/2001	0.89005301	6.418768	6.338358
07/12/2001	0.88528045	6.419823	6.356077
07/06/2002	0.85771893	6.427231	5.971852
09/12/2002	0.83218041	6.363504	5.851075
09/06/2003	0.80827140	6.301306	5.726675
08/12/2003	0.78552254	6.238847	5.385430
26/05/2004	0.76600129	6.157589	5.234346
26/11/2004	0.74604219	6.069247	5.431879
07/12/2004	0.74507190	6.058669	5.510517
07/06/2005	0.72487773	6.015160	5.416925
07/12/2005	0.70545237	5.970608	5.381327
07/06/2006	0.68676842	5.930388	5.216338
07/12/2006	0.66902821	5.883462	4.960739

Date	Reference Rate
02/04/2000	5.400000
14/07/2000	5.950770
07/12/2000	6.277444
07/05/2001	6.340316
06/11/2001	6.418768
07/12/2001	6.419823
07/06/2002	6.427231
09/12/2002	6.363504
09/06/2003	6.301306
08/12/2003	6.238847
26/05/2004	6.157589
26/11/2004	6.069247
07/12/2004	6.058669
07/06/2005	6.015160
07/12/2005	5.970608

Figure 29.6 Output screen

To calculate and display the zero-coupon and forward curves, press the "Construct Curve" button. On the zero curve output form there is a data grid for reference rates. Reference rates are rates that can be manually input or edited, and then compared to the calculated zero rates, input rates or forward rates. This enables the zero construction model to be benchmarked against market data such as bond strips or alternative zero-curve construction methodologies. The user can input any reference rate for any date. To save input time the reference grid can be populated using the input rates, zero rates or forward rates. Selecting the input rates enables the user to compare the calculated spot rates to the bond yields.

When a new zero curve is constructed the reference rates remain unchanged. This allows the user to perform currency or date comparisons for different zero curves.

If the output data is required in a different application, such as Excel or Word, then use the button "Copy Zero Curve Data To the Clipboard" and simply paste it into Excel or Word. This enables the user to further manipulate the application's output.

Instrument valuation

RATE can also be used to value interest-rate swaps and caps and floors.

The swap calculator

The swap calculator returns the value of an interest-rate swap. A standard yield curve definition is enforced after the swap parameters have been captured. This means that RATE can be used to value the same swap against any zero curve. The calculation parameters value date, currency and interpolation do not therefore form part of the swap parameters. The input screen is shown in Figure 29.7.

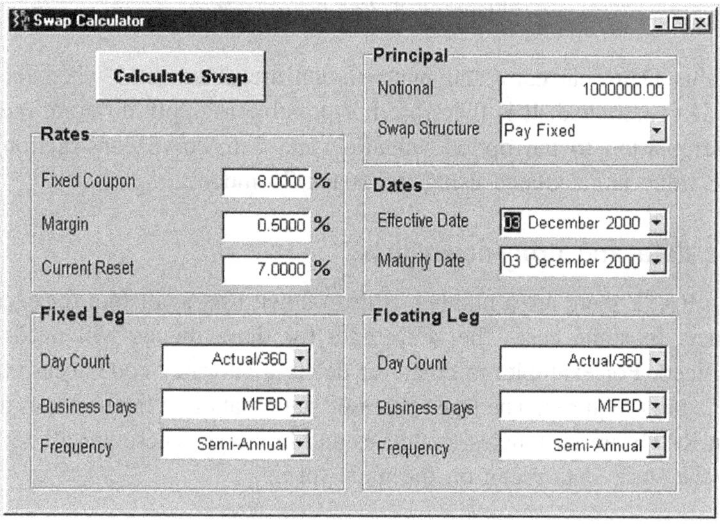

Figure 29.7 Swap input

RATE calculates and displays the cash flows for the fixed leg and floating leg separately. The present value of each leg is determined and aggregated to return the net present value of the swap. Where the effective date precedes the value date then the swap is being valued after it has started accruing interest. Accrued interest for the current coupon is therefore displayed.

Cap / floor calculator

The cap / floor calculator calculates the value of an interest-rate cap/floor based on the selected zero-coupon curve. As with the swap calculator, the cap calculator enforces a standard yield curve definition when the option is valued. The parameter input screen is shown in Figure 29.8.

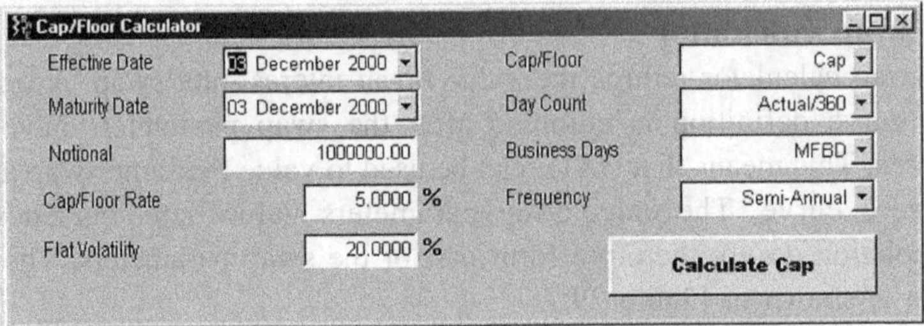

Figure 29.8 Cap Input screen

Value Date, currency and interpolation are determined when the zero curve is constructed. It is therefore not possible to apply different methods of interpolation to the option valuation and zero-curve construction. The option value is calculated using the Black 76 model.

Static data and drop-down lists

Within RATE there are a number of drop-down lists available; for example, currency. In some cases the static data for these menus will need to be maintained. For example, to create or delete a currency code access to this static data is required. The three types of static data that the user can update within RATE are currencies, countries and holidays. These are all accessed using the static data menu on the main form.

Structured finance securities: cash-flow waterfall models

There are two cash-flow waterfall models available on the CD-ROM. These are the:

- ABS Master Trust waterfall model;
- Static balance sheet synthetic CDO model.

They are Microsoft Excel front-end models.

To load the applications, in Windows Explorer go to the relevant directory and then open the Excel file from there.

ABS and RMBS Master Trust structure waterfall cash-flow model

This Microsoft Excel model was written by Suleman Baig and Moorad Choudhry. It can be applied to any multi-tranche structured finance transaction or Master Trust structure. It enables users to model the cash-flows for the payment waterfall for a complex transaction with multiple inputs.

The model can be used to either project or record cash flows relating to an hypothetical Master Trust Structured Transaction. The model has been designed for a term of 29 quarterly periods, but the length and frequency of the transaction can be easily modified through increasing or decreasing the number of columns in each of the worksheets within it. All calculations required to calculate terms and features within the structure are either done so within the model itself (grey cells) or require external data that need to be input by the user (light blue cells). All inputs are consolidated into a single 'Inputs' worksheet. Currently, the model holds dummy data for an hypothetical transaction.

The data required to be entered by the user relates primarily to collateral performance and collections data that would normally be provided by the receivables servicer. That is, data on underlying asset cash-flows, which are usually monitored and recorded by the asset servicer.

The Trustee would normally be expected to use the model to record actual data and calculate bond amortisation and payment flows on each interest payment date.

To project cash flows, anticipated or assumed portfolio performance information would be entered to evaluate the impact on the structure.

The model shows two Series (both issued simultaneously). This is not common practice but is useful for illustrating the interaction between series within the Trust. Of course, the model has flexibility to add further series as they are issued.

Each series has two waterfall worksheets. The first worksheet (labelled as first iteration) shows the initial projected flow of funds. This is completed for each series within the Trust and the level of excess interest or senior obligation shortfall within each series is calculated. The model then re-assigns collections from the (combined) pool and single series available funds are recalculated accordingly. The second iteration waterfall is then the reflection of the actual flows to be effected.

Note amortisation and interest calculation is shown in the Series1Notes and Series2Notes worksheets. Interest and principal is paid out pro-rata within each class (that is, on a per-note basis) as this is the approach adopted by most deals.

The model also features a Principal Deficiency Ledger – which may not feature in all Master Trust transactions – but is useful for the user to see how this form of credit enhancement could be used.

[Chapters 18, 20]

Static synthetic CDO cash-flow waterfall model

This is a working cash-flow waterfall model for an hypothetical synthetic collateralised debt obligation, *Synthetic CDO Ltd,* issue size USD115 million. It was written by Suleman Baig and Moorad Choudhry. The note tranching to this transaction is given in the sheet, along with terms to the deal. The waterfall and associated calculations are on their own tabs in this spreadsheet. The definitions refer to an hypothetical *Offering Circular* (OC) for this transaction, which is not shown.

[Chapters 18, 23]

Microsoft Excel applications

The following spreadsheets are in the directory named "Excel spreadsheets":

- Black–Scholes (B–S) VBA option model, written by Abukar Ali and Moorad Choudhry.

  This is a demonstration of the B–S model to price a vanilla call option. The user enters parameters into the shaded cells.

  [Chapter 13]

- 3-month forward rate calculator, written by Stuart Turner.
  This spreadsheet calculates user-selected term forward rates implied by the 90-day short-term interest rate futures curve. The example given here uses the EuroDollar curve. Shaded cells indicate user-selected inputs.

  [Chapter 13]

- Convertible bond option-adjusted spread (OAS) model, written by Abukar Ali and Moorad Choudhry.

This model demonstrates the OAS technique for pricing a convertible bond. It also calculates parity and delta (convertible bonds are described in Choudhry (2005)). Users input bond parameters in the yellow-shaded cells.

[Chapter 4]

- EuroDollar Futures Strip Hedge, written by Abukar Ali and Moorad Choudhry.

  This worksheet is an educational tool designed to demonstrate the calculation of the hedge required for the holding of a cash bond, when this hedge is constructed using exchange-traded 90-day interest-rate futures contracts. The user can use the worksheet to calculate an approximation of the futures strip required to hedge a long or short position in a cash bond. The spreadsheet also calculates the discount function.

  For illustration, we show the Bloomberg TED page when it has been used to calculate the strip hedge for a $100 million long position in the Treasury $3^{7}/_{8}$% 2013. Note that this example is for a bond whose maturity date extends beyond the maturity of the longest-dated futures contract. If the bond has a maturity date that does not extend beyond a certain contract, then these remaining should not be considered.

  A description of each of the labelled cells in the spreadsheet is given below.

Cell	**Description**
Nominal amount	The nominal value of the bond position being hedged.
Spread	The difference between the bond YTM and the implied futures rate.
Contract	This is the specific contract used in the strip. The designation follows the exchange-traded custom, with H, M, U and Z used to designate contracts expiring in March, June, September and December each year.
Days	The term to maturity of the specified futures contract.
Price	The price of the futures contract.

Rate	The implied 90-day Libor rate on maturity implied by the price of the futures contract
Di	The discount factor derived from the futures contract, given by 1 + (Rate – TED) * Days/360 for spread-adjusted hedging.
Face value	The nominal amount of the bond position.
Present value	The present value of the face value, given by Face value * (1/Di).
Number of contracts	The number of contracts required in the futures strip to hedge the bond holding.

[Chapter 13]

- US Treasury bond repo funding calculator, written by Didier Joannas.

  This spreadsheet is also featured in Chapter 12. It calculates the net funding gain or loss for a two-bond relative value position. In effect, it shows the net breakeven, in terms of basis points, that the trade must make to be profitable. It is currently set up for US Treasury securities; however, the user may easily adjust the relevant cells to bring the worksheet up to date. The list of non-business days is maintained in the Visual Basic module.

  The user enters the bond price, coupon and maturity date in columns B, F and G. Long positions are entered separately to short positions. The repo rate applicable to the bond position is entered at column Q. The net funding gain or loss is shown for each bond against all the other bonds in column S. Note that this means a long position against all short positions, and vice-versa.

  [Chapters 3, 12]

The Excel spreadsheets are designed to be educational tools and instructional models. They may easily be adapted for users' own particular requirements. To load any application, in Windows Explorer go to the "Excel Spreadsheets" directory and then open the Excel file from there.

Reference

Choudhry, M. 2005, *Corporate Bond Markets: Instruments and Applications*, John Wiley & Son, Singapore.

Choudhry, M., Joannas, D., Pienaar, R. and Periera, R. 2005, *Capital Market Instruments: Analysis and Valuation*, 2nd Edition, Palgrave Macmillan, Basingstoke, Hampshire.

Appendix

Financial Markets Arithmetic

In this Appendix we describe the basic building blocks of corporate finance. These include the principles of compounded interest, the time value of money, and future and present values. These concepts are important in all aspects of finance and are a vital ingredient of capital market mathematics. It is essential to have a firm understanding of the main principles before moving on to other areas.

Simple and compound interest

The principles of financial arithmetic have long been used to illustrate that £1 received today is not the same as £1 received at a point in the future. Faced with a choice between receiving £1 today or £1 in one year's time we would not be indifferent, given a rate of interest of, say, 10% and provided that this rate is equal to our required nominal rate. Our choice would be between £1 today or £1 plus 10p – the interest on £1 for one year at 10% per annum. The notion that money has a time value is a basic concept in the analysis of financial instruments. Money has time value because of the opportunity to invest it at a rate of interest.

Simple interest

A loan that has one interest payment on maturity is accruing *simple interest*. On short-term instruments there is usually only the one interest payment on maturity; hence, simple interest is received when the instrument expires. The terminal value of an investment with simple interest is given by (A1.1):

$$FV = PV(1 + r) \qquad \text{(A1.1)}$$

where

FV is the terminal value or *future value*
PV is the initial investment or *present value*
r is the interest rate.

So, for example, if PV is £100, r is 5% and the investment is one year then:

$$\begin{aligned} FV &= £100\ (1 + r) \\ &= £105. \end{aligned}$$

The market convention is to quote interest rates as *annualised* interest rates, which is the interest that is earned if the investment term is one year. Consider a three-month deposit of £100 in a bank, placed at a rate of interest of 6%. In such an example the bank deposit will earn 6% interest for a period of 90 days. As the annual interest gain would be £6, the investor will expect to receive a proportion of this, which is calculated below:

$$£6.00 \times \frac{90}{365}.$$

So the investor will receive £1.479 interest at the end of the term. The total proceeds after the three months is therefore £100 plus £1.479. If we wish to calculate the terminal value of a short-term investment that is accruing simple interest we use the following expression:

$$FV = PV\left(1 + r \times \frac{\text{Days}}{\text{Year}}\right). \tag{A1.2}$$

The fraction $^{\text{Days}}/_{\text{Year}}$ refers to the numerator, which is the number of days the investment runs, divided by the denominator that is the number of days in the year. In the sterling markets the number of days in the year is taken to be 365; however, certain other markets (including the euro currency markets) have a 360-day year convention. For this reason we simply quote the expression as "days" divided by "year" to allow for either convention.

Compound interest

Let us now consider an investment of £100 made for three years, again at a rate of 6%, but this time fixed for three years. At the end of the first year the investor will be credited with interest of £6. Therefore for the second year the interest rate of 6% will be accruing on a principal sum of £106, which means that at the end of year 2 the interest credited will be £6.36. This illustrates how *compounding* works, which is the principle of earning interest on interest. What will the terminal value of our £100 three-year investment be?

In compounding we are seeking to find a *future value* given a *present value,* a *time period* and an *interest rate.* If £100 is invested today (at time t_0) at 6%, then one year later (t_1) the investor will have £100 × (1 + 0.06) = £106. In our example the capital is left in for another two years, so at the end of year 2 (t_2) we will have:

$$
\begin{aligned}
&\pounds 110 \times (1 + 0.06) \times (1 + 0.06) \\
&= \pounds 100 \times (1 + 0.06)^2 \\
&= \pounds 100 \times (1.06)^2 \\
&= \pounds 112.36.
\end{aligned}
$$

The outcome of the process of compounding is the *future value* of the initial amount. We don't have to calculate the terminal value long-hand as we can use the expression in (A1.3).

$$FV = PV\ (1 + r)^n \tag{A1.3}$$

where

r is the periodic rate of interest (expressed as a decimal)
n is the number of periods for which the sum is invested.

In our example the initial £100 investment becomes £110 × $(1 + 0.06)^3$, which is equal to £119.10.

When we compound interest we have to assume that the reinvestment of interest payments during the investment term is at the same rate as the first year's interest. That is why we stated that the 6% rate in our example was *fixed* for three years. We can see, however, that compounding increases our returns compared to investments that accrue only on a simple interest basis. If we had invested £100 for three years fixed at a rate of 6%, but paying on a simple interest basis, our terminal value would be £118, which is £1.10 less than our terminal value using a compound interest basis.

Compounding more than once a year
Now let us consider a deposit of £100 for one year, again at our rate of 6%, but with quarterly interest payments. Such a deposit would accrue interest of £6 in the normal way, but £1.50 would be credited to the account every quarter, and this would then benefit from compounding. Again assuming that we can reinvest at the same rate of 6%, the total return at the end of the year will be:

$$100 \times [(1 + 0.015) \times (1 + 0.015) \times (1 + 0.015) \times (1 + 0.015)] = 100 \times (1 + 0.015)^4$$

which gives us 100 × 1.06136, a terminal value of £106.136. This is some 13 pence more than the terminal value using annual compounded interest. In general, if compounding takes place m times per year, then at the end of n years mn interest payments will have been made and the future value of the principal is given by (A1.4) below:

$$FV = PV\left(1 + \frac{r}{m}\right)^{mn}. \tag{A1.4}$$

As we showed in our example the effect of more frequent compounding is to increase the value of the total return when compared to annual compounding. The effect of more frequent compounding is shown below, where we consider the annualised interest-rate factors, for an annualised rate of 5%.

Compounding frequency	**Interest-rate factor**	
Annual	$(1 + r)$	= 1.050000
Semi-annual	$\left(1 + \frac{r}{2}\right)^2$	= 1.050625
Quarterly	$\left(1 + \frac{r}{4}\right)^4$	= 1.050945
Monthly	$\left(1 + \frac{r}{12}\right)^{12}$	= 1.051162
Daily	$\left(1 + \frac{r}{365}\right)^{365}$	= 1.051267

This shows us that the more frequent the compounding the higher the interest-rate factor. The last case also illustrates how a limit occurs when interest is compounded continuously. Equation (A1.4) can be rewritten as follows:

$$FV = PV\left[\left(1+\frac{r}{m}\right)^{m/r}\right]^{rn}$$
$$= PV\left[\left(1+\frac{1}{m/r}\right)^{m/r}\right]^{rn} \quad \text{(A1.5)}$$
$$= PV\left[\left(1+\frac{1}{n}\right)^{n}\right]^{rn}$$

where $n = m/r$. As compounding becomes continuous and m and hence n approach infinity, the expression in large brackets in (A1.5) above approaches a value known as e, which is shown below.

$$e = \lim_{n\to\infty}\left(1+\frac{1}{n}\right)^{n} = 2.718281 \ldots$$

If we substitute this into (A1.5) this gives us:

$$FV = PVe^{rn} \quad \text{(A1.6)}$$

where we have continuous compounding. In (A1.6) e^{rn} is known as the *exponential function* of rn and it tells us the continuously compounded interest-rate factor. If $r = 5\%$ and $n = 1$ year then:

$$e^{r} = (2.718281)^{0.05} = 1.051271.$$

This is the limit reached with continuous compounding. From our initial example, to illustrate continuous compounding the future value of £100 at the end of three years when the interest rate is 6% is given by:

$$FV = 100e^{(0.06)\times 3}$$
$$= £119.72.$$

Effective interest rates

The interest rate quoted on a deposit or loan is usually the *flat* rate. However, we are often required to compare two interest rates that apply for a similar investment period, but have different interest payment frequencies; for example, a two-year interest rate with interest paid quarterly compared to a two-year rate with semi-annual interest payments. This is normally done by comparing equivalent *annualised* rates. The annualised rate is the interest rate with annual compounding that results in the same return at the end of the period as the rate we are comparing.

The concept of the effective interest rate allows us to state that:

$$PV \times \left(1 + \frac{r}{n}\right)^n = PV \times (1 + aer) \quad \text{(A1.7)}$$

where *aer* is the equivalent annual rate. Therefore if *r* is the interest rate quoted which pays *n* interest payments per year, the *aer* is given by (A1.8):

$$aer = \left[\left(1 + \frac{r}{n}\right)^n - 1\right]. \quad \text{(A1.8)}$$

The equivalent annual interest rate *aer* is known as the *effective* interest rate. We have already referred to the quoted interest rate as the "nominal" interest rate. We can rearrange equation (A1.8) above to give us (A1.9), which allows us to calculate nominal rates.

$$r = [(1 + aer)^{1/n} - 1] \times n \quad \text{(A1.9)}$$

We can see then that the effective rate will be greater than the flat rate if compounding takes place more than once a year. The effective rate is sometimes referred to as the *annualised percentage rate* or APR.

EXAMPLE A1.1 Effective interest rate

Farhana has deposited funds in a building society 1-year fixed rate account with interest quoted at 5%, payable in semi-annual instalments. What is the effective rate that she earns at the end of the period?

$$\left[\left(1 + \frac{0.05}{2}\right)^2 - 1\right] = 5.0625\%$$

Abubakar is quoted a nominal interest rate of 6.40% for a one-year time deposit where the interest is credited at maturity. What is the equivalent rate for the same building society's one-year account that pays interest on a monthly basis?

$$\left[\left(1 + 0.064\right)^{1/12} - 1\right) \times 12 = 6.2196\%$$

Interest-rate conventions

The convention in both wholesale or personal (retail) markets is to quote an annual interest rate. A lender who wishes to earn the interest at the rate quoted has to place his funds on deposit for one year. Annual rates are quoted irrespective of the maturity of a deposit, from overnight to ten years or longer. For example, if one opens a bank account that pays interest at a rate of 3.5%, but then closes it after six months, the actual interest earned will be equal to 1.75% of the sum deposited. The actual return on a three-year building society bond (fixed deposit) that pays 6.75% fixed for three years is 21.65% after three years. The quoted rate is the annual one-year equivalent. An overnight deposit in the wholesale or *interbank* market is still quoted as an annual rate, even though interest is earned for only one day.

The convention of quoting annualised rates is to allow deposits and loans of different maturities and different instruments to be compared on the basis of the interest rate applicable. We must also be careful when comparing interest rates for products that have different payment frequencies. As we have seen from the foregoing paragraphs the actual interest earned will be greater for a deposit earning 6% on a semi-annual basis compared to 6% on an annual basis. The convention in the money markets is to quote the equivalent interest rate applicable when taking into account an instrument's payment frequency.

Value date

In both the money markets and the bond markets, the *value date* of a transaction is the date on which the deal is effected, the date when money changes hands between buyer and seller. It is sometimes referred to as the "settlement date" but the two are not strictly synonymous. The date on which the buyer makes good payment, which is the same date that the seller delivers securities, should always be referred to as the value date.

The standard money market value date is known as *spot* and refers to two business days after trade date, also referred to as "T+2". Same-day settlement is also common in certificate of deposit (CD) and commercial paper (CP) markets, and is known as *cash* settlement or T+0. However, it is possible to deal T+0, T+1, T+2 and T+3 in many markets and instruments as long as both counterparties are agreeable.

For forward dealing and for setting maturity dates, the market convention is to move to the next relevant calendar date under a practice known as *modified following business day*. So a two-month transaction, or a two-month forward transaction, traded on 31 August 2004, would mature (or settle) on 31 October 2004. However, this is a non-business day; ordinarily the maturity or settlement date would move to the next business day, but this changes the month (to November), so it would instead move back to 29 October 2004 as moving forward would change the month. But if both parties are agreeable, a maturity (or settlement) date of 1 November 2004 can be set.

The time value of money

Present values with single payments

The interest rate or discount rate used as part of the present value (price) calculation is key, as it reflects where the instrument is trading in the market and how it is perceived by the market. Earlier we saw how a *future value* could be calculated given a known *present value* and rate of interest. For example, £100 invested today for one year at an interest rate of 6% will generate $100 \times (1 + 0.06) = £106$ at the end of the year. The future value of £100 in this case is £106. We can also say that £100 is the *present value* of £106 in our example.

In equation (A1.3) we established the following future value relationship:

$$FV = PV\,(1 + r)^n \,.$$

By reversing this expression we arrive at the present value (PV) formula (A1.10):

$$PV = \frac{FV}{(1 + r)^n} \qquad \text{(A1.10)}$$

where terms are as before. Equation (A1.10) applies in the case of annual interest payments and enables us to calculate the PV of a known future sum.

EXAMPLE A1.2 Present value

Naseem is saving for a trip around the world after university and needs to have £1,000 in three years' time. He can invest in a building society bond at 7% guaranteed fixed for three years. How much does he need to invest now? To solve this we require the PV of £1,000 received in three years' time.

$$PV = \frac{1000}{(1 + 0.07)^3} = \frac{1000}{1.225043} = 816.29787.$$

Naseem therefore needs to invest £816.30 today.

To calculate the PV for a short-term investment of less than one year we will need to adjust what would have been the interest earned for a whole year by the proportion of days of the investment period. Rearranging the basic equation, we can say that the present value of a known future value is:

$$PV = \frac{FV}{(1 + r \times {}^{\text{Days}}/_{\text{Year}})}. \tag{A1.11}$$

Given a present value and a future value at the end of an investment period, what then is the interest rate earned? We can rearrange the basic equation again to solve for the *yield.*

$$Yield = \left(\frac{FV}{PV} - 1\right) \times \frac{\text{Year}}{\text{Days}} \tag{A1.12}$$

Using equation (A1.12) will give us the interest rate for the actual period. We can then convert this to an effective interest rate using (A1.13).

$$r = \left(1 + Yield \times \frac{\text{Days}}{\text{Year}}\right)^{365/\text{days}} - 1. \tag{A1.13}$$

When interest is compounded more than once a year, the formula for calculating PV is modified, as shown by (A1.14):

$$PV = \frac{FV}{\left(1 + \frac{r}{m}\right)^{mn}} \tag{A1.14}$$

where as before FV is the cash flow at the end of year n, m is the number of times a year interest is compounded, and r is the rate of interest or discount rate. Illustrating this therefore, the PV of £100 that is received at the end of five years at a rate of interest rate of 5%, with quarterly compounding is:

$$PV = \frac{100}{\left(1 + \frac{0.05}{4}\right)^{(4)(5)}}$$

$$= £78.00.$$

Present values with multiple discounting

Present values for short-term investments of under one-year maturity often involve a single interest payment. If there is more than one interest payment, then any discounting needs to take this into account. If discounting takes place m times per year then we can use equation (A1.4) to derive the PV formula as follows:

$$PV = FV\left(1 + \frac{r}{m}\right)^{-mn}. \tag{A1.15}$$

For example, what is the present value of the sum of £1,000 that is to be received in five years where the discount rate is 5% and there is semi-annual discounting?

Using (A1.15) above we see that:

$$PV = 1000\left(1 + \frac{0.05}{2}\right)^{-2 \times 5}$$

$$= £781.20.$$

The effect of more frequent discounting is to lower the PV. As with continuous compounding, the limiting factor is reached with continuous discounting and we can use equation (A1.6) to derive the present value formula for continuous discounting:

$$PV = FVe^{-rn}. \tag{A1.16}$$

Using this expression, if we consider the same example as before but now with continuous discounting, we calculate the PV of £1,000 to be received in five years' time as:

$$PV = 1000e^{-(0.05) \times 5}$$

$$= £778.80.$$

EXAMPLE A1.3 Calculation summaries

Angela invests £250 in a bank account for five years at a rate of 6.75%. What is the future value of this sum assuming annual compounding?

After 180 days Angela decides to close the account and withdraw the cash. What is the terminal value?

$$250 \times (1.0675)^5 = £346.56$$
$$250 \times (1.0675 \times 180/365) = £258.32.$$

To pay off a personal loan Olivia requires £500 in 30 days' time. What must she invest now if she can obtain 12% interest from a bank?

$$500/(1 + 0.12 \times 30/365) = £495.12.$$

If Olivia deposits £1,000 today and receives a total of £1,021 after 90 days, what yield has she earned on the investment?

$$[(1{,}021/1{,}000) - 1] \times 365/90 = 8.52\%.$$

What is the 180-day discount factor earned during this period if the interest rate is 6.15%? What is the 10-year discount factor?

$$1/(1 + 0.0615 \times 180/365) = 0.97056$$
$$1/(1 + 0.0615)^{10} = 0.55055.$$

What is the PV of £100 in 10 years' time at this discount rate?

$$100 \times 0.55055 = £55.06.$$

Multiple cash flows

Future values

Up to now we have considered future values of a single cash flow. Of course the same principles of the time value of money can be applied to a bundle of cash flows. A series of cash flows can be at regular or irregular intervals. If we wish to calculate the total future value of a set of irregular payments made in the future we need to calculate each payment separately and then sum all the cash flows. The formula is represented with the equation given at (A1.17):

$$FV = \sum_{n=1}^{N} C_n \, (1 + r)^{N-n} \tag{A1.17}$$

where C_n is the payment in year n and the symbol Σ means "the sum of". We assume that payment is made and interest credited at the end of each year.

It is much more common to come across a regular stream of future payments. Such a cash flow is known as an *annuity*. In an annuity the payments are identical and so C_n as given in (A1.17) simply becomes C. We can then rearrange (A1.17) as shown below:

$$FV = C \sum_{n=1}^{N} (1 + r)^{N-n}. \tag{A1.18}$$

This equation can be simplified to give us the expression at (A1.19):[1]

$$FV = C \left[\frac{(1 + r)^N - 1}{r}\right]. \tag{A1.19}$$

This formula can be used to calculate the future value of an annuity. For example, if we consider an annuity that pays £500 each year for ten years at a rate of 6%, its future value is given by:

$$FV = 500 \left[\frac{(1.06)^{10} - 1}{0.06}\right] = £6{,}590.40.$$

EXAMPLE A1.4 Calculating pension contributions

We can use the future value equation (A1.19) to calculate the size of contributions required to establish a pension fund on retirement. If we rearrange (A1.19) to obtain the size of the annuity C we obtain:

$$C = FV \left[\frac{r}{(1 + r)^N - 1}\right].$$

[1] If we multiply both sides of (A1.18) by $1 + r$ and then subtract the result from (A1.18) we obtain:

$$FV - (1 + r)\, FV = C\left[\sum_{n=1}^{N}(1 + r)^{N-n} - \sum_{n=1}^{N}(1 + r)^{N-n+1}\right]$$
$$= -C\left[(1 + r)^N - 1\right].$$

Lita wishes to have a savings pool of £250,000 to fund her pension when she retires in 30 years' time. What annual pension contribution is required if the rate of interest is assumed to be a constant 7.9%?

$$C = 250{,}000\left[\frac{0.079}{(1.079)^{30} - 1}\right] = £2247.65.$$

The common definition of an annuity is a continuous stream of cash flows. In practice the pension represented by an annuity is usually paid in monthly instalments, similar to an employed person's annual salary. Certain regular payments compound interest on a more frequent basis than annually, so our formula in (A1.19) needs to be adjusted slightly. If compounding occurs m times each year, then (A1.19) needs to be altered to (A1.20) to allow for this.

$$FV = C\sum_{n=1}^{N}\left(1 + \frac{r}{m}\right)^{m(N-n)} \tag{A1.20}$$

To make calculations simpler we can multiply both sides of (A1.20) by $[1 + (r/m)]$ and subtract the result from (A1.20).[2] Simplifying this will then result in (A1.21) below:

$$FV = C\left[\frac{[1 + (r/m)]^{mn} - 1}{[1 + (r/m)]^{m} - 1}\right]. \tag{A1.21}$$

For example, a 10-year annuity that has annual payments of £5,000 each year, but compounded on a quarterly basis at a rate of 5%, will have a future value of £63,073 as shown below:

$$FV = 5{,}000\left[\frac{[1.025]^{20} - 1}{[1.025]^{2} - 1}\right] = £63{,}073.$$

Where there is continuous compounding, as before, the limiting factor will result in (A1.21) becoming (A1.22):

$$FV = C\left[\frac{e^{rN} - 1}{e^{r} - 1}\right]. \tag{A1.22}$$

[2] The process is:

$$FV - [1 + (r/m)]^{m}\, FV = C\left[\sum_{n=l}^{N}[1 + (r/m)]^{M(N-n)} - \sum_{n=l}^{N}[1 + (r/m)]^{M(N-n)+m}\right]$$
$$= -C\left[(1 + (r/m))^{mN} - 1\right].$$

Equations (A1.21) and (A1.22) can be adjusted yet again to allow for frequent payments together with frequent compounding, but such a stream of cash flows is rarely encountered in practice. For reference, in the case of continuous compounding of continuous payments, the limiting factor expression is as shown in (A1.23):

$$FV = C\left[\frac{e^{rN} - 1}{r}\right]. \tag{A1.23}$$

Present values

Using similar principles as we have employed for calculating future values, we can calculate present values for a stream of multiple of cash flows. The method employed is slightly different according to whether the cash flows are regular or irregular.

For irregular payments we calculate PV by applying the conventional PV formula to each separate cash flow and then summing the present values. This is represented by (A1.24):

$$PV = \sum_{n=1}^{N} C_n(1 + r)^{-n} \tag{A1.24}$$

where C_n is the cash flow made in year n.

Consider a series of annual cash payments made up of £100 in the first year and then increasing by £100 each year until the fifth year. The PV of this cash flow stream is:

$$\begin{aligned} PV &= 100(1.05)^{-1} + 200(1.05)^{-2} + 300(1.05)^{-3} + 400(1.05)^{-4} + 500(1.05)^{-5} \\ &= 95.24 + 181.41 + 259.15 + 329.08 + 391.76 \\ &= £1256.64. \end{aligned}$$

The more frequently encountered type of cash flow stream is an *annuity*, regular annual payments with annual discounting. To calculate the present value of an annuity we can use a variation of (A1.19) as shown in (A1.25):

$$\begin{aligned} PV &= \frac{FV}{(1 + r)^N} \\ &= C\left[\frac{(1 + r)^N - 1}{r}\right]\left[\frac{1}{(1 + r)^N}\right] \\ &= C\left[\frac{1 - (1 + r)^{-N}}{r}\right]. \end{aligned} \tag{A1.25}$$

Consider now an annuity paying £5,000 each year for 20 years at an interest rate of 4.5%. The PV of this annuity is:

$$PV = 5{,}000 \left[\frac{1 - (1.045)^{-20}}{0.045}\right]$$

$$= 65{,}039.68.$$

We illustrated this principle using a 20-year annuity that employed annual discounting. If a cash-flow stream employs more frequent discounting we need to adjust the formula again. If an annuity discounts its cash flows m times each year then the PV of its cash-flow stream is found using the PV-adjusted equation from (A1.21). This becomes (A1.26).

$$PV = \frac{\mathrm{FV}}{\left(1 + \frac{r}{m}\right)^{mN}} = c\left[\frac{1 - [1 + (r/m)]^{mN}}{[1 + (r/m)]^{m} - 1}\right] \qquad \text{(A1.26)}$$

If continuous discounting is employed then this results again in the limiting factor for continuous discounting, so we adjust (A1.26) and the new expression is given in (A1.27):

$$PV = C\left[\frac{1 - e^{-rN}}{e^{r} - 1}\right]. \qquad \text{(A1.27)}$$

The last case to consider is that of the payments stream that has more frequent cash flows in addition to more frequent discounting. Such a payments stream will have m cash flows each year that are also discounted m times per year. To calculate the PV of the cash flows we use (A1.28):

$$PV = \frac{FV}{\left(1 + \frac{r}{m}\right)^{mN}} = C\frac{1 - [1 + (r/m)]^{mN}}{r}. \qquad \text{(A1.28)}$$

The limiting factor for continuous discounting of continuous payments is given by (A1.29):

$$PV = C\left[\frac{1 - e^{-rN}}{r}\right]. \qquad \text{(A1.29)}$$

Payment streams that have cash-flow frequencies greater than annually or semi-annually occur quite often in the markets. To illustrate how we might use (A1.28), consider a mortgage-type loan taken out at the beginning of a period. If the borrower is able to fix the interest rate being charged to the whole life of the mortgage, he or she can calculate the size of the monthly payments that are required to pay off the loan at the end of the period.

For example, consider a repayment mortgage of £76,000 taken out for 25 years at a fixed rate of interest of 6.99%. The monthly repayments that would be charged can be calculated using (A1.28) as shown in (A1.30):

$$C_i = \frac{C}{12} = \frac{PV}{12}\left[\frac{r}{1 - [1 + (r/m)]^{-12 \times N}}\right] \tag{A1.30}$$

where C_i is the size of the monthly payment. Substituting the terms of the mortgage payments in to the equation we obtain:

$$C_i = \frac{76{,}000}{12}\left[\frac{0.0699}{1 - [1 + (0.0699/12)]^{-12 \times 25}}\right] = £536.67.$$

The monthly repayment is therefore £536.67 and includes the interest chargeable in addition to a repayment of some of the principal (hence, the term *repayment* mortgage, as opposed to *endowment* mortgages that only pay off the monthly interest charge). A repayment mortgage is also known as an *amortised* mortgage. An amortised loan is one for which a proportion of the original loan capital is paid off each year. Loans that require the borrower to service the interest charge only each year are known as *straight* or *bullet* loans. It is for this reason that plain vanilla bonds are sometimes known as bullet bonds, since the capital element of a loan raised through a vanilla bond issue is repaid only on maturity.

Perpetual cash flows

The type of annuity that we as individuals are most familiar with is the *annuity pension*, purchased from a life assurance company using the proceeds of a pension fund at the time of retirement. Such an annuity pays a fixed annual cash amount for an undetermined period, usually up until the death of the beneficiary. An annuity with no set finish date is known as a *perpetuity*. As the end date of a perpetuity is unknown we are not able to calculate its PV with exact certainty; however, a characteristic of the term $(1 + r)^{-N}$ is that it approaches zero as N tends to infinity. This fact reduces our PV expression to:

$$PV = \frac{C}{r} \tag{A1.31}$$

and we can use this formula to approximate the present value of a perpetuity. The UK gilt market includes four gilts that have no redemption date, so-called *undated* bonds. The largest issue among the undated gilts is the $3^1/_2$% War Loan, a stock originally issued at the time of the 1914–18 war. This bond pays a coupon of £$3^1/_2$ per £100 nominal of stock. Since the cash-flow structure of this bond matches a perpetual, its PV using (A1.33) when long-dated market interest rates are at, say, 5% would be:

$$PV = \frac{3.5}{0.05} = £70.$$

The PV of the cash-flow stream represented by the War Loan when market rates are 5% would therefore be £70 per £100 nominal of stock. In fact, because this bond pays coupon on a semi-annual basis we should adjust the calculation to account for the more frequent payment of coupons and discounting, so the PV (price) of the bond is more accurately described as:

$$PV = \frac{C/2}{r/2} = \frac{1.75}{0.025}$$

although as we would expect this still gives us a price of £70 per cent!

Discount factors

The calculation of present values from future values is also known as *discounting*. The principles of present and future values demonstrate the concept of the *time value* of money – that in an environment of positive interest rates a sum of money has greater value today than it does at some point in the future because we are able to invest the sum today and earn interest. We will only consider a sum in the future compared to a sum today if we are compensated by being paid interest at a sufficient rate. Discounting future values allows us to compare the value of a future sum with a present sum.

Another way to write the expression in example (A1.14) is to say that we multiply £1,000 by $1/(1.05)^5$, which is the *reciprocal* of $(1.05)^5$ and is denoted in this case as $(1 + 0.05)^{-5}$. The rate of interest r that we use in Example A1.2 is known as the *discount rate* and is the rate we use to *discount* a known future value in order to calculate a present value. We can rearrange equation (A1.14) to give:

$$PV = FV(1 + r)^{-n}$$

and the term $(1 + r)^{-n}$ is known as the n-year discount factor. So we have

$$df_n = (1 + r)^{-n} \tag{A1.32}$$

where df_n is the n-year discount factor.

The three-year discount factor when the discount rate is 9% is:

$$df_n = (1 + 0.09)^{-3} = 0.77218.$$

We can calculate the discount factor for all possible interest rates and time periods to give us a *discount function*. Fortunately we don't need to calculate discount factors ourselves as this has been done for us and a discount table for a range of rates is provided in Table A1.3 on page 1314.

FORMULA SUMMARY

Discount factor with simple interest: $df = \dfrac{1}{(1 + r \times \text{Days}/\text{Year})}$

Discount factor with compound interest: $df_n = \left(\dfrac{1}{1 + r}\right)^n$

$$r = \sqrt[n]{\frac{1}{df}} - 1$$

Earlier we established the continuously compounded interest rate factor as e^{rn}. Using a continuously compounded interest rate therefore we can establish the discount factor to be:

$$df = \frac{1}{1 + (e^{r \times \text{Days}/\text{Year}} - 1)}$$

$$= e^{-r \times \text{Days}/\text{Year}} \tag{A1.33}$$

$$\therefore df_n = e^{-rn}.$$

The continuously compounded discount factor is part of the formula used in option pricing models. It is possible to calculate discount factors from the prices of government bonds. The traditional approach described in most textbooks requires that we first use the price of a bond that has only one remaining coupon, its last one, and calculate a discount factor from this bond's price. We then use this discount factor to calculate the discount factors of bonds with ever-increasing maturities, until we obtain the complete discount function. This method, which is illustrated in the box below, suffers from certain drawbacks and in practice more sophisticated techniques are used, see for example the author's book *Fixed Income Markets* for a discussion of the techniques.

EXAMPLE A1.5 Discount factors

The following hypothetical government bonds pay coupon on a semi-annual basis. Consider the bond prices indicated, and assume that the first bond has precisely six months to maturity, so that it has only one more cash flow to pay, the redemption value and final coupon. Assume further that the remaining bonds mature at precise six-month intervals.

Bond	Price
8% June 2000	101.09
7% December 2000	101.03
7% June 2001	101.44
6.5% December 2001	101.21

The first bond has a redemption payment of 104.00, comprised of the redemption payment and the final coupon payment (remember that this is a semi-annual coupon bond). The present value of this bond is 101.09. This allows us to determine the discount factor of the bond as follows:

$$101.09 = 104.00 \times df_{6\text{-}month}$$
$$0.97202 = df_{6\text{-}month}.$$

This shows that the six-month discount factor is 0.97202. We use the second bond in the table, which has cash flows of 3.50 and 103.50, to calculate the next period discount factor, using the following expression:

$$101.30 = 3.50 \times df_{6\text{-}month} + 103.50 \times df_{1\text{-}year}.$$

We have already calculated the six-month discount factor, and use this to calculate the one-year discount factor from the above expression, which solves to give 0.94327.

We then carry on this procedure for the next bond, leaving us the following discount factors:

Bond	Price	Discount factor
8% June 2000	101.09	0.97202
7% December 2000	101.03	0.94327
7% June 2001	101.44	0.91533
6.5% December 2001	101.21	0.89114

Note how the discount factors progressively reduce in value over an increasing maturity period. Using one of a number of techniques we can graph the set of discount factors above to obtain the two-year discount function. In the same way, if we have government bond prices for all maturities from six months to 30 years, we can obtain the complete discount function for that currency.

The discount function

Discount factors can be calculated for any discount rate that apply to any term to maturity, using the standard formulas. The complete range of discount factors for any particular rate is known as the *discount function.* Figure A1.1 illustrates the discount function when the discount rate selected is 5%. This is obtained by plotting continuous rather than discrete discount factors for a given rate. A discount factor table for selected rates and investment terms is given in Table A1.3.

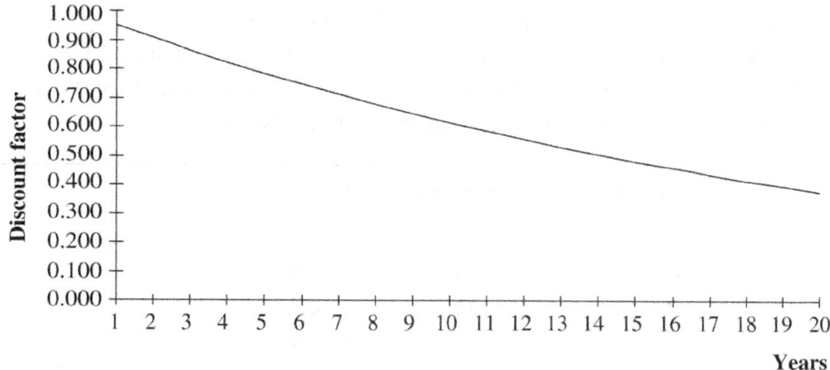

Figure A1.1 Discount function with the rate at 5%

Using Discount factors

An n-period discount factor is the present value of one unit of currency (£1 or \$1) that is payable at the end of period n. Essentially it is the present value relationship expressed in terms of \$1. If $d(n)$ is the n-year discount factor, then the five-year discount factor at a discount rate of 6% is given by:

$$d(5) = \frac{1}{(1 + 0.06)^5} = 0.747258.$$

The set of discount factors for every time period from one day to 30 years or longer is termed the *discount function*. Discount factors may be used to price any financial instrument that is made up of a future cash flow. For example, what would be the value of \$103.50 receivable at the end of six months if the six-month discount factor is 0.98756? The answer is given by:

$$0.98756 \times 103.50 = 102.212.$$

In addition, discount factors may be used to calculate the future value of any present investment. From the example above, \$0.98756 would be worth \$1 in six months' time, so by the same principle a present sum of \$1 would be worth

$$1/d(0.5) = 1/0.98756 = 1.0126$$

at the end of six months.

It is possible to obtain discount factors from current bond prices. Assume a hypothetical set of bonds and bond prices as given in Table A1.1 below, and assume further that the first bond in the table matures in precisely six months' time (these are semi-annual coupon bonds).

Coupon	Maturity date	Price
7%	7-Jun-01	101.65
8%	7-Dec-01	101.89
6%	7-Jun-02	100.75
6.50%	7-Dec-02	100.37

Table A1.1 Hypothetical set of bonds and bond prices

Taking the first bond, this matures in precisely six months' time, and its final cash flow will be 103.50, comprising the \$3.50 final coupon payment and the \$100 redemption payment. The price or present value of this bond is 101.65, which allows us to calculate the six-month discount factor as:

$$d(0.5) \times 103.50 = 101.65$$

which gives $d(0.5)$ equal to 0.98213.

From this first step we can calculate the discount factors for the following six-month periods. The second bond in Table A1.2, the 8% 2001, has the following cash flows:

- \$4 in six months' time
- \$104 in one year's time.

The price of this bond is 101.89, which again is the bond's present value, and this comprises the sum of the present values of the bond's total cash flows. So we are able to set the following:

$$101.89 = 4 \times d(0.5) + 104 \times d(1).$$

However, we already know $d(0.5)$ to be 0.98213, which leaves only one unknown in the above expression. Therefore we may solve for $d(1)$ and this is shown to be 0.94194.

If we carry on with this procedure for the remaining two bonds, using successive discount factors, we obtain the complete set of discount factors as shown in Table A1.2. The continuous function for the two-year period from today is known as the discount function, shown in Figure A1.2.

Coupon	Maturity date	Term (years)	Price	$d(n)$
7%	7-Jun-01	0.5	101.65	0.98213
8%	7-Dec-01	1.0	101.89	0.94194
6%	7-Jun-02	1.5	100.75	0.92211
6.50%	7-Dec-02	2.0	100.37	0.88252

Table A1.2 Discount factors calculated using bootstrapping technique

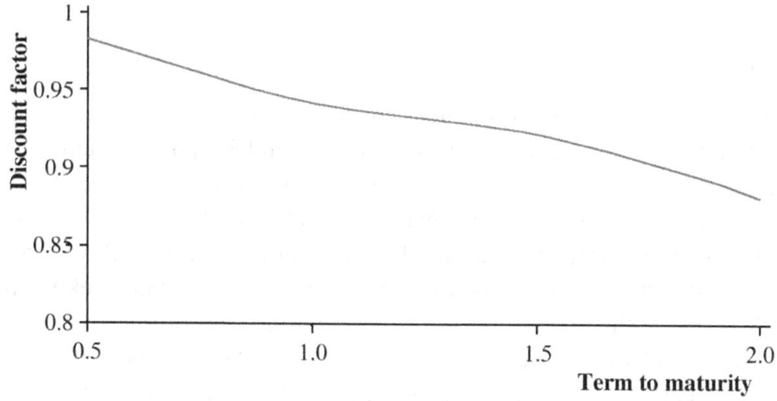

Figure A1.2 Hypothetical discount function

This technique, which is known as *bootstrapping*, is conceptually neat but presents problems when we do not have a set of bonds that mature at precise six-month intervals. In addition, liquidity issues connected with specific individual bonds can also cause complications. However, it is still worth being familiar with this approach.

Note from Figure A1.2 how discount factors decrease with increasing maturity: this is intuitively obvious, since the present value of something to be received in the future diminishes the further into the future we go.

Corporate finance project appraisal

Two common techniques used by corporates and governments to evaluate whether a project is worth undertaking are the *net present value* (NPV) and *internal rate of return* (IRR). Both techniques evaluate the anticipated cash flows associated with a project, using the discounting and present value methods described so far in this Appendix. Generally speaking, it is a company's *cost of capital* that is used as the discount rate in project appraisal, and most companies attempt to ascertain the true cost of their capital as accurately as possible. As most corporate financing is usually a complex mixture of debt and equity this is sometimes problematic. A discussion of cost of capital is outside the scope of this book and we recommend Higson (1995) for readers wishing to know more about this subject.[3]

Net present value (NPV)

In the case of an investment of funds made as part of a project, we would have a series of cash flows of which some would be positive and others negative. Typically, in the early stages of a project we would forecast negative cash flows as a result of investment outflows, followed by positive cash flows as the project began to show a return. Each cash flow can be present valued in the usual way. In project appraisal we would seek to find the PV of the entire stream of cash flows, and the sum of all positive and negative present values added together is the NPV. As the appraisal process takes place before the project is undertaken, the future cash flows that we are concerned with will be estimated forecasts and may not actually be received once the project is underway.

The PV equation is used to show that:

$$NPV = \sum_{n=1}^{N} \frac{C_n}{(1+r)^n} \tag{A1.34}$$

where C_n is the cash flow in the project in period N. The rate r used to discount the cash flows can be the company's cost of capital or the rate of return required by the company to make the project viable.

Companies will apply NPV analysis to expected projected returns because funds invested in any undertaking have a time-related cost, the opportunity cost that is the corporate cost of capital. In effect, NPV measures the PV of the gain achieved from investing in the project (provided that it

[3] Higson, C. (1995), *Business Finance*, Oxford, Butterworth.

is successful!). The general rule of thumb applied is that any project with a positive NPV is worthwhile, whereas those with a negative NPV, discounted at the required rate of return or the cost of capital, should be avoided.

EXAMPLE A1.6 Calculating NPV

What is the NPV of the following set of expected cash flows, discounted at a rate of 15%?

Year 0: –£23,000
Year 1: +£8,000
Year 2: +£8,000
Year 3: +£8,000
Year 4: +11,000

$$\text{NPV} = 23{,}000 - \frac{8{,}000}{(1.15)} + \frac{8{,}000}{(1.15)^2} + \frac{8{,}000}{(1.15)^3} + \frac{11{,}000}{(1.15)^4} = £1{,}554.$$

The internal rate of return (IRR)

The IRR for an investment is the discount rate that equates the PV of the expected cash flows (the NPV) to zero. Using the PV expression we can represent it by the rate r such that:

$$\sum_{n=0}^{N} \frac{C_n}{(1+r)^n} = 0 \qquad \text{(A1.35)}$$

where C_n is the cash flow for the period N, n is the last period in which a cash flow is expected, and Σ denotes the sum of discounted cash flows at the end of periods 0 through n. If the initial cash flow occurs at time 0, equation (A1.35) can be expressed as follows:

$$C_0 = \frac{C_1}{(1+r)} + \frac{C_2}{(1+r)^2} + \dots + \frac{C_N}{(1+r)^N}. \qquad \text{(A1.36)}$$

In corporate finance project appraisal, C_0 is a cash outflow and C_1 to C_N are cash inflows. Thus r is the rate that discounts the stream of future cash flows (C_1 through C_N) to equal the initial outlay at time 0 – C_0. We must therefore assume that the cash flows received subsequently are reinvested to realise the same rate of return as r. Solving for the IRR, r cannot be found analytically and has to be found through numerical iteration, or using a computer or programmable calculator.

To illustrate IRR consider the earlier project cash flows given in Example A1.6. If we wish to find the IRR longhand then we would have to obtain the NPV using different discount rates until we found the rate that gave the NPV equal to zero. The quickest way to do this manually is to select two discount rates, one of which gives a negative NPV and the other a positive NPV, and then *interpolate* between these two rates. This method of solving for IRR is known as an *iterative* process, and involves converging on a solution through trial and error. This is in fact the only way to calculate the IRR for a set of cash flows and it is exactly an iterative process that a computer uses (the computer is just a touch quicker!). If we have two discount rates, say x and y that give positive and negative NPVs respectively for a set of cash flows, the IRR can be estimated using the equation in (A1.37):

$$\text{IRR estimate} = x\% + (y\% - x\%) \times (+ve \text{ NPV value}/[+ve \text{ NPV value} - (-\text{NPV value})]). \quad \text{(A1.37)}$$

EXAMPLE A1.7 IRR calculation

In Example A1.6, using a discount rate of 15% produced a positive NPV. Discounting the cash flows at 19% produces an NPV of –£395. Therefore the estimate for IRR is:

$$15\% + 4\% \times 1554/[1554 - (-395)] = 18.19\%.$$

The IRR is approximately 18.19%. This can be checked using a programmable calculator or spreadsheet programme, or may be checked manually by calculating the NPV of the original cash flows using a discount rate of 18.19%; it should come to £23,000. Using an HP calculator we obtain an IRR of 18.14%.

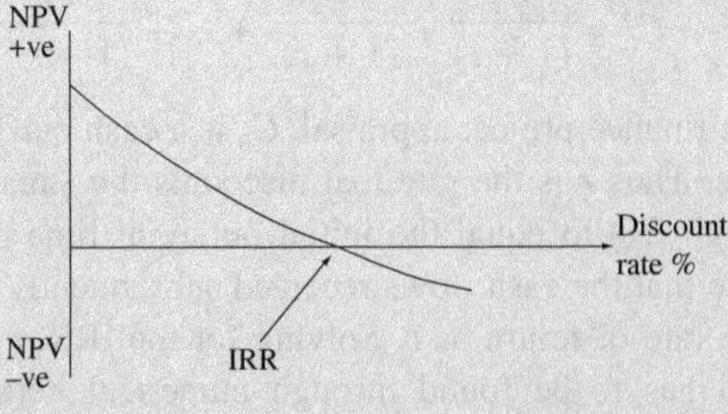

Figure A1.3 Relationship between NPV and IRR

The relationship between the IRR and the NPV of an investment is that while the NPV is the value of the projected returns from the investment using an appropriate discount rate (usually the company's cost of capital); the IRR is the discount rate which results in the NPV being zero. For this reason it is common to hear the IRR referred to as a project's *breakeven* rate. A conventional investment is considered attractive if the IRR exceeds a company's cost of capital, as well as if the NPV is positive. In the context of the bond markets, if we assume that the discount rate applicable does indeed remain constant for the reinvestment of all cash flows arising from a financial instrument, the IRR can then be assumed to be the *yield to maturity* (YTM) for that instrument.

Interpolation and extrapolation

Interest rates in the money markets are always quoted for standard maturities; for example, overnight, "tom next" (the overnight interest rate starting tomorrow, or "tomorrow to the next"), spot next (the overnight rate starting two days forward), one week, one month, two months and so on up to one year. Figure A1.4 shows a typical broker's screen as seen on news services such as Reuters and Telerate.

Dow Jones Markets : martin_g Telerate 4734 Wed Dec 08 09:00:44 1999

08/12 8:54 GMT [GARBAN INTERCAPITAL-EUROPE] 12/08 02:12 4734

	FRA		GBP CDS DEPO	GBP INTERBANK DEP	GBP REPO(GC)	
1X4	6.020-990	O/N	-	5 1/16-4 15/16	-	O/N
2X5	6.110-080	T/N	-	5 3/8 -5 1/4	-	T/N
3X6	6.230-200	1WK	-	5 1/4 -5 1/8	-	1WK
4X7	6.330-300	1MO	5 25/32-5 23/32	5 7/8 -5 13/16	-	2WK
5X8	6.420-390	2MO	5 15/16-5 7/8	5 31/32-5 29/32	-	3WK
6X9	6.510-480	3MO	6-5 15/16	6-5 15/16	-	1MO
9X12	6.760-730	4MO	6 1/32-5 31/32	6 1/32-5 31/32	-	2MO
		5MO	6 1/16- 6	6 1/16- 6	-	3MO
1X7	6.240-210	6MO	6 1/8 -6 1/16	6 5/32-6 3/32	-	4MO
2X8	6.330-300	7MO	6 5/32-6 3/32	6 7/32-6 5/32	-	5MO
3X9	6.420-390	8MO	6 7/32-6 5/32	6 9/32-6 7/32	-	6MO
4X10	6.520-490	9MO	6 9/32-6 7/32	6 5/16-6 1/4	-	9MO
5X11	6.610-580	10M	6 11/32-6 9/32	6 3/8 -6 5/16	-	1YR
6X12	6.700-670	11M	6 13/32-6 11/32	6 7/16-6 3/8		
		12M	6 15/32-6 13/32	6 1/2 -6 7/16		

[FRA 695-2040, EUROSTG 695-2030, GBP REPOS 695-2255]

Figure A1.4 Broker's rates screen

If a bank or corporate customer wishes to deal for non-standard periods, an interbank desk will calculate the rate chargeable for such an "odd date" by *interpolating* between two standard period interest rates. If we assume that the rate for all dates in between two periods increases at the same steady state, we can calculate the required rate using the formula for *straight-line* interpolation, shown in (A1.38):

$$r = r_1 + (r_2 - r_1) \times \frac{n - n_1}{n_1 - n_2} \tag{A1.38}$$

where

r is the required odd-date rate for n days
r_1 is the quoted rate for n_1 days
r_2 is the quoted rate for n_2 days.

Let us imagine that the 1-month (30-day) offered interest rate is 5.25% and that the 2-month (60-day) offered rate is 5.75%. If a customer wishes to borrow money for a 40-day period, what rate should the bank charge? We can calculate the required 40-day rate using the straight-line interpolation process. The increase in interest rates from 30 to 40 days is assumed to be 10/30 of the total increase in rates from 30 to 60 days. The 40-day offered rate would therefore be:

$$5.25 + (5.75 - 5.25) \times 10/30 = 5.4167\%.$$

EXAMPLE A1.8 Interpolation

On an interbank desk Hussein is quoting the 7-day offered rate (the rate at which a bank will *offer* or lend money) at $5^{11}/_{16}\%$, while the 14-day rate is $5^{13}/_{16}\%$. What rate should he quote for the 10-day offered rate?

$$5.6875 + (5.8125 - 5.6875) \times 3/7 = 5.7411\%$$

What about the case of an interest rate for a period that lies just before or just after two known rates and not roughly in between them? When this happens we *extrapolate* between the two known rates, again assuming a straight-line relationship between the two rates and for a period after (or before) the two rates.

EXAMPLE A1.9 Extrapolation

The 1-month offered rate is 5.25% while the 2-month rate is 5.75% as before. What is the 64-day rate?

$$5.25 + (5.75 - 5.25) \times 34/30 = 5.8176\%$$

Interpolation and extrapolation are illustrated graphically in Figure A1.5.

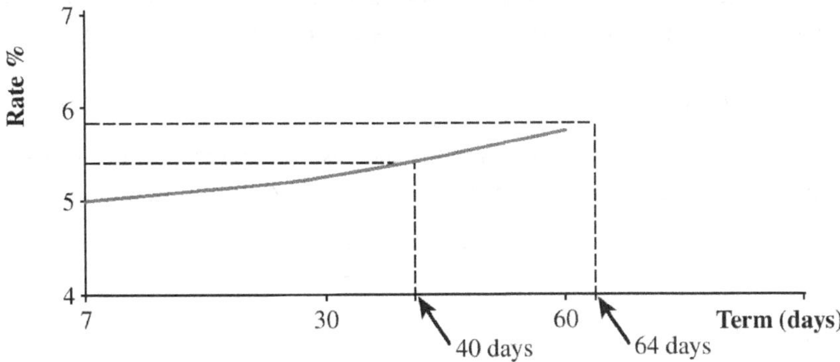

Figure A1.5 Interpolation and extrapolation

Measuring the rate of return

Rates of return are calculated in the market and by investors in order to measure the gain that has been achieved, as well as to compare the gains made by different investments. This is the market convention, presenting the profit made by an investment in percentage return figures rather than actual cash increments. In addition to comparing the performance of different investments, there are three other uses for rates of return.

- *Measuring historical performance*: a frequently used measure of investment performance is the historical rate of return, or the *realised rate of return* on an investment. This is the return that has already been realised, as opposed to return anticipated in the future. In the US market this is also known as the *ex-post* rate of return.
- *Determining future investment*: investors often use historical rates of return to estimate future returns, and to gauge the level of risk associated with a particular security. Over a period of time, because

of the higher associated risk, investors will expect a higher return from a higher risk stock compared to a less volatile one.

- *Estimating the cost of capital*: rates of return are also used to estimate a firm's cost of capital. Corporate decision-makers use their firm's cost of capital when making capital allocation and budget decisions, and one method for estimating the appropriate discount rate to apply in NPV calculations uses the company's historical rate of return on equity.

The rate of return on an investment can be calculated in several ways and we will look at some of the methods in the rest of this section.

Simple rate of return

The simple rate of return measures the increase or decrease in the value of a given investment over a specified period of time. It is given by:

$$R = \frac{P_2 - P_1 + I}{P_1} \tag{A1.39}$$

where

P_1 is the initial value of the investment
P_2 is the investment value at the end of the period
I is the income earned during the investment.

For example, a bond is purchased at a price of £100 and held for a year, during which a coupon of £8 is paid. At the end of the period the bond price is £108. The rate of return is:

$$\frac{108 - 100 + 8}{100} = 0.16 \text{ or } 16\%.$$

The simple rate of return is effective when measuring investment performance that has only one dividend payment at the end of the period. If dividends are paid more frequently or during the period, the measurement loses accuracy.

The time-weighted rate of return

The simple rate of return can be adjusted to account for the timing of dividend or coupon payments and this is known as the *time weighted rate of return* or the *geometric mean rate of return*. If we take P as the initial value of an investment, FV as the final value, C_n as the payment received by the investment in year n and MV_n as the value of the investment when a dividend is received, the time-weighted rate of return is given by (A1.40):

$$(1 + r)^N = \left(\frac{MV_1}{P}\right)\left(\frac{MV_2}{MV_1 + C_1}\right)\left(\frac{MV_3}{MV_2 + C_2}\right)\cdots\left(\frac{FV}{MV_{N-1} + C_{N-1}}\right). \quad \text{(A1.40)}$$

Given that $MV_1/P = (1 + r_1)$ or one plus the return on the investment in the first period, and that $MV_2 / (MV_1 + C_1) = (1 + r_2)$ and so on, the expression can be rewritten as shown in (A1.41):

$$(1 + r)^N = (1 + r_1)(1 + r_2)(1 + r_3) \ldots (1 + r_N). \quad \text{(A1.41)}$$

We can rearrange (A1.41) to solve for r and this gives us (A1.42) as shown:

$$r = [(1 + r_1)(1 + r_2)(1 + r_3) \ldots (1 + r_N)]^{1/T} - 1. \quad \text{(A1.42)}$$

Expression (A1.42) illustrates how the time-weighted return is in fact the *geometric* return of each individual period return.

EXAMPLE A1.10 Time-weighted rate of return calculation

An initial investment of $1,000 is made that subsequently earns $64 at the end of the first year, when the investment was valued at $1,118. At the end of the second year another $64 is earned, when the investment value is $1,250. At the end of the third year the investment value is $1,339. What is the time-weighted rate of return earned by the investment?

$$r = \left[\left(\frac{1{,}118}{1{,}000}\right)\left(\frac{1{,}250}{1{,}118 + 64}\right)\left(\frac{1{,}339}{1{,}250 + 64}\right)\right]^{1/3} - 1$$

$$= [(1.118)(1.0575)(1.019)]^{1/3} - 1 = (1.2047)^{1/3} - 1$$

$$= 0.064 \text{ or } 6.4\%.$$

Inflation-adjusted rate of return

Up to now we have been discussing rates of return calculated as the gain in the nominal cash value of an investment. In certain cases it is desirable to adjust the rate of return calculated on an investment to allow for the effects of inflation. In an inflationary environment the purchasing power of the domestic currency is eroded, so measurement of return can be modified to reflect this. In the United Kingdom, inflation is measured using the *retail prices index* or RPI. The RPI measures the change in price of a specified basket of consumer goods. While RPI is the inflation index itself, there are three key percentage indicators that are used; the *headline* rate of inflation or RPI; the rate of inflation, but excluding mortgage interest payments or RPIX; and inflation excluding any rises in value-added tax rates or RPIY. In the United States the consumer price index, or CPI, measures essentially the same thing.

The rate of inflation in any period can be measured by comparing the levels for two index numbers and is given by (A1.43):

$$i = \frac{RPI_1 - RPI_0}{RPI_1} \tag{A1.43}$$

where

i is the rate of inflation
RPI_0 is the inflation index at the start of the period
RPI_1 is the inflation index at the end of the period.

For example, in June 1998 the United Kingdom's RPI was 163.4 and this had risen to 165.6 in June 1999. Therefore the inflation rate for the period June 1998–June 1999 is calculated as:

$$i = \frac{165.6 - 163.4}{163.4} = 0.01346 \text{ or } 1.355\%.$$

The *real rate of return* is the nominal rate of return adjusted for inflation. It can be calculated using (A1.44):

$$R_{real} = 1 + \frac{R_{nom}}{1 + i} - 1 \tag{A1.44}$$

where

R_{real} is the real rate of return and R_{nom} is the nominal rate of return.

Equation (A1.44) can be approximated by $R_{real} = R_{nom} - i$ and is derived from the Fisher relationship (see Fisher 1930).[4]

Note that if there is zero or very low inflation, the real rate of return will be equal to the nominal rate of return. If investments are made in an inflationary environment and the nominal rate of return is equal to the rate of inflation such that $R_{nom} - i$, then in real terms the rate of return is zero. This often leads to negative returns where rates are very low; for example, with some types of bank accounts. In the United Kingdom current accounts and some deposit and instant access accounts are offered with interest rates below 1%. As the inflation rate has been consistently higher than 1% in the United Kingdom for some time now, account values will be declining in real terms.

Average rates of return

Where an investment is made up of a portfolio of assets the gain on the portfolio is calculated as an average return. An average is also used when measuring the return on a single asset over a period of years. The two main methods used are *arithmetic average* and *geometric average.*

The expression for calculating the average rate of return is given in (A1.45):

$$R_A = \frac{\sum_{t=1}^{m} R_t}{m} \tag{A1.45}$$

where

R_A is the average arithmetic rate of return
t is the length of the period
m is the number of observations.

The geometric method is an averaging method that compounds rates of return. That is, if £1 is invested in the first period, its future value will be $(1 + R_1)$ at the end of the period. We then assume that £$(1 + R_1)$ is invested in the second period, and at the end of period 2 the investment value will have risen to the value at the beginning of period 2 multiplied by the value of £1 invested in period 2. We illustrate this by saying that the investment value at the end of the second period is $(1 + R_1)(1 + R_2)$. More formally we can express the geometric return as:

[4] Fisher, I. 1930, *The Theory of Interest*, Macmillan, New York.

$$R_G = \left[\prod_{t=1}^{m}(1 + R_t)\right]^{1/m} - 1 \qquad \text{(A1.46)}$$

where R_G is the geometric rate of return and the symbol $\prod$ means "take the product of".[5]

The geometric average can be considered to be the actual growth rate of the assets. The arithmetic average should be used, on the other hand, when estimating the average performance across different securities for one period of time. The arithmetic average is also an unbiased estimate of future expected rates of return, and will exceed the geometric average whenever the rates of return are not constant.

Indices

An index is used to measure the rate of return for a basket of securities. In the United Kingdom the most familiar index is the FTSE-100, whose level is faithfully reported daily in the media. The FTSE-100 is made up of the largest 100 stocks, measured by market capitalisation, traded on the London Stock Exchange. The change in its index value can be taken to reflect broadly the overall performance of the stock market, although this is a very large approximation since there are over 5,000 stocks listed on the London market. That said, an index level is often a useful indicator, and it is rare to find an index level rising if the general health of the economy is declining, or vice versa. There is a wide range of indices used across markets internationally, and they are all used to measure historical returns for a group of securities, in the same way that the RPI measures the rise in retail prices. Indices are also used as a benchmark against which to measure a fund manager's performance. They are differentiated in the following three ways:

- by the type of securities included in them, such as equities or bonds, and the sector they are part of (for example, utilities stocks, or emerging markets stocks), as well as the number of securities included in each index;
- by the way the index is adjusted for any changes to its constituent stocks (such as a merger or takeover);
- by the method used to calculate the index level.

[5] For example, $y = \prod_{i=1}^{5} x_i$ means $y = (x_1)(x_2)(x_3)(x_4)(x_5)$.

There are three main types of index: price-weighted, value-weighted and equally weighted indices. Let us look at the way each of these index levels is calculated.

The price-weighted index

In a price-weighted index the value is found by adding all the security prices and dividing by a *divisor*. The value of a price-weighted index at time t is given by (A1.47):

$$I = \frac{1}{\text{divisor}} \sum_{t=1}^{n} P_{i_t} \qquad \text{(A1.47)}$$

where
I is the index level
P_{i_t} is the price of asset i in period t
n is the number of stocks in the index.

The *divisor* is a number that is adjusted periodically for stock dividends and any other corporate actions.

The price-weighted index return is a relatively simple concept. A fund manager who wished to track such an index would simply purchase the same number of shares of each stock in the index. The Dow Jones Industrial Average index in the United States is an example of a price-weighted index. However, this method tends to result in higher priced stocks having greater influence in the level of the index, so it is not very common. The value-weighted index has been designed to remove this bias.

The value-weighted index

A value-weighted index is based on the total market capitalisation of the company whose security is represented in the index. The index level therefore takes into account share value rather than the absolute price level of individual stocks.

The level of a value-weighted index is given by (A1.48):

$$I = \left[\frac{100}{\sum_{n=1}^{N} N_{i_1} P_{i_1}}\right] \sum_{n=1}^{N} N_{i_t} P_{i_t} \qquad \text{(A1.48)}$$

where

N_i is the number of shares of company i at time t
P_i is the price of company i shares at time t.

The numerator 100 is taken to be the starting value of the index. Therefore if calculating the level of the FTSE-100 one would use 1,000 in the numerator, as this index was re-based to 1,000 in 1984.

The level of a value-weighted index is not affected by a corporate action such as a dividend payment or a rights issue, and this is considered to be an advantage of the method over the price-weighted index valuation.

The equal weight index

This index is calculated by assigning the same weight to each constituent security regardless of the security's price or the company's market capitalisation. If a fund manager wished to replicate the performance of an equally weighted index, she would purchase an equal cash amount of each security. There are two ways to calculate the value of an equally weighted index: the arithmetic method and the geometric method. In both cases the rate of return measured for each security over a specific period (usually one day) is measured. The arithmetic method value is given by (A1.49):

$$I = I_{t-1}\left(1 + \frac{1}{n}\sum_{n=1}^{N} R_{i_t}\right) \tag{A1.49}$$

where $\frac{1}{n}\sum R$ is the arithmetic average of the rates of return of all the index securities.

The geometric method, as its name suggests, takes the geometric average of the return for each security in the index over a specified time period. The value is give by:

$$I = I_{t-1}\left[\prod_{n=1}^{N}(1 + R_{i_t})\right]^{1/n}. \tag{A1.50}$$

In general the arithmetic method produces higher values over time compared to the geometric method.

Bond indices

In the same way as the more familiar equity market indices, bond indices measure the return generated by a basket of fixed income stocks. Unlike an equity index such as the Dow or the FTSE-100, however, a bond index presents some complications that may make index valuation problematic. First, since bonds are always approaching in maturity, and because some are redeemed early, the set of bonds in a basket changes more frequently than the shares in an equity index. If we consider an hypothetical international "ten-year benchmark index", as a bond falls to less than, say, eight years maturity, it may be replaced by the current ten-year benchmark bond. This will have different risk characteristics to the bond it replaced and will trade differently in the market as a result. As the constituents of a bond index have to change more frequently, we may not always be comparing like-for-like when we consider historical index values. There is also the issue of bond coupon payments, which make up a significant proportion of a bond's overall return, and which must therefore be incorporated in the index valuation. Nevertheless bond indices are important for the same reason that equity indices are, and form the benchmark against which fund managers' performance is measured. There are also "synthetic" indices whose constituents are structured finance securities, and to which credit derivatives contracts are sometimes linked.

Years	Discount rate (%) 1	2	3	4	5	6	7	8	9	10	12	15	20
1	0.990099	0.980392	0.970874	0.961538	0.952381	0.943396	0.934579	0.925926	0.917431	0.909091	0.892857	0.869565	0.833333
2	0.980296	0.961169	0.942596	0.924556	0.907029	0.889996	0.873439	0.857339	0.841680	0.826446	0.797194	0.756144	0.694444
3	0.970590	0.942322	0.915142	0.888996	0.863838	0.839619	0.816298	0.793832	0.772183	0.751315	0.711780	0.657516	0.578704
4	0.960980	0.923845	0.888487	0.854804	0.822702	0.792094	0.762895	0.735030	0.708425	0.683013	0.635518	0.571753	0.482253
5	0.951466	0.905731	0.862609	0.821927	0.783526	0.747258	0.712986	0.680583	0.649931	0.620921	0.567427	0.497177	0.401878
6	0.942045	0.887971	0.837484	0.790315	0.746215	0.704961	0.666342	0.630170	0.596267	0.564474	0.506631	0.432328	0.334898
7	0.932718	0.870560	0.813092	0.759918	0.710681	0.665057	0.622750	0.583490	0.547034	0.513158	0.452349	0.375937	0.279082
8	0.923483	0.853490	0.789409	0.730690	0.676839	0.627412	0.582009	0.540269	0.501866	0.466507	0.403883	0.326902	0.232568
9	0.914340	0.836755	0.766417	0.702587	0.644609	0.591898	0.543934	0.500249	0.460428	0.424098	0.360610	0.284262	0.193807
10	0.905287	0.820348	0.744094	0.675564	0.613913	0.558395	0.508349	0.463193	0.422411	0.385543	0.321973	0.247185	0.161506
11	0.896324	0.804263	0.722421	0.649581	0.584679	0.526788	0.475093	0.428883	0.387533	0.350494	0.287476	0.214943	0.134588
12	0.887449	0.788493	0.701380	0.624597	0.556837	0.496969	0.444012	0.397114	0.355535	0.318631	0.256675	0.186907	0.112157
13	0.878663	0.773033	0.680951	0.600574	0.530321	0.468839	0.414964	0.367698	0.326179	0.289664	0.229174	0.162528	0.093464
14	0.869963	0.757875	0.661118	0.577475	0.505068	0.442301	0.387817	0.340461	0.299246	0.263331	0.204620	0.141329	0.077887
15	0.861349	0.743015	0.641862	0.555265	0.481017	0.417265	0.362446	0.315242	0.274538	0.239392	0.182696	0.122894	0.064905
16	0.852821	0.728446	0.623167	0.533908	0.458112	0.393646	0.338735	0.291890	0.251870	0.217629	0.163122	0.106865	0.054088
17	0.844377	0.714163	0.605016	0.513373	0.436297	0.371364	0.316574	0.270269	0.231073	0.197845	0.145644	0.092926	0.045073
18	0.836017	0.700159	0.587395	0.493628	0.415521	0.350344	0.295864	0.250249	0.211994	0.179859	0.130040	0.080805	0.037561
19	0.827740	0.686431	0.570286	0.474642	0.395734	0.330513	0.276508	0.231712	0.194490	0.163508	0.116107	0.070265	0.031301
20	0.819544	0.672971	0.553676	0.456387	0.376889	0.311805	0.258419	0.214548	0.178431	0.148644	0.103667	0.061100	0.026084
21	0.811430	0.659776	0.537549	0.438834	0.358942	0.294155	0.241513	0.198656	0.163698	0.135131	0.092560	0.053131	0.021737
22	0.803396	0.646839	0.521893	0.421955	0.341850	0.277505	0.225713	0.183941	0.150182	0.122846	0.082643	0.046201	0.018114
23	0.795442	0.634156	0.506692	0.405726	0.325571	0.261797	0.210947	0.170315	0.137781	0.111678	0.073788	0.040174	0.015095
24	0.787566	0.621721	0.491934	0.390121	0.310068	0.246979	0.197147	0.157699	0.126405	0.101526	0.065882	0.034934	0.012579
25	0.779768	0.609531	0.477606	0.375117	0.295303	0.232999	0.184249	0.146018	0.115968	0.092296	0.058823	0.030378	0.010483
26	0.772048	0.597579	0.463695	0.360689	0.281241	0.219810	0.172195	0.135202	0.106393	0.083905	0.052521	0.026415	0.008735
27	0.764404	0.585862	0.450189	0.346817	0.267848	0.207368	0.160930	0.125187	0.097608	0.076278	0.046894	0.022970	0.007280
28	0.756836	0.574375	0.437077	0.333477	0.255094	0.195630	0.150402	0.115914	0.089548	0.069343	0.041869	0.019974	0.006066
29	0.749342	0.563112	0.424346	0.320651	0.242946	0.184557	0.140563	0.107328	0.082155	0.063039	0.037383	0.017369	0.005055
30	0.741923	0.552071	0.411987	0.308319	0.231377	0.174110	0.131367	0.099377	0.075371	0.057309	0.033378	0.015103	0.004213

Table A1.3 Discount factor table

Glossary

A

A note: A tranche of a structured finance vehicle such as a CDO that is senior to other note tranches.

ABCP: Asset-backed commercial paper.

ABS: Asset-backed security.

Accreting: An accreting principal is one that increases during the life of the deal. See **amortising**, **bullet**.

Accreting swap: Swap whose notional amount increases during the life of the swap (opposite of **amortising** swap).

Accrued interest: The proportion of interest or coupon earned on an investment from the previous coupon payment date until the value date.

Accumulated value: The same as future value.

ACT/360: A day/year count convention taking the number of calendar days in a period and a "year" of 360 days.

ACT/365: A day/year convention taking the number of calendar days in a period and a "year" of 365 days. Under the ISDA definitions used for interest-rate swap documentation, ACT/365 means the same as **ACT/ACT**.

ACT/ACT: A day/year count convention taking the number of calendar days in a period and a year equal to the number of days in the current coupon period multiplied by the coupon frequency. For an interest rate swap, that part of the interest period falling in a leap year is divided by 366 and the remainder is divided by 365.

Add-on factor: Simplified estimate of the potential future increase in the replacement cost, or market value, of a derivative transaction.

Advanced IRB (AIRB): The advanced internal ratings-based approach of the Basel II regulations. The AIRB is one of two internal credit-ratings based approaches allowed under Basel II to calculate regulatory capital requirement for credit risk, with the other being the *foundation* IRB approach. Under AIRB, banks and financial institutions are allowed to provide their own internal data to calculate probability of default, exposure-at-default and loss-given-default. The actual calculations of credit risk based on this data must be undertaken using the Basel II model.

Advanced measurement approach (AMA): The BIS methodology for calculating operational risk capital requirements based on a bank's internal data.

Agent: A participant in the financial markets, such as a broker or a custodian, who undertakes transactions on behalf of (principal) clients.

Aggregated exposure: The gross amount of all types of debt exposure on a banking book or portfolio.

All-in price: See "**dirty price**".

All or nothing: Digital option. This option's **put** (call) pays out a pre-determined amount ("the all") if the index is below (above) the strike price at the option's expiration. The amount by which the underlying **index** is below (above) the **strike** is irrelevant; the payout will be all or nothing.

Alpha: Under Basel II rules for operational risk, *a* or alpha is the multiplier that is used to calculate the operational risk regulatory capital charge. The level is set at 15%. In the fund management industry, a term used to refer to the above-market return generated by a fund, and attributed to the skills of the fund manager.

American: An American-style option is one that may be exercised at any time between trade inception and option expiry.

American option: An option that may be exercised at any time during its life.

Amortising: A financial instrument whose nominal principal amount decreases in size during its life. An amortising principal is one that decreases during the life of a deal, or is repaid in stages during a loan. Amortising an amount over a period of time also means accruing for it pro rata over the period. See **accreting**, **bullet**.

Annuity: An investment providing a series of (generally equal) future cash flows.

Appreciation: An increase in the market value of a currency in terms of other currencies. See **depreciation**, **revaluation**.

Arbitrage: The process of buying securities in one country, currency or market, and selling identical securities in another to take advantage of price differences. When this is carried out simultaneously, it is in theory a risk-free transaction. There are many forms of arbitrage transactions. For instance, in the cash market a bank might issue a money market instrument in one money centre and invest the same amount in another centre at a higher rate, such as an issue of three-month US dollar CDs in the United States at 5.5% and a purchase of three-month Eurodollar CDs at 5.6%. In the futures market arbitrage might involve buying three-month contracts and selling forward six-month contracts.

Arbitrage CDO: A collateralised debt obligation (CDO) that has been issued by an asset manager and in which the collateral is purchased solely for the purpose of securitising it to exploit the difference in yields ("arbitrage") between the underlying market and securitisation market.

Arbitrageur: Someone who undertakes arbitrage trading.

ARCH: (autoregressive conditional heteroscedasticity) A discrete-time model for a random variable. It assumes that variance is stochastic and is a function of the variance of previous time steps and the level of the underlying.

Arithmetic mean: The average.

Asian: An Asian option takes the average value of the underlying over the option's life.

Asian option: *See above.*

Ask: The offered price, in repo transactions the rate at which the market "sells" stock; in other words, the rate at which it pays money on borrowed funds. See **offer**.

Asset: Probable future economic benefit obtained or controlled as a result of past events or transactions. Generally classified as either current or long-term.

Asset allocation: Distribution of investment funds within an asset class or across a range of asset classes for the purpose of diversifying risk or adding value to a portfolio.

Asset and liability management (ALM): The practice of matching the term structure and cash flows of an organisation's asset and liability portfolios to maximise returns and minimise risk. A simple example is a bank using an interest-rate swap to convert a fixed-rate loan (asset) to match the interest basis of its floating-rate deposits (liability).

Asset and liability management committee (ALCO): A committee comprised of (among others) the Head of Treasury, CEO and CFO, which determines overall bank policy and strategy on asset–liability management.

Asset securitisation: The process whereby loans, receivables and other illiquid assets in the balance sheet are packaged into interest-bearing securities that offer attractive investment opportunities.

Asset swap: An interest-rate swap or currency swap used in conjunction with an underlying asset such as a bond investment. See **liability swap**.

Asset swap spread (ASW): The spread over Libor that is received by the person selling the asset swap. This spread reflects the credit quality of the asset.

Asset-backed loan notes (ABN): Another expression for asset-backed securities. See **ABS**.

Asset-backed securities (ABS): Securities that have been issued by a special purpose legal entity (SPV) and which are backed by principal and interest payments on existing assets, which have been sold to the SPV by the deal originator. These assets can include commercial bank loans, credit card loans, auto loans, equipment lease receivables and so on. Also defined as security which is collaterised by specific assets – such as mortgages – rather than by the intangible creditworthiness of the issuer.

Asset-risk benchmark: Benchmark against which the riskiness of a corporation's assets may be measured. In sophisticated corporate risk management strategies the dollar risk of the liability portfolio may be managed against an asset-risk benchmark.

Asset-sensitivity estimates: Estimates of the effect of risk factors on the value of assets.

Assured payment: A payment generated by an irrevocable instruction simultaneously with the movement of securities between counterparty accounts, which occurs for example in CREST/CGO.

At-the-money (ATM): An option is at-the-money if the current value of the underlying is the same as the strike price. See **in-the-money**, **out-of-the-money**.

Auction: A method of issue where institutions submit bids to the issuer on a price or yield basis. Auction rules vary considerably across markets.

Average cap: Also known as an average rate cap, a cap on an average interest rate over a given period rather than on the rate prevailing at the end of the period. See also **average price (rate) option**.

Average life: The weighted-average life of a bond, the estimated time to return principal based on an assumed prepayment speed. It is the average number of years that each unit of unpaid principal remains outstanding.

Average price (rate) option: Option on a currency's average exchange rate or commodity's average spot price in which four variables have to be agreed to between buyer and seller: the premium, the **strike** price, the source of the exchange rate or commodity price data and the sampling interval (each day, for example). At the end of the life of the option the **average spot exchange rate** is calculated and compared with the strike price. A cash payment is then made to the buyer of the option that is equal to the face amount of the option times the difference between the two rates (assuming the option is **in-the-money**; otherwise it expires worthless).

Average worst case exposure: The expression of an exposure in terms of the average of the worst case exposure over a given period.

B

Back-testing: The validation of a model by feeding it historical data and comparing the results with historical reality.

Backwardation: The case when the cash or spot price of a commodity is greater than its forward price. A backwardation occurs when there exists insufficient supply to satisfy nearby demand in a commodity market. The size of the backwardation is determined by differences between supply and demand factors in the nearby positions compared with the same factors on the forward position. It is also known as a *back*. See **contango**.

Balance sheet: Statement of the financial position of an enterprise at a specific point in time, giving assets, liabilities and shareholders' equity.

Balance sheet CDO: A CDO backed by a static pool of assets that were previously on the balance sheet of the originator.

Band: The Exchange Rate Mechanism (ERM II) of the European Union links the currencies of EU members that are not members of the euro, such as Estonia and Malta, in a system that limits the degree of fluctuation of each currency against the euro within a band either side of an agreed par value.

Bank exposure: Under Basel II rules for credit risk exposure capital, this is the exposure arising from exposure to banks and financial institutions under regulatory supervision. It also includes exposure to public-sector bodies that are treated as banks under the Basel II standardised approach, and certain multi-lateral development banks that do not meet the 0% risk-weight of the standardised approach.

Bank for International Settlements (BIS): The international body set up in 1930 to encourage cooperation among central banks and promote stable monetary policy, based in Basel, Switzerland. Its original purpose was to manage the transfer of reparation payments from Germany to various countries under the Treaty of Versailles signed in 1919. Under its later objectives of monetary policy cooperation and coordination it established the Basel I and Basel II rules of regulatory capital requirements.

Banker's acceptance: See **Bill of Exchange.**

Banking book: As described under Bank rules and the EU capital adequacy directives (CAD), a bank's outstanding transactions that relate to customer lending or long-term investments. Includes assets that create exposure to sovereigns, corporates, individuals and other bodies, and that are held primarily to maturity.

Barrier option: A barrier option is one that ceases to exist, or starts to exist, if the underlying reaches a certain barrier level. See **knock in/out**.

Base currency: Exchange rates are quoted in terms of the number of units of one currency (the variable or counter currency) that corresponds to one unit of the other currency (the base currency).

Basel Committee: The Basel committee on banking supervision, a group of central banks and financial institutions from the G10 countries, set up to produce common standards in international banking and hence to reduce systemic risk in the financial system.

Basel rules: The set of rules that require banks to set aside a minimum level of capital to back assets. Now known as Basel I because they are being replaced by new rules (Basel II) from the end of 2007.

Basic indicator approach (BIA): With regard to the Operational Risk capital calculation for Basel II, a method that uses one indicator to represent the entire operational risk for a bank, from which the charge is calculated. The approach uses a single performance measure, such as gross revenue, as the basic indicator.

Basis: The underlying cash-market price minus the futures price. In the case of a bond futures contract, the futures price must be multiplied by the conversion factor for the cash bond in question.

Basis points: In interest-rate quotations, 0.01%.

Basis risk: A form of market risk that arises whenever one kind of risk exposure is hedged with an instrument that behaves in a similar, but not necessarily identical way. For instance, a bank trading desk may use three-month interest rate futures to hedge it commercial paper or a euronote program. Although eurocurrency rates, to which futures prices respond, are well correlated with commercial paper rates they do not always move in lock step. If therefore commercial paper rates move by 10 basis points, but futures prices dropped by only seven basis points, the three-points gap would be the basis risk.

Basis swap: An interest-rate swap where both legs are based on floating-rate payments.

Basis trade: Buying the basis means selling a futures contract and buying the commodity or instrument underlying the futures contract. Selling the basis is the opposite.

Basis trading: Simultaneous trading in a derivative contract (normally a futures contract) and the underlying asset. The purpose of basis trading is to exploit an arbitrage-type profit potential, or to cover a short derivative position. Arbitrage basis trading is designed to take advantage of mispricing of cash and/or futures, or is based on speculation that the basis risk will change.

Basket option: Option based on an underlying basket of bonds, currencies, equities or commodities.

BBA: British Bankers Association.

Bear spread: A spread position taken with the expectation of a fall in value in the underlying.

Bearer bond: A bond for which physical possession of the certificate is proof of ownership. The issuer does not know the identity of the bondholder. Traditionally, the bond carries detachable coupons, one for each interest payment date, which are posted to the issuer when payment is due. At maturity the bond is redeemed by sending in the certificate for repayment. These days bearer bonds are usually settled electronically, and while no register of ownership is kept by the issuer, coupon payments may be made electronically.

Benchmark: A bond whose terms set a standard for the market. The benchmark usually has the greatest liquidity, the highest turnover and is usually the most frequently quoted. It also usually trades expensive to the yield curve, due to higher demand for it among institutional investors.

Beta: In the context of Basel II, Beta or *b* is a fixed percentage defined in the Basel II rules for calculating the regulatory capital charge under the standardised approach for operational risk. The beta relates the level of required capital to the level of the gross income for each of the following eight business lines:

retail banking 12%
asset management 12%
retail brokerage 12%
commercial banking 15%
agency services 15%
corporate finance 18%
trading and sales 18%
payment and sales 18%.

In the equity market, beta is the sensitivity of a stock relative to swings in the overall market. The market has a beta of one, so a stock or portfolio with a beta greater than one will rise or fall more than the overall market, whereas a beta of less than one means that the stock is less volatile.

Bid: The price at which a market-maker will buy bonds. A tight bid–offer spread is indicative of a liquid and competitive market. The bid rate in a repo is the interest rate at which the dealer will borrow the collateral and lend the cash. See **offer**. In the repo market, the repo rate that the cash investor demands from the seller; to "bid" for stock – that is, lend the cash. This is the same terminology and price quote as for CDs. The repo buyer is the cash lender, and has actually traded a *reverse repo*.

Bid–offer: The two-way price at which a market will buy and sell stock.

Big figure: In a foreign exchange quotation, the exchange rate omitting the last two decimal places. For example, when EUR/USD is 1.1910/20, the big figure is 1.19. See **points**.

Bilateral netting: The ability to offset amounts owed to a counterparty under one contract against amounts owed to the same counterparty under another contract; for example, where both transactions are governed by one master agreement. Also known as "**cherry-picking**". Formally defined as an agreement between two counterparties whereby the value of all transactions on which funds are owed is offset against the value of transactions where funds are due, resulting in a single net exposure amount owed by one counterparty to the other. Bilateral netting can cover the entire range of products, including repo, swaps, and options, to produce one net exposure.

Bill: A **bill of exchange** is a payment order written by one person (the drawer) to another, directing the latter (drawee) to pay a certain amount of money at a future date to a third party. A bill of exchange is a bank draft when drawn on a bank. By accepting the draft, a bank agrees to pay the face value of the obligation if the drawer fails to pay, hence the term **bankers acceptance**. A **Treasury bill**, or T-bill, is short-term government paper of up to one year's maturity, sold at a discount to principal value and redeemed at par.

Bill of exchange: A short-term, zero-coupon debt issued by a company to finance commercial trading. If it is guaranteed by a bank, it becomes a banker's acceptance.

Binary default swap: See **digital credit default swap**.

Binomial pricing model: A tool for valuing an option based on building a binomial tree of all the possible paths both up and down that the underlying asset price might take, from start until expiry. It assumes each up or down move is by a given amount.

Binomial tree: A mathematical model to value options, based on the assumption that the value of the underlying can move either up or down a given extent over a given short time. This process is repeated many times to give a large number of possible paths (the "tree") that the value could follow during the option's life.

BIS: Bank for International Settlements.

Black–Scholes: A widely used option-pricing formula devised by Fischer Black and Myron Scholes and published in 1973.

Blended interest-rate swap: Result of adding a forward swap to an existing swap and blending the rates over the total life of the transaction.

Bloomberg: The trading, analytics and news service produced by Bloomberg LP; also used to refer to the terminal itself.

BoE: Bank of England.

Bond basis: An interest rate is quoted on a bond basis if it is on an **ACT/365**, **ACT/ACT** or 30/360 basis. In the short term (for accrued interest, for example), these three are different. Over a whole (non-leap) year, however, they all equate to 1. In general, the expression "bond basis" does not distinguish between them and is calculated as ACT/365. See **money market basis**.

Bonds borrowed: Stock borrowed in a stock-lending transaction.

Bond futures: Contracts traded on a recognised futures exchange that are standardised agreements to buy or sell a fixed nominal amount of a government bond. The contract is based on a "notional" bond, and a specified basket of actual bonds may be delivered against the contract.

Bond-equivalent yield: The yield that would be quoted on a US treasury bond which is trading at par and which has the same economic return and maturity as a given T-bill.

Bond Market Association: Formerly known as the Public Securities Association (PSA), and now the Securities Industry and Financial Markets Association (SIFMA), this is the trade association of the US domestic bond market. As the PSA it produced the original master repo agreement for use in the US dollar market, subsequently used at the basis for the PSA/ISMA master repo agreement used in international repo markets.

Bootstrapping: Building up successive zero-coupon yields from a combination of coupon-bearing yields.

Borrower: In a classic repo, the counterparty that is taking stock, in other words *lending* cash. In stock-lending, the counterparty borrowing a specified security and supplying cash or stock as collateral.

BPV: Basis-point value. The price movement due to a one basis-point change in yield.

Bräss/Fangmeyer: A method for calculating the yield of a bond similar to the **Moosmüller** method, but in the case of bonds that pay coupons more frequently than annually, using a mixture of annual and less than annual *compounding*.

Break forward: A product equivalent to a straightforward option, but structured as a forward deal at an off-market rate that can be reversed at a penalty rate.

Broken date: A maturity date other than the standard ones (such as one week, one, two, three, six and 12 months) normally quoted. Also known as a "cock-date" by FRA traders.

Broker: An intermediary who acts as a broker for repo transactions, either on a matched principal or name-passing basis.

Broker-dealers: Members of stock exchanges who may intermediate between customers and market-makers; may also act as principals, transacting business with customers from their own holdings of stock.

Bull spread: A spread position in options taken with the expectation of a rise in value in the **underlying**.

Bulldog: Sterling domestic bonds issued by non-UK domiciled borrowers. These bonds trade under a similar arrangement to gilts and are settled via the Central Gilts Office (now CREST).

Bullet: A loan/deposit has a bullet maturity if the principal is all repaid at maturity. See **amortising**.

Butterfly: *Either* an option spread that comprises the purchase of a call (or put) combined with the purchase of another call (or put) at a different strike, plus the sale of two calls at a mid-way strike, *or*, a bond spread of one short position and a long position in two other bonds.

Buy/sell-back (Buy/sell-back or sell/buy-back): A sale and spot purchase (for forward settlement) of securities transacted simultaneously. It is not specifically repo but has the same effect and intent, and consists of a simultaneous matching purchase and sale of the same quantity of securities for different value dates. The UK's Gilt Repo Code recommends that buy/sell-backs should only be carried out under a master agreement with the same protections as those in the Gilt Repo Legal Agreement. A buy/sell-back is equivalent to a reverse repo, while a sell/buy-back is equivalent to a repo. Opposite of **sell/buy-back**.

C

Cable: The exchange rate for sterling against the US dollar.

CAD: The European Union's Capital Adequacy Directive.

Calendar spread: The simultaneous purchase/sale of a futures contract for one date and the sale/purchase of a similar futures contract for a different date. See **spread**.

Call option: An option to purchase the commodity or instrument underlying the option. See **put**.

Call price: The price at which the issuer can call in a bond or preferred bond.

Callable bond: A bond that provides the borrower with an option to redeem the issue before the original maturity date. In most cases certain terms are set before the issue, such as the date after which the bond is callable and the price at which the issuer may redeem the bond.

Calling the mark: The process of calling for margin to be reinstated following a mark-to-market revaluation of a repo transaction.

Cancelable swap: Swap in which the payer of the fixed rate has the option, usually exercisable on a specified date, to cancel the deal (see also **swaption**).

Cap: A series of borrower's **IRG**s, designed to protect a borrower against rising interest rates on each of a series of dates.

Capital adequacy: A measure of a bank or financial institution's financial resources to enable it to meet its business and regulatory obligations.

Capital adequacy ratio: A ratio calculated to meet banking regulators' requirements, and made up of the size of a bank's own funds (available capital and reserves) as a proportion of its risky assets (the funds it has lent to credit risky borrowers).

Capital asset pricing model (CAPM): An equity pricing methodology.

Capital market: Long-term market (generally longer than one year) for financial instruments. See **money market**.

Capital ratio: Under Basel I, the minimum ratio of capital to risk-weighted assets. Under Basel II a different approach will apply: the denominator or total risk-weighted assets is determined by multiplying the capital requirements for market risk and operational risk by 12.5 and then adding the result to the sum of risk-weighted assets set for credit risk. Note that 12.5 is the reciprocal of the original Basel I minimum capital ratio of 8%.

Capped option: Option where the holder's ability to profit from a change in value of the underlying is subject to a specified limit.

Caption: Option on a **cap**.

Cash: See **cash market**.

Cash-and-carry: An arbitrage trade in which a trader sells a bond futures contract and simultaneously buys the CTD bond, to lock in perceived mis-pricing in the implied future price of the bond. A reverse cash-and-carry is a purchase of futures against a sale of cash bonds. The key measure to analyse is the repo rate for the CTD, and whether the CTD is expected to be unchanged on futures expiry. For the strategy to be successful the futures contract must be theoretically expensive compared to the cash. The value of the futures contract is determined by reference to the *implied repo rate*; if the implied repo rate is higher than the actual market repo rate, then the futures contract is said to be cheap.

Cash-flow CDO: A CDO that is structured by securitising bonds or loans, undertaken by selling these assets to an issuing company ("SPV") that funds this purchase through the issue of note liabilities. The buyers of the notes take on the credit risk of the securitised assets.

Cash market: The market in full cash instruments, as opposed to derivatives, for which the full nominal value is paid for up front on purchase. The cash market is the underlying market for derivatives contracts.

Cash-driven repo: A repo transaction initiated by a party that wishes to invest cash against security collateral.

Cash flow waterfall: The rules by which the cash flow that the issuer can pay to investors, after all expenses have been paid, is allocated to service issue liabilities and by which the issuer can pay investors in order of seniority.

CBOE: Chicago Board Options Exchange.

CBOT: The Chicago Board of Trade, one of the two futures exchanges in Chicago, United States. It lists the US Treasury bond futures contract, and the 10-year, 5-year and 2-year note contracts, among others.

CD: See **certificate of deposit**.

CDO: Collateralised debt obligation, a structured financial product.

Cedel: Centrale de Livraison de Valeurs Mobilieres; a clearing system for Euro-currency and international bonds. Cedel is located in Luxembourg and is jointly owned by a number of European banks. Now known as **Clearstream**.

Ceiling: The same as *cap*.

Central bank repo: A central bank repo is when the central bank lends funds (provides liquidity) to the market; as such it is a reverse repo in market terms.

Central Gilts Office: The office of the Bank of England which runs the computer-based settlement system for gilt-edged securities and certain other securities (mostly **Bulldog**s) for which the Bank acts as Registrar. It merged with CRESTCo, the London market equity settlement system, in July 2000, and is now known as CREST/CGO or simply CREST.

Central line theorem: The assertion that as sample size, n, increases, the distribution of the mean of a random sample taken from almost any population approaches a normal distribution.

Certificate of deposit (CD): A money market instrument of up to one year's maturity (although CDs of up to five years have been issued) that pays a bullet interest payment on maturity. After issue, CDs can trade freely in the secondary market, the ease of which is a function of the credit quality of the issuer.

CGBR: Central government borrowing requirement.

CGO reference prices: Daily prices of gilt-edged and other securities held in CREST/CGO that are used by CREST/CGO and market-makers in various processes, including revaluing stock loan transactions, calculating total consideration in a repo transaction, and DBV assembly. Now referred to as CREST reference prices or DMO prices (because the prices are published by the UK Debt Management Office).

Cheapest to deliver (CTD): In a bond futures contract, the one underlying bond among all those that are deliverable, which is the most price-efficient for the seller to deliver.

Cherry-picking: See **bilateral netting**.

Classic repo: The term used to refer to a generic sale and repurchase transaction. Originally introduced by ISMA as a term for repo as practised in the US market.

Clean deposit: The same as **time deposit**.

Clean price: The price of a bond excluding accrued coupon. The price quoted in the market for a bond is generally a clean price rather than a **dirty price**.

Clean-up of interest: The practice of transferring repo interest prior to the repo termination date. The most common reason for this is when *close-out and repricing* of a repo transaction takes place.

Clearstream: Formerly CEDEL or its banking arm known as Cedel Bank, the international clearing system owned by a consortium of banks, and which also offers tri-party repo facilities. It was formed following the merger of Cedel with Deutsche Bourse. The German domestic clearing system is known as Clearstream AG, while Eurobonds clear through Clearstream International.

Close-out and repricing: A method of removing mark-to-market credit exposure in a repo and restoring margin balance. It involves terminating the current repo and re-starting it to the original termination date with the margin balance restored.

Close-out netting: The ability to net a portfolio of contracts with a given counterparty in the event of default. See also **bilateral netting**.

Closing leg: The second (terminating) stage of a repo transaction. A repo involves two trades in the same security, one for a near value date and the other for a value date in the future. The closing leg refers to the second trade. Also known as *second* leg, *far* leg, *end* leg, *reverse* leg or *termination* leg.

CMBS: Commercial mortgage-backed security.

CMO: Central Moneymarkets Office which settles transactions in Treasury bills and other money markets instruments, and provides a depository.

CMTM: Current **mark-to-market** value. See **current exposure** and **replacement cost**.

Collar: The simultaneous sale of a *put* (or *call*) *option* and purchase of a call (or put) at different strikes – typically both *out-of-the-money*.

Collateral: Assets or assets of value given up as security in exchange for cash borrowed under a loan. A general term used in the market to cover any securities exchanged in a repo transaction, both initially and subsequently during the period before the repo matures. Used as security against the transfer of cash. Or, in stock-lending, of securities. Under the PSA/ISMA and Gilt Repo Legal agreements, full title to collateral passes from one party to another, the party obtaining title is obliged to deliver back *equivalent* securities.

Collateralised callable notes (CCN): A form of extendible commercial paper (CP) that has two maturity dates, the formal final legal maturity and an earlier maturity date when it is expected to mature in practice.

Collateralised debt obligation (CDO): A multi-asset and multi-tranche debt structure, with the underlying assets comprised of bonds (collateralised bond obligation), loans (collateralised loan obligation) or a mixture of both.

Collateralised loan obligation (CLO): A form of *CDO*.

Collateralised mortgage obligation (CMO): A form of *MBS*.

Collateralised synthetic obligations (CSO): A term for synthetic *CDO*.

Commercial paper (CP): A short-term security issued by a company or bank, generally with a zero coupon.

Commodity swap: Swap where one of the cash flows is based on a fixed value for the underlying commodity and the other is based on a floating index value. The commodity is often oil or natural gas, although copper, gold, other metals and agricultural commodities are also commonly used. The end-users are consumers, who pay a fixed-rate, and the producer.

Competitive bid: A bid for the stock at a price stated by a bidder in an auction. A *non-competitive bid* is a bid where no price is specified; such bids are allotted at the weighted average price of successful competitive bid prices.

Compound interest: When some interest on an investment is paid before maturity and the investor can reinvest it to earn interest on interest, the interest is said to be compounded. Compounding generally assumes that the reinvestment rate is the same as the original rate. See **simple interest**.

Compound option: Option on an option, the first giving the buyer the right, but not the obligation, to buy the second on a specific date at a predetermined price. There are two kinds. One, on currencies, is useful for companies tendering for overseas contracts in a foreign currency. The interest-rate version comprises **captions** and **floortions**.

Consideration: The total price paid in a transaction, including taxes, commissions and (for bonds) accrued interest.

Constant prepayment rate (CPR): An assumed rate used to determine how fast a mortgage or other debt obligation is repaid ahead of its legal maturity.

Contango: The situation when a forward or futures price for something is higher than the spot price (the same as forward premium in foreign exchange). See **backwardation**.

Contingent option: Option where the premium is higher than usual, but is only payable if the value of the underlying reaches a specified level. Also known as a contingent premium option.

Continuous compounding: A mathematical, rather than practical, concept of compound interest where the period of compounding is infinitesimally small.

Contract date: The date on which a transaction is negotiated. See *value date*.

Contract for differences: A deal such as an **FRA** and some futures contracts, where the instrument or commodity effectively bought or sold cannot be delivered; instead, a cash gain or loss is taken by comparing the price dealt with the market price, or an index, at maturity.

Conventional gilts (included double-dated): Gilts on which interest payments and principal repayments are fixed.

Conversion factor: A value assigned by the futures exchange to all bonds deliverable into a futures contract. It is the price at which the bond would have a yield-to-maturity equal to the notional coupon of the futures contract specification. Also known as the *price factor*. The price paid for a bond on delivery is the futures settlement price times the conversion factor.

Convertible bond: A bond that endows on its holder the right to purchase a defined quantity of shares at a defined price. This is achieved by returning the bond to the issuer on maturity (or in some cases earlier), and receiving in return the specified amount of equity. In the absence of a company's bankruptcy or default there will be a floor value to the convertible bond; for example, its redemption value at maturity. In the event that the price of the company's shares rises, the value of the bond will also rise but not necessarily in a perfectly correlated way. The bond has features of both fixed income and equity instruments and these features combined create a return profile akin to that of a call option.

Convertible currency: A currency that may be freely exchanged for other currencies.

Convexity: A measure of the curvature of a bond's price/yield curve (mathematically, [*d*2*P*/*dr*2] / dirty price).

Cooke ratio: The original minimum capital ratio of 8% set under Basel I is sometimes called the Cooke ratio because the Basel Committee chairman at the time was Peter Cooke, a director of the Bank of England.

Correlation matrices: Statistical constructs used in the value-at-risk methodology to measure the degree of relatedness of various market forces.

Corridor: The same as **collar**.

Cost of carry: The net running cost of holding a position (which may be negative); for example, the cost of borrowing cash to buy a bond less the coupon earned on the bond while holding it.

Cost volatility: Volatility relating to operational errors or the fines and losses a business unit may incur. Reflected in excess costs and penalty charges posted to the profit and losses. See also **revenue volatility**.

Counterparty: Generally, from the point of view of a bank or financial market entity, the other side to a financial contract it has entered into. Under Basel II, the entity to which a bank or financial institution has an on- or off-balance sheet exposure.

Counterparty credit risk: The risk of financial loss arising as a result of holding or a contract to which the counterparty fails to fulfil its obligations. Under Basel II this credit risk is made up of three elements:

- the value of the position exposed to default; that is, the credit risk exposure;
- the proportion of this value that is expected to be recovered after the event of default;
- the probability of default itself.

Counterparty risk: The risk that the other side to a transaction will default on payments owed by it during the transaction and/or on maturity.

Counterparty risk-weighting: See **risk-weighting**.

Country risk: The risks, when business is conducted in a particular country, of adverse economic or political conditions arising in that country. More specifically, the credit risk of a financial transaction or instrument arising from such conditions.

Coupon: The interest payment(s) made by the issuer of security to the holders, based on the coupon rate and the face value.

Coupon swap: An interest-rate swap in which one leg is fixed-rate and the other floating-rate.

Cover: To cover an exposure is to deal in such a way as to remove the risk – either reversing the position, or hedging it by dealing in an instrument with a similar but opposite risk profile. Also the amount by how much a bond auction is subscribed.

Covered call/put: The sale of a covered call option is when the option writer also owns the underlying. If the underlying rises in value so that the option is exercised, the writer is protected by his or her position in the underlying. Covered puts are defined analogously. See **naked**.

Covered-interest arbitrage: Creating a loan/deposit in one currency by combining a loan/deposit in another with a forward foreign-exchange swap.

CP: See **commercial paper**.

Credit (or default) risk: The risk that a loss will be incurred if a counterparty to a derivatives transaction does not fulfil its financial obligations in a timely manner.

Credit default swap (CDS): A bilateral financial contract in which one counterparty, known as the protection buyer, pays a premium in the form of a periodic fee, to the other counterparty known as the protection seller. The fee is expressed in basis points of the nominal value of the contract. The contract is written on a reference asset, and in the event of a predefined credit event the protection buyer will deliver the asset to the protection seller, in return for a payment of the nominal value of the contract from the protection seller.

Credit derivative: A *bilateral* contract that isolates credit risk from an underlying specified reference asset and transfers this risk from one party of the contract (the buyer) to the other party (the seller). The seller receives a one-off or periodic premium payment in return for taking on the credit risk. It involves a potential exchange of payments in which at least one of the cash flows is linked to the performance of a specified underlying credit-sensitive asset or liability. The most common credit derivatives are **credit default swaps** and **total return swaps**.

Credit enhancement: A level of investor protection built into a structured finance deal to absorb losses among the underlying assets. This may take the form of cash, "equity" subordinated note tranches, subordinated tranches, cash reserves, excess spread reserve, insurance protection ("wrap") and so on.

Credit-equivalent amount: As part of the calculation of the risk-weighted amount of capital the Bank for International Settlements (BIS) advises each bank to set aside against derivative credit risk, banks must compute a credit-equivalent amount for each derivative transaction. The amount is calculated by summing the *current replacement cost*, or market value, of the instrument and an **add-on factor**.

Credit event: A term used to refer to a number of occurrences that trigger payment under a credit derivative contract. These occurrences include default on payment of interest or principal, bankruptcy, administration and loan restructuring.

Credit-linked note (CLN): A funded credit derivative. Can be regarded as a bond whose final return is linked to the credit performance of a reference entity. See **credit derivative**.

Credit risk: The risk of loss that will be incurred if a counterparty to a transaction does not fulfil its financial obligations under the transaction contract. It also refers to financial loss suffered by a bondholder as a result of default of the issuer of the bond held. Also known as *default risk*.

Credit-risk (or default-risk) exposure: The value of the contract exposed to default. If all transactions are marked-to-market each day, such positive market value is the amount of previously recorded profit that might have to be reversed and recorded as a loss in the event of counterparty default.

Credit spread: The interest-rate spread between two debt issues of similar duration and maturity, reflecting the relative creditworthiness of the issuers.

Credit spread option: A credit derivative contract that confers the option buyer with the right but not the obligation to enter into a credit spread position at a pre-specified spread level. The underlying spread position can be an asset swap, a floating-rate note bond or another credit derivative such as a credit default swap.

Credit swap: See **credit default swap**.

Credit value-at-risk (CVaR): See **Value-at-Risk** (VaR).

CREST: The London equity market electronic book-entry clearing and settlement system, with which the CGO merged in July 2000. The system is operated by CRESTCo and was introduced in 1996.

Cross: See cross-rate.

Cross-currency repo: A repo transaction in which the collateral transferred is denominated in a different currency to that of the cash lent.

Cross-rate: Generally an exchange rate between two currencies, neither of which is the US dollar. In the US market, spot cross is the exchange rate for US dollars against Canadian dollars in its direct form.

CTD: See **cheapest to deliver**.

Cum-dividend: Literally "with dividend", stock that is traded with interest or dividend accrued included in the price.

Cumulative default rate: See **probability-of-default**.

Currency option: The option to buy or sell a specified amount of a given currency at a specified rate at or during a specified time in the future.

Currency swap: An agreement to exchange a series of cash flows determined in one currency, possibly with reference to a particular fixed or floating interest payment schedule, for a series of cash flows based in a different currency. See **interest-rate swap**.

Current assets: Assets that are expected to be used or converted to cash within one year or one operating cycle.

Current exposure: A risk management term referring to current outstanding aggregate interest rate risk.

Current liabilities: Obligations that the firm is expected to settle within one year or one operating cycle.

Current yield: Bond coupon as a proportion of clean price per 100; does not take principal gain/loss or time value of money into account. See **yield to maturity**, **simple yield to maturity**.

Curve fitting: Plotting or estimating the yield curve from market-observed yield data.

Customer repo: A term used in the US Treasury market, where the Federal Reserve Bank of New York places cash in the market on behalf of its customers.

Cylinder: The same as **collar**.

D

DAC-RAP: Delivery against collateral – receipt against payment. Same as DVP.

Daily range: The difference between the high and low points of a single trading day.

Day-count: The convention used to calculate accrued interest on bonds and interest on cash. For UK gilts the accrued interest convention changed to actual/actual from actual/365 on 1 November 1998. For cash, the interest basis in money markets is actual/365 for sterling and actual/360 for US dollar and euro.

DBV (delivery by value): A mechanism whereby a CGO member may borrow from or lend money to another CGO member against overnight gilt collateral. The CGO system automatically selects and delivers securities to a specified aggregate value on the basis of the previous night's CGO reference prices; equivalent securities are returned the following day. The DBV functionality allows the giver and taker of collateral to specify the classes of security to be included within the DBV. The options are: all classes of security held within CGO, including strips and bulldogs; coupon bearing gilts and bulldogs; coupon bearing gilts and strips; only coupon bearing gilts.

DBV repo: A repo transaction in which the delivery of securities is by means of the DBV facility in CREST/CGO.

DEaR: Daily earnings at risk.

Debenture: In the US market, an unsecured domestic bond, backed by the general credit quality of the issuer. Debentures are issued under a trust deed or indenture. In the UK market, a bond that is secured against the general assets of the issuer.

Debt Management Office (DMO): An executive arm of the UK Treasury, responsible for cash management of the government's borrowing requirement. This includes responsibility for issuing government bonds (gilts), a function previously carried out by the Bank of England. The DMO began operations in April 1998.

Debt service coverage ratio (DSCR): A measure of the ability of an entity to service debt liability.

Default: A failure by one party to a contractual agreement to live up to its obligations under the agreement; a breach of contract such as non-payment of debt service interest or principal.

Default correlation: The degree of covariance between the probabilities of default of a given set of counterparties. For example, in a set of counterparties with positive default correlation, a default by one counterparty suggests an increased probability of a default by another counterparty. This statistic cannot be observed in practice, so the market uses proxy indicators, such as equity price correlation, where needed.

Default probability: See **probability-of-default**.

Default risk: See **credit risk**.

Default risk exposure: See **credit-risk exposure**.

Default start options: Options purchased before their "lives" actually commence. A corporation might, for example, decide to pay for a deferred-start option to lock into what it perceives as current advantageous pricing for an option that it knows it will need in the future.

Default-risk exposure: See **credit-risk exposure**.

Deferred strike option: An option where the strike price is established at a future date on the basis of the spot foreign exchange price prevailing at that future date.

Delegation costs: Incentive costs incurred by banks in delegating monitoring activities.

Deliverable bond: One of the bonds which is eligible to be delivered by the seller of a bond futures contract at the contract's maturity, according to the specifications of that particular contract.

Delivery: Transfer of gilts (in settlements) from seller to buyer.

Deliver-out repo: A term for a conventional classic repo where the buyer takes delivery of the collateral.

Delivery repo: A term used in the US market to refer to a repo in which the lender of cash takes actual delivery of the collateral, as opposed to a *hold-in-custody* repo.

Delivery versus payment (DVP): The simultaneous exchange of securities and cash. The assured payment mechanism of the CGO achieves the same protection.

Delta (*δ*): The change in an option's value relative to a change in the underlying's value.

Delta neutral: An option portfolio contracted to have zero delta.

Demand repo: Another term for open repo, a repo trade that has no fixed maturity term, and is renewed at one or both counterparties' agreement each morning.

Depreciation: A decrease in the market value of a currency in terms of other currencies. See **appreciation, devaluation**.

Derivative: Strictly, any financial instrument whose value is derived from another, such as a forward foreign exchange rate, a futures contract, an option, an interest-rate swap and so on. Forward deals to be settled in full are not always called derivatives, however.

Devaluation: An official one-off decrease in the value of a currency in terms of other currencies. See **revaluation, depreciation**.

Diffusion effect: The potential for increase over time of the credit exposure generated by a derivative: as time progresses, there is more likelihood of larger changes in the underlying market variables. Depending on the type and structure of the instrument this effect may be moderated by the **amortisation effect**.

Digital credit default swap: A credit default swap contract in which the payment made by the protection seller on occurrence of a credit event is a fixed predetermined amount. Also known as a **binary default swap**.

Digital option: Unlike simple European and US options, a digital option has fixed payouts and, rather like binary digital circuits, which are either on or off, pays out either this amount or nothing. Digital options can be added together to create assets that exactly mirror index price movements anticipated by investors.

Direct: An exchange rate quotation against the US dollar in which the dollar is the *variable currency* and the other currency is the **base currency**.

Dirty price: The price of a bond including accrued interest. Also known as the "all-in" price.

Discount: The amount by which a currency is cheaper, in terms of another currency, for future delivery than for spot, is the forward discount (in general, a reflection of interest rate differentials between two currencies). If an exchange rate is "at a discount" (without specifying to which of the two currencies this refers), this generally means that the variable currency is at a discount. See **premium**.

Discount factor: A factor by which one multiplies a future known cash flow, to obtain its present value.

Discount house: In the UK money market, originally securities houses that dealt directly with the Bank of England in T-bills and bank bills, or discount instruments; hence, the name. Most discount houses were taken over by international banking groups and the term is no longer used, as the Bank of England deals directly with clearing banks and securities houses.

Discount rate: The method of market quotation for certain securities (US and UK treasury bills, for example), expressing the return on the security as a proportion of the face value of the security received at maturity – as opposed to a yield, which expresses the yield as a proportion of the original investment.

Discount swap: Swap in which the fixed-rate payments are less than the internal rate of return on the swap, the difference being made up at maturity by a balloon payment.

Diversified: A portfolio that has been invested across a range of assets such that its credit risk is minimised. This is achieved by having a mixture of assets whose individual credit risks are uncorrelated with each other.

Diversity score: A Moody's CDO calculation that assigns a numeric value to an asset portfolio that represents the number of uncorrelated assets theoretically in the portfolio. A low diversity score indicates industry and/or geographical concentration and will be penalised in the ratings process.

Dividend discount model: Theoretical estimate of market value that computes the economic or the net present value of future cash flows due to an equity investor.

DMO: The UK Debt Management Office.

DMR: The *Debt Management Report*, published annually by HM Treasury.

Dollar repo: A repo transaction in which collateral returned at the maturity of the trade need not be exactly the same as that originally transferred. This is actually incorporated in the PSA/ISMA GMRA, which states that the obligation is only to return "equivalent" securities. In the US mortgage market it is also known as a *dollar roll*, but there are some detail differences to repo.

Dollar roll: A transaction with a number of similarities to repo, used exclusively for mortgage-backed securities, in the US market.

Down-and-in option: Barrier option where the holder's ability to exercise is activated if the value of the underlying drops below a specified level. See also **up-and-in option**.

Down-and-out-option: Barrier option where the holder's ability to exercise expires if the value of the underlying drops below a specified level.

DRM: Debt and Reserves Management Team in HM Treasury.

Dual currency option: Option allowing the holder to buy either of two currencies.

Dual currency swap: Currency swap where both the interest rates are fixed rates.

Dual strike option: Interest rate option, usually a **cap** or a **floor**, with one floor or ceiling rate for part of the option's life and another for the rest.

Duration: A measure of the weighted average life of a bond or other series of cash flows, using the present values of the cash flows as the weights. See **modified duration** and **Macauley duration**.

Duration gap: Measurement of the interest-rate exposure of an institution.

Duration weighting: The process of using the modified duration value for bonds to calculate the exact nominal holdings in a spread position. This is necessary because £1 million nominal of a two-year bond is not equivalent in interest-rate risk to £1 million of, say, a five-year bond. The modified duration value of the five-year bond will be higher, indicating that its "basis point value" (bpv) will be greater and that, therefore, £1 million worth of this bond represents greater sensitivity to a move in interest rates (risk). As another example, consider a fund manager holding £10 million of five-year bonds. The fund manager wishes to switch into a holding of two-year bonds with the same overall risk position. The basis point values of the bonds are 0.041583 and 0.022898, respectively. The ratio of the basis point values are 0.041583/0.022898 = 1.816. The fund manager, therefore, needs to switch into £10 million × 1.816 = £18.160 million of the two-year bond.

DV01: An acronym for "dollar value of an 01", meaning price value of a basis point. The change in value of a bond or derivative for a 1 basis point change in interest rates. Also known as "Dollar value of a basis point" or DVBP.

DVP: Delivery versus payment, in which the settlement mechanics of a sale or loan of securities against cash is such that the securities and cash are exchanged against each other simultaneously through the same clearing mechanism and neither can be transferred unless the other is.

E

Early exercise: The exercise or assignment of an option prior to expiration.

ECU: The European Currency Unit, a basket composed of European Union currencies, now defunct, following the introduction of the euro currency.

Effective rate: An effective interest rate is the rate that, earned as simple interest over one year, gives the same return as interest paid more frequently than once per year and then compounded. See **nominal rate**.

Efficient frontier method: Technique used by fund managers to allocate assets.

Embedded option: Interest-rate-sensitive option in debt instrument that affects its redemption. Such instruments include **mortgage-backed securities** and **callable bonds**.

End-end: A money market deal commencing on the last working day of a month and lasting for a whole number of months, maturing on the last working day of the correlation.

EONIA: The euro overnight interest-rate reference index, reported daily by the European Banking Federation. It is calculated as the average of the range of overnight interest-rates during the day.

Epsilon (ε): The same as **vega.**

Equity: Generally, the ownership share of a joint-stock company. Also known as a *share*. In the context of structured credit products, the most junior tranche note of a structured credit vehicle, so known as the **equity note**. It is also known as the *first-loss piece*, because losses in the vehicle are taken out of its value first. Its return is comprised of excess return in the vehicle, after all other note liabilities have been paid. For accounting purposes defined as the residual interest in the net assets of an entity that remains after deducting the liabilities.

Equity default swaps (EDS): A swap contract whose payout is linked to the fall in price of a reference equity, similar to a CDS and used to hedge against or speculate on equity price movements.

Equity options: Options on shares of an individual common stock.

Equity warrant: Warranty, usually attached to a bond, entitling the holder purchase share(s).

Equity repo legal agreement: The 1995 PSA/ISMA GMRA when extended to cover equity repo, now stated in Annex IV of the October 2000 agreement.

Equity-linked swap: Swap where one of the cash flows is based on an equity instrument or index, when it is known as an equity index swap.

Equivalent life: The weighted-average life of the principal of a bond where there are partial *redemptions*, using the **present values** of the partial redemptions as the weights.

Equivalent rate: The interest rate that returns the same amount as another quoted interest rate, but at a different compounding basis.

Equivalent securities: A term used in repo to denote that the securities returned must be of identical issue (and *tranche*, where relevant) and nominal value to those repo'ed in.

ERA: See **exchange-rate agreement.**

Eta (η): The same as *vega*.

Euribor: The reference rate for the euro currency, set in Brussels.

Euro: The name for the domestic currency of the European Monetary Union. Not to be confused with **Eurocurrency**.

Euroclear: The international bond and equity clearing system, based in Brussels and owned by a consortium of banks. Euroclear is managed by Morgan Guaranty Trust Company.

Eurocurrency: A Eurocurrency is a currency owned by a non-resident of the country in which the currency is legal tender. Not to be confused with **Euro**.

Euro-issuance: The issue of gilts (or other securities) denominated in Euro.

Euromarket: The international market in which Eurocurrencies are traded.

European: A European *option* is one that may be exercised only at **expiry**. See **American**.

Excess spread: Total cash left over in a securitisation transaction, after paying all costs.

Exchange controls: Regulations restricting the free convertibility of a currency into other currencies.

Exchange-rate agreement: A *contract for differences* based on the movement in a **forward–forward** foreign-exchange swap price. Does not take account of the effect of spot rate changes as an *FXA* does. See **SAFE**.

Exchange-traded: Futures contracts are traded on a futures exchange, as opposed to forward deals, which are **OTC**.

Ex-dividend: The time period before a bond's coupon date when it is traded without its accrued interest payment. This period is usually one or two weeks.

Ex-dividend (xd) date: A bond's record date for the payment of coupons. The coupon payment will be made to the person who is the registered holder of the stock on the xd date. For UK gilts this is seven working days before the coupon date.

Exercise: To exercise an **option** (by the **holder**) is to require the other party (the writer) to fulfil the underlying transaction. Exercise price is the same as **strike** price.

Exotic option: An option that is not plain vanilla; any complex option.

Expected (credit) loss: Estimate of the amount a counterparty is likely to lose as a result of default from a financial contract, with a given level of probability. The expected loss of any position can be derived by combining the distributions of credit exposures, rate of recovery and probabilities of default.

Expected default rate: Estimate of the most likely rate of default of a counterparty expressed as a level of probability.

Expected loss: A statistical measure of the average potential loss expected across a portfolio of assets over a given time period. Under Basel II capital allocation should cover expected losses.

Expected rate of recovery: See **rate of recovery**.

Expiry: An option's expiry is the time after which it can no longer be exercised.

Exposure: Risk to market movements.

Exposure at default (EAD): A Basel II measure for the expected exposure of a bank or financial institution for an asset such as a loan or bond upon default of the issuer. Under the foundation IRB this value is assigned by the Basel Committee, whereas under the advanced IRB it can be set by the firm itself.

Exposure profile: The path of worst case or expected exposures over time. Different instruments reveal quite differently shaped exposures profiles due to the interaction of the diffusion and amortisation effects.

Extinguishable option: Option in which the holder's right to exercise disappears if the value of the underlying passes a specified level. See also **barrier option**.

Extrapolation: The process of estimating a price or rate for a particular value date, from other known prices, when the value date required lies outside the period covered by the known prices. See **interpolation**.

F

Face value: The principal amount of a security generally repaid ("redeemed") all at maturity, but sometimes repaid in stages, on which the **coupon** amounts are calculated.

Failure or **failed trade**: A trade that does not complete because the seller is unable to deliver the stock on time.

FAS 133: The United States Financial Accounting Standards Board (FASB) rule that states that all firms regulated by the Securities and Exchange Commission must mark-to-market their derivatives positions on their balance sheet.

Fed repo: A repo trade entered into between the US Federal Reserve ("Fed") and US Treasury primary dealers, similar to the Bank of England open market operations. The Fed undertakes this in order to supply liquidity to the market. The typical term of a Fed repo is 15 days and is at the Fed funds rate. The collateral accepted is Treasury or Agency securities.

Fence: The same as **collar**.

First-to-Default (FtD): A CDS contract that references a basket of credit names, and which is triggered when a name in the basket experienced a credit event.

First-to-default basket: A credit default swap contract written on a pool or "basket" of reference assets, on which the protection seller sells protection on all the assets, and pays out on occurrence of the first credit event in the basket. There are also 2nd-, 3rd, and *N*th-to-default contracts.

Fixed-coupon repo: Similar to a *dollar repo*, except that the collateral returned must have the same coupon as that originally transferred.

Fixing: See **Libor fixing**.

Flat repo: Repo undertaken with no margin. Also known as *flat basis*.

Flex repo: Classic repo trade in which the lender of cash may draw down the cash supplied in accordance with a schedule agreed at trade inception.

Floating rate: An interest rate set with reference to an external index. Also an instrument paying a floating rate is one where the rate of interest is refixed in line with market conditions at regular intervals, such as every three or six months. In the current market, an exchange rate determined by market forces with no government intervention.

Floating rate CD: CD on which the rate of interest payable is refixed in line with market conditions at regular intervals (usually six months).

Floating rate gilt: Gilt issued with an interest rate adjusted periodically in line with market interbank rates.

Floating rate note (FRN): Capital market instrument on which the rate of interest payable is refixed in line with market conditions at regular intervals (usually three or six months).

Floor: A series of lender's **IRG**s, designed to protect an investor against falling interest rates on each of a series of dates.

Floortion: Option on a **floor**.

Forward: In general, a deal for value later than the normal value date for that particular commodity or instrument. In the foreign exchange market, a forward price is the price quoted for the purchase or sale of one currency against another where the value date is at least one month after the spot date. See **short date**.

Forward band: Zero-cost collar that is one in which the premium payable as a result of buying the cap is offset exactly by that obtained from selling the floor.

Forward break: See **break forward**.

Forward exchange agreement (FXA): A contract for differences designed to create exactly the same economic result as a foreign exchange cash forward–forward deal. See **ERA, SAFE**.

Forward–forward: Short-term exchange of currency deposits. (See also forward–forward deposit.)

Forward–forward deposit: Deposit of cash where the interest rate is effective from a future date (t_1 to a later date, t_2).

Forward–forward yield curve: A yield curve of zero-coupon rates for periods starting at a future point, say, one month or one year from today.

Forward rate agreement (FRA): Short-term interest-rate hedge. Specifically, a contract between buyer and seller for an agreed interest rate on a notional deposit of a specified maturity on a predetermined future date. No principal is exchanged. At maturity the seller pays the buyer the difference if rates have risen above the agreed level, and vice versa.

Forward swap: Swap arranged at the current rate but entered into at some time in the future.

Foundation internal ratings-based approach (FIRB): Under Basel II and its Pillar One framework, the ruling that allows banks and financial institutions to calculate their regulatory capital requirement by using their own internally generated estimate of the probability of default. However, the banks must use BIS-provided values for exposure-at-default and loss-given-default in this calculation.

FRA: See **forward rate agreement**.

Framework document: Sets out the Direct Management Office's responsibilities, objectives and targets; its relationship with the rest of the Treasury; and its accountability as an Executive Agency.

Fraption: Option on a forward-rate agreement. Also known as an interest-rate guarantee.

FRCD: See **floating rate CD**.

FRN: See **floating-rate note**.

FSA: The Financial Services Authority, the body responsible for the regulation of investment business, and the supervision of banks and money market institutions in the United Kingdom. The FSA took over these duties from nine "self-regulatory organisations" that had previously carried out this function, including the Securities and Futures Authority (SFA), which had been responsible for regulation of professional investment business in the City of London. The FSA commenced its duties in 1998.

FTSE-100: Index comprising 100 major UK shares listed on The International Stock Exchange in London. Futures and options on the index are traded at the London International Financial Futures and Options Exchange (**LIFFE**).

Funding reserve: A specified (say, 10 basis points) multiple of the aggregate value of the funding gap, across the maturity structure.

Fungible: A financial instrument that is equivalent in value to another, and easily exchanged or substituted. The best example is cash money, as a £10 note has the same value and is directly exchangeable with another £10 note. A bearer bond also has this quality.

Future: A futures contract is a contract to buy or sell securities or other goods at a future date at a predetermined price. Futures contracts are usually standardised and traded on an exchange.

Futures contract: A deal to buy or sell some financial instrument or commodity for value on a future date. Unlike a *forward* deal, futures contracts are traded only on an exchange (rather than *OTC*), have standardised contract sizes and value dates, and are often only **contract for differences** rather than deliverable.

Future exposure: See **potential exposure**.

Future value: The amount of money achieved in the future, including interest, by investing a given amount of money now. See **time value of money**, **present value**.

G

G7: The "Group of Seven" countries, the United States, Canada, United Kingdom, Germany, France, Italy and Japan.

G10: The Group of Ten, comprising Belgium, Canada, France, Germany, Italy, Japan, the Netherlands, Sweden, Switzerland, United Kingdom and the United States (actually 11 countries).

Gamma (γ): The change in an option's delta relative to a change in the underlying's value.

Gap: The difference in the maturity profile of assets versus liabilities by time bucket. Gives rise to gap risk.

Gap ratio: Ratio of interest-rate sensitive assets to interest-rate sensitive liabilities; used to determine changes in the risk profile of an institution with changes in interest-rate levels.

Gapping: Feature of commodity markets whereby there are large and very rapid price movements to new levels followed by relatively stable prices.

GDP: Gross domestic product, the value of total output produced within a country's borders.

GEMM: A gilt-edged market-maker, a bank or securities house registered with the Bank of England as a market-maker in gilts. A GEMM is required to meet certain obligations as part of its function as a registered market-maker, including making two-way price quotes at all times in all gilts and taking part in gilt auctions. The Debt Management Office now make a distinction between conventional gilt GEMMs and index-linked GEMMs, known as IG GEMMs.

General collateral (GC): Securities, which are not "special", used as collateral against cash borrowing. A repo buyer will accept GC at any time that a specific stock is not quoted as required in the transaction. In the gilts market GC includes DBVs. There is no standard accepted GC in equity repo, although some participants make markets in blue-chip index stocks a quasi-equity GC.

GIC: Guaranteed investment contract. A bank account that pays either a fixed rate for its life, or a fixed spread under Libor for its life.

Gilt: A UK government sterling denominated, listed security issued by HM Treasury with initial maturity of over 365 days when issued. The term "gilt" (or gilt-edged) is a reference to the primary characteristic of gilts as an investment: their security.

Gilt-edged market-maker: See **GEMM**.

GMRA: Global Master Repurchase Agreement, the industry-standard legal agreement describing repo transactions. Issued under the auspices of the Bond Market Association in the US and the International Securities Market Association (ISMA).

GNP: Gross national product, the total monetary value of a country's output, as produced by citizens of that country.

Gold warrant: Naked or attached warrant exercisable into gold at a predetermined price.

Gross basis: The difference between the price of an asset and its implied price given by the price of a futures contract. The gross basis for a government bond futures contract is given by:

$$Basis = P_{bond} - (P_{fut} \times CF)$$

where *CF* is the bond's conversion factor.

Gross redemption yield: The same as **yield to maturity**; "gross" because it does not take tax effects into account.

GRY: See **gross redemption yield**.

Guarantee: A legal obligation in which the guarantor undertakes to repay a third party liability, such as a loan.

Guarantor: A third party to a contract that guarantees the legal obligations under that contract for one party to it, such as repayment of a loan. Such a contract therefore carries a **guarantee**.

H

Haircut: Also known as margin, a reduction measure applied to an asset that is being used as collateral that reduces its accepted market value such that this lower figure is the amount of cash lent against it. The collateral value is therefore given a "haircut", whereas strictly speaking "margin" is the amount over and above the cash loan value that must be added when calculating collateral. In economic terms the effect of both is identical.

Hard stock: Another term for a *special* stock. In the US market the term *hot stock* is also used.

Hedge ratio: The ratio of the size of the position it is necessary to take in a particular instrument as a hedge against another, to the size of the position being hedged.

Hedging: Protecting against the risks arising from potential market movements in exchange rates, interest rates or other variables. See **cover**, **arbitrage**, **speculation**.

Herstatt risk: See **settlement risk**.

High coupon swap: Off-market coupon swap where the coupon is higher than the market rate. The floating-rate payer pays a front-end fee as compensation. Opposite of **low coupon swap**.

Historic rate rollover: A *forward rate swap* in FX where the settlement exchange rate for the near date is based on a historic *off-market* rate rather than the current market rate. This is prohibited by many central banks.

Historic volatility: The actual *volatility* recorded in market prices over a particular period.

Historical simulation methodology: Method of calculating *value-at-risk* (*VaR*) using historical data to assess the likely effect of market moves on a portfolio.

Holder: The holder of an *option* is the party that has purchased it.

Hold in custody (HIC) repo: A repo in which the party that receives cash does not deliver the securities to the counterparty, but segregates them in an internal account for the benefit of the cash provider. In the US market, this is also known as a *trust me* repo.

Hot stock or **hard stock**: A security in high demand, and therefore "special" in the repo market.

Hybrid: A term used to refer to a structure comprising elements of cash and synthetic securitisation. Also a bond that is not conventional or plain vanilla.

I

Icing: The term used to reserve stock, ahead of possibly borrowing it, in the stock-lending market. Stock that has been iced is *open to challenge*.

IDB: Inter-dealer broker, in this context a broker that provides facilities for dealing in bonds between market-makers.

IG: Index-linked gilt whose coupons and final redemption payment are related to the movements in the Retail Price Index (RPI).

Illiquid: An asset that is difficult to trade in a secondary market, either because no buyer or seller is readily available, no price can be determined and/or it cannot be transferred easily to the ownership of a new buyer.

Immunisation: This is the process by which a bond portfolio is created that has an assured return for a specific time horizon irrespective of changes in interest rates. The mechanism underlying immunisation is a portfolio structure that balances the change in the value of a portfolio at the end of the investment horizon (time period) with the return gained from the reinvestment of cash flows from the portfolio. As such, immunisation requires the portfolio manager to offset interest-rate risk and reinvestment risk.

Implied repo rate: The breakeven interest rate at which it is possible to sell a bond *futures contract*, buy a **deliverable bond**, and **repo** the bond out. See **cash-and-carry**.

It is defined as the rate used to measure which stock is the cheapest to deliver (CTD) into the government bond futures contract. The bond with the highest implied repo rate is the CTD bond. It is given by:

$$\frac{P_{fut} - P_{bond}}{P_{bond}} \times \frac{365}{N} \times 100$$

where P_{fut} is the dirty futures price, P_{bond} is the dirty cash price and N is the number of days to expiry of the futures contract. The dirty futures price is the cash inflow from selling the futures contract and the dirty cash price is the cash outflow from simultaneously buying the CTD bond. The term *implied repo rate* is also used, erroneously, to refer to the repo rate "implied" in a sell/buy-back transaction but incorporated in the forward buy-back price.

Implied volatility: The **volatility** used by a dealer to calculate an **option** price; conversely, the volatility implied by the price actually quoted.

Index: A statistical measure of the value of a basket of assets. The constituent assets may be bonds, equities, interest rates or other financial assets. An index is often used as an economic indicator of the group of assets it represents, or as a benchmark against which overall economic performance is measured.

Index option: An **option** whose **underlying** security is an index. Index options enable a trader to bet on the direction of the index.

Index swap: Sometimes the same as a **basis swap**. Otherwise, a swap like an **interest-rate swap** where payments on one or both of the legs are based on the value of an index – such as an equity index, for example. Also, a total return swap contract in which the total return payer pays the counterparty the return on a specified index, such as a bond index or credit reference index.

Indexed notes: Contract whereby the issuer usually assumes the risk of unfavourable price movements in the instrument, commodity or index to which the contract is linked, in exchange for which the issuer can reduce the cost of borrowing (compared with traditional instruments without the risk exposure).

Indexed repo: A repo transaction where the repo rate is linked to an external, specified index such as **Libor**.

Indirect: An exchange rate quotation against the US dollar in which the dollar is the **base currency** and the other currency is the **variable currency**.

Initial margin: The excess either of cash over the value of securities, or of the value of securities over cash in a repo transaction at the time it is executed and subsequently after margin calls.

Interbank: The market in unsecured lending and trading between banks of roughly similar credit quality.

Interest-rate cap: See **cap**.

Interest-rate floor: See **floor**.

Interest-rate guarantee: An **option** on an **FRA**.

Interest-rate option: Option to pay or receive a specified rate of interest on or from a predetermined future date.

Interest-rate swap: An agreement between two parties in which one party pays interest on the agreed notional amount at a specified fixed rate, and the other party pays at a floating rate linked to Libor. Only net cash flows are actually transferred, based on the difference between the fixed rate and the prevailing floating-rate fix. Interest-rate swaps are used to transform the interest-rate basis of an asset or liability. Swaps in liquid currencies such as dollar, sterling and euro can be transacted out to 30 years' maturity, and the swap rate is calculated from the government bond zero-coupon yield curve. May be combined with a **currency swap**.

Intermarket spread: A spread involving futures contracts in one market spread against futures contracts in another market.

Internal rate of return (IRR): The yield necessary to discount a series of cash flows to an NPV of zero.

Internal ratings-based approach (IRB): Under Basel II, the IRB is a procedure used in determining the regulatory capital requirement of a pool of credit exposures. It comprises a classification of exposures by type, with a bank providing risk data for each type. A risk-weighting function allocates a risk-weight for each type, and a bank must meet the minimum requirements set out in the approach in line with the risk-weighting allocated.

Interpolation: The process of estimating a price or rate for value on a particular date by comparing the prices actually quoted for value dates either side. See **extrapolation**.

Intervention: Purchases or sales of currencies in the market by central banks in an attempt to reduce exchange rate fluctuations or to maintain the value of a currency within a particular band, or at a particular level. Similarly, central bank operations in the money markets to maintain interest rates at a certain level.

In-the-money: A **call (put) option** is in-the-money if the underlying is currently more (less) valuable than the **strike** price. See **at-the-money**, **out-of-the-money**.

Intrinsic value: The amount by which an option is in-the-money.

Investment grade: Debt rated at or above BBB– by Standard & Poor's or Baa3 by Moody's.

Investor: A party that is long cash and therefore a purchaser of securities, or lender of money. In a repo transaction, the lender of cash and therefore the taker of collateral.

IRG: See **interest-rate guarantee**.

IRR: See **internal rate of return**.

IRS: See **interest-rate swap**.

ISDA: International Swaps and Derivatives Association.

ISMA: The International Securities Market Association. This association compiled with the PSA (now renamed the Bond Market Association) the PSA/ISMA Global Master Repurchase Agreement.

Issuer risk: Risk to an institution when it holds debt securities issued by another institution. (See also **credit risk**.)

Issuing and paying agent (IPA): An entity responsible for making payments on bond and money market instruments, such as the initial proceeds, coupon payments and redemption proceeds. Generally, a banking institution.

Iteration: The mathematical process of estimating the answer to a problem by seeing how well an estimate fits the data, adjusting the estimate appropriately and trying again, until the answer is close to the actual. Used, for example, in calculating a bond's **yield** from its price.

J

Junk bonds: The common term for high-yield bonds; higher risk, low-rated debt.

K

Kappa (κ): An alternative term to refer to volatility; see **vega**.

Kick-in note: An index-linked hybrid bond whose enhanced return is triggered if the index reaches a certain level above or below where it is when the note is issued.

Knock in/out: A knock out (in) **option** ceases to exist (starts to exist) if the underlying reaches a certain trigger level. See **barrier option**.

L

Lambda (λ): The same as **vega**.

Large exposure: A risk exposure to a bank caused by having a large part of lending made to just one counterparty. Under EU CAD, an extra risk number must be allocated for this risk.

LCH: London Clearing House.

Lender: The provider of collateral in a repo or sell/buy-back, and therefore a *borrower* of cash, or the lender of stock (and taker of collateral) in a stock loan transaction.

Lender option: Floor on a single-period forward rate agreement.

Leptokurtosis: The non-normal distribution of asset-price returns. Refers to a probability distribution that has a fatter tail and a sharper hump than a normal distribution.

Level payment swap: Evens out those fixed-rate payments that would otherwise vary, for example, because of the amortisation of the principal.

Leverage: The ability to control large amounts of an underlying variable for a small initial investment.

Leveraged buy-out (LBO): A mechanism by which a company is purchased, funded by issue of large-scale debt well in excess of the equity behind the deal.

Liability: Probable future sacrifice of economic benefit due to present obligations to transfer assets or provide services to other entities as a result of past events or transactions. Generally classed as either current or long-term.

Liability swap: An interest-rate swap or currency swap used in conjunction with an underlying liability such as a borrowing. See **asset swap**.

Libid: The London Interbank Bid Rate, the rate at which banks will pay for funds in the interbank market.

Libor: The London Interbank Offered Rate, the lending rate for all major currencies up to one-year set at 11 a.m. each day by the British Bankers Association.

Libor fixing: The Libor rate "fixed" by the British Bankers Association (BBA) at 11 a.m. each day, for maturities up to one year.

LIFFE: The London International Financial Futures and Options Exchange, the largest futures exchange in Europe.

Limean: The arithmetic average of Libor and Libid rates.

Limit up/down: Futures prices are generally not allowed to change by more than a specified total amount in a specified time, in order to control risk in very volatile conditions. The maximum movements permitted are referred to as limit up and limit down.

Liquidation: Any transaction that closes out or offsets a futures or options position.

Liquidity: A word describing the ease with which one can undertake transactions in a particular market or instrument. A market where there are always ready buyers and sellers willing to transact at competitive prices is regarded as liquid. In banking, the term is also used to describe the requirement that a portion of a bank's assets be held in short-term risk-free instruments, such as government bonds, T-bills and high-quality CDs.

Liquidity risk: The risk associated with undertaking transactions in illiquid markets, which are characterised by wide bid–offer spreads, lack of transparency, a small number of market-makers and large movements in price after a deal of large size. In the context of banking asset and liability management, the risk of having insufficient funds available to meet a sudden large-scale demand for funds from depositors.

Loan-equivalent amount: Description of derivative exposure that is used to compare the credit risk of derivatives with that of traditional bonds or bank loans.

Lognormal: A variable's **probability distribution** is lognormal if the logarithm of the variable has a normal distribution.

Lognormal distribution: The assumption that the log of today's interest rate, for example, minus the log of yesterday's rate is normally distributed.

Long: A long position is a surplus of purchases over sales of a given currency or asset, or a situation that naturally gives rise to an organisation benefiting from a strengthening of that currency or asset. To a money-market dealer, however, a long position is a surplus of borrowings taken in over money lent out (which gives rise to a benefit if that currency weakens rather than strengthens). See **short**.

Long-dated forward: Forward foreign-exchange contract with a maturity of greater than one year. Some long-dated forwards have maturities as great as 10 years.

Long-term assets: Assets that are expected to provide benefits and services over a period longer than one year.

Long-term Capital Management (LTCM): A US-hedge fund that went bust in 1999.

Long-term liabilities: Obligations to be repaid by the firm more than one year later.

Lookback option: Option that allows the purchaser, at the end of a given period of time, to choose as the rate for exercise any rate that has existed during the option's life.

Loss-given-default (LGD): A calculation of the amount of loss expected to be experienced by an asset default should it default.

Under Basel II the credit loss incurred if an obligor of a bank defaults. LGD includes three types of losses: (i) loss of principal (ii) funding cost loss associated with holding non-performing loans and (iii) operational costs such as cost of collection, legal costs and so on. LGD may be measured in the following ways:

- market LGD, calculated market price of a bond or loan after its issuer has experienced default;
- workout LGD, which is calculated from the cash flows expected from the collection process;
- implied market LGD, which is observed from similar-risk (but not defaulted) bonds or loans.

For Basel II, LGD is reported as a percentage of the exposure-at-default, given as (1 – *RR*) where *RR* is the recovery rate. If any particular loan or exposure is backed by collateral (for example, in a repo), the LGD value is reduced.

Low coupon swap: Tax-driven swap, in which the fixed-rate payments are significantly lower than current market interest rates. The floating-rate payer is compensated by a front-end fee.

LSE: London Stock Exchange.

LTV: Loan-to-value, the ratio of the loan amount over the value of the asset. A lending risk ratio calculated by dividing the total amount of the mortgage or loan by the appraised value of the asset.

M

Macaulay duration: See **duration**.

Manufactured dividend: A payment from the repo buyer to the repo seller during the term of the trade, representing the coupon or dividend received by the temporary owner (repo buyer) of the security being repo'ed. Also applies in a stock loan transaction.

Mapping: The process whereby a Treasury's derivative positions are related to a set of risk "buckets".

Margin: Initial margin is **collateral**, placed by one party with a counterparty at the time of the deal, against the possibility that the market price will move against the first party, thereby leaving the counterparty with a credit risk. Variation margin is a payment or extra collateral transferred subsequently from one party to the other because the market price has moved. Variation margin payment is either in effect a settlement of profit/loss (for example, in the case of a **futures contract**) or the reduction of credit exposure (for example, in the case of a **repo**). In gilt repos, variation margin refers to the fluctuation band or threshold within which the existing collateral's value may vary before further cash or collateral needs to be transferred. In a loan, margin is the extra interest above a **benchmark** (for example, a margin of 0.5% over **Libor**) required by a lender to compensate for the credit risk of that particular borrower.

Margin call: A request following marking-to-market of a repo transaction for the initial margin to be reinstated or, where no initial margin has been taken, to restore the cash/securities ratio to parity.

Margin default rate: See **probability-of-default**.

Margin ratio: A term used in the GMRA and the Equity Legal Agreement, and a term for the initial margin. It is defined as the ratio of the market price of the securities to their purchase price.

Margin transfer: The payment of a **margin call**.

Market comparables: Technique for estimating the fair value of an instrument for which no price is quoted by comparing it with the quoted prices of similar instruments.

Market-maker: Market participant who is committed, explicitly or otherwise, to quoting two-way bid and offer prices at all times in a particular market.

Market risk: Risks related to changes in prices of tradeable macroeconomic variables, such as exchange rate risks.

Mark-to-market: The act of revaluing securities to current market values. Such revaluations should include both coupon accrued on the securities outstanding and interest accrued on the cash.

Matched book: Running a market-making operation in repo. Alternatively, only trading repo to cover your own financing requirements. Also refers to the matching by a repo trader of securities repo'ed in and out. It carries no implications that the trader's position is "matched" in terms of exposure or term to maturity, for example to short-term interest rates, and in fact books are "mismatched" to reflect views on interest rates.

Maturity date: Date on which stock is redeemed.

Mean: Average.

Mezzanine: The intermediate tranche(s) note of a structured credit product such as a CDO or MBS issue, senior to the equity note.

Minmax option: One of the strategies for reducing the cost of options by forgoing some of the potential for gain. The buyer of a currency option, for example, simultaneously sells an option on the same amount of currency but at a different strike price.

MLV: Maximum likely potential increase in value.

Modified duration: A measure of the proportional change in the price of a bond or other series of cash flows, relative to a change in yield. (Mathematically – $[dP/di]$ / dirty price.) See **duration**.

Modified following: The convention that if a value date in the future falls on a non-business day, the value date will be moved to the next following business day, unless this moves the value date to the next month, in which case the value date is moved back to the last previous business day.

Momentum: The strength behind an upward or downward movement in price.

Monetary Policy Committee (MPC): The committee of the Bank of England, staffed by five BoE employees (including the Governor and the Deputy Governor) and four external appointees who are responsible for setting UK interest rates.

Money market: Short-term market (generally up to one year) for financial instruments. See **capital market**.

Money market basis: An interest rate quoted on an ACT/360 basis is said to be on a money market basis. See **bond basis**.

Monte Carlo simulation: Technique used to determine the likely value of a derivative or other contract by simulating the evolution of the underlying variables many times. The discounted *average* outcome of the simulation gives an approximation of the derivative's value. Monte Carlo simulation can be used to estimate the *Value-at-Risk* (VaR) of a portfolio. Here, it generates a simulation of many correlated market movements for the markets to which the portfolio is exposed, and the positions in the portfolio are revalued repeatedly in accordance with the simulated scenarios. This gives a probability distribution of portfolio gains and losses from which the VaR can be determined.

Monte Titoli: The Italian domestic market clearing system.

Moosmüller: A method for calculating the yield of a bond.

Mortgage-backed security (MBS): Security guaranteed by a pool of mortgages, created by the process of securisation.

Moving average convergence/divergence (MACD): The crossing of two exponentially smoothed moving averages that oscillate above and below an equilibrium line.

MTN: Medium-term note.

Multi-index option: Option that gives the holder the right to buy the asset that performs best out of a number of assets (usually two). The investor would typically buy a call allowing him or her to buy the **equity**.

N

Naked: A naked option position is one not protected by an offsetting position in the underlying. See **covered call/put**.

Naked option: An option position in which the writer does not hold the underlying asset.

NAO: National Audit Office.

Negative divergence: When at least two indicators, indexes or averages show conflicting or contradictory trends.

Negotiable: A security that can be bought and sold in a **secondary market** is negotiable.

Net basis: The gross basis of a futures-deliverable bond, adjusted for net carry.

Net interest income (NII): Interest income on all assets held in a banking asset portfolio, net of costs.

Net present value (NPV): The net present value of a series of cash flows is the sum of the present values of each cash flow (some or all of which may be negative).

Netting: The practice of counterparties taking the net exposure of all the trades they have outstanding between them and only settling the net difference. When used in conjunction with a centralised clearing counterparty (similar to a derivatives exchange clearing house), a process that eliminates counterparty credit risk and simplifies stock and cash movements.

NLF: National Loans Fund, the account that brings together all UK government lending and borrowing.

Noise: Fluctuations in the market that can confuse or impede interpretation of market direction.

Nominal amount: Same as **face value** of a security.

Nominal rate: The quoted interest rate, rather than the **effective rate** to which it is equivalent.

Non-deliverable forward: A forward FX contract that does not result in exchange of actual cash currency amounts on maturity, but instead has a single net payment representing the change between the traded forward rate and the spot rate on maturity.

Non-interest-bearing deposits (NIBL): Liabilities of a bank that earn no or very low rates of interest; for example, cheque accounts.

Non-performing: A loan or other asset that is no longer being serviced, or has experienced default.

Non-performing loan (NPL): A loan for which the obligor has not made recent interest payments, or has not paid on maturity or repaid only partially, but which is not yet considered to be in default. An NPL is usually designated as such for a time set by the bank, after which, if it is still non-performing, it will be declared to be in default and recovery processes instituted. This time period can be as little as three months or stretch into years. Also defined as loans that are no longer being serviced by interest payments and/or principal repayment. Typically, a loan is deemed to be an NPL if 90 days has passed since a scheduled payment was missed.

Normal: A normal *probability distribution* is a particular distribution assumed to prevail in a wide variety of circumstances, including the financial markets. Mathematically, it corresponds to the probability density function.

Notional: In a bond futures contract, the bond bought or sold is a standardised non-existent notional bond, as opposed to the actual bonds that are *deliverable* at maturity. **Contracts for differences** also require a notional principal amount on which settlement can be calculated. Otherwise, it is the balance that is used as the basis for calculating interest or credit protection due with respect to an obligation.

Novation: Replacement of a contract or, more usually, a series of contracts with one new contract.

NPV: See **net present value**.

NYSE: New York Stock Exchange.

O

O/N: See **overnight**.

Obligor: A borrower of funds.

Odd date: See **broken date**.

Off-balance sheet: A transaction whose nominal value is not entered on the balance sheet, because the principal amount is not traded. The standard accounting treatment for *contracts for differences*.

Off-balance sheet instruments (OBS): Derivative contracts that are held off the balance sheet, because they are not "cash" assets, and the premium paid to purchase them is a fraction of their notional value.

Off-market: A rate that is not the current market rate.

Off-market coupon swap: Tax-driven swap strategy in which the fixed-rate payments differ significantly from current market rates. There are high and low coupon swaps.

Offer: The price at which a market-maker will sell bonds. Also called "**ask**". In the repo market, the repo rate that the seller is willing to pay on cash received, to "offer" the stock; that is, take the cash.

Open book: A term for a "mismatched" book. However, the term "mismatched" book is not itself generally used by traders.

Open repo: A repo trade with no fixed maturity date, with the daily possibility of terminating the repo or refixing its terms or substituting collateral.

Open to challenge: A request to ice a stock is open to challenge if the party making the icing request has not confirmed the order, and a second party subsequently approaches the stock-lender with a firm request to borrow. The first party retains first option on the stock it has iced.

Opening leg: The first half of a repo transaction. Also known as *start* leg, *first* leg, *near* leg or *onside* leg. See also **closing leg**.

Operational market notice: Sets out the DMO's (previously the bank's) operations and procedures in the gilt market.

Operational risk: Risk of loss occurring due to inadequate systems and control, human error, or management failure.

Opportunity cost: Value of an action that could have been taken if the current action had not been chosen.

Option: The right (but not the obligation) to buy or sell securities at a fixed price within a specified period.

Option forward: See **time option**.

Ordinary least squares (OLS): An econometric technique used to estimate the strength and direction of the relationship between two or more variables.

Originator: In a securitisation transaction, the bank or other entity that is behind the securitisation. Also known as the sponsor. The originating bank directly or indirectly transfers assets in the securitisation, or acts as a sponsor of an asset-backed commercial paper conduit.

Ornstein-Uhlenbeck equation: A standard equation that describes mean reversion. It can be used to characterise and measure commodity price behaviour.

OTC: Over-the-counter. Strictly speaking, any transaction not conducted on a registered stock exchange. Trades conducted via the telephone between banks, and contracts such as FRAs and (non-exchange traded) options are said to be "over-the-counter" instruments. OTC also refers to non-standard instruments or contracts traded privately between two parties; for example, a client with a requirement for a specific risk to be hedged with a tailor-made instrument may enter into an OTC structured trade with a bank that makes markets in such products.

Out-of-the-money: A **call (put) option** is out-of-the-money if the **underlying** is currently less (more) valuable than the strike price. See **at-the-money, in-the-money**.

Outright: An outright (or **forward** outright) is the sale or purchase of one foreign currency against another value on any date other than spot. See **spot, swap, forward, short date**.

Over-the-counter: See **OTC**.

Overborrowed: A position in which a dealer's liabilities (borrowings taken in) are of longer maturity than the assets (loans out).

Over-collateralisation: A capital structure in which assets exceed liabilities.

Over-collateralised: Where the value of collateral exceeds that of the cash lent against it. Used to protect against counterparty and market risk.

Overlent: A position in which a dealer's assets (loans out) are of longer maturity than the liabilities (borrowings taken in).

Overnight: A deal from today until the next working day ("tomorrow").

Overnight index swap (OIS): An interest-rate swap that pays/receives fixed-rate interest on one leg and receives/pays the average of the overnight interest rate on the other leg.

P

p/e ratio: price/earnings ratio.

Pair-off: The netting of consideration and stock in the settlement of two trades (one buy, one sell) in the same security, possible where value dates are identical, to allow settlement of the net differences only.

Paper: Another term for a bond or debt issue.

Par: In foreign exchange, when the **outright** and **spot** exchange rates are equal, the **forward swap** is zero or par. When the price of a security is equal to the face value, usually expressed as 100, it is said to be trading at par. A par swap rate is the current market rate for a fixed **interest-rate swap** against **Libor**.

Par yield curve: A curve plotting maturity against yield for bonds priced at par.

Parity: The official rate of exchange for one currency in terms of another which a government is obliged to maintain by means of intervention.

Participation forward: A product equivalent to a straightforward **option** plus a forward deal, but structured as a forward deal at an **off-market** rate plus the opportunity to benefit partially if the market rate improves.

Path-dependent: A path-dependent **option** is one which depends on what happens to the **underlying** throughout the option's life (such as the **American** or **barrier option**), rather than only at expiry (a **European option**).

Pay-as-you-go (PAUG): A type of CDS contract used when the reference entity is a structured finance security such as an ABS, and whose notional is adjusted to reflect pay-downs and other adjustments to the outstanding balance of the reference security.

Peak exposure: If the worst case or the expected credit risk exposures of an instrument is calculated over time, the resulting graph reveals a credit risk exposure profile. The highest exposure marked out by the profile is the peak exposure generated by the instrument.

Pension: The French domestic market classic repo. Formally documented in law in December 1993, previously known as *pension livrée*.

Periodic resetting swap: Swap where the floating-rate payment is an average of floating rates that have prevailed since the last payment, rather than the interest rate prevailing at the end of the period. For example, the average of six 1-month **Libor** rates rather than one, 6-month Libor rate.

Pillar One: One of the three pillars that comprise the Basel II framework. Pillar One stipulates the methodology for the calculation of the specific capital charges for credit risk and operational risk.

Pillar Two: Pillar Two is part of the Basel II framework and sets out guidelines for supervisory bodies. This includes directions to follow with regard to capital adequacy, internal procedures and risks such as interest-rate risk.

Pillar Three: The market-discipline element of the three-pillar framework behind Basel II, Pillar Three sets out the disclosure requirements for a bank or financial institution to its shareholders and customers.

Pips: See **points**.

Plain vanilla: See **vanilla**.

Points: The last two decimal places in an exchange rate. For example, when EUR/USD is 1.1910/1.1920, the points are 10/20. See **bid figure**.

Pool factor: A value assigned to a tranche of a structured finance security such as an ABS or MBS that is used to determine outstanding market value. As the underlying asset pool experiences paydowns (such as prepayment of a mortgage that is in the underlying pool), the overlying notes are also paid down, usually on a pro-rata basis, to reflect their reduced actual amount. On issue, ABS and MBS notes have a pool factor of 1.0000. As prepayment takes place, the pool factor reduces. To obtain the market value of an ABS or MBS tranche, we multiply the nominal value of the note by the pool factor, and then multiply this value with the dirty price.

Portfolio variance: The square of the **standard deviation** of a portfolio's return from the mean.

Positive cash-flow collar: Collar other than a zero-cost collar.

Potential exposure: Estimate of the future replacement cost, or positive market value, of a derivative transaction. Potential exposure should be calculated using probability analysis based on broad confidence intervals (for example, two standard deviations) over the remaining term of the transaction.

Preference shares: These are a form of corporate financing. They are normally fixed interest shares whose holders have the right to receive dividends ahead of ordinary shareholders. If a company were to go into liquidation, preference shareholders would rank above ordinary shareholders for the repayment of their investment in the company. Preference shares ("prefs") are normally traded within the fixed interest division of a bank or securities house.

Premium: For a bond, the amount by which the price is over par. In the FX market, the amount by which a currency is more expensive, in terms of another currency, for future delivery than for spot, is the forward premium (in general, a reflection of interest-rate differentials between two currencies). If an exchange rate is "at a premium" (without specifying to which of the two currencies this refers), this generally means that the **variable currency** is at a premium. See **discount**.

Present value (PV): The amount of money that needs to be invested now to achieve a given amount in the future when interest is added. See **time value of money**, **future value**.

Pre-settlement risk: As distinct from credit risk arising from intra-day settlement risk, this term describes the risk of loss that might be suffered during the life of the contract if a counterparty to a trade defaulted and if, at the time of default, the instrument had a positive economic value.

Price differential: A term used in the Equity Repo Agreement to describe the accrued return on the cash involved in a repo.

Price-earnings ratio: A ratio giving the price of a stock relative to the earnings per share.

Price factor: See **conversion factor**.

Pricing rate: Another term for repo rate.

Primary market: The market for new debt, into which new bonds are issued. The primary market is made up of borrowers, investors and the investment banks that place new debt into the market, usually with their clients. Bonds that trade after they have been issued are said to be part of the secondary market.

Principal: A party to a repo transaction who acts on their own behalf. Also, a term used to refer to the nominal value of a bond.

Principal protected note: A financial instrument that guarantees repayment of its principal amount (par amount) to investors on maturity or on termination. This feature is often added to higher risk notes such as credit-linked notes referenced to a risky security. The addition of a principal protected feature lowers the coupon that would otherwise be paid to investors in the note.

Probability distribution: The mathematical description of how probable it is that the value of something is less than or equal to a particular level.

Probability-of-default (PD): In general, the probability that an asset will suffer from issuer default over the next 12 months, calculated on historical rates of default among the same class of issuer.

Under Basel II, the statistical measure that a borrower or portfolio of borrowers will default on its financial obligations. Banks and financial institutions must provide to their regulatory authority a measure of PD for each borrower and each borrower of rating, under both the foundation and advanced IRB approaches. PD itself is defined as a conservative view of the long-term average PD for the grade of borrower being assessed. For sovereign exposure, PD is the one-year PD of the borrower grade; for bank and corporate exposures, PD is the greater of either the one-year PD of the borrower grading or 0.03%. The PD of exposures of obligors in default is defined as 100%.

Protection seller: In a credit default swap transaction, the party that accepts the credit risk associated with specified assets. If losses are incurred on the assets, the protection seller makes credit protection payments to the protection buyer. A fee is payable for this protection.

PSA/ISMA Global Master Repurchase Agreement: Developed jointly by PSA and ISMA, this is the market standard documentation for non-dollar repo markets. A revised edition was issued in November 1995. The Gilt Repo Legal Agreement is an amended version of the revised edition (through the inclusion of a Part 2 to its Annex I and modified by a side letter in connection with the upgrade of the CGO service in 1997) designed to meet the needs of the gilt repo market.

PSA: The Public Securities Association. A US-based organisation that developed the market standard documentation for repo in the US domestic market and that developed with the ISMA the Global Master Repurchase Agreement. It changed its name to the Bond Market Association, before merging in July 2006 with the Securities Industry Association to form the Securities Industry and Financial Markets Association (SIFMA).

Put: A put option is an option to sell the commodity or instrument **underlying** the option. See **call option**.

Put-call parity: The theory that demonstrates the relationship between the call price and put price of an option with otherwise identical terms.

PVBP: Present value of a basis point, the change in value of a bond or derivative contract resulting from a 1 basis point change in its yield, or in the level of interest rates. Sometimes used synonymously with **DV01**.

Q

Quanto: An option that has its final payoff linked to two or more underlying assets or reference rates.

Quanto swap: A swap where the payments in one or both legs are based on a measurement (such as the interest rate) in one currency but payable in another currency.

Quasi-coupon date: The regular date for which a **coupon** payment would be scheduled if there were a coupon payable. Used for price/yield calculations for **zero-coupon bond**s.

R

Range forward: A zero-cost collar where the customer is obliged to deal with the same bank at spot if neither limit of the collar is breached at expiry.

Rate of recovery: Estimate of the percentage of the amount exposed to default – that is, the credit-risk exposure – that is likely to be recovered by an institution if a counterparty defaults. The recovery value of a defaulted asset is dependent on its rate of recovery.

Rating: The credit rating of an obligor. This can be a formal rating from an institution such as Moody's, Standard & Poor's or Fitch, or an internal rating assigned by a bank or financial institution based on its own assessment.

Rebate: The fee payable by a borrower of stock in the stock-lending market.

Recall: Where the repo is an open transaction, a request to return repo'ed securities.

Record date: A coupon or other payment due on a security is paid by the issuer to whoever is registered on the record date as being the owner. See **ex-dividend, cum-dividend.**

Recovery rate: See **rate of recovery**.

Redeem: A security is said to be redeemed when the principal is repaid.

Redemption yield: The rate of interest at which all future payments (coupons and redemption) on a bond are discounted so that their total equals the current price of the bond (inversely related to price).

Re-denomination: A change in the currency unit in which the nominal value of a security is expressed (in context, from sterling to euro).

Reduced-cost option: Generic term for options for which there is a reduced premium, either because the buyer undertakes to forgo a percentage of any gain, or because he or she offsets the cost by writing other options (for example, minmax, range forward). See also **zero-cost option**.

Refer: The practice whereby a trader instructs a broker to put "under reference" any prices or rates quoted, meaning that they are no longer "firm" and the broker must refer to the trader before he or she can trade on the price initially quoted.

Register: Record of ownership of securities. For gilts, excluding bearer bonds, entry in an official register confers title.

Registered bond: A bond for which the issuer keeps a record (register) of its owners. Transfer of ownership must be notified and recorded in the register. Interest payments are posted (more usually electronically transferred) to the bondholder.

Registrar's Department: Department of the Bank of England that maintains the register of holdings of gilts.

Regulatory arbitrage: The practice of engaging in financial transactions that provide a benefit that is available due to regulatory requirements of different types and/or ratings of assets.

Regulatory capital: Capital that is obliged to be held by a bank or financial institution to meet regulatory requirements. Defined under Basel I and split into Tier I and Tier II capital, and slightly modified under Basel II with regard to Tier II.

Reinvestment rate: The rate at which interest paid during the life of an investment is reinvested to earn interest on interest, which in practice will generally not be the same as the original yield quoted on the investment.

Relative performance option: Option whose value varies in line with the relative value of two assets.

Replacement cost: The present value of the expected future net cash flows of a derivative instrument. Aside from various conventions dealing with the bid/ask spread, synonymous with the "market value" or "current exposure" of an instrument.

Repo: Usually refers in particular to classic repo. Also used as a term to include classic repos, buy/sell-backs and securities lending.

Repo rate: The return earned on a repo transaction expressed as an interest rate on the cash side of the transaction.

Repo (reverse repo) to maturity: A repo or reverse repo where the security repo'ed matures on the same day as the closing leg.

Repricing: At a variation margin call, when a repo is closed out and re-started to reflect margin delivery. Also used as another term for *marking-to-market.*

Repurchase agreement: See **repo**.

Restructuring: An event of financial modification that is of significance under the terms of a credit derivative contract. Essentially it involves the obligor to a set of loans changing the terms of its obligations, usually due to financial stress, that result in the terms of the obligation becoming less favourable to lenders than previously. Restructuring can take the form of longer term to repay, reduction in principal amount payable, postponement of interest payments, change in priority of payment and so on.

Return on capital employed (ROCE): Measure of the return on capital used in the business.

Return on equity (ROE): The net earning of a company divided by its equity.

Return on net assets (RONA): Measure of the return on the value of the net assets used in the business.

Return on Value-at-Risk (ROVAR): An analysis conducted to determine the relative rates of return on different risks, allowing corporations to compare different risk capital allocations and capital structure decisions effectively.

Revaluation: An official one-off increase in the value of a currency in terms of other currencies. See **devaluation**.

Revenue volatility: Another term for value of income at risk from market fluctuations.

Reverse: See **reverse repo**.

Reverse repo: A repo, but from the point of view of the counterparty taking in collateral. The US AIMR, in its CFA exam syllabus, defines a reverse repo as one undertaken by a corporate customer with a banking counterparty (who engages in repo).

Reversing: Entering into reverse repo, as in "reverse in" securities.

Rho (ρ): The change in an option's value relative to a change in interest rates.

Right of substitution: The right of the party to a repo, which has delivered securities, to substitute equivalent collateral during the life of the repo.

Risk-adjusted return on capital (RAROC): Measure of the return on capital adjusted for the level of risk to which capital has been used, usually by means of incorporating the volatility of the assets whose return is being measured.

Risk reversal: Changing a long (or short) position in a call option to the same position in a put option by selling (or buying) forward, and vice versa.

Risk-free rate: The interest rate payable on an investment that carries zero credit risk. Usually associated with the 90-day T-bill rate.

Risk-weighted asset: Assets that carry an element of credit risk and so must be weighted in accordance with relative risk, for capital adequacy purposes under Basel regulations.

Risk-weighting: The level of risk assigned to a certain type of collateral or counterparts, as used in Basel I capital calculations.

RMBS: Residential mortgage-backed security.

ROA: Return on assets.

Roll: To renew a repo trade at its maturity.

Rollover: See **tom/next** and **roll**. Also refers to a renewal of a loan on its maturity date.

Rump: A gilt issue so designated because it is illiquid, generally because there is a very small nominal amount left in existence.

Running yield: Same as **current yield**.

S

S/N: See **spot/next**.

S/W: See **spot-a-week**.

Safe custody repo: Also known as *safekeeping* repo, where the borrower of cash keeps hold of collateral pledged, placing it in a segregated client account.

Sale and repurchase agreement: The full name for repo.

Secondary market: The market in instruments after they have been issued. Bonds are bought and sold after their initial issue by the borrower, and the marketplace for this buying and selling is referred to as the secondary market. The new issues market is the *primary* market.

Securities and Exchange Commission (SEC): The central regulatory authority in the United States, responsible for policing the financial markets including the bond markets.

Securities lending: The market in borrowing and lending stock, for a fee, against collateral. Also know as stock lending.

Securitisation: The sale of assets, which generate cash flows, from the institution that owns them, to another company that has been specifically set up for the purpose, and the issuing of notes by this second company. These notes are backed by the cash flows from the original assets. The technique was introduced initially as a means of funding for US mortgage banks. Subsequently, the technique was applied to other assets such as credit card payments and leasing receivables. It has also been employed as part of asset–liability management, as a means of managing balance sheet risk. Securitisation allows institutions such as banks and corporates to convert assets that are not readily marketable – such as residential mortgages or car loans – into rated securities that are tradeable in the secondary market. The investors that buy these securities gain an exposure to these types of original assets that they would not otherwise have access to. The technique was first introduced by mortgage banks in the United States during the 1970s. The later synthetic securitisation market is more recent, dating from 1997. The key difference between cash and synthetic securitisation is that in the former, the assets in question are actually sold to a separate legal company known as a **special purpose vehicle** (SPV). This does not occur in a synthetic transaction. We can define securitisation as the process by which illiquid assets of a corporation or a financial institution are transformed into a package of securities backed by these assets; the process of securitisation creates a*sset-backed bonds*.

Security: A financial asset sold initially for cash by a borrowing organisation (the "issuer"). The security is often negotiable and usually has a maturity date when it is redeemed.

Sell/buy-back: A trade economically identical to a classic repo, but conducted as a spot sale and simultaneous repurchase of stock, with the forward repurchase price adjusted to account for interest payable on borrowed funds. The repurchase price is not connected to the actual market price of the stock on repurchase date.

Seller: The counterparty that "sells" collateral in a repo or sell/buy-back; in other words, the party borrowing funds.

Set off: The practice of netting obligations between two counterparties, in the event of default.

Settlement: The process of transferring stock from seller to buyer and arranging the corresponding movement of funds between the two parties.

Settlement bank: A bank that agrees to receive and make assured payments for gilts bought and sold by a CGO member.

Settlement date: Date on which the transfer of gilts and payments occur, usually the next working date after the trade is conducted.

Settlement risk: The risk that occurs when there is a non-simultaneous exchange of value. Also known as "delivery risk" and "Herstatt risk".

Sharpe ratio: A measure of the attractiveness of the return on an asset by comparing how much risk premium the investor can expect it to receive in return for the incremental risk (volatility) the investment carries. It is the ratio of the risk premium to the volatility of the asset.

Short: A short position is a surplus of sales over purchases of a given currency or asset, or a situation that naturally gives rise to an organisation benefiting from a weakening of that currency or asset. To a money market dealer, however, a short position is a surplus of money lent out over borrowings taken in (which give rise to a benefit if that currency strengthens rather than weakens). See **long**.

Short date: The term for short maturity deposits, typically overnight, tom/next, and 2–3 day maturity trades. Sometimes the one-week term will be considered among the short dates.

Simple interest: When interest on an investment is paid all at maturity or not reinvested to earn interest on interest, the interest is said to be simple. See **compound interest**.

Simple yield to maturity: Bond coupon plus principal gain/loss amortised over the time to maturity, as a proportion of the clean price per 100. Does not take time-value of money into account. See **yield to maturity**, **current yield**.

SLN: Secured liquidity notes.

Special: A security which for any reason is sought after in the repo market, thereby enabling any holder of the security to earn incremental income (in excess of the **General collateral** rate) through lending it via a repo transaction. The repo rate for a special will be below the GC rate, as this is the rate the borrower of the cash is paying in returning for supplying the special bond as collateral. An individual security can be in high demand for a variety of reasons; for instance, if there is sudden heavy investor demand for it, or (if it is a benchmark issue) it is required as a hedge against a new issue of similar-maturity paper.

Special purpose vehicle (SPV): A legal entity set up to effect securitisation. Also known as a special purpose company (SPC) or special purpose entity (SPE). Under the securitisation process an *issuer* acquires the assets from the originator. The issuer is usually a company that has been specially set up for the purpose of the securitisation, which is the SPV and is usually domiciled offshore. The creation of an SPV ensures that the underlying asset pool is held separate from the other assets of the originator. This is done so that in the event that the originator is declared bankrupt or insolvent, the assets that have been transferred to the SPV will not be affected. This is known as being bankruptcy-remote. Conversely, if the underlying assets begin to deteriorate in quality and are subject to a ratings downgrade, investors have no recourse to the originator. By holding the assets within an SPV framework, defined in formal legal terms, the financial status and credit rating of the originator becomes almost irrelevant to the bondholders.

Specific: A repo in which the collateral is specified; that is, it is not **GC**. A specific security is not necessarily special.

Speculation: A deal undertaken because the dealer expects prices to move in his or her favour, as opposed to **hedging** or **arbitrage**.

Spot: A deal to be settled on the customary value date for that particular market. In the foreign exchange market this is for value in two working days' time.

Spot-a-week: Money market deposit value spot (T + 2) for one week.

Spot/next: A transaction from **spot** until the next working day.

Spot yield curve: The current zero-coupon yield curve.

Spread: The difference between the bid and offer prices in a quotation. Also a strategy involving the purchase of an instrument and the simultaneous sale of a similar related instrument, such as the purchase of a **call option** at one **strike** and the sale of a call option at a different strike.

Square: A position in which sales exactly match purchases, or in which assets exactly match liabilities. See **long**, **short**. In the money markets, to be "squared off" is to be net zero balance at the clearing bank.

Standard deviation (σ): A measure of how much the values of something fluctuate around its mean value. Defined as the square root of the variance.

Standardised approach (SA): The basic approach to implementing the Basel II capital calculation, based on external credit ratings of balance sheet assets.

Step-down swap: Swap in which the fixed-rate payment decreases over the life of the swap.

Step-up swap: Swap in which the fixed-rate payment increases over the life of the swap.

Stock-driven repo: A repo initiated by a party who is motivated by the need to borrow a specific security or repo out of a specific security for funding purposes. A stock-driven trade usually involves a round nominal amount of stock.

Stock index future: Future on a stock index, allowing a hedge against, or bet on, a broad equity market movement.

Stock index option: Option on a stock index future.

Stock lending: See **securities lending**.

Stock option: Option on an individual stock.

Straddle: A position combining the purchase of both a call and put at the same strike for the same date. See **strangle**.

Strangle: A position combining the purchase of both a call and a put at different strikes for the same date. See **straddle**.

Street: The "street" is a term for the market, originating as "Wall Street". A US term for market convention, so in the US market is the convention for quoting the price or yield for a particular instrument.

Stress testing: An analysis that gives the value of a portfolio under a range of worst case scenarios.

Strike: The strike price or strike rate of an option is the price or rate at which the holder can insist on the underlying transaction being fulfilled.

Strip: A zero-coupon bond that is produced by separating a standard coupon-bearing bond into its constituent principal and interest components. To strip a bond is to separate its principal amount and its coupons and trade each individual cash flow as a separate instrument ("*s*eparately *t*raded and *r*egistered for *i*nterest and *p*rincipal"). Also, a strip of **futures** is a series of short-term futures contracts with consecutive delivery dates, which together create the effect of a longer term instrument (for example, four consecutive 3-month futures contracts as a **hedge** against a one-year swap). A strip of **FRA**s is similar.

Structured investment vehicle (SIV): Investment companies set up as stand-alone, purpose-built legal entities that invest in assets and raise funds in the debt capital markets. They also require an equity share in the total funding, which is the vehicle's capital.

Structured note: A bond that is an over-the-counter (OTC) product that combines a number of elements into a single instrument. It may contain an embedded option, or it may link its return to the performance of another specific asset or index. The liquidity of the secondary market in structured notes is variable.

Substitution: The practice of replacing collateral with another of equivalent credit quality during the term of a repo trade. This is initiated by the supplier of collateral, but must be agreed beforehand by the lender of cash.

Supervisory formula (SF): A BIS-described approach to calculating Basel II capital requirements based on the methodology of the national regulator.

Swap: A foreign exchange swap is the purchase of one currency against another for delivery on one date, with a simultaneous sale to reverse the transaction on another value date. See also **interest-rate swap**, **currency swap**.

Swaption: An option on an interest-rate swap, currency swap.

Switch: Exchanges of one gilt holding for another, sometimes entered into between the DMO and a GEMM as part of the DMO's secondary market operations.

Synthetic: A package of transactions which is economically equivalent to a different transaction. In the structured finance market, a transaction that replicates some of the economic effects of a cash securitisation without recourse to an actual sale of assets, and which involves the use of credit derivatives.

Synthetic CDO: A CDO in which true sale of assets to an SPV does not take place. Rather, the economic effect of transferring the credit risk of the assets is created through the use of credit derivatives that reference the assets.

Synthetic securitisation: Defined by the Basel Committee as a structure with at least two different stratified risk positions or tranches that reflect different degrees of credit risk, where the credit risk of an underlying pool of assets is transferred by means of credit derivatives. The actual assets may not be transferred in ownership, only their credit risk exposure is transferred.

T

T/N: See **tom/next**.

Tail: The exposure to interest rates over a forward–forward period arising from a mismatched position (such as a two-month borrowing against a three-month loan). A forward foreign exchange dealer's exposure to spot movements. The interest-rate *gap* between a deposit and loan (or reverse repo and repo) of differing maturities, representing interest-rate risk.

Tap: The issue of a gilt for exceptional market-management reasons and not on a pre-announced schedule.

TED spread: A term referring to the spread in a trade involving a long/short futures position against a short/long government bond position. Also the futures strip hedge page on Bloomberg. Originally referred to as "Treasury–Eurodollar spread".

Term: The time between the beginning and end of a deal or investment.

Term repo: Repo trades (of a maturity over one day) with a fixed maturity date.

Term structure of interest rates: The plot of zero-coupon interest rates by maturity. Sometimes used synonymously with **yield curve**.

Terminable on demand: A repo trade that may terminated on a daily basis, in other words an *open repo*.

Termination: The maturity date.

Theta (τ): The change in an option's value relative to a change in the time left to expiry.

Tick: The minimum change allowed in a futures price.

Tick value: The change in value of a futures contract for a 1-tick movement in price.

Tier 1 capital: The capital of a bank or financial institution defined as shareholder equity and retained earnings. At least 50% of regulatory capital must be held as Tier 1 capital.

Tier 2 capital: Defined in Basel I but not with a uniform definition in different national jurisdictions. It is generally viewed as the other forms of capital available to a bank or financial institution and so may include long-term subordinated debt, preference shares, undisclosed reserves and hybrid equity capital.

Tier 3 capital: A modification to the original Basel I rules that allowed banks to issue short-term subordinated debt to meet part of their market risk capital requirements. A maximum of 250% of a firm's Tier 1 capital may be issued in this way, subject to the discretion of the national regulator.

Time bucket: The maturity group into which a loan or other exposure is placed. For instance, time buckets of o/n, o/n – one week, one week – three month, three month – six month, six month – 12 month may be calculated, and assets and liabilities placed in buckets according to their maturity.

Time deposit: A non-**negotiable** deposit for a specific term.

Time option: A forward currency deal in which the value date is set to be within a period rather than on a particular day. The customer sets the exact date two working days before settlement.

Time value of money: The concept that a future cash flow can be valued as the amount of money which it is necessary to invest now in order to achieve that cash flow in the future. See **present value**, **future value**.

Today/tomorrow: See **overnight**.

Tom/next: A transaction from the next working day ("tomorrow") until the day after ("next day" – that is, **spot** in the foreign-exchange market).

Total return swap (TRS): A bilateral financial contract in which one party (the total return payer) makes floating-rate payments to the other party (the total return receiver) equal to the total return on a specified asset or index, in return for amounts that generally equal the total return payer's cost of holding the specified asset on its balance sheet. Price appreciation or depreciation may be calculated and exchanged at maturity or on an interim basis. Total return swaps are economically similar to a repo trade, and may be considered as synthetic repos or as a form of credit derivative. However, a total return swap is distinct from a credit default swap in that the floating payments are based on the total economic performance of the specified asset, and are not contingent upon the occurrence of a credit event.

Traded option: Option that is listed on and cleared by an exchange, with standard terms and delivery months.

Trading book: A bank's investment, trading and short-term activity, grouped into the trading book for regulatory capital purposes.

Tranche: In the loan market, one of a series of two or more issues with the same coupon rate and maturity date. The tranches become fungible at a future date, usually just after the first coupon date. In the structured finance market, a term for liability or note in a securitisation transaction.

Transaction risk: Extent to which the value of transactions that have already been agreed is affected by market risk.

Translation risk: An accounting or financial reporting risk where the earnings of a company can be adversely affected due to its method of accounting for foreign earnings.

Transparent: A term used to refer to how clear asset prices are in a market. A transparent market is one in which a majority of market participants are aware of what level a particular bond or instrument is trading.

Treasury bill (T-bill): A short-term security issued by a government, generally with a zero coupon.

Tri-party repo: A repo in which an independent agent bank or clearing house oversees a standard two-party repo transaction. The responsibilities of the triparty agent include maintaining acceptable and adequate collateral and overall maintenance of the outstanding repo trades.

Trigger option: See **barrier option**.

True yield: The yield on a bond that is equivalent to the quoted discount or zero-coupon rate.

Trust account repo: Another term for *safe custody repo*.

Trustee: A third-party specialist appointed to act on behalf of investors.

Tunnel: The same as **collar**.

Tunnel options: Set of collars, typically zero-cost, covering a series of maturities from the current date. They might, for example, be for dates six, 12 or 24 months ahead. The special feature of a tunnel is that the strike price on both sets of options, not just on the options bought, is constant.

U

Uncovered option: When the writer of the option does not own the underlying security. Also known as a **naked option**.

Undated gilts: Gilts for which there is no final date by which the gilt must be redeemed.

Underlying: The cash market asset on which a futures or option contract is written. Also, the reference asset in a credit derivative. Thus, underlying for a bond option is the bond; the underlying for a short-term interest-rate futures contract is typically a three-month deposit.

Underwriting: An arrangement by which a company is guaranteed that an issue of debt (bonds) will raise a given amount of cash. Underwriting is carried out by investment banks, who undertake to purchase any part of the debt issue not taken up by the public. A commission is charged for this service.

Unexpected default rate: The distribution of future default rates is often characterised in terms of an expected default rate (for example, 0.05%) and a worst case default rate (for example, 1.05%). The difference between the worst case default rate and the expected default rate is often termed the "unexpected default" (that is, 1% = 1.05 – 0.05%).

Unexpected loss: The distribution of credit losses associated with a derivative instrument is often characterised in terms of an expected loss or a worst case loss. The unexpected loss associated with an instrument is the difference between these two measures.

Up-and-away option: See **up-and-out option**.

Up-and-out option: Type of barrier option that is extinguished if the value of the underlying goes above a predetermined level. See also **down-and-out option**.

V

Value: The date that the cash is received for stock sold (and vice versa), the value date. Alternatively, the date from which interest begins to commence.

Value-at-Risk (VaR): Formally, the probabilistic bound of market losses over a given period of time (known as the holding period) expressed in terms of a specified degree of certainity (known as the confidence interval). Put more simply, the VaR is the worst case loss that would be expected over the holding period within the probability set out by the confidence interval. Larger losses are possible but with a low probability. For instance, a portfolio whose VaR is $20 million over a one-day holding period, with a 95% confidence interval, would have only a 5% chance of suffering an overnight loss greater than $20 million.

Value date: The date on which a deal is to be consummated. In some bond markets, the value date for coupon accruals can sometimes differ from the settlement date.

Vanilla: A vanilla transaction is a straightforward one.

VaR: See **Value-at-Risk**.

Variable currency: Exchange rates are quoted in terms of the number of units of one currency (the variable or counter currency) which corresponds to one unit of the other currency (the **base currency**).

Variance (σ^2): A measure of how much the values of something fluctuate around its mean value. Defined as the average of $(\text{value} - \text{mean})^2$. See **standard deviation.**

Variance–covariance methodology: Methodology for calculating the VaR of a portfolio as a function of the **volatility** of each asset or liability position in the portfolio and the correlation between the positions.

Variation margin: The band agreed between the parties to a repo transaction at the outset within which the value of the collateral may fluctuate before triggering a right to call for cash or securities to reinstate the initial margin on the repo transaction.

Vega: The change in an option's value relative to a change in the **underlying's volatility**.

Volatility: The standard deviation of the continuously compounded return on the underlying. Volatility is generally annualised. It measures the price fluctuation of an asset or derivative. See **historic volatility**, **implied volatility**.

W

Warrant: A security giving the holder a right to subscribe to a share or bond at a given price and from a certain date. If this right is not exercised before the maturity date, the warrant will expire worthless.

Warrant-driven swap: Swap with a warrant attached allowing the issuer of the fixed-rate bond to go on paying a floating rate in the event that he or she exercises another warrant allowing him or her to prolong the life of the bond.

Weighted average cost (WAC): A term for WACC.

Weighted average cost of capital (WACC): The average cost of capital used in a business, both debt and equity, and which is weighted by the proportion of each type of capital used in the total.

Weighted average life (WAL): The weighted-average life of a portfolio of securities or other assets, each of which has a different term-to-maturity. The weighting is the proportion of nominal value of assets as part of the total portfolio nominal or market value.

Weighted average rate (WAR): The weighted-average cost of all funds borrowed, from all sources, by a business.

When-issued trading: Trading a bond before the issue date; no interest is accrued during this period. Also known as the "grey market".

Worst case (credit risk) exposure: Estimate of the highest positive market value a derivative contract or portfolio is likely to attain at a given moment or period in the future, with a given level of confidence.

Worst case (credit-risk) loss: Estimate of the largest amount a derivative counterparty is likely to lose, with a given level of probability, as a result of default from a derivatives contract or portfolio.

Worst-case default rate: The highest rates of default that are likely to occur at a given moment or period in the future, with a given level of confidence.

Write: To sell an option is to write it. The person selling an option is known as the writer.

Writer: The same as "seller" of an option.

Writing: A generic term for selling or underwriting a contract. For example, the writer of an option is selling to the buyer the option to purchase the underlying asset from the writer at a future date.

X: Used to denote the strike price of an option; sometimes this is denoted using the term *K*.

Yield: The interest rate that can be earned on an investment, currently quoted by the market or implied by the current market price for the investment – as opposed to the coupon paid by an issuer on a security, which is based on the coupon rate and the face value. For a bond, generally the same as yield to maturity unless otherwise specified.

Yield curve: A graphical representation of interest rates plotted against terms to maturity. Most commonly, government bond yields are plotted against their respective maturities. The plot of zero-coupon rates against maturity is known as the *term structure of interest rates*. Only assets of homogenous quality can be used when plotting yields. A *positive* yield curve exhibits an increasing level of interest rates over longer maturity periods, while a *negative* or *inverted* yield curve exhibits diminishing yields over time.

Yield-curve option: Option that allows purchasers to take a view on a yield curve without having to take a view about a market's direction.

Yield-curve swap: Swap in which the index rates of the two interest streams are at different points on the yield curve. Both payments are refixed with the same frequency whatever the index rate.

Yield to equivalent life: The same as **yield to maturity** for a bond with partial redemptions.

Yield to maturity: The **internal rate of return** of a bond – the yield necessary to discount all the bond's cash flows to an **NPV** equal to its current price. See **simple yield to maturity**, **current yield**.

YTM: See **yield to maturity**.

Z

Zero-cost collar: A **collar** where the premiums paid and received are equal, giving a net zero cost.

Zero-cost option: An option structure combining puts and calls, or buys and sells, that result in a zero net premium for the purchaser.

Zero-coupon: A coupon of 0% or zero. Usually used to refer to a **zero-coupon bond** or **strip**.

Zero-coupon bond: Bond on which no coupon is paid. It is either issued at a discount or redeemed at a premium to face value.

Zero-coupon rate: The interest rate on a zero-coupon bond, sometimes called the spot rate. The two terms are not strictly synonymous however; the spot rate refers to the interest rate payable for a term that is infinitesimal, an instantaneous change in time, so in other words it is a theoretical construct. A zero-coupon rate is observable in the market as the rate payable on a zero-coupon bond.

Zero-coupon swap: Swap converting the payment pattern of a zero-coupon bond, either to that of a normal, coupon-paying *fixed-rate* bond or to a **floating rate**.

Zero-coupon yield: The yield returned on a zero-coupon bond.

Zero-premium option: Generic term for options for which there is no premium, either because the buyer undertakes to forgo a percentage of any gain or because he or she offsets the cost by **writing** other options.

Zone A: The categorisation of certain countries under Basel rules; that is, the identification of which sovereign borrowers attract the lowest risk-weighting.

… The New English, for the most part Johnny Rasheed and Shareef C from Surrey, were writing songs about an English day. Beautiful tunes with harmonies and melodies to match, sung with passion and spirit. Shareef C played the guitar liked he'd been born playing it, as for Johnny, well he had so much energy live that if you hooked him up to the national grid you could run London for a week.

The New English….speed, style, soul, and that red, red Harrington. The best. Inspiration and spirit all rolled up into one high-energy ball of real feeling.

This is it! London 1987. Enjoy.

– Nik Slater
sleeve notes to *London 1987 – the definitive New English collection*
March 2001

Index

30/360 convention 164

A

A note 909, 1068
ABCP *see Asset-backed commercial paper*
ABN Amro 86, 114, 128, 238
ABS *see Asset-backed securities*
Acceptance 8, 48, 63, 67-70, 329, 625, 1001, 1026, 1260
Accounting 1, 7, 9, 11, 17, 33, 46, 146, 165, 192, 519, 780, 783, 892-3, 952, 955, 1019, 1244, 1245
Accreting 650, 655
Accreting swap 650, 655
Accrued interest 49, 56, 127, 146, 157, 161-6, 174, 350, 424, 500, 506-7, 520-1, 525, 528, 716-7, 723, 728, 765-6, 778, 810, 984, 1070-1, 1145-6, 1271
Act/360 25, 167, 651, 663-4
  convention 25, 167, 664
Act/365 25, 166-7, 172, 378, 633, 671, 692
Act/Act 166-7, 524
Adjustable-rate mortgage 965, 1012
Agencies 6, 80, 85, 87, 296, 751, 754-6, 759, 781, 807, 809, 827, 865, 883, 898-9, 903, 910, 912-4, 916, 923, 954, 962, 968, 981, 1008, 1034, 1037, 1080, 1094-5, 1119, 1131-2, 1150, 1152, 1185, 1205, 1222, 1232
Agency mortgage-backed securities 968
Agent 72, 92, 116, 122-3, 125, 127, 135, 496, 514-7, 664, 906, 910-1, 929, 934, 1049, 1054, 1132, 1143
All-in price 151, 162, 166, 529, 936
ALCO *see ALM Committee*
ALM *see Asset–liability management*
ALM Committee 209, 211, 254-5, 290, 292-5, 327-35, 337, 611, 833, 1115-7, 1256
  Agenda 292, 328-9
  Objectives 290, 292-4, 833
  Reporting 209, 294, 327-31, 1256
  Responsibility of 254, 293
ALM policies 290
American options 586, 588, 604
Amortisation 219, 273-4, 301, 901, 904, 966, 1005-8, 1017, 1024, 1047, 1192, 1273
Amortising 122, 128, 143, 655, 775, 884-5, 903-4, 961, 996, 1000-1, 1005, 1016-7, 1019, 1030, 1033, 1095, 1114
Amortising bond 143, 1001
Amortising swap 655
Annual payment rate 1004
Annualised 63, 144, 149, 158-9, 161, 168, 201, 388, 390, 419, 501, 592, 621, 867, 976, 984, 989, 1278, 1280-3
  Conventional bonds 987
  Interest rate 63, 144, 388, 390, 419, 501, 867, 984, 1278, 1281-3
  Percentage 63, 161, 976, 1282

Annualised percentage rate 1004, 1007, 1282
Annuity 812-3
Applications
Asset swaps 480, 625, 737, 764
Credit default swaps 772, 774, 792, 808, 1151
Credit-linked notes 772
Total return swaps 779-80, 792
Approaches to pricing 810
Approximate duration 174, 176, 179-80, 182, 185-6, 188, 202, 204, 302, 309, 728, 857, 987-8, 1000, 1016, 1149
APR *see Annualised percentage rate*
Arbitrage 75, 104, 106, 136, 192, 194-5, 309, 320, 324-6, 351, 372, 374, 384, 389, 390, 398, 420, 425-6, 432, 435, 487-8, 532, 545-6, 548, 552, 556, 566, 576, 578, 582, 589-90, 593, 598, 603, 618, 620, 623, 639, 709, 717-23, 737, 775, 812, 821-2, 826, 923, 925-6, 1021, 1029-31, 1033, 1037-8, 1051, 1053, 1059, 1063, 1071, 1079-80, 1091, 1108, 1118, 1122, 1147, 1149, 1151-7, 1197
Collateralised debt obligations 75, 1021, 1029-31, 1037-38, 1051, 1053, 1059, 1063, 1071, 1079-80, 1091, 1108, 1118, 1149, 1151-3, 1156-7
Pricing theory 398
Trading 136, 309, 320, 325, 384, 425, 532, 566, 582, 593, 618, 620, 623, 717-23, 775, 1033, 1037-8, 1079-80, 1118, 1122, 1197
Transactions 104, 398, 420, 425, 532, 552, 556, 582, 593, 603, 925, 1021, 1029, 1031, 1033, 1037-8, 1051, 1053, 1059, 1071, 1108, 1147, 1152
Arbitrage-free pricing 548, 603
Arithmetic 1, 24, 212, 432, 592, 1277, 1309-10, 1312
Average 432, 1309-10, 1312
Ask price 137
Asset-backed bonds 143, 882, 888, 1008, 1016
Asset-backed commercial paper 72, 74-5, 78, 80, 82, 84-8, 97, 226, 881, 892, 921-36, 1149, 1153, 1155-6, 1165, 1189, 1222-3
Conduit 74-5, 78, 84, 86-8, 226, 881, 921-36, 1149, 1153, 1155-6, 1189
Asset-backed securities 75, 116, 143-4, 263, 280, 296, 510, 518, 770, 782-3, 796, 799, 801, 813-21, 826, 828-9, 881, 883-5, 888-9, 893-4, 896, 899-900, 903-5, 913-4, 917, 919, 999-1011, 1016-7, 1019, 1021, 1030, 1032-5, 1044, 1051-5, 1072, 1081, 1095, 1117, 1125, 1130, 1135-6, 1146, 1149, 1152, 1156-7, 1200, 1217-8, 1222, 1229-34, 1263, 1272-3
Asset class 14, 126, 228, 746, 773, 804, 863, 884-5, 908-9, 911, 1015, 1021, 1030, 1032, 1043, 1051, 1077, 1084, 1094-5, 1098, 1114, 1149, 1152, 1171, 1186, 1188, 1195, 1197-200, 1203, 1211, 1225, 1229, 1233, 1239
Credit risk 14, 746, 863, 885, 1015, 1021, 1030, 1032, 1114, 1171, 1198-9, 1229
Asset coverage 910, 974
Asset–liability management 1, 3, 5, 8, 10, 13, 29, 125, 133, 167, 209, 211-6, 218-22, 225-35, 240, 242, 244, 247-56, 260-4, 272-3, 278-9, 289-91, 293-6, 298, 300, 305, 327-35, 339-40, 451, 453, 458, 472-3, 476-7, 491, 539, 563, 569, 582, 610-2, 617, 625, 660, 670, 713, 737, 744-5, 747, 760, 774, 792, 808, 833, 881-2, 887, 893-4, 999, 1008, 1021, 1035, 1038-41, 1059, 1063, 1071, 1112-3, 1147, 1150, 1152-3, 1159, 1165-6, 1182,

1195-6, 1211, 1218, 1222-4, 1230, 1232, 1234, 1241, 1243, 1247-9, 1254, 1256
Funding risk 219, 612, 1063
Function 5, 209, 211, 220, 233, 235, 248, 256, 260-4, 279, 289, 293-4, 298, 305, 327-8, 459, 1008, 1165-6, 1241, 1243, 1254
Gap risk 8, 244, 256
Liquidity risk 8, 211-2, 215-6, 219, 225, 229, 242, 247-9, 253, 260-1, 264, 328, 1248
Risk and return 253
Asset swaps 480, 625, 737, 764
Credit default swaps 737
Spread 480, 737, 764
Asset types 296, 847, 1033, 1152, 1188, 1233
At-the-money 586-7, 606, 687, 857, 859
Auction 62, 316, 318
Issue 62, 316, 318
Auto-loan-backed securities 999-1000
Description 1000
Analysis 999-1000
Average life 127, 274, 800, 804, 900, 903, 908, 915, 967, 976, 982, 985-6, 1005, 1016, 1019, 1040, 1043, 1057, 1118, 1155
Average return 363, 839, 1309
Axa Investment Managers 1119

B

Balance sheet CDO 914, 1021, 1029, 1033, 1037, 1065, 1071-2, 1076, 1113, 1115
Motivation 1029, 1037
Structure 1021, 1029, 1033, 1037, 1065, 1071-2, 1076, 1113, 1115
Structure diagram 1115
Balance sheet management 247, 254, 295-6, 881, 885, 1008, 1039, 1059, 1139, 1159, 1215, 1230
Balloon mortgage 966, 995
Bank asset 11, 883, 949, 1195, 1203, 1211, 1214, 1218, 1223
Bank bills 67
Bank for International Settlements 5, 112, 115, 254, 894, 1071, 1162, 1166-9, 1177, 1179-80, 1185, 1187, 1189, 1195-6, 1199, 1202, 1204, 1209-11, 1214, 1222, 1228, 1235-7, 1239
Bank of England 10, 69, 84, 92, 309, 447, 448, 533
Bank risk 237, 451-2, 455, 478, 530, 1152, 1184-5
Bankers acceptances 48, 67, 69, 70
Banking book 3, 5, 7-8, 220, 241, 249-50, 252-4, 258, 261-2, 267, 273, 275-9, 289, 292, 295, 302, 1169, 1171, 1181, 1188, 1198
Bankruptcy remote 1128
Barings 750-1, 915, 1161-2, 1176, 1234, 1237
Barone-Adesi and Whaley (BAW) model 601, 604
Basel Accord 1167-8, 1177, 1230
Basel I 240, 1200
Basel II 242, 774, 776, 892, 895, 927, 1010, 1147, 1150, 1152, 1161-3, 1166, 1172, 1177-81, 1183-9, 1195-205, 1208-12, 1214-5, 1217-9, 1222-34, 1236, 1239
Bank asset 1195, 1203, 1211, 1214, 1218, 1223
Credit derivative 774, 776, 1203, 1227-9
Example calculations 1195
Impact of 1172, 1195, 1199, 1209-11, 1217, 1225, 1230-4, 1239
Implementation 774, 1162, 1183, 1186, 1196, 1198-9, 1202-3, 1224, 1232, 1239
Internal measurement mechanism 1184

Internal ratings based 1163, 1178-80, 1183, 1185-7, 1189, 1196, 1198-200, 1202-5, 1209-12, 1214-5, 1218, 1222-33, 1239
Pillar 1 1163, 1177-8, 1181, 1197
Pillar 2 1177, 1181, 1183, 1197
Pillar 3 1177, 1181-3, 1197
Risk weights 1178
Securitisation 892, 895, 1010, 1184, 1189, 1196, 1215, 1217-9, 1222, 1229-34
Sovereign debt 1203-5
Standardised approach 927, 1163, 1178, 1180, 1183-5, 1196, 1198-200, 1202, 1204-5, 1209, 1212, 1214-5, 1218, 1222, 1224-6, 1228-3
Three pillars 1163, 1177
Basel Rules 1, 5, 847, 895, 1162, 1165-8, 1171, 1172, 1232
Base rate 244, 366, 400, 456-7, 459-60, 463-8, 658, 966, 981
Basis points 69, 86, 106, 113, 116, 119, 122-6, 167-8, 170-2, 181, 183, 187-8, 191, 193, 198-9, 201, 238, 240-5, 252, 278, 308-9, 311, 314, 318-9, 335, 403, 452, 454, 459-60, 463, 466-8, 472, 474, 477, 480, 482, 486, 510, 520, 524, 535, 541, 567, 573, 576, 613, 627-8, 636, 650, 656, 659, 661, 668-70, 680, 687, 692, 698, 701, 704, 708, 710, 739-40, 742-4, 748, 767, 771-2, 782-4, 788-90, 792, 796, 803, 831, 861, 909, 915, 917, 927-8, 943, 945, 957-9, 979, 990, 1001-2, 1013, 1018, 1026, 1027, 1039, 1041, 1064, 1069, 1086, 1092, 1103, 1276
Basis point value 181-2, 310, 312, 314, 550, 626, 674-5, 677-8, 698-701, 725-6, 741-2744, 986
Basis risk 256, 259, 323, 375, 573, 617, 656, 724, 730, 1166
Basis swaps 625, 656
Basis trading 532, 717, 723
Basket CDS 1069, 1072, 1081, 1085, 1091, 1227
Basket TRS 782
BAW *see Barone-Adesi and Whaley model*
Baxter, M 447
Benchmark 6, 17, 23, 62, 70, 139, 171, 191, 312, 314, 317-20, 344-5, 373, 395, 404, 477, 482, 576, 633, 636-7, 641, 674, 689, 692-3, 718, 753, 760, 784, 788, 866, 909, 977, 981, 996, 1064, 1094, 1163, 1185, 1208, 1248, 1270, 1310, 1313
Bid 52, 60, 62, 102, 104, 108-9, 119, 137, 225, 243, 251, 253, 283, 318, 322, 325, 334, 362, 498, 509, 521, 547, 571-2, 636-7, 659, 679, 703, 720-1, 788, 808, 1131, 1253-4
Bid price 137, 636, 1131
Bid–offer spread 62, 108, 137, 225, 251, 253, 322, 325, 334, 547, 572, 636, 659, 679, 703, 720-1, 788, 1253-4
Binomial
Model 195, 198, 866, 986-7
Process 593
Tree 866
BIS *see Bank for International Settlements*
BISTRO 1063, 1113, 1114
Black 76 model 684, 693, 696, 1272
Black–Derman–Toy 604, 693, 696
Black, F 447, 623
Black–Scholes 590-1, 593-4, 598, 1274
Blended rate 280
Boggiano, K. 1072, 1074
Bonds
Accrued interest 56, 127, 146, 157, 161-6, 350, 424, 520-1, 716-7, 728, 810, 984
Alpine 138
Amortised 966, 1017, 1292

Borrowed/collateral pledged 519-20
Bullet 122, 143, 341, 398, 447, 800, 900, 954, 995, 1000, 1005-6, 1016-7, 1019, 1095, 1292
Callable 190-1, 263, 345, 963, 985, 987, 992
Clean price 146, 161-4, 166, 424, 521, 524, 984
Conventional bonds 142, 352, 917, 987, 1003, 1016
Conventional yield 983
Convertible bonds 235, 518, 524, 782, 931, 937, 1275
Covered bonds 14, 961, 971-4, 1131, 1215-6
Day-count 146, 161, 163-5, 501
Equivalent yield 65, 159, 983-5
Fixed coupon 142, 167, 352, 670, 770
Floating rate 1130
Futures contract 231, 556, 569-70, 583, 674,701, 713, 716-7, 724-30, 741-2, 744, 770, 1275-6
Government bonds 65, 133, 138-9, 142, 146, 151, 157, 241-2, 262, 292, 317, 344, 457, 473, 493, 516, 518, 520, 532, 638, 641-2, 674, 713, 727-8, 744, 814, 847, 982, 1065, 1125-6, 1168, 1170-1, 1294-5
Issue price 142, 1126
Warrant 144, 518
Zero-coupon 142-3, 151-2, 160, 162, 178, 186, 190, 192, 340, 344-5, 349-50, 352-56, 359, 366, 368-71, 384, 387-8, 390, 406, 412-5, 417, 424-6, 429-30, 437, 482, 601, 610, 641-2, 701, 851, 855, 857, 869, 970, 1016, 1018, 1266
Bond Market Association 532
Bond valuation 367, 801
Boot-strapping 351
Borrow/loan vs cash 519
Borrowed funds 67, 297, 325, 522, 628, 853
Borrower 18, 20-1, 48, 67, 69-70, 72, 74, 80, 115, 122-4, 126, 133, 135, 138-9, 144, 250, 259, 274, 297, 323, 391, 393, 495, 513, 516, 524-5, 529, 540, 606-8, 626, 629-31, 652, 655, 668, 670, 751, 754-5, 760, 784, 882, 895, 912, 914-6, 922, 926--8, 961-8, 981, 992, 994-6, 1001, 1024, 1026-7, 1162-3, 1167, 1177-9, 1184, 1187, 1199, 1205-6, 1227, 1244, 1253, 1291-2
BPV *see Basis point value*
Breakeven 126, 172, 310, 314, 351, 362, 372, 374, 522-3, 544-5, 648, 781, 853, 855, 1276, 1303
Principle 351, 362, 372
Rate 126, 522-3, 855, 1303
Brennan and Schwartz 447
British Airways 71-2, 831
British Bankers Association 321, 541, 747
British Petroleum 750
British Telecom 116, 748
Broker-dealer 22, 782-3, 936-7, 943, 948, 958
Brokers 20, 22, 59, 60, 98, 137, 283, 452, 496, 533, 540, 553, 628, 636-7, 658, 689
Brownian motion 418, 594, 602, 605
B–S model 592-5, 597-8, 600-1, 603-6, 609, 622, 1274
B-Spline 410, 1263-4
Building societies 21-2, 56, 136, 219, 236, 242, 289, 387, 394-5, 516, 531, 625, 862, 991, 1182
Bulldog 138
Bullet
Payment 122, 143, 223, 341, 398, 447, 545, 663, 800, 900, 904, 954, 995, 1000, 1005-6, 1016-7, 1019, 1095, 1114, 1292
Bond 142, 231, 239, 311, 502, 630, 740, 882, 1075, 1287

Business lines 4, 11-2, 125, 213, 225-30, 235, 327, 330, 333-4, 745, 833, 1181, 1184, 1199-200, 1202-3, 1235, 1238-9
Butterfly/Barbell 828
Butterfly spread 567
Burghardt, G 623, 704, 710

C

CAD *see Capital adequacy directive*
Calculating spot rate 364, 429
Call feature 143, 199, 967, 985
Call options 601, 624, 680, 857
Call price 599-600
Call protection 995
Call provision 143
Call swaption 680, 682-3, 686
Callable bonds 190, 263, 345, 963, 985
Campbell, J 447
Cap 171, 252, 606-12, 616, 687-8, 1182-3, 1263-5, 1271-2
Capital 1, 3-7, 10-2, 14-5, 18, 29, 31, 33, 35-6, 38, 41, 47, 51, 63, 70, 72, 74, 78, 83, 113, 115, 122, 125, 127, 133, 135, 137-8, 154-5, 172, 222-3, 235-6, 238, 240, 242, 247, 252, 254, 261-2, 281, 290-1, 293, 296-300, 309, 323, 328-30, 335, 337, 339-40, 343, 348, 393, 398, 447-8, 454-5, 477, 489, 493, 495, 499, 517, 532, 562, 603-4, 614, 623, 625-6, 657, 680, 744-5, 748, 755, 760, 774-6, 778-9, 781-2, 784, 805, 840, 847, 866, 875, 882, 887, 893-5, 898, 903, 907, 916, 919, 923, 927, 948-9, 952, 954-5, 957, 972, 1001, 1003, 1011, 1021-2, 1026, 1029, 1031, 1034, 1037-41, 1043, 1051, 1059-60, 1063-9, 1071-3, 1075, 1086, 1088, 1093, 1102-3, 1108, 1110, 1113, 1115, 1118, 1122, 1125, 1127, 1139, 1147-50, 1152-3, 1156, 1161-3, 1165-92, 1172-3, 1175, 1180, 1195-200, 1202, 1204-5, 1207-12, 1214-5, 1217-8, 1220-2, 1224-6, 1228-39, 1249, 1252, 1276-7, 1279, 1292, 1300-1, 1303, 1306
    Adequacy 6, 254, 290, 517, 840, 1029, 1163, 1166, 1168, 1172-3, 1175, 1182, 1185, 1197
    Adequacy ratio 254
    Allocation 916, 1165-6, 1169, 1180-1, 1183, 1306
    Market 1, 12, 14, 47, 63, 74, 133, 135, 137, 138, 222, 339, 340, 343, 393, 398, 447-8, 454, 489, 495, 604, 623, 625, 626, 657, 745, 882, 887, 903, 919, 954, 957, 1026, 1038, 1041, 1043, 1051, 1125, 1148, 1149, 1156, 1165-6, 1199, 1225, 1276-7
    Capital One 297, 1001, 1003
    Ratio 6, 1029, 1197
    Requirements 72, 236, 240, 309, 948, 949, 1063, 1065, 1115, 1139, 1147, 1162, 1163, 1165, 1166, 1167, 1168, 1169, 1171, 1174, 1177, 1178, 1180, 1181, 1182, 1188, 1195, 1197, 1205, 1207, 1208
Capital adequacy directive 532, 928, 1170, 1203
CAPM 603
Caps and floors 582, 602, 606, 608-9, 684, 687, 1271
Cash collateral account 1007
Cash flow
    CDOs 1034
    Waterfall 906, 1009
Cash markets 190, 563
Cash matching 219, 272
Cash value 204, 258, 279, 501, 525, 543, 828, 969, 1308
Cash waterfall process 906
CBOs see *Collateralised bond obligations*
CBOT *see Chicago Board of Trading*
CDOs see *Collateralised debt obligations*

CDO returns 1094
CDS *see Credit default swaps*
CDs see *Certificates of Deposit*
CDS basis 478, 487, 488, 739, 801, 812, 1069
Central Gilts Office 533-4
Certificates of Deposit 18, 47-8, 55-60, 92, 217, 231, 235, 242, 249-50, 257, 259, 262, 292, 307, 309, 328, 518, 532, 534-5, 1165-6
Cheapest-to-deliver 319, 567, 717, 723, 770
Chicago Board of Trading 574, 715-6
Chicago Mercantile Exchange 568, 697
Classic repo 494, 496, 498-506, 508-10, 513, 519, 522, 526, 936
Clean bond 724
Clearing bank 56, 67, 249, 257, 308-9, 751, 966
Clearing house 383, 618, 679-80, 714, 717, 719
Clearing system 92, 515
Clearstream 514, 899
CLNs *see Credit-linked notes*
CLOs *see Collateralised loan obligations*
CMBS *see Commercial mortgage-backed securities*
CMOs *see Collateralised mortgage obligations*
Collars 606
Collateral invested amount 1007
Collateralised bond obligations 1021, 1024, 1030
Collateralised debt obligations 75, 126, 280, 510, 774, 792, 881, 885, 913-4, 936, 947-50, 955, 974, 1021-2, 1024-5, 1028-35, 1037-41, 1043-56, 1059-72, 1074-86, 1088-95, 1098-99, 1102-3, 1107-26, 1135, 1139-40, 1149-53, 1156-7, 1184, 1200, 1229, 1233, 1263, 1272, 1274
  Applications 774, 792, 1038, 1059, 1114, 1151-2, 1263, 1272, 1274
  Risk and return 1094
Collateralised loan obligations 774, 1021, 1022, 1024, 1026, 1030-1, 1037, 1039, 1043, 1061, 1065, 1095-6, 1159
Collateralised mortgage obligations 92, 969, 970, 996, 1003
Collateralised synthetic obligations 1060, 1077, 1083-5, 1090, 1113, 1122, 1128, 1137, 1139
Commercial mortgage-backed securities 946, 954, 968, 994-6, 1055, 1139, 1141, 1159, 1233
Commercial paper 70, 71, 72, 73, 74, 75, 76, 77, 78, 79, 80, 83, 84, 87, 88, 236, 238, 468, 518, 608, 631, 652, 656, 750, 755, 881, 921, 922, 923, 926, 929, 931, 932, 933, 934, 935, 936, 943, 952, 954, 955, 957, 1148, 1149, 1153, 1157, 1222-3, 1283
Complete market 593
Compliance tests 1083
Component 11-2, 87, 155, 164, 179, 191, 204, 249, 328, 367, 560, 625, 765, 767, 836, 1264
Compound interest 1277-9, 1289, 1294
Compounding 161, 373, 545, 552, 664, 1279-82, 1285-7, 1289-90
  Frequency 161, 1280
Conditions of certainty 196
Conduit 74-8, 84, 86-8, 226, 230, 236, 881, 921-7, 929-31, 933, 935-6, 943-7, 952, 955, 995-6, 1149, 1153, 1155-7, 1159, 1189, 1244
Confidence interval 302, 834, 837, 839, 841, 847-50, 860, 865, 1187
Consortium 161
Constant prepayment rate 976-8, 983
Continuous compounding 1281, 1286, 1289-90
Continuous time 415, 417-8, 421, 431-2, 436, 444-5, 447, 563

Contract 8, 22, 29-30, 87, 104, 108-10, 122, 214, 231, 257, 259, 272, 323-4, 329, 375, 379, 383, 424-5, 459, 465, 467, 498-9, 508, 512, 524, 539, 542-3, 545-8, 551-3, 555-77, 582-4, 586, 602-4, 608, 618-20, 629-30, 652, 657-8, 673-80, 697-701, 703-5, 707-9, 711, 713-30, 737, 740-2, 744, 747, 759, 761-3, 767-70, 772-5, 777, 779, 782, 786-91, 796, 798, 800-1, 803-5, 807-8, 811-2, 819-20, 822, 826, 854, 931-3, 935, 937, 946, 950, 952, 954-5, 957, 962, 964-5, 967, 981, 995, 1047, 1049, 1052, 1067, 1072, 1081, 1146, 1217, 1228, 1275-6, 1313
Conversion factor 716-7, 724-6, 728-9, 741-2, 1206
Convexity 172, 183-91, 202-5, 263, 383, 440, 556, 619, 635, 670, 677, 697, 701-6, 708-10, 729, 731, 736-7, 857, 859, 987-8, 992, 1001
  Risk 857
Core deposits 273, 293
Corporate debt 754, 1029, 1065, 1233
Corporate loans 74-5, 792, 883, 893, 922, 1029, 1115, 1121, 1168, 1173, 1198, 1200, 1230
Corporate risk 1224
Correlation 303, 318, 439, 455, 474-5, 558, 684, 701-3, 710, 833-5, 837, 841, 843, 846, 848-50, 853-4, 856, 858-61, 863, 865, 868-70, 872, 877, 1076, 1094, 1100-3, 1107-9, 1111-2, 1135-6, 1189, 1207-8, 1210
  Concept 834, 849
  Estimation of 1111
Cost of capital 281, 328, 477, 1161, 1165, 1300-1, 1303, 1306
Cost of funding 13-4, 86, 260, 263, 279, 299-300, 374, 477, 717, 722, 894, 965, 1030
Counterparty risk 383, 451, 455, 495, 519, 526, 617, 638, 656, 714, 760, 801, 927, 1065, 1122, 1140-1, 1166, 1169-70, 1176, 1217
Coupon
  Rate 57-8, 143, 153, 157, 160, 277, 282, 349, 361, 363, 371, 373, 380, 384, 417, 426, 481-2, 568, 575, 609-10, 641-6, 650, 702-3, 708, 710, 845-6, 855, 970, 996, 1016, 1263
  Yield Curve 73, 139, 160, 199, 277, 339-40, 344-6, 348-56, 360, 362, 364, 367-9, 371, 376-7, 382, 384, 387-8, 390, 406-7, 412, 415-7, 426-29, 436-7, 449, 480-2, 575-6, 633, 658, 671, 701, 710, 723, 731, 856, 986, 991, 1016, 1018, 1263-6, 1271
Covariance 835, 838, 840, 842-4, 849-50, 853, 855, 857
Covenant 128, 806-7, 889, 900
Cox–Ingersoll–Ross 386-7, 390, 437, 447-9, 595, 618-9, 624
Cox, J 447, 449, 623
CP see *Commercial paper*
CPR *see Constant prepayment rate*
Credit analysis 123, 617, 750, 754, 755, 1008, 1214
Credit card receivables 75, 883, 908, 1006, 1008, 1032
Credit default swaps 478-9, 486-8, 737-40, 743-4, 746, 763, 767, 769-76, 786-814, 819-22, 824, 826-31, 949-50, 1011, 1015, 1049, 1064-5, 1067, 1069-72, 1074-8, 1081, 1091, 1099, 1113, 1115, 1117, 1121-3, 1125-6, 1128, 1133, 1135, 1140, 1143, 1146, 1150-1, 1153, 1227-8
  Examples of 802
  Rationale 1151
  Term sheet 1077

Credit derivative 225-6, 263-4, 478-9, 491, 737, 744-8, 750, 759-62, 764, 767-8, 774, 776-7, 779-80, 784-5, 787-8, 792, 794, 796-7, 805-6, 808, 814, 830, 890, 929, 948, 957, 1059-60, 1062-4, 1067-8, 1070-1, 1080-2, 1121-2, 1125, 1130, 1139, 1146, 1184, 1203, 1227-9, 1313
Credit events 746-7, 759, 762, 797, 805-6, 957, 1068, 1080, 1121, 1228
Function 263-4, 779, 787
Valuation of 813
Credit derivative pricing 747, 808
Credit enhancement 70, 76, 883, 885, 888, 890, 899, 901, 905, 922-3, 925-6, 944, 946, 1001, 1003, 1006-8, 1010, 1015, 1032, 1034, 1047-8, 1095, 1110, 1153, 1157, 1222, 1232-3, 1274
Concept 885, 946, 1008
Credit exposure 264, 501, 520, 525, 653, 745, 751, 753, 760, 780, 782, 784, 792, 794-5, 806, 863, 865, 869, 871-2, 877, 948, 1046, 1050, 1060, 1064, 1114, 1123, 1163, 1177, 1216
Credit-linked notes 746, 772, 784-6, 794, 806, 892, 926, 948, 1021, 1035, 1065, 1067-8, 1074-5, 1125, 1140-1, 1143, 1145
Credit option 784, 787-8
Credit rating agencies 751, 755, 781, 883
Credit risk 7-8, 14, 18, 47, 69, 73, 110, 123, 133-4, 139, 193, 211, 239, 241, 244, 247, 253, 263-4, 293, 309, 319, 330, 339, 383, 453, 455, 459, 478, 480, 482, 491, 519, 527, 532, 617, 653, 658, 679, 737, 740, 745-51, 754-5, 758-61, 764, 766, 771-2, 774, 777, 780-1, 784, 792, 794-7, 806, 812, 827, 833, 863-6, 875-6, 885, 890, 895, 948-50, 1015, 1021-2, 1030-2, 1035, 1037, 1044, 1046-7, 1049, 1055, 1059-60, 1062-70, 1072, 1074, 1085, 1090-1, 1093, 1099, 1103, 1107, 1112-5, 1121, 1125, 1127, 1139-41, 1143, 1145, 1150, 1162, 1166-7, 1171, 1177-82, 1187, 1189, 1198,-9, 1206, 1227-9, 1252
Credit Value-at-Risk 491, 748, 758, 833, 864-5, 868, 873
Definition 247, 264
Hedging 8, 239, 264, 453, 491, 617, 679, 737, 774, 863, 1049, 1115, 1166, 1228
Recovery rate 751, 758, 827, 865
Credit spread 563, 574-5, 641, 748, 751, 753, 762, 765, 771, 787-8, 794, 796, 814-6, 822, 868, 1064, 1107, 1110-2, 1155
Swap spread 641
Volatility 563
Credit term structure 790, 1084
CreditMetrics 865-70, 873, 877
Credit-supported commercial paper 72
CREST 92
CRESTCo 92
Cross-currency 324, 520-1, 526, 652, 1049
Cross-rate 101-3, 108
CSOs *see Collateralised synthetic obligations*
Cubic spline 409-10, 439, 441
Cum dividend 162-3
Cumulative gap 259, 294
Cumulative preference shares 1168, 1172
Currency swap 81, 324, 625, 652-3, 675, 892, 954, 1049, 1169, 1174
Current assets 31, 35-6
Current yield 58-9, 61, 154, 175, 177, 189, 345, 418
Curve
Forward 223, 383, 410, 428, 1027, 1270

Yield 10, 56, 73, 94, 96-7, 139, 153, 160, 199, 201, 209, 223-5, 244, 248, 250, 252, 255-6, 259, 262-3, 276-7, 280, 288, 295, 302, 305-7, 309-12, 314-5, 318, 322, 327-8, 339-54, 356, 359-64, 366-71, 376-78, 382-412, 415-7, 422, 426-9, 431, 434, 436-40, 446-9, 451-63, 465-8, 470, 473, 478, 480-2, 486, 560-2, 565-6, 574-6, 596, 605, 618, 633, 636, 638, 642, 648, 655, 658, 661, 671, 673-4, 676, 688, 692-3, 695, 697, 701, 710, 722-3, 730-2, 754, 789, 815, 830-1, 835-7, 861, 869, 986, 991-2, 1002-3, 1016, 1018-9, 1027, 1041, 1084, 1155, 1247, 1263-74
Curve fitting technique 431

D

Daily turnover 534, 659
Das, S 324, 326, 710, 792
Day-count 24-5, 49, 63, 73, 105, 109, 146, 161, 163-5, 172, 189, 375, 378, 501, 525, 543, 546, 632-3, 635-6, 646, 650, 657, 663-4, 1267-8
Basis 63, 146, 161, 164-5, 172, 189, 378, 501, 525, 632, 1268
Convention 657
DBV *see Delivery by value*
Deacon and Derry 429
Dealer CP 73
Dealing sheet 88
Debt capital 35, 41, 47, 135, 138, 339-40, 343, 625-6, 755, 887, 919, 957, 1038, 1165
Debt Management Office 161
Debt service coverage ratio 910, 915
Default
of debt 24, 67, 76, 81, 133, 163, 171-2, 191-3, 199, 236, 250, 296, 369, 383, 388, 413-4, 455, 457, 474, 478, 488-9, 502, 509, 515, 518, 525, 532-3, 553, 638, 653, 658, 737, 746, 748-52, 754, 756-60, 762, 764, 767-9, 771-3, 778-9, 786, 792, 794, 797-8, 806-22, 826-31, 861, 863-66, 868-9, 871-3, 875-7, 889, 895, 900, 910, 912-5, 923, 949-50, 957, 961, 965, 967-8, 972-4, 981, 995-6, 1006, 1011, 1028, 1032, 1034, 1038, 1044, 1046-8, 1050-1, 1055, 1064, 1066-72, 1074-7, 1081-2, 1086, 1088, 1092-5, 1099-103, 1105, 1107-8, 1111-2, 1115, 1117-8, 1122-3, 1135-6, 1145-6, 1157-8, 1163, 1173, 1179, 1184, 1187, 1192, 1198, 1206-8, 1227, 1265
Event 828, 871-3, 1047
Probabilities 810, 812, 814, 817-8, 820, 822, 826-7, 830, 1094, 1100-1, 1198
Risk 24, 133, 191-3, 199, 250, 383, 455, 457, 658, 751, 810, 815, 968, 996, 1032
Delivery by value 518, 534
Delivery date 110, 548, 557, 716, 718, 723
Delta 303, 597, 828, 835-6, 857-9, 1091, 1275
Delta-neutral 828
Hedging 828
Demand deposit 112, 114, 257, 259, 267, 273
Depository 92
Derivative pricing 594
Differential swap 656
Dilution 925
Direct financing 19-21
Direct paper 72
Dirty bond price 162, 172
Dirty price 146, 156, 158, 162-4, 166, 411, 418, 424, 500-1, 506, 521, 524-6, 725, 740, 917
Discount bond 362, 367, 412-3

Discount factor 145-6, 192, 350, 352-6, 368-71, 376-81, 383, 406-8, 411, 419, 422-3, 436, 552-3, 575, 642-6, 648, 650-1, 655, 682-3, 708, 813, 821-2, 826, 1102, 1267, 1276, 1287, 1293-9, 1314
Discount function 192, 369, 371, 378, 381-2, 406, 412, 422-3, 430-1, 435-6, 633, 1263, 1275, 1294-7, 1299
Discount instrument 51, 63, 67, 70, 73, 413, 642, 1018
Discount rate 63-5, 69, 71, 73, 83, 88, 144-5, 149, 152-3, 168, 172, 191-2, 194, 212, 277, 281, 302, 338, 354, 360, 369, 418, 486, 591, 644, 648, 699, 983, 1019, 1103, 1284-7, 1293-4, 1296-7, 1300-3, 1306, 1314
Discounted bond 142, 367
Discounted margin 167-71
Dispersion 184, 195, 758, 1016, 1019
Distribution 292, 302, 591-7, 599, 603, 605, 621, 624, 682-4, 710, 833-9, 844, 847, 849, 858, 863-5, 867-73, 875-8, 1086, 1088, 1099-103, 1106, 1111-2, 1207, 1252
Diversity score 1046-7, 1080, 1089, 1092, 1094, 1117-8, 1123, 1135
Dividend yield 605
Dividend-paying assets 604
Dividends 13, 29, 34, 37, 289, 519, 555, 588, 605, 624, 1173, 1306, 1311
DMO *see Debt management office*
Dollar convexity 204
Dollar duration 183, 730-1, 744
Drift rate 195, 196, 702-3, 70-10
DSCR *see Debt service coverage ratio*
Due diligence 898, 902, 908, 912
Duration 15, 63, 127, 138, 172-91, 201-4, 214, 262-3, 277-8, 294, 298-9, 301-2, 309, 312, 319, 526, 566-7, 574, 635, 671, 703, 725, 727-31, 744, 828, 833, 855-7, 971, 98-3, 985, 987-8, 994, 1000, 1016, 1149
DV01 230-1, 239-40, 244-5, 276, 330, 693, 730, 740-1, 828, 1043

E

Earnings per share 37, 43-5
Econometric 429, 447-9
Economic capital 805, 894, 1022, 1186
ECP *see Eurocommercial paper*
Effective convexity 988
Effective duration 298, 987-8
EL *see Expected loss*
Electronic dealing 496
Embedded option 143, 190, 192, 198-9, 769, 985
Endowment 962, 1292
  Mortgage 962, 1292
EPS 43-5
Equally weighted 836, 1311-2
Equity piece 883, 905, 954, 1039, 1064, 1069, 1093, 1119, 1156, 1232
  Bonds 883, 954, 1064, 1119
Equivalent yield 16, 64-6, 159, 575, 983-5, 989
EU *see European Union*
Euribor 52-4, 240, 459, 553, 608, 631, 676, 917, 1092, 1126, 1129, 1131, 1150
Euro 25, 49, 53, 56, 71-3, 77-8, 80, 85, 92, 101-2, 113, 130-1, 138-9, 142, 149, 151, 157, 163, 165, 178, 276, 340-1, 399, 459, 495, 518, 553-4, 625, 632, 656, 658, 675, 700, 710, 862, 892, 896, 933, 943, 957, 972, 1130-1, 1278
Eurobond 123, 138, 146, 151, 157, 163, 165, 178, 340, 357-9, 373, 495-6, 518, 896, 899
Euroclear 92, 514, 899
Eurocommercial paper 71, 73, 78-80, 926, 931, 1150, 1153, 1157
Eurocurrency 113-4, 631, 675

Eurodollar futures 239-40, 568, 575-6, 579, 623, 698-701, 703-6, 708-10, 1275
European option 586, 588, 605, 681
European Union 138, 341, 403, 1130-1, 1166, 1168, 1173, 1183, 1186, 1195, 1201-3
European Union's Capital Adequacy Directive 1166, 1168
Event risk 896, 1044
Evergreen committed line 927
Excess spread 797, 905, 925-6, 1005-8, 1010, 1013, 1015, 1056, 1093, 1122-3, 1149, 1151, 1153, 1157, 1233
Exchange rates 24, 101, 103-4, 516, 520
Exchange-traded 48, 329, 341, 383, 539, 546, 555, 557, 582, 606, 618-9, 679, 697-8, 705, 713-4, 716, 744, 770, 1122, 1217, 1265, 1275
Ex-dividend date 162-3, 588
Ex-dividend period 163, 165
Exotic
  Currencies 862
  Option 604
Expectations hypothesis 366, 387-93, 395-6, 437-9, 448, 456, 458
Expected credit loss 17, 1093, 1186
Expected inflation 344
Expected loss 833-4, 860, 865, 875, 1050-1, 1099, 1102-3, 1105-7, 1110-2, 1135-6, 1173, 1181, 1186-7, 1207-8
  Measure of 833-4, 1187
  Basel II 1181, 1186-7, 1208
Expected value 437, 594-7, 810, 821, 826, 869, 976
Exponential function 414, 418, 1281
Exponentially weighted moving average 836
Extendable commercial paper 84
Extendable note 84, 86, 87, 88
Extrapolation 578, 1303, 1305

F

Fabozzi, F 184, 296, 325-6, 447, 489, 537, 623, 710, 919, 976, 979, 987, 1239
Face amount 56, 76
Face value 56-8, 61, 63, 69-70, 73, 413, 718, 768, 809-10, 969, 1276
Factors
  Discount 23, 87, 123, 127, 137, 144, 178, 222, 273, 297, 316, 319, 322, 327, 352-5, 369-71, 377-81, 384, 387, 397-9, 406-8, 451, 453-5, 458-9, 472-6, 488, 552, 563, 575, 587-8, 591, 606, 619, 643-6, 648, 650-1, 655, 683, 702, 708, 717, 725, 754, 776, 779, 800-1, 815, 835-7, 860, 863, 872, 876, 883, 890, 893, 910-2, 917, 972, 976, 981-2, 993, 1004, 1038, 1046, 1076, 1094, 1100, 1119, 1151, 1157-8, 1207-8, 1228, 1238, 1254, 1267, 1280, 1293-9
Fair price 144, 146, 147, 150, 353, 368, 595, 721
Fair value 172, 193-4, 196, 199, 466-7, 562, 590-4, 597, 600, 604, 617, 648, 653, 697, 719, 721-4, 746, 948
Fama, E 46, 447, 448, 623
Federal fund 62, 467, 663
Federal Home Loan Corporation 962
Federal National Mortgage Association 962
Federal Reserve 62, 69, 449, 460, 889
Financial engineering 624, 957
Financial institutions 7-8, 22, 71, 112, 261-3, 496, 516, 523, 748, 777, 780, 861, 881, 921, 943, 1095, 1149, 1166
Financial intermediaries 21, 135-7, 536
Financial market 1, 3, 8, 15, 18, 23-4, 101, 135, 211, 398, 447, 473-4, 593, 746, 749, 760, 834, 1243, 1277
Financial sector 135-6

Financial Services Authority 1192, 1214
Financial statement 1, 3, 10, 12-3, 17, 29, 31, 34
 Ratio analysis 1, 29
Financial Times 42-3, 51
First issue 81, 160, 917, 936
First-loss piece 892-3, 896, 904, 907, 1015, 1113, 1115, 1231, 1234
First-order approximation 186
First-to-default 1227
Fitch 751-2, 754, 910, 915, 923, 1204-5, 1231-4
 IBCA 915
Fixed coupon 142, 167, 352, 480, 626, 628, 670, 764, 766-7, 770, 916, 952, 1123, 1182
Fixed income 133-4, 142, 160, 184, 190-1, 326, 386, 406, 447-9, 623, 744, 777, 919, 1239, 1295, 1313
 Investor 133, 160, 191, 386
Fixed interest 113, 142, 254, 625, 628, 631, 657-8, 962
Fixed rate 55, 74, 168, 212, 252, 277, 323, 372, 455, 480, 494, 539, 540, 611, 614-6, 626, 631, 633, 635-6, 646, 650-1, 657-8, 664, 675, 681, 688, 692-3, 698, 700, 855, 922, 962, 979, 1008, 1052-3, 1282, 1292
Fixed to floating 253
Fixed/adjustable hybrid mortgage 966
Flat yield curve 160, 386, 391-2, 397, 561, 986
Flattening of yield curve 295, 861
Floating rate 1053, 1130
 Bonds 1130
 Fixed-rate liability 669, 681
Floors 9, 582, 602, 606, 608-9, 684, 687, 1271
Foreign bond 138
Foreign exchange 8, 101, 108, 110-1, 360, 520, 858
Forward interest rate 108, 325, 344, 396, 398, 539, 566, 593, 606, 610, 618, 684, 702
Forward loan 289
Forward price 105, 109, 320, 325-6, 385, 504-7, 556, 568, 602, 618, 711, 717, 719
Forward rate 19, 48, 104-11, 192-5, 251, 323, 345, 352, 360-67, 369, 371-5, 377-8, 380, 383-5, 388-90, 392-3, 396, 398, 403, 406-7, 409-10, 412, 424-6, 428, 431-9, 446-9, 459, 466-7, 491, 539, 544-6, 556, 558-60, 562, 564-5, 568, 570, 576-8, 609, 618, 640-6, 648, 650-1, 655-6, 658, 676-7, 685, 688, 693, 697, 699-704, 707-10, 854-5, 1263, 1267, 1270, 1274
Forward rate agreements 19, 48, 249, 251-3, 283, 289, 323, 329, 345, 375, 383, 491, 539-55, 558-60, 564, 583, 606, 609-10, 612-3, 618, 631, 639-40, 642, 645, 648, 657, 674, 679-80, 689, 690, 853-5, 1169, 1174
Forward rate notes 142, 167-8, 171-2, 209, 231, 235-6, 477, 670, 1043, 1165
Forward start 223, 288, 385, 425, 680, 699, 704
Forward swaps 107-8, 703-4
Forward yield 339, 343, 360-2, 364, 374, 377, 387, 389, 409, 426-8
Forward yield curve 339, 360, 362, 364, 389, 426-8
FRA position 546, 550, 551
FRAs *see Forward rate agreements*
FRNs *see Forward rate notes*
FSA 1191-2
FtD *see First-to-default*
FTP *see Funds transfer pricing*
FTSE-100 1310, 1312-3
 Funding gap 219, 221, 243, 264, 612
Fully funded CDOs 1076

Fund manager 18, 22, 71, 111-2, 127, 136, 344, 394, 516, 521, 724, 754, 830, 955, 991, 1038, 1063, 1079, 1090, 1095, 1115, 1152, 1156, 1180, 1310-3
Funded credit derivative 747, 761-2, 787-8, 948, 1068, 1121, 1125
Funding rate 155, 171, 230, 243, 250, 254, 272, 482, 510, 782, 927, 943, 958, 1029-30, 1248, 1253-4
Funding risk 219, 236, 238, 612, 1063
Funds transfer pricing 125
Future value 281, 351, 364, 369, 380, 389, 699, 707, 1278-81, 1284-5, 1287-90, 1293, 1297, 1309
Future volatility 473, 592
Futures contract 231, 323, 329, 375, 379, 383, 459, 465, 467, 547, 548, 551, 553, 555-60, 562, 564-70, 572-6, 583, 586, 602-3, 618-20, 630, 673-80, 697-701, 703-9, 711, 713-30, 740-2, 744, 769-70, 1275-6
Futures trading 563, 618
FX *see Foreign exchange*

G

Gamma 857-9
Gap 7-8, 209, 214-24, 226-33, 236, 238-9, 241, 243-4, 247, 249, 252-6, 258-65, 267, 269-79, 288-9, 291-2, 294, 306-7, 323, 328, 330-2, 340, 374, 406, 535, 544-5, 560, 611-2, 614, 856, 1043, 1248
Gap ratio 262-3
Gap risk 8, 216, 231, 239, 243-4, 247, 252, 254, 256, 265, 323, 330, 545, 1043
Gaussian 1100, 1111
GC *see General collateral*
GDP *see Gross domestic product*
GEMMs 533
General collateral 241-5, 307-9, 316-23, 455, 456, 500, 518-9, 527-32, 535, 536, 537, 781
Generic portfolio 1089
Geometric average 389, 432, 645, 658, 1309-10, 1312
GIC *see Guaranteed investment contracts*
Gilt-edged 139, 448, 533-4, 752
Gilts 133, 139, 142-3, 151, 161, 163, 166, 178, 239, 242-3, 308, 311-2, 340, 348, 473, 478-9, 501-2, 520, 532-4, 633, 670, 718, 728, 796, 1064, 1075, 1173, 1293
Ginnie Mae 954, 962
Global capital markets 47, 604, 745, 1051
Global Master Repurchase Agreement 239, 243, 509, 512, 526, 532, 534, 780, 783, 927, 928, 1216
Global note 899
GMRA *see Global Master Repurchase Agreement*
GNMA *see Ginnie Mae*
Government bonds 65, 133, 138-9, 142, 146, 151, 157, 241-2, 262, 292, 317, 344, 457, 473, 493, 516, 518, 520, 532, 638, 641-2, 674, 713, 727-8, 744, 814, 847, 982, 1065, 1125-6, 1168, 1170-1, 1294-5
  Market 139, 143, 341, 369, 400, 406, 495
Government National Mortgage Association 962
GPM *see Graduated payment mortgage*
Graduated payment mortgage 966
Granularity 1219, 1254
Greeks 849
Grid point 259, 267, 276, 411, 412, 844, 845, 846
Gross
  Basis 717, 724
  Price 162
  Redemption 155, 157-8, 340, 356, 1016

Redemption yield 155, 157-8, 340, 356, 1016
Gross domestic product 402, 405
Growing equity mortgage 966
Guarantee 8, 15, 68, 76, 81, 87, 230, 252, 272, 297, 424, 437, 518, 523, 620, 681, 714, 719, 806, 890, 899, 901, 910, 923, 925, 929, 931, 933, 935, 943, 952, 973, 981, 1007, 1037, 1049, 1052, 1064, 1070, 1079-81, 1149, 1171, 1176, 1182, 1184, 1187, 1227, 1284
Guaranteed investment contract 899, 952, 955, 1052, 1053, 1072, 1081, 1115, 1141
GIC *see Guaranteed investment contract*
Guarantor 768, 778, 910, 932-3, 935

H

Haircut 243, 501, 510, 512-3, 521, 525-6, 927-8, 945-6, 1054, 1131, 1149, 1179, 1184, 1216
Hedge ratio 182, 550-1, 567, 574, 670, 673-4, 677-8, 709, 724-5
Hedge size 182
Hedging 8, 179, 181-2, 209, 216, 219, 221, 230-1, 239-41, 244, 249, 254, 256, 260-2, 264, 305, 317, 320, 322-3, 326-30, 332, 375, 384, 388, 451, 453, 457-8, 491, 539, 548-50, 557, 559, 563, 565, 569, 571-2, 574, 582, 610, 617, 624-6, 641, 655-7, 661-2, 668, 670, 673-5, 677-9, 701, 705, 710, 713-4, 723-5, 727-30, 737, 741-2, 744, 750, 773-5, 787, 828, 863, 925, 950, 988, 994, 1049, 1115, 1152-3, 1166, 1228, 1263, 1276
  Approaches 179, 216, 219
  Credit risk 8, 239, 241, 244, 453, 617, 863
  Interest-rate risk 8, 179, 216, 219, 221, 230, 240, 244, 254, 256, 260-2, 264, 323
HIC repo 518-9
High-yield bonds 127, 1033-5, 1052
Historical data 739, 809, 829, 836, 848, 870, 876, 1187
Hold-in-custody 518
Holding period 244, 387-8, 395, 437, 834, 847-8, 876, 986, 989, 992
House price 338, 974
Hull and White 810, 1101
Hull, J 624
Humped yield curve 390, 392-3, 395

I

IBCA 915
Illiquidity 87, 525
IMF *see International Monetary Fund*
Immunised portfolio 179
Implied forward rate 193, 352, 360-1, 365, 367, 369, 373, 380, 388, 560, 568, 577-8, 641, 676, 688
Implied volatility 180, 527, 592, 605-6, 617, 839, 863
Income statement 10, 12, 33, 295
Index 48, 99-100, 142, 167-8, 171-2, 178, 244, 324, 341, 473-6, 494, 608-9, 617, 625-6, 628, 656, 658-9, 664, 693, 713, 788-91, 796, 861, 866, 965, 974, 1053, 1179, 1308, 1310-3
Index swap 48, 99, 100, 244, 341, 625-6, 664, 796
Index-linked 142, 178
  Bond 142, 178
Inflation 142, 283, 289, 307, 344, 390-1, 399, 404, 458-9, 749, 910, 1308-9
  Expectations 283, 307, 344
  Inflation-adjusted 1308
Information technology 67
Initial margin 509, 524-7, 529, 533

Institutional investors 126-8, 136, 300, 394, 495, 524, 750, 909, 991
Insurance 21-2, 38, 56, 112, 136, 297, 338, 394, 524, 531, 582, 590-1, 688, 759, 773-4, 777, 784, 829, 865, 883, 899, 905, 910, 926, 955, 962, 967, 1029, 1032, 1047, 1049, 1052, 1062-3, 1067, 1070, 1072, 1074, 1095, 1115, 1149, 1153, 1182, 1202, 1237, 1239
Integrals 442, 623
Interbank market 242, 267, 307, 317, 320, 334, 383, 453, 473, 478, 530, 532, 927, 1168, 1202, 1283
Interest calculation 49, 164, 166, 543, 1273
Interest income 12-6, 249, 255, 258, 262, 279, 327-9, 332, 610, 615-6, 742, 1152, 1199, 1237
Interest margin 14, 249, 277, 611, 615-6, 999, 1008
Interest-rate
  Gap 307
  Modelling 448
  Option 448
  Risk 8, 127, 172, 176, 179, 183, 184, 190, 211, 212, 216, 219, 220, 221, 230, 240, 244-5, 247, 248, 250, 253-6, 260, 261, 262, 263, 264, 265, 275, 276, 283, 288, 289, 292, 294, 306, 309, 323, 326, 328, 330, 340, 491, 557, 569, 582, 606, 608, 610, 611, 612, 617, 626, 653, 670, 687, 700, 710-1, 732, 737, 740, 744, 764, 780, 833, 954, 987, 1063, 1181, 1182, 1247, 1248
  Swaps 19, 48, 710
  Yield 154, 171
Intermediation 307-8, 322, 746, 760, 1062, 1223
Internal rate of return 130, 153, 155, 1018, 1027, 1300--3
Internal ratings based 1163, 1178-80, 1182-3, 1185-7, 1189, 1196, 1198-200, 1202-6, 1209-12, 1214-5, 1218, 1222-33, 1235, 1239
International market 129, 754
International Monetary Fund 25, 1170
International Securities Identification Number 738, 1093
International Securities Market Association 497, 509, 526, 532-4, 889
International Swap Dealers Association 243, 625, 631, 746, 762-3, 774, 780, 783, 797, 805-6, 808, 1130, 1228
  Definitions 746, 806
Interpolated yield 479, 480, 845-6
Interpolation 157, 379, 383, 407-8, 439, 441, 478, 480, 578, 633, 1267, 1271-2, 1303-5
Interpretation 179, 275, 339, 763, 1100, 1105, 1202
In-the-money 586-7, 591-2, 594-5, 597, 605-6, 613, 617, 680, 683, 788, 986
In-the-money option 605
Intrinsic value 586-9, 849
Inverted yield curve 225, 307, 314, 389, 391-2, 397, 399, 404, 459
Investment
  Banks 12, 14, 17, 22, 56, 73, 136-7, 228, 282, 412, 625, 658, 888, 948, 952, 962, 1041, 1051, 1080, 1157, 1202, 1238, 1244
  Grade 115, 122, 126-7, 510, 752, 800, 829, 890, 901
IRB *see Internal ratings based*
IRR *see Internal rate of return*
Irredeemable bond 150, 177
ISDA *see International Swap Dealers Association*
ISIN *see International Securities Identification Number*
ISMA *see International Securities Market Association*
I-spread 479, 486

Issuance 70-1, 81, 85, 87-8, 115, 238, 457, 899-900, 931, 946, 955, 999-1000, 1012, 1034, 1053, 1128, 1205, 1215, 1217-8

Issue

Price 63, 64, 83, 142, 1126

Proceed 6, 885, 1141

Size 134, 321, 916, 917, 1274

Issuer 18, 47, 70-2, 76, 85-6, 92, 128, 133, 143-4, 146, 154, 163, 198-9, 318, 324, 340, 344, 356, 413, 457, 487, 626, 653, 657, 750-1, 754-5, 760-1, 769, 784-6, 797, 815, 869, 883, 889, 896, 899-905, 908-9, 918, 922, 926, 929, 931-2, 934-5, 944, 947, 969-72, 975, 990, 996, 1001, 1003-8, 1010, 1015, 1026, 1028-9, 1031-2, 1034, 1041, 1043, 1060, 1067-8, 1074-6, 1084-5, 1095, 1115, 1117, 1122, 1125, 1127-31, 1133-4, 1141, 1150, 1170, 1184, 1191-2, 1212, 1215

Issuing process 994

Italy 9, 25, 131, 165, 504, 1202, 1205

J

James and Webber 378, 383, 409, 429

Jarrow, R 326, 448, 711

Jordan 131

Junior

Bonds 901

Class 1127

Loans 775

Notes 883, 901, 904-5, 915

Tranches 797

K

Kessel, I 393, 438, 448

L

Law of no-arbitrage 351, 590, 723

LCH *see London Clearing House*

Legal issue 911, 925

Legal risk 1181

Lending line 114, 295, 969, 1002, 1202

Letters of credit 72, 259, 518, 869, 871, 1001, 1007, 1064, 1125, 1127

Level of default 757, 872, 968, 1093-4

Level-payment fixed-rate mortgage 962

Leveraged buy-out 808

Leveraged investor 155

LGD *see Loss-given default*

Liability-linked swap 668-9

Libid 52, 531, 572, 670, 780

Libor 51-3, 55, 75, 116, 122-7, 167-8, 171, 219, 230, 236, 238, 251-2, 256-7, 307, 320-2, 341, 451, 455-64, 466-8, 470, 472, 477, 480, 510, 521, 531, 537, 541-3, 546-8, 550-1, 557-9, 561, 568, 571-9, 607-8, 612-3, 617, 627-31, 636, 639-41, 643, 651-3, 655-61, 668-9, 671, 675-6, 679-82, 688, 692-3, 700, 705, 707, 711, 719, 738, 740, 742, 748, 750, 764-7, 777-9, 781-3, 787, 792, 794, 796, 802, 855, 908-9, 915, 926-8, 935-7, 943, 945, 952, 957-9, 990, 1013, 1026-8, 1030, 1041, 1051-2, 1054, 1057, 1063-4, 1067, 1069, 1086, 1116, 1119, 1150, 1155, 1252, 1276

Libor-in-arrears swap 655

Life assurance companies 22, 136, 367

LIFFE *see London International Financial Futures Exchange*

Limits 46, 233, 254, 261-2, 265, 267, 289, 329, 516, 589, 782, 833, 839, 860, 862, 865, 874-5, 1150, 1172

Measurement 254,833

Types 1172

Linear interpolation 157, 379, 383, 407-8, 633
Liquidating trusts 995
Liquidation 80, 234-5, 750-1, 758-9, 1167, 1248-50
Liquidity gap 214-7, 220-2, 224, 264-5, 272-3, 277, 1248
Liquidity line 76-7, 84-6, 122, 885, 899, 925-9, 1151, 1153, 1157, 1159, 1187, 1222-3
Liquidity management 8, 87, 220-1, 226, 231, 248, 264-5, 272, 328, 921
Liquidity preference theory 391-3, 396
Lliquidity premium 392, 396-7, 448, 458, 1051
Liquidity ratio 224-5
Liquidity risk 7-8, 211-2, 215-6, 219, 223, 225, 229, 242-3, 247-9, 253, 260-1, 264-5, 328, 455, 835, 876, 1145, 1151, 1248
Loan book 13, 135, 248, 274, 291, 298-301, 774-5, 792, 795, 875, 882, 894, 962, 969, 994, 1026, 1063, 1173-5, 1182
Loan note 895, 944
Loan portfolio 17, 68, 253, 784, 990, 1024, 1029-30, 1037, 1115
Local expectations hypothesis 387, 390, 392
Logarithmic interpolation 407-8
Lognormal distribution 591-3, 597, 603, 605, 621, 682-4, 849
London Clearing House 714
London International Financial Futures Exchange 323, 546, 556-7, 564-6, 675, 699, 713, 717-8
London Stock Exchange 989, 1310
Long bond yield 397
Long cash 22, 307
Long gilt contract 566
Long gilt future 717-8, 730, 744
Long positions 1276
Long-dated bond 136, 160, 388, 394, 397, 770
Long-end 400
Long-term asset 11, 216, 256, 259, 894
Long-term institutional investor 136
Long-term liabilities 31
Loss distribution 867, 872, 1102, 1111
Loss-given default 1187, 1198, 1200, 1206-10, 1214-5, 1227-8
Loss reserves 17, 1186

M

Macaulay duration 175-9, 189, 983
Maintenance margin 714
Managed synthetic CDO 1071, 1080, 1083, 1118, 1137
Mandate to do business 903, 1247
Mapping 844-6, 871, 1046
Margin method 168
Margin swap 656-7
Marginal gap 218, 265, 272
Marginal return 363
Margins 14, 114, 172, 253, 255, 302, 668, 999
  Initial 509, 524-7, 529, 533
  Variation 302
Mark-to-market 7, 239-41, 243, 277, 303, 523, 533, 602, 617-8, 635, 651-2, 709, 794, 850, 857, 864, 866, 933, 957, 1216
Marked-to-market 8, 241, 520, 630, 635, 651, 753, 778, 946, 1053, 1152, 1171, 1216
Market participant 18, 20, 22, 112, 122, 126, 135-6, 211, 320, 339, 344, 366, 394, 408, 434, 493, 495, 501, 515-6, 533, 535-6, 560, 562, 577, 618, 658, 716, 746, 787, 797, 800, 803, 814, 831, 840, 889, 1165-6, 1216

Market risk 8, 14-5, 176, 247, 250, 264, 294, 303, 309, 319, 494, 497, 527, 582, 701, 750, 758, 833-4, 847, 864, 875-6, 946, 1171, 1173, 1182, 1184
Definition 176, 247, 264
Management 8, 247, 264, 294, 582, 750, 833-4, 875-6, 1182
Scope 1182
Market value CDOs 1033-5
Market yield 56, 65, 83, 94, 96-7, 160-1, 340-1, 343, 345, 364, 463, 498
Martingale 421, 593, 623
Master Trust 900, 903-4, 1004, 1011, 1030, 1272-4
Matador 138
Matched book 219-21, 223, 225, 272, 321-2, 792
Matrix 410, 440-1, 756, 840, 842-3, 853-4, 856, 896, 1163, 1178, 1248-9, 1268
Maturity date 48, 56, 61, 65, 68, 70-1, 85, 104, 122, 133-4, 143, 161, 168, 173, 178, 189-90, 220-1, 254, 281, 324, 370-1, 375, 412-3, 415, 510, 513, 521-2, 542, 545-6, 553, 559, 570, 584, 587, 598, 632-3, 635, 640, 646, 652, 672-3, 678, 700, 714, 721, 750, 763-4, 775, 783, 787, 804, 884, 904, 916, 928-9, 933, 935, 945, 959, 963, 969, 995, 1001, 1006, 1013, 1019, 1052, 1055, 1115, 1133, 1150, 1269, 1275-6, 1283, 1298-9
Maturity mismatch 894, 1228
Maturity proceed 58, 351, 510
Maturity value 57, 69, 73, 194, 362, 420, 431, 435, 444-5, 593, 784, 929, 1052
MBNA 297, 1003
MBSs *see Mortgage-backed securities*
McCulloch, D 429, 430, 431, 448, 449
ME screen 59, 482, 693
Mean
Arithmetic 592
Geometric 361
Measurement 167, 183, 185, 188, 190, 254, 277, 294, 748, 750, 758, 833, 835, 837, 857, 860, 867, 875-6, 1167, 1184-6, 1237, 1239, 1306, 1308
Measure of return 155, 159, 160, 340, 345, 1027
Medium-dated bond 727
Medium-term notes 75, 755, 923, 926, 952, 954, 1148, 1150
Merrill Lynch 79, 80, 126, 1125
Merton model 597, 604
Merton, R 448, 624
Mezzanine
Loans 775
Note 928, 1067, 1088, 1151
Tranches 802-3
Microsoft Excel® 189, 196-7, 354-5, 576, 622, 648, 671, 742, 822, 1263, 1272-4
Middle office 231, 233-5, 262, 289, 330, 1241, 1243, 1256
Migration 867, 869, 870, 896, 1157
Mismatch 7, 8, 213, 214, 215, 256, 322, 574, 660, 661, 662, 894, 899, 954, 1227, 1228
Mixed horizon institutional investor 136
MMCV screen 94
MO *see Middle office*
Model risk 1108, 1112
Modelling 279, 294-5, 398, 406, 447-8, 863-5, 871, 908, 910, 912-4, 981, 1095, 1099-100, 1102-3, 1108, 1111, 1169, 1264
Modified duration 175-7, 179-90, 202-4, 263, 277-8, 319, 635, 703, 725, 727-30, 744, 833, 857, 971, 987-8
Monetary policy 283, 399, 402, 455, 494, 496
Monetary Policy Committee 399

Money market CDO 1039, 1041, 1043
Money markets 5, 18-9, 22-4, 47-9, 51, 60, 84, 88, 92, 101-2, 125, 216, 280, 305, 326, 341, 460, 493-4, 496, 535, 539, 544, 546, 556, 559, 563, 565, 606, 623, 625-6, 657-8, 713, 751, 796, 867, 919, 1148, 1165, 1253, 1268, 1283, 1303
Monte Carlo 191, 835-6, 848-50, 860, 876, 1050, 1099, 1101-2, 1111-2
Monte Carlo simulation 835-6, 848-50, 860, 876, 1050, 1099, 1101, 1111-2
Moody's 80, 749, 751-2, 754, 756-8, 762, 792, 806, 809, 865, 896, 910, 915-6, 923, 946, 1013, 1015, 1022, 1061, 1080, 1086, 1094-5, 1116, 1118, 1123, 1126, 1131, 1135-6, 1185, 1204-5, 1216
Mortgage 14, 74-5, 143-4, 191, 194, 259, 274, 279, 296, 298-9, 519, 625-6, 782, 796, 802, 862, 881-4, 887-8, 890-1, 893-5, 898, 908, 910, 914-6, 919, 921-2, 943, 961-95, 1000-1, 1003, 1005, 1009-12, 1016-7, 1019, 1032, 1034, 1051, 1139-41, 1143, 1165, 1171, 1173, 1175, 1181, 1196, 1198-200, 1202, 1215, 1217-8, 1224, 1226-7, 1230, 1233, 1291-2, 1308
Mortgage bond 970-1, 986, 989, 1001
Mortgage interest 970, 981, 1308
Mortgage risk 967
Mortgage term 964, 966
Mortgage-backed bond 191, 194, 274, 279, 796, 888, 963, 968, 970, 976, 979-89, 991-2, 994, 1001, 1005
Mortgage-backed securities 75, 191, 280, 510, 518, 797, 782, 802, 881, 885, 888, 900, 903-5, 913, 915, 936, 961-2, 968, 971, 976, 989, 991, 994, 1003, 1008, 1010-1, 1043, 1051-2, 1095, 1121, 1139-41, 1143, 1145-6, 1157, 1171, 1200
Mortgagor 961, 965, 986
Motivation 46, 236, 805, 885, 887, 896, 921, 948, 1024, 1029, 1030, 1031, 1037, 1051, 1059, 1063, 1165, 1234
MPC 399
MTNs *see Medium-term notes*
Multi-borrower 996
Multiple dealer 1082
Multi-SPV conduit 955
Municipal bond 652

N

Name recognition 116, 750-1
National Cost of Funds Index 965
National Home Loans Corporation 882
Neftci, S 421, 443, 448, 595, 624
Negative
  Amortisation 966
  Carry 155, 722, 974
  Convexity 190, 987, 992, 1001
  Funding 155, 722
  Pledge 1173
  Pledge clause 307, 561, 1173
  Yield curve 399, 1019
Nelson and Siegel 429
Net
  Asset 35, 38-40, 254, 1252, 1258
  Interest 12-4, 16, 163, 255, 258, 262, 279, 610-1, 615-6, 629, 663, 999, 1008, 1199, 1237, 1249, 1252
  Netting 220, 532, 1169, 1227, 1253-4
Net interest margin 14, 611, 613, 615-6, 999, 1008-11, 1013
  Basel II 1010
  Synthetic repackaging 947
Net present value 152, 162, 168, 170, 212, 214, 263, 277, 278-9, 302-3, 549, 642, 646, 648, 650, 652-3, 655, 708, 778, 809, 812, 830-1, 853, 1103, 1271, 1300-3, 1306
Net redemption yield 157
Newton–Raphson method 606

NIBLs 14, 220, 257, 614
NIM *see Net interest margin*
No-arbitrage pricing 104, 398, 556, 589, 590, 593, 620, 709, 723
Nominal amount 124, 151, 199, 282, 310, 314, 323, 498, 500, 503, 506, 521, 528-9, 551, 632-3, 651, 671, 673-4, 762, 936, 950, 993-4, 1031, 1135, 1206, 1275-6
Nominal hedge position 181
Nominal rate 1277, 1282, 1308-9
Nominal value 31, 56, 76, 83, 182, 312, 324, 359, 415, 423, 425, 429, 434, 436, 503, 526, 550, 572, 574-30, 741-2, 761-2, 767-8, 771, 851, 859, 884, 905, 934-6, 945-6, 968-9, 988, 1004, 1049, 1068, 1090, 1141, 1174, 1206, 1275
Non-conventional bond 142
Non-interest bearing liabilities 257, 267
Non-parallel shift 279, 856
Non-performing 259, 883, 895, 898, 995, 1010, 1032, 1226-7
Non-vanilla bond 133, 135, 727, 782
Normal distribution 302, 591-7, 599, 603, 605, 621, 682-4, 833-6, 839, 844, 847, 849, 863-4, 873, 877-8, 1100-1
Note tranching 883, 904, 1054, 1057, 1095, 1116, 1123, 1125, 1274
Notional amount 113, 228, 323, 539-40, 608-9, 628, 631, 655, 687, 776, 790, 809, 827-8, 889, 917-8, 1079, 1100, 1102-3, 1119, 1135, 1206
NPV *see Net present value*

O

OAS *see Option-adjusted spread*
OC *see Offering circular*
OECD *see Organisation for Economic Co-operation and Development*
Off-balance sheet 6, 8, 11, 15-6, 19, 48, 181, 253-4, 256, 259, 277-8, 293, 323-4, 341, 383, 539, 557, 569, 582, 612, 625, 628, 780, 936, 1037, 1063, 1159, 1167, 1169, 1174, 1216
  Instruments 6, 8, 11, 15, 48, 181, 254, 256, 259, 277-8, 293, 323, 341, 383, 539, 569, 582, 625, 780, 1063, 1167, 1169, 1174
Offer price 102, 119, 137, 831
Offering circular 82, 1048, 1049, 1077, 1122, 1135, 1274
Off-market swap 657
OIS *see Overnight-index swap*
OIS swap 342, 658-60, 663-4, 667
OLS *see Ordinary least squares*
One-factor model 623, 1100
On-the-run 318, 320, 753
Open market 69, 493, 495, 496, 534, 658, 780
Operational risk 247, 264, 835, 1177, 1180-4, 1196-200, 1202, 1234-9
Opportunity cost 212, 225, 257, 261, 330, 1244, 1246, 1257, 1259, 1300
Option contracts 582
Option-adjusted spread 190-2, 194-5, 198-201, 263, 449, 624, 985-7, 1274-5
Options 8, 74, 143, 190, 274, 279, 305, 329, 447-8, 473, 563, 582-6, 588, 590, 592, 594, 598, 600-8, 611-3, 617, 623-4, 652, 670, 680, 688, 704, 710-1, 763, 787-8, 857, 922, 932, 936, 985, 1122, 1178, 1183-4, 1206, 1214, 1254, 1265, 1267
  Option-adjusted spread analysis 190-1, 449, 624
  Option book 582, 857-9
  Option element 191, 198-9
  Option pricing 345, 398, 448, 527, 582, 587-91, 601, 617, 623-4, 681, 1264, 1294
  Option risk 257

Ordinary least squares 430
Organisation for Economic Co-operation and Development 1047, 1065, 1071-2, 1074, 1076, 1140, 1170, 1196-7, 1200, 1202-5, 1208-9, 1214, 1227
Origination 136, 298, 1026, 1234
Originator 74, 116, 801, 883-5, 889-92, 896, 898, 901-5, 908, 911-4, 918, 922, 929, 931, 935, 943, 947, 954, 957, 972-3, 1010, 1012, 1015, 1024, 1030-2, 1037-8, 1041, 1046-8, 1059-60, 1062-4, 1067-8, 1072, 1074, 1076-8, 1080, 1083, 1091, 1112, 1114, 1117-8, 1122, 1125, 1139-41, 1143, 1145-6, 1148, 1150, 1153, 1156, 1189, 1217-8, 1229-30, 1232, 1234
OTC *see Over-the-counter*
Out-of-the-money 199, 586-7, 592, 594, 605-6, 612, 687
  Option 592, 605-6
Overnight
  Interest-rate 48, 53, 62, 98-100, 161, 214, 216, 218, 220, 227, 229-30, 234-5, 244, 250, 280, 282-3, 288, 319-21, 325, 332, 341, 459-60, 495, 513, 515, 526, 535-6, 604, 625-6, 657-60, 663-4, 714, 861, 1246, 1248, 1257, 1259, 1283, 1303
Overnight-index swap 48, 99, 100, 244, 341-2, 625-6, 657-64, 667, 689-90, 1248
Over-the-counter 19, 23, 48, 137, 305, 494, 496, 539, 555, 625, 668, 673, 713, 759, 787, 1217, 1265
  Products 759

P

p&l *see Profit & loss*
Par
  Bonds 349
  Value 29, 31, 63, 143, 145, 353, 413, 758, 765-7, 807, 970-1, 1050, 1094, 1123, 1141
  Yield 348-9, 352-3, 356, 361-2, 376, 406, 412, 576, 643, 685
  Yield curve 348-9, 376, 406, 412, 576
Parallel change 262
Parallel shift 256, 259, 263, 276, 278-9, 295, 611, 615-6, 671, 701, 730-1, 856
Parametric 624, 835, 837, 842
Parity 598, 599, 600, 622, 624, 1275
Pass-through 884, 900, 903, 968-71, 976-9, 982, 985, 988, 991, 994, 1001, 1017, 1151
Paying agent 92
Payoff profile 582-5, 787, 857
PD *see Probability of default*
Pension 21-2, 71, 136, 338, 367, 394, 516, 524, 531, 670, 900, 967, 1288-9, 1292
  Fund 21-2, 71, 136, 394, 516, 524, 531, 670, 900, 1288, 1292
Perfect market 398
Performance measure 35, 39, 42
Pfandbriefe 954, 971, 1067, 1075, 1081, 1131, 1216
Physical settlement 92, 714, 761-2, 768-9, 776, 785-6, 798, 1082-3
Plain vanilla bond 142-3, 174, 204, 254, 730, 884, 985, 1005, 1292
Platform 711, 746
Polynomial 408-11, 431
Pool factor 917-8, 1013
Pool insurance 905
Portfolio
  Duration 179
  Management 329, 489, 747, 1055, 1153, 1159
Positive yield curve 224-5, 306, 391, 396, 407, 561, 722, 1019, 1041, 1155
Preference share 6, 41, 758, 1167-8, 1172
Preferred stock 1172

Prepayment
Analysis 976
Model 274, 981
Risk 191, 274, 963, 967, 969, 1000-1, 1181
Present value of a basis point 230, 276-7, 550, 670-4, 730
Price quote 51, 52, 62, 101, 102, 106, 107, 108, 110, 114, 137, 151, 154, 159, 162, 283, 345, 356, 366, 372, 498, 571, 617, 625, 630, 636, 657, 668, 670-4, 692, 730, 744, 770, 985, 1278, 1283, 1304
Price volatility 179, 188, 319, 387, 526, 601, 605, 946, 994, 1179
Price/yield function 202
Price/yield relationship 153, 183-4, 204-5, 857, 993
Pricing
CDO 1150, 1263
CDS 811, 820, 827
Model 546, 586, 590, 592-3, 597, 603-4, 617, 624, 642, 681, 693, 721, 829, 963, 987, 1103, 1263, 1294
Theory 398, 447
Primary
Dealer 92
Market 136-7, 349, 899
Prime rate 62, 256-7, 608, 617, 631, 652, 656, 965
Probability of default 779, 814-9, 821, 863, 871, 1050, 1100, 1145, 1157, 1179-80, 1187, 1198, 1200, 1205-10, 1214, 1225-8
Profit and loss 1, 7, 10, 12, 15, 17, 31, 33-4, 36-8, 40, 43, 231, 238, 241, 584, 618, 629, 698, 701-2, 709, 743, 862-3, 1227, 1241, 1244-9, 1252, 1254, 1257-9
Programme
CP 71-2, 74-6, 81, 8-8, 127, 217, 226, 230, 921-3, 925, 933, 1012, 1057, 1222-3, 1264-5, 1302
Promissory note 70
Protection seller 759, 761-4, 767-70, 776, 784-6, 789-90, 798, 800, 805-6, 809, 950, 1060, 1068-9, 1072, 1113, 1139, 1140, 1228
PSA *see Public Securities Association*
Public Securities Association 532, 533, 977, 978, 979, 980, 981
Put feature 143
Put option 582, 585-6, 588-90, 598-600, 610-1, 787, 858, 1115, 1150, 1267
Put swaption 680, 681, 682
PVBP *see Present value of a basis point*

Q

Quanto option 656
Quote price *see Price quote*
Quoted margin 171, 172

R

Ramp-up period 1034, 1070, 1082
Random variable 303, 418, 1095
Rate of recovery 512, 786, 828, 912
Rate of return 55, 58, 125, 153, 298, 354, 362, 387, 424, 428, 477, 591, 621, 777, 815-6, 1018, 1029, 1300-1, 1305-10, 1312
Rating agencies 6, 80, 85, 87, 751, 755-6, 781, 827, 883, 898-9, 903, 912-4, 954, 1034, 1037, 1094-5, 1131-2, 1150, 1152, 1185, 1222, 1232
Ratio analysis 1, 29, 35-6, 39, 43
Financial statement 1, 29
Recession 39, 41, 222, 399, 402-4, 872, 1105, 1107
Recovery rate 751, 758, 767, 773, 776, 789, 809-10, 813, 817-8, 820-1, 826-31, 865, 868-9, 877, 912-3, 1038, 1047, 1050, 1092, 1094-5, 1100, 1103, 1111, 1136

Redeemable 150, 177-8, 212, 1168
Redemption
  Date 142, 150, 191, 368, 800, 900, 970, 1293
  Payment 142-4, 148, 156, 170, 176, 202, 351-2, 370, 412, 415, 486, 830, 884, 1006, 1017, 1295, 1298
  Value 63, 198, 419, 421, 761, 1295
  Yield 153, 155-60, 168, 184, 190, 194, 201, 314, 340, 343-5, 348, 350, 352-3, 356, 359-62, 383-6, 390, 407, 984-5, 1016, 1018-9
Reference rate 62, 142, 167-8, 170-3, 275, 542-3, 617, 631, 652-3, 663, 855, 965, 1024, 1270
Refinancing burnout 981
Regression
  Analysis 411, 727
  Technique 430-1
Regulation 110, 248, 489, 1161-2, 1166, 1168, 1172, 1190, 1222, 1232, 1239
Regulatory capital 1, 5, 7, 261, 680, 774, 776, 847, 894-5, 898, 907, 949, 952, 955, 1021, 1059-60, 1063-5, 1067, 1072, 1113, 1115, 1122, 1127, 1147, 1150, 1161, 1165-8, 1171-3, 1176, 1185-7, 1196-7, 1199-200, 1202, 1208, 1230-2, 1234
  Basel II 774, 776, 895, 1147, 1150, 1161, 1166, 1172, 1185-7, 1196-7, 1199-200, 1208, 1230-2
Regulatory risk 835
Reinvestment 110, 160, 162, 345-6, 348, 350, 372, 680, 985, 989, 1005, 1016, 1032-3, 1055, 1279, 1303
  Risk 110, 345-6, 348, 350, 985, 1032
Relative value
  Analysis 209, 310, 477, 479, 481-2, 488, 801, 1051
  Trading 309, 311
Rennie, A 447
Repackaging vehicle 890, 947-8
  Mechanics 948
  Secondary market 890
  Structure 890, 947-8
Repacks *see Repackaging vehicle*
Repayment mortgages 961
Repo *see Repurchase agreements*
Repurchase agreements 48, 92, 98, 100, 161, 171-2, 226, 230, 239-44, 264, 283, 288-9, 294, 305-12, 314, 316-26, 345, 383, 400, 455-6, 468, 491, 493-510, 512-37, 534, 537, 540-1, 588, 658-9, 668, 714, 717, 719-22, 738 740, 742, 744, 779-83, 800, 926-9, 936, 943-7, 952, 954, 958, 1053-5, 1057, 1065, 1081, 1130-2, 1134, 1153, 1156-7, 1165-6, 1169-70, 1216, 1276
  Characteristic 668
  Market 172, 307, 308, 311, 314, 316, 318, 321, 326, 493, 494, 495, 496, 509, 519, 521, 524, 533, 534, 535, 537, 540, 720, 782, 800
  Pricing 294, 345, 383, 398, 525, 588, 721
Reserve Bank 449, 1115
Reset date 168, 607, 664, 672, 698, 783, 926, 933, 935, 937, 940, 1024
Residential mortgage-backed security 802, 804, 917-8, 946, 954, 972, 974, 990, 1010-2, 1015, 1043, 1055, 1072, 1139, 1143, 1159, 1200, 1215, 1217, 1233, 1273
Restructuring 86-7, 751, 760, 762-4, 770, 776, 790, 797, 806-7, 1015, 1071, 1118, 1123, 1130, 1228
Retail bank 12-4, 22, 135, 291, 394, 611, 1180, 1196, 1238
Retail price index 1308, 1310
Returns
  On assets 16-7, 74, 247, 250, 263, 300, 922

On capital 1, 3-4, 35, 39, 125, 223, 252, 290-1, 296-8, 329-30, 562, 748, 760, 840, 866, 875, 1037, 1069, 1147, 1161, 1165, 1172, 1224, 1239
On equity 16-7, 35, 39-41, 43, 74, 300, 893, 895, 922, 1069, 1306
Return-to-maturity expectations hypothesis 387, 390
Reverse enquiry 71
Reverse repo 306, 309, 319-22, 496, 500-1, 510, 512, 519, 522-3, 529-30, 658, 740, 742, 952, 954, 1157
Revolving structures 885, 904
Rights issue 1312
Rising yield curve 390
Risk 8, 72, 211-2, 214, 230, 236-7, 240, 243, 245, 247, 254, 261-4, 267, 289-91, 294, 302, 326-9, 451, 453, 527, 582, 608, 610, 617, 626, 674, 679, 687, 710-1, 737, 740, 744-6, 748-50, 758, 774, 779, 792, 815, 833, 835-6, 840-1, 860, 862-4, 873-6, 890, 893, 895, 908, 914, 974, 1022, 1029, 1060, 1062, 1085, 1090, 1107, 1113, 1115, 1141, 1161-2, 1174, 1176, 1179-80, 1182-3, 1185-6, 1196, 1231, 1234, 1237, 1239
Allocation 230, 875, 1180, 1183
Associated 838, 1306
Types 701
Risk capital 840, 1115, 1180, 1196, 1231, 1234, 1237, 1239
Risk management 8, 211-2, 214, 245, 247, 254, 261-4, 267, 289-91, 294, 326-9, 451, 582, 608, 610, 674, 687, 710-1, 737, 745, 748-50, 758, 774, 792, 833, 835, 875-6, 893, 895, 1060, 1062, 1085, 1090, 1113, 1161-2, 1176, 1182-3, 1185-6, 1196, 1239
Risk weights 1168, 1170, 1178, 1217
Risk-free
Interest rate 62, 556, 568, 597-8, 603, 618-9, 622
Yield 63, 815
RiskMetrics 259, 833, 842-5, 848, 854, 856, 858, 877
Risk-return profile 126-7, 296, 337, 478, 896
RMBS *see Residential mortgage-backed security*
ROA *see Returns on assets*
ROC *see Returns on capital*
ROE *see Returns on equity*
Rollover 114, 283, 288, 440
Ross, S 447, 449, 623
RPI *see Retail price index*
RR *see Rate of recovery*
Rubinstein, M 449, 623, 624
Running cost 155
Running yield 154, 177, 418, 721-3

S

S&P *see Standard & Poor's*
Samurai 68-9, 138
Scholes, M 447, 623
SDA *see Standard default assumption*
SEC *see Securities and Exchange Commission*
Secondary market 21, 55, 57-8, 64, 67, 70-1, 115-6, 118, 122, 127, 133, 137-8, 146, 165, 235, 250, 348, 792, 794, 887, 890, 894, 914, 954, 1024, 1026, 1029, 1033, 1094
Second-order measure of interest rate 184
Secured debt 123, 1132, 1214
Securities and Exchange Commission 70
Securities lending 493, 519, 524, 537, 1216
Securities repo conduit 943-7

Securitisation 4-5, 74, 80, 115-6, 126, 247, 264, 295-301, 489, 745, 792, 802-3, 881-96, 898, 901-16, 921-2, 946-7, 962, 970-3, 990, 996, 1002, 1008-11, 1013, 1015, 1021, 1032, 1039, 1059-60, 1062-4, 1070, 1077, 1086, 1091, 1095, 1098, 1113-4, 1118, 1125, 1139, 1151, 1165, 1174, 1184, 1189, 1196, 1215, 1217-9, 1222, 1229-34
  Applications 792, 891, 921, 1038, 1059, 1114, 1151
  Balance sheet management 247, 295-6, 881, 885, 1008, 1039, 1059, 1139, 1215, 1230
  Basel II 892, 895, 1010, 1184, 1189, 1196, 1215, 1217-9, 1222, 1229-34
  Cash flow waterfall 906, 1009
  Definition 247, 264, 971
  Funding tool 885
Security 19, 65, 72, 77, 81, 127, 147, 171, 192, 199, 201, 263, 298, 318, 320, 360, 413, 419, 421, 479, 495, 498, 510, 514-5, 519, 522, 528, 566, 589, 593-4, 625, 670, 777, 784, 798, 805, 809, 889, 895, 903, 910, 923, 925, 929, 937, 944-7, 957, 961-2, 968-73, 977-9, 982-3, 985-9, 991, 994, 1003, 1019, 1055, 1064, 1093, 1128, 1132, 1134, 1136, 1219, 1222, 1305, 1311-2
Segmentation 393, 395
Sell/buy-back 496, 504-9, 526, 532
Semi-annual rates 608, 643, 652, 655-6, 668
Senior note class 905
Seniority 758, 769, 869, 883, 950, 1117, 1219
Sensitivity 16, 172-3, 179, 184, 214, 250, 258, 262, 276-9, 291, 294, 302-3, 332, 570, 606, 611-2, 670, 703, 725, 730, 835, 837, 982, 987-8, 1047, 1107-9, 1112, 1188
Sequential pay 901, 994
Series of notes 143, 219, 350, 388, 390, 406, 409, 447-8, 563, 607, 639, 641, 648, 657, 663, 788, 810, 820, 857, 860, 868, 877, 881, 904, 949-50, 994, 1005, 1011-3, 1024, 1030, 1032, 1041, 1043, 1130, 1140, 1273, 1287, 1290, 1300
Servicing
  Fee 16, 965, 1071, 1093
Settlement
  Cash 558, 562, 602, 700, 713-4, 761-2, 768-9, 776, 786, 797-8, 807, 1134, 1283
  Date 61, 101, 146, 163, 171-2, 189, 360, 498, 521, 542-8, 550-1, 553, 700, 1267, 1283-4
  Physical 92, 714, 761-2, 768-9, 776, 785-6, 798, 1082-3
  System 92, 496, 506
Share price 42-4, 46, 291, 588
Shiller, R 449
Short cash 22, 221, 307
Short duration 63
Short position 181, 267, 275, 312, 318, 320, 322, 420, 493, 495, 530-1, 544, 556, 582-4, 603, 630-1, 643, 700-1, 708, 720, 724, 781, 855, 957, 1275-6
Short rate 385, 419-20, 422, 426, 605
Short-end 345, 393, 400, 605, 1038, 1041
Short-term instruments 74, 136-7, 262, 388, 1277
Short-term interest rate futures 19, 48, 1274
Simple
  Interest 161, 543, 1277-9, 1294
  Margin 172
  Yield 161, 341
Simulation modelling 294-5, 1095
Simulation VaR 848
Single asset 751, 767, 839, 1309
Single monthly mortality rate 976

Single payment 412, 682-3, 899, 1284
Single-tranche 1084-6, 1088-92
CDO 1084-6, 1089-90, 1092
SIVs *see Structured investment vehicles*
Skewed distribution 864
Skewness 877
SMM *see Single monthly mortality rate*
Soft bullet 900, 904
SONIA swap 657-9
Sovereign 18, 47-8, 133, 138-9, 209, 231, 235, 239-40, 473, 771, 777, 796, 835, 1021, 1046, 1055, 1064, 1072, 1152, 1170, 1178-9, 1184-5, 1200, 1203-6, 1208-10, 1212, 1214, 1216, 1218, 1227-8
Credit risk 796
Debt 1072, 1203-5, 1216
Risk 835, 1178
Spain 9, 25, 98, 131, 138, 165, 971
SPC *see Special purpose company*
SPE *see Special purpose entity*
SPV *see Special purpose vehicle*
Special purpose company 890, 1001
Special purpose entity 890
Spot
Exchange rate 101, 104, 652
Market 112, 360
Price 107-8, 504, 506, 555, 602-3
Rate 102, 104, 106-11, 192, 194-5, 201, 352, 356, 359-61, 363-9, 383-4, 388-90, 392-3, 396-7, 406, 410, 421-2, 426, 428-9, 431-39, 444-6, 481-2, 546, 550, 576, 633, 641-2, 644, 650, 682-3, 708, 822, 1016, 1270
Rate discount 682-3
Yield 349-50, 352, 354, 361-4, 367-9, 372, 389, 481
Spot rate curve 359, 366, 369, 383, 426, 428
Spot yield curve 349, 350, 354, 364, 368, 369, 481
Spread
Duration 172, 184, 189-90, 730
Risk 219, 751, 753
Spread Option 684-5
Concept 685
SPV 74, 80-1, 88, 296, 301, 786-7, 797, 884, 888-93, 895-6, 899, 901-4, 909-12, 914-15, 921-3, 927, 931, 944, 947-8, 950, 952, 955, 957, 962, 972, 989, 1001, 1010, 1021, 1030-2, 1038, 1047, 1049, 1053, 1060, 1062, 1067, 1069-72, 1074-5, 1078-83, 1085-6, 1113, 1115, 1123, 1125, 1127-9, 1139-41, 1143, 1157
Stand-alone trust 1003
Standard & Poors 80, 489, 749, 751-2, 754, 756, 759, 762, 910, 916, 923, 105-7, 1131, 1157-8, 1185, 1204-5, 1211, 1216
Standard Chartered 862
Standard default assumption 981
Standard deviation 592, 594, 596, 621, 703, 758, 835, 837-43, 846-7, 850, 860, 868-9, 874, 876, 1107, 1111-2
Standardised approach 927, 1163, 1178, 1180, 1183-5, 1196, 1198-200, 1202, 1204-5, 1209, 1212, 1214-6, 1218, 1222, 1224-6, 1228-31, 1237-8
Static
Cash flow model 983, 987
Spread 360, 1016, 1018-9
Statistical concept 834
Statistics 274, 449, 874, 1157
Steepening 295, 861, 1002
Stein, E. & J. 1072
Sterling 24, 49, 51, 55-7, 60, 63, 67, 80, 84, 92-6, 101-2, 105, 109, 129, 138, 148-51, 167, 172, 231, 240, 244, 276, 320-1, 323-4, 340-1, 356, 399-400-3, 454, 458-60, 463, 466-7, 478-9, 501, 520-1, 534-6, 546-7,

552, 557-9, 564-7, 570-1, 576, 618, 625, 629, 632, 638-9, 653, 656, 658-9, 674-5, 680, 688, 699, 707, 727, 730, 788, 972, 1005, 1278
Stochastic
Behaviour of interest rate 397
Differential 418, 624
Process 398, 435-6, 595, 623, 876-7, 1095
Stock lending 264, 316, 524, 532-5
Straddles 781
Straight line 407
Strategies 250-2, 295, 322, 372, 390, 447, 620, 710, 720, 1038, 1182
Stress scenarios 1047-8, 1231
Stress testing 292, 860-3
Strike price 585-9, 591, 594, 597-9, 601, 606, 609, 612, 622, 680, 770, 787, 932
Stripped mortgage-backed securities 968
Strips 143, 151, 239-40, 242-3, 346, 412, 415, 993, 1270
Structure diagram 88, 929, 944, 950, 989, 1015, 1056, 1078, 1115, 1148
Structured Credit Product 489, 745-6, 748, 794, 891, 929, 957
Structured finance 75, 510, 746, 782, 796-7, 801, 803-4, 896, 917, 927, 931, 943, 948, 954, 1021, 1051, 1079, 1114, 1121, 1151-2, 1156-7, 1159, 1200, 1203, 1217, 1219-22, 1229-30, 1272-3, 1313
Structured finance securities 75, 746, 797, 803, 896, 917, 943, 948, 954, 1121, 1151-2, 1157, 1203, 1217, 1220-1, 1272, 1313
ABCP 72, 74-5, 78, 80, 82, 84-8, 97, 226, 881, 892, 921-36, 1149, 1153, 1155-6, 1165, 1189, 1222-3
ABS 75, 116, 143-4, 263, 280, 296, 510, 518, 770, 782-3, 796, 799, 801, 813-21, 826, 828-9, 881, 883-5, 888-9, 893-4, 896, 899-900, 903-5, 913-4, 917, 919, 999-1011, 1016-7, 1019, 1021, 1030, 1032-5, 1044, 1051-5, 1072, 1081, 1095, 1117, 1125, 1130, 1135-6, 1146, 1149, 1152, 1156-7, 1200, 1217-8, 1222, 1229-34, 1263, 1272-3
CDOs 75, 126, 280, 510, 774, 792, 881, 885, 913-4, 936, 947-50, 955, 974, 1021-2, 1024-5, 1028-35, 1037-41, 1043-56, 1059-72, 1074-86, 1088-95, 1098-99, 1102-3, 1107-26, 1135, 1139-40, 1149-53, 1156-7, 1184, 1200, 1229, 1233, 1263, 1272, 1274
SIVs 881, 885, 923, 925-6, 1053, 1147-53, 1155-6
Structured investment vehicles 881, 885, 923, 925-6, 1053, 1147-53, 1155-6
Example 882
Rationale 1148, 1151
Structured notes 794
Structured product 74, 769, 772, 786, 794, 948, 1038, 1095, 1125, 1165
Structuring 86-7, 214, 230, 792, 888, 901, 908, 914, 950, 972, 1031, 1038, 1041, 1046, 1069, 1091, 1110, 1112, 1118, 1234
Subordinated bonds 1168
Subordinated debt 6, 298-9, 885, 1148, 1150, 1167-8, 1173, 1182, 1211, 1215, 1249, 1252
Sundaresan, S 414, 449, 888, 919
Swap pricing 640-1, 646, 650, 653, 808, 812, 1103
Swap rate 93, 378, 380-1, 383, 451-3, 455, 458, 473-4, 477-9, 486, 627, 635-6, 639-41, 643-45, 650, 653, 655, 657-8, 669, 677, 679, 681-2, 684-6, 688-9, 693, 697-8, 700, 703-4, 707-8, 765-7, 856, 1263

Swap spread 108, 209, 295, 403, 451, 453-8, 472-82, 487, 636-8, 641, 689, 737-8, 861, 1028, 1069, 1191
Swaps 8, 19, 48, 74, 81, 98-100, 107-9, 230, 240, 244, 249, 253, 305, 324-6, 329, 341-2, 345-6, 378, 383, 403-4, 451-3, 455, 457, 478-80, 486, 491, 494, 553, 568, 582-3, 610, 618, 624-6, 629-32, 636-42, 652-3, 656-60, 668, 670, 672-5, 679-81, 687, 689, 692-3, 697-8, 702-4, 709-11, 737, 746, 764, 767, 771, 773, 777, 780, 792, 794, 806-7, 821, 851, 855, 869, 922, 937, 949-50, 954, 1011, 1048-9, 1063-4, 1067, 1074, 1076-7, 1081, 1099, 1117, 1146, 1174, 1216, 1271
Swaption 680-88, 693, 696
Sweden 131, 165
Switzerland 5, 25, 131, 138, 165, 1167
Syndicate 113-23, 125, 127, 748, 773-6, 792, 954, 1026, 1028, 1030, 1091
Syndicated loans 113-4, 748, 773, 774, 775, 792, 954, 1026
Synthetic assets 890, 1118, 1121, 1151
Synthetic CDOs 774, 792, 1043, 1059-60, 1063-4, 1071, 1080, 1083, 1090, 1091, 1095, 1113, 1139
Synthetic CLOs 774
Synthetic conduits 929
Synthetic funding structures 952, 955
Synthetic liabilities 1080
Synthetic repackaging 947
Synthetic securities 954
Synthetic securitisation 489, 888, 912, 921, 1011, 1013, 1059-60, 1070, 1113, 1125, 1184, 1229
Synthetic structure 746, 769, 794, 926, 929, 952, 1031, 1038, 1060, 1062-3, 1070, 1125

T

Taxation 34, 238, 240, 891
  Considerations 891
Taylor expansion 186, 202, 204
T-bill 18-9, 23-4, 47-8, 62-5, 69, 73, 76, 93, 167, 217, 235, 249-50, 292, 295, 345, 419, 421, 498, 526, 574, 588, 617, 631, 652, 787, 1115, 1117, 1175
Technical analysis 563
Technical default 751, 754, 759, 762, 771, 861
TED spread 574-6
Telerate 98, 110, 663, 1303
Term premium 209, 225, 451, 458-60, 463, 465-8, 470, 472, 477, 1248-50, 1252
  Fair value 466-7
Term sheet 81, 123, 927, 929, 931, 933, 935, 1077, 1127
Term structure
  of interest rate 192, 250, 340, 350, 352, 368, 406, 412, 414, 417, 436, 447-9, 1149
Term to maturity 55, 82, 88, 155, 172-3, 178, 190, 241, 340, 345-6, 348-50, 353, 360, 367, 387, 392, 396, 403, 408, 413, 430, 513, 556, 591, 635, 641, 671, 763, 806, 815, 882, 962, 982, 985-6, 995, 1095, 1136, 1275, 1296
Testing 292, 391, 438, 516, 860-3
The Economist 248, 399, 449, 746
Theoretical 65, 137, 192, 274, 349-50, 371, 383-4, 388, 426, 555, 559-62, 566, 600, 602, 639, 677, 708, 718, 723, 803, 808-9, 830-1, 1249
Theory of Financial Decision Making 386, 448, 624
Third party 76, 496, 893, 913, 1132, 1141, 1143, 1237

Tick
Size 557
Value 551, 557-9, 564, 567, 574, 675, 699, 708-9, 716, 718
Time bucket 212, 216, 218-20, 231-2, 259, 275-6, 332, 335
Time deposit 60, 114, 567, 1282
Time horizon 136-7, 273, 310, 566, 744, 756, 864-5, 867, 869, 1157, 1187
Time period 133, 217-8, 234-5, 258, 277, 335, 354, 369, 391, 406, 434, 444, 540, 542-3, 545, 588, 595, 620, 762, 801, 834-5, 847, 871, 1279, 1297, 1312
Time value
of money 135, 154-5, 260, 1277, 1284, 1287, 1293
Time-weighted rate of return 354, 1306-7
to call 199, 527, 922, 996
Total return 19, 136, 173, 230, 374, 390, 437, 494, 546, 746, 777, 778, 779, 780, 781, 794, 796, 912, 925, 933, 936, 989, 992, 1002, 1067, 1081, 1119, 1121, 1280
Total return swaps 19, 230, 240, 494, 746, 777-80, 782, 792, 912, 925-6, 933-4, 936, 952, 1067, 1081, 1118-9, 1121
Trade bill 67
Trading
At a discount 178, 722-3
Book 3, 5, 7-8, 14-5, 234, 237, 241, 834-5, 845, 847-8, 857, 1163, 1169, 1171, 1173, 1177, 1181, 1198
Flat 163
Strategy 340, 619-20, 720, 723
Traditional
ALM 261, 327
Approach 144, 249, 261, 279, 1294
Tranche 118-22, 124, 775, 794, 797-8, 800, 802-4, 883, 885, 892, 903-4, 907-8, 915, 917, 948-50, 989, 1002, 1004, 1011-4, 1031-2, 1034, 1037-9, 1041, 1043-4, 1048-51, 1054, 1067, 1072, 1076, 1079, 1084-6, 1088-92, 1099, 1102-3, 1105-15, 1122, 1126, 1140-1, 1146, 1148, 1151, 1153, 1196, 1200, 1217-22, 1229-34, 1273
Transaction cost 297, 398, 593, 603, 619, 1070
Treasury
Bills 18
Bonds 72, 240, 326, 1000, 1067
Notes 239
Procedures 1243
Spread 478, 480, 1051
Strip 239, 412, 415
Tri-party repo 496, 514-7
TRSs *see Total Return Swaps*
Trustee 81, 889, 892, 898, 900, 910, 913, 1049, 1054, 1117, 1123, 1125, 1129, 1132-4, 1137, 1273
Twist 256
Two-way price 20, 108, 109, 154
Two-way quote 137

U

UK gilts 133, 163, 239, 308, 311, 340, 473, 478, 479, 502, 532, 718, 728, 796
Repo market 172, 307, 308, 311, 314, 316, 318, 321, 326, 493, 494, 495, 496, 509, 519, 521, 524, 533, 534, 535, 537, 540, 720, 782, 800
UL *see Unexpected loss*
Unbiased expectations hypothesis 366, 387-92, 395-6, 438-9
Undated bond 150, 1168, 1293

Underlying asset 75-7, 85-7, 116, 263, 303, 321-2, 543, 555-6, 568, 574, 582, 584-95, 597-8, 600, 602-3, 605-6, 609, 618, 620, 622, 624, 668, 713-4, 718-9, 721-4, 727, 761, 764-5, 767, 774-9, 784, 787, 797-8, 800, 805-8, 810, 850, 857-8, 860, 863, 872, 876, 883-4, 889-90, 892-3, 895, 898, 900-2, 905, 909, 912-3, 915-8, 923, 925-6, 928, 932-3, 937, 944, 947, 949, 952, 954, 972, 974, 979, 985-6, 990, 992-6, 1001, 1009-10, 1012, 1015-6, 1021-2, 1024, 1030-2, 1037-8, 1044, 1046-50, 1053-4, 1056, 1060, 1065, 1067, 1069-70, 1072, 1075, 1080, 1093, 1095, 1099, 1118, 1155, 1218-9, 1229, 1233, 1267-9, 1273
Underwriter 317, 457, 915, 1054
Underwriting 73, 123, 344, 903
Unexpected loss 1186-7
  Basel II 1186-7
  Measurement of 1186
Unfunded CDO 1065, 1076
Unfunded synthetic CDO 949, 1077-8
Unsecured debt 1132, 1214
US Treasuries 133, 163, 239, 346, 369, 473, 502, 526, 1053

V

Valuation 30, 42-46, 133, 143, 192, 194, 199, 258, 294, 367, 423, 480, 489, 513, 516, 549, 553, 555, 600, 604-5, 623-4, 635, 640-1, 646, 648, 651-3, 655, 681, 683, 685, 693-4, 696, 746, 782, 801, 810, 812-3, 849, 852, 862, 868-9, 967, 974, 976, 985, 987, 1027, 1046, 1172, 1190-1, 1246, 1264, 1271-2, 1276, 1312-3
Value date 24-5, 53, 105, 146, 163, 166, 498-500, 504, 510, 512, 559, 783, 935, 1267-9, 1271-2, 1283
Value-at-Risk 15, 176, 259, 261, 263-4, 294, 302-3, 330, 491, 748, 750, 758, 833-68, 873-4, 876, 1171, 1187
  Applications 491, 833, 835, 843, 849, 857, 873
  Assessment 750
  Calculation of 833, 840, 851, 1171
  Concept 330, 748
  Confidence level 302, 837, 839, 841, 847, 848-50, 860, 865, 1187
  Correlation 303, 833-40, 842-5, 848-50, 853-4, 856, 858, 860-1, 863, 865, 868,
  Credit VaR 748, 758, 833, 865, 868
  Definition 176
  For credit risk 863, 1187
  Historical VaR 848
  Methodology 15, 259, 758, 833, 842, 848, 856, 863, 874
  Types 847
Van Deventer, Donald 165, 429, 447, 449
Vanilla
  Bond 133, 135, 142-3, 174, 178, 190, 194, 204, 254, 349, 670, 673, 727, 730, 782, 784, 884, 985, 992, 994-5, 1005, 1292
  Swap 324, 635, 641, 655, 657, 692
VaR *see Value-at-Risk*
Variable rate 142, 168, 171, 259, 626, 855, 965-6
  Gap 259
Variance 329, 594, 603, 624, 835, 837-44, 846, 849-50, 853-5, 857, 859, 1100, 1135
Variation
  Margin 505, 509, 525, 527-8, 532, 551, 574, 680, 714, 1055
Vasicek, O 623

Volatility 127, 137, 172, 179-80, 188-9, 195-6, 198-9, 241, 244, 249, 255, 261, 273, 293, 295, 302-3, 319, 329, 360, 387, 457, 473-6, 526-7, 535, 563, 587, 591-3, 598, 600-1, 605-6, 610, 613, 617, 622-4, 638, 682-3, 686, 688, 693, 702, 704, 708, 725, 727-9, 779, 833-4, 836-40, 842-6, 848-50, 852-3, 856-9, 863, 866-7, 869-70, 872-3, 876-7, 908, 946, 979, 986, 993, 1016, 1051, 1179

Voting right 29, 519, 780

W

WACC *see Weighted-average cost of capital*

Waggoner, S 429, 449

WAL *see Weighted-average life*

Warrant 144, 237, 491, 518, 584, 1248

Weaknesses 260, 604

Webber, N 448

Weighted-average
- Cost of capital 280-2, 286
- Life 804, 900, 903, 982, 1155, 1159

Weiner process 418, 594

Whole-loan repo 519

Windas, T 449, 624

Withholding tax 138, 157, 407, 775, 891, 959

World Bank 955

Writer of options 217, 317, 457, 582, 586-7, 590, 680, 763, 787, 915, 1054

www.yieldcurve.com 10

ee bond 138

Yield
- Analysis 118-21, 148, 160, 170, 1019, 1027
- Calculation 147, 158, 161, 168, 170, 1018

Yield curve 56, 73, 94, 96-7, 139, 160, 199, 201, 209, 223-5, 244, 248, 250, 252, 255-6, 259, 262-3, 276-7, 280, 288, 295, 305-7, 309-12, 314-5, 318, 322, 327-8, 339-54, 356, 360, 362, 364, 367-9, 371, 376-8, 382, 384-410, 412, 415-7, 426-9, 431, 436-8, 440, 447-453, 456-60, 463, 468, 470, 480-2, 560-2, 565-6, 574-6, 605, 618, 633, 636, 638, 642, 658, 671, 674, 693, 697, 701, 710, 722-3, 730-1, 754, 815, 856, 861, 986, 991, 1002-3, 1016, 1018-9, 1027, 1041, 1155, 1263-8, 1271-2
- Definition 322

Yield spread 191, 201, 309-11, 314, 356-60, 403, 477, 562, 638, 727, 802, 986, 1001, 1018-9, 1041, 1051, 1068, 1095, 1205, 1215

Yield to maturity 153, 155-6, 158-61, 167, 174, 179-80, 184, 189, 192, 199, 340, 343, 345-6, 348-9, 354-6, 408, 413-4, 417-8, 478, 481, 717, 742, 984, 1016, 1018-9, 1266, 1275, 1303
- Calculation 160-1, 481

YTM *see Yield to maturity*

Z

Zero gap 258

Zero rate 480, 531, 1267, 1270

Zero-coupon 71, 108, 110, 142-3, 151-2, 160, 162, 178, 182, 186, 190, 192, 195, 277, 281-2, 339-40, 344-5, 349, 350, 352-6, 359-63, 365-9, 371, 373, 376-7, 379-1, 383-4, 387-8, 390, 406, 412-7, 420-2, 424-7, 429-30, 434-7, 445, 480-2, 552, 555, 568, 575-6, 598, 600-1, 609-10, 633, 640-2, 644-6, 648, 650, 658, 685, 688, 697, 700-3, 707-10, 731-2, 845-6, 851, 855, 857, 869, 970, 993, 1016, 1018, 1263-6, 1270-1

Bond 142-3, 151-2, 162, 178, 182, 186, 190, 192, 195, 345, 349-50, 352-3, 359-60, 362, 365-6, 368, 371, 384, 387-8, 390, 406, 412-3, 415, 420-2, 424-6, 429-30, 434-7, 445, 555, 575, 598, 600-1, 640-2, 700-1, 703, 707, 709, 857, 970, 993, 1016

Curve 352, 363, 376, 480-1, 633, 648, 731-2, 869

Yield 340, 344, 349-50, 352, 355, 362, 376-7, 384, 390, 406, 414-7, 481, 576, 642, 646, 697, 701, 1018

Zero-volatility 360, 1016

Spread 360, 1016

Z-spread 478, 481, 482, 483, 486, 487, 737, 738, 743, 1016